Annotated Sample Student Papers

Annotated Student Research Papers

A note about the cover Literature matters because it reminds us that even though every person has a unique story, we are all connected. This eye-catching cover by artist Jill Hoy captures some of the vibrant diversity that makes both life and literature so fascinating.

Making Literature Matter

AN ANTHOLOGY
FOR READERS AND WRITERS

Making Literature Matter

AN ANTHOLOGY
FOR READERS AND WRITERS

SEVENTH EDITION

John Schilb
Indiana University

John Clifford
University of North Carolina at Wilmington

bedford/st.martin's
Macmillan Learning
Boston | New York

For Bedford/St. Martin's
Vice President, Editorial, Macmillan Learning Humanities: Edwin Hill
Senior Program Director for English: Leasa Burton
Program Manager: John E. Sullivan III
Executive Marketing Manager, Readers and Literature: Joy Fisher Williams
Director of Content Development: Jane Knetzger
Developmental Editor: Alicia Young
Content Project Manager: Louis C. Bruno Jr.
Senior Workflow Project Supervisor: Joe Ford
Production Supervisor: Robin Besofsky
Media Project Manager: Allison Hart
Manager of Publishing Services: Andrea Cava
Project Management: Lumina Datamatics, Inc.
Composition: Lumina Datamatics, Inc.
Photo Editors: Hilary Newman, Angela Boehler
Photo Researcher: Candice Cheesman/Lumina Datamatics, Inc.
Text Permissions Manager: Kalina Ingham
Text Permissions Researcher: Jen Roach/Lumina Datamatics, Inc.
Senior Art Director: Anna Palchik
Text Design: Jean Hammond
Cover Design: John Callahan
Cover Image: Jill Hoy, *Seals.* Photo, Stuart Mullenberg Photography, LLC. Reproduced with permission of Jill Hoy and Caroline Fenn.
Printing and Binding: Edwards Brothers Malloy

Manufactured in the United States of America.

2 1 0 9 8 7

f e d c b a

For information, write: Bedford/St. Martin's, 75 Arlington Street, Boston, MA 02116

ISBN 978-1-319-05472-4

Acknowledgments

Text acknowledgments and copyrights appear at the back of the book on pages 1323–1332, which constitute an extension of the copyright page. Art acknowledgments and copyrights appear on the same page as the art selections they cover.

Preface for Instructors

Preparing the seventh edition of *Making Literature Matter* reminds us that we began work on the first edition more than two decades ago. We designed our book for college courses needing a text that could play dual roles: as a literature anthology and as a writing guide. Given the book's many adoptions, instructors appear to find that it achieves both purposes. Yet with each new edition, we aim to do more than maintenance. We re-tailor the book to address emerging trends. One of the trends we have grappled with in recent years is how to capture the sustained attention of students who are incessantly beguiled by their smartphones and the abundant distractions of the Internet. What can a book or teacher do to make literature matter for a digital generation—students who move fast and revel in various media? In choosing literature for our book, we hunt for works that will engage them. We strive to provoke their thoughts and stir their imaginations. Similarly, we aim to ensure that our advice about writing helps students articulate their ideas, even if they do this through a mélange of postmodern devices. We survey teachers who have actually used our text, asking them how it can better serve their classes. At the same time, we track new movements in literature and in literary criticism. We note changes in composition studies, including innovative technologies in the field. We observe what's now occurring in introductory college courses. Above all, we study how they teach writing, reading, and research. In short, we conduct our own research.

This edition does retain key elements of its predecessors. Basically, Part One performs the functions it has fulfilled before. The opening chapters define *literature* and identify strategies for reading it closely. The rest of the section chiefly presents ways to *write* about literature. Throughout, Part One offers guidance in this art, drawing on numerous student essays for examples. We focus especially on composing *arguments*. As in previous editions, we point out that arguments needn't be mere rants. We note that when college courses ask students to write arguments, usually they want more than screeds. Rather, they seek essays that are civil, thoughtful, and well supported, so that readers can see how the writer's main claim makes sense. We describe how, in their encounters with literature, students can move from their initial responses into this process of persuasion. We identify for them specific steps that arguing about literature involves. We teach them how to pinpoint an issue, take a position, tap evidence, and spell out their logic, so that other people will respect their view. As in previous editions, Part One then turns to the main kinds of literature featured in

Part Two: poetry, short stories, plays, and essays. We identify each genre's typical elements, stressing the major role these can play in literary interpretation. Part One then provides detailed assistance with research-based papers, which courses in literature and composition often require. We discuss various sorts of investigative projects, explaining how to find, deploy, and cite sources. Finally, for this edition, Part One concludes with a new Chapter 7, "Writing with Critical Approaches to Literature." This material was included as an appendix in previous editions; we moved it up into the text to make it more visible and relevant for both students and teachers and expanded it to cover more schools of thought.

Part Two of the book remains essentially a collection of literature. Again, the selections appear in chapters focused on thematic topics: families; love; freedom and confinement; crime and justice; and journeys. These subjects quickly interest students due to their obvious relevance. As before, we organize each chapter into small clusters of works. This arrangement encourages comparison and contrast: students grow more aware of similarities *and* more conscious of a text's distinct traits. Every cluster in Part Two remains packed with questions and writing assignments, offering students numerous issues to pursue. Each chapter features five types of clusters that promote special kinds of inquiry. One type gathers works by the same author, such as Emily Dickinson and Langston Hughes. In a second group, a single work, such as Sylvia Plath's "Daddy," is followed by professional critics' comments on it. A third cluster puts a work in cultural context by juxtaposing it with other documents; a favorite example is Ralph Ellison's story "Battle Royal" with accompanying texts by Booker T. Washington, W. E. B. DuBois, and Gunnar Myrdal. The fourth type places works on related subjects from different genres in conversation with one another. The fifth type—new to this edition—presents literary works that explore current issues, such as immigration and capital punishment, accompanied by arguments on the issue.

This seventh edition, however, mixes continuity with change. In other words, we have engaged in revision ourselves. The book includes several new features, which reflect our attention to developments in literature, curricula, technology, and the larger world.

New to the Seventh Edition

The revisions in the second edition reflect the many useful suggestions of our users and reviewers as well as our own attempts to integrate new developments in literature and composition studies, along with current social, cultural, scientific, and technological issues.

Much literature that is new to the book. Bearing in mind the world's ever-increasing diversity, we have added stirring contemporary selections by writers such as Geeta Kothari, Karen Russell, Alexander Weinstein, Kristin Valdez Quade, T. Coraghessan Boyle, Chad Abushnab, Rivka Galchen, Ted Chiang, David Hernandez, and Meghan Daum. We also revive older texts that merit renewed notice—classic works by the likes of Vladimir Nabokov, Langston Hughes, Edgar Allan Poe, Michel Foucault, W. H. Auden, and Ryūnosuke Akutagawa.

Several new topics for clusters. New clusters in the anthology emphasize current world issues. For example, we group three essays that contemplate governmental surveillance, and a play by Ida Fink is paired with a short story by Ryūnosuke Akutagawa in a cluster that explores the experience of bearing witness to horrific events. Other new selections appear in clusters that touch on perpetual human concerns. For example, Geeta Kothari joins David Sedaris and Ruth Reichl in a cluster of essays reflecting on the role that food plays in family life. A story by Alexander Weinstein is paired with a Shirley Jackson classic in a cluster that examines how tradition can be a trap. A short story by Karen Russell appears alongside a Seamus Heaney poem, and both explore impossible love.

"Literature and Current Issues" clusters link literary works to contemporary debates. Responding to reviewers' comments that students often find it difficult to see how literature is relevant to the world they live in, we have created a new kind of cluster that connects a literary selection to arguments raised by contemporary issues. Examples include a poem about narcissism by Tony Hoagland, accompanied by essays on millennials' alleged self-obsession; a poem by Jimmy Santiago Baca, with essays debating whether immigrants take jobs from native-born workers; a story by Ursula K. Le Guin, with essays exploring the cost of one person's happiness; a Sherman Alexie poem, with debates on capital punishment.

More strategies for critical reading, and opportunities to practice them. Chapter 4 on the reading process now includes a section on how to get ideas for writing by tracing characters' emotions, demonstrating how the strategy can be applied to Edward Hirsch's poem "Execution." The chapter now concludes with an additional poem (T. S. Eliot's "The Love Song of J. Alfred Prufrock") and story (Allison Alsup's "Old Houses") on which students can attempt the array of close-reading strategies they have learned in the chapter.

Necessary additions and updates to the chapter on research and documentation. In Chapter 6, treatment of research includes more information about using sources and avoiding plagiarism as well as citation and documentation coverage that reflects the latest MLA guidelines published in the eight edition of *The MLA Style Manual* (2016).

A new chapter in "Writing with Critical Approaches to Literature." This material existed as an appendix in previous editions of *Making Literature Matter*, but due to its popularity, we moved it into the text chapters and added discussions of affect theory, performance theory, cognitive theory, and thing theory.

An Instructor's Manual Is Available for Download

You may want to access the instructor's manual, *Resources for Teaching Making Literature Matter: An Anthology for Readers and Writers*, Seventh Edition, through the online catalog page; visit **macmillanlearning.com**. Prepared by John Schilb, John Clifford, Joyce Hollingsworth, and Laura Sparks, these instructor resources include sample syllabi; advice (including an annotated bibliography for further research) on teaching literature, composition, and argumentation; and, especially, substantial commentaries on the individual literary works throughout the book to aid class preparation and discussion.

Acknowledgments

As always, the staff at Bedford/St. Martin's has coached us with a rare blend of insight, vision, practicality, wit, and warmth. The utter epitome of these virtues is Steve Scipione, who remains our invaluable mentor and friend. Karen Henry is also a stalwart and perceptive guide, and we also give thanks to Leasa Burton, Senior Program Director for English, and Edwin Hill, Vice President of Editorial for the Humanities at Macmillan Learning. We are grateful as well to a hardworking editor, Alicia Young; a diligent associate editor, Julia Domenicucci; and an industrious editorial assistant, Aubrea Bailis. For their editorial vision in earlier editions of *Making Literature Matter*, we thank Charles Christensen, Joan Feinberg, and Denise Wydra. In production, we are grateful to Lou Bruno, Andrea Cava, and Michael Granger. In the permissions department, text permissions manager Kalina Ingham, permissions editor Jen Roach, photo researcher Candice Cheesman, and photo research manager Angela Boehler expertly and efficiently negotiated and obtained reprint rights.

Once more, we thank Janet E. Gardner, formerly of the University of Massachusetts at Dartmouth, for her contributions to the chapter on research; Joyce Hollingsworth of the University of North Carolina at Wilmington for her previous work on the instructor's manual; and Laura Sparks for the work on the instructor's manual for this edition.

As always, John Schilb is indebted to his former University of Maryland colleague Jeanne Fahnestock and his current colleagues at Indiana University, especially Christine Farris and Kathy Smith. John Clifford would like to thank Sheri Malman for her invaluable assistance with this project, especially her professional editing.

Of course, we remain grateful as well to the instructors who have commented on various editions over the years—especially to those who have adopted the book, some for many editions. For their extremely helpful responses, we thank Liz Ann Baez Aguilar, San Antonio College; Jonathan Alexander, University of California, Irvine; Donna Allen, Erie Community College; Julie Aipperspach Anderson, Texas A&M University; Virginia Anderson, University of Texas at Austin; Liana Andreasen, South Texas College; Sonja L. Andrus, Collin County Community College; Joe Argent, Gaston College; Andrew Armond, Belmont Abbey College; Carolyn Baker, San Antonio College; Rance G. Baker, San Antonio College; Barbara Barnard, Hunter College; Charles Bateman, Essex County College; Linda Bensel-Meyers, University of Tennessee, Knoxville; Professor Alexander V. Bernal, San Antonio College; Elaine Boothby, South River High School; Colleen Brooks-Edgar, South Texas College; Christy Brown, Mission College; Carole Bruzzano, Montclair State University; Susan Buchler, Montgomery County Community College; Christopher Cartright, Armstrong State University;

Elizabeth L. Cobb, Chapman University; Robin Coffelt, University of North Texas; Chauna Craig, Indiana University of Pennsylvania; Timothy R. Cramer, Santa Monica College; Jacob Crane, Bentley University; Michael A. Cronin, Northern Oklahoma College; Janet Dale, Georgia College; Rosemary B. Day, Central New Mexico Community College–Montoya Campus; Thomas Deans, Kansas State University; Kevin J. H. Dettmar, Pomona College; Jennifer Diffley, Orange Coast College; Jennifer Dorfield, Westfield State College; Michael Doyle, Blue Ridge Community College; Penelope Dugan, Richard Stockton, College of New Jersey; Thomas Dukes, University of Akron; Mary Dutterer, Howard Community College; Kelly Edmisten, University of North Carolina at Wilmington; Lauren Edmondson, Northern Virginia Community College; Leigh Edwards, Florida State University; Monika Elbert, Montclair State University; Irene R. Fairley, Northeastern University; John Funk, Bishop Chatard High School; Joli Furnari, Montclair State University; Katie Frank, Yavapai College; Selma Goldstein, Rider University; Martha K. Goodman, Central Virginia Community College; Christopher Gould, University of North Carolina at Wilmington; Maureen Groome, Brevard Community College; Chad Hammett, Texas State University; John Hansen, Mohave Community College; Martin Harris, Belmont Abbey College; William Harrison, Northern Virginia Community College; Iris Rose Hart, Santa Fe Community College; Glenn Hatcher, Gaston College; Denise Haughian, University of Wisconsin-Stout; Carol Peterson Haviland, California State University, San Bernardino; H. Suzanne Heagy, Fairmont State University; Ana Hernandez, Miami-Dade College–Wolfson; John Heyda, Miami University–Middletown; Jeff Hoogeveen, Lincoln University; Richard Dean Hovey, Pima Community College; Karen Howard, Volunteer State Community College; Clark Hutton, Volunteer State Community College; Joan Kellerman, University of Massachusetts–Dartmouth; Sabine A. Klein, Purdue University; Gerard Lambert, Miami Dade College; Sonya Lancaster, University of Kansas; Kasee Clifton Laster, Ashland University; Marianne Layer, Armstrong Atlantic State University; Michael J. Lee, Montgomery County Community College; Margaret Lindgren, University of Cincinnati; Donna Long, Fairmont State University; Linda Lovell, Northwest Arkansas Community College; Irma Luna, San Antonio College; Betty Mandeville, Volunteer State Community College; Henry Margenau, Montclair State University; Kelly Martin, Collin County Community College; Phillip Mayfield, Fullerton College; Miles S. McCrimmon, J. Sargeant Reynolds Community College; Christopher McDermott, University of Georgia; Mandy McDougal, Volunteer State Community College; Terence McNulty, Middlesex Community College; Itzi Meztli, Slippery Rock University; Rebecca Millan, South Texas College; Deborah Church Miller, University of Georgia; Sharmila Nambiar, South Texas College; Steven Newman, University of Nebraska–Omaha; Dana Nichols, Gainesville State College; Jim O'Loughlin, University of Northern Iowa; Gordon O'Neal, Collin County Community College; Christine Peter, University of Massachusetts–Dartmouth; Brenton Phillips, Cloud County Community College; Jacqueline Regan, Montclair State University; Kathleen Reiman, Yavapai College; Nancy Lawson Remler, Armstrong Atlantic State University; Jim Richey, Tyler Junior College; David Rollison, College of Marin; Jane Rosecrans, J. Sargeant Reynolds Community

College; Teri Rosen, Hunter College; Lisa Roy-Davis, Collin County Community College; Donna Samet, Broward Community College; Jamie Sanchez, Volunteer State Community College; Daniel Schierenbeck, University of Central Missouri; Meryl F. Schwartz, Lakeland Community College; Pauline Scott, Alabama State University; Julie Segedy, Chabot College; Lucia Seranyan, Northern Virginia Community College, Woodbridge Campus; Kimberly Alford Singh, Northern Virginia Community College; Jason Skipper, Miami University at Oxford; Jennifer Smith, Miami University at Oxford; Debra L. Snyder, Livingstone College; Jamieson Spencer, St. Louis Community College; Pam Stinson, Northern Oklahoma College; Douglas Strayer, Henry Ford Community College; Sarah Syrjanen, Florida State University; Jonathan Taylor, Ferris State University; J. D. Thayer, Gonzaga University; Julie Tilton, San Bernardino Valley College; Larry A. Van Meter, Texas A&M University; William Verrone, University of North Carolina at Wilmington; Bradley Waltman, College of Southern Nevada; Phillippe West, Concordia University; C. White-Elliott, College of the Desert; Sharon Winn, Northeastern State University; Bertha Wise, Oklahoma City Community College; Pauline G. Woodward, Endicott College; Gulnar Zaman, Northern Virginia Community College; James H. Zorn, Bergen Community College; and our anonymous reviewer from Montclair State University.

Through all editions of *Making Literature Matter*, three things have stayed the same: what matters most to John Schilb is Wendy Elliot; what matters most to John Clifford is Janet Ellerby; and we dedicate this book to them.

John Schilb, Indiana University
John Clifford, University of North Carolina at Wilmington

We're All In. As Always.

Bedford/St. Martin's is as passionately committed to the discipline of English as ever, working hard to provide support and services that make it easier for you to teach your course your way.

Find **community support** at the Bedford/St. Martin's English Community (**community.macmillan.com**), where you can follow our *Bits* blog for new teaching ideas, download titles from our professional resource series, and review projects in the pipeline.

Choose **curriculum solutions** that offer flexible custom options, combining our carefully developed print and digital resources, acclaimed works from Macmillan's trade imprints, and your own course or program materials to provide the exact resources your students need.

Rely on **outstanding service** from your Bedford/St. Martin's sales representative and editorial team. Contact us or visit macmillanlearning.com to learn more about any of the options below.

Choose from alternative formats of *Making Literature Matter*. Bedford/St. Martin's offers a range of popular e-Book formats. For details of our e-Book partners, visit **macmillanlearning.com/ebooks**.

***Assign* LaunchPad Solo for Literature*—the online, interactive guide to close reading*—at launchpadworks.com.** To get the most out of *Making Literature Matter: An Anthology for Readers and Writers*, assign it with *LaunchPad Solo for Literature*, which can be packaged at **a significant discount**. With easy-to-use and easy-to-assign modules, reading comprehension quizzes, and engaging author videos, *LaunchPad Solo for Literature* guides students through three common assignment types: responding to a reading, drawing connections between two or more texts, and instructor-led collaborative close reading. Get all of our great resources and activities in one fully customizable space online; then use our tools with your own content. To learn more about how you can use *LaunchPad Solo for Literature* in your course, please see pages xv–xvi of this Preface.

Package one of our best-selling brief handbooks at a discount. Do you need a pocket-sized handbook for your course? Package *Easy Writer* by Andrea Lunsford or *A Pocket Style Manual* by Diana Hacker and Nancy Sommers with this text at a 20 percent discount. For more information, go to **macmillanlearning.com**.

Teach longer works at a nice price. Volumes in our literary reprint series—Bedford College Editions, Bedford Cultural Editions, Case Studies in Contemporary Criticism, Case Studies in Critical Controversy, the Bedford Series in History and Culture, and the Bedford Shakespeare Series—can be shrink-wrapped with *Making Literature Matter: An Anthology for Readers and Writers* at a discount. For a complete list of available titles, visit **macmillanlearning.com.**

Trade up and save 50 percent. Add more value and choice to your students' learning experiences by packaging their Bedford/St. Martin's textbook with one of a thousand titles from our sister publishers, including Farrar, Straus and Giroux and St. Martin's Press—at a discount of 50 percent off the regular price. Visit **macmillanlearning.com/tradeup** for details.

Engage your students with digital assignments. *Teaching Literature with Digital Technology* is a collection of digital assignments, each created by a contributor in the fields of literature and composition. Edited by Seattle-based scholar and teacher Tim Hetland and available as a print text or e-Book, this resource for instructors invites students to become knowledge-makers as it introduces creative uses of social media, digital tools, podcasts, multimodal assignments, and digital archives to learn about literature. Sample assignments can be viewed in the Professional Resources folder on the Macmillan English Community site. To order the print text, use ISBN 978-1-4576-2948-8; to order the e-Book, use ISBN 978-1-3190-7643-6.

Order content for your course management system. Content cartridges for the most common course management systems—Blackboard, Canvas, Angel, Moodle, Sakai, and Desire2Learn—allow you to easily download Bedford/St. Martin's digital materials for your course. For more information, visit **macmillanlearning.com**.

LaunchPad Solo
macmillan learning

PAIRING *MAKING LITERATURE MATTER* WITH *LAUNCHPAD SOLO FOR LITERATURE* HELPS STUDENTS SUCCEED.

Available at a significant discount when packaged with *Making Literature Matter, LaunchPad Solo for Literature* gets to the heart of close reading. It offers a set of online materials that help beginning literature students learn and practice close reading and critical thinking skills in an interactive environment.

To package *LaunchPad Solo for Literature*, use ISBN 978-1-319-07191-2.

How can *LaunchPad Solo for Literature* enhance your course?

IT HELPS STUDENTS COME PREPARED TO CLASS. Assign one of almost 500 reading comprehension quizzes on commonly taught stories, poems, plays, and essays to ensure that your students complete and understand their reading. For homework assignments, have students work through close reading modules that will prepare them for lively, informed classroom discussions.

IT GIVES STUDENTS HANDS-ON PRACTICE IN CLOSE READING. Easy-to-use and easy-to-assign modules based on widely taught literary selections guide students through three common assignment types:

- *Respond to a Reading* Questions in the margins that refer to specific passages in a publisher-provided literary work prompt students to read carefully and think critically about key issues raised by the text.
- *Draw Connections* Students read and compare two or more publisher-provided texts that illuminate each other. Students can download these texts, which have been annotated to highlight key moments and contextual information, and respond in writing to a series of questions that highlight important similarities and differences between and among the texts.

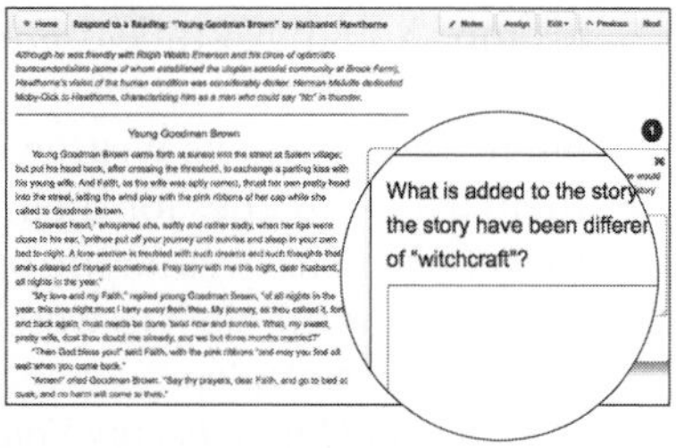

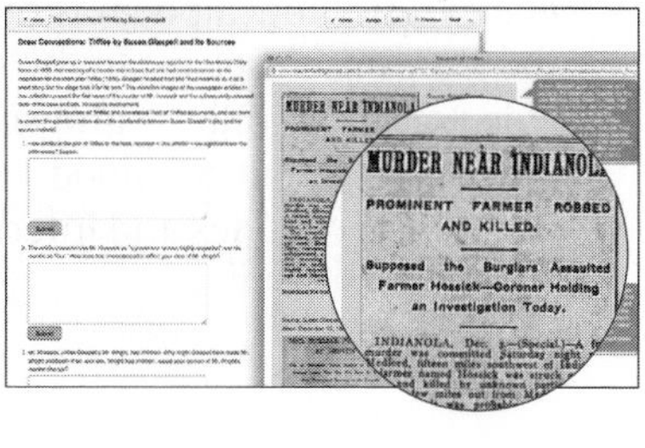

To explore *LaunchPad Solo for Literature*,
visit **launchpadworks.com**.

- *Collaborate on a Reading* Instructors can upload their favorite text or choose from over 200 publisher-provided texts to create a customized lesson on close reading. Using the highlighting tools and Notes feature in LaunchPad, the instructor can post notes or questions about specific passages or issues in a text, prompting students to respond with their own comments, questions, or observations. Students can also respond to each other, further collaborating and deepening their understanding of a text.

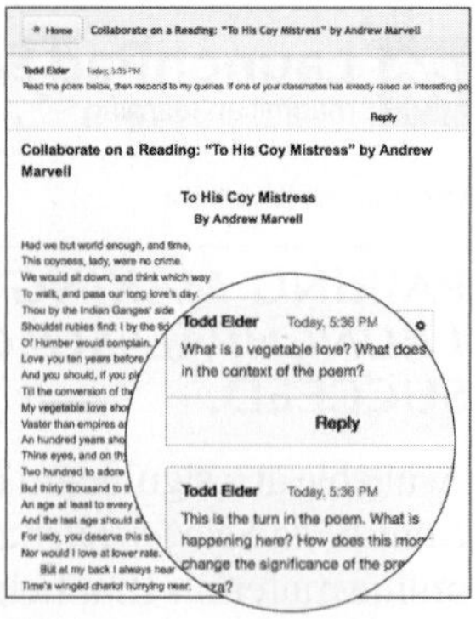

IT LETS YOU CREATE MULTIMEDIA ASSIGNMENTS ABOUT LITERATURE. *LaunchPad Solo for Literature* enables you to embed videos, including favorite selections from YouTube, directly into your digital course. Whether you want students to analyze a Shakespearean scene, listen to W. B. Yeats reading his poems, or compare *The Great Gatsby* in print and on film, the tools are at your fingertips. You can annotate these videos for your students, or ask them to leave their own comments directly on the video content itself. Consider some of these assignment suggestions:

- *Create a Dialogue around an Assignment.* Some projects are complicated because they involve many choices and stages. Record yourself explaining the project, and upload the video to the Video Assignment tool. Require students to comment by asking a question or by proposing a topic.
- *Critique a Video as a Group.* Embed a video from YouTube or from another source. In your assignment instructions, provide discussion questions. Require students to add 2–3 comments on the video that respond to the prompt. You may grade this assignment with a rubric.
- *Collaborate on Acting out a Scene from a Play.* Although students most often study plays as written texts, it can be fun and informative to have them act out scenes for their classmates. Assign small groups of students to record themselves acting out their favorite scene from a play and upload the video for the class to watch. You can add your feedback and comments directly on the video.
- *Compare and Share Poems Your Students Read Aloud.* Sound is essential in poetry, and how a poem is read can be as important to understanding as the words themselves. Invite students to record themselves—either using video or audio only—and share the results with the class. Consider giving each student a "mood" for their reading, so that the class can hear how different tones and interpretations affect their response to the poem.

Brief Contents

Contents

PART TWO Literature and Its Issues

Contents by Genre

Stories

Poems

Plays

Essays

Critical Commentaries

Cultural Contexts

Arguments on Current Issues

Full-Color Images

Making Literature Matter

AN ANTHOLOGY
FOR READERS AND WRITERS

PART ONE

Working with Literature

CHAPTER 1

What Is Literature? How and Why Does It Matter?

The title of this book, *Making Literature Matter*, may seem curious to you. Presumably your school assumes that literature already matters, for otherwise it would hardly offer courses in the subject. Quite possibly you are taking this course because you think literature is important or hope it will become so for you. But with our title, we want to emphasize that literature does not exist in a social vacuum. Rather, literature is part of human relationships; people *make* literature matter to other people. We are especially concerned with how you can make literature matter to others as well as to yourself. Above all, we point out ways you can argue about literature, both in class discussions and in your own writing.

Here is a poem that has engaged many readers, judging by how often it has appeared in literature anthologies since its first publication in 1963. The author is James Wright (1927–1980), who was born and raised in the industrial town of Martin's Ferry, Ohio, and won the Pulitzer Prize for poetry in 1972. Many of Wright's poems deal with the working-class life he experienced. Early in his career as a poet, he wrote in conventional forms, but later he became much more experimental. The following poem, perhaps Wright's most famous, is a case in point. The poem's speaker, you will see, comes to a judgment about whether he's managed to make his very existence matter.

JAMES WRIGHT

Lying in a Hammock at William Duffy's Farm in Pine Island, Minnesota

Over my head, I see the bronze butterfly,
Asleep on the black trunk,
Blowing like a leaf in green shadow.
Down the ravine behind the empty house,
The cowbells follow one another
Into the distances of the afternoon.
To my right,

In a field of sunlight between two pines,
The droppings of last year's horses
Blaze up into golden stones.
I lean back, as the evening darkens and comes on.
A chicken hawk floats over, looking for home.
I have wasted my life. *[1963]*

Did the last line startle you? For many readers, Wright's poem is memorable because its conclusion is unexpected, even jarring. At first glance, nothing in the speaker's description of his surroundings justifies his blunt self-condemnation at the end. If anything, the previous lines evoke rural tranquility, so that a more predictable finish would be "I am now at peace." Instead, the speaker suddenly criticizes himself. Intrigued by this mysterious move, readers usually look at the whole poem again, studying it for signs of growing despair. Often they debate with one another how the ending does relate to preceding lines. Thus, although the poem's speaker implies his life hasn't mattered, the poem itself has mattered to readers, plunging them into lively exchanges over how to interpret Wright's text.

We present Wright's poem to begin pointing out how literature can matter to people. We will keep referring to the poem in this introduction. But now we turn to three big questions:

- How have people defined *literature*?
- Why study literature in a college writing course?
- What can *you* do to make literature matter to others?

How Have People Defined *Literature*?

Asked to define *literature*, most people would include Wright's text, along with other poems. In addition to poetry, they would say *literature* encompasses fiction (novels as well as short stories) and drama. But limiting the term's scope to these genres can be misleading, for they are rooted in everyday life. Often they employ ordinary forms of talk, although they may play with such expressions and blend them with less common ones. Someone lying in a hammock may, in fact, recite details of the landscape—especially if he or she is talking to someone else on a cell phone, as is common nowadays. And quite possibly you have heard someone proclaim "I have wasted my life" or make a similar declaration. In any case, surely much of Wright's language is familiar to you, even if you haven't seen it arranged into these particular phrases and lines.

The genres regarded as literary are tied in other ways to everyday behavior. For instance, things function as symbols not only in poems but also in daily conversation. Even people who aren't poets have little trouble associating shadows, evening, darkness, and hawks with death. (In the case of Wright's poem, the issue then becomes whether the text supports or complicates this association.) Hammocks, too, are often treated as meaningful images. They are familiar symbols of "taking it easy." (With Wright's poem, the issue again becomes whether the speaker's hammock signifies *more* than just leisure.)

Throughout the day, then, it can be said that people put literary genres into practice. Perhaps you have commented on certain situations by quoting a song lyric or citing words from a poem, story, or play. Surely you are poetic in the sense that you use metaphors in your everyday conversations. After all, most of us are capable, as Wright's speaker is, of comparing a butterfly to a leaf (even if we aren't apt to compare horse droppings to "golden stones"). Probably you are often theatrical as well, carrying out various kinds of scripts and performing any number of roles. Furthermore, probably you are engaged in storytelling no matter how little fiction you actually write. Imagine this familiar situation: you are late for a meeting with friends because you got stuck in traffic, and now you must explain to them your delay. Your explanation may well become a tale of suspense, with you the hero racing against time to escape the bumper-to-bumper horde. As writer Joan Didion has observed, "We tell ourselves stories in order to live." Almost all of us spin narratives day after day because doing so helps us meaningfully frame our lives. (Unfortunately, the story that Wright's speaker tells is "I have wasted my life." Nevertheless, it's a means for interpreting his existence, and maybe somehow it helps him keep on living.)

You may admit that literature is grounded in real life and yet still tend to apply the term only to written texts of fiction, poetry, and drama. But this tendency is distinctly modern, for the term *literature* has not always been applied so restrictively. *Literature* was at first a characteristic of *readers*. From the term's emergence in the fourteenth century to the middle of the eighteenth, *literature* was more or less a synonym for *literacy*. People of literature were assumed to be well read.

In the late eighteenth century, however, the term's meaning changed. Increasingly it referred to books and other printed texts rather than to people who read them. At the beginning of this shift, the scope of literature was broad, encompassing nearly all public writing. But as the nineteenth century proceeded, the term's range shrank. More and more people considered literature to be imaginative or creative writing, which they distinguished from nonfiction. This trend did take years to build; in the early 1900s, literature anthologies still featured essays as well as excerpts from histories and biographies. By the mid-1900s, though, the narrower definition of literature prevailed.

This limited definition has become vulnerable. From the early 1970s, a number of literature faculty have called for widening it. In 1979, for instance, a National Endowment for the Humanities–Modern Language Association institute entitled "Women's Nontraditional Literature" applied the term *literature* to genres that had not been thought of as such. Participants studied essays, letters, diaries, autobiographies, and oral testimonies. To each of these genres, women have contributed much; in fact, the institute's participants concluded that a literature curriculum slights many works by women if it focuses on fiction, poetry, and drama alone.

Of course, even within these three categories, the term *literature* has been selectively applied. Take the case of novelist and short-story writer Stephen King, whose books have sold millions of copies. Despite his commercial success, a lot of readers—including some of his fans—refuse to call King's writing literature.

They assume that to call something literature is to say that it has artistic merit, and for them King's tales of horror fall short.

Yet people who use the term *literature* as a compliment may still disagree about whether a certain text deserves it. Plenty of readers do praise King's writing as literature, even as others deem it simply entertainment. In short, artistic standards differ. To be sure, some works have been constantly admired through the years; regarded as classics, they are frequently taught in literature classes. *Hamlet* and other plays by William Shakespeare are obvious examples. But in the last twenty years, much controversy has arisen over the *literary canon*, those works taught again and again. Are there good reasons why the canon has consisted mostly of works by white men? Or have the principles of selection been skewed by sexism and racism? Should the canon be changed to accommodate a greater range of authors? Or should literary studies resist having any canon at all? These questions have provoked various answers and continued debate.

Also in question are attempts to separate literature from *nonfiction*. Much nonfiction shows imagination and relies on devices found in novels, short stories, poems, and plays. The last few years have seen the emergence of the term *creative nonfiction* as a synonym for essays, autobiographies, histories, and journalistic accounts that use evocative language and strong narratives. Conversely, works of fiction, poetry, and drama may center on real-life events. For example, beginning with James Wright's "Lying in a Hammock," several of the poems in our book can easily be seen as autobiographical. Perhaps you have suspected already that the speaker in Wright's poem is Wright himself. In numerous interviews, Wright admitted as much. He acknowledged that he based the poem on his own experience of lying in a hammock, which really did lead him to think "I have wasted my life."

A note of caution is in order. While testimony such as Wright's can be illuminating, it should be used prudently. In crucial respects, Wright's poem still differs from Wright's life. The text is a representation of his experience, not the experience itself. His particular choice and arrangement of words continue to merit study, especially because he could have depicted his experience in plenty of other ways. As critic Charles Altieri notes, important to specify are the ways in which a poem is "binding the forms of syntax to the possibilities of feeling." Keep in mind, too, that the author of a work is not always the ideal guide to it. After all, the work may matter to its readers by raising for them issues and ideas that the author did not foresee. Besides, often the author's comments about the text leave certain aspects of it unexplained. Though Wright disclosed his poem's origins, readers must still decide how to connect its various images to its final line. Even so, "Lying in a Hammock" confirms that a literary work can stem from actual circumstances, whatever use the reader makes of facts about them.

Some people argue, however, that literature about real events is still "literary" because it inspires contemplation rather than action. This view of literature has traditionally been summed up as "art for art's sake." This notion brushes aside, however, all the poems, novels, short stories, and plays that encourage audiences to undertake certain acts. Included in our book, for example, is Sherman Alexie's "Capital Punishment," a poem designed to spark resistance to the death penalty. True, not every poem is so conspicuously action-oriented. Wright's "Lying in a

Hammock" seems more geared toward reflection, especially because the speaker is physically reclining while he observes nature and ponders his life. But readers may take even this poem as an incitement to change their behavior, so that they can feel they have not wasted their own lives.

In our book, we resist endorsing a single definition of *literature.* Rather, we encourage you to review and perhaps rethink what the term means to you. At the same time, to expand the realm of literature, we include several essays in addition to short stories, poems, and plays. We also present numerous critical commentaries as well as various historical documents. Throughout the book, we invite you to make connections among these different kinds of texts. You need not treat them as altogether separate species.

What Makes Literature "Literature"?

We have suggested that, in some respects, literature can resemble other writing. So, too, can it resemble ordinary speech. Still, literature can be viewed as a distinct category, even if controversies arise over what specific texts belong to it. Usually, works classified as literature permit the reader to treat their characters as imaginary. Just as often, these works' use of language is especially skillful and challenging. Through their style, they dramatically depict people, situations, and settings, emotionally drawing their readers in. At the same time, many of the words in such texts can have more than one meaning. They might be ambiguous, symbolic, or metaphorical. Furthermore, the main characters are often complicated, even mysterious. Their acts, relationships, and motives defy simple diagnosis. Typically, just as complex is any "lesson" these works teach. They illuminate life, but they do so by showing how it resists reduction to clichés or other slogans. Furthermore, the basic design of these works may not be immediately clear. Their patterns may be detectable only after repeated reading. Overall, a literary work tends to make its readers *analyze* it, *interpret* it. They may then disagree about its meaning and impact. Indeed, we hope that our own literary selections will spark debates in your class.

To point out a literary work's special features, we turn to a poem that dramatizes the exasperation many people feel when wildlife destroys their farms, gardens, or yards. Entitled "Woodchucks," the poem is by Maxine Kumin (1925–2014) and appears in her 1982 collection *Our Ground Time Here Will Be Brief.*

MAXINE KUMIN

Woodchucks

Gassing the woodchucks didn't turn out right.
The knockout bomb from the Feed and Grain Exchange
was featured as merciful, quick at the bone
and the case we had against them was airtight,
both exits shoehorned shut with puddingstone,°
but they had a sub-sub-basement out of range.

5 puddingstone: Cement mixed with pebbles.

Next morning they turned up again, no worse
for the cyanide than we for our cigarettes
and state-store Scotch, all of us up to scratch.
They brought down the marigolds as a matter of course
and then took over the vegetable patch
nipping the broccoli shoots, beheading the carrots.

The food from our mouths, I said, righteously thrilling
to the feel of the .22, the bullets' neat noses.
I, a lapsed pacifist fallen from grace
puffed with Darwinian° pieties for killing,
now drew a bead on the littlest woodchuck's face.
He died down in the everbearing roses.

Ten minutes later I dropped the mother. She
flipflopped in the air and fell, her needle teeth
still hooked in a leaf of early Swiss chard.
Another baby next. O one-two-three
the murderer inside me rose up hard,
the hawkeye killer came on stage forthwith.

There's one chuck left. Old wily fellow, he keeps
me cocked and ready day after day after day.
All night I hunt his humped-up form. I dream
I sight along the barrel in my sleep.
If only they'd all consented to die unseen
gassed underground the quiet Nazi way. *[1972]*

16 Darwinian: Charles Darwin (1809–1882), an English naturalist who first theorized about evolution and natural selection.

☰ THINKING ABOUT THE TEXT

Here are just a few of the questions that "Woodchucks" provokes. Choose one of them. Then, take ten minutes or so and freewrite an answer to it, supporting your statements with specific words from the poem.

1. In line 4, the word *case* evidently refers to a method of entrapping the woodchucks, but probably it also refers to the speaker's reasons for hunting them. How good are her reasons? What might be the "case" for *not* killing these animals?
2. What key changes — psychological as well as physical — does the speaker go through in her campaign to get rid of the woodchucks?
3. To what extent does the speaker suggest that her feelings are mixed and even in conflict?
4. Presumably the last line alludes to the mass exterminations of the Holocaust. What would you say to someone who argues that this is an inappropriate, even tasteless, way to end a poem about woodchucks?

Of course, Kumin is by no means the only person who has ever written about the ethical and practical issues involved in killing woodchucks. For example, in a lengthy June 5, 2008, *New York Times* article entitled "Peter Rabbit Must Die," reporter Joyce Wadler tells stories about various people she interviewed who had to decide whether and how to exterminate woodchucks or other invaders of their turf. In 2013, a Wisconsin legislator drafted legislation that would remove woodchucks from the state's protected species list and permit hunting or trapping of them ten months out of the year. As you might expect, his proposed bill proved controversial; numerous bloggers argued for and against it. And woodchucks, for the present, still remain a protected species on the state's most recent published list (2015). But Kumin's poem differs from a news report, a statute, or an opinion piece about woodchucks in ways that for many readers would establish it as more literary:

- While news articles such as Wadler's are arranged in paragraphs, "Woodchucks" proceeds through stanzas. This kind of structure, common in poetry, draws attention to words that begin and end lines.
- Like many poems, Kumin's also includes words that stand out because they rhyme (e.g., "scratch" and "patch," "grace" and "face"), virtually echo (e.g., "Gassing" and "gassed"), or begin with the same sound, a pattern known as alliteration (e.g., "bomb" and "bone," "food" and "feel," "neat" and "noses").
- In addition, some words in this poem seem to have multiple meanings. For example, "right" in the first line can mean not only "efficient" but also "ethical," just as "airtight" can mean "perfect" in a *practical* sense as well as "indisputable" in a *philosophical* sense.
- In reading Wadler's article or the legislator's bill or the blogs debating it, you are apt to be chiefly aware of these texts' *content*. Most readers of Kumin's poem are at least as concerned with its *form*. Most of them would linger over the language of "Woodchucks" more than they would over the news report's style. Noteworthy, for instance, is how the speaker looks back ironically on her own language ("The food from our mouths, I said, righteously thrilling"), thereby casting doubt on its logic. And of course, her concluding analogy to the Nazis jolts; it pushes readers to wonder how much the entire poem has been about Hitler's genocidal regime.
- Many news articles describe their subjects' thoughts rather broadly. For instance, the typical person in Wadler's piece is someone who wants to get rid of intrusive woodchucks but looks for humane ways of doing the deed. Kumin's speaker, on the other hand, seems to go through a complex series of psychological stages; her thoughts seem more intricate than those of Wadler's interviewees.
- Kumin's speaker, like many characters in literature, is hard to pigeonhole. Wadler identifies her interview subjects as particular individuals, but like many reporters she ultimately seems more interested in them as examples of basic human types. Describing an artist who actually spoke

to the woodchucks on his property—warning them to flee before he shot them—she says that this man's tale "is not as unusual as some would like to believe." She thereby suggests that he is a common sort of person afflicted by pests: the sensitive soul driven to fight back. Similarly, in describing some opponents of the proposed Wisconsin bill who attended a hearing about it, Associated Press reporter Todd Richmond labeled them as merely "a handful of animal lovers" who were "blasting the measure." Hardly a profile of psychological depth! Given the words that Kumin's speaker uses and the various patterns they take, her speaker requires more figuring out.

- Whereas news writers surely expect you to assume that their interviewees are real, you don't have to take Kumin's speaker as such. This figure may reflect the poet's own experience to some extent, for Kumin operated a farm in New Hampshire and so perhaps hunted pests herself. Still, you are free to see her central character as fictive. This possibility enables you to speculate long and broadly about the speaker's psyche—including ideas and feelings of hers that she may not be quite aware of. Notice that after referring to "we," she eventually shifts to "I," a change that may be unconscious but that nonetheless implies she has become personally obsessed. Because you can see the poem's speaker as imaginary, you are also free to entertain various responses to her. If she were an actual person—someone you knew or might someday meet—you might feel compelled to make a single, fast judgment about her. The poem, however, lets you access her thinking while not pressuring you to decide quickly how ethical she is. Your attitudes toward her can shift, clash, and blend more than if her acts had real-life effects. In this respect, "Woodchucks" is a thought experiment, as are most literary works. Still, in exercising your interpretive powers, such texts help you cope with the world. They heighten your awareness of the ways in which it, too, demands careful study.

We are *not* saying that poems are always superior to news reports and other true-life texts. That would be an excessive claim. But, as "Woodchucks" demonstrates, literary works often lead you to grapple with more extensive and trickier questions—thereby offering you much to address in your own writing.

To help you think further about what distinguishes literature from other writing, let's turn to a short fictional piece. Its author, Ted Chiang (b. 1967), is primarily known as a writer of science fiction. His 1998 short story "Story of Your Life" won the prestigious Nebula and Theodore Sturgeon Memorial Awards; it is also the basis of the 2016 film *Arrival.* The following work by Chiang originally accompanied a video installation by the team of Jennifer Allora and Guillermo Calzadilla. On multiple screens, these artists provocatively juxtaposed pictures of Puerto Rico's Arecibo radio telescope with images of an endangered parrot species in a neighboring forest. Chiang's text was then published in *e-flux journal* and subsequently chosen for *The Best American Short Stories 2016.* As you read, consider these questions: Do you consider Chiang's text to be *literature*? Why, or why not? You might bear in mind a comment that another writer of fiction, Lydia

Davis, made in a 2008 interview with *The Believer* magazine. "It's a hard thing to define," she remarked, "but to be simple about it, I would say a story has to have a bit of narrative, if only 'she says,' and then enough of a creation of a different time and place to transport the reader." By your own standards, is "The Great Silence" indeed a *story*? Why, or why not?

TED CHIANG

The Great Silence

The humans use Arecibo to look for extraterrestrial intelligence. Their desire to make a connection is so strong that they've created an ear capable of hearing across the universe.

But I and my fellow parrots are right here. Why aren't they interested in listening to our voices?

We're a nonhuman species capable of communicating with them. Aren't we exactly what humans are looking for?

*

The universe is so vast that intelligent life must surely have arisen many times. The universe is also so old that even one technological species would have had time to expand and fill the galaxy. Yet there is no sign of life anywhere except on Earth. Humans call this the Fermi paradox.

One proposed solution to the Fermi paradox is that intelligent species actively try to conceal their presence, to avoid being targeted by hostile invaders.

Speaking as a member of a species that has been driven nearly to extinction by humans, I can attest that this is a wise strategy.

It makes sense to remain quiet and avoid attracting attention.

*

The Fermi paradox is sometimes known as the Great Silence. The universe ought to be a cacophony of voices, but instead it's disconcertingly quiet.

Some humans theorize that intelligent species go extinct before they can expand into outer space. If they're correct, then the hush of the night sky is the silence of a graveyard.

Hundreds of years ago, my kind was so plentiful that the Rio Abajo forest resounded with our voices. Now we're almost gone. Soon this rainforest may be as silent as the rest of the universe.

*

There was an African Grey Parrot named Alex. He was famous for his cognitive abilities. Famous among humans, that is.

A human researcher named Irene Pepperberg spent thirty years studying Alex. She found that not only did Alex know the words for shapes and colors, he actually understood the concepts of shape and color.

Many scientists were skeptical that a bird could grasp abstract concepts. Humans like to think they're unique. But eventually Pepperberg convinced them that Alex wasn't just repeating words, that he understood what he was saying.

Out of all my cousins, Alex was the one who came closest to being taken seriously as a communication partner by humans.

Alex died suddenly, when he was still relatively young. The evening before he died, Alex said to Pepperberg, "You be good. I love you."

If humans are looking for a connection with a non-human intelligence, what more can they ask for than that?

*

Every parrot has a unique call that it uses to identify itself; biologists refer to this as the parrot's "contact call."

In 1974, astronomers used Arecibo to broadcast a message into outer space intended to demonstrate human intelligence. That was humanity's contact call.

In the wild, parrots address each other by name. One bird imitates another's contact call to get the other bird's attention.

If humans ever detect the Arecibo message being sent back to Earth, they will know someone is trying to get their attention.

*

Parrots are vocal learners: we can learn to make new sounds after we've heard them. It's an ability that few animals possess. A dog may understand dozens of commands, but it will never do anything but bark.

Humans are vocal learners, too. We have that in common. So humans and parrots share a special relationship with sound. We don't simply cry out. We pronounce. We enunciate.

Perhaps that's why humans built Arecibo the way they did. A receiver doesn't have to be a transmitter, but Arecibo is both. It's an ear for listening, and a mouth for speaking.

*

Humans have lived alongside parrots for thousands of years, and only recently have they considered the possibility that we might be intelligent.

I suppose I can't blame them. We parrots used to think humans weren't very bright. It's hard to make sense of behavior that's so different from your own.

But parrots are more similar to humans than any extraterrestrial species will be, and humans can observe us up close; they can look us in the eye. How do they expect to recognize an alien intelligence if all they can do is eavesdrop from a hundred light years away?

*

It's no coincidence that "aspiration" means both hope and the act of breathing.

When we speak, we use the breath in our lungs to give our thoughts a physical form. The sounds we make are simultaneously our intentions and our life force.

I speak, therefore I am. Vocal learners, like parrots and humans, are perhaps the only ones who fully comprehend the truth of this.

*

There's a pleasure that comes with shaping sounds with your mouth. It's so primal and visceral that throughout their history, humans have considered the activity a pathway to the divine.

Pythagorean mystics believed that vowels represented the music of the spheres, and chanted to draw power from them.

Pentecostal Christians believe that when they speak in tongues, they're speaking the language used by angels in Heaven.

Brahmin Hindus believe that by reciting mantras, they're strengthening the building blocks of reality.

Only a species of vocal learners would ascribe such importance to sound in their mythologies. We parrots can appreciate that.

*

According to Hindu mythology, the universe was created with a sound: "Om." It's a syllable that contains within it everything that ever was and everything that will be.

When the Arecibo telescope is pointed at the space between stars, it hears a faint hum.

Astronomers call that the "cosmic microwave background." It's the residual radiation of the Big Bang, the explosion that created the universe fourteen billion years ago.

But you can also think of it as a barely audible reverberation of that original "Om." That syllable was so resonant that the night sky will keep vibrating for as long as the universe exists.

When Arecibo is not listening to anything else, it hears the voice of creation.

*

We Puerto Rican Parrots have our own myths. They're simpler than human mythology, but I think humans would take pleasure from them.

Alas, our myths are being lost as my species dies out. I doubt the humans will have deciphered our language before we're gone.

So the extinction of my species doesn't just mean the loss of a group of birds. It's also the disappearance of our language, our rituals, our traditions. It's the silencing of our voice.

*

Human activity has brought my kind to the brink of extinction, but I don't blame them for it. They didn't do it maliciously. They just weren't paying attention.

And humans create such beautiful myths; what imaginations they have. Perhaps that's why their aspirations are so immense. Look at Arecibo. Any species who can build such a thing must have greatness within it.

My species probably won't be here for much longer; it's likely that we'll die before our time and join the Great Silence. But before we go, we are sending a message to humanity. We just hope the telescope at Arecibo will enable them to hear it.

The message is this:

You be good. I love you. *[2015]*

Why Study Literature in a College Writing Course?

We assume you are reading this book in a course aimed at helping you write. Quite likely the course is meant to prepare you for writing assignments throughout college, including papers in fields beyond English. It's natural to wonder how reading literature serves this purpose.

Much academic writing is, in fact, based on reading. You'll find the two interconnected in course after course. Many classes will ask you to produce essays that analyze published texts. To *analyze* means going beyond your first impressions, carefully noting a text's ideas, techniques, and effects. You'll also find yourself needing to *synthesize*: that is, to trace how the text is patterned, as well as how it relates to other works. Together, these acts of analysis and synthesis have been called reading *closely*, a process we explain and model in Chapter 2. We encourage you to practice this method with the selections in our book.

Often, college courses will ask you to write about some text that isn't easily understood. The purpose of your paper will be to help other readers of the text grasp its meanings and, perhaps, judge its worth. Literature is a good training ground for these skills of interpretation and evaluation. The poems, stories, plays, and essays in this book repeatedly invite inquiry. They don't settle for delivering simple straightforward messages. Rather, they offer puzzles, complications, metaphors, symbols, and mysteries, thereby recognizing that life is complex. In particular, literary works encourage you to ponder the multiple dimensions of language: how, for example, a word's meaning can vary depending on context. Furthermore, much literature can help you understand your own life and conduct it better. In this capacity, literature serves as "equipment for living," scholar-critic Kenneth Burke's description of its function.

Some people *dislike* literature because they find it too vague and indirect. They resent that it often forces them to figure out symbols and implications when they would rather have ideas presented outright. Perhaps you wish the speaker in Wright's poem had made clear why his observations prompted him to criticize himself. But in life, truth can be complicated and elusive. In many ways, literature is most realistic when it suggests the same. Besides, many readers—perhaps including you—appreciate literature most when it resists simple decoding, forcing them to adopt new assumptions and learn new methods of analysis. Indeed, throughout this book we suggest that the most interesting and profitable conversations about literature are those in which the issues are not easily resolved. One of the best things your course can provide you and your classmates is the chance to exchange insights about texts such as Wright's.

We have been suggesting that one value of studying literature in a writing class is that it often engages not just thought but feeling. The two interweave so that readers find themselves engaging in interpretation and evaluation because they *care* about lives depicted in the text. Most of the works in this book appeal to your emotions, encouraging you to identify with certain characters, to be disturbed by others, and to wonder what happens next in the plot. Indeed, many readers of literature prize the moments that make them them laugh or cry or gasp as well as think. To be sure, it can be argued that the most worthwhile literature gets us to comprehend, and perhaps even appreciate, certain kinds of people who would normally confuse or disturb us. Perhaps you would never say to yourself, "I have wasted my life"; all the same, you may find it valuable to analyze how Wright's speaker reaches this conclusion. "When it's the real thing," critic Frank Lentricchia suggests, "literature enlarges us, strips the film of familiarity from the world; creates bonds of sympathy with all kinds, even with evil characters, who we learn are all in the family." This "enlargement" is both intellectual *and* emotional.

Finally, writing about literature is good training for other fields because literary analysis often involves taking an interdisciplinary perspective. A typical interpretation of James Wright's poem, for example, will bring in principles of psychology to explain the speaker's frame of mind. Similarly, to evaluate his statement "I have wasted my life," readers find themselves grappling with the philosophical question of what constitutes a "productive" or "good" life. Moreover, the poem's farm setting has economic, political, historical, and sociological significance, for much less of the world's population performs agricultural labor than was the case a century ago. Wright's brief text can even play a role in studies of cross-cultural relationships, for as Sven Birkerts has pointed out, the poem is one of several experiments the poet tried with Chinese literary forms.

What Can *You* Do to Make Literature Matter to Others?

In an 1895 essay called "The Art of Fiction," the American novelist, short-story writer, and critic Henry James wrote, "Art lives upon discussion, upon experiment, upon curiosity, upon variety of attempt, upon the exchange of views and the comparison of standpoints." Certainly James was suggesting that the creators of literature play a big role in making it matter. But he was suggesting, too, that plenty of other people contribute to literature's impact. Today, these people include publishers, printers, agents, advertisers, librarians, professional reviewers, bookstore staff, Internet chat groups, and even show-business figures such as Oprah Winfrey, who has interested millions of viewers in participating in her "book club." Teachers of literature also make it matter—or at least they try to. Perhaps your parents or other family members have contributed to your appreciation of certain literary texts; many adults introduce their children and grandchildren to books they loved when young. Moreover, friends often recommend works of literature to one another.

Again, we concede that some people think of literature negatively, believing that it matters in a way they don't like. The ancient Greek philosopher Plato wanted to ban poets from his ideal republic because he thought they merely imitated truth. Throughout subsequent history, various groups have tried to abolish or censor much literature. In communities across the contemporary United States, pressure groups have succeeded in removing particular novels from library shelves, including classics such as Mark Twain's *Adventures of Huckleberry Finn* and J. D. Salinger's *The Catcher in the Rye*. History has also seen many writers killed, jailed, or harassed for their work. In recent years, the most conspicuous example of such persecution has been the Ayatollah Khomeini's indictment of author Salman Rushdie. In 1989, the ayatollah was so enraged by the portrayal of Islam in Rushdie's novel *The Satanic Verses* that he commanded his followers to hunt Rushdie down and slay him. Even after the ayatollah died, Rushdie was in danger, for the *fatwa* against him remained in effect. Not until eight years after the original edict did the Iranian government back away from it. At present, Rushdie still enjoys only a limited measure of safety, and the affair stands as a reminder that some writers risk their lives. Ironically, the ayatollah's execution order was a sort of homage to literature, a fearsome way of crediting it with the power to shape thinking.

Our book aims to help you join the conversations that Henry James saw as nourishing literature. More specifically, our book focuses on helping you argue about literature, whether your audience is your classmates, your teacher, or other people. While arguments involve real or potential disagreement, they need not be waged like wars. When we use the term *argument* in this book, we have in mind civilized efforts through which people try to make their views persuasive. When you argue about literature, you are carefully reasoning with others, helping them see how a certain text should matter to them.

In particular, we have much to say about you as a writer. A key goal of your course, we assume, is to help you compose more effective texts of your own. By writing arguments about literature, you make it matter to others. Moreover, you learn about yourself as you analyze a literary text and negotiate other readers' views of it. We emphasize that, at its best, arguing is a process of inquiry for everyone involved. Both you and your audience may wind up changing your minds.

WRITING ASSIGNMENTS

1. Write a brief essay in which you explain what you value in literature by focusing on why you like a particular literary work. Don't worry about whether you are defining *literature* correctly. This exercise will help you begin to review the values you hold as you read a work that you regard as literary.
2. Sometimes a literary work matters to you in one way when you first read it and in another way when you read it again. Write a brief essay in which you discuss a work that you interpreted differently when you reread it. What significance did it have for you the first time? What was its significance later? What about your life changed between the two readings? If you cannot think of a literary work, choose a film you have seen.
3. Write a brief essay in which you identify the values that a previous literature teacher of yours seemed to hold. Be sure to identify, too, ways in which the teacher expressed these values. You may want to bring up one or more specific events that took place in the teacher's classroom.
4. Many bookstores sell computer-instruction manuals. Examine one of these. Do you consider it literature? Write a brief essay answering this question. Be sure to explain how you are defining *literature* and to refer to the manual's specific features.

5. Visit a bookstore at your school or in your town. Spend at least half an hour looking at books in various sections of the store, noting how the publishers of these works try to make them matter. Look at such things as the books' physical formats, the language on their covers, and any introductory material they include. Write a brief essay in which you identify and evaluate the strategies for "mattering" used by at least three of these books.
6. Visit a Web site that includes readers' comments about particular works of fiction. A good example is www.amazon.com, a commercial online "bookstore." Another good site is Oprah Winfrey's, www.oprah.com, which features extensive exchanges about novels she has chosen for her "book club." At whatever site you visit, choose a novel or short-story collection that has attracted many reader comments. Write a brief essay in which you identify the values that seem reflected in the comments. In what respects does literature seem to matter to these readers? What do they evidently hope to find in it?

SUMMING UP: WHAT IS LITERATURE?

- **Literature encompasses poetry, fiction, and plays — but may also encompass other genres, such as nonfiction essays.** This book does not endorse a single definition of *literature* but encourages you to review and perhaps rethink what the term means to you. (pp. 3–4)
- **Literary texts tend to show certain characteristics more than other texts, such as news articles, do.** For example, they call attention to their form; they explore the multiple meanings of words; they present psychological complexity; and they require interpretation. (pp. 7–11)
- **Studying literature in a college writing course makes sense for several reasons.** Many other courses require you to write about reading; literature offers you ground for developing skills of interpretation and evaluation that many college writing assignments demand; literature serves as "equipment for living"; reading it engages both thought and feeling; and literary analysis is often interdisciplinary. (pp. 14–15)
- **The *literary canon* — works taught again and again as great art — is nowadays being reevaluated.** (p. 5)
- **Understanding literature involves collaboration with other readers and comparison with other texts.** (pp. 14–15)
- **Thinking about literature is enhanced and clarified by writing about it.** (p. 16)
- **The most effective arguments about literature involve inquiry, not rancor and battle.** (p. 16)

CHAPTER 2

How to Read Closely

Courses in many disciplines ask for *close reading*. But literature classes strongly emphasize it — one reason they are good preparation for other fields. Nevertheless, the steps involved in close reading are not always clear to students. Perhaps you have been told to engage in this process without knowing what it entails. Because close reading is central to literary studies, plays a big role in other courses, and yet remains murky for many students, this chapter both explains it and models it.

If you are taking a course that asks you to *write* about the literary works you study, close reading of them will help you form ideas about them worth spreading to *your* audiences. Such reading will also help you decide what details of these texts will best support your points about them. So, as we proceed to explain close reading, we treat it mainly as what some would call a method of invention. It's a way for you, as a *writer*, to discover things to say about literature.

Basic Strategies for Close Reading

Actually, close reading consists of not one strategy but several. All of them can help you gain insights into a literary work, which you might then convey through your writing. You need not follow these strategies in the order we list them here, but try each of them.

1. Make predictions as you read. That is, guess what will happen and how the text will turn out. If you wind up being surprised, fine. You may get a richer understanding of the text as you reflect on how it *defies* your expectations.

2. Reread the text. Reread the text several times, focusing each time on a different element of the text and using at least one of these occasions to read aloud. Few readers of a literary work can immediately see everything important and interesting in it. You greatly increase your chances of getting ideas about a text if you read it again and again. At first, you may be preoccupied with following the plot or with figuring out the text's main theme. Only by examining the text repeatedly may you notice several of its other aspects, including features that really stir your thoughts. But don't try to study everything in the text each time you look at it. Use each reading of it to study just one characteristic. In an early stage, for example, you might trace the text's repetitions, and then you might use a later reading to pinpoint its ambiguous words. This division of labor can, in the end, generate many insights that a less focused approach would not.

Reading all of the text or portions of it out loud gives you a better sense of how the text is manipulating language. Reading aloud is especially useful in the case of poems, for you may detect rhymes or soundalike words that you would not notice when reading silently.

3. Test the text against your own experiences. Keep in mind your experiences, beliefs, assumptions, and values as you read the text, but note ways that it challenges or complicates these things. When you first read a particular literary work, your interpretations and judgments are bound to be influenced by your personal background. This includes your beliefs, assumptions, and values, as well as things that have happened to you. Indeed, many people read a literary work hoping they can personally identify with the characters, situations, and views it presents. This is an understandable goal. Pay attention, though, to details of the text that do *not* match your life and current thinking. After all, the author may be deliberately challenging or complicating readers' habitual attitudes. In any case, parts of the text that are hard to identify with will often provide you with great subjects when you write about the work. Bear in mind, though, that you will not interest your readers if you simply criticize characters in the work or sneer at other elements of it. In particular, try not to sum up characters with negative labels such as *immoral*, *weird*, or *sick*. These terms often strike readers as reflecting mere prejudice—a poor substitute for careful analysis of human complexity.

4. Look for patterns in the text and disruptions of them. Many a literary work is organized by various patterns, which may not be evident on first reading. In fact, you might not detect a number of these patterns until you read the text several times. You may even see these better if you move back and forth in the text instead of just reading it straight through. Typically, a literary work's patterns include repetitions of words and of actions; oppositions; words similar or related in meaning; and technical methods of organization (such as rhyme schemes or frequent use of flashbacks). Just as important to note are moments in the text that are inconsistent with one or more of its patterns. Locate and think about places where the work makes a significant shift in meaning, imagery, tone, plot, a character's behavior, narrative point of view, or even physical format (for example, a change in rhyme scheme).

5. Note ambiguities. These are places where the text's meaning is not crystal clear and therefore calls for interpretation: for example, words that can have more than one definition; symbols that have multiple implications; and actions that suggest various things about a character.

6. Consider the author's alternatives. That is, think about what the author *could* have done and yet did not do. The author of a literary work faces all sorts of decisions in composing it. And as you study the work, you will have more to say about it if you think about those choices. Try, then, to compare the author's handling of particular passages to other possible treatments of them. By considering, for example, why the author chose a certain word over others, you may better detect implications and effects of the author's actual language. Similarly, by reflecting on how the author *might* have portrayed a certain character more simplistically, you strengthen your ability to analyze the character's variety of traits.

7. Ask questions. As you read, generate questions that have more than one possible answer. When we first read a literary work, most of us try to get comfortable with it. We search for passages that are clear; we groan when we encounter ones that are mysterious or confusing. Sooner or later, though, we must confront puzzles in the text if we are to analyze it in depth. Furthermore, if we plan to *write* about the text, we are more likely to come up with ideas worth communicating to our readers if we present ourselves as helping them deal with matters *not* immediately clear. After all, our audience will not need our analysis if it centers on what's obvious. Therefore, list multiple questions that the work raises for you, especially ones that have various possible answers. Then, if you focus on addressing one of these questions in your writing—providing and supporting your own particular answer to it—your readers will find value in turning to *your* text. Furthermore, when you come across literary passages that seem easy to understand, consider how they might actually involve more than one possible meaning. Even little words may prove ambiguous and, therefore, worth analyzing in your writing. Of course, you may have to consult a dictionary in order to see the different meanings that a word can have.

The questions you come up with need hardly be restricted to matters of the work's "theme." After all, most any literary text worth studying can't be reduced to a single message. Often, such texts play with multiple ideas, perhaps emphasizing tensions among them. Therefore, it may make more sense for you to refer to a work's *themes*. Actually, as we have been suggesting throughout our catalog of reading strategies, any literary text has several other features. As a writer, you may wind up with much more to say about a literary work if you consider one or more of these other elements: for example, facts obscured or absent in the text; possible definitions of key words; symbols; patterns; evaluations to be made of the characters or the overall work; the text's historical and cultural context; the text's genre; its relevance to current political debates; and cause-effect relationships. In the next chapter, we explain these elements at greater length, identifying them as *issues* you might write about.

8. Jot down possible answers. Even while reading the text, begin developing and pulling together your thoughts by informally writing about it. See if you can generate not only good questions but also tentative answers to them. Writing need not be the final outcome of your reflections on a literary work. You can jot down ideas about the text even as you first encounter it. Such informal, preliminary writing can actually help you generate insights into the text that you would not have achieved simply by scanning it. The following are some of the specific things you might do:

- *Make notes in the text itself.* A common method is to mark key passages, either by underlining these passages or by running a highlighter over them. Both ways of marking are popular because they help readers recall main features of the text. But use these techniques moderately if you use them at all, for marking lots of passages will leave you unable to distinguish the really important parts of the text. Also, try "talking back" to the text in its margins. Next to particular passages, you might jot down words of your own, indicating any feelings and questions you have about those parts. On any page of the text, you might circle related words and then draw lines between these words to emphasize their connection. If a word or an idea shows up on numerous pages, you might circle it each time. Furthermore, try cross-referencing by listing on at least one page the numbers of all those pages where the word or idea appears.

- *As you read the text, occasionally look away from it and jot down anything in it you recall.* This memory exercise lets you review your developing impressions of the text. When you turn back to its actual words, you may find that you have distorted or overlooked aspects of it that you should take into account.
- *At various moments in your reading, freewrite about the text for ten minutes or so.* Spontaneously explore your preliminary thoughts and feelings about it, as well as any personal experiences the text leads you to recall. One logical moment to do freewriting is when you have finished reading the text. But you do not have to wait until then; as you read, you might pause occasionally to freewrite. This way, you give yourself an opportunity to develop and review your thoughts about the text early on.
- *Create a "dialectical notebook."* So named by composition theorist Ann Berthoff, it involves using pages of your regular notebook in a particular way. On each page, draw a line down the middle to create two columns. In the left column, list various details of the text: specifically, words, images, characters, and events that strike you. In the right column, jot down for each detail one or more sentences indicating *why* you were drawn to it. Take as many pages as you need to record and reflect on your observations. You can also use the two-column format to carry out a dialogue with yourself about the text. This is an especially good way to ponder aspects of the text that you find confusing, mysterious, or complex.
- *Play with the text by revising it.* Doing so will make you more aware of options that the author rejected and will give you a better sense of the moves that the author chose to make. Specifically, you might rearrange parts of the text, add to it, change some of its words, or shift its narrative point of view. After you revise the text, compare your alternative version with the original, considering especially differences in their effects.

Close Readings of a Poem

To demonstrate what it means to read closely, we present observations that various students made about a poem. Even before you look at the students' comments, try doing what they did. We asked each of them to read the poem several times (step 2, pp. 18–19). More specifically, they devoted each of their readings to a particular element of the poem:

- First, they focused on how it fulfilled or defied their predictions.
- Then, they considered how the poem matched and diverged from their personal backgrounds.
- They then traced the poem's patterns, as well as breaks from these.
- They noted places where the poem is puzzling, ambiguous, or unclear.
- Next, they identified at least one choice that the poem's author faced.
- They then settled on questions that have more than one possible answer and that therefore might be worth addressing in a formal essay about the poem.
- Finally, pulling their thoughts together, they came up with tentative answers to these questions, which they might then have developed in a formal essay.

Again, the order of these stages is not the only one possible; the important thing is to go through them all. At each stage of their reading, the students also did a few minutes of freewriting, using this strategy to develop thoughts about whatever element was their focus. Following the poem are excerpts from these informal reflections.

The poem is by Sharon Olds (b. 1942), who teaches at New York University and has produced many volumes of verse. "Summer Solstice, New York City" appears in her 1987 book, *The Gold Cell.* Again, like most of the other literature we include in Part One, the poem deals with work—in this case, efforts by New York City police to prevent a suicide.

SHARON OLDS

Summer Solstice, New York City

By the end of the longest day of the year he could not stand it,
he went up the iron stairs through the roof of the building
and over the soft, tarry surface
to the edge, put one leg over the complex green tin cornice
and said if they came a step closer that was it.
Then the huge machinery of the earth began to work for his life,
the cops came in their suits blue-gray as the sky on a cloudy evening,
and one put on a bullet-proof vest, a
black shell around his own life,
life of his children's father, in case
the man was armed, and one, slung with a
rope like the sign of his bounden duty,
came up out of a hole in the top of the neighboring building
like the gold hole they say is in the top of the head,
and began to lurk toward the man who wanted to die.
The tallest cop approached him directly,

softly, slowly, talking to him, talking, talking,
while the man's leg hung over the lip of the next world
and the crowd gathered in the street, silent, and the
hairy net with its implacable grid was
unfolded near the curb and spread out and
stretched as the sheet is prepared to receive at birth.
Then they all came a little closer
where he squatted next to his death, his shirt
glowing its milky glow like something
growing in a dish at night in the dark in a lab and then
everything stopped
as his body jerked and he
stepped down from the parapet and went toward them
and they closed on him, I thought they were going to
beat him up, as a mother whose child has been
lost will scream at the child when it's found, they
took him by the arms and held him up and
leaned him against the wall of the chimney and the
tall cop lit a cigarette
in his own mouth, and gave it to him, and
then they all lit cigarettes, and the
red, glowing ends burned like the
tiny campfires we lit at night
back at the beginning of the world. *[1987]*

Applying the Strategies

MAKE PREDICTIONS

KATHERINE: I was really tense as I read this poem because I thought the man would jump at the end and then we would get a horrible description of him splattering on the sidewalk. I didn't predict the cops would succeed in talking him out of it. When the poet says he "jerked," that could easily have been the start of his jumping, but thank God he is instead stepping back. I'm glad that they persuaded him to remain alive.

MARIA: I was like the poem's speaker expecting that they would physically grab him and treat him roughly, and so I was surprised when they were nice to him and even offered him a cigarette.

TREVOR: I predicted that the poem would end with the man still on the edge of the building deciding whether or not to jump off, because I think that in a way it would be neat to leave us guessing whether he's really going to do it. I wasn't all that surprised when he pulled back and joined the cops, because that was certainly one possible outcome. However, I was surprised when the author had them smoking cigarettes at the end like "at the beginning of the world." I didn't expect that image of prehistoric people to show up here at the end.

REFLECT ON ONE'S PERSONAL BACKGROUND

JAMES: It's hard for me to sympathize with someone who commits suicide, especially because someone at my high school killed himself and all of his friends and family were terribly saddened by what he did. I think that no matter how bad things get for you, there's a way out if only you look for it. Suicide is no answer, and it hurts the people you leave behind. So I'm glad that the man in this poem winds up not committing suicide. If he had, I would have thought less of him.

CARLA: I vaguely remember seeing some movies in which a character stands on a ledge and thinks about jumping off it. In real life, I've never seen something like that. What this poem most brings to my mind are reports I heard about people jumping off the World Trade Towers to escape being killed by fire. Of course, they died anyway. As I recall, TV didn't show these people jumping, out of respect for them I guess, and I'm glad that I didn't have to see this happen. Still, I'm aware that it did. Anyway, the man thinking about suicide in this poem isn't facing the same situation. He can easily live if he wants to.

BOB: I guess the police are obligated to try rescuing the man even if they have to risk their own lives. I've never been in this position, so I'm not sure how I'd feel if I'd been assigned to save the man in this poem. Though I disapprove of suicide, maybe I wouldn't have the guts to try confronting him on the edge of the building, and I'm not sure I could talk to him calmly, because if he did jump he might take me down with him. I admire the ability of these cops to stay cool and talk him into joining them. I'm also impressed that they then treat him like a friend instead of like a potentially violent nutcase that they have to get under control through force. If it were me, I think I might want to throw him to the ground and pin his arms so that he wouldn't try something like that again.

READ FOR PATTERNS AND FOR BREAKS IN PATTERNS

DOMINICK: This may be too little a thing to think about, but I notice that the word "it" is repeated in the beginning section of the poem. The first line ends with "it," and line 5 does also. I'm not sure what is meant by "it" in "he could not stand it." Obviously on one level "it" here means his life, but he seems to have something specific about his life in mind when he says this, but we don't learn what he's specifically thinking of. The second "it" seems to refer to the fact that he will kill himself if they come closer. But that reference too isn't as clear as it might be. I see that later on "it" comes up again as a word for the cigarette that the cop gives to the man (after lighting it in his own mouth, yuck!). Maybe we're supposed to connect this "it" to the "its" at the start.

BOB: After the middle of the poem we start to get a lot of birth imagery. The word "birth" is even stated, and a little later there's the image of something "growing" in a lab dish.

JARED: "World" is repeated. In the middle of the poem, there's a reference to "the next world," and the very last word of the poem is "world," meaning the world where we currently live.

COURTNEY: I found a number of references to children. There are the words "his children's father," and then toward the end the word "child" is repeated, though this time it's a mother's child. And then the last line refers to "the beginning of the world," as if the world is a child that has just been born.

FRANK: It's funny that the word "end" is one of the first words of the poem, and then the word "beginning" is one of its last words. I can more easily imagine the reverse. Anyway, "end" and "beginning" are opposites that the poet seems to want us to think about. Come to think of it, there is mention of "ends" near the conclusion, but these are the "ends" of the men's cigarettes and not the end of the world.

ALEX: The word "day" appears in the first line (it's "the longest day of the year"), but later there is the word "night" ("growing in a dish at night"), and then "night" is in the next-to-last line. Ironically, things get brighter (the man decides to live) as the poem moves from "day" to "night."

PAUL: As the poem moves along, there's a shift in pronouns. In the first half or so, we get forms of "he" and "they." Then the word "I" suddenly appears, and then the next-to-last line has the word "we."

READ FOR PUZZLES, AMBIGUITIES, AND UNCLEAR MOMENTS

KATHERINE: I just don't learn enough about this man's thinking to know why he's even planning to kill himself. This is something the poem doesn't make clear. But I guess the "I" of the poem doesn't know the man's thinking either, and meanwhile she's in the position of possibly witnessing the man falling to the pavement! Maybe the author doesn't tell us exactly why the man wants to commit suicide because we can then identify more easily with him. We can think about moments when we were incredibly unhappy, whether or not we were depressed by the same things he is.

TIM: We're told that the cop approaching the man is doing a lot of talking, but we don't find out what he specifically says, even though this may have played a big role in getting the man to step back and live.

HILLARY: The gold hole sounds like something from folklore, but I don't know the background.

RACHEL: I'm wondering how much we're supposed to focus on the speaker's reactions to what's going on, or whether we should think more about the man and the policemen.

READ FOR THE AUTHOR'S CHOICES

KATHERINE: Olds could have had the man jump and die. Even if this poem is based on a real incident where the man decided to live, she could have changed what happened. Also, if she still went with the rescue version, she could have had the policemen treat the man roughly after they rescued him.

PAUL: The word "I" could have appeared more often throughout the poem, especially because the poem is written from the point of view of someone observing this suicide attempt.

TIM: We might have been told why the man was thinking of killing himself and what the cops said to him. I realize this information would be hard for the speaker of the poem to give us, since she's just observing the whole business from the street below. Still, maybe Olds could have found a way of telling us at least a little more about what the men on the roof were saying and thinking.

BOB: The author didn't have to use birth images. She could have described this event without them. In fact, death imagery seems more appropriate when a poem is about a possible suicide.

GENERATE QUESTIONS THAT HAVE MORE THAN ONE POSSIBLE ANSWER

JENNIFER: What might the poet be trying to convey when she ends the poem with the image of "the beginning of the world"? The last line really captures my attention.

PAUL: What should we conclude when the pronouns shift from "he" and "they" to "I" and finally "we"?

VICTORIA: How should we interpret the poem's repeated references to children and to parents (both father and mother)?

BOB: How important are the cops as characters in this poem?

STATE TENTATIVE ANSWERS

JENNIFER: Maybe the poet is telling us that each time you overcome depression and decide to go on living, it's like the rebirth of the world, and you're rejoining a "we" in the sense of rejoining the rest of humanity.

PAUL: I believe that the speaker comes to identify with the man and his rescuers and then sees herself and them as all part of a common humanity, as if we all have to decide when to risk our lives and when to preserve them.

VICTORIA: In a paper, I could argue that these child and parent references are used by Olds to suggest that even as adults, we sometimes act like children and sometimes have to act like a parent, but Olds evidently prefers that we not act like a very stern parent.

BOB: The cops are very important in this poem. So much of it is about what they do and how they maybe feel. They're required to save the guy, they're part of "huge machinery," and one of them might end up sacrificing the "life of his children's father" just in order to rescue someone who wants to kill himself anyway, but then the cops turn out to be quite sympathetic toward the guy. There's even this odd religious-type moment with the sharing of a cigarette and then all the men lighting up. I think I would focus my paper on how the cops do their duty to preserve life even when they probably didn't want to, and then something spiritual happens because they didn't give up on the job they were assigned.

DAN: If I'm remembering correctly, the summer solstice is a turning point in the year, and you could say that there's a turning point in this poem when the man steps down from the ledge and chooses not to die. After the summer solstice we're heading toward winter, which is associated with death, but psychologically the poem goes in the opposite direction.

Think about your own developing understanding of Olds's poem. What aspect of it might you focus on in a formal essay? What's a claim that you might make? To us, the students' claims we have quoted seem promising topics for papers. Nevertheless, they could probably stand some polishing and further reflection. After all, they are the outcome of freewriting—an exploratory phase. In any case, what we want to stress is that you are more likely to get ideas about a literary work if you use the reading strategies that this group of students applied.

Reading Closely by Annotating

When you use such strategies, you may come up with several observations about the literary work you are reading. You may even find it helpful to record them directly on the text. Then, by reviewing the points you have annotated and connecting them to one another, you will provide yourself with a solid foundation for a paper. Here we demonstrate this process by showing how student Kara Lundquist annotated a poem by the noted writer and editor X. J. Kennedy (b. 1929) and then composed a possible opening paragraph for an essay about it.

X. J. KENNEDY

Death of a Window Washer

He dropped the way you'd slam an obstinate sash, — *Window washer is given no name.*

His split belt like a shade unrolling, flapping. — *Did his body "split" when he hit the ground? Poem avoids gruesome details to focus mostly on bystanders.*

Forgotten on his account, the mindless copying

Machine ran scores of memos no one wanted.

Heads stared from every floor, noon traffic halted
As though transformed to stone. Cops sealed the block
With sawhorse barricades, laid canvas cover.
Nuns crossed themselves, flies went on being alive,
A broker counted ten shares sold as five,
And by coincidence a digital clock
Stopped in front of a second it couldn't leap over.

Struck wordless by his tumble from the sky
To their feet, two lovers held fast to each other
Uttering cries. But he had made no cry.
He'd made the city pause briefly to suffer
His taking ample room for once. In rather
A tedious while the rinsed street, left to dry,
Unlatched its gates that passersby might pass.
Why did he live and die? His legacy
Is mute: one final gleaming pane of glass.

Alliteration: What do "c" words suggest?

Nuns' reaction different from insects'. But are the humans here much more sensitive?

Echoes "account" in line 3. Did the dead man count (matter)?

Do people prefer to "leap over" deaths like this?

At first seems to mean "experience pain," then seems to mean "put up with."

"Tedious" to whom? People soon get impatient for the body to go.

Unusual to ask why he lived in the first place.

Relates to "wordless" in line 12 and "no cry" in line 14.

"Pane of glass " (clear vision) seems opposite of "mute." Connect "pane" to "pain"?

[2007]

Here is the paragraph that Kara composed, based on her annotations.

X. J. Kennedy's poem "Death of a Window Washer" emphasizes not the title character's horrible accident, but rather how bystanders react to it. The poem suggests that although people may be *momentarily* affected by the death of an ordinary person whom they do not know, eventually they want to resume their own lives and pay him little attention. The specific situation that the poem dramatizes is the accidental plunge of a window washer from a city building. Certainly this incident shocks, at first, the passersby who witness it. Even though "flies went on being alive," various human beings are disturbed by the man's sudden death. But as the poem proceeds, the city's inhabitants want to go back to their personal pursuits. A turning point in the poem is the word "suffer," which the speaker uses to describe the city dwellers at the end of line 15. This word might, at first, lead the reader to believe that they are tormented by the window washer's accident. But in the next line, it becomes clear that they are "suffering" in the sense that they are impatiently waiting for his corpse to be removed. Rather than permanently grieve over his having "passed" (i.e., died), they want to "pass" his body (line 18) and take up their daily existence once again. Therefore, although his death has been highly visible to them, they don't really bother to learn anything about him. His life is *not* revealed to them like the reality behind a "gleaming pane of glass." The speaker's concluding use of this image is, in fact, ironic.

Kara's annotations and this paragraph based on them are merely examples of what could be noted about Kennedy's poem. A different reader might flag other elements, such as the various features of Kennedy's technical craft. For instance, his sentences often spill over from one line to the next. This interruption in the syntax at the end of the line is known as enjambment, which creates a brief pause in the reading, which seems highly appropriate for a poem about a plunge. More puzzling is Kennedy's decision to rhyme just in certain spots—what might he be aiming to emphasize there?

Further Strategies for Close Reading

IDENTIFY CHARACTERS' EMOTIONS

Your feelings about the characters in a literary work can help you write a paper about it. Especially useful to consider is *why* you view these people as you do. What specific aspects of their thinking and conduct affect your attitudes toward them? You will have more material for the paper, though, if you also examine how the characters feel. With this strategy of close reading, you patiently and carefully identify *their* emotions, not simply your own. This analysis can even wind up giving you your paper's key idea—what, in our next chapter, we will call its *main claim*.

As you pinpoint the characters' passions and moods, try not to judge these right away. Emotions that may at first seem obnoxious or odd can have interesting roots. Also, they may be stages in complex mental journeys. A character may display numerous feelings, including ones that conflict, and undergo major changes of heart. Bear in mind, too, that many people in literature repress or mask their real desires, so the reader must infer their true inner states. Identify as well any emotions that characters significantly *lack*. Noting what feelings they *might* have had helps you pinpoint those they express.

We invite you to practice this method of analysis with the following poem. "Execution" is by the veteran poet Edward Hirsch (b. 1950) and appeared in his 1989 book *The Night Parade* as well as in a 2010 retrospective on his career, *The Living Fire: New and Selected Poems*. As you read the text, try to specify the emotions of the speaker and his main subject, his former coach. We follow up the poem with specific questions about their feelings. Then, to demonstrate the potential benefit of this approach to literature, we present a few ideas that student Courtney Reeves came up with when she applied it to "Execution." The insights she gained helped her eventually construct the introduction to an essay she wrote on the poem.

EDWARD HIRSCH

Execution

The last time I saw my high school football coach
He had cancer stenciled into his face
Like pencil marks from the sun, like intricate
Drawings on the chalkboard, small *x*'s and *o*'s
That he copied down in a neat numerical hand
Before practice in the morning. By day's end
The board was a spiderweb of options and counters,
Blasts and sweeps, a constellation of players
Shining under his favorite word, *Execution*,
Underlined in the upper right-hand corner of things.
He believed in football like a new religion
And had perfect unquestioning faith in the fundamentals
Of blocking and tackling, the idea of warfare
Without suffering or death, the concept of teammates
Moving in harmony like the planets—and yet
Our awkward adolescent bodies were always canceling
The flawless beauty of Saturday afternoons in September,
Falling away from the particular grace of autumn,
The clear weather, the ideal game he imagined.
And so he drove us through punishing drills
On weekday afternoons, and doubled our practice time,
And challenged us to hammer him with forearms,
And devised elaborate, last-second plays—a flea-
Flicker, a triple reverse—to save us from defeat.
Almost always they worked. He despised losing
And loved winning more than his own body, maybe even
More than himself. But the last time I saw him
He looked wobbly and stunned by illness,
And I remembered the game in my senior year
When we met a downstate team who loved hitting
More than we did, who battered us all afternoon
With a vengeance, who destroyed us with timing
And power, with deadly, impersonal authority,
Machine-like fury, perfect execution. *[1989]*

≡ THINKING ABOUT THE TEXT

1. To what extent does the speaker seem grief-stricken about his coach's mortal illness? Point to specific words in the text that influence your answer.
2. In line 11, the speaker says of the coach, "He believed in football like a new religion." What values would someone like the coach need to have in order to feel so passionately about this sport? Why might someone who regards "football like a new religion" not necessarily feel the same way about baseball or basketball?
3. In line 25, the speaker says that the coach "despised losing." How, if at all, did he reveal this attitude to his players? Identify specific words that help you address this question.
4. What other words in the poem indicate to you how the coach, during the speaker's youth, felt about high school football?
5. Where, if anywhere, does the speaker indicate how the players felt about the coach back then? Where, if anywhere, is the speaker evasive about what the players' attitudes toward the coach were?
6. In line 28, the speaker says that the coach now "looked wobbly and stunned by illness." What, evidently, was the coach feeling about his misfortune?
7. How does the speaker seem to feel about the football game he recalls at the end of the poem?
8. The title word, "execution," appears twice in the poem. Do these two appearances reflect the same emotion, or different ones? Explain.
9. If the title of this poem were the name of an emotion, what emotion would you think appropriate?

After examining the characters' emotions, Courtney Reeves formed these ideas for her paper on the poem. We italicize her references to emotions.

The speaker does not openly express *sorrow* for his former coach when he finds him both *physically and mentally suffering* from cancer. Nor is it clear that the speaker was ever extremely *fond* of the coach, although probably he *respected* him when he played for him. In general, the poem is not a blatant *sympathy* card for the coach. Instead, it seems chiefly a philosophical reflection, carried out with some *sadness*. The speaker seems mostly to *brood* about the ironies of the coach's present situation, including how these ironies apply to the speaker himself. Noticing that the coach now looks *"wobbly and stunned,"* the speaker obviously thinks that a big reason he appears this way is that cancer has physically attacked him. The speaker also seems to believe that the disease has *psychologically thrown the coach off balance*, in at least two respects. First, although the coach is surely aware that his cancer may kill him, he cannot know for certain how long he actually has to live. The title of the poem, "Execution," refers in one sense to killing that is swift and scheduled, but the coach has now entered a period of *scary* unpredictability about his fate. Second, the coach's look of *unsteadiness and confusion* results from his lifelong belief that people can overcome their limits through skillful physical performances, another sense of the word "execution." This was a goal that the coach *strived for* when he pushed the speaker and his fellow players to achieve a perfect "execution" of plays that would enable them to defeat all opposing teams. Having cancer *shocks* the coach by showing him that he was naive in making football "a new religion" in which proper training of the body would mean success not only on the field but throughout life. He discovers that even though the game of football usually lacks real "suffering and death," these things strike all of us eventually, and that even though he "loved winning more than his own body," he depended on his body's health. The speaker, on the other hand, does not seem "wobbly and stunned" by what has happened to the coach. He suggests that during his boyhood he himself saw the reality of human limits with greater clarity and *detachment* than the coach did. Perhaps, though, the speaker is with *at least a bit of desperation* trying to ward off death by writing this well-"executed" poem about it, just as the coach *frenziedly* wrote marks on the blackboard to help the team "execute" plays.

IDENTIFY SPEECH ACTS

Another way to read a literary text closely and get ideas about it is to identify the **speech acts** in it. Speech acts are things that the characters *do* with words. Try to specify what types of behavior characters engage in as they talk, as well as the effects they aim to have on their listeners. These performances often reveal key aspects of their personalities, features you might overlook if you focus just on their physical acts. When you study their verbal expressions as dramatic gestures, you also provide yourself with more material for a paper—including, perhaps, for its main claim.

Of course, for many speech acts in literature—and for many in real life—there is no single, clearly correct label. How best to describe them is a matter of interpretation. When you read about one of these acts, several terms for it may occur to you, leaving you to decide which fits best.

For examples of speech acts, let's return briefly to Sharon Olds's poem "Summer Solstice, New York City." In line 5, the man on the roof who contemplates suicide tells the people attempting to stop him that "if they came a step closer that was it." You can easily call his words a *warning*. Later, the poem's speaker admits that she wondered whether the police officers would react angrily to the man,

> . . . as a mother whose child has been
> lost will scream at the child when it's found . . . (lines 31–32)

You might say that she envisions their strongly *scolding* him. Actually, though, their behavior toward him is gentler from the start. Early on, the poem's speaker observes that

> The tallest cop approached him directly,
> softly, slowly, talking to him, talking, talking (lines 16–17)

Although neither you nor the poem's speaker knows what exactly the officer is saying, you can guess what he is *doing* as he talks to the man. What label would you apply to this speech act? What does he evidently hope to achieve through it?

Theorists of speech acts have compiled long lists of them, and probably you can think of plenty on your own. Below, we list just a few kinds. For clarity's sake, all of our sample sentences begin with "I," but each of these acts can take other forms.

- The speaker maintains that something is in fact the case.

  Claiming: I *claim* that Brad and Angelina are on the brink of reuniting.

  Concluding: I *conclude* from the data that gender differences are trivial.

  Arguing: I *argue* that victim impact statements deserve more attention in trials.

- The speaker tries to make the hearer carry out the speaker's wish.

  Requesting: I *request* that you turn off your cell phones.

  Demanding: I *demand* that you stop seeing him.

  Recommending: I *recommend* that you drive us home by taking the shortcut.

- The speaker states an intention to do something.

  Promising: I *promise* to get home by 5:00 p.m.

  Guaranteeing: I *guarantee* that I will fix your car by tomorrow.

  Warning: I *warn* you I will call the police if you do not leave right now.

- The speaker establishes a new state of affairs.

  Declaring: I *declare* you the winner of the race.

  Firing: I hereby *fire* you from this company.

  Approving: I hereby *approve* your application for a driver's license.

- The speaker acknowledges that he or she holds a particular attitude toward something.

  Apologizing: I *apologize* to you for my behavior last night.

  Congratulating: I *congratulate* you on your promotion.

  Protesting: I *protest* your decision to extend the school year.

In addition, many speech acts are best identified by their actual effect on the listener, whether or not it is the impact that the speaker was striving for. Here are some examples: *humiliation, intimidation, scaring, harassment, persuading,* and *misleading.*

A few other things are important to bear in mind:

- Someone may pretend to engage in a particular kind of speech act and yet not fulfill one of its normal conditions: for example, an *apology* may not be sincere; the speaker may not really have the authority to *fire* workers.
- A speech act may not be the kind that it first appears to be: for example, when the head of a corporation seems to make a *suggestion,* the staff might take it as an *order.*

- Often you can better grasp the nature of a particular speech act if you identify options that the speaker rejected—things that the speaker *might* have done but decided not to. For instance, the police officers in Olds's poem *might* have scolded the man on the roof; instead, they chose to talk with him in a friendlier way.
- Most scholars who study "speech acts" extend this term to cover *various* media (not just speech) and *various* communicative signs (not just words). For examples of how broadly the term can be applied, look at photographs that you and other people have posted on Facebook or similar sites. Which of these images strike you as performing the following acts? (Note that an image can have more than one function.)

commemorating	advertising
mourning	denying
announcing	protesting
arguing	bragging
joking	warning

To practice analyzing speech acts in literature, read the following story, "Orientation." As you read, try to come up with names for the speech acts you find in it. Afterward, we will pose some questions that help you do this. Then, to demonstrate the potential benefit of this approach, we present a few ideas that student Eva Berlin came up with when she applied it to "Orientation." The insights she gained helped her eventually construct the introduction to an essay she wrote on the story.

DANIEL OROZCO

Orientation

The son of Nicaraguan immigrants, California-born Daniel Orozco (b. 1957) currently teaches at the University of Idaho. His award-winning short fiction has appeared in a variety of magazines, including Harper's *and* Zoetrope, *and has been collected in* Orientation and Other Stories *(2011). He received a B.A. from Stanford University, an M.A. from San Francisco State University, and an M.F.A. from the University of Washington. He has also held a writing fellowship at Stanford. "Orientation" was originally published in a 1994 issue of* Seattle Review *and was subsequently selected for* The Best American Short Stories 1995.

Those are the offices and these are the cubicles. That's my cubicle there, and this is your cubicle. This is your phone. Never answer your phone. Let the Voicemail System answer it. This is your Voicemail System Manual. There are no personal phone calls allowed. We do, however, allow for emergencies. If you must make an emergency phone call, ask your supervisor first. If you can't find your supervisor, ask Phillip Spiers, who sits over there. He'll check with Clarissa Nicks, who sits over there. If you make an emergency phone call without asking, you may be let go.

These are your IN and OUT boxes. All the forms in your in box must be logged in by the date shown in the upper left-hand corner, initialed by you in the upper right-hand corner, and distributed to the Processing Analyst whose name is numerically coded in the lower left-hand corner. The lower right-hand corner is left blank. Here's your Processing Analyst Numerical Code Index. And here's your Forms Processing Procedures Manual.

You must pace your work. What do I mean? I'm glad you asked that. We pace our work according to the eight-hour workday. If you have twelve hours of work in your IN box, for example, you must compress that work into the eight-hour day. If you have one hour of work in your IN box, you must expand that work to fill the eight-hour day. That was a good question. Feel free to ask questions. Ask too many questions, however, and you may be let go.

That is our receptionist. She is a temp. We go through receptionists here. They quit with alarming frequency. Be polite and civil to the temps. Learn their names, and invite them to lunch occasionally. But don't get close to them, as it only makes it more difficult when they leave. And they always leave. You can be sure of that.

The men's room is over there. The women's room is over there. John LaFoun- 5
taine, who sits over there, uses the women's room occasionally. He says it is accidental. We know better, but we let it pass. John LaFountaine is harmless, his forays into the forbidden territory of the women's room simply a benign thrill, a faint blip on the dull flat line of his life.

Russell Nash, who sits in the cubicle to your left, is in love with Amanda Pierce, who sits in the cubicle to your right. They ride the same bus together after work. For Amanda Pierce, it is just a tedious bus ride made less tedious by the idle nattering of Russell Nash. But for Russell Nash, it is the highlight of his day. It is the highlight of his life. Russell Nash has put on forty pounds, and grows fatter with each passing month, nibbling on chips and cookies while peeking glumly over the partitions at Amanda Pierce, and gorging himself at home on cold pizza and ice cream while watching adult videos on TV.

Amanda Pierce, in the cubicle to your right, has a six-year-old son named Jamie, who is autistic. Her cubicle is plastered from top to bottom with the boy's crayon artwork — sheet after sheet of precisely drawn concentric circles and ellipses, in black and yellow. She rotates them every other Friday. Be sure to comment on them. Amanda Pierce also has a husband, who is a lawyer. He subjects her to an escalating array of painful and humiliating sex games, to which Amanda Pierce reluctantly submits. She comes to work exhausted and freshly wounded each morning, wincing from the abrasions on her breasts, or the bruises on her abdomen, or the second-degree burns on the backs of her thighs.

But we're not supposed to know any of this. Do not let on. If you let on, you may be let go.

Amanda Pierce, who tolerates Russell Nash, is in love with Albert Bosch, whose office is over there. Albert Bosch, who only dimly registers Amanda Pierce's existence, has eyes only for Ellie Tapper, who sits over there. Ellie Tapper, who hates Albert Bosch, would walk through fire for Curtis Lance. But Curtis Lance hates Ellie Tapper. Isn't the world a funny place? Not in the ha-ha sense, of course.

Anika Bloom sits in that cubicle. Last year, while reviewing quarterly reports 10
in a meeting with Barry Hacker, Anika Bloom's left palm began to bleed. She fell into a trance, stared into her hand, and told Barry Hacker when and how his wife would die. We laughed it off. She was, after all, a new employee. But Barry Hacker's wife is dead. So unless you want to know exactly when and how you'll die, never talk to Anika Bloom.

Colin Heavey sits in that cubicle over there. He was new once, just like you. We warned him about Anika Bloom. But at last year's Christmas Potluck, he felt sorry for her when he saw that no one was talking to her. Colin Heavey brought her a drink. He hasn't been himself since. Colin Heavey is doomed. There's nothing he can do about it, and we are powerless to help him. Stay away from Colin Heavey. Never give any of your work to him. If he asks to do something, tell him you have to check with me. If he asks again, tell him I haven't gotten back to you.

This is the Fire Exit. There are several on this floor, and they are marked accordingly. We have a Floor Evacuation Review every three months, and an Escape Route Quiz once a month. We have our Biannual Fire Drill twice a year, and our Annual Earthquake Drill once a year. These are precautions only. These things never happen.

For your information, we have a comprehensive health plan. Any catastrophic illness, any unforeseen tragedy is completely covered. All dependents are completely covered. Larry Bagdikian, who sits over there, has six daughters. If anything were to happen to any of his girls, or to all of them, if all six were to simultaneously fall victim to illness or injury—stricken with a hideous degenerative muscle disease or some rare toxic blood disorder, sprayed with semiautomatic gunfire while on a class field trip, or attacked in their bunk beds by some prowling nocturnal lunatic—if any of this were to pass, Larry's girls would all be taken care of. Larry Bagdikian would not have to pay one dime. He would have nothing to worry about.

We also have a generous vacation and sick leave policy. We have an excellent disability insurance plan. We have a stable and profitable pension fund. We get group discounts for the symphony, and block seating at the ballpark. We get commuter ticket books for the bridge. We have Direct Deposit. We are all members of Costco.

This is our kitchenette. And this, this is our Mr. Coffee. We have a coffee pool, 15
into which we each pay two dollars a week for coffee, filters, sugar, and CoffeeMate. If you prefer Cremora or half-and-half to CoffeeMate, there is a special pool for three dollars a week. If you prefer Sweet 'n Low to sugar, there is a special pool for two-fifty a week. We do not do decaf. You are allowed to join the coffee pool of your choice, but you are not allowed to touch the Mr. Coffee.

This is the microwave oven. You are allowed to *heat* food in the microwave oven. You are not, however, allowed to *cook* food in the microwave oven.

We get one hour for lunch. We also get one fifteen-minute break in the morning, and one fifteen-minute break in the afternoon. Always take your breaks. If you skip a break, it is gone forever. For your information, your break is a privilege, not a right. If you abuse the break policy, we are authorized to rescind your breaks. Lunch, however, is a right, not a privilege. If you abuse the lunch policy, our hands will be tied, and we will be forced to look the other way. We will not enjoy that.

This is the refrigerator. You may put your lunch in it. Barry Hacker, who sits over there, steals food from this refrigerator. His petty theft is an outlet for his grief. Last New Year's Eve, while kissing his wife, a blood vessel burst in her brain. Barry Hacker's wife was two months pregnant at the time, and lingered in a coma for half a year before dying. It was a tragic loss for Barry Hacker. He hasn't been himself since. Barry Hacker's wife was a beautiful woman. She was also completely covered. Barry Hacker did not have to pay one dime. But his dead wife haunts him. She haunts all of us. We have seen her, reflected in the monitors of our computers, moving past our cubicles. We have seen the dim shadow of her face in our photocopies. She pencils herself in in the receptionist's appointment book, with the notation: To see Barry Hacker. She has left messages in the receptionist's Voicemail box, messages garbled by the electronic chirrups and buzzes in the phone line, her voice echoing from an immense distance within the ambient hum. But the voice is hers. And beneath her voice, beneath the tidal *whoosh* of static and hiss, the gurgling and crying of a baby can be heard.

In any case, if you bring a lunch, put a little something extra in the bag for Barry Hacker. We have four Barrys in this office. Isn't that a coincidence?

This is Matthew Payne's office. He is our Unit Manager, and his door is always 20
closed. We have never seen him, and you will never see him. But he is here. You can be sure of that. He is all around us.

This is the Custodian's Closet. You have no business in the Custodian's Closet.

And this, this is our Supplies Cabinet. If you need supplies, see Curtis Lance. He will log you in on the Supplies Cabinet Authorization Log, then give you a Supplies Authorization Slip. Present your pink copy of the Supplies Authorization Slip to Ellie Tapper. She will log you in on the Supplies Cabinet Key Log, then give you the key. Because the Supplies Cabinet is located outside the Unit Manager's office, you must be very quiet. Gather your supplies quietly. The Supplies Cabinet is divided into four sections. Section One contains letterhead stationery, blank paper and envelopes, memo and note pads, and so on. Section Two contains pens and pencils and typewriter and printer ribbons, and the like. In Section Three we have erasers, correction fluids, transparent tapes, glue sticks, et cetera. And in Section Four we have paper clips and push pins and scissors and razor blades. And here are the spare blades for the shredder. Do not touch the shredder, which is located over there. The shredder is of no concern to you.

Gwendolyn Stich sits in that office there. She is crazy about penguins, and collects penguin knickknacks: penguin posters and coffee mugs and stationery, penguin stuffed animals, penguin jewelry, penguin sweaters and T-shirts and socks. She has a pair of penguin fuzzy slippers she wears when working late at the office. She has a tape cassette of penguin sounds which she listens to for relaxation. Her favorite colors are black and white. She has personalized license plates that read PEN GWEN. Every morning, she passes through all the cubicles to wish each of us a *good* morning. She brings Danish on Wednesdays for Hump

Day morning break, and doughnuts on Fridays for TGIF afternoon break. She organizes the Annual Christmas Potluck, and is in charge of the Birthday List. Gwendolyn Stich's door is always open to all of us. She will always lend an ear, and put in a good word for you; she will always give you a hand, or the shirt off her back, or a shoulder to cry on. Because her door is always open, she hides and cries in a stall in the women's room. And John LaFountaine—who, enthralled when a woman enters, sits quietly in his stall with his knees to his chest—John LaFountaine has heard her vomiting in there. We have come upon Gwendolyn Stich huddled in the stairwell, shivering in the updraft, sipping a Diet Mr. Pibb and hugging her knees. She does not let any of this interfere with her work. If it interfered with her work, she might have to be let go.

Kevin Howard sits in that cubicle over there. He is a serial killer, the one they call the Carpet Cutter, responsible for the mutilations across town. We're not supposed to know that, so do not let on. Don't worry. His compulsion inflicts itself on strangers only, and the routine established is elaborate and unwavering. The victim must be a white male, a young adult no older than thirty, heavyset, with dark hair and eyes, and the like. The victim must be chosen at random, before sunset, from a public place; the victim is followed home, and must put up a struggle; et cetera. The carnage inflicted is precise: the angle and direction of the incisions; the layering of skin and muscle tissue; the rearrangement of the visceral organs; and so on. Kevin Howard does not let any of this interfere with his work. He is, in fact, our fastest typist. He types as if he were on fire. He has a secret crush on Gwendolyn Stich, and leaves a red-foil-wrapped Hershey's Kiss on her desk every afternoon. But he hates Anika Bloom, and keeps well away from her. In his presence, she has uncontrollable fits of shaking and trembling. Her left palm does not stop bleeding.

In any case, when Kevin Howard gets caught, act surprised. Say that he 25
seemed like a nice person, a bit of a loner, perhaps, but always quiet and polite.

This is the photocopier room. And this, this is our view. It faces southwest. West is down there, toward the water. North is back there. Because we are on the seventeenth floor, we are afforded a magnificent view. Isn't it beautiful? It overlooks the park, where the tops of those trees are. You can see a segment of the bay between those two buildings there. You can see the sun set in the gap between those two buildings over there. You can see this building reflected in the glass panels of that building across the way. There. See? That's you, waving. And look there. There's Anika Bloom in the kitchenette, waving back.

Enjoy this view while photocopying. If you have problems with the photocopier, see Russell Nash. If you have any questions, ask your supervisor. If you can't find your supervisor, ask Phillip Spiers. He sits over there. He'll check with Clarissa Nicks. She sits over there. If you can't find them, feel free to ask me. That's my cubicle. I sit in there. *[1994]*

☰ THINKING ABOUT THE TEXT

1. Let's return to the story's first paragraph. It seems to feature a variety of speech acts. How would you describe what the speaker is doing in each sentence?

2. What are the various speech acts that the speaker performs in paragraph 3?
3. Discussing Colin Heavey, the speaker says, "We warned him about Anika Bloom" (para. 11). Where in this orientation does the speaker seem to be *warning* the listener? List some specific examples of this speech act.
4. Where, if anywhere, in the story does the speaker seem to engage in the speech act of *gossiping*? Define what this term means to you. How would you distinguish *gossiping* from mere reporting of information?
5. In paragraph 7, the speaker recommends that the listener "comment on" the artwork of Amanda Pierce's son. Presumably it would be impolite to *criticize* these drawings. What other speech acts might the new employee perform when observing them? The speaker also orders the listener to "not let on" that Amanda suffers from spousal abuse. What speech acts could occur if "letting on" were allowed? To whom might they be addressed?
6. In paragraph 13, the speaker praises the firm's "comprehensive health plan." In explaining how it might apply to Larry Bagdikian, however, what else is he doing besides *praising*?
7. In paragraph 18, what might the speaker be doing when he tells the listener that Barry Hacker's deceased wife "haunts all of us"? He claims that "She pencils herself in in the receptionist's appointment book, with the notation: To see Barry Hacker." What speech act might this notation be?
8. What kind of speech act is the statement at the end of paragraph 22, "The shredder is of no concern to you"?
9. In paragraph 23, the speaker says of Gwendolyn Stich that "every morning, she passes through all the cubicles to wish each of us a *good* morning." What kind of speech act is she performing when she does this? In the same paragraph, the speaker reports that Gwendolyn has moments of great emotional distress. What, if anything, does his account of her suffering make you think about the wish she expresses to everyone each day?
10. Why, in paragraph 24, might the speaker tell the listener not to "let on" that Kevin Howard is a serial killer? When the speaker then says "Don't worry," why might he want to reassure the listener that Kevin poses no threat to the office staff?
11. The last sentence in the story is "I sit in there." What would you say to someone who argues that Orozco should have ended not with a simple declaration of fact but with a more dramatic speech act?
12. Orozco reports that since his story was published, "it has even been included in an employee orientation manual, which is either very funny or very disturbing." Why might a company use the story this way? How might it expect new employees to react? Does the orientation in this story

resemble other orientations with which you are familiar? In what ways? Consider the kinds of advice given and language used.

13. What assumptions do you make about the speaker's audience, that is, the listener being oriented? Imagine this person's reaction at a few particular moments of the story.

After considering the speech acts that occur in the story, Eva Berlin formed these ideas for her paper on it. We italicize her references to verbal behavior.

An orientation is something like a course syllabus. Usually, someone who *orients* a company's new employees *explains* to them the firm's policies; *points out* various areas and facilities of the office; *introduces* them to other members of the staff; and in general *welcomes* them to their new workplace while *teaching* them about it. The speaker in Orozco's story does these things, but he performs more specific speech acts that together might disturb his listener and a lot of the story's readers. Although he *praises* the listener for *asking* "a good question" and *encourages* this person to *raise* even more, he immediately *warns* the listener not to go overboard with inquisitiveness: "*Ask* too many questions, however, and you may be let go" (para. 3). The last four words even become a refrain in the story as it proceeds. At other times, his warnings come across as *threats* that are especially sinister in their vagueness: "If you abuse the lunch policy, our hands will be tied, and we will be forced to look the other way. We will not enjoy that" (para. 17). At other times, he *commands* the listener to perform, or avoid performing, certain acts: for example, "You must pace your work" (para. 3); "Be sure to *comment* on" Jamie's artwork (para. 7); "Stay away from Colin Heavey" (para. 11); "You have no business in the Custodian's Closet" (para. 21); "Gather your supplies quietly" (para. 22); "Do not touch the shredder" (para. 22); "act surprised" (para. 25). Perhaps some readers will regard him as *giving advice*, but he makes these statements so crisply and authoritatively that they seem more like *orders*. Curiously, he doesn't always follow these *orders* himself. Right after *disclosing* to the listener awful details of how Amanda Pierce's husband abuses her, he *commands* the listener to "not *let on*" about these details, even though he himself has just "*let on*" about them (para. 8). Overall, he seems to enjoy *gossiping* about the mostly horrible lives of his co-workers, as if he relishes their misery. Even as he *praises* the company's health plan, *citing* as an example the good coverage that Larry Bagdikian receives, he energetically *elaborates* gruesome details of the calamities that may strike Larry and his family. Interestingly, he *calmly reports* Kevin Howard's murders without *expressing alarm* about them, as if the crimes entertain him rather than scare him. The same goes for his *account* of how Barry Hacker's wife haunts the office. Besides *sketching* eerie biographies of his colleagues, the speaker proves capable of *criticizing* them; he seems to *express outright contempt* when he *labels* John LaFountaine's visits to the women's room as "a faint blip on the dull flat line of his life" (para. 5).

It seems significant that although the speaker *describes* the office as if he is in charge of it, he works in a cubicle, just as his listener will. He does not occupy the suite that a top executive would. In fact, there is no solid indication that the speaker has much power in the company. His rank is certainly lower than that of his Unit Manager, Matthew Payne, whom he has never even had the privilege of seeing. Through his *warnings, commands, gossiping,* and *criticizing,* he may be trying to *assert through words* a power that he does not really hold within the company's hierarchy. In a sense, his verbal behavior may be a series of *attempts to console himself* for his actual lack of power.

Using Topics of Literary Studies to Get Ideas

You can also get ideas about the text if, as you read it, you consider how it deals with **topics** that have preoccupied literary studies as a profession. Some of these topics have interested the discipline for many years. One example is work, a common subject of the literature in Part One. Traditionally, literary studies has also been concerned with the chapter topics in Part Two: family relations, love, freedom and confinement, crime and justice, and journeys. Moreover, the discipline has long called attention to topics that are essentially classic conflicts: for example, innocence versus experience, free will versus fate or determinism, the individual versus society, nature versus culture, and eternity versus the passing time.

Over the last few years, however, literary studies has turned to several new concerns. For instance, quite a few literary critics now consider the ways in which literary texts are often *about* reading, writing, interpretation, and evaluation. Critics increasingly refer to some of the following subjects in their analysis of literature:

- Traits that significantly shape human identity, including gender, race, ethnic background, social class, sexual orientation, cultural background, nationality, and historical context
- Representations of groups, including stereotypes held by others
- Acknowledgments — or denials — of differences among human beings
- Divisions, conflicts, and multiple forces *within* the self
- Boundaries, including the processes through which these are created, preserved, and challenged
- Politics and ideology, including the various forms that power and authority can take; acts of domination, oppression, exclusion, and appropriation; and acts of subversion, resistance, and parody
- Ways that carnivals and other festivities challenge or preserve social order
- Distinctions between what's universal and what's historically or culturally specific
- Relations between the public and the private, the social and the personal
- Relations between the apparently central and the apparently marginal

- Relations between what's supposedly normal and what's supposedly abnormal
- Relations between "high" culture and "low" (that is, mass or popular) culture
- Economic and technological developments, as well as their effects
- The role of performance in everyday life
- Values—ethical, aesthetic, religious, professional, and institutional
- Desire and pleasure
- The body
- The unconscious
- Memory, including public commemorations as well as personal memory
- Material things, including common physical objects

If you find that a literary text touches on one of these topics, try next to determine how the work specifically addresses that topic. Perhaps you will consider the topic an element of the text's themes. In any case, remember that, by itself, a topic is not the same as a theme. While a topic can usually be expressed in a word or a short phrase, a theme is a whole claim or assertion that you believe the text makes.

Actually, the topics we have identified may be most worth consulting when you have just begun analyzing a literary text and are far from establishing a theme. By using these topics, you can generate preliminary questions about the text, various issues you can then explore.

To demonstrate how these topics can stimulate inquiry, we apply some of them to the following poem, "Night Waitress." It is from the 1986 book *Ghost Memory*, by the late American poet Lynda Hull (1954–1994). Hull had been developing an impressive career in literature when she died in a car accident. This poem is also about work, the speaker being the night waitress of the title.

LYNDA HULL

Night Waitress

Reflected in the plate glass, the pies
look like clouds drifting off my shoulder.
I'm telling myself my face has character,
not beauty. It's my mother's Slavic face.
She washed the floor on hands and knees
below the Black Madonna, praying
to her god of sorrows and visions
who's not here tonight when I lay out the plates,
small planets, the cups and moons of saucers.
At this hour the men all look
as if they'd never had mothers.
They do not see me. I bring the cups.
I bring the silver. There's the man

who leans over the jukebox nightly
pressing the combinations
of numbers. I would not stop him
if he touched me, but it's only songs
of risky love he leans into. The cook sings
with the jukebox, a moan and sizzle
into the grill. On his forehead
a tattooed cross furrows,
diminished when he frowns. He sings words
dragged up from the bottom of his lungs.
I want a song that rolls
through the night like a big Cadillac
past factories to the refineries
squatting on the bay, round and shiny
as the coffee urn warming my palm.
Sometimes when coffee cruises my mind
visiting the most remote way stations,
I think of my room as a calm arrival
each book and lamp in its place. The calendar
on my wall predicts no disaster
only another white square waiting
to be filled like the desire that fills
jail cells, the old arrest
that makes me stare out the window or want
to try every bar down the street.
When I walk out of here in the morning
my mouth is bitter with sleeplessness.
Men surge to the factories and I'm too tired
to look. Fingers grip lunch box handles,
belt buckles gleam, wind riffles my uniform
and it's not romantic when the sun unlids
the end of the avenue. I'm fading
in the morning's insinuations
collecting in the crevices of buildings,
in wrinkles, in every fault
of this frail machinery.

[1986]

A WRITING EXERCISE

After you read "Night Waitress," do a ten-minute freewrite in which you try to identify how the poem relates to one or more of the topics mentioned on pages 41–42.

We think that several of the topics now popular in literary studies are relevant to Hull's poem. Here are a few possibilities, along with questions that these topics can generate.

Gender. The speaker alludes to conventional roles through which men and women relate to each other. When the speaker declares that "at this hour the men all look / as if they'd never had mothers," she indicates that women have often played a maternal role for men. Furthermore, she implies that often women have been the primary caretaker of their sons. (Notice that she makes no reference to fathers.) What is the effect of this attention to women as mothers of men? In most of the poem, the speaker refers to men as potential lovers. Yet even as she suggests she would like a sexual relationship with a man, she suggests as well that she has had trouble establishing worthwhile attachments. Why has she had such difficulty, do you think? Does the problem seem due to her personality alone, or do you sense larger forces shaping her situation? Notice, too, that the poem refers to the factory workers as male, while the woman who speaks is a waitress. To what extent does American society perpetuate a gendered division of labor?

Ethnic background. Near the start of the poem, the speaker refers to her "mother's Slavic face" and points out that her mother served "the Black Madonna," a religious icon popular in Central European countries such as the Czech Republic and Poland. What is the effect of these particular ethnic references? To pursue this line of inquiry, probably you will need to do research into the Black Madonna, whether in a library or on the Internet.

Social class. In part, considering social class means thinking about people's ability to obtain material goods. When the speaker compares her ideal song to "a big Cadillac," she implies that she doesn't currently possess such a luxurious car. At the same time, she is expressing her desire for the song, not the car. Why might the song be more important to her right now? Social class is also a matter of how various workplaces are related to one another. This poem evokes a restaurant, factories, refineries, and bars. How are these settings connected as parts of American society? Think, too, about how you would label the social class of the various occupations the poem mentions. What would you say is the social class of a waitress? To what classes would you assign people who work in factories and refineries? Who, for the most part, are the social classes that have to work at night?

Sexual orientation. The speaker of "Night Waitress" seems heterosexual, an orientation often regarded as the only legitimate one. Because almost all societies have made heterosexuality the norm, a lot of people forget that it is a particular orientation and that not everyone identifies with it. Within literary studies, gay and lesbian critics have pointed out that a literary work may seem to deal with sexuality in general but may actually refer just to heterosexuality. Perhaps "Night Waitress" is examining heterosexuality as a specific social force. If so, how might the speaker's discontent be related to heterosexuality's influence as a particular institution? Keep in mind that you don't have to assume anything about the author's sexuality as you pursue such a question. In fact, heterosexuality may be a more important topic in Hull's poem than she intended.

Divisions, conflicts, and multiple forces within the self. The poem's beginning indicates that the speaker experiences herself as divided. The first four lines reveal that she feels pride and disappointment in her mirror image: "I'm telling myself my face has character, / not beauty." Later she indicates that within her mind are "remote way stations" that she visits only on occasion. Furthermore, she seems to contradict herself. Although she initially refers to her room as "a calm arrival," she goes on to describe that place negatively, as empty and confined. Early in the evening, she seems sexually attracted to the man playing the jukebox ("I would not stop him / if he touched me"), but by morning her mood is "not romantic" and she is "too tired / to look" at the male factory workers. What may be the significance of these paradoxes?

Boundaries. In the first line, the speaker is apparently looking at a window, and later she reveals that at times she feels driven to "stare out the window" of her room. What should a reader make of these two references to such a common boundary? When the speaker observes that the men in the restaurant "do not see me," she indicates that a boundary exists between them and her. Do you think she is merely being paranoid, or do you suspect that the men are indeed ignoring her? If they *are* oblivious to her, how do you explain their behavior? Still another boundary explored in the poem is the line between night and day. What happens when the speaker crosses this line? What can night, day, and the boundary between them signify? You might also consider what the author of a literary work does with its technical boundaries. Often a poem creates boundaries in its breaks between stanzas. Yet "Night Waitress" is a continuous, unbroken text; what is the effect of Hull's making it so? At the same time, Hull doesn't always respect sentence boundaries in her lines. At several points in the poem, sentences spill over from one line to another. This poetic technique is called **enjambment**; what is its effect here?

Politics and ideology. When, in referring to the jukebox man, the speaker declares that "I would not stop him / if he touched me," she can be taken to imply that male customers often flirt with waitresses. How might flirtation be seen as involving power, authority, and even outright domination? Do you see the poem as commenting on such things? Earlier we raised issues of social class; these can be seen as political issues, too. How would you describe a society in which some people have "a big Cadillac" and others do not?

Carnivals and other festivities. Although the poem does not refer to a "carnival" in any sense of that word, it does mention bars, which today are regarded by many people as places of festive retreat from work. What adjectives would you use to describe the speaker when she says that sometimes she wants "to try every bar down the street"?

Distinctions between what is universal and what is historically or culturally specific. Try to identify anything that is historically or culturally specific about this poem's setting. Certainly the word *Slavic* and the reference to the Black Madonna indicate that the speaker has a particular background. You might also note her description of the restaurant, her use of the Cadillac as a metaphor, and her mention of the "factories" and the "refineries" that are "squatting on the bay." Although a wide range of places might fit these details, the poem's setting does not seem universal. Indeed, many readers are attracted to literature *because* it deals with specific landscapes, people, and plots. Nevertheless, these same readers usually expect to get some larger, more widely applicable meanings out of literature even as they are engaged by its specific details. Are you inclined to draw general conclusions from "Night Waitress"? If so, what general meanings do you find in it? What sorts of people do you think might learn something about themselves from reading this poem?

Relations between the public and the private, the social and the personal. The speaker of "Night Waitress" works in a very public place, a restaurant. Yet she seems to feel isolated there, trapped in her own private world. How did she come to experience public life this way, do you think? Later, she initially seems to value her room as a private retreat, calling it "a calm arrival," but then she describes it as a place so lonely that it leads her to "stare out the window or want / to try every bar down the street." How, then, would you ultimately describe the relations between the speaker's public life and her private one? In addressing this issue, probably you need to consider whether the speaker's difficulties are merely personal or reflect a larger social disorder. When, at the end of the poem, she refers to "this frail machinery," is she referring just to herself, or is she suggesting that this phrase applies to her society in general? If she is indeed making a social observation, what do you sense are the "faults" in her society? Who else might be "fading"?

Relations between "high" culture and "low" culture. Although the speaker does not identify the "songs / of risky love" playing on the jukebox, surely they are examples of what is called low, mass, or popular culture. Just as a lot of us are moved by such music when we hear it, so the jukebox player and the cook are engaged by it. In contrast, the poem itself can be considered an example of high culture. Often poetry is regarded as a serious art even by people who don't read it. In what ways, if any, does this poem conceivably resemble the songs it mentions? Given that author Lynda Hull is in essence playing with combinations of words, can we compare her with "the man / who leans over the jukebox nightly / pressing the combinations / of numbers"? (Actually, *numbers* has been a poetic term; centuries ago, it was commonly used as a synonym for the rhythms of poems.)

The role of performance in everyday life. The most conspicuous performer in this poem is the cook, who "sings words / dragged up from the bottom of his lungs." But in everyday life, people often perform in the sense of taking on certain roles, even disguising their real personalities. Do you see such instances of performing in this poem? If so, where? Notice that the speaker wears a uniform; can that be considered a costume she wears while performing as a waitress?

Religious values. The speaker clearly refers to religion when she recalls her mother's devotion to the Black Madonna, behavior that involved "praying / to her god of sorrows and visions." And although that god is "not here tonight," the speaker's description of waitressing has ritualistic overtones reminiscent of religious ceremonies. When she says, "I bring the cups. / I bring the silver," she could almost be describing preparations for Communion. In fact, she depicts the cook as wearing a religious emblem: "On his forehead / a tattooed cross furrows, /

diminished when he frowns." What do you make of all this religious imagery? Might the speaker be trying to pursue certain religious values? Can she be reasonably described as looking for salvation?

Desire and pleasure. The speaker explicitly mentions the word *desire* when she describes the emptiness she feels in her room, a feeling of desolation "that makes me stare out the window or want / to try every bar down the street." These lines may lead you to believe that her desire is basically sexual. Yet when the speaker uses the words *I want* earlier in the poem, she expresses her wish for "a song that rolls / through the night like a big Cadillac." Here, her longing does not appear sexual in nature. Is the speaker referring to at least two kinds of desire, then? Or do you see her as afflicted with basically one kind?

The body. A notable feature of this poem is its attention to body parts. The speaker mentions her "shoulder," her "face," her mother's "face," her mother's "hands and knees," the cook's "forehead," his "lungs," her "palm," the "way stations" of her "mind," her "mouth," the factory workers' "fingers," and their "belt buckles." At the same time, the speaker never describes any particular body as a whole. What is the effect of this emphasis on mere parts? Does it connect in any way to the speaker's ultimate "fading"?

Memory. Already we have noted the speaker's reference to her mother at the start of the poem. In what way, if any, is it significant that she engages in recollection? What circumstances in her life might have prompted the speaker to look back at the past?

Material things. The speaker mentions cups, plates, saucers, and silverware. Evidently she's careful to "lay out" (line 8) these items in a particular order. Similarly, she reports, the room where she lives has "each book and lamp in its place" (line 32). What do you conclude from her neat ordering of these objects? Note that the only "warming" she feels in the poem comes from "the coffee urn" (line 28). Is there a possibility of her ever feeling warmth from a human being? "Box" appears multiple times: as part of the word "jukebox" (brought up twice, in lines 14 and 19) and as part of the phrase "lunch box" (line 42). With this repetition, perhaps Hull is encouraging her readers to connect "jukebox" and "lunch box" in some meaningful way. The first seems a means of entertainment, the second an object taken to work or school. But they're both part of the speaker's world; what should readers infer from that fact?

≡ A WRITING EXERCISE

We have applied several topics from our list to Lynda Hull's poem "Night Waitress." Now see you how can apply topics from the list to other literature. Next, we present two texts: the first is a famous poem, the second is a recent award-winning short story. Try to come up with several questions about one or both of these works, referring to topics on our list. Then select at least one of the questions you have formulated, and freewrite for ten minutes in response to it.

T. S. ELIOT

The Love Song of J. Alfred Prufrock

One of the most respected intellectuals of his time, Thomas Stearns Eliot (1888–1965) was a poet, playwright (Murder in the Cathedral), *and critic* (The Sacred Wood). *His poem* "The Waste Land" *(1922), considered a modernist masterpiece, is perhaps the last century's most influential poem. The long-running Broadway play* Cats *is based on some of Eliot's lighter poems. Born in America and educated at Harvard, Eliot lived his mature life in England. He was awarded the Nobel Prize for literature in 1948.*

S'io credesse che mia risposta fosse
A persona che mai tornasse al mondo,
Questa fiamma staria senza più scosse.
Ma perciocchè giammai di questo fondo
Non tornò vivo alcun, s'i'odo il vero,
Senza tema d'infamia ti rispondo.°

Let us go then, you and I,
When the evening is spread out against the sky
Like a patient etherized upon a table;
Let us go, through certain half-deserted streets,
The muttering retreats
Of restless nights in one-night cheap hotels
And sawdust restaurants with oyster-shells:
Streets that follow like a tedious argument
Of insidious intent
To lead you to an overwhelming question . . .
Oh, do not ask, "What is it?"
Let us go and make our visit.

In the room the women come and go
Talking of Michelangelo.

The yellow fog that rubs its back upon the window panes,
The yellow smoke that rubs its muzzle on the window panes
Licked its tongue into the corners of the evening,
Lingered upon the pools that stand in drains,
Let fall upon its back the soot that falls from chimneys,
Slipped by the terrace, made a sudden leap,
And seeing that it was a soft October night,
Curled once about the house, and fell asleep.

And indeed there will be time°
For the yellow smoke that slides along the street,

23 there will be time: An allusion to Ecclesiastes 3:1–8: "To everything there is a season, and a time to every purpose under heaven." **EPIGRAPH: S'io . . . rispondo:** In Dante's *Inferno,* a sufferer in hell says, "If I thought I was talking to someone who might return to Earth, this flame would cease; but if what I have heard is true, no one does return; therefore, I can speak to you without fear of infamy."

Rubbing its back upon the window panes;
There will be time, there will be time
To prepare a face to meet the faces that you meet;
There will be time to murder and create,
And time for all the works and days° of hands
That lift and drop a question on your plate:
Time for you and time for me,
And time yet for a hundred indecisions,
And for a hundred visions and revisions,
Before the taking of a toast and tea.
In the room the women come and go
Talking of Michelangelo.
    And indeed there will be time
To wonder, "Do I dare?" and, "Do I dare?"—
Time to turn back and descend the stair,
With a bald spot in the middle of my hair—
(They will say: "How his hair is growing thin!")
My morning coat, my collar mounting firmly to the chin,
My necktie rich and modest, but asserted by a simple pin—
(They will say: "But how his arms and legs are thin!")
Do I dare
Disturb the universe?
In a minute there is time
For decisions and revisions which a minute will reverse.

    For I have known them all already, known them all:
Have known the evenings, mornings, afternoons,
I have measured out my life with coffee spoons;
I know the voices dying with a dying fall
Beneath the music from a farther room.
    So how should I presume?

    And I have known the eyes already, known them all—
The eyes that fix you in a formulated phrase,
And when I am formulated, sprawling on a pin,
When I am pinned and wriggling on the wall,
Then how should I begin
To spit out all the butt-ends of my days and ways?
    And how should I presume?

    And I have known the arms already, known them all—
Arms that are braceleted and white and bare
(But in the lamplight, downed with light brown hair!)
    Is it perfume from a dress
    That makes me so digress?
Arms that lie along a table, or wrap about a shawl.

29 works and days: Hesiod's eighth-century B.C.E. poem gave practical advice.

And should I then presume?
And how should I begin?

Shall I say, I have gone at dusk through narrow streets,
And watched the smoke that rises from the pipes
Of lonely men in shirtsleeves, leaning out of windows? . . .
I should have been a pair of ragged claws
Scuttling across the floors of silent seas.

And the afternoon, the evening, sleeps so peacefully!
Smoothed by long fingers,
Asleep . . . tired . . . or it malingers,
Stretched on the floor, here beside you and me.
Should I, after tea and cakes and ices,
Have the strength to force the moment to its crisis?
But though I have wept and fasted, wept and prayed,
Though I have seen my head (grown slightly bald) brought in upon a platter,°
I am no prophet—and here's no great matter;
I have seen the moment of my greatness flicker,
And I have seen the eternal Footman hold my coat, and snicker,
And in short, I was afraid.

And would it have been worth it, after all,
After the cups, the marmalade, the tea,
Among the porcelain, among some talk of you and me,
Would it have been worth while
To have bitten off the matter with a smile,
To have squeezed the universe into a ball
To roll it toward some overwhelming question,
To say: "I am Lazarus,° come from the dead,
Come back to tell you all, I shall tell you all"—
If one, settling a pillow by her head,
Should say: "That is not what I meant at all;
That is not it, at all."

And would it have been worth it, after all,
Would it have been worth while,
After the sunsets and the dooryards and the sprinkled streets,
After the novels, after the teacups, after the skirts that trail along the floor—
And this, and so much more?—
It is impossible to say just what I mean!
But as if a magic lantern° threw the nerves in patterns on a screen:
Would it have been worth while

82 head . . . platter: Like John the Baptist (Matt. 14:1–12). **94 "I am Lazarus":** Raised from the dead by Jesus. **105 magic lantern:** Precursor of the slide projector.

If one, settling a pillow or throwing off a shawl,
And turning toward the window, should say:
    "That is not it at all,
    That is not what I meant, at all."

No! I am not Prince Hamlet, nor was meant to be;
Am an attendant lord,° one that will do
To swell a progress,° start a scene or two
Advise the prince: withal, an easy tool,
Deferential, glad to be of use,
Politic, cautious, and meticulous;
Full of high sentence, but a bit obtuse;
At times, indeed, almost ridiculous—
Almost, at times, the Fool.
I grow old . . . I grow old . . .
I shall wear the bottoms of my trowsers rolled.

    Shall I part my hair behind?° Do I dare to eat a peach?°
I shall wear white flannel trowsers, and walk upon the beach.
I have heard the mermaids singing, each to each.

I do not think that they will sing to me.

I have seen them riding seaward on the waves,
Combing the white hair of the waves blown back
When the wind blows the water white and black.

We have lingered in the chambers of the sea
By seagirls wreathed with seaweed red and brown,
Till human voices wake us, and we drown. *[1917]*

112 attendant lord: Like Polonius in Shakespeare's *Hamlet.* **113 progress:** State procession. **121–22 trowsers rolled . . . part my hair behind:** The latest fashion; **eat a peach:** Considered a risky fruit.

ALLISON ALSUP

Old Houses

A native of the San Francisco Bay Area, Allison Alsup lives in New Orleans where she writes and teaches creative writing. Her story "Old Houses," based on an unsolved crime on the street where she grew up, was selected for the 2014 O. Henry Prize Stories. In addition to fiction, she also writes about New Orleans bars and cocktails and is the co-author of The French Quarter Drinking Companion.

As they gather for the spring block party on the Peabodys' extra lot, the residents of Hillcrest Way think how lucky they are to live in old houses and among the kind of people who understand old houses and their architecture—Tudor, Colonial, Spanish Mediterranean. Every house on the street is different but in keeping with the neighborhood, scaled and proportioned. *Houses that know who they are*, Dennis Petersen calls them in an effort to distinguish them from the ones down the hill. The homes on the roads below are smaller, built on stingier lots and in some cases, built too late to have the kind of distinct identity that old houses do. His own house is Norman, the first on the block, and built over a century ago.

The latecomers make their way down the sidewalks towards the Peabodys' lot, the women holding cheese trays and pasta salads, the men bottles of wine. They are all grateful to Richard and Katherine for having purchased the lot and for having saved it from the builders. They have seen what developers can do. When fire swept through the hills across town, the builders razed everything and erected rows of white boxes with no room for gardens or yards for children to play in. So after they place their offerings on the folding table buffet on the Peabodys' lawn, they all compliment Katherine on her growing collection of irises. They note, as always, with genuine delight, how the lot opens the view in just the right spot: a slice of steel blue bay and beyond, the studded grid of downtown San Francisco. The view is better, they note, from *this* side.

They are fond of the phrase *original to the house*. Moldings and in-laid oak floors original to the house. Built-in cabinets, box beams, coved ceilings and stained glass original to the house. Bannisters, mullions, muntins, french doors, glass knobs, telephone niches, carved mantles, fireplace grates, chandeliers, porthole windows and *working* shutters, all original to the house. The little bedroom on the ground floor, original to the house. All the old houses on Hillcrest have one—just a few steps from the kitchen and the back stairs. They don't call it a maid's room, except in private. Of course, no one has a maid anymore, only a woman who cleans and a gardener who comes once a week to mow and round up the leaves. Live-ins are for those in the hills above, people who can't be bothered to walk their own dogs.

In some of their houses, the little room has been converted into an office, sometimes into a discreet spot for the television. Five years ago, the Welshes lined the back wall with double-glazed windows and made a music studio where he could play the violin and she the French horn. The children played too, before they went to college and moved away. Since their remodel, Judith Goldman times her evening walks to coincide with the Welshes' practice hour; sometimes Suzanne Collier joins her and they share news of their daughters who attend neighboring colleges in Massachusetts. Sometimes however, Judith prefers to walk alone. The faint sound of the Russian composers and the sight of the cool evening fog weaving through the tall pines makes her think of summers spent as a girl in upstate New York. She had her own little room remade into a library complete with a gas fireplace and matching highback chairs. When she closes the door, her husband knows not to bother her.

They stand clustered about the grass, sampling salads and refilling wine glasses. They like to think about all that their houses have witnessed. They all know the story of the Petersens' house—built for a bachelor sea captain at the turn of the last century. Of course, there had been sea captains then. They all agree that with his thick sweaters and ruddy face, Dennis Petersen does indeed resemble a sea captain.

You never own an old house, they agree, you just safeguard it for the next generation.

By this, they mean their children, the eldest of whom have scattered. And really, given the way prices and taxes have risen, inheriting a house on Hillcrest is the next generation's only hope for an old house in a good neighborhood. Of course, they themselves will never leave. They'll have to be carried out feet first, they say, though they are careful to speak softly so that the old doctor won't hear. His house, just across the street from the Peabodys' lawn, rises above the thick clump of Katherine's yellow irises. He is very old now and must decline the invitations to the block party. He sends his wishes from behind the closed curtains of his white stucco Spanish Mediterranean. They do not say so, but the other residents of Hillcrest are relieved. They have never understood why he chose to stay after what happened. They wouldn't have been able to.

Occasionally, an article appears in the paper, marking the tenth, twentieth, now thirtieth anniversary of the killings—the doctor's first wife and older daughter, home from college for a visit between semesters. The case remains unsolved; the articles end with the usual plea for information. They have written to the paper and asked that the name Hillcrest be withheld from the article; it gives the wrong impression of the neighborhood. But of course, the paper still prints the street name and inevitably one of their kids learns of the crimes and they're forced to tell the version they've agreed upon. They assure their children all this happened long before they moved in, another era really. They're more careful now. It's why Madeleine Welsh was right to phone the police about the stranger looking over the Colliers' garden gate. Below them is a different city, where hooded youths with guns roam the flat streets. There isn't a wall between them and the rest of the world. They must all watch out for one another. It's why the block parties are so important. Still, what's past is past.

They omit certain details. They don't tell the children the way the killer bound the two women with their own stockings or what he did to the girl. They don't mention that it was the younger daughter, the one still in high school, who walked home from class to find her mother and sister on the living room floor just a few feet from the piano. Nor do they say that the front door had not been forced open or that the prime suspect lived just two doors down, in what is now the Dillingers' house: a shaggy-haired, hollow-eyed teenage boy whose second story window faced the doctor's house. They do not admit what they have all imagined from the black-and-white photo of the victims reprinted in the paper each year: the scrubbed co-ed opening the door, her pressed miniskirt, her straight smile and full brunette hair. *Please, come in.* They especially do not like to think about that. As parents, they have aimed to instill good manners in their own children. The police investigated, but couldn't make a case against the boy. That hasn't changed, the adults agree. Even with all the technology now, they have no faith in the cops. Instead they tell their children, That was long time ago. They've learned to be more careful now. They watch out for one another.

Everyone claps encouragement as James and Madeleine Welsh arrive carrying their instruments in black armored cases. Each year they learn a new piece just for the party. James has never told his wife this, but he believes their music placates ghosts. Nor has Suzanne Collier ever revealed that years ago, after she saw the girl's picture in the paper, she began to hear odd noises. She said nothing of it, even to Anne Dillinger, who had confided that she once hired a woman to burn sage in every room of their house. Judith Goldman keeps most thoughts to herself. Sometimes when she closes the door to her small library, she sits in her highback chair and thinks about when the house was new. She imagines the young girls who once slept in her little room. She pictures their raw fingers and plain faces, the way they rose from narrow beds early in the morning to pin back mopstraight hair and light the fireplace. She imagines the routine of their days, cooking and cleaning for a family not their own, and how the girls must have longed for the few dark hours to themselves in this tiny room. She thinks of her own daughter, now three thousand miles away in a little dorm room. When Judith calls, her daughter does not seem relieved to hear from her or interested in news from the neighborhood. Judith doesn't understand it, but she detects accusation, even disdain, in her daughter's voice.

Wine glasses are refilled, then everyone quiets as James and Madeleine settle their music stand on the grass. Anne Dillinger gently guides her husband away from the spinach dip. The first tendrils of the evening fog have crept in and some of the women slip on jackets they have knowingly brought. There is a general murmur about *San Francisco summers*. And there's a breeze; the sheet music ripples. Dennis Petersen steps forward and with thick, pink fingers, steadies the sheets. His tall frame looms to the side of the metal stand and they all smile, certain that in a past life, he held the pitted wood of a ship's wheel with the same measured calm.

Keeping their backs to the doctor's house, they tell themselves that any place as old as Hillcrest has stories. All old houses do. It's part of their character. The older neighbors stand smiling as the younger parents gather their children, pull them close and whisper, *Listen*. Then Madeleine's lips nestle into the brass mouthpiece of her horn, and James lowers his bow to the strings. *[2012]*

SUMMING UP: READING CLOSELY

- ***Close reading* is a process that consists of several strategies, all of which can help you get ideas about a literary work for an essay you will write.** These strategies include making predictions as you read; rereading the text with a different focus each time; reading aloud; comparing the text with your personal experience; tracing patterns and breaks from them; noting ambiguities; considering the author's alternatives; generating questions; and formulating a tentative claim. (pp. 18–21)
- **Close reading is aided by several *writing* strategies.** These include commenting in the text's margins; note-taking; freewriting; creating a "dialectical notebook"; and playfully revising the text. (pp. 20–21)
- **To generate ideas about a literary text, consider its characters' emotions and speech acts, as well as how the text deals with topics that have preoccupied literary studies.** (pp. 41–42)

CHAPTER 3

How to Make Arguments about Literature

The fourth word in this chapter's title may puzzle you. Why would we want you to *argue*? Are we really inviting you to yell or sneer? The word *arguing* may remind you of spats you regret. Most everyone has suffered arguments like these. They arise in the media all the time. Talk-radio hosts and their callers mix strong opinion with insult. Television's political panels routinely lapse into squabbles; guests feel required to clash. Quarrels explode on daytime talkfests; couples fight over who's cheated on whom. Online forums are plagued by "trolls," writers who crudely mock others' posts. No wonder many people define *arguing* as combat. It often seems like war.

What Is Argument?

In this book, we define *arguing* in a positive sense. We ask you to think of it as a calm, courteous process in which you

identify a subject of current or possible debate;

analyze why you view the subject the way you do;

address others who may not share your view; and

try to persuade them that your view is worth accepting or at least makes sense.

This better kind of arguing occurs at various times and places. You may try to coax friends who dread horror films into joining you at *Saw 12*. In class, you may need to explain the logic of your stand on climate change. Beyond campus, you may advocate for social causes. For instance, you might petition your city to launch recycling sites.

Let's face it: to argue *is* to disagree, or to air views not all may hold. Still, at its best, arguing is an *alternative* to war. It's *not* a contest you try to "win" by insisting you're right. To argue well is to state your ideas, support them, and negotiate objections to them, all the while maintaining a civil tone. In an ideal argument, you note principles you share with your critics. You treat fairly ideas different from yours. When these seem wise, you adjust your thinking. The whole process leads you to test your beliefs. "The real argument," Phillip Lopate observes, "should be with yourself." Columnist David Brooks goes even further: "If you write in a way that suggests combative certitude," he warns, "you may gradually smother the inner chaos that will be the source of lifelong freshness and creativity." In their own fashion, these writers point to something important about argument: at its best, it teaches you about yourself and your world, while alerting you to what you still must learn.

Students regularly encounter this kind of arguing in college. Academic subjects aren't just pools of information. They go beyond proven facts. Disciplines grapple with uncertainties: problems, questions, and conflicts they haven't yet solved. Physicists disagree about the origins of the universe. Historians write conflicting accounts of Hitler's Germany; they debate how much his extreme anti-Semitism was traditional there. Two sociologists may scan the same figures on poverty and make different inferences from them. Typically, scholars draw conclusions that are open to challenge. They must explain why their judgments are sound. They expect to engage in reasoned debate with their colleagues. They see this as their field's best chance for truth.

In your classes, expect disagreements. They're crucial to learning in college. Often, classmates will voice ideas you don't immediately accept. Just as often, they'll hesitate to adopt some opinion of yours. Authors you read will deal with controversies, from their own points of view. As a writer yourself, you will enter debates and have to defend your stands.

No one naturally excels at this type of arguing. It takes practice. Our book is a series of opportunities to become skilled in this art. In Part Two, each chapter ends with arguments about a single subject. We then invite you to add your slant. Our book's chief springboard for argument, though, is works of literature. Those we include don't deliver simple, straightforward messages. They offer puzzles, complications, metaphors, symbols, and mysteries. In short, they stress life's complexity. They especially encourage you to ponder multiple dimensions of language: how, for example, shifts of context can change a word's meaning. Each of our literary works calls for you to interpret. As you read the text, you must figure out various features of it. Then, other readers may not see the text as you see it. So next, you'll *argue* for your view. Often you'll do so by composing essays and perhaps online posts. In the rest of this chapter, we offer strategies you can employ to argue about literature as a writer.

As we discuss this process, we refer to arguments that might be made about the following story, Jamaica Kincaid's "Girl." It first appeared in *The New Yorker* in 1978 and was later reprinted in her first book, a 1984 collection of short stories entitled *At the Bottom of the River.*

JAMAICA KINCAID

Girl

Originally named Elaine Potter Richardson, Jamaica Kincaid (b. 1949) was born on the island of Antigua in the West Indies. At the time, Antigua was a British colony. Kincaid lived there until she was seventeen, when she emigrated to the United States. Soon she became a nanny for the family of Michael Arlen, television critic for The New

Yorker. *Eventually, the magazine published her own short stories and, during the early 1990s, her gardening columns. Although she continues to live in the United States, almost all of her writing deals with her native land. In particular, she has written about Antiguan women growing up under British domination. She has published the novels* Annie John *(1985),* Lucy *(1990),* Autobiography of My Mother *(1996), and* Mr. Potter *(2002). Her books of nonfiction include* A Small Place, *an analysis of Antigua (1988); a memoir,* My Brother *(1997);* My Garden (Book) *(1999); and* Talk Stories *(2001), a collection of brief observations that she originally wrote for* The New Yorker. *In 2009, she was inducted into the American Academy of Arts and Sciences and is currently a professor of literature at Claremont McKenna College in California. Her latest book is a novel,* See Now Then *(2013).*

Wash the white clothes on Monday and put them on the stone heap; wash the color clothes on Tuesday and put them on the clothesline to dry; don't walk barehead in the hot sun; cook pumpkin fritters in very hot sweet oil; soak your little cloths right after you take them off; when buying cotton to make yourself a nice blouse, be sure that it doesn't have gum on it, because that way it won't hold up well after a wash; soak salt fish overnight before you cook it; is it true that you sing benna° in Sunday school?; always eat your food in such a way that it won't turn someone else's stomach; on Sundays try to walk like a lady and not like the slut you are so bent on becoming; don't sing benna in Sunday school; you mustn't speak to wharf-rat boys, not even to give directions; don't eat fruits on the street—flies will follow you; *but I don't sing benna on Sundays at all and never in Sunday school*; this is how to sew on a button; this is how to make a button-hole for the button you have just sewed on; this is how to hem a dress when you see the hem coming down and so to prevent yourself from looking like the slut I know you are so bent on becoming; this is how you iron your father's khaki shirt so that it doesn't have a crease; this is how you iron your father's khaki pants so that they don't have a crease; this is how you grow okra—far from the house, because okra tree harbors red ants; when you are growing dasheen,° make sure it gets plenty of water or else it makes your throat itch when you are eating it; this is how you sweep a corner; this is how you sweep a whole house; this is how you sweep a yard; this is how you smile to someone you don't like too much; this is how you smile to someone you don't like at all; this is how you smile to someone you like completely; this is how you set a table for tea; this is how you set a table for dinner; this is how you set a table for dinner with an important guest; this is how you set a table for lunch; this is how you set a table for breakfast; this is how to behave in the presence of men who don't know you very well, and this way they won't recognize immediately the slut I have warned you against becoming; be sure to wash every day, even if it is with your own spit; don't squat down to play marbles—you are not a boy, you know; don't pick people's flowers—you might catch something; don't throw stones at blackbirds, because it might not be a

7 benna: Calypso music. **dasheen:** A kind of taro plant.

blackbird at all; this is how to make a bread pudding; this is how to make doukona;° this is how to make pepper pot; this is how to make a good medicine for a cold; this is how to make a good medicine to throw away a child before it even becomes a child; this is how to catch a fish; this is how to throw back a fish you don't like, and that way something bad won't fall on you; this is how to bully a man; this is how a man bullies you; this is how to love a man, and if this doesn't work there are other ways, and if they don't work don't feel too bad about giving up; this is how to spit up in the air if you feel like it, and this is how to move quick so that it doesn't fall on you; this is how to make ends meet; always squeeze bread to make sure it's fresh; *but what if the baker won't let me feel the bread?*; you mean to say that after all you are really going to be the kind of woman who the baker won't let near the bread? *[1978]*

31 doukona: A spicy plantain pudding.

THINKING ABOUT THE TEXT

1. Is "Girl" really a story? What characteristics of a story come to mind as you consider this issue?
2. Describe the culture depicted in "Girl" as well as the role of females in that culture. Is either the culture or the role of females in it different from what you are familiar with? Explain.
3. Do you think that the instructions to this girl are all given on the same occasion? Why, or why not? Who do you suppose is giving the instructions? Would you say that the instructor is oppressive or domineering? Identify some of the assumptions behind your position.
4. What effect does Kincaid achieve by making this text a single long sentence? By having the girl speak at only two brief moments?
5. At one point, the girl is shown "how to make a good medicine to throw away a child before it even becomes a child" (lines 33–34). What do you think of the instructor's willingness to give such advice? What do you conclude from its position in the text between "how to make a good medicine for a cold" (line 33) and "how to catch a fish" (line 35)? Does the order of the various pieces of advice matter? Could Kincaid have presented them in a different order without changing their effects?

Strategies for Making Arguments about Literature

Arguing is a form of **rhetoric**. This is a term from ancient Greek. It means writing, speech, and visual images used for a certain purpose: to affect how people think and act. Rhetorical texts don't just convey a message. They aim to *shape* beliefs and conduct. Often they're efforts to *alter* these things. Say you write an essay interpreting Jamaica Kincaid's "Girl"; you will be engaging in rhetoric if you try to change the minds of people who currently hold views of the story other than yours.

A related term is **the rhetorical situation**. It's the specific context you have in mind when you engage in rhetoric. Major circumstances include the following:

- **The particular topic you choose.** If you are writing about "Girl" for your teacher and classmates, have they previously discussed the story? If they have, you won't be introducing a new subject to them. If they haven't, you may have to explain why you are bringing up the story now.

  Of course, the topic of an argument may already interest the public at large. The December 2012 massacre of children in Newtown, Connecticut, immediately provoked disputes over gun control, school safety, mental illness, and screen violence. Other writers must alert their readers to their subject or remind them of it. This was the situation for legal scholars Woodrow Hartzog and Evan Selinger in 2013, when they posted an online argument about Facebook. At the time, people worried about Facebook's dangers to privacy. They felt the site wouldn't securely protect users' personal data. In their argument, Hartzog and Selinger deliberately shift to another subject. They recommend thinking less about *privacy* and more about *obscurity*, which they note is a word "rarely used" in debates about Facebook's risks. To them, *privacy* is so vague a concept that brooding about how the site guards it is futile. They call for pushing Facebook to keep personal facts *obscure*: "hard to obtain or understand" when cyberstalkers hunt for them.
- **The main readers, listeners, or viewers you decide to address.** As we have suggested, these people may be other members of the class you're currently in. In the wider world, writers often have to decide to what specific groups they are directing their arguments. In 2003, for example, architecture critic Paul Goldberger wrote an article complaining that cell phones made their users less sensitive to the physical realities of urban settings. Goldberger chose to publish his argument in *Metropolis*, a city-oriented magazine. Its mission statement declares that it "examines contemporary life through design," featuring articles that "range from the sprawling urban environment to intimate living spaces to small objects of everyday lives." This magazine also seeks to put design in "economic, environmental, social, cultural, political, and technological contexts." Readers of *Metropolis* would not be surprised, therefore, for the magazine to include an opinion piece about cell phones' impact on cities. Perhaps Goldberger hoped his piece would someday circulate more widely, as it now does on the Web. But surely his target group loomed in his mind as he decided on content, form, and words.
- **Possible "channels" for the text.** These include available institutions, media, and genres. To spark a crusade against guerilla leader Joseph Kony—who has kidnapped children and made them serve in his army—Jason Russell chose to make a video documentary exposing his atrocities. (As you may know, the film went viral when Russell posted it

online.) Even if you write an interpretive essay about "Girl" for a college class, you might do more than submit it in print to your teacher. Other possibilities include submitting it electronically; posting it online in a class forum; using it as the basis for a YouTube video; or incorporating parts of it into a multimedia class presentation (an activity we discuss at the end of Chapter 6).

Current politicians fling the word "rhetoric" as an insult. They accuse their rivals of indulging in it. They treat the word with contempt because they think it means windy exaggeration. But before the modern age, it meant something nobler. Rhetoric was the valuable attempt to *influence* readers, listeners, or viewers. In this sense, almost all of us resort to rhetoric daily. We need to learn rhetorical strategies if we're to have impact on others. For centuries, then, schools have seen rhetoric as a vital art. They've deemed it important to study, practice, and teach. In ancient Greece and Rome as well as Renaissance Europe, it was a core academic subject. American colleges of the nineteenth century also made it central. This focus survives in many courses today, especially ones about writing or speech. Our book reflects this commitment to rhetoric, especially through our advice about writing.

Within the field of rhetoric, arguments are a more specific category. Those you make about literature involve eight basic elements. You attempt to **persuade** an **audience** to accept your **claims** regarding an **issue**. To achieve this aim, you present **evidence**, explain your **reasoning**, rely on **assumptions**, and make other kinds of **appeals**. The boldfaced words play key roles in this book; we mention them often. Here we explain what we mean by each, beginning with *issue* and then moving to *claims, persuasion, audience, evidence, reasoning, assumptions*, and *appeals*. Throughout our discussion, we refer to Kincaid's story "Girl."

IDENTIFY AN ISSUE

An **issue** is something about which people have disagreed or might disagree. Even as you read a text, you can try to guess what features of it will lead to disagreements in class. You may sense that your own reaction to certain aspects of the text is heavily influenced by your background and values, which other students may not share. Some parts of the text may leave you with conflicting ideas or mixed feelings, as if half of you disagrees with the other half. At moments like these, you come to realize what topics are issues for you, and next you can urge the rest of your class to see these topics as issues, too.

An issue is best defined as a question with no obvious, immediate answer. Thus, you can start identifying issues by noting questions that occur to you as you read. Perhaps this question-posing approach to texts is new for you. Often readers demand that a text be clear, and they get annoyed if it leaves them puzzled. Certain writing ought to be immediately clear in meaning; think of operating instructions on a plane's emergency doors. But the value of a literary work often lies in the work's complexities, which can lead readers to reexamine their own ways of perceiving the world. Also, your discussions and papers about literature are likely to be most useful when they go beyond the obvious to deal with more challenging matters. When your class begins talking about a work, you may feel obliged to stay quiet if you have no firm statements to make. But you can contribute a lot by bringing up questions that occurred to you as you read. Especially worth raising are questions that continue to haunt you.

In any case, when you write an argument about a literary text, readers should find your main issue *significant*. It must be a question they believe is worth caring about. Sometimes they'll immediately see its value. But often you'll need to explain what's *at stake*—how the answer to this question can significantly affect one's understanding of the text. Scholars of rhetoric describe this task as establishing the issue's *exigence*.

A possible issue with Jamaica Kincaid's "Girl" concerns how much affection the main speaker has for the girl she addresses. A logical hypothesis is that these two are mother and daughter, but to what degree is the speaker showing motherly love? In fact, people may disagree over how to define this term. What does it mean to *you*?

You may feel unable to answer questions like these. But again, you achieve much when you simply formulate questions and bring them up in class. As other students help you ponder them, you will grow better able to explore issues through writing as well as through conversation.

You are more likely to come up with questions about a text if you assume that for every decision the writer made, alternatives existed. In "Girl," Kincaid might have given her title character more of a speaking voice. She might have divided the story into multiple sections rather than present it in one long paragraph. When you begin to explore why authors made the choices they did, you also begin to examine the effects of those choices.

Next we identify ten kinds of issues that arise in literature courses. Our list will help you detect the issues that come up in your class and discover others to bring up in discussions or in your writing. The list does not include every kind of issue; you may think of others. Moreover, you may find that an issue can fit into more than one of the categories we name. But when you do have an issue that seems hard to classify, try to assign it to a single category, if only for the time being. You will then have some initial guidance for your reading, class discussions, and writing. If you later feel that the issue belongs to another category, you can shift your focus.

1. Issues of fact. Rarely does a work of literature provide complete information about its characters and events. Rather, literature is usually marked by what literary theorist Wolfgang Iser calls "gaps," moments when certain facts are omitted or obscured. At such times, readers may give various answers to the question, What is happening in this text? Readers tackle questions of fact only if they suspect that their answers will affect their overall view of a text. It may not matter, for example, that we fail to learn the exact age of Kincaid's title character. More consequential seems the question of whether the story's main speaker actually presented all her lessons at the same time. Imagine a reader who believes this is indeed the case. Imagine a second reader who believes that the speaker delivered these lessons at various times but that the girl is remembering them as one continuous monologue. How might these two readers see the whole story differently because of their different assumptions?

2. Issues of theme. You may be familiar with the term **theme** from other literature courses. By *theme* critics usually mean the main claim that an author seems to be making with his or her text. Sometimes a theme is defined in terms of a single word—for example, *work* or *love*. But such words are really mere topics. Identifying the topics addressed by a text can be a useful way of starting to analyze that text, and earlier in Part One we list several topics that currently preoccupy literary studies. A text's theme, however, is best seen as an assertion that you need at least one whole sentence to express.

With many texts, an issue of theme arises because readers can easily disagree about the text's main idea. In literature classes, such disagreements often occur, in part because literary works tend to express their themes indirectly. This is especially the case with a story like "Girl," in which the main speaker's views are not necessarily the same as the author's. Readers of the story may give various answers to the question, What is the author ultimately saying? Perhaps some readers will take Kincaid to imply that mothers always know best. Other readers may conclude that Kincaid thinks that excessively controlling mothers are damaging to children.

If you try to express a text's theme, avoid making a statement that is so general that it could apply to many other works. Arguing that Kincaid's theme is "Girls are pressured to fit stereotyped roles" does not get at her story's details. On the other hand, do not let a text's details restrict you so much that you make the theme seem relevant only to a small group. If you argue that Kincaid's theme is "Antiguan women are domineering," then the many readers who are *not* from Antigua will wonder why they should care. In short, try to express themes as *mid-level generalizations.* With Kincaid's story, one possible theme is "In some cultures, women prepare girls for adulthood by teaching them to follow conventions *and* to assert themselves." A statement like this seems both attentive to Kincaid's specific text and applicable to a large portion of humanity. You are free to challenge this version of Kincaid's theme by proposing an alternative. Moreover, even if you do accept this statement as her theme, you are then free to decide whether it is a sound observation. Identifying a theme is one thing; evaluating it is another.

Keep in mind that a theme ties together various parts of a text. Focusing on a single passage, even if it seems thematic, may lead you to ignore other passages that a statement of theme should encompass. For instance, the last words of "Girl" may tempt you to believe that its theme is "Be the kind of woman who feels the bread." Yet in other parts of the story, the main speaker seems to be calling for a compliant attitude. You need to take these moments into account as well.

Often you will sense a work's theme but still have to decide whether to state it as an **observation** or as a **recommendation**. You would be doing the first, for example, if you expressed Kincaid's theme as we did above: "In some cultures, women prepare girls for adulthood by teaching them to follow conventions *and* to assert themselves." You would be doing the second if you said Kincaid's theme is "Women should teach girls to follow conventions *and* to assert themselves." Indeed, people who depict a theme as a recommendation often use a word like *should*. Neither way of expressing a theme is necessarily better than the other. But notice that each way conjures up a particular image of the author. Reporting Kincaid's theme as an observation suggests that she is writing as a psychologist, a philosopher, or some other analyst of human nature. Reporting her theme as a recommendation suggests that she is writing as a teacher, preacher, manager, or coach: someone who is telling her readers what to do. Your decision about how to phrase a theme will depend in part on which image of the author you think is appropriate.

You risk obscuring the intellectual, emotional, and stylistic richness of a text if you insist on reducing it to a single message. Try stating the text's theme as a problem for which there is no easy solution, which suggests that the text is complex. For instance, if you say that Kincaid's theme is "In some cultures, women who prepare girls for adulthood are caught in a contradiction between wanting to empower them and wanting to keep them safe," you position yourself to address various elements of the story.

Also weigh the possibility that a text is conveying more than one theme. If you plan to associate the text with any theme at all, you might refer to *a* theme of the text rather than *the* theme of the text. Your use of the term *theme* would still have implications. Above all, you would still be suggesting that you have identified one of the text's major points. Subsequently, you might have to defend this claim, showing how the point you have identified is indeed central to the text.

Issues of theme have loomed large in literary studies. We hope that you will find them useful to pursue. But because references to theme are so common in literary studies, students sometimes forget that there are other kinds of issues. As you move through this list, you may find some that interest you more.

3. Issues of definition. In arguments about literature, issues of **definition** arise most often when readers try to decide what an author means by a particular word. Consider the title of Kincaid's story; what does it mean to be a "girl" in this particular culture? Notice that an issue of definition can arise even with ordinary language.

4. Issues of symbolism. In literary studies, an issue of **symbolism** usually centers on a particular image. In question are the image's meaning and purpose, including whether the image is more than just a detail. Notice that "Girl" concludes with the image of bread; indeed, "bread" is the story's very last word. You can take this reference literally, thinking just about the physical product that bread is, but you might want to argue that Kincaid is prodding her readers to consider symbolic associations often made with this food. For example, bread has traditionally been taken to represent the very spirit of life itself.

5. Issues of pattern. With issues of **pattern**, you observe how a text is organized and try to determine how certain parts of the text relate to other parts. But think, too, about the meaning and purpose of any pattern you find, especially since readers may disagree about the pattern's significance. Also ponder the implications of any moment when a text *breaks* with a pattern it has been following. Disruptions of a pattern may be as important as the pattern itself.

A conspicuous pattern in "Girl" is the main speaker's series of commands, which includes repeated use of the words *this is how*. Indeed, **repetition** is a common pattern in literature. Yet at two points in Kincaid's story, the speaker is interrupted by italicized protests from the girl: "*but I don't sing benna on Sundays at all and never in Sunday school*" (lines 11–12) and "*but what if the baker won't let me feel the bread?*" (line 41). What should we conclude about the main speaker from her string of orders? What should we conclude about the girl from her two disruptions? Readers may have various answers to these questions.

A text's apparent oppositions are also patterns that may be debated. An example in "Girl" is the distinction that the main speaker makes in lines 8–9 between being "a lady" and being a "slut." What contrasting values and behavior does she seem to associate with these terms? What sorts of young woman might these two categories leave out? Again, different answers to such questions are possible.

6. Issues of evaluation. Consciously or unconsciously, **evaluation** always plays a central role in reading. When you read a work of literature, you evaluate its ideas and the actions of its characters. You judge, too, the views you assume the author is promoting. Moreover, you gauge the artistic quality of the text.

Specifically, you engage in three kinds of evaluation as you read. One kind is *philosophical*: you decide whether a particular idea or action is wise. Another kind is *ethical*: you decide whether an idea or action is morally good. The third kind is *aesthetic*: you decide whether the work as a whole or parts of the text succeed as art. Another reader may disagree with your criteria for wisdom, morality, and art; people's standards often differ. It is not surprising, then, that in the study of literature issues of evaluation come up frequently.

Sometimes you may have trouble distinguishing the three types of judgment from each other. Philosophical evaluation, ethical evaluation, and aesthetic evaluation can overlap. Probably the first two operate in the mind of a reader who is judging the advice given by the main speaker in "Girl." This reader may, for instance, find the speaker insensitive: that is, neither smart nor humane. Moreover, if this reader thinks Kincaid sympathizes with the speaker, then he or she may consider "Girl" flawed as a work of art. Keep in mind, however, that you can admire many aspects of a literary work even if you disagree with the ideas you see the author promoting. Someone may relish Kincaid's colorful language regardless of the views presented in the story.

But whose works should be taught? Many scholars argue that literary studies have focused too much on white male authors, and some refuse to assume that the works of these authors are great and universally relevant. They criticize the long neglect of female and minority writers like Kincaid, a black woman born and raised in the West Indies. In part because of these scholars' arguments, "Girl" now appears in many literature anthologies. Yet other people continue to prize "classics" by William Shakespeare, John Milton, and William Blake. This ongoing debate about the literature curriculum includes disagreements about the worth of recent texts. After all, contemporary literature has yet to pass a "test of time." Does Kincaid's 1978 story deserve to be anthologized and taught? *We* think so and have included "Girl" in our own book. What, though, is *your* evaluation of it? Also, what particular standards have you used to judge it?

7. Issues of historical and cultural context. Plenty of literary works have engaged readers who are quite unlike their authors. These readers may include much-later generations and inhabitants of distant lands. Nevertheless, an author's own **historical and cultural context** may significantly shape his or her text. Consider Jamaica Kincaid's use of her past in "Girl." Though she has lived in the United States since she was seventeen, she evidently tapped memories of her childhood on Antigua to write this story and to represent the island's culture. Since many of the story's readers would be unfamiliar with Antigua, she had to decide what aspects of it to acquaint them with. What features of it does she emphasize, and what features does she downplay or omit? When Kincaid was born, Antiguans were under British control, and many labored hard for little money. Do these historical facts matter in "Girl"? If so, in what conceivable ways? Notice that answering such political and economic questions usually requires research. Even then, answers may be complicated. Indeed, rarely does a literary text straightforwardly reflect its author's background. Debate arises over how text and context relate.

We provide some background for each literary work we present to help you begin to situate it historically and culturally. In Chapter 6, we explain how to put literature in context, especially by doing research in the library and on the Internet. For now, we want to emphasize that contextualizing a work involves more than just piling up facts about its origin. In the study of literature, issues of historical and cultural context are often issues of *relevance*: *which* facts about a work's creation are important for readers to know, and *how* would awareness of these facts help readers better understand the work? Readers can inform themselves about a particular author's life, for instance, but they may disagree about the extent to which a given text is autobiographical.

Perhaps you like to connect a literary work with its author's own life. The author of the story we have been discussing apparently drew to some extent on her personal experiences. You may be tempted, therefore, to think that "Girl" consists of advice Kincaid herself received. Yet when you assert that a work is thoroughly autobiographical, you risk overlooking aspects of the text that depart from the author's own experiences, impressions, and beliefs. We are not urging you to refrain from ever connecting the author's text to the author's life. Rather, we are pointing out that whatever links you forge may be the subject of debate.

Even the term *history* can be defined in various ways. When you refer to a work's historical context, you need to clarify whether you are examining (1) the life of the work's author; (2) the time period in which it was written; (3) any time period mentioned within the text; (4) its subsequent reception, including responses to it by later generations; or (5) the forms in which the work has been published, which may involve changes in its spelling, punctuation, wording, and overall appearance.

8. Issues of genre. So far, we have been identifying categories of issues. Issues of **genre** are *about* categorization, for they involve determining what *kind* of text a particular work is. You might categorize "Girl" as belonging to the short-story genre, but someone might disagree because it seems to lack a conventional plot. This debate would involve deciding what the essential characteristics of a "short story" are. Even if you argue that Kincaid's text belongs to this genre, you can attempt to classify it more precisely by aiming for a term that better sums up its content and form. Issues of genre often arise with such further classification.

A literary text may relate in some way to a characteristic of ordinary, real-life interactions. In key respects, "Girl" belongs to the parental-advice genre. Try, though, to distinguish between text genre and real-life genre. Kincaid's story can be categorized as *an exploration of how gender roles are reinforced*. In any case, you may find that two or more labels are appropriate for a particular text. For instance, besides the category we've just mentioned, you might label "Girl" as *assembled memories*—if, that is, you believe the title character is *recollecting* bits of advice she received on various occasions. You would then have to decide whether these two labels are equally helpful. Much of the time, issues of genre are issues of priority. Readers debate not whether a certain label for a work is appropriate but whether that label is the best.

9. Issues of social policy. In many works of literature, writers have attempted to instigate social reform by exposing defects in their cultures and encouraging specific cures. A famous example is Upton Sinclair's 1906 novel, *The Jungle*, which vividly depicts horrible conditions in Chicago's stockyards and thereby led the meat-processing plant owners to adopt more humane and hygienic practices. Even a work of literature that is not blatantly political or that seems rooted in the distant past may make you conscious of your own society's problems and possible solutions to them. Yet you and your classmates may propose different definitions of and solutions for cultural problems. The result is what we call issues of **social policy**.

Sometimes your position on an issue of social policy will affect how you read a certain literary work. For example, your view on how girls and boys should be educated may affect your response to Kincaid's story. Even if current issues of social policy do not influence your original reading of a work, you can still use the work to raise such issues in your writing or in class discussion. Imagine discussing Kincaid's story at a meeting of junior high school teachers. What policies might the story be used to promote there?

10. Issues of cause and effect. Issues of **causality** are common in literary studies. Often they arise as readers present different explanations for a character's behavior. Why does the girl in Kincaid's story protest at two particular moments? Remember that even a work's narrator or main speaker is a character with motives worth analyzing.

Such questions can be rephrased to center on the author. For instance, you can ask why Kincaid ends her story by having the characters speak about feeling the bread. If you look back at our discussion of these ten types of issues, you may see that most issues can be phrased as questions about the author's purposes. But remember your options. Focusing on authorial intent in a given case may not be as useful as sticking with another type of issue. Or you may turn a question about authorial intent into a question about authorial **effect**. How should readers react when Kincaid ends her story the way she does? You can address questions like this without sounding as if you know exactly what the author intended.

MAKE A CLAIM

You may not be used to calling things you say or write *claims.* But even when you utter a simple observation about the weather—for instance, "It's beginning to rain"—you are making a claim. Basically, a **claim** is a statement that is spoken or written so that others will consider it to be true. With this definition in mind, you may start noticing claims everywhere. Most of us make lots of them every day. Furthermore, most of our claims are accepted as true by the people to whom we make them. Imagine how difficult life would be if the opposite were the case; human beings would be perpetually anxious if they distrusted almost everything they were told.

At times, though, claims do conflict with other claims. In a literature course, disagreements inevitably arise. Again, try not to let disagreements scare you. You can learn a lot from encountering views other than yours and from having to support your own. Moreover, exciting talk can occur as your class negotiates differences of opinion.

Recall that we defined an *issue* as a question with various debatable answers. *Claims*, as we use the term, are the debatable answers. For examples of claims in literary studies, look back at our explanations of ten kinds of issues. In that discussion, we mentioned possible claims about "Girl": e.g., that Kincaid's theme is "Women should teach girls to follow conventions *and* to assert themselves," that the final image of bread is symbolic, and that the story's genre is assembled memories. These claims are debatable because in each case at least one other position is possible.

In literature classes, two types of claims are especially common. To criticize Kincaid's main speaker is to engage in **evaluation**. To identify themes of "Girl" is to engage in **interpretation**. Conventionally, interpretation is the kind of analysis that depends on hypotheses rather than simple observation of plain fact. Throughout this book, we refer to the practice of interpreting a work or certain aspects of it. Admittedly, sometimes you may have trouble distinguishing interpretation from evaluation. When you evaluate some feature of a work or make an overall judgment of that work, probably you are operating with a certain interpretation as well, even if you do not make that interpretation explicit. Similarly, when you interpret part of a work or the text as a whole, probably you have already decided whether the text is worth figuring out. Nevertheless, the two types of claims differ in their emphases. When you attempt to interpret a work, you are mostly analyzing it; when you attempt to evaluate the work, you are mostly judging it.

In class discussions, other students may resist a claim you make about a literary work. Naturally, you may choose to defend your view at length. But remain open to the possibility of changing your mind, either by modifying your claim somehow or by shifting completely to another one. Also, entertain the possibility that a view different from yours is just as reasonable, even if you do not share it.

In much of your writing for your course, you will be identifying an issue and making one main claim about it, which can be called your **thesis**. As you attempt to support your main claim, you will make a number of smaller claims. In drafts of your paper, welcome opportunities to test the claims you make in it. Review your claims with classmates to help you determine how persuasive your thinking is. You will be left with a stronger sense of what you must do to make your paper credible.

AIM TO PERSUADE

As we have noted, argument is often associated with arrogant insistence. Many assume that if two people are arguing, they are each demanding to be seen as correct. At its best, however, argument involves careful efforts to persuade. When you make such an effort, you indicate that you believe your claims, even if you remain open to revising them. You indicate as well that you would like others to agree with you. Yet to attempt **persuasion** is to concede that you must support your claims if others are to value them.

As you have probably discovered on many occasions, swaying people who hold views different from yours can be difficult. You will not always be able to change their minds, yet you may still convince them that your claims are at least reasonable. Moreover, the process of trying to persuade others will compel you to clarify your ideas, to review why you hold them, and to analyze the people you aim to affect.

CONSIDER YOUR AUDIENCE

When you hear the word **audience**, perhaps you think first of people attending plays, concerts, movies, or lectures. Yet *audience* also describes readers, including the people who read your writing. Not everything you write is for other people's eyes; in this course, you may produce notes, journal entries, and even full-length drafts that only you will see. From time to time in the course, however, you will do public writing. On these occasions, you will be trying to persuade your audience to accept whatever claims you make.

These occasions will require you to consider more than just your subject matter. If you are truly to persuade your readers, you must take them into account. Unfortunately, you will not be able to find out everything about your audience beforehand. Moreover, you will have to study the ways in which your readers differ from one another. Usually, though, you will be able to identify some of their common values, experiences, and assumptions. Having this knowledge will strengthen your ability to make a case they appreciate.

In analyzing a work of literature, you may try to identify its *implied reader*: that is, the type of person that the work seems to address. Remember, too, that people may have read the work in manuscript or when it was first published.

Finally, the work may have had innumerable readers since. Often we ask you to write about a text's effect on you and to compare your reaction with your classmates'.

You can introduce your essay's main claim by referring to the audience you're focusing on:

- Readers you disagree with

  While some readers may feel that the main speaker in "Girl" loves the title character, the tone of this adult woman suggests that she does not care much for the girl at all.

- Hasty, superficial readers

  Because the main speaker in "Girl" gives many instructions that suggest she is very much in control of her life, readers may overlook signs that she *hasn't* entirely mastered her existence but instead is trying to cope as best she can.

- Puzzled readers

  Many readers may wonder why the girl's father is barely mentioned in Kincaid's story. Kincaid evidently wants us to think more about how mother-daughter relationships treat men, including fathers, as outsiders.

- Your own divided self

  While at first I thought that the main speaker is a cold and perhaps even bitter "teacher," I have concluded that she does feel warm toward the title character and genuinely cares about the girl's welfare.

Above all, you may wonder how familiar your readers already are with the text you are analyzing. Perhaps your teacher will resolve your uncertainty, telling you exactly how much your audience knows about the text. Then again, you may be left to guess. Should you presume that your audience is totally unfamiliar with the text? This approach is risky, for it may lead you to spend a lot of your paper merely summarizing the text rather than analyzing it. A better move is to write as if your audience is at least a bit more knowledgeable. Here is a good rule of thumb: *assume that your audience has, in fact, read the text but that you need to recall for this group any features of the text that are crucial to your argument.* Although probably your paper will still include summary, the amount you provide will be limited, and your own ideas will be more prominent.

GATHER AND PRESENT EVIDENCE

Evidence is the support that you give your claims so that others will accept them. What sort of evidence you must provide depends on what your audience requires to be persuaded. When you make claims during class discussions, your classmates and instructor might ask you follow-up questions, thereby suggesting what you must do to convince them. As a writer, you might often find yourself having to guess your readers' standards of evidence. Naturally, your guesses will be influenced by any prior experiences you have had with your audience. Moreover, you may have opportunities to review drafts with some of its members.

When you make an argument about literature, the evidence most valued by your audience is likely to be details from the work itself. Direct quotations from the text are powerful indications that your claims are well grounded. But when you quote, you need to avoid willful selectivity. If, when writing about Kincaid's story, you quote the girl's question "*but what if the baker won't let me feel the bread?*" without acknowledging the main speaker's response, you may come across as misrepresenting the text. In general, quoting from various parts of a text will help you give your readers the impression that you are being accurate.

If you make claims about the historical or cultural context of a work, your evidence may include facts about its original circumstances. You may be drawn to the author's own experiences and statements, believing these shed light on the text. But again, use such materials cautiously, for they are not always strong evidence for your claims. People are not obliged to accept the author's declaration of his or her intent as a guide to the finished work. Some people may feel that the author's statement of intention was deliberately misleading, while others may claim that the author failed to understand his or her own achievement.

EXPLAIN YOUR REASONING

Philosopher Gary Gutting observes that "facts alone are necessary but not sufficient for a good argument. As important as getting the facts right is putting the facts into a comprehensible logical structure that supports your conclusion." This advice can help you as you strive to persuade others through writing. Besides evidence, your readers will expect you to show careful **reasoning**. Ideally, they'll come away feeling that your ideas truly connect. They should sense that your main claim derives from your other ones. The steps in your logic should be clear in your essay's organization. Otherwise, you may confuse your audience—especially if you crawl through the literary work chronologically, commenting on each of its lines. Perhaps your main claim is that although "Girl" is a collection of the title character's assorted memories—bits of advice that the main speaker gave her on multiple occasions—these bits resemble one another so much that they have come to haunt her as a single monologue. An essay that simply plods through the story won't help you develop this idea. Probably you should first identify for your audience some ways in which the speaker's instructions do seem to have been uttered at various times rather than at a single moment. You should then explain the psychological nature of the girl's memory—her recalling these directions as a single speech. In general, alert your audience to your stages of thought.

IDENTIFY YOUR ASSUMPTIONS

Assumptions behind an argument may be numerous and debatable. That's why we single them out as an element here. One category is beliefs about the audience's experiences. If you suspect that your readers are quite unfamiliar with cultures like Antigua's, then your essay will have to spell out explicitly at least some of its distinctive features.

Another potentially significant set of assumptions has to do with your values, which often reflect your own particular life. For instance, you may want to condemn the speaker in "Girl" as a "bad" mother because your own is nicer. But this criticism would require more support than just your personal experience. You'd need to explain why *various* people should apply it to the speaker—whatever their particular mothers are like. In general, be cautious with the labels you give literary figures. If you describe characters with strongly judgmental words like *bad, crazy, normal,* or *good,* your readers may think you are showing your own prejudices and upbringing. Often they'll seek more precise and moderate language, believing it is more faithful to the actual text.

A third type of assumption is what rhetorical theory calls *warrants*. This term refers to the writer's beliefs about what can serve as evidence. Imagine, for example, that a paper of yours on Kincaid's story cites the main speaker's final phrase ("the kind of woman who the baker won't let near the bread") as evidence that she basically desires the girl to become an assertive adult. You would be relying on at least two warrants: (1) the assumption that, in a short story, a speaker's concluding words probably convey her central goal; and (2) the assumption that demanding to feel a merchant's wares is a show of strength. Of course, your readers might question these premises; you need to anticipate whether you'll have to state and defend them.

Once you state your warrants for a claim you are making, your audience may go further, asking you to identify assumptions supporting the warrants themselves. But more frequently you will have to decide how much you should mention your warrants in the first place. In class discussion, usually your classmates' and instructor's responses to your claims will indicate how much you have to spell out your assumptions. When you write, you have to rely more on your own judgment of what your audience requires. If you suspect that your readers will find your evidence unusual, you should identify your warrants at length. If, however, your readers are bound to accept your evidence, then a presentation of warrants may simply distract them. Again, reviewing drafts of your paper with potential readers will help you determine what to do.

MAKE USE OF APPEALS

To make their arguments persuasive, writers employ three basic kinds of appeals. Rhetorical theory calls them **logos**, **ethos**, and **pathos**, terms drawn from ancient Greek. In practice, they don't always play equal roles. An argument may depend on one or two of these strategies, not the entire trio. But all three are potential resources.

In a way, we've already introduced **logos**. The term refers to the logical substance of an arguer's case. When you rely on logos, you focus on showing that your claims are sound. You do this by emphasizing your evidence and your reasons. Most audiences will demand anyway that these features be strong. No surprise, then, that logos is the most common type of appeal.

Ethos often operates, too. When applied to writing, this term refers to the image you project as an author. Actually, there are two types of ethos. One is your audience's image of you before you present your analysis. It's your prior reputation. When Paul Goldberger published his article in *Metropolis*, many of its readers already knew that he is a leading, Pulitzer Prize–winning critic of architecture. Their awareness would incline them to respect his argument against cell phones, whether or not they agreed with him. Advertisers have reputational ethos in mind when they hire celebrities for endorsements. The hope is that you'll join Weight Watchers because Oprah Winfrey did. This ethos also comes into play with self-help manuals. Often their covers boast that the writer is an academic. You're supposed to buy *How to Find Lovers by Loving Yourself* because its author has a Ph.D.

Sadly, most of us aren't famous or highly credentialed. Yet there's a second kind of ethos. It's the picture of you that people form as they read your text. To gain their trust, you should patiently lay out your claims, reasons, and evidence. When arguers are scornful, some of their audience may object. John Burt points out a problem that Stephen Douglas's ethos created in his famous debates with Abraham Lincoln. When the two men competed for a U.S. Senate seat in 1858, the main issue was slavery. On this topic, Douglas planned to come across as a seeker of compromise. But on stage, he fiercely insulted Lincoln, showing nastiness and no tact. As Burt observes, "Douglas's own management of his case was so intemperate, so inflammatory, and so personal that whatever case one could make for his position, he himself was the last person who could plausibly carry the day for that case." Sometimes anger *is* right, especially when injustice must be noticed and stopped. But for much of your writing, especially in college, a less combative tone will serve better.

Writers enhance their ethos through **concessions** and **qualifications**. Concessions are kind acknowledgments of interpretations other than yours. Your readers will appreciate your noting in the first place that these views can exist. You will look even better if you treat such alternatives with respect. Try to admit that they're not entirely wrong. For instance, you may want to argue that Kincaid's main speaker holds men in contempt. Even so, consider granting that other readers of the story may see the character differently. You might admit that at moments she suggests her listener should accept male power. Of course, you would still proceed to argue your own claim about her. But you'll have dealt admirably with a rival idea.

In the same spirit, you might *qualify* your generalizations so that you don't come across as proclaiming them to be absolute facts. In rhetorical theory, qualifications aren't credentials for a job. They are two kinds of words. One kind helps writers strengthen their claims. A common example is the word *very*, as in a sentence like "Cell phones are very bad for cities' sense of community." The second kind of qualification has the opposite effect. Words in this category weaken a claim. They help writers sound cautious, often an attractive trait. Rather than declare that "the speaker is scornful toward men," you might say that this is *probably* her attitude or that it *seems* to be her stance. Similar terms that have the nice effect of making you sound careful include *maybe*, *perhaps*, and *possibly*.

These words suggest that the writer isn't self-righteously certain; with them, you project restraint.

Pathos is an appeal to the heart. You find it in charities' ads. Many show photos of suffering children—kids who are hungry, injured, or poor. These pictures are meant to rouse pity. If they succeed, viewers sob and donate. At other times, pathos stirs fear. Activists warn that if society ignores them, apocalypse will come. Pathos-filled arguments aren't dry in tone. Their language expresses *moods*. It targets its audience's *emotions*. When you write such arguments, you push readers to *feel* the stakes of your issue. You hope they'll *passionately* favor your claims. Sure, you risk sounding excessive: too sad, too mad, too scared, or too hurt. But pathos can be a respectable tool, as well as a powerful one. Plenty of subjects even demand an emotional tone. Readers expect essays on genocide to anguish over the victims. Further, pathos can join logos and ethos. Arguments that move readers may also awe them with logic; the author's image may impress them, too.

So, in writing an essay about Kincaid's story, you might refer to the "intimidating" voice of the main speaker. But keep such language limited. If you constantly vent your own passions, you may weaken your argument about the story. If you say that you find the speaker "creepy" and "monstrous" and "inhuman" and "despicable" and "loathsome" and "absolutely un-motherly," you may bother your readers. They might think that language like this conveys far more about *you*. Probably they'd want more details of the story and fewer bursts of your feelings. Again, emotional words *can* play a role in your argument. They may well add to its force. But they're effective only when you supply them in small doses.

A Sample Student Argument about Literature

The following essay demonstrates several of the strategies we have discussed. Its student author had read Kincaid's "Girl" in a course on composition and literature. Her assignment was to write an argument paper about a specific element of the story. She chose to raise an issue and develop a claim about its ending.

Ann Schumwalt
English 102
Professor Peretti
3 February ----

The Mother's Mixed Messages in "Girl"

In Jamaica Kincaid's story "Girl," the speaker is evidently a mother trying to teach her daughter how to behave. The story is basically a single-paragraph speech in which the mother gives various commands, instructions, and lessons, apparently in an effort at training her child to become what their culture considers a proper young woman. Only twice does the daughter herself interrupt the mother's monologue. It's interesting that the second break occurs near the end of the story. Right after the mother orders her to "always squeeze bread to make sure it's fresh," the daughter asks, *"but what if the baker won't let me feel the bread?"* (line 40). There is only one more sentence before the story concludes: the mother responds by asking, "you mean to say that after all you are really going to be the kind of woman who the baker won't let near the bread?" (40–42). Faced with this final exchange, many readers may wonder why author Kincaid chooses to make it the story's conclusion. It could have appeared earlier in the text, and Kincaid might have ended with any of the mother's statements that now come before it. This ending also feels *in*conclusive, for the very last words are a question that does not receive an answer. What, therefore, is Kincaid trying to emphasize with this puzzling finish? A closer look at its language, as well as at other words of the text, suggests that Kincaid is deliberately making us uncertain about whether the mother's stern training will indeed help her daughter become strong enough to survive in their society. The mother may *believe* that she is providing sufficient survival skills, but Kincaid encourages readers to suspect that she is actually *dis*empowering her daughter, not letting her develop the willpower she needs to endure.

Refers to puzzled readers, as a way of bringing up the main issue. The essay will help these readers with the "closer look" it proceeds to offer.

Introduces the essay's main issue (a cause and effect one) as a question.

The essay's main claim.

When the mother commands her daughter to squeeze the bread, probably she sees herself as pushing her to take charge of her life rather than meekly accept other people's treatment of her. To squeeze something is to perform a vigorous, self-assertive action, and in this case it would involve testing the baker's product instead of just accepting it. Earlier in the text, the mother offers a few other hints that she wishes the daughter to be aggressive, not passive. For example, she advises her on "how to make a good medicine to throw away a child before it even becomes a child" (33–34); on "how to bully a man" (35–38); and on "how to spit up in the air if you feel like it" (38). A number of readers may infer, too, that even when she is telling the daughter how to perform household chores like washing, ironing, setting meals, and sweeping, she is fostering her independence by enabling her to handle basic demands of daily existence.

Because Ann is mainly concerned with the story's ending, she starts her paper with it, rather than moving chronologically through Kincaid's text.

Qualifies this statement rather than expressing it as an absolute fact.

Draws evidence from the text's actual words.

Acknowledges existence of another possible interpretation.

But in crucial ways, the mother presses her daughter to play a subservient role in society. More specifically, she attempts to imprison her in a model of femininity that allows for men to dominate. Emphasizing that "you are not a boy, you know" (29), she demands that she "try to walk like a lady" (8) and take care of her father's clothes. The various chores that she expects her daughter to perform would make life easier for the male head of the household. Moreover, they

Pathos used with the negatively emotional words presses, subservient, imprison, and dominate. Evidence then offered to support such language.

seem duties that a boy would not be required to fulfill. Similarly, the mother hopes to restrict the daughter's sexual behavior. Repeatedly she warns her "to prevent yourself from looking like the slut I know you are so bent on becoming" (14–15). Again, it is doubtful that a boy would receive warnings like this. Like the United States, perhaps the culture reflected in this story even lacks a masculine equivalent of the derogatory term "slut."

A reasonable assumption.

An assumption, though qualified with the word perhaps.

At the end, I admit, the mother seems to associate her daughter with an image of power. She implies that the girl should become "the kind of woman" whom the baker *does* "let near the bread" so that she can test it by squeezing it (41–42). But even here, actually, the mother does not envision her daughter as actively taking charge. In the scenario she sketches, the baker *allows* the girl to feel the bread. In order to touch it, she must get his permission, rather than straightforwardly exert her own authority. Moreover, she first has to be a certain sort of woman; otherwise, she has not earned the right to examine his product. What type of woman is this? While some readers may argue that the mother wants her daughter to be an *assertive* female, many of the directions she has already given her would greatly limit her sphere of action, leaving her to be a relatively unadventurous housekeeping "lady." Evidently the mother feels that the baker will give her daughter access to the bread only if she is a basically tame and polite version of womanhood.

Concession.

The mother may not realize that she is conveying mixed messages to her child. If we, as readers, take her to be hoping that her daughter becomes empowered *and* subservient, we may be spotting a contradiction that the mother herself is not conscious of. But the daughter may be aware of it. Perhaps the daughter is, in fact, now a grown-up woman who is trying to make sense of the paradoxical pieces of advice her mother gave her during her adolescence. The mother may have offered these supposed bits of wisdom at various different times, but the daughter is now remembering them all as one speech and struggling to figure out their implications. Kincaid's decision to conclude the story with a question mark may be her way of indicating that even in adulthood, the daughter still has not determined whether her mother wanted to *liberate* her or *confine* her. We can regard the daughter as someone who is still attempting to "read" her mother's intentions. As actual readers of this story, we would then be in the same position as she is, having to come up with our own interpretation of what her mother wanted her to do and be.

"May not" is a qualification, indicating that Ann is less than sure what the mother thinks.

Even the text's punctuation may be significant.

Works Cited

Kincaid, Jamaica. "Girl." *Making Literature Matter: An Anthology for Readers and Writers,* edited by John Schilb and John Clifford, 7th ed., Bedford/St. Martin's, 2018, pp. 58–59.

Looking at Literature as Argument

Much of this book concerns arguing *about* literature. But many works of literature can be said to present arguments themselves. Admittedly, not all of literature can be seen as containing or making arguments, but occasionally you will find that associating a literary text with argument opens up productive lines of inquiry. Moreover, as you argue about literature, arguments *within* literature can help you see how you might persuade others.

Some works lay out an argument that the author obviously approves of. For an example, let us turn to the following poem. It was written around 1652 by John Milton (1608–1674), a poet who played a leading role in England's Puritan revolution. Seeking to make dominant their own version of Christianity, the Puritans executed King Charles I and installed their leader, Oliver Cromwell, as head of state. Milton wrote "When I consider how my light is spent" while working as an official in Cromwell's government. This is an autobiographical poem and refers to Milton's growing blindness, which threatened to prevent him from serving both his political leader and his religious one, God. The poem is often referred to as Milton's "Sonnet XIX." True sonnets consist of fourteen lines with different rhyme patterns depending on the type. Sonnet XIX is a Petrarchan sonnet, which usually rhymes the first eight lines (the octave) ABBA, ABBA and the next six (the sestet) CDE, CDE.

JOHN MILTON

When I consider how my light is spent

When I consider how my light is spent,
    Ere half my days in this dark world and wide,
    And that one talent which is death to hide
Lodged with me useless, though my soul more bent
To serve therewith my Maker, and present
    My true account, lest He returning chide;
    "Doth God exact day-labor, light denied?"
I fondly ask. But Patience, to prevent
That murmur, soon replies, "God doth not need
    Either man's work or His own gifts. Who best
    Bear His mild yoke, they serve Him best. His state
Is kingly: thousands at His bidding speed,
    And post o'er land and ocean without rest;
    They also serve who only stand and wait."

[c. 1652]

The speaker does not actually spell out his warrants. Consider, however, his reference to Christ's parable of the talents (Luke 19.12–27). In the ancient Middle East, a *talent* was a unit of money. In the parable, a servant is scolded by his master for hoarding the one talent that his master had given him. By telling this story, Christ implies that people should make use of the gifts afforded them by God. For the speaker in Milton's poem, the parable has a lot of authority. Evidently he feels that he should carry out its lesson. In effect, then, the parable has indeed become a warrant for him: that is, a basis for finding his blindness cause for lament.

Who, exactly, is the speaker's audience? Perhaps he is not addressing anyone in particular. Or perhaps the speaker's mind is divided and one side of it is addressing the other. Or perhaps the speaker is addressing God, even though he refers to God in the third person. Given that the speaker is answered by Patience, perhaps he means to address *that* figure, although Patience may actually be just a part of him rather than an altogether separate being.

At any rate, Patience takes the speaker for an audience in responding. And while Patience does not provide evidence, let alone warrants, Patience does make claims about God and his followers. Furthermore, Milton as author seems to endorse Patience's claims; apparently he is using the poem to advance them. Besides pointing out *how* God is served, Milton suggests that God *ought* to be served, even if God lets bad things happen to good people like Milton.

Every author can be considered an audience for his or her own writing, but some authors write expressly to engage in a dialogue with themselves. Perhaps Milton wrote his poem partly to convince himself that his religion was still valid and his life still worth living. Significantly, he did not publish the poem until about twenty years later. Yet because he did publish it eventually, at some point he must have contemplated a larger audience for it. The first readers of the poem would have been a relatively small segment of the English population: those literate and prosperous enough to have access to books of poetry. In addition, a number of the poem's first readers would have shared Milton's religious beliefs. Perhaps, however, Milton felt that even the faith of this band had to be bolstered. For one thing, not every Protestant of the time would have shared Milton's enthusiasm for the Puritan government. Recall that this regime executed the king, supposedly replacing him with the rule of God. Milton's words "His state / Is kingly" can be seen as an effort to persuade readers that the Puritans did put God on England's throne.

Certain arguments made in literary texts may or may not have the author's endorsement. Faced with a conflict of ideas, readers must engage in interpretation, forced to decide which position is apt to be the author's own view. A classic example is "Mending Wall," a famous poem by Robert Frost (1874–1963), from his 1914 book, *North of Boston*. Troubled by his neighbor's desire to repair the wall between their farms, the poem's speaker argues against its necessity, but literary critics have long debated whether Frost agrees with the speaker's claims and reasons. How persuasive do you find them?

ROBERT FROST

Mending Wall

Something there is that doesn't love a wall,
That sends the frozen-ground-swell under it,
And spills the upper boulders in the sun;
And makes gaps even two can pass abreast.
The work of hunters is another thing:
I have come after them and made repair
Where they have left not one stone on a stone,
But they would have the rabbit out of hiding,
To please the yelping dogs. The gaps I mean,
No one has seen them made or heard them made,
But at spring mending-time we find them there.
I let my neighbor know beyond the hill;
And on a day we meet to walk the line
And set the wall between us once again.
We keep the wall between us as we go.
To each the boulders that have fallen to each.
And some are loaves and some so nearly balls
We have to use a spell to make them balance:
"Stay where you are until our backs are turned!"
We wear our fingers rough with handling them.
Oh, just another kind of outdoor game,
One on a side. It comes to little more:
There where it is we do not need the wall:
He is all pine and I am apple orchard.
My apple trees will never get across
And eat the cones under his pines, I tell him.
He only says, "Good fences make good neighbors."
Spring is the mischief in me, and I wonder
If I could put a notion in his head:
"*Why* do they make good neighbors? Isn't it
Where there are cows? But here there are no cows.
Before I built a wall I'd ask to know
What I was walling in or walling out,
And to whom I was like to give offense.
Something there is that doesn't love a wall,
That wants it down." I could say "Elves" to him,
But it's not elves exactly, and I'd rather
He said it for himself. I see him there
Bringing a stone grasped firmly by the top
In each hand, like an old-stone savage armed.
He moves in darkness as it seems to me,
Not of woods only and the shade of trees.
He will not go behind his father's saying,

And he likes having thought of it so well
He says again, "Good fences make good neighbors." [1914]

Other works of literature argue indirectly. At first, they may not look like efforts to persuade, but most readers will eventually guess that the author is making a case. An example is the following poem. W. H. Auden wrote "Refugee Blues" in 1939, a time when many Jews were trapped in Hitler's Germany. The poem's speaker belongs to this beleaguered group. So does the person that the speaker addresses. This community struggled to find asylum elsewhere. Yet most other countries—the United States included—took few or none of them in. The poem is certainly a cry of despair over these Jews' plight. But Auden is also arguing for a policy change. He is calling for nations to offer these people a home. As you read his poem, consider the refugees of today. What, specifically, might *their* "blues" be about?

W. H. AUDEN

Refugee Blues

Say this city has ten million souls,
Some are living in mansions, some are living in holes:
Yet there's no place for us, my dear, yet there's no place for us.

Once we had a country and we thought it fair,
Look in the atlas and you'll find it there:
We cannot go there now, my dear, we cannot go there now.

In the village churchyard there grows an old yew,
Every spring it blossoms anew:
Old passports can't do that, my dear, old passports can't do that.

The consul banged the table and said,
"If you've got no passport you're officially dead":
But we are still alive, my dear, but we are still alive.

Went to a committee; they offered me a chair;
Asked me politely to return next year:
But where shall we go to-day, my dear, but where shall we go to-day?

Came to a public meeting; the speaker got up and said;
"If we let them in, they will steal our daily bread":
He was talking of you and me, my dear, he was talking of you and me.

Thought I heard the thunder rumbling in the sky;
It was Hitler over Europe, saying, "They must die":
O we were in his mind, my dear, O we were in his mind.

Saw a poodle in a jacket fastened with a pin,
Saw a door opened and a cat let in:
But they weren't German Jews, my dear, but they weren't German Jews.

Went down the harbour and stood upon the quay,
Saw the fish swimming as if they were free:
Only ten feet away, my dear, only ten feet away.

Walked through a wood, saw the birds in the trees;
They had no politicians and sang at their ease:
They weren't the human race, my dear, they weren't the human race.

Dreamed I saw a building with a thousand floors,
A thousand windows and a thousand doors:
Not one of them was ours, my dear, not one of them was ours.

Stood on a great plain in the falling snow;
Ten thousand soldiers marched to and fro:
Looking for you and me, my dear, looking for you and me.

[1939]

Literature and Current Issues

When you read a literary work, you may find it doesn't make arguments. Nevertheless, it may help you grasp current issues. It may even help you form claims about them. To play this role, the work needn't be recent. Ancient tragedies can shed light on politics today. However old the text, literature may give you insights into contemporary debates. In turn, these debates may help you understand a work of literature better. They may lead you to notice aspects of it you'd otherwise neglect.

Here, we present a 2015 short story about a current practice: the public shaming of individuals and organizations. They suffer mass scorn for things they've said or done. These scoldings usually occur via social media like Twitter. Such denunciations are popular; each week, new ones erupt. Yet increasingly these assaults are criticized themselves. Not only do they provoke howls of protest from their targets, but they also elicit concerned warnings from a growing number of cultural commentators who point out that these attacks are often harmful, unfair, and mean. To give you a sense of this emerging debate, we follow the story with two nonfiction texts about public shaming today. By putting the story in "conversation" with these works, we suggest ways of connecting literature to real-life disputes.

The story's author, Rivka Galchen (b. 1976), was born in Toronto, Canada, but she has lived in the United States since she was a child. Although she holds an M.D. degree with a specialization in psychiatry, she has pursued a literary career. Besides earning an M.F.A. in creative writing at Columbia University, she has published a novel, *Atmospheric Disturbances* (2008), and a collection of short stories, *American Innovations* (2014). She has also written several pieces of journalism. "Usl at the Stadium" first appeared in the October 12, 2015, issue of *The New Yorker*. Galchen based the story on an actual series of events.

RIVKA GALCHEN

Usl at the Stadium

The game on Sunday had a 2 P.M. start, and Usl was featured on the Jumbotron intermittently from 4:02 to 4:09. By eight-thirty, his home phone was ringing. His home phone never rang. It was a holdover from another time. His mother had told him that it was essential, a matter of safety—for hurricanes, or blackouts, or terrorist attacks. You never knew what could happen until it happened. She had insisted on paying the bill so that Usl would keep the landline. She had pleaded, "Please grant me permission to protect my child," and so he had.

The landline was ringing because Usl had become an Internet sensation. Usl had been sleeping when he appeared on the Jumbotron at the Yankees game; the cameras and the commentators had turned on Usl numerous times, and at length, and he had slept through it all. It wasn't until the voices of strangers over that old-fashioned telephone alerted him that he understood how widely watched his sleep had been. Now a gentle feminine voice pitched him: "What we're thinking is that you come into the office and we'll take a top-quality, nice photo of you. We really love the idea that you get a chance to present yourself. You'll recapture control over your image."

Usl looked online to reconfirm who he was in the eyes of the world:

> Fatty cow that needs two seats at all time and represent symbol of failure

had been posted one minute earlier in the comments section under a YouTube clip. The clip had more than seventy thousand views. Wasn't it really just footage of a man dreaming? No one seemed to see it that way. Usl was only twenty-eight years old—could his life already be ruined? Could he save it? Usl told the woman on the phone that he needed to think about her idea, that he would call her back.

He called Gregory.

5 "People at a newspaper are not your allies," Gregory said. Gregory was Usl's friend but also his boss. Usl worked the buyback end of Gregory's storefront diamond-district place. Customers ascended the back stairs to consult with Usl about their old jewelry, and Usl weighed, assessed, proposed prices, bought. Gregory liked to say that it was a sultanate there on the second floor; the sultan was Usl. Now Gregory said, "These are people who demeaned Eliot Spitzer over private issues, who—"

"But people are saying untrue things about me—"

"You'll be extending the time that you're at the center of attention—"

"If you were me—"

"I'm not you. I'm not interested in fame. I am me. I'm interested in coming to work. I hope you're not thinking of not coming in to work tomorrow."

10 The angle of the camera in the footage was particularly unflattering—distorting, really. It wasn't a strong likeness.

Usl called the voice from the newspaper back. "I will come in."

The now slightly less kind-sounding woman informed Usl that if he made it in before 11 A.M. they would run the photo online the same day.

Usl trembled.

Or was the trembling elsewhere?

They had found his cell-phone number?

"I love you!" the text message read. It was his mother. "You are a great and successful and handsome and very good and nice man!!!" Even she had seen the footage? Usl's mother was very loving, had always been very loving. Good mothers are bad mothers, Usl thought. Only bad, mean mothers prepare you for what is to come. If Usl was ever a mother, whatever, a father, he wanted to be a bad one.

More calls came in, through the night, from television programs that had once seemed to occur in inaccessible lands but that turned out to be really less than thirty minutes away; they would send a car service. Usl couldn't sleep. When, as a child, he encountered characters six feet tall, fuzzy, offering hugs, or flyers, or hot dogs, he had been frightened. He unplugged the phone.

Then there was a knock at the door. Was he O. J. Simpson? They were pursuing him everywhere.

"It's me! It's Berge!"

Berge was Usl's neighbor. Usl let him in.

Berge said, "You've had a huge piece of luck. Huge. I know you may not see it, but this is the luckiest day of your life."

"I'm very tired," Usl said, and then felt ambushed by fresh shame—after all, why was he so tired? "People laugh, but I was sleeping because I haven't been getting my sleep. When you don't sleep, you're not yourself. When you don't sleep, you find yourself sleeping all the time."

"You're going to sue," Berge declared. Sue somebody. Berge would figure it out. He wouldn't charge—he would just take fifteen per cent upon collection. Did Usl feel damaged? Yes, Usl did feel damaged. Then there should be damages. Berge had recently passed the bar. He wasn't lying about that, Usl thought. Berge often shared his magazines with Usl; he was a nice guy, basically.

"But I can't sue thousands of people," Usl said. "It's thousands of people who have damaged me." He caught a glimpse of his screen:

He's dreaming of cupcakes.

"No, thousands wouldn't be sensible," Berge said. "We'll sue the Yankees."

"But I love the Yankees."

"We'll sue the Stadium."

"I love the Stadium. I've been happy there."

"You're very stressed. Let me figure it out for you."

By 1 A.M., Berge had prepared papers for Usl to sign—Berge was also a notary, he said—naming a broadcasting corporation. "They won't take it personally," Berge assured him. "It's business."

By Tuesday, views of the YouTube footage had exceeded a million. Usl abandoned the Internet, turned on the radio for escape, and there learned that he, Usl, was a too sensitive behemoth who needed to be *#&$ed in his cookie-dough face; also, that he should eat celery. Normally, if you heard people talking about you on the radio it meant that you were crazy, since of course no one on the radio was talking about you, and if you thought that people on the radio were talking about you, as had happened to Usl's uncle, then you were supposed to go see somebody, a professional. Usl didn't want to see anybody.

"Gold resists attacks by almost all individual acids" appeared on his cell phone. A year earlier he had subscribed to GemFacts by text; at first it had bothered him, the repeated disappointment of thinking a person had contacted him and then discovering it was just an impersonal update.

Usl called Gregory again. "I can't come in today," he said.

"Take a joke," Gregory said. "They're talking things they don't know. Have those talkers ever handled gold rings like they were chickpeas? They're nobodies. So what if they say you're fat. You are fat. I'm also fat. It's not like it's not true."

Gregory was a cheerful man, and the son of a Holocaust survivor; he had six 35
children, and he sometimes wore a T-shirt that read, "I Have the Body of a God: Buddha." "If you wanted to not be fat, you would be not fat," he said.

"It's not just that," Usl said. The two sports announcers, Mike and Mike—voices Usl knew well, had thought of as friends of his, in a way—had said of sleeping Usl the kinds of things that people say. Unpleasant things. But the words of those false friends had then bloomed into much worse words, typed up by viewers whose numbers were growing without perceptible limit. Usl was reading:

> Please rid us of your nasty pimpled ass and put a shotgun in your mouth tonight, I'll buy the shells
>
> Then:
>
> He is a waste of decent seats, he can sleep at the nachos stand and give a real fan a view, lol

Usl said to Gregory, "What really bothers me is that they think I don't appreciate baseball. They think I don't understand what's at stake."

"Sure. It's suicide or sniper," Gregory said. "And you don't want to be a sniper—I get it—so instead you feel really bad, you turn it on yourself. So as not to kill people. But it's also not suicide or sniper: it's just get your pants on and get on with your day. Do I have a chicken for an employee? I need a man. It's man or pansy, it's—"

Usl hung up. 40

Usl had been unemployed for seventeen months when he got the job with Gregory. When he started working, his mother gave him a polished blue stone to keep in his pocket, to ward off evil. Mock if you want, but the stone had worked. Usl had been enjoying his job for more than a year now. He had even made a flyer on how to detect fake gold. The magnet test was overrated, the flyer explained. In Usl's years of experience (even though it had been less than one when he made the flyer), he had seen plenty of non-magnetic fake gold; recognizing real gold versus fake was about getting a feel for the weight of the thing in your hands.

That flyer of Usl's had been downloaded from his open Facebook page a hundred and seventy-three times.

That had seemed like a big number. It had brought attention to Gregory's shop. Gregory kept a poster of faces with various expressions on the office wall—it was something the Chinese restaurant nearby had given them—and Gregory had written Usl's name under the face labeled "Triumphant." He had done this after an eighty-four-year-old woman, who had bought gold every birthday of her life, brought it all in to sell after seeing a horoscope that read, "Even a Gemini needs to slow down a bit once in a while, and with your ruler Mercury still moving retrograde this is the ideal time." She explained to Usl that she had visited several buyback places. She chose Usl. Because she trusted him, because she could see his goodness in the way that his hands were not bossy or deceptive. Usl had never before thought about his hands. But he did think, then, that it was true what she had said, that they were good hands.

By midday Tuesday, Usl had understood a few things. One was that he should have been in contact with his mother. Usl had not gone to the paper to be photographed; Usl had ceased to answer either of his phones. But his mother was in the papers; his mother had been photographed. In her own home, sitting in her armchair, with a red geranium plant at her side. In the caption, she was quoted: "He was very tired, because he had been working very hard. He is my son of gold." In the article, she was asked about Usl's name, which some people had said was short for "useless." She said that, no, that was not the case, that Usl had been the nickname of Usl's grandfather, Warhel, a beautiful soul who had died during a flu outbreak when he was only thirty-four. And, as for Usl himself, Usl was not a nickname, Usl was his full proper name, it was enough.

Usl called his mother.

"Someone had to tell them about the real you," she said. "Here you are—this celebrity—but the celebrity is this person who isn't you. They made me look very old in that picture, because of the green lighting, but I'm O.K. with that, because a mother has to fix what is said about her son, whatever the cost."

"Nothing's fixed," Usl said. He had the feeling, as he often did with his mother, that he was speaking to a ghost poorly educated about the present.

"They thought you were drunk," she went on. "Many people thought that. You can't let them think that—it will affect your future employment. I explained that you drink only Diet Coke."

That bit about the Diet Coke wasn't true, but Usl let it pass. "You're destroying me," he said, albeit softly.

The truth was, Usl knew, that the photograph of his mother was not as damaging as the papers that Berge had filed on his behalf.

> Who gets paid 10 million to sleep there like a fat ass. FUCK YOU FATTY.

Berge had asked for nine million dollars in damages, not ten; of course the commenters had the details wrong, had everything wrong. Usl should have followed his old rule: no decisions after midnight. It was said that the filing was full of misspellings and grammatical errors.

> What a loser. And now he's suing? Double loser. His suit is the only thing that brought the world's attention to him. Triple loser. And if there is any justice on this earth, this case will be tossed out and he'll be ridiculed and humiliated all over. We're dealing with a quadruple loser at the very least, folks.

Berge was always full of ideas. One should stay away from people with ideas.

> Americas pre-occupation with sports is obscene. Can't tell you how many kids I know can recite batting averages, game plays, but don't know the first 5 books of the Bible. Nor could they recite an account beyond Noah's Ark, and when they do its Hollywoodized to the point of recognizable gibberish. They Idolize these players, who in turn Idolize Money. Then these Sports-gods humiliate their fans, and their fans try to capitalize, and the lawyers capitalize. Who ends up loosing?

Ignominy was the only type of celebrity around. At least for Usl and everyone he knew.

"I love you," his mother texted again. "I love you very much. I love you very, very much. You are a strong man. They are trying to hunt down and destroy you. But you are a cheetah."

And then, automated delivery: "Gold is unaffected by oxygen at any temperature." If only.

Say what you will, Usl wanted to get a slice. Why not? He would leave his apartment. He could do it. Usl stepped into the elevator, which today smelled like urine; also there were bugs sun-printed in the case of the light fixture. He normally enjoyed his elevator; it had a mechanical floor-indicator arrow that still worked. It was classy. Just as he himself was classy. That was the truth. He worked with gold, which did not rust.

As he stepped out of the building, he saw three of his neighbors playing dominoes. One held up a newspaper and shook it at him, in fellowship or menace, he didn't know. He had more than once dreamed of everyone recognizing him, of extending a series of half waves to acknowledge his fellows with respect as he passed them on the street; now he walked by his neighbors quickly, panting slightly.

He ordered a slice of pepper-and-mushroom. The server put a slice of pepperoni on a paper plate. Usl re-stated what he wanted—pepper-and-mushroom. Mexican pop was playing loudly. The server had a red bandanna tied back over his thick black hair. Always Mexicans at the Italian places, Usl thought. The server squinted at Usl. A squint of recognition? "Pep-per-and-mush-room," Usl reënunciated. The guy gave him a second slice. "Just one slice," Usl said. "Just the pepper-and-mushroom. No pepperoni."

It was worked out. Nobody had shouted. A triumph.

"Yo, thanks," Usl said.

"Yo? It's not the barrio, man," the server said. "Be polite."

People were disgusting. You gave your heart, you tried to be considerate, and who cared? They thought Usl could be pushed around. Why did it seem so clear that he could be pushed around? How did they know? Other people slept at baseball games. The games were sometimes boring. There were commercials between innings, and also commercials mid-inning. The batters took their time getting to the box, as if nothing else in the world, no one else in the world, existed. It was selfish, really. There were millions and millions and millions of other people who were treated with more respect than Usl. Maybe billions. Some of them stupid, some fat, some ugly, whatever it was, but that was the truth, Usl didn't invent it. Who did they think they were—Brad Pitt? They couldn't all be Brad Pitt. If Brad Pitt had criticized him, that would be a different thing.

One day they weren't going to have Usl to kick around anymore. One day they'd be sorry. This was among the things that he hadn't said. That he kept not saying. He had not assumed another identity, or his own, and pursued the pursuers online. Oh, he had been tempted, but that was what the Others would do. He had not told the Others what he thought of them.

Usl was finishing his pizza when a man in an orange T-shirt and a hard hat, holding a large soda in one hand, made eye contact with him. Then he raised a fist in the air and shouted, "Yankees!"

Instinctively, Usl raised his fist in return. As if in the childishly imagined kingdom of fellowship and dignity.

"It's you, right?" the hard-hat man said.

Usl said, "No."

But already the man in the hard hat was signaling to others around him, shouting, calling things out. The hats were gathering.

Usl could find a small makeshift hut in the woods, not far from a beach. He had seen one once; he was going to go and live there. When the time seemed right, in maybe ten or fifteen years, he would return to civilization. He would be very fit, from living a life in nature. He would say his name was Dave. He would tell people how they should live. They would listen.

But he at least owed Gregory notice that he would be leaving, that he would be gone forever, sort of. Also, his paycheck would be useful. He was owed eight days. Truth be told, he wanted to run the idea by Gregory. Gregory, he realized, was like a dad to him. He would get his blessing.

Just in front of Gregory's, as Usl was staring at his phone—"You are my star and my sunshine!"—someone tapped him on the shoulder.

By primal reflex, Usl nearly hit the man, shouted, defending his body.

The man was saying, "Hey, hey, hey, sorry. I was just saying hello."

Usl looked up fully from his phone and realized it was Andre, the guy who regularly stood in front of Gregory's, handing out flyers for the business. Andre was a very slim and fairly straightforwardly good-looking black man; his appearance, today, seemed like a reproach. Usl said, "I apologize, I'm in such a high state of alert."

"A silver alert?" Andre asked.

"A what?" Usl said, his fear returning.

"Forget it, relax, forget it. I meant on your phone."

"What's silver, what's alert?" Usl said. Was he being asked about Google Alerts? About GemFacts? How was everyone allowed inside his head, his computer, his phone, his dreams.

"Like a silver alert, for when old people go missing," Andre said. "Amber alert for when a kid is missing, silver for old people. I think there's other colors, too. Sorry, I know you're under stress. It's just been on my mind. I was wondering how you get one of those alerts sent out. Like, once we found my mom near where the buses are parked, between Ninth and Tenth Avenues. She had no idea how to get home. She lives right near here, but she gets lost. And I'm not in a total panic about her, but she's not answering my calls this morning, so I was asking. Is your mom old? Is she right in the head?"

Andre had always seemed to Usl like a man with girlfriends, never like a man with a mom. Usl still had the polished good-luck stone from his mother. She was always trying, she was still trying. Usl said, "You could go look for her."

"Tell Gregory I'm back in thirty minutes," Andre said.

"They're nobodies, Usl," Gregory said when he went inside. "They are small, small people who can't find their own dicks because they are so small."

"You're a terrible man, Gregory. You're one of them."

"I'm just trying to cheer you up."

"By being a monster."

"Not nice."

"You're like a disease. For all I know, you started the comments about me. What do I know? Evil isn't choosy. For all I know, you gave them my phone number." Usl had yelled at no one yet; he was now yelling at Gregory. He found that he had quite a lot to say. He said Gregory didn't even care about Andre's mom.

"You know what, Usl? I'm going to tell you something that maybe you don't want to hear."

Usl was ready for it.

Gregory said, "I'm going to tell you that I love you, and that I care for you."

Usl began to cry. He cried a little more. Eventually he said, "I'm just so tired. When I'm tired, I make bad decisions."

"I understand," Gregory said. "You know, scientists used to ask, Why do we sleep? What is the purpose of sleep? But then other scientists said that these are the wrong questions. The question is, Why are we so often awake? What is the purpose of being awake? I mean, besides for ten minutes of eating, a little bit of romance. Once that's over, why are we not immediately again asleep?"

Gregory went on, "And so I said to myself one day, about this sleep question: This is the answer to the problem of evil. The question isn't, Why is there evil? The question is, Why is there good? I mean, it's not, Why is there the bubonic plague and Putin? It's, Why is there spring and love and barbecue? Why is there ever an unrequired kind act? Look, I'm just telling you how I go about my life, because I am old and you are still young. There isn't supposed to be any gold in the crust of the earth. It's a very heavy element. All the gold should be in the molten core. Unreachable for us. So why do we keep finding gold in the crust? How did it get there? Some people say it's meteorites that fell, that crashed, and that this catastrophe splashed up gold. That's the only reason we come across it. I don't subscribe to this theory. But I am sharing it with you."

Usl's sleep at the baseball game had been a sweet one. Sifting past and beyond the ensuing terror, he found that he could remember that sleep, he could remember his dream. He had been at a really nice desk, of a dark, well-polished wood. He recognized the desk; it had made an appearance in real life. When he was just a kid — a real kid, not a twenty-eight-year-old who felt like a kid but a twelve- or thirteen-year-old who really was that — he had been delivering something to a lawyer, to a proper lawyer. That lawyer had sat at such a desk. But before he saw it little Usl had waited outside the lawyer's office, outside but inside, inside the outer chamber, in the air-conditioning, and the secretary, a gentle-faced woman who looked a little bit like the pretty woman who drove a taxi in that old TV show, had asked him if he wanted some water. She had brought him some, in a cone-shaped paper cup, from the water cooler. This, Usl thought, must be real life. He must have been thirsty at the game. He must have been waiting. *[2015]*

Galchen's story is fiction. But when she wrote about Usl, she had a real person in mind. In April 2014, Andrew Rector fell asleep while attending a Yankees/Red Sox game. Repeatedly, the stadium's jumbotron screen showed his sprawled, slumbering body. Countless viewers at home saw this spectacle as well, for the game was televised on ESPN. Soon, pictures of the snoozing man appeared online, receiving millions of hits. A similar number of messages about him swept through social media. Many of these messages mocked him. They ridiculed not only Rector's napping but also his considerable weight. He garnered even more scorn when he sued the ESPN commentators for damages. His suit was thrown out of court, however, just before Galchen's story appeared. By that time, his mother reported, Rector had left the country. He could no longer bear the American public's contempt.

Rector's experience isn't unusual. Nowadays, public shaming happens over and over. The weapons include social media, smartphone cameras, and Web sites like YouTube. The trend has grown so big that it's captured the attention of journalists. One such reporter is Jon Ronson (b. 1967). Originally from Wales, he's a veteran investigator of offbeat topics. His books include *Them: Adventures with Extremists* (2001), *The Psychopath Test: A Journey Through the Madness Industry* (2011), and *The Men Who Stare at Goats* (2004), which became a feature film. In 2015, Ronson published a book about the practice of shaming. Its title, *So You've Been Publicly Shamed*, may someday apply to all of us. Meanwhile, he researched his book by talking with people whom the title already fits.

Evidently, Ronson didn't speak with Andrew Rector, the model for Galchen's character Usl. Probably Rector's case was too recent for him to include in his book. Still, Ronson's discussion of shaming provides a context for Galchen's story. To help you connect the story with the real shamings Ronson describes, we offer the following excerpt from an article he wrote. Published in the February 12, 2015, issue of the *New York Times Magazine*, the article is a preview of Ronson's book. As its title indicates, much of this piece focuses on the case of Justine Sacco.

JON RONSON

From *"How One Stupid Tweet Blew Up Justine Sacco's Life"*

As she made the long journey from New York to South Africa, to visit family during the holidays in 2013, Justine Sacco, 30 years old and the senior director of corporate communications at IAC, began tweeting acerbic little jokes about the indignities of travel. There was one about a fellow passenger on the flight from John F. Kennedy International Airport:

" 'Weird German Dude: You're in First Class. It's 2014. Get some deodorant.'—Inner monologue as I inhale BO. Thank God for pharmaceuticals."

Then, during her layover at Heathrow:

"Chilly—cucumber sandwiches—bad teeth. Back in London!"

And on Dec. 20, before the final leg of her trip to Cape Town: 5

"Going to Africa. Hope I don't get AIDS. Just kidding. I'm white!"

She chuckled to herself as she pressed send on this last one, then wandered around Heathrow's international terminal for half an hour, sporadically checking her phone. No one replied, which didn't surprise her. She had only 170 Twitter followers.

Sacco boarded the plane. It was an 11-hour flight, so she slept. When the plane landed in Cape Town and was taxiing on the runway, she turned on her phone. Right away, she got a text from someone she hadn't spoken to since high school: "I'm so sorry to see what's happening." Sacco looked at it, baffled.

Then another text: "You need to call me immediately." It was from her best friend, Hannah. Then her phone exploded with more texts and alerts. And then it rang. It was Hannah. "You're the No. 1 worldwide trend on Twitter right now," she said.

Sacco's Twitter feed had become a horror show. "In light of @JustineSacco 10 disgusting racist tweet, I'm donating to @care today" and "How did @JustineSacco get a PR job?! Her level of racist ignorance belongs on Fox News. #AIDS can affect anyone!" and "I'm an IAC employee and I don't want @JustineSacco doing any communications on our behalf ever again. Ever." And then one from her employer, IAC, the corporate owner of The Daily Beast, OKCupid and Vimeo: "This is an outrageous, offensive comment. Employee in question currently unreachable on an intl flight." The anger soon turned to excitement: "All I want for Christmas is to see @JustineSacco's face when her plane lands and she checks her inbox/voicemail" and "Oh man, @JustineSacco is going to have the most painful phone-turning-on moment ever when her plane lands" and "We are about to watch this @JustineSacco bitch get fired. In REAL time. Before she even KNOWS she's getting fired."

The furor over Sacco's tweet had become not just an ideological crusade against her perceived bigotry but also a form of idle entertainment. Her complete ignorance of her predicament for those 11 hours lent the episode both dramatic irony and a pleasing narrative arc. As Sacco's flight traversed the length of Africa, a hashtag began to trend worldwide: #HasJustineLandedYet. "Seriously.

I just want to go home to go to bed, but everyone at the bar is SO into #HasJustineLandedYet. Can't look away. Can't leave" and "Right, is there no one in Cape Town going to the airport to tweet her arrival? Come on, Twitter! I'd like pictures #HasJustineLandedYet."

A Twitter user did indeed go to the airport to tweet her arrival. He took her photograph and posted it online. "Yup," he wrote, "@JustineSacco HAS in fact landed at Cape Town International. She's decided to wear sunnies as a disguise."

By the time Sacco had touched down, tens of thousands of angry tweets had been sent in response to her joke. Hannah, meanwhile, frantically deleted her friend's tweet and her account—Sacco didn't want to look—but it was far too late. "Sorry @JustineSacco," wrote one Twitter user, "your tweet lives on forever."

In the early days of Twitter, I was a keen shamer. When newspaper columnists made racist or homophobic statements, I joined the pile-on. Sometimes I led it. The journalist A.A. Gill once wrote a column about shooting a baboon on safari in Tanzania: "I'm told they can be tricky to shoot. They run up trees, hang on for grim life. They die hard, baboons. But not this one. A soft-nosed .357 blew his lungs out." Gill did the deed because he "wanted to get a sense of what it might be like to kill someone, a stranger."

I was among the first people to alert social media. (This was because Gill 15
always gave my television documentaries bad reviews, so I tended to keep a vigilant eye on things he could be got for.) Within minutes, it was everywhere. Amid the hundreds of congratulatory messages I received, one stuck out: "Were you a bully at school?"

Still, in those early days, the collective fury felt righteous, powerful and effective. It felt as if hierarchies were being dismantled, as if justice were being democratized. As time passed, though, I watched these shame campaigns multiply, to the point that they targeted not just powerful institutions and public figures but really anyone perceived to have done something offensive. I also began to marvel at the disconnect between the severity of the crime and the gleeful savagery of the punishment. It almost felt as if shamings were now happening for their own sake, as if they were following a script.

Eventually I started to wonder about the recipients of our shamings, the real humans who were the virtual targets of these campaigns. So for the past two years, I've been interviewing individuals like Justine Sacco: everyday people pilloried brutally, most often for posting some poorly considered joke on social media. Whenever possible, I have met them in person, to truly grasp the emotional toll at the other end of our screens. The people I met were mostly unemployed, fired for their transgressions, and they seemed broken somehow—deeply confused and traumatized. . . .

Late one afternoon last year, I met Justine Sacco in New York, at a restaurant in Chelsea called Cookshop. Dressed in rather chic business attire, Sacco ordered a glass of white wine. Just three weeks had passed since her trip to Africa, and she was still a person of interest to the media. Websites had already ransacked her Twitter feed for more horrors. (For example, "I had a sex dream about an autistic kid last night," from 2012, was unearthed by BuzzFeed in the article "16 Tweets

Justine Sacco Regrets.") A New York Post photographer had been following her to the gym.

"Only an insane person would think that white people don't get AIDS," she told me. It was about the first thing she said to me when we sat down.

Sacco had been three hours or so into her flight when retweets of her joke 20
began to overwhelm my Twitter feed. I could understand why some people found it offensive. Read literally, she said that white people don't get AIDS, but it seems doubtful many interpreted it that way. More likely it was her apparently gleeful flaunting of her privilege that angered people. But after thinking about her tweet for a few seconds more, I began to suspect that it wasn't racist but a reflexive critique of white privilege—on our tendency to naïvely imagine ourselves immune from life's horrors. Sacco, like Stone, had been yanked violently out of the context of her small social circle. Right?

"To me it was so insane of a comment for anyone to make," she said. "I thought there was no way that anyone could possibly think it was literal." (She would later write me an email to elaborate on this point. "Unfortunately, I am not a character on 'South Park' or a comedian, so I had no business commenting on the epidemic in such a politically incorrect manner on a public platform," she wrote. "To put it simply, I wasn't trying to raise awareness of AIDS or piss off the world or ruin my life. Living in America puts us in a bit of a bubble when it comes to what is going on in the third world. I was making fun of that bubble.")

I would be the only person she spoke to on the record about what happened to her, she said. It was just too harrowing—and "as a publicist," inadvisable—but she felt it was necessary, to show how "crazy" her situation was, how her punishment simply didn't fit the crime.

"I cried out my body weight in the first 24 hours," she told me. "It was incredibly traumatic. You don't sleep. You wake up in the middle of the night forgetting where you are." She released an apology statement and cut short her vacation. Workers were threatening to strike at the hotels she had booked if she showed up. She was told no one could guarantee her safety.

Her extended family in South Africa were African National Congress supporters—the party of Nelson Mandela. They were longtime activists for racial equality. When Justine arrived at the family home from the airport, one of the first things her aunt said to her was: "This is not what our family stands for. And now, by association, you've almost tarnished the family."

As she told me this, Sacco started to cry. I sat looking at her for a moment. 25
Then I tried to improve the mood. I told her that "sometimes, things need to reach a brutal nadir before people see sense."

"Wow," she said. She dried her eyes. "Of all the things I could have been in society's collective consciousness, it never struck me that I'd end up a brutal nadir."

She glanced at her watch. It was nearly 6 P.M. The reason she wanted to meet me at this restaurant, and that she was wearing her work clothes, was that it was only a few blocks away from her office. At 6, she was due in there to clean out her desk.

"All of a sudden you don't know what you're supposed to do," she said. "If I don't start making steps to reclaim my identity and remind myself of who I am on a daily basis, then I might lose myself."

The restaurant's manager approached our table. She sat down next to Sacco, fixed her with a look and said something in such a low volume I couldn't hear it, only Sacco's reply: "Oh, you think I'm going to be grateful for this?"

We agreed to meet again, but not for several months. She was determined to prove that she could turn her life around. "I can't just sit at home and watch movies every day and cry and feel sorry for myself," she said. "I'm going to come back."

After she left, Sacco later told me, she got only as far as the lobby of her office building before she broke down crying. . . .

Recently, I wrote to Sacco to tell her I was putting her story in The Times, and I asked her to meet me one final time to update me on her life. Her response was speedy. "No way." She explained that she had a new job in communications, though she wouldn't say where. She said, "Anything that puts the spotlight on me is a negative."

It was a profound reversal for Sacco. When I first met her, she was desperate to tell the tens of thousands of people who tore her apart how they had wronged her and to repair what remained of her public persona. But perhaps she had now come to understand that her shaming wasn't really about her at all. Social media is so perfectly designed to manipulate our desire for approval, and that is what led to her undoing. Her tormentors were instantly congratulated as they took Sacco down, bit by bit, and so they continued to do so. Their motivation was much the same as Sacco's own—a bid for the attention of strangers—as she milled about Heathrow, hoping to amuse people she couldn't see. *[2015]*

In this article and in his book, Ronson feels sorry for Justine Sacco. He thinks she was foolish to send her notorious tweet, but he doesn't believe she deserved the abuse she received. Indeed, Ronson came to sympathize with many of his interview subjects. For him, they were victims more than villains. He started to doubt the morality of shamers. Often, he sensed, their crusades are reckless and cruel.

Some cultural observers, though, defend public shaming, or at least they endorse certain types. Among these advocates is Jennifer Jacquet, a scholar and social activist. Jacquet earned a Ph.D. in natural resources management and environmental studies at the University of British Columbia. Currently she is an assistant professor of environmental studies at New York University, where she is also affiliated with the Stern School of Business. In 2015, she published a book titled *Is Shame Necessary?: New Uses for an Old Tool*. Jacquet would agree with Ronson that many kinds of shaming are awful. But in her book, she argues that other kinds have worth. On behalf of wildlife preservation, she herself has joined efforts to shame environmentally insensitive firms. In her view, there really are "new uses for an old tool." Of course, she wants to ensure that these uses are good, so she lays out principles she hopes shamers will heed. Here, in this excerpt from her book, she explains one.

JENNIFER JACQUET

From *Is Shame Necessary?*

Effective shaming should focus on a transgression for which there is no threat of a more severe or formal form of punishment. If there is a formal system of sanctioning in place—if, for example, there were a U.S. law that made voting compulsory (as there is in Australia)—there would be no need to mobilize the audience, and using shame might even be a waste of attention. The crowd itself might even find this to be a waste of its time. A Texas man filmed his neighbor vandalizing his car and not only used it against him in court, but also posted the footage online. Why publicize this crime and further shame the neighbor? The Texas man didn't need the help of the crowd for punishment—there was a system in place to punish the transgression.

When there is no legal mechanism or no enforcement of laws, then shaming moves up the list of options for social control. There were no laws regulating how AIG had to spend the government bailout money, just as there were no laws that prohibited banks from using bailout money for banker bonuses. Financial executives received almost $20 billion in bonuses in 2008, after a $245 billion government bailout. Citigroup proposed to buy a $50 million corporate jet in early 2009, shortly after receiving $45 billion in taxpayer funds. The courts could not find anything illegal in this behavior, but days later, President Obama said that Citigroup "should know better" and called the bonuses "shameful."

Occupy Wall Street was a signal that even though the legal system had not found that the banks had acted outside the law, many people felt the banks had done something wrong. Had more than one lone investment banker gone to prison after the 2008 financial crisis—as hundreds did during the last fraud-filled financial crisis, in the 1980s, which was one-seventieth the size of the one in 2008—we would have probably seen less shaming used against financial institutions and their employees. The Occupy Wall Street movement claimed some modest accomplishments—banks abandoned plans for debit-card fees, the government established a new agency to protect consumers from the financial sector, and the meme of "the one percent" was born. It also served as a reminder that when there are no formal avenues to punishment, society still has shame up its sleeve.

Law professor Toni Massaro has argued against shaming on the grounds that "shaming may convey the message that drunk drivers, child molesters, and the other offenders subjected to these penalties are less than human" and that they "deserve our contempt." In those specific cases, Massaro could be correct. But when shaming is used against bankers or nonvoters or against companies like Google, Amazon, and Starbucks for their offshore tax havens, it's not because society sees them as "less than human" (although in the case of the corporations, they might be) but because there is no alternative. For the same reason, states are left with shaming delinquent taxpayers because, unlike the federal government, states have almost no other means of recourse. (The State of California can confiscate only second homes and luxury vehicles, and only after a big legal brouhaha.)

It's not that shaming is preferable; it's just that, in some cases, shaming is all 5
we have. When fishermen in southern Chile are seen in areas that the

community has designated as marine protected areas, other fishermen write the transgressors' names on a big sign in town that says LOS CASTIGADOS ("THE PUNISHED"). The fishermen are group-policing the area and using shame because there are no formal sanctions. International law instruments like the Universal Declaration of Human Rights have no formal avenues for punishment, so shaming is one of the main tactics of enforcement. Kenneth Roth, executive director of Human Rights Watch, wrote, "The strength of organizations like Human Rights Watch is not their rhetorical voice but their shaming methodology—their ability to investigate misconduct and expose it to public opprobrium."

Sometimes formal punishment will never be implemented, and shaming can encourage better behavior. It is not likely, for instance, that highly salty or otherwise unhealthy foods will ever be outlawed—nor that we would want them to be. Yet we also grapple with the problems associated with unhealthy diets. Research shows that shaming might help reduce consumption of unhealthy foods—not by shaming the consumers, but by shaming the foods, that is, singling out the most egregious products that they might purchase. Researchers labeled some foods at a hospital kiosk "less healthy" and sales of healthier items increased by 6 percent. Beginning in 1993, the Finnish government required a label on foods with high salt content, which led to a significant decrease in overall salt consumption.

[2015]

THINKING ABOUT THE TEXT

We encourage you to link Galchen's story with the issues that Ronson and Jacquet raise. You might, through writing or discussion, tackle these specific questions.

1. Photographs of Andrew Rector sleeping at the stadium are readily available online. We could have used one of them to illustrate Galchen's story. But we chose not to. What would *your* decision have been? What would be the arguments for and against reproducing Rector's image in this book?
2. To what extent is Galchen's portrayal of Usl sympathetic? Is Ronson's portrayal of Justine Sacco equally so? Refer to specific passages in both texts.
3. Although the title character of Galchen's story has a real-life counterpart, she uses her freedom as a writer of fiction to invent certain details. How does Usl's mother play a significant role in the story? Why do you think Galchen gives Usl the particular job he has? What does she emphasize about Usl's lawsuit? What should readers make of the story's last word, "waiting"?
4. What would you say to someone who argues that the stadium jumbotron's repeated close-ups of Rector were an invasion of privacy?
5. Many of the shaming messages directed at Rector—and evidently at Usl, too—refer to his being overweight. Do you think that the shamers would be less scornful toward someone who was thinner? Why, or why not? To what extent, and in what ways, are overweight people nowadays made to feel ashamed?

6. What examples of public shaming can *you* think of? How similar are these cases to what Andrew Rector, Galchen's character Usl, and Justine Sacco experienced?
7. What would you say to someone who argues that social media companies like Twitter should exercise more control over content that insults people?
8. What do you think motivates shamers to send insulting messages about people they don't know and have never heard of before?
9. What advice would you give people who have been publicly shamed, such as Andrew Rector, Galchen's character Usl, and Justine Sacco?
10. In our excerpt from her book, Jacquet identifies one principle that shamers should follow if their act of shaming is to have value. In your own words, what is that principle? What principles would you add?
11. Jacquet says, "It's not that shaming is preferable; it's just that, in some cases, shaming is all we have." To what extent do you agree with her? Explain your reasoning.

SUMMING UP: MAKING ARGUMENTS ABOUT LITERATURE

- **The art of arguing is part of the tradition known as *rhetoric*. The *rhetorical situation* includes your particular topic, your audience, and the "channels" you employ. (pp. 59–61)**
- **When you argue, you attempt to *persuade* an *audience* to accept your *claims* regarding an *issue* by presenting *evidence*, explaining your *reasoning*, relying on *assumptions*, and making other kinds of *appeals*. (p. 57)**
- **An *issue* is something about which people have disagreed or might disagree.** Defined as questions with no obvious, immediate answers, ten kinds of issues that arise in literature courses are those of (1) fact, (2) theme, (3) definition, (4) symbolism, (5) pattern, (6) evaluation, (7) historical and cultural context, (8) genre, (9) social policy, and (10) cause and effect. (pp. 62–68)
- ***Claims* are the debatable answers to an issue.** In literature classes, two common types of claims are those of interpretation and those of evaluation. (pp. 68–69)
- **The art of persuasion involves trying to change people's minds.** You should convince them that your claims are at least reasonable. (p. 69)

SUMMING UP: MAKING ARGUMENTS ABOUT LITERATURE

- **The term *audience* applies to the people who read your writing.** If you are to persuade them, you must take into account their common values, experiences, and assumptions, not just focus on your subject matter. To introduce your main claim about a literary work, you might refer to readers of it who disagree with you; hasty, superficial readers; puzzled readers; or your own divided self. (pp. 69–70)
- ***Evidence* is the support that you give your claims so that others will accept them.** When you make an argument about a literary work, your readers expect you to support your case with details in the text. (pp. 70–71)
- **To persuade your audience, you need to show clearly your process of reasoning.** Methodically lay out your claims as well as the logic that connects them. (p. 69)
- ***Assumptions* are beliefs of yours that support your argument and that you may have to acknowledge as well as defend.** They include (1) beliefs about your audience's experiences; (2) values you hold; and (3) warrants, which are reasons you have for considering certain things evidence. (pp. 71–72)
- ***Appeals* in arguments fall into three main categories.** These are *logos*, the logical substance of the case; *ethos*, the image of the arguer that the audience gets; and *pathos*, the stirring of emotion. To create a positive ethos, you might make several concessions and qualifications. (pp. 71–73)
- **Some literary works can be said to present arguments themselves.** Certain characters make claims, often in debate with one another, through characterization, plot, and image, and other works indicate that the author is arguing for a certain position. (pp. 77–80)

CHAPTER 4

The Writing Process

In Chapter 5, we discuss how to write about each of the four literary genres featured in this book. Here, however, we suggest how to write about a literary work of any genre. To make our advice concrete, we mostly trace what one student did as she worked on a writing assignment for a course much like yours. Each student chose a single poem from the syllabus and wrote a 600-word argument paper on it for a general audience. We focus on the writing process of a student named Abby Hazelton.

Ultimately, Abby chose to write about William Wordsworth's "The Solitary Reaper." In his own day, Wordsworth (1770–1850) was poet laureate of England, and he continues to be regarded as a major British Romantic poet. He and fellow poet Samuel Taylor Coleridge collaborated on *Lyrical Ballads* (1798), a collection of verse that became a landmark of Romantic poetry. In his preface to the second edition two years later, Wordsworth famously defined *poetry* as "emotion recollected in tranquillity," contended that it should draw on "common life," and called for it to incorporate "language really used by men." Like many other Romantics, Wordsworth celebrated scenes of nature and country life, while deploring the increasing spread of cities. "The Solitary Reaper" appeared in his 1807 *Poems in Two Volumes.*

Before examining Abby's writing process, read Wordsworth's poem.

WILLIAM WORDSWORTH

The Solitary Reaper

Behold her, single in the field,
    Yon solitary Highland Lass!
Reaping and singing by herself;
    Stop here, or gently pass!
Alone she cuts and binds the grain,
And sings a melancholy strain;
O listen! for the Vale profound
Is overflowing with the sound.

No Nightingale did ever chaunt
    More welcome notes to weary bands

Of travellers in some shady haunt,
    Among Arabian sands:
A voice so thrilling ne'er was heard
In spring-time from the Cuckoo-bird,
Breaking the silence of the seas
Among the farthest Hebrides.

Will no one tell me what she sings?—
    Perhaps the plaintive numbers flow
For old, unhappy, far-off things,
    And battles long ago:
Or is it some more humble lay,
Familiar matter of to-day?
Some natural sorrow, loss, or pain,
That has been, and may be again?

Whate'er the theme, the Maiden sang
    As if her song could have no ending;
I saw her singing at her work,
    And o'er the sickle bending;—
I listen'd, motionless and still;
And, as I mounted up the hill,
The music in my heart I bore,
Long after it was heard no more. *[1807]*

Once she chose to write about Wordsworth's poem for her paper, Abby engaged in four sorts of activities: (1) exploring, (2) planning, (3) composing, and (4) revising. As we describe each, keep in mind that these activities need not be consecutive. Abby moved back and forth among them as she worked on her assignment.

Strategies for Exploring

As you read a literary work, you are bound to interpret and judge it. Yet not all reading is close reading, which can also be called **critical reading**. This process involves carefully and self-consciously analyzing various aspects of a text, including its meanings, its effects, and its treatment of typical elements of its genre. When you read a work closely and critically, you also note questions it raises for you—issues you might explore further in class discussion and writing. Indeed, close reading is a process of self-reflection. During this process, you monitor your own response to the text and try to identify why you see the text the way you do.

Exploring, the first stage of writing an essay about literature, is this particular process of reading. As we explain in Chapter 2, it specifically involves the following:

- Making predictions as you read
- Rereading the text with a different focus each time, including at least one stage in which you read aloud
- Comparing the text with your personal experience

- Tracing patterns and breaks from these patterns
- Noting ambiguities
- Considering the author's alternatives
- Generating questions
- Considering how the text deals with topics that have preoccupied literary studies
- Formulating a tentative claim
- Using informal writing to move through all these steps, including commenting in the text's margins; note-taking; freewriting; creating a "dialectical notebook"; and playfully revising the text

A WRITING EXERCISE

Do at least ten minutes of freewriting about Wordsworth's poem, keeping it nearby so that you can consult it if you need to. In particular, try to raise questions about the poem, and consider which of these may be worth addressing in a more formal paper.

Here is an excerpt from Abby's freewriting.

I see that this poem consists of four stanzas, each of which is eight lines long. But these stanzas have different emphases. The first stanza is a series of commands. The speaker tells people to "Behold," "Stop here, or gently pass," and "listen." The second stanza mainly describes the reaper. The third stanza is basically a bunch of questions. The fourth is the speaker's recollection of his experience in general. So I could write a paper about how this poem changes as it moves along and why the stanzas shift in emphasis. But one problem with a paper like that is that it might get me bogged down in mechanically moving from stanza to stanza. I don't want that to happen. Another thing I could do is answer one of the speaker's own questions, which are about what kind of song the reaper is singing. Evidently this "Highland Lass" is using a Scottish dialect that he doesn't understand. But I'm just as ignorant as he is about the song. I guess I'm more likely to contribute some analysis of my own if I come up with a question myself. I'm struck by the fact that he doesn't give us much sense of the reaper's song. There's no way that a printed poem could convey the reaper's tune, but still. And the words are foreign to the speaker. But I'm surprised that he doesn't make a little effort to convey at least some of the song's lyrics even if they're foreign words that he might hear wrong or misspell. How can I as a reader join him in experiencing the beauty of her song if I don't learn any of its words? I wonder if we're supposed to see the poem as being more about the speaker than about the reaper. More specifically, maybe we're supposed to be a little disturbed that he's a British intellectual who is making a spectacle out of a foreign woman from the working class. At any rate, he seems bent on controlling this experience even as he invites us to share it. Another question for me is, Why does he shift from present tense to past tense in the last stanza? This change is really curious to me. I don't see anything earlier on that prepares me for it. First, we're led to believe that the speaker is observing the reaper right then and there, but at the end he speaks as if this occurred in the past, though maybe the recent past. This inconsistency in the time frame makes me think that in some important way the overall poem is about time. At any rate, I'm drawn to the inconsistency because it's so blatant. If I wrote about it, I might still devote a paragraph to each stanza, but I'd be starting with the last one and referring back to the others in order to explain that stanza. What I still have to figure out, though, is what exactly the poem is saying about time when it makes the shift of tense.

Freewriting enabled Abby to raise several questions. At the same time, she realized that her paper could not deal with everything that puzzled her. When you first get an assignment like hers, you may fear that you will have nothing to say. But you will come up with a lot of material if, like Abby, you take time for exploration. As we have suggested, it's a process of examining potential subjects through writing, discussion, and just plain thinking. One of your challenges will be to choose among the various issues you have formulated. At the end of this excerpt from her freewriting, Abby is on the verge of choosing to analyze the poem's shift of tense in its final stanza. For her, this shift is an interesting change from a pattern, the poem's previous uses of present tense. Abby has not yet decided how to explain this shift; at the moment, it remains for her a mystery. But her paper would achieve little if it focused just on aspects of the poem that are easy to interpret. Though Abby has more thinking to do about the poem's shift of tense, it seems a promising subject for her precisely because it puzzles her.

Strategies for Planning

Planning for an assignment like Abby's involves five main activities:

1. Choosing the text you will analyze
2. Identifying your audience
3. Identifying the main issue, claim, and evidence you will present
4. Identifying your assumptions
5. Determining how you will organize your argument, including how you will demonstrate your process of reasoning

CHOOSE A TEXT

Abby considered several poems before choosing one for her paper. She settled on Wordsworth's for five reasons. First, it was a text that left her with plenty of questions. Second, she believed that these questions could be issues for other readers. Third, she felt increasingly able to *argue* about the poem — that is, to make and support claims about it. Fourth, she believed that she could adequately analyze the poem within the assignment's word limit. Finally, Wordsworth's poem drew her because she had heard about the Romantic movement in English literature and was curious to study an example of it.

Faced with the same assignment, you might choose a different poem than Abby did. Still, the principles that she followed are useful. Think about them whenever you are free to decide which texts you will write about. With some assignments, of course, you may need a while to decide which text is best for you. And later, after you have made your decision, you may want to make a switch. For example, you may find yourself changing your mind once you have done a complete draft. Frustrated by the text you have chosen, you may realize that another inspires you more. If so, consider making a substitution. Naturally, you will feel more able to switch if you have ample time left to write the paper, so avoid waiting to start your paper just before it is due.

IDENTIFY YOUR AUDIENCE

To determine what your readers will see as an issue and to make your claims about it persuasive to them, you need to develop an audience profile. Perhaps your instructor will specify your audience. You may be asked, for example, to imagine yourself writing for a particular group in a particular situation. If you were Abby, how would you analyze "The Solitary Reaper" for an orchestra wanting to know what this poem implies about music? Even when not required of you, such an exercise can be fun and thought-provoking for you as you plan a paper.

Most often, though, instructors ask students to write for a "general" audience, the readership that Abby was asked to address. Assume that a general audience is one that will want evidence for your claims. While this audience will include your instructor, let it also include your classmates, since in class discussions they will be an audience for you whenever you speak. Besides, your class may engage in peer review, with students giving one another feedback on their drafts.

IDENTIFY YOUR ISSUE, CLAIM, AND EVIDENCE

When you have written papers for previous classes, you may have been most concerned with coming up with a thesis. Maybe you did not encounter the term *issue* at all. But good planning for a paper does entail identifying the main issue you will address. Once you have sensed what that issue is, try phrasing it as a question. If the answer would be obvious to your readers, be cautious, for you really do not have an issue if the problem you are raising can be easily resolved.

Also, try to identify what *kind* of issue you will focus on. For help, look at our list of various types (pp. 62–67). Within "The Solitary Reaper," the speaker raises an issue of fact: he wants to know what sort of song the reaper is singing. But as someone writing about Wordsworth's poem, Abby wanted to focus on another kind of issue, which she decided is best regarded as an issue of pattern. More precisely, she thought her main question might be, What should we conclude from the inconsistency in pattern that occurs when the final stanza shifts to past tense? To be sure, Abby recognized that addressing this issue would lead to issues of theme and of cause and effect, for she would have to consider why Wordsworth shifts tenses and how the shift relates to his overall subject.

Now that she had identified her main issue, Abby had to determine her main claim. Perhaps you have grown comfortable with the term *thesis* and want to keep using it. Fine. Bear in mind, though, that your thesis is the main *claim* you will make and proceed to support. And when, as Abby did, you put your main issue as a question, then your main claim is your answer to that question. Sometimes you will come up with question and answer simultaneously. Once in a while, you may even settle on your answer first, not being certain yet how to word the question. Whatever the case, planning for your paper involves articulating both the question (the issue) and the answer (your main claim). Try actually writing both down, making sure to phrase your main issue as a question and your main claim as the answer. Again, Abby's main issue was, What should we conclude from the inconsistency in pattern that occurs when the final stanza shifts to past tense? After much thought, she expressed her main claim this way:

> One possible justification for the shift to past tense is that it reminds us of the speaker's inability to halt the passage of time. He would like to freeze his encounter with the reaper, keeping it always in the present. But as the shift in tense indicates, time goes on, making the encounter part of the speaker's past. Perhaps, therefore, the poem's real subject is the idea that time is always in flux.

Audiences usually want evidence, and as we noted earlier, most arguments you write about literature will need to cite details of the work itself. Because direct quotation is usually an effective move, Abby planned to elaborate her claim by citing several of Wordsworth's references to time. Remember, though, that you need to avoid seeming willfully selective when you quote. While Abby expected to quote from Wordsworth's last stanza, she also knew she had to relate it to earlier lines so that her readers would see her as illuminating the basic subject of the whole poem. In particular, she looked for language in the first three stanzas that might hint at the speaker's lack of control over time, thereby previewing the last stanza's emphasis.

IDENTIFY YOUR ASSUMPTIONS

Often, to think about particular challenges of your paper is to think about your assumptions. Remember that a big category of assumptions is warrants; these are what lead you to call certain things evidence for your claims. Abby knew that one of her warrants was an assumption about Wordsworth himself — that he was not being sloppy when he shifted tenses in his last stanza. Rarely will your paper need to admit all the warrants on which it relies. Most of the time, your task will be to guess which warrants your readers do want stated. Abby felt there was at least one warrant she would have to spell out — her belief that the poem's verb tenses reveal something about the speaker's state of mind.

DETERMINE YOUR ORGANIZATION

To make sure their texts seem organized and demonstrate their process of reasoning, most writers first do an **outline**, a list of their key points in the order they will appear. Outlines are indeed a good idea, but bear in mind that there are various kinds. One popular type, which you may already know, is the **sentence outline**. As the name implies, it lists the writer's key points in sentence form. Its advantages are obvious: this kind of outline forces you to develop a detailed picture of your argument's major steps, and it leaves you with sentences you can then incorporate into your paper. Unfortunately, sentence outlines tend to discourage flexibility. Because they demand much thought and energy, you may hesitate to revise them, even if you come to feel your paper would work better with a new structure.

A second, equally familiar outline is the **topic outline**, a list in which the writer uses a few words to signify the main subjects that he or she will discuss. Because it is sketchy, this kind of outline allows writers to go back and change plans if necessary. Nevertheless, a topic outline may fail to provide all the guidance a writer needs.

We find a third type useful: a **rhetorical purpose outline**. As with the first two, you list the major sections of your paper. Next, you briefly indicate two things for each section: the effect you want it to have on your audience, and how you will achieve that effect. Here is the rhetorical purpose outline that Abby devised for her paper.

INTRODUCTION

The audience needs to know the text I'll discuss.	I'll identify Wordsworth's poem.
The audience must know my main issue.	I'll point out that the poem is puzzling in its shift of tenses at the end.
The audience must know my main claim.	I'll argue that the shift to past tense suggests that the poem's real subject is the inability of human beings to halt the passage of time.

ANALYSIS OF THE POEM'S FINAL STANZA

The audience needs to see in detail how the final stanza's shift to past tense signals the speaker's inability to control the passage of time.	I will point out not only the shift of tense but also other words in the last stanza that imply time moves on. I will note as well that music is an especially fleeting medium, so the reaper's song was bound to fade.

ANALYSIS OF THE PRECEDING STANZAS

To accept that the passage of time is the poem's real concern, the audience must see that the preceding stanzas hint at this subject.	I will analyze the first three stanzas in turn, showing how each implies the speaker is frustrated over his inability to control time.

CONCLUSION

The audience may need to be clearer about what I consider the ultimate *tone* of the poem.	I will say that although the poem can be thought of as a warm tribute to the singing reaper, the final emphasis on the passage of time is pessimistic in tone, and the speaker winds up as "solitary" as the reaper.

For your own rhetorical purpose outlines, you may want to use phrases rather than sentences. If you do use sentences, as Abby did, you do not have to write all that many. Note that Abby wrote relatively few as she stated the effects she would aim for and her strategies for achieving those effects. Thus, she was not tremendously invested in preserving her original outline. She felt free to change it if it failed to prove helpful.

Strategies for Composing

Composing is not always distinguishable from exploring, planning, and revising. As you prepare for your paper, you may jot down words or whole sentences. Once you begin a draft, you may alter that draft in several ways before you complete it. You may be especially prone to making changes in drafts if you use a computer, for word processing enables you to jump around in your text, revisiting and revising what you have written.

Still, most writers feel that doing a draft is an activity in its own right, and a major one at that. The next chapter presents various tips for writing about specific genres, and Chapter 6 discusses writing research-based papers. Meanwhile, here are some tips to help you with composing in general.

DECIDE ON A TITLE

You may be inclined to let your **title** be the same as that of the text you discuss. Were you to write about Wordsworth's poem, then, you would be calling your own paper "The Solitary Reaper." But often such mimicry backfires. For one thing, it may lead your readers to think that you are unoriginal and perhaps even lazy. Also, you risk confusing your audience, since your paper would actually be *about* Wordsworth's poem rather than being the poem itself. So take the time to come up with a title of your own. Certainly it may announce the text you will focus on, but let it do more. In particular, use your title to indicate the main claim you will be making. With just a few words, you can preview the argument to come.

MAKE CHOICES ABOUT YOUR STYLE

Perhaps you have been told to "sound like yourself" when you write. Yet that can be a difficult demand (especially if you are not sure what your "self" is really like). Above all, the **style** you choose depends on your audience and purpose. In writing an argument for a general audience, probably you would do best to avoid the extremes of pomposity and breezy informality. Try to stick with words you know well, and if you do want to use some that are only hazily familiar to you, check their dictionary definitions first.

At some point in our lives, probably all of us have been warned not to use *I* in our writing. In the course you are taking, however, you may be asked to write about your experiences. If so, you will find *I* hard to avoid. Whether to use it does become a real question when you get assignments like Abby's, which require you chiefly to make an argument about a text. Since you are supposed to focus on that text, your readers may be disconcerted if you keep referring to yourself. Even so, you need not assume that your personal life is irrelevant to the task. Your opening paragraph might refer to your personal encounters with the text, as a way of establishing the issue you will discuss. A personal anecdote might serve as a forceful conclusion to your paper. Moreover, before you reach the conclusion, you might orient your readers to the structure of your paper by using certain expressions that feature the word *I*: for example, *As I suggested earlier, As I have noted, As I argue later.* In general, you may be justified in saying *I* at certain moments. When tempted to use this pronoun, though, consider whether it really is your best move.

Arguments about literature are most compelling when supported by quotations, but be careful not to quote excessively. If you constantly repeat other people's words, providing few of your own, your readers will hardly get a sense of you as an author. Moreover, a paper full of quotation marks is hard to read. Make sure to quote selectively, remembering that sometimes you can simply paraphrase. When you do quote, try to cite only the words you need. You do not have to reproduce a whole line or sentence if one word is enough to support your point.

When summarizing what happens in a literary work, be careful not to shift tenses as you go along. Your reader may be confused if you shift back and forth between past and present. We suggest that you stick primarily to the present tense, which is the tense that literary critics customarily employ. For example, instead of saying that the speaker *praised* the lass, say that he *praises* her.

DRAFT AN INTRODUCTION

As a general principle, use your introduction to identify as quickly and efficiently as possible

- the main text that you will analyze;
- the main issue about it that you will address; and
- the main claim that you will develop in response to that issue.

Don't waste time with grand philosophical statements such as "Society doesn't always appreciate the work that everyone does," or "Over the centuries, much literature has been about work," or "William Wordsworth was a great British Romantic poet."

Remember that your main issue should be a significant question with no obvious answer. Try using one or more of the following strategies to establish that issue at the start of your essay:

- **State the issue as, indeed, a question.** For example: "Why, conceivably, does Wordsworth shift to the past tense in his poem's final stanza?"
- **Apply a word like *puzzling, confusing, mysterious,* or *curious* to whatever feature your issue will be about.** For example: "Because Wordsworth uses present tense for much of the poem, it is puzzling that he turns to past tense at the very end."
- **Through personal reference, state that you were first puzzled by a particular feature of the work but are now able to interpret it.** For example: "At first, I was confused when Wordsworth shifted to the past tense, but now I have arrived at a possible explanation for this move."
- **Indicate that you aim to help other readers of the work, who may have trouble understanding the feature of it you will focus on.** For example: "Quite a few readers of Wordsworth's poem may have difficulty seeing why he shifts to the past tense at the end. There is, however, a possible explanation for this move."
- **Indicate that you will express disagreement with existing or possible interpretations.** For example: "While some readers of Wordsworth's poem may feel that his shift to the past tense shows a wonderful ability to preserve his experience with the reaper, a more plausible interpretation is that it shows his isolation after meeting her."

LIMIT PLOT SUMMARY

Short stories and plays spin tales. So do many poems and essays. But if you are writing about a literary text that is narrative in form, don't spend much of your paper just summarizing the narrative. Developing a genuine argument about the work involves more than recounting its plot. Here are strategies you can use to limit this:

- **Assume that your reader knows the basic plot and needs only a few brief reminders of its key elements.**

- **Keep in mind that your main purpose is to put forth, explain, and support a *claim* about the text — your answer to some question you raise about it.**
- **After your introduction, try to begin each new paragraph with a subclaim that helps you develop your main claim.** Use the rest of the paragraph to elaborate and provide evidence for this subclaim. *Don't* begin a paragraph simply by recording a plot incident, for doing so is liable to bog you down in sheer summary.
- **Instead of reciting plot details, write about how the work you are analyzing is *constructed*.** Make observations about specific methods that the author uses to present the story, including techniques of organization and characterization. For example, rather than say "The speaker in Wordsworth's poem wonders what the woman is singing," state and develop a point like "Wordsworth chooses not to translate the woman's song for us; instead, he depicts the speaker as not knowing her words, so that the poem becomes mostly about the effect of her song as sheer musical notes."
- **Instead of turning frequently to plot details, try to linger on some of the author's specific language, exploring possible definitions of particular words.** For example, rather than say "The speaker in Wordsworth's poem remembers the woman's music," examine possible meanings of the word *bore* in the poem's next-to-last line, "The music in my heart I bore." *Bore* can simply mean "carried," and probably that is one meaning that Wordsworth has in mind here. But it can also mean "engraved, deeply inscribed," and perhaps Wordsworth wants us to think of this definition, too.

DECIDE HOW TO REFER TO THE AUTHOR'S LIFE AND INTENTIONS

Be cautious about relating the work to the author's life. Sometimes a certain character within the work may indeed express the author's own views, but don't simply assume that a character speaks for the author. Even the *I* of a first-person poem may differ significantly from its creator. True, many literary works are at least somewhat autobiographical, based on one or more aspects of the author's life. Nevertheless, even works that are largely autobiographical may not be entirely so. Besides, knowledge of the author's life won't always help you figure out his or her text. Wordsworth may have derived "The Solitary Reaper" from a personal encounter, but we must still interpret the particular poem he proceeded to write. So,

- **Be careful in linking a work to the author's own circumstances.** Such connections can be legitimate, but the more you push them, the more you may risk distorting the work's exact design. You also risk neglecting the author's artistic achievement. Not everyone who hears a reaper sing could turn this event into a poem!

Much of what you write about a literary work will reflect your understanding of its author's intentions. Needless to say, you can't peer into the author's mind. Rather, you'll make hypotheses about the author's aims. So,

- **Sometimes, at least, admit that you are guessing at what the author thought.** Often, your reader will assume that you are speculating about the author's aims, but your argument about them can be more persuasive if, at times, you acknowledge that you're trying to come up with the best hypothesis rather than stating an absolute fact. Take care, however, to explain why your guesses are logical.
- **If you suspect that the author might object to your view of the text, feel free to acknowledge such possible disagreements.** In fact, many theorists argue that a literary work may differ from how its author sees it. They refuse, therefore, to treat the author as an absolute authority on the work. D. H. Lawrence's advice was "Trust the tale, not the teller." Even if Lawrence is right, of course, you must show how *your* interpretation of a text manages to make sense of it.
- **Feel free to concede that your analysis of the work isn't the only reasonable one.** You can develop your main claim about a literary work partly by noting and addressing ways in which other readers may disagree with you about it. Bear in mind, though, that you will annoy your own audience if you come across as dogmatic. Be as fair as you can to views different from yours. Actually, your readers will appreciate it if at times you concede that yours is not the only reasonable interpretation. You can even specify one or more alternatives. Of course, you would still try to make a case for *your* explanation, perhaps by saying why it is *more plausible* or *more helpful* than its rivals. But speak of these competitors with respect, instead of just dismissing them with scorn.

RECOGNIZE AND AVOID LOGICAL FALLACIES

Although arguments presented in literary texts are often not logical, your arguments about these texts should be. Readers do not expect a poem's speaker, for example, to present cogently reasoned arguments to her lover, nor do they expect a lament for the lost passions of youth to be anything but subjective. But different kinds of writing have different conventions. What works in poetry may not be appropriate in an argument. The kinds of serious arguments you are expected to create cannot be successful using heartfelt emotion alone. When you write about literature, shaky thinking might cause your audience to dismiss your ideas. Your claims and the assumptions behind them should be clear and reasoned. If they are not, you might be committing a **fallacy**, a common term for unsound reasoning.

In the next several paragraphs, we discuss typical logical fallacies. Some of them are especially relevant to literary studies, and for all of them we provide examples related to "The Solitary Reaper." We do not want you to brood over this list, seeing it as a catalog of sins to which you might fall prey. If you constantly fear being accused of fallacies, you might be too paralyzed to make claims at all! In our discussion of fallacies, we also identify circumstances in which your audience might *not* object to a particular fallacy. In addition, we suggest how a writer might revise such claims to be more persuasive. Indeed, the main value in studying fallacies is to identify ways you might develop arguments more effectively.

One of the most common fallacies, ***ad hominem*** (Latin: "toward the man"), is probably the easiest to commit because it is the hardest to resist. Instead of doing the hard work of analyzing the claim and the evidence, we simply ignore them and attack the character of the person making the argument. Instead of trying to figure out what is going on in a complex work of literature, we say, "How can you take seriously a poem about love written by a manic depressive who commits suicide?" It is best to focus on the message, not the messenger.

A related fallacy, **begging the question** (a kind of circular reasoning in which the statement being argued is already assumed to have been decided) is also involved in this example since it is assumed (not proved) that unstable poets cannot have cogent insights about love.

In writing about "The Solitary Reaper," a classmate of Abby's ignored whatever argument the poem is making and focused on Wordsworth's credibility as an observer: "British intellectuals have been either romanticizing or degrading country people for centuries. Whatever Wordsworth thinks about the 'Highland Lass' is almost certainly wrong." First of all, the speaker of the poem should not be automatically equated with the poet. When they write, poets and fictional writers construct personae that may or may not reflect their own views. Second, attacking Wordsworth is a fallacy for several reasons. It first has to be demonstrated that the poet is a British intellectual, that intellectuals have consistently misrepresented rural people, and that the speaker has done so in this particular case. The classmate should revise her claim so that it deals with the words in the text, not her view of the poet's credibility.

Professional historians, mathematicians, and philosophers usually cite other professionals working in their field; that is, they **appeal to authority** to bolster their credibility. Disciplinary knowledge is created by a community of scholars who cite the ideas of its members as evidence for their claims. The warrant is that recognized authorities know what they are talking about. Quoting them is persuasive. But not completely: appeals to authority can also be fallacious. Literary critics, like other thinkers, often disagree. Just citing an expert does not conclusively prove your claim. A classmate of Abby's, for example, quoted a critic, Ian Lancashire, who says that the narrator "transcends the limitations of mortality," but the student did not give his own reasons or his own evidence for thinking this way. This appeal to critical authority without giving reasons or evidence is a fallacy because a sound argument would at least have to consider other critics. An argument is a reasoning process in which claims are supported, not simply asserted, even if they come from an expert.

A related fallacy involves using quotations from unreliable sources. Although the Internet is often a valuable tool, students sometimes use it uncritically. If you went to the search engine Google and entered Wordsworth's "The Solitary Reaper," you would quickly find Ian Lancashire's essay; and since he is a professor at the University of Toronto with many publications on this and other Romantic topics, citing him is appropriate. But some of the commentators noted by the Google search are students, perhaps English majors who have written a paper for a course on the Romantic poets. Using them as authorities would damage your judgment and credibility.

Equally harmful to the soundness of your argument is to rely too heavily on personal experience as evidence for your claim. Personal experience can sometimes be compelling and authoritative. Indeed, many critics have successfully used their own experiences with discrimination to create cogent arguments. But they rarely rely exclusively on personal experience. Instead they blend relevant experience with textual and critical specifics. Telling your readers that "The Solitary Reaper" is factually flawed because you never saw harvesters work alone when you worked on your uncle's farm would be a fallacy.

Actually, the previous example of using personal experience as authority is also unsound because the personal sample is too small to warrant a reasonable conclusion. It is hard to convince your audience if you claim too much based on limited experience. A student arguing that "The Solitary Reaper" demonstrates that field workers are melancholy would be committing a **hasty generalization** fallacy. Simply claiming less would improve the argument. In fact, this student might change the focus of her argument by doing research on other poems by Wordsworth, finding several that deal with young women in nature. Using "She Dwelt among Untrodden Ways" and "She Was a Phantom of Delight," the student might argue that Wordsworth is so enraptured by the natural world that he often blurs the boundaries between people and nature.

Another common fallacy is ***post hoc, ergo propter hoc*** (Latin: "because of this, then that"). Few of us escape this error in cause and effect. Many superstitions probably began because of this fallacy. A man breaks a mirror and bad luck follows. Did the mirror cause the bad luck? Logic says no, but the next day he breaks a leg, and a week later his car is stolen. The coincidence is often too tempting to resist. Does smoking marijuana lead to hard drugs? Logic says no, since you could argue just as plausibly that almost anything (carrots, beer, coffee) that comes before could be said to cause what comes after. Unless a clear, logical link between the two events is demonstrated, you might be accused of the *post hoc* fallacy.

In writing about "The Solitary Reaper," you might want to argue that the "melancholy strain" the traveler heard caused him to have a deeper appreciation for the beauty and mystery of rural people. But perhaps the narrator held such an opinion for a long time, or perhaps this is just one of dozens of such encounters that the poet remembers fondly. A sounder argument would focus on the cause and effect that do seem to be in the text: the mystery of the song's content adds to the emotional response the poet has.

Most of us commit a version of the **intentional fallacy** when we defend ourselves against someone we offended by saying, "That's not what I meant. It was just a joke." The problem arises because we are not always able to carry out our intentions. Perhaps our language is not precise enough, or perhaps our intention to be sincere or honest or witty gets mixed up with other intentions we have to sound intelligent, confident, or impressive. Students are often surprised when teachers tell them that a writer's stated intentions cannot be taken as the final word on a poem's meaning. "Wordsworth knows the poem better than anyone else" is an understandable retort. But that might not be the case. Wordsworth might not be the most astute reader of his own work. And he may not be fully aware of all that he intended. A student would be committing an intentional fallacy by arguing that "The Solitary Reaper" is written in the language used by the common man because Wordsworth says so in his preface to *Lyrical Ballads.* While this student should be commended for doing extra research, another student might point out that "Vale profound," "plaintive numbers," and "humble lay" seem conventionally poetic. Like others, this fallacy is easily revised by claiming less: "Most of 'The Solitary Reaper' is written in simple diction to approximate the language used by ordinary people."

When you try to destroy someone's argument by ignoring their main point and focusing on something marginal, you are attacking a **straw man**. The student who argues that we should dismiss Wordsworth's credibility as an observer because of "his absurd declaration that 'a voice so thrilling ne'er was heard'" is committing the straw man fallacy. While it is probably true that the song he hears is not the most thrilling in the history of the world, this is hardly Wordsworth's main point. Writers gain more credibility if they deal with a writer's strongest or main claim.

A favorite tactic of traditionalists trying to hold the line against change, the **slippery slope** fallacy is used to claim that if we allow one thing to happen, then slipping into catastrophe is just around the corner. If we do not prevent students from wearing gangsta rap fashions, gangs will eventually roam the hallways; if we allow the morning-after pill, sexual anarchy will follow. A small step is seen as precipitating an avalanche.

The following claim by a student anticipates something that simply is not logically called for: "Although Wordsworth probably means well, his praise for the 'Highland Lass' is a dangerous move since she is probably illiterate and full of rural biases and superstitions. His failure to discriminate will lead to loss of judgment and standards." Again, claiming less improves the argument: Wordsworth is less interested in the content ("Whate'er the theme") than in the "music in my heart," an emotional response that we hope does not carry over into his views on medicine, engineering, and economics.

We are all guilty at times of the fallacy of **oversimplification** — of not seeing the inevitable complexity of things. At the risk of committing a hasty generalization ourselves, it is probably the case that your instructor will be impressed if you look for complexity in literary texts and in your arguments. Seeing complexity is a consequence of hard thinking. There are rarely two sides to a question. More likely, there are a dozen plausible and reasonable perspectives. The cliché that the truth often appears in shades of gray rather than in black and white gets at the idea that simple solutions are often the result of shallow thinking.

Complexity is not what the following claim reveals: "'The Solitary Reaper' is a poem about a traveler who hears a young girl 'singing by herself,' and like a catchy ad, the tune stays with him." Being exposed to other viewpoints in class discussions and in peer-group revision can help this student avoid oversimplifying the experience Wordsworth has, one that touches on issues of mortality, the mysteries of emotional response, the purpose of poetry, and the power of the natural world. When Henry David Thoreau, the author of *Walden* (1854), urged his contemporaries to live simply, he was talking about their lifestyles, not their thinking.

Non sequitur is a general catchall fallacy that means "it does not follow." Some principle of logic has been violated when we make a claim that the evidence cannot support. In "The Solitary Reaper," it does not follow that because the Highland Lass "sings a melancholy strain," she herself is sad. She could be happy, absentminded, or simply bored. Perhaps the song is a conventional ballad typically sung by workers to pass the time. Revising this fallacy, like many of the others, involves setting aside time in the revision process to look again at your claims and the assumptions behind them, carefully and objectively making a clear connection between your claim and the evidence you say supports it.

First Draft of a Student Paper

The following is Abby's first complete draft of her paper. Eventually, she revised this draft after a group of her classmates reviewed it and after she reflected further on it herself. For the moment, though, read this first version, and decide what you would have said to her about it.

Abby Hazelton
Professor Ramsey
English 102
4 March - - - -

The Passage of Time in
"The Solitary Reaper"

William Wordsworth, one of the most famous writers in the movement known as British Romanticism, liked to write about beautiful features of the countryside. In his poem "The Solitary Reaper," the speaker enthuses over a girl who sings as she works in the fields. Yet although he is enraptured by her "melancholy strain," (line 6), he is unsure what it is *about* because she is using a Scottish dialect that he cannot understand. By contrast, the subject of the poem seems much clearer. The very title of the poem refers to the singing girl, and the subsequent lines repeatedly praise her song as wonderfully haunting. Nevertheless, the poem has puzzling aspects. Many readers are likely to wonder if they are supposed to find the speaker guilty of cultural and class superiority when he, as a British intellectual, treats a Scottish peasant girl as a spectacle. Another issue, the one I focus on in my paper, arises when the final stanza shifts to past tense. In the first three stanzas, the speaker uses present tense, as if he is currently observing the singer whom he describes. In the concluding stanza, however, the speaker uses verbs such as "sang" (25), "saw" (27), and "listen'd" (29), as if he is *recalling* his encounter with her. How can we explain this inconsistency? One possible justification for the final shift to past tense is that it reminds us of the speaker's inability to halt the passage of time. Even though he would like to freeze the encounter, time goes on. Perhaps, therefore, the poem's real subject is the idea that time is always in flux. Indeed, even before the final stanza, the speaker betrays an awareness that he can't bend time to his will.

Simply by virtue of the shift to past tense, the last stanza indicates that time goes on despite the speaker's wishes. But other elements of this stanza convey the same notion. Recalling his experience of the girl's singing, the speaker reports that he was "motionless and still" (29), yet in the very next line he admits that he eventually moved: "I mounted up the hill" (30). When the speaker says that "the Maiden sang / As if her song could have no ending" (25–26), the words "As if" are significant, implying that the song did end for him in reality. Similarly, the poem itself has to end at some point. In fact, it concludes with the words "no more," which stress that the singer and her song now belong to the speaker's past (32). Only in his "heart" (31), apparently, can he retain them. Furthermore, the medium of print can never convey the sound of music. In fact, prior to recording technology, music was the most fleeting of media, its notes fading with each new moment. By seeking to transmit music, the speaker ensures that he will wind up being frustrated by time.

Even if the final stanza's shift of tense is jarring, the first three stanzas give hints that the speaker will end up defeated by time. Significantly, the poem's very first word is "Behold" (1). In issuing this command, the speaker evidently hopes that other people will abandon all motion and gaze at the singer, basking in her song. The speaker reinforces this call for paralysis with the command that begins line 4: "Stop here." Yet, as if acknowledging limits to his control, he adds "or gently pass!" (4). Besides referring to other human beings, these commands seem directed at time itself. The speaker hopes that time, too, will "Stop" and "Behold." Even at this point in the poem, however, he realizes that time is inclined to "pass," in which case he hopes that it will at least move on "gently" (4).

The second stanza is chiefly concerned with space. Comparing the girl's song to other sounds, the speaker ranges from "Arabian sands" (12) to "the seas / Among the farthest Hebrides" (15–16). In the third stanza, however, he focuses again on time. Trying to determine the subject of the song, he expresses uncertainty about its time frame. He wonders whether the song concerns "old, unhappy, far-off things / And battles long ago" (19–20) or instead deals with "Familiar matter of to-day" (22). Moreover, even if he suspects the song's subject is "Some natural sorrow, loss, or pain" (23), he is unsure whether this experience of despair is confined to the past ("has been") or will reoccur ("may be again") (24). Whichever of the possibilities he raises is true, the speaker is clearly limited in his ability to figure out the song's relation to time. In other words, he cannot force time into a meaningful pattern, let alone prevent its passing.

By the end of the poem, the speaker seems as "solitary" as the reaper. In addition to losing his experience with her as time moves on, he is isolated in other ways.

This situation seems to leave the speaker as "solitary" as the reaper. Throughout the poem, actually, we don't see him in the company of others. His opening "Behold" is directed at no one in particular. Furthermore, we can't be sure he is speaking to actual passersby or, rather, to the poem's hypothetical future readers. Nor, for all his praise of the singer, does he apparently talk to her. Rather, he gives the impression that he keeps at a distance. Even if he did try to converse with the reaper, he himself would still be "solitary" in the sense of failing to understand her language and failing to communicate her song to his readers. He does not even bother trying to reproduce some of the song's words. Therefore, despite the speaker's enchantment over the reaper, this poem is ultimately pessimistic. The speaker is left only with his memories of a wonderful experience. He has lost the experience itself.

Works Cited

Wordsworth, William. "The Solitary Reaper." *Making Literature Matter: An Anthology for Readers and Writers*, edited by John Schilb and John Clifford, 7th ed., Bedford/St. Martin's, 2018, pp. 98–99.

Strategies for Revising

Most first drafts are far from perfect. Even experienced professional writers often have to revise their work. Besides making changes on their own, many of them solicit feedback from others. In various workplaces, writing is collaborative, with coauthors exchanging ideas as they try to improve a piece. Remain open to the possibility that your draft needs changes, perhaps several. Of course, you are more apt to revise extensively if you have given yourself enough time. Conversely, you will not feel able to change much of your paper if it is due the next day. You will also limit your ability to revise if you work only with your original manuscript, scribbling possible changes between the lines. This practice amounts to conservatism, for it encourages you to keep passages that really ought to be overhauled.

You may have trouble, however, improving a draft if you are checking many things in it at once. Therefore, read the draft repeatedly, looking at a different aspect of it each time. A good way to begin is to outline the paper you have written and then compare that outline with your original one. If the two outlines differ, your draft may or may not need adjusting; perhaps you were wise to swerve from your original plan. In any case, you should ponder your departures from that plan, considering whether they were for the best.

If, like Abby, you are writing an argument paper, our Checklist for Revising box has some topics and questions you might apply as you review your first draft. Some of these considerations overlap. Nevertheless, take them in turn rather than all at once.

A CHECKLIST FOR REVISING

Logic

- Will my audience see that the issue I am focusing on is indeed an issue?
- Will the audience be able to follow the logic of my argument?
- Is the logic as persuasive as it might be? Is there more evidence I can provide? Do I need to identify more of my assumptions?
- Have I addressed all of my audience's potential concerns?

Organization

- Does my introduction identify the issue that I will focus on? Does it state my main claim?
- Will my audience be able to detect and follow the stages of my argument?
- Does the order of my paragraphs seem purposeful rather than arbitrary?
- Have I done all I can to signal connections within and between sentences? Within and between paragraphs?
- Have I avoided getting bogged down in mere summary?
- Will my conclusion satisfy readers? Does it leave any key questions dangling?

Clarity

- Does my title offer a good preview of my argument?
- Will each of my sentences be immediately clear?
- Am I sure how to define each word that I have used?

Emphasis

- Have I put key points in prominent places?
- Have I worded each sentence for maximum impact? In particular, is each sentence as concise as possible? Do I use active verbs whenever I can?

Style

- Are my tone and level of vocabulary appropriate?
- Will my audience think me fair-minded? Should I make any more concessions?
- Do I use any mannerisms that may distract my readers?
- Have I used any expressions that may annoy or offend?
- Is there anything else I can do to make my paper readable and interesting?

A CHECKLIST FOR REVISING

Grammar

- Is each of my sentences grammatically correct?
- Have I punctuated properly?

Physical Appearance

- Have I followed the proper format for quotations, notes, and bibliography?
- Are there any typographical errors?

We list these considerations from most to least important. When revising a draft, think first about matters of logic, organization, and clarity. There is little point in fixing the grammar of particular sentences if you are going to drop them later because they fail to advance your argument.

As we noted, a group of Abby's classmates discussed her draft. Most of these students seemed to like her overall argument, including her main issue and claim. Having been similarly confused by the poem's shift of tense, they appreciated the light that Abby shed on it. They were impressed by her willingness to examine the poem's specific words. They especially liked her closing analogy between the reaper and the speaker himself. Nevertheless, the group made several comments about Abby's paper that she took as suggestions for improvement. Ultimately, she decided that the following changes were in order.

1. She should make her introduction more concise. The first draft is so long and dense that it may confuse readers instead of helping them sense the paper's main concerns. This problem is common to first drafts. In this preliminary phase, many writers worry that they will fail to generate *enough* words; they are hardly thinking about how to restrain themselves. Moreover, the writer of a first draft may still be unsure about the paper's whole argument, so the introduction often lacks a sharp focus. After Abby finished and reviewed her first draft, she saw ways of making her introduction tighter.

2. She should rearrange paragraphs. After her introduction, Abby discussed the poem's last stanza in more detail. Then she moved back to stanza 1. Next, just before her paper's conclusion, she analyzed stanzas 2 and 3. Abby thought that the structure of her paper moved logically from the obvious to the hidden: the poem's last stanza emphasized the passage of time, and the earlier stanzas touched on this subject more subtly. Yet Abby's method of organization frustrated her classmates. They thought her paper would be easier to follow if, after the introduction, it moved chronologically through the poem. For them, her discussion of stanzas 2 and 3 seemed especially mislocated. Though she had positioned this discussion as her paper's climax, her classmates did not sense it to be her most significant and compelling moment of insight. Most important, they believed, were her comments on the *final* stanza, for that seemed to them the most important part of Wordsworth's poem. In other words, they thought the climax of the paper would be stronger if it focused on the climax of the poem. Abby hesitated to adopt her classmates' recommendation, but eventually she did so. When you read her final version, see if you like her rearrangement of paragraphs. Sometimes, though not always, a paper about a literary work seems more coherent if it does follow the work's chronological structure. And papers should indeed build to a climax, even if readers disagree about what its content should be.

3. She should reconsider her claim that "this poem is ultimately pessimistic." Abby's classmates thought this claim did not fully account for the poem's last two lines: "The music in my heart I bore, / Long after it was heard no more" (31–32). While they agreed with her that the words "no more" emphasize that the singer has faded into the past, they disagreed that her song is lost as well, for it remains in the speaker's "heart." They noted that Abby had acknowledged this fact, but they felt she had done so too briefly and dismissively. In addition, one student encouraged her to think about poetry and music as ways of keeping memories alive. More specifically, he suggested that the speaker of "The Solitary Reaper" is Wordsworth himself, who is using this poem to preserve his memory of an actual encounter. After studying the poem again, Abby decided that her classmates' ideas had merit, and she incorporated them into her revision. Of course, such advice is not always worth heeding. Still, writers should accept the invitation to look more closely at whatever text they are analyzing.

Revised Draft of a Student Paper

Here is the new version of the paper that Abby wrote. Attached to it are marginal comments by us that call your attention to her strategies.

Abby Hazelton
Professor Ramsey
English 102
11 March ----

Title clearly indicates the particular work being analyzed and the aspect to be focused on

The Passage of Time in
"The Solitary Reaper"

In William Wordsworth's poem "The Solitary Reaper," the speaker enthuses over a girl who sings as she works in the fields. Throughout the poem, his rapture is evident. Yet in the last stanza, he makes a puzzling move, shifting to past tense after using present tense in the previous three stanzas. No longer does he seem to be currently observing the singer he describes; rather, now he seems to be *recalling* his encounter with her. One possible justification for this shift in tense is

Immediately refers to specific detail of text.

With "puzzling," signals issue to be addressed.

that it reminds us of the speaker's inability to halt the passage of time. Even though he would like to freeze the encounter, time goes on. Perhaps, therefore, the poem's real theme is that time is always in flux. Indeed, even before the final stanza, the speaker betrays an awareness that he can't bend time to his will.

Identifies the main claim.

Connects feature of the poem to be focused on to other parts of it.

Significantly, the poem's very first word is "Behold" (line 1). In issuing this command, the speaker evidently hopes that other people will abandon all motion and gaze at the singer. The speaker reinforces this call for paralysis with the command that begins line 4: "Stop here." Yet, as if acknowledging limits to his control, he adds "or gently pass!" (4). Besides referring to other human beings, these commands seem directed at time itself. The speaker hopes that time, too, will "Stop" and "Behold." Even at this point in the poem, however, he realizes that time is inclined to "pass," in which case he hopes that it will at least move on "gently."

Analyzes an implication of the poem's particular language rather than just beginning with a plot detail.

Develops point that even the poem's early stanzas show concern about the passage of time that final stanza emphasizes.

The second stanza is chiefly concerned with space. Comparing the girl's song to other sounds, the speaker ranges from "Arabian sands" (12) to "the seas / Among the farthest Hebrides" (15–16). In the third stanza, however, he focuses again on time. Trying to determine the subject of her song, he expresses uncertainty about its time frame. He wonders whether the song concerns "old, unhappy, far-off things / And battles long ago" (19–20) or instead deals with "Familiar matter of to-day" (22). Moreover, even if he suspects the song's subject is "Some natural sorrow, loss, or pain" (23), he is unsure whether this experience of despair is confined to the past ("has been") or will reoccur ("may be again") (24). Whichever of the possibilities he raises is true, the speaker is clearly limited in his ability to figure out the song's relation to time. In other words, he cannot force time into a meaningful pattern, let alone prevent its passing.

Moves chronologically through the poem, carefully pointing out how second stanza differs from the first.

Makes distinctions among stanzas' topics. Returns to main claim of the essay.

Refers to actual words of poem to support points.

Ends paragraph by reminding us what main claim is.

Simply by virtue of the shift to past tense, the last stanza indicates that time goes on despite the speaker's wishes. But other elements of the stanza convey this same notion. Recalling his experience of the girl's singing, the speaker reports that he was "motionless and still" (29), yet in the very next line he admits that he eventually moved: "I mounted up the hill" (30). When the speaker says that "the Maiden sang / As if her song could have no ending" (25–26), the words "As if" are significant, implying that the song did end for him in reality. Similarly, the poem itself has to end at some point. In fact, it concludes with the words "no more" (32), which stress that the singer and her song now belong to the speaker's past. Only in his "heart" (31), apparently, can he retain them.

Directs attention to part of poem with which she is most concerned.

Traces implications of poem's words, especially as these are related to main issue and claim.

This situation seems to leave the speaker as "solitary" as the reaper. Throughout the poem, actually, we don't see him in the company of others. His opening "Behold" is directed at no one in particular. Furthermore, we can't be sure he is speaking to actual passersby or, rather, to the poem's hypothetical future readers. Nor, for all his praise of the singer, does he apparently talk to her. Rather, he gives the impression that he keeps at a distance. Even if he did converse with the reaper, he himself would still be "solitary" in the sense of failing to understand her dialect and failing to communicate her words to his readers. As things stand, he is apparently unable or unwilling to reproduce any of the song's lyrics. Just as important, the medium of print can never convey the sounds of music. In fact, prior to recording technology, music was the most fleeting of media, its notes fading with each new moment. By seeking to transmit music, the speaker ensures that he will wind up being frustrated by time.

Connects last stanza to other parts of poem.

Several observations support idea that the speaker is isolated.

Concludes climactic paragraph with substantial analysis.

Yet perhaps the singer and her song are preserved in more than just the speaker's "heart." It can be argued that they are also preserved by the poem, if only to a limited extent. More generally, we can say that literature is a means by which human beings partially succeed in perpetuating things. This idea seems quite relevant to "The Solitary Reaper" if we suppose that the speaker is the poet himself and that he actually witnessed the scene he describes. If we make such assumptions, we can see Wordsworth as analogous to the speaker. After all, both engage in commemorative verbal art. Because time passes, the "strain[s]" that Wordsworth and the singer produce in their efforts to preserve time are bound to be "melancholy" (6). Still, their art matters, for through it they are imaginatively "[r]eaping" (3) experiences that would otherwise fade.

Signals that she is simply making a suggestion here, rather than asserting a definite new point.

Concluding paragraph reminds us of main issue and claim, but goes beyond mere repetition to bring up some new suggestions.

Works Cited

Wordsworth, William. "The Solitary Reaper." *Making Literature Matter: An Anthology for Readers and Writers*, edited by John Schilb and John Clifford, 7th ed., Bedford/St. Martin's, 2018, pp. 98–99.

To us, Abby's revision is more persuasive and compelling than her first draft. In particular, she has nicely complicated her claim about the poem's "pessimism." Nevertheless, we would hesitate to call this revision the definitive version of her paper. Maybe you have thought of things Abby could do to make it even more effective. In presenting her two drafts, we mainly want to emphasize the importance of revision. We hope, too, that you will remember our specific tips as you work on your own writing.

Strategies for Writing a Comparative Paper

Much writing about literature *compares* two or more texts. After all, you can gain many insights into a text by noting how it resembles and differs from others. In this section we offer specific advice for writing a comparative paper, a task you may be assigned in your course. We also present a sample paper that models strategies of comparative writing.

To aid our discussion, we ask that you read the following two poems. The first, "Two Trees," appears in the 2009 verse collection *Rain* by Don Paterson (b. 1963), a Scottish writer who is also a jazz musician, a professor at the University of St. Andrews, and the poetry editor for the publisher Picador Macmillan. Next comes "Regarding History," a poem from the 2005 book *Trill & Mordent* by Luisa A. Igloria (b. 1961), a Filipina American writer who is a professor of English and creative writing at Old Dominion University in Norfolk, Virginia.

DON PATERSON

Two Trees

One morning, Don Miguel got out of bed
with one idea rooted in his head:
to graft his orange to his lemon tree.
It took him the whole day to work them free,
lay open their sides, and lash them tight.
For twelve months, from the shame or from the fright
they put forth nothing; but one day there appeared
two lights in the dark leaves. Over the years
the limbs would get themselves so tangled up
each bough looked like it gave a double crop,
and not one kid in the village didn't know
the magic tree in Miguel's patio.

The man who bought the house had had no dream
so who can say what dark malicious whim
led him to take his axe and split the bole
along its fused seam, and then dig two holes.
And no, they did not die from solitude;
nor did their branches bear a sterile fruit;
nor did their unhealed flanks weep every spring
for those four yards that lost them everything
as each strained on its shackled root to face
the other's empty, intricate embrace.
They were trees, and trees don't weep or ache or shout.
And trees are all this poem is about.

[2009]

LUISA A. IGLORIA

Regarding History

A pair of trees on one side of the walk, leaning
now into the wind in a stance we'd call involuntary —
I can see them from the kitchen window, as I take meat
out of the oven and hold my palms above the crust, darkened
with burnt sugar. Nailed with cloves, small earth of flesh
still smoldering from its furnace. In truth I want to take it
into the garden and bury it in soil. There are times
I grow weary of coaxing music from silence, silence
from the circularity of logic, logic from the artifact.
Then, the possibilities of sunlight are less attractive
than baying at the moon. I want to take your face
in my hands, grow sweet from what it tells, tend
how it leans and turns, trellis or vine of morning-glory.
I wish for limbs pared to muscle, to climb away from
chance and all its missed appointments, its half-drunk
cups of coffee. Tell me what I'll find, in this
early period at the beginning of a century.
Tell me what I'll find, stumbling into a boat
and pushing off into the year's last dark hours. *[2005]*

LIST SIMILARITIES AND DIFFERENCES

A class like yours sensed value in comparing Paterson's poem with Igloria's. So the students proceeded to brainstorm lists of specific similarities and differences — something you might do to start analyzing texts you bring together. For these two poems, the class came up with the following comparisons:

SIMILARITIES

In both poems, a prominent role is played by a real pair of trees, and their relation to each other seems important.

Both poems describe labor. In Paterson's, it's the labor of joining and then separating the trees; in Igloria's, it's the labor of cooking, burying, coaxing, climbing, and "pushing off."

The word *limbs* appears in both poems.

Both poems contain many words that have negative connotations. Paterson's poem includes words such as *shame, fright, dark malicious whim, die, sterile, unhealed, weep, strained, shackled, empty,* and *ache,* while Igloria's poem includes words such as *darkened, burnt, Nailed, bury, weary, missed,* and *dark*.

More specifically, both poems contain words associated with death.

Both poems refer to the time frame of a year, with Paterson's mentioning "twelve months" and Igloria's concluding with "the year's last dark hours."

DIFFERENCES

The speaker in Igloria's poem uses first person, indicated by the pronoun *I*, while the speaker in Paterson's poem is no specific, identifiable person.

Paterson's poem does, however, name a particular character (Don Miguel) and refers to several other people (kids in the village, the man who chopped apart the trees), while the only people in Igloria's poem seem to be "I" and "you."

Paterson's poem centers on a particular image, the two trees, whereas Igloria's poem has other images besides the pair of trees.

Paterson's poem seems more like a narrative; it tells a story. Igloria's poem seems to be more the expression of the speaker's mood.

While Igloria's speaker is clearly interested in the pair of trees as metaphors for her relationship with "you," Paterson's poem leaves readers to interpret whether and how the two trees have metaphorical implications.

"Two Trees" rhymes, but "Regarding History" does not.

"Regarding History" seems in many respects a love poem, but "Two Trees" is hard to see in that way.

"Two Trees" comments on the fact that it is a poem, but "Regarding History" does not.

"Regarding History" ends with its speaker wanting to know something ("Tell me what I'll find"), but "Two Trees" may leave its readers wanting to know something: whether we're supposed to accept its speaker's claim that "trees are all this poem is about."

As you plan your own comparative paper, lists such as these can help you organize your thoughts. To be sure, this class did not immediately think of all the similarities and differences it ended up noting. Usually, going beyond obvious points of comparison is a gradual process, for which you should give yourself plenty of time. Similarly, once you have made lists such as the one above, take time to decide which similarities and differences truly merit your attention. At most, only a few can be part of your paper's main issue and claim.

CONSIDER "WEIGHTING" YOUR COMPARISON

Unfortunately, many students writing a comparative analysis are content to put forth main claims such as these:

There are many similarities and differences between "Two Trees" and "Regarding History."

While "Two Trees" and "Regarding History" have many similarities, in many ways they are also different.

While "Two Trees" and "Regarding History" are different in many ways, they are similar in others.

Several problems arise with these common methods of introducing a comparative paper. For one thing, they give the reader no preview of the specific ideas to come. Indeed, they could have been written by someone who never bothered to read the two poems, for any two texts are similar in certain ways and different in others. Furthermore, these sorts of claims leave no meaningful and compelling way of organizing the paper. Rather, they encourage the writer to proceed arbitrarily, noting miscellaneous similarities and differences on impulse. More precisely, claims such as these fail to identify the *issue* driving the paper. Why compare Paterson's and Igloria's poems in the first place? Comparison is a means to an end, not an end in itself. What important question is the writer using these two texts to answer? In short, what's at stake?

A more fruitful approach, we think, is to write a *weighted* comparative analysis—that is, an argument chiefly concerned with *one* text more than others. When professional literary critics compare two texts, often they mainly want to answer a question about just one of them. They bring in the second text because they believe that doing so helps them address the issue they are raising about their key text. True, a good paper can result even when you treat equally all texts you discuss. But you might write a paper that seems more purposeful and coherent if you focus basically on one work, using comparisons to resolve some issue concerning it.

A Student Comparative Paper

The following paper by student Jeremy Cooper demonstrates weighted comparative analysis. The author refers to Igloria's "Regarding History" along with Paterson's "Two Trees," but he is mostly concerned with Paterson's poem. He brings up Igloria's poem not to do comparison for its own sake but to address a question he has about Paterson's text.

Jeremy Cooper
Professor Budnoy
English 102
15 October ----

Title does not merely repeat title of the poem to be analyzed. Moreover, title specifies what aspect of that poem he will examine.

Don Paterson's Criticism of Nature's Owners

Until its last two lines, Don Paterson's poem "Two Trees" tells a fairly straightforward story. The title refers to an orange tree and a lemon tree that stood next to each other on an estate. The speaker in the poem recalls how these trees were treated by two different owners of the property. The first owner, Don Miguel, successfully grafted the trees together. The

First sentence refers to poem he will focus on, his primary text.

next owner, a man unnamed by the speaker, separated them with an axe. Given the speaker's clear description of these events, most readers would probably have no trouble understanding what happened to the trees. But the poem's concluding pair of lines is puzzling:

Signals issue that the paper will address.

> They were trees, and trees don't weep or ache or shout.
> And trees are all this poem is about. (23–24)

On the surface, the word "all" seems equivalent to "merely." If this is the case, readers might feel that Paterson is encouraging them to take a limited view of his poem, seeing it as concerned with nothing more than trees. They would then feel *dis*couraged from looking for additional significance or meaning in his text. But this interpretation of Paterson's focus risks making his poem appear relatively trivial, an impression that he surely does not want to create. A likelier possibility is that the speaker is being ironic in his final declaration, stating the word "all" sarcastically. Such a tone might then move readers to question whether the poem is simply about trees. They might feel compelled to consider how its real subject is something else. Indeed, the poem's actual main topic seems to be the regrettable attitudes that human beings take toward nature when they are able to own it.

Introductory paragraph ends by stating the claim about the primary text that the paper will support and develop.

Trees play a major role in Paterson's poem, as their presence in the title suggests. In the first of the poem's two stanzas, the speaker describes Don Miguel's effort to fuse the orange tree and the lemon tree together, something that he evidently managed to accomplish so well that the trees became hard to distinguish from each other: "the limbs would get themselves so tangled up / each bough looked like it gave a double crop" (9–10). In the second stanza, the speaker turns to describing how the next owner of the trees did the opposite thing to them, splitting them apart (15–16). The poem presents no other scenic feature to compete with the two trees for the reader's attention. The speaker just briefly mentions a bed (1), a patio (12), a house (13), and an axe (15).

That the focus is very much on the trees becomes even more apparent if we compare this poem with another in which two trees figure, Luisa A. Igloria's "Regarding History." Igloria's poem begins with "A pair of trees on one side of the walk, leaning / now into the wind in a stance we'd call involuntary" (1–2). Later, the speaker seems to have these two trees still in mind when she says that she wants to hold her lover's face and feel "how it leans and turns, trellis or vine of morning-glory" (13). The close relation of the word "leans" in this line to "leaning" (1) in the earlier one implies that the

This is a secondary text, which he uses to reinforce the point he has just made about his primary text.

trees remain a meaningful symbol for her throughout the poem. But, unlike Paterson's speaker, Igloria's turns her thoughts to a number of images other than trees. For example, besides her beloved's face, she thinks of food she has just prepared ("meat / out of the oven" [3–4], which she has evidently "Nailed with cloves" [5]), her garden (7), sunlight (10), the moon (11), muscle (14), coffee (16), and a boat (18). Basically, the two trees in this poem are just part of its many elements. By contrast, the pair of trees in Paterson's poem is much more prominent.

The question then becomes what we as readers should make of their central role in that poem. Some of us may be inclined to see Paterson's trees as a metaphor, their physical existence being less significant than something else they represent. The pair of trees in "Regarding History" do seem metaphorical, functioning in the speaker's mind as stand-ins for a human relationship. When she observes that the trees are "leaning / now into the wind in a stance we'd call involuntary" (1–2), she appears to be actually thinking of her relationship with her beloved. Specifically, she seems worried about pressures on their relationship that threaten their ability to keep it steady. This concern of hers comes up again later, when she expresses a desire "to take your face" (11) and "tend / how it leans and turns" (12–13). Here, too, she evidently feels that her connection to her loved one is challenged by outside forces. As in her earlier remark about the trees, she fears that she will not be able to protect her relationship from influences that will make her and her lover do "involuntary" (2) things. In comparison, though, the two trees in Paterson's poem do not appear to have a metaphorical function. In the first place, the speaker of "Two Trees" lacks a distinct personality, so that the poem does not encourage readers to interpret the trees he mentions as representing thoughts or feelings of his. Whereas Igloria's speaker dominates "Regarding History" with her clearly marked hopes and concerns, Paterson's speaker writes largely like a reporter narrating news events. Moreover, when he tells what the two property owners did to the trees, he describes these actions so precisely and concretely that he makes it hard for readers to consider the trees as symbolic rather than physical. Also, in such lines as "they did not die from solitude" (17) and "nor did their unhealed flanks weep every spring" (19) the speaker seems to be reminding the reader that they are, in fact, basically vegetation rather than images of something in the human mind. If anything, these lines discourage the reader from interpreting the trees as metaphors.

He has identified a possible interpretation but now offers a different one, which he proceeds to argue for.

He uses comparison with his secondary text to support his argument about his primary text.

But if the two trees in Paterson's poem come across mainly as real elements of nature, the attitudes that their owners show toward them are nevertheless significant. Actually, the poem's main subject is not the trees of the title, but the intense and disturbing emotions that drove Don Miguel and the later owner to handle them roughly. The feelings that led the second owner to separate the trees seem villainous. The speaker suggests that this man "had had no dream" (13) but instead acted on some mysterious "dark malicious whim" that compelled him to "split" them apart (14–15), leaving their flanks "unhealed" (19) and their roots "shackled" (21). This language gives the impression of a plantation owner in the pre–Civil War American South, the type of person who cruelly divided slave families and kept their members separated in bondage. Because the poem ends with the physical stress inflicted upon the trees by their second owner, some readers may be more bothered by this man's behavior than they are by Don Miguel's. They might even appreciate Don Miguel's interest in uniting the trees, especially because his labor resulted in the heartening picture of "two lights in the dark leaves" (8). But the language used to describe his actions, too, is mostly negative. The words "lay open" (5), "lash them tight" (5), "shame" (6), "fright" (6), and "tangled up" (9) imply traumatic destruction, even rape, rather than blissful harmony. In his willingness to manipulate the trees, Don Miguel therefore seems no better than the man who replaced him. Furthermore, Don Miguel's behavior toward the trees did not have the excuse of being carefully thought-out and planned. He simply awoke "with one idea rooted in his head: / to graft his orange to his lemon tree" (2–3). Just as the word "Don" in the first line is an indication that he is a man of power in his community, so the repetition of the word "his" in this line suggests that he felt able to perform surgery on the trees merely because he owned them. Both of the men in the poem avoided thinking of what was best for the trees. Instead, both preferred to exercise the authority they had as possessors of the trees, no matter how abusive their handling of the trees might be. The speaker in Igloria's poem calls attention to what she currently *lacks* or is *unable* to do, through statements like "I want to take your face" (11), "I wish for limbs pared to muscle" (14), and "Tell me what I'll find" (18). Furthermore, she does not possess the two trees that figure in "Regarding History." Rather, she is a mere observer of them: "I can see them from the kitchen window" (3). In Paterson's poem, on the other hand, Don Miguel and the second man treat their trees violently and are able to do so because the trees are legally theirs.

He is working with the claim he put forth in his introduction.

Again, he acknowledges the possibility of an interpretation different from his, before advancing his view.

Once more, he uses comparison with his secondary text to reinforce his argument about his primary text.

Paterson does not end his poem by directly indicating what he thinks is the proper way of treating trees like those of his title. He does not clearly offer some sort of prescription for their care. Many readers may, nevertheless, come away from the poem concluding that human beings should avoid tampering with trees and, more generally, should leave nature alone as often as possible. In any case, Paterson's central purpose seems to be to make us more aware that when humans own some of nature, they may treat it arrogantly, whether in the pursuit of unity (Don Miguel's aim when he fuses the trees) or separation (the second man's goal when he breaks them apart).

He suggests that this interpretation is possible but that he is more interested in getting his readers to accept his main claim about the poem: the idea he returns to in his final sentence.

Works Cited

Igloria, Luisa A. "Regarding History." Schilb and Clifford, p. 122.

Paterson, Don. "Two Trees." Schilb and Clifford, p. 121.

Schilb, John, and John Clifford, editors. *Making Literature Matter: An Anthology for Readers and Writers.* 7th ed., Bedford/St. Martin's, 2018.

Jeremy gains much from comparing "Two Trees" with "Regarding History." In paragraph 3, the analysis of the modest role that trees play in Igloria's poem bolsters Jeremy's claim that they are the core of Paterson's poem. In paragraph 4, the discussion of how Igloria uses trees as metaphors strengthens Jeremy's point that Paterson's trees are literal. In paragraph 5, the observation that Igloria's speaker is *not* an owner of trees helps Jeremy stress that Paterson's men possess them. Obviously, though, Jeremy focuses his paper on Paterson's poem, not on both. By concentrating chiefly on "Two Trees," he enables himself to develop a tight and logical argument, whereas focusing on both poems would encourage him to roam through similarities and differences at random.

Perhaps you know the advice usually given about how to organize a comparative paper. Traditionally, writers aiming to compare two texts learn of two options: (1) discuss one text and then move to the other, comparing it with the first; (2) discuss the texts together, noting each of their similarities and differences in turn. Both of these alternatives make sense and provide a ready-made structure for your paper; either can result in a coherent essay. Still, a weighted analysis such as Jeremy's — an analysis that focuses on one text more than another — is more likely than either of the alternatives to seem the logical evolution of a pointed claim.

SUMMING UP: THE WRITING PROCESS

- **Writing an argument about a literary work involves *exploring, planning, composing,* and *revising.*** (pp. 99–118)
- ***Exploring* requires you to read the work closely, noting questions it raises for you.** Does the text confirm your predictions about it? Does rereading it change your mind? How does it compare with your personal experience? What patterns, and breaks from these patterns, do you find? What ambiguities? What were the author's alternatives? How does the text deal with common topics in literary studies? What is a tentative claim you can make about it? (pp. 99–101)
- ***Planning* combines several activities.** These include selecting a text to write about; envisioning your audience; identifying your main issue, claim, and evidence as you anticipate challenges to them; deciding what warrants to use; and determining how you will organize your argument. (pp. 101–05)
- **Keep in mind the following tips when you are *composing* a draft.**

  Decide on a title that previews your main claim. (pp. 105–06)

  Choose a style that fits your audience and purpose. (p. 106)

  Draft an introduction that identifies as quickly and efficiently as possible the main text you will analyze, your main issue, and your main claim. (p. 107)

  Limit plot summary. (pp. 107–08)

  Decide how you will refer to the author's life and intentions. (pp. 108–09)

  Recognize and avoid logical fallacies. (pp. 109–13)
- ***Revising* is a process.** Read your draft repeatedly, looking at a different aspect of it each time, in particular its logic, organization, clarity, emphases, style, grammar, and physical appearance. (pp. 116–117)
- **Be cautious about relating the work to its author's life, and be alert to fallacious reasoning in your arguments and those of others.** (pp. 115–18)
- **Feel free to concede that your analysis of a literary work is not the only reasonable interpretation of it.** (p. 122)
- **Favor *weighted* comparison if you are writing a paper that compares two or more literary works.** (pp. 123–24)

CHAPTER 5

Writing about Literary Genres

At the beginning of Chapter 1, we discussed how literary works are often understood as examples of particular **genres** (kinds or types of writing). While acknowledging that most readers think of literature as comprising the genres of fiction, poetry, and drama, we invited you to think of nonfiction (such as historical writing), creative nonfiction (such as autobiography and memoir), and essays (sometimes including argumentative prose) as literature, too. In this chapter, we present elements of literary analysis for the genres of fiction, poetry, drama, and the essay, and show how various students have used those elements to generate writing about literary works. You will notice that many of these elements are useful in thinking about most genres, but different genres make different use of elements, emphasizing some more than others. We also devote a section to writing about poems and pictures; over the centuries, many poets have been prompted to create their art in response to visual images created by other kinds of artists.

Writing about Stories

Short stories can be said to resemble novels. Above all, both are works of fiction. Yet the difference in length matters. As William Trevor, a veteran writer of short stories, has observed, short fiction is "the art of the glimpse; it deals in echoes and reverberations; craftily it withholds information. Novels tell all. Short stories tell as little as they dare." Maybe Trevor overstates the situation when he claims that novels reveal everything. All sorts of texts feature what literary theorist Wolfgang Iser calls "gaps." Still, Trevor is right to emphasize that short stories usually tell much less than novels do. They demand that you understand and evaluate characters on the basis of just a few details and events. In this respect, short stories resemble poems. Both tend to rely on compression rather than expansion, seeking to affect their audience with a sharply limited number of words.

Short stories' focused use of language can make the experience of reading them wonderfully intense. Furthermore, you may end up considering important human issues as you try to interpret the "glimpses" they provide. Precisely because short stories "tell as little as they dare," they offer you much to ponder as you proceed to write about them.

In discussing the writing process, we refer often to the story that follows. Published in 1941, "A Visit of Charity" is by a pioneer of American short fiction,

Eudora Welty (1909–2001). She spent her life chiefly in her hometown of Jackson, Mississippi, and most of her writing is set in the American South.

EUDORA WELTY

A Visit of Charity

It was mid-morning—a very cold, bright day. Holding a potted plant before her, a girl of fourteen jumped off the bus in front of the Old Ladies' Home, on the outskirts of town. She wore a red coat, and her straight yellow hair was hanging down loose from the pointed white cap all the little girls were wearing that year. She stopped for a moment beside one of the prickly dark shrubs with which the city had beautified the Home, and then proceeded slowly toward the building, which was of whitewashed brick and reflected the winter sunlight like a block of ice. As she walked vaguely up the steps she shifted the small pot from hand to hand; then she had to set it down and remove her mittens before she could open the heavy door.

"I'm a Campfire Girl. . . . I have to pay a visit to some old lady," she told the nurse at the desk. This was a woman in a white uniform who looked as if she were cold; she had close-cut hair which stood up on the very top of her head exactly like a sea wave. Marian, the little girl, did not tell her that this visit would give her a minimum of only three points in her score.

"Acquainted with any of our residents?" asked the nurse. She lifted one eyebrow and spoke like a man.

"With any old ladies? No—but—that is, any of them will do," Marian stammered. With her free hand she pushed her hair behind her ears, as she did when it was time to study Science.

The nurse shrugged and rose. "You have a nice *multiflora cineraria*° there," 5
she remarked as she walked ahead down the hall of closed doors to pick out an old lady.

There was loose, bulging linoleum on the floor. Marian felt as if she were walking on the waves, but the nurse paid no attention to it. There was a smell in the hall like the interior of a clock. Everything was silent until, behind one of the doors, an old lady of some kind cleared her throat like a sheep bleating. This decided the nurse. Stopping in her tracks, she first extended her arm, bent her elbow, and leaned forward from the hips—all to examine the watch strapped to her wrist; then she gave a loud double-rap on the door.

"There are two in each room," the nurse remarked over her shoulder.

"Two what?" asked Marian without thinking. The sound like a sheep's bleating almost made her turn around and run back.

One old woman was pulling the door open in short, gradual jerks, and when she saw the nurse a strange smile forced her old face dangerously awry. Marian, suddenly propelled by the strong, impatient arm of the nurse, saw next the

multiflora cineraria: A houseplant with brightly colored flowers and heart-shaped leaves.

side-face of another old woman, even older, who was lying flat in bed with a cap on and a counterpane° drawn up to her chin.

"Visitor," said the nurse, and after one more shove she was off up the hall.

Marian stood tongue-tied; both hands held the potted plant. The old woman, still with that terrible, square smile (which was a smile of welcome) stamped on her bony face, was waiting. . . . Perhaps she said something. The old woman in bed said nothing at all, and she did not look around.

Suddenly Marian saw a hand, quick as a bird claw, reach up in the air and pluck the white cap off her head. At the same time, another claw to match drew her all the way into the room, and the next moment the door closed behind her.

"My, my, my," said the old lady at her side.

Marian stood enclosed by a bed, a washstand, and a chair; the tiny room had altogether too much furniture. Everything smelled wet—even the bare floor. She held on to the back of the chair, which was wicker and felt soft and damp. Her heart beat more and more slowly, her hands got colder and colder, and she could not hear whether the old women were saying anything or not. She could not see them very clearly. How dark it was! The window shade was down, and the only door was shut. Marian looked at the ceiling. . . . It was like being caught in a robbers' cave, just before one was murdered.

"Did you come to be our little girl for a while?" the first robber asked.

Then something was snatched from Marian's hand—the little potted plant.

"Flowers!" screamed the old woman. She stood holding the pot in an undecided way. "Pretty flowers," she added.

Then the old woman in bed cleared her throat and spoke. "They are not pretty," she said, still without looking around, but very distinctly.

Marian suddenly pitched against the chair and sat down in it.

"Pretty flowers," the first old woman insisted. "Pretty—pretty . . ."

Marian wished she had the little pot back for just a moment—she had forgotten to look at the plant herself before giving it away. What did it look like?

"Stinkweeds," said the other old woman sharply. She had a bunchy white forehead and red eyes like a sheep. Now she turned them toward Marian. The fogginess seemed to rise in her throat again, and she bleated, "Who—are—you?"

To her surprise, Marian could not remember her name. "I'm a Campfire Girl," she said finally.

"Watch out for the germs," said the old woman like a sheep, not addressing anyone.

"One came out last month to see us," said the first old woman.

A sheep or a germ? wondered Marian dreamily, holding on to the chair.

"Did not!" cried the other old woman.

"Did so! Read to us out of the Bible, and we enjoyed it!" screamed the first.

"Who enjoyed it!" said the woman in bed. Her mouth was unexpectedly small and sorrowful, like a pet's.

"We enjoyed it," insisted the other. "You enjoyed it—I enjoyed it."

counterpane: Bedspread.

"We all enjoyed it," said Marian, without realizing that she had said a word.

The first old woman had just finished putting the potted plant high, high on the top of the wardrobe, where it could hardly be seen from below. Marian wondered how she had ever succeeded in placing it there, how she could ever have reached so high.

"You mustn't pay any attention to old Addie," she now said to the little girl. "She's ailing today."

"Will you shut your mouth?" said the woman in bed. "I am not."

"You're a story."

"I can't stay but a minute—really, I can't," said Marian suddenly. She looked down at the wet floor and thought that if she were sick in here they would have to let her go.

With much to-do the first old woman sat down in a rocking chair—still another piece of furniture!—and began to rock. With the fingers of one hand she touched a very dirty cameo pin on her chest. "What do you do at school?" she asked.

"I don't know . . ." said Marian. She tried to think but she could not.

"Oh, but the flowers are beautiful," the old woman whispered. She seemed to rock faster and faster; Marian did not see how anyone could rock so fast.

"Ugly," said the woman in bed.

"If we bring flowers—" Marian began, and then fell silent. She had almost said that if Campfire Girls brought flowers to the Old Ladies' Home, the visit would count one extra point, and if they took a Bible with them on the bus and read it to the old ladies, it counted double. But the old woman had not listened, anyway; she was rocking and watching the other one, who watched back from the bed.

"Poor Addie is ailing. She has to take medicine—see?" she said, pointing a horny finger at a row of bottles on the table, and rocking so high that her black comfort shoes lifted off the floor like a little child's.

"I am no more sick than you are," said the woman in bed.

"Oh, yes you are!"

"I just got more sense than you have, that's all," said the other old woman, nodding her head.

"That's only the contrary way she talks when *you all* come," said the first old lady with sudden intimacy. She stopped the rocker with a neat pat of her feet and leaned toward Marian. Her hand reached over—it felt like a petunia leaf, clinging and just a little sticky.

"Will you hush! Will you hush!" cried the other one.

Marian leaned back rigidly in her chair.

"When I was a little girl like you, I went to school and all," said the old woman in the same intimate, menacing voice. "Not here—another town . . ."

"Hush!" said the sick woman. "You never went to school. You never came and you never went. You never were anything—only here. You never were born! You don't know anything. Your head is empty, your heart and hands and your old black purse are all empty, even that little old box that you brought with you you brought empty—you showed it to me. And yet you talk, talk, talk, talk, talk all the time until I think I'm losing my mind! Who are you? You're a stranger—a perfect stranger! Don't you know you're a stranger? Is it possible that they have actually done a thing like this to anyone—sent them in a stranger to talk, and rock, and tell away her whole long rigmarole? Do they seriously suppose that I'll be able to keep it up, day in, day out, night in, night out, living in the same room with a terrible old woman—forever?"

Marian saw the old woman's eyes grow bright and turn toward her. This old woman was looking at her with despair and calculation in her face. Her small lips suddenly dropped apart, and exposed a half circle of false teeth with tan gums.

"Come here, I want to tell you something," she whispered. "Come here!"

Marian was trembling, and her heart nearly stopped beating altogether for a moment.

"Now, now, Addie," said the first old woman. "That's not polite. Do you know what's really the matter with old Addie today?" She, too, looked at Marian; one of her eyelids dropped low.

"The matter?" the child repeated stupidly. "What's the matter with her?"

"Why, she's mad because it's her birthday!" said the first old woman, beginning to rock again and giving a little crow as though she had answered her own riddle.

"It is not, it is not!" screamed the old woman in bed. "It is not my birthday, no one knows when that is but myself, and will you please be quiet and say nothing more, or I'll go straight out of my mind!" She turned her eyes toward Marian again, and presently she said in the soft, foggy voice, "When the worst comes to the worst, I ring this bell, and the nurse comes." One of her hands was drawn out from under the patched counterpane—a thin little hand with enormous black freckles. With a finger which would not hold still she pointed to a little bell on the table among the bottles.

"How old are you?" Marian breathed. Now she could see the old woman in bed very closely and plainly, and very abruptly, from all sides, as in dreams. She wondered about her—she wondered for a moment as though there was nothing else in the world to wonder about. It was the first time such a thing had happened to Marian.

"I won't tell!"

The old face on the pillow, where Marian was bending over it, slowly gathered and collapsed. Soft whimpers came out of the small open mouth. It was a sheep that she sounded like—a little lamb. Marian's face drew very close, the yellow hair hung forward.

"She's crying!" She turned a bright, burning face up to the first old woman.

"That's Addie for you," the old woman said spitefully.

Marian jumped up and moved toward the door. For the second time, the claw almost touched her hair, but it was not quick enough. The little girl put her cap on.

"Well, it was a real visit," said the old woman, following Marian through the doorway and all the way out into the hall. Then from behind she suddenly clutched the child with her sharp little fingers. In an affected, high-pitched whine she cried, "Oh, little girl, have you a penny to spare for a poor old woman that's not got anything of her own? We don't have a thing in the world—not a penny for candy—not a thing! Little girl, just a nickel—a penny—"

Marian pulled violently against the old hands for a moment before she was 65
free. Then she ran down the hall, without looking behind her and without looking at the nurse, who was reading *Field & Stream* at her desk. The nurse, after another triple motion to consult her wrist watch, asked automatically the question put to visitors in all institutions: "Won't you stay and have dinner with *us*?"

Marian never replied. She pushed the heavy door open into the cold air and ran down the steps.

Under the prickly shrub she stooped and quickly, without being seen, retrieved a red apple she had hidden there.

Her yellow hair under the white cap, her scarlet coat, her bare knees all flashed in the sunlight as she ran to meet the big bus rocketing through the street.

"Wait for me!" she shouted. As though at an imperial command, the bus ground to a stop.

She jumped on and took a big bite out of the apple. *[1941]* 70

A Student's Personal Response to the Story

Here is some freewriting a student did about the story you just read. By simply jotting down some observations and questions, she provided herself with the seeds of a paper.

> I'm not sure which character I should be sympathizing with in Welty's story. Right away I disliked the girl because she wasn't really interested in seeing the old women. I don't know why the story is called "A Visit of Charity," since she just wanted to get more points. And yet I have to admit that when I was younger I was sort of like her. I remember one time when my church youth group had to sing Christmas carols at an old folks' home, and I was uneasy about having to meet all these ancient men and women I didn't know, some of whom could barely walk or talk. It's funny, because I was always comfortable around my grandparents, but I have to confess that being around all those old people at once spooked me a little. I smiled a lot at them and joined in the singing and helped hand out candy canes afterward. But I couldn't wait to leave. Once I did, I felt proud of myself for going there, but I guess I also felt a little guilty because I didn't really want to be there at all. So, maybe I'm being hypocritical when I criticize the girl in Welty's story for insensitivity. Anyway, I expected that Welty would present in a good light any old women that Marian encountered, just to emphasize that Marian was being unkind and that it's really sad for people to have to live in a retirement home (or senior citizens' center or whatever they're calling such places nowadays). And yet the two old women she meets are cranky and unpleasant. Even the receptionist doesn't come off all that good. If I were Marian, I probably would have left even sooner

than she did! Maybe Welty didn't want us to sympathize with anyone in the story, and maybe that's OK. I tend to want a story to make at least some of the characters sympathetic, but maybe it's unfair of me to demand that. Still, I'm wondering if I'm not appreciating Welty's characters enough. When the two old women argue, should we side with one of them, or are we supposed to be bothered by them both? Are we supposed to think any better of the girl by the time she leaves? The apple she eats immediately made me think of the Adam and Eve story, but I don't know what I'm supposed to do with that parallel.

The Elements of Short Fiction

Whether discussing them in class or writing about them, you will improve your ability to analyze stories like Welty's if you grow familiar with typical elements of short fiction. These elements include plot and structure, point of view, characters, setting, imagery, language, and theme.

PLOT AND STRUCTURE

For many readers, the most important element in any work of fiction is **plot**. As they turn the pages of a story, their main question is, What will happen next? In reading Welty's story, quite possibly you wanted to know how Marian's visit to the rest home would turn out. Indeed, plots usually center on human beings, who can be seen as engaging in actions, as being acted upon, or both. You might describe Marian as acting, noting among other things that she "jumped off the bus" (para. 1); that "she shifted the small pot from hand to hand" (para. 1); that "she pushed her hair behind her ears" (para. 4); that her "face drew very close" to Addie's (para. 60); that she "jumped up and moved toward the door" (para. 63); that she "pulled violently against the old hands" of the other elderly woman (para. 65); that "she ran to meet the big bus" (para. 68); and that she "jumped on and took a big bite out of the apple" (para. 70). But you might also describe her as being affected by other forces. For example, she is "suddenly propelled by the strong, impatient arm of the nurse" (para. 9); the "claw" of the first old woman "drew her all the way into the room" (para. 11); and she repeats the two women's language "without realizing that she had said a word" (para. 31). In any case, most short stories put characters into high-pressure situations, whether for dark or comic effect. To earn the merit points she desires, Marian has to contend with the feuding roommates.

Besides physical events, a short story may involve psychological developments. Welty's heroine goes through mental changes during her visit. One is that her interest in the two women grows; they are no longer just a dutiful task to her. This change is indicated best by a particular word: "wondered." When the women discuss a previous visitor, Marian "wondered" about the animal imagery suddenly filling her mind (para. 26). When the first old woman perches the plant "high on the top of the wardrobe," the girl "wondered how she had ever succeeded in placing it there" (para. 32). Then, as Marian gazes upon the bedridden

Addie, "She wondered about her—she wondered for a moment as though there was nothing else in the world to wonder about" (para. 58). As if to emphasize that the girl is experiencing a psychological transition, the narrator reports: "It was the first time such a thing had happened to Marian" (para. 58). Many stories do show characters undergoing complete or partial conversions. Meanwhile, a number of stories include characters who stick to their beliefs but gain a new perspective on them.

Does Marian's encounter with the two women have something to do with her ultimately biting the apple and leaping onto the bus? If so, what's the specific connection? Questions like these bring up relations of cause and effect, terms that often figure in discussions of plot. The novelist and short-story writer E. M. Forster refers to them in defining the term *plot* itself. To Forster, a plot is not simply one incident after another, such as "the king died and then the queen died." Rather, it is a situation or a whole chain of events in which there are reasons *why* characters behave as they do. Forster's example: "The king died, and then the queen died of grief."

Writers of short stories do not always make cause and effect immediately clear. Another possible plot, Forster suggests, is "The queen died, no one knew why, until it was discovered that it was through grief at the death of the king." In this scenario, all of the characters lack information about the queen's true psychology for a while, and perhaps the reader is in the dark as well. Indeed, many short stories leave the reader ignorant for a spell. For instance, only near the conclusion of her story does Welty reveal that before entering the rest home, Marian had put an apple under the shrub. Why does the author withhold this key fact from you? Perhaps Welty was silent about the apple because, had she reported it right away, its echoes of Eve might have overshadowed your interpretation of the story as you read. Worth considering are issues of effect: what the characters' behavior makes you think of them and what impact the author's strategies have on you.

When you summarize a story's plot, you may be inclined to put events in chronological order. But remember that short stories are not always linear. Alice Adams, author of many short stories, offered a more detailed outline of their typical **structure**. She proposed the formula ABDCE: these letters stand for **action, background, development, climax**, and **ending**. More precisely, Adams's formula begins a story with an action, follows that action with some background information, and then moves the plot forward in time through a major turning point and toward some sort of resolution. Not all writers of short stories follow this scheme. In fact, Adams did not always stick to it. Certainly a lot of short stories combine her background and development stages, moving the plot along while offering details of their characters' pasts. And sometimes a story will have several turning points rather than a single distinct climax. But by keeping Adams's formula in mind, if only as a common way to construct short stories, you will be better prepared to recognize how a story departs from chronological order.

The first paragraph of Welty's story seems to be centered on *action*. Marian arrives at the Old Ladies' Home and prepares to enter it. Even so, Welty provides some basic information in this paragraph, describing Marian and the rest home as if the reader is unfamiliar with both. Yet only in the second paragraph do you learn Marian's name and the purpose of her visit. Therefore, Welty can be said to obey Adams's formula, beginning with *action* and then moving to *background*. Note, however, that the second paragraph features *development* as well. By explaining to the receptionist who she is and why she is there, Marian takes a step closer to the central event, her meeting with the two roommates. The remainder of the story keeps moving forward in time.

What about *climax*, Adams's fourth term? Traditionally, the climax of a story has been defined as a peak moment of drama appearing near the end. Also, it is usually thought of as a point when at least one character commits a significant act, experiences a significant change, makes a significant discovery, learns a significant lesson, or perhaps does all these things. With Welty's story, you could argue that the climax is when Marian asks Addie her age, meets with refusal, sees Addie crying, and tries to bolt. Certainly this is a dramatic moment, involving intense display of emotion resulting in Marian's departure. But, as we noted, Marian also experiences inner change. When she looks on Addie "as though there was nothing else in the world to wonder about," this is "the first time such a thing had happened to Marian."

Adams's term *ending* may seem unnecessary. Why would anyone have to be reminded that stories end? Yet a story's climax may engage readers so much that they overlook whatever follows. If the climax of Welty's story is Marian's conversation with the tearful Addie, then the ending is basically in four parts: the plea that Addie's roommate makes to Marian as she is leaving; Marian's final encounter with the receptionist; Marian's retrieval of the apple; and her escape on the bus, where she bites into the apple. Keep in mind that the ending of a story may relate somehow to its beginning. The ending of Welty's "A Visit of Charity," for instance, brings the story full circle. Whereas at the start Marian gets off a bus, hides the apple, and meets the receptionist, at the conclusion she rushes by the receptionist, recovers the apple, and boards another bus. However a story ends, ask yourself if any of the characters have changed at some point between start and finish. Does the conclusion of the story indicate that at least one person has developed in some way, or does it leave you with the feeling of lives frozen since the start? As Welty's story ends, readers may have various opinions about Marian. Some may find that she has not been changed all that much by her visit to the home, while others may feel that it has helped her mature.

A common organizational device in short stories is **repetition**. It takes various forms. First, a story may repeat words, as Welty's story does with its multiple uses of the word "wondered." Second, a story may repeatedly refer to a certain image, as you see with Welty's images of the plant and the apple. Third, a story may involve repeated actions. In "A Visit of Charity," the two roommates repeatedly argue; Marian travels by bus at the beginning and at the end; and the nurse consults her wristwatch both when Marian arrives and when she leaves.

POINT OF VIEW

A short story may be told from a particular character's perspective or **point of view**. When it is written in the **first person**—narrated by someone using the pronoun *I* or, more rarely, *we*—you have to decide how much to accept the narrator's point of view, keeping in mind that the narrator may be psychologically complex. How objective does the narrator seem in depicting other people and events? In what ways, if any, do the narrator's perceptions seem influenced by his or her personal experiences, circumstances, feelings, values, and beliefs? Does the narrator seem to have changed in any way since the events recalled? How reasonable do the narrator's judgments seem? At what moments, if any, do you find yourself disagreeing with the narrator's view of things?

Not every short story is narrated by an identifiable person. Many of them are told by what has been traditionally called an **omniscient narrator**. The word *omniscient* means "all-knowing" and is often used as an adjective for God. An omniscient narrator is usually a seemingly all-knowing, objective voice. This is the kind of voice at work in Welty's story, right from the first paragraph. There, Marian is described in an authoritatively matter-of-fact tone that appears detached from her: "Holding a potted plant before her, a girl of fourteen jumped off the bus in front of the Old Ladies' Home." Keep in mind, though, that a story may rely primarily on an omniscient narrator and yet at some points seem immersed in a character's perspective. This, too, is the case with Welty's story. Consider the following passage about Marian:

> Everything smelled wet—even the bare floor. She held on to the back of the chair, which was wicker and felt soft and damp. Her heart beat more and more slowly, her hands got colder and colder, and she could not hear whether the old women were saying anything or not. She could not see them very clearly. How dark it was! The window shade was down, and the only door was shut. Marian looked at the ceiling. . . . It was like being caught in a robbers' cave, just before one was murdered.

The passage remains in the third person, referring to "she" rather than to "I." Nevertheless, the passage seems intimately in touch with Marian's physical sensations. Indeed, the sentence "How dark it was!" seems something that Marian would say to herself. Similarly, the analogy to the robbers' cave may be Marian's own personal perception, and as such, the analogy may reveal more about her own state of mind than about the room. Many literary critics use the term **free indirect style** for moments like this, when a narrator otherwise omniscient conveys a particular character's viewpoint by resorting to the character's own language.

Throughout this book, we encourage you to analyze an author's strategies by considering the options that he or she faced. You may better understand a short story's point of view if you think about the available alternatives. For example, how would you have reacted to Welty's story if it had focused on Addie's perceptions more than on Marian's?

CHARACTERS

Although we have been discussing plots, we have also referred to the people caught up in them. Any analysis you do of a short story will reflect your understanding and evaluation of its **characters**. Rarely does the author of a story provide you with extended, enormously detailed biographies. Rather, you see the story's characters at select moments of their lives. To quote William Trevor again, the short story is "the art of the glimpse."

You may want to judge characters according to how easily you can identify with them. Yet there is little reason for you to read works that merely reinforce your prejudices. Furthermore, you may overlook the potential richness of a story if you insist that its characters fit your usual standards of behavior. An author can teach you much by introducing you to the complexity of people you might automatically praise or condemn in real life. Many of us would immediately condemn someone reluctant to help old women, but Welty encourages us to analyze carefully the girl in her story rather than just denounce her. You may be tempted to dismiss the roommates in Welty's story as unpleasant, even "sick"; in any case, take the story as an opportunity to explore *why* women in a rest home may express discontent.

One thing to consider about the characters in a story is what each basically desires. At the beginning of Welty's story, for example, Marian is hardly visiting the Old Ladies' Home out of "charity," despite that word's presence in the story's title. Rather, Marian hopes to earn points as a Campfire Girl. Again, characters in a story may change, so consider whether the particular characters you are examining alter their thinking. Perhaps you feel that Marian's visit broadens her vision of life; then again, perhaps you conclude that she remains much the same.

Reading a short story involves relating its characters to one another. In part, you'll need to determine their relative importance. Even a seemingly minor character can perform some noteworthy function; the nurse in "A Visit of Charity" not only ushers Marian in and out but also marks time. Nevertheless, any reader will try to identify a story's *main* figures. When a particular character seems the focus, he or she is referred to as the story's **protagonist**. Many readers would say that Marian is the protagonist of "A Visit of Charity." When the protagonist is in notable conflict with another character, this foe is referred to as the **antagonist**. Because Marian initially finds both roommates unpleasant, you may want to call them her antagonists. But it's not a word that you *must* apply to some character in a story; the work can have a protagonist and yet *not* include an opponent. Moreover, as a story proceeds, characters may alter their relationships with one another. Marian grows more conscious of the tensions *between* the roommates, and then for a moment she sympathizes with Addie. It is possible, too, for one character to be ambivalent toward another, feeling both drawn *and* opposed to that person. Perhaps the roommates have a love-hate relationship, needing each other's company even as they bicker. As perhaps you have found in your own experience, human relationships are often far from simple. Works of literature can prove especially interesting when they suggest as much.

What power and influence people achieve may depend on particular traits of theirs. These include their gender, social class, race, ethnic background, nationality, sexual orientation, age, and the kind of work they do. Because these attributes may greatly affect a person's life, pay attention to them as you analyze characters. For instance, in Welty's story, all the characters are female. How might their gender matter? How might the story's dynamics have differed if it had featured at least one man? Another element of the story is its gap in ages: while the roommates are old, Marian is barely a teenager. What, over their years of living, might the two women have learned that the girl doesn't know yet?

Typically, characters express views of one another, and you have to decide how accurate these are. Some characters will seem wise observers of humanity. Others will strike you as making distorted statements about the world, revealing little more than their own biases and quirks. And some characters will seem to fall in the middle, coming across as partly objective and partly subjective. On occasion, you and your classmates may find yourselves debating which category a particular character fits. One interesting case is Welty's character Addie. Look again at the speech in which she berates her roommate:

> "Hush!" said the sick woman. "You never went to school. You never came and you never went. You never were anything—only here. You never were born! You don't know anything. Your head is empty, your heart and hands and your old black purse are all empty, even that little old box that you brought with you you brought empty—you showed it to me. And yet you talk, talk, talk, talk, talk all the time until I think I'm losing my mind! Who are you? You're a stranger—a perfect stranger! Don't you know you're a stranger? Is it possible that they have actually done a thing like this to anyone—sent them in a stranger to talk, and rock, and tell away her whole long rigmarole? Do they seriously suppose that I'll be able to keep it up, day in, day out, night in, night out, living in the same room with a terrible old woman—forever?"

Some may argue that this speech is merely an unreasonable rant, indicating Addie's dour mood rather than her roommate's true nature. (For one thing, contrary to Addie's declaration, the roommate must have been born!) Yet it can also be argued that Addie shrewdly diagnoses her situation. Perhaps statements like "you never were born," "your head is empty," and "you're a stranger" are true in a metaphorical sense.

SETTING

Usually a short story enables readers to examine how people behave in concrete circumstances. The characters are located in a particular place or **setting**. Moreover, they are shown at particular moments in their personal histories. Sometimes the story goes further, referring to them as living at a certain point in world history.

As the word *sometimes* implies, short stories vary in the precision with which they identify their settings. They differ as well in the importance of their setting. Sometimes location serves as a mere backdrop for the plot. At other times, the setting can be a looming presence. When Welty's character Marian visits the Old Ladies' Home, we get her vivid impressions of it. Even when a story's setting seems ordinary, it may become filled with drama and meaning as the plot develops. One way of analyzing characters is to consider how they accommodate themselves—or fail to accommodate themselves—to their surroundings. The two roommates in Welty's story are evidently frustrated with living in the Old Ladies' Home, and they take out their frustration on each other.

IMAGERY

Just like poems, short stories often use **imagery** to convey meaning. Sometimes a character in the story may interpret a particular image just the way you do. Some stories, though, include images that you and the characters may analyze quite differently. One example is the apple in Welty's story. Whereas Marian probably views the apple as just something to eat, many readers would make other associations with it, thinking in particular of the apple that Adam and Eve ate from the tree of knowledge in the Garden of Eden. By the end of Welty's story, perhaps Marian has indeed become like Adam and Eve, in that she has lost her innocence and grown more aware that human beings age. At any rate, many readers would call Marian's apple a **symbol**. Traditionally, that is the term for an image seen as representing some concept or concepts. Again, Marian herself probably does not view her apple as symbolic; indeed, characters within stories rarely use the word *symbol* at all.

Images may appear in the form of metaphors or other figures of speech. For example, when Marian enters the Old Ladies' Home, she experiences "a smell in the hall like the interior of a clock." Welty soon builds on the clock image as she describes the receptionist checking her wristwatch, an action that this character repeats near the end. Welty's whole story can be said to deal with time and its effects, both on the old and on the young.

Images in short stories usually appeal to the reader's visual sense. Most often, they are things you can picture in your mind. Yet stories are not limited to rendering visual impressions. They may refer to other senses, too, as when Welty's young heroine notices the odor in the hall.

LANGUAGE

Everything about short stories we have discussed so far concerns **language**. After all, works of literature are constructed entirely out of words. Here, however, we call your attention to three specific uses of language in stories: title, predominant style, and dialogue.

A story's **title** may be just as important as any words in the text. Not always will the relevance of the title be immediately clear to you. Usually you have to read a story all the way through before you can sense fully how its title applies. In any case, play with the title in your mind, considering its various possible meanings and implications. In analyzing the title of Welty's "A Visit of Charity," you may find it helpful to think about this famous passage from the King James translation of the New Testament: "And now abideth faith, hope, charity, these three; but the greatest of these is charity" (1 Corinthians 13:13). You may also want to look up the word *charity* in a dictionary.

Not all short stories have a uniform **style**. Some feature various tones, dialects, vocabularies, and levels of formality. Welty's story incorporates different types of speech almost from its start. When, using rather formal language, the nurse asks Marian, "Acquainted with any of our residents?" (para. 3), the girl puts this question more plainly: "With any old ladies?" (para. 4). Stories that do have a predominant style are often told in the first person, thus giving the impression of a presiding "voice." Charlotte Perkins Gilman's "The Yellow Wallpaper (pp. 248–60) teems with the anguished expressions of its beleaguered narrator.

Dialogue may serve more than one purpose in a short story. By reporting various things, characters may provide you with necessary background for the plot. In Welty's story, it's only from the roommates' fragmentary remarks that Marian—and the reader—can learn anything about their lives up until now. Actually, dialogue can also be thought of as an action in itself, moving the plot along. Try to identify the particular kinds of acts that characters perform when they speak. When the first roommate asks the departing Marian for a coin, she seems to be begging, but perhaps she is also doing whatever she can to hold the girl there; her having "clutched the child" (para. 64) suggests as much. Indeed, dialogue may function to reveal shifts in characters' relations with one another.

THEME

We have already discussed the term **theme** on pages 63–64. There, we identified issues of theme as one kind of issue that comes up in literary studies. At the same time, we suggested that the term *theme* applies to various literary genres, not just short stories. Later in this chapter, we examine theme in connection with poems, plays, and essays. Here, though, we consider theme as an element of short fiction. In doing so, we review some points from our earlier discussion, applying them now to Welty's story.

Recall that we defined the theme of a work as the main claim it seems to make. Furthermore, we identified it as an assertion, a proposition, or a statement rather than as a single word. "Charity" is obviously a *topic* of Welty's story, but because it is just one word, it is not an adequate expression of the story's *theme*. The following exercise invites you to consider just what that theme may be.

1. Try to state a text's theme as a midlevel generalization. If you were to put it in very broad terms, your audience would see it as fitting a great many works besides the one you have read. If you went to the opposite extreme, tying the theme completely to specific details of the text, your audience might think the theme irrelevant to their own lives.

The phrase "the moral of the story" suggests that a story can usually be reduced to a single message, often a principle of ethics or religion. Plenty of examples can be cited to support this suggestion. In the New Testament, for instance, Jesus tells stories—they are called *parables*—to convey some of his key ideas. In any number of cultures today, stories are used to teach children elements of good conduct. Moreover, people often determine the significance of a real-life event by building a story from it and by drawing a moral from it at the same time. These two processes conspicuously dovetailed when England's Princess Diana was killed in a car crash. Given that she died fleeing photographers, many people saw her entire life story as that of a woman hounded by the media. The moral was simultaneous and clear: thou shalt honor the right to privacy.

It is possible to lose sight of a story's theme by placing too much emphasis on minor details of the text. The more common temptation, however, is to turn a story's theme into an all-too-general cliché. Actually, a story is often most interesting when it *complicates* some widely held idea that it seemed ready to endorse. Therefore, a useful exercise is to start with a general thematic statement about the story and then make it increasingly specific. With "A Visit of Charity," for example, you might begin by supposing that a theme is "Everyone must give up their dreams of innocence and paradise, just as Adam and Eve did." Your next step would be to identify the specific spin that Welty's story gives this idea. How does her story differ from others on this theme? Note, for instance, that Marian comes literally face to face with the mortality of women much older than she is, and that the experience fills her momentarily with "wonder." Try to rephrase our version of Welty's theme so that it seems more in touch with these specific details of the text.

2. A theme of a text may be related to its title. It may also be expressed by some statement made within the text. But often various parts of the text merit consideration as you try to determine its theme.

In our discussion of a short story's language, we called attention to the potential significance of its title. The title may serve as a guide to the story's theme. What clues, if any, do you find in the title "A Visit of Charity"? Of course, determining a story's theme entails going beyond the title. You have to read, and usually reread, the entire text. In doing so, you may come across a statement that seems a candidate for the theme because it is a philosophical generalization. Nevertheless, take the time to consider whether the story's essence is indeed captured by this statement alone.

3. You can state a text's theme either as an observation or as a recommendation. Each way of putting it evokes a certain image of the text's author. When you state the theme as an **observation**, you depict the author as a psychologist, a philosopher, or some other kind of analyst. When you state the theme as a **recommendation**—which often involves your using the word *should*—you depict the author as a teacher, preacher, manager, or coach. That is, the author comes across as telling readers what to do.

As we have noted, stories are often used to teach lessons. Moreover, often the lessons are recommendations for action, capable of being phrased as "Do X" or "Do not do X." The alternative is to make a generalization about some state of affairs. When you try to express a particular story's theme, which of these two options should you follow? There are several things to consider in making your decision. First is your personal comfort: do you feel at ease with both ways of stating the theme, or is one of these ways more to your taste? Also worth pondering is the impression you want to give of the author: do you want to portray this person as a maker of recommendations, or do you want to assign the author a more modest role? Which of these two identities do you prefer for Welty?

4. Consider stating a text's theme as a problem. That way, you are more apt to convey the complexity and drama of the text.

We have suggested that short stories often pivot around conflicts between people and conflicts within people. Perhaps the most interesting stories are ones that pose conflicts not easily resolved. Probably you will be more faithful to such a text if you phrase its theme as a problem. In the case of Welty's story, for example, you might state the theme as follows: "Young people may sense an older person's infirmity, but, especially if that person is a stranger, they may as yet lack sufficient maturity and confidence to stay and help."

5. Rather than refer to *the* theme of a text, you might refer to *a* theme of the text, implying that the text has more than one. You would still be suggesting that you have identified a central idea of the text. Subsequently, you might have to defend your claim.

Unlike the average novel, the typical short story pivots around only a few ideas. Yet you need not insist that the story you are analyzing has a single theme. The shortest piece of short fiction may have more than one, and your audience may well appreciate your admitting this. One theme of Welty's story may be that none of us can escape the passage of time. The old roommates aside, teenaged Marian seems on the brink of adulthood, and her concluding bus ride suggests that she is moving further into it. But additional themes are possible. A second idea, dramatized by the roommates' feud, may be that old age can test a person's spirit even as it hurts the person's body. Of course, to call either of these ideas a theme of the story is still to make a claim that requires support.

Perhaps the biggest challenge you will face in writing about short stories is to avoid long stretches of plot summary. Selected details of the plot will often serve as key evidence for you. You will need to describe such moments from the story you are discussing, even if your audience has already read it. But your readers are apt to be frustrated if you just repeat plot at length. They will feel that they may as well turn back to the story itself rather than linger with your rehash. Your paper is worth your readers' time only if you provide insights of your own, *analyzing* the story rather than just *summarizing* it.

To understand what analysis of a short story involves, let's turn to student Tanya Vincent. Assigned to write an argument paper about a short story, Tanya decided to focus on Welty's. She realized that for her paper to be effective, she had to come up with an issue worth addressing, a claim about that issue, and evidence for that claim. Moreover, she had to be prepared to identify her process of reasoning and her assumptions.

For most writing assignments, settling on an issue will be your most important preliminary step. Without a driving question, you will have difficulty producing fresh, organized, and sustained analysis. For her paper on "A Visit of Charity," Tanya chose to address this issue: What does the story suggest *charity* can mean? In part, she was drawn to this question because the word *charity* appears in the story's title and because it comes up in the famous passage from 1 Corinthians 13 that we quoted earlier. But the question also enticed her because Welty's protagonist doesn't appear truly compassionate. A conventional definition of *charity* is that it is an expression of a sincere desire to help people. Given that Marian appears to lack this desire, is Welty's title ironic? Or does charity in some *other* sense of the word operate in the story? Tanya realized that she would be tackling an issue of definition. She would need to examine various possible meanings of "charity" and determine which are relevant to specific details of Welty's text.

A paper about a short story doesn't have to mention explicitly all the elements of short fiction we've identified. Nevertheless, thinking of these elements can help you plan such a paper, providing you with some preliminary terms for your analysis. Tanya perceived that her paper would be very much about characters and plot; it might also dwell upon imagery and language. She knew, too, that she would be more apt to persuade her readers if she included quotations from the story. Yet, as with plot summary, quoting should be limited, so that the paper seems an original argument—not a recycling of the literary work's own words. Tanya sensed that practically every sentence of Welty's story could be quoted and then interpreted. At the same time, she realized that she should quote only *some* words, not all.

Final Draft of a Student Paper

Here is Tanya's final draft of her paper about "A Visit of Charity." As you read it, keep in mind that it emerged only after she had done several preliminary drafts, in consultation with some of her classmates as well as her instructor. Although Tanya's paper is a good example of how to write about a short story, most drafts can stand to be revised further. What do you think Tanya has done well in her paper? If she planned to do yet another revision, what suggestions would you make?

Tanya Vincent
Professor Stein
English 1A
3 November ----

The Real Meaning of "Charity"
in "A Visit of Charity"

Many people would define the word "charity" as an act in which an individual or institution sincerely offers material or spiritual comfort to someone less fortunate. In this respect, charity is a form of love. Such is the meaning implied in the King James translation of the most famous statement about charity, 1 Corinthians 13.13: "And now abideth faith, hope, charity, these three; but the greatest of these is charity." In fact, some other translations of this biblical passage use "love" instead of "charity," thereby suggesting that the two terms are more or less equivalent. But Marian, the protagonist of Eudora Welty's short story "A Visit of Charity," does not appear to demonstrate this concept of charity when she visits

An assumption, but seems a reasonable one.

the Old Ladies' Home. She gives no indication that she sincerely cares about any of its residents. Rather, she approaches the visit as a mechanical task that she must perform to raise her standing as a Campfire Girl. Nor does she seem to become much more empathetic after spending time at the Home. Several readers of the story, therefore, might think its title ironic.

Starts to introduce her issue and claim by referring to readers who are possibly superficial.

This view may, however, be too limited. Welty may be encouraging us to move past our familiar concept of "charity" and give the word a meaning that *can* apply to her text in a nonironic way. It is true that Marian does not act lovingly or even compassionately on her trip to the Home. Yet maybe her brief moments with the two elderly roommates provide charity to Marian herself, making her a beneficiary of it rather than a donor of it. After all, her encounter with the two women helps to make her at least a bit more aware of the stresses that old age can bring. Charity in *this* sense would mean the providing of a necessary lesson about what life can be like as an adult. Even though the two roommates do not intend to be benevolent teachers of the girl, her meeting with them has some value, for it gives her a preview of realities she will have to deal with more extensively as she grows up.

A qualification. Tanya holds back from claiming certainty about Welty's intentions.

Introduction ends with main issue (a definitional kind) and main claim.

When we first meet her in the story, Marian seems anything but passionately devoted to improving life for the Home's inhabitants. Probably "Old Ladies' Home" is not the building's real name to begin with, but instead Marian's own insensitive designation. Clearly she looks upon her visit as a chore. To her, it is just something she must do to earn points. Later, we readers learn that she has even computed the specific amounts available to her: "She had almost said that if Campfire Girls brought flowers to the Old Ladies' Home, the visit would count one extra point, and if they took a Bible with them on the bus and read it to the old ladies, it counted double" (133). When, back at the story's start, she introduces herself to the nurse, she does not even pretend to be a true Angel of Mercy pursuing a higher spiritual purpose: "I'm a Campfire Girl. . . . I have to pay a visit to some old lady" (131). So indifferent is she to the Home's aged occupants that she candidly announces "any of them will do" (131). When she does meet with the two roommates, she chooses not to stay long with them. Nor does she offer charity in a traditional sense when one of the roommates begs. While the woman asks, "have you a penny to spare for a poor old woman that's not got anything of her own?" (135), Marian is anxious to flee. Nor, when she does leave the pair, is her exit gradual, patient, and kind: she

Concession to readers who have trouble finding "charity" in the story.

"jumped up and moved toward the door"; "pulled violently against the old hands"; "ran down the hall, without looking behind her and without looking at the nurse"; "quickly . . . retrieved a red apple"; "ran to meet the big bus"; "shouted" at the bus; and "jumped on" (135). These frenzied motions indicate that Marian is ultimately *repelled* by the two women, not drawn to them as clients for her kindness.

Here and elsewhere in the paper, Tanya quotes from Welty's text.

Nevertheless, perhaps Marian's experience with them confers a sort of charity upon *her* by alerting her to facts she will eventually have to face. When she first meets the roommate who is supposedly healthier, she is struck by the "terrible, square smile (which was a smile of welcome) stamped on her bony face" (132). This seems more an image of death than of life, suggesting that Marian is beginning to grow conscious of mortality. This implication gets even stronger when Marian comes to the bed of the sicker woman, Addie: "She wondered about her — she wondered for a moment as though there was nothing else in the world to wonder about. It was the first time such a thing had happened to Marian" (134). More precisely, Marian seems to discover that people soon to die may become a mixture of helplessness and fierce self-assertion. To the girl, Addie repeatedly comes across as a sheep or lamb, a species of animal traditionally associated with innocence. Even before she enters the room, Marian twice experiences Addie's voice as that of a sheep "bleating" (131), and at Addie's bedside she mentally compares the tearful, suffering woman to "a little lamb" (134). Yet Addie is also someone capable not only of refusing to tell her age, but also of berating her roommate: "And yet you talk, talk, talk, talk, talk all the time until I think I'm losing my mind!" (134). In turn, the object of this scorn displays to Marian a similar blend of powerlessness and ferocity. "In an affected, high-pitched whine," this roommate refers to herself as "a poor old woman," but at the same time "she suddenly clutched the child with her sharp little fingers" (134). Indeed, if Addie comes across to Marian as a sheep or lamb, the girl senses right from the start of the meeting that the other woman is an aggressive bird: "Suddenly Marian saw a hand, quick as a bird claw, reach up in the air and pluck the white cap off her head" (132). In general, neither of the roommates fits the sentimental stereotype of the sweet old lady. But their difference from this image is precisely what can be educational for Marian. Their nearness to death, and the complex behavior they show in response to their fate,

Transition to development of main claim.

As earlier, with "wondered," Tanya shows attention to repetition.

are matters that the girl will have to contend with a lot once she herself becomes a full-fledged adult.

While admitting that the sentence about "the first time" appears significant, some readers may doubt that Marian learns anything from this experience. Their skepticism would be understandable, given that she does not philosophize at length about the visit and ends it rather speedily. Welty does, however, suggest the stirrings of mental change in Marian by drawing our attention to the bodily disorientation she goes through in the old women's room. Immediately upon meeting them, she "stood tongue-tied" (132). Soon, "her heart beat more and more slowly, her hands got colder and colder, and she could not hear whether the old women were saying anything or not" (132). Moreover, "she could not see them very clearly" (132). A moment later, she winds up "pitched against the chair" (132) and forgets her own name. Eventually "her heart nearly stopped beating altogether" (134). These disabilities, though temporary, indicate that at *some* level of consciousness, Marian is having perceptions that she did not have before. Specifically, she seems to have glimmers of how death increasingly enters people's lives as they age.

Concession to readers with a different view.

The story's very last sentence further suggests that Marian either learns this lesson or vaguely intuits it. By taking "a big bite out of the apple" (135), she resembles Adam and Eve, whose own eating of an apple resulted in their becoming mortal. But in writing her story, Welty may also have had in mind a second biblical passage. Occurring just two lines before the famous statement about charity I have quoted, it is a well-known review of life's journey: "When I was a child, I spake as a child, I understood as a child, I thought as a child: but when I became a man, I put away childish things" (1 Corinthians 13.11). Although Marian is female, the line can still apply to her. Before her visit to the Home, she has been "a child," and she acts that way for much of her time there. But the visit may make her more inclined to "put away childish things," in which case she herself would receive a form of charity from it.

Again, acknowledges that she can't be certain about Welty's thinking.

Work Cited

Welty, Eudora. "A Visit of Charity." *Making Literature Matter: An Anthology for Readers and Writers*, edited by John Schilb and John Clifford. 7th ed., Bedford/St. Martin's, 2018, pp. 131–35.

SUMMING UP: WRITING ABOUT SHORT STORIES

- **Short stories require you to understand and evaluate them on the basis of just a few details and events.**
- **Think carefully about the title and its possible meanings and implications.**
- **The elements of short fiction include *plot* and *structure*, *point of view*, *characters*, *setting*, *imagery*, *language*, and *theme*.**
- ***Plot* and *structure* are related, but plots usually center on human beings and their actions, and structure often follows the ABDCE formula (action, background, development, climax, ending).** (pp. 137–38)
- ***Points of view* vary and include first person and omniscient.** (pp. 135–36)
- **As you analyze and evaluate the *characters* in a short story** (pp. 139–40), **consider these questions:**

  What does each character desire?

  How do the characters, even minor characters, relate to one another?

  Can you identify a protagonist and an antagonist?

  How are the characters' lives affected by traits such as gender, class, race, ethnicity, nationality, sexual orientation, and occupation?

  Can you trust the accuracy of the views the characters have of one another?

  How does the characters' dialogue function – does it provide background, advance the plot, reveal shifts in characters' relations, or what?
- ***Setting* provides a context for actions.** One way of analyzing characters is to consider how they do or do not accommodate themselves to their surroundings. (p. 141)
- ***Images* appeal to the reader's senses – usually the visual sense – and may appear in the form of metaphors and other figures of speech.** (p. 142)
- **The language of a short story may have various meanings and implications.** Think about the potential significance not only of its title, but also of its style and dialogue. (pp. 142–43)
- **A *theme* of a short story is a claim it seems to make, best identified as an assertion, a proposition, or a statement. In your writing, try to state the theme as a midlevel generalization, either as an observation, as a recommendation, or as a problem.** (pp. 143–46)
- **In writing an argument about a short story, remember to formulate an issue worth addressing.** (pp. 144–45)

Writing about Poems

Some students are put off by poetry, perhaps because their early experiences with it were discouraging. They imagine that poems have deep hidden meanings they can't uncover. Maybe their high-school English teacher always had the right interpretation, and they rarely did. This need not be the case. Poetry can be accessible to all readers.

The problem is often a confusion about the nature of poetry, since poetry is more compressed than prose. Poetry focuses more on connotative, emotional, or associative meanings and conveys meaning more through suggestion, indirection, and the use of metaphor, symbol, and imagery than prose does. It seldom hands us a specific meaning. Poetic texts suggest certain possibilities, but the reader completes the transaction. Part of the meaning comes from the writer, part from the text itself, and part from the reader. Even students who are the same age, race, religion, and ethnicity are not duplicates of one another. Each has unique experiences, family histories, and emotional lives. If thirty people read a poem about conformity or responsibility, all thirty will have varying views about these concepts, even though they will probably have some commonalities. (Most societies are so saturated with shared cultural experiences that it is nearly impossible to avoid some overlap in responses.)

In a good class discussion, then, we should be aware that even though we might be members of the same culture, each of us reads from a unique perspective, a perspective that might also shift from time to time. If a woman reads a poem about childbirth, her identity as a female will seem more relevant than if she were reading a poem about death, a more universal experience. In other words, how we read a poem and how significant and meaningful the poem is for us depends both on the content of the poem and on our specific circumstances. Suppose you are fourteen when you first read a poem about dating; you would likely have very different responses rereading it at nineteen, twenty-five, and fifty. We read poems through our experiences. As we gain new experiences, our readings change.

One reason to respond in writing to your first reading is to be able to separate your first thoughts from those of your classmates. They too will bring their own experiences, values, and ideas to the discussion. In the give-and-take of open discussion, it may be difficult to remember what you first said. Of course, the point of a classroom discussion is not simply to defend your initial response, for then you would be denying yourself the benefit of other people's ideas. A good discussion should open up the poem, allow you to see it from multiple viewpoints, and enable you to expand your perspective, to see how others make sense of the world.

This rich mixture of the poet's text, the reader's response, and discussion among several readers can create new possibilities of meaning. Even more than fiction or drama, poetry encourages creative readings that can be simultaneously true to the text and to the reader. A lively class discussion can uncover a dozen or more plausible interpretations of a poem, each backed up with valid evidence both from the poem and from the reader's experience. You may try to persuade others that your views about the poem are correct; others may do the same to you. This negotiation is at the heart of a liberal, democratic education. In fact, maybe the most respected and repeated notion about being well-educated is the ability to empathize with another's point of view, to see as another sees. Reading, discussing, and writing about poetry can help you become a person who can both create meaning and understand and appreciate how others do. This is one important way literature matters.

The following three poems are about work—about the joys and sorrows, the satisfactions and frustrations of physical labor. Some people might think of poets as intellectuals who are far removed from the experiences of the working class, but this is not the case. Indeed, many poets were themselves brought up in working-class homes and know firsthand the dignity and value of such work. Even among poets who do not toil with their hands, few lack the imaginative empathy that would allow them to write perceptively about firefighters and factory workers, cleaning women and mill workers. These three poems are especially relevant today when physical work is becoming less and less a reality among middle-class Americans. Poems that matter are poems about real life—about love and death, about pain and loss, about beauty and hope. These three poems about work are about all of these and more.

The first poem, Mary Oliver's (b. 1935) "Singapore," appeared in *House of Light* (1992). She has won a Pulitzer Prize for her poetry. "Blackberries" is by Yusef Komunyakaa (b. 1947), who has become known for exploring various aspects of African American experience; the poem is from *Magic City* (1992). Edwin Arlington Robinson's "The Mill" is the oldest poem in the cluster. Robinson (1869–1935) is considered the first major poet of twentieth-century America.

MARY OLIVER

Singapore

In Singapore, in the airport,
a darkness was ripped from my eyes.
In the women's restroom, one compartment stood open.
A woman knelt there, washing something
    in the white bowl.

Disgust argued in my stomach
and I felt, in my pocket, for my ticket.

A poem should always have birds in it.
Kingfishers, say, with their bold eyes and gaudy wings.
Rivers are pleasant, and of course trees.
A waterfall, or if that's not possible, a fountain
    rising and falling.
A person wants to stand in a happy place, in a poem.

When the woman turned I could not answer her face.
Her beauty and her embarrassment struggled together, and
    neither could win.

(continued on page 153, after the insert)

PORTFOLIO

Comparing Poems and Pictures

Although literature and visual art may seem quite different media, they have often been closely connected. For one thing, any page of literature is a visual image, whether or not readers are always conscious of this fact. Also, most publishers of literature carefully design the covers of their books, aiming to lure readers. Specific genres and authors, however, have forged even stronger relations between literature and art. Beginning in classical times and continuing today, many poems have precisely described existing paintings and sculptures; this tradition of verse is called **ekphrasis**. In the late eighteenth century, William Blake made highly ornamental engravings of his poems, so that they were striking works of art and not just written texts. In the nineteenth century, many novels included illustrations, a tradition evident today in children's picture books. At present, perhaps you are a fan of **graphic novels**: comic books that combine words and images to tell stories aimed at adults.

Aside from this history of connections, comparing a literary text with an image is a good mental exercise. The process can help you acquire more insights into each work. Given this possibility, we present several pairings of poems and works of art. Every pairing deals with one of the topics addressed in Parts One and Two of this book: work, family, love, freedom and confinement, crime and justice, and journeys. In some cases, the literary text was written in response to its accompanying image. In other cases, we connect a poem and an image for the first time, inviting you to trace their similarities and differences. With any of these pairings, comparison can help you generate ideas for writing, a principle we stress throughout this book.

Analyzing Visual Art

You can better understand a work of visual art — and develop ideas for an essay about it — if you raise certain questions about it and try to answer them. These questions apply to various types of pictures. Bear in mind that even photographs are not mere reproductions of reality. People who create them are, consciously or not, choosing their subject and figuring out how best to represent it. Especially in the age of digital technologies such as Photoshop, images caught by the camera can be tweaked in all sorts of ways. Moreover, the scene depicted might be a staged fantasy in the first place.

Here are questions to ask yourself as you examine a picture with an eye to analyzing it:

1. **What details do you see in the picture?** Besides recognizable objects and figures (human beings or animals), consider shapes, colors, lighting, and shading. Do not list just the picture's most prominent elements, for those that at first seem trivial may turn out to be important for you.
2. **What are aspects of the picture's style — the artist's particular way of handling the subject?** Among other things, consider what the artist does and does not allow the viewer to see; how realistic or abstract the work seems; and whether anyone in the picture looks directly at the viewer.
3. **How has the artist organized the picture?** Note especially patterns of resemblance and contrast. Think, too, about whether the picture's design directs the viewer's attention to a particular part of it.
4. **What mood does the picture evoke?** Consider emotions that you experience as a viewer, as well as those that seem to be felt by any living figures in the scene.
5. **What is at least one detail of the picture that strikes you as puzzling (and therefore especially in need of interpretation)?**
6. **Does the picture seem to tell a story or appear to be part of a story that has already begun and will continue?**
7. **How does the picture relate to its title and (where applicable) to its caption?**
8. **What are some options that the artist could have explored but did not pursue?**

Writing an Essay That Compares Literature and Art

Before you write an essay comparing a work of literature with a work of art, collect as many details as you can about each. The questions above can help you do this with the artwork. For aid in gathering observations about the literary text, see Chapter 2, How to Read Closely, especially the section on Basic Strategies for Close Reading. Then, as you proceed to write, keep the following principles especially in mind:

- **You do not have to give equal space to each work.** Rather, you may prefer to come up with an issue and a main claim by focusing on interpreting *one* of the works: either the literary text *or* the visual image. Your secondary work will still play some role in the essay, but your primary one will receive greater attention. The result will be what in Chapter 4 we call a *weighted* comparison. (See that chapter for more tips.)
- **Assume that your reader is at least somewhat familiar with both the literary work and the image but needs to be reminded of their basic details.** In particular, help your audience *visualize* the art you discuss.
- **Refer at least sometimes to the author of the literary work and to the artist who created the image.** Doing so will help you analyze how their productions involve particular strategies of representation — attempts to affect audiences in particular ways.

A Sample Paper Comparing a Poem and a Picture

To give you a better idea of what an essay comparing literature and art looks like, we present a paper by student Karl Magnusson. He connects Edward Hopper's painting *Office at Night* to a prose poem of the same title by Rolando Perez. This pairing is the first in our color plates section. As you will see, Karl's essay is a weighted comparison; it focuses mostly on Perez's poem.

Karl Magnusson
Professor Kemper
English W350
May 16, ----

Lack of Motion and Speech in
Rolando Perez's "Office at Night"

Edward Hopper's painting *Office at Night* depicts a man and a woman working in the kind of setting indicated by the title. The man is apparently the boss of the woman, who seems to be his secretary. He sits at a desk by an open window, studying a document that he holds in front of him. She is positioned to the left and slightly to the rear of him. More precisely, she stands at a filing cabinet with her right hand resting on an open drawer. Their respective postures suggest that she is waiting to hear what he will say next. Perhaps she has just asked him a question and he is thinking about how to answer, or perhaps she is simply expecting him, as her superior, to issue her a new order. In any case, viewers of the painting are free to interpret their interaction, and different spectators might come up with different ideas about what these people really mean to each other. Indeed, not everyone would conceive their relationship to be what Rolando Perez imagines it as being in his poem about Hopper's artwork. Also entitled "Office at Night," Perez's poem speculates that the man and woman have a romantic interest in each other that neither he nor she can express. Furthermore, the poem conveys their reticence in terms that have often been used to describe the medium of painting in general.

Immediately refers to the painting and then proceeds to summarize its key details.

Now turns to the poem, which will be the primary work in this weighted comparison.

This is the essay's main claim, which is about the poem.

The poem draws attention more to the self-repression of the boss. The secretary, too, evidently does not feel able to speak frankly about their emotions, perhaps because she is after all his employee. But the text tends to focus on *his* reluctance to reveal that he is enamored of her. This mixture of lust and hesitation is evident right near the start of the poem. There, just before describing the secretary's alluring clothes, the poem's speaker wonders, "How many times did he [the boss] dream of this very same scenario" (lines 1–2). The implication is that the boss has entertained sensual visions of his employee in his mind while

Proceeds to support the main argument with specific lines from the poem.

doing nothing to bring them about. He merely fantasizes a romance with her, not actually helping it come to life. Soon after, the reader learns that *she* had to prompt *him* to "open the window" (line 5) and let fresh air in. Evidently she wishes to stimulate their senses and admit their real feelings, but this is behavior that he apparently would never "have dared" (4) to engage in on his own. Later, he resists actually inviting her to take their office working relationship in a romantic direction. Although he apparently considers the possibility that "he would do something, he would act, produce the right combination of words" (14–15) to initiate a courtship, he remains silent and still. The implication is that he is restrained by the memory of his previous disappointments in love — "too many truths in the past" (17). Whatever specific episodes in his past he is thinking of, the result is that "now history holds him back" (17). Rather than "suggest[ing] that they lock up and go for a drink somewhere" (16), he stays emotionally locked up, not letting his true attachment to her emerge.

In describing physical details of the office, the poem's speaker sums up the couple's inability to be emotionally open with each other. In part, the speaker does this by sometimes using images of motion that underscore by contrast how the man and woman fail to act on their feelings. The "patch of light" that "touches them both . . . lightly, very lightly . . . as with fingertips" (10–12) is a reminder that these two people do not physically touch each other at all. The phrase "gently carried there by the wind" (8) — used in reference to a piece of paper on the floor — indirectly emphasizes that the couple will not let themselves be carried away by passion. When, however, near the end of the poem, the speaker describes the paper as "timidly undisturbed" (20), the symbolism is more direct: the word "timidly" seems to fit the couple as well, for they have been too scared to confess their emotional bond. Moreover, the speaker's observation that "he hasn't moved, and she hasn't moved" (18–19) directly reinforces their *psychological* paralysis. The poem's final phrase, "wounded and frozen infinity" (20), is not just an overview of this late-night office environment. The speaker is also indicating the basic state of the couple's relationship. They are "wounded" in the sense that they suffer unfulfilled desires for each other. They are "frozen" in the sense that they cannot reveal these desires. The word "infinity" implies that, given their inertia, their situation is unlikely to change.

Not every poem about Hopper's *Office at Night* painting would necessarily focus on its two human figures. Nor would every poem about the painting necessarily depict their relationship in the way that Perez's does. Indeed, a distinctive feature of his poem is that his portrait of the couple attributes to them characteristics often associated with the medium of painting itself. Aware, like most people, that figures in a painting do not move, Perez takes this fact and makes it an element of the couple's behavior. The static nature of painting in general is echoed in their paralytic inhibition. Furthermore, just as people in paintings do not speak aloud, so the couple in Perez's poem resist articulating what they really feel. Also, just as viewers of a painting have to guess the thoughts of anyone shown in it, so Perez's man and woman force themselves to guess what is on each other's mind.

Perez could be seen as tolerating and even encouraging affairs between bosses and their secretaries. In this respect, his text seems more in keeping with the world of 1940, the year Hopper painted *Office at Night*. Back then, expressions of love between a manager and a subordinate might have been smiled upon, perceived as what the poem's speaker calls "the correct combination of words" and "the correct series of reactions" (15–16). The same expressions now, however, might be condemned as politically and even legally *in*correct. Certainly government and company policies on sexual harassment warn executives not to seduce the employees who serve them. Nevertheless, it would be unfair simply to dismiss Perez's poem or Hopper's painting as outdated, especially because the audiences for these works do not have to take them as being just about romance in the office. Both the poem and the painting allow for interpretations that see the couple as universal — as people who might exist anywhere. In this case, their reticence toward each other would be a widespread human problem: the difficulty of communicating the stirrings of one's heart.

The concluding paragraph does not simply repeat what has already been said. It touches on a new subject: changes in policies on office affairs.

Works Cited

Hopper, Edward. *Office at Night*. 1940, Walker Art Center, Minneapolis. Schilb and Clifford, Portfolio F.

Perez, Rolando. "Office at Night." Schilb and Clifford, Portfolio F–G.

Schilb, John, and John Clifford, editors. *Making Literature Matter: An Anthology for Readers and Writers*. 7th ed., Bedford/St. Martin's, 2018.

Edward Hopper, *Office at Night*. 1940. Oil on canvas. 30-5/16 × 33-15/16 × 2-3/4″ framed. Collection Walker Art Center, Minneapolis. Gift of the T. B. Walker Foundation, Gilbert M. Walker Fund, 1948.

ROLANDO PEREZ

Office at Night

It is past nine o'clock, and she has stayed late to help him. How many times did he dream of this very same scenario: her standing there in her tight blue dress, with her black pumps and flesh-colored stockings. And now it has finally happened. Without him having to ask — not that he would have dared — she volunteered all on her own.

He had to "open the window."

"This office at night is a bit stuffy."

A sheet of paper that once lay on top of other papers on his desk, now lies on the green carpet — to his right — gently carried there by the wind. Standing at a black filing cabinet, searching for some old bills, she has noticed the paper lying on the floor. The desk lamp throws a shadow on the desk, and illuminates his hands. And a patch of light, reflected on the wall, touches them both . . . lightly, very lightly . . . as with finger tips.

Will she bend over to pick it up?

If only the phone beside him would ring, then he would do something, he would act, produce the correct combination of words that would elicit the correct series of reactions from her. He might even suggest that they lock up and go for a drink somewhere. But having heard too many truths in the past, now history holds him back. In his suit, with his shirt buttoned to the top, and his tie still on, he hasn't moved, and she hasn't moved; and the wind-swept paper will stay on the floor, halfway between his desk and her cabinet, timidly undisturbed, in this wounded and frozen infinity.

[2002]

Edward Hopper, *Conference at Night*. The Roland P. Murdock Collection, Wichita Art Museum, Wichita, Kansas.

VICTORIA CHANG

Edward Hopper's *Conference at Night*

The man sitting on the desk seems to have no eyes or they are closed or they have
been dug out the man sitting on the table sits in a way of a boss or perhaps he wants

to be the boss and the woman and man can help him the desks have nothing on
them but two wooden boards they hold shadows and the man no papers no tacks

the man has no stacks of anything the room can't be his office it is a morgue for
desks people that have left laid off fired sacked axed let go why let go of the past

why must the past too be given a notice why can't we live in the past in our best
dresses the woman looks like a man maybe she will be a boss or maybe

it's better to look like a woman but act like a man a boss once told me never to
act like a woman the woman stares beyond the man the man on the desk looks

between the man and woman whatever they are conferencing about has passed is
the past the pair helped the man become the boss he lost touch with the pair who

lost touch with each other who were both laid off

[2011]

Gustav Klimt, *The Kiss*. 1907–1908. Oesterreichische Galerie im Belvedere, Vienna, Austria. Photo Credit: Erich Lessing/Art Resource, NY.

LAWRENCE FERLINGHETTI

Short Story on a Painting of Gustav Klimt

They are kneeling upright on a flowered bed
  He
    has just caught her there
                  and holds her still
    Her gown
         has slipped down
                      off her shoulder
He has an urgent hunger
           His dark head
                 bends to hers
                      hungrily
And the woman the woman
  turns her tangerine lips from his
     one hand like the head of a dead swan
        draped down over
                      his heavy neck
           the fingers
              strangely crimped
                    tightly together
   her other arm doubled up
         against her tight breast

her hand a languid claw
clutching his hand
which would turn her mouth
to his
her long dress made
of multicolored blossoms
quilted on gold
her Titian hair
with blue stars in it
And his gold
harlequin robe
checkered with
dark squares
Gold garlands
stream down over
her bare calves &
tensed feet
Nearby there must be
a jeweled tree
with glass leaves aglitter
in the gold air
It must be
morning
in a faraway place somewhere
They
are silent together
as in a flowered field
upon the summer couch
which must be hers
And he holds her still
so passionately
holds her head to his
so gently so insistently
to make her turn
her lips to his
Her eyes are closed
like folded petals
She
will not open
He
is not the One

[1976]

Edvard Munch, *The Scream*. © 2014 The Munch Museum/The Munch-Ellingsen Group/Artists Rights Society (ARS), NY. Photo credit: The Art Archive at Art Resource, NY.

MAY MILLER

The Scream

I am a woman controlled,
Remember this; I never scream,
Yet I stood a form apart
Watching my other frenzied self
Beaten by words and wounds
Make in silence a mighty scream—
A scream that the wind took up
And thrust through the bars of night
Beyond all reason's final rim.
Out where the sea's last murmur dies
And the gull's cry has no sound,
Out where city voices fade,
Stilled in a lyric sleep
Where silence is its own design,
My scream hovered a ghost denied
Wanting the shape of lips.

[1975]

Frida Kahlo, *Frida and Diego Rivera*. 1931. Oil on canvas. 99 × 78.7 cm. San Francisco Museum of Modern Art, Albert M. Bender Collection, gift of Albert M. Bender; © Banco de Mexico Diego Rivera & Frida Kahlo Museums Trust, Mexico, D.F./Artists Rights Society (ARS), New York.

DAVID DOMINGUEZ

Wedding Portrait

Yesterday afternoon, I hung a framed print in the living room—
a task that took two head-throbbing hours.
It's a wedding portrait that we love: *Frida and Diego Rivera*.
I wonder how two people could consistently hurt each other,
but still feel love so deeply as their bones turned into dust?
Before Frida died, she painted a watermelon still life;
before his death, Diego did too.
I want to believe that those paintings were composed
during parallel moments because of their undying devotion.
If I close my eyes, I can see melon wedges left like
centerpieces except for the slice
Diego put on the table's corner—
one piece of fruit pecked at by a dove
that passed through a window.

I know that I won't be building a bookshelf anytime soon
and that the chances of me constructing a roll-top desk
are as slim as me building an Adirondack chair that sits plumb,
but I'm good with the spackle and putty knives in my tool belt.
The knots in my back might not be there
if I had listened to her suggestions,
and I could well have done without two hours of silence
over a few holes in the wall.
But somehow, life has its ways of working things out.
This afternoon, I shut the blinds,
turned off the TV, lights, and phone,
and massaged my wife's feet to fight off a migraine—
her second one this week despite
the prophylactics and pain killers that we store in the breadbox.
For once, I'd like to experience what she feels:
nausea, blindness, and pain that strike
when the cranial vessels dilate,
fill with blood, leak, and make the brain swell.
Earlier, an MRI triggered the reaction as it mapped her head
with electrical current, gradient magnets, and radio waves
hammering her floundering eyes.
For now, we have our room, the bed frame, and the mattress
where she lies as I knead her toes.
Come nightfall, I hope that we'll sit in the patio and watch
the breeze stirring the lemon, lime, and orange trees
that I planted along the back fence.
On certain nights, the moon turns our lawn
into green acrylic where we sip Syrah and mint tea
until all we know is the sound
of our breathing among the whispering leaves. *[2010]*

Rembrandt van Rijn, *Self Portrait at the Age of 63*. 1669. Oil on canvas, 86 × 70.5 cm. National Gallery, London. Photo Credit: © National Gallery, London/Art Resource, NY.

LINDA PASTAN

Ethics

In ethics class so many years ago
our teacher asked this question every fall:
if there were a fire in a museum
which would you save, a Rembrandt painting
or an old woman who hadn't many
years left anyhow? Restless on hard chairs
caring little for pictures or old age
we'd opt one year for life, the next for art
and always half-heartedly. Sometimes
the woman borrowed my grandmother's face
leaving her usual kitchen to wander
some drafty, half-imagined museum.
One year, feeling clever, I replied
why not let the woman decide herself?
Linda, the teacher would report, eschews
the burdens of responsibility.
This fall in a real museum I stand
before a real Rembrandt, old woman,
or nearly so, myself. The colors
within this frame are darker than autumn,
darker even than winter — the browns of earth,
though earth's most radiant elements burn
through the canvas. I know now that woman
and painting and season are almost one
and all beyond saving by children. *[1980]*

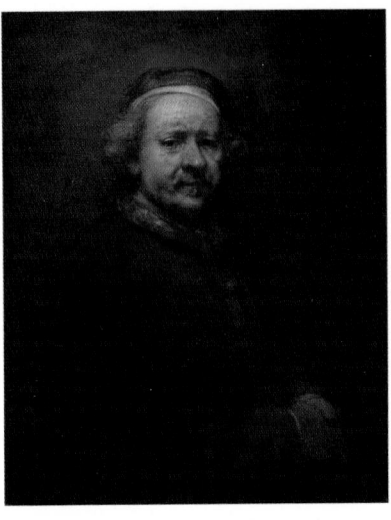

Jacob Lawrence, *They Were Very Poor.*

SANDRA GILBERT

Jacob Lawrence's "They Were Very Poor"

and they bowed in their poverty & their
difference over
the blank bowl & platter

they had, the brooding
board where no bread
was—

& they lost the past of yams, melons, greens,
rabbit loins, chicken legs, squirrels, & all
the Big House stuff

they stole amid storms of chains,
hails of whips, black bits
in the mouth,

they lost the salt & sweet of that
food, they lost the sour & bitter
of the god who had

forgotten them, they lost the hot dead
air in the cabins, the weevils, the blood, the mice
whispering through the bins, the wind

howling as the trains blasted
northward, & what was left was only
the bowl of empty

color & the sky-bright wall
& the great cauldron
dangling from the danger

of a new nail.

She smiled and I smiled. What kind of nonsense is this?
Everybody needs a job.
Yes, a person wants to stand in a happy place, in a poem.
But first we must watch her as she stares down at her labor,
which is dull enough.
She is washing the tops of the airport ashtrays, as big as
hubcaps, with a blue rag.
Her small hands turn the metal, scrubbing and rinsing.
She does not work slowly, nor quickly, but like a river.
Her dark hair is like the wing of a bird.

I don't doubt for a moment that she loves her life.
And I want her to rise up from the crust and the slop
and fly down to the river.
This probably won't happen.
But maybe it will.
If the world were only pain and logic, who would want it?

Of course, it isn't.
Neither do I mean anything miraculous, but only
the light that can shine out of a life. I mean
the way she unfolded and refolded the blue cloth,
the way her smile was only for my sake; I mean
the way this poem is filled with trees, and birds. *[1992]*

YUSEF KOMUNYAKAA

Blackberries

They left my hands like a printer's
Or thief's before a police blotter
& pulled me into early morning's
Terrestrial sweetness, so thick
The damp ground was consecrated
Where they fell among a garland of thorns.

Although I could smell old lime-covered
History, at ten I'd still hold out my hands
& berries fell into them. Eating from one
& filling a half gallon with the other,
I ate the mythology & dreamt
Of pies & cobbler, almost

Needful as forgiveness. My bird dog Spot
Eyed blue jays & thrashers. The mud frogs
In rich blackness, hid from daylight.
An hour later, beside City Limits Road
I balanced a gleaming can in each hand,

Limboed between worlds, repeating *one dollar.*
The big blue car made me sweat.
Wintertime crawled out of the windows.
When I leaned closer I saw the boy
& girl my age, in the wide back seat
Smirking, & it was then I remembered my fingers
Burning with thorns among berries too ripe to touch. *[1992]*

EDWIN ARLINGTON ROBINSON

The Mill

The miller's wife had waited long,
  The tea was cold, the fire was dead;
And there might yet be nothing wrong
  In how he went and what he said:
"There are no millers any more,"
  Was all that she had heard him say;
And he had lingered at the door
  So long that it seemed yesterday.

Sick with fear that had no form
  She knew that she was there at last;
And in the mill there was a warm
  And mealy fragrance of the past.
What else there was would only seem
  To say again what he had meant;
And what was hanging from a beam
  Would not have heeded where she went.

And if she thought it followed her,
  She may have reasoned in the dark
That one way of the few there were
  Would hide her and would leave no mark:
Black water, smooth above the weir
  Like starry velvet in the night,
Though ruffled once, would soon appear
  The same as ever to the sight. *[1920]*

A Student's Personal Responses to the Poems

The following are selections from the response journal of student Michaela Fiorucci, who chose to focus on boundaries—on the various divisions we set up between ourselves and other people, such as income, race, gender, sexual preference, and religion. It seemed to her an interesting way to talk about work since Michaela had observed barriers of all kinds between workers at her job at the university.

Using an explorative strategy, Michaela did some freewriting on the three poems, hoping to discover an argument about boundaries that might fit. The following are selections from her response journal.

> In "Singapore," there is a clear boundary between the middle-class American tourist and the cleaning lady, so much so that at first the narrator says, "Disgust argued in my stomach." The cleaning woman also seems to believe in a barrier and continues to work in a steady way. The narrator finally sees beauty in her dedication to her work. When the narrator does see beauty in her work habits, it helps close the barrier between them. There are also the issues of boundaries between fantasy and reality and between a world of pain and logic and one with birds and rivers. But at the end these boundaries also seem to be closing.
>
> In "Blackberries," the young boy seems to be living in a rural paradise, beyond the city boundaries, outside the usual urban and suburban environment. He lives in a land of bird dogs, jays, thrashers, and mud frogs. He makes comparisons between blackness and light that seem to anticipate the economic boundary that appears in the last stanza, the one between the poor boy and the rich kids in the car. It is this division between the children in air-conditioned comfort and the narrator on the outside looking in that seems to be the main point of this poem. Some boundaries cause us pain.
>
> "The Mill" tells the sad story of a miller who could not see a boundary between himself and his job. When he tells his wife "there are no millers any more," he is really saying that his life is over; he has no reason to live. And so he crosses the boundary between life and death. Tragically, his wife also has difficulty seeing herself outside her role as wife and housekeeper, and so she also crosses that ultimate boundary. She does so, however, in a completely different way: she drowns herself, so no one will know. She passes through life's boundary without leaving a trace.

After reading these brief freewrites to her response group, Michaela still didn't have a focus, but she liked the idea that boundaries, like walls, sometimes serve a purpose and sometimes they don't. She remembered a discussion of Robert Frost's "Mending Wall" from another course that focused on negotiating the walls we build between us. Her professor liked this idea since it helped her considerably narrow the concept of boundaries.

After reviewing her freewriting, Michaela wrote the following first draft and read it to her response group. She then discussed with her instructor her plans for a revision. Her instructor made a number of specific and general comments. After reading her first draft, what feedback would you give Michaela? Her revision appears later in this chapter on pp. 164–66.

First Draft of a Student Paper

Michaela Fiorucci
Mr. Hardy
English 102
15 April - - - -

Boundaries in Robinson, Komunyakaa, and Oliver

Although most sophomores I know at school value their privacy, they also want to create intimate relationships. It is often hard to reconcile these two impulses. Most middle-class students are lucky enough to have their own rooms, private enclaves against annoying sisters and brothers, intrusive mothers and fathers. But a room is also more than a physical boundary; it is also a symbolic assertion of identity. It says, "I'm separate from others, even within the closeness of the family." Such a commitment to physical privacy might be innocent enough, but it does contain dangerous seeds, especially when extended beyond the home to neighborhoods. When different ethnic groups want boundaries between them, it is no longer innocent. When the upper classes need to be separated from workers because they see each other as radically different, a dangerous boundary has been erected.

It would be reductive, however, to say all boundaries need to be erased. Edwin Arlington Robinson's "The Mill" is a good example of the dangerous consequences of a missing boundary. The poem narrates the sad story of a farm couple who commit suicide — the husband because he feels useless, the wife because she can't imagine life without her husband. During my first few readings, I was struck by the lack of communication between the couple. He must have been depressed for a long time, but it seems they never discussed his feelings. Keeping an emotional distance from others was probably a typical part of the way men and women dealt with each other a hundred years ago. It was a boundary not to be crossed. Apparently he could not say, "I feel terrible that I am going to lose my job." And his wife accepts his reticence, even though he might have been having second thoughts as he "lingered at the door" (line 7). Clearly this is a boundary that should have been breached. But after several readings I began to realize that the boundary that should have been established wasn't — the idea that a person's value or worth is synonymous with his or her identity is dehumanizing. And it probably isn't something that just happened in the past. Nor is the equally dehumanizing idea that a wife is nothing without her husband. When the miller's wife decides to "leave no mark" (20) by jumping into the pond, she is admitting she is not a worthwhile person by herself. Both identify totally with a role that in my view should be only one aspect of a complex human life. The final barrier she crosses, from life to death, is symbolically represented in the poem as a feminine domestic gesture: she doesn't want to leave a mess. The boundaries of person and occupation should be made clear; the arbitrary boundaries between genders should not.

When the narrator in Yusef Komunyakaa's "Blackberries" claims that he is "Limboed between worlds" (18), he means the rural paradise of "Terrestrial sweetness" (4) and "rich blackness" (15) he temporarily lives in versus the commercial, urban work that "made me sweat" (19). He has constructed a boundary between the ancient picking of berries and the technology of automobiles, between a natural closeness with nature and the artificial "Wintertime crawled out of the windows" (20). Even though the narrator is only ten, he senses the sensual joys of being one with nature. He seems to reject "old lime-covered / History" (7–8) in favor of "mythology" (11), which seems to suggest a conscious rejection or maybe repression of the contemporary world. But this boundary cannot stand. He needs the outside world to survive, and when the car approaches, it is the modern world and all its pluses and minuses that draw near. When he looks in, he sees "Smirking" (23) children; he sees class prejudice, hierarchy, and economic reality. The smirkers of the world are in charge. This realization dissolves the protective boundary around his Garden of Eden, and he feels physical pain. But really he feels the pain of initiation, the pain of having to cross a boundary he wanted to delay as long as possible. Although we can sympathize with the young narrator, he would probably have fared better by not making his boundary so extreme.

The narrator in Mary Oliver's "Singapore" at first sees a significant boundary between herself as a middle-class traveler and a cleaning woman washing a toilet. It is a separation we might all make, given our socialization to see this kind of physical labor as degrading. College-educated people in America have a tendency to see themselves as distinct from workers. For most, a woman washing something in a compartment is beyond the pale, a clear indication that the woman is other. But Oliver does have some conflicting ideas since she says a "Disgust argued in my stomach" (6). Since we are also socialized to be tolerant and open-minded, she knows she shouldn't think this way. And since she is also a writer with ideas about how a poem should "always have birds in it" (8), she looks harder at the cleaning woman, finally seeing in her face, in her hair, and in the way she works slowly, "like a river" (25), the positive aspects she probably wants to find. Oliver does not simply accept the boundaries that her culture constructs but negotiates with herself, eventually seeing that "light . . . can shine out of a life" (35) even where we do not expect it. In the woman's careful folding and unfolding of her blue work cloth and in her smile, Oliver eclipses the social boundary and ends up with a life-affirming vision "filled with trees, and birds" (38).

Works Cited

Komunyakaa, Yusef. "Blackberries." Schilb and Clifford, pp. 153–54.

Oliver, Mary. "Singapore." Schilb and Clifford, pp. 152–53.

Robinson, Edwin Arlington. "The Mill." Schilb and Clifford, p. 154

Schilb, John, and John Clifford, editors. *Making Literature Matter: Anthology for Readers and Writers*, 7th ed., Bedford/St. Martin's, 2018.

The Elements of Poetry

SPEAKER AND TONE

The voice we hear in a poem could be the poet's, but it is better to think of the speaker as an artistic construction — perhaps a **persona** (mask) for the poet or perhaps a character who does not resemble the poet at all. For example, the speaker in Lynda Hull's "Night Waitress" (pp. 42–43) is not the poet herself but a struggling worker. In large part, to describe any poem's speaker is to pinpoint the person's tone or attitude. Sometimes this is hard to discern. The tone could be ironic or sentimental, joyful or morose, or a combination of emotions. To get a precise sense of it, read the poem aloud, actually performing the speaker's role. Bear in mind that his or her tone may change over the course of the poem. For instance, as the speaker in Yusef Komunyakaa's "Blackberries" recalls a day in his childhood when he picked fruit and then tried to sell it on a highway, he shifts from nostalgia (remembering "Terrestrial sweetness") to bitter recognition of class bias (the "Smirking" of the children who passed him in their car).

The narrator of "The Mill" immediately creates a somber, foreboding tone of anxiety and dread with the tea is "cold" and the fire is "dead," which also foreshadows the death of the miller. Likewise, his brief statement that "there are no millers any more" reinforces and intensifies the sense of impending doom that permeates the plot and theme of the poem. And, of course, such a grim tone is warranted by the dual suicides. Interestingly, the ominous tone of the poem noticeably shifts in the last four lines to one of quiet smooth repose as the once ruffled pond appears "like starry velvet in the night." Perhaps the miller and his wife are finally at peace.

DICTION AND SYNTAX

Although we would all agree that poets rely on the meaning of words to express their feelings and their ideas, what words mean is no simple matter. Perplexed over what a poet might have intended, we often consult a dictionary. And that certainly might help demystify a puzzling passage. But poetry is often more about complicating than clarifying. Most poets are more interested in opening up words than pinning them down. Unlike journalists or science writers, poets often intend to be ambiguous. They like a word's possibilities, its rich emotional overtones. That's one reason readers see in poems different things; one reader may think of the line "Wintertime crawled out of the window" as meaning air conditioning and another as meaning the chilly arrogance and distaste of the privileged for laborers. Komunyakaa knows exactly what he meant by "wintertime."

Looking up "wintertime" in the dictionary would give us the denotative meaning, which wouldn't be much help here. But the emotional overtones or associations for individual readers give us the complex multiplicity that poets hope will enrich the poem's meaning. When in "Singapore," for example, the narrator says "a darkness was ripped from my eyes," the objective denotative meaning is probably not what she is after. More likely Oliver is counting on the more subjective, emotional associations of "darkness." Perhaps lack of understanding or ignorance is suggested. Perhaps intolerance or fear of otherness comes to mind. And in the background lie all the negative associations of the unknown, the uncertainty and the danger of things unseen. These are the word's connotations, and they are crucial to the evocative suggestiveness of poems. Oliver wants readers to allow connotation to do its work in expanding and personalizing the meaning of words. In this sense, the word *darkness* contains within it infinite subjective and cultural possibilities.

The same is true for "light" in line 38 of the last stanza. It is the connotative possibilities that infuse "light" with significance, especially when contrasted with the darkness of the first stanza. Seen in the context of the poem, "light" might suggest beauty or integrity or perhaps dedication, commitment, or the ability to find in work something valuable and beautiful. For religious readers, "light" might suggest the beauty and worthiness of each human soul, while for the political thinkers, the dedication and skill of laborers might come to mind. What other connotations can you suggest for these two words?

The last line of the poem offers a clear distinction between denotation and connotation when Oliver says, "this poem is filled with trees, and birds." Literally, of course, trees and birds do not fill the page (except for the actual words), but if we think of trees and birds connoting or suggesting delicate beauty or the majesty of nature or perhaps simply positive and pleasant thoughts, then through her diction, Oliver's meaning is both clarified and expanded.

FIGURES OF SPEECH

When we use figures of speech, we mean something other than the words' literal meaning. In the first sentence of "Singapore," Mary Oliver writes that "a darkness was ripped from my eyes." This direct comparison is a **metaphor**. Had she been more indirect, she might have written "it was like a darkness . . . ," a common literary device called a **simile**. Poets use metaphors and similes to help us see in a fresh perspective. Comparing love to a rose encourages us to think differently about love, helping us see its delicate beauty. Of course, today that comparison is no longer novel and can even be a cliché, suggesting that a writer is not trying to be original and is settling instead for an easy comparison. When Robert Burns wrote "my love is like a red, red rose" more than two hundred years ago, it was a fresh comparison that excited new ways of looking at love. Indeed, some theorists, like the contemporary American philosopher Richard Rorty, think that metaphors can change our ways of looking at the world. Our thinking about time, for example, might be different if we didn't think with linear metaphors about the past being behind us and the future up ahead. What if, as some American Indian languages do, ours used a circular metaphor, having just one day that constantly repeated itself? Would our perceptions of time change?

What if Mary Oliver had begun her poem by saying that "a misunderstanding was corrected," instead of "a darkness was ripped from my eyes"? Her metaphor is not only more dramatic and memorable but also more suggestive. Darkness deepens the idea of lack of knowledge, suggesting not only intellectual blindness but also a host of negative connotations that readers might associate with the dark. Fresh metaphors can be expansive and illuminating. They help us understand the world differently.

Oliver creatively uses metaphors and similes throughout "Singapore." "Disgust argued" is an interesting metaphor or perhaps a **personification**, in which the speaker's stomach is given the ability to argue. She interrupts her observation of the cleaning woman in the third stanza to make a comment on the function of poetry itself, claiming that poems should have birds, rivers, and trees in them. Is she suggesting metaphorically that poems should be pleasant? Is that the only thing birds, rivers, and trees suggest to you?

She returns to the woman, and they exchange glances. Apparently the speaker is struggling with her own socialization that sees this kind of physical labor as demeaning. She directly describes the woman's "scrubbing and rinsing" but then returns to similes, describing her work as being "like a river" and her hair "like the wing of a bird." These comparisons seem for a moment to clarify the event for the speaker, helping her see this seemingly oppressive job positively. Amazingly, she wants the woman actually to become a bird and "rise up from the crust and the slop and fly."

But in the final stanza, she reminds us that she isn't really expecting that kind of physical miracle; instead, she wants to remind us that how we describe the woman working controls how we feel about her. If we see the folding and unfolding of her washcloth metaphorically, then we might see her differently; we might see her natural dignity, her beauty, and how her "light" was able to illuminate the speaker's "darkness."

Sometimes the poet chooses words like *darkness* and *light* that are so rich in texture that they can be examined as both metaphor and connotation. Such words might also be thought of as examples of synecdoche or metonymy. **Synecdoche** substitutes part of something for the whole, as in "I love my new wheels" referring to a car. **Metonymy** substitutes something associated with a thing, as in "Hollywood is resisting censorship" for the entire film industry. Oliver's "eyes" might be a synecdoche for her mind, and "darkness" and "light" can be metonymies for ignorance and beauty. Locate examples in our three poems of metaphor, connotation, synecdoche, and metonymy, if you can.

Although students often seem perplexed when professors find hidden **symbols** in poems, writers rarely plant such puzzling images deep in the recesses of their texts. The best symbols grow naturally out of the meaning-making process that readers go through. In the context of a particular poem, symbols are usually objects that can stand for general ideas. And like metaphors and similes, they suggest different things to different readers. The whale in *Moby-Dick*, for example, can be read as a symbol for implacable evil or perhaps the mysteries of the universe. In "Singapore," the specific event of the speaker watching a woman washing ashtrays in a toilet could be symbolic of anything we find unpleasant or strange or alien. And the whole event, including her eventual understanding, could easily be an **allegory** or extended symbol for the necessity for all of us to transcend our cultural socialization to understand other cultures and other attitudes toward working.

SOUND

The English poet Alexander Pope hoped that poetry's **sound** could become "an echo to [its] sense," that what the ear hears would reinforce what the mind understands. To many people, **rhyme** is the most recognizable aspect of poetry. The matching of final vowel and consonant sounds can make a poem trite or interesting. The now-familiar rhyming of "moon" and "June" with "swoon" suggests a poet who will settle for a cliché rather than do the hard work of being fresh. Rhyme, of course, is pleasing to the ear and makes the poem easier to remember, but it also gives the poem psychological force. Most contemporary poets choose not to rhyme, preferring the flexibility and freedom of free verse. But sound is still a high priority.

One of the most famous and effective examples of how sound can "echo" its sense is found in Robert Frost's "Stopping by Woods on a Snowy Evening," especially in the last two stanzas:

> He gives his harness bells a shake
> To ask if there is some mistake.
> The only other sound's the sweep
> Of easy wind and downy flake.
> The woods are lovely, dark and deep,
> But I have promises to keep,
> And miles to go before I sleep,
> And miles to go before I sleep.

Skilled poets like Frost use **alliteration** to connect words near each other by repeating the consonant sound. A variation, **assonance**, repeats vowel sounds. Frost obviously and subtly employs these sound techniques to echo both theme and mood. The alliterative -*s*'s in "shake," "some," "sound's," and "sweep" also connect the meaning of these words, which are also reinforced by the -*s*'s in "gives," "his," "harness," "bells," "asks," "is," "mistake," "sound's," and "easy." And when alliteration is combined with the assonance of "sweep" and "easy," as well as "downy" and "sound's," visual, tactile, and aural images are joined to create a soothing, restful, and idyllic scene of beauty and peace. All of these choices prepare the reader for the -*e*'s of "keep" and "deep" and the -*s*'s of the repeated "woods," "promises," "miles," and "sleep." In this way, the serenity and retreat of the woods are verbally and thematically contrasted with the demands of life's duties, culminating in the deadly temptation to escape responsibility by entering the winter woods.

Notice how Mary Oliver uses alliteration in her first stanza to link "women's," "woman," "washing," and "white." Komunyakaa's first stanza, too, links "printers," "police," and "pulled" as well as "they," "thief's," "Terrestrial," "thick," and "thorns." What effect do these and other elements of sound have on the impact and meaning of the poems?

RHYTHM AND METER

Many poets in the early twentieth century chose to have their poems rhyme. Edwin Arlington Robinson's "The Mill" employs a typical **rhyme scheme** in which in each stanza the last words in lines 1 and 3 sound the same and the last words in lines 2 and 4 sound the same. We indicate such a pattern with letters—*abab.* The second half of the first stanza would then be *cdcd* and so forth.

Rhythm in poetry refers to the beat, a series of stresses, pauses, and accents. We are powerfully attuned to rhythm, whether it is our own heartbeat or the throb of the bass guitar in a rock band. When we pronounce a word, we give more **stress** (breath, emphasis) to some syllables than to others. When these stresses occur at a regular interval over, say, a line of poetry, we refer to it as **meter**. When we scan a line of poetry, we try to mark its stresses and pauses. We use ´ to indicate a stressed syllable and ˘ for an unstressed one. The basic measuring unit for these stressed and unstressed syllables in English is the **foot**. There are four usual feet: *iambic, trochaic, anapestic,* and *dactylic.* An **iamb** is an unstressed syllable followed by a stressed one, as in "thĕ woóds." Reversed we have a **trochee**, as in "tígĕr." An **anapest** contains three syllables that are unstressed, then unstressed, then stressed, as in "Whĕn thĕ blúe / wăve rŏlls nightlў / ŏn deép Galileé." The reverse, the **dactyl**, can be heard in the Mother Goose rhyme, "Pússў cát, / pússў cát / whére hăve yŏu / beén?" If you look at the first four lines of "The Mill" again, you can hear a regular beat of iambs:

> Thĕ míll / ĕr's wífe / hăd wáit / ĕd lóng,
> Thĕ téa / wăs cóld, / thĕ fíre / wăs deád;
> Ănd thére / mĭght yét / bĕ nóth / ĭng wróng
> Ĭn hów / hĕ wént / ănd whát / hĕ saíd:

Depending on the number of feet, we give lines various names. If a line contains one foot, it is a **monometer**; two, a **dimeter**; three, a **trimeter**; four, a **tetrameter**; five, a **pentameter**; six, a **hexameter**; seven, a **heptameter**; and eight, an **octometer**. So Robinson's lines are iambic tetrameter. Most lines in Shakespeare's sonnets are iambic pentameter, or five iambs.

Note the punctuation in Robinson's poem. When a line ends with a comma, we are meant to pause very briefly; when a line ends with a period (end stop), we pause a bit longer. But when there is no punctuation (line 7), we are meant to continue on until the end of the next line. This is known as

enjambment. These poetic techniques improve the sound and flow of the poem and enhance the thoughts and feelings that give poetry its memorable depth and meaningfulness.

THEME

Some readers are fond of extracting ideas from poems, claiming, for example, that the theme of "Blackberries" is the loss of innocence or that the theme of "The Mill" is the loss of identity. In a sense, these thematic observations are plausible enough, but they are limiting and misleading. "Blackberries" certainly seems to have something to do with the interruption of a certain view about physical labor, but the significance for each reader might be much more specific, having to do with the Garden of Eden; hierarchy in society; the arrogance of the rich; or sensitivity, cruelty, and dignity. "The Mill" could also be about gender relations, economic cruelty, or the responsibility of communities. Reducing a complex, ambiguous poem to a bald statement robs the poem of its evocative power, its mystery, and its art.

Some critics stress the response of readers; others care only for what the text itself says; still others are concerned with the social and cultural implications of the poem's meaning. Psychoanalytic readers may see poems as reflections of the psychological health or illness of the poet; source-hunting or intertextual readers want to find references and hints of other literary works hidden deep within the poem. Feminist readers may find sexism, Marxists may find economic injustice, and gay and lesbian readers may find heterosexual bias. Readers can and will find in texts a whole range of issues. Perhaps we find what we are looking for, or we find what matters most to us.

This does not mean that we should think of committed readers as biased or as distorting the text to fulfill their own agenda, although biased or distorted readings are not rare. In a literature course, readers are entitled to read poems according to their own interpretations as long as they follow the general convention of academic discourse. That is, it is possible to make a reasonable case that "Blackberries" is really about rejecting contemporary technology in favor of rural life. The reason that some themes sound more plausible than others is that these critics marshal their evidence from the text and their own experience. Usually the evidence that fits best wins: if you can persuade others that you have significant textual support for your theme and if you present a balanced and judicious persona, you can usually carry the day. Poems almost always have several reasonable themes. The critic's job is to argue for a theme that seems to make the most sense in relation to the support. Often the same evidence can be used to bolster different themes because themes are really just higher-level generalizations than the particulars found in the text. Critics use the concrete elements of a poem to make more general abstract statements. In "Blackberries," for example, the same textual support could be used to uphold a theme about the cruelty of children or the more general notion of an initiation in a class-conscious culture or the even more general idea of the inevitable loss of innocence.

Revised Draft of a Student Paper

Michaela Fiorucci
Mr. Hardy
English 102
25 April - - - -

Negotiating Boundaries

Although most college students value their privacy, they also want to create intimate relationships; it is often hard to reconcile these two impulses. Most middle-class students are lucky enough to have their own bedrooms, private enclaves against annoying sisters and brothers, intrusive mothers and fathers. But such boundaries are more than physical barriers; they are also a symbolic assertion of identity. They say, "I'm separate from you even within the closeness of our family." Such a commitment to physical privacy might be innocent enough, but it does contain dangerous seeds, especially when extended beyond the home to neighborhoods. When different ethnic groups want boundaries between them, it is no longer innocent. When the upper classes want to be separated from workers because they see each other as radically different, a dangerously undemocratic boundary has been erected. Boundaries clearly serve a protective function, but unneeded ones can also prevent us from helping and understanding each other. Writers like Edwin Arlington Robinson, Yusef Komunyakaa, and Mary Oliver understand that we must negotiate boundaries, building them when they increase privacy and self-worth and bridging them when human solidarity can be enhanced.

Creates context about boundaries, moving from the personal to neighborhoods and beyond.

Announces her focus on need to negotiate.

It would be reductive to say that boundaries are either good or bad, since their value depends so much on context. Robinson's "The Mill" is a good example of the dangerous consequences of a failure to cross a boundary that should not exist and then a failure to establish a boundary where one should exist. The poem narrates the sad story of a farm couple who commit suicide — the husband because he feels useless, the wife because she can't imagine life without her husband. A contemporary reader is struck by the lack of communication between the couple. He must have been depressed for a long time, but it seems they never discussed his feelings. Keeping such an emotional boundary between husband and wife was probably typical of the way men and women dealt with each other one hundred years ago. Apparently it was a constructed barrier that few could cross. He simply could not bare his

Begins first concrete supporting example.

Example of harmful tradition boundary.

heart by saying, "I feel terrible that I am going to lose my job." And his wife accepts his reticence, even though he might have been having second thoughts as he "lingered at the door" (line 7). Clearly this is a boundary that should have been breached. The time for their solidarity was before he kills himself, not after.

After several readings it is clear that the boundary that should have been established wasn't. The miller is the victim of the demeaning idea that a person's worth is synonymous with his or her occupation. When his job disappears, so must he. Although Robinson's tone is flat, we sense his frustration with the inevitability of this grim tragedy, one that is compounded by the equally dehumanizing idea that a wife cannot exist without her husband. When the miller's wife decides to "leave no mark" (20) by jumping into the pond, she is admitting that she is useless outside her matrimonial role. Both identify with a role that should be only one aspect of a complex human life. The final barrier she crosses, from life to death, is symbolically represented in the poem as a feminine domestic gesture: she doesn't want to leave a mess. She continues as a housewife even in death. The boundaries between a person and occupation should be clear, but the arbitrary boundaries between husbands and wives should continue to be eradicated.

Concrete reference to poems strengthens argument.

Concludes paragraph with example of a boundary needing negotiating.

When the ten-year-old narrator in "Blackberries" claims that he is "Limboed between worlds" (18), he means the rural paradise of "Terrestrial sweetness" (4) and "rich blackness" (15) he temporarily lives in versus the commercial urban world that seems to make him anxious. He has constructed a boundary between the ancient task of picking berries and the modern technology of automobiles, between a closeness with nature and the artificial air-conditioning of the car. Although the narrator enjoys being one with nature, he seems to be cutting himself off from the realities of the world. He seems to reject "old lime-covered / History" (7–8) in favor of "mythology" (11), which seems to suggest a conscious rejection of the present. But this is a boundary that cannot stand. He needs the outside world to survive financially, and so when the car approaches, it is the modern world and all its complexity that draws near. When he looks into the car, he sees "Smirking" (23) children; he sees class prejudice, hierarchy, and economic reality. The smirkers of the world are in charge. It is this realization that dissolves the protective boundary around his Garden of Eden; consequently, he feels physical pain, but it is really the pain of initiation into reality that he feels. He must now cross a boundary he tried to delay.

Second concrete example of problematic boundary.

Notes consequences of not negotiating.

Although we can sympathize with the young narrator, like the couple in "The Mill," he would have been better off not making his boundary so extreme.

Connection to previous poem increases essay's unity.

The narrator in Mary Oliver's "Singapore" also imagines that she sees a significant boundary, here between herself as a middle-class traveler and a cleaning woman laboring over a toilet. It is a separation we might all make, given our socialization in America to consider this kind of physical labor as degrading. College-educated people have a tendency to see themselves as distinct from the working class. For many, a woman washing an ashtray in a toilet bowl is beyond the pale, a clear indication that the woman is Other. But Oliver does not simply give into her cultural conditioning; she contests the boundary, asserting that a "Disgust argued in my stomach"(6). Since part of our democratic socialization is also to be tolerant and open-minded, Oliver knows that she shouldn't stereotype workers. And since she is also a writer with ideas about how a poem should "always have birds in it" (8), she looks hard at the cleaning woman, finally seeing in her face, in her hair, and in the way she works, slowly "like a river" (25), the positive aspects of the woman that most of us would probably miss.

Third concrete example of boundaries.

Explicit example of negotiating a boundary.

Oliver does not simply accept the boundaries that her culture constructs. Instead, she negotiates internally, eventually seeing that a "light . . . can shine out of a life" (35) even where we would not expect it. In the woman's careful folding and unfolding of her blue work cloth and in her smile, Oliver sees a beauty that helps her eclipse a social boundary, ending with a life-affirming vision "filled with trees, and birds" (38). Such an insight does not come easily to us because we usually accept our given cultural boundaries. The miller and his wife are tragically unequipped to bridge the divide between them. Likewise, the boy in "Blackberries" is unable to sustain his fantasy boundaries. Oliver's traveler, however, struggles to negotiate boundaries and is thereby able to increase human solidarity even across class structures and cultures.

Notes benefits of breaching a boundary.

Concludes by uniting all 3 poems in support of claim.

Works Cited

Komunyakaa, Yusef. "Blackberries." Schilb and Clifford, pp. 153–54.

Oliver, Mary. "Singapore." Schilb and Clifford, pp. 152–53.

Robinson, Edwin Arlington. "The Mill." Schilb and Clifford, p. 154.

Schilb, John, and John Clifford, editors. *Making Literature Matter: An Anthology for Readers and Writers*. 7th ed., Bedford/St. Martin's, 2018.

SUMMING UP: WRITING ABOUT POEMS

- **The elements of poetry include *speaker* and *tone*, *diction* and *syntax*, *figures of speech*, *sound*, *rhythm* and *meter*, and *theme*.**
- **Identify the speaker and tone.** The voice we hear in a poem is often a *persona* — a "mask" that could be the poet's real voice or a complete fiction. Paying attention to the speaker's tone — his or her attitude — illuminates a poem's meaning. (p. 158)
- **Be aware of the complexities of *diction* and *syntax*.** In poetry, the connotations or emotional and personal associations of the diction — word choice — often suggest more than the literal meaning of the words. Poetry is more compressed and indirect than prose, so meaning is often suggested through connotation, metaphor, and imagery and is seldom finite. The order of the words — syntax — can be varied and experimented with to amplify and complicate meaning. (pp. 158–59)
- **Major figures of speech include *metaphor* and *symbols*.** A metaphor is a dramatic direct comparison — "Love is a rose," "Faith is a sea" — that poets use to help readers see and think differently and creatively. Similes ("My love is like a red, red rose") are more indirect, but no less suggestive. Symbols suggest general ideas. They reinforce or extend the poem's possible meanings and rarely point in one direction. (pp. 159–61)
- ***Sound*, *rhythm*, and *meter* work together to give a poem psychological force.** How a poem sounds is often overlooked, perhaps because modern poems often do not rhyme. *Alliteration*, for example, connects words and enhances meaning. As in music, rhythm adds to the meaning of poetry, encircling the thoughts and feeling that give poetry depth and meaning. (pp. 161–63)
- **Don't expect a poem's theme to be straightforward or clear-cut.** Strong poems are rich, complex, and often ambiguous. Narrow theme statements such as "'Blackberries' is about the loss of innocence" are often misleading and limiting. Although this statement is plausible enough, a number of other ideas are certainly possible. Be wary of reducing a poem's theme to a bold statement that robs the poem of its subtlety and evocative power. (p. 163)
- **Arguing successfully that your interpretation is worth considering depends largely on the validity of your evidence.** Poems almost always have several reasonable themes. We can argue strongly for a theme, however, if we can support our claim. The critic who presents the best evidence for a particular theme in a balanced and judicious way is often the most persuasive. (p. 163)

Writing about Plays

Most plays incorporate elements also found in short fiction, such as plot, characterization, dialogue, setting, and theme. But, in contrast to short fiction and other literary genres, plays are typically enacted live, in front of an audience. Theater professionals distinguish between the written *script* of a play and its actual *performances*. When you write about a play, you may wind up saying little or nothing about performances of it. When you first read and analyze a play, however, try to imagine ways of staging it. You might even research past productions of the play, noting how scenery, costumes, and lighting—as well as particular actors—were used.

Because a play is usually meant to be staged, its readers are rarely its only interpreters. Audiences at productions of the play also ponder its meanings. So, too, do members of the casts; no doubt you have heard of actors "interpreting" their parts. When a play is put on, even members of the backstage team are involved in interpreting it. The technical designers' choices of sets, costumes, and lighting reflect their ideas about the play, while the director works with cast and crew to implement a particular vision of it. No matter what the author of the script intended, theater is a collaborative art: all of the key figures involved in a play's production are *active* interpreters of the play, in that they influence the audience's understanding and experience of it. Therefore, you can develop good ideas when you read a play if you imagine yourself directing a production of it. More specifically, think what you would say to the actors as you guide them through their parts. As you engage in this thought experiment, you will see that you have options, for even directors keen on staying faithful to the script know it can be staged in any number of ways. Perhaps your course will give you and other students the chance to perform a scene together; if so, you will be deciding what interpretation of the scene to set forth.

To help you understand how to write about plays, we will refer often to the one-act play that follows. *The Stronger* was first performed in 1889. Its Swedish author, August Strindberg (1849–1912), is widely acknowledged as a founder of modern drama. Throughout his career, Strindberg experimented with a variety of theatrical styles. With this particular play, an encounter between two actresses, he dared to have one of the women speak and the other remain silent.

AUGUST STRINDBERG

The Stronger

Translated by Edith and Warner Oland

CHARACTERS

MRS. X, *an actress, married*
MISS Y, *an actress, unmarried*
A WAITRESS

SCENE: *The corner of a ladies' café. Two little iron tables, a red velvet sofa, several chairs. Enter Mrs. X, dressed in winter clothes, carrying a Japanese basket on her arm.*

Miss Y sits with a half-empty beer bottle before her, reading an illustrated paper, which she changes later for another.

MRS. X: Good afternoon, Amelie. You're sitting here alone on Christmas eve like a poor bachelor!

Miss Y looks up, nods, and resumes her reading.

MRS. X: Do you know it really hurts me to see you like this, alone, in a café, and on Christmas eve, too. It makes me feel as I did one time when I saw a bridal party in a Paris restaurant, and the bride sat reading a comic paper, while the groom played billiards with the witnesses. Huh, thought I, with such a beginning, what will follow, and what will be the end? He played billiards on his wedding eve! *(Miss Y starts to speak.)* And she read a comic paper, you mean? Well, they are not altogether the same thing.

A waitress enters, places a cup of chocolate before Mrs. X, and goes out.

MRS. X: You know what, Amelie! I believe you would have done better to have kept him! Do you remember, I was the first to say "Forgive him"? Do you remember that? You would be married now and have a home. Remember that Christmas when you went out to visit your fiancé's parents in the country? How you gloried in the happiness of home life and really longed to quit the theater forever? Yes, Amelie dear, home is the best of all, the theater next and children—well, you don't understand that.

Miss Y looks up scornfully.

Mrs. X sips a few spoonfuls out of the cup, then opens her basket and shows Christmas presents.

MRS. X: Now you shall see what I bought for my piggywigs. *(Takes up a doll.)* Look at this! This is for Lisa, ha! Do you see how she can roll her eyes and turn her head, eh? And here is Maja's popgun. *(Loads it and shoots at Miss Y.)*

Miss Y makes a startled gesture.

MRS. X: Did I frighten you? Do you think I would like to shoot you, eh? On my soul, if I don't think you did! If you wanted to shoot *me* it wouldn't be so surprising, because I stood in your way—and I know you can never forget that—although I was absolutely innocent. You still believe I intrigued and got you out of the Stora theater, but I didn't. I didn't do that, although you think so. Well, it doesn't make any difference what I say to you. You still believe I did it. *(Takes up a pair of embroidered slippers.)* And these are for my better half. I embroidered them myself—I can't bear tulips, but he wants tulips on everything.

Miss Y looks up ironically and curiously.

MRS. X *(putting a hand in each slipper)*: What little feet Bob has! What? And you should see what a splendid stride he has! You've never seen him in slippers!

(Miss Y laughs aloud.) Look! *(She makes the slippers walk on the table. Miss Y laughs loudly.)* And when he is grumpy he stamps like this with his foot. "What! damn those servants who can never learn to make coffee. Oh, now those creatures haven't trimmed the lamp wick properly!" And then there are draughts on the floor and his feet are cold. "Ugh, how cold it is; the stupid idiots can never keep the fire going." *(She rubs the slippers together, one sole over the other.)*

Miss Y shrieks with laughter.

MRS. X: And then he comes home and has to hunt for his slippers which Marie has stuck under the chiffonier—oh, but it's sinful to sit here and make fun of one's husband this way when he is kind and a good little man. You ought to have had such a husband, Amelie. What are you laughing at? What? What? And you see he's true to me. Yes, I'm sure of that, because he told me himself—what are you laughing at?—that when I was touring in Norway that that brazen Frédérique came and wanted to seduce him! Can you fancy anything so infamous? *(Pause.)* I'd have torn her eyes out if she had come to see him when I was at home. *(Pause.)* It was lucky that Bob told me about it himself and that it didn't reach me through gossip. *(Pause.)* But would you believe it, Frédérique wasn't the only one! I don't know why, but the women are crazy about my husband. They must think he has influence about getting them theatrical engagements, because he is connected with the government. Perhaps you were after him yourself. I didn't use to trust you any too much. But now I know he never bothered his head about you, and you always seemed to have a grudge against him someway.

Pause. They look at each other in a puzzled way.

Come and see us this evening, Amelie, and show us that you're not put out with us,—not put out with me at any rate. I don't know, but I think it would be uncomfortable to have you for an enemy. Perhaps it's because I stood in your way or—I really—don't know why—in particular.

Pause. Miss Y stares at Mrs. X curiously.

MRS. X *(thoughtfully)*: Our acquaintance has been so queer. When I saw you for the first time I was afraid of you, so afraid that I didn't dare let you out of my sight; no matter when or where, I always found myself near you—I didn't dare have you for an enemy, so I became your friend. But there was always discord when you came to our house, because I saw that my husband couldn't endure you, and the whole thing seemed as awry to me as an ill-fitting gown—and I did all I could to make him friendly toward you, but with no success until you became engaged. Then came a violent friendship between you, so that it looked all at once as though you both dared show your real feelings only when you were secure—and then—how was it later? I didn't get jealous—strange to say! And I remember at the christening, when you acted as godmother, I made him kiss you—he did so, and you became so confused—as it were; I didn't notice it then—didn't think about it later, either—have never thought about it until—now! *(Rises suddenly.)*

Why are you silent? You haven't said a word this whole time, but you have let me go on talking! You have sat there, and your eyes have reeled out of me all these thoughts which lay like raw silk in its cocoon—thoughts—suspicious thoughts, perhaps. Let me see—why did you break your engagement? Why do you never come to our house any more? Why won't you come to see us tonight?

Miss Y appears as if about to speak.

MRS. X: Hush, you needn't speak—I understand it all! It was because—and because—and because! Yes, yes! Now all the accounts balance. That's it. Fie, I won't sit at the same table with you. *(Moves her things to another table.)* That's the reason I had to embroider tulips—which I hate—on his slippers, because you are fond of tulips; that's why *(Throws slippers on the floor.)* we go to Lake Mälarn in the summer, because you don't like salt water; that's why my boy is named Eskil—because it's your father's name; that's why I wear your colors, read your authors, eat your favorite dishes, drink your drinks—chocolate, for instance; that's why—oh—my God—it's terrible, when I think about it; it's terrible. Everything, everything came from you to me, even your passions. Your soul crept into mine, like a worm into an apple, ate and ate, bored and bored, until nothing was left but the rind and a little black dust within. I wanted to get away from you, but I couldn't; you lay like a snake and charmed me with your black eyes; I felt that when I lifted my wings they only dragged me down; I lay in the water with bound feet, and the stronger I strove to keep up the deeper I worked myself down, down, until I sank to the bottom, where you lay like a giant crab to clutch me in your claws—and there I am lying now.

I hate you, hate you, hate you! And you only sit there silent—silent and indifferent; indifferent whether it's new moon or waning moon, Christmas or New Year's, whether others are happy or unhappy; without power to hate or to love; as quiet as a stork by a rat hole—you couldn't scent your prey and capture it, but you could lie in wait for it! You sit here in your corner of the café—did you know it's called "The Rat Trap" for you?—and read the papers to see if misfortune hasn't befallen someone, to see if someone hasn't been given notice at the theater, perhaps; you sit here and calculate about your next victim and reckon on your chances of recompense like a pilot in a shipwreck. Poor Amelie, I pity you, nevertheless, because I know you are unhappy, unhappy like one who has been wounded, and angry because you are wounded. I can't be angry with you, no matter how much I want to be—because you come out the weaker one. Yes, all that with Bob doesn't trouble me. What is that to me, after all? And what difference does it make whether I learned to drink chocolate from you or someone else. *(Sips a spoonful from her cup.)*

Besides, chocolate is very healthful. And if you taught me how to dress—*tant mieux!*°—that has only made me more attractive to my husband; so you lost

tant mieux: So much the better (French).

and I won there. Well, judging by certain signs, I believe you have already lost him; and you certainly intended that I should leave him—do as you did with your fiancé and regret as you now regret; but, you see, I don't do that—we mustn't be too exacting. And why should I take only what no one else wants?

Perhaps, take it all in all, I am at this moment the stronger one. You received nothing from me, but you gave me much. And now I seem like a thief since you have awakened and find I possess what is your loss. How could it be otherwise when everything is worthless and sterile in your hands? You can never keep a man's love with your tulips and your passions—but I can keep it. You can't learn how to live from your authors, as I have learned. You have no little Eskil to cherish, even if your father's name was Eskil. And why are you always silent, silent, silent? I thought that was strength, but perhaps it is because you have nothing to say! Because you never think about anything! *(Rises and picks up slippers.)*

Now I'm going home—and take the tulips with me—*your* tulips! You are unable to learn from another; you can't bend—therefore, you broke like a dry stalk. But I won't break! Thank you, Amelie, for all your good lessons. Thanks for teaching my husband how to love. Now I'm going home to love him. *(Goes.)* *[1889]*

A Student's Personal Response to the Play

Trish Carlisle was enrolled in a class that read and discussed Strindberg's *The Stronger*. Below is some freewriting that Trish did about the play.

Near the end of Strindberg's play, Mrs. X says that "I am at this moment the stronger one." But is she? I guess that depends on what Strindberg meant by "the stronger" when he gave his play that title. As I was reading, I started to think that the stronger woman is actually the silent one, Miss Y, because she seems to have more self-control than Mrs. X does. I mean, Miss Y doesn't apparently feel that she has to make long, loud speeches in defense of her way of life. I can even believe that with her silence she is manipulating Mrs. X into getting fairly hysterical. Also, I guess we're to think that Amelie has managed to lure away Mrs. X's husband, at least for a while. Furthermore, we don't have to believe Mrs. X when at the end she claims that she has triumphed over Miss Y. Maybe people who have really succeeded in life don't need to proclaim that they have, as Mrs. X does.

Nevertheless, I can see why some students in this class feel that Mrs. X is in fact the stronger. If she has her husband back and wants her husband back, and if Miss Y is really without companionship at the end and has even lost her job at the theater, then probably Mrs. X is entitled to crow. Was Strindberg being deliberately unclear? Did he want

> his audience to make up their own minds about who is stronger? Maybe neither of these women is strong, because each of them seems dependent on a man, and Mrs. X's husband may not even be such a great person in the first place. If I were Mrs. X, maybe I wouldn't even take him back. I guess someone could say that it's Mrs. X's husband who is the stronger, since he has managed to make the two women fight over him while he enjoys his creature comforts. Anyway, Strindberg makes us guess what he is really like. Because he's offstage, he's just as silent as Miss Y is, although his wife imitates his voice at one point.
>
> In a way, I feel that this play is too short. I want it to go on longer so that I can be sure how to analyze the two women and the man. But I realize that one of the reasons the play is dramatic is that it's brief. I might not be interested in it if it didn't leave me hanging. And it's also theatrical because Miss Y is silent even as Mrs. X lashes out at her. I wonder what the play would be like if we could hear Miss Y's thoughts in a sort of voice-over, like we find in some movies. It's interesting to me that the play is *about* actresses. I wonder if these characters are still "performing" with each other even if they're not acting in a theater at the moment.

Trish's freewriting would eventually help her develop ideas for a paper in which she had to analyze Strindberg's play. Compare your responses to the play with hers. Did the same issues come up for you? How do you feel about the women characters? What, if anything, do you wish the playwright had made clearer? What would you advise Trish to think about as she moved from freewriting to drafting a paper?

The Elements of Drama

You strengthen your ability to write about plays if you grow familiar with typical elements of drama. These elements include plot and structure, characterization, stage directions and setting, imagery, language, and theme.

PLOT AND STRUCTURE

Most plays, like most short stories, have a **plot**. When you read them, you find yourself following a narrative, a sequence of interrelated events. Even plays as short as *The Stronger* feature a plot, though the onstage action occurs in just one place and takes just a little while. As with short fiction, the reader of a play is often anxious to know how the events will turn out. The reader may especially feel this way when the play contains a mystery that characters are trying to solve. In Strindberg's play, for example, Mrs. X is apparently bent on discovering what relation her husband has had with her friend.

In summarizing the play, you might choose to depict the plot as a detective story. Then again, you might prefer to emphasize the characters' emotional conflicts as you describe how the play proceeds. In fact, there are various ways you can describe Strindberg's plot; just bear in mind that your account should be grounded in actual details of the text. However you summarize a play will reflect your sense of which characters are central to it. Is the offstage husband Bob in *The Stronger* as important as the two women onstage? More important than they are? Less important? Your summary will also reflect your sense of which characters have power. Do you think the two women in Strindberg's drama equally influence that play's events? In addition, your summary ought to acknowledge the human motives that drive the play's action. Why do you think Mrs. X feels compelled to confront Miss Y?

Summarizing the plot of a play can mean arranging its events chronologically. Yet bear in mind that some of the play's important events may have occurred in the characters' pasts. In many plays, actually, characters learn things about the past that they did not know and must now try to accept. For example, important events mentioned in *The Stronger* take place before the play begins. By the time the curtain rises, Miss Y's close relationship with Bob is well in the past. A typical summary would begin with the events on stage, but you could also summarize Strindberg's play as a chronicle of the relationship that precedes the scene in the café.

In discussing the structure of short stories, we noted that many of them follow Alice Adams's formula *ABDCE* (Action, Background, Development, Climax, and Ending). This scheme, however, does not fit many plays. In a sense, the average play is entirely Action, for its performers are constantly engaged in physical movement of various sorts. Furthermore, as we have been suggesting, information about Background can surface quite often as the play's characters talk. Yet the terms Development, Climax, and Ending do seem appropriate for many plays. Certainly the plot of *The Stronger* develops, as Mrs. X becomes increasingly hostile to Miss Y. Certainly the play can be said to reach a Climax, a moment of great significance and intensity, when Mrs. X moves to another table and declares her hatred for Miss Y. The term *Ending* can also apply to this play, although readers may disagree about exactly when its Climax turns into its Ending. Certainly Mrs. X is in a different state of mind at the play's last moment; at that point, she stops haranguing Miss Y and leaves, declaring that she will save her own marriage.

Like short stories, plays often use repetition as an organizational device. The characters in a play may repeat certain words; Mrs. X's variations on "silence" multiply as Miss Y retreats from interacting with her. Also, a play may show repeated actions, such as Mrs. X's interruptions of Miss Y. In addition, a play may suggest that the onstage situation echoes previous events, as when Mrs. X alludes to confrontations between her husband and Miss Y in the past.

The Stronger is a short, one-act play. But many other plays are longer and divided conspicuously into subsections. The ancient Greek drama *Antigone* alternates choral sections with scenes involving only the title character and her uncle Creon. All of Shakespeare's plays, and most modern ones, are divided into acts, which are often further divided into scenes. Even within a one-act play, however, you can detect various stages in the action. This task is easier when the one-act play is fairly lengthy, but even a very short play like *The Stronger* can be broken down into stages, although you will have to decide exactly what those stages are.

CHARACTERS

Many short stories have a narrator who reveals the characters' inner thoughts. Most plays, however, have no narrator at all. To figure out what the characters think, you must study what they *say* and how they *move*, if the author has indeed provided stage directions. To be sure, some characters say a great deal, leaving you with several clues to their psyche. If you are familiar with Shakespeare's lengthy play *Hamlet*, you may recall that it contains thousands of lines. Moreover, when the title character is alone on stage making long speeches to the audience, he seems to be baring his very soul. Yet despite such moments, Hamlet's mental state remains far from clear; scholars continue to debate his sanity. Thus, as a reader of *Hamlet* and other plays, you have much room for interpretation. Often you will have to decide whether to accept the judgments that characters express about one another. For example, how fair and accurate does Strindberg's Mrs. X seem to you as she berates Miss Y?

As with short stories, a good step toward analyzing a play's characters is to consider what each desires. The drama or comedy of many plays arises when the desires of one character conflict with those of another. Strindberg's Mrs. X feels that Miss Y has been a threat to her marriage, and while we cannot be sure of Miss Y's thoughts, evidently she is determined not to answer Mrs. X's charges. At the end of the play, the women's conflict seems to endure, even though Mrs. X proclaims victory. Many other plays end with characters managing to resolve conflict because one or more of them experiences a change of heart. Whatever the play you are studying, consider whether any of its characters change. Is any character's thinking transformed? If so, whose?

The main character of a play is often referred to as its **protagonist**, and a character who notably opposes this person is often referred to as the **antagonist**. As you might guess without even reading Shakespeare's play, Prince Hamlet is the protagonist of *Hamlet*; his uncle Claudius, who succeeded Hamlet's father to the throne of Denmark, serves as his antagonist. To be sure, applying these terms may be tricky or impossible in some instances. The two women in *The Stronger* oppose each other, but each can be called the protagonist and each can be called the antagonist. Can you think of other plays you have read in which the protagonist and antagonist are not readily identifiable?

In discussing the elements of short fiction, we referred to point of view, the perspective from which a story is told. Since very few plays are narrated, the term *point of view* fits this genre less well. While it is possible to claim that much of Shakespeare's *Hamlet* reflects the title character's point of view, he is offstage for stretches, and the audience may focus on other characters even when he appears. Also, do not overlook the possible significance of characters who are not physically present. A character may be important even when he or she never appears onstage. In *The Stronger*, the two women's conflict is partly about Mrs. X's unseen husband.

In most plays, characters' lives are influenced by their social standing, which in turn is influenced by particular traits of theirs. These may include their gender, their social class, their race, their ethnic background, their nationality, their sexual orientation, and the kind of work they do. Obviously *The Stronger* deals with gender relationships. Mrs. X defines herself in gendered terms: wife, mother, and insecure lover in competition with a rival for her husband's affections. But there are elements of social class too—of the circumstances of upper-middle-class Swedish women in Stockholm in the late nineteenth century—that may require research.

STAGE DIRECTIONS AND SETTING

When analyzing a script, pay attention to the staging directions it gives, and try to imagine additional ways that the actors might move around. Through a slight physical movement, performers can indicate important developments in their characters' thoughts. When Mrs. X fires a popgun at Miss Y, audience members may flinch in surprised sympathy with Miss Y's "startled gesture." But they may be just as startled by Miss Y's mirthful response, culminating in a "shriek of laughter," when Mrs. X uses her husband's slippers to mime and mock him. Is Miss Y's laughter hysterical, or knowing, or something else? How does it set up the "puzzled," curious looks Mrs. X and Miss Y exchange moments later?

You can get a better sense of how a play might be staged if you research its actual production history. Granted, finding out about its previous stagings may be difficult. But at the very least, you can discover some of the theatrical conventions that must have shaped presentations of the play, even one that is centuries old. Consider Sophocles' classical tragedy *Antigone* and Shakespeare's *Hamlet*, canonical plays that you may have read or seen performed in films or theater. While classical scholars would like to learn more about early performances of *Antigone*, they already know that it and other ancient Greek plays were staged in open-air arenas. They know, too, that *Antigone*'s Chorus turned in unison at particular moments, and that the whole cast wore large masks. Although the premiere of *Hamlet* was not videotaped, Shakespeare scholars are sure that, like other productions in Renaissance England, it made spare use of scenery and featured an all-male cast. By contrast, *The Stronger* is anchored in the nineteenth-century realist tradition that values in literary works an accurate and plausible presentation of everyday life and events.

Some plays can be staged in any number of styles and still work well. Shakespeare wrote *Hamlet* back in Renaissance England, but quite a few successful productions of it have been set in later times, such as late-nineteenth-century England. Even modern plays that seem to call for realist productions can be staged in a variety of ways. Note Strindberg's description of the setting for *The Stronger*: "The corner of a ladies' café. Two little iron tables, a red velvet sofa, several chairs." Many productions of this play have remained within the conventions of realism, striving to make the audience believe that it is seeing a late-nineteenth-century Stockholm café. But a production of *The Stronger* may present the audience with only a few pieces of furniture that barely evoke the café. Furthermore, the production might have Mrs. X's husband physically hover in the background, as if he were a ghost haunting both women's minds. You may feel that such a production would horribly distort Strindberg's drama; a boldly experimental staging of a play can indeed become a virtual rewriting of it. Nevertheless, remember that productions of a play may be more diverse in style than the script would indicate.

Remember, too, that a particular theater's architecture may affect a production team's decisions. Realism's illusion of the "fourth wall" works best on a proscenium stage, which is the kind probably most familiar to you. In brief, a proscenium is a boxlike space where the actors perform in front of the entire audience. In a proscenium production of *The Stronger*, the ladies' café can be depicted in great detail. The performing spaces at some theaters, however, are "in the round": that is, the audience completely encircles the stage. What would have to be done with the café then? List some items in the café that an "in the round" staging could accommodate.

In referring to possible ways of staging a play, we have inevitably been referring as well to its setting. A play may not be all that precise in describing its setting; Strindberg provides set designers with few guidelines for creating his Stockholm café. More significant, perhaps, than the place of the action is its *timing*: Mrs. X finds Miss Y sitting alone on Christmas eve. Yet a play may stress to its audience that its characters are located in particular places, at particular moments in their personal histories or at a particular moment in *world* history. For example, *The Stronger* calls attention to the fact that it is set in a ladies' café, a female space. Are there gendered public arenas today where Mrs. X might play out her conflict with Miss Y? Could the play be set in a women's locker room? What would happen if the setting were not for women only?

You can learn much about a play's characters by studying how they accommodate themselves—or fail to accommodate themselves—to their settings. When Strindberg's Mrs. X can no longer bear sitting next to Miss Y, her shift to another table dramatically signifies her feelings. Of course, much of the drama in Strindberg's play occurs because there is a *single* setting, in which at least one character feels confined. Other plays employ a wider variety of settings to dramatize their characters' lives.

IMAGERY

When plays use images to convey meaning, sometimes they do so through dialogue. At the beginning of *The Stronger*, for instance, Mrs. X recalls "a bridal party in a Paris restaurant," where "the bride sat reading a comic paper, while the groom played billiards with the witnesses." The play proceeds to become very much about divisions between husband and wife; moreover, the two women engage in a tense "game" that seems analogous to billiards. But just as often, a play's meaningful images are physically presented in the staging: through gestures, costumes, lighting, and props. For instance, consider the slippers embroidered with tulips that Mrs. X flourishes early in the play. The slippers and the tulips gain meaning as the play progresses. The audience may be ever more inclined to see them as *symbolic*. *Symbol* is the term traditionally used for an image that represents some concept or concepts.

Keep in mind that *you* may interpret an image differently than the characters within the play do. When Strindberg's Mrs. X refers to billiards, she may not think at all that she will be playing an analogous game with Miss Y. You, however, may make this connection, especially as the play proceeds.

LANGUAGE

As we have been suggesting, a play's meaning and impact may be apparent only when the play is physically staged. Nevertheless, you can learn much from studying the language in its script. For example, the play's very title may be important. At the climax of Strindberg's play, Mrs. X even refers to herself as "the stronger." Obviously the playwright is encouraging audiences to think about the title's implications. Yet not always will the meaning of a play's title be immediately clear. In her freewriting, Trish wonders how to define "stronger" and which of Strindberg's characters fit the term. Even if you think the title of a play is easily explainable, pause to see whether that title can actually lead to an issue of definition. In other words, don't take the title for granted.

In most plays, language is a matter of dialogue. The audience tries to figure out the play by focusing on how the characters address one another. But remember that the pauses or silences within a play may be just as important as its dialogue. In fact, a director may *add* moments of silence that the script does not explicitly demand. In many plays, however, the author does specify moments when one or more characters significantly fail to speak. *The Stronger* is a prominent example: Miss Y is notably silent throughout the play, and as a reader you probably find yourself wondering why she is. Ironically, the play's *absence* of true dialogue serves to remind us that plays usually *depend* on dialogue.

Consider this moment in *The Stronger* when Miss Y fails to speak:

> MRS. X: . . . Why are you silent? You haven't said a word this whole time, but you have let me go on talking! You have sat there, and your eyes have reeled out of me all these thoughts which lay like raw silk in its cocoon—thoughts—suspicious thoughts, perhaps. Let me see—why did you break your engagement? Why do you never come to our house any more? Why won't you come to see us tonight?
>
> *Miss Y appears as if about to speak.*
>
> MRS. X: Hush, you needn't speak—I understand it all! . . .

An interesting discussion might result from imagining what Miss Y might have said had she not been cut off. It's also worth reflecting on what Strindberg conceivably gains by *not* having Miss Y speak at that moment.

THEME

We have already discussed *theme* in short fiction (pp. 143–46), and here we will build on some points from our earlier discussion. Again, a *theme* is the main claim—an assertion, a proposition, or a statement—that a work seems to make.

As with other literary genres, try to state a play's theme as a midlevel generalization. If expressed in very broad terms, it will seem to fit many other works besides the one you have read; if narrowly tied to the play's characters and their particular situation, it will seem irrelevant to most other people's lives. With *The Stronger*, an example of a very broad theme would be "Women should not fight over a man." At the opposite extreme, a too-narrow theme would be "Women should behave well toward each other on Christmas eve, even if one of them has slept with the other's husband." If you are formulating Strindberg's theme, you might *start* with the broad generalization we have cited and then try to narrow it to a midlevel one. You might even think of ways that Strindberg's play *complicates* that broad generalization. What might, in fact, be a good midlevel generalization in Strindberg's case?

As we have noted, the very title of *The Stronger* seems significant. Indeed, a play's theme may be related to its title or to some other parts of the text. Nevertheless, be wary of couching the theme in terms drawn solely from the title or from some passage within the text. The play's theme may not be reducible to these words alone. Remember that the title of Strindberg's play can give rise to issues of definition in the first place.

You can state a play's theme as an observation or as a recommendation. With Strindberg's play, an observation-type theme would be "Marriage and career may disrupt relations between women." A recommendation-type theme would be either the broad or narrow generalization that we cited above. Neither way of stating the theme is automatically preferable, but remain aware of the different tones and effects they may carry. Consider, too, the possibility of stating the theme as a problem, as in this example: "We may be inclined to defend our marriages when they seem threatened, but in our defense we may cling to illusions that can easily shatter." Furthermore, consider the possibility of referring to *a* theme of the play rather than *the* theme, thereby acknowledging the possibility that the play is making several important claims.

When you write about a play, certainly you will refer to the text of it, its **script**. But probably the play was meant to be staged, and most likely it has been. Thus, you might refer to actual productions of it and to ways it can be performed. Remember, though, that different productions of the play may stress different meanings and create different effects. In your paper, you might discuss how much room for interpretation the script allows those who would stage it. For any paper you write about the play, look beyond the characters' dialogue and study whatever stage directions the script gives.

Undoubtedly your paper will have to offer some plot summary, even if your audience has already read the play. After all, certain details of the plot will be important support for your points. But, as with papers about short fiction, keep the amount of plot summary small, mentioning only events in the play that are crucial to your overall argument. Your reader should feel that you are analyzing the play rather than just recounting it.

To understand more what analysis of a play involves, let's return to Trish Carlisle, the student whose freewriting you read earlier. Trish was assigned to write a 600-word paper about Strindberg's *The Stronger*. She was asked to imagine herself writing to a particular audience: performers rehearsing a production of the play she chose. More specifically, she was to identify and address some question that these performers might have, an issue that might be bothering them as they prepared to put on the play. Trish knew that, besides presenting an issue, her paper would have to make a main claim and support it with evidence. Moreover, the paper might have to spell out some of the warrants or assumptions behind her evidence.

Because finding an issue was such an important part of the assignment, Trish decided to review her freewriting about Strindberg's play, noting questions she had raised there about it. Trish saw that the chief issue posed for her by *The Stronger* was "Which character is the stronger?" Nevertheless, Trish recognized that the issue "Which character is the stronger?" still left her with various decisions to make. For one thing, she had to decide what kind of an issue she would call it. Trish saw that it could be considered an issue of fact, an issue of evaluation, or an issue of definition. Although it could fit into all of these categories, Trish knew that the category she chose would influence the direction of her paper. Eventually she decided to treat "Which character is the stronger?" as primarily an issue of definition, because she figured that, no matter what, she would be devoting much of her paper to defining *stronger* as a term.

Of course, there are many different senses in which someone may be "stronger" than someone else. Your best friend may be a stronger tennis player than you, in the sense that he or she always beats you at that game. But you may be a stronger student than your friend, in the sense that you get better grades in school. In the case of Strindberg's play, Trish came to see that a paper focused on which character is *morally* stronger would differ from one focused on who is *emotionally* stronger, and these papers would differ in turn from one focused on which character is *politically* stronger, more able to impose his or her will. These reflections led Trish to revise her issue somewhat. She decided to address the question "Which particular sense of the word 'stronger' is most relevant to Strindberg's play?" In part, Trish came up with this reformulation of her issue because she realized that the two women feuding in the play are actresses, and that they behave as actresses even when they are not professionally performing. Trish's answer to her revised question was that the play encourages the audience to consider which woman is the stronger *actress*—which woman is more able, that is, to convey her preferred version of reality.

When you write about a play, you may have to be selective, for your paper may not be able to accommodate all the ideas and issues that occur to you. Trish was not sure which woman in Strindberg's play is the stronger actress. She felt that a case can be made for Mrs. X or Miss Y; indeed, she suspected that Strindberg was letting his audience decide. But she decided that her paper was not obligated to resolve this matter; she could simply mention the various possible positions in her final paragraph. In the body of her paper, Trish felt she would contribute much if she focused on addressing her main issue with her main claim. Again, her main issue was "Which particular sense of the word 'stronger' is most relevant to Strindberg's play?" Her main claim was that "The play is chiefly concerned with which woman is the stronger actress, 'stronger' here meaning 'more able to convey one's version of reality.'"

Although a paper about a play need not explicitly mention the elements of plays we have identified, thinking about these elements can provide you with a good springboard for analysis. Trish saw that her paper would be very much concerned with the title of Strindberg's play, especially as that title applied to the characters. Also, she would have to refer to stage directions and imagery, because Miss Y's silence leaves the reader having to look at her physical movements and the play's props for clues to her thinking. The play does not really include dialogue, a term that implies people talking with each other. Nevertheless, Trish saw that there are utterances in the script that she could refer to, especially as she made points about the play's lone speaker, Mrs. X. Indeed, a persuasive paper about a play is one that quotes from characters' lines and perhaps from the stage directions, too. Yet the paper needs to quote selectively, for a paper chock full of quotations may obscure instead of enhance the writer's argument.

Final Draft of a Student Paper

Here is Trish's final draft of her paper about *The Stronger*. It emerged out of several drafts, and after Trish had consulted classmates and her instructor. As you read this version of her paper, note its strengths, but also think of any suggestions that might help Trish make the paper even better.

Trish Carlisle
Professor Zelinsky
English 102
28 April ----

Which Is the Stronger Actress
in August Strindberg's Play?

You have asked me to help you solve difficulties you may be experiencing with August Strindberg's script for *The Stronger* as you prepare to play the roles of Mrs. X and Miss Y. These female characters seem harder to judge than the three women who are the focus of Susan Glaspell's play *Trifles*, the play you are performing next month. Obviously, Glaspell is pushing us to think well of Mrs. Hale, Mrs. Peters, and Minnie Wright. The two women in Strindberg's play are another matter; in particular, you have probably been wondering which of these two women Strindberg thinks of as "the stronger." If you knew which character he had in mind with that term, you might play the roles accordingly. As things stand, however, Strindberg's use of the term in his title is pretty ambiguous. It is not even clear, at least not immediately, which particular sense of the word *stronger* is most relevant to the play. I suggest that the play is chiefly concerned with which character is the stronger actress. In making this claim, I am defining *stronger* as "more able to convey one's version of reality."

Identifies main issue

States main claim

You may feel that Strindberg is clarifying his use of the word *stronger* when he has Mrs. X bring up the word in the long speech that ends the play. In that final speech, she declares to Miss Y that "I am . . . the stronger one" (172) and that Miss Y's silence is not the "strength" that Mrs. X previously thought it was. At this point in the play, Mrs. X is evidently defining *stronger* as "more able to keep things, especially a man." She feels that she is the stronger because she is going home to her husband, while Miss Y is forced to be alone on Christmas Eve. Yet there is little reason to believe that Mrs. X is using the word *stronger* in the sense that the playwright has chiefly in mind. Furthermore, there is little reason to believe that Mrs. X is an accurate judge of the two women's situations. Perhaps she is telling herself that she is stronger because she simply needs to believe that she is. Similarly, perhaps she is telling herself that she now has control over her husband when in actuality he may still be emotionally attached to Miss Y. In addition, because Miss Y does not speak and because Mrs. X sweeps out without giving her any further opportunity to do so, we don't know if Miss Y agrees with Mrs. X's last speech.

Since Mrs. X's final use of the word *stronger* is so questionable, we are justified in thinking of other ways that the term might be applied. In thinking about this play, I have entertained the idea that the stronger character is actually Mrs. X's husband Bob, for he has two women fighting over him and also apparently has the creature comforts that servants provide. But now I tend to think that the term applies to one or both of the two women. Unfortunately, we are not given many facts about them, for it is a brief one-act play and one of the major characters does not even speak.° But as we try to figure out how Strindberg is defining the term *stronger*, we should notice one fact that we are indeed given: each of these women is an actress. Both of them have worked at Stockholm's Grand Theater, although apparently Mrs. X got Miss Y fired from the company. Furthermore, Mrs. X engages in a bit of theatrical illusion when she scares Miss Y by firing the toy pistol at her. Soon after, Mrs. X plays the role of her own husband when she puts her hands in the slippers she has bought for him and imitates not only his walk but also the way he scolds his servants. Miss Y even laughs at this "performance," as if she is being an appreciative audience for it. In addition, if Mrs. X is right about there being an adulterous affair between her husband and Miss Y, then those two people have basically been performing an act for Mrs. X. It is possible, too, that Mrs. X has not been quite so naïve; perhaps she has deliberately come to the café in order to confront Miss Y about the affair and to proclaim ultimate victory over her. In that case, Mrs. X is performing as someone more innocent than she really is. On the other hand, Miss Y might be using her silence as an actress would, manipulating her audience's feelings by behaving in a theatrical way.

Because we do know that these women are professional actresses, and because Strindberg gives us several hints that they are performing

even speak: Returns to main claim.

right there in the café, we should feel encouraged to think that he is raising the question of which is the stronger *actress*. Of course, we would still have to decide how he is defining the term *stronger*. But if he does have in mind the women's careers and behavior as actresses, then he seems to be defining *stronger* as "more able to convey one's version of reality." Obviously Mrs. X is putting forth her own version of reality in her final speech, although we do not know how close her version comes to the actual truth. Again, we cannot be sure of Miss Y's thoughts because she does not express them in words; nevertheless, she can be said to work at influencing Mrs. X's version of reality by making strategic use of silence.

I realize°- that the claim I am making does not solve every problem you might have with the play as you prepare to perform it. Frankly, I am not sure who *is* the stronger actress. I suspect that Strindberg is being deliberately ambiguous; he wants the performers to act in a way that will let each member of the audience arrive at his or her own opinion. Still, if you accept my claim, each of you will think of yourself as playing the part of an actress who is trying to shape the other woman's sense of reality.

Works Cited

Strindberg, August. "The Stronger." Translated by Edith and Warner Oland, *Making Literature Matter: An Anthology for Readers and Writers*, edited by John Schilb and John Clifford, 7th ed., Bedford/St. Martin's, 2018, pp. 168–72.

SUMMING UP: WRITING ABOUT PLAYS

- **Consider the differences between page and stage.** Theater professionals distinguish between a play's written script and its actual performances, so consider how any play you are analyzing has been or might be staged. Try to imagine yourself as its director, thinking about how you would guide the actors through their parts. (pp. 173–74)
- **The elements of drama include *plot* and *structure*, *characters*, *stage directions* and *setting*, *imagery*, *language*, and *theme*.**
- **The *plot* and *structure* of plays often resemble those of stories.** Like short stories, plays often feature plot development, a climax, a significant ending, and repetitions of words and situations. (pp. 173–74)
- ***Characters* in plays function like characters in stories.** As such, they can often be analyzed by asking the same questions (see Summing Up on pp. 175–76). A difference is that most plays lack a narrator and even a central point of view; you have to figure out the characters' thoughts from dialogue and movement.

(continued on next page)

I realize: Acknowledges there are remaining issues.

SUMMING UP: WRITING ABOUT PLAYS *(continued)*

- **When analyzing a script, pay attention to its *stage directions*, and imagine other ways that the actors might move around.** (pp. 175–76)
- **While some plays do not describe their *setting* precisely, others stress that they are occurring in particular places or moments.** As with short stories, you can learn much about a play's characters by examining how they accommodate themselves — or fail to accommodate themselves — to their settings. (pp. 176–77)
- ***Images* are often conveyed through words and stagecraft** — through dialogue, gestures, costumes, lighting, and props. (pp. 177–78)
- **Most plays rely on dialogue as their most important *language*,** making their audience figure things out from how the characters address one another. Pauses or silences may be important as well. (p. 178)
- **The *theme* of a play is the main claim — an assertion, a proposition, or a statement — that it seems to make.** As when writing about short stories, try to state the theme as a midlevel generalization, either as an observation or as a recommendation. By specifically wording the theme as a problem, you may better convey the complexity and drama of the play. (pp. 178–81)
- **When you write about a play, remember to formulate an issue worth addressing, a claim about that issue, and evidence for that claim, besides preparing to identify your warrants.** Keep in mind that you will refer to its script, but you might also discuss how much room for interpretation the script allows those who would stage it.

Writing about Essays

Many readers do not realize that nonfiction is a literary genre. They believe that writing about information and facts, science and technology, history and biography, memories and arguments is far different from writing traditional literary works such as sonnets, short stories, and plays. But what counts as literature is often more a matter of tradition and perspective than a matter of content, language, or merit. Many contemporary critics have noticed that definitions of literature are quite subjective, even arbitrary. We are told that literature must move us emotionally; it must contain imaginative, extraordinary language; it must deal with profound, timeless, and universal themes. If these claims are true of poems, stories, and plays, they might also be true of essays, autobiographies, memoirs, speeches, and historical writing.

Essays demand as much of a reader's attention as fiction, drama, and poetry do. They also demand a reader's active participation. And as with more conventional literature, the intellectual, emotional, and aesthetic rewards of attentively reading essays are significant.

Writing about essays in college is best done as a process that begins with careful reading and a first response and ends with editing and proofreading. Author Henry David Thoreau once noted that books should be read with the same care and deliberation with which they were written. This is as true for essays as it is for complex modern poetry. Few people, even professionals, can read a text and write cogently about it the first time. Writing well about essays—actively participating in a cycle of reading, reflecting, and writing—takes as much energy and discipline as writing about other genres. And the results are always worth it.

The essay presented here deals with women and work—more specifically, with the struggles of gifted African American women in a context of poverty and oppression. "Many Rivers to Cross" by June Jordan (1936–2002) was the keynote address at a 1981 conference on "Women and Work" held at Barnard College in New York City. In the speech, Jordan recalls the suicide of her mother fifteen years earlier. Her essay uses an autobiographical narrative as evidence for her argument about the necessity for women to be strong. In this sense, the essay is inductive as it moves from specifics to a generalization rather than the more typical deductive approach, which begins with a claim that is then supported. What are the advantages and disadvantages of Jordan's structure?

JUNE JORDAN

Many Rivers to Cross

When my mother killed herself I was looking for a job. That was fifteen years ago. I had no money and no food. On the pleasure side I was down to my last pack of Pall Malls plus half a bottle of J and B. I needed to find work because I needed to be able fully to support myself and my eight-year-old son, very fast. My plan was to raise enough big bucks so that I could take an okay apartment inside an acceptable public school district, by September. That deadline left me less than three months to turn my fortunes right side up.

It seemed that I had everything to do at once. Somehow, I must move all of our things, mostly books and toys, out of the housing project before the rent fell due, again. I must do this without letting my neighbors know because destitution and divorce added up to personal shame, and failure. Those same neighbors had looked upon my husband and me as an ideal young couple, in many ways: inseparable, doting, ambitious. They had kept me busy and laughing in the hard weeks following my husband's departure for graduate school in Chicago; they had been the ones to remember him warmly through teasing remarks and questions all that long year that I remained alone, waiting for his return while I became the "temporary," sole breadwinner of our peculiar long-distance family by telephone. They had been the ones who kindly stopped the teasing and the queries when the year ended and my husband, the father of my child, did not come back. They never asked me and I never told them what that meant, altogether. I don't think I really knew.

I could see how my husband would proceed more or less naturally from graduate school to a professional occupation of his choice, just as he had shifted rather easily from me, his wife, to another man's wife—another woman. What I could not see was how I should go forward, now, in any natural, coherent way. As a mother without a husband, as a poet without a publisher, a freelance journalist without assignment, a city planner without a contract, it seemed to me that several incontestable and conflicting necessities had suddenly eliminated the whole realm of choice from my life.

My husband and I agreed that he would have the divorce that he wanted, and I would have the child. This ordinary settlement is, as millions of women will testify, as absurd as saying, "I'll give you a call, you handle everything else." At any rate, as my lawyer explained, the law then was the same as the law today; the courts would surely award me a reasonable amount of the father's income as child support, but the courts would also insist that they could not enforce their own decree. In other words, according to the law, what a father owes to his child is not serious compared to what a man owes to the bank for a car, or a vacation. Hence, as they say, it is extremely regrettable but nonetheless true that the courts cannot garnish a father's salary, nor freeze his account, nor seize his property on behalf of his children, in our society. Apparently this is because a child is not a car or a couch or a boat. (I would suppose this is the very best available definition of the difference between an American child and a car.)

Anyway, I wanted to get out of the projects as quickly as possible. But I was 5
going to need help because I couldn't bend down and I couldn't carry anything heavy and I couldn't let my parents know about these problems because I didn't want to fight with them about the reasons behind the problems—which was the same reason I couldn't walk around or sit up straight to read or write without vomiting and acute abdominal pain. My parents would have evaluated that reason as a terrible secret compounded by a terrible crime; once again an unmarried woman, I had, nevertheless, become pregnant. What's more I had tried to interrupt this pregnancy even though this particular effort required not only one but a total of three abortions—each of them illegal and amazingly expensive, as well as, evidently, somewhat poorly executed.

My mother, against my father's furious rejections of me and what he viewed as my failure, offered what she could; she had no money herself but there was space in the old brownstone of my childhood. I would live with them during the summer while I pursued my crash schedule for cash, and she would spend as much time with Christopher, her only and beloved grandchild, as her worsening but partially undiagnosed illness allowed.

After she suffered a stroke, her serenely imposing figure had shrunk into an unevenly balanced, starved shell of chronic disorder. In the last two years, her physical condition had forced her retirement from nursing, and she spent most of her days on a makeshift cot pushed against the wall of the dining room next to the kitchen. She could do very few things for herself, besides snack on crackers, or pour ready-made juice into a cup and then drink it.

In June, 1966, I moved from the projects into my parents' house with the help of a woman named Mrs. Hazel Griffin. Since my teens, she had been my hairdresser. Every day, all day, she stood on her feet, washing and straightening hair in her crowded shop, the Arch of Beauty. Mrs. Griffin had never been married, had never finished high school, and she ran the Arch of Beauty with an imperturbable and contagious sense of success. She had a daughter as old as I who worked alongside her mother, coddling customer fantasy into confidence. Gradually, Mrs. Griffin and I became close; as my own mother became more and more bedridden and demoralized, Mrs. Griffin extended herself—dropping by my parents' house to make dinner for them, or calling me to wish me good luck on a special freelance venture, and so forth. It was Mrs. Griffin who closed her shop for a whole day and drove all the way from Brooklyn to my housing project apartment in Queens. It was Mrs. Griffin who packed me up, so to speak, and carried me and the boxes back to Brooklyn, back to the house of my parents. It was Mrs. Griffin who ignored my father standing hateful at the top of the stone steps of the house and not saying a word of thanks and not once relieving her of a single load she wrestled up the stairs and past him. My father hated Mrs. Griffin because he was proud and because she was a stranger of mercy. My father hated Mrs. Griffin because he was like that sometimes: hateful and crazy.

My father alternated between weeping bouts of self-pity and storm explosions of wrath against the gods apparently determined to ruin him. These were his alternating reactions to my mother's increasing enfeeblement, her stoic depression. I think he was scared; who would take care of him? Would she get well again and make everything all right again?

This is how we organized the brownstone; I fixed a room for my son on the 10
top floor of the house. I slept on the parlor floor in the front room. My father slept on the same floor, in the back. My mother stayed downstairs.

About a week after moving in, my mother asked me about the progress of my plans. I told her things were not terrific but that there were two different planning jobs I hoped to secure within a few days. One of them involved a study of new towns in Sweden and the other one involved an analysis of the social consequences of a huge hydro-electric dam under construction in Ghana. My mother stared at me uncomprehendingly and then urged me to look for work in the local post office. We bitterly argued about what she dismissed as my "high-falutin" ideas and, I believe, that was the last substantial conversation between us.

From my first memory of him, my father had always worked at the post office. His favorite was the night shift, which brought him home usually between three and four o'clock in the morning.

It was hot. I finally fell asleep that night, a few nights after the argument between my mother and myself. She seemed to be rallying; that afternoon, she and my son had spent a long time in the backyard, oblivious to the heat and the mosquitoes. They were both tired but peaceful when they noisily re-entered the house, holding hands awkwardly.

But someone was knocking at the door to my room. Why should I wake up? It would be impossible to fall asleep again. It was so hot. The knocking continued. I switched on the light by the bed: 3:30 A.M. It must be my father. Furious, I pulled on a pair of shorts and a t-shirt. "What do you want? What's the matter?" I asked him, through the door. Had he gone berserk? What could he have to talk about at that ridiculous hour?

"OK, all right," I said, rubbing my eyes awake as I stepped to the door and opened it. "What?"

To my surprise, my father stood there looking very uncertain.

"It's your mother," he told me, in a burly, formal voice. "I think she's dead, but I'm not sure." He was avoiding my eyes.

"What do you mean," I answered.

"I want you to go downstairs and figure it out."

I could not believe what he was saying to me. "You want me to figure out if my mother is dead or alive?"

"I can't tell! I don't know!!" he shouted angrily.

"Jesus Christ," I muttered, angry and beside myself.

I turned and glanced about my room, wondering if I could find anything to carry with me on this mission; what do you use to determine a life or a death? I couldn't see anything obvious that might be useful.

"I'll wait up here," my father said. "You call up and let me know."

I could not believe it; a man married to a woman more than forty years and he can't tell if she's alive or dead and he wakes up his kid and tells her, "You figure it out."

I was at the bottom of the stairs. I halted just outside the dining room where my mother slept. Suppose she really was dead? Suppose my father was not just being crazy and hateful? "Naw," I shook my head and confidently entered the room.

"Momma?!" I called, aloud. At the edge of the cot, my mother was leaning forward, one arm braced to hoist her body up. She was trying to stand up! I rushed over. "Wait. Here, I'll help you!" I said.

And I reached out my hands to give her a lift. The body of my mother was stiff. She was not yet cold, but she was stiff. Maybe I had come downstairs just in time! I tried to loosen her arms, to change her position, to ease her into lying down.

"Momma!" I kept saying. "Momma, listen to me! It's OK! I'm here and everything. Just relax. Relax! Give me a hand, now. I'm trying to help you lie down!"

Her body did not relax. She did not answer me. But she was not cold. Her eyes were not shut.

From upstairs my father was yelling, "Is she dead? Is she dead?"

"No!" I screamed at him. "No! She's not dead!"

At this, my father tore down the stairs and into the room. Then he braked.

"Milly?" he called out, tentative. Then he shouted at me and banged around the walls. "You damn fool. Don't you see now she's gone. Now she's gone!" We began to argue.

"She's alive! Call the doctor!"

"No!"

"Yes!"

At last my father left the room to call the doctor.

I straightened up. I felt completely exhausted from trying to gain a response from my mother. There she was, stiff on the edge of her bed, just about to stand up. Her lips were set, determined. She would manage it, but by herself. I could not help. Her eyes fixed on some point below the floor.

"Momma!" I shook her hard as I could to rouse her into focus. Now she fell 40 back on the cot, but frozen and in the wrong position. It hit me that she might be dead. She might be dead.

My father reappeared at the door. He would not come any closer. "Dr. Davis says he will come. And he call the police."

The police? Would they know if my mother was dead or alive? Who would know?

I went to the phone and called my aunt. "Come quick," I said. "My father thinks Momma has died but she's here but she's stiff."

Soon the house was weird and ugly and crowded and I thought I was losing my mind.

Three white policemen stood around telling me my mother was dead. "How 45 do you know?" I asked, and they shrugged and then they repeated themselves. And the doctor never came. But my aunt came and my uncle and they said she was dead.

After a conference with the cops, my aunt disappeared and when she came back she held a bottle in one of her hands. She and the police whispered together some more. Then one of the cops said, "Don't worry about it. We won't say anything." My aunt signalled me to follow her into the hallway where she let me understand that, in fact, my mother had committed suicide.

I could not assimilate this information: suicide.

I broke away from my aunt and ran to the telephone. I called a friend of mine, a woman who talked back loud to me so that I could realize my growing hysteria, and check it. Then I called my cousin Valerie who lived in Harlem; she woke up instantly and urged me to come right away.

I hurried to the top floor and stood my sleeping son on his feet. I wanted to get him out of this house of death more than I ever wanted anything. He could not stand by himself so I carried him down the two flights to the street and laid him on the backseat and then took off.

At Valerie's, my son continued to sleep, so we put him to bed, closed the door, 50 and talked. My cousin made me eat eggs, drink whiskey, and shower. She would take care of Christopher, she said. I should go back and deal with the situation in Brooklyn.

When I arrived, the house was absolutely full of women from the church dressed as though they were going to Sunday communion. It seemed to me they were, every one of them, wearing hats and gloves and drinking coffee and solemnly addressing invitations to a funeral and I could not find my mother anywhere and I could not find an empty spot in the house where I could sit down and smoke a cigarette.

My mother was dead.

Feeling completely out of place, I headed for the front door, ready to leave. My father grabbed my shoulder from behind and forcibly spun me around.

"You see this?" he smiled, waving a large document in the air. "This am insurance paper for you!" He waved it into my face. "Your mother, she left you insurance, see?"

I watched him. 55

"But I gwine burn it in the furnace before I give it you to t'row away on trash!"

"Is that money?" I demanded. "Did my mother leave me money?"

"Eh-heh!" he laughed. "And you don't get it from me. Not today, not tomorrow. Not until I dead and buried!"

My father grabbed for my arm and I swung away from him. He hit me on my head and I hit back. We were fighting.

Suddenly, the ladies from the church bustled about and pushed, horrified, 60
between us. This was a sin, they said, for a father and a child to fight in the house of the dead and the mother not yet in the ground! Such a good woman she was, they said. She was a good woman, a good woman, they all agreed. Out of respect for the memory of this good woman, in deference to my mother who had committed suicide, the ladies shook their hats and insisted we should not fight; I should not fight with my father.

Utterly disgusted and disoriented, I went back to Harlem. By the time I reached my cousin's place I had begun to bleed, heavily. Valerie said I was hemorrhaging so she called up her boyfriend and the two of them hobbled me into Harlem Hospital.

I don't know how long I remained unconscious, but when I opened my eyes I found myself on the women's ward, with an intravenous setup feeding into my arm. After a while, Valerie showed up. Christopher was fine, she told me; my friends were taking turns with him. Whatever I did, I should not admit I'd had an abortion or I'd get her into trouble, and myself in trouble. Just play dumb and rest. I'd have to stay on the ward for several days. My mother's funeral was tomorrow afternoon. What did I want her to tell people to explain why I wouldn't be there? She meant, what lie?

I thought about it and I decided I had nothing to say; if I couldn't tell the truth then the hell with it.

I lay in that bed at Harlem Hospital, thinking and sleeping. I wanted to get well.

I wanted to be strong. I never wanted to be weak again as long as I lived. 65
I thought about my mother and her suicide and I thought about how my father could not tell whether she was dead or alive.

I wanted to get well and what I wanted to do as soon as I was strong again, actually, what I wanted to do was I wanted to live my life so that people would know unmistakably that I am alive, so that when I finally die people will know the difference for sure between my living and my death.

And I thought about the idea of my mother as a good woman and I rejected that, because I don't see why it's a good thing when you give up, or when you cooperate with those who hate you or when you polish and iron and mend and endlessly mollify for the sake of the people who love the way that you kill yourself day by day silently.

And I think all of this is really about women and work. Certainly this is all about me as a woman and my life work. I mean I am not sure my mother's suicide was something extraordinary. Perhaps most women must deal with a similar inheritance, the legacy of a woman whose death you cannot possibly pinpoint because she died so many, many times and because, even before she became your mother, the life of that woman was taken; I say it was taken away.

And really it was to honor my mother that I did fight with my father, that man who could not tell the living from the dead.

And really it is to honor Mrs. Hazel Griffin and my cousin Valerie and all 70
the women I love, including myself, that I am working for the courage to admit the truth that Bertolt Brecht has written; he says, "It takes courage to say that the good were defeated not because they were good, but because they were weak."

I cherish the mercy and the grace of women's work. But I know there is new work that we must undertake as well: that new work will make defeat detestable to us. That new women's work will mean we will not die trying to stand up: we will live that way: standing up.

I came too late to help my mother to her feet.

By way of everlasting thanks to all of the women who have helped me to stay alive I am working never to be late again. *[1985]*

A Student's Personal Response to the Essay

Isla Bravo wrote in her journal:

> It was shocking to read about Jordan's mother's suicide in the first sentence of "Many Rivers to Cross." I expected the rest of the essay to be about only that one event, but she went on to talk about everything else that was going on in her life around that time first. It is hard to understand how she managed everything in her life. She is out of money and needs to find a way to improve her financial status in just three months. My family may not have everything we've ever wanted, but we've always done pretty well, and I never worried about where we lived.
>
> Even though I have never had to struggle the way Jordan did, I can relate to her descriptions of her friends and neighbors. They all help her out the best they can when her husband leaves her and then when her mother dies. These are the people that she really appreciates in her life. They are the same kind of people that brought food to my parents when my grandmother died. These are the people that she loves, and she creates her own sort of family despite the fact that her father is so mean to her. These are people with whom she creates relationships that aren't defined by specific standards created by society.
>
> When Jordan says that her mother's death may not be extraordinary, that maybe every woman watches someone die over and over, she is really talking about all the little things that can wear a lot of women down and cause their deaths a long time before they actually die. She

can't even tell that her mother is dead because she's been wearing down for so long. The image of her mother looking as if she was "just about to stand up" made me think of my grandmother's funeral and how she looked like she was sleeping rather than dead. For Jordan the image of her mother in that sort of paralysis is also an image of her possible future. It is strange to think of someone whose life has been so hard on them that their death doesn't create a jarring difference.

Jordan seems to be trying to keep herself from wearing down just like her mother at the end. Women are given roles by society that prevent them from being able to really enjoy their lives. She uses her other friends and family as models for how to survive. She has a friend who calms her down on the phone, a cousin that gives her advice in the hospital, and more that take care of her son when she can't. Mrs. Griffin is a good example of the type of person she wants to be. She has to work hard to avoid becoming her mother. It seems as if she is motivated by guilt because she wasn't able to help her mother when she says, "I came too late to help my mother to her feet." Even though it wasn't her fault that her mother put up with so much, it certainly makes her determined to prevent her life from ending up the same way her mother's did.

The Elements of Essays

First impressions are valuable, but writing intelligently about essays should not be completely spontaneous. We can be personal and insightful, but persuading others about the validity of our reading takes a more focused and textually informed presentation. The following discussion of the basic elements of the essay is meant to increase your ability to analyze and write about essays. The elements include voice, style, structure, and ideas.

VOICE

When we read the first few sentences of an essay, we usually hear the narrator's **voice**: we hear a person speaking to us, and we begin to notice if he or she sounds friendly or hostile, stuffy or casual, self-assured or tentative. The voice might be austere and technical or personal and flamboyant. The voice may be intimate or remote. It may be sincere, hectoring, hysterical, meditative, or ironic. The possibilities are endless.

We usually get a sense of the writer's voice from the **tone** the writer projects. In the first paragraph of Jordan's essay, we get a sense of the speaker's voice through the direct and forthright tone that she takes, beginning with the disturbing assertion that her mother killed herself and that she herself was destitute. She is also not afraid to admit that her cigarettes and scotch were running low and informal enough to use "big bucks" and "okay" (para. 1). This is not someone who will be putting on airs or who will skirt the bare-bones truth of her situation, however unflattering or unpleasant.

Given the situation she describes, it is not surprising that Jordan's tone would occasionally be sarcastic and ironic, as when she describes the "difference between an American child and a car" (para. 4) and her abortions as "somewhat poorly executed" (para. 5).

Jordan's concerned and bewildered voice over the death of her mother and the revelation of her suicide turns to anger and outrage over the insensitive and selfish response of her father. And then while recovering in the hospital, Jordan's voice and tone shift drastically with "I wanted to be strong" (para. 65). She is now assertive, confident, and committed. Rejecting any sentimental thoughts of her deceased mother, she is determined not to be as weak as her mother. And so she boldly promises that she is now committed to the "new work that we must undertake" (para. 71). This new work, she asserts in a voice brimming with hope and determination, means that she will live "standing up" (para. 71).

When we speak of a writer's persona, we mean a kind of performance mask or stance the writer assumes. Writers are trying to construct a persona that will serve their purposes. Voice and tone are techniques that help writers create an appropriate persona.

STYLE

We all have stylish friends. They look good. Their shoes and pants and shirts seem to complement each other perfectly. It's not that they are color-coordinated—that would be too obvious for them—it's something more subtle. They seem to make just the right choices. When they go to a party, to the movies, or to school, they have a personal style that is their own.

Writers also have **style**. They make specific choices in words, in syntax and sentence length, in diction, in metaphors, even in sentence beginnings and endings. Writers use parallelism, balance, formal diction, poetic language, even sentence fragments to create their own styles.

Jordan's first three dramatic sentences are a good example of how she adapts her style to the content. Here she uses short, direct sentences to announce her predicament, but then her sentences get longer and more complex. Notice in the second paragraph her cumulative sentence ("Those same neighbors . . ."). In this pattern, writers make a statement and then add modifiers after a colon or a comma that can be words (as in this case) or long phrases. Notice the next long, compound sentence. She then ends the paragraph with a short simple assertion. Skilled writers like Jordan vary their sentence length and type as well as the imaginative ways they begin their sentences. Notice, for example, the different ways Jordan begins her paragraphs. Also notice the way Jordan crafts transitions between paragraphs, sometimes with a simple word ("Anyway" in para. 5), or a pronoun ("This" in para. 10), or a conjunction ("And" in paras. 67–70), or a phrase ("About . . ." in para. 11).

STRUCTURE

The way essayists put their work together is not mysterious. The best writers create a **structure** to fit their needs. Most do not have a prearranged structure in mind or feel the need to obey the composition rules many students think they have to follow: topic sentence first and three examples following. Writers of essays aren't inclined to follow formulas. Essayists begin and end as they see fit; they give explicit topic sentences or create narratives that imply themes; they begin with an assertion and support it, or vice versa. Essayists are inventors of structures that fit the occasion and their own way of seeing the world. The thought of the essay significantly influences its structure. Like the relationship between mind and body, form and thought are inseparable.

Jordan's plan, of course, is to begin her argument with a detailed autobiographical narrative focused on her mother's suicide. After setting the scene with her husband abandoning her and the necessity to move into her childhood home, Jordan focuses on the relationship between her egregious bullying father and her weak mother. And then, after detailing in excruciating detail the night of her mother's death, Jordan begins the generalizations that are at the heart of her argument, which is, essentially: my mother was weak and that cost her her life, and I'm not going to let that happen to me.

IDEAS

All writers have something on their minds when they write. That seems especially true when writers decide to put their **ideas** into a nonfictional form such as the essay. Of course, lots of ideas fill poems and short stories too, but they are usually expressed more indirectly. Although essays seem more idea-driven, this does not mean that as readers we have a responsibility to extract the precise idea or argument the writer had in mind. That may not even be possible since in the creative process of all writing, ideas get modified or changed. Sometimes a writer's original intention is significantly transformed; sometimes writers are not fully conscious of all their hidden intentions. Regardless, readers of essays are not simply miners unearthing hidden meanings; they are more like coproducers. And in creating that meaning, ideas are central.

Of course, Jordan has been developing ideas from the very beginning of her essay. It seems as if she becomes more focused on ideas per se when her narrative concludes at the hospital, but her comments about her husband starting in paragraph 2 clearly develop the idea that choice has been systematically eliminated from her life, and by implication the lives of all working-class women. Paragraph 4 also focuses on the unfairness of the courts and their favorable bias toward men. But the primary emphasis on ideas happens with "I wanted to be strong" in paragraph 65, with Jordan's manifesto-like assertion in the same paragraph that she was never going to "be weak again as long as I lived." Interestingly, she cites the fight with her father, who could not tell the difference between the living and the dead, as a metaphor for the larger fight of all women to assert that a change is coming in the lives of women, that new women will live "standing up" (para. 71). And Jordan's concluding idea in the last sentence announces a new solidarity, a new community of women who will help each other be independent. And now, some thirty years later, Jordan's ideas have proven to be prescient.

Final Draft of a Student Paper

After writing journal entries and a freewrite, Isla planned her essay and then wrote a draft. She used responses from several students in a small-group workshop and from her instructor to help her revise her essay, sharpening her focus and supporting her claims more explicitly. Here is Isla's final version.

Isla Bravo
Ms. Hollingsworth
English 201
21 April ----

Resisting Women's Roles

June Jordan takes a strongly feminist stance against the roles women are forced to contend with in her essay "Many Rivers to Cross." She begins the essay from her experience as a woman who has conformed to the social expectations of a wife, daughter, and mother. Her commitment to these roles has left her as a single mother who is contending with an unwanted pregnancy, forced to care for a dying mother and a belligerent father, and without a place of her own to live or work. This essay supports my argument that women need to establish their independence and not allow society to control their lives. This argument is substantiated by Jordan's exploration of her own defiance of society's conventions regarding the roles for women as wife, daughter, and mother in an attempt to preserve herself from the restrictions that destroyed her mother.

Clear, explicit claim with her plan to support.

Women are expected by society to place their families before their careers, and part of this sacrifice includes aiding their husband's careers in lieu of their own. Jordan portrays herself as an example of how this convention is detrimental to a woman's ability to survive on her own. Jordan sacrifices her own professional ambition to her husband's pursuit of his career. The ensuing complications depict the limitations and perils of the idea that women must always place their own careers behind their husbands'. Rather than specifically condemning this social expectation, she provides an illustration of the destruction it can cause. Her own career is a secondary priority, subjugated to her roles as a supportive wife and mother, while her husband pursues graduate school in another city and has an affair with another man's wife. Jordan squanders a year of her life waiting for her husband's return and becomes "a mother without a husband, . . . a poet without a publisher, a freelance journalist without assignment, a city planner without a contract" (186). She abides by the social

Gives concrete examples of negative consequences of following convention.

Qualifies her objections.

conventions that insist she support her husband, and her life remains in stasis until he steps out of his own commitments. By living her life under the social guidelines for a wife, she allows herself to be exploited for her husband's convenience. Her needs are supplanted by her husband's, and his abandonment leaves her embarrassed and destitute.

Another concrete example supporting need for independence.

Jordan's depiction of her parents' relationship illustrates the generational quality of these social conventions. Her parents' relationship foreshadows the potential outcome of her marriage if it continues. Her parents' relationship is wholly restricted to the typical gender roles they both inherit from society. Her mother subjugates her own life only to the needs of her husband, a sacrifice he expects from her. This historical relationship becomes clear when Jordan describes her father's response to her mother's fatal illness when she says, "I think he was scared; who would take care of him? Would she get well again and make everything all right again?" (187). The fact that his concern was about his own life — "who would take care of him?" — makes it clear that their relationship revolved around only his own comfort. Jordan is desperate to prevent her own life from following this path.

Concludes paragraph with reference to claim.

Another concrete example of societal expectations.

Jordan's relationship with her father explores another aspect of the expectations placed on women by society, that of a daughter. Jordan's father's reliance on her mother for all of his comfort turns onto Jordan when her mother is no longer able to fulfill these duties. Jordan's role as his daughter, her most important function, is dynamically portrayed when her father forces her to check her mother's body to see if she is alive because he is incapable or unwilling to do it himself. He says to her, "I'll wait up here. . . . You call up and let me know" (188), only to yell at her inaccurate determination. His anger appears to stem more from the disruption to his own life rather than from the loss of his wife; he is angry rather than sad. He appears almost offended by her death and his daughter's failure to provide him with the level of comfort he craves for his life. His own expectations for the superior role in the household have been created by a male-dominated society and have been enforced by the manner in which his wife seems to have fulfilled those expectations as well. The role of a dutiful child is not by itself destructive until it begins to take precedence in this destructive manner. His expectation is that Jordan should take on the role of caregiver, waiting on him despite any reluctance on her part and regardless of the animosity that exists between them.

Qualifies her objections before reinforcing objections to harmful social convention.

Another concrete example supporting her claim.

Jordan also defies social conventions by her unwillingness to become a mother again to the new baby she's carrying. She attempts to abort the child several times until she finally does lose the baby. Jordan describes the advice she receives from a friend in the hospital: "Whatever I did, I should not admit I'd had an abortion or I'd get her into trouble, and myself in trouble" (190). The possibility that Jordan does not want to be a mother to another child is abhorrent to the social standards that have formed her life and surroundings. Motherhood is the expected career for a woman, and her choice to not have another baby is a direct rejection of those standards.

As a woman in this particular culture, she has certain designated assignments of work that include being a daughter, wife, and mother. She rejects a caretaker role for her father, her marriage has dissolved, and she has an abortion. These portrayals do not suggest a rejection of these roles in their entirety; rather, they explicitly show how they can become harmful if they force women into situations they might have avoided if not for these societal pressures. From this point, she is able to look toward her own career and her own needs. The role society imposes on her as a woman puts her in a position that deemphasizes her own ambitions and preferences. The end of her mother's life is the catalyst that forces her to fully recognize the restrictions that she has been living with and that her mother succumbed to until her death. Jordan says, "I came too late to help my mother to her feet. . . . I am working never to be late again" (191). She wants to free herself from the limiting standards for women in society and hopefully free other women to be independent and assertive.

Reviews her assigned roles and her objections.

Gives context for her defiance of social expectations.

Concludes by reinforcing and extending her claim to all women.

Work Cited

Jordan, June. "Many Rivers to Cross." *Making Literature Matter: An Anthology for Readers and Writers*, edited by John Schilb and John Clifford, 7th ed., Bedford/St. Martin's, 2018, pp. 185–91.

SUMMING UP: WRITING ABOUT ESSAYS

- **Essays (and nonfiction) use language as imaginatively and effectively as other genres of literature.** Essays should – like stories, poems, and plays – be read with care and deliberation and written about with energy and discipline. (p. 192)
- **The elements of essays include *voice*, *style*, *structure*, and *ideas*.**
- **In essays, *voice* is important.** The writer's voice (which might be sincere, ironic, or meditative) can convey the tone a writer projects. But even in essays, writers might assume a persona that serves their purposes. (pp. 192–93)
- **The *style* and *structure* of essays often provide useful models for writers.** Noticing how essays are put together, how sentences and paragraphs follow one another logically, can lead to the writing of well-organized and stylish essays. (pp. 193–94)
- **As in all genres, *ideas* are crucial, but they seem especially prominent in essays.** (p. 194)
- **Argumentative essays model effective ways to make arguments.** It is often valuable to analyze argumentative essays for the ways that writers make claims about issues, support their claims with evidence, and project a good image of themselves. (p. 194)

CHAPTER 6

Writing Researched Arguments

Maybe the word *research* makes you anxious. It gives many people qualms. It brings to mind for them big and complex assignments in high school. Back then, they experienced "the research paper" as a major challenge. It loomed for them as a hurdle, one they struggled to leap. Often they couldn't figure out its rationale. Why do all this labor? Why hunt for materials, base a long essay on them, then end with a formatted bibliography? Such toil can prove overwhelming. A student might lose sight of its point.

Take heart. Research needn't be a daunting and valueless exercise. Indeed, it's become a common and rewarding pursuit. Millions now own devices that make the process easy. Just by tapping on keyboards or smartphones, they mine the Web's vast data. We bet you cruise cyberspace for answers to lots of questions. You might not call these voyages *research*, but that is what they are. Of course, frequently you're looking for a less-than-momentous fact: where to buy hoverboards, when the next *Star Wars* movie premieres, who's performing at local clubs, what folks think of your town's new restaurant, how your school's football team ranks. But probably you also turn to the Internet for more crucial knowledge. You may seek details about a disease that afflicts a family member. You may wish to compare online mortgage rates. A job you hold may require you to monitor several Web sites, gleaning data that will help your firm serve its clientele. Maybe you assist a nonprofit cause that's quite Internet-oriented; many of them search online for possible donors and allies. In general, the digital era is an age of research. It's a tool people use to manage their day.

Nevertheless, we can imagine you saying something like this: "OK, I realize now that I do research every day. But I'm still not confident I can do academic research—the kind of research that college teachers want. And I'm by no means sure I can turn it into essays—the kind of writing they expect." We understand the concern you may feel about these tasks. In the rest of this chapter, we explain and demonstrate ways to handle them.

Here at the start, we stress this fact: most college instructors don't assign something called "the research paper." They consider this label too vague. Yes, they'll require essays based on personal research. But they'll be more precise about the goal. Most often, they'll want you to compose researched *arguments*. You'll write essays addressed to an audience. You'll raise issues and put forth claims. You'll offer evidence and reasons. And you'll do research to prepare for this kind of writing. You'll seek materials that will help you build a persuasive case.

If you'll mainly write about a particular work, that's your **primary source**. Your other findings are your **secondary sources**. Some may prove not as useful as you predicted. Leave them out of your essay; don't sweat to jam them in. The rest of your sources should each play a clear role in your text. You'll have to decide their functions. Overall, use your essay to **synthesize** your sources. Put them in conversation. Make plain how they relate to one another; show how they connect to *your* chief issue and claim.

Begin Your Research by Giving It Direction

As you start your research, you may know already what your essay will argue. Certainty can be an advantage, productively steering your hunt. But it risks narrowing your scope. You may settle for sources that just reinforce your existing ideas. Research should expand your thinking. Let it be a means of inquiry. Even if you're sure of the claim you'll make, stay open to changing your mind. Consider the claim a hypothesis that your research will test. Don't stick with findings that preserve views you currently hold. Look for materials that may send you down exciting new paths.

Of course, your opening mood might be different. Perhaps you'll be hazy about your topic. You may not know what research to do. Still, you can give it direction. If you've chosen a particular literary work to write about, read it several times. If it's in this book, review what we tell you about its author. Take a look at our questions and comments about it. Then ask questions of your own about the work. Strive to come up with a question whose answer isn't obvious—an issue that demands you conduct research.

Another strategy is to list keywords: terms that occur to you as you study the work. These can become your search terms. The list below is an example. It concerns Charlotte Perkins Gilman's "The Yellow Wallpaper," an 1892 story based partly on the writer's life. Heading the list are the story's title and the author's name. They're followed by terms that often arise when the story is discussed in class. For research on Gilman's tale, these items could serve as guides:

- "The Yellow Wallpaper"
- Charlotte Perkins Gilman
- Nineteenth-century theories about women's health, psychology, and work
- Nineteenth-century American feminism
- Nineteenth-century fiction by American women
- The rest cure
- Postpartum depression
- Psychological abuse
- S. Weir Mitchell (Gilman's doctor in real life)
- Woman-centered horror stories as a genre
- The *New England Magazine*
- Nineteenth-century American periodicals

No item on the list is a *claim* about Gilman's story. Finding and developing a claim would be a goal of your research. But any of the terms could be a point of departure for you. They are words you would put in a search box to launch your probe.

Search for Sources in the Library and Online

Once you have your topic in mind and perhaps sketched a tentative claim, begin looking for research sources. Many different types of sources for literary research are available, and the types you will need will depend largely on the type of claim you choose to defend. If your issue is primarily one of interpretation — about the theme, patterns, or symbolism of the text, for instance — you will most likely need to consult literary criticism to see what has been said in the past about the literature you are discussing. If your issue concerns historical or cultural context, including issues of social policy, you may need to consult newspapers, magazines, and similar sorts of cultural documents. Some topics might require several different types of sources.

Not many years ago, for most people the word *research* was synonymous with hours spent in the library hunting for books and articles. For many students today, *research* has become synonymous with the Internet, which they turn to in the belief that everything is available online. But this is simply not true. Many of the best and most reliable sources are still available only in print. In particular, lots of potentially useful books haven't been digitized yet. They remain in your school library, so you'll have to go there if you hope to read them. The library may also house relevant documents and scholarly journals that aren't online. The library's computerized **catalog** will alert you to its holdings, helping you locate useful texts. Typically, the catalog entry for a book lists various subject headings for it. By clicking on a heading, you'll find other books on that topic. When you go to the library's shelves for a book, browse through neighboring volumes, for perhaps they also address your subject of study.

Of course, a wealth of information is available on the Internet. As with the library, your goal is to find useful information efficiently, evaluate it carefully, and employ it effectively in your paper. Unfortunately, and unlike a library's sources, information on the Internet is not indexed and organized to make it easily accessible to researchers. Many students go right away to Wikipedia, hoping to find most of their needed data there. Indeed, a Wikipedia entry may contain some useful facts. Nevertheless, you shouldn't accept on faith everything that the entry says. It's the product of anonymous people, many of whom may not really be experts on the subject they claim to know. Wikipedia can be a decent *starting* point for online searches, especially because it provides links to Web sites that may be more authoritative. But many teachers will object if you depend on Wikipedia itself as a source. Consider it a launch pad, not a destination.

You will need to do a certain amount of "surfing" if you are to find appropriate online materials for your project. A number of **search engines** (programs for finding information) are designed to help you track down materials on the Web. If you are an old hand on the Internet, probably you can depend on search engines that have served you well in the past. Bear in mind, however, that relying on just one search engine may not lead you to all the sources that would benefit you. Many students pursuing a research topic go immediately to Google. They type their subject into the box, click a mouse, and expect to see terrific sources pop right up on-screen. Yet often this search method proves exasperating. For one thing, it may succeed all *too* well in generating items. Our five sample researched arguments discuss "The Yellow Wallpaper"; a Google search using this title elicits around 628,000 results. The first paper also deals with postpartum depression; if you Google this term, you'll come up with roughly 3,820,000 results. Even if you combine "The Yellow Wallpaper" with "postpartum depression," you'll get roughly 6,110 results. It can take forever to sift through these avalanches for whatever gems they contain. Faced with such landslides, some writers just pounce on the first few results they obtain. But "first" doesn't necessarily mean "best." An ideal article may surface late in a Google list.

You can narrow your results by adding words to your search, making it more exact. Or you might turn to Google Scholar, which sticks with academic texts. There, combining "The Yellow Wallpaper" with "postpartum depression" produces about 125 results. This is certainly a more manageable number. Still, Google addiction will limit you as a researcher. See what other Web sites can do for you. If your college or university makes available to you sites such as JSTOR, Academic Search Premier, and Project Muse, these will give you access to hundreds of scholarly journals and books. The Internet service LexisNexis offers current articles from newspapers and magazines, as well as transcripts of radio and TV broadcasts.

When you take a course, find out what search engines serve its field. For literary research, a great one is the ***MLA International Bibliography***, sponsored by the Modern Language Association (MLA) and carried by many schools. It lists books and articles on a wide range of topics in literary studies. Later in this chapter are sample researched arguments by students who used MLA's service. They looked for sources related to "The Yellow Wallpaper." For instance, Sarah Michaels was curious how the story might add to current debates about postpartum depression. Therefore, one of her search terms was this disorder's name. Typing it into the MLA search box, she found a useful article on how TV reports the problem. Katie Johnson was focused on literary criticism about Gilman's story. Using its title to search with, she found analyses of the tale.

Like most search engines, MLA's enables you to filter. Say you're looking for studies of "The Yellow Wallpaper." Once you insert this title into MLA's search box, you can restrict the results to articles published in journals. You can also have the results appear in reverse chronological order, so that the most recent articles come first. They'll mention older articles and books that have proven important, and you could turn to those next.

In several journals, each article is prefaced by a summary called an **abstract**. This overview, usually a paragraph, immediately tells you the article's main claim. Whenever you discover an article or book relevant to your project, examine its bibliography as well. Often, this will have the heading **Works Cited**. Likely to be listed there are other texts you'll find useful. In general, scholars refer to previous works on their subject. They extend, challenge, or refine their predecessors' claims. Notice how they treat these prior views. You'll get a sense of the conversation your topic has already stirred. You may also see how to join this dialogue with ideas of your own.

Evaluate the Sources

Whatever method you use to locate your research materials, remember that not all sources are created equal. Take care to **evaluate** those you come across. When tempted to use a writer's work, ask yourself the following: What do I want my audience to think about this person? Often, you'll hope your readers will accept him or her as some sort of authority. In a way, you have to think about **ethos**, a term we discussed in Chapters 3 and 4. There, you may recall, we defined *ethos* as the image that an author projects. Many writers try to be persuasive by constructing an admirable ethos—a version of themselves that will impress their readers. Similarly, when you incorporate sources into a researched argument, you will often want your audience to respect them. These sources may not agree with one another—heck, *you* may not agree with them all—but they'll need to have recognizable expertise. Otherwise, why should your readers pay attention to them?

Suppose you plan to write a research paper on "The Yellow Wallpaper." An online search leads you to an analysis of the story. You might refer to this study in your essay. But you need to determine whether the author is someone your readers would take seriously. You have to look for credentials. Perhaps the writer is a professor publishing in a scholarly journal. Maybe, like Paul Goldberger in Chapter 3, this person is an award-winning authority in a certain field (in this case, architecture). Another writer in the same chapter, Jennifer Jacquet, is a veteran evironmentalist affiliated with a disitnguished univesity. Sometimes you can learn writers' professional status by visiting the Web sites of institutions they work for. At any rate, be skeptical when a Web post's author is shrouded in mystery. The views expressed may be interesting, but if their advocate is a phantom, you can't expect your readers to care about them. Useful to bear in mind is the famous *New Yorker* magazine cartoon about the digital age. One canine, perched at a computer, tells another that "on the Internet, nobody knows you're a dog." In short, the Web can fool you. Although someone posting on it is probably human, hunt for details of the person's background. Your audience will expect you to have this information about a source, even if you don't include every bit of it in your paper.

A teacher may require a number of your sources to be articles from "peer-reviewed" academic journals. Such journals publish a manuscript only after it has been evaluated by experts in its subject. Usually, a journal's Web site will indicate whether it falls into this category. Some search engines have a feature that, when you activate it, confines your results to peer-reviewed works. For example, both Academic Search Premier and the MLA International Bibliography enable you to restrict your search this way. Most books published by academic and university presses have also been peer reviewed. Of course, even when it doesn't come with this label, a book or an article may still be worth consulting. In many popular newspapers (such as the *New York Times* and the *Washington Post*) and magazines (such as *The New Yorker* and the *Atlantic*), you'll find thoughtful, well-grounded reports and opinion pieces.

In general, you should ask the following basic questions of your sources: (1) Is the information recent, and if not, is the validity of the information likely to have changed significantly over time? (2) How credible is the author? Is he or she a recognized expert on the subject? (3) Is the source published by an established, respectable press, or does it appear in a well-respected journal or periodical (the *Los Angeles Times* has more credibility than the *National Enquirer*, for example) or Web site (one supported by a university or library, for instance)? (4) Based on what you've learned about responsible argument, do the arguments in your source seem sound, fair, and thoughtful? Is the evidence convincing? Is the development of the argument logical?

You increase your own credibility with your audience by using the most reliable research materials available to you, so do not just stick with whatever comes to hand if you have the opportunity to find a stronger source.

Record Your Sources' Key Details

As your research proceeds, record your discoveries. In a computer file or handwritten notes, jot down key details of each source. Don't expect that you'll simply recall this information. Memory is imperfect; data can fade from your mind.

Above all, specify each source by using bibliographical form. You'll then have an entry ready to put in your essay's Works Cited section. In a literature course, the format you'll usually follow is that of the MLA. Later in this chapter, we explain MLA's guidelines at length. At the moment, here are sample MLA-formatted entries by the two students we've mentioned. Sarah, who found the article about postpartum depression, logged it in her notes this way:

> Dubriwny, Tasha N. "Television News Coverage of Postpartum Disorders and the Politics of Medicalization." *Feminist Media Studies*, vol. 10, no. 3, Sept. 2010, pp. 285–303.

Katie, who investigated literary criticism, recorded one of her articles as follows:

> Johnson, Greg. "Gilman's Gothic Allegory: Rage and Redemption in 'The Yellow Wallpaper.'" *Studies in Short Fiction*, vol. 26, no. 4, Fall 1989, pp. 521–30.

What else about a source might you write down? You have several options.

A *summary* of the source—one or two sentences indicating in your own words the author's main claim. Such summaries guarantee that you understand the gist of an author's argument and (since they are in your own words) can readily be incorporated in your paper. You might think of a summary as a restatement of the author's principal claim, perhaps with a brief indication of the types of supporting evidence he or she marshals. You can also write summaries of supporting points—subsections of an author's argument—if they seem applicable to your paper. A summary should not, however, include quotations, exhaustive detail about subpoints, or a list of all the evidence in a given source. A summary is meant to provide a succinct overview—to demonstrate that you have grasped a point and convey it to your readers.

A possible summary of Durbriwny's article:

> In the period of 2000–2007, television reports on postpartum disorders used expert and personal testimonies to depict these disorders as the medical problems of individuals. It is more appropriate, however, to put these conditions in a social context, for the women suffering from them are actually challenging the destructive cultural stereotype of the "good" mother.

A possible summary of Johnson's article:

> The heroine of "The Yellow Wallpaper" emerges not as a pathetic madwoman, but as someone who asserts her freedom and creativity by imagining a Gothic fantasy for herself and writing about it in her diary.

***Quotations* (with page numbers) that you might incorporate into your essay.** A quotation may be a word, a phrase, a sentence, or an entire passage.

A striking sentence in Dubriwny's article:

> Women's varied emotions and behaviors during the postpartum period — their feelings of anger, distress, sadness, and guilt as well as happiness — point to a substantial gap between the lived reality of mothering and the discourse of essential/good motherhood. (287)

A memorable sentence from Johnson:

> Thus as the story progresses, the heroine follows both her childlike promptings and her artistic faith in creating a Gothic alternative to the stifling daylight world of her husband and the society at large. (524)

***Paraphrasing* (with page numbers) that you might incorporate in your essay.** A paraphrase puts a statement in new words. Think of it as a translation that attempts to convey the basic idea of the original passage. It has two advantages over a quotation. First, an accurate paraphrase proves that you understand the material you've read. Second, a paraphrase is easier to integrate into your essay than a quotation, since it is already written in your own words and style. When you paraphrase, you need to identify the original page number, just as you do with quotations.

A statement by Dubriwny:

> Unfortunately, the struggle over the definition of postpartum disorders is, in television news, not much of a struggle at all, as only a few voices exist to challenge the complete medicalization of postpartum disorders. (299)

A possible paraphrase of Dubriwny's statement:

> Sadly, televised reports tend to depict postpartum depression and similar maladies as medical problems, rarely giving air time to activists who propose other ways of understanding such conditions (299).

A statement by Johnson, about Gilman's heroine:

> Her experience should finally be viewed not as a final catastrophe but as a terrifying, necessary stage in her progress toward self-identity and personal achievement. (523)

A possible paraphrase of Johnson's statement:

> At the end of the story, the heroine may seem doomed but actually is not, for she has to engage in such frightening behavior if she is eventually to become a fulfilled, accomplished individual (523).

Texts and other materials with which the source is in conversation. When you note these, you put the source in context. You become more aware of the issues that the source addresses.

> Dubriwny analyzes how postpartum disorders were represented in television reports from 2000 to 2007. She focuses on a selection of tapes available in the Vanderbilt Television News Archives. They're her primary source. Motivating her research was recent public attention to certain events, including Andrea Yates's murder of her children and Tom Cruise's disapproval of Brooke Shields's reliance on antidepressants. Dubriwny is influenced, too, by advocacy groups and sociologists who critique the role that dominant models of motherhood play in diagnoses of postpartum conditions. Also driving her to write is the relative lack of scholarship on the biases that shape media representations of these disorders.

> Johnson takes Gilman's story as his primary source. He argues that its heroine's behavior at the end is a creative, self-affirming protest against the patriarchal society that her husband represents. Johnson opposes interpretations of the story that see the heroine as simply mad. But when he cites specific studies of the story, he tends to choose those that support his view. He also develops his claim by referring to Gilman's nonfiction autobiographical writings; to other women writers (Emily Dickinson, Charlotte Bronte, Sylvia Plath); and to scholarship on the Gothic literary tradition.

Strategies for Integrating Sources

Throughout your research, you'll aim to evolve an argument of your own. It's something *you'll* contribute to discussions taking place. The student essays at the conclusion of this chapter are examples. Each recruits sources to advance a claim that the student herself has produced.

Once you've finished your research, take time to reflect. If you've come up with an issue and claim, think about them again. In light of all your findings, is your argument still good? Does it need fine-tuning? Should you even change topics? Maybe, though, you remain unsure what to argue. To gain focus, review the issues your sources raise. What debates do they participate in? What sides in these debates do *you* favor? What issues do these debates ignore or slight? For help in getting ideas, you might also review the categories of issues we present on pages 61–68 of Chapter 3.

As you draft your essay, show that you're using your sources. Don't let them overshadow *your* contribution. They should clearly serve your argument, not crowd it out. Whenever you summarize, paraphrase, or quote, identify your source's function. Indicate the role it plays in a conversation you run. If you've taken many notes in your research, your essay may not have room for all. Cast aside those that fail to help.

Use direct quotations sparingly. Hordes of them make for choppy reading and may obscure your ideas. When you're tempted to quote, consider paraphrasing instead. If you still feel that quoting is necessary, try to limit the number of words. Perhaps you needn't quote an entire sentence or passage. A bit of phrasing may suffice. Here are examples of selective quotation.

Original (from Dubriwny's article):

> The medical experts interviewed in the news coverage engage in a process of decontextualizing postpartum distress. What I mean is that the experts take the distress out of the social context of mothering and focus almost solely on biological causes of postpartum disorders. (290)

Limited quoting:

> Dubriwny is concerned that TV reports on postpartum conditions use medical authorities to emphasize "biological causes" rather than "the social context of mothering" (290).

Original (from Johnson's article):

> Two of the story's major structural devices are its contrasting of the husband's daylight world and his wife's nocturnal fantasy, and the religious imagery by which she highlights the liberating and redemptive qualities of her experience. (523)

Limited quoting:

> Johnson contends that although the heroine seems tormented, she actually finds her interaction with the wallpaper "liberating and redemptive" (523).

When quoting up to four lines of prose or three lines of poetry, integrate the quotation directly into your paragraph, enclosing the quoted material in double quotation marks and checking to make sure that the quotation accurately reflects the original. Longer quotations are set off from the text by starting a new line and indenting one inch on the left margin only; these are called **block quotations**. For these, quotation marks are omitted since the indention is enough to indicate that the material is a quotation. Examples of the correct format for both long and short quotations appear in Katie Johnson's paper (pp. 224–27).

When a short quotation is from a poem, line breaks in the poem are indicated by slash marks, with single spaces on either side. The following example demonstrates the format for a short quotation, in this case from Yusef Komunyakaa's poem "Blackberries" (featured in Chapter 5). The numbers in parentheses specify which lines in the poem are being quoted:

> The poem's speaker recalls the scene as sinister, noting: "The big blue car made me sweat. / Wintertime crawled out of the windows" (19–20).

While it is essential to quote accurately, sometimes you may need to alter a quotation slightly, either by deleting text for brevity or by adding or changing text to incorporate it grammatically. If you delete words from a quotation, indicate the deletion by inserting an ellipsis (three periods with spaces between them), as demonstrated by the following quotation from Robert Frost's poem "Mending Wall" (Chapter 3):

> The speaker makes his neighbor sound warlike, describing him as "Bringing a stone . . . / In each hand, like an old-stone savage armed" (39–40).

If you need to change or add words for clarity or grammatical correctness, indicate the changes with square brackets. If, for instance, you wanted to clarify the meaning of "They" in Komunyakaa's opening line "They left my hands like a printer's," you could do so like this:

> The speaker recalls that "[The blackberries] left my hands like a printer's" (1).

No quotation is self-sufficient. Nor is its meaning always self-evident. When you put a quotation in your essay, help your audience see why it's there. Introduce it clearly. Follow it with any additional explanation it needs. The longer the quotation, the more analysis readers want.

Avoid Plagiarism

Plagiarism is a serious violation of academic standards. Most colleges have policies that explain how they define and treat it. You should learn your institution's guidelines. But there are general rules of thumb to follow when you quote, summarize, or paraphrase. The major one is this: indicate clearly which ideas are yours and which are other people's. You commit **plagiarism** if you claim credit for another person's thoughts. Even if you put them in your own words, they came from someone else. If you don't attribute these ideas to their source, you mislead your readers. You betray your audience's trust.

To see better what we mean, look at the sentence below, which is on page 527 of Greg Johnson's article about Gilman's "The Yellow Wallpaper." Johnson refers to the story's heroine, who records her distress in her diary:

> An experienced writer, she understands the healing power which inheres in the act of writing and recognizes intuitively that her physician husband's rest cure can lead only to her psychic degeneration.

You would be committing plagiarism if you presented Johnson's sentence—or parts of it—as your own prose:

> We should remember that the heroine is an experienced writer. She understands intuitively the healing power that writing has. Indeed, writing in her diary is a means by which she tries to head off the degeneration of her mind that her physician husband's rest cure will cause.

You would also be plagiarizing if you paraphrased Johnson's sentence without noting that it's his:

> A veteran crafter of prose, the heroine perceives that her journal-keeping is important for her mental health. At some level of consciousness, she also realizes that the treatment her doctor spouse is putting her through will result in the decay of her mind.

Here is a way you could quote from Johnson's sentence, give him credit for it, identify its page number, and make clear what you're doing with him as a source:

> Many analysts of the story overlook the fact that its narrator writes. Specifically, she maintains a diary of her ordeal. As Greg Johnson points out, her journal-keeping has for her a "healing power," whereas the treatment her husband is putting her through "can lead only to her psychic degeneration" (527). Johnson may be overestimating how perceptive the narrator is when he claims that "she understands" (527) the diary's therapeutic function. Perhaps she isn't as aware of its value as he thinks. Still, writing is a resource for her as she tries to cope with the medical treatment her husband inflicts.

Sometimes authors unintentionally plagiarize. They forget that certain ideas they recorded during their research are actually quotations or paraphrases. Nevertheless, most readers will see "accidental" plagiarism as still plagiarism. So be precise in your research notes. Put within quotation marks anything you copy. The moment your notes quote or restate someone else's words, jot down information about the source. Of course, you should record the page number, but do even more. Include all the details you'll need for a Works Cited entry, because your essay may end up referring to the source. In general, equip yourself to give credit.

What *does not* need to be referenced is **common knowledge**: factual information that the average reader can be expected to know or that is readily available in many easily accessible sources. For example, it is common knowledge that Charlotte Perkins Gilman was an American writer. It is also common knowledge that she was born in 1860 and died in 1935, even though most people would have to look that information up in an encyclopedia or a biographical dictionary to verify it.

Strategies for Documenting Sources (MLA Format)

Documentation is the means by which you give credit to the authors of all primary and secondary sources cited within a researched argument. It serves two principal purposes: (1) it allows your readers to find out more about the origin of the ideas you present, and (2) it protects you from charges of plagiarism. Every academic discipline follows slightly different conventions for documentation, but the method most commonly used for writing about literature is the format devised by the MLA. This documentation method encompasses **in-text citations**, which briefly identify within the body of your paper the source of a particular quotation, summary, or paraphrase, and a bibliography, called **Works Cited**, which gives more complete publication information.

While mastering the precise requirements of MLA punctuation and format can be time consuming and even frustrating, getting them right adds immeasurably to the professionalism of a finished paper. More detailed information, including special circumstances and documentation styles for types of sources not covered here, will be found in the *MLA Handbook for Writers of Research Papers*, Eighth Edition (Modern Language Association, 2016). Of course, if your instructor requests that you follow a different documentation method, you should follow his or her instructions instead.

MLA IN-TEXT CITATION

Each time you include information from any outside source—whether in the form of a summary, a paraphrase, or a quotation—you must provide your reader with a brief reference indicating the author and page number of the original. This reference directs the reader to the Works Cited list, where more complete information is available.

There are two basic methods for in-text citation. The first, and usually preferable, method is to include the author's name in the text of your essay and note the page number in parentheses at the end of the citation. The following paraphrase and quotation from "The Yellow Wallpaper" show the format to be followed for this method. Note that the page number (without the abbreviation "p." or additional punctuation) is enclosed within parentheses and that the final punctuation for the sentence occurs after the parenthetical reference, effectively making the reference part of the preceding sentence. For a direct quotation, the closing quotation marks come before the page reference, but the final period is still saved until after the reference.

> Gilman's narrator believes her husband trivializes her disorder (249).

> Gilman's narrator sadly reports that her husband considers her disorder to be just "a slight hysterical tendency" (249).

The method is similar for long quotations (those set off from the main text of your essay). The only differences are that the final punctuation mark comes before the parenthetical page reference, and that the quotation is not enclosed within quotation marks.

In those cases where citing the author's name in your text would be awkward or difficult, you may include both the author's last name and the page reference in the parenthetical citation. The following example draws a quotation from Greg Johnson's article about Gilman's story.

According to one interpreter of the story, the heroine's final behavior is a "necessary stage in her progress toward self-identity and personal achievement" (Johnson 523).

If you cite more than one work by the same author, you must specify from which of these works each citation comes. Many Internet sources don't number their pages; the parenthetical reference needs to include only the author's last name (or, if the work is anonymous, an identifying title.) In the case of poems, use line numbers (rather than page numbers) if they're provided, and precede your first use of a line number with the word "line." If the poem lacks line numbers, cite it by giving the page number. But if the poem is just one page long, you don't need to cite any numbers within your text. The page number must appear, though, in your Works Cited.

MLA WORKS CITED

The second feature of the MLA format is the Works Cited list, or bibliography. This list should begin on a new page of your paper and should be double-spaced throughout and use hanging indention, which means that all lines except the first are indented one-half inch. The list is alphabetized by author's last name (or by the title in the case of anonymous works) and includes every primary and secondary source referred to in your paper. The format for the most common types of entries is given below. If any of the information called for is unavailable for a particular source, simply skip that element and keep the rest of the entry as close as possible to the given format. An anonymous work, for instance, skips the author's name and is alphabetized under the title.

DIRECTORY TO MLA WORKS-CITED ENTRIES

(continued on next page)

DIRECTORY TO MLA WORKS-CITED ENTRIES
(continued)

Books

Here are typical elements of a book citation, in the order they should appear:

1. The author, last name first. If the book has an editor rather than an author, put the last name first but then add a comma and the word "editor." An author might be corporate; in that case, put the name of the organization.
2. The full title, in italics. If the book has a subtitle, put a colon between title and subtitle.
3. If the book has both an author and an editor, now put the words "edited by" and then the editor's name.
4. If the book has a translator, now put the words "translated by" and the translator's name.
5. If the book is in an edition other than the first, put the edition number.
6. Put the name of the publisher. If the publisher is a university, abbreviate "University" as "U" and Press as "P": for example, U of Chicago P or Indiana UP.
7. Put the year of publication.

Rules of punctuation: Follow the author's name with a period. Do the same for the book's full title. Usually, in the rest of the entry, your chief form of punctuation will be a comma. If you use a period again, it will be for abbreviations and for the entry's final punctuation mark. There are a few exceptions to this rule, which we will point out later.

A book by a single author or editor.

Cima, Gay Gibson. *Performing Women: Female Characters, Male Playwrights, and the Modern Stage*. Cornell UP, 1993.

Booth, Wayne C. *The Rhetoric of Fiction*. 2nd ed., U of Chicago P, 1983.
Tucker, Robert C., editor. *The Marx-Engels Reader*. Norton, 1972.
O'Connor, Flannery. *The Habit of Being: Letters of Flannery O'Connor*. Edited by Sally Fitzgerald, Farrar, Straus, and Giroux, 1979.

A book with multiple authors or editors. If there are two, identify the additional person by first and last name. If there are three or more, just give the first person's name followed by "et al." (al. being the abbreviation for the Latin word *alia*).

Leeming, David, and Jake Page. *God: Myths of the Male Divine*. Oxford UP, 1996.
Arrow, Kenneth Joseph, et al., editors. *Education in a Research University*. Stanford UP, 1996.

A book with a corporate author.

National Conference on Undergraduate Research. *Proceedings of the National Conference on Undergraduate Research*. U of North Carolina, 1995.

A recent edition of a book originally published much earlier. If you want your reader to know the first publication date, give it a sentence of its own after the book's title.

Bronte, Emily. *Wuthering Heights*. 1847. Penguin Classics, 2002.

Short Works from Collections and Anthologies

Many scholarly books are collections of articles on a single topic by several different authors. When you cite an article from such a collection, include the information given below. The format is the same for works of literature that appear in an anthology, such as this one:

1. The name of the author(s) of the article or literary work.
2. The title of the short work, enclosed in quotation marks.
3. The title of the anthology, italicized.
4. The name(s) of the editor(s) of the collection or anthology.
5. All relevant publication information, in the same order and format as it would appear in a book citation.
6. The inclusive page numbers for the shorter work.
7. The medium of publication.

A single work from a collection or an anthology. Begin with the author of the single work, and then the work's title. Follow this with the book's title, its editor, and other information you would normally provide for a book. Conclude the entry with the page numbers of the single work.

Kirk, Russell. "Eliot's Christian Imagination." *The Placing of T. S. Eliot*, edited by Jewel Spears Brooker, U of Missouri P, 1991, pp. 136–44.
Silko, Leslie Marmon. "Yellow Woman." *The Story and Its Writer: An Introduction to Short Fiction*, edited by Ann Charters, 9th ed., Bedford/St. Martin's, 2015, pp. 1209–15.

Multiple works from the same collection or anthology. Write a single general entry that provides full publication information for the collection or anthology as a whole. The entry for each shorter work then contains only its author and title, the names of the book's editors, and the page numbers of the shorter work, with all of these facts separated by commas.

Charters, Ann, editor. *The Story and Its Writer: An Introduction to Short Fiction*. 9th ed., Bedford/St. Martin's, 2015.

Faulkner, William. "A Rose for Emily." Charters, pp. 409–15.

Multiple Works by the Same Author

If you cite more than one work by a single author, alphabetize the individual works by title. Give the author's full name only for the first citation in the Works Cited. Any subsequent entry for that author begins not with the name but with three hyphens followed by a period.

Faulkner, William. "A Rose for Emily." *The Story and Its Writer: An Introduction to Short Fiction*, edited by Ann Charters, 9th ed., Bedford/St. Martin's, 2015, pp. 454–60.

---. *The Sound and the Fury*. Modern Library, 1956.

Works in Periodicals

When you cite articles and other short works from journals, magazines, or newspapers, include the following information, in the given order and format:

1. The name(s) of the author(s) of the short work, as for a book publication.
2. The title of the short work, in quotation marks.
3. The title of the periodical, italicized.
4. The volume number, issue number, and date of the issue. See the model citations below for examples of how to abbreviate volume, number, and date in the citations.
5. The page numbers of the short work.

Rules of punctuation: Follow the author's name with a period. Do the same for the short work's title. Usually, in the rest of the entry, your chief form of punctuation will be a comma. If you use a period again, it will be for abbreviations and for the entry's final punctuation mark. There are a few exceptions to this rule, which we will point out later.

A work in a scholarly journal. Publication information for works from scholarly and professional journals should include the volume number, the issue number, the month or season of the issue, and the year.

Charles, Casey. "Gender Trouble in *Twelfth Night*." *Theatre Journal*, vol. 49, no. 2, May 1997, pp. 121–41.

An article in a magazine. Publication information for articles in general-circulation magazines includes the month(s) of publication for a monthly (or bimonthly), or the date (day, abbreviated month, then year) for a weekly or biweekly.

Cowley, Malcolm. "It Took a Village." *Utne Reader*, Nov.-Dec. 1997, pp. 48–49.

Kolbert, Elizabeth. "Unnatural Selection." *New Yorker*, 18 April 2016, pp. 22–28.

An article in a newspaper. When citing an article from a newspaper, include the date (day, abbreviated month, year), followed by the edition, the section number, or the section letter (if applicable).

Bray, Hiawatha. "New FCC Rules Draw Criticism." *Boston Globe*, 17 May 2016, p. C2.

A book review in a scholarly journal.

Hawkins, Ty. Review of *Vietnam and Beyond: Tim O'Brien and the Power of Storytelling*, by Stefania Ciocia. *Studies in the Novel*, Vol. 45, No. 4, Winter 2013, pp. 705–07.

A book review in a magazine.

Plumly, Stanley. Review of *Those Who Write for Immortality: Romantic Reputations and the Dream of Lasting Fame*, by H. J. Jackson. *The American Scholar*, vol. 84, no. 2, Spring 2015, pp. 152–53.

A book review in a newspaper.

Yardley, Jonathan. Review of *One Matchless Time: A Life of William Faulkner*, by Jay Parini. *The Washington Post*, 24 Oct. 2004, p. T2.

Online Sources

Documentation for online sources should include as much of the following information as possible, in the order and format specified:

1. The name(s) of the author(s), as for a book publication.
2. The title of the work accessed, in quotation marks. For e-mails and postings, the title is the subject line.
3. The title of the periodical, italicized.
4. The volume number, issue number, and date of the issue. See the model citations below for examples of how to abbreviate volume, number, and date in the citations.
5. The URL or, better yet, the DOI. The letters "DOI" stand for "digital object identifier." A DOI is a permanent tag, enabling an online source to be located even when the URL changes. Not every Internet document has a DOI, but if you can find one for your source, list that rather than the URL. Lowercase is preferred for **doi** entries in the actual citation.
6. If there is no date of issue, you may indicate the date you accessed the site, e.g., "Accessed 2 May 2018."

Rules of punctuation: Follow the author's name with a period. Do the same for the work's title. Usually, in the rest of the entry, your chief form of punctuation will be a comma. If you use a period again, it will be for abbreviations and for the entry's final punctuation mark. There are a few exceptions to this rule, which we will point out later.

An article in an online journal.

Abowitz, Richard. "The Hughes Blues." *The Smart Set*, 2 Mar. 2016, http://thesmartset.com/the-langston-hughes-blues/.

An article in a print journal that you access through an online database. Provide all the information you would give if you were citing the print version of the article. End this section with a period. Then put the name of the database (in italics), a comma, the URL or the DOI, and a final period.

De Baerdemaeker, Ruben. "Performative Patterns in Hemingway's 'Soldier's Home.'" *The Hemingway Review*, vol. 27, no. 1, Fall 2007, pp. 55–73. *Project Muse*, doi: 10.1353/hem.2007.0017.

A book review that appears online.

Livingston, James. Review of *The Age of the Crisis of Man*, by Mark Greif. *Bookforum*, 9 Mar. 2015, http://www.bookforum.com/review/14328.

A comment posted at a Web site. Begin the entry with whatever name the commenter has used. Then write "Comment on," followed by the title (in quotation marks) of the text that the comment responds to. Next, using commas, give the title of the journal or Web site where the comment appears, followed by the date that the comment was posted, the time it was posted (if available), and the URL.

Stefan. Comment on "How Should We Live in a Diverse Society?" *Pandaemonium*, 4 May 2016, 10:25 p.m., https://kenanmalik.wordpress.com/2016/05/02/how-should-we-live-in-a-diverse-society/.

A contribution to a listserv or similar online forum. In this case, the title is the subject line.

Bean, Joyce. "Re: Is fiction w/ community as subject still viable?" *Writing Program Administration*, 10 May 2016, 12:08 p.m., https://lists.asu.edu/cgi-bin/wa?A2=ind1605&L=WPA-L&D=0&P=149100.

An e-mail message. Again, the title is the subject line. Then you should identify who received the message, along with the date it arrived.

Hardy, Rachel. "Re: Flannery O'Connor's stories." Received by Jacob Ravitz, 5 Apr. 2018.

An online video, such as those available at YouTube. For an entry like this, you have options. Your choices should reflect what you want to stress. Note the following options for citing a certain YouTube video. The first example starts with the video's title, which would surely help your readers track down the video. But if you wish to stress the title *and* acknowledge who posted the video, you could include that person's name, as our second example does. Maybe, though, you'll want to emphasize the video's director; our third example begins with his name and production role.

"A Conversation with Tobias Wolff Directed by Lawrence Bridges." *YouTube*, 30 Nov. 2013, https://www.youtube.com/watch?v=0MZ3oKPFf90.

"A Conversation with Tobias Wolff Directed by Lawrence Bridges." *YouTube*, posted by Lawrence Bridges, 30 Nov. 2013, https://www.youtube.com/watch?v=0MZ3oKPFf90.

Bridges, Lawrence, director. "A Conversation with Tobias Wolff Directed by Lawrence Bridges." *YouTube*, 30 Nov. 2013, https://www.youtube.com/watch?v=0MZ3oKPFf90.

Citation Formats for Other Kinds of Sources

An interview you conducted. In the author slot, identify the person you interviewed. Follow this information with "Personal interview," a comma, and the interview's date.

McCorkle, Patrick. Personal interview, 12 Mar. 2018.

An episode of a television series. Begin with the episode's title. Using commas, follow this with the series title, the season and episode numbers, the network or production company, and the date of first airing. Our first example refers to the notorious "red wedding" episode of the TV series *Game of Thrones*. If you want to call attention to particular contributors, you can do so by adding information about them as our second example does.

"The Rains of Castamere." *Game of Thrones*, season 3, episode 9, HBO, 2 June 2013.

"The Rains of Castamere." *Game of Thrones*, created by David Benioff and D. B. Weiss, performances by Richard Madden, Michelle Fairley, and Oona Chaplin, season 3, episode 9, HBO, 2 June 2013.

A film. Many film citations indicate title and director. Depending on which you want to emphasize, you can begin with either. Our first and second examples show these options. If you want to call attention to other contributors, you can do so by adding information about them as our third example does. In any case, end your entry by identifying the main production company and the year of first release.

The Dark Knight. Directed by Christopher Nolan, Warner Bros., 2008.

Nolan, Christopher, director. *The Dark Knight*, Warner Bros., 2008.

The Dark Knight. Directed by Christopher Nolan, performances by Christian Bale and Heath Ledger, Warner Bros, 2008.

A Note on Endnotes

Occasionally, you may have an idea or find a piece of information that seems important to your paper but that you just cannot work in smoothly without interrupting the flow of ideas. Such information can be included in the form of **endnotes**. A small superscript number in your text signals a note, and the notes themselves appear on a separate page at the end of your paper, before the Works Cited. Often, endnotes point readers to sources that they can then investigate if they wish. Any source mentioned in an endnote must be listed in the Works Cited.

Five Annotated Student Researched Arguments

We end this chapter with five researched arguments written by students. All of the essays refer to Charlotte Perkins Gilman's short story "The Yellow Wallpaper." But they model different ways to write about it. In order, the essays are:

- A researched argument that uses a literary work to examine a social issue
- A researched argument that deals with existing interpretations of a literary work
- A researched argument that analyzes a literary work through the framework of a particular theorist
- A researched argument that places a literary work in historical and cultural context
- A researched argument that places a literary work in a multimedia context

Each argument demonstrates strategies we've discussed. Each also shows how to cite sources using MLA format. We annotate these essays in their margins, with comments that point out specific moves they make. After each essay, we review how it uses its sources. You'll see that the authors draw on research to create a conversation. They synthesize their findings as they build a case of their own.

A RESEARCHED ARGUMENT THAT USES A LITERARY WORK TO EXAMINE SOCIAL ISSUES

Some research papers mention a literary work but then focus on examining a social issue related to that work. An example of such a paper is the following essay by student Sarah Michaels. To prepare for writing her paper, Sarah consulted numerous sources, and she turns to them during the course of her essay. The chief danger in a project like this is that it will become a mere "data dump"—that is, a paper in which the writer uncritically cites one source after another without really making an original argument. In writing an essay like Sarah's, be sure to identify your main issue and claim clearly. Present yourself as someone who is genuinely *testing* your sources, determining the specific ways in which they are relevant to your argument. Keep in mind that even if you are representing a source as useful, you can indicate how its ideas need to be further complicated. With at least some of your sources, analyze specific terms they employ, lingering over their language. Moreover, try to relate your sources to one another. We think Sarah accomplishes all these objectives. Even if you disagree, aim to practice her strategies yourself.

Sarah Michaels
Professor Swain
English L202
21 May ----

"The Yellow Wallpaper" as a Guide to Social Factors in Postpartum Depression

In 2005, actor Brooke Shields's memoir *Down Came the Rain: My Journey through Postpartum Depression* drew much public attention to the psychological problem mentioned in its subtitle.[1] But during the last couple of decades, postpartum depression has been the subject of reports by many medical institutions and media outlets. By now, lots of people other than health professionals are aware of this problem and can at least roughly define it. If asked, most of them would probably say that although it can exhibit varying degrees of severity, postpartum depression is basically a state of despair suffered by a significant number of women who have just given birth. This is, in fact, the main image of it presented in a recent document about it, an October 2010 report by Marian Earls and a committee of the American Academy of Pediatrics. Besides explaining what postpartum depression is, the report urges pediatricians and other primary care providers to screen new mothers for it. Given that many members of the public already know that the problem is widespread, the report has not sparked much disagreement. Responding to it in the online magazine *Slate*, however, Emily Anthes does challenge its almost total emphasis on mothers. She argues that the Academy's committee makes a questionable assumption in writing as if only females are traumatized by birth. In her article entitled "Dads Get Blue, Too," she criticizes the report's authors for not acknowledging at greater length that new fathers can experience postpartum depression as well.[2] More generally, her article suggests that discussions of this disorder can be skewed by ideological views that need to be recognized. But more than a century ago, Charlotte Perkins Gilman's story "The Yellow Wallpaper" made pretty much the same point by showing how a woman diagnosed with a label like postpartum depression is a victim of her domestic

Calls attention to an endnote.

Quickly identifies social issue that the paper will focus on.

Introduces the literary work that the paper will relate to the social issue.

circumstances and her society's ideas about gender, not just a person who has become ill on her own. When juxtaposed with the Academy's report, Gilman's 1892 tale is a reminder that today's doctors should look beyond an individual woman's symptoms of post-birth distress, because the social arrangements in which she lives may significantly affect her health.

The term *postpartum depression* has for a long time appeared in analyses of "The Yellow Wallpaper" and of the personal experience that Gilman based the story on. Veronica Makowsky points out that this clinical phrase has even "become a critical commonplace" (329) in studies of the relationship between the story and Gilman's life. Gilman does not, however, actually use the term *postpartum depression* in the tale. Instead, the heroine's husband, John, declares that she suffers from "temporary nervous depression — a slight hysterical tendency" (249), and the character herself refers to her "nervous troubles" (250). Nor does Gilman bring up the term in her accounts of the real-life despair she went through when she gave birth to her daughter. In her essay "Why I Wrote 'The Yellow Wallpaper,'" she recalls being tormented much of her life by "a severe and continuous nervous breakdown tending to melancholia" (261). In her book-length autobiography *The Living of Charlotte Perkins Gilman*, she describes herself as suffering from "nervous prostration" (90). Indeed, the *Oxford English Dictionary*'s entry for *postpartum depression* indicates that the term was not recorded until 1929, when it showed up in an issue of the *American Journal of Psychiatry*.

Concedes that the term is used by scholars rather than by the author herself.

Nevertheless, the phrase does seem to fit the condition of Gilman's narrator. According to the American Academy of Pediatrics report, the symptoms of postpartum depression can range from "crying, worrying, sadness, anxiety, and mood swings" to more disturbing signs like "paranoia, mood shifts, hallucinations, [and] delusions" (1033). Gilman's character can be said to display most of these things once her child is born. At the estate that is the story's setting, she has trouble sleeping, she comes to doubt her husband's love, and, most dramatically, she rips off the wallpaper in her bedroom to free a woman whom she imagines wanting to creep away.

Directly connects language of the report to the story.

But simply labeling the heroine's distress as postpartum depression risks ignoring the conditions surrounding her that contribute to her suffering. Commenting on "The Yellow Wallpaper," literary critic Paula A. Treichler points out that a medical diagnosis can block understanding of "social, cultural, and economic practices" (69), even though these may support the doctor's claim to expertise, play a role in the

Uses another interpreter of the story to advance this paper's argument.

patient's anguish, and become more important to confront than the patient's individual pain.[3] In Gilman's story, John uses his social authority as physician and husband to control his wife. Specifically, he isolates her on the estate and makes her give up real activity, just as Gilman's real-life doctor, S. Weir Mitchell, demanded that she rest. As a result, the heroine feels obligated to surrender to the stereotypical passive female role, even though she would welcome more interaction with others and suspects that "congenial work, with excitement and change, would do me good" (249). When she proceeds to hallucinate the woman in the wallpaper, this is something that she is *driven* to do by John's assertion of masculine power, just as Weir Mitchell's prescription for inertia drove Gilman "near the border line of utter mental ruin" ("Why" 792).

Key quote from the story.

With "The Yellow Wallpaper" in mind, readers of the American Academy of Pediatrics report might examine how it downplays what Treichler calls "social, cultural, and economic practices" in its focus on diagnosing postpartum depression in women. Although the report does note that "Paternal depression is estimated at 6%" (1032), it does not linger on this fairly significant figure. In addition, the committee mentions only in passing that while "as many as 12% of all pregnant or postpartum women experience depression in a given year," the percentage is twice as much "for low-income women" (1032). Similarly brief is the recognition that "Eighteen percent of fathers of children in Early Head Start had symptoms of depression" (1033), a distinctly high figure that again suggests one's social class can affect one's health. Nor does the report develop its brief notice that possible causes of postpartum depression include "domestic violence" (1034), which would be a serious problem in the patient's environment rather than a malfunction within the patient herself. Instead of insisting that "Treatment must address the mother-child dyad relationship" (1036), the committee might also have called for addressing the chance that the mother suffers from a lack of money or the presence of an abusive partner.

Uses the story to examine the issue raised by the report.

Paper works with specific examples and language from the report.

Juxtaposing Gilman's story with the Academy's report does not mean that readers of this recent document about postpartum depression have to declare its authors evil. The attitudes and recommendations of the committee are not as morally disturbing as those of Gilman's character John. But her story should encourage the report's readers to notice where, in its call for screening women for postpartum depression, it risks screening *out* social influences on people diagnosed with this clinical problem.

Heads off possible misunderstanding.

Endnotes

The endnotes provide additional information not easily incorporated into the paper's main text.

[1] Shields also discussed her postpartum depression in a *New York Times* op-ed column, in which she defended herself against actor Tom Cruise's charge that she should have relied on vitamins and exercise rather than on the prescription drug Paxil.

[2] For an article that supports Anthes's attention to fathers even though she does not mention it, see Kim and Swain.

[3] For an article that expresses a position like Treichler's, see Dubriwny's critique of how modern-day TV news broadcasts represent postpartum disorders.

Works Cited

Anthes, Emily. "Dads Get Blue, Too." *Slate*, 4 Nov. 2010, http://slate.com/articles/double_x/doubleex/2010/11/dads_gett_blue_too.html.

Citation for an online article.

Dubriwny, Tasha N. "Television News Coverage of Postpartum Disorders and the Politics of Medicalization." *Feminist Media Studies*, vol. 10, no. 3, Sept. 2010, pp. 285–303.

Earls, Marian F., and the Committee on Psychosocial Aspects of Child and Family Health. "Clinical Report: Incorporating Recognition and Management of Perinatal and Postpartum Depression into Pediatric Practice. *Pediatrics*, vol. 26, no. 5, Nov. 2010, pp. 1032–38, doi: 10.1542/peds.2010-2348.

Gilman, Charlotte Perkins. *The Living of Charlotte Perkins Gilman: An Autobiography*. 1935. Arno Press, 1972.

Citation for a book.

---. "Why I Wrote 'The Yellow Wallpaper.'" 1913. Schilb and Clifford, pp. 260–61.

Note style for multiple works by same author. Note, too, that when you cite more than one work from the same book, you give each book its own entry and cite each work from it in the shorthand form you see here.

---. "The Yellow Wallpaper." 1892. Schilb and Clifford, pp. 247–60.

Kim, Pilyoung, and James E. Swain. "Sad Dads: Paternal Postpartum Depression." *Psychiatry*, Feb. 2007, pp. 36–47.

Makowsky, Veronica. "Fear of Feeling and the Turn-of-the-Century Woman of Letters." *American Literary History*, vol. 5, no. 2, Summer 1993, pp. 326–34.

Schilb, John, and John Clifford, editors. *Making Literature Matter: An Anthology for Readers and Writers*. 7th ed., Bedford/St. Martin's, 2018.

Shields, Brooke. *Down Came the Rain: My Journey through Postpartum Depression*. Hyperion, 2005.

---. "War of Words." *New York Times*, 1 July 2005, late ed., p. A17.

Treichler, Paula A. "Escaping the Sentence: Diagnosis and Discourse in 'The Yellow Wallpaper.'" *Tulsa Studies in Women's Literature*, vol. 3, nos. 1–2, Spring-Autumn 1984, pp. 61–77.

Citation for a print article.

HOW SARAH USES HER SOURCES

Sarah's primary source. The October 2010 report on postpartum depression by the Earls Committee of the American Academy of Pediatrics; Sarah's argument is mainly a critique of this report

Gilman, "The Yellow Wallpaper." To point out social contexts that the Earls Committee ignored

Shields. To indicate that postpartum depression has become a big public issue (so that the topic deserves the attention Sarah will give it)

Anthes. To indicate that the Committee's report has received *some* criticism (which Sarah will add to)

Makowsky. To confirm that it's not unusual for literary critics to associate Gilman and her story with postpartum depression

Gilman, autobiographical nonfiction. To acknowledge that Gilman herself didn't use the term *postpartum depression*, though it now seems applicable to her and her story

Treichler. To support Sarah's focus on the social contexts of postpartum depression

Kim and Swain. To reinforce the argument made by Anthes (whom Sarah uses to suggest that criticism of the Earls Committee report is appropriate)

Dubriwny. To support Sarah's focus on the social contexts of postpartum depression

A RESEARCHED ARGUMENT THAT DEALS WITH EXISTING INTERPRETATIONS OF A LITERARY WORK

A researched writing assignment may require you to develop a claim about a literary work by relating your analysis to previous interpretations of the text. In the following essay, student Katie Johnson makes an argument about Charlotte Perkins Gilman's story "The Yellow Wallpaper" by incorporating statements made by people who have already written about it. To prepare for writing her essay, she especially consulted the *MLA International Bibliography*, through which she located several published articles about Gilman's tale. The bibliographies of these articles led her to still more interpretations of the story. The biggest challenge in writing an essay like this is to stay focused on developing an idea of your own rather than just inserting and echoing opinions held by others. Katie ended up examining an element of Gilman's story that she felt had not been adequately noted, let alone properly interpreted, by literary critics. As her essay proceeds, therefore, she does not simply agree with all the interpreters she cites. She treats with respect, however, those she finds fault with, civilly pointing out how her own thoughts differ. In addition, she clearly takes seriously the specific language of the critics she mentions, pondering their actual words rather than superficially summarizing their views.

Katie Johnson
Professor Van Wyck
English L141
5 May ----

The Meaning of the Husband's Fainting
in "The Yellow Wallpaper"

At the end of Charlotte Perkins Gilman's short story "The Yellow Wallpaper," the narrator is in a state that many people observing her would consider madness. She has torn off the wallpaper in her room and now seems proud of being able to "creep smoothly on the floor" (259). Her outwardly bizarre behavior at this point, along with her telling of the whole story beforehand, has led most literary critics to focus on analyzing her final conduct, as if it was the only really noteworthy feature of this concluding scene. Just as striking, however, is the final behavior of the narrator's husband, John. Up until the ending, he has acted as an authority on his wife's medical condition, and he has tried to assert power by always telling her what to do. At the conclusion, though, his mastery plainly vanishes. After finding the key to his wife's room, letting himself in, and beholding her crawling, he faints. Both the narrator and her husband end up on the floor. The narrator herself is highly aware of John's collapse, as she shows when she complains that "I had to creep over him every time!" (260). Because John's fainting is a dramatic reversal of his previous behavior and resembles the narrator's final physical position, it is surprising that only some literary critics have bothered to comment on John's breakdown, and even then the comments are relatively few. This neglect is a shame because, through John's fainting, Gilman seems to imply that he is left without any clear gender role to support him when his wife defies his manly effort to keep her what his society would consider sane.

Concisely summarizes the story's conclusion in first paragraph, which ends by stating main claim the essay will develop.

Until the last scene, John has repeatedly attempted to control his wife in the way that his society would expect of a man. This effort of his is reinforced by the professional standing he has achieved as a doctor. His masculine authority is interconnected with his medical authority. As we readers are made aware, he does not succeed in thoroughly bending his wife's will to his. Much of her narration is about her secret rebellion against him, which takes the form of imagining women trapped in the wallpaper of her room. Despite her hidden thoughts, however, he is often issuing commands to her, and she finds it hard to resist his domination. She admits to us that "I take pains to control myself—before him, at least, and that makes me very tired" (249). His attempts at enforcing his power over her include shutting her up in an odd country house in the first place. When she expresses suspicion of the estate, he simply "laughs" and "scoffs" (249), as he seems to do whenever she reveals independent thinking. She also says that he "hardly lets me stir without special direction" and gives her "a schedule prescription for each hour in the day" (249). Furthermore, he discourages her from writing, does not want to let her have visitors, and refuses to leave the estate when she informs him that she is not getting any better. Actually, he treats her more like his child than his wife, which is revealed when he asks "What is it, little girl?" (254) one night when she wakes up bothered by the wallpaper. All in all, he fits the nineteenth-century image of the ideal man as someone who gives his wife orders and expects her to follow them, though John tries to disguise his bossiness by declaring that he loves her and is looking out for her best interests.

The literary critics who do write about John's fainting at the end of the story tend to see it as a moment of irony, because in their view this masculine authority figure winds up physically collapsing in a way that is stereotypically associated with women. For example, Carol Margaret Davison states that when John faints, he is "assuming the traditional role of frail female" (66). Greg Johnson describes John's fall as "Gilman's witty inversion of a conventional heroine's confrontation with Gothic terror" (529), and similarly, Beverly A. Hume says that what happens is that John is "altering his conventional role as a soothing, masculine figure to that of a stereotypically weak nineteenth-century female" (478). These comments are not unreasonable, because during the nineteenth century, fainting was indeed something that women were believed to do more often than men. But a pair of literary critics has made another observation that, even though it sounds like the ones I have just quoted, points in a different direction that seems worth pursuing. Sandra M. Gilbert and Susan Gubar refer to John's fainting as an "unmasculine swoon of surprise" (91). They sound as if they are saying that he now seems feminine, but actually the word "unmasculine" simply indicates that he is no

Synthesizes comments from critics, combining them to indicate the pattern she finds in interpretations of the story.

Does not flatly declare critics wrong but will develop an idea they have not mentioned.

longer acting like a stereotypical male, so that readers of the story have to wonder whether he has any kind of identity left to him now. In fact, John's fainting seems like a total falling apart, as if he has become incapable of performing any further role at all, whether it is stereotypically feminine or masculine. Though his wife is creeping, at least she is still able to move, whereas he lies paralyzed. Overall, he appears to suffer a complete loss of identity rather than take on a female identity. Because his wife has fallen into what he sees as madness despite his efforts to control her, he experiences a shattering of his male ego, the result being not that he is left with a "womanly" self but that he now lacks any sense of self at all. Just as he has only leased the estate instead of owning it, so too has his personhood proven impermanent because his ability to treat his wife as his property has apparently gone. At the very end of the story, the narrator even refers to her husband merely as "that man" (260), suggesting that he is no longer recognizable as an individual human being.

Carefully analyzes a particular word that this pair of critics uses. Rest of paragraph develops main claim.

More than one literary critic has argued that John has suffered a loss of power only momentarily and that he will soon dominate his wife just as much as he did before. Judith Fetterley contends that "when John recovers from his faint, he will put her in a prison from which there will be no escape" (164), and Paula Treichler claims that

> As the ending of her narrative, her madness will no doubt commit her to more intense medical treatment, perhaps to the dreaded Weir Mitchell of whom her husband has spoken. The surrender of patriarchy is only temporary; her husband has merely fainted, after all, not died, and will no doubt move swiftly and severely to deal with her. Her individual escape is temporary and compromised. (67)

Because quotation from Treichler is somewhat lengthy, Katie puts it in block form.

Unfortunately, Gilman did not write a sequel called "The Yellow Wallpaper: The Next Day" to let us know exactly what happens to the couple after the husband wakes up. Fetterley and Treichler might have been right if the events of this story had taken place in real life and involved a real married couple. Though it was based on Gilman's actual situation,[1] the story should be treated as a work of fiction, and Gilman has chosen to conclude it by showing John as physically overcome. If she had wanted to suggest that he will quickly regain power, presumably she would have done so. As the text stands, the final scene emphasizes his new weakness, not signs of a strength that will soon be restored to him.

Synthesizes two critics' observations, putting them together as examples of a view that she questions.

Directs readers to endnote.

Disagrees with two critics but carefully explains why and avoids using hostile tone.

Although both the husband and the wife are in a bad physical state at the end, we as readers do not have to sympathize with them equally. Especially by having the wife narrate the story, Gilman has designed it so that we are encouraged to care far more about her than about John. A lot of readers might even feel joy at his collapse, regarding it as the bringing down of a tyrant. In any case, his fainting is worth paying attention to as a sign that he has experienced a loss of masculine power that leaves him unable to function as any kind of self.

Uses final paragraph not only to restate main claim but also to add the point that readers of story do not have to feel as sorry for John as they do for his wife.

Endnote

[1] Gilman recalls the personal experience that motivated her to write her story in her essay "Why I Wrote 'The Yellow Wallpaper.'"

Endnote provides information that could not be easily integrated into main text of essay.

Works Cited

Davison, Carol Margaret. "Haunted House/Haunted Heroine: Female Gothic Closets in 'The Yellow Wallpaper.'" *Women's Studies*, vol. 33, no. 1, Jan.–Feb. 2004, pp. 47–75.

Citation for article in scholarly journal.

Fetterley, Judith. "Reading about Reading: 'A Jury of Her Peers,' 'The Murders in the Rue Morgue,' and 'The Yellow Wallpaper.'" *Gender and Reading: Essays on Readers, Texts, and Contexts*, edited by Elizabeth A. Flynn and Patrocinio P. Schweickart, Johns Hopkins UP, 1986, pp. 147–64.

Citation for work in anthology.

Gilbert, Sandra M., and Susan Gubar. *The Madwoman in the Attic: The Woman Writer and the Nineteenth-Century Literary Imagination*. Yale UP, 1979.

Citation for book.

Gilman, Charlotte Perkins. "Why I Wrote 'The Yellow Wallpaper.'" 1913. Schilb and Clifford, pp. 260–61.

---. "The Yellow Wallpaper." 1892. Schilb and Clifford, pp. 247–60.

Note style for multiple works by the same author. Note, too, that when you cite more than one work from the same book, you give the book its own entry and then cite each work from it in the shorthand form you see here.

Hume, Beverly A. "Gilman's 'Interminable Grotesque': The Narrator of 'The Yellow Wallpaper.'" *Studies in Short Fiction*, vol. 28, no. 4, Fall 1991, pp. 477–84.

Johnson, Greg. "Gilman's Gothic Allegory: Rage and Redemption in 'The Yellow Wallpaper.'" *Studies in Short Fiction*, vol. 26, no. 4, Fall 1989, pp. 521–30.

Schilb, John, and John Clifford, editors. *Making Literature Matter: An Anthology for Readers and Writers*. 7th ed., Bedford/St. Martin's, 2018.

Citation for anthology.

Treichler, Paula A. "Escaping the Sentence: Diagnosis and Discourse in 'The Yellow Wallpaper.'" *Tulsa Studies in Women's Literature*, vol. 3, nos. 1–2, Spring–Autumn 1984, pp. 61–77.

HOW KATIE USES HER SOURCES

Katie's primary source. Gilman's "The Yellow Wallpaper"; Katie's argument is mainly an interpretation of the story's ending, specifically the husband's fainting

Davison, Johnson, Hume. To indicate a perspective that Katie doesn't quite accept and will go beyond

Gilbert and Gubar. To indicate a perspective that seems close to Katie's own but isn't really the same as hers

Fetterley, Treichler. To indicate an interpretation of the story's ending that Katie disagrees with

Gilman, article on her writing of the story. To acknowledge that the story has roots in real life

A RESEARCHED ARGUMENT THAT ANALYZES A LITERARY WORK THROUGH THE FRAMEWORK OF A PARTICULAR THEORIST

In Chapter 7, we explain how to write a research paper that takes one of the critical approaches now popular in literary theory. Some research papers, however, make an argument about a literary work by applying to it the ideas of a single theorist. Often, this is someone whose concepts have already influenced many scholars. Perhaps this person has even pioneered an entire field of thought. Examples include the father of psychoanalysis, Sigmund Freud; the founder of Marxist theory, Karl Marx; leading voices of existentialism such as Friedrich Nietzsche and Martin Heidegger; and the modern feminist writer Virginia Woolf.

If you attempt a paper like this, the theorist you choose might not have read the literary work you discuss. Even so, his or her ideas can illuminate it. Of course, you need to summarize the theorist's thinking in a manner that is both helpful and concise. Instead of just offering scattered, random passages from this person's writing, try to provide an efficient overview of the theorist's basic *framework*: that is, the main ideas that this figure contributes. You will especially want to specify the ideas that are most helpful for interpreting your chosen literary text. In essence, you will be using these concepts as a *lens*. Your paper can, however, admit that the theorist's principles do not cover *everything* important in the text. Probably you will be more credible to your reader if you concede that while the theorist's framework is useful, it provides a less-than-exact explanation. In fact, you will be seen more as developing a claim of your own if you point out the *limits* of the theorist's ideas along with their strengths. This is what student Jacob Grobowicz does in the following paper. His essay applies to "The Yellow Wallpaper" the ideas of the late Michel Foucault, a French theorist whose writings about modern power relations have inspired scholars in the social sciences and humanities. But Jacob does not simply quote from Foucault's writings. Instead, he critically examines the lens he provides, arguing that it clarifies major parts of the story but does not account for them all.

Jacob Grobowicz
Professor Burke
English L202
10 May - - - -

Using Foucault to Understand Disciplinary Power
in Gilman's "The Yellow Wallpaper"

Michel Foucault provides a useful framework for understanding the narrator's experiences in Charlotte Perkins Gilman's 1892 short story "The Yellow Wallpaper." More specifically, the theory of power that Foucault puts forth in his book *Discipline and Punish*[1] sheds light on the narrator's frustration with the "rest cure" that her husband makes her undergo. Of course, any perspective on a literary work may neglect some aspects of it. As a slant on Gilman's story, Foucault's book does have limits. In particular, *Discipline and Punish* does not pay much attention to gender, a significant element of the narrator's life. Still, quite relevant to her situation is Foucault's central argument in the book, which is that "discipline" is the main form of power in the modern age.

Directs reader to an endnote.

Immediately establishes what literary work the paper will focus on, as well as what theorist and what specific text by that theorist.

The paper's main claim, which identifies which of the theorist's concepts the paper will apply to the story.

When Foucault refers to "discipline" in his book, he has two meanings of the term in mind, though he sees them as closely related to each other. First, human beings have become "disciplined" in the sense that they feel pressured to follow the standards held by all sorts of authorities. According to his historical account, power was previously associated with the figure of the king. Judges were a narrow group of officials who carried out the will of the monarch by punishing blatant violators of the law. Foucault also points out that the punishment usually took the form of physical imprisonment. The emphasis was on confinement of the criminal's body, not on reform of the criminal's soul. Foucault views the modern era, however, as a major shift from this state of affairs. He declares that nowadays, the administrators of power are more widespread: "The judges of normality are everywhere. We are in the society of the teacher-judge, the doctor-judge, the educator-judge, the 'social-worker' judge" (304). Furthermore, these figures look beyond sheer criminals and try to control all humanity. In fact, they aim to mold human beings' basic thinking, a goal they pursue by getting people to adopt conformist ideas and values promoted by various fields of expertise. Increasingly, Foucault claims, human beings are kept in place through forms of training, knowledge, and examination that are developed and advanced by academic and professional

Begins a two-paragraph section that summarizes relevant details of theorist's framework and defines a key term of his.

specialties — "disciplines" in the second sense of the word. Foucault argues that although these fields pose as benevolent "sciences of man," they actually participate in "the modern play of coercion over bodies, gestures and behavior" (191).

Discipline and Power stresses this idea by spending many pages on the image of the Panopticon. This is a model for a prison, proposed in the nineteenth century by British philosopher Jeremy Bentham. He envisioned a penitentiary with a central tower whose guards could observe all of the surrounding cells. The prisoners would feel constantly threatened by the tower's gaze, even though they could not be sure when the building was actually occupied. Eventually, their insecurity would drive them to monitor and restrict their conduct on their own, thereby doing the guards' work. Foucault brings up the Panopticon to argue that while institutions still engage in external surveillance — watching people in various ways — fields of expertise now serve dominant forces by leading people to engage in *self*-surveillance. In this respect, power can be said to *produce* the self rather than simply repress it.

Of all the experts that Foucault mentions in *Discipline and Power*, the one most significant to the narrator of "The Yellow Wallpaper" is "the doctor-judge." Suffering from a depression that seems related to her having recently given birth, she is in the hands of a physician named John who is also her husband. His diagnosis of her is reinforced by her brother, who is a doctor as well. Moreover, when the narrator fails to get physically better as fast as John would like, he threatens to deliver her over to S. Weir Mitchell, the real-life medical expert whose rest cure proved unendurable to Gilman herself. By linking three physicians to each other — John, the brother, and Weir Mitchell — Gilman suggests that her heroine must cope with principles and values imposed on her by the field of medicine in general, which Foucault calls attention to as a discipline that manipulates people's identities in the name of health. In John's view, his spouse is not experiencing any serious discontentment with her life, even though the reader senses that she is, in fact, distressed at having to accommodate herself to the roles of wife and mother as defined by the field of medicine specifically and by society overall. Proclaiming that she is afflicted by simply "a slight hysterical tendency" (249), John prevents himself from learning "how much I really suffer" (250). Relying on his alleged expertise as a representative of his profession, he values his own clinical precision over her vague reports of unease: "He has no patience with faith, an intense horror of superstition, and he scoffs openly at any talk of things not to be felt and seen and put down in figures" (248). Foucault might say that

Paper now begins directly connecting theorist's ideas to specific details of the story.

John wishes for his wife to discipline herself, which involves her obeying the policies that John derives from his scientific background. Indeed, at two different points in the story, she comments that he is basically focused on her achieving "self-control" (pp. 249, 254).

It is important for the reader to note that John is not an outright monster in his treatment of the narrator. He does not physically abuse her, at least not in any dramatic way. In fact, even when he is condescending toward her, he seems to believe sincerely that he has her best interests at heart. In an article that interprets the story with Foucault's ideas in mind, John S. Bak overstates the case when he argues that the narrator's husband subjects her to "a dehumanizing imprisonment" (40) and "resembles the penal officers of the eighteenth-century psychiatric wards or penitentiaries" (42). Although he isolates her on a country estate, he does not virtually lock her up and physically torment her, as Bak implies. While much of the plot takes place in a single room, she is free to roam the estate, and it is *she* who denies *him* access to the room for a brief spell at the end. Explaining in his book how power now operates, Foucault points out that it tends to present itself not as a crude, blatant instrument of punishment but as a means of enlightened reform.

Heads off possible misunderstanding.

Takes a position on an article that has already applied the theorist's ideas to the story.

Foucault does believe, however, that agents of power like John are presumptuous in assuming that they can produce better human beings through their guidance. So, too, Gilman's narrator does not find that her husband's professional advice is helping her to grow healthier. Inwardly, she disagrees with him when he commands her to avoid physical activity, for she supposes that "congenial work, with excitement and change, would do me good" (249). Though "he hates to have me write a word" (250), she defies him by secretly writing down the story of her lingering unhappiness and tension. Similarly, she tries to conceal from him her inability to comply with his demand that she get plenty of sleep. Eventually, rather than automatically following his prescriptions, she finds herself "getting a little afraid of John" (256). She moves from believing that "he loves me so" (254) to suspecting that in his interrogations of her, he has merely "pretended to be very loving and kind" (258). Of course, the most dramatic form that her alienation from him takes is her preoccupation with the woman she sees lurking behind her room's wallpaper. The narrator's effort to free the woman — including her violent tearing of the paper — vividly demonstrates that Gilman's heroine hopes to escape the forces of domination that her husband symbolizes. She is not as capable as Foucault is of coming up with a full-fledged theory of the modern disciplinary society that her husband represents, but intuitively she associates him

Resumes connecting the theorist's ideas directly to the story.

with this kind of world, and in essence she protests against it as she strips the paper off.

While Foucault's *Discipline and Punish* provides much context for Gilman's story, it does not offer an adequate account of how lives like the narrator's are affected by their gender. In order to be complete, an analysis of "The Yellow Wallpaper" would have to acknowledge that the narrator's womanhood does matter to the plot. When she originally comes to the estate, clearly she is distressed by her society's expectation that as a mother she will be the prime nurturer of her newborn child. Then, the patriarchal authority that John enjoys in that society as her husband encourages him to tell her what is good for her. His demand that she rest instead of work is no doubt supported by their culture's belief that women of her upper-middle-class standing are not supposed to perform much physical labor in the first place. Most likely Foucault was aware that gender has usually been a key variable in modern society's power structures, and there is no reason to think he would simply ignore how it bears on Gilman's story. But because *Discipline and Punish* does not give gender much attention, its significance for Gilman's narrator is a topic that Foucault leaves other, more explicitly feminist perspectives to discover.

Points out limits of this framework, rather than simply matching it to the story.

Some feminist theorists have criticized Foucault not only for neglecting gender but also for failing to develop any model of resistance to domination. For example, Nancy C. M. Hartsock faults him for leaving people with no method of escaping "passivity and immobility," no "hope of transcendence" over "the ways humans have been subjugated" (45). Nor does Gilman offer in her story a clear notion of what resistance to unjust power would look like. One feature of "The Yellow Wallpaper" that has much been debated is whether the narrator's destruction of the wallpaper and her crawling on the floor are a truly effective challenge to disciplinary society. Readers who might otherwise agree on many elements of the story have disagreed on this issue. While Bak, for example, claims that ultimately the narrator "is successful at freeing herself from her male-imposed shackles" (40), Paula A. Treichler argues that "the surrender of patriarchy is only temporary" and that "her madness will no doubt commit her to more intense medical treatment, perhaps to the dreaded Weir Mitchell of whom her husband has spoken" (67). It is possible that Gilman was being deliberately ambiguous with her ending, wishing to provoke discussion about how to define worthwhile resistance instead of attempting to settle the question herself. In any case, Foucault's *Discipline and Punish* sheds light on a lot of her story even if it keeps Gilman's readers wondering exactly what her narrator should have done.

Concluding paragraph connects the theorist to the story by briefly bringing up new topic, resistance.

Endnote

[1] *Discipline and Punish* is not the only text by Foucault that can help in analyzing Gilman's story. Another possible work is his book *Madness and Civilization: A History of Insanity in the Age of Reason*, which can be useful for understanding the psychological problems of Gilman's narrator. *Discipline and Punish* is especially good, however, at explaining how power relationships throughout modern societies like the narrator's involve academic and professional disciplines of various sorts.

Endnote provides additional information that is not easily incorporated into main body of the paper.

Works Cited

Bak, John S. "Escaping the Jaundiced Eye: Foucauldian Panopticism in Charlotte Perkins Gilman's 'The Yellow Wallpaper.'" *Studies in Short Fiction*, vol. 31, no. 1, Winter 2010, pp. 39–46.

Foucault, Michel. *Discipline and Punish: The Birth of the Prison*. Translated by Alan Sheridan, Vintage Books, 1979.

- - - . *Madness and Civilization: A History of Insanity in the Age of Reason*. Translated by Richard Howard, Vintage Books, 1988.

Gilman, Charlotte Perkins. "The Yellow Wallpaper." *Making Literature Matter: An Anthology for Readers and Writers*, edited by John Schilb and John Clifford, 7th ed., Bedford/St. Martin's, 2018, pp. 247–60.

Hartsock, Nancy C. M. "Postmodernism and Political Change: Issues for Feminist Theory." *Feminist Interpretations of Michel Foucault*, edited by Susan J. Hekman, Pennsylvania State UP, 1996, pp. 39–55.

Treichler, Paula A. "Escaping the Sentence: Diagnosis and Discourse in 'The Yellow Wallpaper.'" *Tulsa Studies in Women's Literature*, vol. 3, no. 1–2, Spring-Autumn 1984, pp. 61–77.

Citation for scholarly article.

Citation for book. Note style for multiple works by same author.

Citation for work in an anthology.

HOW JACOB USES HIS SOURCES

Jacob's primary sources. Gilman's "The Yellow Wallpaper" and Foucault's *Discipline and Punish*. Jacob puts Gilman's story in "dialogue" with Foucault's book. More specifically, he draws heavily on Foucault's ideas to emphasize that John, the physician and husband of Gilman's narrator, tries to make her a "disciplined" woman

Bak. To point out that (1) that some interpreters of Gilman's story suggest John literally imprisons his wife, and (2) that some interpreters of the story think that its narrator finally achieves genuine freedom

Hartsock. To indicate that some theorists criticize Foucault for not proposing any real way to escape domination

(continued on next page)

HOW JACOB USES HIS SOURCES (continued)

Treichler. To point out that some interpreters of the story think its narrator does *not* escape patriarchal control

Foucault, *Madness and Civilization*. To acknowledge that *Discipline and Punish* isn't the only book by Foucault that illuminates the distress of Gilman's narrator

A RESEARCHED ARGUMENT THAT PLACES A LITERARY WORK IN HISTORICAL AND CULTURAL CONTEXT

When scholars do research on a literary work, often they aim to place it in its original situation. They investigate the background from which it emerged. How can they relate the work to its historical and cultural context? This is the basic issue they pursue. Perhaps you'll write a researched argument that addresses this question by applying it to a literary text you've read. If so, you'll probably make use of various sources. But you'll need to develop a claim of your own. The following essay demonstrates how. Brittany Thomas connects Gilman's "The Yellow Wallpaper" to its original era. In order to do this, she examined autobiographical nonfiction by Gilman. She studied as well a lecture by S. Weir Mitchell, Gilman's doctor. She also consulted scholarship on nineteenth-century medical treatments of women. Gradually, she came to focus on the "rest cure" Gilman suffered. After all, it was the ordeal that led Gilman to write her tale. Brittany realized the story leaves out a feature of this therapy: the massages that it usually involved. She suspected that this omission was deliberate. Her essay states and elaborates a claim about it. She argues that Gilman probably wanted to stress the narrator's isolation from human touch.

Brittany Thomas
Professor Schneebaum
English L202
25 April ----

The Relative Absence of the Human Touch
in "The Yellow Wallpaper"

In her essay "Why I Wrote 'The Yellow Wallpaper,'" Charlotte Perkins Gilman reveals that her famous story was inspired by a personal depression that got worse when she underwent a "rest cure" prescribed to her by "a noted specialist in nervous diseases, the best known in the country" (261). Though she does not name this doctor in the essay, we are aware today that he was S. Weir Mitchell, a name that she actually brings up briefly in "The Yellow Wallpaper." The rest cure that the story's narrator

Immediately mentions one of her sources, but only to set up main claim about Gilman's story, which she states at end of paragraph.

goes through, however, does not seem to have all the features that Weir Mitchell's did. Interestingly, neither by reading the essay nor by reading Gilman's story would you realize that Weir Mitchell's treatment involved massage. The question for an interpreter of the story thus becomes, Why did Gilman leave massage out of "The Yellow Wallpaper"? Because we can only guess at her intentions, perhaps a better way of putting the question is this: What is the effect of omitting massage from the story? One important consequence is that there is less of a literal human touch in the story than there might have been, and so the heroine's alienation from others and her withdrawal into fantasy seem stronger than they might have been.

Using question form helps signal cause/effect issue that the essay will address.

This is the essay's main claim

Weir Mitchell himself seems to have regarded massage as a very big component of his rest cure. He gives it a lot of attention in his 1904 lecture "The Evolution of the Rest Treatment." There he describes at length two cases, one of a man and one of a woman, where he found out that rubbing the body helped the person overcome depression. He recalls arriving at the conclusion "that massage was a tonic of extraordinary value" (264), and he continues his lecture by giving a brief account of the larger world history of what he terms "this invaluable therapeutic measure" (265). Evidently Weir Mitchell did not perform massage himself; in his lecture, he describes having others do it for him. Perhaps he thought that if he personally rubbed a patient's body, he would run the risk of being accused of a sexual advance. Despite his use of stand-ins for him, he clearly considered massage a necessary feature of his rest cure. One reason was that he thought the depressed person's body needed some form of physical stimulation, which the person would not otherwise be getting by lying around so much of the time. He states in his lecture that massage was something that "enabled me to use rest in bed without causing the injurious effects of unassisted rest" (235). Probably this method also reflected a more general belief of his, which Jane F. Thrailkill describes as the assumption "that the efficacy of his cure lay in its treatment of a patient's material body, not in what we might now term the psychological effects of isolation or of his own charismatic presence" (532). Thrailkill goes on to point out that Weir Mitchell was not alone in this belief: "[T]he medical wisdom of the day . . . conceived of a patient as a conceptually inert bundle of physiological processes" (552).[1] Massage was a means of helpfully manipulating the physique, which for Weir Mitchell and other doctors of his era was the main source of difficulties that today might be seen as chiefly mental.

Briefly summarizes Weir Mitchell's lecture, focusing on his remarks about massage rather than spending additional time on other topics of his speech.

Analyzes at length one particular source, Weir Mitchell's lecture.

Square brackets indicate alteration of text being quoted. Ellipses indicate words deleted from original text.

Given that massage was so important to Weir Mitchell, it is significant that Gilman's references to it are not consistent. She does recall being massaged when she discusses how Weir Mitchell treated her medically in her autobiography *The Living of Charlotte Perkins Gilman*. In that book, she says that besides being "put to bed and kept there," she was "fed, bathed, [and] rubbed" (96). She does not refer to massage, however, in "Why I Wrote 'The Yellow Wallpaper.'" More important for interpretations of the story, she does not make massage part of "The Yellow Wallpaper" itself. It plays no role at all in the plot. The elements of the rest cure that come up in the story are, instead, physical seclusion and forced abandonment of work.

Synthesis of three texts, comparing what they do with the topic of massage. More specifically, compares Gilman's autobiography, Gilman's essay on writing the story, and the story itself.

If massage were a major element of the rest cure that the narrator goes through in "The Yellow Wallpaper," the story would probably feature a lot more human touching than it presently does. The way the story is written, the heroine experiences relatively little physical contact with other people, or at least she does not tell us that she is having much of this. What is especially interesting is that we do not find many instances of her being physically touched by her husband, John. There are, in fact, a few places in the text where he does touch her. She says that when she informs him that she is disturbed by the wallpaper, "he took me in his arms and called me a blessed little goose" (251). When she weeps because he will not leave the house to visit relatives, "dear John gathered me up in his arms, and just carried me upstairs and laid me on the bed, and sat by me and read to me till it tired my head" (254). When she complains that he is wrong to think she is getting better, he gives her "a big hug" and says "'Bless her little heart! . . . she shall be as sick as she pleases!'" (255). Yet his moments of touching her not only are very few but also reflect his insensitivity toward her. His folding her in his arms seems an effort to control her and trivialize her protests, not an expression of genuine love. Moreover, she takes no real comfort from his touch. If this amounts to rubbing her, then from her point of view, he is rubbing her the wrong way. Again, however, massage is significantly absent from this story, and because what touches there are seem so few and inhumane, readers are led to feel that the narrator is pretty much alone in her concerns. She has only the imaginary woman in the wallpaper to bond with, and she seems drawn to that woman in large part because her human companions have no true understanding of the distress that caused her to need some sort of cure in the first place.

In effect, admits it would be misleading to claim there are no instances of touching in the story. Proceeds to bring together (to synthesize) various examples of such contact.

Accounts for details of story that might seem to conflict with main claim.

In calling attention to the role of massage in S. Weir Mitchell's rest cure, I do not mean to minimize the importance of his treatment's other components. The physical rest he demanded of his patients was certainly a big element of the cure, so that we can easily see why Gilman made it central to her story. In his lecture, Weir Mitchell also points out that he applied electrical charges to the patient's body. Historians of women's health Barbara Ehrenreich and Deirdre English argue that Weir Mitchell relied heavily as well on "the technique of healing by *command*" (119, emphasis in original), constantly and firmly giving orders to his patients so that they felt obligated to obey his wishes and to get better on the precise schedule he had in mind. Massage certainly figured, however, in Weir Mitchell's mode of treatment, including his handling of Gilman's own case, so that her omission of it from "The Yellow Wallpaper" seems a deliberate strategy for giving other things emphasis. Above all, the quite limited role of human touching in the story serves to make readers highly aware that the narrator is without the loving, intimate company she really needs to recover from her depression.

Heads off possible misunderstanding of argument; dealing with it enables her to write a concluding paragraph that does more than just repeat main claim.

Endnote

[1] Thrailkill spends much of her article tracing how an emphasis on treating depression through physical means (the approach taken by Weir Mitchell) gave way late in the nineteenth century to a more psychological and verbal form of therapy (such as Sigmund Freud practiced).

Endnote provides information that could not be easily integrated into main text of the essay.

Works Cited

Ehrenreich, Barbara, and Deirdre English. *For Her Own Good: 150 Years of the Experts' Advice to Women*. Doubleday-Anchor, 1978.

Gilman, Charlotte Perkins. *The Living of Charlotte Perkins Gilman: An Autobiography*. 1935. Arno Press, 1972.

---. "Why I Wrote 'The Yellow Wallpaper.'" 1913. Schilb and Clifford, pp. 260–61.

---. "The Yellow Wallpaper." 1892. Schilb and Clifford, pp. 247–60.

Making Literature Matter: An Anthology for Readers and Writers. 7th ed., Bedford/St. Martin's, 2018.

Thrailkill, Jane F. "Doctoring 'The Yellow Wallpaper.'" *ELH*, vol. 69, no. 2, Summer 2002, pp. 525–66.

Weir Mitchell, S. Excerpt from "The Evolution of the Rest Treatment." 1904. Schilb and Clifford, pp. 262–65.

Citation for book.

Note style for multiple works by same author.

When you cite more than one work from the same book, you give the book its own entry and cite each work from it in the shorthand form you see here.

Citation for anthology.

Citation for scholarly article.

HOW BRITTANY USES HER SOURCES

Brittany's primary source. Gilman's "The Yellow Wallpaper"; Brittany's argument is mainly a consideration of why Gilman left massage out of the story

Mitchell. To indicate that Gilman's own doctor valued massage as a therapeutic measure, even if he used other methods as well

Gilman, autobiography. To prove that Mitchell used massage in treating Gilman

Gilman, article on her writing of the story. (1) To emphasize that Gilman based her story on Mitchell's treatment of her; (2) to acknowledge that Gilman didn't always mention that massage was one of Mitchell's tools

Thrailkill. To emphasize that massage was an important tool for Mitchell and reflected a basic medical belief of his era

Ehrenreich and English. To acknowledge that massage wasn't Mitchell's only method

A RESEARCHED ARGUMENT THAT PLACES A LITERARY WORK IN A MULTIMEDIA CONTEXT

Increasingly, scholars do research on a literary work by tracing its appearances in, or connections to, various media. These modes can include visual forms such as photographs, films, electronic screens, and print advertisements or illustrations. Music and other kinds of sounds may prove relevant as well. At the start of this book's color portfolio, we present a sample paper that analyzes a poem based on a specific painting. Here, though, is a student essay that develops a claim about "The Yellow Wallpaper." It does so by referring to illustrations that appeared in the January 1892 issue of the *New England Magazine*, where Gilman's story was first published. The paper's author, Kyra Blaylock, was able to access this long-ago issue on the Web. She then examined all of the pictures in it. Of course, she was especially interested in the illustrations that accompanied Gilman's work. But she realized that she could usefully compare one of the Gilman images with another picture: an illustration for the story that preceded Gilman's in the magazine. Kyra reproduces both images at the end of her paper. Alternatively, she might have included them *within* her text, perhaps by reducing their size. Important to notice, in any case, is that she does not simply lay out these pictures for her reader to study. Her essay carefully describes them and probes implications of their details.

Kyra Blaylock
Professor Michaels
English L202
16 May - - - -

Different Kinds of Horrifying Images in
"The Yellow Wallpaper" and "A Salem Witch"

Charlotte Perkins Gilman's short story "The Yellow Wallpaper" was originally published in the January 1892 issue of the *New England Magazine*. At the time, many people saw it as a tale of horror. In a 1996 article that traces the history of the story's reception, Julie Bates Dock and her coauthors report that several of its initial readers were scared by Gilman's text. For example, reviewer Anne Montgomerie found the story "a perfect crescendo of horror," and famous literary critic William Dean Howells observed that Gilman manages to "freeze our young blood" (qtd. in Dock et al. 59).[1] But not all horror stories are alike. They may differ in their means of making their audiences shudder. This possibility becomes evident if we compare Gilman's story to the one immediately preceding it in the same issue of the *New England Magazine*, Edith Mary Norris's "A Salem Witch."

Uses a source to document first reactions; directs this paper's reader to an endnote.

Like Gilman, Norris centers her story on an oppressed woman. She sets her tale in late-seventeenth-century Salem, during that city's notorious witch trials. The heroine, Margaret, is unjustly charged with witchcraft, after being accused of it by a rival for her fiancé's affections. Although the fiancé, Rafe, cannot prevent Margaret from dying of despair, he is an attractive figure who genuinely cares for her. By contrast, Gilman sets her tale in what is for her the present age, the late nineteenth century. Furthermore, her narrator is persecuted by her husband, a doctor who forbids her to do meaningful work and who consequently helps drive her mad. Unlike Rafe, he proves insensitive to the heroine, and in the end, he collapses in fright when she asserts female power. In general, "A Salem Witch" situates horror in the nation's distant past, and it disturbs its audience by depicting a woman who unfairly and fatally suffers despite a good man's love. "The Yellow Wallpaper," on the other hand, locates horror in contemporary times and disturbs its audience by presenting a woman who subdues an obnoxious husband. In other words, the horror evoked by Gilman's story had *feminist* implications for her era, whereas other examples of the horror genre — including one in the very same magazine issue — were not as politically daring. This difference shows up in the illustrations that accompanied Norris's and Gilman's stories when they appeared together. The contrast emerges especially in the pictures depicting the stories' climaxes.

Briefly summarizes Gilman's story and the other that the paper will focus on.

This is the paper's main claim, which involves comparing two particular visual images.

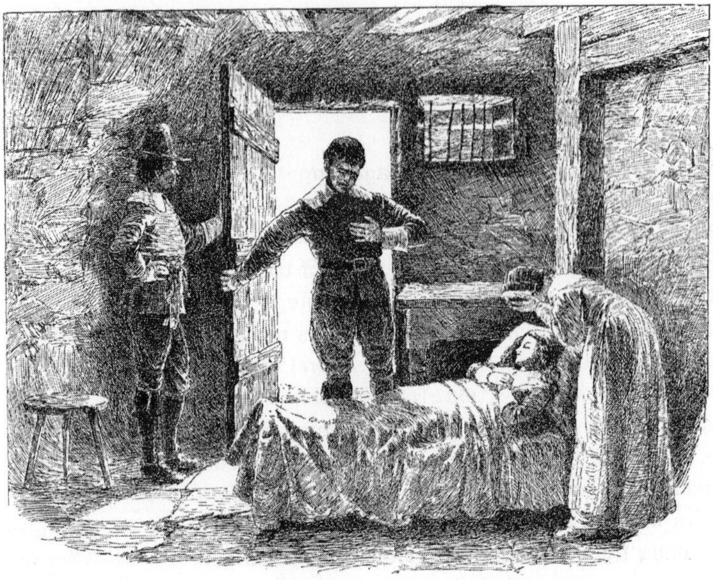
"His strong frame shook with an agony too deep for words."

Figure 1
Courtesy of Cornell University Library, Making of America Digital Collection.

The *New England Magazine*'s illustration for the climax of "A Salem Witch" (645, fig. 1)[2] juxtaposes male dominance with female passivity. Rafe stands imposingly inside Margaret's prison door as she lies dead in bed. Having been declared guilty of witchcraft, she was scheduled to be executed; no matter what, she was doomed. But Rafe finds her already destroyed by psychological pain. The tableau seems to bear out Edgar Allan Poe's famous remark that "the death . . . of a beautiful woman is unquestionably the most poetical topic in the world." Of course, Poe's comment would trouble many people today, for it suggests that good literature depends upon female characters playing the victim role. In the picture for Norris's story, Rafe is certainly a victim as well, for he has lost his beloved. Nevertheless, he remains vividly alive, as is noted by the picture's caption: "His strong frame shook with an agony too deep for words." Physically, he remains erect and mighty, looming at the picture's center, while Margaret is stretched out lifeless below him. Even her sister, Dorcas, who has been nursing Margaret and now leans over her body, bows beneath Rafe rather than standing at his level. To be sure, Margaret seems bathed in light, as if she is bound for heaven, while Rafe is consumed by a darkness that signifies abiding sorrow. But Rafe still seems more powerful than Margaret in this continuing capacity to *feel*. Indeed, he dramatically expresses his mental "agony" by placing his hand on his

Directs the reader to an endnote, and the paragraph proceeds not only to describe one of the images but also to analyze its details.

Ellipses indicate words deleted from original text.

heart and gazing with grief at his beloved's corpse. At the same time, his inability to verbalize his emotions — their being "too deep for words" — fits another masculine stereotype: the stoic, reserved John Wayne figure that many of us know from Western films. Rafe and Margaret do appear similarly pious: Rafe's hand-on-heart gesture seems religiously inspired, and Margaret's dead hands are folded in a prayerful way. But if she is headed toward divine reward, she has nonetheless been mortally punished on earth, while Rafe can still protest against the society that condemned her. By the end of the story, his protest takes the form of abandoning Salem for Europe. In the illustration, however, he serves as a living witness of Margaret's tragedy. As we look at him in the picture, we also see the horror of her death through his eyes.

Transition to description and analysis of the second image.

The illustration for the climax of "The Yellow Wallpaper" (656; fig. 2) reverses this gender dynamic. It shows the female narrator leaning over, and gazing down at, her husband John's sprawled body. Frustrated by her supposedly "therapeutic" confinement, she has been tearing down her room's wallpaper to free the woman she detects in it. Distressed by her action, John has fainted, no longer capable of coolly playing the self-confident medical expert. He hardly displays Rafe's "strong frame"; rather, he seems as stricken as Margaret. His outstretched hands seem to grasp for help. As the narrator bends over him, placing her hands on his ribcage and head, she may even be viewed as a champion wrestler determined to keep him pinned down. Long strands of her hair dangle across his torso, as if to confirm that *she* is in control. Only *her* face is fully visible, while his is partly squashed on the floor. Moreover, we cannot tell from her face whether she even recognizes him. Indeed, within the text itself, she seems to regard him as a bothersome stranger: "Now why should that man have fainted? But he did, and right across my path by the wall, so that I had to creep over him every time!" (260). Because the illustration is a static image, it is unable to depict the narrator's "creeping"; inevitably it must show her as frozen rather than as striving to move past John. In this respect, the picture does not quite convey her sense that he is now just a barrier to her progress. Nevertheless, the drawing implies that she is subverting the social order, for at least temporarily, this woman is exerting power over a man. She enacts a fantasy of woman's liberation that many readers of the magazine would surely find shockingly new.

Acknowledges an interpretation different from the paper's own.

In their horror at the heroine's revolt, some of these readers may have wished that patriarchy be restored. That is, they may have viewed the illustration as a warning that bizarre and awful consequences will occur if men fail to keep women in their

Figure 2
Courtesy of Cornell University Library, Making of America Digital Collection.

"proper" place. This response would turn "The Yellow Wallpaper" into a cautionary *anti*-feminist tract. But such a reaction would ignore much of Gilman's written text: in particular, her clear effort to show John as oblivious to the emotional needs of the heroine. John not only "laughs at" his wife, but also tells her that "the very worst thing [she] can do is to think about [her] condition" (249) and that her restless discontent "is a false and foolish fancy" (255). In Norris's story, by contrast, Margaret is chiefly betrayed by another *woman*, who calls her a witch in an attempt to steal Rafe away from her. Although the husband in Gilman's story is not an outright, moustache-twirling villain, he is a major source of her distress. When Gilman has him faint at the end of the story, his collapse seems the comeuppance of a husband who has been arrogant, not kind, toward his spouse. He has failed to demonstrate the love that Rafe shows Margaret in "A Salem Witch." With "The Yellow Wallpaper," therefore, Gilman seems chiefly out to horrify her readers by dramatizing how masculine authority thwarts women's freedom to the point where they must gain power in whatever way they can, even if their self-assertion comes at men's expense. By placing "A Salem Witch" in the distant past, by killing Margaret off, and by leaving Rafe alive with his "strong frame," Norris does not challenge her present society nearly as much as Gilman does. Comparing the two climactic illustrations makes the difference in their political stances apparent.

Concludes by explaining how the paper's interpretation accounts for more of the story's written text.

Endnotes

Endnotes provide information that could not be easily integrated into main text of the essay.

[1]Dock and her coauthors add that at least some early readers of "The Yellow Wallpaper" did not see it *only* as a horror story. Indeed, these scholars argue that a number of readers found feminist messages in Gilman's tale well before the present women's movement did.

[2]The deathbed scene is not the *final* illustration for Norris's story in the magazine. At the conclusion of the story, there appears a picture of the coastal cottage in England where Rafe and Dorcas eventually go to live.

Works Cited

Dock, Julie Bates, et al. "'But One Expects That': Charlotte Perkins Gilman's 'The Yellow Wallpaper' and the Shifting Light of Scholarship." *PMLA*, vol. 111, no. 1, Jan. 1996, pp. 52–65.

Gilman, Charlotte Perkins. "The Yellow Wallpaper." *New England Magazine*, Jan. 1892, pp. 647–56. *Making of America*, Cornell U Library, ebooks .library.cornell.edu/m/moa/. Accessed 27 Nov. 2013. Also in *Making Literature Matter: An Anthology for Readers and Writers*, 7th ed., edited by John Schilb and John Clifford, Bedford/St. Martin's, 2018, pp. 247–60.

Norris, Edith Mary. "A Salem Witch." *New England Magazine*, Jan. 1892, pp. 638–46. *Making of America*, Cornell U Library, ebooks.library.cornell.edu/m/moa/. Accessed 27 Nov. 2013.

Poe, Edgar Allan. "The Philosophy of Composition." 1846. *Project Gutenberg Ebook of Edgar Allan Poe's Complete Poetical Works*, www. publicliterature.org/pdf/10031.pdf.

Citation for article in scholarly journal.

Two citations of the work needed here: (1) Its location in this print anthology; (2) the work's original publication, now available on the Web, which features an illustration that the paper refers to.

Citation for work available on the Web.

HOW KYRA USES HER SOURCES

Kyra's primary source. "The Yellow Wallpaper" as it first appeared. Kyra compares one of the story's original illustrations with a picture for another story in the same issue. This comparison helps Kyra argue that Gilman's narrator is unusual in challenging masculine authority

Dock, et al. To point out that many original readers of Gilman's story saw it as belonging to the horror genre

Norris. To show that a story preceding Gilman's in the same issue offered a more benevolent image of masculinity

Poe. To indicate that the heroine of Norris' story fits a stereotype of the beautiful woman who dies, whereas Gilman's heroine survives

MAKING A MULTIMEDIA PRESENTATION ABOUT A LITERARY WORK

College courses often require class presentations. Besides writing about a work of literature, you may have to make a speech about it. Moreover, your talk might employ media other than your spoken words. Kyra Blaylock's paper on "The Yellow Wallpaper" examines drawings that accompanied Gilman's story when it debuted. If Kyra gave a speech based on her essay, she could display these sketches during it. Similarly, a speech by you can use visual images to illustrate, support, or connect your ideas. These images might include photographs, paintings, film clips, YouTube videos, advertisements, diagrams, or screen captures from Web sites. They might include, too, bits of text you want your audience to notice, such as literary quotations, dictionary entries, timelines, headlines, captions, and tweets. An additional medium you can turn to is sound, including music recordings and historic news broadcasts. Don't forget, either, the possibility of using props. American Girl dolls can vividly demonstrate how nineteenth-century women like Gilman's narrator were expected to look.

Whatever media you enlist, a speech about a literary work demands careful planning. Here are some specific tips:

- You may annoy your audience if you just loosely string together assorted facts, images, and details. You need to decide on a structure for your talk—a way to make it seem organized and compelling. One good plan is to frame your speech as an *argument*. This would involve stating an issue and main claim at the outset. Then you would develop and support the claim, pointing out your evidence and reasons. You may also need to admit and defend certain assumptions you hold. Alternatively, you might frame your talk as a *mystery*. You might begin by identifying a difficult question or problem, and then lead your listeners to a solution.
- Visual technology, such as PowerPoint or Prezi, can prove valuable. But make sure that all of your slides play meaningful roles in your presentation. Don't waste time on displays that just amuse or dazzle; each image needs to serve a clear and genuine purpose. Keep in mind that the slides in your talk may not merit equal attention. Some you might show quickly; others you might linger on. In general, planning your speech entails deciding how you will *pace* it. Which parts of it can you race through? Which require longer discussion?
- Limit the number of words you put on a slide, for otherwise your audience may need to spend much time and effort to read them. Make the words large enough to be visible in the first place; don't make people squint. If you do have to show lengthy passages, you might distribute them on handouts.
- Determine how to maintain eye contact with your audience. You may lose their interest if you constantly look at a script or just repeat words already up on screen. You might speak instead from notes written on cards.
- Your presentation will engage people more if you involve them in an activity. It can be one that also helps you understand your audience

better. For example, they might briefly freewrite on your topic, jotting down things they currently know or assume about it. You might then have volunteers read a few of their sentences aloud.

- You may want to have a bottle of water at hand, in case your mouth gets dry. Your audience is unlikely to be bothered by an occasional sip. But don't indulge in prolonged, dramatic swigs, as if giving a speech is the same as running a marathon.
- Rehearse your speech several times. This practice will enable you to gauge how long your presentation will take—an important matter if you must stick to a certain time limit. If you plan to use technology, test it beforehand, making sure that it will actually function.

Perhaps your presentation will be a *group* effort rather than a speech you make on your own. Here are some suggestions to help you and your partners collaborate:

- When you first meet as a group, be sure to exchange contact information (e.g., e-mail addresses and phone numbers). Also, try to set up at least a tentative schedule: dates and times when you will meet in person or share work-in-progress through e-mails.
- As early as possible, the group should decide what each member's tasks will be, both in preparing the speech and in actually making it. The goal should be a roughly equal division of labor, based on what each member specifically wants to research and speak about. The group may find value in appointing a "team manager": someone who will monitor the planning and keep everyone informed about how this process is going.
- Rehearsal is always important, but especially for a group. If each member of your team prepares part of the presentation, everyone should then gather for several run-throughs of it, to make sure that its various elements mesh.
- Ideally, each member will come to the group's meetings, take on tasks, and perform them well. But this doesn't always happen. Someone may wind up missing in action. If a member skips meetings or assigned duties, the rest of the group can do more than simply wring their hands. They can adjust their plans, proceed without the person, and tell their instructor what's happened.

SUMMING UP: WRITING RESEARCHED ARGUMENTS

- ***Plan* your research.** (pp. 200–06)

  Identify an issue to pursue.

  Investigate electronic sources such as Internet Web sites, using more than one search engine; investigate print sources as well.

(continued on next page)

SUMMING UP: WRITING RESEARCHED ARGUMENTS *(continued)*

Take time to evaluate the materials you discover.

Keep yourself well organized.

Record everything that may prove useful later — do not risk plagiarism by failing to distinguish between your own ideas and those of others.

- **Start composing by revisiting your tentative main claim, taking into account what you have learned through research.** (p. 206)

  Keep organized, and subdivide and arrange your notes in logical order.

  Focus on constructing an argument of your own, using secondary sources to support your claims and evidence.

  Follow MLA conventions for format and style.

- **Document your sources by following MLA guidelines.** (pp. 209–18)
- **For a research paper that uses a literary work to examine social issues, deals with existing interpretations of it, interprets it through the framework of a particular theorist, places it in a historical or cultural context, or relates it to visual images, be sure to make an argument of your own. This entails raising an issue and making a claim about the work.** (pp. 219–34)
- **For a multimedia presentation on a literary work, aim to engage your audience by clearly organizing your remarks; using technology in helpful and meaningful ways; maintaining eye contact; and perhaps incorporating an activity. For a group presentation, establish a planning schedule and try to divide labor fairly. For any presentation you give, rehearse.** (238–44)

Cultural Contexts: Charlotte Perkins Gilman's "The Yellow Wallpaper"

CHARLOTTE PERKINS GILMAN, "The Yellow Wallpaper"

CULTURAL CONTEXTS:
CHARLOTTE PERKINS GILMAN, "Why I Wrote 'The Yellow Wallpaper' "

S. WEIR MITCHELL, From "*THE EVOLUTION OF THE REST TREATMENT*"

JOHN HARVEY KELLOGG, From *THE LADIES' GUIDE IN HEALTH AND DISEASE*

When doctors make a medical or psychiatric diagnosis, they pinpoint their patient's condition but also often accept or reject their society's definition of *health*. The social context of diagnoses seems especially worth considering when a particular condition afflicts one gender much more than the other. Today, many more women than men appear to suffer from depression, anorexia, bulimia, and dissociative identity disorder. Why? Perhaps traditional female roles encourage these illnesses; perhaps gender bias affects how doctors label and treat them. Charlotte Perkins Gilman raised both these possibilities in her 1892 short story "The Yellow Wallpaper." In her own life, the consequences from her egregious treatment were not as serious as she depicts in her story. But Gilman was the exception. Many women suffered terribly from doctors who ignored the cultural causes of depression. Besides Gilman's story, we include her account of why she wrote it, an excerpt from a lecture by Silas Weir Mitchell about his cure, and some advice about motherhood from John Kellogg, another influential doctor of the time.

BEFORE YOU READ

How is mental illness depicted in movies and television shows you have seen? Which representations of mental illness have you appreciated the most? Which have you especially disliked? State your criteria for these judgments.

CHARLOTTE PERKINS GILMAN
The Yellow Wallpaper

Charlotte Perkins Gilman (1860–1935) was a major activist and theorist in America's first wave of feminism. During her lifetime, she was chiefly known for her 1898 book Women and Economics. *In it she argued that women should not be confined to the household and made economically dependent on men. Gilman also advanced such ideas through her many public-speaking appearances and her magazine* The Forerunner, *which she edited from 1909 to 1916. Gilman wrote many articles and works of fiction for The Forerunner, including a tale called* Herland *(1915) in which she envisioned an all-female utopia. Today, however, Gilman is*

Charlotte Perkins Gilman.
Fotosearch/Getty Images

best known for her short story "The Yellow Wallpaper," which she published first in an 1892 issue of the New England Magazine. *The story is based on Gilman's struggle with depression after the birth of her daughter Katharine in 1885. Seeking help for emotional turmoil, Gilman consulted the eminent neurologist Silas Weir Mitchell, who prescribed his famous "rest cure." This treatment, which forbade Gilman to work, actually worsened her distress. She improved only after she moved to California, divorced her husband, let him raise Katharine with his new wife, married someone else, and plunged fully into a literary and political career. As Gilman noted in her posthumously published autobiography,* The Living of Charlotte Perkins Gilman *(1935), she never fully recovered from the debilitation that had led her to Dr. Mitchell, but she ultimately managed to be enormously productive. Although "The Yellow Wallpaper" is a work of fiction rather than a factual account of her experience with Mitchell, Gilman used the story to criticize the doctor's patriarchal approach as well as society's efforts to keep women passive.*

It is very seldom that mere ordinary people like John and myself secure ancestral halls for the summer.

A colonial mansion, a hereditary estate, I would say a haunted house and reach the height of romantic felicity—but that would be asking too much of fate!

Still I will proudly declare that there is something queer about it.

Else, why should it be let so cheaply? And why have stood so long untenanted?

John laughs at me, of course, but one expects that in marriage.

John is practical in the extreme. He has no patience with faith, an intense horror of superstition, and he scoffs openly at any talk of things not to be felt and seen and put down in figures.

John is a physician, and *perhaps*—(I would not say it to a living soul, of course, but this is dead paper and a great relief to my mind)—*perhaps* that is one reason I do not get well faster.

You see, he does not believe I am sick!

And what can one do?

If a physician of high standing, and one's own husband, assures friends and relatives that there is really nothing the matter with one but temporary nervous depression—a slight hysterical tendency°—what is one to do?

My brother is also a physician, and also of high standing, and he says the same thing.

So I take phosphates or phosphites—whichever it is, and tonics, and journeys, and air, and exercise, and am absolutely forbidden to "work" until I am well again.

Personally, I disagree with their ideas.

Personally, I believe that congenial work, with excitement and change, would do me good.

But what is one to do?

I did write for a while in spite of them; but it *does* exhaust me a good deal—having to be so sly about it, or else meet with heavy opposition.

I sometimes fancy that in my condition if I had less opposition and more society and stimulus—but John says the very worst thing I can do is to think about my condition, and I confess it always makes me feel bad.

So I will let it alone and talk about the house.

The most beautiful place! It is quite alone, standing well back from the road, quite three miles from the village. It makes me think of English places that you read about, for there are hedges and walls and gates that lock, and lots of separate little houses for the gardeners and people.

There is a *delicious* garden! I never saw such a garden—large and shady, full of box-bordered paths, and lined with long grape-covered arbors with seats under them.

There were greenhouses, too, but they are all broken now.

There was some legal trouble, I believe, something about the heirs and coheirs; anyhow, the place has been empty for years.

hysterical tendency: It was common among Victorian doctors to believe women had an innate tendency to be overly emotional; now a discredited assumption.

That spoils my ghostliness, I am afraid, but I don't care—there is something strange about the house—I can feel it.

I even said so to John one moonlight evening, but he said what I felt was a *draught*, and shut the window.

I get unreasonably angry with John sometimes. I'm sure I never used to be so sensitive. I think it is due to this nervous condition.

But John says if I feel so, I shall neglect proper self-control; so I take pains to control myself—before him, at least, and that makes me very tired.

I don't like our room a bit. I wanted one downstairs that opened on the piazza and had roses all over the window, and such pretty old-fashioned chintz hangings! but John would not hear of it.

He said there was only one window and not room for two beds, and no near room for him if he took another.

He is very careful and loving, and hardly lets me stir without special direction.

I have a schedule prescription for each hour in the day; he takes all care from me, and so I feel basely ungrateful not to value it more.

He said we came here solely on my account, that I was to have perfect rest and all the air I could get. "Your exercise depends on your strength, my dear," said he, "and your food somewhat on your appetite; but air you can absorb all the time." So we took the nursery at the top of the house.

It is a big, airy room, the whole floor nearly, with windows that look all ways, and air and sunshine galore. It was nursery first and then playroom and gymnasium, I should judge; for the windows are barred for little children, and there are rings and things in the walls.

The paint and paper look as if a boys' school had used it. It is stripped off—the paper—in great patches all around the head of my bed, about as far as I can reach, and in a great place on the other side of the room low down. I never saw a worse paper in my life.

One of those sprawling flamboyant patterns committing every artistic sin.

It is dull enough to confuse the eye in following, pronounced enough to constantly irritate and provoke study, and when you follow the lame uncertain curves for a little distance they suddenly commit suicide—plunge off at outrageous angles, destroy themselves in unheard of contradictions.

The color is repellant, almost revolting; a smouldering unclean yellow, strangely faded by the slow-turning sunlight.

It is a dull yet lurid orange in some places, a sickly sulphur tint in others.

No wonder the children hated it! I should hate it myself if I had to live in this room long.

There comes John, and I must put this away,—he hates to have me write a word.

We have been here two weeks, and I haven't felt like writing before, since that first day.

I am sitting by the window now, up in this atrocious nursery, and there is nothing to hinder my writing as much as I please, save lack of strength.

John is away all day, and even some nights when his cases are serious.

I am glad my case is not serious!

But these nervous troubles are dreadfully depressing.

John does not know how much I really suffer. He knows there is no *reason* to suffer, and that satisfies him.

Of course it is only nervousness. It does weigh on me so not to do my duty in any way!

I meant to be such a help to John, such a real rest and comfort, and here I am a comparative burden already!

Nobody would believe what an effort it is to do what little I am able, — to dress and entertain, and order things.

It is fortunate Mary is so good with the baby. Such a dear baby!

And yet I *cannot* be with him, it makes me so nervous.

I suppose John never was nervous in his life. He laughs at me so about this wallpaper!

At first he meant to repaper the room, but afterward he said that I was letting it get the better of me, and that nothing was worse for a nervous patient than to give way to such fancies.

He said that after the wallpaper was changed it would be the heavy bedstead, and then the barred windows, and then that gate at the head of the stairs, and so on.

"You know the place is doing you good," he said, "and really, dear, I don't care to renovate the house just for a three months' rental."

"Then do let us go downstairs," I said, "there are such pretty rooms there."

Then he took me in his arms and called me a blessed little goose, and said he would go down cellar, if I wished, and have it whitewashed into the bargain.

But he is right enough about the beds and windows and things.

It is an airy and comfortable room as anyone need wish, and, of course, I would not be so silly as to make him uncomfortable just for a whim.

I'm really getting quite fond of the big room, all but that horrid paper.

Out of one window I can see the garden, those mysterious deepshaded arbors, the riotous old-fashioned flowers, and bushes and gnarly trees.

Out of another I get a lovely view of the bay and a little private wharf belonging to the estate. There is a beautiful shaded lane that runs down there from the house. I always fancy I see people walking in these numerous paths and arbors, but John has cautioned me not to give way to fancy in the least. He says that with my imaginative power and habit of story-making, a nervous weakness like mine is sure to lead to all manner of excited fancies, and that I ought to use my will and good sense to check the tendency. So I try.

I think sometimes that if I were only well enough to write a little it would relieve the press of ideas and rest me.

But I find I get pretty tired when I try.

It is so discouraging not to have any advice and companionship about my work. When I get really well, John says we will ask Cousin Henry and Julia down for a long visit; but he says he would as soon put fireworks in my pillow-case as to let me have those stimulating people about now.

I wish I could get well faster.

But I must not think about that. This paper looks to me as if it *knew* what a vicious influence it had!

There is a recurrent spot where the pattern lolls like a broken neck and two bulbous eyes stare at you upside down.

I get positively angry with the impertinence of it and the everlastingness. Up and down and sideways they crawl, and those absurd, unblinking eyes are everywhere. There is one place where two breadths didn't match, and the eyes go all up and down the line, one a little higher than the other.

I never saw so much expression in an inanimate thing before, and we all know how much expression they have! I used to lie awake as a child and get more entertainment and terror out of blank walls and plain furniture than most children could find in a toy-store.

I remember what a kindly wink the knobs of our big, old bureau used to have, and there was one chair that always seemed like a strong friend.

I used to feel that if any of the other things looked too fierce I could always hop into that chair and be safe.

The furniture in this room is no worse than inharmonious, however, for we had to bring it all from downstairs. I suppose when this was used as a playroom they had to take the nursery things out, and no wonder! I never saw such ravages as the children have made here.

The wallpaper, as I said before, is torn off in spots, and it sticketh closer than a brother—they must have had perseverance as well as hatred.

Then the floor is scratched and gouged and splintered, the plaster itself is dug out here and there, and this great heavy bed, which is all we found in the room, looks as if it had been through the wars.

But I don't mind it a bit—only the paper.

There comes John's sister. Such a dear girl as she is, and so careful of me! I must not let her find me writing.

She is a perfect and enthusiastic housekeeper, and hopes for no better profession. I verily believe she thinks it is the writing which made me sick!

But I can write when she is out, and see her a long way off from these windows.

There is one that commands the road, a lovely shaded winding road, and one that just looks off over the country. A lovely country, too, full of great elms and velvet meadows.

This wallpaper has a kind of sub-pattern in a different shade, a particularly irritating one, for you can only see it in certain lights, and not clearly then.

But in the places where it isn't faded and where the sun is just so—I can see a strange, provoking, formless sort of figure, that seems to skulk about behind that silly and conspicuous front design.

There's sister on the stairs!

Well, the Fourth of July is over! The people are all gone and I am tired out. John thought it might do me good to see a little company, so we just had mother and Nellie and the children down for a week.

Of course I didn't do a thing. Jennie sees to everything now.

But it tired me all the same.

John says if I don't pick up faster he shall send me to Weir Mitchell° in the fall.

But I don't want to go there at all. I had a friend who was in his hands once, and she says he is just like John and my brother, only more so!

Besides, it is such an undertaking to go so far.

I don't feel as if it was worthwhile to turn my hand over for anything, and I'm getting dreadfully fretful and querulous.

I cry at nothing, and cry most of the time.

Of course I don't when John is here, or anybody else, but when I am alone.

And I am alone a good deal just now. John is kept in town very often by serious cases, and Jennie is good and lets me alone when I want her to.

So I walk a little in the garden or down that lovely lane, sit on the porch under the roses, and lie down up here a good deal.

I'm getting really fond of the room in spite of the wallpaper. Perhaps *because* of the wallpaper.

It dwells in my mind so!

I lie here on this great immovable bed—it is nailed down, I believe—and follow that pattern about by the hour. It is as good as gymnastics, I assure you. I start, we'll say, at the bottom, down in the corner over there where it has not been touched, and I determine for the thousandth time that I *will* follow that pointless pattern to some sort of a conclusion.

I know a little of the principle of design, and I know this thing was not arranged on any laws of radiation, or alternation, or repetition, or symmetry, or anything else that I ever heard of.

It is repeated, of course, by the breadths, but not otherwise.

Looked at in one way each breadth stands alone, the bloated curves and flourishes—a kind of "debased Romanesque" with *delirium tremens*—go waddling up and down in isolated columns of fatuity.

But, on the other hand, they connect diagonally, and the sprawling outlines run off in great slanting waves of optic horror, like a lot of wallowing seaweeds in full chase.

The whole thing goes horizontally, too, at least it seems so, and I exhaust myself in trying to distinguish the order of its going in that direction.

They have used a horizontal breadth for a frieze, and that adds wonderfully to the confusion.

There is one end of the room where it is almost intact, and there, when the crosslights fade and the low sun shines directly upon it, I can almost fancy radiation after all,—the interminable grotesques seem to form around a common center and rush off in headlong plunges of equal distraction.

It makes me tired to follow it. I will take a nap I guess.

* * *

Weir Mitchell: Dr. S. Weir Mitchell (1829–1914) was an eminent Philadelphia neurologist who advocated "rest cures" for nervous disorders. He was the author of *Diseases of the Nervous System, Especially of Women* (1881).

I don't know why I should write this. 105

I don't want to.

I don't feel able.

And I know John would think it absurd. But I *must* say what I feel and think in some way—it is such a relief!

But the effort is getting to be greater than the relief.

Half the time now I am awfully lazy, and lie down ever so much. 110

John says I mustn't lose my strength, and has me take cod liver oil and lots of tonics and things, to say nothing of ale and wine and rare meat.

Dear John! He loves me very dearly, and hates to have me sick. I tried to have a real earnest reasonable talk with him the other day, and tell him how I wish he would let me go and make a visit to Cousin Henry and Julia.

But he said I wasn't able to go, nor able to stand it after I got there; and I did not make out a very good case for myself, for I was crying before I had finished.

It is getting to be a great effort for me to think straight. Just this nervous weakness I suppose.

And dear John gathered me up in his arms, and just carried me upstairs and 115 laid me on the bed, and sat by me and read to me till it tired my head.

He said I was his darling and his comfort and all he had, and that I must take care of myself for his sake, and keep well.

He says no one but myself can help me out of it, that I must use my will and self-control and not let any silly fancies run away with me.

There's one comfort, the baby is well and happy, and does not have to occupy this nursery with the horrid wallpaper.

If we had not used it, that blessed child would have! What a fortunate escape! Why, I wouldn't have a child of mine, an impressionable little thing, live in such a room for worlds.

I never thought of it before, but it is lucky that John kept me here after all, I 120 can stand it so much easier than a baby, you see.

Of course I never mention it to them any more—I am too wise, but I keep watch of it all the same.

There are things in the wallpaper that nobody knows but me, or ever will.

Behind that outside pattern the dim shapes get clearer every day.

It is always the same shape, only very numerous.

And it is like a woman stooping down and creeping about behind that pat- 125 tern. I don't like it a bit. I wonder—I begin to think—I wish John would take me away from here!

It is so hard to talk with John about my case, because he is so wise, and because he loves me so.

But I tried it last night.

It was moonlight. The moon shines in all around just as the sun does.

I hate to see it sometimes, it creeps so slowly, and always comes in by one window or another.

John was asleep and I hated to waken him, so I kept still and watched the 130 moonlight on that undulating wallpaper till I felt creepy.

The faint figure behind seemed to shake the pattern, just as if she wanted to get out.

I got up softly and went to feel and see if the paper *did* move, and when I came back John was awake.

"What is it, little girl?" he said. "Don't go walking about like that—you'll get cold."

I thought it was a good time to talk, so I told him that I really was not gaining here, and that I wished he would take me away.

"Why, darling!" said he, "our lease will be up in three weeks, and I can't see how to leave before.

"The repairs are not done at home, and I cannot possibly leave town just now. Of course if you were in any danger, I could and would, but you really are better, dear, whether you can see it or not. I am a doctor, dear, and I know. You are gaining flesh and color, your appetite is better, I feel really much easier about you."

"I don't weigh a bit more," said I, "nor as much; and my appetite may be better in the evening when you are here but it is worse in the morning when you are away!"

"Bless her little heart!" said he with a big hug, "she shall be as sick as she pleases! But now let's improve the shining hours by going to sleep, and talk about it in the morning!"

"And you won't go away?" I asked gloomily.

"Why, how can I, dear? It is only three weeks more and then we will take a nice little trip of a few days while Jennie is getting the house ready. Really dear you are better!"

"Better in body perhaps—" I began, and stopped short, for he sat up straight and looked at me with such a stern, reproachful look that I could not say another word.

"My darling," said he, "I beg you, for my sake and for our child's sake, as well as for your own, that you will never for one instant let that idea enter your mind! There is nothing so dangerous, so fascinating, to a temperament like yours. It is a false and foolish fancy. Can you trust me as a physician when I tell you so?"

So of course I said no more on that score, and we went to sleep before long. He thought I was asleep first, but I wasn't, and lay there for hours trying to decide whether that front pattern and the back pattern really did move together or separately.

On a pattern like this, by daylight, there is a lack of sequence, a defiance of law, that is a constant irritant to a normal mind.

The color is hideous enough, and unreliable enough, and infuriating enough, but the pattern is torturing.

You think you have mastered it, but just as you get well underway in following, it turns a back-somersault and there you are. It slaps you in the face, knocks you down, and tramples upon you. It is like a bad dream.

The outside pattern is a florid arabesque, reminding one of a fungus. If you can imagine a toadstool in joints, an interminable string of toadstools, budding and sprouting in endless convolutions—why, that is something like it.

That is, sometimes!

There is one marked peculiarity about this paper, a thing nobody seems to notice but myself, and that is that it changes as the light changes.

When the sun shoots in through the east window—I always watch for that 150
first long, straight ray—it changes so quickly that I never can quite believe it.

That is why I watch it always.

By moonlight—the moon shines in all night when there is a moon—I wouldn't know it was the same paper.

At night in any kind of light, in twilight, candlelight, lamplight, and worst of all by moonlight, it becomes bars! The outside pattern I mean, and the woman behind it is as plain as can be.

I didn't realize for a long time what the thing was that showed behind, that dim sub-pattern, but now I am quite sure it is a woman.

By daylight she is subdued, quiet. I fancy it is the pattern that keeps her so 155
still. It is so puzzling. It keeps me quiet by the hour.

I lie down ever so much now. John says it is good for me, and to sleep all I can.

Indeed he started the habit by making me lie down for an hour after each meal.

It is a very bad habit I am convinced, for you see I don't sleep.

And that cultivates deceit, for I don't tell them I'm awake—O, no!

The fact is I am getting a little afraid of John. 160

He seems very queer sometimes, and even Jennie has an inexplicable look.

It strikes me occasionally, just as a scientific hypothesis,—that perhaps it is the paper!

I have watched John when he did not know I was looking, and come into the room suddenly on the most innocent excuses, and I've caught him several times *looking at the paper*! And Jennie too. I caught Jennie with her hand on it once.

She didn't know I was in the room, and when I asked her in a quiet, a very quiet voice, with the most restrained manner possible, what she was doing with the paper—she turned around as if she had been caught stealing, and looked quite angry—asked me why I should frighten her so!

Then she said that the paper stained everything it touched, that she had 165
found yellow smooches on all my clothes and John's, and she wished we would be more careful!

Did not that sound innocent? But I know she was studying that pattern, and I am determined that nobody shall find it out but myself!

Life is very much more exciting now than it used to be. You see I have something more to expect, to look forward to, to watch. I really do eat better, and am more quiet than I was.

John is so pleased to see me improve! He laughed a little the other day, and said I seemed to be flourishing in spite of my wallpaper.

I turned it off with a laugh. I had no intention of telling him it was *because* of the wallpaper—he would make fun of me. He might even want to take me away.

I don't want to leave now until I have found it out. There is a week more, and I think that will be enough.

I'm feeling ever so much better! I don't sleep much at night, for it is so interesting to watch developments; but I sleep a good deal in the daytime.

In the daytime it is tiresome and perplexing.

There are always new shoots on the fungus, and new shades of yellow all over it. I cannot keep count of them, though I have tried conscientiously.

It is the strangest yellow, that wallpaper! It makes me think of all the yellow things I ever saw—not beautiful ones like buttercups, but old foul, bad yellow things.

But there is something else about that paper—the smell! I noticed it the moment we came into the room, but with so much air and sun it was not bad. Now we have had a week of fog and rain, and whether the windows are open or not, the smell is here.

It creeps all over the house.

I find it hovering in the dining-room, skulking in the parlor, hiding in the hall, lying in wait for me on the stairs.

It gets into my hair.

Even when I go to ride, if I turn my head suddenly and surprise it—there is that smell!

Such a peculiar odor, too! I have spent hours in trying to analyze it, to find what it smelled like.

It is not bad—at first, and very gentle, but quite the subtlest, most enduring odor I ever met.

In this damp weather it is awful, I wake up in the night and find it hanging over me.

It used to disturb me at first. I thought seriously of burning the house—to reach the smell.

But now I am used to it. The only thing I can think of that it is like is the *color* of the paper! A yellow smell.

There is a very funny mark on this wall, low down, near the mopboard. A streak that runs round the room. It goes behind every piece of furniture, except the bed, a long, straight, even *smooch,* as if it had been rubbed over and over.

I wonder how it was done and who did it, and what they did it for. Round and round and round—round and round and round—it makes me dizzy!

I really have discovered something at last.

Through watching so much at night, when it changes so, I have finally found out.

The front pattern *does* move—and no wonder! The woman behind shakes it!

Sometimes I think there are a great many women behind, and sometimes only one, and she crawls around fast, and her crawling shakes it all over.

Then in the very bright spots she keeps still, and in the very shady spots she just takes hold of the bars and shakes them hard.

And she is all the time trying to climb through. But nobody could climb through that pattern—it strangles so; I think that is why it has so many heads.

They get through, and then the pattern strangles them off and turns them upside down, and makes their eyes white!

If those heads were covered or taken off it would not be half so bad.

I think that woman gets out in the daytime! 195

And I'll tell you why—privately—I've seen her!

I can see her out of every one of my windows!

It is the same woman, I know, for she is always creeping, and most women do not creep by daylight.

I see her in that long shaded lane, creeping up and down. I see her in those dark grape arbors, creeping all around the garden.

I see her on that long road under the trees, creeping along, and when a carriage comes she hides under the blackberry vines. 200

I don't blame her a bit. It must be very humiliating to be caught creeping by daylight!

I always lock the door when I creep by daylight. I can't do it at night, for I know John would suspect something at once.

And John is so queer now, that I don't want to irritate him. I wish he would take another room! Besides, I don't want anybody to get that woman out at night but myself.

I often wonder if I could see her out of all the windows at once.

But, turn as fast as I can, I can only see out of one at one time. 205

And though I always see her, she *may* be able to creep faster than I can turn!

I have watched her sometimes away off in the open country, creeping as fast as a cloud shadow in a high wind.

If only that top pattern could be gotten off from the under one! I mean to try it, little by little.

I have found out another funny thing, but I shan't tell it this time! It does not do to trust people too much.

There are only two more days to get this paper off, and I believe John is beginning to notice. I don't like the look in his eyes. 210

And I heard him ask Jennie a lot of professional questions, about me. She had a very good report to give.

She said I slept a good deal in the daytime.

John knows I don't sleep very well at night, for all I'm so quiet!

He asked me all sorts of questions too, and pretended to be very loving and kind.

As if I couldn't see through him! 215

Still, I don't wonder he acts so, sleeping under this paper for three months.

It only interests me, but I feel sure John and Jennie are secretly affected by it.

Hurrah! This is the last day, but it is enough. John is to stay in town over night, and won't be out until this evening.

Jennie wanted to sleep with me—the sly thing! But I told her I should undoubtedly rest better for a night all alone.

That was clever, for really I wasn't alone a bit! As soon as it was moonlight and that poor thing began to crawl and shake the pattern, I got up and ran to help her.

I pulled and she shook, I shook and she pulled, and before morning we had peeled off yards of that paper.

A strip about as high as my head and half around the room.

And then when the sun came and that awful pattern began to laugh at me, I declared I would finish it to-day!

We go away to-morrow, and they are moving all my furniture down again to leave things as they were before.

Jennie looked at the wall in amazement, but I told her merrily that I did it out of pure spite at the vicious thing.

She laughed and said she wouldn't mind doing it herself, but I must not get tired.

How she betrayed herself that time!

But I am here, and no person touches this paper but me,—not *alive*!

She tried to get me out of the room—it was too patent! But I said it was so quiet and empty and clean now that I believed I would lie down again and sleep all I could, and not to wake me even for dinner—I would call when I woke.

So now she is gone, and the servants are gone, and the things are gone, and there is nothing left but that great bedstead nailed down, with the canvas mattress we found on it.

We shall sleep downstairs to-night, and take the boat home to-morrow.

I quite enjoy the room, now it is bare again.

How those children did tear about here!

This bedstead is fairly gnawed!

But I must get to work.

I have locked the door and thrown the key down into the front path.

I don't want to go out, and I don't want to have anybody come in, till John comes.

I want to astonish him.

I've got a rope up here that even Jennie did not find. If that woman does get out, and tries to get away, I can tie her!

But I forgot I could not reach far without anything to stand on!

This bed will *not* move!

I tried to lift and push it until I was lame, and then I got so angry I bit off a little piece at one corner—but it hurt my teeth.

Then I peeled off all the paper I could reach standing on the floor. It sticks horribly and the pattern just enjoys it! All those strangled heads and bulbous eyes and waddling fungus growths just shriek with derision!

I am getting angry enough to do something desperate. To jump out of the window would be admirable exercise, but the bars are too strong even to try.

Besides I wouldn't do it. Of course not. I know well enough that a step like that is improper and might be misconstrued.

I don't like to *look* out of the windows even—there are so many of those creeping women, and they creep so fast.

I wonder if they all come out of that wallpaper as I did?

But I am securely fastened now by my well-hidden rope—you don't get *me* out in the road there!

I suppose I shall have to get back behind the pattern when it comes night, and that is hard!

It is so pleasant to be out in this great room and creep around as I please!

I don't want to go outside. I won't, even if Jennie asks me to.

For outside you have to creep on the ground, and everything is green instead of yellow.

But here I can creep smoothly on the floor, and my shoulder just fits in that long smooch around the wall, so I cannot lose my way.

Why, there's John at the door!

It is no use, young man, you can't open it!

How he does call and pound!

Now he's crying for an axe.

It would be a shame to break down that beautiful door!

"John dear!" said I in the gentlest voice, "the key is down by the front steps, under a plantain leaf!"

That silenced him for a few moments.

Then he said—very quietly indeed, "Open the door, my darling!"

"I can't," said I. "The key is down by the front door under a plantain leaf!"

And then I said it again, several times, very gently and slowly, and said it so often that he had to go and see, and he got it of course, and came in. He stopped short by the door.

"What is the matter?" he cried. "For God's sake, what are you doing!"

I kept on creeping just the same, but I looked at him over my shoulder.

"I've got out at last," said I, "in spite of you and Jane. And I've pulled off most of the paper, so you can't put me back!"

Now why should that man have fainted? But he did, and right across my path by the wall, so that I had to creep over him every time! *[1892]*

THINKING ABOUT THE TEXT

1. What psychological stages does the narrator go through as the story progresses?
2. How does the wallpaper function as a symbol in this story? What do you conclude about the narrator when she becomes increasingly interested in the woman she finds there?
3. Explain your ultimate view of the narrator by using specific details of the story and by identifying some of the warrants or assumptions behind your opinion. Do you admire her? Sympathize with her? Recoil from her? What would you say to someone who simply dismisses her as crazy?

4. The story is narrated in the present tense. Would its effect be different if it were narrated in the past tense? Why, or why not?
5. In real life, Gilman's husband and her doctor were two separate people. In the story, the narrator's husband is her doctor as well. Why do you think Gilman made this change? What is the effect of her combining husband and doctor?

CHARLOTTE PERKINS GILMAN

Why I Wrote "The Yellow Wallpaper"

Gilman published the following piece in the October 1913 issue of her magazine, The Forerunner.

Many and many a reader has asked that. When the story first came out, in the *New England Magazine* about 1891, a Boston physician made protest in *The Transcript.* Such a story ought not to be written, he said; it was enough to drive anyone mad to read it.

Another physician, in Kansas I think, wrote to say that it was the best description of incipient insanity he had ever seen, and—begging my pardon—had I been there?

Now the story of the story is this:

For many years I suffered from a severe and continuous nervous breakdown tending to melancholia—and beyond. During about the third year of this trouble I went, in devout faith and some faint stir of hope, to a noted specialist in nervous diseases, the best known in the country. This wise man put me to bed and applied the rest cure, to which a still good physique responded so promptly that, he concluded there was nothing much the matter with me, and sent me home with solemn advice to "live as domestic a life as far as possible," to "have but two hours' intellectual life a day," and "never to touch pen, brush, or pencil again as long as I lived." This was in 1887.

I went home and obeyed those directions for some three months, and came 5
so near the border line of utter mental ruin that I could see over.

Then, using the remnants of intelligence that remained, and helped by a wise friend, I cast the noted specialist's advice to the winds and went to work again—work, the normal life of every human being; work, in which is joy and growth and service, without which one is a pauper and a parasite; ultimately recovering some measure of power.

Being naturally moved to rejoicing by this narrow escape, I wrote *The Yellow Wallpaper*, with its embellishments and additions to carry out the ideal (I never had hallucinations or objections to my mural decorations) and sent a copy to the physician who so nearly drove me mad. He never acknowledged it.

The little book is valued by alienists° and as a good specimen of one kind of literature. It has to my knowledge saved one woman from a similar fate—so terrifying her family that they let her out into normal activity and she recovered.

But the best result is this. Many years later I was told that the great specialist had admitted to friends of his that he had altered his treatment of neurasthenia since reading *The Yellow Wallpaper.*

It was not intended to drive people crazy, but to save people from being driven 10
crazy, and it worked. *[1913]*

alienists: Nineteenth-century term for psychiatrists.

THINKING ABOUT THE TEXT

1. S. Weir Mitchell was the "noted specialist in nervous diseases" (para. 4) whom Gilman mentions. Yet she does not identify him by name. Why not, do you think? Some historians argue that, contrary to Gilman's claim here, Mitchell continued to believe his "rest cure" valid. Does this issue of fact matter to your judgment of her piece? Why, or why not?
2. Look again at Gilman's last sentence. Do you believe that her story could indeed "save people from being driven crazy"? Why, or why not?
3. Does this piece as a whole affect your interpretation and opinion of Gilman's story? Why, or why not? In general, how much do you think readers of a story should know about its author's life?

S. WEIR MITCHELL

From *The Evolution of the Rest Treatment*

Charlotte Perkins Gilman sought help from Silas Weir Mitchell (1829–1914) because he was a well-known and highly respected physician who had treated many women's mental problems. Mitchell developed his "rest cure" while serving as an army surgeon during the Civil War. Ironically, like Gilman, he was also a writer. Besides producing numerous monographs on medical subjects, he published many short stories and novels. The following is an excerpt from a lecture that Mitchell gave to the Philadelphia Neurological Society in 1904, twelve years after "The Yellow Wallpaper" appeared. As you will see, Mitchell was still enthusiastic about his "rest cure," although he had changed it in certain respects since devising it.

I have been asked to come here to-night to speak to you on some subject connected with nervous disease. I had hoped to have had ready a fitting paper for so notable an occasion, but have been prevented by public engagements and private business so as to make it quite impossible. I have, therefore, been driven to ask whether it would be agreeable if I should speak in regard to the mode in which the treatment of disease by rest was evolved. This being favorably received, I am here this evening to say a few words on that subject.

You all know full well that the art of cure rests upon a number of sciences, and that what we do in medicine, we cannot always explain, and that our methods are far from having the accuracy involved in the term *scientific*. Very often, however, it is found that what comes to us through some accident or popular use and proves of value, is defensible in the end by scientific explanatory research. This was the case as regards the treatment I shall briefly consider for you to-night.

The first indication I ever had of the great value of mere rest in disease, was during the Civil War, when there fell into the hands of Doctors Morehouse, Keen, and myself, a great many cases of what we called acute exhaustion. These were men, who, being tired by much marching, gave out suddenly at the end of some unusual exertion, and remained for weeks, perhaps months, in a pitiable state of what we should call today, Neurasthenia. In these war cases, it came on with strange abruptness. It was more extreme and also more certainly curable than are most of the graver male cases which now we are called on to treat.

I have seen nothing exactly like it in civil experience, but the combination of malaria, excessive exertion, and exposure provided cases such as no one sees today. Complete rest and plentiful diet usually brought these men up again and in many instances enabled them to return to the front.

5 In 1872 I had charge of a man who had locomotor ataxia° with extreme pain in the extremities, and while making some unusual exertion, he broke his right thigh. This confined him to his bed for three months, and the day he got up, he broke his left thigh. This involved another three months of rest. At the end of that time he confessed with satisfaction that his ataxia was better, and that he was, as he remained thereafter, free from pain. I learned from this, and two other cases, that in ataxia the bones are brittle, and I learned also that rest in bed is valuable in a proportion of such cases. You may perceive that my attention was thus twice drawn towards the fact that mere rest had certain therapeutic values.

In 1874 Mrs. G., of B——, Maine, came to see me in the month of January. I have described her case elsewhere, so that it is needless to go into detail here, except to say that she was a lady of ample means, with no special troubles or annoyances, but completely exhausted by having had children in rapid succession and from having undertaken to do charitable and other work to an extent far beyond her strength. When first I saw this tall woman, large, gaunt, weighing under a hundred pounds, her complexion pale and acneous, and heard her story, I was for a time in a state of such therapeutic despair as usually fell upon physicians of that day when called upon to treat such cases. She had been to Spas, to physicians of the utmost eminence, passed through the hands of gynecologists, worn spinal supporters, and taken every tonic known to the books. When I saw her she was unable to walk up stairs. Her exercise was limited to moving feebly up and down her room, a dozen times a day. She slept little and, being very intelligent, felt deeply her inability to read or write. Any such use of the eyes caused headache and nausea. Conversation tired her, and she had by degrees accepted a life of isolation. She was able partially to digest and retain her meals if she lay down in a noiseless and darkened room. Any disturbance or the least excitement, in short, any effort, caused nausea and immediate rejection of her meal. With care she could retain enough food to preserve her

ataxia: An inability to control muscular movements that is symptomatic of some nervous diseases.

life and hardly to do more. Anemia, which we had then no accurate means of measuring, had been met by half a dozen forms of iron, all of which were said to produce headache, and generally to disagree with her. Naturally enough, her case had been pronounced to be hysteria, but calling names may relieve a doctor and comfort him in failure, but does not always assist the patient, and to my mind there was more of a general condition of nervous excitability due to the extreme of weakness than I should have been satisfied to label with the apologetic label hysteria.

I sat beside this woman day after day, hearing her pitiful story, and distressed that a woman, young, once handsome, and with every means of enjoyment in life should be condemned to what she had been told was a state of hopeless invalidism. After my third or fourth visit, with a deep sense that everything had been done for her that able men could with reason suggest, and many things which reason never could have suggested, she said to me that I appeared to have nothing to offer which had not been tried over and over again. I asked her for another day before she gave up the hope which had brought her to me. The night brought counsel. The following morning I said to her, if you are at rest you appear to digest your meals better. "Yes," she said. "I have been told that on that account I ought to lie in bed. It has been tried, but when I remain in bed for a few days, I lose all appetite, have intense constipation, and get up feeling weaker than when I went to bed. Please do not ask me to go to bed." Nevertheless, I did, and a week in bed justified her statements. She threw up her meals undigested, and was manifestly worse for my experiment. Sometimes the emesis° was mere regurgitation, sometimes there was nausea and violent straining, with consequent extreme exhaustion. She declared that unless she had the small exercise of walking up and down her room, she was infallibly worse. I was here between two difficulties. That she needed rest I saw, that she required some form of exercise I also saw. How could I unite the two?

As I sat beside her, with a keen sense of defeat, it suddenly occurred to me that some time before, I had seen a man, known as a layer on of hands, use very rough rubbing for a gentleman who was in a state of general paresis.° Mr. S. had asked me if I objected to this man rubbing him. I said no, and that I should like to see him do so, as he had relieved, to my knowledge, cases of rheumatic stiffness. I was present at two sittings and saw this man rub my patient. He kept him sitting in a chair at the time and was very rough and violent like the quacks now known as osteopaths. I told him he had injured my patient by his extreme roughness, and that if he rubbed him at all he must be more gentle. He took the hint and as a result there was every time a notable but temporary gain. Struck with this, I tried to have rubbing used on spinal cases, but those who tried to do the work were inefficient, and I made no constant use of it. It remained, however, on my mind, and recurred to me as I sat beside this wreck of a useful and once vigorous woman. The thought was fertile. I asked myself why rubbing might not prove competent to do for the muscles and tardy circulation what voluntary exercise does. I said to myself, this may be exercise without exertion, and wondered why I had not long before had this pregnant view of the matter.

emesis: Vomiting.
paresis: Brain syphilis.

Suffice it to say that I brought a young woman to Mrs. G.'s bedside and told her how I thought she ought to be rubbed. The girl was clever, and developed talent in that direction, and afterwards became the first of that great number of people who have since made a livelihood by massage. I watched the rubbing two or three times, giving instructions, in fact developing out of the clumsy massage I had seen, the manual of a therapeutic means, at that time entirely new to me. A few days later I fell upon the idea of giving electric passive exercise and cautiously added this second agency. Meanwhile, as she had always done best when secluded, I insisted on entire rest and shut out friends, relatives, books, and letters. I had some faith that I should succeed. In ten days I was sure the woman had found a new tonic, hope, and blossomed like a rose. Her symptoms passed away one by one. I was soon able to add to her diet, to feed her between meals, to give her malt daily, and, after a time, to conceal in it full doses of pyro-phosphates of iron. First, then, I had found two means which enabled me to use rest in bed without causing the injurious effects of unassisted rest; secondly, I had discovered that massage was a tonic of extraordinary value; thirdly, I had learned that with this combination of seclusion, massage, and electricity, I could overfeed the patient until I had brought her into a state of entire health. I learned later the care which had to be exercised in getting these patients out of bed. But this does not concern us now. In two months she gained forty pounds and was a cheerful, blooming woman, fit to do as she pleased. She has remained, save for time's ravage, what I made her.

It may strike you as interesting that for a while I was not fully aware of the 10
enormous value of a therapeutic discovery which employed no new agents, but owed its usefulness to a combination of means more or less well known.

Simple rest as a treatment had been suggested, but not in this class of cases. Massage has a long history. Used, I think, as a luxury by the Orientals for ages, it was employed by Ling in 1813. It never attained perfection in the hands of the Swedes, nor do they to-day understand the proper use of this agent. It was over and over recognized in Germany, but never generally accepted. In France, at a later period, Dreyfus, in 1841, wrote upon it and advised its use, as did Recamier and Lainé in 1868. Two at least of these authors thought it useful as a general agent, but no one seems to have accepted their views, nor was its value as a tonic spoken of in the books on therapeutics or recommended on any text-book as a powerful toning agent. It was used here in the Rest Treatment, and this, I think, gave it vogue and caused the familiar use of this invaluable therapeutic measure.

A word before I close. My first case left me in May, 1874, and shortly afterwards I began to employ the same method in other cases, being careful to choose only those which seemed best suited to it. My first mention in print of the treatment was in 1875, in the Sequin Lectures, Vol. 1, No. 4, "Rest in the Treatment of Disease." In that paper I first described Mrs. G.'s case. My second paper was in 1877, an address before the Medico-Chirurgical faculty of Maryland, and the same year I printed my book on "Rest Treatment." The one mistake in the book was the title. I was, however, so impressed at the time by the extraordinary gain in flesh and blood under this treatment that I made it too prominent in the title of the book. Let me say that for a long time the new treatment was received with the utmost incredulity. When I spoke in my papers of the people who had gained half a pound a day or more, my results were questioned and ridiculed in this city as approaching charlatanism. At a later date in England some physicians were equally wanting in foresight and courtesy. It seems incredible that any man who was a member of the British Medical Association could have said that he would rather see his patients not get well than have them cured by such a method as that. It was several years before it was taken up by Professor Goodell, and it was a longer time in making its way in Europe when by mere accident it came to be first used by Professor William Playfair.

I suffered keenly at that time from this unfair criticism, as any sensitive man must have done, for some who were eminent in the profession said of it and of me things which were most inconsiderate. Over and over in consultation I was rejected with ill-concealed scorn. I made no reply to my critics. I knew that time would justify me: I have added a long since accepted means of helping those whom before my day few helped. This is a sufficient reward for silence, patience, and self-faith. I fancy that there are in this room many who have profited for themselves and their patients by the thought which evolved the Rest Treatment as I sat by the bedside of my first rest case in 1874. Playfair said of it at the British Association that he had nothing to add to it and nothing to omit, and to this day no one has differed as to his verdict.

How fully the use of massage has been justified by the later scientific studies of Lauder Brunton, myself, and others you all know. It is one of the most scientific of remedial methods. *[1904]*

THINKING ABOUT THE TEXT

1. How would you describe Mitchell's tone in this lecture? What self-image does he seem to cultivate? Support your answers by referring to specific words in the text.
2. Why does Mitchell consider Mrs. G.'s case significant? In what ways does she resemble Gilman and the narrator of Gilman's story?
3. Mitchell indicates that his patients have included male as well as female hysterics. Are we therefore justified in concluding that gender did not matter much in his application of the "rest cure"? Why, or why not?

JOHN HARVEY KELLOGG
From *The Ladies' Guide in Health and Disease*

John Harvey Kellogg (1852–1943) was an American physician who wrote much advice about how to discipline one's sexual desires and, in the case of women, how to be a good mother. As founder and superintendent of the Battle Creek Sanitarium in Michigan, Dr. Kellogg urged that his patients eat cereals as part of their treatment, and eventually, his brother established the cereal company that bears their family name. Dr. Kellogg's keen interest in cereals and health foods is satirized in T. Coraghessan Boyle's 1993 novel, The Road to Wellville, *and the film based on that book. The following piece is an excerpt from Kellogg's 1882* Ladies' Guide in Health and Disease: Girlhood, Maidenhood, Wifehood, Motherhood. *In this selection, he virtually equates womanhood with motherhood and discusses what a woman must do to produce outstanding children. Kellogg's advice reflects the view that much of his society held about women—or at least about middle- and upper-class white women. His discussion of "puerperal mania" is especially relevant to Gilman's story.*

The special influence of the mother begins with the moment of conception. In fact it is possible that the mental condition at the time of the generative act has much to do with determining the character of the child, though it is generally conceded that at this time the influence of the father is greater than that of the mother. Any number of instances have occurred in which a drunken father has impressed upon his child the condition of his nervous system to such a degree as to render permanent in the child the staggering gait and maudlin manner which in his own case was a transient condition induced by the poisonous influence of alcohol. A child born as the result of a union in which both parents were in a state of beastly intoxication was idiotic.

Another fact might be added to impress the importance that the new being should be supplied from the very beginning of its existence with the very best conditions possible. Indeed, it is desirable to go back still further, and secure a proper preparation for the important function of maternity. The qualities which go to make up individuality of character are the result of the summing up of a long line of influences, too subtle and too varied to admit of full control, but still, to some degree at least, subject to management. The dominance of law is nowhere more evident than in the relation of ante-natal influences to character.

The hap-hazard way in which human beings are generated leaves no room for surprise that the race should deteriorate. No stock-breeder would expect anything but ruin should he allow his animals to propagate with no attention to their physical conditions or previous preparation.

Finding herself in a pregnant condition, the mother should not yield to the depressing influences which often crowd upon her. The anxieties and fears which women sometimes yield themselves to, grow with encouragement, until they become so absorbed as to be capable of producing a profoundly evil impression on the child. The true mother who is prepared for the functions of maternity, will welcome the evidence of pregnancy, and joyfully enter upon the Heaven-given task of molding a human character, of bringing into the world a new being whose life-history may involve the destinies of nations, or change the current of human thought for generations to come.

The pregnant mother should cultivate cheerfulness of mind and calmness 5
of temper, but should avoid excitements of all kinds, such as theatrical performances, public contests of various descriptions, etc. Anger, envy, irritability of temper, and, in fact, all the passions and propensities should be held in check. The fickleness of desire and the constantly varying whims which characterize the pregnant state in some women should not be regarded as uncontrollable, and to be yielded to as the only means of appeasing them. The mother should be gently

encouraged to resist such tendencies when they become at all marked, and to assist her in the effort, her husband should endeavor to engage her mind by interesting conversation, reading, and various harmless and pleasant diversions.

If it is desired that the child should possess a special aptitude for any particular art or pursuit, during the period of pregnancy the mother's mind should be constantly directed in this channel. If artistic taste or skill is the trait desired, the mother should be surrounded by works of art of a high order of merit. She should read art, think art, talk, and write about art, and if possible, herself engage in the close practical study of some one or more branches of art, as painting, drawing, etching, or modeling. If ability for authorship is desired, then the mother should devote herself assiduously to literature. It is not claimed that by following these suggestions any mother can make of her children great artists or authors at will; but it is certain that by this means the greatest possibilities in individual cases can be attained; and it is certain that decided results have been secured by close attention to the principles laid down. It should be understood, however, that not merely a formal and desultory effort on the part of the mother is what is required. The theme selected must completely absorb her mind. It must be the one idea of her waking thoughts and the model on which is formed the dreams of her sleeping hours.

The question of diet during pregnancy as before stated is a vitally important one as regards the interests of the child. A diet into which enters largely such unwholesome articles as mustard, pepper, hot sauces, spices, and other stimulating condiments, engenders a love for stimulants in the disposition of the infant. Tea and coffee, especially if used to excess, undoubtedly tend in the same direction. We firmly believe that we have, in the facts first stated, the key to the constant increase in the consumption of ardent spirits. The children of the present generation inherit from their condiment-consuming, tea-, coffee-, and liquor-drinking, and tobacco-using parents, not simply a readiness for the acquirement of the habits mentioned, but a propensity for the use of stimulants which in persons of weak will-power and those whose circumstances are not the most favorable, becomes irresistible.

The present generation is also suffering in consequence of the impoverished diet of its parents. The modern custom of bolting the flour from the different grains has deprived millions of infants and children of the necessary supply of bone-making material, thus giving rise to a greatly increased frequency of the various diseases which arise from imperfect bony structure, as rickets, caries, premature decay of the teeth, etc. The proper remedy is the disuse of fine-flour bread and all other bolted grain preparations. Graham-flour bread, oatmeal, cracked wheat, and similar preparations, should be relied upon as the leading articles of diet. Supplemented by milk, the whole-grain preparations constitute a complete form of nourishment, and render a large amount of animal food not only unnecessary but really harmful on account of its stimulating character. It is by no means so necessary as is generally supposed that meat, fish, fowl, and flesh in various forms should constitute a large element of the dietary of the pregnant or nursing mother in order to furnish adequate nourishment for the developing child. We have seen the happiest results follow the employment of a strictly vegetarian dietary, and do not hesitate to advise moderation in the use of flesh food, though we do not recommend the entire discontinuance of its use by the pregnant mother who has been accustomed to use it freely.

A nursing mother should at once suspend nursing if she discovers that pregnancy has again occurred. The continuance of nursing under such circumstances is to the disadvantage of three individuals, the mother, the infant at the breast, and the developing child.

Sexual indulgence during pregnancy may be suspended with decided benefit to both mother and child. The most ancient medical writers call attention to the fact that by the practice of continence° during gestation, the pains of childbirth are greatly mitigated. The injurious influences upon the child of the gratification of the passions during the period when its character is being formed, is undoubtedly much greater than is usually supposed. We have no doubt that this is a common cause of the transmission of libidinous tendencies to the child; and that the tendency to abortion is induced by sexual indulgence has long been a well-established fact. The females of most animals resolutely resist the advances of the males during this period, being guided in harmony with natural law by their natural instincts which have been less perverted in them than in human beings. The practice of continence during pregnancy is also enforced in the harems of the East, which fact leads to the practice of abortion among women of this class who are desirous of remaining the special favorites of the common husband.

The general health of the mother must be kept up in every way. It is especially important that the regularity of the bowels should be maintained. Proper diet and as much physical exercise as can be taken are the best means for accomplishing this. When constipation is allowed to exist, the infant as well as the mother suffers. The effete products which should be promptly removed from the body, being long retained, are certain to find their way back into the system again, poisoning not only the blood of the mother but that of the developing fetus. . . .

Puerperal Mania.—This form of mental disease is most apt to show itself about two weeks after delivery. Although, fortunately, of not very frequent occurrence, it is a most serious disorder when it does occur, and hence we may with propriety introduce the following somewhat lengthy, but most graphic description of the disease from the pen of Dr. Ramsbotham, an eminent English physician:—

"In mania there is almost always, at the very commencement, a troubled, agitated, and hurried manner, a restless eye, an unnaturally anxious, suspicious, and unpleasing expression of face;—sometimes it is pallid, at others more flushed than usual;—an unaccustomed irritability of temper, and impatience of control or contradiction; a vacillation of purpose, or loss of memory; sometimes a rapid succession of contradictory orders are issued, or a paroxysm of excessive anger is excited about the merest trifle. Occasionally, one of the first indications will be a sullen obstinacy, or listlessness and stubborn silence. The patient lies on her back, and can by no means be persuaded to reply to the questions of her attendants, or she will repeat them, as an echo, until, all at once, without any apparent cause, she will

continence: Chastity, abstinence, or restraint.

break out into a torrent of language more or less incoherent, and her words will follow each other with surprising rapidity. These symptoms will sometimes show themselves rather suddenly, on the patient's awakening from a disturbed and unrefreshing sleep, or they may supervene more slowly when she has been harassed with wakefulness for three or four previous nights in succession, or perhaps ever since her delivery. She will very likely then become impressed with the idea that some evil has befallen her husband, or, what is still more usual, her child; that it is dead or stolen; and if it be brought to her, nothing can persuade her it is her own; she supposes it to belong to somebody else; or she will fancy that her husband is unfaithful to her, or that he and those about her have conspired to poison her. Those persons who are naturally the objects of her deepest and most devout affection, are regarded by her with jealousy, suspicion, and hatred. This is particularly remarkable with regard to her newly born infant; and I have known many instances where attempts have been made to destroy it when it has been incautiously left within her power. Sometimes, though rarely, may be observed a great anxiety regarding the termination of her own case, or a firm conviction that she is speedily about to die. I have observed upon occasions a constant movement of the lips, while the mouth was shut; or the patient is incessantly rubbing the inside of her lips with her fingers, or thrusting them far back into her mouth; and if questions are asked, particularly if she be desired to put out her tongue, she will often compress the lips forcibly together, as if with an obstinate determination of resistance. One peculiarity attending some cases of puerperal mania is the immorality and obscenity of the expressions uttered; they are often such, indeed, as to excite our astonishment that women in a respectable station of society could ever have become acquainted with such language."

The insanity of childbirth differs from that of pregnancy in that in the latter cases the patient is almost always melancholy,° while in the former there is active mania. Derangement of the digestive organs is a constant accompaniment of the disease.

If the patient has no previous or hereditary tendency to insanity, the prospect of a quite speedy recovery is good. The result is seldom immediately fatal, but the patient not infrequently remains in a condition of mental unsoundness for months or even years, and sometimes permanently. 20

Treatment: When there is reason to suspect a liability to puerperal mania from previous mental disease or from hereditary influence, much can be done to ward off an attack. Special attention must be paid to the digestive organs, which should be regulated by proper food and simple means to aid digestion. The tendency to sleeplessness must be combatted by careful nursing, light massage at night, rubbing of the spine, alternate hot and cold applications to the spine, cooling the head by cloths wrung out of cold water, and the use of the warm bath at bed time. These measures are often successful in securing sleep when all other measures fail.

The patient must be kept very quiet. Visitors, even if near relatives, must not be allowed when the patient is at all nervous or disturbed, and it is best to exclude

melancholy: Mental state characterized by severe depression, somatic problems, and hallucinations or delusions.

nearly every one from the sick-room with the exception of the nurse, who should be a competent and experienced person.

When the attack has really begun, the patient must have the most vigilant watchcare, not being left alone for a moment. It is much better to care for the patient at home, when possible to do so efficiently, than to take her to an asylum.

When evidences of returning rationality appear, the greatest care must be exercised to prevent too great excitement. Sometimes a change of air, if the patient is sufficiently strong, physically, will at this period prove eminently beneficial. A visit from a dear friend will sometimes afford a needed stimulus to the dormant faculties. Such cases as these of course require intelligent medical supervision.

[1882]

THINKING ABOUT THE TEXT

1. What specific responsibilities does Kellogg assign to women? What are some key assumptions he makes about them?
2. Quite possibly Kellogg would have said that the narrator of Gilman's story suffers from puerperal mania. What details of the story would support this diagnosis? What significant details of the narrator's life, if any, would Kellogg be ignoring if he saw her as *merely* a case of puerperal mania?
3. If Kellogg's advice were published today, what parts of it do you think readers would accept? What parts do you think many readers would reject?

WRITING ABOUT ISSUES

1. After reading the three essays given here, research women's psychological disorders of the nineteenth century and write an essay that argues that those "disorders" were the result of male attitudes toward women.
2. Research the term *female hysteria* and write a report that includes the ideas of S. Weir Mitchell and other prominent nineteenth-century doctors. Include in your report your evaluation of their credibility.
3. Research how mental illness was diagnosed and treated within a particular period of American history. Then, write an essay that argues for seeing the culture of that period as an influence on how mental illness was conceived then.
4. Research such contemporary psychological problems as depression, bulimia, anorexia, and dissociative identity disorders. Write an essay that tries to explain why these diseases seem to affect mostly women.

CHAPTER 7

Writing with Critical Approaches to Literature

Exploring the topics of literary criticism can help readers understand the various ways literature can matter. One popular way to investigate critical approaches to literature is to group critics into schools. Critics who are concerned primarily with equality for women, for example, are often classified as feminist critics, and those concerned with the responses of readers are classified as reader-response critics. Likewise, critics who focus on the unconscious are said to belong to the psychoanalytic school, and those who analyze class conflicts belong to the Marxist school.

Classifying critics in this way is probably more convenient than precise. Few critics like to be pigeonholed or thought predictable, and many professional readers tend to be eclectic—that is, they use ideas from various schools to help them illuminate the text. Nevertheless, knowing something about contemporary schools of criticism can make you a more informed reader and help literature matter to you even more.

There is a commonsense belief that words mean just what they say—that to understand a certain passage in a text a reader simply needs to know what the words mean. But meaning is rarely straightforward. Scholars have been arguing over the meaning of passages in the Bible, in the Constitution, and in Shakespeare's plays for centuries without reaching agreement. Pinning down the exact meaning of words like *sin*, *justice*, and *love* is almost impossible, but even more daunting is the unacknowledged theory of reading that each person brings to any text, including literature. Some people who read the Bible or the Constitution, for example, believe in the literal meaning of the words, and some think the real meaning lies in the original intention of the writer, while others believe that the only meaning we can be sure of is our own perspective. For these latter readers, there is no objective meaning, and no absolutely true meaning is possible.

Indeed, a good deal of what a text means depends on the perspective that readers bring with them. Passages can be read effectively from numerous points of view. A generation ago most English professors taught their students to pay attention to the internal aspects of a poem and not to the poem's larger social and political contexts. So oppositions, irony, paradox, and coherence—not gender equality or social justice—were topics of discussion. Proponents of this approach were said to belong to the New Critical school. In the last twenty-five years or so, however, professors have put much more emphasis on the external aspects of interpretation, stressing social, political, cultural, sexual, and gender-based perspectives. Each one of these perspectives can give us a valuable window on a text, helping us see the rich possibilities of literature. Even though each approach can provide insights into a text, it can also be blind to other textual elements. When we read in too focused a way, we can sometimes miss the opportunity to see what others see.

In this chapter, however, we want to present our interpretation in a clear, logical, and reflective manner as we take a position and try to persuade others of its reasonableness. Since there are many possible lenses to see a text through, you can be sure your classmates will see things differently. Part of the excitement and challenge of making arguments that matter is your ability to analyze and clarify your ideas, gather and organize your evidence, and present your claim in carefully revised and edited prose.

Contemporary Schools of Criticism

The following fourteen approaches are just a few of the many different literary schools or perspectives a reader can use in engaging a text. Think of them as intellectual tools or informed lenses that you can employ to enhance your interpretation of a particular literary text:

- New Criticism
- Feminist criticism
- Psychoanalytic criticism
- Marxist criticism
- Deconstruction
- Reader-response criticism
- Postcolonial criticism
- New Historicism
- Queer theory
- Object-oriented criticism
- Cognitive criticism
- Affective criticism
- Performance-oriented criticism
- Rhetorical criticism

NEW CRITICISM

New Criticism was developed about seventy years ago as a way to focus on "the text itself." Although it is no longer as popular as it once was, some of its principles are still widely accepted, especially the use of specific examples from the text as evidence for a particular interpretation. Sometimes called *close reading*, this approach does not see either the writer's intention or the reader's personal response as relevant. It is also uninterested in the text's social context, the spirit of the age, or its relevance to issues of gender, social justice, or oppression.

These critics are interested, for example, in a poem's internal structure, images, symbols, metaphors, point of view, plot, and characterizations. Emphasis is placed on literary language—on the ways connotation, ambiguity, irony, and paradox all reinforce the meaning. In fact, *how* a poem means is inseparable from *what* it means. The primary method for judging the worth of a piece of literature is its organic unity or the complex way all the elements of a text contribute to the poem's meaning.

Critics often argue that their interpretations are the most consistent with textual evidence. A popular approach is to note the oppositions in the text and to focus on tensions, ironies, and paradoxes. Typically a paradox early in the text is shown at the end not to be that contradictory after all. The critic then argues that all the elements of the text can be seen as contributing to this resolution.

FEMINIST CRITICISM

Feminist criticism developed during the 1970s as an outgrowth of a resurgent women's movement. The goals of the feminist critic and the feminist political activist are similar—to contest the patriarchal point of view as the standard for all moral, aesthetic, political, and intellectual judgments and to assert that gender roles are primarily learned, not universal. They hope to uncover and challenge essentialist attitudes that hold it is normal for women to be kept in domestic, secondary, and subservient roles, and they affirm the value of a woman's experiences and perspectives in understanding the world. Recently both female and male critics have become interested in gender studies, a branch of theory concerned with the ways cultural practices socialize us to act in certain ways because of our gender. Focused primarily on issues of identity, gender criticism looks at the ways characters in literary texts are represented, or how they are constructed in a particular culture as feminine or masculine. Like the broader area of feminism, many gender specialists hope that studying the arbitrary ways we are expected to dress, walk, talk, and behave can help us widen the conventional notions of gender.

PSYCHOANALYTIC CRITICISM

Psychoanalytic criticism began with Sigmund Freud's theories of the unconscious, especially the numerous repressed wounds, fears, unresolved conflicts, and guilty desires from childhood that can significantly affect behavior and mental health in our adult lives. Freud developed the tripart division of the mind into the ego (the conscious self), the superego (the site of what our culture has taught us about good and bad), and the id (the primitive unconscious and source of our sexual drive). Psychoanalytic critics often see literature as a kind of dream, filled with symbolic elements that often mask their real meaning. Freud also theorized that young males were threatened by their fathers in the competition for the affection of their mothers. Critics are alert to the complex ways this Oedipal drama unfolds in literature.

MARXIST CRITICISM

Marxist criticism is based on the political and economic theories of Karl Marx. Marxists think that a society is propelled by its economy, which is manipulated by a class system. Most people, especially blue-collar workers (the proletariat), do not understand the complex ways their lives are subject to economic forces beyond their control. This false consciousness about history and material well-being prevents workers from seeing that their values have been socially constructed to keep them in their place. What most interests contemporary Marxists is the way ideology shapes our consciousness. And since literature both represents and projects ideology, Marxist critics see it as a way to unmask our limited view of society's structures.

DECONSTRUCTION

Deconstruction is really more a philosophical movement than a school of literary criticism, but many of its techniques have been used by Marxist and feminist literary critics to uncover important concepts they believe are hidden in texts. Made famous by the French philosopher Jacques Derrida, deconstruction's main tenet is that Western thought has divided the world into binary opposites. To gain a semblance of control over the complexity of human experience, we have constructed a worldview in which good is clearly at one end of a continuum and bad at the other. Additional examples of binary opposites include masculine and feminine, freedom and slavery, objective and subjective, mind and body, and presence and absence. According to Derrida, however, this arbitrary and illusory construct simply reflects the specific ideology of one culture. Far from being opposed to each other, masculinity and femininity, for example, are intimately interconnected, and traces of the feminine are to be found within the masculine. The concepts need each other for meaning to occur, an idea referred to as *différance*. Derrida also notes that language, far from being a neutral medium of communication, is infused with our biases, assumptions, and values — which leads some of us to refer to sexually active women as "sluts" and to sexually active men as "studs." One term ("sluts") is marginalized, and the other ("studs") is privileged because our culture grants men more power than women in shaping the language that benefits them.

Thus, language filters, distorts, and alters our perception of the world. For deconstructors or deconstructive critics, language is not stable or reliable, and when closely scrutinized, it becomes slippery and ambiguous, constantly overflowing with implications, associations, and contradictions. For Derrida, this endless freeplay of meaning suggests that language is always changing, always in flux — especially so when we understand that words can be viewed from almost endless points of view or contexts. That is why deconstructionists claim that texts (or individuals or systems of thought) have no fixed definition, no center, no absolute meaning. And so one way to deconstruct or lay bare the arbitrary construction of a text is to show that the oppositions in the text are not really absolutely opposed, that outsiders can be seen to be insiders, and that words that seem to mean one thing can mean many things.

READER-RESPONSE CRITICISM

Reader-response criticism is often misunderstood to be simply giving one's opinion about a text: "I liked it," "I hate happy endings," "I think the characters were unrealistic." But reader-response criticism is actually more interested in why readers have certain responses. The central assumption is that texts do not come alive and do not mean anything until active readers engage them with specific assumptions about what reading is. New Critics think a reader's response is irrelevant because a text's meaning is timeless. But response critics, including feminists and Marxists, maintain that what a text means cannot be separated from the reading process used by readers as they draw on personal and literary experiences to make meaning. In other words, the text is not an object but an event that occurs in readers over time.

Response criticism includes critics who think that the reader's contribution to the making of meaning is quite small as well as critics who think that readers play a primary role in the process. Louise Rosenblatt is a moderate response critic since she thinks the contributions are about equal. Her transactive theory claims that the text guides our response, like a printed musical score that we adjust as we move through the text. She allows for a range of acceptable meanings as long as she can find reasonable textual support in the writing.

Response critics like Stanley Fish downplay individual responses, focusing instead on how communities influence our responses to texts. We probably all belong to a number of these interpretive communities (such as churches, universities, neighborhoods, political parties, and social class) and have internalized their interpretive strategies, their discourse, or their way of reading texts of all kinds. Fish's point is that we all come to texts already predisposed to read them in a certain way: we do not interpret stories, but we create them by using the reading tools and cultural assumptions we bring with us. Our reading then reveals what is in us more than what is in the text. We find what we expect to see.

POSTCOLONIAL CRITICISM

Postcolonial criticism, like feminist criticism, has developed because of the dramatic shrinking of the world and the increasing multicultural cast of our own country. It is mainly interested in the ways nineteenth-century European political domination affects the lives of people living in former colonies, especially the way the dominant culture becomes the norm and those without power are portrayed as inferior. Postcolonial critics often look for stereotypes in texts as well as in characters whose self-image has been damaged by being forced to see themselves as Other, as less than. As oppressed people try to negotiate life in both the dominant and the oppressed cultures, they can develop a double consciousness that leads to feelings of alienation and deep conflicts.

Literary critics often argue that being caught between the demands of two cultures — one dominant and privileged, the other marginalized and scorned — causes a character to be "unhomed," a psychological refugee who is uncomfortable everywhere.

NEW HISTORICISM

New Historicism was developed because critics were dissatisfied with the old historicism, a long-standing traditional approach that viewed history simply as a background for understanding the literary text. History was thought to be an accurate record of what happened because the professional historian used objective and proven methods. But most literary critics no longer hold to this view of history. Instead, history is now thought to be just one perspective among many possibilities, inevitably subjective and biased. Influenced by the theorist Michel Foucault, history is seen as one of many discourses that can shed light on the past. But the dominant view is that all of us, including historians, writers, and critics, live in a particular culture and cannot escape its influences. And since these social, cultural, literary, economic, and political influences are all interrelated, all texts can tell us something important. Stories, histories, diaries, laws, speeches, newspapers, and magazines are all relevant. Culture permeates all texts, influencing everyone to see society's view of reality, of what's right and wrong and which values, assumptions, and truths are acceptable. Critics and historians try to interpret a vast web of interconnected discourses and forces in order to understand an era. Naturally, since many of these forces are competing for power, critics are always looking for power struggles among discourses. Think of the present struggle over the amount of influence religion should have in politics or who has the right to marry. Literature is one of the texts in a culture that shapes our views and which critics investigate to unearth these competing ideas.

QUEER THEORY

Influenced by the social, cultural, and academic advances of feminist theory in the 1980s, gay and lesbian critics in the 1990s began to join the critical conversation taking place in universities. Besides uncovering the possible homosexuality or bisexuality of canonical authors (such as Christopher Marlowe, Willa Cather, Emily Dickinson, and Henry James), these critics sought to reveal and discredit long-held stereotypes of gay and lesbian fictional characters. By challenging the homophobic prejudice they found in literature and society, lesbian and gay critics hoped to raise awareness of the complex ways society privileges heterosexual behavior and marginalizes any deviation from its norms. Adrienne Rich, an influential lesbian theorist, popularized the term "compulsive heterosexuality" to suggest the subtle and explicit ways the dominant straight culture unthinkingly socializes us to see heterosexuality as a given, the taken-for-granted default sexual identity for all. As a result, same-sex relationships suffer the disempowering injustices allotted to those judged abnormal. Therefore another concern of gay and lesbian critics has been to suggest that sexual identity is not a stable or an absolute given. Again, Adrienne Rich is helpful with her idea of a "lesbian continuum" where sexual identity is not absolute but is best seen as contextual and fluid, ranging from young girls holding hands (homosocial), to same-sex flirting and kissing (homoerotic), to genital sex (homosexual).

The idea of sexual identity as fluid and contingent can be seen as a bridge to Queer Theory, an umbrella term that became popular in the 1990s in the Lesbian-Gay-Bisexual-Transgender-Questioning-Intersex-Asexual (LGBTQIA) community. Although *queer* had been a term of homophobic abuse, it was rehabilitated to refer to whatever is at odds with the norm, the accepted, and the dominant. Practitioners of queer theory want to challenge the many institutions in which heteronormativity is so deeply embedded. Like deconstructionists, queer theorists do not believe in stable identities; consequently, they always debunk and question conventional gender identity and roles. Performance is more important than what you are; action counts, not biology.

OBJECT-ORIENTED CRITICISM

Object-oriented criticism is a new force in literary studies. It focuses on how we confront, produce, consume, and exchange material things. Indeed, another name for this approach is Thing Theory. It doesn't assume that all things referred to in literature are symbols. Rather, it examines what characters *do* with objects they encounter. These include clothes, furniture, money, cars, weapons, sports equipment, jewelry, huge industrial machinery, kitchen utensils, and other household tools. Many object-oriented interpretations are responses to environmental issues. They trace, for instance, how landscapes are altered—often harmed—by human artifacts. Also relevant is the global spread of capitalism. An object-focused approach might study how characters lust for luxuries instead of just aiming to satisfy basic needs. Often, this type of criticism is driven as well by technological trends. Wireless devices now cram our homes, our schools, our offices, our places of leisure, and our hands. It's a network called the Internet of Things. Object-oriented critics note signs of this trend in current texts. They also look for ancestors of it in earlier literature. Some of these critics examine, too, the physical forms of texts. After all, literature thrives now on multiple platforms, such as e-readers, audiobooks, smartphones, and traditional print.

COGNITIVE CRITICISM

Cognitive criticism borrows from recent research in psychology. Specifically, it draws on studies of the mind's basic operations—the mental processes through which we cope with the world. This approach to literature seeks to identify characters' frameworks for understanding and interacting with people. Although this approach is concerned with brains, it doesn't neglect bodies. It considers how the mind envisions, guides, and responds to the body's movements. A number of cognitive critics note how literature's metaphors often stem from physical acts and sensations. Take, for example, the concept of spiritual, moral, or intellectual progress as a "journey." This notion derives from common experience; often we head toward a place that we hope is better than where we've been.

Many cognitive critics endorse a certain principle of neuroscience. It's called **Theory of Mind**. This term refers to the assumptions and guesses we make about other people. A character whose Theory of Mind is sound can infer—often predict—what others know, believe, or wish. A character who lacks a sound Theory of Mind is oblivious to people's real thoughts. When we read literature, we each apply our own Theory of Mind, especially in analyzing characters. Cognitive critics don't always focus, though, on individuals. Sometimes they study how a literary text depicts a collective mind's activity: for instance, a community's gossip.

We also apply our Theory of Mind when, from the words of a literary work, we guess its author's intentions. In part, we try to identify features of the **storyworld** we face. This term refers to the physical and cultural environments the author presents. If the video game you're playing is set in a fantasy landscape, you try to detect as soon as you can the main principles of this storyworld. You do the same with sci-fi novels about colonies in space. We rely on our Theory of Mind even with fiction set in real places. Such works still build a storyworld whose features we must detect. A novel set in today's Houston will stress certain aspects of the city while paying little or no attention to others. As readers, we need to determine the form this particular Houston takes.

AFFECTIVE CRITICISM

Affect is another word for emotion. Affective critics study the feelings that a literary work expresses, depicts, and provokes. One of their major concerns is the work's emotional impact. They're interested in how, and for what purpose, the text stirs readers' hearts. Often these critics ponder how, by stirring emotions, literature sparks political action. Harriet Beecher Stowe's novel *Uncle Tom's Cabin* is a famous case; though plainly sentimental in depicting slavery's victims, it drove many readers to join the abolitionist cause. When focused on characters, affective criticism sees their emotions as clues to their values, beliefs, and wishes. This approach tries to be precise in labeling their feelings. It carefully distinguishes, say, between anger, resentment, distrust, disgust, annoyance, and discontent. Affective critics inspired by feminism challenge crude gender stereotypes; they don't assume women are emotionally driven and that men are devoted to logic. Many of these critics argue, in fact, that emotion and reason can blend. They tend to analyze how characters are complex mixtures of both and in ways not tied to one gender.

Like cognitive criticism, studies of affect in literature don't stick with individuals. Several of these studies trace how a particular feeling spreads from person to person. You yourself may know actual cases; the mass hysteria of Salem's witch trials is a famous one. Teresa Brennan, a leading affective critic, has even titled a book of hers *The Transmission of Affect*. She emphasizes that in fiction, as well as in real life, feelings can prove contagious.

PERFORMANCE-ORIENTED CRITICISM

The word *performance* has long been familiar to readers of drama. They've associated it with how a play might be staged and how the actors might play their parts. But recently critics have applied the term to additional literary genres, including short stories, novels, essays, and poems. In this broader use, however, *performance* has multiple definitions. It's important to know what meaning of the word a critic has in mind. Sometimes the focus is on how a character executes a task: for example, the character's athletic or job performance. At other times, the critic equates *performance* with deception, as when characters pretend to be people they're not. The term *performance* can also refer to theatrical behavior in everyday life. Characters can be said to *perform* when they tell a story, make a joke, or mock the quirks of someone else, even when their "audience" is just a small group of friends. A number of literary critics go further. They hold that a person's ordinary routines can be called performances, too. Some even claim we perform our identity, for we present ourselves as certain types of people through the actions we often repeat. A critic who subscribes to this theory might focus on a character's habits, noting how they define that person's self.

RHETORICAL CRITICISM

Our book emphasizes the art of argument. In Chapter 3, we noted that this art belongs to a larger, centuries-old tradition known as **rhetoric**. We defined *rhetoric* as writing, speech, and visual images designed to shape people's behavior and beliefs. So, a rhetorical approach to literature might focus on a character's attempt to persuade. This attempt might not be a structured argument packed with reasons and proof. Often characters try to sway their audience less elaborately. Still, the methods they use are worth analyzing. A bit more broadly, a rhetorical critic might study a literary work's *speech acts*. We explained what these are in Chapter 2. In brief, they're the various moves that characters perform with words, especially to influence other people. Examples include promising, requesting, demanding, apologizing, firing, warning, and bragging.

Rhetorical criticism can also be applied to writers. James Wood points out that authors of realistic fiction are engaged in persuasion. As they spin their plots, they're trying "to convince us that this could have happened." Wood's remark fits as well creators of fantasy, horror, or sci-fi. They coax their audience to accept the imaginative worlds they construct. Rhetorical approaches to a text might go on to study its writer's other purposes. Often the critic identifies first the writer's techniques and then ponders why the writer used them. Such analysis may involve considering the writer's options. What strategies *could* this author have used? Why did the author choose certain strategies and reject certain others?

Working with the Critical Approaches

Keep these brief descriptions of the critical approaches in mind as you read the following story by James Joyce, one of the most important writers of the twentieth century. Joyce (1882–1941) was born in Ireland, although he spent most of his life in self-imposed exile on the European continent. "Counterparts" is from *Dubliners* (1914), a collection of stories set in the Irish city of his childhood years. (For more by James Joyce, see "Araby," on p. 500 and "Eveline" at the end of this chapter.)

JAMES JOYCE

Counterparts

The bell rang furiously and, when Miss Parker went to the tube, a furious voice called out in a piercing North of Ireland accent:

—Send Farrington here!

Miss Parker returned to her machine, saying to a man who was writing at a desk:

—Mr Alleyne wants you upstairs.

The man muttered *Blast him!* under his breath and pushed back his chair to 5
stand up. When he stood up he was tall and of great bulk. He had a hanging face, dark wine-coloured, with fair eyebrows and moustache: his eyes bulged forward slightly and the whites of them were dirty. He lifted up the counter and, passing by the clients, went out of the office with a heavy step.

He went heavily upstairs until he came to the second landing, where a door bore a brass plate with the inscription *Mr Alleyne.* Here he halted, puffing with labor and vexation, and knocked. The shrill voice cried:

—Come in!

The man entered Mr Alleyne's room. Simultaneously Mr Alleyne, a little man wearing gold-rimmed glasses on a cleanshaven face, shot his head up over a pile of documents. The head itself was so pink and hairless that it seemed like a large egg reposing on the papers. Mr Alleyne did not lose a moment:

—Farrington? What is the meaning of this? Why have I always to complain of you? May I ask you why you haven't made a copy of that contract between Bodley and Kirwan? I told you it must be ready by four o'clock.

—But Mr Shelley said, sir— 10

—*Mr Shelley said, sir.* . . . Kindly attend to what I say and not to what *Mr Shelley says, sir.* You have always some excuse or another for shirking work. Let me tell you that if the contract is not copied before this evening I'll lay the matter before Mr Crosbie. . . . Do you hear me now?

—Yes, sir.

—Do you hear me now? . . . Ay and another little matter! I might as well be talking to the wall as talking to you. Understand once for all that you get a half an hour for your lunch and not an hour and a half. How many courses do you want, I'd like to know. . . . Do you mind me, now?

—Yes, sir.

Mr Alleyne bent his head again upon his pile of papers. The man stared 15
fixedly at the polished skull which directed the affairs of Crosbie & Alleyne, gauging its fragility. A spasm of rage gripped his throat for a few moments and then passed, leaving after it a sharp sensation of thirst. The man recognized the sensation and felt that he must have a good night's drinking. The middle of the month was passed and, if he could get the copy done in time, Mr Alleyne might give him an order on the cashier. He stood still, gazing fixedly at the head upon the pile of papers. Suddenly Mr Alleyne began to upset all the papers, searching for something. Then, as if he had been unaware of the man's presence till that moment, he shot up his head again, saying:

—Eh? Are you going to stand there all day? Upon my word, Farrington, you take things easy!

—I was waiting to see . . .

—Very good, you needn't wait to see. Go downstairs and do your work.

The man walked heavily towards the door and, as he went out of the room, he heard Mr Alleyne cry after him that if the contract was not copied by evening Mr Crosbie would hear of the matter.

He returned to his desk in the lower office and counted the sheets which 20
remained to be copied. He took up his pen and dipped it in the ink but he continued to stare stupidly at the last words he had written: *In no case shall the said Bernard Bodley be.* . . . The evening was falling and in a few minutes they would be lighting the gas: then he could write. He felt that he must slake the thirst in his throat. He stood up from his desk and, lifting the counter as before, passed out of the office. As he was passing out the chief clerk looked at him inquiringly.

—It's all right, Mr Shelley, said the man, pointing with his finger to indicate the objective of his journey.

The chief clerk glanced at the hat-rack but, seeing the row complete, offered no remark. As soon as he was on the landing the man pulled a shepherd's plaid cap out of his pocket, put it on his head and ran quickly down the rickety stairs. From the street door he walked on furtively on the inner side of the path towards the corner and all at once dived into a doorway. He was now safe in the dark snug of O'Neill's shop, and, filling up the little window that looked into the bar with his inflamed face, the color of dark wine or dark meat, he called out:

—Here, Pat, give us a g.p., like a good fellow.

The curate brought him a glass of plain porter. The man drank it at a gulp and asked for a caraway seed. He put his penny on the counter and, leaving the curate to grope for it in the gloom, retreated out of the snug as furtively as he had entered it.

Darkness, accompanied by a thick fog, was gaining upon the dusk of 25
February and the lamps in Eustace Street had been lit. The man went up by the houses until he reached the door of the office, wondering whether he could finish his copy in time. On the stairs a moist pungent odor of perfumes saluted his nose: evidently Miss Delacour had come while he was out in O'Neill's. He crammed his cap back again into his pocket and re-entered the office assuming an air of absent-mindedness.

—Mr Alleyne has been calling for you, said the chief clerk severely. Where were you?

The man glanced at the two clients who were standing at the counter as if to intimate that their presence prevented him from answering. As the clients were both male the chief clerk allowed himself a laugh.

—I know that game, he said. Five times in one day is a little bit. . . . Well, you better look sharp and get a copy of our correspondence in the Delacour case for Mr Alleyne.

This address in the presence of the public, his run upstairs, and the porter he had gulped down so hastily confused the man and, as he sat down at his desk to get what was required, he realized how hopeless was the task of finishing his copy of the contract before half past five. The dark damp night was coming and he longed to spend it in the bars, drinking with his friends amid the glare of gas and the clatter of glasses. He got out the Delacour correspondence and passed out of the office. He hoped Mr Alleyne would not discover that the last two letters were missing.

The moist pungent perfume lay all the way up to Mr Alleyne's room. Miss Delacour was a middle-aged woman of Jewish appearance. Mr Alleyne was said to be sweet on her or on her money. She came to the office often and stayed a long time when she came. She was sitting beside his desk now in an aroma of perfumes, smoothing the handle of her umbrella, and nodding the great black feather in her hat. Mr Alleyne had swivelled his chair round to face her and thrown his right foot jauntily upon his left knee. The man put the correspondence on the desk and bowed respectfully but neither Mr Alleyne nor Miss Delacour took any notice of his bow. Mr Alleyne tapped a finger on the correspondence and then flicked it towards him as if to say: *That's all right: you can go.*

The man returned to the lower office and sat down again at his desk. He stared intently at the incomplete phrase: *In no case shall the said Bernard Bodley be* . . . and thought how strange it was that the last three words began with the same letter. The chief clerk began to hurry Miss Parker, saying she would never have the letters typed in time for post. The man listened to the clicking of the machine for a few minutes and then set to work to finish his copy. But his head was not clear and his mind wandered away to the glare and rattle of the public-house. It was a night for hot punches. He struggled on with his copy, but when the clock struck five he had still fourteen pages to write. Blast it! He couldn't finish it in time. He longed to execrate aloud, to bring his fist down on something violently. He was so enraged that he wrote *Bernard Bernard* instead of *Bernard Bodley* and had to begin again on a clean sheet.

He felt strong enough to clear out the whole office singlehanded. His body ached to do something, to rush out and revel in violence. All the indignities of his life enraged him. . . . Could he ask the cashier privately for an advance? No, the cashier was no good, no damn good: he wouldn't give an advance. . . . He knew where he would meet the boys: Leonard and O'Halloran and Nosey Flynn. The barometer of his emotional nature was set for a spell of riot.

His imagination had so abstracted him that his name was called twice before he answered. Mr Alleyne and Miss Delacour were standing outside the counter and all the clerks had turned round in anticipation of something. The man got up from his desk. Mr Alleyne began a tirade of abuse, saying that two letters were missing. The man answered that he knew nothing about them, that he had made a faithful copy. The tirade continued: it was so bitter and violent that the man could hardly restrain his fist from descending upon the head of the manikin before him.

—I know nothing about any other two letters, he said stupidly.

—*You—know—nothing.* Of course you know nothing, said Mr Alleyne. Tell me, he added, glancing first for approval to the lady beside him, do you take me for a fool? Do you think me an utter fool?

The man glanced from the lady's face to the little egg-shaped head and back again; and, almost before he was aware of it, his tongue had found a felicitous moment:

—I don't think, sir, he said, that that's a fair question to put to me.

There was a pause in the very breathing of the clerks. Everyone was astounded (the author of the witticism no less than his neighbors) and Miss Delacour, who was a stout amiable person, began to smile broadly. Mr Alleyne flushed to the hue of a wild rose and his mouth twitched with a dwarf's passion. He shook his fist in the man's face till it seemed to vibrate like the knob of some electric machine:

—You impertinent ruffian! You impertinent ruffian! I'll make short work of you! Wait till you see! You'll apologize to me for your impertinence or you'll quit the office instanter! You'll quit this, I'm telling you, or you'll apologize to me!

He stood in a doorway opposite the office watching to see if the cashier would come out alone. All the clerks passed out and finally the cashier came out with the chief clerk. It was no use trying to say a word to him when he was with the chief clerk. The man felt that his position was bad enough. He had been obliged to offer an abject apology to Mr Alleyne for his impertinence but he knew what a hornet's nest the office would be for him. He could remember the way in which Mr Alleyne had hounded little Peake out of the office in order to make room for his own nephew. He felt savage and thirsty and revengeful, annoyed with himself and with everyone else. Mr Alleyne would never give him an hour's rest; his life would be a hell to him. He had made a proper fool of himself this time. Could he not keep his tongue in his cheek? But they had never pulled together from the first, he and Mr Alleyne, ever since the day Mr Alleyne had overheard him mimicking his North of Ireland accent to amuse Higgins and Miss Parker: that had been the beginning of it. He might have tried Higgins for the money, but sure Higgins never had anything for himself. A man with two establishments to keep up, of course he couldn't. . . .

He felt his great body again aching for the comfort of the public-house. The fog had begun to chill him and he wondered could he touch Pat in O'Neill's. He could not touch him for more than a bob—and a bob was no use. Yet he must get money somewhere or other: he had spent his last penny for the g.p. and soon it would be too late for getting money anywhere. Suddenly, as he was fingering his watch-chain, he thought of Terry Kelly's pawn-office in Fleet Street. That was the dart! Why didn't he think of it sooner?

He went through the narrow alley of Temple Bar quickly, muttering to himself that they could all go to hell because he was going to have a good night of it. The clerk in Terry Kelly's said *A crown!* but the consignor held out for six shillings; and in the end the six shillings was allowed him literally. He came out of the pawn-office joyfully, making a little cylinder of the coins between his thumb and fingers. In Westmoreland Street the footpaths were crowded with young men and women returning from business and ragged urchins ran here and there yelling out the names of the evening editions. The man passed through the crowd, looking on the spectacle generally with proud satisfaction and staring masterfully at the office-girls. His head was full of the noises of tram-gongs and swishing trolleys and his nose already sniffed the curling fumes of punch. As he walked on he preconsidered the terms in which he would narrate the incident to the boys:

—So, I just looked at him—coolly, you know, and looked at her. Then I looked back at him again—taking my time, you know. *I don't think that that's a fair question to put to me,* says I.

Nosey Flynn was sitting up in his usual corner of Davy Byrne's and, when he heard the story, he stood Farrington a half-one, saying it was as smart a thing as ever he heard. Farrington stood a drink in his turn. After a while O'Halloran and Paddy Leonard came in and the story was repeated to them. O'Halloran stood tailors of malt, hot, all round and told the story of the retort he had made to the chief clerk when he was in Callan's of Fownes's Street; but, as the retort was after the manner of the liberal shepherds in the eclogues, he had to admit that it was not so clever as Farrington's retort. At this Farrington told the boys to polish off that and have another.

Just as they were naming their poisons who should come in but Higgins! Of course he had to join in with the others. The men asked him to give his version of it, and he did so with great vivacity for the sight of five small hot whiskies was very exhilarating. Everyone roared laughing when he showed the way in which Mr Alleyne shook his fist in Farrington's face. Then he imitated Farrington, saying, *And here was my nabs, as cool as you please,* while Farrington looked at the company out of his heavy dirty eyes, smiling and at times drawing forth stray drops of liquor from his moustache with the aid of his lower lip.

When that round was over there was a pause. O'Halloran had money but neither of the other two seemed to have any; so the whole party left the shop somewhat regretfully. At the corner of Duke Street Higgins and Nosey Flynn bevelled off to the left while the other three turned back towards the city. Rain was drizzling down on the cold streets and, when they reached the Ballast Office, Farrington suggested the Scotch House. The bar was full of men and loud with the noise of tongues and glasses. The three men pushed past the whining matchsellers at the door and formed a little party at the corner of the counter. They began to exchange stories. Leonard introduced them to a young fellow named Weathers who was performing at the Tivoli as an acrobat and knockabout *artiste.* Farrington stood a drink all round. Weathers said he would take a small Irish and Apollinaris. Farrington, who had definite notions of what was what, asked the boys would they have an Apollinaris too; but the boys told Tim to make theirs hot. The talk became theatrical. O'Halloran stood a round and then Farrington stood another round, Weathers protesting that the hospitality was too Irish. He promised to get them in behind the scenes and introduce them to some nice girls. O'Halloran said that he and Leonard would go but that Farrington wouldn't go because he was a married man; and Farrington's heavy dirty eyes leered at the company in token that he understood he was being chaffed. Weathers made them all have just one little tincture at his expense and promised to meet them later on at Mulligan's in Poolbeg Street.

When the Scotch House closed they went round to Mulligan's. They went into the parlor at the back and O'Halloran ordered small hot specials all round. They were all beginning to feel mellow. Farrington was just standing another round when Weathers came back. Much to Farrington's relief he drank a glass of bitter this time. Funds were running low but they had enough to keep them going. Presently two young women with big hats and a young man in a check suit came in and sat at a table close by. Weathers saluted them and told the company that they were out of the Tivoli. Farrington's eyes wandered at every moment in the direction of one of the young women. There was something striking in her appearance. An immense scarf of peacock-blue muslin was wound round her hat and knotted in a great bow under her chin; and she wore bright yellow gloves, reaching to the elbow. Farrington gazed admiringly at the plump arm which she moved very often and with much grace; and when, after a little time, she answered his gaze he admired still more her large dark brown eyes. The oblique staring expression in them fascinated him. She glanced at him once or twice and, when the party was leaving the room, she brushed against his chair and said *O, pardon!* in a London accent. He watched her leave the room in the hope that she would look back at him, but he was disappointed. He cursed his want of money and cursed all the rounds he had stood, particularly all the whiskies and Apollinaris which he had stood to Weathers. If there was one thing that he hated it was a sponge. He was so angry that he lost count of the conversation of his friends.

When Paddy Leonard called him he found that they were talking about feats of strength. Weathers was showing his biceps muscle to the company and boasting so much that the other two had called on Farrington to uphold the national honor. Farrington pulled up his sleeve accordingly and showed his biceps muscle to the company. The two arms were examined and compared and finally it was agreed to have a trial of strength. The table was cleared and the two men rested their elbows on it, clasping hands. When Paddy Leonard said *Go!* each was to try to bring down the other's hand on to the table. Farrington looked very serious and determined.

The trial began. After about thirty seconds Weathers brought his opponent's hand slowly down on to the table. Farrington's dark wine-coloured face flushed darker still with anger and humiliation at having been defeated by such a stripling.

—You're not to put the weight of your body behind it. Play fair, he said. 50

—Who's not playing fair? said the other.

—Come on again. The two best out of three.

The trial began again. The veins stood out on Farrington's forehead, and the pallor of Weathers' complexion changed to peony. Their hands and arms trembled under the stress. After a long struggle Weathers again brought his opponent's hand slowly on to the table. There was a murmur of applause from the spectators. The curate, who was standing beside the table, nodded his red head towards the victor and said with loutish familiarity:

—Ah! that's the knack!

—What the hell do you know about it? said Farrington fiercely, turning on 55
the man. What do you put in your gab for?

—Sh, sh! said O'Halloran, observing the violent expression of Farrington's face. Pony up, boys. We'll have just one little smahan more and then we'll be off.

A very sullen-faced man stood at the corner of O'Connell Bridge waiting for the little Sandymount tram to take him home. He was full of smouldering anger and revengefulness. He felt humiliated and discontented; he did not even feel drunk; and he had only twopence in his pocket. He cursed everything. He had done for himself in the office, pawned his watch, spent all his money; and he had not even got drunk. He began to feel thirsty again and he longed to be back again in the hot reeking public-house. He had lost his reputation as a strong man, having been defeated twice by a mere boy. His heart swelled with fury and, when he thought of the woman in the big hat who had brushed against him and said *Pardon!* his fury nearly choked him.

His tram let him down at Shelbourne Road and he steered his great body along in the shadow of the wall of the barracks. He loathed returning to his home. When he went in by the side-door he found the kitchen empty and the kitchen fire nearly out. He bawled upstairs:

—Ada! Ada!

His wife was a little sharp-faced woman who bullied her husband when he was sober and was bullied by him when he was drunk. They had five children. A little boy came running down the stairs.

—Who is that? said the man, peering through the darkness.

—Me, pa.

—Who are you? Charlie?

—No, pa. Tom.

—Where's your mother?

—She's out at the chapel.

—That's right. . . . Did she think of leaving any dinner for me?

—Yes, pa. I—

—Light the lamp. What do you mean by having the place in darkness? Are the other children in bed?

The man sat down heavily on one of the chairs while the little boy lit the lamp. He began to mimic his son's flat accent, saying half to himself: *At the chapel. At the chapel, if you please!* When the lamp was lit he banged his fist on the table and shouted:

—What's for my dinner?

—I'm going . . . to cook it, pa, said the little boy.

The man jumped up furiously and pointed to the fire.

—On that fire! You let the fire out! By God, I'll teach you to do that again!

He took a step to the door and seized the walking-stick which was standing behind it.

—I'll teach you to let the fire out! he said, rolling up his sleeve in order to give his arm free play.

The little boy cried *O, pa!* and ran whimpering round the table, but the man followed him and caught him by the coat. The little boy looked about him wildly but, seeing no way of escape fell upon his knees.

—Now, you'll let the fire out the next time! said the man, striking at him viciously with the stick. Take that, you little whelp!

The boy uttered a squeal of pain as the stick cut his thigh. He clasped his hands together in the air and his voice shook with fright.

—O, pa! he cried. Don't beat me, pa! And I'll . . . I'll say a *Hail Mary* for you. . . . I'll say a *Hail Mary* for you, pa, if you don't beat me. . . . I'll say a *Hail Mary*. . . .

[1914]

A thorough critical analysis of "Counterparts" using any one of these approaches would take dozens of pages. The following are brief suggestions for how such a reading might proceed.

NEW CRITICISM

A New Critic might want to demonstrate the multiple ways the title holds the narrative together, giving it unity and coherence—for example, Farrington and his son Tom are counterparts since Tom is the victim of his father's bullying just as Farrington is bullied by Mr. Alleyne at work. You can also probably spot other counterparts: Farrington and his wife, for example, trade off bullying each other, and their means of escaping from the drudgery of their lives, the bar and the church, are also parallel. And naturally when Weathers, the acrobat, defeats the much larger Farrington in arm wrestling, we are reminded of the verbal beating Farrington must endure from his equally diminutive boss, Mr. Alleyne. New Critics are fond of finding the ways all the elements of a text reinforce one another.

A New Critic might argue that these counterparts or oppositions introduce tensions into the story from the first few lines when the "bell rang furiously" for Farrington to report to Mr. Alleyne for a dressing-down. The irony is that Farrington is big and Alleyne is small, that Farrington is powerful and Alleyne is fragile as an egg. But it is Mr. Alleyne who breaks Farrington; it is Farrington who is weak. Throughout the story, tensions, oppositions, and ironies continue, for example, when Farrington is defeated by the smaller Weathers. In the last scene, the tension is finally resolved when the larger Farrington beats his small son, making him a counterpart to both Alleyne and Weathers in oppressing the weak. The final evidence that Farrington is ethically powerless is cruelly obvious as the son promises to pray for his abusing father.

FEMINIST CRITICISM

Feminist critics and their first cousins, gender critics, would naturally be struck by the violent masculinity of Farrington, his fantasies of riot and abuse, his savage feelings of revenge, and his "smouldering anger" (para. 57). Farrington is depicted not only as crude and brutish but also as a kind of perverse stereotype of male vanity, self-centeredness, and irresponsibility. His obsession with obtaining money for drinking completely disregards his role as the provider for a large family, and, of course, the beatings of his son are a cruel parody of his role as paternal protector. And if he had not wasted his money on drink, Farrington would also be a womanizer ("Farrington's eyes wandered at every moment in the direction of one of the young women," para. 47). Gender critics would be interested in the social and cultural mechanisms that could construct such primitive masculinity.

A reasonable argument might focus on the representation of women in the story. Miss Parker, Miss Delacour, Farrington's wife, and the performer Farrington sees in the bar are marginal characters. One student made the following claim: "The women in Farrington's world, and Irish society in general, have no agency: they are prevented from taking an active part in determining their lives and futures." Another student argued differently, saying, "While women in general are oppressed by the raw and brutal masculinity represented by Farrington, the women in this story do hold a degree of power over men." Based on their own analysis and interpretations, these students demonstrated that there was reasonable textual evidence to support their claims.

PSYCHOANALYTIC CRITICISM

A psychoanalytic critic would first notice the extreme pattern of behavior Farrington exhibits, as he repeatedly withdraws from his adult work responsibilities and as he fantasizes about being physically violent against his supervisors. Critics would argue that such behavior is typical of Farrington's repressed wounds and his unresolved conflicts with his own father. Farrington seems to be playing out painful childhood experiences. Given the violent displacement (taking it out on someone else) visited on Tom, we can imagine that Farrington is beating not only his boss, Mr. Alleyne, but also perhaps his own abusive father. The fantasies at work in Farrington also suggest the psychological defense of projection, since Farrington is blaming his problems on Mr. Alleyne and his job. Although his tasks do seem to be tedious, they certainly cannot account for his "spasm of rage" (para. 15) or his desire "to clear out the whole office singlehanded" (para. 32). When Farrington feels "humiliated and discontented" (para. 57), it is only in part because of his immediate context. It is the return of the repressed that plagues Farrington, a resurfacing of a buried pain. These ideas should also be tied to Farrington's death wish, especially his stunningly self-destructive behavior at work. Freudian critics would also argue that these specific actions are related to other core issues that would include intense loss of self-esteem, fear of intimacy, and betrayal.

MARXIST CRITICISM

A Marxist critic would be interested in focusing on the specific historical moment of "Counterparts" and not on Farrington's individual psyche, which can only distract us from the real force that affects human experience—the economic system in which Farrington is trapped. Economic power—not the Oedipal drama or gender—is the crucial human motivator. Farrington's material circumstances and not timeless values are the key to understanding his behavior. The real battle lines are drawn between Crosbie and Alleyne (the "haves") and Farrington (a "have-not")—that is, between the bourgeoisie and the proletariat, between those who control economic resources and those who perform the labor that fills the coffers of the rich. In a Marxist analysis, critics would argue that Farrington is a victim of class warfare. His desperation, his humiliation, his rage, his cruel violence are all traceable to classism—an ideology that determines people's worth according to their economic class. Although Farrington does appear shiftless and irresponsible, it is not because of his class; it is because of the meaninglessness of his work and the demeaning hierarchy that keeps him at the bottom. In his alienation, he reverts to a primitive physical masculinity, a false consciousness that only further diminishes his sense of his worth.

Marxists are often interested in what lies beneath the text in its political unconscious. To get at the unconscious, Marxists, like psychoanalytic critics, look for symptoms on the surface that suggest problems beneath. Typically, such symptomatic readings reveal class conflicts that authors are sometimes unaware of themselves. Marxist critics might debate whether Joyce himself understood that the root cause of Farrington's aberrant behavior was economic and not psychological. This makes sense since for Marxists both reader and writer are under the sway of the same ideological system that they see as natural.

One student made the following claim: "Farrington's role as proletarian results in his feelings of inferiority, resentment over lack of entitlement, and an expectation of disappointment." This same student, like many Marxist critics who see the function of literature through a pragmatic lens, concluded her essay with an appeal toward change, arguing that "The remedy does not lie in changing Farrington's consciousness, but rather in changing the economic and political discourse of power that has constituted him."

DECONSTRUCTION

One of many possible deconstructions of "Counterparts" would involve focusing on a troubling or puzzling point called an *aporia*. Some deconstructive critics have looked at the incomplete phrase that Farrington copies, "*In no case shall the said Bernard Bodley be . . .*" as an aporia, an ambiguous and not completely understandable textual puzzle but one that might be a way into the story's meaning. The oppositions that are being deconstructed or laid bare here are *presence* and *absence*, *word* and *reality*. Working off the implications of the title "Counterparts," Bernard Bodley can be seen as a double or counterpart for Farrington, a character like Bodley whose existence is in doubt. Although Farrington's size suggests that he is very much physically present, his behavior might suggest otherwise. He spends his time copying other people's words and has a compelling need to repeat the narrative of his encounter with Mr. Alleyne, as if he must demonstrate his own existence through repetition. He does not have a viable inner life, an authentic identity. Farrington's essence is not present but absent. His identity is insubstantial. He tries to fill the emptiness at the center of his being with camaraderie and potency, but his efforts produce the opposite—escape, loneliness, and weakness. In other words, the said Farrington does not really exist and cannot be. In this way, we can deconstruct "Counterparts" as a story in which presence is absence, strength is weakness, Farrington's actions lead only to paralysis and repetition, and Farrington's frustration with his impotence makes his oppressors more powerful.

One student working with similar interpretations of "Counterparts" noted other oppositions, especially between male and female, escape and confinement. She argued that Farrington spends most of his time trying to avoid being thought of as stereotypically feminine. However, the more exaggerated his masculine aggression, drinking, violence, and irresponsibility become, the weaker, the more stereotypically feminine he becomes. Similarly, the more Farrington tries to escape, the more ensnared he is. In this way, the student argued, our conventional understandings of these opposing terms are deconstructed, so that we are no longer confident about the meaning of escape, masculinity, or strength.

READER-RESPONSE CRITICISM

Willa Ervinman, a student, was asked to respond to the story by using Stanley Fish's ideas and noting the conflicts between the interpretive or discourse communities Willa belonged to and those depicted in the story. The following are excerpts from her response journal:

> I was upset by Farrington's lack of responsibility at work. He is completely unreliable and demonstrates very little self-esteem. He must know that the people he works with consider him a slacker and a fake. I was raised in a middle-class home where both my parents worked hard in a bank from 9 to 5. Just the idea that they would sneak out of work to drink in dark bars is absurd. My belief in the discourse of middle-class responsibility or perhaps the Protestant work ethic makes it almost impossible for me to see Farrington with sympathy even though I can see that his work is probably completely mechanical and unfulfilling. . . .
>
> Farrington's domestic violence against his son is such a violation of the discourse of domesticity that it is hard to understand any other response. Someone in my response group thought that Farrington was a victim of his working-class discourse of masculinity. I can see how he was humiliated by the smaller men, Mr. Alleyne and Weathers, but beating his innocent son as a kind of revenge cannot be forgiven. My grandmother tells me that it was common for children to be physically punished in her day, but in the interpretive community I was raised in, there is no excuse for domestic violence. It is more than a character flaw; it is criminal behavior, and I judge Farrington to be a social menace, beyond compassion.

Willa went on to argue that Farrington's violent behavior is inexcusable, interpreting our current understandings of domestic violence and responsible masculinity as evidence. She blended this personal view with textual support. Her warrant for her claim was that historical circumstances and norms should not be used to excuse reprehensible behavior.

POSTCOLONIAL CRITICISM

"Counterparts" was written in the early twentieth century at a time when the Ireland Joyce writes about was still a colony of the British Empire. Farrington is, then, a colonial subject and subject to political domination. At the story's opening, Farrington, a Catholic from the south of Ireland, is summoned by a "furious voice" from Northern Ireland, a stronghold of British sympathy and Protestant domination. The tension is announced early because it is crucial to Farrington's behavior and his internalized and colonized mindset. Many colonials have a negative self-image because they are alienated from their own indigenous culture. Indeed, Farrington seems completely ill suited to the office copying task he is relegated to. He seems more suited to some physical endeavor, but given the difficult economics of Dublin, he probably has few career options.

Farrington is the Other in the discourse of colonialism, and he is made to seem inferior at every turn, from the verbal lashing of Mr. Alleyne to the physical defeat by Weathers, who is probably British. Symbolically, Farrington tries to resist his subjugation by the British establishment but fails. He is what postcolonial theorists refer to as *unhomed* or *displaced*. He is uncomfortable at work, in the bars where he seeks solace, and finally in his ultimate refuge, a place unprepared even to feed him. Indeed, in an act likely to perpetuate abuse upon future generations, Farrington turns on his own family, becoming, through his enraged attack on his child Tom, a metaphor for the conflicted, tormented, and defeated Ireland. When a colonial is not "at home" even in his own home, he is truly in psychological agony and exile. Joyce represents the trauma of British domination through one subject's self-destructive and self-hating journey, a journey made even more cruelly ironic by Farrington's attack—in a mimicry of British aggression and injustice—on his own subjected son.

NEW HISTORICISM

A critic influenced by Foucault and New Historicism might argue that Farrington is a victim of an inflexible discourse of masculinity, that he has been socialized by working-class norms of how a man should behave to such an extent that he cannot change. Growing up in a working-class culture, Farrington would have received high marks among his peers for his size and strength, just as Mr. Alleyne would be diminished in status for his. And in another context, say, on a construction site, Farrington's sense of masculinity might be a plus. But in an office, his aggressive masculinity is a liability. In all cultures, people are subject to multiple discourses that pull them one way then another. Farrington's sarcasm, his drinking, his longing for camaraderie, and his resorting to violence to solve problems are the results of being too enmeshed in a discourse of masculinity from working-class Dublin and not enough in the middle-class business assumptions about discipline, responsibility, and concentration. Farrington is defeated at work, in the pubs, and at home because he is unable to move from one discourse to another. He is stuck in a subject position that only reinforces his powerlessness. His self-esteem is so damaged by the end of the story that he even violates his own code of masculinity by beating a defenseless child.

QUEER THEORY

Because queer theorists are as concerned with gender identities as they are with sexuality, they would be interested in the asymmetrical power relationship between Farrington's "great bulk" (para. 5) and Mr. Allyne's "little man" with a "pink and hairless head" (para. 8). Farrington is surely performing as a queer character when he betrays his traditional masculine role by being thoroughly emasculated at work; he is incompetent at simple tasks, and his status in the hierarchy is diminishing. And the reader knows that Farrington's occupation as a copier will soon be obsolete, replaced by legions of female typists. He is a queer figure in a queer job. However, his sexuality is less of an issue than the idea that heterosexuality as a pervasive and rigid institution causes Farrington intense humiliation and anguish as he fails at every traditional (albeit arbitrary) masculine standard.

Farrington seeks solace and escape from his newfound queerness in the male homosocial pubs of Dublin. Here he does seem to perform masterfully with the retelling of his witty put-down of his boss. But the reader is well aware that Farrington has queered the real narrative of his confrontation with Mr. Allyne. In actuality, he was forced to apologize abjectly for his remarks and will pay dearly for not knowing his place. It is also here in his beloved pub space that he receives the greatest blow to what remains of his masculinity. He is humiliated in a contest of strength by an "artiste," "a mere boy" (para. 56).

When as an alienated outcast he returns home in rage and anger, and "viciously" (para. 78) beats his own son in a traditionally female space, the kitchen, his impotence is complete. In a good example of fluid gender roles, his wife, Ada, "who bullied [Farrington] when he was sober and was bullied by him when he was drunk" (para. 60) temporarily abandons her traditional role of caring for him. Their relationship is indeed queer. Farrington's performative queerness is never clearer than in his final violent undoing of the conventional role of the protective father, making a mockery of masculine decency, compassion, and fairness.

Alert to the inconsistencies, contradictions, and ambiguities of conventional gender behaviors, protocols, and values, queer theorists offer provocative and enriching readings that remind readers how easy it is to oversimplify the bewildering complexities of being men and women.

OBJECT-ORIENTED CRITICISM

An object-oriented critic might begin to analyze the story by listing physical things it brings up. The list might include items that seem trivial at first. A class studying "Counterparts" drew up an inventory of its objects and these turned out to be quite a large set of props. It included a bell, a tube, a counter, papers, desks, a pen, a typewriter, hats, an umbrella, a watch, coins, drinking glasses, chairs, tables, a scarf, trams, a walking-stick, and more. The most sinister of these objects is the walking-stick, which Farrington uses to beat his son. How ironic that a tool designed to help becomes a means of punishment! How ironic, too, that the stick thus resembles the story's opening bell, which "furiously" rings to express the manager's rage.

But the class sought additional ways to connect the story's things. The students decided to pinpoint the items that Farrington holds in his hands. As he moves through his evening in Dublin, what does he exchange for what? The class was especially drawn to paragraph 42, where Farrington pawns his watch for six shillings and plans to spend them on liquor. His surrender of the watch suggests that keeping time isn't important to him, though his office insists on sticking to a schedule. Nor does he care to possess for long the coins he gets in return; instead, he craves the glasses of alcohol he can use them to buy. The class discussed the values revealed in what he does with these objects. Students realized that one possible claim would go something like this: "When he pawns the watch to get coins that he spends on liquor for his friends and himself, Farrington shows that he mainly values drunken companionship, which briefly helps him ignore the world where time and money matter." The story contains other things that a critic might fruitfully analyze. Notable, too, is that in only one scene does Farrington's hand touch a person. It's when he arm-wrestles Weathers: a combat, not a union of hearts.

COGNITIVE CRITICISM

When Mr. Alleyne first scolds him, Farrington feels a "rage" that leads to "a sharp sensation of thirst." Farrington automatically thinks his body is telling him "that he must have a good night's drinking" (para. 15). Farrington's conclusion would interest cognitive critics, for they like to examine how the mind decodes the body's signals. They wouldn't assume that Farrington analyzes his thirst correctly. They would be apt to point out other ways his mind could interpret it. They might argue that Farrington isn't reflective enough—that he fails to consider what he's *really* thirsting for. (Respect? Power? Love?)

Cognitive critics would also note when Farrington exercises his Theory of Mind. These are moments when he guesses what others think or predicts their conduct. An example is when he departs from the office in search of alcohol. If he removes his usual hat from the rack, he assumes, the chief clerk will know he's leaving. So, Farrington keeps his hat there, slips out of the office, and dons another cap he's concealed. Later, he relies on his Theory of Mind when a friend makes a joke about him. Because Farrington trusts his mates, he doesn't take the jab seriously: "he understood he was being chafffed" (para. 46).

But a more striking passage is paragraph 40. There, Farrington makes several inferences about people he knows. He believes that the cashier won't give him money in the chief clerk's presence. He suspects that Higgins won't feel able to offer him cash. He assumes that his apology to Mr. Alleyne is futile—that the manager has long resented him and will, in the future, harass him. Interestingly, we don't witness Farrington's apology. We learn about it only when he later reflects upon it. Joyce reveals what Farrington *thinks* about his apology, rather than showing us the act itself. Joyce thereby supports an idea voiced by the ancient philosopher Epictetus: "it is not events that disturb people, it is their judgments concerning them." Many cognitive critics would agree, and they would see this moment in "Counterparts" as an example.

Just as ripe for a cognitive approach is paragraph 45. There, Farrington becomes sexually interested in the actress sitting near him. Furthermore, he thinks she might feel the same way. Yet his guess proves wrong: "He watched her leave the room in hopes that she would look back at him, but he was disappointed." A cognitive critic might argue for a claim like this: "Farrington's mistaken hypothesis about the woman's thinking suggests that his Theory of Mind fails him when it confronts someone very different from him: in this case, someone who is female, English, youthful, artistic, and possibly from a higher class."

Cognitive critics would be interested, too, in how we read "Counterparts." They would say we deploy our own Theory of Mind in our reading process. For instance, we notice and ponder key aspects of the storyworld. If we're familiar with Dublin, we'll know Joyce refers to real streets. Various readers may pay attention to sensory details. To evoke the city, Joyce uses more than just visual images. He mentions smells: Miss Delacour's "moist pungent perfume" (para. 30); Farrington's beloved "curling fumes of punch" (para. 42). He mentions sounds, including "the noises of tram-gongs and swishing trolleys" (para. 42) as well as "the noise of tongues and glasses" (para. 46). Yet Joyce overwhelmingly identifies Dublin with a particular kind of establishment: the pub. Farrington cherishes the drunken conviviality of taverns. So, once he leaves work, he mainly visits bars. Only near the end is there reference to another Dublin institution: the church. We're reminded of it when Farrington learns that his wife is "out at the chapel" (para. 66). At the time Joyce wrote "Counterparts," many Dubliners would have despised how he paints their city. They would think he over-emphasizes its saloons while slighting its houses of worship. Joyce might have admitted being selective in crafting the text's storyworld. He might have said that it reflects *Farrington*'s view of Dublin—what this particular character values about the city. Joyce himself had a broader and deeper knowledge of his home town. Though he left it to pursue his writing career, he knew Dublin in all its variety, and he remembered it in great detail.

Some cognitive critics would study Joyce's metaphors. They would be especially interested in ones based on the human body. For example, Farrington walks with a "heavy step" (para. 5); then goes "heavily upstairs" (para. 6); later moves "heavily towards the door" (para. 19); and, near the end, "heavily" plops on a chair (para. 70). The repeated references to his physical weight imply something about his psyche: this eager bar-hopper is spiritually crushed. The same thing is suggested when, upon returning home, Farrington is "peering through the darkness" (para. 61). Joyce is aware that for all human eyes, darkness is an obstacle. So, he makes darkness a metaphor for this character's mind. It represents Farrington's mental lack of vision. Farrington doesn't really understand himself or his family's worth.

AFFECTIVE CRITICISM

Struggling with the pressures of his job, Farrington looks forward to drinking with his friends. Joyce describes his anticipation this way: "The barometer of his emotional nature was set for a spell of riot." The word "emotional" would interest affective critics, who'd find many subsequent references to emotions in the story. These critics might also be interested in the word "riot." For Farrington, it means barroom fun, but it can also signify the intense mixture of feelings that churns in him during the night. Some of the feelings are positive. Farrington gazes at passers-by with "proud satisfaction" (para. 42). He shares the delight of his friends as their revels begin: "Everyone roared with laughter" (para. 45). More often, though, Farrington seethes with anger, even rage. These two words appear several times in the text. An affective critic would probably seek to know *why* Farrington boils so often. What's the basic cause of his fury?

For an answer, the critic might turn to paragraph 57. There, while Farrington reviews his evening, he's "full of smouldering anger and revengefulness." The paragraph ends with his memory of one particular incident: "when he thought of the woman with the big hat who had brushed against him and said *Pardon!* his fury nearly choked him." It's significant that the paragraph climaxes with this event. Farrington's encounter with the woman is a clue to the source of his frequent wrath. An affective critic might claim that Farrington boils when he feels his dignity's lost. Support for such a hypothesis comes even earlier, in paragraph 32: "All the indignities of his life enraged him." Surely Farrington overreacts to the woman's treatment of him. She's not mean to him; she apologizes to him. But because he anticipated more warmth from her, he sees her as snidely indifferent. She's an unexpected blow to his pride. Perhaps her indifference especially galls him because it occurs outside his office. He's familiar with "indignities" at work, but the way she treats him in the pub is a shock to his ego.

PERFORMANCE-ORIENTED CRITICISM

If we look for performances in the story, we can find plenty. Literally, the cast of characters includes three who work in show business: the acrobat Weathers and the two women who, like him, perform at the Tivoli. If we define *performance* as execution of a task, we might focus on one or more of the following botches: (1) Farrington's unsuccessful attempt to meet his boss's demands; (2) Farrington's defeats at arm-wrestling; (3) Tom Farrington's failure to maintain the fire, a lapse that sparks his father's rage. If we define *performance* as deceit, we have another example: it's when Farrington pretends to his colleagues that he hasn't gone out for a drink. He leaves his regular hat on the rack to suggest he's still at work; he swallows a caraway seed to hide his liquor breath. But Farrington and his mates also "perform" when they jokingly re-enact his retort to Mr. Alleyne. Here *performance* refers to forms of entertainment in daily life. The story's narrator even connects the men's barroom humor to show business: "The talk became theatrical" (para. 46). This definition of *performance* fits as well Farrington's behavior at home, when he cruelly begins "to mimic his son's flat accent" (para. 70).

We can apply the word *performance*, too, to Farrington's self-presentation. How does he "act out" or "stage" the image that he wants to project? Significantly, when Weathers defeats him at arm-wrestling, Farrington concludes that he's "lost his reputation as a strong man" (para. 56). Here he indicates the impression he hopes to convey. But what *is* "a strong man"? At this particular moment, Farrington defines him as a hardy athlete. Earlier he assumes "a strong man" also casts off his woes, by drinking with friends who respect him. By contrast, Farrington feels undermined by the woman in the bar. At his office, too, he lacks power: Alleyne declares him incompetent and calls him an "insolent ruffian" (para. 39). And even at home, Farrington can't always rule; his wife "bullied her husband when he was sober" (para. 60). At the end of the story, therefore, Farrington yearns to assert his ideal self-image. He's out to prove that, despite his setbacks, he's indeed "a strong man"—a figure who wields physical *and* social authority. But the only way he thinks he can do this is to thrash his son! An alternative, one student proposed, would be to drop the "strong man" ideal and perform a different identity: that of a anti-capitalist rebel. Farrington would then fight the overall system that keeps him a lowly clerk. The student's claim demonstrates how a performance-oriented approach can mesh with feminist and Marxist approaches.

RHETORICAL CRITICISM

To a rhetorical critic, the story may notably *lack* arguments. None of its characters makes an extensive effort to persuade. When Mr. Alleyne asks Farrington: "Do you think me an utter fool?" (para. 37), Farrington briefly states what could be called a claim: "I don't think, sir, he said, that that's a fair question to put to me" (para. 39). But to Alleyne this is an insult, not an argument, and he angrily rebukes Farrington for it. Later, Farrington's friends prod him to arm-wrestle Weathers by bringing up Ireland's "national honor" (para. 48). But Farrington doesn't need convincing; he's ready to compete. Overall, the story emphasizes how arguing is *discouraged*. Alleyne's status lets him boss Farrington around; he needn't listen to backtalk from the man. Tom Farrington can't soften his father's heart; he can only suffer his blows.

Still, the story depicts speech acts that rhetorical critics would note. For example, Alleyne shoos Farrington out of his office and later demands he apologize. Farrington begs Pat for a drink; bargains with the pawnbroker; scolds the man who praises Weathers' victory; and scolds Tom at home. The story ends with a cry from Tom that's a promise and a plea: he swears that he'll say a Hail Mary for his father if Farrington will stop beating him. This final speech act led one student to propose an interesting claim: Farrington's own conduct throughout the story is a plea for recognition; when he strikes out at people, he's actually begging to be treated with dignity.

A rhetorical approach might examine Joyce's strategies as a writer. These include his ways of making the setting and characters seem real. For instance, the critic might note Joyce's use of actual street names. Credible, too, are his precise and vivid descriptions, such as "The veins stood out on Farrington's forehead, and the pallor of Weathers' complexion changed to peony" (para. 33). Some of Joyce's other techniques require interpretation; it's not immediately clear why he uses them. Take his method of narration. The story is told in third person; the narrator is an observer who's all-knowing and often detached. Note, for example, this description of Farrington in paragraph 5: "When he stood up he was tall and of great bulk." Similar is this statement about him in paragraph 57: "A very sullen-faced man stood at the corner of O'Connell Bridge waiting for the little Sandymount tram to take him home." More specifically, though, Joyce's narrative method is *free indirect style*. As we explained in Chapter 5, the term refers to a certain kind of third-person storytelling. At moments, the narrator conveys a character's own perceptions by using words that the character would use. From time to time, "Counterparts" seems to provide direct access to Farrington's thoughts. We get the sense that he's talking to himself. An example is this passage: "Could he ask the cashier privately for an advance? No, the cashier was no good, no damn good: he wouldn't give an advance" (para. 32). Another example is this passage later on: "Mr. Alleyne would never give him an hour's rest; his life would be a hell to him. He had made a proper fool of himself this time. Could he not keep his tongue in his cheek?" (para. 40). Overall, the narration goes back and forth: sometimes describing Farrington from a distance, sometimes zooming into his mind. Besides identifying this process, a rhetorical critic would consider its aims. For what purposes does Joyce tell the story this way? A class decided that this narrative method serves two of his likely goals. In much of his work, Joyce deliberately challenges rosy conceptions of Dublin — views that focus fondly on its charm. He aims to make his readers acknowledge the city's less glamorous folk. When "Counterparts" describes Farrington from a distance, we notice him as a social type. We see Dublin includes imperfect people like him. Yet clearly Joyce wants us to see as well how someone like Farrington *thinks*. When the story provides his own words and perspective, we grasp what makes him tick.

Sample Student Essay

The following essay was written by a first-year student using a postcolonial perspective.

Molly Frye
Prof. Christine Hardee
English 102
10 May - - - -

A Refugee at Home

It is difficult to argue that Farrington, the main character in James Joyce's "Counterparts," should be seen in a sympathetic light. After all, he seems an extreme stereotype of an aggressive, irresponsible drinker. Although his character traits certainly do not conform to our modern standards of mature masculinity, I want to argue that although we do not want to condone Farrington's brutal behavior, we can find it understandable. As an Irish subject in the British Empire, Farrington is more sinned against than sinner, more victim than victimizer. Farrington is not simply an obnoxious male since his actions can be understood as stemming from his colonial consciousness in struggling vainly against his powerlessness. His frustrations are especially clear in the three spaces Farrington inhabits: his office, the bars, and his home.

After setting up a context, states her claim supported by three examples.

Farrington's first appearance is telling. Because of his poor job performance, his boss demands to see him: "Send Farrington here!" Farrington, who most often is referred to as "the man," mutters his first words, "Blast him!" This typical antagonistic relationship in a colonial context foreshadows the rest of the story. Farrington is the working-class subject caught in a menial and unsatisfying job he can never complete under a boss who has social and cultural power. This counterpart relationship is similar to the positions of Ireland and England where the colony is disparaged and oppressed by the empire. In his office run by Protestants loyal to the British, Farrington is ironically "tall and of great bulk," while his boss, Mr. Alleyne, is "a little man" whose head, "pink and hairless," resembles a "large egg." Farrington's only asset, his size and strength, is irrelevant because he is so economically and socially weak. This disparity only increases Farrington's frustration and precipitates fantasies of violence against his oppressor. When Mr. Alleyne rebukes him, "Do you mind me now," Farrington is sent into a "spasm of rage." He cannot, of course, act on his aggressive urges, so he represses these feelings by rationalizing that he must have a "good night's drinking." Thus begins a pattern of self-destructive behavior that only increases Farrington's marginal position in society.

First concrete example of Farrington as frustrated colonial subject.

Transition to explanation of Farrington's failures at work.

Farrington is so uncomfortable at work, a postcolonial condition known as being unhomed, that he cannot concentrate on anything but drinking. He seems quite unsuited for the tedious task of copying legal documents, staring "stupidly at the last words he has written," knowing he will never finish his task, never advance, never get anywhere. Farrington is paralyzed by his alienation. He feels his only recourse is sneaking out to drink, which only exacerbates his poverty and powerlessness. When he attempts to cover up his inability to concentrate and finish copying letters for Mr. Alleyne, he is caught and confronted. Instead of acknowledging his underling position, he attempts a witticism which, of course, backfires. Even though he is forced to apologize, his job now seems in jeopardy. Mr. Alleyne humiliates him by calling him an "impertinent ruffian," a status that seems to him the most he can hope for. As a colonial subject, Farrington is plagued by a double consciousness. He longs for the masculine status his physical strength should give him in his working-class culture, but he must suffer indignities at the hands of Mr. Alleyne because of his inability to perform a simple task a competent child could do. Farrington should probably be working in construction as a laborer, not an office worker where discipline, patience, and mental concentration are necessary.

Uses postcolonial ideas to explain Farrington's behavior.

When Farrington finally leaves work, he expects to find some solace in the Dublin pubs. He has hocked his watch for drinking

Transition to second example of Farrington as colonized.

money, a clear indication of how desperate he is to escape the confines of regimented office work. The camaraderie of Paddy Leonard and Nosey Flynn is temporary, and Farrington is not at home in these public spaces either. He runs out of money he would have spent drinking and womanizing, and he is finally humiliated by another small British man. Called on to "uphold the national honor," Farrington's loss in an arm-wrestling contest with Weathers leaves him "full of smouldering anger and revengefulness. He is humiliated and discontented . . . His heart swelled with fury. . . ." His longing for escape from the confinement and disappointment of work has taken a disastrous turn. Farrington's already damaged self-esteem is degraded, and his repressed anger at his oppressor is near the breaking point. Perhaps his self-destructive behavior can be redirected at his home, his last possibility for comfort and acceptance.

Transition to last example.

For the unhomed colonized, however, this is not to be. Farrington enters the kitchen to find it symbolically empty, "the fire nearly out." His wife is at chapel, his five children in bed, and his dinner is cold. His agonies continue. Having internalized the humiliations suffered at work and in the pubs, Farrington has no resources left. And so in a bitter irony, he beats his son for not attending to the fire, "striking at him viciously with a stick. 'Take that, you little whelp!'" Farrington the oppressed becomes Farrington the oppressor. His role as provider and protector is cruelly turned upside-down. Farrington compensates for his defeats at the hands of Mr. Alleyne and Weathers by beating his son, and in doing so, mimics the cycle of oppression prevalent in countries dominated by the empire. Farrington is not only a cog in the bureaucratic wheel at work; he is also a pathetic, but understandable cog crushed by the wheel of power even in his own home.

Uses all three examples in concluding.

Works Cited

Joyce, James. "Counterparts." 1914. *Making Literature Matter: An Anthology for Readers and Writers*, 7th ed., edited by John Schilb and John Clifford, Bedford/St. Martin's, 2018, pp. 241–300.

FOR THINKING AND WRITING

1. Using a feminist critique of Joyce, one student claimed that "Joyce's text indulges dominance over submission." Do you think there is textual evidence to support this assertion?
2. How might various approaches interpret these lines from "Counterparts"?
   - "The man passed through the crowd, looking on the spectacle generally with proud satisfaction and staring masterfully at the office-girls" (para. 42).

- "His heart swelled with fury and, when he thought of the woman in the big hat who had brushed against him and said *Pardon!* his fury nearly choked him" (para. 57).
- "What's for my dinner?" (para. 71).

3. Influenced by New Critical ideas, one student wrote, "'Counterparts' is filled with parallel scenes and emotions that reflect one another." What textual evidence would help support this notion?
4. Engaging in a Marxist critique, one student wrote, "His unfair work conditions so distract him that he does not even know the names of his children." What is the warrant behind such an assertion? What work conditions might the student think "fair"?
5. Using a New Historicist approach, what might you learn about this story from doing research on the elementary-school curriculum in Dublin, the pay scale in a law office, the legal rights of women, the laws on domestic violence, the unemployment rate? What other practices and texts do you think would illuminate the story?
6. What's an object in the story that you've come to think is more significant than you first realized? Explain your change of mind.
7. Expand the story by adding a couple of paragraphs that describe Mrs. Farrington's return home from church. Convey *her* perspective on the marriage. What might be a Theory of Mind she relies on? What emotions might she feel? What sort of performance might she engage in? After your new ending, write a paragraph or two about the choices you made in composing it.
8. Besides free indirect style, what techniques used by Joyce might a rhetorical critic focus on?

A WRITING EXERCISE

Now you try. After reading the following story, construct an argument influenced by one or more of the following critical approaches: postcolonial, Marxist, reader-response, or feminist.

JAMES JOYCE
Eveline

Like "Counterparts," "Eveline" is from Dubliners *(1914). For more by James Joyce, see his story "Araby" on page 507.*

She sat at the window watching the evening invade the avenue. Her head was leaned against the window curtains and in her nostrils was the odor of dusty cretonne. She was tired.

Few people passed. The man out of the last house passed on his way home; she heard his footsteps clacking along the concrete pavement and afterwards crunching on the cinder path before the new red houses. One time there used to be a field there in which they used to play every evening with other people's children. Then a man from Belfast bought the field and built houses in it—not like their little brown houses but bright brick houses with shining roofs. The children of the avenue used to play together in that field—the Devines, the Waters, the Dunns, little Keogh the cripple, she and her brothers and sisters. Ernest, however, never played: he was too grown up. Her father used often to hunt them in out of the field with his blackthorn stick; but usually little Keogh used to keep *nix* and call out when he saw her father coming. Still they seemed to have been rather happy then. Her father was not so bad then; and besides, her mother was alive. That was a long time ago; she and her brothers and sisters were all grown up; her mother was dead. Tizzie Dunn was dead, too, and the Waters had gone back to England. Everything changes. Now she was going to go away like the others, to leave her home.

Home! She looked round the room, reviewing all its familiar objects which she had dusted once a week for so many years, wondering where on earth all the dust came from. Perhaps she would never see again those familiar objects from which she had never dreamed of being divided. And yet during all those years she had never found out the name of the priest whose yellowing photograph hung on the wall above the broken harmonium beside the colored print of the promises made to Blessed Margaret Mary Alacoque. He had been a school friend of her father. Whenever he showed the photograph to a visitor her father used to pass it with a casual word:

—He is in Melbourne now.

She had consented to go away, to leave her home. Was that wise? She tried to 5
weigh each side of the question. In her home anyway she had shelter and food; she had those whom she had known all her life about her. Of course she had to work hard both in the house and at business. What would they say of her in the Stores when they found out that she had run away with a fellow? Say she was a fool, perhaps; and her place would be filled up by advertisement. Miss Gavan would be glad. She had always had an edge on her, especially whenever there were people listening.

—Miss Hill, don't you see these ladies are waiting?

—Look lively, Miss Hill, please.

She would not cry many tears at leaving the Stores.

But in her new home, in a distant unknown country, it would not be like that. Then she would be married—she, Eveline. People would treat her with respect then. She would not be treated as her mother had been. Even now, though she was over nineteen, she sometimes felt herself in danger of her father's violence. She knew it was that that had given her the palpitations. When they were growing up he had never gone for her, like he used to go for Harry and Ernest, because she was a girl; but latterly he had begun to threaten her and say what he would do to her only for her dead mother's sake. And now she had nobody to protect her. Ernest was dead and Harry, who was in the church decorating business, was nearly always down somewhere in the country. Besides, the invariable squabble for money on Saturday nights had begun to weary her unspeakably. She always gave her entire wages—seven shillings—and Harry always sent up what he could but the trouble was to get any money from her father. He said she used to squander the money, that she had no head, that he wasn't going to give her his hard-earned money to throw about the streets, and much more, for he was usually fairly bad of a Saturday night. In the end he would give her the money and ask her had she any intention of buying Sunday's dinner. Then she had to rush out as quickly as she could and do her marketing, holding her black leather purse tightly in her hand as she elbowed her way through the crowds and returning home late under her load of provisions. She had hard work to keep the house together and to see that the two young children who had been left to her charge went to school regularly and got their meals regularly. It was hard work—a hard life—but now that she was about to leave it she did not find it a wholly undesirable life.

She was about to explore another life with Frank. Frank was very kind, 10
manly, open-hearted. She was to go away with him by the night-boat to be his wife and to live with him in Buenos Aires where he had a home waiting for her. How well she remembered the first time she had seen him; he was lodging in a house on the main road where she used to visit. It seemed a few weeks ago. He was standing at the gate, his peaked cap pushed back on his head and his hair tumbled forward over a face of bronze. Then they had come to know each other. He used to meet her outside the Stores every evening and see her home. He took her to see *The Bohemian Girl* and she felt elated as she sat in an unaccustomed part of the theater with him. He was awfully fond of music and sang a little. People knew that they were courting and, when he sang about the lass that loves a sailor, she always felt pleasantly confused. He used to call her Poppens out of fun. First of all it had been an excitement for her to have a fellow and then she had begun to like him. He had tales of distant countries. He had started as a deck boy at a pound a month on a ship of the Allan Line going out to Canada. He told her the names of the ships he had been on and the names of the different services. He had sailed through the Straits of Magellan and he told her stories of the terrible Patagonians. He had fallen on his feet in Buenos Aires, he said, and had come over to the old country just for a holiday. Of course, her father had found out the affair and had forbidden her to have anything to say to him.

—I know these sailor chaps, he said.

One day he had quarreled with Frank and after that she had to meet her lover secretly.

The evening deepened in the avenue. The white of two letters in her lap grew indistinct. One was to Harry; the other was to her father. Ernest had been her favorite but she liked Harry too. Her father was becoming old lately, she noticed; he would miss her. Sometimes he could be very nice. Not long before, when she had been laid up for a day, he had read her out a ghost story and made toast for her at the fire. Another day, when their mother was alive, they had all gone for a picnic to the Hill of Howth. She remembered her father putting on her mother's bonnet to make the children laugh.

Her time was running out but she continued to sit by the window, leaning her head against the window curtain, inhaling the odor of dusty cretonne. Down far in the avenue she could hear a street organ playing. She knew the air. Strange that it should come that very night to remind her of the promise to her mother, her promise to keep the home together as long as she could. She remembered the last night of her mother's illness; she was again in the close dark room at the other side of the hall and outside she heard a melancholy air of Italy. The organ-player had been ordered to go away and given sixpence. She remembered her father strutting back into the sickroom saying:

—Damned Italians! coming over here! 15

As she mused the pitiful vision of her mother's life laid its spell on the very quick of her being—that life of commonplace sacrifices closing in final craziness. She trembled as she heard again her mother's voice saying constantly with foolish insistence:

—Derevaun Seraun! Derevaun Seraun!°

She stood up in a sudden impulse of terror. Escape! She must escape! Frank would save her. He would give her life, perhaps love, too. But she wanted to live. Why should she be unhappy? She had a right to happiness. Frank would take her in his arms, fold her in his arms. He would save her.

She stood among the swaying crowd in the station at the North Wall. He held her hand and she knew that he was speaking to her, saying something about the passage over and over again. The station was full of soldiers with brown baggages. Through the wide doors of the sheds she caught a glimpse of the black mass of the boat, lying in beside the quay wall, with illumined portholes. She answered nothing. She felt her cheek pale and cold and, out of a maze of distress, she prayed to God to direct her, to show her what was her duty. The boat blew a long mournful whistle into the mist. If she went, tomorrow she would be on the sea with Frank, steaming toward Buenos Aires. Their passage had been booked. Could she still draw back after all he had done for her? Her distress awoke a nausea in her body and she kept moving her lips in silent fervent prayer.

A bell clanged upon her heart. She felt him seize her hand: 20

—Come!

All the seas of the world tumbled about her heart. He was drawing her into them: he would drown her. She gripped with both hands at the iron railing.

—Come!

No! No! No! It was impossible. Her hands clutched the iron in frenzy. Amid the seas she sent a cry of anguish!

—Eveline! Evvy! 25

He rushed beyond the barrier and called to her to follow. He was shouted at to go on but he still called to her. She set her white face to him, passive, like a helpless animal. Her eyes gave him no sign of love or farewell or recognition.

[1914]

Derevaun Seraun!: Gaelic for "The end of pleasure is pain."

FOR THINKING AND WRITING

1. There is a French expression that says to understand all is to forgive all. Given the ending of "Eveline," argue for or against this idea.
2. Compare "Counterparts" and "Eveline" (see "Strategies for Writing a Comparative Paper," p. 121), arguing that Joyce has or has not prepared us for the endings.

PART TWO

Literature and Its Issues

CHAPTER 8

Families

In the not-too-distant past, family life was the focal point of our emotional existence, the center of all our important psychological successes and failures. It was common for several generations to live together in the same town and even the same home. Grandparents, aunts, and uncles were an intimate part of daily life, not just relatives one saw during the holidays. Besides the usual emotional drama that always takes place between parents and children, there were the additional tensions that inevitably arise when the values of the old clash with those of the young. Of course, there was also the comforting emotional support available from more than just a mother and father as well as the sense of belonging and bonding with the many aunts, uncles, and cousins that usually lived nearby.

As extended families become less common, the emotional stakes of home life seem higher than ever. Since we rely on one another more in today's nuclear family, our sense of disappointment, our sense of rejection, and our sense of unworthiness can be more acute. During childhood, the drama of family life can stamp an indelible mark on our psyches, leaving psychological scars that make safe passage into adulthood difficult. Our status within the family can also offer us a sense of worth and confidence that leads to contentment and success later on. For all of us, however, family life is composed not of psychological and sociological generalities but, rather, of our one-to-one relationships with fathers, sisters, grandmothers. Writers often give us imaginative, honest, and illuminating charts of their successes and failures in negotiating both the calm and the choppy waters of our family journeys. The following clusters do not hope to be complete or representative of your experiences. We do hope, however, that in reading and discussing these poems and stories, you will find them an interesting and provocative catalyst for you to delve into the joys and sorrows of your own life in a family.

The chapter opens with four poems about reconnecting with fathers, followed by loving, honest, and humorous snapshots of grandparents. The third cluster records the difficulties of gays and lesbians in families, followed by three critical comments on Sylvia Plath's brilliant classic, "Daddy." The next grouping examines stories that reveal the tension that often arises between mothers and daughters. Then a pair of stories focus on two boys searching for a reasonable father. In the eighth cluster we introduce a new idea of joining a work of literature with current societal concerns. In this case, we present a variation of the age-old struggle between fathers and sons, with religious extremism complicating the issue. Next we pair Ernest Hemingway's "Soldier's Home"—a story about a soldier trying to reconnect with his family after the trauma of war—with three essays that amplify its cultural contexts. The penultimate cluster presents three memoirs about food and family, followed by a story and nonfictional narrative about the sometimes critical decision people have to make about parenthood.

Reconciling with Fathers: Poems

LUCILLE CLIFTON, "forgiving my father"

ROBERT HAYDEN, "Those Winter Sundays"

THEODORE ROETHKE, "My Papa's Waltz"

LI-YOUNG LEE, "My Father, in Heaven, Is Reading Out Loud"

In childhood, our emotions are often intense. Fears about life arise because we feel so powerless. For some of us, our fathers held all the power. Fathers may use their power in various ways—some to control or abuse, others to comfort and protect. We form perceptions about our fathers from these early memories. Often we become judgmental about their failures in the world or their failures as parents. As we grow older, we sometimes come to terms with our fathers and see them simply as human beings with strengths and weaknesses. But it is not always simple; some wounds may be too deep for us to reconcile. The four poets in this cluster approach memories of their fathers with different perspectives and purposes: to forgive their fathers and perhaps themselves, to remember fondly, to come to a closure, to relive a past that still haunts them, to come to terms with loss.

BEFORE YOU READ

Make a list of four strong memories about your father from your childhood. Are the memories positive or not? Can you remember how you felt then? Is it different from how you feel now? How can you explain the difference?

LUCILLE CLIFTON

forgiving my father

Lucille Clifton (1936–2010) was born in a small town near Buffalo, New York. She attended Howard University and Fredonia State Teacher's College and taught poetry at a number of universities. Her numerous awards for writing include two creative writing fellowships from the National Endowment for the Arts (1970 and 1973), two Pulitzer Prize nominations (for Good Woman: Poems and a Memoir *and for* Next, *both in 1988), several major poetry awards, and an Emmy. The mother of six, Clifton has written fifteen children's books. She was a former poet laureate of Maryland and the Distinguished Professor of Humanities at St. Mary's College. "Forgiving my father" is from her 1980 book,* Two-Headed Woman. Voices, *her most recent book, was published in 2008.*

it is friday. we have come
to the paying of the bills.
all week you have stood in my dreams
like a ghost, asking for more time

but today is payday, payday old man,
my mother's hand opens in her early grave
and i hold it out like a good daughter.

there is no more time for you. there will
never be time enough daddy daddy old lecher
old liar. i wish you were rich so i could take it all
and give the lady what she was due
but you were the son of a needy father,
the father of a needy son,
you gave her all you had
which was nothing. you have already given her
all you had.

you are the pocket that was going to open
and come up empty any friday.
you were each other's bad bargain, not mine.
daddy old pauper old prisoner, old dead man
what am i doing here collecting?
you lie side by side in debtor's boxes
and no accounting will open them up. *[1980]*

THINKING ABOUT THE TEXT

1. How might you answer the question in line 21? Are the last two lines of the poem a kind of answer? Is there some way we can "collect" from the dead?
2. Should we bury the dead — that is, should we let the past go and let bygones be bygones? Or is it necessary to settle old scores? What do you think Clifton's answer would be?
3. How consistently does Clifton use the payday analogy? Make a list of words that reinforce her overall scheme.
4. Would you think differently about the speaker's father if Clifton had written "elderly one" instead of "old man" (line 5) or "old playboy / old fibber" instead of "old lecher / old liar" (lines 9–10)?
5. Some readers look for tensions or contradictions early in a poem, hoping they will be resolved at the end. Does this poem end in a resolution of paying up and forgiving?

ROBERT HAYDEN

Those Winter Sundays

Born in Detroit, Michigan, African American poet Robert Hayden (1913–1980) grew up in a poor neighborhood where his natural parents left him with family friends.

He grew up with the Hayden name, not discovering his original name until he was forty. Hayden attended Detroit City College (now Wayne State University) from 1932 to 1936, worked in the Federal Writer's Project, and later earned his M.A. at the University of Michigan in 1944. He taught at Fisk University from 1946 to 1968 and at the University of Michigan from 1968 to 1980 and published several collections of poetry. Although his poems sometimes contain autobiographical elements, Hayden is primarily a formalist poet who preferred that his poems not be limited to personal or ethnic interpretations. "Those Winter Sundays" is from Angle of Ascent *(1966).*

Sundays too my father got up early
and put his clothes on in the blueblack cold,
then with cracked hands that ached
from labor in the weekday weather made
banked fires blaze. No one ever thanked him.

I'd wake and hear the cold splintering, breaking.
When the rooms were warm, he'd call,
and slowly I would rise and dress,
fearing the chronic angers of that house,

Speaking indifferently to him,
who had driven out the cold
and polished my good shoes as well.
What did I know, what did I know
of love's austere and lonely offices?

[1962]

THINKING ABOUT THE TEXT

1. Is the concluding question meant rhetorically—that is, is the answer so obvious that no real reply is expected? Write a response that you think the son might give now.
2. Why did the children never thank their father? Is this common? What specific things might you thank your father (or mother) for? Do parents have basic responsibilities to their children that do not warrant thanks?
3. Is there evidence that the son loves his father now? Did he then? Why did he speak "indifferently" (line 10) to his father? Is it clear what the "chronic angers" (line 9) are? Should it be?
4. How might you fill in the gaps here? For example, how old do you think the boy is? How old is the father? What kind of a job might he have? What else can you infer?
5. What is the speaker's tone? Is he hoping for your understanding? Your sympathy? Are we responsible for the things we do in childhood? Is this speaker repentant or simply explaining?

MAKING COMPARISONS

1. What degrees of forgiveness do you see in Clifton's and Hayden's poems?
2. Writing a poem for one's father seems different from writing a poem about him. Explain this statement in reference to these poems.
3. Compare the purpose of the questions in each poem. How might each poet answer the other poet's questions?

THEODORE ROETHKE

My Papa's Waltz

Born in Saginaw, Michigan, Theodore Roethke (1908–1963) was strongly influenced by childhood experiences with his father, a usually stern man who sold plants and flowers and who kept a large greenhouse, the setting for many of Roethke's poems. Roethke was educated at the University of Michigan, took courses at Harvard, and taught at several universities before becoming poet-in-residence at the University of Washington in 1948. Roethke's books include The Lost Son and Other Poems *(1949), the source for "My Papa's Waltz";* The Waking *(1953), which won a Pulitzer Prize; and* Words for the Wind *(1958), which won the National Book Award. Roethke's intensely personal style ensures his place among the most influential postmodern American poets.*

The whiskey on your breath
Could make a small boy dizzy;
But I hung on like death:
Such waltzing was not easy.

We romped until the pans
Slid from the kitchen shelf;
My mother's countenance
Could not unfrown itself.

The hand that held my wrist
Was battered on one knuckle;
At every step you missed
My right ear scraped a buckle.

You beat time on my head
With a palm caked hard by dirt,
Then waltzed me off to bed
Still clinging to your shirt.

[1948]

THINKING ABOUT THE TEXT

1. Is the narrator looking back at his father with fondness? Bitterness?
2. Would the poem make a different impression if we changed "romped" (line 5) to "fought" and "waltzing" (line 4) to "dancing"?

3. Why did the boy hang on and cling to his father? From fear? From affection?
4. What is the mother's role here? How would you characterize her frown?
5. Readers often have a negative view of the relationship represented here, but many change their minds, seeing some positive aspects to the father and son's waltz. How might you account for this revision?

MAKING COMPARISONS

1. Would you have read this poem differently if the poet had used Clifton's title "forgiving my father"?
2. How would you compare the tone of Roethke's poem with that of Hayden's? Do they miss their fathers?
3. Would you say that Roethke has more complex feelings about his father, whereas Clifton and Hayden seem clearer?

LI-YOUNG LEE

My Father, in Heaven, Is Reading Out Loud

Li-Young Lee (b. 1959) was born in Indonesia to Chinese parents. His father taught medicine and philosophy in Jakarta. During a purge of ethnic Chinese, Lee's father was imprisoned because of his Western interests. He eventually escaped, and the family finally settled in Pittsburgh, where his father became a Presbyterian minister. Lee graduated from the University of Pittsburgh in 1979. He has won many prizes for his poetry, from Rose *(1986) to* Book of My Nights *(2001). His latest book is* Behind My Eyes *(2009). He lives in Chicago with his wife and two sons.*

My father, in heaven, is reading out loud
to himself Psalms or news. Now he ponders what
he's read. No. He is listening for the sound
of children in the yard. Was that laughing
or crying? So much depends upon the
answer, for either he will go on reading,
or he'll run to save a child's day from grief.
As it is in heaven, so it was on earth.

Because my father walked the earth with a grave,
determined rhythm, my shoulders ached
from his gaze. Because my father's shoulders
ached from the pulling of oars, my life now moves
with a powerful back-and-forth rhythm:
nostalgia, speculation. Because he
made me recite a book a month, I forget
everything as soon as I read it. And knowledge
never comes but while I'm mid-stride a flight
of stairs, or lost a moment on some avenue.

A remarkable disappointment to him,
I am like anyone who arrives late
in the millennium and is unable
to stay to the end of days. The world's
beginnings are obscure to me, its outcomes
inaccessible. I don't understand
the source of starlight, or starlight's destinations.
And already another year slides out
of balance. But I don't disparage scholars;
my father was one and I loved him,
who packed his books once, and all of our belongings,
then sat down to await instruction
from his god, yes, but also from a radio.
At the doorway, I watched, and I suddenly
knew he was one like me, who got my learning
under a lintel; he was one of the powerless,
to whom knowledge came while he sat among
suitcases, boxes, old newspapers, string.

He did not decide peace or war, home or exile,
escape by land or escape by sea.
He waited merely, as always someone
waits, far, near, here, hereafter, to find out:
is it praise or lament hidden in the next moment? *[1990]*

THINKING ABOUT THE TEXT

1. Lee begins his poem by speculating that his father is either reading or listening. What does this suggest about the narrator's view of his father?
2. What influence does Lee suggest his father had on him in stanza 2? Is it positive or negative or both?
3. When Lee says that his father awaited "instruction / from his god, yes, but also from a radio" (lines 30–31), what is he suggesting?
4. Does Lee finally identify with his father? In what way?
5. Would you interpret the last stanza as reconciliation? Be specific about the resolution that Lee comes to.

MAKING COMPARISONS

1. Unlike Hayden and Roethke, Lee explicitly says he loved his father. What other differences do you note?
2. Is this view of his father more or less balanced than the other three poets?
3. Which of the previous three fathers does Lee's seem most like?

WRITING ABOUT ISSUES

1. Choose one of the four preceding poems to argue that our feelings for our fathers are complex, not simple.
2. In *Words* (1964), Jean-Paul Sartre writes that "there is no good father, that is the rule." Use examples from the four poems to argue that this is, or is not, the case.
3. Do you think all children leave childhood or adolescence with unresolved tensions in their relationships with their fathers? Write a personal narrative that confronts this idea.
4. Locate at least three more poems that deal with memories of fathers. Write a brief report, noting the similarities to the four poems presented here.

Grandparents and Legacies: Poems

NIKKI GIOVANNI, "Legacies"

LINDA HOGAN, "Heritage"

GARY SOTO, "Behind Grandma's House"

ALBERTO RÍOS, "Mi Abuelo"

JUDITH ORTIZ COFER, "Claims"

In contemporary middle-class America, the influence, even the presence, of our grandparents has waned. They often live elsewhere, perhaps in retirement communities or nursing homes. But this was not always the case. Grandparents in the past, and in traditional households even today, were active members of the family, exerting influence on the daily decisions of everyday life, from diet to childrearing. Some of this was beneficial: grandparents gave children a personal understanding of their cultural traditions as well as the benefit of their accumulated wisdom. But they could also create tension in families where change and progress conflicted with the habits and attitudes of the past. The following five poets present us with different perspectives on their grandparents, some loving and proud, others less positive, and one quite funny.

BEFORE YOU READ

What specific memories do you have of your grandparents? What role do you think they should play in a family's life? What effects might the segregation of the elderly have on a society?

NIKKI GIOVANNI

Legacies

Raised near Cincinnati, Ohio, Nikki Giovanni (b. 1943) returned as a teenager to her birthplace and spiritual home in Knoxville, Tennessee, where she experienced the strong influence of her grandmother, Louvenia Watson. She studied at the University of Cincinnati from 1961 to 1963 and earned a B.A. at Fisk University in 1967. She also attended the University of Pennsylvania School of Social Work (1967) and Columbia University School of the Arts (1968). She has taught at a number of universities, since 1987 at Virginia Polytechnic Institute, where she is a professor of English. Her poetry, essays, and works for children reflect her commitment to African American community, family, and womanhood. Her books include Quilting the Black-Eyed Pea: Poems and Not Quite Poems *(2002). Her most recent books are* On My Journey Now: Looking at African American History through the Spirituals *(2006),* Acolytes *(2007), and* Bicycles: Love Poems *(2009). "Legacies" is from Giovanni's 1972 book,* My House.

her grandmother called her from the playground
"yes, ma'am"
"i want chu to learn how to make rolls," said the old
woman proudly
but the little girl didn't want
to learn how because she knew
even if she couldn't say it that
that would mean when the old one died she would be less
dependent on her spirit so
she said
"i don't want to know how to make no rolls"
with her lips poked out
and the old woman wiped her hands on
her apron saying "lord
these children"
and neither of them ever
said what they meant
and i guess nobody ever does *[1972]*

THINKING ABOUT THE TEXT

1. Does the dialogue in Giovanni's poem reveal the true feelings of the grandmother and the girl? Be explicit about what is really going on in their minds. Is the girl superstitious?
2. Is it true that "nobody" (line 18) says what she really means? Do you? Is this an indication of honesty or something else—say, tact or convention? Are poets more likely to tell the truth?
3. What makes this piece a poem? Would you prefer more metaphors or similes, allusions, or flowery language? Is *proudly* (line 4) an important word here?
4. Change the grandmother's words to those that reflect more of what is in her heart. Might the girl respond differently if the grandmother were more forthright?
5. The title is only referred to obliquely. Why? What does it refer to? Is contemporary society concerned with legacies? Are you? Are they important or irrelevant?

LINDA HOGAN

Heritage

Born in 1947 in Denver, Colorado, Linda Hogan calls on her Chickasaw heritage to interpret environmental, antinuclear, and other spiritual and societal issues. Her published works include poems, stories, screenplays, essays, and novels. Her novel Power *(1998) has been praised for its beauty of language, mythical structure, and allegorical power. Her works include* The Woman Who Watches Over the World: A Native Memoir *(2001) and* Sightings: The Gray Whales' Mysterious Journey *(2002). Her many honors include an American Book Award for* Seeing through the Sun *(1985), a Colorado Book Award and a Pulitzer nomination for* The Book of Medicines *(1993), fellowships from the Guggenheim Foundation and the National Endowment for the Arts, and a Lannan Award. Hogan received her M.A. from the University of Colorado at Boulder, where she currently teaches creative writing. "Heritage" is from her 1978 book titled* Calling Myself Home.

From my mother, the antique mirror
where I watch my face take on her lines.
She left me the smell of baking bread
to warm fine hairs in my nostrils,
she left the large white breasts that weigh down
my body.

From my father I take his brown eyes,
the plague of locusts that leveled our crops,
they flew in formation like buzzards.

From my uncle the whittled wood
that rattles like bones
and is white
and smells like all our old houses
that are no longer there. He was the man
who sang old chants to me, the words
my father was told not to remember.

From my grandfather who never spoke
I learned to fear silence.
I learned to kill a snake
when you're begging for rain.

And Grandmother, blue-eyed woman
whose skin was brown,
she used snuff.
When her coffee can full of black saliva
spilled on me
it was like the brown cloud of grasshoppers
that leveled her fields.
It was the brown stain
that covered my white shirt,
my whiteness a shame.
That sweet black liquid like the food
she chewed up and spit into my father's mouth
when he was an infant.
It was the brown earth of Oklahoma

stained with oil.
She said tobacco would purge your body of poisons.
It has more medicine than stones and knives
against your enemies.
That tobacco is the dark night that covers me.

She said it is wise to eat the flesh of deer
so you will be swift and travel over many miles.
She told me how our tribe has always followed a stick
that pointed west
that pointed east.
From my family I have learned the secrets
of never having a home.

[1978]

THINKING ABOUT THE TEXT

1. The last sentence seems to contain a contradiction. "From my family I have learned the secrets" might lead you to expect something positive. But maybe the last phrase is not meant to be positive. What is your reading of Hogan's conclusion?
2. What does the narrator learn from her mother? Her father? Her uncle? Her grandfather? Her grandmother? What kinds of things did you learn from your family members? Use concrete images.
3. Why does she say "my whiteness a shame" (line 30)? Is this a racial comment?
4. Examine the "black saliva" section in lines 21 to 39. Does it start off negatively? Does it change? Explain.
5. We all learn things from our families, both positive and negative. Is Hogan giving a balanced account? Should she? Would you? Do poets have any responsibility to the larger culture? Or should they just follow their own inner vision?

MAKING COMPARISONS

1. Compare Hogan's grandfather to Giovanni's grandmother.
2. Describe the ways the tone of "Heritage" differs from Giovanni's poem.
3. What indications of cultural differences do you find in these two poems?

GARY SOTO

Behind Grandma's House

Born in 1952 in Fresno, California, Gary Soto gives voice to San Joaquin Valley agricultural workers whose deprivations have been part of his experience and social awareness from an early age. After graduating with honors from California State University in 1974, Soto went on to earn an M.F.A. in creative writing from the University of California at Irvine in 1976 and to teach in the university system. He has received numerous writing awards, including the distinction of being the first writer identifying himself as Chicano to be nominated for a Pulitzer Prize. A young adult novel, The Afterlife, *was published in 2003. A book of poems,* One Kind of Faith *(2003), was cited as confirming Soto's "immense talent." His latest book of poems is* Partly Cloudy *(2009). His Mexican American heritage continues to be central to his work. The poem reprinted here is from Soto's 1985 book,* Black Hair.

At ten I wanted fame. I had a comb
And two Coke bottles, a tube of Bryl-creem.
I borrowed a dog, one with
Mismatched eyes and a happy tongue,
And wanted to prove I was tough
In the alley, kicking over trash cans,
A dull chime of tuna cans falling.
I hurled light bulbs like grenades
And men teachers held their heads,
Fingers of blood lengthening
On the ground. I flicked rocks at cats,
Their goofy faces spurred with foxtails.
I kicked fences. I shooed pigeons.
I broke a branch from a flowering peach
And frightened ants with a stream of piss.
I said "Shit," "Fuck you," and "No way
Daddy-O" to an imaginary priest
Until grandma came into the alley,
Her apron flapping in a breeze,
Her hair mussed, and said, "Let me help you,"
And punched me between the eyes. *[1985]*

THINKING ABOUT THE TEXT

1. Were you glad or disturbed when the narrator's grandmother hit him? Does he deserve it? Are you angry or sympathetic to his attempts to be tough? Do you understand why he wants to appear older? Is this normal?
2. What did you want at age ten? Did your grandparents know your desires? Did they support you? Did they ever set you straight? Are our grandparents' values too dated to matter?
3. Are the concrete details meaningful to you? Does the profanity help Soto achieve authenticity, or is it unnecessary?
4. Does the speaker learn something here, or is this just a snapshot of an event?
5. How would you describe our culture's ideas of the different roles of parents and grandparents? Do grandparents in today's culture have less influence than in the past? Is this a good thing or not?

MAKING COMPARISONS

1. Is Soto more or less respectful of his grandparent than the writers of the previous two poems?
2. Is this a gendered poem? That is, could a female see herself in a comparable situation? Are the Giovanni and Hogan poems gendered?
3. How might the portraits of grandmothers given here be stereotypical or not?

ALBERTO RÍOS

Mi Abuelo°

Alberto Ríos (b. 1952) has said that being bilingual is like going through life with a pair of binoculars; having at least two words for everything opens one's eyes to the world. Ríos is a person of the border in several ways: his father was from Chiapas, Mexico, and his mother from Lancashire, England. He grew up in the city of Nogales, Arizona, where he could stand with one foot in the United States and the other in Mexico; as a writer, he crosses the line between poetry and prose, having written seven books of poetry, three collections of short stories, and a memoir. He is an instructor of creative writing and since 1994 the Regents Professor of English at Arizona State University, where he has taught since 1982. He received his B.A. (1974) and his M.F.A. in creative writing (1979) from the University of Arizona. His work appears in 175 anthologies, including the Norton Anthology of Modern Poetry, *and his awards include fellowships from the Guggenheim Foundation and the National Endowment for the Arts and the 1982 Walt Whitman Award for* Whispering to Fool the Wind. *A recent book of poems,* The Smallest Muscle in the Human Body *(2002), was a finalist for the National Book Award. His latest book of poems is* A Small Story about the Sky *(2015).*

Where my grandfather is is in the ground
where you can hear the future
like an Indian with his ear at the tracks.
A pipe leads down to him so that sometimes
he whispers what will happen to a man
in town or how he will meet the best
dressed woman tomorrow and how the best
man at her wedding will chew the ground
next to her. Mi abuelo is the man
who speaks through all the mouths in my house.
An echo of me hitting the pipe sometimes
to stop him from saying *my hair is a*

Mi Abuelo: My grandfather (Spanish).

sieve is the only other sound. It is a phrase
that among all others is the best,
he says, and *my hair is a sieve* is sometimes
repeated for hours out of the ground
when I let him, which is not often.
An abuelo should be much more than a man
like you! He stops then, and speaks: *I am a man*
who has served ants with the attitude
of a waiter, who has made each smile as only
an ant who is fat can, and they liked me best,
but there is nothing left. Yet I know he ground
green coffee beans as a child, and sometimes
he will talk about his wife, and sometimes
about when he was deaf and a man
cured him by mail and he heard groundhogs
talking, or about how he walked with a cane
he chewed on when he got hungry.
At best, mi abuelo is a liar.
I see an old picture of him at nani's with an
off-white yellow center mustache and sometimes
that's all I know for sure. He talks best
about these hills, *slowest waves*, and where this man
is going, and I'm convinced his hair is a sieve,
that his fever is cooled now underground.
Mi abuelo is an ordinary man.
I look down the pipe, sometimes, and see a
ripple-topped stream in its best suit, in the ground. *[1990]*

THINKING ABOUT THE TEXT

1. The narrator seems ambivalent about his abuelo. What specific things does he know about him? Can you tell his attitude toward him? How do you read the line "At best, mi abuelo is a liar" (line 30)? What might the worst be?
2. When the grandfather speaks from the grave (*"I am a man . . ."*) (lines 19–23), he seems odd indeed. Is he a bit crazy, or do you see meaning in his ant speech?
3. What does Ríos mean when he writes that his abuelo "speaks through all the mouths in my house" (line 10)? Could this be a positive notion?
4. Ríos seems convinced that his grandfather's "fever is cooled now" (line 36). Should we take this literally?
5. Do you agree that Ríos wants to continue conversing with his dead abuelo? Why? Can we see this as a metaphor?

≡ MAKING COMPARISONS

1. Compare Ríos's attitude toward his grandfather with the attitudes shown in the poems by Giovanni, Hogan, and Soto.
2. Which of the grandparents featured in these poems would you like to meet? Why?
3. Do all the poems have a sense that grandparents possess some special experience or knowledge?

JUDITH ORTIZ COFER
Claims

Judith Ortiz Cofer (1952–2016) was born in Puerto Rico but spent most of her childhood traveling between Paterson, New Jersey, and Hormiqueros, Puerto Rico. The constant shifting of languages and cultures influenced most of her early work, especially two volumes of poetry: Reaching for the Mainland *and* Terms of Survival, *both published in 1987. Her first novel,* The Line of the Sun *(1989), the first novel ever published by the University of Georgia Press, was widely praised and was nominated for the Pulitzer Prize. Her themes center on the pressures of migratory life and the cultural importance of male-female relationships.* Woman in Front of the Sun *was published in 2000.* A Love Story Beginning in Spanish *was published in 2005. Her latest work is* Lessons from a Writer's Life *(2011).*

Last time I saw her, Grandmother
had grown seamed as a Bedouin tent.
She had claimed the right
to sleep alone, to own
her nights, to never bear
the weight of sex again nor to accept
its gift of comfort, for the luxury
of stretching her bones.
She'd carried eight children,
three had sunk in her belly, *naufragos*°
she called them, shipwrecked babies
drowned in her black waters.
Children are made in the night and
steal your days
for the rest of your life, amen. She said this
to each of her daughters in turn. Once she had made a pact
with man and nature and kept it. Now like the sea,
she is claiming back her territory.

[1987]

10 naufragos: Victims of shipwrecks (Spanish).

THINKING ABOUT THE TEXT

1. To whom does the title refer?
2. What is the pact the grandmother made with "man and nature" (line 17)?
3. Comment on the simile "like the sea" Cofer uses in the last sentence. Has the reader been prepared for that comparison? Why, or why not?
4. What parts do duty and responsibility play in the grandmother's life? Does her quote (lines 13–15) suggest a negative view of children or sex?
5. Do you think the grandmother's response is typical or unusual?

MAKING COMPARISONS

1. Is Cofer's attitude toward her grandmother more or less respectful than the other poets here?
2. Compare Cofer's grandmother with Soto's.
3. Which of the grandparents portrayed here might make the same decision about sex as Cofer's grandmother?

WRITING ABOUT ISSUES

1. Pick one of the five preceding poems, and argue that it offers an appropriate view of grandparents.
2. Pick two of these poems, and argue that something of value is learned in each.
3. Which poem comes closest to your own experiences? Write a narrative that demonstrates this.
4. Do some research on over-sixty-five communities from a sociological point of view. Write a report about your findings. Include the impact of such places on the family and on the larger culture. Do you think they are a positive development or not?

Gays and Lesbians in Families: Poems

ESSEX HEMPHILL, "Commitments"

AUDRE LORDE, "Who Said It Was Simple"

MINNIE BRUCE PRATT, "Two Small-Sized Girls"

RICHARD BLANCO, "Queer Theory: According to My Grandmother"

The late Essex Hemphill was gay, as is Richard Blanco; the late Audre Lorde was a lesbian, as is Minnie Bruce Pratt. All four writers in this cluster remind their audience that families may have gay or lesbian members, but the families depicted in most literature, films, television shows, and songs are heterosexual. Indeed, much of American society prefers this image. Throughout history, plenty of gays and lesbians have concealed their sexual identities from their families, fearing rejection. Families that do have gay or lesbian members may refuse to admit the fact, although most have grown more accepting of their loved ones' differences.

As increasing numbers of gays and lesbians "come out of the closet," many are also publicly claiming the term *family*. They seek acceptance by the families they were raised in and the right to form and raise families of their own. Some worked hard to get same-sex marriage legalized. In all these efforts, they have quite a few heterosexual allies, but they face heterosexual resistance too. In the 1990s, a lesbian mother, Sharon Bottoms, lost custody of her children for that reason. Also, gays and lesbians are far from winning a universal right to adopt. In 2004, Massachusetts became the first state to legalize same-sex marriage, but as arguments about it raged throughout the United States, the federal government sought to discourage it by passing the Defense of Marriage Act in 1996, and several states passed laws against it. But in June 2013 the Supreme Court passed two landmark decisions, ruling that a law denying same-sex couples federal benefits was unconstitutional and that same-sex marriages in California could continue as legal. In June 2015, the Supreme Court ruled that same-sex marriage was legal in every state and U.S. territory. Gays and lesbians still face difficulties with adoption and foster parenting, although there are indications that societal attitudes here are changing, albeit slowly. Consider your own position on these matters as you read the following poems. Each refers to American society's widespread assumption that families are heterosexual; each also points out the suffering that can result from this belief.

BEFORE YOU READ

What, at present, is your attitude toward gays and lesbians? Try to identify specific people, experiences, and institutions that have shaped your view. If it has changed over the years, explain how. Finally, describe an occasion that made you quite conscious of the attitude you now hold.

ESSEX HEMPHILL

Commitments

Before his untimely death from AIDS-related complications, Essex Hemphill (1957–1995) explored through prose, poetry, and film what it meant to live as a black gay man. The following poem comes from his 1992 book Ceremonies: Prose and Poetry. *His other books include a collection he edited,* Brother to Brother: New Writings by Black Gay Men *(1991). Hemphill also appeared in the documentaries* Looking for Langston *and* Tongues Untied.

I will always be there.
When the silence is exhumed.
When the photographs are examined
I will be pictured smiling
among siblings, parents,
nieces and nephews.

In the background of the photographs
the hazy smoke of barbecue,
a checkered red-and-white tablecloth
laden with blackened chicken,
glistening ribs, paper plates,
bottles of beer, and pop.

In the photos
the smallest children
are held by their parents.
My arms are empty, or around
the shoulders of unsuspecting aunts
expecting to throw rice at me someday.

Or picture tinsel, candles,
ornamented, imitation trees,
or another table, this one
set for Thanksgiving,
a turkey steaming the lens.

My arms are empty
in those photos, too,
so empty they would break

around a lover.
I am always there
for critical emergencies,
graduations,
the middle of the night.

I am the invisible son.
In the family photos
nothing appears out of character.
I smile as I serve my duty.

[1992]

THINKING ABOUT THE TEXT

1. The speaker begins with the announcement "I will always be there," and yet later he says "I am the invisible son" (line 32). How can these two statements be reconciled? In the second line, he uses the word *exhumed*. Look up this word in a dictionary. What do you infer from the speaker's use of it?
2. Unlike the other stanzas, the second lacks verbs. Should Hemphill have included at least one verb there for the sake of consistency? Why, or why not? Is the scene described in the second stanza characteristic of your own family? Note similarities and differences.
3. What do you think the speaker means when he describes his arms in the photographs as "so empty they would break / around a lover" (lines 26-27)?
4. In line 34, the speaker refers to "character." How does he seem to define the term? He concludes the poem by noting, "I smile as I serve my duty." Should this line be taken as an indication of how he really feels about his family commitments? Why, or why not?
5. List some commitments that you think the speaker's family should be making toward him. What overall attitude of yours toward the family does your list suggest? What is your overall attitude toward the speaker?

AUDRE LORDE

Who Said It Was Simple

Audre Lorde (1934–1992), a prolific writer and speaker, was also active in the civil rights, women's, and gay and lesbian movements. She published several books of poetry, including Cables to Rage *(1970);* From a Land Where Other People Live *(1973), where the following poem appeared;* The New York Head Shop and Museum *(1974);* Coal *(1976);* The Black Unicorn *(1978); and* Our Dead behind Us *(1986). In addition, she wrote several works of nonfiction, including a memoir,* Zami: A New Spelling of My Name *(1982); a collection of essays and speeches,* Sister Outsider *(1984); and an account of her struggle with breast cancer,* The Cancer Journals *(1980). Her last book was* The Marvelous Arithmetic of Distance *(1993). Although Lorde was a lesbian, she had two children and described herself as "black, lesbian, mother, warrior, poet." Lorde was quite controversial, as she saw a clear link among sexism, racism, and homophobia. The key issue for her was mainstream culture's intolerance of difference. This issue alienated her from many white feminists who thought solidarity was crucial. Although Lorde certainly believed in sisterhood, for her the metaphor of family had its limits, as the following poem suggests.*

There are so many roots to the tree of anger
that sometimes the branches shatter
before they bear.

Sitting in Nedicks
the women rally before they march
discussing the problematic girls

they hire to make them free.
An almost white counterman passes
a waiting brother to serve them first
and the ladies neither notice nor reject
the slighter pleasures of their slavery.
But I who am bound by my mirror
as well as my bed
see causes in colour
as well as sex

and sit here wondering
which me will survive
all these liberations.

[1973]

THINKING ABOUT THE TEXT

1. What is the thematic focus that Lorde announces with the tree metaphor of the first three lines?
2. What does the counterman do, and why does that annoy the speaker?
3. Why does Lorde use such a strong word as *slavery* (line 11) to describe the women at the counter who are served before the "brother"?
4. What does Lorde mean by being "bound by my mirror / as well as my bed" (lines 12–13)?
5. Do you see irony in Lorde's final stanza? Do you think Lorde is using "liberations" (line 18) sarcastically?

MAKING COMPARISONS

1. Explain how both Lorde and Hemphill use the idea of invisibility.
2. Lorde mentions anger. Do you think Hemphill is angry, or do you sense other emotions?
3. Lorde was the mother of two children. Do you think that gave her a different perspective when protesting for gay rights?

MINNIE BRUCE PRATT

Two Small-Sized Girls

Minnie Bruce Pratt (b. 1946) has long been active in the women's movement. Her prose writings include Rebellion: Essays, 1980–1991 *(1991) and a 1995 volume of short pieces titled* S/HE. *As a poet, she has published* The Sound of One Fork *(1981);* Crime against Nature *(1990), which won the prestigious Lamont Prize of the American Academy of Poets; and* We Say We Love Each Other *(1992). Her latest books are* Walking Back Up Depot Street *(1999),* The Dirt She Ate *(2003), and* Inside the Money Machine *(2011). In divorce proceedings, Pratt lost custody of her two sons because she is a lesbian. Many of the poems in* Crime against Nature, *including the following, refer to this experience.*

1

Two small-sized girls, hunched in the corn crib,
skin prickly with heat and dust. We rustle
in the corn husks and grab rough cobs gnawed
empty as bone. We twist them with papery shreds.
Anyone passing would say we're making our dolls.

Almost sisters, like our mothers, we turn and shake
the shriveled beings. We are not playing at babies.
We are doing, single-minded, what we've been watching
our grandmother do. We are making someone. We hunker
on splintered grey planks older than our mothers,
and ignore how the sun blazes across us, the straw husks,
the old door swung open for the new corn of the summer.

2

Here's the cherry spool bed from her old room,
the white bedspread crocheted by Grandma,
rough straw baskets hanging on the blank wall,
snapshots from her last trip home, ramshackle
houses eaten up by kudzu. The same past
haunts us. We have ended up in the same present

where I sit crosslegged with advice on how to keep
her children from being seized by their father
ten years after I lost my own. The charge then:
crime against nature, going too far with women,
and not going back to men. And hers? Wanting
to have her small garden the way she wanted it,
and wanting to go her own way. The memory:

> Her father's garden, immense rows of corn,
> cantaloupe and melon squiggling, us squatting,
> late afternoon, cool in the four o'clocks;
> waiting for them to open, making up stories,
> anything might happen, waiting in the garden.

3

So much for the power of my ideas about oppression
and her disinterest in them. In fact we've ended
in the same place. Made wrong, knowing we've done
nothing wrong:

Like the afternoon we burned up
the backyard, wanting to see some fire.
The match's seed opened into straw, paper,
then bushes, like enormous red and orange
lantana flowers. We chased the abrupt power
blooming around us down to charred straw,
and Grandma bathed us, scorched and ashy,
never saying a word.

Despite our raw hearts,
guilt from men who used our going to take our children,
we know we've done nothing wrong, to twist and search
for the kernels of fire deep in the body's shaken husk. *[1990]*

THINKING ABOUT THE TEXT

1. Do you think any behavior deserves to be called a "crime against nature" (line 22)? Explain your reasoning.
2. Ironically, one pattern in Pratt's poem is nature imagery. Do you consider some or all of this imagery to be symbolic, or do you accept the images simply as details of a physical scene? Refer to specific examples.
3. Compare the three sections of the poem. What are their common elements? How do they significantly differ from one another? Why does the speaker believe that she and her cousin have "ended / in the same place" (lines 32–33)?
4. How would you describe the two girls' relationship to their grandmother? Support your answer with specific details from the text.
5. Do you think this poem is an affirmation of family ties? A criticism of them? Both? Again, refer to specific details.

MAKING COMPARISONS

1. Compare the tone of the three speakers in Hemphill's, Lorde's, and Pratt's poems.
2. Do you get the impression that all three speakers in this cluster are searching for Pratt's "kernels of fire deep in the body's shaken husk" (line 46)? Show how these words are or are not relevant in each case.
3. Do you sympathize with any of the three speakers more than the others? Why, or why not?

RICHARD BLANCO

Queer Theory: According to My Grandmother

Richard Blanco (b. 1968) was born in Madrid and emigrated to Miami as an infant with his Cuban exiled family. He graduated from Florida International University with a B.S. in civil engineering and later received an M.F.A. in 1997. He was the fifth poet, first Latino, and first openly gay person to read at a presidential inauguration. At Barack Obama's second inauguration, Blanco read "One Today," a poem that affirms America's collective identity. He has taught at Georgetown and American Universities and continues to practice as a civil engineer in his home in Bethel, Maine. The following poem is taken from Looking for the Gulf Motel *(2012), published by the University of Pittsburgh Press. One critic notes that Blanco is "a virtuoso of art and craft who juggles the subjective and the objective beautifully."*

Never drink soda with a straw—
  milk shakes? Maybe.
Stop eyeing your mother's Avon catalog,
and the men's underwear in those Sears flyers.
  I've seen you . . .
Stay out of her Tupperware parties
and her perfume bottles—don't let her kiss you,
  she kisses you much too much.
Avoid hugging men, but if you must,
  pat them real hard
  on the back, even
  if it's your father.
Must you keep that cat? Don't pet him so much.
  Why don't you like dogs?
Never play house, even if you're the husband.
Quit hanging with that Henry kid, he's too pale,
  and I don't care what you call them
  those GI Joes of his
  are dolls.
Don't draw rainbows or flowers or sunsets.
  I've seen you . . .
Don't draw at all—no coloring books either.
Put away your crayons, your Play-Doh, your Legos.
  Where are your Hot Wheels,
  your laser gun and handcuffs,
  the knives I gave you?
Never fly a kite or roller skate, but light
  all the firecrackers you want,
  kill all the lizards you can, cut up worms—
  feed them to that cat of yours.
Don't sit *Indian* style with your legs crossed—
  you're no Indian.
Stop click-clacking your sandals—
  you're no girl.
For God's sake, never pee sitting down.
  I've seen you . . .
Never take a bubble bath or wash your hair
with shampoo—shampoo is for women.

So is conditioner.
So is mousse.
So is hand lotion.
Never file your nails or blow-dry your hair—
go to the barber shop with your grandfather—
you're not *unisex*.
Stay out of the kitchen. Men don't cook—
they eat. Eat anything you want, except:
deviled eggs
Blow Pops
croissants (Bagels? Maybe.)
cucumber sandwiches
petit fours
Don't watch *Bewitched* or *I Dream of Jeannie*.
Don't stare at *The Six-Million Dollar Man*.
I've seen you . . .
Never dance alone in your room:
Donna Summer, Barry Manilow, the Captain
and Tennille, Bette Midler, and all musicals—
forbidden.
Posters of kittens, *Star Wars*, or the Eiffel Tower—
forbidden.
Those fancy books on architecture and art—
I threw them in the trash.
You can't wear cologne or puka shells
and I better not catch you in clogs.
If I see you in a ponytail—I'll cut it off.
What? No, you can't pierce your ear,
left or right side—
I don't care—
you will not look like a goddamn queer,
I've seen you . . .
even if you are one. *[2012]*

THINKING ABOUT THE TEXT

1. Blanco's grandmother has a fairly extensive forbidden list. Which ones surprised you, and why? Are some of these dated? Is the "gayness" of other items on the list unclear?
2. The grandmother seems to have fairly old-fashioned notions about what boys and girls should and should not do. How would you describe her version of male and female behavior?
3. How might the last three lines be seen as a compromise on the grandmother's part? Although egregious stereotyping is a serious topic, Blanco's poem is also meant to be humorous. Wherein does the humor lie? Is it effective?

4. The grandmother's assumption, not uncommon among some uneducated people, is that gay men like the same things that stereotypical girls do. How does this poem support that view? Where do you think such a misconception comes from? Does our culture encourage such views?
5. Perhaps Blanco is somewhat hyperbolic about his grandmother's forbidden list. Which items seem unlikely to have actually caught the grandmother's attention? Why might Blanco have included them?

MAKING COMPARISONS

1. Compare the idea of "being oneself" in these four poems.
2. In her poem, Pratt uses the phrase "we know we've done nothing wrong." How would Essex Hemphill and Richard Blanco have responded to this idea?
3. What are the major ideas you see in these four poems?

WRITING ABOUT ISSUES

1. Choose Hemphill's, Lorde's, or Pratt's poem, and write an essay arguing for or against a position held by someone in the poem. The person can be the speaker. Support your argument with specific details and examples.
2. Choose two of the poems in this cluster, and write an essay comparing how commitments figure in them. Be sure to cite specific words from each poem.
3. In the next week, observe and jot down things on your campus that you think might disturb a gay or lesbian student. (If you are a gay or lesbian student, you may have already thought about such matters.) Then write an essay addressing the issue of whether your campus is inviting to gay and lesbian students. In arguing for your position on this issue, refer to some of the observations you made. If you wish, refer as well to one or more of the poems in this cluster.
4. Even after the Supreme Court ruled in June 2015 that same-sex marriage is a constitutional right that invalidates all existing state bans, a number of states have passed "religious freedom" bills allowing businesses, religious institutions, and state government employees the right to refuse service to LGBT people. Investigate the issues in this debate and write an essay in which you put forward your own position.

Exorcising the Dead: Critical Commentaries on a Poem

SYLVIA PLATH, "Daddy"

CRITICAL COMMENTARIES:
LYNDA K. BUNDTZEN, From *Plath's Incarnations*
STEVEN GOULD AXELROD, From *Sylvia Plath: The Wound and the Cure of Words*

TIM KENDALL, From *Sylvia Plath: A Critical Study*

As contradictory as it might seem, we sometimes get angry when someone close to us dies. Psychologists tell us that anger is a healthy emotion in the mourning process, following sorrow and preceding acceptance: it is painful to miss loved ones, and we resent it. We might even direct the anger at them, feeling as if they are responsible for depriving us of their love. Sometimes, however, this anger lingers on long after the normal grieving process is over. Perhaps the attachment was abnormally strong, or perhaps the survivor's own life is too unstable to allow him or her to reach the final acceptance stage.

In the following poem, Sylvia Plath writes about her dead father as if he were a terrible person, even though as a young girl she seems to have adored him. Perhaps she is trying to expel his memory so she can find peace; perhaps she is using the poem as an occasion to express a deeper meaning about authority or influence from the past. Regardless, the poem is a powerful, strange, and passionate work of art. Following the poem, we include four critical essays that focus on autobiographical questions while also extending the critical discussion.

Each of the three critics presented here constructs arguments about "Daddy" after an obviously careful reading of Plath's poem. Each makes focused assertions that are supported with detailed references to tone, diction, syntax, rhyme, meter, metaphor, alliteration, symbol, and theme—all the elements discussed in Writing about Poems (p. 151). Note how scrupulously all three cite words, lines, and passages to create an informed, judicious, and disciplined persona and hence a convincing argument.

BEFORE YOU READ

Does it make sense to you that we might get angry at those who die because they have somehow deserted us? Do you think we have to "work out" the tensions between us and our parents before we can move into adulthood? Might it be healthy to exaggerate the difficulties of our childhood in poems and stories?

SYLVIA PLATH

Daddy

Born to middle-class parents in suburban New York, Sylvia Plath (1932–1963) became known as an intensely emotional "confessional" poet whose work is primarily autobiographical. Her father, a professor of biology and German, died when she was eight, the year her first poem was published. She graduated with honors from Smith College in 1950, after an internship at Mademoiselle *and a suicide attempt in her junior year, experiences described in her novel* The Bell Jar *(1963). She won a Fulbright Scholarship to study at Cambridge University, in England, where she met and married poet Ted Hughes. The couple had two children; the marriage ended the year before her suicide in 1963. "Daddy" is from* Ariel, *published posthumously in 1965.*

You do not do, you do not do
Any more, black shoe
In which I have lived like a foot
For thirty years, poor and white,
Barely daring to breathe or Achoo.

Daddy, I have had to kill you.
You died before I had time—
Marble-heavy, a bag full of God,
Ghastly statue with one gray toe
Big as a Frisco seal

And a head in the freakish Atlantic
Where it pours bean green over blue
In the waters off beautiful Nauset.° *Cape Cod inlet*
I used to pray to recover you.
Ach, du.° *Oh, you*

In the German tongue, in the Polish Town°
Scraped flat by the roller
Of wars, wars, wars.
But the name of the town is common.
My Polack friend

Says there are a dozen or two.
So I never could tell where you
Put your foot, your root,
I never could talk to you.
The tongue stuck in my jaw.

It stuck in a barb wire snare.
Ich, ich, ich, ich,° *I, I, I, I*
I could hardly speak.
I thought every German was you.
And the language obscene

An engine, an engine
Chuffing me off like a Jew.
A Jew to Dachau, Auschwitz, Belsen.°
I began to talk like a Jew.
I think I may well be a Jew.

The snows of the Tyrol, the clear beer of Vienna
Are not very pure or true.
With my gypsy-ancestress and my weird luck

16 Polish Town: Plath's father was born in Granbow, Poland. **33 Dachau . . . Belsen:** Nazi death camps in World War II.

And my Taroc° pack and my Taroc pack
I may be a bit of a Jew.

I have always been scared of *you*,
With your Luftwaffe,° your gobbledygoo.
And your neat mustache
And your Aryan eye, bright blue.
Panzer-man, panzer-man,° O You—

Not God but a swastika
So black no sky could squeak through.
Every woman adores a Fascist,
The boot in the face, the brute
Brute heart of a brute like you.

You stand at the blackboard, daddy,
In the picture I have of you,
A cleft in your chin instead of your foot
But no less a devil for that, no not
Any less the black man who

Bit my pretty red heart in two.
I was ten when they buried you.
At twenty I tried to die
And get back, back, back to you.
I thought even the bones would do

But they pulled me out of the sack,
And they stuck me together with glue.
And then I knew what to do.
I made a model of you,
A man in black with a Meinkampf° look

And a love of the rack and the screw.
And I said I do, I do.
So daddy, I'm finally through.
The black telephone's off at the root,
The voices just can't worm through.

If I've killed one man, I've killed two—
The vampire who said he was you
And drank my blood for a year,
Seven years, if you want to know.
Daddy, you can lie back now.

There's a stake in your fat black heart
And the villagers never liked you.

39 Taroc: Tarot cards used to tell fortunes. The practice may have originated among the early Jewish Cabalists and was then widely adopted by European Gypsies during the Middle Ages. **42 Luftwaffe:** World War II German air force. **45 panzer-man:** A member of the German armored vehicle division. **65 Meinkampf:** Hitler's autobiography (*My Struggle*).

They are dancing and stamping on you.
They always *knew* it was you.
Daddy, daddy, you bastard, I'm through. *[1962]*

THINKING ABOUT THE TEXT

1. Can this poem be seen as a series of arguments for why Plath has to forget her father? What complaints does the speaker seem to have against her father?
2. Some psychologists claim that we all have a love-hate relationship with our parents. Do you agree? Would Plath's speaker agree?
3. How effective is it for the speaker to compare herself to a Jew in Hitler's Germany? What other similes and metaphors are used to refer to her father? Do they work, or are they too extreme? Perhaps Plath wants them to be outrageous. Why might she?
4. Plath combines childhood rhymes and words with brutal images. What effect does this have on you? Why do you think Plath does this? What odd stylistic features can you point to here?
5. Why do you think it is necessary for the speaker to be finally "through" with her father? Is it normal young adult rebelliousness? What else might it be?

LYNDA K. BUNDTZEN

From *Plath's Incarnations*

Educated at the University of Minnesota, where she earned a B.A. in 1968, and the University of Chicago, where she earned a Ph.D. in 1972, Lynda Bundtzen (b. 1947) teaches at Williams College. A Renaissance scholar with a strong interest in women's issues, she teaches and writes on subjects that range from Shakespeare to Thelma and Louise. Plath's Incarnations *was published in 1983. Her latest book is* The Other Ariel *(2001).*

In "Daddy," Plath is conscious of her complicity in creating and worshiping a father-colossus.

> You stand at the blackboard, daddy,
> In the picture I have of you,
> A cleft in your chin instead of your foot
> But no less a devil for that, no not
> Any less the black man who
>
> Bit my pretty red heart in two.
> I was ten when they buried you.
> At twenty I tried to die
> And get back, back, back to you.
> I thought even the bones would do.

The photograph is of an ordinary man, a teacher, with a cleft chin. She imaginatively transforms him into a devil who broke her heart, and she tells her audience precisely what she is doing. As Plath describes "Daddy," it is "spoken by a girl with an Electra complex. Her father died while she thought he was God. Her case is complicated by the fact that her father was also a Nazi and her mother very possibly part Jewish. In the daughter the two strains marry and paralyze each other — she has to act out the awful little allegory once over before she is free of it." The poem is a figurative drama about mourning — about the human impulse to keep a dead loved one alive emotionally. And it is about mourning gone haywire — a morbid inability to let go of the dead. The child was unready for her father's death, which is why, she says, she must kill him a second time. She resurrected Daddy and sustained his unnatural existence in her psyche as a vampire, sacrificing her own life's blood, her vitality, to a dead man. The worship of this father-god, she now realizes, is self-destructive.

There is nothing unconscious about the poem; instead it seems to force into consciousness the child's dread and love for the father, so that these feelings may be resolved. Plath skillfully evokes the child's world with her own versions of Mother Goose rhymes. Like the "old woman who lived in a shoe and had so many children she didn't know what to do," she has tried to live in the confines of the black shoe that is Daddy. Like Chicken Little, waiting for the sky to fall in, she lives under an omnipresent swastika "So black no sky could squeak through." And Daddy is a fallen giant toppled over and smothering, it seems, the entire United States. He has one grey toe (recalling Otto Plath's gangrened appendage) dangling like a Frisco seal in the Pacific and his head lies in the Atlantic.

The Mother Goose rhythms gradually build to a goose step march as the mourning process turns inward. She feels more than sorrow, now guilt, for Daddy's death and this guilt leads to feelings of inadequacy, acts of self-abasement, and finally self-murder. Nothing she can do will appease the guilt: she tries to learn his language; she tries to kill herself; she marries a man in his image. It will not do.

The self-hatred must be turned outward again into "*You* do not do" by a very self-conscious transformation of a mild-mannered professor into an active oppressor. Her emotional paralysis is acted out as a struggle between Nazi man and Jewess, and, I would argue, the Jewess wins. The poem builds toward the imaginary stake driving, the dancing and stamping and "Daddy, daddy, you bastard, I'm through." Not necessarily through with life, as many critics have read this line, but through with the paralysis, powerlessness, guilt. At last Daddy — the Nazi Daddy she frightened herself with, and not the real one, the professor — is at rest.

5 Plath's control over ambivalent feelings toward her father is probably the result of their availability for conscious artistic manipulation. She had already written several poems about her dead father when she composed "Daddy," and we also know from a conversation recorded by Steiner that she had "worked through" her emotions in therapy. "She talked freely about her father's death when she was nine and her reactions to it. 'He was an autocrat,' she recalled.

'I adored and despised him, and I probably wished many times that he were dead. When he obliged me and died, I imagined that I had killed him.' " The result in "Daddy" is a powerful and remarkably accessible allegory about her adoration and dread, which ends in emotional catharsis. *[1983]*

STEVEN GOULD AXELROD
From *Sylvia Plath: The Wound and the Cure of Words*

An expert in nineteenth- and twentieth-century American poetry, Steven Gould Axelrod (b. 1944) was educated at the University of California at Los Angeles and served as chair of the English Department at the University of California at Riverside, where he received a Distinguished Teaching Award in 1989. His publications include book-length works on modern and contemporary poets. Sylvia Plath: The Wound and the Cure of Words *was published in 1990.*

The covert protest of "The Colossus" eventually transformed itself into the overt rebellion of "Daddy." Although this poem too has traditionally been read as "personal" or "confessional," Margaret Homans has more recently suggested that it concerns a woman's dislocated relations to speech. Plath herself introduced it on the BBC as the opposite of confession, as a constructed fiction: "Here is a poem spoken by a girl with an Electra complex. Her father died while she thought he was God. Her case is complicated by the fact that her father was also a Nazi and her mother very possibly part Jewish. In the daughter the two strains marry and paralyze each other—she has to act out the awful little allegory once over before she is free of it." We might interpret this preface as an accurate retelling of the poem; or we might regard it as a case of an author's estrangement from her text, on the order of Coleridge's preface to "Kubla Khan" in which he claims to be unable to finish the poem, having forgotten what it was about. However we interpret Plath's preface, we must agree that "Daddy" is dramatic and allegorical, since its details depart freely from the facts of her biography. In this poem she again figures her unresolved conflicts with paternal authority as a textual issue. Significantly, her father was a published writer, and his successor, her husband, was also a writer. Her preface asserts that the poem concerns a young woman's paralyzing self-division, which she can defeat only through allegorical representation. Recalling that paralysis was one of Plath's main tropes for literary incapacity, we begin to see that the poem evokes the female poet's anxiety of authorship and specifically Plath's strategy of delivering herself from that anxiety by making it the topic of her discourse. Viewed from this perspective, "Daddy" enacts the woman poet's struggle with "daddy-poetry." It represents her effort to eject the "buried male muse" from her invention process and the "jealous gods" from her audience.

Plath wrote "Daddy" several months after Hughes left her, on the day she learned that he had agreed to a divorce. George Brown and Tirril Harris have shown that early loss makes one especially vulnerable to subsequent loss, and Plath seems to have defended against depression by almost literally throwing herself into her poetry. She followed "Daddy" with a host of poems that she considered her greatest achievement to date: "Medusa," "The Jailer," "Lady Lazarus," "Ariel," the bee sequence, and others. The letters she wrote to her mother and brother on the day of "Daddy," and then again four days later, brim with a sense of artistic self-discovery: "Writing like mad. . . . Terrific stuff, as if domesticity had choked me." Composing at the "still blue, almost eternal hour before the baby's cry, before the glassy music of the milkman, settling his bottles," she experienced an enormous surge in creative energy. Yet she also expressed feelings of misery: "The half year ahead seems like a lifetime, and the half behind an endless hell." She was again contemplating things German: a trip to the Austrian Alps, a renewed effort to learn the language. If "German" was Randall Jarrell's "favorite country," it was not hers, yet it returned to her discourse like clockwork at times of psychic distress. Clearly Plath was attempting to find and to evoke in her art what she could not find or communicate in her life. She wished to compensate for her fragmenting social existence by investing herself in her texts: "Hope, when free, to write myself out of this hole." Desperately eager to sacrifice her "flesh," which was "wasted," to her "mind and spirit," which were "fine," she wrote "Daddy" to demonstrate the existence of her voice, which had been silent or subservient for so long. She wrote it to prove her "genius."

Plath projected her struggle for textual identity onto the figure of a partly Jewish young woman who learns to express her anger at the patriarch and at his language of male mastery, which is as foreign to her as German, as "obscene" as murder, and as meaningless as "gobbledygoo." The patriarch's death "off beautiful Nauset" recalls Plath's journal entry in which she associated the "green seaweeded water" at "Nauset Light" with "the deadness of a being . . . who no longer creates." Daddy's deadness—suggesting Plath's unwillingness to let her father, her education, her library, or her husband inhibit her any longer—inspires the poem's speaker to her moment of illumination. At a basic level, "Daddy" concerns its own violent, transgressive birth as a text, its origin in a culture that regards it as illegitimate—a judgment the speaker hurls back on the patriarch himself when she labels *him* a bastard. Plath's unaccommodating worldview, which was validated by much in her childhood and adult experience, led her to understand literary tradition not as an expanding universe of beneficial influence . . . but as a closed universe in which every addition required a corresponding subtraction—a Spencerian agon in which only the fittest survived. If Plath's speaker was to be born as a poet, a patriarch must die.

As in "The Colossus," the father here appears as a force or an object rather than as a person. Initially he takes the form of an immense "black shoe," capable of stamping on his victim. Immediately thereafter he becomes a marble "statue," cousin to the monolith of the earlier poem. He then transforms into Nazi Germany, the archetypal totalitarian state. When the protagonist mentions Daddy's "boot in the face," she may be alluding to Orwell's comment in *1984*, "If you want a picture of the future, imagine a boot stomping on a human face—forever." Eventually the father declines in stature from God to a devil to a dying vampire. Perhaps he shrinks under the force of his victim's denunciation, which de-creates him as a power as it creates him as figure. But whatever his size, he never assumes human dimensions, aspirations, and relations—except when posing as a teacher in a photograph. Like the colossus, he remains figurative and symbolic, not individual.

Nevertheless, the male figure of "Daddy" does differ significantly from that 5
of "The Colossus." In the earlier poem, which emphasizes his lips, mouth, throat, tongue, and voice, the colossus allegorically represents the power of speech, however fragmented and resistant to the protagonist's ministrations. In the later poem Daddy remains silent, apart from the gobbledygoo attributed to him once. He uses his mouth primarily for biting and for drinking blood. The poem emphasizes his feet and, implicitly, his phallus. He is a "black shoe," a statue with "one gray toe," a "boot." The speaker, estranged from him by fear, could never tell where he put his "foot," his "root." Furthermore, she is herself silenced by his shoe: "I never could talk to you." Daddy is no "male muse," not even one in ruins, but frankly a male censor. His boot in the face of "every woman" is presumably lodged in her mouth. He stands for all the elements in the literary situation and in the female ephebe's internalization of it, that prevent her from producing any words at all, even copied or subservient ones. Appropriately, Daddy can be killed only by being stamped on: he lives and dies by force, not language. If "The Colossus" tells a tale of the patriarch's speech, his grunts and brays, "Daddy" tells a tale of the daughter's effort to speak.

Thus we are led to another important difference between the two poems. The "I" of "The Colossus" acquires her identity only through serving her "father," whereas the "I" of "Daddy" actuates her gift only through opposition to him. The latter poem precisely inscribes the plot of Plath's dream novel of 1958: "a girl's search for her dead father—for an outside authority which must be developed, instead, from the inside." As the child of a Nazi, the girl could "hardly speak," but as a Jew she begins "to talk" and to acquire an identity. In Plath's allegory, the outsider Jew corresponds to "the rebel, the artist, the odd," and particularly to the woman artist. Otto Rank's *Beyond Psychology*, which had a lasting influence on her, explicitly compares women to Jews, since "woman ... has suffered from the very beginning a fate similar to that of the Jew, namely, suppression, slavery, confinement, and subsequent persecution." Rank, whose discourse I would consider tainted by anti-Semitism, argues that Jews speak a language of pessimistic "self-hatred" that differs essentially from the language of the majority cultures in which they find themselves. He analogously, though more sympathetically, argues that woman speaks in a language different from man's, and that as a result of man's denial of woman's world, "woman's 'native tongue' has hitherto been unknown or at least unheard." Although Rank's essentializing of woman's "nature" lapses into the sexist clichés of his time ("intuitive," "irrational"), his idea of linguistic difference based on gender and his analogy between Jewish and female speech seem to have embedded themselves in the substructure of "Daddy" (and in many of Plath's other texts as well). For Plath, as later for Adrienne Rich, the Holocaust and the patriarchy's silencing of women were linked outcomes of the masculinist interpretation of the world. Political insurrection and female self-assertion also interlaced symbolically. In "Daddy," Plath's speaker finds her voice and motive by identifying herself as antithetical to her Fascist father. Rather than getting the colossus "glued" and properly jointed, she wishes to stick herself "together with glue," an act that seems to require her father's dismemberment. Previously devoted to the patriarch—both in "The Colossus" and in memories evoked in "Daddy" of trying to "get back" to him—she now seeks only to escape from him and to see him destroyed.

Plath has unleashed the anger, normal in mourning as well as in revolt, that she suppressed in the earlier poem. But she has done so at a cost. Let us consider her childlike speaking voice. The language of "Daddy," beginning with its title, is often regressive. The "I" articulates herself by moving backward in time, using the language of nursery rhymes and fairy tales (the little old woman who lived in a shoe, the black man of the forest). Such language accords with a child's conception of the world, not an adult's. Plath's assault on the language of "daddy-poetry" has turned inward, on the language of her own poem, which teeters precariously on the edge of a preverbal abyss—represented by the eerie, keening "oo" sound with which a majority of the verses end. And then let us consider the play on "through" at the poem's conclusion. Although that last line allows for multiple readings, one interpretation is that the "I" has unconsciously carried out her father's wish: her discourse, by transforming itself into cathartic oversimplifications, has undone itself.

Yet the poem does contain its verbal violence by means more productive than silence. In a letter to her brother, Plath referred to "Daddy" as "gruesome," while on almost the same day she described it to A. Alvarez as a piece of "light verse." She later read it on the BBC in a highly ironic tone of voice. The poem's unique spell derives from its rhetorical complexity: its variegated and perhaps bizarre fusion of the horrendous and the comic. . . . [I]t both shares and remains detached from the fixation of its protagonist. The protagonist herself seems detached from her own fixation. She is "split in the most complex fashion," as Plath wrote of Ivan Karamazov in her Smith College honors thesis. Plath's speaker uses potentially self-mocking melodramatic terms to describe both her opponent ("so black no sky could squeak through") and herself ("poor and white"). While this aboriginal speaker quite literally expresses black-and-white thinking, her civilized double possesses a sensibility sophisticated enough to subject such thinking to irony. Thus the poem expresses feelings that it simultaneously parodies—it may be parodying the very idea of feeling. The tension between erudition and simplicity in the speaker's voice appears in her pairings that juxtapose adult with childlike diction: "breathe or Achoo," "your Luftwaffe, your gobbledygoo." She can expound such adult topics as Taroc packs, Viennese beer, and Tyrolean snowfall; can specify death camps by name; and can employ an adult vocabulary of "recover," "ancestress," "Aryan," "*Meinkampf*," "obscene," and "bastard." Yet she also has recourse to a more primitive lexicon that includes "chuffing," "your fat black heart," and "my pretty red heart." She proves herself capable of careful intellectual discriminations ("so I never could tell"), conventionalized description ("beautiful Nauset"), and moral analogy ("if I've killed one man, I've killed two"), while also exhibiting regressive fantasies (vampires), repetitions ("wars,

wars, wars"), and inarticulateness ("panzer-man, panzer-man, O You—"). She oscillates between calm reflection ("You stand at the blackboard, daddy, / In the picture I have of you") and mad incoherence ("Ich, ich, ich, ich"). Her sophisticated language puts her wild language in an ironic perspective, removing the discourse from the control of the archaic self who understands experience only in extreme terms.

The ironies in "Daddy" proliferate in unexpected ways, however. When the speaker proclaims categorically that "every woman adores a Fascist," she is subjecting her victimization to irony by suggesting that sufferers choose, or at least accommodate themselves to, their suffering. But she is also subjecting her authority to irony, since her claim about "every woman" is transparently false. It simply parodies patriarchal commonplaces, such as those advanced . . . concerning "feminine masochism." The adult, sophisticated self seems to be speaking here: Who else would have the confidence to make a sociological generalization? Yet the content of the assertion, if taken straightforwardly, returns us to the regressive self who is dominated by extravagant emotions she cannot begin to understand. Plath's mother wished that Plath would write about "decent, courageous people," and she herself heard an inner voice demanding that she be a perfect "paragon" in her language and feeling. But in the speaker of "Daddy," she inscribed the opposite of such a paragon: a divided self whose veneer of civilization is breached and infected by unhealthy instincts.

10 Plath's irony cuts both ways. At the same time that the speaker's sophisticated voice undercuts her childish voice, reducing its melodrama to comedy, the childish or maddened voice undercuts the pretensions of the sophisticated voice, revealing the extremity of suffering masked by its ironies. While demonstrating the inadequacy of thinking and feeling in opposites, the poem implies that such a mode can locate truths denied more complex cognitive and affective systems. The very moderation of the normal adult intelligence, its tolerance of ambiguity, its defenses against the primal energies of the id, results in falsification. Reflecting Schiller's idea that the creative artist experiences a "momentary and passing madness" (quoted by Freud in a passage of *The Interpretation of Dreams* that Plath underscored), "Daddy" gives voice to that madness. Yet the poem's sophisticated awareness, its comic vision, probably wins out in the end, since the poem concludes by curtailing the power of its extreme discourse. . . . Furthermore, Plath distanced herself from the poem's aboriginal voice by introducing her text as "a poem spoken by a girl with an Electra complex"—that is, as a study of the *girl's* pathology rather than her father's—and as an allegory that will "free" her from that pathology. She also distanced herself by reading the poem in a tone that emphasized its irony. And finally, she distanced herself by laying the poem's wild voice permanently to rest after October. The aboriginal vision was indeed purged. "Daddy" represents not Dickinson's madness that is divinest sense, but rather an entry into a style of discourse and a mastery of it. The poem realizes the trope of suffering by means of an inherent irony that both questions and validates the trope in the same gestures, and that finally allows the speaker to conclude the discourse and to remove herself from the trope with a sense of completion rather than wrenching, since the irony was present from the very beginning.

Plath's poetic revolt in "Daddy" liberated her pent-up creativity, but the momentary success sustained her little more than self-sacrifice had done. "Daddy" became another stage in her development, an unrepeatable experiment, a vocal opening that closed itself at once. The poem is not only an elegy for the power of "daddy-poetry" but for the powers of speech Plath discovered in composing it.

When we consider "Daddy" generically, a further range of implications presents itself. Although we could profitably consider the poem as the dramatic monologue Plath called it in her BBC broadcast, let us regard it instead as the kind of poem most readers have taken it to be: a domestic poem. I have chosen this term, rather than M. L. Rosenthal's better-known "confessional poem" or the more neutral "autobiographical poem," because "confessional poem" implies a confession rather than a making (though Steven Hoffman and Lawrence Kramer have recently indicated the mode's conventions) and because "autobiographical poem" is too general for our purpose. I shall define the domestic poem as one that represents and comments on a protagonist's relationship to one or more family members, usually a parent, child, or spouse. To focus our discussion even further, I shall emphasize poetry that specifically concerns a father. *[1990]*

TIM KENDALL

From *Sylvia Plath: A Critical Study*

Tim Kendall edits Thumbscrew *and is the author of* Paul Muldoon *(1996). He received an Eric Gregory Award for his poetry in 1997 and appears in the* Oxford Poets 2000 *anthology. He was the Thomas Chatterton British Academy Lecturer for 2001 at the University of Bristol and is currently a professor of English Literature at the University of Exeter. In 2005, Kendall was awarded the lucrative Philip Leverhulme Prize. This selection is from a book he published in 2001.*

Plath's journals . . . indicate that as late as December 1958, the poet was seriously considering a Ph.D. in psychology: "Awesome to confront a program of study which is so monumental: all human experience."[1] The previous day Plath had discovered in Freud's *Mourning and Melancholia* "an almost exact description of my feelings and reasons for suicide."[2] She felt creatively vindicated when she found parallels between her own life and writings and those of Freud and Jung: "All this relates in a most meaningful way my instinctive images with perfectly valid psychological analysis. However, I am the victim, rather than the analyst."[3] In these examples, experience precedes the psychoanalytical explanation; Freud and Jung confirm what Plath already knows. Despite her emphasis on victimhood, such passages show how she transforms herself into her own case history, becoming simultaneously victim and analyst. The same dual role is apparent in "Daddy," which Plath introduces for BBC radio in terms of Freudian allegory:

> Here is a poem spoken by a girl with an Electra complex. Her father died while she thought he was God. Her case is complicated by the fact that her

father was also a Nazi and her mother very possibly part Jewish. In the daughter the two strains marry and paralyze each other—she has to act out the awful little allegory once over before she is free of it.

"Daddy," built on poetic repetition, is therefore a poem about a compulsion to repeat, and its psychology is characterized according to Freudian principles. Repetition necessitates performance—the speaker must "*act out* the awful little allegory once over" in order to escape it. Whether she does succeed in escaping depends on the poem's ambivalent last line: "Daddy, daddy, you bastard, I'm through." "I'm through" can mean (especially to an American ear) "I've had enough of you," but it also means "I've got away from you, I'm free of you," or "I'm done for, I'm beaten," or even "I've finished what I have to say." The speaker's ability to free herself from the urge to repeat remains in the balance.

These dilemmas and uncertainties can be traced back, as Plath suggests, to Freud's accounts of compulsive behavior. "Daddy" adopts a Freudian understanding of infantile sexuality (the Electra complex), a Freudian belief in transference (the vampire-husband "said he was you," and the father also shifts identities), and a Freudian attitude towards repetitive behavior. In a passage from *Beyond the Pleasure Principle* which might conveniently serve to diagnose the speaker of "Daddy," Freud argues that,

> The patient cannot remember the whole of what is repressed in him, and what he cannot remember may be precisely the essential part of it. Thus he acquires no sense of the conviction of the correctness of the construction that has been communicated to him. He is obliged to *repeat* the repressed material as a contemporary experience instead of, as the physician would prefer to see, *remembering* it as something belonging to the past. These reproductions, which emerge with such unwished-for exactitude, always have as their subject some portion of infantile sexual life—of the Oedipus complex, that is, and its derivatives; and they are invariably acted out in the sphere of the transference, of the patient's relation to the physician.[4]

This illuminates Plath's attempts to persuade the dead father to communicate. The refusal of the father-figure, in his various transferred roles of colossus, Nazi, teacher, and vampire, to become "something belonging to the past" is evident in the speaker's need to kill him repeatedly. He must be imaginatively disinterred in order to be killed again, and even as one of the undead, he must be destroyed with a stake in his heart. This repetitive pattern of disappearance and return represents Plath's version of the *fort-da* game as famously described in *Beyond the Pleasure Principle,* where the child's repeated and "long-drawn-out 'o-o-o-o' " is only a slight vowel modulation away from the "oo" repetitions of "Daddy." The father-figure is a "contemporary experience," not a memory; and, as Freud explains, the reason for his continuing presence lies in the speaker's "infantile sexual life." The father's early death ensures that she cannot progress, and her sense of selfhood is stutteringly confined within a compulsion to repeat:

> I never could talk to you.
> The tongue stuck in my jaw.

> It stuck in a barb wire snare.
> Ich, ich, ich, ich,
> I could hardly speak.

Repetition occurs when Plath's speaker gets stuck in the barb wire snare of communication with her father. She is unable to move beyond the self. This proposes a more fundamental understanding of repetitive words and phrases than those suggested by Blessing or Shapiro. "Daddy" implies that each local repetition, whatever its microcosmic effects, symptomizes a larger behavioral pattern of repetition compulsion. The poem's title, the "oo" rhymes, and the nursery-rhyme rhythms all reinforce this suggestion of a mind struggling to free itself from the need to repeat infantile trauma. Such infantilism, exhibited by an adult persona, contributes to the poem's transgressive humor: Plath read "Daddy" aloud to a friend, reports Anne Stevenson, "in a mocking, comical voice that made both women fall about with laughter."[5]

Psychoanalyzing the speaker of "Daddy" in the Freudian terms proposed by Plath herself is a valuable exercise which carries important implications for *Ariel*'s use of repetition, but it still does not settle the nature of the poet's complex relationship to the "girl with an Electra complex." Plath's introduction for radio seems to reverse the pattern in her journals: now Freud becomes a source as much as an explanation. Her introduction also reverses the reader's experience of the poem. "Daddy" conveys a power and an intimacy which challenge any hygienic separation of poet and poetic voice. With such contradictory evidence, the gulf between poet and persona, cold-blooded technique and blood-hot emotion, analyst and victim, seems unbridgeable. If these divisions can be successfully reconciled, it is through Plath's emphasis on performance and repetition. Freud's account of repetition compulsion shares with Plath's description of "Daddy" a crucial verb: just as Plath's persona must "act out the awful little allegory," so Freud notes that the Oedipus complex and its derivatives are "invariably acted out in the sphere of the transference." Repetition guarantees performance, and performance requires an audience. Freud notes, as if glossing "Daddy," that "the artistic play and artistic imitation carried out by adults, which, unlike children's, are aimed at an audience, do not spare the spectators (for instance, in tragedy) the most painful experiences and can yet be felt by them as highly enjoyable." Plath categorized "Daddy" as "light verse,"[6] a genre which W. H. Auden considered to be "written for performance."[7] "Daddy" may be written for performance, but it pushes the "painful experiences" and the entertainment value to extremes which many readers find intolerable. Freud's Aristotelian concern—why is tragedy pleasurable?—also seems a valid question to ask of Plath's poem: "Daddy" derives its aesthetic pleasures from incest, patricide, suicide, and the Nazi extermination camps.

These taboo-breaking juxtapositions of personal and private realms help explain the poem's notoriety. However, controversy over "Daddy" always returns eventually to Plath's relationship with her persona. Seamus Heaney's principled objection, for example, discerns no difference at all:

> A poem like "Daddy," however brilliant a *tour de force* it can be acknowledged to be, and however its violence and vindictiveness can be understood or

> excused in light of the poet's parental and marital relations, remains, nevertheless, so entangled in biographical circumstances and rampages so permissively in the history of other people's sorrows that it simply withdraws its rights to our sympathy.[8]

Heaney's pointed phrase "rampages so permissively" might be disputed as an unfair rhetorical flourish, especially in the context of Plath's hard-earned Emersonian desire to assimilate and her wider theological explorations. But Heaney's most revealing word is his last: "sympathy." Heaney refers to one aspect of Aristotelian catharsis—pity for the suffering of others—which he claims that "Daddy" fails to earn. It is not surprising that his critical decorum should come into conflict with a poem which is so consciously and manifestly indecorous. Heaney reads "Daddy" purely as the protest of the poet-victim, who behaves vindictively because of her difficult parental and marital relations. This fails to credit Plath with the self-awareness to be acting deliberately—to be performing. In "Daddy" Plath seeks no one's "sympathy"; she has once more become victim and analyst, the girl with the Electra complex and the physician who diagnoses her condition. Plath wonders in her journal whether "our desire to investigate psychology [is] a desire to get Beuscher's [her psychiatrist's] power and handle it ourselves."[9] "Daddy," as her introduction makes clear, represents a poetic handling of that power. Freud states that the patient must acquire "some degree of aloofness."[10] "Daddy" is the work of a poet so aloof as to render allegorical, act out, and psychoanalyze, her own mental history. *[2001]*

Notes

1. Sylvia Plath, *The Journals of Sylvia Plath, 1950–1962*, ed. Karen V. Kukil (London: Faber & Faber, 2000), p. 452.
2. Ibid., p. 447.
3. Ibid., p. 514.
4. S. Freud, *Beyond the Pleasure Principle*, tr. and ed. J. Strachey (Hogarth, 1961), p. 12.
5. A. Stevenson, *Bitter Fame: A Life of Sylvia Plath* (Viking, 1989), p. 277.
6. A. Alvarez, "Sylvia Plath," in C. Newman (ed.), *The Art of Sylvia Plath* (Indiana UP, 1970), p. 66.
7. W. H. Auden (ed.), *The Oxford Book of Light Verse* (OUP, 1938), p. ix.
8. S. Heaney, "The Indefatigable Hoof-taps: Sylvia Plath," *The Government of the Tongue* (Faber, 1988), p. 165.
9. *Journals*, p. 449.
10. *Beyond the Pleasure Principle*, p. 13.

MAKING COMPARISONS

1. "Daddy" seems to be a protest, but some critics see it as more than that. Which of the three commentaries makes the best case that it is more than a revolt against the speaker's father?
2. Which critic seems to answer most of the perplexing questions of this poem—for example, the father as Nazi, the father as vampire, the childlike rhythms, the speaker's vengefulness, her viciousness?

3. Do these critics make any similar points? How might you describe them? What is their most striking difference?

WRITING ABOUT ISSUES

1. Choose one of the critical commentaries in this cluster and argue that the textual evidence supporting its assertions is, or is not, adequate.
2. Imagine you are Sylvia Plath. After reading these three essays, write a letter to a literary journal either attacking or praising these critics.
3. Write an essay arguing that your own reading of "Daddy" makes more sense than those of Bundtzen, Axelrod, or Kendall. Assume that the audience for the criticism is your class.
4. There are dozens of critical commentaries on Plath's "Daddy." Some were written soon after the poem's publication; others are quite recent. Locate an early piece of criticism, and compare it to one published in the past few years. Do these critics make similar or different points? Is one more concerned with the text, with gender issues, with cultural concerns, or with what other critics say? Write a brief comparison of the two, explaining your evidence.

Mothers and Daughters: Stories

TILLIE OLSEN, "I Stand Here Ironing"

AMY TAN, "Two Kinds"

ALICE WALKER, "Everyday Use"

We all know stories of parents who want to mold their children, stories of mothers and fathers who push their reluctant children to be fashion models or beauty queens or Little League stars. Some studies of adults playing musical instruments in orchestras say the biggest factor in their success was the commitment of their parents. But we also hear about tennis prodigies who burn out at sixteen because of parental pressure. Mothers and daughters have always struggled with each other over life goals and identity. How much guidance is enough? How much is too much? What is a reasonable balance between preparing a child for life's challenges and shaping a child to act out the mother's fantasy or her internal vision of what the good life is? And no matter where parents fall on this continuum, are there childhood events so powerful that we cannot get beyond them? The following three stories chart the difficulties mothers and daughters have with each other and with the social and cultural forces that influence our destiny.

BEFORE YOU READ

Are your parents responsible for your successes? Your failures? Do you wish that your parents had pushed you to succeed more insistently? Are you annoyed that your parents set unreasonable standards for you?

TILLIE OLSEN

I Stand Here Ironing

Born in Omaha, Nebraska, to Russian immigrants of Jewish descent and socialist views, Tillie Olsen (1912–2007) was an activist in social and political causes all of her life, often choosing family, work, union, feminist, or other political causes over writing. Although her publishing record is short, its quality is greatly admired. In addition to critically respected short stories, Olsen wrote a novel, Yonnondio *(1974), which paints a vivid picture of a coal-mining family during the Depression. Her essay collection,* Silences *(1978), stimulated debate about class and gender as factors in the creation of literature and led both directly and indirectly to the revived interest in works by women writers. The mother of four daughters, Olsen often wrote about generational relationships within families. "I Stand Here Ironing" is from her 1961 collection of stories,* Tell Me a Riddle.

I stand here ironing, and what you asked me moves tormented back and forth with the iron.

"I wish you would manage the time to come in and talk with me about your daughter. I'm sure you can help me understand her. She's a youngster who needs help and whom I'm deeply interested in helping."

"Who needs help." . . . Even if I came, what good would it do? You think because I am her mother I have a key, or that in some way you could use me as a key? She has lived for nineteen years. There is all that life that has happened outside of me, beyond me.

And when is there time to remember, to sift, to weigh, to estimate, to total? I will start and there will be an interruption and I will have to gather it all together again. Or I will become engulfed with all I did or did not do, with what should have been and what cannot be helped.

She was a beautiful baby. The first and only one of our five that was beautiful at birth. You do not guess how new and uneasy her tenancy in her now-loveliness. You did not know her all those years she was thought homely, or see her poring over her baby pictures, making me tell her over and over how beautiful she had been—and would be, I would tell her—and was now, to the seeing eye. But the seeing eyes were few or nonexistent. Including mine. 5

I nursed her. They feel that's important nowadays. I nursed all the children, but with her, with all the fierce rigidity of first motherhood, I did like the books then said. Though her cries battered me to trembling and my breasts ached with swollenness, I waited till the clock decreed.

Why do I put that first? I do not even know if it matters, or if it explains anything.

She was a beautiful baby. She blew shining bubbles of sound. She loved motion, loved light, loved color and music and textures. She would lie on the floor in her blue overalls patting the surface so hard in ecstasy her hands and feet would blur. She was a miracle to me, but when she was eight months old I had to leave her daytimes with the woman downstairs to whom she was no miracle at all, for I worked or looked for work and for Emily's father, who "could no longer endure" (he wrote in his good-bye note) "sharing want with us."

I was nineteen. It was the pre-relief, pre-WPA world of the depression. I would start running as soon as I got off the streetcar, running up the stairs, the place smelling sour, and awake or asleep to startle awake, when she saw me she would break into a clogged weeping that could not be comforted, a weeping I can hear yet.

After a while I found a job hashing at night so I could be with her days, and it was better. But it came to where I had to bring her to his family and leave her. 10

It took a long time to raise the money for her fare back. Then she got chicken pox and I had to wait longer. When she finally came, I hardly knew her, walking quick and nervous like her father, looking like her father, thin, and dressed in a shoddy red that yellowed her skin and glared at the pockmarks. All the baby loveliness gone.

She was two. Old enough for nursery school they said, and I did not know then what I know now—the fatigue of the long day, and the lacerations of group life in the kinds of nurseries that are only parking places for children.

Except that it would have made no difference if I had known. It was the only place there was. It was the only way we could be together, the only way I could hold a job.

And even without knowing, I knew. I knew the teacher that was evil because all these years it has curdled into my memory, the little boy hunched in the corner, her rasp, "why aren't you outside, because Alvin hits you? that's no reason, go out, scaredy." I knew Emily hated it even if she did not clutch and implore "don't go Mommy" like the other children, mornings.

She always had a reason why we should stay home. Momma, you look 15
sick. Momma, I feel sick. Momma, the teachers aren't there today, they're sick. Momma, we can't go, there was a fire there last night. Momma, it's a holiday today, no school, they told me.

But never a direct protest, never rebellion. I think of our others in their three-, four-year-oldness—the explosions, the tempers, the denunciations, the demands—and I feel suddenly ill. I put the iron down. What in me demanded that goodness in her? And what was the cost, the cost to her of such goodness?

The old man living in the back once said in his gentle way: "You should smile at Emily more when you look at her." What *was* in my face when I looked at her? I loved her. There were all the acts of love.

It was only with the others I remembered what he said, and it was the face of joy, and not of care or tightness or worry I turned to them—too late for Emily. She does not smile easily, let alone almost always as her brothers and sisters do. Her face is closed and sombre, but when she wants, how fluid. You must have seen it in her pantomimes, you spoke of her rare gift for comedy on the stage that rouses laughter out of the audience so dear they applaud and applaud and do not want to let her go.

Where does it come from, that comedy? There was none of it in her when she came back to me that second time, after I had to send her away again. She had a new daddy now to learn to love, and I think perhaps it was a better time.

Except when we left her alone nights, telling ourselves she was old enough. 20

"Can't you go some other time, Mommy, like tomorrow?" she would ask. "Will it be just a little while you'll be gone? Do you promise?"

The time we came back, the front door open, the clock on the floor in the hall. She rigid awake. "It wasn't just a little while. I didn't cry. Three times I called you, just three times, and then I ran downstairs to open the door so you could come faster. The clock talked loud. I threw it away, it scared me what it talked."

She said the clock talked loud again that night I went to the hospital to have Susan. She was delirious with the fever that comes before red measles, but she was fully conscious all the week I was gone and the week after we were home when she could not come near the new baby or me.

She did not get well. She stayed skeleton thin, not wanting to eat, and night after night she had nightmares. She would call for me, and I would rouse from exhaustion to sleepily call back: "You're all right, darling, go to sleep, it's just a dream," and if she still called, in a sterner voice, "now go to sleep, Emily, there's nothing to hurt you." Twice, only twice, when I had to get up for Susan anyhow, I went in to sit with her.

Now when it is too late (as if she would let me hold her and comfort her like I 25
do the others) I get up and go to her at once at her moan or restless stirring. "Are you awake, Emily? Can I get you something?" And the answer is always the same: "No, I'm all right, go back to sleep, Mother."

They persuaded me at the clinic to send her away to a convalescent home in the country where "she can have the kind of food and care you can't manage for her, and you'll be free to concentrate on the new baby." They still send children to that place. I see pictures on the society page of sleek young women planning affairs to raise money for it, or dancing at the affairs, or decorating Easter eggs or filling Christmas stockings for the children.

They never have a picture of the children so I do not know if the girls still wear those gigantic red bows and the ravaged looks on the every other Sunday when parents can come to visit "unless otherwise notified"—as we were notified the first six weeks.

Oh it is a handsome place, green lawns and tall trees and fluted flower beds. High up on the balconies of each cottage the children stand, the girls in their red bows and white dresses, the boys in white suits and giant red ties. The parents stand below shrieking up to be heard and the children shriek down to be heard, and between them the invisible wall "Not To Be Contaminated by Parental Germs or Physical Affection."

There was a tiny girl who always stood hand in hand with Emily. Her parents never came. One visit she was gone. "They moved her to Rose Cottage," Emily shouted in explanation. "They don't like you to love anybody here."

She wrote once a week, the labored writing of a seven-year-old. "I am fine. 30
How is the baby. If I write my leter nicly I will have a star. Love." There never was a star. We wrote every other day, letters she could never hold or keep but only hear read—once. "We simply do not have room for children to keep any personal possessions," they patiently explained when we pieced one Sunday's shrieking together to plead how much it would mean to Emily, who loved so to keep things, to be allowed to keep her letters and cards.

Each visit she looked frailer. "She isn't eating," they told us.

(They had runny eggs for breakfast or mush with lumps, Emily said later, I'd hold it in my mouth and not swallow. Nothing ever tasted good, just when they had chicken.)

It took us eight months to get her released home, and only the fact that she gained back so little of her seven lost pounds convinced the social worker.

I used to try to hold and love her after she came back, but her body would stay stiff, and after a while she'd push away. She ate little. Food sickened her, and I think much of life too. Oh she had physical lightness and brightness, twinkling by on skates, bouncing like a ball up and down up and down over the jump rope, skimming over the hill; but these were momentary.

She fretted about her appearance, thin and dark and foreign-looking at a 35
time when every little girl was supposed to look or thought she should look like a chubby blonde replica of Shirley Temple. The doorbell sometimes rang for her, but no one seemed to come and play in the house or to be a best friend. Maybe because we moved so much.

There was a boy she loved painfully through two school semesters. Months later she told me how she had taken pennies from my purse to buy him candy. "Licorice was his favorite and I brought him some every day, but he still liked Jennifer better'n me. Why, Mommy?" The kind of question for which there is no answer.

School was a worry for her. She was not glib or quick in a world where glibness and quickness were easily confused with ability to learn. To her overworked and exasperated teachers she was an overconscientious "slow learner" who kept trying to catch up and was absent entirely too often.

I let her be absent, though sometimes the illness was imaginary. How different from my now-strictness about attendance with the others. I wasn't working. We had a new baby. I was home anyhow. Sometimes, after Susan grew old enough, I would keep her home from school, too, to have them all together.

Mostly Emily had asthma, and her breathing, harsh and labored, would fill the house with a curiously tranquil sound. I would bring the two old dresser mirrors and her boxes of collections to her bed. She would select beads and single earrings, bottle tops and shells, dried flowers and pebbles, old postcards and scraps, all sorts of oddments; then she and Susan would play Kingdom, setting up landscapes and furniture, peopling them with action.

Those were the only times of peaceful companionship between her and Susan. I have edged away from it, that poisonous feeling between them, that terrible balancing of hurts and needs I had to do between the two, and did so badly, those earlier years.

Oh there were conflicts between the others too, each one human, needing, demanding, hurting, taking—but only between Emily and Susan, no, Emily toward Susan that corroding resentment. It seems so obvious on the surface, yet it is not obvious; Susan, the second child, Susan, golden- and curly-haired and chubby, quick and articulate and assured, everything in appearance and manner Emily was not; Susan, not able to resist Emily's precious things, losing or sometimes clumsily breaking them; Susan telling jokes and riddles to company for applause while Emily sat silent (to say to me later: that was *my* riddle, Mother, I told it to Susan); Susan, who for all the five years' difference in age was just a year behind Emily in developing physically.

I am glad for that slow physical development that widened the difference between her and her contemporaries, though she suffered over it. She was too vulnerable for that terrible world of youthful competition, of preening and parading, of constant measuring of yourself against every other, of envy, "If I had that copper hair," "If I had that skin. . . ." She tormented herself enough about not looking like the others, there was enough of unsureness, the having to be conscious of words before you speak, the constant caring—what are they thinking of me? without having it all magnified by the merciless physical drives.

Ronnie is calling. He is wet and I change him. It is rare there is such a cry now. That time of motherhood is almost behind me when the ear is not one's own but must always be racked and listening for the child cry, the child call. We sit for a while and I hold him, looking out over the city spread in charcoal with its soft aisles of light. "*Shoogily,*" he breathes and curls closer. I carry him back to bed, asleep. *Shoogily.* A funny word, a family word, inherited from Emily, invented by her to say: *comfort.*

In this and other ways she leaves her seal, I say aloud. And startle at my saying it. What do I mean? What did I start to gather together, to try and make coherent? I was at the terrible, growing years. War years. I do not remember them well.

I was working, there were four smaller ones now, there was not time for her. She had to help be a mother, and housekeeper, and shopper. She had to get her seal. Mornings of crisis and near hysteria trying to get lunches packed, hair combed, coats and shoes found, everyone to school or Child Care on time, the baby ready for transportation. And always the paper scribbled on by a smaller one, the book looked at by Susan then mislaid, the homework not done. Running out to that huge school where she was one, she was lost, she was a drop; suffering over the unpreparedness, stammering and unsure in her classes.

There was so little time left at night after the kids were bedded down. She would struggle over books, always eating (it was in those years she developed her enormous appetite that is legendary in our family) and I would be ironing, or preparing food for the next day, or writing V-mail to Bill, or tending the baby. Sometimes, to make me laugh, or out of her despair, she would imitate happenings or types at school.

I think I said once: "Why don't you do something like this in the school amateur show?" One morning she phoned me at work, hardly understandable through the weeping: "Mother, I did it. I won, I won; they gave me first prize; they clapped and clapped and wouldn't let me go."

Now suddenly she was Somebody, and as imprisoned in her difference as she had been in anonymity.

She began to be asked to perform at other high schools, even in colleges, then at city and statewide affairs. The first one we went to, I only recognized her that first moment when thin, shy, she almost drowned herself into the curtains. Then: Was this Emily? The control, the command, the convulsing and deadly clowning, the spell, then the roaring, stamping audience, unwilling to let this rare and precious laughter out of their lives.

Afterwards: You ought to do something about her with a gift like that—but without money or knowing how, what does one do? We have left it all to her, and the gift has so often eddied inside, clogged and clotted, as been used and growing.

She is coming. She runs up the stairs two at a time with her light graceful step, and I know she is happy tonight. Whatever it was that occasioned your call did not happen today.

"Aren't you ever going to finish the ironing, Mother? Whistler painted his mother in a rocker. I'd have to paint mine standing over an ironing board." This is one of her communicative nights and she tells me everything and nothing as she fixes herself a plate of food out of the icebox.

She is so lovely. Why did you want me to come in at all? Why were you concerned? She will find her way.

She starts up the stairs to bed. "Don't get me up with the rest in the morning." "But I thought you were having midterms." "Oh, those," she comes back in, kisses me, and says quite lightly, "in a couple of years when we'll all be atom-dead they won't matter a bit."

She has said it before. She *believes* it. But because I have been dredging the past, and all that compounds a human being is so heavy and meaningful in me, I cannot endure it tonight.

I will never total it all. I will never come in to say: She was a child seldom smiled at. Her father left me before she was a year old. I had to work her first six years when there was work, or I sent her home and to his relatives. There were years she had care she hated. She was dark and thin and foreign-looking in a world where the prestige went to blondeness and curly hair and dimples, she was slow where glibness was prized. She was a child of anxious, not proud, love. We were poor and could not afford for her the soil of easy growth. I was a young mother, I was a distracted mother. There were other children pushing up, demanding. Her younger sister seemed all that she was not. There were years she did not want me to touch her. She kept too much in herself, her life was such she had to keep too much in herself. My wisdom came too late. She has much to her and probably little will come of it. She is a child of her age, of depression, of war, of fear.

Let her be. So all that is in her will not bloom—but in how many does it? There is still enough left to live by. Only help her to know—help make it so there is cause for her to know—that she is more than this dress on the ironing board, helpless before the iron. *[1961]*

THINKING ABOUT THE TEXT

1. Is Olsen's last paragraph optimistic or pessimistic about personal destiny? Is there some support in the story for both perspectives?
2. There is an old expression: "To know all is to forgive all." Does this statement apply to "I Stand Here Ironing"? Some critics want to privilege personal responsibility; others, social conditions. Do you blame Emily's mother? Or is she just a victim?
3. How might this story be different if told from Emily's perspective? From Susan's? From Emily's teacher's? What are the advantages and disadvantages of writing a story from one character's point of view?
4. How would you describe the voice or voices we hear in the story? What qualities, dimensions, or emotions can you infer? Does one dominate? Are you sympathetic to this voice? Is that what Olsen wanted?
5. Do you agree with the mother's decision not to visit the school for a conference? What are her reasons? Are they sound? What do you think the teacher wants to discuss? How involved in a child's life should a teacher be?

AMY TAN

Two Kinds

Born to Chinese immigrants in Oakland, California, Amy Tan (b. 1952) weaves intricate stories about generational and intercultural relationships among women in families, basing much of her writing on her own family history. She earned a double B.A., in English and linguistics, and an M.A. in linguistics at San Jose State University. Her novels dealing with mother-daughter relationships, The Joy Luck Club *(1989) and* The Kitchen God's Wife *(1991), have received awards and critical acclaim.* The Hundred Secret Senses *(1995) explores the relationship between sisters who grew up in different cultures. Her latest novel is* Valley of Amazement *(2013), and another book is a collection of nonfiction,* The Opposite of Fate *(2003). "Two Kinds" is excerpted from* The Joy Luck Club.

My mother believed you could be anything you wanted to be in America. You could open a restaurant. You could work for the government and get good retirement. You could buy a house with almost no money down. You could become rich. You could become instantly famous.

"Of course you can be prodigy, too," my mother told me when I was nine. "You can be best anything. What does Auntie Lindo know? Her daughter, she is only best tricky."

America was where all my mother's hopes lay. She had come here in 1949 after losing everything in China: her mother and father, her family home, her first husband, and two daughters, twin baby girls. But she never looked back with regret. There were so many ways for things to get better.

We didn't immediately pick the right kind of prodigy. At first my mother thought I could be a Chinese Shirley Temple. We'd watch Shirley's old movies on TV as though they were training films. My mother would poke my arm and say, "*Ni kan*"—You watch. And I would see Shirley tapping her feet, or singing a sailor song, or pursing her lips into a very round O while saying, "Oh my goodness."

"*Ni kan,*" said my mother as Shirley's eyes flooded with tears. "You already 5
know how. Don't need talent for crying!"

Soon after my mother got this idea about Shirley Temple, she took me to a beauty training school in the Mission district and put me in the hands of a student who could barely hold the scissors without shaking. Instead of getting big fat curls, I emerged with an uneven mass of crinkly black fuzz. My mother dragged me off to the bathroom and tried to wet down my hair.

"You look like Negro Chinese," she lamented, as if I had done this on purpose.

The instructor of the beauty training school had to lop off these soggy clumps to make my hair even again. "Peter Pan is very popular these days," the instructor assured my mother. I now had hair the length of a boy's, with straight-across bangs that hung at a slant two inches above my eyebrows. I liked the haircut and it made me actually look forward to my future fame.

In fact, in the beginning, I was just as excited as my mother, maybe even more so. I pictured this prodigy part of me as many different images, trying each one on for size. I was a dainty ballerina girl standing by the curtains, waiting to hear the right music that would send me floating on my tiptoes. I was like the Christ child lifted out of the straw manger, crying with holy indignity. I was Cinderella stepping from her pumpkin carriage with sparkly cartoon music filling the air.

In all of my imaginings, I was filled with a sense that I would soon become 10
perfect. My mother and father would adore me. I would be beyond reproach. I would never feel the need to sulk for anything.

But sometimes the prodigy in me became impatient. "If you don't hurry up and get me out of here, I'm disappearing for good," it warned. "And then you'll always be nothing."

Every night after dinner, my mother and I would sit at the Formica kitchen table. She would present new tests, taking her examples from stories of amazing children she had read in *Ripley's Believe It or Not*, or *Good Housekeeping*, *Reader's Digest*, and a dozen other magazines she kept in a pile in our bathroom. My mother got these magazines from people whose houses she cleaned. And since she cleaned many houses each week, we had a great assortment. She would look through them all, searching for stories about remarkable children.

The first night she brought out a story about a three-year-old boy who knew the capitals of all the states and even most of the European countries. A teacher was quoted as saying the little boy could also pronounce the names of the foreign cities correctly.

"What's the capital of Finland?" my mother asked me, looking at the magazine story.

All I knew was the capital of California, because Sacramento was the name 15
of the street we lived on in Chinatown. "Nairobi!" I guessed, saying the most foreign word I could think of. She checked to see if that was possibly one way to pronounce "Helsinki" before showing me the answer.

The tests got harder—multiplying numbers in my head, finding the queen of hearts in a deck of cards, trying to stand on my head without using my hands, predicting the daily temperatures in Los Angeles, New York, and London.

One night I had to look at a page from the Bible for three minutes and then report everything I could remember. "Now Jehoshaphat had riches and honor in abundance and . . . that's all I remember, Ma," I said.

And after seeing my mother's disappointed face once again, something inside of me began to die. I hated the tests, the raised hopes and failed expectations. Before going to bed that night, I looked in the mirror above the bathroom sink and when I saw only my face staring back—and that it would always be this ordinary face—I began to cry. Such a sad, ugly girl! I made high-pitched noises like a crazed animal, trying to scratch out the face in the mirror.

And then I saw what seemed to be the prodigy side of me—because I had never seen that face before. I looked at my reflection, blinking so I could see more clearly. The girl staring back at me was angry, powerful. This girl and I were the same. I had new thoughts, willful thoughts, or rather thoughts filled with lots of won'ts. I won't let her change me, I promised myself. I won't be what I'm not.

So now on nights when my mother presented her tests, I performed listlessly, 20
my head propped on one arm. I pretended to be bored. And I was. I got so bored I started counting the bellows of the foghorns out on the bay while my mother drilled me in other areas. The sound was comforting and reminded me of the cow jumping over the moon. And the next day, I played a game with myself, seeing if my mother would give up on me before eight bellows. After a while I usually counted only one, maybe two bellows at most. At last she was beginning to give up hope.

Two or three months had gone by without any mention of my being a prodigy again. And then one day my mother was watching *The Ed Sullivan Show* on TV. The TV was old and the sound kept shorting out. Every time my mother got halfway up from the sofa to adjust the set, the sound would go back on and Ed would be talking. As soon as she sat down, Ed would go silent again. She got up, the TV broke into loud piano music. She sat down. Silence. Up and down, back and forth, quiet and loud. It was like a stiff embraceless dance between her and the TV set. Finally she stood by the set with her hand on the sound dial.

She seemed entranced by the music, a little frenzied piano piece with this mesmerizing quality, sort of quick passages and then teasing lilting ones before it returned to the quick playful parts.

"*Ni kan,*" my mother said, calling me over with hurried hand gestures. "Look here."

I could see why my mother was fascinated by the music. It was being pounded out by a little Chinese girl, about nine years old, with a Peter Pan haircut. The girl had the sauciness of a Shirley Temple. She was proudly modest like a proper Chinese child. And she also did this fancy sweep of a curtsy, so that the fluffy skirt of her white dress cascaded slowly to the floor like the petals of a large carnation.

In spite of these warning signs, I wasn't worried. Our family had no piano 25
and we couldn't afford to buy one, let alone reams of sheet music and piano lessons. So I could be generous in my comments when my mother bad-mouthed the little girl on TV.

"Play note right, but doesn't sound good! No singing sound," complained my mother.

"What are you picking on her for?" I said carelessly. "She's pretty good. Maybe she's not the best, but she's trying hard." I knew almost immediately I would be sorry I said that.

"Just like you," she said. "Not the best. Because you not trying." She gave a little huff as she let go of the sound dial and sat down on the sofa.

The little Chinese girl sat down also to play an encore of "Anitra's Dance" by Grieg. I remember the song, because later on I had to learn how to play it.

Three days after watching *The Ed Sullivan Show*, my mother told me what my 30
schedule would be for piano lessons and piano practice. She had talked to Mr. Chong, who lived on the first floor of our apartment building. Mr. Chong was a retired piano teacher and my mother had traded housecleaning services for weekly lessons and a piano for me to practice on every day, two hours a day, from four until six.

When my mother told me this, I felt as though I had been sent to hell. I whined and then kicked my foot a little when I couldn't stand it anymore.

"Why don't you like me the way I am? I'm *not* a genius! I can't play the piano. And even if I could, I wouldn't go on TV if you paid me a million dollars!" I cried.

My mother slapped me. "Who ask you be genius?" she shouted. "Only ask you be your best. For you sake. You think I want you be genius? Hnnh! What for! Who ask you!"

"So ungrateful," I heard her mutter in Chinese. "If she had as much talent as she has temper, she would be famous now."

Mr. Chong, whom I secretly nicknamed Old Chong, was very strange, 35
always tapping his fingers to the silent music of an invisible orchestra. He looked

ancient in my eyes. He had lost most of the hair on top of his head and he wore thick glasses and had eyes that always looked tired and sleepy. But he must have been younger than I thought, since he lived with his mother and was not yet married.

I met Old Lady Chong once and that was enough. She had this peculiar smell like a baby that had done something in its pants. And her fingers felt like a dead person's, like an old peach I once found in the back of the refrigerator; the skin just slid off the meat when I picked it up.

I soon found out why Old Chong had retired from teaching piano. He was deaf. "Like Beethoven!" he shouted to me. "We're both listening only in our head!" And he would start to conduct his frantic silent sonatas.

Our lessons went like this. He would open the book and point to different things, explaining their purpose: "Key! Treble! Bass! No sharps or flats! So this is C major! Listen now and play after me!"

And then he would play the C scale a few times, a simple chord, and then, as if inspired by an old, unreachable itch, he gradually added more notes and running trills and a pounding bass until the music was really something quite grand.

I would play after him, the simple scale, the simple chord, and then I just played some nonsense that sounded like a cat running up and down on top of garbage cans. Old Chong smiled and applauded and then said, "Very good! But now you must learn to keep time!"

So that's how I discovered that Old Chong's eyes were too slow to keep up with the wrong notes I was playing. He went through the motions in half-time. To help me keep rhythm, he stood behind me, pushing down on my right shoulder for every beat. He balanced pennies on top of my wrists so I would keep them still as I slowly played scales and arpeggios. He had me curve my hand around an apple and keep that shape when playing chords. He marched stiffly to show me how to make each finger dance up and down, staccato like an obedient little soldier.

He taught me all these things, and that was how I also learned I could be lazy and get away with mistakes, lots of mistakes. If I hit the wrong notes because I hadn't practiced enough, I never corrected myself. I just kept playing in rhythm. And Old Chong kept conducting his own private reverie.

So maybe I never really gave myself a fair chance. I did pick up the basics pretty quickly, and I might have become a good pianist at that young age. But I was so determined not to try, not to be anybody different that I learned to play only the most ear-splitting preludes, the most discordant hymns.

Over the next year, I practiced like this, dutifully in my own way. And then one day I heard my mother and her friend Lindo Jong both talking in a loud bragging tone of voice so others could hear. It was after church, and I was leaning against the brick wall wearing a dress with stiff white petticoats. Auntie Lindo's daughter, Waverly, who was about my age, was standing farther down the wall about five feet away. We had grown up together and shared all the closeness of two sisters squabbling over crayons and dolls. In other words, for the most part, we hated each other. I thought she was snotty. Waverly Jong had gained a certain amount of fame as "Chinatown's Littlest Chinese Chess Champion."

45 "She bring home too many trophy," lamented Auntie Lindo that Sunday. "All day she play chess. All day I have no time do nothing but dust off her winnings." She threw a scolding look at Waverly, who pretended not to see her.

"You lucky you don't have this problem," said Auntie Lindo with a sigh to my mother.

And my mother squared her shoulders and bragged: "Our problem worser than yours. If we ask Jing-mei wash dish, she hear nothing but music. It's like you can't stop this natural talent."

And right then, I was determined to put a stop to her foolish pride.

A few weeks later, Old Chong and my mother conspired to have me play in a talent show which would be held in the church hall. By then, my parents had saved up enough to buy me a secondhand piano, a black Wurlitzer spinet with a scarred bench. It was the showpiece of our living room.

50 For the talent show, I was to play a piece called "Pleading Child" from Schumann's *Scenes from Childhood*. It was a simple, moody piece that sounded more difficult than it was. I was supposed to memorize the whole thing, playing the repeat parts twice to make the piece sound longer. But I dawdled over it, playing a few bars and then cheating, looking up to see what notes followed. I never really listened to what I was playing. I daydreamed about being somewhere else, about being someone else.

The part I liked to practice best was the fancy curtsy: right foot out, touch the rose on the carpet with a pointed foot, sweep to the side, left leg bends, look up and smile.

My parents invited all the couples from the Joy Luck Club to witness my debut. Auntie Lindo and Uncle Tin were there. Waverly and her two older brothers had also come. The first two rows were filled with children both younger and older than I was. The littlest ones got to go first. They recited simple nursery rhymes, squawked out tunes on miniature violins, twirled Hula Hoops, pranced in pink ballet tutus, and when they bowed or curtsied, the audience would sigh in unison, "Awww," and then clap enthusiastically.

When my turn came, I was very confident. I remember my childish excitement. It was as if I knew, without a doubt, that the prodigy side of me really did exist. I had no fear whatsoever, no nervousness. I remember thinking to myself, This is it! This is it! I looked out over the audience, at my mother's blank face, my father's yawn, Auntie Lindo's stiff-lipped smile, Waverly's sulky expression. I had on a white dress layered with sheets of lace, and a pink bow in my Peter Pan haircut. As I sat down I envisioned people jumping to their feet and Ed Sullivan rushing up to introduce me to everyone on TV.

And I started to play. It was so beautiful. I was so caught up in how lovely I looked that at first I didn't worry how I would sound. So it was a surprise to me when I hit the first wrong note and I realized something didn't sound quite right. And then I hit another and another followed that. A chill started at the top of my head and began to trickle down. Yet I couldn't stop playing, as though my hands were bewitched. I kept thinking my fingers would adjust themselves back, like a train switching to the right track. I played this strange jumble through two repeats, the sour notes staying with me all the way to the end.

When I stood up, I discovered my legs were shaking. Maybe I had just been nervous and the audience, like Old Chong, had seen me go through the right motions and had not heard anything wrong at all. I swept my right foot out, went down on my knee, looked up and smiled. The room was quiet, except for Old Chong, who was beaming and shouting, "Bravo! Bravo! Well done!" But then I saw my mother's face, her stricken face. The audience clapped weakly, and as I walked back to my chair, with my whole face quivering as I tried not to cry, I heard a little boy whisper loudly to his mother, "That was awful," and the mother whispered back, "Well, she certainly tried." 55

And now I realized how many people were in the audience, the whole world it seemed. I was aware of eyes burning into my back. I felt the shame of my mother and father as they sat stiffly throughout the rest of the show.

We could have escaped during intermission. Pride and some strange sense of honor must have anchored my parents to their chairs. And so we watched it all: the eighteen-year-old boy with a fake mustache who did a magic show and juggled flaming hoops while riding a unicycle. The breasted girl with white makeup who sang from *Madama Butterfly* and got honorable mention. And the eleven-year-old boy who won first prize playing a tricky violin song that sounded like a busy bee.

After the show, the Hsus, the Jongs, and the St. Clairs from the Joy Luck Club came up to my mother and father.

"Lots of talented kids," Auntie Lindo said vaguely, smiling broadly.

"That was somethin' else," said my father, and I wondered if he was referring to me in a humorous way, or whether he even remembered what I had done. 60

Waverly looked at me and shrugged her shoulders. "You aren't a genius like me," she said matter-of-factly. And if I hadn't felt so bad, I would have pulled her braids and punched her stomach.

But my mother's expression was what devastated me: a quiet, blank look that said she had lost everything. I felt the same way, and it seemed as if everybody were now coming up, like gawkers at the scene of an accident, to see what parts were actually missing. When we got on the bus to go home, my father was humming the busy-bee tune and my mother was silent. I kept thinking she wanted to wait until we got home before shouting at me. But when my father unlocked the door to our apartment, my mother walked in and then went to the back, into the bedroom. No accusations. No blame. And in a way, I felt disappointed. I had been waiting for her to start shouting, so I could shout back and cry and blame her for all my misery.

I assumed my talent-show fiasco meant I never had to play the piano again. But two days later, after school, my mother came out of the kitchen and saw me watching TV.

"Four clock," she reminded me as if it were any other day. I was stunned, as though she were asking me to go through the talent-show torture again. I wedged myself more tightly in front of the TV.

"Turn off TV," she called from the kitchen five minutes later. 65

I didn't budge. And then I decided. I didn't have to do what my mother said anymore. I wasn't her slave. This wasn't China. I had listened to her before and look what happened. She was the stupid one.

She came out from the kitchen and stood in the arched entryway of the living room. "Four clock," she said once again, louder.

"I'm not going to play anymore," I said nonchalantly. "Why should I? I'm not a genius."

She walked over and stood in front of the TV. I saw her chest was heaving up and down in an angry way.

"No!" I said, and I now felt stronger, as if my true self had finally emerged. So 70
this was what had been inside me all along.

"No! I won't!" I screamed.

She yanked me by the arm, pulled me off the floor, snapped off the TV. She was frighteningly strong, half pulling, half carrying me toward the piano as I kicked the throw rugs under my feet. She lifted me up and onto the hard bench. I was sobbing by now, looking at her bitterly. Her chest was heaving even more and her mouth was open, smiling crazily as if she were pleased I was crying.

"You want me to be someone that I'm not!" I sobbed. "I'll never be the kind of daughter you want me to be!"

"Only two kinds of daughters," she shouted in Chinese. "Those who are obedient and those who follow their own mind! Only one kind of daughter can live in this house. Obedient daughter!"

"Then I wish I wasn't your daughter. I wish you weren't my mother," 75
I shouted. As I said these things I got scared. I felt like worms and toads and slimy things were crawling out of my chest, but it also felt good, as if this awful side of me had surfaced, at last.

"Too late change this," said my mother shrilly.

And I could sense her anger rising to its breaking point. I wanted to see it spill over. And that's when I remembered the babies she had lost in China, the ones we never talked about. "Then I wish I'd never been born!" I shouted. "I wish I were dead! Like them."

It was as if I had said the magic words, Alakazam!—and her face went blank, her mouth closed, her arms went slack, and she backed out of the room, stunned, as if she were blowing away like a small brown leaf, thin, brittle, lifeless.

It was not the only disappointment my mother felt in me. In the years that followed, I failed her so many times, each time asserting my own will, my right to fall short of expectations. I didn't get straight As. I didn't become class president. I didn't get into Stanford. I dropped out of college.

For unlike my mother, I did not believe I could be anything I wanted to be. I 80
could only be me.

And for all those years, we never talked about the disaster at the recital or my terrible accusations afterward at the piano bench. All that remained unchecked, like a betrayal that was now unspeakable. So I never found a way to ask her why she had hoped for something so large that failure was inevitable.

And even worse, I never asked her what frightened me the most: Why had she given up hope?

For after our struggle at the piano, she never mentioned my playing again. The lessons stopped, the lid to the piano was closed, shutting out the dust, my misery, and her dreams.

So she surprised me. A few years ago, she offered to give me the piano, for my thirtieth birthday. I had not played in all those years. I saw the offer as a sign of forgiveness, a tremendous burden removed.

"Are you sure?" I asked shyly. "I mean, won't you and Dad miss it?" 85

"No, this your piano," she said firmly. "Always your piano. You only one can play."

"Well, I probably can't play anymore," I said. "It's been years."

"You pick up fast," said my mother, as if she knew this was certain. "You have natural talent. You could been genius if you want to."

"No I couldn't."

"You just not trying," said my mother. And she was neither angry nor sad. 90 She said it as if to announce a fact that could never be disproved. "Take it," she said.

But I didn't at first. It was enough that she had offered it to me. And after that, every time I saw it in my parents' living room, standing in front of the bay windows, it made me feel proud, as if it were a shiny trophy I had won back.

Last week I sent a tuner over to my parents' apartment and had the piano reconditioned, for purely sentimental reasons. My mother had died a few months before and I had been getting things in order for my father, a little bit at a time. I put the jewelry in special silk pouches. The sweaters she had knitted in yellow, pink, bright orange—all the colors I hated—I put those in moth-proof boxes. I found some old Chinese silk dresses, the kind with little slits up the sides. I rubbed the old silk against my skin, then wrapped them in tissue and decided to take them home with me.

After I had the piano tuned, I opened the lid and touched the keys. It sounded even richer than I remembered. Really, it was a very good piano. Inside the bench were the same exercise notes with handwritten scales, the same secondhand music books with their covers held together with yellow tape.

I opened up the Schumann book to the dark little piece I had played at the recital. It was on the left-hand side of the page, "Pleading Child." It looked more difficult than I remembered. I played a few bars, surprised at how easily the notes came back to me.

And for the first time, or so it seemed, I noticed the piece on the right-hand 95 side. It was called "Perfectly Contented." I tried to play this one as well. It had a lighter melody but the same flowing rhythm and turned out to be quite easy. "Pleading Child" was shorter but slower; "Perfectly Contented" was longer but faster. And after I played them both a few times, I realized they were two halves of the same song.

[1989]

☰ THINKING ABOUT THE TEXT

1. Most sons and daughters struggle to establish their own identities. Does this seem true in "Two Kinds"? Does the cultural difference between the immigrant mother and Americanized daughter intensify their struggle? Do you think you have different goals in life than your parents do?
2. Do you agree with the mother's belief that "you could be anything you wanted to be in America" (para. 1)? Does race matter? Gender? Ethnicity? Religion? Sexual orientation?
3. What do you believe each character learned from the argument at the piano bench the day after the recital?
4. How does Tan establish the differing personalities of her characters? Through details? Dialogue? Anecdotes? Do the main characters change significantly? Does she tell us or show us?
5. Do you sympathize with the mother or with the daughter? Should parents channel their children toward selected activities? Or should parents let their children choose their own paths? Can parents push their children too much? Why would they do this?

☰ MAKING COMPARISONS

1. Do you think Emily's mother in Olsen's story would want to be like the Chinese mother if given the opportunity? Which mother would you prefer to have? Why?
2. One mother seems to do too little, the other too much. Is this your reading of the two stories? Is the lesson of Olsen's and Tan's stories that mothers can't win no matter what they do? Or do you have a more optimistic interpretation?
3. Which daughter's life seems more difficult? How possible is it to say from the outside looking in?

ALICE WALKER

Everyday Use

A native of Eatonton, Georgia, Alice Walker (b. 1944) attended Spelman College and received her B.A. from Sarah Lawrence College in 1965. During the 1960s, she was active in the civil rights movement, an experience reflected in her 1976 novel Meridian *and in her autobiographical book,* The Way Forward Is with a Broken Heart *(2000). Walker is accomplished in many genres, and her essays, short stories, novels, and poems are widely read. She is perhaps best known for the novel* The Color Purple *(1976), which earned her both a Pulitzer Prize and an American Book Award and was made into a movie. Terming herself a "womanist" rather than a feminist in the essays of* In Search of Our Mothers' Gardens *(1983), Walker has confronted many issues concerning women, including abusive relationships, lesbian love, and the horrors of ritual genital mutilation in some African societies. Her daughter, Rebecca, has written her own memoir,* Black, White and Jewish, *dealing with her childhood and adolescence as the daughter of Alice Walker and activist lawyer Mel Leventhal, to whom Walker was married for nine years, after meeting him during voter registration drives in Mississippi in 1967. The short story "Everyday Use," from the collection* In Love and Trouble: Stories of Black Women *(1973), deals with definitions of history, heritage, and value in a changing world for African Americans in the mid-twentieth century. Her recent work includes a novel,* Now Is the Time to Open Your Heart *(2004);* We Are the Ones We've Been Waiting For *(2006), "a book of spiritual ruminations with a progressive political edge"; and* Hard Times Require Serious Dancing: New Poems *(2010). Her most recent collection is* The World Will Follow Joy: Turning Madness into Flowers *(2014).*

I will wait for her in the yard that Maggie and I made so clean and wavy yesterday afternoon. A yard like this is more comfortable than most people know. It is not just a yard. It is like an extended living room. When the hard clay is swept clean as a floor and the fine sand around the edges lined with tiny, irregular grooves anyone can come and sit and look up into the elm tree and wait for the breezes that never come inside the house.

Maggie will be nervous until after her sister goes: she will stand hopelessly in corners homely and ashamed of the burn scars down her arms and legs, eyeing her sister with a mixture of envy and awe. She thinks her sister has held life always in the palm of one hand, that "no" is a word the world never learned to say to her.

You've no doubt seen those TV shows where the child who has "made it" is confronted, as a surprise, by her own mother and father, tottering in weakly from backstage. (A pleasant surprise, of course: What would they do if parent and child came on the show only to curse out and insult each other?) On TV mother and child embrace and smile into each other's faces. Sometimes the mother and father weep, the child wraps them in her arms and leans across the table to tell how she would not have made it without their help. I have seen these programs.

Sometimes I dream a dream in which Dee and I are suddenly brought together on a TV program of this sort. Out of a dark and soft-seated limousine I am ushered into a bright room filled with many people. There I meet a smiling, gray, sporty man like Johnny Carson who shakes my hand and tells me what a fine girl I have. Then we are on the stage and Dee is embracing me with tears in her eyes. She pins on my dress a large orchid, even though she has told me once that she thinks orchids are tacky flowers.

In real life I am a large, big-boned woman with rough, man-working hands. 5
In the winter I wear flannel nightgowns to bed and overalls during the day. I can kill and clean a hog as mercilessly as a man. My fat keeps me hot in zero weather. I can work outside all day, breaking ice to get water for washing; I can eat pork liver

cooked over the open fire minutes after it comes steaming from the hog. One winter I knocked a bull calf straight in the brain between the eyes with a sledge hammer and had the meat hung up to chill before nightfall. But of course all this does not show on television. I am the way my daughter would want me to be: a hundred pounds lighter, my skin like an uncooked barley pancake. My hair glistens in the hot bright lights. Johnny Carson has much to do to keep up with my quick and witty tongue.

But that is a mistake. I know even before I wake up. Who ever knew a Johnson with a quick tongue? Who can even imagine me looking a strange white man in the eye? It seems to me I have talked to them always with one foot raised in flight, with my head turned in whichever way is farthest from them. Dee, though. She would always look anyone in the eye. Hesitation was no part of her nature.

"How do I look, Mama?" Maggie says, showing just enough of her thin body enveloped in pink skirt and red blouse for me to know she's there, almost hidden by the door.

"Come out into the yard," I say.

Have you ever seen a lame animal, perhaps a dog run over by some careless person rich enough to own a car, sidle up to someone who is ignorant enough to be kind to him? That is the way my Maggie walks. She has been like this, chin on chest, eyes on ground, feet in shuffle, ever since the fire that burned the other house to the ground.

Dee is lighter than Maggie, with nicer hair and a fuller figure. She's a woman 10
now, though sometimes I forget. How long ago was it that the other house burned? Ten, twelve years? Sometimes I can still hear the flames and feel Maggie's arms sticking to me, her hair smoking and her dress falling off her in little black papery flakes. Her eyes seemed stretched open, blazed open by the flames reflected in them. And Dee. I see her standing off under the sweet gum tree she used to dig gum out of; a look of concentration on her face as she watched the last dingy gray board of the house fall in toward the red-hot brick chimney. Why don't you do a dance around the ashes? I'd wanted to ask her. She had hated the house that much.

I used to think she hated Maggie, too. But that was before we raised the money, the church and me, to send her to Augusta to school. She used to read to us without pity; forcing words, lies, other folks' habits, whole lives upon us two, sitting trapped and ignorant underneath her voice. She washed us in a river of make-believe, burned us with a lot of knowledge we didn't necessarily need to know. Pressed us to her with the serious way she read, to shove us away at just the moment, like dimwits, we seemed about to understand.

Dee wanted nice things. A yellow organdy dress to wear to her graduation from high school; black pumps to match a green suit she'd made from an old suit somebody gave me. She was determined to stare down any disaster in her efforts. Her eyelids would not flicker for minutes at a time. Often I fought off the temptation to shake her. At sixteen she had a style of her own: and knew what style was.

I never had an education myself. After second grade the school was closed down. Don't ask me why: in 1927 colored asked fewer questions than they do now. Sometimes Maggie reads to me. She stumbles along good-naturedly but can't see well. She knows she is not bright. Like good looks and money, quickness passed her by. She will marry John Thomas (who has mossy teeth in an earnest face) and then I'll be free to sit here and I guess just sing church songs to myself. Although I never was a good singer. Never could carry a tune. I was always better at a man's job. I used to love to milk till I was hooked in the side in '49. Cows are soothing and slow and don't bother you, unless you try to milk them the wrong way.

I have deliberately turned my back on the house. It is three rooms, just like the one that burned, except the roof is tin; they don't make shingle roofs any more. There are no real windows, just some holes cut in the sides, like the portholes in a ship, but not round and not square, with rawhide holding the shutters up on the outside. This house is in a pasture, too, like the other one. No doubt when Dee sees it she will want to tear it down. She wrote me once that no matter where we "choose" to live, she will manage to come see us. But she will never bring her friends. Maggie and I thought about this and Maggie asked me, "Mama, when did Dee ever *have* any friends?"

She had a few. Furtive boys in pink shirts hanging about on washday after 15
school. Nervous girls who never laughed. Impressed with her they worshiped the well-turned phrase, the cute shape, the scalding humor that erupted like bubbles in lye. She read to them.

When she was courting Jimmy T she didn't have much time to pay to us, but turned all her faultfinding power on him. He *flew* to marry a cheap gal from a family of ignorant flashy people. She hardly had time to recompose herself.

* * *

When she comes I will meet—but there they are!

Maggie attempts to make a dash for the house, in her shuffling way, but I stay her with my hand. "Come back here," I say. And she stops and tries to dig a well in the sand with her toe.

It is hard to see them clearly through the strong sun. But even the first glimpse of leg out of the car tells me it is Dee. Her feet were always neat-looking, as if God himself had shaped them with a certain style. From the other side of the car comes a short, stocky man. Hair is all over his head a foot long and hanging from his chin like a kinky mule tail. I hear Maggie suck in her breath. "Uhnnnh," is what it sounds like. Like when you see the wriggling end of a snake just in front of your foot on the road. "Uhnnnh."

Dee next. A dress down to the ground, in this hot weather. A dress so loud it 20
hurts my eyes. There are yellows and oranges enough to throw back the light of the sun. I feel my whole face warming from the heat waves it throws out. Earrings gold, too, and hanging down to her shoulders. Bracelets dangling and making noises when she moves her arm up to shake the folds of the dress out of her armpits. The dress is loose and flows, and as she walks closer, I like it. I hear Maggie go "Uhnnnh" again. It is her sister's hair. It stands straight up like the wool on a sheep. It is black as night and around the edges are two long pigtails that rope about like small lizards disappearing behind her ears.

"Wa-su-zo-Tean-o!" she says, coming on in that gliding way the dress makes her move. The short stocky fellow with the hair to his navel is all grinning and he follows up with "Asalamalakim, my mother and sister!" He moves to hug Maggie but she falls back, right up against the back of my chair. I feel her trembling there and when I look up I see the perspiration falling off her chin.

"Don't get up," says Dee. Since I am stout it takes something of a push. You can see me trying to move a second or two before I make it. She turns, showing white heels through her sandals, and goes back to the car. Out she peeks next with a Polaroid. She stoops down quickly and lines up picture after picture of me sitting there in front of the house with Maggie cowering behind me. She never takes a shot without making sure the house is included. When a cow comes nibbling around the edge of the yard she snaps it and me and Maggie *and* the house. Then she puts the Polaroid in the back seat of the car, and comes up and kisses me on the forehead.

Meanwhile Asalamalakim is going through the motions with Maggie's hand. Maggie's hand is as limp as a fish, and probably as cold, despite the sweat, and she keeps trying to pull it back. It looks like Asalamalakim wants to shake hands but wants to do it fancy. Or maybe he don't know how people shake hands. Anyhow, he soon gives up on Maggie.

"Well," I say. "Dee."

"No, Mama," she says. "Not 'Dee,' Wangero Leewanika Kemanjo!" 25

"What happened to 'Dee'?" I wanted to know.

"She's dead," Wangero said. "I couldn't bear it any longer being named after the people who oppress me."

"You know as well as me you was named after your aunt Dicie," I said. Dicie is my sister. She named Dee. We called her "Big Dee" after Dee was born.

"But who was *she* named after?" asked Wangero.

"I guess after Grandma Dee," I said. 30

"And who was she named after?" asked Wangero.

"Her mother," I said, and saw Wangero was getting tired. "That's about as far back as I can trace it," I said. Though, in fact, I probably could have carried it back beyond the Civil War through the branches.

"Well," said Asalamalakim, "there you are."

"Uhnnnh," I heard Maggie say.

"There I was not," I said, "before 'Dicie' cropped up in our family, so why should I try to trace it that far back?" 35

He just stood there grinning, looking down on me like somebody inspecting a Model A car. Every once in a while he and Wangero sent eye signals over my head.

"How do you pronounce this name?" I asked.

"You don't have to call me by it if you don't want to," said Wangero.

"Why shouldn't I?" I asked. "If that's what you want us to call you, we'll call you."

"I know it might sound awkward at first," said Wangero. 40

"I'll get used to it," I said. "Ream it out again."

Well, soon we got the name out of the way. Asalamalakim had a name twice as long and three times as hard. After I tripped over it two or three times he told me to just call him Hakim-a-barber. I wanted to ask him was he a barber, but I didn't really think he was, so I didn't ask.

"You must belong to those beef-cattle peoples down the road," I said. They said "Asalamalakim" when they met you, too, but they didn't shake hands. Always too busy: feeding the cattle, fixing the fences, putting up salt-lick shelters, throwing down hay. When the white folks poisoned some of the herd the men stayed up all night with rifles in their hands. I walked a mile and a half just to see the sight.

Hakim-a-barber said, "I accept some of their doctrines, but farming and raising cattle is not my style." (They didn't tell me, and I didn't ask, whether Wangero [Dee] had really gone and married him.)

We sat down to eat and right away he said he didn't eat collards and pork was unclean. Wangero, though, went on through the chitlins and corn bread, the greens and everything else. She talked a blue streak over the sweet potatoes. Everything delighted her. Even the fact that we still used the benches her daddy made for the table when we couldn't afford to buy chairs.

"Oh, Mama!" she cried. Then turned to Hakim-a-barber. "I never knew how lovely these benches are. You can feel the rump prints," she said, running her hands underneath her and along the bench. Then she gave a sigh and her hand closed over Grandma Dee's butter dish. "That's it!" she said. "I knew there was something I wanted to ask you if I could have." She jumped up from the table and went over in the corner where the churn stood, the milk in it clabber by now. She looked at the churn and looked at it.

"This churn top is what I need," she said. "Didn't Uncle Buddy whittle it out of a tree you all used to have?"

"Yes," I said.

"Uh huh," she said happily. "And I want the dasher, too."

"Uncle Buddy whittle that, too?" asked the barber.

Dee (Wangero) looked up at me.

"Aunt Dee's first husband whittled the dash," said Maggie so low you almost couldn't hear her. "His name was Henry, but they called him Stash."

"Maggie's brain is like an elephant's," Wangero said, laughing. "I can use the churn top as a centerpiece for the alcove table," she said, sliding a plate over the churn, "and I'll think of something artistic to do with the dasher."

When she finished wrapping the dasher the handle stuck out. I took it for a moment in my hands. You didn't even have to look close to see where hands pushing the dasher up and down to make butter had left a kind of sink in the wood. In fact, there were a lot of small sinks; you could see where thumbs and fingers had sunk into the wood. It was beautiful light yellow wood, from a tree that grew in the yard where Big Dee and Stash had lived.

After dinner Dee (Wangero) went to the trunk at the foot of my bed and started rifling through it. Maggie hung back in the kitchen over the dishpan. Out came Wangero with two quilts. They had been pieced by Grandma Dee and then Big Dee and me had hung them on the quilt frames on the front porch and quilted them. One was in the Lone Star pattern. The other was Walk Around the Mountain. In both of them were scraps of dresses Grandma Dee had worn fifty and more years ago. Bits and pieces of Grandpa Jarrell's paisley shirts. And one teeny faded blue piece, about the size of a penny matchbox, that was from Great Grandpa Ezra's uniform that he wore in the Civil War.

"Mama," Wangero said sweet as a bird. "Can I have these old quilts?"

I heard something fall in the kitchen, and a minute later the kitchen door slammed.

"Why don't you take one or two of the others?" I asked. "These old things was just done by me and Big Dee from some tops your grandma pieced before she died."

"No," said Wangero. "I don't want those. They are stitched around the borders by machine."

"That'll make them last better," I said. 60

"That's not the point," said Wangero. "These are all pieces of dresses Grandma used to wear. She did all this stitching by hand. Imagine!" She held the quilts securely in her arms, stroking them.

"Some of the pieces, like those lavender ones, come from old clothes her mother handed down to her," I said, moving up to touch the quilts. Dee (Wangero) moved back just enough so that I couldn't reach the quilts. They already belonged to her.

"Imagine!" she breathed again, clutching them closely to her bosom.

"The truth is," I said, "I promised to give them quilts to Maggie, for when she marries John Thomas."

She gasped like a bee had stung her. 65

"Maggie can't appreciate these quilts!" she said. "She'd probably be backward enough to put them to everyday use."

"I reckon she would," I said. "God knows I been saving 'em for long enough with nobody using 'em. I hope she will!" I didn't want to bring up how I had offered Dee (Wangero) a quilt when she went away to college. Then she had told me they were old-fashioned, out of style.

"But they're *priceless*!" she was saying now, furiously; for she has a temper. "Maggie would put them on the bed and in five years they'd be in rags. Less than that!"

"She can always make some more," I said. "Maggie knows how to quilt." 70

Dee (Wangero) looked at me with hatred. "You just will not understand. The point is these quilts, *these* quilts!"

"Well," I said, stumped. "What would *you* do with them?"

"Hang them," she said. As if that was the only thing you *could* do with quilts.

Maggie by now was standing in the door. I could almost hear the sound her feet made as they scraped over each other.

"She can have them, Mama," she said, like somebody used to never winning anything, or having anything reserved for her. "I can 'member Grandma Dee without the quilts."

I looked at her hard. She had filled her bottom lip with checkerberry snuff 75
and it gave her face a kind of dopey, hangdog look. It was Grandma Dee and Big Dee who taught her how to quilt herself. She stood there with her scarred hands hidden in the folds of her skirt. She looked at her sister with something like fear

but she wasn't mad at her. This was Maggie's portion. This was the way she knew God to work.

When I looked at her like that something hit me in the top of my head and ran down to the soles of my feet. Just like when I'm in church and the spirit of God touches me and I get happy and shout. I did something I never had done before: hugged Maggie to me, then dragged her on into the room, snatched the quilts out of Miss Wangero's hands and dumped them into Maggie's lap. Maggie just sat there on my bed with her mouth open.

"Take one or two of the others," I said to Dee.

But she turned without a word and went out to Hakim-a-barber.

"You just don't understand," she said, as Maggie and I came out to the car.

"What don't I understand?" I wanted to know. 80

"Your heritage," she said. And then she turned to Maggie, kissed her, and said, "You ought to try to make something of yourself, too, Maggie. It's really a new day for us. But from the way you and Mama still live you'd never know it."

She put on some sunglasses that hid everything above the tip of her nose and her chin.

Maggie smiled; maybe at the sunglasses. But a real smile, not scared. After we watched the car dust settle I asked Maggie to bring me a dip of snuff. And then the two of us sat there just enjoying, until it was time to go in the house and go to bed. *[1973]*

≡ THINKING ABOUT THE TEXT

1. Be specific in arguing that Mama is more sympathetic to Maggie than to Dee. Is Mama hostile to Dee? What values are involved in the tension between Mama and Dee and Maggie?
2. Although many students seem to prefer Maggie to Dee, most would probably rather be Dee than Maggie. Is this true for you? Why?
3. Do you think Walker is against "getting back to one's roots"? Does she give a balanced characterization of Maggie? Of Dee? How might she portray Dee if she wanted to be more positive about her? Less positive?
4. Do you think it helps or hinders the social fabric to affirm ethnic differences? Do you think America is a melting pot? Is a quilt a better symbol to capture our diversity? Can you suggest another metaphor?
5. Do you think most mothers would side with daughters with whom they are more politically or culturally sympathetic? What might be the deciding factor? Are most mothers equally supportive of each of their children?

≡ MAKING COMPARISONS

1. How do you think Maggie would fare if she were the first child in "I Stand Here Ironing"? In "Two Kinds"?
2. Which relationship in the stories in this cluster is closest to your own? Explain.

3. Which one of the five daughters seems the kindest? The smartest? The most ambitious? The most troubled? The most likely to succeed? To find love? Do you think the mothers are responsible for how their daughters turn out?

WRITING ABOUT ISSUES

1. After reading Olsen's story, as Emily's teacher, write a letter to Emily's mother persuading her that she should still come in for a conference. Acknowledge her excuses and her side of the issue, but offer objections.
2. Write a brief essay arguing that each of the mothers presented in Olsen's, Tan's, and Walker's stories is either a good or a bad model for parenting.
3. Write a personal-experience narrative about a time when your parents pushed you too hard or too little or wanted you to be someone you thought you were not. Conclude with your present view of the consequences of their action.
4. Ask six males and six females if they feel their parents tried to shape their personalities, behavior, choice of friends, and so forth. Were the parents' efforts successful? Do the sons and daughters resent it now? Conclude your brief report with some generalizations, including how relevant gender is.

Longing for a Father: Stories

JOHN CHEEVER, "REUNION"

DAGOBERTO GILB, "UNCLE ROCK"

Psychologically inclined critics seem to have no trouble unearthing subtle searches for father figures in literature and films of all sorts. They should have no problem finding that theme in the two stories printed here. Their interest, of course, is not idiosyncratic since the ideal father figure as a wise, strong, and caring protector is a staple of American cultural imagination. And while that might be the case for some, many fathers are decidedly less saintly. It's common for writers, perhaps drawing on their own experiences, to focus on the ways fictional fathers compare to the lofty, and perhaps unfair, iconic all-knowing, all-caring image. Growing-up narratives often deal with the tension between childhood expectations for the perfect father and the sometimes disappointing and painful reality. In these two stories, one boy is bitterly disappointed, while the other gradually comes to learn a lesson about the differences between his boyish views of masculinity and being a good partner and husband.

BEFORE YOU READ

What was your view of what made a good father when you were ten? How about at fifteen? What about now?

JOHN CHEEVER

Reunion

John Cheever (1912–1982), known as the "Chekhov of the suburbs," is widely regarded as one of the most significant short story writers of the twentieth century. Cheever left his private high school at age seventeen and wrote about it in a story called "Expelled" when he was eighteen. It was published in the New Republic. *After serving in the army, Cheever moved to New York City and published "The Enormous Radio," in* The New Yorker *in 1947, which was the beginning of a long and successful career.* The Wapshot Chronicle *was published in 1957 and* Bullet Park *in 1969. During this time, Cheever struggled for years with alcoholic depression. In March 1977, Cheever was featured on the cover of* Newsweek *as the author of Falconer, "a great American novel."* Stories of John Cheever *(1978) became one of the most successful story collections ever, winning numerous awards for its poised, elegant prose, and insightful perspective on American life.*

The last time I saw my father was in Grand Central Station. I was going from my grandmother's in the Adirondacks to a cottage on the Cape that my mother had rented, and I wrote my father that I would be in New York between trains for an hour and a half, and asked if we could have lunch together. His secretary wrote to say that he would meet me at the information booth at noon, and at twelve o'clock sharp I saw him coming through the crowd. He was a stranger to me—my mother divorced him three years ago and I hadn't been with him since—but as soon as I saw him I felt that he was my father, my flesh and blood, my future and my doom. I knew that when I was grown I would be something like him; I would have to plan my campaigns within his limitations. He was a big, good-looking man, and I was terribly happy to see him again. He struck me on the back and shook my hand. "Hi Charlie," he said, "Hi, boy. I'd like to take you up to my club, but it's in the Sixties, and if you have to catch an early train I guess we'd better get something to eat around here." He put his arm around me, and I smelled my father the way my mother sniffs a rose. It was a rich compound of whiskey, after shave lotion, shoe polish, woolens, and the rankness of a mature male. I hoped that someone would see us together. I wished that we could be photographed. I wanted some record of our having been together.

We went out of the station and up a side street to a restaurant. It was still very early, and the place was empty. The bartender was quarreling with a delivery boy, and there was one very old waiter in a red coat down by the kitchen door. We sat down, and my father hailed the waiter in a loud voice. *"Kellner°!"* he shouted. *"Garçon°! Cameriere°! You!"* His boisterousness in the empty restaurant seemed out of place. "Could we have a little service here!" he shouted. "Chop-chop." Then he clapped his hands. This caught the waiter's attention, and he shuffled over to our table.

"Were you clapping your hands at me?" he asked.

"Calm down, calm down, *sommelier°*," my father said. "If it isn't too much to ask of you—if it wouldn't be too much above and beyond the call of duty, we would like a couple of Beefeater Gibsons°."

"I don't like to be clapped at," the waiter said. 5

"I should have brought my whistle," my father said. "I have a whistle that is audible only to the ears of old waiters. Now, take out your little pad and your little pencil and see if you can get this straight: two Beefeater Gibsons. Repeat after me: two Beefeater Gibsons."

"I think you'd better go somewhere else," the waiter said quietly.

"That," said my father, "is one of the most brilliant suggestions I have ever heard. Come on, Charlie, let's get the hell out of here."

I followed my father out of that restaurant and into another. He was not so boisterous this time. Our drinks came, and he cross-questioned me about the baseball season. He then struck the edge of his empty glass with his knife and began shouting again. *"Garçon! Kellner! Cameriere! You!* Could we trouble you to bring us two more of the same?"

"How old is the boy?" the waiter asked. 10

"That," my father said, "is none of your God-damned business."

"I'm sorry, sir," the waiter said, "but I won't serve the boy another drink."

Kellner: Barkeep; waiter (German). ***Garçon:*** Waiter (French). ***Cameriere:*** Waiter (Italian). ***Sommelier:*** Wine steward. **Beefeater Gibson:** A martini made with Beefeater gin.

"Well, I have some news for you," my father said. "I have some very interesting news for you. This doesn't happen to be the only restaurant in New York. They've opened another on the corner. C'mon, Charlie."

He paid the bill, and I followed him out of that restaurant into another. Here the waiters wore pink jackets like hunting coats, and there was a lot of horse tack on the walls. We sat down, and my father began to shout again.

"Master of the hounds! Tallyhoo and all that sort of thing. We'd like a little something in the way of a stirrup cup. Namely, two Bibson Geefeaters."

"Two Bibson Geefeaters?" the waiter asked, smiling.

"You know damned well what I want," my father said angrily. "I want two Beefeater Gibsons, and make it snappy. Things have changed in jolly old England. So my friend the duke tells me. Let's see what England can produce in the way of a cocktail."

"This isn't England," the waiter said.

"Don't argue with me," my father said. "Just do as you're told."

"I just thought you might like to know where you are," the waiter said.

"If there is one thing I cannot tolerate," my father said, "it is an impudent domestic. C'mon, Charlie."

The fourth place we went to was Italian. "*Buon giorno,*" my father said. "*Per favore, possiamo avere*° *due cocktail americani*°, *forti, forti. Molto gin, poco vermut.*"

"I don't understand Italian," the waiter said.

"Oh, come off it," my father said. "You understand Italian, and you know damned well you do. *Vogliamo due cocktail americani. Subito.*"

The waiter left us and spoke with the captain, who came over to our table and said, "I'm sorry, sir, but this table is reserved."

"All right," my father said. "Get us another table."

"All the tables are reserved," the captain said.

"I get it," my father said. "You don't desire our patronage. Is that it? Well, the hell with you. *Vada all'inferno*°. Let's go, Charlie."

"I have to get my train," I said.

"I'm sorry, sonny," my father said. "I'm terribly sorry." He put his arm around me and pressed me against him. "I'll walk you back to the station. If there had only been time to go up to my club."

"That's all right, Daddy," I said.

"I'll get you a paper," he said. "I'll get you a paper to read on the train."

Then he went up to a newsstand and said, "Kind sir, will you be good enough to favor me with one of your God-damned, no-good, ten-cent afternoon papers?" The clerk turned away from him and stared at a magazine cover. "Is it asking too much, kind sir," my father said, "is it asking too much for you to sell me one of your disgusting specimens of yellow journalism°?"

"I have to go, Daddy," I said. "It's late."

Per favore possiamo avere: Please can we have ... (Italian). ***Due cocktail americani:*** Two American cocktails (Italian). ***Vada all' inferno:*** Go to hell (Italian). **Yellow journalism:** A style of newspaper reporting that emphasizes sensationalism over facts.

"Now, just wait a second, sonny," he said. "Just wait a second. I want to get a rise out of this chap." 35

"Goodbye, Daddy," I said, and I went down the stairs and got my train, and that was the last time I saw my father. *[1978]*

THINKING ABOUT THE TEXT

1. Filling in the gaps in this story, why do you think Charlie's mother divorced his father? Why hasn't Charlie seen his father in three years? Why hasn't he seen him since?
2. How would you characterize the father's behavior? Do you think his son's presence might have affected him?
3. How does the son's comment that he was "terribly happy to see him" (para. 2) and his calling his father "Daddy" (paras. 35–40) affect your attitude toward the father's behavior? Why does he hope that someone will "see us together" (para. 2)?
4. Explain what you think the son means when he says, "I would have to plan my campaigns within his limitations" (para. 2). Seen as an initiation story, what is it the boy learns from his reunion?
5. Why is the last thing his father says to him significant? The narrator, of course, is remembering an incident from his past. What do you think his attitude is toward this incident? What specific details suggest his attitude?

DAGOBERTO GILB

Uncle Rock

Dagoberto Gilb (b. 1950) was born in Los Angeles and raised by a single mother, a Mexican woman who came to the United States illegally. He graduated from the University of Santa Barbara, where he also received a master's degree in religious studies in 1976. His first full book of stories, The Magic of Blood, *was published in 1993 by the University of New Mexico Press. Recent books include a collection of stories,* Before the End, After the Beginning *(2011), and a novel,* The Flowers *(2008). He has won numerous awards, including a Guggenheim and the PEN/Hemingway and PEN/Faulkner Awards. The following story first appeared in* The New Yorker *and was selected for the PEN/O. Henry Prize Stories 2012. He lives in Austin, Texas.*

In the morning, at his favorite restaurant, Erick got to order his favorite American food, sausage and eggs and hash-brown *papitas*° fried crunchy on top. He'd be sitting there, eating with his mother, not bothering anybody, and life was good, when a man started changing it all. Most of the time it was just a man staring too much—but then one would come over. Friendly, he'd put his thick hands on the

papitas: In Spanish, "little potato": a potato pancake, not American-style french fries.

table as if he were touching water, and squat low, so that he was at sitting level, as though he were being so polite, and he'd smile, with coffee-and-tobacco-stained teeth. He might wear a bolo tie and speak in a drawl. Or he might have a tan uniform on, a company logo on the back, an oval name patch on the front. Or he'd be in a nothing-special work shirt, white or striped, with a couple of pens clipped onto the left side pocket, tucked into a pair of jeans or chinos that were morning-clean still, with a pair of scuffed work boots that laced up higher than regular shoes. He'd say something about her earrings, or her bracelet, or her hair, or her eyes, and if she had on her white uniform how nice it looked on her. Or he'd come right out with it and tell her how pretty she was, how he couldn't keep himself from walking up, speaking to her directly, and could they talk again? Then he'd wink at Erick. Such a fine-looking boy! How old is he, eight or nine? Erick wasn't even small for an eleven-year-old. He tightened his jaw then, slanted his eyes up from his plate at his mom and not the man, definitely not this man he did not care for. Erick drove a fork into a goopy American egg yolk and bled it into his American potatoes. She wouldn't offer the man Erick's correct age, either, saying only that he was growing too fast.

She almost always gave the man her number if he was wearing a suit. Not a sports coat but a buttoned suit with a starched white shirt and a pinned tie meant something to her. Once in a while, Erick saw one of these men again at the front door of the apartment in Silverlake. The man winked at Erick as if they were buddies. Grabbed his shoulder or arm, squeezed the muscle against the bone. What did Erick want to be when he grew up? A cop, a jet-airplane mechanic, a travel agent, a court reporter? A dog groomer? Erick stood there, because his mom said that he shouldn't be impolite. His mom's date said he wanted to take Erick along with them sometime. The three of them. What kind of places did Erick think were fun? Erick said nothing. He never said anything when the men were around, and not because of his English, even if that was the excuse his mother gave for his silence. He didn't talk to any of the men and he didn't talk much to his mom, either. Finally they took off, and Erick's night was his alone. He raced to the grocery store and bought half a gallon of chocolate ice cream. When he got back, he turned on the TV, scooted up real close, as close as he could, and ate his dinner with a soup spoon. He was away from all the men. Even though a man had given the TV to them. He was a salesman in an appliance store who'd bragged that a rich customer had given it to him and so why shouldn't he give it to Erick's mom, who couldn't afford such a good TV otherwise?

When his mom was working as a restaurant hostess, and was going to marry the owner, Erick ate hot-fudge sundaes and drank chocolate shakes. When she worked at a trucking company, the owner of all the trucks told her he was getting a divorce. Erick climbed into the rigs, with their rooms full of dials and levers in the sky. Then she started working in an engineer's office. There was no food or fun there, but even he could see the money. He was not supposed to touch anything, but what was there to touch — the tubes full of paper? He and his mom were invited to the engineer's house, where he had two horses and a stable, a swimming pool, and two convertible sports cars. The engineer's family was there: his grown children, his gray-haired parents. They all sat down for dinner in a dining room that seemed bigger than Erick's apartment, with three candelabras on the table, and a tablecloth and cloth napkins. Erick's mom took him aside to tell him to be well mannered at the table and polite to everyone. Erick hadn't said anything. He never spoke anyway, so how could he have said anything wrong? She leaned into his ear and said that she wanted them to know that he spoke English. That whole dinner he was silent, chewing quietly, taking the smallest bites, because he didn't want them to think he liked their food.

When she got upset about days like that, she told Erick that she wished they could just go back home. She was tired of worrying. "Back," for Erick, meant mostly the stories he'd heard from her, which never sounded so good to him: She'd had to share a room with her brothers and sisters. They didn't have toilets. They didn't have electricity. Sometimes they didn't have enough food. He saw this Mexico as if it were the backdrop of a movie on afternoon TV, where children walked around barefoot in the dirt or on broken sidewalks and small men wore wide-brimmed straw hats and baggy white shirts and pants. The women went to church all the time and prayed to alcoved saints and, heads down, fearful, counted rosary beads. There were rocks everywhere, and scorpions and tarantulas and rattlesnakes, and vultures and no trees and not much water, and skinny dogs and donkeys, and ugly bad guys with guns and bullet vests who rode laughing into town to drink and shoot off their pistols and rifles, as if it were the Fourth of July, driving their horses all over town like dirt bikes on desert dunes. When they spoke English, they had stupid accents—his mom didn't have an accent like theirs. It didn't make sense to him that Mexico would only be like that, but what if it was close? He lived on paved, lighted city streets, and a bicycle ride away were the Asian drugstore and the Armenian grocery store and the corner where black Cubans drank coffee and talked Dodgers baseball.

5 When he was in bed, where he sometimes prayed, he thanked God for his mom, who he loved, and he apologized to Him for not talking to her, or to anyone, really, except his friend Albert, and he apologized for her never going to church and for his never taking Holy Communion, as Albert did—though only to God would he admit that he wanted to because Albert did. He prayed for good to come, for his mom and for him, since God was like magic, and happiness might come the way of early morning, in the trees and bushes full of sparrows next to his open window, louder and louder when he listened hard, eyes closed.

The engineer wouldn't have mattered if Erick hadn't told Albert that he was his dad. Albert had just moved into the apartment next door and lived with both his mother and his father, and since Albert's mother already didn't like Erick's mom, Erick told him that his new dad was an engineer. Erick actually believed it, too, and thought that he might even get his own horse. When that didn't happen, and his mom was lying on her bed in the middle of the day, blowing her nose, because she didn't have the job anymore, that was when Roque came around again. Roque was nobody—or he was anybody. He wasn't special, he wasn't not. He tried to speak English to Erick, thinking that was the reason Erick didn't say anything when he was there. And Erick had to tell Albert that Roque was his uncle, because the engineer was supposed to be his new dad any minute. Uncle Rock, Erick said.

His mom's brother, he told Albert. Roque worked at night and was around during the day, and one day he offered Erick and Albert a ride. When his mom got in the car, she scooted all the way over to Roque on the bench seat. Who was supposed to be her brother, Erick's Uncle Rock. Albert didn't say anything, but he saw what had happened, and that was it for Erick. Albert had parents, grandparents, and a brother and a sister, and he'd hang out only when one of his cousins wasn't coming by. Erick didn't need a friend like him.

What if she married Roque, his mom asked him one day soon afterward. She told Erick that they would move away from the apartment in Silverlake to a better neighborhood. He did want to move, but he wished that it weren't because of Uncle Rock. It wasn't just because Roque didn't have a swimming pool or horses or a big ranch house. There wasn't much to criticize except that he was always too willing and nice, too considerate, too generous. He wore nothing flashy or expensive, just ordinary clothes that were clean and ironed, and shoes he kept shined. He combed and parted his hair neatly. He didn't have a buzzcut like the men who didn't like kids. He moved slow, he talked slow, as quiet as night. He only ever said yes to Erick's mom. How could she not like him for that? He loved her so much—anybody could see his pride when he was with her. He signed checks and gave her cash. He knocked on their door carrying cans and fruit and meat. He was there when she asked, gone when she asked, back whenever, grateful. He took her out to restaurants on Sunset, to the movies in Hollywood, or on drives to the beach in rich Santa Monica.

Roque knew that Erick loved baseball. Did Roque like baseball? It was doubtful that he cared even a little bit—he didn't listen to games on the radio or TV, and he never looked at a newspaper. He loved boxing, though. He knew the names of all the Mexican fighters as if they lived here, as if they were Dodgers players, like Steve Sax or Steve Yeager, Dusty Baker, Kenny Landreaux or Mike Marshall, Pedro Guerrero. Roque did know about Fernando Valenzuela, as everyone did, even his mom, which is why she agreed to let Roque take them to a game. What Mexican didn't love Fernando? Dodger Stadium was close to their apartment. He'd been there once with Albert and his family—well, outside it, on a nearby hill, to see the fireworks for Fourth of July. His mom decided that all three of them would go on a Saturday afternoon, since Saturday night, Erick thought, she might want to go somewhere else, even with somebody else.

Roque, of course, didn't know who the Phillies were. He knew nothing about the strikeouts by Steve Carlton or the home runs by Mike Schmidt. He'd never heard of Pete Rose. It wasn't that Erick knew very much, either, but there was nothing that Roque could talk to him about, if they were to talk.

If Erick showed his excitement when they drove up to Dodger Stadium and 10
parked, his mom and Roque didn't really notice it. They sat in the bleachers, and for him the green of the field was a magic light; the stadium decks surrounding them seemed as far away as Rome. His body was somewhere it had never been before. The fifth inning? That's how late they were. Or were they right on time, because they weren't even sure they were sitting in the right seats yet when he heard the crack of the ball, saw the crowd around them rising as it came at them.

Erick saw the ball. He had to stand and move and stretch his arms and want that ball until it hit his bare hands and stayed there. Everybody saw him catch it with no bobble. He felt all the eyes and voices around him as if they were every set of eyes and every voice in the stadium. His mom was saying something, and Roque, too, and then, finally, it was just him and that ball and his stinging hands. He wasn't even sure if it had been hit by Pete Guerrero. He thought for sure it had been, but he didn't ask. He didn't watch the game then—he couldn't. He didn't care who won. He stared at his official National League ball, reimagining what had happened. He ate a hot dog and drank a soda and he sucked the salted peanuts and the wooden spoon from his chocolate-malt ice cream. He rubbed the bumpy seams of his home-run ball.

Game over, they were the last to leave. People were hanging around, not going straight to their cars. Roque didn't want to leave. He didn't want to end it so quickly, Erick thought, while he still had her with him. Then one of the Phillies came out of the stadium door and people swarmed—boys mostly, but also men and some women and girls—and they got autographs before the player climbed onto the team's bus. Joe Morgan, they said. Then Garry Maddox appeared. Erick clutched the ball but he didn't have a pen. He just watched, his back to the gray bus the Phillies were getting into.

Then a window slid open. *Hey, big man,* a voice said. Erick really wasn't sure. *Gimme the ball, la pelota,* the face in the bus said. *I'll have it signed, comprendes? Échalo*°, just toss it to me. Erick obeyed. He tossed it up to the hand that was reaching out. The window closed. The ball was gone a while, so long that his mom came up to him, worried that he'd lost it. The window slid open again and the voice spoke to her. *We got the ball, Mom. It's not lost, just a few more.* When the window opened once more, this time the ball was there. *Catch.* There were all kinds of signatures on it, though none that he could really recognize except for Joe Morgan and Pete Rose.

Then the voice offered more, and the hand threw something at him. *For your mom, O.K.? Comprendes?* Erick stared at the asphalt lot where the object lay, as if he'd never seen a folded-up piece of paper before. *Para tu mamá, bueno?*° He picked it up, and he started to walk over to his mom and Roque, who were so busy talking they hadn't noticed anything. Then he stopped. He opened the note himself. No one had said he couldn't read it. It said, *I'd like to get to know you. You are muy linda. Very beautiful and sexy. I don't speak Spanish very good, may be you speak better English, pero No Importa. Would you come by tonite and let me buy you a drink?* There was a phone number and a hotel-room number. A name, too. A name that came at him the way that the home run had.

Erick couldn't hear. He could see only his mom ahead of him. She was talking to Roque, Roque was talking to her. Roque was the proudest man, full of joy because he was with her. It wasn't his fault he wasn't an engineer. Now Erick could hear again. Like sparrows hunting seed, boys gathered round the bus, calling out, while the voice in the bus was yelling at him, *Hey, big guy! Give it to her!* Erick had the ball in one hand and the note in the other. By the time he reached

Comprendes Echalo?: Do you understand? ***para tu mama, bueno?:*** For your Mom, OK?

his mom and Roque, the note was already somewhere on the asphalt parking lot. *Look,* he said in a full voice. *They all signed the ball.* [2010]

THINKING ABOUT THE TEXT

1. What are some reasons that Erick doesn't speak throughout the story? Why does he finally speak in the last line of the story?
2. This could be thought of as a coming-of-age narrative for Erick. What does he come to understand about adult life, especially men and women? How does his view of men change?
3. Why does Erick say he doesn't need a friend like Albert? What does Erick fear? What does he hope for?
4. What are Roque's strengths and weaknesses according to Erick? Does he change his mind about these? What is the significance of Uncle Rock becoming Roque?
5. Why does Erick throw the note from the ballplayer away? How can this be seen as a positive move for Erick?

MAKING COMPARISONS

1. How are ideas about masculinity dealt with in these two stories?
2. What do both boys learn about men in these stories? Why, for example, are they disappointed in male behavior?
3. What might Erick think of Charlie's father? What might Charlie's father think of Roque?

WRITING ABOUT ISSUES

1. Argue that Erick does or does not learn something important about adult relationships.
2. Argue that both stories are about a search for an appropriate father figure.
3. Argue that unpacking the titles of these two stories is a way to understand significant ideas about masculine role models.
4. Write an argument, based on your personal experience and on your familiarity with novels, films, and television shows, about appropriate role models for fatherhood provided by American culture.

Literature and Current Issues: Why Do Children Rebel against Parental Expectations?

HANIF KUREISHI, "My Son, the Fanatic"

ARGUMENTS ON THE ISSUE:
ROGER COHEN, "Why ISIS Trumps Freedom"

ABDELKADER BENALI, "From Teenage Angst to Jihad"

Parents the world over hope that their children will flourish in society. They want them to be happy, to be successful, and to lead meaningful, productive lives. And the dream of most working-class parents is that their children can move into the middle class, with all the material and cultural advantages they were not able to provide. Not only is that the American Dream; it is a universal hope. Although the following story takes place in England, it could have happened here. In fact, it has, a multitude of times. Our story, however, explores the difficulties that ensue when the child not only rejects the parent's dream but also rejects the entire culture's values and behavior. For the child, the parent's dream is a nightmare. We are familiar with the children who grew up in the 1960s in both England and America who rejected the materialism of their parents, at least for a while. But when religion is at the heart of the rebellion against the parents, the problem is more intense. The father in the following story hopes that his son will adopt Western values, but the son has recently become a devout Muslim with hostile attitudes toward all things Western. The father is baffled and frustrated and finally quite angry. There seems to be no room for compromise. Roger Cohen and Abdelkader Benali provide some insight into why young Muslims like Ali, raised in the West, might reject its values in favor of a fundamentalism that seems to want to return to a pre-industrial society of religious zealotry. Speaking from experience as a Muslim raised in Europe, Abdelkader Benali sheds light on the difficulty of living in a secular culture. Both essays were written after the deadly attack on the satirical French magazine, *Charlie Hebdo*, by radical Islamists but before the massacre in Paris in November 2015 by ISIS (stands for Islamic State in Iraq and Syria; militant group known for its brutal terrorist attacks). The need to understand the chasm between Western modernity and religious extremism has never been as crucial.

BEFORE YOU READ

What does the word *fanatic* mean to you? Do you know people whom you would label as fanatics? What is it about their behavior that makes you think of them in this way? Are there any reasons that someone might label you a fanatic?

David Levenson/
Getty Images

HANIF KUREISHI

My Son, the Fanatic

Of British and Pakistani descent, Hanif Kureishi was born in Kent, England, in 1954. Although he has written several plays, he is best known for his fiction and screenplays. Much of his work deals with the struggles of South Asian immigrants and their families as they face the tensions of Great Britain's increasingly multicultural society. Kureishi's novels include The Buddha of Suburbia *(1990),* The Black Album *(1995),* Intimacy *(1998),* Gabriel's Gift *(2001), and* The Body *(2004). His script for the movie* My Beautiful Laundrette *(1986), which he based on his story of the same title, was nominated for an Academy Award and won a New York Film Critics' Award. His most recent screenplays include* Venus *(2007) and the* Black Album *(2009). His most recent work is the novel* The Last Word *(2014) and the short story collection* Love + Hate: Stories and Essays *(2015). The following story first appeared in a 1994 issue of* The New Yorker. *It was later included in his first collection of short fiction,* Love in a Blue Time *(1997). Subsequently, he wrote a screen adaptation of the story, and this film version, also titled* My Son the Fanatic, *was released in 1998.*

Surreptitiously the father began going into his son's bedroom. He would sit there for hours, rousing himself only to seek clues. What bewildered him was that Ali was getting tidier. Instead of the usual tangle of clothes, books, cricket bats, video games, the room was becoming neat and ordered; spaces began appearing where before there had been only mess.

Initially Parvez had been pleased: his son was outgrowing his teenage attitudes. But one day, beside the dustbin, Parvez found a torn bag which contained not only old toys, but computer discs, video tapes, new books, and fashionable clothes the boy had bought just a few months before. Also without explanation, Ali had parted from the English girlfriend who used to come often to the house. His old friends had stopped ringing.

For reasons he didn't himself understand, Parvez wasn't able to bring up the subject of Ali's unusual behavior. He was aware that he had become slightly afraid of his son, who, alongside his silences, was developing a sharp tongue. One remark Parvez did make, "You don't play your guitar any more," elicited the mysterious but conclusive reply, "There are more important things to be done."

Yet Parvez felt his son's eccentricity as an injustice. He had always been aware of the pitfalls which other men's sons had fallen into in England. And so, for Ali he had worked long hours and spent a lot of money paying for his education as an accountant. He had bought him good suits, all the books he required, and a computer. And now the boy was throwing his possessions out!

The TV, video, and sound system followed the guitar. Soon the room was 5
practically bare. Even the unhappy walls bore marks where Ali's pictures had been removed.

Parvez couldn't sleep; he went more to the whisky bottle, even when he was at work. He realized it was imperative to discuss the matter with someone sympathetic.

Parvez had been a taxi driver for twenty years. Half that time he'd worked for the same firm. Like him, most of the other drivers were Punjabis. They preferred to work at night, the roads were clearer and the money better. They slept during the day, avoiding their wives. Together they led almost a boy's life in the cabbies' office, playing cards and practical jokes, exchanging lewd stories, eating together, and discussing politics and their problems.

But Parvez had been unable to bring this subject up with his friends. He was too ashamed. And he was afraid, too, that they would blame him for the wrong turning his boy had taken, just as he had blamed other fathers whose sons had taken to running around with bad girls, truanting from school, and joining gangs.

For years Parvez had boasted to the other men about how Ali excelled at cricket, swimming, and football, and how attentive a scholar he was, getting straight A's in most subjects. Was it asking too much for Ali to get a good job now, marry the right girl, and start a family? Once this happened, Parvez would be happy. His dreams of doing well in England would have come true. Where had he gone wrong?

But one night, sitting in the taxi office on busted chairs with his two closest 10
friends watching a Sylvester Stallone film, he broke his silence.

"I can't understand it!" he burst out. "Everything is going from his room. And I can't talk to him any more. We were not father and son — we were brothers! Where has he gone? Why is he torturing me!"

And Parvez put his head in his hands.

Even as he poured out his account the men shook their heads and gave one another knowing glances. From their grave looks Parvez realized they understood the situation. "Tell me what is happening!" he demanded.

The reply was almost triumphant. They had guessed something was going wrong. Now it was clear. Ali was taking drugs and selling his possessions to pay for them. That was why his bedroom was emptying.

"What must I do then?" 15

Parvez's friends instructed him to watch Ali scrupulously and then be severe with him, before the boy went mad, overdosed, or murdered someone.

Parvez staggered out into the early morning air, terrified they were right. His boy — the drug addict killer!

To his relief he found Bettina sitting in his car.

Usually the last customers of the night were local "brasses" or prostitutes. The taxi drivers knew them well, often driving them to liaisons. At the end of the girls' shifts, the men would ferry them home, though sometimes the women would join them for a drinking session in the office. Occasionally the drivers would go with the girls. "A ride in exchange for a ride," it was called.

Bettina had known Parvez for three years. She lived outside the town and 20 on the long drive home, where she sat not in the passenger seat but beside him, Parvez had talked to her about his life and hopes, just as she talked about hers. They saw each other most nights.

He could talk to her about things he'd never be able to discuss with his own wife. Bettina, in turn, always reported on her night's activities. He liked to know where she was and with whom. Once he had rescued her from a violent client, and since then they had come to care for one another.

Though Bettina had never met the boy, she heard about Ali continually. That late night, when he told Bettina that he suspected Ali was on drugs, she judged neither the boy nor his father, but became businesslike and told him what to watch for.

"It's all in the eyes," she said. They might be bloodshot; the pupils might be dilated; he might look tired. He could be liable to sweats, or sudden mood changes. "Okay?"

Parvez began his vigil gratefully. Now he knew what the problem might be, he felt better. And surely, he figured, things couldn't have gone too far? With Bettina's help he would soon sort it out.

He watched each mouthful the boy took. He sat beside him at every oppor- 25 tunity and looked into his eyes. When he could he took the boy's hand, checking his temperature. If the boy wasn't at home Parvez was active, looking under the carpet, in his drawers, behind the empty wardrobe, sniffing, inspecting, probing. He knew what to look for: Bettina had drawn pictures of capsules, syringes, pills, powders, rocks.

Every night she waited to hear news of what he'd witnessed.

After a few days of constant observation, Parvez was able to report that although the boy had given up sports, he seemed healthy, with clear eyes. He didn't, as his father expected, flinch guiltily from his gaze. In fact the boy's mood was alert and steady in this sense: as well as being sullen, he was very watchful. He returned his father's long looks with more than a hint of criticism, of reproach even, so much so that Parvez began to feel that it was he who was in the wrong, and not the boy!

"And there's nothing else physically different?" Bettina asked.

"No!" Parvez thought for a moment. "But he is growing a beard."

One night, after sitting with Bettina in an all-night coffee shop, Parvez came home particularly late. Reluctantly he and Bettina had abandoned their only explanation, the drug theory, for Parvez had found nothing resembling any drug in Ali's room. Besides, Ali wasn't selling his belongings. He threw them out, gave them away, or donated them to charity shops.

Standing in the hall, Parvez heard his boy's alarm clock go off. Parvez hurried into his bedroom where his wife was still awake, sewing in bed. He ordered her to sit down and keep quiet, though she had neither stood up nor said a word. From this post, and with her watching him curiously, he observed his son through the crack in the door.

The boy went into the bathroom to wash. When he returned to his room Parvez sprang across the hall and set his ear at Ali's door. A muttering sound came from within. Parvez was puzzled but relieved.

Once this clue had been established, Parvez watched him at other times. The boy was praying. Without fail, when he was at home, he prayed five times a day.

Parvez had grown up in Lahore where all the boys had been taught the Koran. To stop him falling asleep when he studied, the Moulvi° had attached a piece of string to the ceiling and tied it to Parvez's hair, so that if his head fell forward, he would instantly awake. After this indignity Parvez had avoided all religions. Not that the other taxi drivers had more respect. In fact they made jokes about the local mullahs° walking around with their caps and beards, thinking they could tell people how to live, while their eyes roved over the boys and girls in their care.

Parvez described to Bettina what he had discovered. He informed the men in the taxi office. The friends, who had been so curious before, now became oddly silent. They could hardly condemn the boy for his devotions.

Parvez decided to take a night off and go out with the boy. They could talk things over. He wanted to hear how things were going at college; he wanted to tell him stories about their family in Pakistan. More than anything he yearned to understand how Ali had discovered the "spiritual dimension," as Bettina described it.

To Parvez's surprise, the boy refused to accompany him. He claimed he had an appointment. Parvez had to insist that no appointment could be more important than that of a son with his father.

Moulvi: Islamic religious scholar who might perform the function of a teacher.
mullahs: Muslims with religious education, who often hold supervisory positions within Islam.

The next day, Parvez went immediately to the street where Bettina stood in the rain wearing high heels, a short skirt, and a long mac on top, which she would open hopefully at passing cars.

"Get in, get in!" he said.

They drove out across the moors and parked at the spot where on better days, with a view unimpeded for many miles by nothing but wild deer and horses, they'd lie back, with their eyes half closed, saying "This is the life." This time Parvez was trembling. Bettina put her arms around him.

"What's happened?"

"I've just had the worst experience of my life."

As Bettina rubbed his head Parvez told her that the previous evening he and Ali had gone to a restaurant. As they studied the menu, the waiter, whom Parvez knew, brought him his usual whisky and water. Parvez had been so nervous he had even prepared a question. He was going to ask Ali if he was worried about his imminent exams. But first, wanting to relax, he loosened his tie, crunched a popadom,° and took a long drink.

Before Parvez could speak, Ali made a face.

"Don't you know it's wrong to drink alcohol?" he said.

"He spoke to me very harshly," Parvez told Bettina. "I was about to castigate the boy for being insolent, but managed to control myself."

He had explained patiently to Ali that for years he had worked more than ten hours a day, that he had few enjoyments or hobbies and never went on holiday. Surely it wasn't a crime to have a drink when he wanted one?

"But it is forbidden," the boy said.

Parvez shrugged, "I know."

"And so is gambling, isn't it."

"Yes. But surely we are only human?"

Each time Parvez took a drink, the boy winced, or made a fastidious face as an accompaniment. This made Parvez drink more quickly. The waiter, wanting to please his friend, brought another glass of whisky. Parvez knew he was getting drunk, but he couldn't stop himself. Ali had a horrible look on his face, full of disgust and censure. It was as if he hated his father.

Halfway through the meal Parvez suddenly lost his temper and threw a plate on the floor. He had felt like ripping the cloth from the table, but the waiters and other customers were staring at him. Yet he wouldn't stand for his own son telling him the difference between right and wrong. He knew he wasn't a bad man. He had a conscience. There were a few things of which he was ashamed, but on the whole he had lived a decent life.

"When have I had time to be wicked?" he asked Ali.

In a low monotonous voice the boy explained that Parvez had not, in fact, lived a good life. He had broken countless rules of the Koran.

"For instance?" Parvez demanded.

Ali hadn't needed time to think. As if he had been waiting for this moment, he asked his father if he didn't relish pork pies?

popadom: Unleavened bread made from lentils and shaped like a disc.

"Well . . ."

Parvez couldn't deny that he loved crispy bacon smothered with mushrooms and mustard and sandwiched between slices of fried bread. In fact he ate this for breakfast every morning.

Ali then reminded Parvez that he had ordered his own wife to cook pork sausages, saying to her, "You're not in the village now, this is England. We have to fit in!"

Parvez was so annoyed and perplexed by this attack that he called for more drink.

"The problem is this," the boy said. He leaned across the table. For the first time that night his eyes were alive. "You are too implicated in Western civilization."

Parvez burped; he thought he was going to choke. "Implicated!" he said. "But we live here!"

"The Western materialists hate us," Ali said. "Papa, how can you love something which hates you?"

"What is the answer then?" Parvez said miserably. "According to you."

Ali addressed his father fluently, as if Parvez were a rowdy crowd that had to be quelled and convinced. The Law of Islam would rule the world; the skin of the infidel would burn off again and again; the Jews and Christers would be routed. The West was a sink of hypocrites, adulterers, homosexuals, drug takers, and prostitutes.

As Ali talked, Parvez looked out of the window as if to check that they were still in London.

"My people have taken enough. If the persecution doesn't stop there will be *jihad.* I, and millions of others, will gladly give our lives for the cause."

"But why, why?" Parvez said.

"For us the reward will be in paradise."

"Paradise!"

Finally, as Parvez's eyes filled with tears, the boy urged him to mend his ways.

"How is that possible?" Parvez asked.

"Pray," Ali said. "Pray beside me."

Parvez called for the bill and ushered his boy out of the restaurant as soon as he was able. He couldn't take any more. Ali sounded as if he'd swallowed someone else's voice.

On the way home the boy sat in the back of the taxi, as if he were a customer.

"What has made you like this?" Parvez asked him, afraid that somehow he was to blame for all this. "Is there a particular event which has influenced you?"

"Living in this country."

"But I love England," Parvez said, watching his boy in the mirror. "They let you do almost anything here."

"That is the problem," he replied.

For the first time in years Parvez couldn't see straight. He knocked the side of the car against a lorry, ripping off the wing mirror. They were lucky not to have been stopped by the police: Parvez would have lost his license and therefore his job.

Getting out of the car back at the house, Parvez stumbled and fell in the road, scraping his hands and ripping his trousers. He managed to haul himself up. The boy didn't even offer him his hand.

Parvez told Bettina he was now willing to pray, if that was what the boy wanted, if that would dislodge the pitiless look from his eyes.

"But what I object to," he said, "is being told by my own son that I am going to hell!"

What finished Parvez off was that the boy had said he was giving up accountancy. When Parvez had asked why, Ali had said sarcastically that it was obvious.

"Western education cultivates an antireligious attitude."

And, according to Ali, in the world of accountants it was usual to meet women, drink alcohol, and practice usury.

"But it's well-paid work," Parvez argued. "For years you've been preparing!"

Ali said he was going to begin to work in prisons, with poor Muslims who were struggling to maintain their purity in the face of corruption. Finally, at the end of the evening, as Ali was going to bed, he had asked his father why he didn't have a beard, or at least a mustache.

"I feel as if I've lost my son," Parvez told Bettina. "I can't bear to be looked at as if I'm a criminal. I've decided what to do."

"What is it?"

"I'm going to tell him to pick up his prayer mat and get out of my house. It will be the hardest thing I've ever done, but tonight I'm going to do it."

"But you mustn't give up on him," said Bettina. "Many young people fall into cults and superstitious groups. It doesn't mean they'll always feel the same way."

She said Parvez had to stick by his boy, giving support, until he came through.

Parvez was persuaded that she was right, even though he didn't feel like giving his son more love when he had hardly been thanked for all he had already given.

Nevertheless, Parvez tried to endure his son's looks and reproaches. He attempted to make conversation about his beliefs. But if Parvez ventured any criticism, Ali always had a brusque reply. On one occasion Ali accused Parvez of "grovelling" to the whites; in contrast, he explained, he was not "inferior," there was more to the world than the West, though the West always thought it was best.

"How is it you know that?" Parvez said, "seeing as you've never left England?"

Ali replied with a look of contempt.

One night, having ensured there was no alcohol on his breath, Parvez sat down at the kitchen table with Ali. He hoped Ali would compliment him on the beard he was growing but Ali didn't appear to notice.

The previous day Parvez had been telling Bettina that he thought people in the West sometimes felt inwardly empty and that people needed a philosophy to live by.

"Yes," said Bettina. "That's the answer. You must tell him what your philosophy of life is. Then he will understand that there are other beliefs."

After some fatiguing consideration, Parvez was ready to begin. The boy watched him as if he expected nothing.

Haltingly Parvez said that people had to treat one another with respect, particularly children their parents. This did seem, for a moment, to affect the boy. Heartened, Parvez continued. In his view this life was all there was and when you died you rotted in the earth. "Grass and flowers will grow out of me, but something of me will live on — "

"How?"

"In other people. I will continue — in you." At this the boy appeared a little distressed. "And your grandchildren," Parvez added for good measure. "But while I am here on earth I want to make the best of it. And I want you to, as well!"

"What d'you mean by 'make the best of it'?" asked the boy.

"Well," said Parvez. "For a start . . . you should enjoy yourself. Yes. Enjoy yourself without hurting others."

Ali said that enjoyment was a "bottomless pit."

"But I don't mean enjoyment like that!" said Parvez. "I mean the beauty of living!"

"All over the world our people are oppressed," was the boy's reply.

"I know," Parvez replied, not entirely sure who "our people" were, "but still — life is for living!"

Ali said, "Real morality has existed for hundreds of years. Around the world millions and millions of people share my beliefs. Are you saying you are right and they are all wrong?"

Ali looked at his father with such aggressive confidence that Parvez could say no more.

One evening Bettina was sitting in Parvez's car, after visiting a client, when they passed a boy on the street.

"That's my son," Parvez said suddenly. They were on the other side of town, in a poor district, where there were two mosques.

Parvez set his face hard.

Bettina turned to watch him. "Slow down then, slow down!" She said, "He's good-looking. Reminds me of you. But with a more determined face. Please, can't we stop?"

"What for?"

"I'd like to talk to him."

Parvez turned the cab round and stopped beside the boy.

"Coming home?" Parvez asked. "It's quite a way."

The sullen boy shrugged and got into the back seat. Bettina sat in the front. Parvez became aware of Bettina's short skirt, gaudy rings and ice-blue eyeshadow. He became conscious that the smell of her perfume, which he loved, filled the cab. He opened the window.

While Parvez drove as fast as he could, Bettina said gently to Ali, "Where have you been?"

"The mosque," he said.

"And how are you getting on at college? Are you working hard?"

"Who are you to ask me these questions?" he said, looking out of the window. Then they hit bad traffic and the car came to a standstill.

By now Bettina had inadvertently laid her hand on Parvez's shoulder. She said, "Your father, who is a good man, is very worried about you. You know he loves you more than his own life."

"You say he loves me," the boy said.

"Yes!" said Bettina.

"Then why is he letting a woman like you touch him like that?" 130

If Bettina looked at the boy in anger, he looked back at her with twice as much cold fury.

She said, "What kind of woman am I that deserves to be spoken to like that?"

"You know," he said. "Now let me out."

"Never," Parvez replied.

"Don't worry, I'm getting out," Bettina said. 135

"No, don't!" said Parvez. But even as the car moved she opened the door, threw herself out, and ran away across the road. Parvez shouted after her several times, but she had gone.

Parvez took Ali back to the house, saying nothing more to him. Ali went straight to his room. Parvez was unable to read the paper, watch television, or even sit down. He kept pouring himself drinks.

At last he went upstairs and paced up and down outside Ali's room. When, finally, he opened the door, Ali was praying. The boy didn't even glance his way.

Parvez kicked him over. Then he dragged the boy up by his shirt and hit him. The boy fell back. Parvez hit him again. The boy's face was bloody. Parvez was panting. He knew that the boy was unreachable, but he struck him nonetheless. The boy neither covered himself nor retaliated; there was no fear in his eyes. He only said, through his split lip: "So who's the fanatic now?" *[1994]*

☰ THINKING ABOUT THE TEXT

1. Not until a few pages into the story do we learn what is really going on with Ali. Until then, we share his father's mystification. Why do you think Kureishi does not tell us sooner about Ali's turn to religion?
2. Ali says, "The Western materialists hate us" (para. 64). Is this true? His father then asks, "What is the answer then? . . . According to you" (para. 65). How do you respond to Ali's answer?
3. What specific ideals and principles are in conflict as the father and son argue with each other? Can these differences be negotiated, or are they irreconcilable?
4. What should we conclude about Parvez's relationship with Bettina? What would you say to someone who faults Parvez for committing adultery with a prostitute? Is Parvez's relationship an individual one, or does it say something about Western values?
5. Do you approve of Parvez's behavior when he beats his son at the story's end? Why, or why not? Is Ali's response to the beating correct—that is, do you think the father has become a fanatic?

ROGER COHEN

Why ISIS Trumps Freedom

Roger Cohen (1955), a regular columnist for the New York Times, *was born in London and graduated from Oxford University in 1977 with degrees in history and French. He began his career with the* Wall Street Journal *covering Italy and Beirut. He joined the* New York Times *in 1990 and covered the Bosnian War. He later wrote about his experience in* Hearts Grown Brutal *(1998), which was highly praised. He has won numerous awards and prizes for his journalism and articles on the Middle East. In 2012 Cohen won a Lifetime Achievement award for journalistic excellence. The following essay appeared in the* New York Times *on August 13, 2015.*

What leads young European Muslims in the thousands to give up lives in France, Britain or Germany, enlist in the ranks of the movement calling itself the Islamic State, and dedicate themselves to the unlikely aim of establishing a caliphate backed by digital propaganda?

The honest answer is that we don't know why a 20-something Briton with a degree in computer engineering or a young Frenchman from a Norman village reaches a psychological tipping point.

Zealotry of any kind subsumes the difficulty of individual choices into the exalted collective submission of dedication to a cause. Your mission is set. It is presented as a great one with great rewards. Goodbye, tough calls. Goodbye, loneliness.

Islamic State has been adept in exploiting the alienation felt by many young Muslims, from the "quartiers" of Paris to the back streets of Bradford. It offers to give meaning, whether in this life or the next, to meaningless lives.

The group has benefited from active support by online jihadi preachers 5
and from tacit backing, or at least acquiescence, from imams in some mosques who are inclined, in the words of Prime Minister David Cameron of Britain, to "quietly condone." It has manipulated anger over America's wars in Iraq and Afghanistan, over Abu Ghraib and Guantánamo, over Shia ascendancy in the Middle East, over bleak existences on the margins of European society.

Still, the explanations fall short. Plenty of people experience great hardship or prejudice without opting to behead infidels and apostates, practice codified rape on teenage nonbelievers, and pursue the establishment of God's rule on earth through his chosen caliph and in accordance with Shariah law.

Every effort of Western societies, particularly since 9/11, to curb the metastasizing jihadi ideology that threatens them has failed. Some of the organizations that grew out of that ideology have been hurt. But the ideas behind them, rooted in a violent rejection of modernity (but not all its tools, witness the Islamic State's slick use of the Internet) and in an extreme, literalist interpretation of certain teachings of Sunni Islam, have proved of unquenchable appeal.

It's a long way from Yorkshire to Raqqa in eastern Syria, yet some young British Muslims make the trip. Other recruits arrive from Saudi Arabia and Russia, Libya and Australia. The Islamic State has demonstrated very broad outreach. It is clearly tapping into something deep. Perhaps that something is at root a yearning to be released from the burden of freedom.

Western societies have been going ever further in freeing their citizens' choices—in releasing them from ties of tradition or religion, in allowing people to marry whom they want and divorce as often as they want, have sex with whom they want, die when they want and generally do what they want. There are few, if any, moral boundaries left.

10 In this context, radical Islam offers salvation, or at least purpose, in the form of a life whose moral parameters are strictly set, whose daily habits are prescribed, whose satisfaction of everyday needs is assured and whose rejection of freedom is unequivocal. By taking away freedom, the Islamic State lifts a psychological weight on its young followers adrift on the margins of European society.

Mark Lilla, in an essay this year in the *New York Review of Books* on the French novelist Michel Houellebecq's "Submission" (whose central character, a disaffected literature professor, ultimately chooses to convert to Islam) made this important point:

"The qualities that Houellebecq projects onto Islam are no different from those that the religious right ever since the French Revolution has attributed to premodern Christendom—strong families, moral education, social order, a sense of place, a meaningful death, and, above all, the will to persist as a culture. And he shows a real understanding of those—from the radical nativist on the far right to radical Islamists—who despise the present and dream of stepping back in history to recover what they imagine was lost."

Lilla concluded that Houellebecq sees France in the grip of "a crisis that was set off two centuries ago when Europeans made a wager on history: that the more they extended human freedom, the happier they would be. For him, that wager has been lost. And so the continent is adrift and susceptible to a much older temptation, to submit to those claiming to speak for God."

In Europe right now, those speaking most ardently for God tend to be Muslims. Some of them have spoken out bravely against the Islamic State. A majority see the movement as a betrayal of their religion. But the jihadi temptation to escape from freedom into all-answering zealotry is there and will not soon be curbed.

15 It is interesting that another foe of the West, President Vladimir Putin, attacks its culture from a similar standpoint: as irreligious, decadent and relativist, and intent on globalizing these "subversive" values, often under the cover of democracy promotion, freedom and human rights.

The great victory in 1989 was of freedom. But every triumph stirs a counterforce. The road to Raqqa is the road from freedom's burden. *[2015]*

THINKING ABOUT THE TEXT

1. Although Cohen says he doesn't exactly know the answer to his opening question, what are some possible answers?
2. Give specific examples of what Cohen refers to as "the burden of freedom." How might this apply to your own experiences or your friends?
3. How does radical Islam benefit from or exploit this burden?

4. Presumably "1989" in the last paragraph refers to the fall of the Berlin Wall and the subsequent dissolution of the Soviet empire. How is this related to Cohen's point about Muslims?
5. What "counter forces" to freedom have you noticed in America? What reasons can you give, and what might be some solutions?

MAKING COMPARISONS

1. How might Ali's behavior be understandable in light of Cohen's third and fourth paragraphs?
2. Why might Ali agree with Putin's attack on the West?
3. How does Cohen's ninth paragraph relate to Ali and his father?

ABDELKADER BENALI

From Teenage Angst to Jihad

Abdelkader Benali (b. 1975), a Dutch writer and journalist, was born in Morocco and grew up in Rotterdam. He has been described as one of the Netherlands' leading writers. His first novel, Wedding of the Sea *(1996), was critically acclaimed. His latest books are* My Mother's Voice *(2009) and* The Museum of Lost Loved Ones *(2009). The following essay appeared in the* New York Times *on January 13, 2015.*

Something snapped. I was 13 years old, dreaming of books and girls and nothing else—a healthy Dutch kid with a Moroccan background who freewheeled through life. Then something happened that made me feel different from the pack. One day in history class, the fatwa against Salman Rushdie became the subject. Our teacher talked about freedom of expression; I talked about insulting the Prophet. There was an awkward silence. What was that Abdelkader guy talking about? Fatwhat?

But our teacher, Mr. Fok, understood me. He claimed the fatwa didn't make sense. How could somebody be offended by fiction? How could using one's imagination lead to the death sentence?

I remember standing up, my voice rising as I struggled to make an argument about the holiness of the Prophet to me and my community. And the more Mr. Fok responded with cold and rational analysis the angrier I got. Didn't he get that this was about more than reason and common sense? Didn't he get that mocking the Prophet was a moral crime?

My classmates looked at me like a madman. By then I was standing and shouting. I'd never felt such anger before. This wasn't about a novel, this was about me. About us. I wanted revenge. Mr. Fok just looked at me, amazed by my temper and a bit annoyed, and dismissed me from class.

For the first time in my life I felt what it meant to be Muslim. I didn't want to feel 5
that way. I wanted to blend in, to look normal like the other kids in my class. After the frustration and anger ebbed, I felt shame—for letting my religion down, letting my family down, letting myself down. Shame for an anger I didn't understand.

I grew up in a relatively traditional Moroccan family. We observed Ramadan but my father rarely went to the mosque. There were two books in our house, the Quran and the phone book. We never looked at either of them.

We didn't talk much about the fatwa but it was impossible to ignore. Muslims were marching through the streets of Rotterdam. It was the first time we felt seen as part of a community that had questions to answer: Which side are you on? Why are you offended? Where does this anger come from? Can Islam coexist with Western values?

The world didn't stop reminding me I was a Muslim. My name, my background, my skin, my family and the events unfolding in the world all led to more self-questioning.

Islam told me God is One and the Prophet is his messenger. Adhere to the five pillars and all will be well. But we were living in a non-Muslim country. But I wasn't Dutch, nor was I secular. I had to find a way to reconcile my religious background with a secular world. I felt orphaned.

And resolving that dilemma is much harder in a secular society that seems to 10
have stopped struggling with these big questions altogether.

In the end, I didn't find the answers in holy texts. I found them in literature.

I read Kafka's "Metamorphosis" and Camus' "The Plague." I thought back on my younger days lashing out against *The Satanic Verses.* I remembered sneaking into a bookshop and seeing the book piled up ready to be read but my English was insufficient to understand it. The book turned me away; the curiosity stayed.

When I was 17, I found *The Satanic Verses* tucked away in a school library. I grabbed it, started reading and was mesmerized. Here was a young man struggling with his faith in a faithless world—an immigrant son from a deeply religious home thrown into a world where everything is embraced and nothing is sacred. It confirmed what I had felt deep inside: a free and open society is a threat to religious people. Their religion will be mocked—sometimes even suppressed—and this will provoke anger.

And now it's happening again. The rise of extremists who lure young Muslims in the West with visions of Islamic utopia is creating nausea among European Muslims. Boys and girls are leaving their families and being converted into killing machines. They are leaving not from Baghdad but from Brussels and The Hague. We insist that this can't be our Islam and if this is Islam we don't want it. But I know from my own experience that the lure of extremism can be very powerful when you grow up in a world where the media and everyone around you seems to mock and insult your culture.

And European governments are not helping fight extremism by giving in to 15
Islamophobia cooked up by right-wing populists. What I see is a lack of courage to embrace the Muslims of Europe as genuinely European—as citizens like everyone else.

One of the first people the terrorists in Paris killed was one of us: Mustapha Ourrad, and Algerian-born copy editor at *Charlie Hebdo*. Then they killed another Muslim: the police officer, Ahmed Merabet. The killers didn't take mercy on them. In the name of Islam they killed Muslims. And every time a European Muslim sees that image of Mr. Merabet's last moments, he sees himself lying there on the cold pavement. Helpless. And the next question will be: What will I say tomorrow at work or at school?

What happened last week is not about lack of humor, or a failure to understand caricature. Nor is it about hatred of the West. It's about anger taking a wrong turn.

What makes us human and creative is our doubt. But doubt on its own can turn into anger and fundamentalism.

As the French writer Michel Houellebecq said in an interview: "People cannot live without God. Life becomes unbearable." The terrorists found their God in a godless society. *Charlie Hebdo* mocked their God by declaring him nothing more than a cartoon. They came back to rescue their God and left 12 dead behind. They fell prey to a powerful delusion.

It was the same delusion I felt as a teenager: that by attacking the messenger 20
your anger will disappear and you will be victorious. But the only way to conquer your anger is to understand where its roots lie. For me the freedom to doubt, to not choose sides and to feel empathy for characters and people with whom I disagree was liberating. Today I still embrace my Islamic background, but without the dogma, repression and strict adherence to ritual.

Since 9/11, so many European Muslims have also doubted their belonging. Do they belong to the Paris of Voltaire or the Mecca of Muhammad? It's the wrong question.

Muslims are every bit as European as the Roma, gays, intellectuals, farmers and factory workers. We have been in Europe for centuries and politicians and the press must stop acting is if we arrived yesterday. We are here to stay. *[2015]*

THINKING ABOUT THE TEXT

1. Explain the narrator's anger as a young adolescent. What were the sources of anger for you at that age? Your friends?
2. What is Benali's argument for why the terrorists strike? What is his solution?
3. What part does "reason and common sense" play in the controversy over moral values?
4. Explain the implications of Benali's statement: "I had to find a way to reconcile my religious background with a secular world" for him and for the Evangelicals in America.
5. Argue for or against Houellebecq's statement: "People cannot live without God. Life becomes unbearable." What do some people substitute for God?

MAKING COMPARISONS

1. What are the similarities and difference between Ali and Abdelkader growing up?
2. Explain why Benali's fourteenth paragraph might explain Ali's behavior.
3. Compare the statements of Michel Houellebecq in both Cohen and Benali.

WRITING ABOUT THE ISSUES

1. Cohen argues that one of the West's most prized attributes—freedom—is the very thing radical Muslims hate. Argue that this does or doesn't help to explain Ali's behavior.
2. Write an essay that analyzes the arguments of Cohen and Benali about the root causes of terrorism.
3. In the story, of course, Ali does not become a terrorist. But might he? Write an essay using Cohen and Benali that argues one way or the other.
4. Research the controversy over either *Charlie Hebdo* or *The Satanic Verses*. Find out the issues involved and what arguments were put forth by both sides. Write an argument that joins the controversy with your own point of view. Be sure to give fair treatment to the opposition.

A Troubled Freedom: Cultural Contexts for a Story

ERNEST HEMINGWAY, "Soldier's Home"

CULTURAL CONTEXTS:

JAMES M. HUTCHISSON, From *Ernest Hemingway: A New Life*

LEICESTER HEMINGWAY, From *My Brother, Ernest Hemingway*

CAROLINE ALEXANDER, "The Shock of War"

Among the earliest narratives in literature are those that chart the perilous journey of the soldier from home to battle and then home again. Although most of us probably assume that the physical dangers of war are the most harrowing, it is sometimes the case that, for returning warriors, the transition to a previous life can be even more gruesomely traumatic. The anticipated freedom from war is often a bitter disappointment as the inevitable psychological scars of war do not heal fast enough, if at all. Soldiers, having experienced the horrors of war, return significantly changed. They are often so afflicted by trauma that their families are bewildered and powerless to help. Writers since Homer have given us vivid stories of the troubled freedom damaged soldiers and their anxious families endure when the transition from war to home goes badly.

Ernest Hemingway's classic tale highlights the difficulties an alienated soldier has reconnecting with his family after World War I. Following "Soldier's Home," we present three cultural contexts that help us understand Hemingway's actual wartime experiences and why his story's main character had such a troubled homecoming. We follow an excerpt from a recent biography of Hemingway, focusing on his ambulance experience in Italy and his return home to Oak Park, with reminiscence from Hemingway's brother, Leicester. We then include an essay that sheds light on what Hemingway's contemporaries called "shell shock" and what we now know was PTSD.

ERNEST HEMINGWAY

Soldier's Home

One of the most influential writers of the first half of the twentieth century, Ernest Hemingway (1898–1961) was born in a suburb of Chicago but felt most alive at his parents' summer home in the woods of Michigan, where he could indulge his enthusiastic love of hunting, fishing, and camping. After high school, where he was an active and excellent student, Hemingway decided to become a journalist instead of going to college and worked successfully for the Kansas City Star. *He signed up as an ambulance driver for the Red Cross during World War I and was seriously wounded in Italy. After moving to Paris after the war, he wrote his first important book,* In Our Time *(1925). It was well received, and the next year* The Sun Also Rises, *about the "lost generation," made him a celebrity. He published several popular novels, including* For Whom the Bell Tolls *(1949) and* The Old Man and the Sea *(1952). He received the Nobel Prize for literature in 1954 and committed suicide after difficult mental and physical problems. Always full of contradictions, Hemingway was at once an inveterate sportsman and an omnivorous reader; he loved life while also being obsessed with death, especially his father's suicide. Most people think of him as a famous and intensely masculine writer of adventure tales of big game hunting, fishing, and war. While this is true, he was also a dedicated and intricate stylist of great delicacy and power. The following story is a good example of Hemingway's technique. He was a believer in compression, using an analogy to an iceberg to explain his narrative method: "There is seven-eighths of it under water for every part that shows." His laconic style continues to influence today's writers.*

Krebs went to the war from a Methodist college in Kansas. There is a picture which shows him among his fraternity brothers, all of them wearing exactly the same height and style collar. He enlisted in the Marines in 1917 and did not return to the United States until the second division returned from the Rhine in the summer of 1919.

There is a picture which shows him on the Rhine with two German girls and another corporal. Krebs and the corporal look too big for their uniforms. The German girls are not beautiful. The Rhine does not show in the picture.

By the time Krebs returned to his home town in Oklahoma the greeting of heroes was over. He came back much too late. The men from the town who had been drafted had all been welcomed elaborately on their return. There had been a great deal of hysteria. Now the reaction had set in. People seemed to think it was rather ridiculous for Krebs to be getting back so late, years after the war was over.

At first Krebs, who had been at Belleau Wood, Soissons, the Champagne, St. Mihiel, and in the Argonne° did not want to talk about the war at all. Later he felt the need to talk but no one wanted to hear about it. His town had heard too many atrocity stories to be thrilled by actualities. Krebs found that to be listened to at all he had to lie, and after he had done this twice he, too, had a reaction against the war and against talking about it. A distaste for everything that had happened to him in the war set in because of the lies he had told. All of the times that had been able to make him feel cool and clear inside himself when he thought of them; the times so long back when he had done the one thing, the only thing for a man to do, easily and naturally, when he might have done something else, now lost their cool, valuable quality and then were lost themselves.

His lies were quite unimportant lies and consisted in attributing to himself 5
things other men had seen, done, or heard of, and stating as facts certain apocryphal incidents familiar to all soldiers. Even his lies were not sensational at the pool room. His acquaintances, who had heard detailed accounts of German women found chained to machine guns in the Argonne forest and who could not comprehend, or were barred by their patriotism from interest in, any German machine gunners who were not chained, were not thrilled by his stories.

Belleau Wood . . . Argonne: Battle sites in World War I.

Krebs acquired the nausea in regard to experience that is the result of untruth or exaggeration, and when he occasionally met another man who had really been a soldier and they talked a few minutes in the dressing room at a dance he fell into the easy pose of the old soldier among other soldiers: that he had been badly, sickeningly frightened all the time. In this way he lost everything.

During this time, it was late summer, he was sleeping late in bed, getting up to walk down town to the library to get a book, eating lunch at home, reading on the front porch until he became bored, and then walking down through the town to spend the hottest hours of the day in the cool dark of the pool room. He loved to play pool.

In the evening he practiced on his clarinet, strolled down town, read, and went to bed. He was still a hero to his two young sisters. His mother would have given him breakfast in bed if he had wanted it. She often came in when he was in bed and asked him to tell her about the war, but her attention always wandered. His father was noncommittal.

Before Krebs went away to the war he had never been allowed to drive the family motor car. His father was in the real estate business and always wanted the car to be at his command when he required it to take clients out into the country to show them a piece of farm property. The car always stood outside the First National Bank building where his father had an office on the second floor. Now, after the war, it was still the same car.

Nothing was changed in the town except that the young girls had grown up. 10
But they lived in such a complicated world of already defined alliances and shifting feuds that Krebs did not feel the energy or the courage to break into it. He liked to look at them, though. There were so many good-looking young girls. Most of them had their hair cut short. When he went away only little girls wore their hair like that or girls that were fast. They all wore sweaters and shirt waists with round Dutch collars. It was a pattern. He liked to look at them from the front porch as they walked on the other side of the street. He liked to watch them walking under the shade of the trees. He liked the round Dutch collars above their sweaters. He liked their silk stockings and flat shoes. He liked their bobbed hair and the way they walked.

When he was in town their appeal to him was not very strong. He did not like them when he saw them in the Greek's ice cream parlor. He did not want them themselves really. They were too complicated. There was something else. Vaguely he wanted a girl but he did not want to have to work to get her. He would have liked to have a girl but he did not want to have to spend a long time getting her. He did not want to get into the intrigue and the politics. He did not want to have to do any courting. He did not want to tell any more lies. It wasn't worth it.

He did not want any consequences. He did not want any consequences ever again. He wanted to live alone without consequences. Besides he did not really need a girl. The army had taught him that. It was all right to pose as though you had to have a girl. Nearly everybody did that. But it wasn't true. You did not need a girl. That was the funny thing. First a fellow boasted how girls mean nothing to him, that he never thought of them, that they could not touch him. Then a fellow boasted that he could not get along without girls, that he had to have them all the time, that he could not go to sleep without them.

That was all a lie. It was all a lie both ways. You did not need a girl unless you thought about them. He learned that in the army. Then sooner or later you always got one. When you were really ripe for a girl you always got one. You did not have to think about it. Sooner or later it would come. He had learned that in the army.

Now he would have liked a girl if she had come to him and not wanted to talk. But here at home it was all too complicated. He knew he could never get through it all again. It was not worth the trouble. That was the thing about French girls and German girls. There was not all this talking. You couldn't talk much and you did not need to talk. It was simple and you were friends. He thought about France and then he began to think about Germany. On the whole he had liked Germany better. He did not want to leave Germany. He did not want to come home. Still, he had come home. He sat on the front porch.

He liked the girls that were walking along the other side of the street. He liked the look of them much better than the French girls or the German girls. But the world they were in was not the world he was in. He would like to have one of them. But it was not worth it. They were such a nice pattern. He liked the pattern. It was exciting. But he would not go through all the talking. He did not want one badly enough. He liked to look at them all, though. It was not worth it. Not now when things were getting good again.

He sat there on the porch reading a book on the war. It was a history and he was reading about all the engagements he had been in. It was the most interesting reading he had ever done. He wished there were more maps. He looked forward with a good feeling to reading all the really good histories when they would come out with good detail maps. Now he was really learning about the war. He had been a good soldier. That made a difference.

One morning after he had been home about a month his mother came into his bedroom and sat on the bed. She smoothed her apron.

"I had a talk with your father last night, Harold," she said. "and he is willing for you to take the car out in the evenings."

"Yeah?" said Krebs, who was not fully awake. "Take the car out? Yeah?"

"Yes. Your father has felt for some time that you should be able to take the car out in the evenings whenever you wished but we only talked it over last night."

"I'll bet you made him," Krebs said.

"No. It was your father's suggestion that we talk the matter over."

"Yeah. I'll bet you made him," Krebs sat up in bed.

"Will you come down to breakfast, Harold?" his mother said.

"As soon as I get my clothes on," Krebs said.

His mother went out of the room and he could hear her frying something downstairs while he washed, shaved, and dressed to go down into the dining-room for breakfast. While he was eating breakfast his sister brought in the mail.

"Well, Hare," she said. "You old sleepyhead. What do you ever get up for?"

Krebs looked at her. He liked her. She was his best sister.

"Have you got the paper?" he asked.

She handed him the *Kansas City Star* and he shucked off its brown wrapper and opened it to the sporting page. He folded the *Star* open and propped it against the water pitcher with his cereal dish to steady it, so he could read while he ate.

"Harold," his mother stood in the kitchen doorway, "Harold, please don't muss up the paper. Your father can't read his *Star* if it's been mussed."

"I won't muss it," Krebs said.

His sister sat down at the table and watched him while he read.

"We're playing indoor over at school this afternoon," she said. "I'm going to pitch."

"Good," said Krebs. "How's the old wing?"

"I can pitch better than lots of the boys. I tell them all you taught me. The other girls aren't much good."

"Yeah?" said Krebs.

"I tell them all you're my beau. Aren't you my beau, Hare?"

"You bet."

"Couldn't your brother really be your beau just because he's your brother?"

"I don't know."

"Sure you know. Couldn't you be my beau, Hare, if I was old enough and if you wanted to?"

"Sure. You're my girl now."

"Am I really your girl?"

"Sure."

"Do you love me?"

"Uh, huh."

"Will you love me always?"

"Sure."

"Will you come over and watch me play indoor?"

"Maybe."

"Aw, Hare, you don't love me. If you loved me, you'd want to come over and watch me play indoor."

Krebs's mother came into the dining-room from the kitchen. She carried a plate with two fried eggs and some crisp bacon on it and a plate of buckwheat cakes.

"You run along, Helen," she said. "I want to talk to Harold."

She put the eggs and bacon down in front of him and brought in a jug of maple syrup for the buckwheat cakes. Then she sat down across the table from Krebs.

"I wish you'd put down the paper a minute, Harold," she said.

Krebs took down the paper and folded it.

"Have you decided what you are going to do yet, Harold?" his mother said, taking off her glasses.

"No," said Krebs.

"Don't you think it's about time?" His mother did not say this in a mean way. She seemed worried.

"I hadn't thought about it," Krebs said.

"God has some work for everyone to do," his mother said. "There can be no idle hands in His Kingdom."

"I'm not in His Kingdom," Krebs said.

"We are all of us in His Kingdom."

Krebs felt embarrassed and resentful as always.

"I've worried about you so much, Harold," his mother went on. "I know the temptations you must have been exposed to. I know how weak men are. I know what your own dear grandfather, my own father, told us about the Civil War and I have prayed for you. I pray for you all day long, Harold."

Krebs looked at the bacon fat hardening on his plate.

"Your father is worried, too," his mother went on. "He thinks you have lost your ambition, that you haven't got a definite aim in life. Charley Simmons, who is just your age, has a good job and is going to be married. The boys are all settling down; they're all determined to get somewhere; you can see that boys like Charley Simmons are on their way to being really a credit to the community."

Krebs said nothing.

"Don't look that way, Harold," his mother said. "You know we love you and I want to tell you for your own good how matters stand. Your father does not want to hamper your freedom. He thinks you should be allowed to drive the car. If you want to take some of the nice girls out riding with you, we are only too pleased. We want you to enjoy yourself. But you are going to have to settle down to work, Harold. Your father doesn't care what you start in at. All work is honorable as he says. But you've got to make a start at something. He asked me to speak to you this morning and then you can stop in and see him at his office."

"Is that all?" Krebs said.

"Yes. Don't you love your mother, dear boy?"

"No," Krebs said.

His mother looked at him across the table. Her eyes were shiny. She started crying.

"I don't love anybody," Krebs said.

It wasn't any good. He couldn't tell her, he couldn't make her see it. It was silly to have said it. He had only hurt her. He went over and took hold of her arm. She was crying with her head in her hands.

"I didn't mean it," he said. "I was just angry at something. I didn't mean I didn't love you."

His mother went on crying. Krebs put his arm on her shoulder.

"Can't you believe me, mother?"

His mother shook her head.

"Please, please, mother. Please believe me."

"All right," his mother said chokily. She looked up at him. "I believe you, Harold."

Krebs kissed her hair. She put her face up to him.

"I'm your mother," she said. "I held you next to my heart when you were a tiny baby."

Krebs felt sick and vaguely nauseated.

"I know, Mummy," he said. "I'll try and be a good boy for you."

"Would you kneel and pray with me, Harold?" his mother asked.

They knelt down beside the dining-room table and Krebs's mother prayed.

"Now, you pray, Harold," she said.

"I can't," Krebs said.

"Try, Harold."

"I can't."

"Do you want me to pray for you?"

"Yes."

So his mother prayed for him and then they stood up and Krebs kissed his 95
mother and went out of the house. He had tried so to keep his life from being complicated. Still, none of it had touched him. He had felt sorry for his mother and she had made him lie. He would go to Kansas City and get a job and she would feel all right about it. There would be one more scene maybe before he got away. He would not go down to his father's office. He would miss that one. He wanted his life to go smoothly. It had just gotten going that way. Well, that was all over now, anyway. He would go over to the schoolyard and watch Helen play indoor baseball.

[1925]

THINKING ABOUT THE TEXT

1. Why does Krebs stay in Europe so long? Why is Krebs upset with himself? What specific behaviors does he regret?
2. Why doesn't Krebs want a close relationship with the girls he watches? In what way might this be quite understandable?
3. What does Krebs mean by his frequent use of "complicated"?
4. What seems to be Krebs's plan for the future? Why does he feel he must leave home? How might he be successful?
5. What specific details could you use to argue that Hemingway means Krebs to be or not to be a sympathetic figure?

JAMES M. HUTCHISSON

From *Ernest Hemingway: A New Life*

James M. Hutchisson was born in Washington, D.C., and received his B.A. in English from Radford College in 1982. He was granted a Ph.D. in nineteenth- and twentieth-century literature from the University of Delaware in 1987. He has published widely and is the author of The Rise of Sinclair Lewis *(Penn State, 1996). He is currently a professor of English and Director of Graduate Studies at the Citadel in Charleston, South Carolina.*

On the afternoon of 7 July, Hemingway rode out on his bicycle with rations of black coffee, chocolate bars, and peanut butter for the men at the front, only a few miles away. When he got there, he heard a rumor that there was going to be an offensive that night. He talked the troops into letting him come back to the line that evening to see for himself. At about 12:30 in the morning, 8 July, hunkered down in the trenches, Hemingway saw a flash in the sky. An Austrian mortar shell sped toward them—basically a can full of pieces of junk steel that burst on contact. The shell hit the post where Hemingway was standing. He was knocked down by the hot blast and temporarily lost consciousness.

When he recovered, he did a very brave thing. The precise details have varied over time as the teller of the tale (often Hemingway himself) alternately exaggerated or mangled attempts to relive history; because of Hemingway's inherent boastfulness, many have also doubted some of his claims. But there is no question that what Hemingway did next was heroic. His friend Ted Brumback told Hemingway's parents what happened in a letter: "The concussion of the explosion knocked him unconscious and buried him in earth. There was an Italian between Ernest and the shell. He was instantly killed, while another, standing a few feet away, had both his legs blown off. A third Italian was badly wounded and this one Ernest, after he had regained consciousness, picked up on his back and carried to the first aid dugout." The X-rays later showed that, in addition to being hit by shrapnel from the mortar shell, Hemingway's legs had also been raked with machine-gun fire, which he variously compared to being stung repeatedly by wasps or getting smacked in the leg with an icy snowball. When he was blown up, he later recalled, he felt life go out of him and go off and then come back.

Medics took him to a barn where the roof had been shot off. He lay there in agony for two hours, staring up at the night sky and wondering if he was going to die. Then he was transported to a first-aid station at Fornaci and given morphine for the pain. A priest passing by assumed he was near death and administered last rites. Then he was moved yet again: first to the town hall and then to a dressing station in the local school, before finally being carried away by ambulance to a field hospital in Casier, in the Treviso province. There, doctors removed 227 pieces of shrapnel from his body. The bullets from the machine guns, however, had to remain lodged in his right kneecap until he could be sent to Milan for surgery. For his actions, Hemingway earned a formal commendation from the Red Cross and a citation from the Italian government, along with its second-highest decoration, the Medaglia d'Argento al Valore Militare. The citation read: "Gravely wounded by numerous pieces of shrapnel from an enemy shell, with an admirable spirit of brotherhood, before taking care of himself, he rendered generous assistance to the Italian soldiers more seriously wounded by the same explosion and did not allow himself to be carried elsewhere until they had been evacuated." Although a noncombatant, Hemingway nonetheless became a bona fide war hero. He was not, however, the first American wounded in Italy, as some have believed.

He felt guilty about the medal, thinking he did not deserve it. His feelings of survivor's guilt would carry over, some years later, into such stories as "Soldier's Home," about the shell-shocked Harold Krebs, and "Now I Lay Me," in which Nick Adams lies awake at night in the hospital with the feeling that if he shut his eyes he would never wake up and that his soul would leave his body. Hemingway began to appreciate the uncertainty of the unknown, of what lay beyond him on the other side, if indeed there was another side. He began to recognize that living with the anticipation of death was truly horrifying; it made life arduous and at times seemingly unendurable. Dying, however, was an easy solution to stress and pain. He began to believe that it took great force of will not to bend to the power of the seductive siren call of death. This perspective became the bedrock of Hemingway's philosophy.

His letters home during his recuperation, therefore, are full of a jocosity meant to hide his guilt at not being obliterated in the blast. In his first letter, Hemingway called the incident "getting bunged up," and detailed with great enthusiasm all of the "really swell" collection of battlefield souvenirs that he had amassed. He then went on to say, "It's the next best thing to getting killed and reading your own obituary," "Well I can now hold up my hand and say I've been shelled by high explosive, shrapnel, and gas. . . . Maybe I'll get a hand grenade later," and "So we took off my trousers and the old limbs were still there." Some have argued that these letters are disingenuous—deliberately couched in a cavalier tone in order not to upset his parents about his brush with death. But with the advantage of hindsight, one can see this as the beginning of Hemingway's pattern of deflection and deflation—of diverting his true feelings and replacing them with audacious indifference, of describing momentous experiences with casual understatement. . . .

A hero's welcome awaited Hemingway when his steamer docked at New York Harbor on 21 January 1919. News of the supposed first-wounded boy in the war had reached the States ahead of him, and, to Hemingway's surprise, waiting at the pier was a reporter from the *New York Sun*. Hemingway surely could not have anticipated this and must not have known what he was expected to say. He recovered quickly, however, and described the attack in which he'd been wounded. The reporter took it all in, nodding eagerly, waiting for more. And then, probably caught up in a whirlwind of emotion, Hemingway embellished the story, figuring that the brush with death gave him license to exaggerate a bit. Someone so young surely enjoyed the novelty of being an instant celebrity as well.

The false additions were, as one might expect from a nineteen-year-old, not very credible, but the press, eager for a good story, loved it, and Hemingway started to realize what good copy he could make if he stretched the truth. So he told the reporter that after the medics had pulled thirty-two pieces of shrapnel from his head and body, they told him he would need perhaps a dozen more operations over the coming year. Hemingway said that he didn't think this would be necessary—that the doctors were worrywarts and were exaggerating his potential incapacity—and that, bored after lying about the hospital, he had returned to the front and kept fighting until the armistice. Seizing a good opportunity, Hemingway then announced that he was looking for work. In addition to his wartime adventures, he touted his experience as a newsman in Kansas City and said that any New York paper that "wants a man who is not afraid of work and wounds" should let him know what was on offer. No opportunities came his way, however, despite the page 8 headline that appeared the following day: "Has 227 Wounds, but Is Looking for Job: Kansas City Boy First to Return from Italian Front."

From a public show to a private moment: at the Lasalle Street station in Chicago a few days later, where Ed and Marcelline° met his train, the mood could not have been more different or more subdued. An anxious parent waited on the cold platform. As the train rolled in, Ed caught a glimpse of his son wearing a khaki uniform and a black cape, and he rushed to the stairs that descended from the side of the car. His father and sister saw not the returning hero but the young boy who had stepped into an arena of ugly, traumatizing violence. "Here boy!—Here," Ed said, "lean on me!" And they started out of the station, down another long flight of stairs. Hemingway shrugged off the pain, but his father, the physician, knew that he was hurting, and when they arrived home in Oak Park, Hemingway gave in.

Hemingway was suffering from post-traumatic stress disorder. It was called shell shock at the time, but the name was not the only difference. Shell-shocked soldiers were thought to be mentally able to pull themselves out of their depression, that it was an emotional rather than a medical condition. Soldiers were left to fight their own mental battles. As a result, many never recovered. More than eighty thousand cases of shell shock were reported during the war, and by 1927 there were still more than sixty-five thousand men in mental hospitals worldwide as a result of the condition. Today, victims of PTSD are treated pharmaceutically. No such option existed for Hemingway, and he suffered from the effects of nearly dying for the rest of his life. He lost his emotional balance, developed conflicting and ambivalent relationships with friends, family members, and lovers, and suffered great insecurity about his noncombatant role in the war.

10 PTSD is an anxiety disorder that develops after one is exposed to a terrifying event that presents grave physical danger. It is severe and can continue to the point that the person affected is plagued by widespread psychological trauma. Hemingway manifested the key symptoms: he was unaffectionate, especially with people he used to be close to, such as his sisters; he was irritable and aggressive; he was easily startled; and he had trouble sleeping. (If he went out at night, Ursula° faithfully waited up for him, knowing that he would be frightened in the darkness of his bedroom. She sometimes even slept with him to calm his anxiety). Today, many victims of PTSD undergo counseling in which they relive the experience in a therapeutic setting, sometimes involving trusted friends or family members in reliving the event with them. Hemingway kept to himself and did not talk about the event in honest, straightforward terms. When he did talk about it, he made it into the stuff of fiction. Because he never received proper treatment, Hemingway battled depression, insecurity, aggression, and—later in life—paranoia. Lingering physical injuries from the blast went unnoticed and eventually, in combination with other injuries, evolved into serious physical and mental illnesses. These were all factors that finally drove him to suicide at a relatively young age.

As Michael Reynolds notes in *The Young Hemingway*, no one at the time with mental illness would have gone to see a doctor, as this would have been seen as a sign of weakness. Moreover, depression and mental instability ran in the family. Ed twice left the family for short stays in New Orleans to repair his shattered

Ed and Marcelline: Hemingway's father and older sister. **Ursula:** One of Hemingway's younger sisters.

nerves (in 1903 and again in 1908). Moreover, as Reynolds puts it, "Insomnia, erratic blood pressure, blinding headaches and severe depression were the genetic inheritance° of Ernest Hemingway, his sisters and brothers."

Neither Ed nor Grace recognized the severity of their son's illness. Then, when Hemingway received the shocking news from Agnes° that she was engaged to someone else, he grew worse. For the next several months, he more or less took to his bed. In the mornings, bundled up in the Red Cross comforter he had brought home as a souvenir, he would sleep and read. In the afternoons, he would take a bit of exercise, then return to his third-floor retreat after an early supper. According to his sister Madelaine° ("Sunny"), then fourteen, he would stow bottles of various liqueurs behind the books on the shelves and imbibe when he felt the need. The alcohol, combined with the natural depressive effects of his trauma, made things worse. He would even press a drink on Sunny when she came upstairs to check on him. When she refused, he would drop the matter, but he told her again and again not to let the conformity of Oak Park keep her from experiencing life. "Don't be afraid to taste all the other things in life that aren't here in Oak Park," he would say. "There's a whole big world out there full of people who really feel things. . . . Sometimes I think we only half live over here." And then he would seem to trail off, back into his depressive stupor. Marcelline understood what her brother was thinking and feeling: "For Ernest it must have been something like being put in a box with the cover nailed down to come home to conventional, suburban Oak Park living, after his own vivid experiences."

The effects of Hemingway's brush with death cannot be overestimated. Being wounded, leaving Italy, returning home, losing Agnes, and having to go through a painful physical and emotional recuperation—all of these things constituted the formative period in Hemingway's life. They produced two overarching and contradictory results; the first was the primal wound that never went away psychologically and that would manifest itself in various iterations throughout his life, leading eventually to his clinical depression and suicide. But they also, ironically, gave him a boost that he would not otherwise have had. Like the love affair with Agnes, Hemingway's being wounded provided him the opportunity to shape himself in an image that would prove enduringly appealing, and it gave him something to write about that would appear over and over again, in different symbolic forms, throughout his career. The stress produced by these conflicting impulses exacerbated some of his worst characteristics: his anxiety and insecurity, his harshness toward himself, and his snap judgments and mistreatment of others. It also gave him a taste for violence and danger that would never abate.

genetic inheritance: Hemingway suffered from hemochromatosis, a condition that causes the body to absorb too much iron. The condition is hereditary and caused the various symptoms that Hemingway exhibited before his suicide in 1961. **Agnes:** Agnes von Kurowsky Stanfield was an American nurse stationed in Milan during World War I. Hemingway was one of her patients. The two fell in love and planned to marry, but just a couple of months after Hemingway returned to the United States, Kurowsky wrote to tell him she was engaged to someone else. Hemingway based the character Catherine Barkley in *A Farewell to Arms* on Kurowsky. **Madelaine:** Another of Hemingway's younger sisters.

The extent of Hemingway's celebrity became clear to him during this time, when parties and gala celebrations were held in his honor. He launched himself into lengthy rounds of public appearances, telling his story, showing off his medals, and talking about what he'd seen on the battlefield. Hemingway wore his Red Cross uniform, and he polished these performances into engaging narrative accounts. Speaking to church groups, social clubs, high school societies, and literally anyone who invited him, Hemingway would show up in his field uniform and pass around his torn, bullet-riddled trousers, urging his listeners to count the number of holes in them. He made a sobering impression on his audiences. Frank Platt, his former English teacher, recalled that "it was a very impressive evening" when Hemingway spoke to a school assembly: "they felt that this man had been through the war and these were the dents of his armor."

15 Yet Hemingway continued to doubt the extent of his heroism because he had not been, technically, a soldier. Time and again he would seize opportunities to serve near battle—in the Spanish Civil War, in China, and in World War II—as if to make up for his noncombatant status in the Great War. Occasionally, however, he would let down his guard and confide to his male friends more honestly how he felt. "You know and I know," he wrote his former commander, Jim Gamble, two months after returning to Oak Park, "that all the real heroes are dead. If I had been a really game guy I would have gotten myself killed off." But Hemingway never let such candor penetrate the finely filamented scrim in which he wrapped his public image. It was a defensive measure to which he clung tightly for the rest of his life.

THINKING ABOUT THE TEXT

1. Clearly Hutchisson does not stick strictly to an objective account of the events of Hemingway's life. Comment on his interpretation and speculation about the psychological consequences of Hemingway's wartime experience.
2. Comment on ideas of Hemingway's boastfulness and guilt in Hutchisson and Krebs' in "Soldier's Home."
3. What anecdotes about Hemingway's return to Oak Park in Hutchisson seem relevant to understanding Krebs' behavior?

LEICESTER HEMINGWAY

From *My Brother, Ernest Hemingway*

Leicester Hemingway (1915–1982) was the younger brother of Ernest Hemingway. He was a successful author, writing six books including a novel, The Sound of the Trumpet *(1953). His 1961 biography of his brother was widely praised. In 1982, while suffering from a serious illness, he committed suicide, like his brother, with a gunshot to the head.*

Ernest was mustered out of the Red Cross while still in Europe. It took nearly a month to get back to Oak Park. His return there was anticipated with much the same excitement that stirred Tennessee as the residents there waited for Sergeant York.

"The night that Ernie came home from the war" was a moment in family history. Our two youngest sisters were allowed to stay up. And at about nine o'clock I was even awakened on purpose—an action unthinkable except in case of disaster and maybe not then. All the lights in the house were on. Out in the dining room, hot chocolate was served nobody said a word about holding off on the marshmallows. Ernest stood around being kissed and back-slapped while the neighbors came hurrying as the word spread. I was hoisted up onto his shoulders and Carol, the next youngest, insisted on being lifted up too. It was pretty glorious stuff being kid brother to the guy who had personally helped make the world safe for democracy. And I was not the only one who saw him in that light.

By February 1, 1919, the *Oak Parker* had an interview with Ernest, written by Roselle Dean, listing his enemy contact as "wounded three times when he went with a motor truck into the front lines to distribute cigarettes and block chocolate to the soldiers. In No Man's Land, he was at an observation post when a big shell came in and burst, hitting him and killing two Italian soldiers at his side. This felled the young hero, deeply implanting shot in both knees. As soon as he was able to crawl, however, and still under fire, he picked up a wounded man and carried him on his back to the Italian trenches, despite the fact that he was knocked down twice by machine gun fire, which struck him in the left thigh and right foot. In all, Lieutenant Hemingway received thirty-two 45-caliber bullets in his limbs and hands, all of which have been removed except one in the left limb which the young warrior is inclined to foster as a souvenir—if his surgeon-father does not deprive him of this novel keepsake. . . . Lieutenant Hemingway submitted to having twenty-eight bullets extracted without taking an anaesthetic. His only voluntary comment on the war is that it was great sport and he is ready to go on the job if it ever happens again."

Though his voluntary comments may have been limited, Ernest managed to keep a straight face while letting the stories grow. He allowed his modest mask to be lifted from time to time and almost every time some new glory was disclosed. It was a splendid triumph for the young man so recently regarded by his family as an irresponsible gray sheep who would not settle down.

During those first months that he was home, Ernest gave a wonderful party 5
for Sunny and her friends. Old-timers at Oak Park still remember it. He brought a captured Austrian star-shell pistol and more than a half-dozen shells down from his room. A lot of time had passed in the years since the game warden had scared him into running. He seemed as unconcerned about the legality of shooting such a weapon in the heart of Oak Park as he was about the danger of it. Out in the back yard he raised the muzzle of this great pistol with its foot-long barrel and 4-gauge bore.

"Blame!" A thin, fiery line arced into the sky. Five seconds later a great white light burst out and slowly, ever so slowly, it drifted down over on Grove Avenue.

The next shot allowed for more windage. By the time he had fired red, blue, green, and white lights, the still-burning star shells were landing back in our own yard. Two of them that burned small holes in the grass were gleefully stamped out. The neighborhood kids were greatly impressed. So was everyone in our family. For years the pockmarks where the flares had burned into the ground remained in the back yard. Ernest's luck was running so good then that no other fires were started in the area. The empty shells, almost twice the diameter of 12-gauge shotgun shells, smelled deliciously of burned powder for years afterward.

In mid-March, Ernest was still riding the crest. He addressed the assembly of Oak Park High School and gave it all that he had. The front-page story in the *Trapeze*, by editor Edwin Wells, put into the harsh light of print some of what may well have been said in jest.

> Lieutenant Ernest M. Hemingway '17, late of the Italian Ambulance Service of the American Red Cross and then of the Italian Army, spoke of his experiences in Italy at assembly last Friday. Caroline Bagley, a classmate of the speaker, introduced him to an audience the greater part of which already knew him.
>
> "Stein," as he has been nicknamed, had lost none of the manner of 10
> speech which made his Ring Lardner letters for the *Trapeze* of several years ago so interesting. He told of his experiences first in a quiet sector in the Lower Piave and last in the final big Italian drive.
>
> He seemed especially interested in a division of the Italian Army called "Arditi." "These men," he said, "had been confined in the Italian penal institutions, having committed some slight mistake such as—well—murder or arson, and were released on the condition that they would serve in this division which was used by the government for shock troops.
>
> "Armed only with revolvers, hand grenades, and two-bladed short swords, they attacked, frequently stripped to the waist. Their customary loss in an engagement was about two-thirds."
>
> On the day of which Lieutenant Hemingway was speaking, they came up in camions, the whole regiment singing a song which from any other body of men would have meant three months in jail. Hemingway sang the song for the audience in Italian and then translated it. Several hours after their initial engagement with the enemy, Lieutenant Hemingway saw a wounded captain being brought back to a field hospital in an ambulance.
>
> "He had been shot in the chest but had plugged the holes with cigarettes and gone on fighting. On his way to the hospital he amused himself by throwing hand grenades into the ditch just to see them go off. This illustrates the spirit of these men."
>
> At the time he was wounded Lieutenant Hemingway was assigned to the 15
> 69th Regiment of Infantry. He was with several Italians in an advanced listening post. It was at night but the enemy had probably noticed them, for he dropped a trench mortar shell, which consists of a gallon can filled with explosive and slugs, into the hole in which they were.
>
> "When the thing exploded," Lieutenant Hemingway said, "it seemed as if I was moving off somewhere in a sort of red din. I said to myself, 'Gee! Stein, you're dead,' and then I began to feel myself pulling back to earth. Then I woke up. The sand bags had caved in on my legs and at first I felt disappointed that I had not been wounded. The other soldiers had retreated

> leaving me and several others for dead. One of these soldiers who was left started crying. So I knew he was alive and told him to shut up. The Austrians seemed determined to wipe out this one outpost. They had star shells out and their trench searchlights were trying to locate us.
>
> "I picked up the wounded man and started back toward the trenches. As I got up to walk, my knee cap felt warm and sticky, so I knew I'd been touched. Just before we reached the trench their searchlight spotted us and they turned a machine gun on us. One got me in the thigh. It felt just like a snowball, so hard and coming with such force it knocked me down. We started on, but just as we reached the trench and were about to jump in, another bullet hit me, this time in the foot. It tumbled me and my wounded man all in a heap in the trench, and when I came to again I was in a dugout. Two soldiers had just come to the conclusion that I was to 'pass out shortly.' By some arguing I was able to convince them that they were wrong."
>
> So Lieutenant Hemingway told his modest story of the incident for which he was awarded the highest decoration given by the Italian Government. In addition to his medals, one of which was conferred personally by the King of Italy, Lieutenant Hemingway has a captured Austrian automatic revolver, a gas mask, and his punctured trousers. Besides these trophies he has his field equipment which he wore into the assembly hall.
>
> While in Oak Park High he was prominent in the school's activities. He was on the *Trapeze* staff for two years and was one of the editors in his last year. Always interested in athletics, he won his monogram in football and was manager of the track team.

In much of this, Ernest was definitely kidding the kids and was taken, 20
apparently, seriously. But he was also under increasing pressure about his uncertain future. Our parents had harbored definite hopes that this fling at soldiering had taught him a lesson, that now he would suddenly show a keen interest in some "sensible" way of life. But if nothing else, Ernest had begun a legend to live up to — one that would never be so easy that it would be less than a challenge.

Not all of Ernest's wounds were physical. Like hundreds of thousands of other soldiers before and since, he had received some psychic shock. He was plagued by insomnia and couldn't sleep unless he had a light in his room. To his friend Guy Hickok he described how he felt when the mortar shell exploded. "I felt my soul or something coming right out of my body like you'd pull a silk handkerchief out of a pocket by one corner. It flew around and then came back and went in again and I wasn't dead any more."

The older bartender in "A Clean Well-Lighted Place" knew something of that feeling. Nick Adams says in "Now I Lay Me," "If I could have a light I was not afraid to sleep, because I knew my soul would only go out of me if it were dark."

In those first months Ernest's welcome home had all the genuine reverence due a national hero, within the confines of Oak Park. At home he was enshrined in his third-floor room. The steep climb could not have been easy for him, but it probably helped to strengthen that trick knee. And in his room he had war souvenirs, pictures of Europe, maps, uniforms, guns, bayonets, medals, an unexploded live hand grenade, and a secret bottle to pass around to friends who came to visit. On rare and wondrous occasions I was allowed to follow the clumping footsteps up the back stairs to the third floor. I watched in awe while Ernest and his friends handled the guns, sighted them out the windows, snapped their actions, and asked questions. Besides the Austrian star-shell pistol he had brought back an Austrian Mannlicher carbine with a straight-pull bolt.

"That's a sniper's rifle," he told me. "I killed the sniper who was using it to pick off our troops from up in a tree."

25 It baffled me, young as I was, that he bothered to tell me these marvelous stories only when he had other friends around. But he gave me a shiny medal with a portrait of King Victor Emmanuel on it, which hung from a red-and-green ribbon. And for a long time I refused to go out of the house without that medal pinned to the front of my shirt. I was the only kid I knew whose brother had been in the war in Italy, and I had the medal that could prove it. In those days I didn't know the only American units in Italy until the war was nearly over were Red Cross units.

THINKING ABOUT THE TEXT

1. Compare the character of Krebs to that of Hemingway as presented by his brother. What are the similarities and differences?
2. Comment on the fictional and nonfictional aspects of the piece from *the Trapeze.* How might the events mentioned have worked their way into "Soldier's Home"?
3. What other aspects of Leicester's account might shed light on Hemingway's short story?

CAROLINE ALEXANDER

The Shock of War

Caroline Alexander (1956) was born in Florida to British parents. She studied philosophy and theology at Oxford as a Rhodes Scholar. She received a PhD. in classics from Columbia University. She has written a number of books, including The War That Killed Achilles: The True Story of Homer's Iliad and the Trojan War *(2009) and* The Bounty: The True Story of the Mutiny on the Bounty *(2004).*

In September 1914, at the very outset of the great war, a dreadful rumor arose. It was said that at the Battle of the Marne, east of Paris, soldiers on the front line had been discovered standing at their posts in all the dutiful military postures—but not alive. "Every normal attitude of life was imitated by these dead men," according to the patriotic serial *The Times History of the War,* published in 1916. "The illusion was so complete that often the living would speak to the dead before they realized the true state of affairs." "Asphyxia," caused by the powerful new high-explosive shells, was the cause for the phenomenon—or so it was claimed. That such an outlandish story could gain credence was not surprising: notwithstanding the massive cannon fire of previous ages, and even automatic weaponry unveiled in the American Civil War, nothing like this thunderous new artillery firepower had been seen before. A battery of mobile 75mm field guns, the pride of the French Army, could, for example, sweep ten acres of terrain, 435 yards deep, in less than 50 seconds; 432,000 shells had been fired in a five-day period of the September engagement on the Marne. The rumor emanating from there reflected the instinctive dread aroused by such monstrous innovation. Surely—it only made sense—such a machine must cause dark, invisible forces to pass through the air and destroy men's brains.

Shrapnel from mortars, grenades and, above all, artillery projectile bombs, or shells, would account for an estimated 60 percent of the 9.7 million military fatalities of World War I. And, eerily mirroring the mythic premonition of the Marne, it was soon observed that many soldiers arriving at the casualty clearing stations who had been exposed to exploding shells, although clearly damaged, bore no visible wounds. Rather, they appeared to be suffering from a remarkable state of shock caused by blast force. This new type of injury, a British medical report concluded, appeared to be "the result of the actual explosion itself, and not merely of the missiles set in motion by it." In other words, it appeared that some dark, invisible force had in fact passed through the air and was inflicting novel and peculiar damage to men's brains.

"Shell shock," the term that would come to define the phenomenon, first appeared in the British medical journal *The Lancet* in February 1915, only six months after the commencement of the war. In a landmark article, Capt. Charles Myers of the Royal Army Medical Corps noted "the remarkably close similarity" of symptoms in three soldiers who had each been exposed to exploding shells: Case 1 had endured six or seven shells exploding around him; Case 2 had been buried under earth for 18 hours after a shell collapsed his trench; Case 3 had been blown off a pile of bricks 15 feet high. All three men exhibited symptoms of "reduced visual fields," loss of smell and taste, and some loss of memory. "Comment on these cases seems superfluous," Myers concluded, after documenting in detail the symptoms of each. "They appear to constitute a definite class among others arising from the effects of shell-shock."

Early medical opinion took the common-sense view that the damage was "commotional," or related to the severe concussive motion of the shaken brain in the soldier's skull. Shell shock, then, was initially deemed to be a physical injury, and the shellshocked soldier was thus entitled to a distinguishing "wound stripe" for his uniform, and to possible discharge and a war pension. But by 1916, military and medical authorities were convinced that many soldiers exhibiting the characteristic symptoms—trembling "rather like a jelly shaking"; headache; tinnitus, or ringing in the ear; dizziness; poor concentration; confusion; loss of memory; and disorders of sleep—had been nowhere near exploding shells. Rather, their condition was one of "neurasthenia," or weakness of the nerves—in laymen's terms, a nervous breakdown precipitated by the dreadful stress of war.

Organic injury from blast force? Or neurasthenia, a psychiatric disorder inflicted by the terrors of modern warfare? Unhappily, the single term "shell shock" encompassed both conditions. Yet it was a nervous age, the early 20th century, for the still-recent assault of industrial technology upon age-old sensibilities had given rise to a variety of nervous afflictions. As the war dragged on, medical opinion increasingly came to reflect recent advances in psychiatry, and the majority of shell shock cases were perceived as emotional collapse in the face of the unprecedented and hardly imaginable horrors of trench warfare. There was a convenient practical outcome to this assessment; if the disorder was nervous and not physical, the shellshocked soldier did not warrant a wound stripe, and if unwounded, could be returned to the front.

The experience of being exposed to blast force, or being "blown-up," in the phrase of the time, is evoked powerfully and often in the medical case notes, memoirs and letters of this era. "There was a sound like the roar of an express train, coming nearer at tremendous speed with a loud singing, wailing noise," recalled a young American Red Cross volunteer in 1916, describing an incoming artillery round. "It kept coming and coming and I wondered when it would ever burst. Then when it seemed right on top of us, it did, with a shattering crash that made the earth tremble. It was terrible. The concussion felt like a blow in the face, the stomach and all over; it was like being struck unexpectedly by a huge wave in the ocean." Exploding at a distant 200 yards, the shell had gouged a hole in the earth "as big as a small room."

By 1917, medical officers were instructed to avoid the term "shell shock," and to designate probable cases as "Not Yet Diagnosed (Nervous)." Processed to a psychiatric unit, the soldier was assessed by a specialist as either "shell shock (wound)" or "shell shock (sick)," the latter diagnosis being given if the soldier had not been close to an explosion. Transferred to a treatment center in Britain or France, the invalided soldier was placed under the care of neurology specialists and recuperated until discharged or returned to the front. Officers might enjoy a final period of convalescence before being disgorged back into the maw of the war or the working world, gaining strength at some smaller, often privately funded treatment center—some quiet, remote place such as Lennel House, in Coldstream, in the Scottish Borders country. . . .

Life at Lennel was conducted in the familiar and subtly strict routine of the well-run country house, with meals at set times, leisurely pursuits and tea on the terrace. Lady Clementine's° family mixed freely with the officer guests, her youngest daughter, "Kitty," who was only 1 year old when the war broke out, being a special favorite. Kept busy throughout the day with country walks, chummy conversation, piano playing, table tennis, fishing, golfing and bicycling, and semiformal meals, each officer nonetheless retired at night to his private room and here confronted, starkly and alone, the condition that had brought him this peaceful interlude in the first place.

Lady Clementine: Lennel was run by Major Walter and Lady Clementine Waring.

"Has vivid dreams of war episodes—feels as if sinking down in bed"; "Sleeping well but walks in sleep: has never done this before: dreams of France"; "Insomnia with vivid dreams of fighting"; and "Dreams mainly of dead Germans . . . Got terribly guilty conscience over having killed Huns."

The terse medical case notes, averaging some three pages per patient, introduce each officer by name and age, cite his civilian address as well as regiment and service details, and include a brief section for "Family History," which typically noted whether his parents were still alive, any familial history of nervous disorders and if a brother had been killed in the war. Education, professional life and an assessment of the officer's temperament before his breakdown were also duly chronicled. Captain Kyle, for example, age 23 and in service for three years and three months at the time of admittance to Lennel had previously been a "Keen athlete, enjoyed life thoroughly, no nerves." Brigadier General McLaren had also been "Keen on outdoor sports"—always the benchmark of British mental health—but had "Not very many friends."

Many treatments abounded for the neurasthenic soldier. The most notorious were undoubtedly Dr. Lewis Yealland's electric shock therapies, conducted at the National Hospital for Paralysed and Epileptic, at Queen Square, London, where he claimed his cure "had been applied to upwards of 250 cases" (an unknown number of which were civilian). Yealland asserted that his treatment cured all the most common "hysterical disorders of warfare"—the shaking and trembling and stammering, the paralysis and disorders of speech—sometimes in a single suspect half-hour session. Electric heat baths, milk diets, hypnotism, clamps and machines that mechanically forced stubborn limbs out of their frozen position were other strategies. As the war settled in, and shell shock—both commotional and emotional—became recognized as one of its primary afflictions, treatment became more sympathetic. Rest, peace and quiet, and modest rehabilitative activities became the established regimen of care, sometimes accompanied by psychotherapy sessions, the skillful administration of which varied from institution to institution and practitioner to practitioner.

While the officers at Lennel were clearly under medical supervision, it is not evident what specific treatments they received. Lady Clementine's approach was practical and common-sensical. She was, according to her grandson Sir Ilay, an early advocate of occupational therapy—keeping busy. Painting, in particular, seems to have been encouraged, and a surviving photograph in a family album shows Lennel's mess hall ringed with heraldic shields, each officer having been instructed by Lady Clementine to paint his family coat of arms. (And if they didn't have one? "I expect they made one up," Sir llay recalled, amused.) But beyond the nature of the men's treatment, of course, was the larger, central, burning question of what, really, was the matter.

The symptoms recorded in the case notes, familiar from literature of the time, are clear enough: "palpitations—Fear of fainting . . . feeling of suffocation, of constriction in throat"; "Now feels worn out & has pain in region of heart"; "Depression—Overreaction—Insomnia—Headaches"; nervousness, lassitude, being upset by sudden noise"; "Patient fears gunfire, death and the dark . . . In periods of wakefulness he visualizes mutilations he has seen, and feels the terror of heavy fire"; "Depressed from incapacity to deal with easy subjects & suffered much from eye pain." And there is the case of Second Lieutenant Bertwistle, with two years of service in the 27th Australian Infantry, although only 20 years of age, whose face wears a "puzzled expression" and who exhibits a "marked defect of recent and remote memory." "His mental content appears to be puerile. He is docile," according to the records that accompanied him from the Royal Victoria Military Hospital in Netley, on England's south coast.

The official Report of the War Office Committee of Enquiry Into "Shell-Shock" made at war's end gravely concluded that "shell-shock resolves itself into two categories: (1) Concussion or commotional shock; and (2) Emotional shock" and of these "It was given in evidence that the victims of concussion shock, following a shell burst, formed a relatively small proportion (5 to 10 percent)." The evidence about damage from "concussion shock" was largely anecdotal, based heavily upon the observations of senior officers in the field, many of whom, veterans of earlier wars, were clearly skeptical of any newfangled attempt to explain what, to their mind, was simple loss of nerve: "New divisions often got 'shell shock' because they imagined it was the proper thing in European warfare," Maj. Pritchard Taylor, a much-decorated officer, observed. On the other hand, a consultant in neuropsychiatry to the American Expeditionary Force reported a much higher percentage of concussion shock: 50 percent to 60 percent of shell shock cases at his base hospital stated they had "lost consciousness or memory after having been blown over by a shell." Unfortunately, information about the circumstances of such injuries was highly haphazard. In theory, medical officers were instructed to state on a patient's casualty form whether he had been close to an exploding shell, but in the messy, frantic practice of processing multiple casualties at hard-pressed field stations, this all-important detail was usually omitted.

Case notes from Lennel, however, record that a remarkable number of the 15
"neurasthenic" officers were casualties of direct, savage blast force: "Perfectly well till knocked over at Varennes . . . after this he couldn't sleep for weeks on end"; "He has been blown up several times—and has lately found his nerve was getting shaken." In case after case, the officer is buried, thrown, stunned, concussed by exploding shells. Lieutenant Graves had gone straight from Gallipoli "into line & through Somme." In fighting around Beaumont Hamel in France, a shell had landed "quite close & blew him up." Dazed, he was helped to the company dugout, after which he "Managed to carry on for some days," although an ominous "Weakness of R[ight] side was developing steadily." Ironically, it was precisely the soldier's ability "to carry on" that had aroused skepticism over the real nature of his malady.

The extent to which blast force was responsible for shell shock is of more than historic interest. According to a Rand Corporation study, 19 percent of U.S. troops sent to Iraq and Afghanistan, about 380,000, may have sustained brain injuries from explosive devices—a fact that has prompted comparisons with the British experience at the Somme in 1916. In 2009, the U.S. Defense Advanced Research Projects Agency (DARPA) made public the results of a two-year, $10 million study of the effects of blast force on the human brain—and in doing so, not only advanced the prospect of modern treatment but cast new light on the old shell shock conundrum.

The study revealed that limited traumatic brain injury (TBI) may manifest no overt evidence of trauma — the patient may not even be aware an injury has been sustained. Diagnosis of TBI is additionally vexed by the clinical features — difficulty concentrating, sleep disturbances, altered moods — that it shares with post-traumatic stress disorder (PTSD), a psychiatric syndrome caused by exposure to traumatic events. "Someone could have a brain injury and be looking like it was PTSD," says Col. Geoffrey Ling, the director of the DARPA study.

Differentiation between the two conditions — PTSD and TBI, or the "emotional" versus "commotional" puzzle of World War I — will be enhanced by the study's most important find: that at low levels the blast-exposed brain remains structurally intact, but is injured by inflammation. This exciting prospect of a clinical diagnosis was presaged by the observation in World War I that spinal fluid drawn from men who had been "blown up" revealed changes in protein cells. "They were actually pretty insightful," Ling says of the early medics. "Your proteins, by and large, are immunoglobulins, which basically are inflammatory. So they were ahead of their time."

"You can never tell how a man is going to do in action," a senior officer had observed in the War Office Committee report of 1922, and it was this searing truth of self-discovery that the patients at Lennel feared. They were betrayed by the stammering and trembling they could not control, the distressing lack of focus, their unmanly depression and lassitude. No list of clinical symptoms, such as the written records preserve, can do justice to the affliction of the shellshocked patient. This is more effectively evoked in the dreadful medical training films of the war, which capture the discordant twitching, uncontrollable shaking and haunting vacant stares. "Certainly one met people who were — different," Sir Ilay recalled gently, speaking of damaged veterans he had seen as a boy, "and it was explained of their being in the war. But we were all brought up to show good manners, not to upset."

Possibly, it was social training, not medical, that enabled Lady Clementine to assist and solace the damaged men who made their way to Lennel. If she was unsettled by the sights and sounds that filled her home, she does not seem to have let on. That she and her instinctive treatment were beneficial is evident from what is perhaps the most remarkable feature of the Lennel archive — the letters the officers wrote to their hostess upon leaving.

"I am quite unable adequately to express my gratitude to you for your kindness and hospitality to me," wrote Lieutenant Craven, as if giving thanks for a pleasant weekend in the country. Most letters, however, run to several pages, their eager anecdotes and their expressions of anxieties and doubt give evidence of the sincerity of the writer's feeling. "I got such a deep breath of 'Lennel,' while I was reading your letter," wrote one officer from the Somme in December 1916, "& I'll bet you had your tennis shoes on, & no hat, & a short skirt, & had probably just come in from a walk across the wet fields"; "Did you really and truly mean that I would be welcome at Lennel if I ever get the opportunity for another visit?" one officer asked yearningly.

A number of the letters are written from hotels while awaiting the results of medical boards. Most hoped for light duty—the dignity of continued service but without the dreaded liabilities. "The Medical Board sent me down here for two months light duty after which I must return to the fray!" writes Lieutenant Jacob, and, as a wistful postscript; "Did you ever finish that jolly Japanese puzzle picture?!" For some, the rush of the outside world came at them too fast: "I have been annoyed quite a lot at little things & my stammer has returned," one officer confided. Several write from other hospitals; "I had not the remotest idea of how & when I came here," Lieutenant Spencer wrote to Lady Clementine. "I do not know what really happened when I took ill but I do sincerely hope that you will forgive me if I was the cause of any unpleasant situation or inconvenience."

At war's end, the legions of shellshocked veterans dispersed into the mists of history. One catches glimpses of them, however, through a variety of oblique lenses. They crop up in a range of fiction of the era, hallucinating in the streets of London, or selling stockings door to door in provincial towns, their casual evocation indicating their familiarity to the contemporary reader.

THINKING ABOUT THE TEXT

1. How does this account shed light on Krebs's behavior?
2. How is it probable that the WWI era's views of masculinity contributed to the culture's perspective on "shell shock"?
3. If you could enter a time machine and go back to 1917, what could you be able to tell Hemingway and Krebs about their symptoms that might be helpful?

WRITING ABOUT ISSUES

1. Look up articles about the "Lost Generation" and in an essay, argue that this idea helps readers better understand both Hemingway and Krebs.
2. Creative writing teachers often implore their students to write "what they know." Write an essay which explores the pluses and minuses of this advice, focusing on "Soldier's Home."
3. Read "A Very Short Story" (available online) and write an essay that compares this story to Hemingway's actual experience with his first serious love, Agnes von Kurowsky, a nurse he met in Italy.
4. Read another story about a returning veteran—for example, Tim O'Brien's "Speaking of Courage" or Louise Erdrich's "The Red Convertible"—and compare the ideas raised there to Hemingway's.

Food in Families: Essays

RUTH REICHL, "The Queen of Mold"

DAVID SEDARIS, "Tasteless"

GEETA KOTHARI, "If You Are What You Eat, Then What Am I?"

Food occupies a ubiquitous and central place in the customs and rituals of all cultures. If the pragmatic reasons are obvious, perhaps the innumerable variations in the types of food and the complex and often inscrutable manner of its consumption are not so clear. Professionally trained anthropologists believe you can tell a lot about a culture by studying its eating habits, but even casual observers know that what you eat and how you eat it are windows into personality. And we all have stories of how we first encounter food. Perhaps some of the earliest stories we can remember revolve around our behavior at the family dinner table. As a source of despair or pleasure, these memories form many of the narratives we tell about ourselves over a lifetime. It is no wonder then, that memoirists tell many stories about how food shaped their lives. In the three selections here, one is by a noted food critic, one by an acclaimed humorist, and the other by a well-received novelist. All three offer interesting and insightful accounts of how food influenced their lives.

BEFORE YOU READ

In one way or another, food is part of the stories all families tell. Recall stories you've heard someone in your family tell or perhaps ones you've told yourself. What do these stories say about your family or about your view of your family?

RUTH REICHL

The Queen of Mold

Ruth Reichl (b. 1948), one of America's most famous food writers, was born in Greenwich Village in New York City. She graduated from the University of Michigan in 1970 with an M.A. in art history. She and her husband moved to Berkeley, California, and took part in the culinary revolution happening there. She became the food and restaurant critic for the Los Angeles Times *and later the* New York Times. *She has won the James Beard Award (restaurant criticism's highest honor) four times. Her most recent paperback is* For you, Mom. Finally. *(2009). The following is taken from her successful first memoir,* Tender at the Bone: Growing Up at the Table *(1998).*

This is a true story.

Imagine a New York City apartment at six in the morning. It is a modest apartment in Greenwich Village. Coffee is bubbling in an electric percolator. On the table is a basket of rye bread, an entire coffee cake, a few cheeses, a platter of cold cuts. My mother has been making breakfast—a major meal in our house, one where we sit down to fresh orange juice every morning, clink our glasses as if they held wine, and toast each other with "Cheerio. Have a nice day."

Right now she is the only one awake, but she is getting impatient for the day to begin and she cranks WQXR up a little louder on the radio, hoping that the noise will rouse everyone else. But Dad and I are good sleepers, and when the sounds of martial music have no effect she barges into the bedroom and shakes my father awake.

"Darling," she says, "I need you. Get up and come into the kitchen."

My father, a sweet and accommodating person, shuffles sleepily down the hall. He is wearing loose pajamas, and the strand of hair he combs over his bald spot stands straight up. He leans against the sink, holding on to it a little, and obediently opens his mouth when my mother says, "Try this."

Later, when he told the story, he attempted to convey the awfulness of what she had given him. The first time he said that it tasted like cat toes and rotted barley, but over the years the description got better. Two years later it had turned into pigs' snouts and mud and five years later he had refined the flavor into a mixture of antique anchovies and moldy chocolate.

Whatever it tasted like, he said it was the worst thing he had ever had in his mouth, so terrible that it was impossible to swallow, so terrible that he leaned over and spit it into the sink and then grabbed the coffeepot, put the spout into his mouth, and tried to eradicate the flavor.

My mother stood there watching all this. When my father finally put the coffeepot down she smiled and said, "Just as I thought. Spoiled!"

And then she threw the mess into the garbage can and sat down to drink her orange juice.

For the longest time I thought I had made this story up. But my brother insists that my father told it often, and with a certain amount of pride. As far as I know, my mother was never embarrassed by the telling, never even knew that she should have been. It was just the way she was.

Which was taste-blind and unafraid of rot. "Oh, it's just a little mold," I can remember her saying on the many occasions she scraped the fuzzy blue stuff off some concoction before serving what was left for dinner. She had an iron stomach and was incapable of understanding that other people did not.

This taught me many things. The first was that food could be dangerous, especially to those who loved it. I took this very seriously. My parents entertained a great deal, and before I was ten I had appointed myself guardian of the guests. My mission was to keep Mom from killing anybody who came to dinner.

Her friends seemed surprisingly unaware that they took their lives in their hands each time they ate with us. They chalked their ailments up to the weather, the flu, or one of my mother's more unusual dishes. "No more sea urchins for me," I imagined Burt Langner saying to his wife, Ruth, after a dinner at our house, "they just don't agree with me." Little did he know that it was not the sea urchins that had made him ill, but that bargain beef my mother had found so irresistible.

"I can make a meal out of anything," Mom told her friends proudly. She liked to brag about "Everything Stew," a dish invented while she was concocting a casserole out of a two-week-old turkey carcass. (The very fact that my mother confessed to cooking with two-week-old turkey says a lot about her.) She put the turkey and a half can of mushroom soup into the pot. Then she began rummaging around in the refrigerator. She found some leftover broccoli and added that. A few carrots went in, and then a half carton of sour cream. In a hurry, as usual, she added green beans and cranberry sauce. And then, somehow, half an apple pie slipped into the dish. Mom looked momentarily horrified. Then she shrugged and said, "Who knows? Maybe it will be good." And she began throwing everything in the refrigerator in along with it—leftover pâté, some cheese ends, a few squishy tomatoes.

That night I set up camp in the dining room. I was particularly worried about the big eaters, and I stared at my favorite people as they approached the buffet, willing them away from the casserole. I actually stood directly in front of Burt Langner so he couldn't reach the turkey disaster. I loved him, and I knew that he loved food.

Unknowingly I had started sorting people by their tastes. Like a hearing child born to deaf parents, I was shaped by my mother's handicap, discovering that food could be a way of making sense of the world.

At first I paid attention only to taste, storing away the knowledge that my father preferred salt to sugar and my mother had a sweet tooth. Later I also began to note how people ate, and where. My brother liked fancy food in fine surroundings, my father only cared about the company, and Mom would eat anything so long as the location was exotic. I was slowly discovering that if you watched people as they ate, you could find out who they were.

Then I began listening to the way people talked about food, looking for clues to their personalities. "What is she really saying?" I asked myself when Mom bragged about the invention of her famous corned beef ham.

"I was giving a party," she'd begin, "and as usual I left everything for the last minute." Here she'd look at her audience, laughing softly at herself. "I asked Ernst to do the shopping, but you know how absentminded he is! Instead of picking up a ham he brought me corned beef." She'd look pointedly at Dad, who would look properly sheepish.

"What could I do?" Mom asked. "I had people coming in a couple of hours. I had no choice. I simply pretended it was a ham." With that Dad would look admiringly at my mother, pick up his carving knife, and start serving the masterpiece. *[1998]*

MIRIAM REICHL'S CORNED BEEF HAM

4 pounds whole corned beef
5 bay leaves
1 onion, chopped
1 tablespoon prepared mustard
¼ cup brown sugar
Whole cloves
1 can (1 pound 15 ounces) spiced peaches

Cover corned beef with water in a large pot. Add bay leaves and onion. Cook over medium heat about 3 hours, until meat is very tender.

While meat is cooking, mix mustard and brown sugar.

Preheat oven to 325°.

Take meat from water and remove all visible fat. Insert cloves into meat as if it were ham. Cover the meat with the mustard mixture and bake 1 hour, basting frequently with the peach syrup.

Surround meat with spiced peaches and serve.

Serves 6.

THINKING ABOUT THE TEXT

1. What does Reichl's father's changing description tell you about the nature of many details in memoirs?
2. How would you unpack the comment Reichl makes about her mother: "It was just the way she was" (para. 10)?
3. Why is "The Queen of Mold" an appropriate title for this brief essay?
4. What do you think Reichl means when she says, "I was shaped by my mother's handicap, discovering that food could be a way of making sense of the world" (para. 16)? Give an example of this from your own experience.
5. What does the final anecdote say about Reichl's parents?

DAVID SEDARIS

Tasteless

David Sedaris (b. 1956) is one of America's most famous humorists. His books have sold seven million copies. Sedaris was born in Binghamton, New York, and grew up in Raleigh, North Carolina. He graduated from the School of the Art Institute of Chicago in 1987. While he was performing in a Chicago club, he was discovered by Ira Glass, current host of the National Public Radio program This American Life. *Sedaris's radio essays made him famous. His first book of stories and essays,* Barrel Fever, *was published in 1994. In 2001,* Time *magazine named him "Humorist of the Year."* Dress Your Family in Corduroy and Denim *rose to number one on the* New York Times *nonfiction best-seller list in June 2004. Sedaris's most recent book,* Let's Explore Diabetes with Owls, *was published in April 2013.*

One of the things they promise when you quit smoking is that food will regain its flavor. Taste buds paved beneath decades of tar will spring back to life, and an entire sense will be restored. I thought it would be like putting on a pair of glasses—something dramatic that makes you say, "Whoa!"—but it's been six months now, and I have yet to notice any significant change.

Part of the problem might be me. I've always been in touch with my stomach, but my mouth and I don't really speak. Oh, it chews all right. It helps me form words and holds stuff when my hands are full, but it doesn't do any of these things very well. It's third-rate at best—fifth if you take my teeth into consideration.

Even before I started smoking, I was not a remarkably attentive eater. "Great fried fish," I'd say to my mother, only to discover that I was eating a chicken breast or, just as likely, a veal cutlet. She might as well have done away with names and identified our meals by color: "Golden brown." "Red." "Beige with some pink in it."

I am a shoveller, a quantity man, and I like to keep going until I feel sick. It's how a prisoner might eat, one arm maneuvering the fork and the other encircling the plate like a fence: head lowered close to my food, eyes darting this way and that; even if I don't particularly like it, it's *mine*, God damn it.

Some of this has to do with coming from a large family. Always afraid that I 5
wouldn't get enough, I'd start worrying about more long before I finished what was in front of me. We'd be at the dinner table, and, convict-like, out of one side of my mouth, I'd whisper to my sister Amy.

"What'll you take for that chicken leg?"

"You mean my barbecued rib?"

"Call it what you like, just give me your asking price."

"Oh gosh," she'd say. "A quarter?"

"Twenty-five cents! What do you think this is—a restaurant?" 10

She'd raise the baton of meat to her face and examine it for flaws. "A dime."

"A nickel," I'd say, and before she could argue I'd have snatched it away.

I should have been enormous, the size of a panda, but I think that the fear of going without—the anxiety that this produced—acted like a kind of furnace, and burned off the calories before I could gain weight. Even after learning how to make my own meals, I remained, if not skinny, then at least average. My older sister Lisa and I were in elementary school when our mother bought us our first cookbook. The recipes were fairly simple—lots of Jell-O-based desserts and a wheel-shaped meat loaf cooked in an angel-food-cake pan. This last one was miraculous to me. "A meat loaf—with a hole in it!" I kept saying. I guess I thought that as it baked the cavity would fill itself with rubies or butterscotch pudding. How else to explain my disappointment the first dozen times I made it?

In high school, I started cooking pizzas—"from scratch," I liked to say, "the ol' fashioned way." On Saturday afternoons, I'd make my dough, place it in a cloth-covered bowl, and set it in the linen closet to rise. We'd have our dinner at seven or so, and four hours later, just as "Shock Theater," our local horror-movie program, came on, I'd put my pizzas in the oven. It might have been all right if this were just *part* of my evening, but it was everything: all I knew about being young had canned Parmesan cheese on it. While my classmates were taking acid and having sex in their cars, I was arranging sausage buttons and sliced peppers into smiley faces.

"The next one should look mad," my younger brother would say. And, as 15
proof of my versatility, I would create a frown.

To make it all that much sadder, things never got any better than this. Never again would I take so many chances or feel such giddy confidence in my abilities. This is not to say that I stopped cooking, just that I stopped trying.

Between the year that I left my parents' house and the year that I met Hugh, I made myself dinner just about every night. I generally alternated between three or four simple meals, but if forced to name my signature dish I'd probably have gone with my Chicken and Linguine with Grease on It. I don't know that I ever had an actual recipe; rather, like my Steak and Linguine with Blood on It, I just sort of played it by ear. The good thing about those meals was that they had only two ingredients. Anything more than that and I'm like Hugh's mother buying Christmas presents. "I look at the list, I go to the store, and then I just freeze," she says.

I suggest that it's nothing to get worked up about, and see in her eyes the look I give when someone says, "It's only a dinner party," or "Can we have something *with* the Chicken and Linguine with Grease on It?"

I cook for myself when I'm alone; otherwise, Hugh takes care of it, and happily, too. People tell me that he's a real chef, and something about the way they say it, a tone of respect and envy, leads me to believe them. I know that the dinners he prepares are correct. If something is supposed to be hot, it is. If it looks rust-colored in pictures, it looks rust-colored on the plate. I'm always happy to eat Hugh's cooking, but when it comes to truly tasting, to discerning the subtleties I hear others talking about, it's as if my tongue were wearing a mitten.

That's why fine restaurants are wasted on me. I suppose I can appreciate the 20
lighting, or the speed with which my water glass is refilled, but, as far as the food is concerned, if I can't distinguish between a peach and an apricot I really can't tell the difference between an excellent truffle and a mediocre one. Then, too, the more you pay the less they generally give you to eat. French friends visiting the United States are floored by the size of the portions. "Plates the size of hubcaps!" they cry. "No wonder the Americans are so fat."

"I know," I say. "Isn't it awful?" Then I think of Claim Jumper, a California-based chain that serves a massive hamburger called the Widow Maker. I ordered a side of creamed spinach there, and it came in what looked like a mixing bowl. It was like being miniaturized, shrunk to the height of a leprechaun or a doll and dropped in the dining room of regular-sized people. Even the salt and pepper shakers seemed enormous. I ate at Claim Jumper only once, and it was the first time in years that I didn't corral my plate. For starters, my arm wasn't long enough, but even if it had been I wouldn't have felt the need. There was plenty to go around, some of it brown, some of it green, and some a color I've come to think of, almost dreamily, as enough. *[2013]*

≡ THINKING ABOUT THE TEXT

1. What does Sedaris claim is the result of growing up in a large family? Is this meant to be taken at face value or is he being hyperbolic for humorous effect?
2. What is the relationship between the opening two paragraphs and the closing sentence?

3. Sedaris is noted for his humor. Point out two or three places where you think he is deliberately funny. How does this increase or decrease the content of the text?
4. What is the effect of Sedaris's self-deprecating humor? Does it increase or decrease his narrative persona?
5. What is the point of his anecdote about his partner's mother? Is being a good cook a matter of attitude or personality? What answer does the story suggest?

MAKING COMPARISONS

1. Compare the attitudes of both narrators toward cooking as a child.
2. How would Sedaris as a child have fared if he'd had Reichl's mother?
3. Compare the significance of the titles in each memoir.

GEETA KOTHARI

If You Are What You Eat, then What Am I?

Geeta Kothari teaches in the Writing Program at the University of Pittsburgh. She is the nonfiction editor at the Kenyon Review *and the editor of the anthology* Did My Mamma Like to Dance? and Other Stories about Mothers and Daughters *(1994). Her fiction and nonfiction have appeared in* the Kenyon Review, Best American Essays, *and* the Massachusetts Review.

To belong is to understand the tacit codes of the people you live with.
MICHAEL IGNATIEFF, *Blood and Belonging*

I

The first time my mother and I open a can of tuna, I am nine years old. We stand in the doorway of the kitchen, in semi-darkness, the can tilted toward daylight. I want to eat what the kids at school eat: bologna, hot dogs, salami—foods my parents find repugnant because they contain pork and meat by-products, crushed bone and hair glued together by chemicals and fat. Although she has never been able to tolerate the smell of fish, my mother buys the tuna, hoping to satisfy my longing for American food.

Indians, of course, do not eat such things.

The tuna smells fishy, which surprises me because I can't remember anyone's tuna sandwich actually smelling like fish. And the tuna in those sandwiches doesn't look like this, pink and shiny, like an internal organ. In fact, this looks similar to the bad foods my mother doesn't want me to eat. She is silent, holding her face away from the can while peering into it like a half-blind bird.

"What's wrong with it?" I ask.

She has no idea. My mother does not know that the tuna everyone else's 5
mothers made for them was tuna *salad*.

"Do you think it's botulism?"

I have never seen botulism, but I have read about it, just as I have read about but never eaten steak and kidney pie.

There is so much my parents don't know. They are not like other parents, and they disappoint me and my sister. They are supposed to help us negotiate the world outside, teach us the signs, the clues to proper behavior: what to eat and how to eat it.

We have expectations, and my parents fail to meet them, especially my mother, who works full time. I don't understand what it means, to have a mother who works outside and inside the home; I notice only the ways in which she disappoints me. She doesn't show up for school plays. She doesn't make chocolate-frosted cupcakes for my class. At night, if I want her attention, I have to sit in the kitchen and talk to her while she cooks the evening meal, attentive to every third or fourth word I say.

We throw the tuna away. This time my mother is disappointed. I go to school 10
with tuna eaters. I see their sandwiches, yet cannot explain the discrepancy between them and the stinking, oily fish in my mother's hand. We do not understand so many things, my mother and I.

II

On weekends, we eat fried chicken from Woolworth's on the back steps of my father's first-floor office in Murray Hill. The back steps face a small patch of garden-hedges, a couple of skinny trees, and gravel instead of grass. We can see the back window of the apartment my parents and I lived in until my sister was born. There, the doorman watched my mother, several months pregnant and wearing a sari, slip on the ice in front of the building.

My sister and I pretend we are in the country, where our American friends all have houses. We eat glazed doughnuts, also from Woolworth's, and French fries with catsup.

III

My mother takes a catering class and learns that Miracle Whip and mustard are healthier than mayonnaise. She learns to make egg salad with chopped celery, deviled eggs dusted with paprika, a cream cheese spread with bits of fresh ginger and watercress, chicken liver pâté, and little brown and white checkerboard sandwiches that we have only once. She makes chicken *á la king* in puff pastry shells and eggplant parmesan. She acquires smooth wooden paddles, whose purpose is never clear, two different egg slicers, several wooden spoons, icing tubes, cookie cutters, and an electric mixer.

IV

I learn to make tuna salad by watching a friend. My sister never acquires a taste for it. Instead, she craves:

bologna
hot dogs
bacon
sausages

and a range of unidentifiable meat products forbidden by my parents. Their restrictions are not about sacred cows, as everyone around us assumes; in a pinch, we are allowed hamburgers, though lamb burgers are preferable. A "pinch" means choosing not to draw attention to ourselves as outsiders, impolite visitors who won't eat what their host serves. But bologna is still taboo.

V

Things my sister refuses to eat: butter, veal, anything with *jeera*. The babysitter 15
tries to feed her butter sandwiches, threatens her with them, makes her cry in fear and disgust. My mother does not disappoint her; she does not believe in forcing us to eat, in using food as a weapon. In addition to pbj, my sister likes pasta and marinara sauce, bologna and Wonder bread (when she can get it), and fried egg sandwiches with turkey, cheese, and horseradish. Her tastes, once established, are predictable.

VI

When we visit our relatives in India, food prepared outside the house is carefully monitored. In the hot, sticky monsoon months in New Delhi and Bombay, we cannot eat ice cream, salad, cold food, or any fruit that can't be peeled. Definitely no meat. People die from amoebic dysentery, unexplained fevers, strange boils on their bodies. We drink boiled water only, no ice. No sweets except for jalebi, thin fried twists of dough in dripping hot sugar syrup. If we're caught outside with nothing to drink, Fanta, Limca, Thums Up (after Coca-Cola is thrown out by Mrs. Gandhi) will do. Hot tea sweetened with sugar, served with thick creamy buffalo milk, is preferable. It should be boiled, to kill the germs on the cup.

My mother talks about "back home" as a safe place, a silk cocoon frozen in time where we are sheltered by family and friends. Back home, my sister and I do not argue about food with my parents. Home is where they know all the rules. We trust them to guide us safely through the maze of city streets for which they have no map, and we trust them to feed and take care of us, the way parents should.

Finally, though, one of us will get sick, hungry for the food we see our cousins and friends eating, too thirsty to ask for a straw, too polite to insist on properly boiled water.

At my uncle's diner in New Delhi, someone hands me a plate of aloo tikki, fried potato patties filled with mashed channa dal and served with a sweet and a sour chutney. The channa, mixed with hot chilies and spices, burns my tongue and throat. I reach for my Fanta, discard the paper straw, and gulp the sweet orange soda down, huge draughts that sting rather than soothe.

When I throw up later that day (or is it the next morning, when a stomach- 20
ache wakes me from deep sleep?), I cry over the frustration of being singled out, not from the pain my mother assumes I'm feeling as she holds my hair back from my face. The taste of orange lingers in my mouth, and I remember my lips touching the cold glass of the Fanta bottle.

At that moment, more than anything, I want to be like my cousins.

VII

In New York, at the first Indian restaurant in our neighborhood, my father orders with confidence, and my sister and I play with the silverware until the steaming plates of lamb biryani arrive.

What is Indian food? my friends ask, their noses crinkling up.

Later, this restaurant is run out of business by the new Indo-Pak-Bangladeshi combinations up and down the street, which serve similar food. They use plastic cutlery and Styrofoam cups. They do not distinguish between North and South Indian cooking, or between Indian, Pakistani, and Bangladeshi cooking, and their customers do not care. The food is fast, cheap, and tasty. Dosa, a rice flour crepe stuffed with masala potato, appears on the same trays as chicken makhani.

Now my friends want to know, Do you eat curry at home? 25

One time, my mother makes lamb vindaloo for guests. Like dosa, this is a South Indian dish, one that my Punjabi mother has to learn from a cookbook. For us, she cooks everyday food—yellow dal, rice, chappati, bhaji. Lentils, rice, bread, and vegetables. She has never referred to anything on our table as "curry" or "curried," but I know she has made chicken curry for guests. Vindaloo, she explains, is a curry too. I understand, then, that curry is a dish created for guests, outsiders, a food for people who eat in restaurants.

VIII

I have inherited brown eyes, black hair, a long nose with a crooked bridge, and soft teeth with thin enamel. I am in my twenties, moving to a city far from my parents, before it occurs to me that jeera, the spice my sister avoids, must have an English name. I have to learn that haldi = turmeric, methi = fenugreek. What to make with fenugreek, I do not know. My grandmother used to make methi roti for our breakfast, corn bread with fresh fenugreek leaves served with a lump of homemade butter. No one makes it now that she's gone, though once in a while my mother will get a craving for it and produce a facsimile ("The corn meal here is wrong.") that only highlights what she's really missing: the smells and tastes of her mother's house.

I will never make my grandmother's methi roti or even my mother's unsatisfactory imitation of it. I attempt chapati; it takes six hours, three phone calls home, and leaves me with an aching back. I have to write translations down: jeera = cumin. My memory is unreliable. But I have always known garam = hot.

IX

My mother learns how to make brownies and apple pie. My father makes only Indian food, except for loaves of heavy, sweet, brown bread that I eat with thin slices of American cheese and lettuce. The recipe is a secret, passed on to him by a woman at work. Years later, when he finally gives it to me, when I finally ask for it, I end up with three bricks of gluten that even the birds and my husband won't eat.

X

My parents send me to boarding school, outside of London. They imagine that I will overcome my shyness and find a place for myself in this all-girls' school. They have never lived in England, but as former subjects of the British Empire, they find London familiar, comfortable in a way New York—my mother's home for over twenty years by now—is not. Americans still don't know what to call us; their Indians live on reservations, not in Manhattan. Because they understand the English, my parents believe the English understand us.

I poke at my first school lunch—thin, overworked pastry in a puddle of lumpy gravy. The lumps are chewy mushrooms, maybe, or overcooked shrimp. "What is this?" I don't want to ask, but I can't go on eating without knowing.

"Steak and kidney pie."

The girl next to me, red-haired, freckled, watches me take a bite from my plate. She has been put in charge of me, the new girl, and I follow her around all day, a foreigner at the mercy of a reluctant and angry tour guide. She is not used to explaining what is perfectly and utterly natural.

"What, you've never had steak and kidney pie? Bloody hell."

My classmates scoff, then marvel, then laugh at my ignorance. After a year, I understand what is on my plate: sausage rolls, blood pudding, Spam, roast beef in a thin, greasy gravy, all the bacon and sausage I could possibly want. My parents do not expect me to starve.

The girls at school expect conformity; it has been bred into them, through years of uniforms and strict rules about proper behavior. I am thirteen and contrary, even as I yearn for acceptance. I declare myself a vegetarian and doom myself to a diet of cauliflower cheese and baked beans on toast. The administration does not question my decision; they assume it's for vague, undefined religious reasons, although my father, the doctor, tells them it's for my health. My reasons, from this distance of many years, remain murky to me.

Perhaps I am my parents' daughter after all.

XI

When she is three, sitting on my cousin's lap in Bombay, my sister reaches for his plate and puts a chili in her mouth. She wants to be like the grown-ups who dip green chilies in coarse salt and eat them like any other vegetable. She howls inconsolable animal pain for what must be hours. She doesn't have the vocabulary for the oily heat that stings her mouth and tongue, burns a trail through her small tender body. Only hot, sticky tears on my father's shoulder.

As an adult, she eats red chili paste, mango pickle, kimchee, foods that make my eyes water and my stomach gurgle. My tastes are milder. I order raita at Indian restaurants and ask for food that won't sear the roof of my mouth and scar the insides of my cheeks. The waiters nod, and their eyes shift—a slight once-over that indicates they don't believe me. I am Indian, aren't I? My father seems to agree with them. He tells me I'm asking for the impossible, as if he believes the recipes are immutable, written in stone during the passage from India to America.

XII

I look around my boyfriend's freezer one day and find meat: pork chops, ground beef, chicken pieces, Italian sausage. Ham in the refrigerator, next to the homemade Bolognese sauce. Tupperware filled with chili made from ground beef and pork.

He smells different from me. Foreign. Strange.

I marry him anyway.

He has inherited blue eyes that turn gray in bad weather, light brown hair, a sharp pointy nose, and excellent teeth. He learns to make chili with ground turkey and tofu, tomato sauce with red wine and portobello mushrooms, roast chicken with rosemary and slivers of garlic under the skin.

He eats steak when we are in separate cities, roast beef at his mother's house, hamburgers at work. Sometimes I smell them on his skin. I hope he doesn't notice me turning my face, a cheek instead of my lips, my nose wrinkled at the unfamiliar, musky smell.

XIII

And then I realize I don't want to be a person who can find Indian food only in restaurants. One day, my parents will be gone, and I will long for the foods of my childhood, the way they long for theirs. I prepare for this day the way people on TV prepare for the end of the world. They gather canned goods they will never eat while I stockpile recipes I cannot replicate. I am frantic, disorganized, grabbing what I can, filing scribbled notes haphazardly. I regret the tastes I've forgotten, the meals I have inhaled without a thought. I worry that I've come to this realization too late.

XIV

Who told my mother about Brie? One day we were eating Velveeta, the next day Brie, Gouda, Camembert, Port Salut, Havarti with caraway, Danish fontina, string cheese made with sheep's milk. Who opened the door to these foreigners that sit on the refrigerator shelf next to last night's dal?

Back home, there is one cheese only, which comes in a tin, looks like Bakelite, and tastes best when melted.

And how do we go from Chef Boyardee to fresh pasta and homemade sauce, made with Redpack tomatoes, crushed garlic, and dried oregano? Macaroni and cheese, made with fresh cheddar and whole milk, sprinkled with bread crumbs and paprika. Fresh eggplant and ricotta ravioli, baked with marinara sauce and fresh mozzarella.

My mother will never cook beef or pork in her kitchen, and the foods she knew in her childhood are unavailable. Because the only alternative to the supermarket, with its TV dinners and canned foods, is the gourmet Italian deli across the street, by default our meals become socially acceptable.

XV

If I really want to make myself sick, I worry that my husband will one day leave me for a meat-eater, for someone familiar who doesn't sniff him suspiciously for signs of alimentary infidelity.

XVI

Indians eat lentils. I understand this as absolute, a decree from an unidentifiable authority that watches and judges me.

So what does it mean that I cannot replicate my mother's dal? She and my father show me repeatedly, in their kitchen, in my kitchen. They coach me over the phone, buy me the best cookbooks, and finally write down their secrets. Things I'm supposed to know but don't. Recipes that should be, by now, engraved on my heart.

Living far from the comfort of people who require no explanation for what I do and who I am, I crave the foods we have shared. My mother convinces me that moong is the easiest dal to prepare, and yet it fails me every time: bland, watery, a sickly greenish-yellow mush. These imperfect imitations remind me only of what I'm missing.

But I have never been fond of moong dal. At my mother's table it is the last thing I reach for. Now I worry that this antipathy toward dal signals something deeper, that somehow I am not my parents' daughter, not Indian, and because I cannot bear the touch and smell of raw meat, though I can eat it cooked (charred, dry, and overdone), I am not American either.

I worry about a lifetime purgatory in Indian restaurants where I will complain that all the food looks and tastes the same because they've used the same masala.

XVII

About the tuna and her attempts to feed us, my mother laughs. She says, "You were never fussy. You ate everything I made and never complained."

My mother is at the stove, wearing only her blouse and petticoat, her sari carefully folded and hung in the closet. She does not believe a girl's place is in the kitchen, but she expects me to know that too much hing can ruin a meal, to know without being told, without having to ask or write it down. Hing = asafoetida.

She remembers the catering class. "Oh, that class. You know, I had to give it up when we got to lobster. I just couldn't stand the way it looked."

She says this apologetically, as if she has deprived us, as if she suspects that hav- 60
ing a mother who could feed us lobster would have changed the course of our lives.

Intellectually, she understands that only certain people regularly eat lobster, people with money or those who live in Maine, or both. In her catering class there were people without jobs for whom preparing lobster was a part of their professional training as caterers. Like us, they wouldn't be eating lobster at home. For my mother, however, lobster was just another American food, like tuna—different, strange, not natural yet somehow essential to belonging.

I learned how to prepare and eat lobster from the same girl who taught me tuna salad. I ate bacon at her house, too. And one day this girl, with her houses in the country and Martha's Vineyard, asked me how my uncle was going to pick me up from the airport in Bombay. In 1973, she was surprised to hear that he used a car, not an elephant. At home, my parents and I laughed, and though I never knew for sure if she was making fun of me, I still wanted her friendship.

My parents were afraid my sister and I would learn to despise the foods they loved, replace them with bologna and bacon and lose our taste for masala. For my mother, giving up her disgust of lobster, with its hard exterior and foreign smell, would mean renouncing some essential difference. It would mean becoming, decidedly, definitely, American—unafraid of meat in all its forms, able to consume large quantities of protein at any given meal. My willingness to toss a living being into boiling water and then get past its ugly appearance to the rich meat inside must mean to my mother that I am, somehow, someone she is not.

But I haven't eaten lobster in years. In my kitchen cupboards, there is a thirteen-pound bag of basmati rice, jars of lime pickle, mango pickle, and ghee, cans of tuna and anchovies, canned soups, coconut milk, and tomatoes, rice noodles, several kinds of pasta, dried mushrooms, and unlabeled bottles of spices: haldi, jeera, hing. When my husband tries to help me cook, he cannot identify all the spices. He gets confused when I forget their English names and remarks that my expectations of him are unreasonable.

I am my parents' daughter. Like them, I expect knowledge to pass from me to 65
my husband without one word of explanation or translation. I want him to know what I know, see what I see, without having to tell him exactly what it is. I want to believe that recipes never change. *[1999]*

THINKING ABOUT THE TEXT

1. Explain the significance of the title. In what sense are you what you eat?
2. Describe a childhood experience where you ate somewhere different from your usual diet. What was different about the food? What was your

response at the time? What is your take on that event today? Can you see similarities to Kothari's experience?

3. Kothari says her mother did not believe in "using food as a weapon." What does she mean? Describe a personal experience or one you witnessed where this was the case.
4. What is Kothari's point when she says her tour guide at boarding school "is not used to explaining what is perfectly and utterly natural"? Have you had a similar experience?
5. Explain the significance of the first sentence of the last paragraph. Give an example from your own experience where knowledge was passed to you "without one word of explanation or translation."

MAKING COMPARISONS

1. Compare the mothers' attitudes toward food in Reichl's and Kothari's memoirs.
2. Compare Reichl's and Kothari's attitudes toward their mothers.
3. Point out moments of insight in these three memoirs that seemed surprising or impressive.

WRITING ABOUT ISSUES

1. Based on your own experience, agree or disagree with Reichl's observation that, "if you watched people as they ate, you could find out who they were" (para. 17).
2. Write an essay that researches the cultural significance of the "family meal" in at least two societies.
3. Read a chapter in Reichl's *Tender at the Bone* other than "The Queen of Mold" and discuss the significance of food in Reichl's early life.
4. Write an essay that argues that food is more or less significant in present-day America than it was in your childhood.

Critical Decisions about Parenthood: Across Genres

MAXINE HONG KINGSTON, "No Name Woman" (essay)

DAVID FOSTER WALLACE, "Good People" (story)

Ambitious politicians are not the only voices extolling the virtues of family life. Millennia of images and narratives have socialized us to accept the naturalness of motherhood and fatherhood and to see parenthood as a concept that is nearly beyond critique, beyond questioning. We look askance at those who fail in their roles as loving, supportive parents—and sometimes even at couples who decide that they do not want children or at least not as a result of a particular pregnancy. Even though the right to terminate a pregnancy is still an emotionally contested political and ethical issue, there is almost universal condemnation—in America, at least—for parents who harm infants. Our culture does not seem to forgive such behavior, often condemning it regardless of the circumstances. However, in Kingston's harrowing tale, the circumstances are so oppressive that Kingston's aunt seems a set-upon victim without recourse. Her critical decision is, of course, tragically haunting, but we also wonder how many choices she really has.

The couple in Wallace's story does have choices, even if they are not easy or clear. Although the narrative is told in the third person, the focus is on Lane's consciousness, on his troubled thinking about the predicament he and Sheri are in. As in Kingston's tale, the confluence of religious mores, cultural norms, and emotional complexity give the story a rich intensity as the couple struggles to do the right thing.

BEFORE YOU READ

Recall a difficult decision you had to make. To what extent were cultural, religious, and family expectations influential?

MAXINE HONG KINGSTON

No Name Woman

Born in Stockton, California, to Chinese immigrants, Maxine Hong Kingston's (b. 1940) first language was Say Yup, a dialect of Cantonese. As a member of a close-knit community, many of whose members came from the same village in China, she was immersed in the storytelling tradition of her particular Chinese culture and soon became a gifted writer in her second language, English. Winning eleven scholarships, Kingston began her education at the University of California at Berkeley as an engineering major but soon moved into English literature, receiving her B.A. in 1962 and her teaching certificate in 1965. After teaching in Hawaii for ten years, Kingston published her first book, The Woman Warrior: Memoirs of a Girlhood among Ghosts *(1976), from which the following selection comes. This volume won the National Book Critics Circle Award for nonfiction. Kingston's reinterpretation of oral traditions*

Jack Sotomayor / Getty Images

is continued in her later works, including Tripmaster Monkey: His Fake Book *(1989),* Hawai'i One Summer *(1998),* To Be a Poet *(2003),* The Fifth Book of Peace *(2003), an edited volume of contemporary soldiers' memoirs entitled* Veterans of War, Veterans of Peace *(2006), and* I Love a Broad Margin to My Life *(2011), a book of poems.*

"You must not tell anyone," my mother said, "what I am about to tell you. In China your father had a sister who killed herself. She jumped into the family well. We say that your father has all brothers because it is as if she had never been born.

"In 1924 just a few days after our village celebrated seventeen hurry-up weddings—to make sure that every young man who went 'out on the road' would responsibly come home—your father and his brothers and your grandfather and his brothers and your aunt's new husband sailed for America, the Gold Mountain. It was your grandfather's last trip. Those lucky enough to get contracts waved good-bye from the decks. They fed and guarded the stowaways and helped them off in Cuba, New York, Bali, Hawaii. 'We'll meet in California next year,' they said. All of them sent money home.

"I remember looking at your aunt one day when she and I were dressing; I had not noticed before that she had such a protruding melon of a stomach. But I did not think, 'She's pregnant,' until she began to look like other pregnant women, her shirt pulling and the white tops of her black pants showing. She could not have been pregnant, you see, because her husband had been gone for years. No one said anything. We did not discuss it. In early summer she was ready to have the child, long after the time when it could have been possible.

"The village had also been counting. On the night the baby was to be born the villagers raided our house. Some were crying. Like a great saw, teeth strung with lights, files of people walked zigzag across our land, tearing the rice. Their lanterns doubled in the disturbed black water, which drained away through the broken bunds. As the villagers closed in, we could see that some of them, probably men and women we knew well, wore white masks. The people with long hair hung it over their faces. Women with short hair made it stand up on end. Some had tied white bands around their foreheads, arms, and legs.

5 "At first they threw mud and rocks at the house. Then they threw eggs and began slaughtering our stock. We could hear the animals scream their deaths—the roosters, the pigs, a last great roar from the ox. Familiar wild heads flared in our night windows; the villagers encircled us. Some of the faces stopped to peer at us, their eyes rushing like searchlights. The hands flattened against the panes, framed heads, and left red prints.

"The villagers broke in the front and the back doors at the same time, even though we had not locked the doors against them. Their knives dripped with the blood of our animals. They smeared blood on the doors and walls. One woman swung a chicken, whose throat she had slit, splattering blood in red arcs about her. We stood together in the middle of our house, in the family hall with the pictures and tables of the ancestors around us, and looked straight ahead.

"At that time the house had only two wings. When the men came back, we would build two more to enclose our courtyard and a third one to begin a second courtyard. The villagers pushed through both wings, even your grandparents' rooms, to find your aunt's, which was also mine until the men returned. From this room a new wing for one of the younger families would grow. They ripped up her clothes and shoes and broke her combs, grinding them underfoot. They tore her work from the loom. They scattered the cooking fire and rolled the new weaving in it. We could hear them in the kitchen breaking our bowls and banging the pots. They overturned the great waist-high earthenware jugs; duck eggs, pickled fruits, vegetables burst out and mixed in acrid torrents. The old woman from the next field swept a broom through the air and loosed the spirits-of-the-broom over our heads. 'Pig.' 'Ghost.' 'Pig,' they sobbed and scolded while they ruined our house.

"When they left, they took sugar and oranges to bless themselves. They cut pieces from the dead animals. Some of them took bowls that were not broken and clothes that were not torn. Afterward we swept up the rice and sewed it back up into sacks. But the smells from the spilled preserves lasted. Your aunt gave birth in the pigsty that night. The next morning when I went for the water, I found her and the baby plugging up the family well.

"Don't let your father know that I told you. He denies her. Now that you have started to menstruate, what happened to her could happen to you. Don't humiliate us. You wouldn't like to be forgotten as if you had never been born. The villagers are watchful."

Whenever she had to warn us about life, my mother told stories that ran 10
like this one, a story to grow up on. She tested our strength to establish realities. Those in the emigrant generations who could not reassert brute survival died young and far from home. Those of us in the first American generations have had to figure out how the invisible world the emigrants built around our childhoods fits in solid America.

The emigrants confused the gods by diverting their curses, misleading them with crooked streets and false names. They must try to confuse their offspring as well, who, I suppose, threaten them in similar ways—always trying to get things straight, always trying to name the unspeakable. The Chinese I know hide their names; sojourners take new names when their lives change and guard their real names with silence.

Chinese-Americans, when you try to understand what things in you are Chinese, how do you separate what is peculiar to childhood, to poverty, insanities, one family, your mother who marked your growing with stories, from what is Chinese? What is Chinese tradition and what is the movies?

If I want to learn what clothes my aunt wore, whether flashy or ordinary, I would have to begin, "Remember Father's drowned-in-the-well sister?" I cannot ask that. My mother has told me once and for all the useful parts. She will add nothing unless powered by Necessity, a riverbank that guides her life. She plants vegetable gardens rather than lawns; she carries the odd-shaped tomatoes home from the fields and eats food left for the gods.

Whenever we did frivolous things, we used up energy; we flew high kites. We children came up off the ground over the melting cones our parents brought home from work and the American movie on New Year's Day—*Oh, You Beautiful Doll* with Betty Grable one year, and *She Wore a Yellow Ribbon* with John Wayne another year. After the one carnival ride each, we paid in guilt; our tired father counted his change on the dark walk home.

Adultery is extravagance. Could people who hatch their own chicks and eat 15
the embryos and the heads for delicacies and boil the feet in vinegar for party food, leaving only the gravel, eating even the gizzard lining—could such people engender a prodigal aunt? To be a woman, to have a daughter in starvation time was a waste enough. My aunt could not have been the lone romantic who gave up everything for sex. Women in the old China did not choose. Some man had commanded her to lie with him and be his secret evil. I wonder whether he masked himself when he joined the raid on her family.

Perhaps she had encountered him in the fields or on the mountain where the daughters-in-law collected fuel. Or perhaps he first noticed her in the marketplace. He was not a stranger because the village housed no strangers. She had to have dealings with him other than sex. Perhaps he worked an adjoining field, or he sold her the cloth for the dress she sewed and wore. His demand must have surprised, then terrified her. She obeyed him; she always did as she was told.

When the family found a young man in the next village to be her husband, she had stood tractably beside the best rooster, his proxy, and promised before they met that she would be his forever. She was lucky that he was her age and she would be the first wife, an advantage secure now. The night she first saw him, he had sex with her. Then he left for America. She had almost forgotten what he looked like. When she tried to envision him, she only saw the black and white face in the group photograph the men had had taken before leaving.

The other man was not, after all, much different from her husband. They both gave orders: she followed. "If you tell your family, I'll beat you. I'll kill you. Be here again next week." No one talked sex, ever. And she might have separated the rapes from the rest of living if only she did not have to buy her oil from him or gather wood in the same forest. I want her fear to have lasted just as long as rape lasted so that the fear could have been contained. No drawn-out fear. But women at sex hazarded birth and hence lifetimes. The fear did not stop but permeated everywhere. She told the man, "I think I'm pregnant." He organized the raid against her.

On nights when my mother and father talked about their life back home, sometimes they mentioned an "outcast table" whose business they still seemed to be settling, their voices tight. In a commensal tradition, where food is precious, the powerful older people made wrongdoers eat alone. Instead of letting them start separate new lives like the Japanese, who could become samurais and geishas, the Chinese family, faces averted but eyes glowering sideways, hung on to the offenders and fed them leftovers. My aunt must have lived in the same house as my parents and eaten at an outcast table. My mother spoke about the raid as if she had seen it, when she and my aunt, a daughter-in-law to a different household, should not have been living together at all. Daughters-in-law lived with their husbands' parents, not their own; a synonym for marriage in Chinese is "taking a daughter-in-law." Her husband's parents could have sold her, mortgaged her, stoned her. But they had sent her back to her own mother and father, a mysterious act hinting at disgraces not told me. Perhaps they had thrown her out to deflect the avengers.

She was the only daughter; her four brothers went with her father, husband, 20
and uncles "out on the road" and for some years became Western men. When the goods were divided among the family, three of the brothers took land, and the youngest, my father, chose an education. After my grandparents gave their daughter away to her husband's family, they had dispensed all the adventure and all the property. They expected her alone to keep the traditional ways, which her brothers, now among the barbarians, could fumble without detection. The heavy, deep-rooted women were to maintain the past against the flood, safe for returning. But the rare urge west had fixed upon our family, and so my aunt crossed boundaries not delineated in space.

The work of preservation demands that the feelings playing about in one's guts not be turned into action. Just watch their passing like cherry blossoms. But perhaps my aunt, my forerunner, caught in a slow life, let dreams grow and fade and after some months or years went toward what persisted. Fear at the enormities of the forbidden kept her desires delicate, wire and bone. She looked at a man because she liked the way the hair was tucked behind his ears, or she liked the question-mark line of a long torso curving at the shoulder and straight at the hip. For warm eyes or a soft voice or a slow walk—that's all—a few hairs, a line, a brightness, a sound, a pace, she gave up family. She offered us up for a charm that vanished with tiredness, a pigtail that didn't toss when the wind died. Why, the wrong lighting could erase the dearest thing about him.

It could very well have been, however, that my aunt did not take subtle enjoyment of her friend, but, a wild woman, kept rollicking company. Imagining her free with sex doesn't fit, though. I don't know any women like that, or men either. Unless I see her life branching into mine, she gives me no ancestral help.

To sustain her being in love, she often worked at herself in the mirror, guessing at the colors and shapes that would interest him, changing them frequently in order to hit on the right combination. She wanted him to look back.

On a farm near the sea, a woman who tended her appearance reaped a reputation for eccentricity. All the married women blunt-cut their hair in flaps about their ears or pulled it back in tight buns. No nonsense. Neither style blew easily into heart-catching tangles. And at their weddings they displayed themselves in their long hair for the last time. "It brushed the backs of my knees," my mother tells me. "It was braided, and even so, it brushed the backs of my knees."

25 At the mirror my aunt combined individuality into her bob. A bun could have been contrived to escape into black streamers blowing in the wind or in quiet wisps about her face, but only the older women in our picture album wear buns. She brushed her hair back from her forehead, tucking the flaps behind her ears. She looped a piece of thread, knotted into a circle between her index fingers and thumbs, and ran the double strand across her forehead. When she closed her fingers as if she were making a pair of shadow geese bite, the string twisted together catching the little hairs. Then she pulled the thread away from her skin, ripping the hairs out neatly, her eyes watering from the needles of pain. Opening her fingers, she cleaned the thread, then rolled it along her hairline and the tops of her eyebrows. My mother did the same to me and my sisters and herself. I used to believe that the expression "caught by the short hairs" meant a captive held with a depilatory string. It especially hurt at the temples, but my mother said we were lucky we didn't have to have our feet bound when we were seven. Sisters used to sit on their beds and cry together, she said, as their mothers or their slave removed the bandages for a few minutes each night and let the blood gush back into their veins. I hope that the man my aunt loved appreciated a smooth brow, that he wasn't just a tits-and-ass man.

Once my aunt found a freckle on her chin, at a spot that the almanac said predestined her for unhappiness. She dug it out with a hot needle and washed the wound with peroxide.

More attention to her looks than these pullings of hairs and pickings at spots would have caused gossip among the villagers. They owned work clothes and good clothes, and they wore good clothes for feasting the new seasons. But since a woman combing her hair hexes beginnings, my aunt rarely found an occasion to look her best. Women looked like great sea snails—the corded wood, babies, and laundry they carried were the whorls on their backs. The Chinese did not admire a bent back; goddesses and warriors stood straight. Still there must have been a marvelous freeing of beauty when a worker laid down her burden and stretched and arched.

Such commonplace loveliness, however, was not enough for my aunt. She dreamed of a lover for the fifteen days of New Year's, the time for families to exchange visits, money, and food. She plied her secret comb. And sure enough she cursed the year, the family, the village, and herself.

Even as her hair lured her imminent lover, many other men looked at her. Uncles, cousins, nephews, brothers would have looked, too, had they been home between journeys. Perhaps they had already been restraining their curiosity, and they left, fearful that their glances, like a field of nesting birds, might be startled and caught. Poverty hurt, and that was their first reason for leaving. But another, final reason for leaving the crowded house was the never-said.

30 She may have been unusually beloved, the precious only daughter, spoiled and mirror gazing because of the affection the family lavished on her. When her husband left, they welcomed the chance to take her back from the in-laws; she could live like the little daughter for just a while longer. There are stories that my grandfather was different from other people, "crazy ever since the little Jap bayoneted him in the head." He used to put his naked penis on the dinner table, laughing. And one day he brought home a baby girl, wrapped up inside his brown Western-style greatcoat. He had traded one of his sons, probably my father, the youngest, for her. My grandmother made him trade back. When he finally got a daughter of his own, he doted on her. They must have all loved her, except perhaps my father, the only brother who never went back to China, having once been traded for a girl.

Brothers and sisters, newly men and women, had to efface their sexual color and present plain miens. Disturbing hair and eyes, a smile like no other, threatened the ideal of five generations living under one roof. To focus blurs, people shouted face to face and yelled from room to room. The immigrants I know have loud voices, unmodulated to American tones even after years away from the village where they called their friendships out across the fields. I have not been able to stop my mother's screams in public libraries or over telephones. Walking erect (knees straight, toes pointed forward, not pigeon-toed, which is Chinese-feminine) and speaking in an inaudible voice, I have tried to turn myself American-feminine. Chinese communication was loud, public. Only sick people had to whisper. But at the dinner table, where the family members came nearest one another, no one could talk, not the outcasts nor any eaters. Every word that falls from the mouth is a coin lost. Silently they gave and accepted food with both hands. A preoccupied child who took his bowl with one hand got a sideways glare. A complete moment of total attention is due everyone alike. Children and lovers have no singularity here, but my aunt used a secret voice, a separate attentiveness.

She kept the man's name to herself throughout her labor and dying; she did not accuse him that he be punished with her. To save her inseminator's name she gave silent birth.

He may have been somebody in her own household, but intercourse with a man outside the family would have been no less abhorrent. All the village were kinsmen, and the titles shouted in loud country voices never let kinship be forgotten. Any man within visiting distance would have been neutralized as a lover — "brother," "younger brother," "older brother" — one hundred and fifteen relationship titles. Parents researched birth charts probably not so much to assure good fortune as to circumvent incest in a population that has but one hundred surnames. Everybody has eight million relatives. How useless then sexual mannerisms, how dangerous.

As if it came from an atavism deeper than fear, I used to add "brother" silently to boys' names. It hexed the boys, who would or would not ask me to dance, and made them less scary and as familiar and deserving of benevolence as girls.

But, of course, I hexed myself also — no dates. I should have stood up, both 35
arms waving, and shouted out across libraries, "Hey, you! Love me back." I had no idea, though, how to make attraction selective, how to control its direction and magnitude. If I made myself American-pretty so that the five or six Chinese boys in the class fell in love with me, everyone else — the Caucasian, Negro, and Japanese boys — would too. Sisterliness, dignified and honorable, made much more sense.

Attraction eludes control so stubbornly that whole societies designed to organize relationships among people cannot keep order, not even when they bind people to one another from childhood and raise them together. Among the very poor and the wealthy, brothers married their adopted sisters, like doves. Our family allowed some romance, paying adult brides' prices and providing dowries so that their sons and daughters could marry strangers. Marriage promises to turn strangers into friendly relatives — a nation of siblings.

In the village structure, spirits shimmered among the live creatures, balanced and held in equilibrium by time and land. But one human being flaring up into violence could open up a black hole, a maelstrom that pulled in the sky. The frightened villagers, who depended on one another to maintain the real, went to my aunt to show her a personal, physical representation of the break she had made in the "roundness." Misallying couples snapped off the future, which was to be embodied in true offspring. The villagers punished her for acting as if she could have a private life, secret and apart from them.

If my aunt had betrayed the family at a time of large grain yields and peace, when many boys were born, and wings were being built on many houses, perhaps, she might have escaped such severe punishment. But the men — hungry, greedy, tired of planting in dry soil — had been forced to leave the village in order to send food-money home. There were ghost plagues, bandit plagues, wars with the Japanese, floods. My Chinese brother and sister had died of an unknown sickness. Adultery, perhaps only a mistake during good times, became a crime when the village needed food.

The round moon cakes and round doorways, the round tables of graduated size that fit one roundness inside another, round windows and rice bowls — these talismans had lost their power to warn this family of the law: a family must be whole, faithfully keeping the descent line by having sons to feed the old and the dead, who in turn look after the family. The villagers came to show my aunt and her lover-in-hiding a broken house. The villagers were speeding up the circling of events because she was too shortsighted to see that her infidelity had already harmed the village, that waves of consequences would return unpredictably, sometimes in disguise, as now, to hurt her. This roundness had to be made coin-sized so that she would see its circumference: punish her at the birth of her baby. Awaken her to the inexorable. People who refused fatalism because they could invent small resources insisted on culpability. Deny accidents and wrest fault from the stars.

After the villagers left, their lanterns now scattering in various directions 40
toward home, the family broke their silence and cursed her. "Aiaa, we're going to die. Death is coming. Death is coming. Look what you've done. You've killed us. Ghost! Dead ghost! Ghost! You've never been born." She ran out into the fields, far enough from the house so that she could no longer hear their voices, and pressed herself against the earth, her own land no more. When she felt the birth coming, she thought that she had been hurt. Her body seized together. "They've hurt me too much," she thought. "This is gall, and it will kill me." With forehead and knees against the earth, her body convulsed and then relaxed. She turned on her back, lay on the ground. The black well of sky and stars went out and out and out forever; her body and her complexity seemed to disappear. She was one of the stars, a bright dot in blackness, without home, without a companion, in eternal cold and silence. An agoraphobia rose in her, speeding higher and higher, bigger and bigger; she would not be able to contain it; there would be no end to fear.

Flayed, unprotected against space, she felt pain return, focusing her body. This pain chilled her—a cold, steady kind of surface pain. Inside, spasmodically, the other pain, the pain of the child, heated her. For hours she lay on the ground, alternately body and space. Sometimes a vision of normal comfort obliterated reality: she saw the family in the evening gambling at the dinner table, the young people massaging their elders' backs. She saw them congratulating one another, high joy on the mornings the rice shoots came up. When these pictures burst, the stars drew yet further apart. Black space opened.

She got to her feet to fight better and remembered that old-fashioned women gave birth in their pigsties to fool the jealous, pain-dealing gods, who do not snatch piglets. Before the next spasms could stop her, she ran to the pigsty, each step a rushing out into emptiness. She climbed over the fence and knelt in the dirt. It was good to have a fence enclosing her, a tribal person alone.

Laboring, this woman who had carried her child as a foreign growth that sickened her every day, expelled it at last. She reached down to touch the hot, wet, moving mass, surely smaller than anything human, and could feel that it was human after all—fingers, toes, nails, nose. She pulled it up on to her belly, and it lay curled there, butt in the air, feet precisely tucked one under the other. She opened her loose shirt and buttoned the child inside. After resting, it squirmed and thrashed and she pushed it up to her breast. It turned its head this way and that until it found her nipple. There, it made little snuffling noises. She clenched her teeth at its preciousness, lovely as a young calf, a piglet, a little dog.

She may have gone to the pigsty as a last act of responsibility: she would protect this child as she had protected its father. It would look after her soul, leaving supplies on her grave. But how would this tiny child without family find her grave when there would be no marker for her anywhere, neither in the earth nor the family hall? No one would give her a family hall name. She had taken the child with her into the wastes. At its birth the two of them had felt the same raw pain of separation, a wound that only the family pressing tight could close. A child with no descent line would not soften her life but only trail after her, ghostlike, begging her to give it purpose. At dawn the villagers on their way to the fields would stand around the fence and look.

Full of milk, the little ghost slept. When it awoke, she hardened her breasts 45
against the milk that crying loosens. Toward morning she picked up the baby and walked to the well.

Carrying the baby to the well shows loving. Otherwise abandon it. Turn its face into the mud. Mothers who love their children take them along. It was probably a girl; there is some hope of forgiveness for boys.

"Don't tell anyone you had an aunt. Your father does not want to hear her name. She has never been born." I have believed that sex was unspeakable and words so strong and fathers so frail that "aunt" would do my father mysterious harm. I have thought that my family, having settled among immigrants who had also been their neighbors in the ancestral land, needed to clean their name, and a wrong word would incite the kinspeople even here. But there is more to this silence: they want me to participate in her punishment. And I have.

In the twenty years since I heard this story I have not asked for details nor said my aunt's name; I do not know it. People who can comfort the dead can also chase after them to hurt them further—a reverse ancestor worship. The real punishment was not the raid swiftly inflicted by the villagers, but the family's deliberately forgetting her. Her betrayal so maddened them, they saw to it that she would suffer forever, even after death. Always hungry, always needing, she would have to beg food from other ghosts, snatch and steal it from those whose living descendants give them gifts. She would have to fight the ghosts massed at crossroads for the buns a few thoughtful citizens leave to decoy her away from village and home so that the ancestral spirits could feast unharassed. At peace, they could act like gods, not ghosts, their descent lines providing them with paper suits and dresses, spirit money, paper houses, paper automobiles, chicken, meat, and rice into eternity—essences delivered up in smoke and flames, steam and incense rising from each rice bowl. In an attempt to make the Chinese care for people outside the family, Chairman Mao encourages us now to give our paper replicas to the spirits of outstanding soldiers and workers, no matter whose ancestors they may be. My aunt remains forever hungry. Goods are not distributed evenly among the dead.

My aunt haunts me—her ghost drawn to me because now, after fifty years of neglect, I alone devote pages of paper to her, though not origamied into houses and clothes. I do not think she always means me well. I am telling on her, and she was a spite suicide, drowning herself in the drinking water. The Chinese are always very frightened of the drowned one, whose weeping ghost, wet hair hanging and skin bloated, waits silently by the water to pull down a substitute.

[1976]

≡ THINKING ABOUT THE TEXT

1. This cautionary tale is meant to persuade Kingston to conform to her parents' values. What is the argument behind the narrative the mother tells? Does it make sense to you? What might be a contemporary argument in a middle-class American family?
2. Were you ever put at an "outcast table" (para. 19) or anything comparable in your house or school? Have you ever heard of such a ritual? What did happen when you were punished? What kinds of things were you punished for? Why do you think these specific things were chosen?
3. Is this also a tale about gender inequality? How does Kingston suggest this? How are relations between men and women portrayed here?
4. How do ghosts and spirits function in this essay? Which parts of this piece seem true to you, and which seem fictional? Why do you suppose Kingston blends these elements?
5. Sexual mores change over time and from country to country. What specifically about the aunt's context made her transgression so severe? How would her "crime" be viewed in contemporary America? Why? What do you think an ideal response would be?

DAVID FOSTER WALLACE

Good People

David Foster Wallace (1962–2008) was born in Ithaca, New York, and later went to elementary and high school in Urbana, Illinois. His parents were both college professors and after receiving degrees from Amherst College and the University of Arizona and publishing Infinite Jest *(1991), a highly regarded novel, he eventually became a professor at Pomona College in Claremont, California, in 2002. He received the prestigious MacArthur Fellowship in 1997 and was working on a novel,* The Pale King, *when he committed suicide, having suffered from depression since his late adolescence. Although the short story, "Good People," published here seems fairly straightforward and clearly written, most of his critically acclaimed fiction features long multi-clause sentences, jargon, various voices and modes of writing, and extensive footnotes and endnotes. Wallace hoped to write "morally passionate, passionately moral fiction" that might help readers "become less alone inside." He is generally considered to be one of the most influential and innovative writers of his generation.*

They were up on a picnic table at that park by the lake, by the edge of the lake, with part of a downed tree in the shallows half hidden by the bank. Lane A. Dean, Jr., and his girlfriend, both in bluejeans and button-up shirts. They sat up on the table's top portion and had their shoes on the bench part that people sat on to picnic or fellowship together in carefree times. They'd gone to different high schools but the same junior college, where they had met in campus ministries. It was springtime, and the park's grass was very green and the air suffused with honeysuckle and lilacs both, which was almost too much. There were bees, and the angle of the sun made the water of the shallows look dark. There had been more storms that week, with some downed trees and the sound of chainsaws all up and down his parents' street. Their postures on the picnic table were both the same forward kind with their shoulders rounded and elbows on their knees. In this position the girl rocked slightly and once put her face in her hands, but she was not crying. Lane was very still and immobile and looking past the bank at the downed tree in the shallows and its ball of exposed roots going all directions and the tree's cloud of branches all half in the water. The only other individual nearby was a dozen spaced tables away, by himself, standing upright. Looking at the torn-up hole in the ground there where the tree had gone over. It was still early yet and all the shadows wheeling right and shortening. The girl wore a thin old checked cotton shirt with pearl-colored snaps with the long sleeves down and always smelled very good and clean, like someone you could trust and care about even if you weren't in love. Lane Dean had liked the smell of her right away. His mother called her *down to earth* and liked her, thought she was good people, you could tell—she made this evident in little ways. The shallows lapped from different directions at the tree as if almost teething on it. Sometimes when alone and thinking or struggling to turn a matter over to Jesus Christ in prayer, he would find himself putting his fist in his palm and turning it slightly as if still playing and pounding his glove to stay sharp and alert in center. He did not do this now; it would be cruel and indecent to do this now. The older individual stood beside his picnic table—he was at it but not sitting—and looked also out of place in a suit coat or jacket and the kind of men's hat Lane's grandfather wore in photos as a young insurance man. He appeared to be looking across the lake. If he moved, Lane didn't see it. He looked more like a picture than a man. There were not any ducks in view.

One thing Lane Dean did was reassure her again that he'd go with her and be there with her. It was one of the few safe or decent things he could really say. The second time he said it again now she shook her head and laughed in an unhappy way that was more just air out her nose. Her real laugh was different. Where he'd be was the waiting room, she said. That he'd be thinking about her and feeling bad for her, she knew, but he couldn't be in there with her. This was so obviously true that he felt like a ninny that he'd kept on about it and now knew what she had thought every time he went and said it—it hadn't brought her comfort or eased the burden at all. The worse he felt, the stiller he sat. The whole thing felt balanced on a knife or wire; if he moved to put his arm up or touch her the whole thing could tip over. He hated himself for sitting so frozen. He could almost visualize himself tiptoeing past something explosive. A big stupid-looking tiptoe, like in a cartoon. The whole last black week had been this way and it was wrong. He knew it was wrong, knew something was required of him that was not this terrible frozen care and caution, but he pretended to himself he did not know what it was that was required. He pretended it had no name. He pretended that not saying aloud what he knew to be right and true was for her sake, was for the sake of her needs and feelings. He also worked dock and routing at UPS, on top of school, but had traded to get the day off after they'd decided together. Two days before, he had awakened very early and tried to pray but could not. He was freezing more and more solid, he felt like, but he had not thought of his father or the blank frozenness of his father, even in church, which had once filled him with such pity. This was the truth. Lane Dean, Jr., felt sun on one arm as he pictured in his mind an image of himself on a train, waving mechanically to something that got smaller and smaller as the train pulled away. His father and his mother's father had the same birthday, a Cancer. Sheri's hair was colored an almost corn blond, very clean, the skin through her central part pink in the sunlight. They'd sat here long enough that only their right side was shaded now. He could look at her head, but not at her. Different parts of him felt unconnected to each other. She was smarter than him and they both knew it. It wasn't just school—Lane Dean was in accounting and business and did all right; he was hanging in there. She was a year older, twenty, but it was also more—she had always seemed to Lane to be on good terms with her life in a way that age could not account for. His mother had put it that she *knew what it is she wanted*, which was nursing and not an easy program at Peoria Junior College, and plus she worked hostessing at the Embers and had bought her own car. She was serious in a way Lane liked. She had a cousin that died when she was thirteen, fourteen, that she'd loved and been close with. She only talked about it that once. He liked her smell and her downy arms and the way she exclaimed when something made her laugh. He had liked just being with her and talking to her. She was serious in her faith and values in a way that Lane had liked and now, sitting here with her on the table, found himself afraid of. This was an awful thing. He was starting to believe that he might not be serious in his faith. He might be somewhat of a hypocrite, like the Assyrians in Isaiah, which would be a far graver sin than the appointment—he had decided he believed this. He was desperate to be good people, to still be able to feel he was good. He rarely before now had thought of damnation and Hell—that part of it didn't speak to his spirit—and in worship services he more just tuned himself out and tolerated Hell when it came up, the same way you tolerate the job you've got to have to save up for what it is you want. Her tennis shoes had little things doodled on them from sitting in her class lectures. She stayed looking down like that. Little notes or reading assignments in Bic in her neat round hand on the rubber elements around the sneaker's rim. Lane A. Dean, looking now at her inclined head's side's barrettes in the shape of blue ladybugs. The appointment was for afternoon, but when the doorbell had rung so early and his mother'd called to him up the stairs, he had known, and a terrible kind of blankness had commenced falling through him.

He told her that he did not know what to do. That he knew if he was the salesman of it and forced it upon her that was awful and wrong. But he was trying to understand—they'd prayed on it and talked it through from every different angle. Lane said how sorry she knew he was, and that if he was wrong in believing they'd truly decided together when they decided to make the appointment she should please tell him, because he thought he knew how she must have felt as it got closer and closer and how she must be so scared, but that what he couldn't tell was if it was more than that. He was totally still except for moving his mouth, it felt like. She did not reply. That if they needed to pray on it more and talk it through, then he was here, he was ready, he said. The appointment could get moved back; if she just said the word they could call and push it back to take more time to be sure in the decision. It was still so early in it — they both knew that, he said. This was true, that he felt this way, and yet he also knew he was also trying to say things that would get her to open up and say enough back that he could see her and read her heart and know what to say to get her to go through with it. He knew this without admitting to himself that this was what he wanted, for it would make him a hypocrite and liar. He knew, in some locked-up little part of him, why it was that he'd gone to no one to open up and seek their life counsel, not Pastor Steve or the prayer partners at campus ministries, not his UPS friends or the spiritual counselling available through his parents' old church. But he did not know why Sheri herself had not gone to Pastor Steve — he could not read her heart. She was blank and hidden. He so fervently wished it never happened. He felt like he knew now why it was a true sin and not just a leftover rule from past society. He felt like he had been brought low by it and humbled and now did believe that the rules were there for a reason. That the rules were concerned with him personally, as an individual. He promised God he had learned his lesson. But what if that, too, was a hollow promise, from a hypocrite who repented only after, who promised submission but really only wanted a reprieve? He might not even know his own heart or be able to read and know himself. He kept thinking also of 1 Timothy and the hypocrite therein who *disputeth over words*. He felt a terrible inner resistance but could not feel what it was that it resisted. This was the truth. All the different angles and ways they had come at the decision together did not ever include it — the word — for had he once said it, avowed that he did love her, loved Sheri Fisher, then it all would have been transformed. It would not be a different stance or angle, but a difference in the very thing they were praying and deciding on together. Sometimes they had prayed together over the phone, in a kind of half code in case anybody accidentally picked up the extension. She continued to sit as if thinking, in the pose of thinking, like that one statue. They were right up next to each other on the table. He was looking over past her at the tree in the water. But he could not say he did: it was not true.

But neither did he ever open up and tell her straight out he did not love her. This might be his *lie by omission*. This might be the frozen resistance — were he to look right at her and tell her he didn't, she would keep the appointment and go. He knew this. Something in him, though, some terrible weakness or lack of values, could not tell her. It felt like a muscle he did not have. He didn't know why; he just could not do it, or even pray to do it. She believed he was good, serious in his values. Part of him seemed willing to more or less just about lie to someone with that kind of faith and trust, and what did that make him? How could such a type of individual even pray? What it really felt like was a taste of the reality of what might be meant by Hell. Lane Dean had never believed in Hell as a lake of fire or a loving God consigning folks to a burning lake of fire — he knew in his heart this was not true. What he believed in was a living God of compassion and love and the possibility of a personal relationship with Jesus Christ through whom this love was enacted in human time. But sitting here beside this girl as unknown to him now as outer space, waiting for whatever she might say to unfreeze him, now he felt like he could see the edge or outline of what a real vision of Hell might be. It was of two great and terrible armies within himself, opposed and facing each other, silent. There would be battle but no victor. Or never a battle—the armies would stay like that, motionless, looking across at each other, and seeing therein something so different and alien from themselves that they could not understand, could not hear each other's speech as even words or read anything from what their face looked like, frozen like that, opposed and uncomprehending, for all human time. Two-hearted, a hypocrite to yourself either way.

When he moved his head, a part of the lake further out flashed with sun— 5
the water up close wasn't black now, and you could see into the shallows and see that all the water was moving but gently, this way and that—and in this same way he besought to return to himself as Sheri moved her leg and started to turn beside him. He could see the man in the suit and gray hat standing motionless now at the lake's rim, holding something under one arm and looking across at the opposite side where a row of little forms on camp chairs sat in a way that meant they had lines in the water for crappie—which mostly only your blacks from the East Side ever did—and the little white shape at the row's end a Styrofoam creel. In his moment or time at the lake now just to come, Lane Dean first felt he could take this all in whole: everything seemed distinctly lit, for the circle of the pin oak's shade had rotated off all the way, and they sat now in sun with their shadow a two-headed thing in the grass before them. He was looking or gazing again at where the downed tree's branches seemed to all bend so sharply just under the shallows' surface when he was given to know that through all this frozen silence he'd despised he had, in truth, been praying, or some little part of his heart he could not hear had, for he was answered now with a type of vision, what he would later call within his own mind a vision or *moment of grace*. He was not a hypocrite, just broken and split off like all men. Later on, he believed that what happened was he'd had a moment of almost seeing them both as Jesus saw them—as blind but groping, wanting to please God despite their inborn fallen nature. For in that same given moment he saw, quick as light, into Sheri's heart, and was made to know what would occur here as she finished turning to him and the man in the hat watched the fishing and the downed elm shed cells into the water. This down-to-earth girl that smelled good and wanted to be a nurse would take and hold one of his hands in both of hers to unfreeze him and make him look at her, and she would say that she cannot do it. That she is sorry she did not know this sooner, that she hadn't meant to lie—she agreed because she'd wanted to believe that she could, but she cannot. That she will carry this and have it; she has to. With her gaze clear and steady. That all night last night she prayed and searched inside herself and decided this is what love commands of her. That Lane should please please sweetie let her finish. That listen—this is her own decision and obliges him to nothing. That she knows he does not love her, not that way, has known it all this time, and that it's all right. That it is as it is and it's all right. She will carry this, and have it, and love it and make no claim on Lane except his good wishes and respecting what she has to do. That she releases him, all claim, and hopes he finishes up at P.J.C. and does so good in his life and has all joy and

good things. Her voice will be clear and steady, and she will be lying, for Lane has been given to read her heart. To see through her. One of the opposite side's blacks raises his arm in what may be greeting, or waving off a bee. There is a mower cutting grass someplace off behind them. It will be a terrible, last-ditch gamble born out of the desperation in Sheri Fisher's soul, the knowledge that she can neither do this thing today nor carry a child alone and shame her family. Her values blocked the way either way, Lane could see, and she has no other options or choice—this lie is not a sin. Galatians 4:16, *Have I then become your enemy?* She is gambling that he is good. There on the table, neither frozen nor yet moving, Lane Dean, Jr., sees all this, and is moved with pity, and also with something more, something without any name he knows, that is given to him in the form of a question that never once in all the long week's thinking and division had even so much as occurred—why is he so sure he doesn't love her? Why is one kind of love any different? What if he has no earthly idea what love is? What would even Jesus do? For it was just now he felt her two small strong soft hands on his, to turn him. What if he was just afraid, if the truth was no more than this, and if what to pray for was not even love but simple courage, to meet both her eyes as she says it and trust his heart? *[2007]*

THINKING ABOUT THE TEXT

1. What happens to Lane during his "moment of grace"? How would you define "good" in the title?
2. What is the significance of the much repeated word "frozen"? What relevance do some of the other details in the story have, for example, the man by the lake; the fallen tree; references to his father and other specific details?
3. Describe Lane's conflicted and evolving notions about whether he loves Sheri or not. How do love and courage connect for him, or do they? Why does Wallace never use the word "abortion," even though the procedure lies at the emotional heart of his story?
4. What is your take on the final decision Lane and Sheri might make? What evidence can you cite to support your position? Why doesn't Foster have Sheri speak, especially given that the decision is ultimately hers to make?
5. How well do you think Lane knows Sheri's heart? How well does he know his own? Do you think he is sensitive enough to her needs? Is he serious about doing the right thing? What other considerations do you think he should be thinking about?

MAKING COMPARISONS

1. What impact do community values play in the decision Kingston's aunt makes and the process Lane and Sheri are involved in?

2. How would you describe the concept of freedom of choice in both texts?
3. Sexual mores change over time and from country to country. What seem to be similarities and difference in the contexts of these two stories?

WRITING ABOUT ISSUES

1. Write a brief argument from one of the villager's point of view in Kingston's story, justifying the attack. How would you respond to that argument?
2. Write an argument about the significance economic vulnerability, religious values, and community tradition play in the decisions faced by Kingston's aunt and Lane and Sheri.
3. Write an essay that answers the following: Do the story and the essay accomplish Wallace's hope that writing be "morally passionate, [and] passionately moral"? If so, how do they accomplish this? If not, why not? Do they help readers "become less alone inside"? Why or why not?
4. Read Ernest Hemingway's brief story "Hills Like White Elephants." There are clear echoes of this tale in "Good People." Speculate about the outcome of both stories and argue whether either couple are good people.

CHAPTER 9

Love

Our culture makes many claims about love: stories of the rejected lover who dies of a broken heart abound. Modern kings give up the throne, ancient cities go to war—all for love. Love is thought to be such a powerful emotion that its loss may even make one want to die or to kill. (In some countries, finding one's wife or husband in bed with a lover is a legal excuse for murder.) Men and women seem willing to radically change their lives to be near their beloved. These are a few examples of love's powerful influence on our behavior and our understanding of who we are.

Yet a serious discussion about the nature of love is often frustratingly difficult. We can all make a list of things we love: a cold beer in summer, a great science-fiction film, a new car, a quiet dinner with a good friend, a walk in fresh snow, a football game when our favorite team comes from behind for a dramatic victory. We love our parents, our siblings, our best friends. How can one word cover such diversity?

When we try to generalize about love, we find ourselves relying on specific incidents because giving examples is easier than giving definitions. If clarifying the essence of love seems difficult, perhaps it is because our stories, myths, and songs are filled with contradictions. Love conquers all, we say, but doesn't love fade? We profess our undying love, but divorce statistics soar. Love is complex and frustrating to pin down. Our culture even identifies different types of love: true love, platonic love, maternal love, erotic love. Yet opinions about love are strong; we all have evidence for what it is and isn't that we find persuasive.

But the evidence we find so convincing is influenced by cultural assumptions, probably more than we know. It would be naive to claim otherwise when we are bombarded with so many movies, songs, and stories about love. Indeed, some critics argue that romantic love is only a socially constructed illusion, merely an elaborate rationalization for physical desire. Once the carnal attraction fades, we get restless. At least, this is one argument, and probably not a popular one among college students in search of love. Because we know what we feel about those we love, we often grow impatient with other people's perspectives. We are likely to ignore friends who say, "He wouldn't treat you like that if he really loved you." Perhaps nothing arouses our interest more than a discussion of our hopes and dreams about love.

Our engagement with stories and poems about love is equally complex and ambivalent. Although the stories in this chapter often illuminate the sometimes dark passageways we take in our romantic journeys, there is no consensus about the final destination. Arguing about love stories engages us as much as it may also baffle us. As you read, rely on your own experience, ethical positions, and literary judgment in determining whether specific characters are indeed in love, whether they should continue their relationship, whether they need more commitment or less. The wise and the foolish seem equally perplexed in matters of the heart.

The first five clusters comprise poems about love. Four expressions of true love, three passionate love poems, three poems about melancholy love, and two poems about seductions lead up to Matthew Arnold's haunting "Dover Beach" and three cultural contexts for thinking about the poem. The following cluster presents a variety of arguments on narcissism using Tony Hoaglund's poem, "What Narcissism Means to Me," as a point of departure. Three stories of romantic illusion are next, followed by stories about love by two twentieth-century masters, William Faulkner and Raymond Carver. One of the world's greatest plays about jealousy, *Othello*, is next along with three interesting critical commentaries. Two essays that argue the value of marriage comprise the penultimate cluster. And a poem and a story about the mysterious "bog people" conclude the chapter.

True Love: Poems

WILLIAM SHAKESPEARE, "Let me not to the marriage of true minds"

JOHN KEATS, "Bright Star"

ELIZABETH BARRETT BROWNING, "How Do I Love Thee?"

E. E. CUMMINGS, "somewhere i have never travelled"

Think about the term *true love.* Why *true*? Does *love* need this modification? Isn't love supposed to be true? Is there a *false* love? Or is something else implied that *love* doesn't convey by itself? Might it be something like *the one-and-only*? Some writers seem committed to the idea that true love lasts forever, for better or worse, regardless of circumstances. Is this just a fantasy, something we hope will be true? Or is it a reality, delivered to those who are lucky or who work hard to make it true? See if you agree with the four poets in this cluster, some of whom are direct and clear about the possibilities of true love, while others take a more indirect, even playful tone.

BEFORE YOU READ

Do you believe in true love? How would you describe it? How has the idea been portrayed in books and films you are familiar with?

WILLIAM SHAKESPEARE

Let me not to the marriage of true minds

William Shakespeare (1564–1616) is best known to modern readers as a dramatist; however, there is evidence that both he and his contemporaries valued his poetry above the plays. In 1598, for example, a writer praised Shakespeare's "sugared sonnets among his private friends." As with other aspects of his life and work, questions about how much autobiographical significance to attach to Shakespeare's subject matter continue to arise. Regardless of the discussion, there can be no doubt that the sonnets attributed to Shakespeare, at times directed to a man and at others directed to a woman, address the subject of love. Sonnet 116, which was written in 1609 and proposes a "marriage of true minds," is no exception.

Let me not to the marriage of true minds,
Admit impediments. Love is not love
Which alters when it alteration finds,
Or bends with the remover to remove:
Oh, no! it is an ever-fixèd mark,

That looks on tempests and is never shaken;
It is the star to every wandering bark,° *small ship*
Whose worth's unknown, although his height be taken.
Love's not Time's fool, though rosy lips and cheeks
Within his bending sickle's compass come;
Love alters not with his brief hours and weeks,
But bears it out even to the edge of doom.
If this be error and upon me proved,
I never writ, nor no man ever loved. *[1609]*

THINKING ABOUT THE TEXT

1. Why would you be pleased if your beloved wrote you this sonnet? Is he professing his love or giving a definition of true love as unchanging?
2. What if love didn't last "even to the edge of doom" (line 12)? Why might it then be ordinary?
3. Shakespeare uses images to describe true love. Which one strikes you as apt? Can you suggest an image of your own?
4. The concluding couplet seems to be saying something like "I'm absolutely right." Do you think Shakespeare is? Can you think of a situation in which love should bend or alter?
5. The world seems to demonstrate that true love seldom lasts forever. Why then do writers of all kinds profess the opposite? If you really believe that true love does not exist, would you still marry? If your beloved asked you if your love would last forever, would you truthfully answer, "Only time will tell"?

JOHN KEATS

Bright Star

John Keats (1795–1821) was born into a working-class family. He hoped to be a physician but decided that poetry was his calling. His narrative poem Endymion *(1818) received poor reviews, but he was totally committed to his work. He was stricken with tuberculosis shortly after the poem's publication and went to Italy to recover. He died in Rome at age twenty-five.*

In 2009, Jane Campion directed Bright Star, *a film based on the last three years of Keats's life. The film focuses on his intense relationship with Fanny Brawne. Lines from many of his most famous poems are recited, including "La Belle Dame Sans Merci" and "Ode on Melancholy," as well as lines from his poetic letters to Fanny. On his tombstone is his own inscription: "Here lies one whose name was writ in water." Today Keats is considered one of literature's greatest poets.*

Bright star, would I were stedfast as thou art—
Not in lone splendour hung aloft the night
And watching, with eternal lids apart,
Like nature's patient, sleepless Eremite,° *A Christian hermit*
The moving waters at their priestlike task
Of pure ablution round earth's human shores,
Or gazing on the new soft-fallen mask
Of snow upon the mountains and the moors—
No—yet still stedfast, still unchangeable,
Pillow'd upon my fair love's ripening breast,
To feel for ever its soft fall and swell,
Awake for ever in a sweet unrest,
Still, still to hear her tender-taken breath,
And so live ever—or else swoon to death. *[1819]*

☰ THINKING ABOUT THE TEXT

1. Discuss how the speaker wants to be like the bright star in some ways, but not in others.
2. Is the speaker trying to stop time (as the pop star Jim Croce sang, "If I could save time in a bottle"), or is he hoping that his love will never change?
3. "Sweet unrest" (line 12) seems to be a contradiction. Is it? What is Keats trying to get at?
4. Is it psychologically healthy to want to have an unchanging love for someone forever? Is it realistic? Is it simply a kind of ritual to say such things?
5. Keats was quite sickly at the end of his short life. Do you think awareness of his serious illness influenced the theme of his poem?

☰ MAKING COMPARISONS

1. Compare the images of change that both Shakespeare and Keats use.
2. Compare Shakespeare's and Keats's use of the star metaphor.
3. Do both poets have similar notions of true love?

ELIZABETH BARRETT BROWNING

How Do I Love Thee?

Elizabeth Barrett Browning (1806–1861) was a prominent Victorian poet whose work was well received in England and the United States. She was raised in a wealthy family and was a studious, precocious child who read widely in classic and contemporary literature. Her first collection of poems, An Essay on Mind, with Other Poems, *was published in 1826. Elizabeth battled illness her whole life and often depended on opium and morphine. She married the poet Robert Browning in 1846, and they moved to Italy for her health. They had a son nicknamed Pen. Two verse novels,* Aurora Leigh *(1856) and* Sonnets from the Portuguese *(1850), which are both still highly regarded works, made her famous. "How Do I Love Thee?" is the popular title of the forty-third of her* Sonnets from the Portuguese.

How do I love thee? Let me count the ways.
I love thee to the depth and breath and height
My soul can reach, when feeling out of sight
For the ends of being and ideal grace.
I love thee to the level of every day's
Most quiet need, by sun and candle-light.
I love thee freely, as men strive for right.
I love thee purely, as they turn from praise.
I love thee with the passion put to use
In my old griefs, and with my childhood's faith.
I love thee with a love I seemed to lose
With my lost saints. I love thee with the breath,
Smiles, tears, of all my life; and, if God choose,
I shall but love thee better after death.

[1845]

THINKING ABOUT THE TEXT

1. Explain the lines, ". . . when feeling out of sight / For the ends of being and ideal grace" (lines 3–4).
2. How would you translate ". . . to the level of every day's / Most quiet need, by sun and candle-light" (lines 5–6) into everyday prose?
3. How would you define these terms that Browning uses: "freely" (line 7), "purely" (line 8), and "childhood's faith" (line 10)?
4. How do you interpret Browning's idea that she loves with a love "I seemed to lose / With my lost saints" (lines 11–12)?
5. What other topics besides love are considered in Browning's sonnet?

MAKING COMPARISONS

1. How would you describe the kind of love Browning writes about? Spiritual, physical, erotic, platonic, sentimental? Compare this love to that in Shakespeare and Keats.
2. Compare the theme of Browning's poem with Keats's and Shakespeare's themes.
3. How is death dealt with in these poems?

E. E. CUMMINGS

somewhere i have never travelled

E. E. Cummings is the pen name of Edward Estlin Cummings (1894–1962), and though he experimented with language on every level, he did not legally change his name to lowercase and preferred the usual uppercase. Born in Cambridge, Massachusetts, and educated at Harvard, he tried his hand at essays, plays, and other types of prose; in fact, it was a novel based on a World War I concentration camp experience in France, The Enormous Room *(1922), that first brought Cummings attention. It is his poetry, however, that most readers immediately recognize for its eccentric use of typography and punctuation, its wordplay and slang usage, its jazz rhythms, and its childlike foregrounding of the concrete above the abstract. Cummings hated pretension and would only agree to deliver the prestigious Eliot lectures at Harvard in 1953 if they were called nonlectures. His two large volumes of* The Complete Poems, *1913–1962, published in 1972, include humor, understated satire, and celebrations of love and sex.*

somewhere i have never travelled, gladly beyond
any experience, your eyes have their silence:
in your most frail gesture are things which enclose me,
or which i cannot touch because they are too near
your slightest look easily will unclose me
though i have closed myself as fingers,
you open always petal by petal myself as Spring opens
(touching skilfully, mysteriously) her first rose
or if your wish be to close me, i and
my life will shut very beautifully, suddenly,

as when the heart of this flower imagines
the snow carefully everywhere descending;

nothing which we are to perceive in this world equals
the power of your intense fragility: whose texture
compels me with the colour of its countries,
rendering death and forever with each breathing

(i do not know what it is about you that closes
and opens; only something in me understands
the voice of your eyes is deeper than all roses)
nobody, not even the rain, has such small hands *[1931]*

≡ THINKING ABOUT THE TEXT

1. In your own words, what is Cummings saying about the effect love has on him? Is this hyperbolic? Why?
2. Does love open us up? In what ways? Can you give a personal example of what a strong feeling did to you?

3. Is this a poem about love or obsession or romantic infatuation? What is the difference?
4. What do you think "the power of your intense fragility" (line 14) might mean? Is this a contradiction?
5. When Cummings says "something in me understands" (line 18), what might he mean? Is love located inside us somewhere? In our hearts? Our brains?

≡ MAKING COMPARISONS

1. Is Cummings's flower imagery more effective than the images that Shakespeare and Keats use?
2. Is this poem closer in theme to Keats's poem or to Browning's?
3. What do you imagine Shakespeare and Keats would think about Cummings's sentence structure? His images?

≡ WRITING ABOUT ISSUES

1. Translate the Cummings poem into concrete prose. Try not to use images; just explain the individual lines as simply as you can.
2. Write a comparison of the effects these four poems had on you.
3. Write a position paper arguing for or against the reality of true love. Make reference to two of the poems given here.
4. Find three more love poems by William Shakespeare or John Keats and write a report about the issues of love that this poet raises.

Passionate Love: Poems

MICHAEL S. HARPER, "Discovery"

SUSAN MINOT, "My Husband's Back"

DEREK WALCOTT, "Love After Love"

A brief online search will turn up scores of sites about love in all its variety and complexity. There are three types or five types or seven types, depending on the site. The Greeks started this confusing classification with eros, or unconditional love, and storge, or affectionate love. The list goes on: mania, infatuation, puppy love, and so forth. Although we have used the term passionate love for these three poems, you might want to think about how you would label the deep feelings in Harper's, Minot's, and Walcott's poems. Look up the Greek's idea of a healthy version of self-love, Philacitia, before reading Walcott's poem.

BEFORE YOU READ

Describe recent examples of passionate love you have read about or seen on television or in films.

MICHAEL S. HARPER

Discovery

Born in Brooklyn, New York, in 1951 to working-class parents, Michael S. Harper and his family soon moved to a predominantly white Los Angeles neighborhood. While attending college in Los Angeles, he worked as a postal worker, where he met educated black men like his father who came of age before the civil rights movement and had not been able to advance economically. Harper received an M.F.A. from the University of Iowa's creative writing program. His first book of poems, Dear John, Dear Coltrane *(1970), from which this selection is taken, was nominated for the National Book Award. He has received many writing awards, including a Guggenheim. Among his ten books of poetry are* Songlines in Michaeltree: New and Collected Poems *(2000) and* Use Trouble *(2009). He is a professor of English at Brown University.*

We lay together, darkness all around,
I listen to her constant breath,
and when I thought she slept,
I too fell asleep.
But something stirred me, why I . . .
she was staring at me with her eyes,
her breasts still sturdy,
her thigh warming mine.

And I, a little shaken as she stroked
my skin and kissed my brow,
reached for the light turned on,
feeling for the heat which would
reveal how long she had looked
and cared.
The bulb was hot. It burned my hand. *[1970]*

THINKING ABOUT THE TEXT

1. The last sentence seems literal. But how might you read it metaphorically?
2. Why do you think Harper used the ellipsis in line 5? Is this an effective device, or should he have tried to say what the "something" was?
3. Why was the speaker "a little shaken" (line 9)? Would you feel that way in a similar situation, or would your response be something else? Surprise? Satisfaction?
4. Why did he want to know "how long she had looked / and cared" (lines 13–14)? Why might it matter to him? Would it to you?
5. Would you interpret the staring as evidence of passionate love? Would you interpret the speaker's behavior as true love or something else?

SUSAN MINOT

My Husband's Back

Susan Minot (b. 1956) was born in Boston and grew up in Manchester-by-the-Sea, Massachusetts. She studied writing and painting at Brown University and received an M.F.A. from Columbia University. Minot was an editor of the literary journal Grant Street. *Her first book,* Monkeys *(1986), is a collection of nine stories about a large New England family. Minot's female protagonists are searching for love, usually unsuccessfully. Her best-selling collection* Lust and Other Stories *(1989) focuses on romantic love, although one critic cautions readers not to "look for a happy, mutual, heterosexual relationship in Minot. You will not find it." Her novel* Evening *(1998) was made into a popular film in 2007 starring Vanessa Redgrave, Meryl Streep, and Claire Danes. Her novel about war-torn Africa,* Thirty Girls, *was published in 2014. A volume of her verse,* Poems 4am, *was published in 2002. The women in these poems seem more optimistic about love than do those in her fiction.*

Sunday evening.
Breakdown hour. Weeping into
a pot of burnt rice. Sun dimmed
like a light bulb gone out

behind a gray lawn of snow.
The baby flushed with the flu
asleep on a pillow.
The fire won't catch.
The wet wood's caked
with ice. Sitting
on the couch my spine
collides with all its bones
and I watch my husband
peer past the glass grate
and blow.
His back in a snug plaid shirt
gray and white
leaning into the woodstove
is firm and compact
like a young man's back.

And the giant world which swirls
in my head
stopping most thought
suddenly ceases
to spin. It sits
right there, the back I love,
animal and gamine,° leaning
on one arm.
I could crawl on it forever
the one point in the world
turns out
I have traveled everywhere
to get to. *[2005]*

gamine: Untamed and mischievous.

THINKING ABOUT THE TEXT

1. Why is the speaker "Weeping" (line 2)? Is she unhappy? Frustrated? Overwhelmed?
2. Why does "the giant world" (line 21) cease to spin?
3. What do you think the speaker means in the last two lines when she says she has "traveled everywhere / to get to" (lines 32–33)?
4. Do you think being in love can help a person deal with global tragedies? Domestic frustration? Cosmic gloom?
5. Do you think Minot's feelings of love are momentary, caused by the "Breakdown hour" (line 2)?

MAKING COMPARISONS

1. Which of the two characters in "Discovery" might Minot's narrator be? Why?
2. Compare the use of light bulbs in these two poems.
3. How would you describe the two women's attitudes toward love?

DEREK WALCOTT

Love After Love

Derek Walcott (1930–2017) was born in Saint Lucia in the West Indies. He trained as a painter and his work was exhibited in New York City. He published his first poem at fourteen and went on to publish over two dozen collections. The most highly praised are Omeros *(1990) and* Midsummer *(1984). His latest book is* The Poetry of Derek Walcott *(1948–2013). He has won numerous awards including a MacArthur Fellowship, the Queen's gold Medal for Poetry in 1988, and the Nobel Prize in Literature in 1992. The Nobel committee described his work as "a poetic oeuvre of great luminosity."*

The time will come
when, with elation
you will greet yourself arriving
at your own door, in your own mirror
and each will smile at the other's welcome,

and say, sit here. Eat.
You will love again the stranger who was your self.
Give wine. Give bread. Give back your heart
to itself, to the stranger who has loved you

all your life, whom you ignored
for another, who knows you by heart.
Take down the love letters from the bookshelf,

the photographs, the desperate notes,
peel your own image from the mirror.
Sit. Feast on your life.

THINKING ABOUT THE TEXT

1. What is the significance of the title?
2. Who is the "stranger" (line 9)? Why does the narrator say "give back your heart" (line 8)?
3. Is the narrator addressing the reader? What specific advice is given?
4. Explain the line "Feast on your life" (line 15).
5. Aristotle said that "all friendly feelings for others are an extension of a man's feeling for himself." How does this apply to this poem?

MAKING COMPARISONS

1. All three poems can be said to be about passionate love but in very different ways. Explain.
2. How might the speaker in "Discovery" appreciate Walcott's poem in a way that Minot's narrator would not?
3. How would you rate these poems in terms of being optimistic or pessimistic about love?

WRITING ABOUT ISSUES

1. Write an essay that discusses the complexity of passionate love in these three poems.
2. Argue for or against Minot's narrator's belief that love can be an antidote to life's difficulties.
3. Argue that the passion exhibited by Harper's partner and Minot's narrator is good or bad for a relationship.
4. Argue that there is or isn't a difference between Philacitia and Narcissism. Give concrete examples from novels, films, and even your experience?

Melancholy Loves: Poems

EDNA ST. VINCENT MILLAY, "What Lips My Lips Have Kissed, and Where, and Why"

W. H. AUDEN, "Funeral Blues"

ROBIN BECKER, "Morning Poem"

It is not uncommon, of course, for a romantic relationship to evolve from intense physical attraction or erotic love in the beginning to sadness or melancholy at the end. Naturally, poets have written about all stages of love in all their complexity, from joy and wonder to resignation and despair. Few of us would prefer to suffer than to exult in love, but perhaps Tennyson's lines " 'Tis better to have loved and lost than never to have loved at all" capture the pragmatic attitude that understands that love is a risk worth taking. Although at different times in history melancholy was embraced as an appropriate attitude toward the vagaries of love, most of us probably hope to recover, not wallow in the sorrow of a failed romance. In our selections, Edna St. Vincent Millay and W. H. Auden offer us memorable variations on love lost, whereas Robin Becker's narrator tries to deal with the implications of "while nothing lasts" even in the midst of a passionate affair.

BEFORE YOU READ

How might communicating grief help people cope? Is there a difference between writing a poem, which could be private or public, and joining a community of mourners in a support group or on Facebook? In what other ways do people grieve? How do you prefer to mourn?

EDNA ST. VINCENT MILLAY

What Lips My Lips Have Kissed, and Where, and Why

Edna St. Vincent Millay (1892–1950) was born in Rockland, Maine. Her mother encouraged her to be ambitious and self-sufficient and taught her about literature at an early age. On the strength of her early poems, Millay won a scholarship to Vassar, where she became a romantic legend for breaking the "hearts of half the undergraduate class." She also soon became wildly famous for her love poetry, giving readings in large auditoriums across the country, much like a contemporary rock star. She was openly bisexual, and her fame, talent, beauty, and bohemian aura were said to have driven her many admirers to distraction. A biography by Nancy Milford, Savage Beauty *(2001), quotes from dozens of letters to Millay, whining, pleading, and groveling for her favors. Milford writes that "she gave the Jazz Age its lyric voice." In fact, we still use a phrase that Salon.com says Millay "invented to describe a life of impudent abandon":*

My candle burns at both ends;
It will not last the night;

But oh, my foes, and oh, my friends—
It gives a lovely light!

Once called "the greatest female poet since Sappho," Millay's reputation in academic circles has fallen off somewhat. Perhaps her work seems a bit obvious compared to the cerebral and allusive free verse of poets like T. S. Eliot. But some critics still think of her as America's "most illustrious love poet." The title poem of Renascence and Other Poems *(1917) ranks as a landmark of modern literature, and the collection itself is ranked fifth on the New York Public Library's Books of the Century. The following poem is from* Collected Poems *(1956).*

What lips my lips have kissed, and where, and why,
I have forgotten, and what arms have lain
Under my head till morning; but the rain
Is full of ghosts tonight, that tap and sigh
Upon the glass and listen for reply,
And in my heart there stirs a quiet pain
For unremembered lads that not again
Will turn to me at midnight with a cry.
Thus in winter stands the lonely tree,
Nor knows what birds have vanished one by one,
Yet knows its boughs more silent than before:
I cannot say what loves have come and gone,
I only know that summer sang in me
A little while, that in me sings no more. *[1923]*

THINKING ABOUT THE TEXT

1. What is it the speaker misses if she can't remember who her lovers were?
2. What does Millay mean by "a quiet pain" (line 6)?
3. Is Millay the "lonely tree" in winter (line 9)? Does it surprise you that she was only thirty-one when she wrote this poem?
4. Do you read the last two lines as saying that the speaker is no longer in love?
5. How would you describe the tone of this poem? Is it wistful or nostalgic? Appropriate? Regretful or sentimental? Bittersweet or simply sad?

W. H. AUDEN

Funeral Blues

Wystan Hugh Auden (1907–1973) was born in England and is widely regarded as the finest English poet of the twentieth century. Yet he moved to the United States in 1939, became an American citizen, and spent his remaining years living alternately in this country and in Austria. Auden's reputation as a poet soared in the 1930s, especially with the publication of his second book, Poems *(1930). In this period of his career, he was much influenced by psychoanalysis and Marxism. During the late 1930s, his leftist sympathies led him to join what was ultimately a losing cause, the fight against Fascist rebels in Spain. The following poem has several titles and versions, including "Stop All the Clocks" and a text with five stanzas. Auden intended this poem to be sung by the soprano Hedli Anderson, but the lyric has taken on a life of its own and has evolved into perhaps the most frequently read elegy at funerals in English-speaking countries. From the innumerable postings online, it is clear that it beautifully and lucidly describes our deep sense of loss at the death of a loved one.*

Stop all the clocks, cut off the telephone.
Prevent the dog from barking with a juicy bone,
Silence the pianos and with muffled drum
Bring out the coffin, let the mourners come.

Let aeroplanes circle moaning overhead
Scribbling in the sky the message He is Dead,
Put crêpe bows round the white necks of the public doves,
Let the traffic policemen wear black cotton gloves.
He was my North, my South, my East and West,
My working week and my Sunday rest
My noon, my midnight, my talk, my song;
I thought that love would last forever, I was wrong.

The stars are not wanted now; put out every one,
Pack up the moon and dismantle the sun.
Pour away the ocean and sweep up the wood;
For nothing now can ever come to any good. *[1940]*

≡ THINKING ABOUT THE TEXT

1. What is it about this poem that makes it so universally popular?
2. What images in the poem seem most poignant to you?
3. Auden employs hyperbole throughout the poem. Is this an effective device since we are not meant to take his thoughts literally?
4. Are thoughts like those presented here normal for the grieving process?
5. Given the despair of the last line, why do you think so many people read this poem at funerals?

ROBIN BECKER

Morning Poem

Robin Becker (b. 1951) was born in Philadelphia, Pennsylvania, and received her B.A. (1973) and M.A. (1976) from Boston University. She taught for many years at the Massachusetts Institute of Technology. She has been teaching at Penn State since 1994. She has published seven books of poetry, including Domain of Perfect Affection *(2006), a collection informed by feminist and lesbian sympathies. She was appointed Penn State Laureate in 2010. The noted poet Maxine Kumin says Becker's poetry has a "controlled ironic intelligence."*

Listen. It's morning. Soon I'll see your hand reach
for my watch, the water will agitate in the kettle,
but listen. Traffic. I want your dreams first. And
to slide my leg beneath yours before the day opens.
Wait. We slept late. You'll be moody, the phone
will ring, someone wanting something. Let me put
my hands in your hair. Who I was last night I would
be again. This is how the future holds me, how depression
wakes with us; my body shelters it. Let me
put my head on your breast. I know nothing lasts.
I would try to hold you back, not out of meanness
but fear. Oh my practical, my worldly-wise. You
know how the body falters, falls in on itself. Tell me
that we will never want from each other what we
cannot have. Lie. It's morning. *[2008]*

THINKING ABOUT THE TEXT

1. Why does the speaker say that "depression wakes with us" (lines 8–9)?
2. What does the narrator mean by "I would try to hold you back" (line 11)?
3. How do the following words or phrases suggest the narrator's mood: "watch," "agitate," "Traffic," "slept late," "moody," "the phone will ring" (lines 2–6)?
4. How might "lie" in the last line be ambiguous? How is the meaning of the phrase "It's morning" in the last line different from the opening line?
5. What do you think the narrator means when she says "who I was last night I would / be again" (lines 7–8)?

MAKING COMPARISONS

1. Compare the use of night in these poems.
2. Compare the line "I know nothing lasts" (line 10) in "Morning Poem" with the last two lines of Millay's poem.
3. Compare the attitudes of the two narrators toward loss.

WRITING ABOUT ISSUES

1. Translate Millay's and Auden's poems into prose. Write a brief essay that explains the ways these two poems are different than the prose translations.

2. Write a brief essay that argues that Millay has or does not have a healthier attitude toward love affairs than either Becker or Neruda.
3. Argue that the attitude of one of these poets toward love affairs is closer to that of today's college students than the others. Refer to specific lines or ideas in all three poems.
4. Read John Keats's classic poem "Ode on Melancholy," and write an essay that compares Keats's views on melancholic love with Auden's.

Seductive Arguments: Poems

JOHN DONNE, "The Flea"

ANDREW MARVELL, "To His Coy Mistress"

Surely the idea of men trying to convince women to sleep with them is neither new nor surprising. As the line from the Talking Heads has it, "Same as it ever was." Naturally such impulses have found their way into literature, from the Greeks to the present. It was the Roman poet Horace, after all, who made famous the term *carpe diem*, or "seize the day," an attitude that became quite popular among poets in the seventeenth century. Their rhetorical strategy was simple: sleep with me before time runs out. If the logic is somewhat dubious, their poetic sophistication and inventiveness perhaps make up for the flawed logic. And, of course, women at the time were expected to be virgins until marriage, and their marriage prospects and options in general were seriously diminished if they were not. Perhaps the most famous of these poems is Andrew Marvell's "To His Coy Mistress." And while not technically a carpe diem poem, John Donne's obvious seductive intentions have made "The Flea" famous for its wildly imaginative attempts to bring logic to his physical urges.

BEFORE YOU READ

Are seduction poems (or songs or letters) effective? Is such an offer more effectively made in person? What would the difference be? Could you say some things in a letter, say, that you couldn't (or wouldn't) say in person?

JOHN DONNE

The Flea

Long regarded as a major English writer, John Donne (1572–1631) was also trained as a lawyer and clergyman. Around 1594, he converted from Catholicism to Anglicanism; in 1615, he was ordained; and in 1621, he was appointed to the prestigious position of dean of St. Paul's Cathedral in London. Today, his sermons continue to be studied as literature, yet he is more known for his poetry. When he was a young man, he often wrote about love, but later he focused on religious themes. In the following classic poem—a complex combination of poetic sophistication and persuasive rhetoric (if somewhat ridiculous logic)—the narrator tries to convince a lady to sleep with him. His clever and seemingly serious argument hinges on a flea having bitten both the speaker and his mistress, and thus their blood is joined. Actually, at the time, it was believed that blood was exchanged during intercourse. The speaker's insistence is both amusing and shocking.

Mark but this flea, and mark in this,
How little that which thou deniest me is;

It sucked me first, and now sucks thee,
And in this flea our two bloods mingled be;
Thou know'st that this cannot be said
A sin, nor shame, nor loss of maidenhead,
    Yet this enjoys before it woo,
    And pampered swells with one blood made of two,
    And this, alas, is more than we would do.

Oh stay, three lives in one flea spare,
Where we almost, nay more than married are.
This flea is you and I, and this
Our mariage bed, and marriage temple is;
Though parents grudge, and you, w'are met,
And cloistered in these living walls of jet.
    Though use make you apt to kill me,
    Let not to that, self-murder added be,
    And sacrilege, three sins in killing three.

Cruel and sudden, hast thou since
Purpled thy nail, in blood of innocence?
Wherein could this flea guilty be,
Except in that drop which it sucked from thee?
Yet thou triumph'st, and say'st that thou
Find'st not thy self, nor me the weaker now;
    'Tis true; then learn how false, fears be:
    Just so much honor, when thou yield'st to me,
    Will waste, as this flea's death took life from thee. *[1633]*

THINKING ABOUT THE TEXT

1. Using straightforward prose, explain why the narrator thinks his mistress should have sex with him.
2. Besides "kill" and "death," words often used in Donne's time for sexual intercourse, what other terms in the poem have a sexual connotation or double meaning?
3. Choose several metaphors in the poem and explain their significance.
4. How does the narrator turn the argument against his beloved in the conclusion?
5. Probably not many women either then or now would be persuaded by this argument. The narrator seems so clever and sophisticated that he must know that. Do you agree? Are his motives as simple as they seem? What might his thinking be? Since it appears that his love might have killed the flea ("Purpled thy nail, in blood of innocence" [line 20]), what do you imagine her response to him is?

ANDREW MARVELL

To His Coy Mistress

Andrew Marvell (1621–1678) was famous in his own time as an adroit politician and a writer of satire, but modern readers admire him for the style and content of his lyric, metaphysical poetry. Born into a Protestant family, Marvell was tolerant of Catholicism from a young age, and his willingness to somehow circumvent the religious prejudices of seventeenth-century England allowed his continued success. He traveled to Holland, France, Italy, and Spain—possibly to avoid the English civil war as a young man and undoubtedly to spy for England in later years. He tutored Cromwell's ward and later served on his Council of State but was influential enough during the Restoration to get his fellow poet and mentor, John Milton, released from prison. Although admired by the Romantic poets of the early nineteenth century, Marvell's poetry (much of it published after his death) was revived in the twentieth century by T. S. Eliot and has been widely read for its ironic approach to the conventions of love.

Had we but world enough, and time,
This coyness, lady, were no crime.
We would sit down, and think which way
To walk, and pass our long love's day.
Thou by the Indian Ganges'° side
Shouldst rubies find; I by the tide
Of Humber° would complain.° I would
Love you ten years before the Flood,
And you should, if you please, refuse
Till the conversion of the Jews.
My vegetable love should grow°
Vaster than empires, and more slow;
An hundred years should go to praise
Thine eyes and on thy forehead gaze,
Two hundred to adore each breast,
But thirty thousand to the rest:
An age at least to every part,
And the last age should show your heart.
For, lady, you deserve this state,
Nor would I love at lower rate.
    But at my back I always hear
Time's wingèd chariot hurrying near;
And yonder all before us lie
Deserts of vast eternity.

5 Ganges: A river in India sacred to the Hindus. **7 Humber:** An estuary that flows through Marvell's native town, Hull. **complain:** Sing love songs. **11 My vegetable love . . . grow:** A slow, insensible growth, like that of a vegetable.

Thy beauty shall no more be found,
Nor in thy marble vault shall sound
My echoing song; then worms shall try
That long preserved virginity,
And your quaint honor turn to dust,
And into ashes all my lust.
The grave's a fine and private place,
But none, I think, do there embrace.
Now, therefore, while the youthful hue
Sits on thy skin like morning dew,
And while thy willing soul transpires°
At every pore with instant fires,
Now let us sport us while we may,
And now, like amorous birds of prey,
Rather at once our time devour
Than languish in his slow-chapped° power.
Let us roll all our strength and all
Our sweetness up into one ball,
And tear our pleasures with rough strife
Thorough° the iron gates of life.
Thus, though we cannot make our sun
Stand still, yet we will make him run.

[1681]

35 transpires: Breathes forth. **40 slow-chapped:** Slow-jawed. **44 Thorough:** Through.

THINKING ABOUT THE TEXT

1. Considered as both an intellectual and an emotional argument, what is the narrator's goal, and what specific claims does he make? Are they convincing? Do you think they were in 1681? Do you think women three hundred years ago worried about virginity? Why?
2. What does this poem say about the needs of Marvell's audience? What assumptions about women does the poem make?
3. How many sections does this poem have? What is the purpose of each? How is the concluding couplet in each related to that section? Is the rhyme scheme related to the meaning of these couplets?
4. Is the speaker passionate? Sincere? How do you make such a decision? Do you look at his language or at his message?
5. Some feminist readers see in the last ten lines a kind of indirect threat, a suggestion of force through the use of violent images. Is this a plausible reading? If this is the case, what do you now think of the narrator's pleading?

MAKING COMPARISONS

1. Compare the logic of seduction in Donne's and Marvell's poems.
2. Compare the use of a woman's honor in both poems.
3. Compare the tone of both poems. Is one more likely to achieve its goal than the other?

WRITING ABOUT ISSUES

1. Make an argument about the effectiveness of a contemporary song or poem that aims to seduce through logic and wit. Discuss its strategies and compare them to those in "The Flea" and / or "To His Coy Mistress."
2. Write a letter to Donne or Marvell explaining why contemporary readers of his poem might find his proposal objectionable.
3. Do the narrators of Donne's and Marvell's poems remind you of any figures from contemporary popular culture—television characters, film or music idols, characters in video games, celebrities who are always cropping up in tabloids? If so, write an essay that will persuade others to see the similarities.
4. Argue that contemporary social networks like Facebook and Twitter make verbal seduction easier or more difficult.

Literature and Current Issues: Are Millennials Narcissists?

TONY HOAGLAND, "What Narcissism Means to Me"

ARGUMENTS ON THE ISSUE:

BROOKE LEA FOSTER, "The Persistent Myth of the Narcissistic Millennial"

EMILY ESFAHANI SMITH AND JENNIFER AAKER, "Millennial Searchers"

COLSON WHITEHEAD, "How 'You Do You' Perfectly Captures Our Narcissistic Culture"

STEVE KELLEY AND JEFF PARKER, "You Know the Great Thing about Selfies?"

The original Narcissist didn't fare too well. According to Ovid, a first-century B.C.E. writer, Narcissus was a young man so handsome that all the young nymphs fell in love with him. In this myth, he wanders into the woods, sees his reflection in a pool for the first time, and tries to kiss his image. But he cannot have his heart's desire and soon dies of despair. Hence, our belief that a narcissist is filled with excessive and destructive self-love. Narcissists for centuries have been thought to be lazy, self-centered, and arrogant. This idea persists in the widespread accusation that Millennials are self-absorbed, selfish narcissists, interested in selfies, instant gratification, and insatiable consumerism.

However, a distinction should be made between the use of narcissism by psychological professionals as a personality disorder and its popular use by cultural critics, politicians, and bloggers. For a psychiatrist, narcissists are filled with grandiosity, feeling entitled to extraordinary privileges and showing no empathy for people. They cannot tolerate criticism; they dominate conversations and generally feel superior. When cultural critics say Millennials are narcissistic, they rarely mean they are psychologically ill, rather that they are self-absorbed and vain, too interested in self-gratification, perhaps a little too self-important and selfish.

But there is a further distinction to be made between good narcissism and bad narcissism. This is a debate that has been going on ever since Freud considered narcissism to be primarily a female problem. Naturally that is not an accepted view today. But the question of whether narcissism is good or bad is still a lively and unsettled matter among professionals and cultural critics. For example, Elizabeth Lunbeck in *The Americanization of Narcissism* (2014) claims that charismatic leaders demonstrate good narcissism. She admits that there is bad narcissism, being arrogant and demanding, for example. But good narcissism gives a boost to your self-esteem and makes you vivacious and creative. In fact, it helps you to love. This, then, is the focus of this cluster: the debate between these two kinds of narcissism. And more specifically, are Millennials narcissistic or just normal young people?

We begin with a poem by Tony Hoagland that some readers see as a defense of narcissism, while others read his poem as a critique. Our four arguments are equally divided. The first two pieces argue that the accusations of narcissism in young people are not only unwarranted but that narcissism itself is not so bad. That is not the case with the piece by Whitehead and the comic by Kelley and Parker. For them narcissism is rampant in the culture and harmful. So the question is: Are Millennials self-deluded narcissists or socially conscious optimists?

BEFORE YOU READ

The Narcissistic Personality Inventory asks which is more applicable to you: "Compliments embarrass me" versus "I like to be complimented," and "I am more capable than other people," versus "There is a lot that I can learn from other people." How would you answer? Do you think this is a fair way to judge if someone is narcissistic or not? Why?

TONY HOAGLAND

What Narcissism Means to Me

Tony Hoagland (b. 1953) is an American poet who teaches at the University of Houston and the M.F.A. program at Warren Wilson College. He was born in Fort Bragg, North Carolina. He has a B.A. from the University of Iowa and an M.F.A. from the University of Arizona. His widely published and highly praised poetry is known for its witty take on American life. His latest collection is Application for Release from the Dream *(2015). His collection* What Narcissism Means to Me *(2003) was a finalist for the National Book Critics Circle Award.*

There's Socialism and Communism and Capitalism
said Neal,
and there's Feminism and Hedonism,
        and there's Catholicism and Bipedalism and Consumerism,

but I think Narcissism is the system
that means the most to me

and Sylvia said that in Neal's case
narcissism represented a heroic achievement in positive thinking.

And Ann,
who calls everybody Sweetie pie
        whether she cares for them or not,

Ann lit a cigarette and said, Only miserable people will tell you
        that love has to be deserved,

and when I heard that, a distant chime went off for me,

remembering a time when I believed
        that I could simply live without it

Neal had grilled the corn and sliced the onions
                into thick white disks,
                and piled the wet green pickles
                                up in stacks like coins
        and his chef's cap was leaning sideways like a mushroom cloud.

Then Ethan said that in his opinion,
if you're going to mess around with self-love
        you shouldn't just rush into a relationship,

and Sylvia was weeping softly now, looking down
        into her wine cooler and potato chips,

and then the hamburgers were done, just as
the sunset in the background started
            cutting through the charcoal clouds

exposing their insides—black,
streaked dark red,
        like a slab of scorched, rare steak,

delicious but unhealthy,
or, depending upon your perspective,
                unhealthy but delicious,

—the way that, deep inside the misery
        of daily life,
            love lies bleeding.

[2003]

THINKING ABOUT THE TEXT

1. What does Neal mean when he says narcissism "means the most to me"? Is he a narcissist?
2. How might narcissism be a "heroic achievement in positive thinking"?
3. Ann says only "miserable people" think that "love has to be deserved." What does this have to do with narcissism? Do you think love has to be deserved? Is this true for maternal love? Romantic love? Why?
4. The narrator remembers a time when he could not live without love (line 16). Is this self-love? Or the love of another? What difference does it make?
5. The poem ends with an analogy between love and a slab of steak. Explain what you think this means. How might this be related to narcissism?

BROOK LEA FOSTER

The Persistent Myth of the Narcissistic Millennial

Brook Lea Foster (b. 1975) is a journalist focusing on health, education, and lifestyle issues. She has worked as an editor and writer at the Boston Globe *and* Sunday Magazine. *Her articles have appeared in such places as the* New York Times, The Atlantic, *and* Psychology Today. *She also has written books on parenting, including* For Goodness Sex *(2014).*

A few months ago, the news went viral that the American Psychiatric Association had classified "taking selfies" as a sign of a mental disorder. It lit up Facebook and Twitter until it was revealed that the article was a hoax.

But still, I doubt I'm the only one that has felt at least a tiny sense of self-loathing after, say, posting a photo of myself on Facebook. Deep down, taking a "selfie" doesn't just feel like capturing a moment—it also feels like capturing myself at my most vain.

In his pop-psychology book *The Narcissist Next Door: Understanding the Monster in Your Family, in Your Office, in Your Bed—in Your World,* published in September, author and *Time* editor at large Jeffrey Kluger argues that the popularity of the "selfie" is just one way that our culture is becoming more narcissistic. In fact, he says, narcissistic behaviors today aren't just more accepted; they're celebrated. "We've become accustomed to preeners and posers who don't have anything to offer except themselves and their need to be on the public stage," he says. The egocentric antics of figures like Donald Trump or Kim Kardashian, for example, make our own narcissistic proclivities seem more palatable by comparison, and social media only instigates the desire for attention. Facebook, to a narcissist, can be like an open bar to a drunk.

But Kluger also devotes a chunk of his book to what's become a tired argument: The idea that Millennials—the generation that came of age with selfies and Facebook and the Kardashians—are the most self-absorbed generation of all. "Plenty of people are narcissistic in our society," Kluger says, "but Millennials are doing these things on a pandemic level."

Of course they are. They're young and full of themselves, like every other generation that's come before them was at some point. But are Millennials any more narcissistic than, say, the Baby Boomers, who were once considered the most self-obsessed cohort of their time? Consider the 1976 cover story of *New York Magazine*, in which Tom Wolfe declared the '70s "The Me Decade." One could argue that every generation seems a little more narcissistic than the last, puffing out its chest and going out into the world with an overabundance of self-confidence, swagger, even a bit of arrogance. These traits are simply hallmarks of early adulthood—it's often the first time people are putting themselves out there, applying for first jobs and meeting potential life partners. Overconfidence is how people muscle through the big changes.

Whether it's *Time*'s 2013 cover story "The Me, Me, Me Generation" or Kluger's book, the same statistics are cited as proof of Millennial narcissism. In a 2008 study published in the *Journal of Personality*, San Diego State University psychology professor Jean Twenge found that narcissistic behaviors among college students studied over a 27-year period had increased significantly from the 1970s. A second study published in 2008 by the National Institutes of Health showed that 9.4 percent of 20- to 29-year-olds exhibit extreme narcissism, compared with 3.2 percent of those older than 65.

But there's a problem with all of this evidence: The data is unreliable. "It's incredibly unfair to call Millennials narcissistic, or to say they're more so than previous generations," says Jeffrey Jensen Arnett, a professor of psychology at Clark University and author of *Getting to 30: A Parent's Guide to the Twentysomething Years*. Arnett has devoted a significant amount of time and research to disproving the statistics that San Diego State's Twenge has built a career on. He says that her assertion that narcissistic behaviors among young people have risen 30 percent is flimsy, since she's basing it around data collected from the 40-question Narcissistic Personality Inventory (NPI), the results of which leave quite a bit up for interpretation. For example, does agreement with statements like "I am assertive" or "I wish I were more assertive" measure narcissism, self-esteem, or leadership?

Culturally, narcissism has become a catchphrase of sorts for traits people deem unpleasant or unlikable in a person, similar to how people will say they have obsessive-compulsive disorder just because they're fastidious or detail-oriented, rather than because they meet the actual clinical diagnosis. If you love to talk about yourself, but you also show empathy for others, you're not a narcissist. If you're extremely confident at work but you're good at accepting criticism, you're probably not a narcissist either.

In fact, according to the APA, only about 1 percent of people would meet the textbook definition of narcissism. Instead, many people today exhibit something called "subclinical narcissism," which Kluger describes as a kind of narcissism lite. It's the co-worker who loves to talk about herself, the friend at the cocktail party who entertains a crowd with his self-absorbed (but funny) stories, the sibling that consistently shows up empty-handed at holidays. They are people who channel their love of themselves into a kind of infectious self-confidence, leading them to believe that it's their world and everyone else is living in it.

Part of the problem with diagnosing narcissism is that it's easy to confuse it 10
with other types of behaviors, as Arnett alluded to. Here's another ambiguous set of NPI statements: "The thought of ruling the world frightens the hell out of me," or "If I ruled the world it would be a better place." Arnett says: "I could see a 19-year-old chuckling at the idea of ruling the world and checking it off on the NPI. On the inventory, there are things that are narcissism, things that are clearly not narcissism, and things that are ridiculous. But altogether, it's uninterpretable."

Also dubious is the methodology used in the study out of the NIH. To investigate whether twentysomethings were more narcissistic than those over 65, researchers sat down with both age groups and interviewed them about their narcissistic behaviors. But here's the rub: While the younger people polled were asked about their current lives, those over 65 were asked to remember how they behaved decades ago—not an entirely reliable account of whether or not they acted in a narcissistic manner.

Other studies have directly contradicted the idea that Millennials are the most narcissistic of previous generations. In a large survey of high-school seniors across several decades, psychologist M. Brent Donnellan (now at Texas A&M University) found little change when looking at the Millennial generation's ideas about self-esteem, individualism, or life satisfaction compared to young people in the past. And when psychology researchers at the University of Illinois compared narcissism rates with age and life stages in another 2010 study, they found that narcissistic behavior was related not to generation, but to age-related developmental stages. "This leads to the conclusion that every generation is Generation Me, as every generation of younger people are more narcissistic than their elders," the researchers wrote.

Perhaps today's young people are products, rather than drivers, of the cultural saturation of narcissism that Kluger describes. They're not leading the charge—they're simply evolving with the times, just as their parents, siblings, and grandparents are. Maybe Kluger is right: Maybe we're *all* just a little more into ourselves than we used to be.

And for those uniquely self-centered, narcissistic Millennials, well, researchers say they're actually a lot less selfish than popular reports make it seem. While Twenge alleges that the increase in narcissism has promoted a generational trend toward "more extrinsic values (money, image, and fame) and away from intrinsic values (community feeling, affiliation, and self-acceptance)," other researchers, including Arnett, have found the opposite. In a recent survey of 18- to 29-year olds, 80 percent agreed with the statement, "It is more important for me to enjoy my job than to make a lot of money," while 86 percent agreed that "It is important to me to have a career that does some good in the world." And a 2010 survey of high school seniors found that from 1976 to 2006, "there were no meaningful changes in egotism, self-enhancement, individualism, self-esteem."

So they love the selfie? Let them. Says Arnett: "In many other ways, this is an exceptionally generous generation." 15 *[2014]*

≡ THINKING ABOUT THE TEXT

1. How does Foster use selfies to make a distinction between being narcissistic and being vain? What do you think the distinction is?
2. How does Foster rebut the evidence used by her opposition, especially Jean Twenge and Jeffrey Kluger?
3. What does Foster mean that narcissism has become a "catchphrase"? Do you think this is the case? Why?
4. How does Foster's concluding paragraph sum up her claim?
5. Why do you think people refer to young people, especially high school and college students, as narcissistic? How would you define that term?

≡ MAKING COMPARISONS

1. How are Hoagland's and Foster's takes on narcissism different or similar?
2. How is Foster's response to Ethan's assertion that "if you're going to mess around with self-love/you shouldn't just rush into a relationship" narcissistic or not?
3. Is Hoagland saying narcissism is bad? Is Foster saying narcissism is good? Why?

EMILY ESFAHANI SMITH AND JENNIFER L. AAKER

Millennial Searchers

Emily Esfahani Smith (b. 1988) writes about psychology and cultures. She is the Manners and Morals columnist at The New Criterion. *Her articles have appeared in* The Atlantic, The New Criterion, *and the* New York Times. *She was born in Switzerland and grew up in Montreal. She graduated from Dartmouth College.*

Jennifer L. Aaker (b. 1967) is a professor of Marketing at Stanford Graduate School of Business. She was born in Palo Alto, California. She studied at the University of California, Berkeley, graduating with a B.A. in 1989. She received a Ph.D. from Stanford in Marketing and Psychology in 1995. She has published widely, focusing on happiness, social media, and time. Her books include. The Power of Stories *(with A. Smith and B. McCarthy, 2013) and* The Dragonfly Effect: Quick, Effective and Powerful Ways to Use Social Media to Drive Social Change *(with A. Smith, 2010).*

For Viktor Frankl, the Holocaust survivor who wrote the best-selling book "Man's Search for Meaning," the call to answer life's ultimate question came early. When he was a high school student, one of his science teachers declared to the class,

"Life is nothing more than a combustion process, a process of oxidation." But Frankl would have none of it. "Sir, if this is so," he cried, jumping out of his chair, "then what can be the meaning of life?"

The teenage Frankl made this statement nearly a hundred years ago — but he had more in common with today's young people than we might assume.

Today's young adults born after 1980, known as Generation Y or the millennial generation, are the most educated generation in American history and, like the baby boomers, one of the largest. Yet since the Great Recession of 2008, they have been having a hard time. They are facing one of the worst job markets in decades. They are in debt. Many of them are unemployed. The income gap between old and young Americans is widening. To give you a sense of their lot, when you search "are millennials" in Google, the search options that come up include: "are millennials selfish," "are millennials lazy," and "are millennials narcissistic."

Do we have a lost generation on our hands? In our classes, among our peers, and through our research, we are seeing that millennials are not so much a lost generation as a generation in flux. Chastened by these tough economic times, today's young adults have been forced to rethink success so that it's less about material prosperity and more about something else.

5 And what is that something else? Many researchers believe that millennials are focusing more on happiness than prior generations, and that the younger ones in that age cohort are doing so even more than the older ones who did not take the brunt of the recession. Rather than chasing the money, they appear to want a career that makes them happy — a job that combines the perks of Google with the flexibility of a start-up.

But a closer look at the data paints a slightly different picture. Millennials appear to be more interested in living lives defined by meaning than by what some would call happiness. They report being less focused on financial success than they are on making a difference. A 2011 report commissioned by the Career Advisory Board and conducted by Harris Interactive, found that the No. 1 factor that young adults ages 21 to 31 wanted in a successful career was a sense of meaning. Though their managers, according to the study, continue to think that millennials are primarily motivated by money, nearly three-quarters of the young adults surveyed said that "meaningful work was among the three most important factors defining career success."

Meaning, of course, is a mercurial concept. But it's one that social scientists have made real progress understanding and measuring in recent years. Social psychologists define meaning as a cognitive and emotional assessment of the degree to which we feel our lives have purpose, value and impact. In our joint research, we are looking closely at what the building blocks of a meaningful life are. Although meaning is subjective — signifying different things to different people — a defining feature is connection to something bigger than the self. People who lead meaningful lives feel connected to others, to work, to a life purpose, and to the world itself. There is no one meaning of life, but rather, many sources of meaning that we all experience day to day, moment to moment, in the form of these connections.

It's also important to understand what meaning is not. Having a sense of meaning is not the same as feeling happy. In a new longitudinal study done by one of us, Jennifer L. Aaker, with Roy F. Baumeister, Kathleen D. Vohs and Emily N. Garbinsky, 397 Americans were followed over a monthlong period and asked the degree to which they considered their lives to be meaningful and happy, as well as beliefs and values they held, and what type of choices they had made in their lives.

It turns out that people can reliably assess the extent to which their lives have meaning, much in the same way that people can assess their degree of life satisfaction or happiness. Although a meaningful life and a happy life overlap in certain ways, they are ultimately quite different. Those who reported having a meaningful life saw themselves as more other-oriented—by being, more specifically, a "giver." People who said that doing things for others was important to them reported having more meaning in their lives.

10 This was in stark contrast to those who reported having a happy life. Happiness was associated with being more self-oriented—by being a "taker." People felt happy, in a superficial sense, when they got what they wanted, and not necessarily when they put others first, which can be stressful and requires sacrificing what you want for what others want. Having children, for instance, is associated with high meaning but lower happiness.

When individuals adopt what we call a meaning mind-set—that is, they seek connections, give to others, and orient themselves to a larger purpose— clear benefits can result, including improved psychological well-being, more creativity, and enhanced work performance. Workers who find their jobs meaningful are more engaged and less likely to leave their current positions.

Further, this mind-set affects what types of careers millennials search for. Today's young adults are hoping to go into careers that make an enduring impact on others. Last spring, when the National Society of High School Scholars, a global honor society for high school students, asked more than 9,000 top students and recent graduates what they wanted to do with their lives, they found that these recession-era millennials favored careers in health care and government. Of the top 25 companies they wanted to pursue out of a list of more than 200, eight were in health care or at hospitals while six were in government or the military. St. Jude Children's Research Hospital came in as the No. 1 place these millennials wanted to work. "The focus on helping others is what millennials are responding to," James W. Lewis, the chief executive of the honor society, told Forbes.

Some studies have suggested that millennials are narcissistic and flaky in their professional and personal lives, and are more selfish than prior generations. But new data suggests that these negative trends are starting to reverse. In a study published this summer in the journal *Social Psychological and Personality Science,* the researchers Heejung Park, Jean M. Twenge and Patricia M. Greenfield looked at surveys that have, each year since the 1970s, tracked the attitudes of hundreds of thousands of 12th graders. Although concern for others had been decreasing among high school seniors and certain markers of materialism—like valuing expensive products such as cars—had been increasing for nearly four decades, these trends began to reverse after 2008. Whereas older millennials showed a concern for meaning, the younger millennials who came of age during the Great Recession started reporting more concern for others and less interest in material goods.

This data reflects a broader pattern. Between 1976 and 2010, high school seniors expressed more concern for others during times of economic hardship, and less concern for others during times of economic prosperity. During times of hardship, young people more frequently look outward to others and the world at large.

Of course, nobody likes living through tough economic times—and the mil- 15
lennials have been dealt a tough hand. But at the same time, there are certain benefits to economic deprivation. Millennials have been forced to reconsider what a successful life constitutes. By focusing on making a positive difference in the lives of others, rather than on more materialistic markers of success, they are setting themselves up for the meaningful life they yearn to have—the very thing that Frankl realized makes life worth living. *[2013]*

THINKING ABOUT THE TEXT

1. What distinction do the authors make between happiness and meaning? How is this connected to narcissism?
2. What careers do Millennials tend to go in for, and how is this connected to narcissism?
3. How do the authors rebut the opposition who say Millennials are "narcissistic and flaky"?
4. Describe the connection the authors make between the economy and narcissism.
5. What is the claim made by the authors and how do they support it?

MAKING COMPARISONS

1. How do the authors differ from the ideas of Jean Twenge? How does Foster differ with Jean Twenge?
2. Compare the claims of Hoagland, Foster, and Smith/Aaker.
3. Compare the idea of doing "good" in the world in the two essays.

COLSON WHITEHEAD

How "You Do You" Perfectly Captures Our Narcissistic Culture

Colson Whitehead (b. 1969) was born in New York City and graduated from Harvard College in 1991. His first novel, The Intuitionist *(1999), was reviewed by John Updike, who called it "ambitious," "scintillating," and "strikingly original." His latest novel,* The Underground Railroad *(2016), has won the National Book Award and the Pultizer Prize. His essays have appeared in the* New York Times, Harpers, The New Yorker, *and others. His account of high-stakes poker,* The Nobel Hustle: Poker, Beef Jerky and Death, *was published in 2014. He was awarded a MacArthur Fellowship in 2002.*

You will recall the fable of the Scorpion and the Frog. The Scorpion needs a ride across the river. The waters are rising on account of climate change, or perhaps he has been priced out of his burrow, who knows? The exact reason is lost in the fog of pre-modernity. The Frog is afraid that the Scorpion will sting him, but his would-be passenger reassures him that they would both die if that happened. That would be crazy. Sure enough, halfway across, the Scorpion stings the Frog. Just before they drown, the Scorpion says, "Aren't you going to ask why I did that?" And the Frog croaks, "You do you."

We don't all partake of the same slang menu—you say "pop," I say "soda," and we'll all get properly sorted on Judgment Day. Wherever you hail from, you'll recognize "You do you" and "Do you" as contemporary versions of that life-affirming chestnut "Just be yourself." It's the gift of encouragement from one person to another, what we tell children on the first day of kindergarten, how we reassure buddies as they primp for a blind date or rehearse asking for a raise. You do you, as if we could be anyone else. Depending on your essential qualities, this song of oneself is cause for joy or tragedy.

You've also come across that expression's siblings, like the defensive, arms-crossed "Haters gonna hate" or the perpetually shrugging "It is what it is." Like black holes, they are inviolable. All criticism is destroyed when it hits the horizon of their circular logic, and not even light can escape their immense gravity. In a world where the selfie has become our dominant art form, tautological phrases like "You do you" and its tribe provide a philosophical scaffolding for our ever-evolving, ever more complicated narcissism.

William Safire, writing in these pages in 2006, coined a word for these self-justifying constructions: "tautophrases." This was in the midst of his investigation into the ubiquity of "It is what it is," as evidenced in its use by cultural specimens as disparate as Britney Spears and Scott McClellan, a press secretary for President George W. Bush. (Pause to reminisce.) Whether the subject is an imperfect situation to be endured ("The new coffee in the break room is the pits") or an existential conundrum ("My body is a bunch of atoms working in brief harmony before death returns them to the universe"), "It is what it is" effectively ends the discussion so that we can stop, nod in solemn agreement and move on.

According to Safire, "It is what it is" has many tautophrasal relatives and 5
ancestors. "What's done is done," "What will be will be." The striking thing about his examples is how many of them preserve and burnish the established order. When God informs Moses, "I am that I am," he is telling the prophet, "Look, get off my back, I'm God." I've never argued with a bush, burning or otherwise, but I imagine they're quite persuasive. "Boys will be boys" and "A man's gotta do what a man's gotta do" excuse mischief and usually worse, reinforcing the dominant masculine code. It's doubtful that "I just discovered penicillin!" or "Publishing

Willa Cather's 'My Antonia' was the most satisfying moment of my career" elicited a gruff "A man's gotta do what a man's gotta do," but perhaps I am cynical. Popeye's "I yam what I yam," however, remains what it has always been—the pathetic ravings of a man who claims superstrength, when it is obvious to everyone else in the room that spinach merely ameliorates the symptoms of an undiagnosed vitamin deficiency. A scurvy dog, indeed.

While the word "tautophrase" didn't take off, the phenomenon it described blossomed, abetted by hip-hop. Sure, philosophical resignation has been a part of the music as far back as 1984, when Run-D.M.C. reeled off a litany of misfortune—"Unemployment at a record high/People coming, people going, people born to die"—and underscored it with a weary, "It's like that/and that's the way it is." But grandiosity, narcissism and artful braggadocio have also been integral to hip-hop from the start, whether they were the fruit of a supercharged sense of self or a coping mechanism for a deleterious urban environment. As with everything interesting in black culture, hip-hop's swaggering tautophrases have been digested and regurgitated by the mainstream. Last year, Taylor Swift somewhat boringly testified that not only are "Haters gonna hate," they're gonna "hate hate hate" exponentially, presumably in direct proportion to her lack of culpability. Instead of serving the establishment (monotheism, patriarchal energies), the modern tautophrase empowers the individual. Regardless of how shallow that individual is.

"Do you" certainly sallies forth from black vernacular, even if the nature of its mundane parts makes its origin Google-proof. The phrase is affection conferred by another person: a "+1," wrapped inside a fav, tucked inside a like. "Game recognizes game" reflects love of oneself, a kiss upon a mirror. It fixes the observed in his or her place while flattering the speaker: "I'm calling you out for possessing a particular set of skills" (in lovemaking, basketball or macramé), for I, too, am blessed with those very same skills. It takes one to know one.

Haters hate; that's them doing them. No matter how saintly you are, the kittens rescued and orphanages saved from demolition, people yearn to bring you down. Classify your antagonists as haters, however, and your flaws are absolved by their greater sin of envy. Obviously, the haters have other qualities apart from their hatred, but such thinking goes against the very nature of the hermetic tautophrase, which refuses intrusion into the bubble of its logic. The hated-upon must resist lines of inquiry, like "Haters are inclined to hate, but perhaps I have contributed to this situation somehow by frustrating that natural impulse in all human beings, that of empathy, however submerged that impulse is in this deadened, modern world." To do otherwise would be to acknowledge your own monstrosity.

Which brings us to the problem of what happens when the person in question is not just an ordinary plodder, a high-school-age Todd or Alissa preening in the mall's food court, but a true villain. What if, like the Scorpion, your you is not so good? "There's been so much blood lately—should I cut back maybe on the pillaging today?" The lieutenant gestures with his longbow: "You do you, Genghis." "Should I take this pistol with me on the 1 train?" The voice in his head that sounds weirdly like his mother's says, "Do you, Bernie Goetz."

And if the person happens to be the leader of the free world?

It just so happened that the president appeared in a BuzzFeed-produced "Obamacare" video in February called "Things Everyone Does but Doesn't Talk About." The video was aimed at uninsured young people, urging them to enroll at Healthcare.gov before the deadline, and featured Obama practicing "Top Gun" faces in front of the mirror, using a selfie stick and shooting an imaginary jump shot. In short, running through a series of contemporary solipsistic gestures. The video ended with a junior White House staff member walking in on the president midcavort. "Can I live?" Obama asked. Be a normal person for just a moment? "You do you," the staff member said, with the insouciance that is a hallmark of the millennial tribe.

These colloquial shenanigans irritated the op-ed page of *The Wall Street Journal.* " 'You do you' is the ultimate self-referential slogan for the ultimate self-referential presidency," the writer fumed. "It's the 'Be yourself' piety of our age turned into a political license by Mr. Obama to do as he pleases." According to *The Journal,* Obama's millennial affectations and his age-inappropriate preening provide context for the rise of ISIS, our crummy foreign policy, immigration amnesty's wrong turn. "You do you," taken to its extreme, provides justification for every global bad actor. The invasion of Ukraine is Putin being Putin, Iran's nuclear ambitions Khamenei being Khamenei.

Haters gonna hate.

While it's true that running for president requires a healthy amount of self-regard—"What the heck, I can rule 300 million people, been thinking about it, and I'm up to the task"—the tautophrase I most associate with the White House is "It is what it is." No matter what you do, no matter the sincerity of your intentions, the stinger is coming out, and now look what you've done: drone-borne collateral damage to bystanders thousands of miles away and children with empty bellies within walking distance. The job is murder, quick by gun sight or slow like despair, in brutal magnitudes. It's a job that makes the tautology decouple from a circle, like a serpent spitting out its tail, to become a straight, blunt declarative: It is what happens. It is the world. It simply is.

We have enough vision and resources to be the Frog, generous and steadfast, and more than enough poison to play the Scorpion, true to our natures. Either way, the waters will take us. Given the rising, merciless It that you and I face day in and day out, surely haters are the least of our worries. Might as well do you. Perform the impersonation of your best self.

Maybe you'll get it right this time. *[2015]*

☰ THINKING ABOUT THE TEXT

1. What is the connection Whitehead makes between "tautophrases" and narcissism?
2. Which one of the tautophrases Whitehead cites have you or your friends used? What did you mean? Should "whatever" be placed among these phrases? Does this word mean something specific, or is it contextual?

3. What is Whitehead's claim about these phrases? Is he overstating their significance? Do you think "It is what it is" is a way to avoid responsibility for the status quo? Give reasons from your own experience.
4. What is Whitehead's specific objection to the phrase "you do you"? When Whitehead says toward the essay's end, (after " . . . Khamenei being Khamenei"), "Haters gonna hate," what does he mean? Is this ironic, sarcastic, or straightforward? Is this an effective technique? Why?
5. Whitehead comes back to the Scorpion and the Frog tale in his conclusion. Paraphrase the point he is making about this story in the last two paragraphs. What connection does this have to narcissism?

MAKING COMPARISONS

1. Whitehead suggests that certain phrases are narcissistic and a kind of denial. What connection might this have to Hoagland's poem?
2. Compare the tone of the three essays. Which seems more effective? Why?
3. Compare the conclusion all three essayists come to about narcissism.

STEVE KELLEY AND JEFF PARKER

You Know the Great Thing about Selfies?

Steve Kelley drew comics for two Dartmouth College newspapers until he graduated with honors in 1981. His first professional job began that same year at the San Diego Union Tribune, *where he stayed for two decades. Following this, Kelley became a staff editorial cartoonist for the* New Orleans Times-Picayune *until 2012. His editorial cartoons have won several awards, and he was a finalist for the 1999 Pulitzer Prize in editorial cartooning. In addition to writing Dustin, Kelley writes comedy and stand-up routines.*

Jeff Parker first drew cartoons for Florida Environments *in 1989 before moving to the* Orlando Business Journal *in 1990. From 1992 to 2013, he drew editorial cartoons for his hometown newspaper,* Florida Today. *He has earned several awards from the editorial cartoon community and since 1992 is published in Pelican Books's* Best Editorial Cartoons *of the Year annually. Currently, Parker draws* Dustin *and assists with Mike Peters's comic* Mother Goose and Grimm. *In 2010,* Dustin *was awarded the National Cartoonists Society Reuben Award for Best Newspaper Comic Strip. The strip follows a 23-year-old millennial, Dustin, who moves home after college, unemployed and unmotivated to change that status.*

Dustin
YOU KNOW THE GREAT THING ABOUT SELFIES?
NO...
CLICK
10-8
©2016 Steve Kelley & Jeff Parker, Dist. by King Features Syndicate, Inc.
KELLEY and PARKER
dustincomics.com
IF YOU EVER WONDER WHAT A NARCISSIST LOOKS LIKE, YOU'VE GOT COUNTLESS PICTURES OF ONE RIGHT THERE ON YOUR PHONE....

[2016]

THINKING ABOUT THE TEXT

1. What argument do Kelley and Parker make in this comic?
2. Consider how the millennial and the adult couple are portrayed. Do either the millennial or the couple seem happier than the other? What are each of them doing? What are they wearing? Now compare how they are drawn between the two panels. What might this imply about the creators' message?
3. How would you change the cartoon to be more critical of the millennial or the couple?
4. Editorial cartoons often comment on current issues and trends. How does the conversation around millennials and narcissism fit this? How does it not?
5. The man and woman pictured are Helen and Ed, the parents of the 23-year-old Dustin this comic strip is named for. Does knowing this change your interpretation of the scene?

MAKING COMPARISONS

1. Compare the use of selfies in the three essays and the comic.
2. This comic assumes a connection between selfies and narcissism. How does this compare to Hoagland's depiction of narcissism?
3. How does Foster's essay about "the persistent myth of the narcissistic millennial" relate to this comic? What similarities and differences do you see between the two?

WRITING ABOUT ISSUES

1. Write an essay that argues that Hoagland's poem is a defense or an accusation of narcissism. Include at least two of our essays in your argument.
2. Research the history of narcissism, explaining how professional psychologists disagreed over its meaning and whether it is an illness or not.
3. Find another article on narcissism and Millennials (for example, "Are Millennials 'Deluded Narcissists'?") and explain how this argument is similar to or different than the ones included here.
4. Read "Selfie" by Joan Acocella in *The New Yorker* (May 12, 2014) and argue that the "middle position" on narcissism does or does not make more sense than the positions given in our four arguments.

Love as a Haven: Cultural Contexts for a Poem

MATTHEW ARNOLD, "Dover Beach"

CULTURAL CONTEXTS:
CHARLES DICKENS, From *Hard Times*

FRIEDRICH ENGELS, From *The Condition of the Working Class in England*

JAMES ELI ADAMS, "Narrating Nature: Darwin"

Considered one of the greatest poems of the Victorian period, Matthew Arnold's "Dover Beach" expresses the spiritual malaise troubling many educated people in the middle of the nineteenth century. Although England was becoming the most powerful country in the world, there were serious social problems left unattended as it focused on its empire. And Matthew Arnold was keenly aware of them. He was educated to be an educational reformer, to promote a rich intellectual and ethical spirit in English society. Moral and social issues were crucial for him, and he championed the study of the best that was said and thought. But there was such a class division in England that only a small fraction of the population was able to reap the rewards Arnold thought a humanistic education could deliver. Such injustice troubled him.

Industrialization brought power and wealth to some and great poverty to many others. It is difficult to educate children when they are starving and cold. Prostitution was also a huge social problem, compounded by disease and poverty. Child labor was also widespread, and hundreds of thousands of nine- and ten-year-olds were working sixty hours a week under gruesomely unsafe and brutal conditions. To add to Arnold's ethical discomfort, scientific advances in geology and biology seemed to many to be in direct contradiction to the natural history found in the first book of the Bible, Genesis. Scientific evidence was demonstrating that the earth was millions of years old, not six thousand. Although his ideas had been well-known in scientific circles for a while, Charles Darwin's *On the Origin of the Species* (1859) dealt a blow to traditional religious ideas of creation with the theory that all life had evolved over millions of years through a process that put an emphasis on chance and randomness over a clear divine plan. If the Bible was so wrong about these facts, perhaps the whole basis of Christianity should be called into question. Such thoughts produced a crisis of faith for many thinkers like Arnold.

"Dover Beach" reflects a sense of spiritual ambiguity and abandonment as Arnold contemplates the "turbid ebb and flow / Of human misery." Although a progressive who supported objective scientific investigation and discovery, Arnold was disturbed by the reality that we might be on our own in the universe. He hears the "melancholy, long, withdrawing roar" of traditional faith and looks to love for solace in a world that is not as simple and comforting as it once seemed. And so, like so many before and after him, he hopes that love, or maybe simply loyalty, can be an antidote to his discontented soul. Although many critics see the other person in the room with Arnold as the reader, feminists object that the person never speaks, just listens. Such a patriarchal view, that women should comfort men in their world-weariness was quite common in Victorian England but is problematic in today's world where men and women must confront the disturbing issues of the day equally.

We have included three cultural contexts for Arnold's poem that address some of the issues troubling Arnold and his contemporaries—one by the novelist Charles Dickens who, like Arnold, opposed the kind of utilitarian education portrayed in the opening chapters of *Hard Times*. Friedrich Engels gives us an eyewitness account of the kind of poverty that Arnold would have seen everywhere. And, finally, a brief selection from *A History of Victorian Literature* comments on the impact of evolution.

BEFORE YOU READ

How does our culture promote the idea that love is an antidote to a depressing world? What social, political, or scientific issue would you say affects your generation the most?

MATTHEW ARNOLD

Dover Beach

Victorian poet Matthew Arnold (1822–1889) was the eldest son of Thomas Arnold, an influential clergyman and historian and headmaster of Rugby, one of England's most prestigious college preparatory schools. He grew up in an educational milieu in which religious, political, and social issues were discussed in depth. He went on to Oxford, where he eventually achieved success despite his irreverence and eccentricity. In 1851, he became an inspector of schools and served in this capacity for thirty-five years. He drew on his experiences with people of diverse social classes to become a keen critic of British education and culture, and he expressed his views of society in critical essays on literary, social, and religious issues as well as in poems. "Dover Beach" may have been written during the months just before or just after Arnold's marriage and honeymoon, which included a ferry ride from Dover, England, to Calais, France.

The sea is calm tonight.
The tide is full, the moon lies fair
Upon the straits;—on the French coast the light
Gleams and is gone; the cliffs of England stand,
Glimmering and vast, out in the tranquil bay.
Come to the window, sweet is the night-air!
Only, from the long line of spray
Where the sea meets the moon-blanched land,
Listen! you hear the grating roar
Of pebbles which the waves draw back, and fling,

Rischgitz/Getty Images

At their return, up the high strand,
Begin, and cease, and then again begin,
With tremulous cadence slow, and bring
The eternal note of sadness in.

Sophocles long ago
Heard it on the Aegean, and it brought
Into his mind the turbid ebb and flow
Of human misery;° we
Find also in the sound a thought,
Hearing it by this distant northern sea.

The Sea of Faith
Was once, too, at the full, and round earth's shore
Lay like the folds of a bright girdle furled.
But now I only hear
Its melancholy, long, withdrawing roar,
Retreating, to the breath
Of the night-wind, down the vast edges drear
And naked shingles° of the world.

15–18 Sophocles . . . misery: In *Antigone*, Sophocles compares the disasters that beset the house of Oedipus to a mounting tide. **28 shingles:** Pebble beach.

Ah, love, let us be true
To one another! for the world, which seems
To lie before us like a land of dreams,
So various, so beautiful, so new,
Hath really neither joy, nor love, nor light,
Nor certitude, nor peace, nor help for pain;
And we are here as on a darkling plain
Swept with confused alarms of struggle and flight,
Where ignorant armies clash by night.

[1867]

THINKING ABOUT THE TEXT

1. In trying to re-create this scene—say, for a movie script—what would you have the lovers look like? Where would the couple be positioned? If you were the director, how would you explain the scene to the actors—that is, what is the speaker saying? Put another way, what argument is being made?
2. Arnold uses the sea as a metaphor. What do you think it represents? What other metaphors and similes are used? Are they effective in making his point?
3. What specifically triggers Arnold's despondency? What was comforting about the "Sea of Faith"? What do you think Arnold meant by the sentence beginning with "But now I only hear . . ." (line 24)?
4. In the film *The Anniversary Party*, Kevin Kline's character reads the last stanza of this poem to a couple celebrating their sixth wedding anniversary. Some critics saw it as an ironic joke, others as a parody of a "sweet" love poem. What is it about the poem that seems to make it inappropriate for such an occasion? Would you send it to your beloved? Why, or why not?
5. What specific reasons does the speaker give for the lovers to be true to each other, beginning with "for the world" (line 30)? Is this an attitude you share? Do you know others who agree? Is this an extreme position? What would the opposite view be? Is this extreme, as well? How does this poem express a contemporary feeling? If you were Arnold's editor, what changes would you suggest to reflect contemporary ideas about relationships between lovers?

CHARLES DICKENS

From *Hard Times*

Charles Dickens (1812–1870), one of the most famous, prolific, and respected novelists in English literature, was born into a family of modest means and had to begin work at twelve years old, an event that would have a profound effect on his thinking and writing. The appalling conditions he experienced find their way into his great novels, including Oliver Twist, David Copperfield, *and* Great Expectations. *Most of his novels were commercially successful as serializations in monthly magazines, which was a common means of publishing at the time. At the height of his fame, Dickens travelled widely, giving readings in Europe and America. He read voraciously and was intensely interested in the political and social issues of the day. The excerpt here, the first two chapters of* Hard Times *(1859), is a parody-like critique of Jeremy Bentham's utilitarianism, which promoted the idea of the greatest happiness for the greatest number. Like Matthew Arnold, Dickens opposed an education of bare facts, a dehumanized education that did little else but prepare children for the further dehumanization of the factory. On his tomb in Poet's Corner in Westminster Abbey is inscribed the following: "He was a sympathiser to the poor, the sick, and the oppressed; and by his death, one of England's greatest writers is lost to the world."*

"Now, what I want is, Facts. Teach these boys and girls nothing but Facts. Facts alone are wanted in life. Plant nothing else, and root out everything else. You can only form the minds of reasoning animals upon Facts: nothing else will ever be of any service to them. This is the principle on which I bring up my own children, and this is the principle on which I bring up these children. Stick to Facts, sir!"

The scene was a plain, bare, monotonous vault of a school-room, and the speaker's square forefinger emphasized his observations by underscoring every sentence with a line on the schoolmaster's sleeve. The emphasis was helped by the speaker's square wall of a forehead, which had his eyebrows for its base, while his eyes found commodious cellarage in two dark caves, overshadowed by the wall. The emphasis was helped by the speaker's mouth, which was wide, thin, and hard set. The emphasis was helped by the speaker's voice, which was inflexible, dry, and dictatorial. The emphasis was helped by the speaker's hair, which bristled on the skirts of his bald head, a plantation of firs to keep the wind from its shining surface, all covered with knobs, like the crust of a plum pie, as if the head had scarcely warehouse-room for the hard facts stored inside. The speaker's obstinate carriage, square coat, square legs, square shoulders, — nay, his very neckcloth, trained to take him by the throat with an unaccommodating grasp, like a stubborn fact, as it was, — all helped the emphasis.

"In this life, we want nothing but Facts, sir; nothing but Facts!"

The speaker, and the schoolmaster, and the third grown person present, all backed a little, and swept with their eyes the inclined plane of little vessels then and there arranged in order, ready to have imperial gallons of facts poured into them until they were full to the brim. [. . .]

* * *

Thomas Gradgrind, sir. A man of realities. A man of facts and calculations. 5
A man who proceeds upon the principle that two and two are four, and nothing over, and who is not to be talked into allowing for anything over. Thomas Gradgrind, sir — peremptorily Thomas — Thomas Gradgrind. With a rule and a pair of scales, and the multiplication table always in his pocket, sir, ready to weigh and measure any parcel of human nature, and tell you exactly what it

comes to. It is a mere question of figures, a case of simple arithmetic. You might hope to get some other nonsensical belief into the head of George Gradgrind, or Augustus Gradgrind, or John Gradgrind, or Joseph Gradgrind (all supposititious, non-existent persons), but into the head of Thomas Gradgrind—no, sir!

In such terms Mr. Gradgrind always mentally introduced himself, whether to his private circle of acquaintance, or to the public in general. In such terms, no doubt, substituting the words "boys and girls," for "sir," Thomas Gradgrind now presented Thomas Gradgrind to the little pitchers before him, who were to be filled so full of facts.

Indeed, as he eagerly sparkled at them from the cellarage before mentioned, he seemed a kind of cannon loaded to the muzzle with facts, and prepared to blow them clean out of the regions of childhood at one discharge. He seemed a galvanizing apparatus, too, charged with a grim mechanical substitute for the tender young imaginations that were to be stormed away.

"Girl number twenty," said Mr. Gradgrind, squarely pointing with his square forefinger, "I don't know that girl. Who is that girl?"

"Sissy Jupe, sir," explained number twenty, blushing, standing up, and curtseying.

"Sissy is not a name," said Mr. Gradgrind. "Don't call yourself Sissy. Call yourself Cecilia."

"It's father as calls me Sissy, sir," returned the young girl in a trembling voice, and with another curtsey.

"Then he has no business to do it," said Mr. Gradgrind. "Tell him he mustn't. Cecilia Jupe. Let me see. What is your father?"

"He belongs to the horse-riding, if you please, sir."

Mr. Gradgrind frowned, and waved off the objectionable calling with his hand.

"We don't want to know anything about that, here. You mustn't tell us about that, here. Your father breaks horses, don't he?"

"If you please, sir, when they can get any to break, they do break horses in the ring, sir."

"You mustn't tell us about the ring, here. Very well, then. Describe your father as a horsebreaker. He doctors sick horses, I dare say?"

"Oh yes, sir."

"Very well, then. He is a veterinary surgeon, a farrier, and horsebreaker. Give me your definition of a horse."

(Sissy Jupe thrown into the greatest alarm by this demand.)

"Girl number twenty unable to define a horse!" said Mr. Gradgrind, for the general behoof of all the little pitchers. "Girl number twenty possessed of no facts, in reference to one of the commonest of animals! Some boy's definition of a horse. Bitzer, yours."

The square finger, moving here and there, lighted suddenly on Bitzer, perhaps because he chanced to sit in the same ray of sunlight which, darting in at one of the bare windows of the intensely white-washed room, irradiated Sissy. For, the boys and girls sat on the face of the inclined plane in two compact bodies, divided up the centre by a narrow interval; and Sissy, being at the corner of a row on the sunny side, came in for the beginning of a sunbeam, of which Bitzer, being at the corner of a row on the other side, a few rows in advance, caught the end. But, whereas the girl was so dark-eyed and dark-haired, that she seemed to receive a deeper and more lustrous colour from the sun, when it shone upon her, the boy was so light-eyed and light-haired that the self-same rays appeared to draw out of him what little colour he ever possessed. His cold eyes would hardly have been eyes, but for the short ends of lashes which, by bringing them into immediate contrast with something paler than themselves, expressed their form. His short-cropped hair might have been a mere continuation of the sandy freckles on his forehead and face. His skin was so unwholesomely deficient in the natural tinge, that he looked as though, if he were cut, he would bleed white.

"Bitzer," said Thomas Gradgrind. "Your definition of a horse."

"Quadruped. Graminivorous. Forty teeth, namely twenty-four grinders, four eye-teeth, and twelve incisive. Sheds coat in the spring; in marshy countries, sheds hoofs, too. Hoofs hard, but requiring to be shod with iron. Age known by marks in mouth." Thus (and much more) Bitzer.

"Now girl number twenty," said Mr. Gradgrind. "You know what a horse is."

She curtseyed again, and would have blushed deeper, if she could have blushed deeper than she had blushed all this time. Bitzer, after rapidly blinking at Thomas Gradgrind with both eyes at once, and so catching the light upon his quivering ends of lashes that they looked like the antennæ of busy insects, put his knuckles to his freckled forehead, and sat down again.

The third gentleman now stepped forth. A mighty man at cutting and drying, he was; a government officer; in his way (and in most other people's too), a professed pugilist; always in training, always with a system to force down the general throat like a bolus, always to be heard of at the bar of his little Public-office, ready to fight all England. To continue in fistic phraseology, he had a genius for coming up to the scratch, wherever and whatever it was, and proving himself an ugly customer. He would go in and damage any subject whatever with his right, follow up with his left, stop, exchange, counter, bore his opponent (he always fought All England) to the ropes, and fall upon him neatly. He was certain to knock the wind out of common sense, and render that unlucky adversary deaf to the call of time. And he had it in charge from high authority to bring about the great public-office Millennium, when Commissioners should reign upon earth.

"Very well," said this gentleman, briskly smiling, and folding his arms. "That's a horse. Now, let me ask you girls and boys, Would you paper a room with representations of horses?"

After a pause, one half of the children cried in chorus, "Yes, sir!" Upon which the other half, seeing in the gentleman's face that Yes was wrong, cried out in chorus, "No, sir"—as the custom is, in these examinations.

"Of course, No. Why wouldn't you?"

A pause. One corpulent slow boy, with a wheezy manner of breathing, ventured the answer, Because he wouldn't paper a room at all, but would paint it.

"You *must* paper it," said the gentleman, rather warmly.

"You must paper it," said Thomas Gradgrind, "whether you like it or not. Don't tell us you wouldn't paper it. What do you mean, boy?"

"I'll explain to you, then," said the gentleman, after another and a dismal pause, "why you wouldn't paper a room with representations of horses. Do you ever see horses walking up and down the sides of rooms in reality—in fact? Do you?"

"Yes, sir!" from one half. "No, sir!" from the other.

"Of course no," said the gentleman, with an indignant look at the wrong half. "Why, then, you are not to see anywhere, what you don't see in fact; you are not to have anywhere, what you don't have in fact. What is called Taste, is only another name for Fact." Thomas Gradgrind nodded his approbation.

"This is a new principle, a discovery, a great discovery," said the gentleman. "Now, I'll try you again. Suppose you were going to carpet a room. Would you use a carpet having a representation of flowers upon it?"

There being a general conviction by this time that "No, sir!" was always the right answer to this gentleman, the chorus of No was very strong. Only a few feeble stragglers said Yes: among them Sissy Jupe.

"Girl number twenty," said the gentleman, smiling in the calm strength of knowledge.

Sissy blushed, and stood up.

"So you would carpet your room—or your husband's room, if you were a grown woman, and had a husband—with representations of flowers, would you?" said the gentleman. "Why would you?"

"If you please, sir, I am very fond of flowers," returned the girl.

"And is that why you would put tables and chairs upon them, and have people walking over them with heavy boots?"

"It wouldn't hurt them, sir. They wouldn't crush and wither, if you please, sir. They would be the pictures of what was very pretty and pleasant, and I would fancy—"

"Ay, ay, ay! But you mustn't fancy," cried the gentleman, quite elated by coming so happily to his point. "That's it! You are never to fancy."

"You are not, Cecilia Jupe," Thomas Gradgrind solemnly repeated, "to do anything of that kind."

"Fact, fact, fact!" said the gentleman. And "Fact, fact, fact!" repeated Thomas Gradgrind.

"You are to be in all things regulated and governed," said the gentleman, "by fact. We hope to have, before long, a board of fact, composed of commissioners of fact, who will force the people to be a people of fact, and of nothing but fact. You must discard the word Fancy altogether. You have nothing to do with it. You are not to have, in any object of use or ornament, what would be a contradiction in fact. You don't walk upon flowers in fact; you cannot be allowed to walk upon flowers in carpets. You don't find that foreign birds and butterflies come and perch upon your crockery; you cannot be permitted to paint foreign birds and butterflies upon your crockery. You never meet with quadrupeds going up and down walls; you must not have quadrupeds represented upon walls. You must use," said the gentleman, "for all these purposes, combinations and modifications (in primary colours) of mathematical figures which are susceptible of proof and demonstration. This is the new discovery. This is fact. This is taste."

The girl curtseyed, and sat down. She was very young, and she looked as if she were frightened by the matter-of-fact prospect the world afforded.

50 "Now, if Mr. M'Choakumchild," said the gentleman, "will proceed to give his first lesson here, Mr. Gradgrind, I shall be happy, at your request, to observe his mode of procedure."

Mr. Gradgrind was much obliged. "Mr. M'Choakumchild, we only wait for you."

So, Mr. M'Choakumchild began in his best manner. He and some one hundred and forty other schoolmasters, had been lately turned at the same time, in the same factory, on the same principles, like so many pianoforte legs. He had been put through an immense variety of paces, and had answered volumes of head-breaking questions. Orthography, etymology, syntax, and prosody, biography, astronomy, geography, and general cosmography, the sciences of compound proportion, algebra, land-surveying and levelling, vocal music, and drawing from models, were all at the ends of his ten chilled fingers. He had worked his stony way into Her Majesty's most Honourable Privy Council's Schedule B, and had taken the bloom off the higher branches of mathematics and physical science, French, German, Latin, and Greek. He knew all about all the Water Sheds of all the world (whatever they are), and all the histories of all the peoples, and all the names of all the rivers and mountains, and all the productions, manners, and customs of all the countries, and all their boundaries and bearings on the two and thirty points of the compass. Ah, rather overdone, M'Choakumchild. If he had only learnt a little less, how infinitely better he might have taught much more! *[1859]*

THINKING ABOUT THE TEXT

1. What is ironic about Sissy not being able to define a horse to Gradgrind's satisfaction? Why is Bitzer's definition more appealing to Gradgrind?
2. What do you think Dickens means by "Ah . . . M'Choakumchild. If he had only learnt a little less, how infinitely better he might have taught much more!" (para. 52)?
3. What is your reading of the last question in the selection? How does Dickens make it fairly obvious that he means us to laugh (wince?) at the two educators?

FRIEDRICH ENGELS

From *The Condition of the Working Class in England*

Friedrich Engels (1820–1895) was born in Germany to wealthy parents who expected him to have a career in business. But early on, Engels had a strong interest in revolutionary politics. When he was twenty-two, his father sent him to Manchester, England, to learn the textile business. Instead, he met a young radical, Mary Burns, who gave him a tour of the horrors of environmental destruction, child labor, and numbing poverty in the slums of Manchester. His observations became the influential text from which our selection is taken. Engels went on to collaborate with Karl Marx on The German Ideology *(1846; published 1932) and* The Communist Manifesto *(1848) and to help him write* Das Kapital *(1867). Engels is considered one of the great social scientists and political theorists of the nineteenth century.*

I may mention just here that the mills almost all adjoin the rivers or the different canals that ramify throughout the city, before I proceed at once to describe the labouring quarters. First of all, there is the old town of Manchester, which lies between the northern boundary of the commercial district and the Irk. Here the streets, even the better ones, are narrow and winding, as Todd Street, Long Millgate, Withy Grove, and Shude Hill, the houses dirty, old, and tumbledown, and the construction of the side streets utterly horrible. Going from the Old Church to Long Millgate, the stroller has at once a row of old-fashioned houses at the right, of which not one has kept its original level; these are remnants of the old pre-manufacturing Manchester, whose former inhabitants have removed with their descendants into better-built districts, and have left the houses, which were not good enough for them, to a population strongly mixed with Irish blood. Here one is in an almost undisguised working-men's quarter, for even the shops and beerhouses hardly take the trouble to exhibit a trifling degree of cleanliness. But all this is nothing in comparison with the courts and lanes which lie behind, to which access can be gained only through covered passages, in which no two human beings can pass at the same time. Of the irregular cramming together of dwellings in ways which defy all rational plan, of the tangle in which they are crowded literally one upon the other, it is impossible to convey an idea. And it is not the buildings surviving from the old times of Manchester which are to blame for this; the confusion has only recently reached its height when every scrap of space left by the old way of building has been filled up and patched over until not a foot of land is left to be further occupied.

The south bank of the Irk is here very steep and between fifteen and thirty feet high. On this declivitous hillside there are planted three rows of houses, of which the lowest rise directly out of the river, while the front walls of the highest stand on the crest of the hill in Long Millgate. Among them are mills on the river, in short, the method of construction is as crowded and disorderly here as in the lower part of Long Millgate. Right and left a multitude of covered passages lead from the main street into numerous courts, and he who turns in thither gets into a filth and disgusting grime, the equal of which is not to be found—especially in the courts which lead down to the Irk, and which contain unqualifiedly the most horrible dwellings which I have yet beheld. In one of these courts there stands directly at the entrance, at the end of the covered passage, a privy without a door, so dirty that the inhabitants can pass into and out of the court only by passing through foul pools of stagnant urine and excrement. This is the first court on the Irk above Ducie Bridge—in case any one should care to look into it. Below it on the river there are several tanneries which fill the whole neighbourhood with the stench of animal putrefaction. Below Ducie Bridge the only entrance to most of the houses is by means of narrow, dirty stairs and over heaps of refuse and filth. The first court below Ducie Bridge, known as Allen's Court, was in such a state at the time of the cholera that the sanitary police ordered it evacuated, swept, and disinfected with chloride of lime. Dr. Kay gives a terrible description of the state of this court at that time. Since then, it seems to have been partially torn away and rebuilt; at least looking down from Ducie Bridge, the passer-by sees several ruined walls and heaps of débris with some newer houses. The view from this bridge, mercifully concealed from mortals of small stature by a parapet as high as a man, is characteristic for the whole district. At the bottom flows, or rather stagnates, the Irk, a narrow, coal-black, foul-smelling stream, full of débris and refuse, which it deposits on the shallower right bank. In dry weather, a long string of the most disgusting, blackish-green, slime pools are left standing on this bank, from the depths of which bubbles of miasmatic gas constantly arise and give forth a stench unendurable even on the bridge forty or fifty feet above the surface of the stream. But besides this, the stream itself is checked every few paces by high weirs, behind which slime and refuse accumulate and rot in thick masses. Above the bridge are tanneries, bonemills, and gasworks, from which all drains and refuse find their way into the Irk, which receives further the contents of all the neighbouring sewers and privies. It may be easily imagined, therefore, what sort of residue the stream deposits. Below the bridge you look upon the piles of débris, the refuse, filth, and offal from the courts on the steep left bank; here each house is packed close behind its neighbour and a piece of each is visible, all black, smoky, crumbling, ancient, with broken panes and window frames. The background is furnished by old barrack-like factory buildings. On the lower right bank stands a long row of houses and mills; the second house being a ruin without a roof, piled with débris; the third stands so low that the lowest floor is uninhabitable, and therefore without windows or doors. Here the background embraces the pauper burial-ground, the station of the Liverpool and Leeds railway, and, in the rear of this, the Workhouse, the "Poor-Law Bastille" of Manchester, which, like a citadel, looks threateningly down from behind its high walls and parapets on the hilltop, upon the working-people's quarter below.

Above Ducie Bridge, the left bank grows more flat and the right bank steeper, but the condition of the dwellings on both banks grows worse rather than better. He who turns to the left here from the main street, Long Millgate, is lost; he wanders from one court to another, turns countless corners, passes nothing but narrow, filthy nooks and alleys, until after a few minutes he has lost all clue, and knows not whither to turn. Everywhere half or wholly ruined buildings, some of them actually uninhabited, which means a great deal here; rarely a wooden or stone floor to be seen in the houses, almost uniformly broken, ill-fitting windows and doors, and a state of filth! Everywhere heaps of débris, refuse, and offal; standing pools for gutters, and a stench which alone would make it impossible for a human being in any degree civilised to live in such a district. The newly-built extension of the Leeds railway, which crosses the Irk here, has swept away some of these courts and lanes, laying others completely open to view. Immediately under the railway bridge there stands a court, the filth and horrors of which surpass all the others by far, just because it was hitherto so shut off, so secluded that the way to it could not be found without a good deal of trouble. I should never have discovered it myself, without the breaks made by the railway, though I thought I knew this whole region thoroughly. Passing along a rough bank, among stakes and washing-lines, one penetrates into this chaos of small one-storied, one-roomed huts, in most of which there is no artificial floor; kitchen, living and sleeping-room all in one. In such a hole, scarcely five feet long by six broad, I found two beds—and such bedsteads and beds!—which, with a staircase and chimney-place, exactly filled the room. In several others I found absolutely nothing, while the door stood open, and the inhabitants leaned against it. Everywhere before the doors refuse and offal; that any sort of pavement lay underneath could not be seen but only felt, here and there, with the feet. This whole collection of cattle-sheds for human beings was surrounded on two sides by houses and a factory, and on the third by the river, and besides the narrow stair up the bank, a narrow doorway alone led out into another almost equally ill-built, ill-kept labyrinth of dwellings.

Enough! The whole side of the Irk is built in this way, a planless, knotted chaos of houses, more or less on the verge of uninhabitableness, whose unclean interiors fully correspond with their filthy external surroundings. And how could the people be clean with no proper opportunity for satisfying the most natural and ordinary wants? Privies are so rare here that they are either filled up every day, or are too remote for most of the inhabitants to use. How can people wash when they have only the dirty Irk water at hand, while pumps and water pipes can be found in decent parts of the city alone? In truth, it cannot be charged to the account of these helots of modern society if their dwellings are not more cleanly than the pig-sties which are here and there to be seen among them. The landlords are not ashamed to let dwellings like the six or seven cellars on the quay directly below Scotland Bridge, the floors of which stand at least two feet below the low-water level of the Irk that flows not six feet away from them; or like the upper floor of the corner-house on the opposite shore directly above the bridge, where the ground floor, utterly uninhabitable, stands deprived of all fittings for doors and windows, a case by no means rare in this region, when this open ground floor is used as a privy by the whole neighbourhood for want of other facilities! *[1844]*

THINKING ABOUT THE TEXT

1. What specific details of Engels's description of the slums would have upset Matthew Arnold?
2. What indication of the class conflicts, which Engels would highlight in later books, is most present here?
3. Where is Engels's rage at these deplorable conditions most clear?

JAMES ELI ADAMS

Narrating Nature: Darwin

James Eli Adams (b. 1956) is a professor of English at Columbia University. He received degrees from the Massachusetts Institute of Technology and Oxford University and his Ph.D. from Cornell University in 1987. He writes on a range of issues in Victorian studies. He is the general editor of the Encyclopedia of the Victorian Era, *among many other books and articles. The following excerpt is from* A History of Victorian Literature *(2009), named by Choice as an Outstanding Academic Book.*

Even as Mill was inveighing against intellectual cowardice and the decline of individual genius, a country squire was putting the final touches on arguably the most daring and unsettling book of the century. Charles Darwin's *On the Origin of Species By Means of Natural Selection, or Preservation of Favoured Races in the Struggle for Life* (1859) has had an impact so far-ranging and many-faceted that it confounds brief summary. Darwin's theory did not constitute a radical break with prevailing science; evolution had been "in the air" for decades, so much so that Tennyson's In Memoriam (much influenced by Chamber's Vestiges of Creation) seemed to be arguing with Darwin a decade before the Origin appeared. Indeed, Darwin was spurred to write up his long-pondered theory (the main ideas were in place as early as 1839) only after a fellow naturalist, A. R. Wallace, presented a paper anticipating some of its central claims. Darwin's theory also was far from the first to undermine the idea of divine creation most influentially set forth in Genesis. The geologist Charles Lyell, on whom Darwin drew heavily, during the 1830s had argued that natural forces acted uniformly over time, constantly reshaping the face of the planet, and left an ongoing history of its power in "the evidence of the rocks"!—a record which included those fossils of extinct species that so haunted Tennyson. As John Tyndall in his 1874 Belfast address would put it, "the strength of the doctrine of Evolution consists, not in an experimental demonstration . . . but in its general harmony with scientific thought" (Tyndall 1905: ii.206). Indeed, Darwin lacked any concept of genetics, and thus any plausible account of why variations occurred (as distinct from how they might establish new species). Thus at the heart of this theory, as critics pointed out, there was something of a black box. But Darwin nonetheless provided the most intricate, persuasive, and lucid account to date not only of extinction but also of the emergence of new species over time. The Newtonian world did not change; Darwinian nature was inherently, emphatically historical.

Darwin, then, tells a compelling story, a narrative at once expansive and intricately detailed, which reached all of educated Britain, and was appropriated to many, often conflicting ends. The idea of "struggle" between different species and their environment seemed to some commentators readily transferable to the analysis of society. This was a superficially plausible gesture (and one encouraged by Darwin's own subtitle). Darwin's theory resembles an extension to the animal and vegetable world of laissez-faire economics, or the intellectual marketplace of Millian liberalism. Thus Herbert Spencer, most influentially, coined the phrase "survival of the fittest" in order to describe social competition—with the clear implication that class hierarchies were underwritten by nature itself. In *The Principles of Sociology* (1876), Spencer (1820–1903) argued that societies are themselves organisms that evolve from "primitive" to more complex forms. This view would have an enormous impact in emergent sciences of anthropology and sociology, which typically formulated schemes of racial and cultural development grounded on a similar logic. But Spencer, like many commentators since, smuggled into his evolutionary scheme a sense of direction that Darwinian evolution does not provide. Spencer's "social Darwinism" (which persists in some forms of "evolutionary psychology") is closer to earlier Lamarckian schemes, whereby (for example) giraffes develop long necks in order to reach more food. This suggestion that evolutionary changes arise to meet a pre-existent need obscures one of the most disconcerting aspects of Darwin's theory: evolution offers no overarching direction, no governing telos. The present moment is not the culmination of the past, but one moment in an endless process of change. An animal happened to appear with a longer neck than its fellows, which in a particular milieu made it better adapted to survival; the same variation in another environment might prove fatal. The new species is "better" only in a strenuously relativist sense: the word that Darwin uses is not "progress" but "adaptation." As T. H. Huxley would insist in a famous 1893 essay, evolution provides no ethics.

Clearly this randomness was as much a blow to traditional faith as was the more obvious conflict with biblical schemes of creation. Yet Darwin's theory also provided a narrative model, as recent commentators have pointed out, that had much in common with those engaging a more familiar storyteller, the novelist. Not only does Darwinian theory incorporate history, it takes up familiar mythic themes of transformation and metamorphosis; it foregrounds the idea of kinship; it puts great stress (unlike, say, classical mechanics) on the particularity of the world, its sheer abundance and variety, as well as its subtle gradations and modulations (Beer 2000). Perhaps most suggestively, Darwinism discovers unifying structure without teleology. Victorian novelists likewise began with the assumption that the world they described was intelligible and coherent. But the efforts to embody that coherence in novelistic form—most obviously through coincidence and other residues of the so-called "providential plot"—were increasingly liable to seem either unrealistic, too obvious a simplification of the flux of experience, or to seem a deadening abridgement of human agency, in which the power of choice was thoroughly circumscribed by external forces. Thus Darwin leads back to another version of Mill's worry, which is also Estella's: we are not free, you and I. It would be some while before this impact was fully grasped by poets and novelists, but in the latter decades of the century, the impact would be immense. *[2009]*

THINKING ABOUT THE TEXT

1. What are some ways in which Darwin's famous text was interpreted then and now? How do you think Matthew Arnold read Darwin?
2. How do you think religious Victorians responded to what Adams calls "one of the most disconcerting aspects of Darwin's theory: evolution offers no overarching direction, no governing telos" (para. 2)?

3. How might Adams's notion of Darwinian randomness have influenced "Dover Beach"? How might the idea he mentions in the penultimate sentence, "we are not free, you and I" have affected Arnold's outlook?

≡ WRITING ABOUT ISSUES

1. Write an argument based on Thomas H. Huxley's famous observation in an 1893 essay: "Evolution provides no ethics."
2. Write an analysis of "Dover Beach" that traces the narrator's thinking through the different sections of the poem. Be explicit about his concerns and his possible remedy.
3. Argue that love should or should not be used as a haven against the world. Refer to "Dover Beach" and other texts or films to support your claims.

Romantic Dreams: Stories

JAMES JOYCE, "Araby"

JOHN UPDIKE, "A & P"

LESLIE MARMON SILKO, "Yellow Woman"

Although centuries old, the cliché that the human heart is a mystery still seems valid. We still wonder if falling in love is natural: Is love our inborn impulse to seek romance, or is it simply a physical attraction spurred on by our evolutionary need to procreate? Perhaps Western culture has socialized us to believe in the power of romantic love and the often irrational behavior that follows. Might it serve some deep psychological need to find a substitute for a beloved parent? Is it a giving emotion? A selfish one? Is it a psychological malady or the one thing worth giving up everything for? Do we need to believe in it whether or not it exists? Since we are often driven to irrational behavior, delusions, and heartbreak, might we be better off without romantic love? Or might life without it be intolerably flat?

In the following cluster, three fiction writers explore the ways romantic love can sometimes cloud judgment, encouraging us to act against our best interests.

Joyce shows us a boy in the throes of romantic idealism; Updike gives us a memorable picture of how an indifferent world responds to romantic gestures; and Silko shows us a woman torn between myth and reality.

BEFORE YOU READ

Can people be truly happy without being in love? Is there one person in the world who is your true love? Or are there only certain types of people you could love? If your love didn't make you "float on a cloud," would you be disappointed? Is true love unconditional? Have you ever been fooled by romantic dreams?

JAMES JOYCE

Araby

James Joyce (1882–1941) is regarded as one of the most innovative and influential writers of the modernist movement of the early twentieth century. His use of interior monologue, wordplay, complex allusions, and other techniques variously delighted, offended, or puzzled readers. Joyce's work demanded attention and was often subject to censorship during his lifetime. A Portrait of the Artist as a Young Man *(1916), set in Joyce's native Dublin, is largely autobiographical. Like his hero at the end of the novel, Joyce left Ireland at the age of twenty to spend the remainder of his life in Paris and other European cities. His long, complex novel* Ulysses *(1922), also set in Dublin, takes the reader through one day in the life of its protagonist and his city. In "Araby," published in* Dubliners *(1914), as in other stories in the collection, Joyce pictures the limited life of his character and leads him toward a sudden insight, or epiphany.*

North Richmond Street, being blind, was a quiet street except at the hour when the Christian Brothers' School set the boys free. An uninhabited house of two storeys stood at the blind end, detached from its neighbors in a square ground. The other houses of the street, conscious of decent lives within them, gazed at one another with brown imperturbable faces.

The former tenant of our house, a priest, had died in the back drawing-room. Air, musty from having been long enclosed, hung in all the rooms, and the waste room behind the kitchen was littered with old useless papers. Among these I found a few paper-covered books, the pages of which were curled and damp: *The Abbot*, by Walter Scott, *The Devout Communicant*, and *The Memoirs of Vidocq*. I liked the last best because its leaves were yellow. The wild garden behind the house contained a central apple-tree and a few straggling bushes under one of which I found the late tenant's rusty bicycle-pump. He had been a very charitable priest; in his will he had left all his money to institutions and the furniture of his house to his sister.

When the short days of winter came dusk fell before we had well eaten our dinners. When we met in the street the houses had grown sombre. The space of sky above us was the color of ever-changing violet and towards it the lamps of the street lifted their feeble lanterns. The cold air stung us and we played till our bodies glowed. Our shouts echoed in the silent street. The career of our play brought us through the dark muddy lanes behind the houses where we ran the gauntlet of the rough tribes from the cottages, to the back doors of the dark dripping gardens where odors arose from the ashpits, to the dark odorous stables where a coachman smoothed and combed the horse or shook music from the buckled harness. When we returned to the street light from the kitchen windows had filled the areas. If my uncle was seen turning the corner we hid in the shadow until we had seen him safely housed. Or if Mangan's sister came out on the doorstep to call her brother in to his tea we watched her from our shadow peer up and down the street. We waited to see whether she would remain or go in and, if she remained, we left our shadow and walked up to Mangan's steps resignedly. She was waiting for us, her figure defined by the light from the half-opened door. Her brother always teased her before he obeyed and I stood by the railings looking at her. Her dress swung as she moved her body and the soft rope of her hair tossed from side to side.

Every morning I lay on the floor in the front parlor watching her door. The blind was pulled down to within an inch of the sash so that I could not be seen. When she came out on the doorstep my heart leaped. I ran to the hall, seized my books, and followed her. I kept her brown figure always in my eye and, when we came near the point at which our ways diverged, I quickened my pace and passed her. This happened morning after morning. I had never spoken to her, except for a few casual words, and yet her name was like a summons to all my foolish blood.

Her image accompanied me even in places the most hostile to romance. On 5
Saturday evenings when my aunt went marketing I had to go to carry some of the parcels. We walked through the flaring streets, jostled by drunken men and bargaining women, amid the curses of laborers, the shrill litanies of shop-boys who stood on guard by the barrel of pigs' cheeks, the nasal chanting of street-singers,

who sang a *come-all-you* about O'Donovan Rossa,° or a ballad about the troubles in our native land. These noises converged in a single sensation of life for me: I imagined that I bore my chalice safely through a throng of foes. Her name sprang to my lips at moments in strange prayers and praises which I myself did not understand. My eyes were often full of tears (I could not tell why) and at times a flood from my heart seemed to pour itself out into my bosom. I thought little of the future. I did not know whether I would ever speak to her or not or, if I spoke to her, how I could tell her of my confused adoration. But my body was like a harp and her words and gestures were like fingers running upon the wires.

One evening I went into the back drawing-room in which the priest had died. It was a dark rainy evening and there was no sound in the house. Through one of the broken panes I heard the rain impinge upon the earth, the fine incessant needles of water playing in the sodden beds. Some distant lamp or lighted window gleamed below me. I was thankful that I could see so little. All my senses seemed to desire to veil themselves and, feeling that I was about to slip from them, I pressed the palms of my hands together until they trembled, murmuring: "*O love! O love!*" many times.

At last she spoke to me. When she addressed the first words to me I was so confused that I did not know what to answer. She asked me was I going to *Araby*. I forgot whether I answered yes or no. It would be a splendid bazaar, she said she would love to go.

"And why can't you?" I asked.

While she spoke she turned a silver bracelet round and round her wrist. She could not go, she said, because there would be a retreat that week in her convent. Her brother and two other boys were fighting for their caps and I was alone at the railings. She held one of the spikes, bowing her head towards me. The light from the lamp opposite our door caught the white curve of her neck, lit up her hair that rested there and, falling, lit up the hand upon the railing. It fell over one side of her dress and caught the white border of a petticoat, just visible as she stood at ease.

"It's well for you," she said. 10

"If I go," I said, "I will bring you something."

What innumerable follies laid waste my waking and sleeping thoughts after that evening! I wished to annihilate the tedious intervening days. I chafed against the work of school. At night in my bedroom and by day in the classroom her image came between me and the page I strove to read. The syllables of the word *Araby* were called to me through the silence in which my soul luxuriated and cast an Eastern enchantment over me. I asked for leave to go to the bazaar on Saturday night. My aunt was surprised and hoped it was not some Freemason° affair. I answered few questions in class. I watched my master's face pass from amiability to sternness; he hoped I was not beginning to idle. I could not call my wandering thoughts together. I had hardly any patience with the serious work of life which, now that it stood between me and my desire, seemed to me child's play, ugly monotonous child's play.

O'Donovan Rossa: Jeremiah O'Donovan (1831–1915) was nicknamed "Dynamite Rossa" for advocating violent means to achieve Irish independence.
Freemason: A Protestant fraternal society that was in the past viewed by Catholics as hostile.

On Saturday morning I reminded my uncle that I wished to go to the bazaar in the evening. He was fussing at the hallstand, looking for the hat-brush, and answered me curtly:

"Yes, boy, I know."

As he was in the hall I could not go into the front parlor and lie at the window. I left the house in bad humor and walked slowly towards the school. The air was pitilessly raw and already my heart misgave me.

When I came home to dinner my uncle had not yet been home. Still it was early. I sat staring at the clock for some time and, when its ticking began to irritate me, I left the room. I mounted the staircase and gained the upper part of the house. The high cold empty gloomy rooms liberated me and I went from room to room singing. From the front window I saw my companions playing below in the street. Their cries reached me weakened and indistinct and, leaning my forehead against the cool glass, I looked over at the dark house where she lived. I may have stood there for an hour, seeing nothing but the brown-clad figure cast by my imagination, touched discreetly by the lamplight at the curved neck, at the hand upon the railings, and at the border below the dress.

When I came downstairs again I found Mrs. Mercer sitting at the fire. She was an old garrulous woman, a pawnbroker's widow, who collected used stamps for some pious purpose. I had to endure the gossip of the tea-table. The meal was prolonged beyond an hour and still my uncle did not come. Mrs. Mercer stood up to go: she was sorry she couldn't wait any longer, but it was after eight o'clock and she did not like to be out late, as the night air was bad for her. When she had gone I began to walk up and down the room, clenching my fists. My aunt said:

"I'm afraid you may put off your bazaar for this night of Our Lord."

At nine o'clock I heard my uncle's latchkey in the halldoor. I heard him talking to himself and heard the hallstand rocking when it had received the weight of his overcoat. I could interpret these signs. When he was midway through his dinner I asked him to give me the money to go to the bazaar. He had forgotten.

"The people are in bed and after their first sleep now," he said.

I did not smile. My aunt said to him energetically:

"Can't you give him the money and let him go? You've kept him late enough as it is."

My uncle said he was very sorry he had forgotten. He said he believed in the old saying: "All work and no play makes Jack a dull boy." He asked me where I was going and, when I had told him a second time he asked me did I know *The Arab's Farewell to His Steed.* When I left the kitchen he was about to recite the opening lines of the piece to my aunt.

I held a florin° tightly in my hand as I strode down Buckingham Street towards the station. The sight of the streets thronged with buyers and glaring with gas recalled to me the purpose of my journey. I took my seat in a third-class carriage of a deserted train. After an intolerable delay the train moved out of the station slowly. It crept onward among ruinous houses and over the twinkling

florin: A silver coin worth two shillings.

river. At Westland Row Station a crowd of people pressed to the carriage doors; but the porters moved them back, saying that it was a special train for the bazaar. I remained alone in the bare carriage. In a few minutes the train drew up beside an improvised wooden platform. I passed out on to the road and saw by the lighted dial of a clock that it was ten minutes to ten. In front of me was a large building which displayed the magical name.

I could not find any sixpenny entrance and, fearing that the bazaar would be closed, I passed in quickly through a turnstile, handing a shilling to a weary-looking man. I found myself in a big hall girdled at half its height by a gallery. Nearly all the stalls were closed and the greater part of the hall was in darkness. I recognized a silence like that which pervades a church after a service. I walked into the center of the bazaar timidly. A few people were gathered about the stalls which were still open. Before a curtain, over which the words *Café Chantant* were written in colored lamps, two men were counting money on a salver. I listened to the fall of the coins.

Remembering with difficulty why I had come I went over to one of the stalls and examined porcelain vases and flowered tea-sets. At the door of the stall a young lady was talking and laughing with two young gentlemen. I remarked their English accents and listened vaguely to their conversation.

"O, I never said such a thing!"

"O, but you did!"

"O, but I didn't!"

"Didn't she say that?"

"Yes. I heard her."

"O, there's a . . . fib!"

Observing me the young lady came over and asked me did I wish to buy anything. The tone of her voice was not encouraging; she seemed to have spoken to me out of a sense of duty. I looked humbly at the great jars that stood like eastern guards at either side of the dark entrance to the stall and murmured:

"No, thank you."

The young lady changed the position of one of the vases and went back to the two young men. They began to talk of the same subject. Once or twice the young lady glanced at me over her shoulder.

I lingered before her stall, though I knew my stay was useless, to make my interest in her wares seem the more real. Then I turned away slowly and walked down the middle of the bazaar. I allowed the two pennies to fall against the sixpence in my pocket. I heard a voice call from one end of the gallery that the light was out. The upper part of the hall was now completely dark.

Gazing up into the darkness I saw myself as a creature driven and derided by vanity; and my eyes burned with anguish and anger. *[1914]*

THINKING ABOUT THE TEXT

1. Why do the boy's eyes burn with anguish and anger? Has he learned something about romantic love? Was he in love with Mangan's sister? Give evidence.

2. If this story is partly autobiographical, what is Joyce's attitude toward his younger self? Are you sympathetic or critical of your own initiations into the complexities of relationships?
3. Reread the first and last paragraphs. In what ways might they be connected?
4. Find examples of religious imagery. What do you think is its purpose?
5. Do you think the boy's quest has symbolic meaning? Do you think cultures can also search for something?

JOHN UPDIKE
A & P

John Updike (1932–2009) was born in Shillington, Pennsylvania, an only child of a father who taught high-school algebra and a mother who wrote short stories and novels. After graduating from Harvard, Updike studied art in England and later joined the staff of The New Yorker. *In 1959, he published his first novel,* The Poorhouse Fair, *and moved to Massachusetts. His many novels are notable for their lyrical and accurate depiction of the details and concerns of modern America.* Rabbit Run *(1960) and the sequels* Rabbit Redux *(1971),* Rabbit Is Rich *(1981), and* Rabbit at Rest *(1990) are considered important and insightful records of American life. His other works include the novels* Villages *(2004) and* Terrorist *(2006);* Due Considerations: Essays and Criticism *(2007);* The Maples Stories *(2009); and* Hub Fans Bid Kid Adieu: John Updike on Ted Williams *(2010). "A & P" comes from* Pigeon Feathers and Other Stories *(1962).*

In walks these three girls in nothing but bathing suits. I'm in the third checkout slot, with my back to the door, so I don't see them until they're over by the bread. The one that caught my eye first was the one in the plaid green two-piece. She was a chunky kid, with a good tan and a sweet broad soft-looking can with those two crescents of white just under it, where the sun never seems to hit, at the top of the backs of her legs. I stood there with my hand on a box of HiHo crackers trying to remember if I rang it up or not. I ring it up again and the customer starts giving me hell. She's one of these cash-register-watchers, a witch about fifty with rouge on her cheekbones and no eyebrows, and I know it made her day to trip me up. She'd been watching cash registers for fifty years and probably never seen a mistake before.

By the time I got her feathers smoothed and her goodies into a bag—she gives me a little snort in passing, if she'd been born at the right time they would have burned her over in Salem—by the time I get her on her way the girls had circled around the bread and were coming back, without a pushcart, back my way along the counters, in the aisle between the checkouts and the Special bins. They didn't even have shoes on. There was this chunky one, with the two-piece—it was bright green and the seams on the bra were still sharp and her belly was still pretty pale so I guessed she just got it (the suit)—there was this one, with one of those chubby berry-faces, the lips all bunched together under her nose, this one, and a tall one, with black hair that hadn't quite frizzed right, and one of these sunburns right across under the eyes, and a chin that was too long—you know, the kind of girl other girls think is very "striking" and "attractive" but never quite makes it, as they very well know, which is why they like her so much—and then the third one, that wasn't quite so tall. She was the queen. She kind of led them, the other two peeking around and making their shoulders round. She didn't look around, not this queen, she just walked straight on slowly, on these long white prima-donna legs. She came down a little hard on her heels, as if she didn't walk in her bare feet that much, putting down her heels and then letting the weight move along to her toes as if she was testing the floor with every step, putting a little deliberate extra action into it. You never know for sure how girls' minds work (do you really think it's a mind in there or just a little buzz like a bee in a glass jar?) but you got the idea she had talked the other two into coming in here with her, and now she was showing them how to do it, walk slow and hold yourself straight.

She had on a kind of dirty-pink—beige maybe, I don't know—bathing suit with a little nubble all over it, and what got me, the straps were down. They were off her shoulders looped loose around the cool tops of her arms, and I guess as a result the suit had slipped a little on her, so all around the top of the cloth there was this shining rim. If it hadn't been there you wouldn't have known there could have been anything whiter than those shoulders. With the straps pushed off, there was nothing between the top of the suit and the top of her head except just *her*, this clean bare plane of the top of her chest down from the shoulder bones like a dented sheet of metal tilted in the light. I mean, it was more than pretty.

She had sort of oaky hair that the sun and salt had bleached, done up in a bun that was unravelling, and a kind of prim face. Walking into the A & P with your straps down, I suppose it's the only kind of face you *can* have. She held her head so high her neck, coming up out of those white shoulders, looked kind of stretched, but I didn't mind. The longer her neck was, the more of her there was.

She must have felt in the corner of her eye me and over my shoulder Stokesie 5
in the second slot watching, but she didn't tip. Not this queen. She kept her eyes moving across the racks, and stopped, and turned so slow it made my stomach rub the inside of my apron, and buzzed to the other two, who kind of huddled against her for relief, and then they all three of them went up the cat-and-dog-food-breakfast-cereal-macaroni-rice-raisins-seasonings-spreads-spaghetti-soft-drinks-crackers-and-cookies aisle. From the third slot I look straight up this aisle to the meat counter, and I watched them all the way. The fat one with the tan sort of fumbled with the cookies, but on second thought she put the package back. The sheep pushing their carts down the aisle—the girls were walking against the usual traffic (not that we have one-way signs or anything)—were pretty hilarious. You could see them, when Queenie's white shoulders dawned on them, kind of jerk, or hop, or hiccup, but their eyes snapped back to their own baskets and on they pushed. I bet you could set off dynamite in an A & P and the people would by and large keep reaching and checking oatmeal off their lists and muttering "Let me see, there was a third thing, began with A, asparagus, no, ah, yes,

applesauce!" or whatever it is they do mutter. But there was no doubt, this jiggled them. A few houseslaves in pin curlers even looked around after pushing their carts past to make sure what they had seen was correct.

You know, it's one thing to have a girl in a bathing suit down on the beach, where what with the glare nobody can look at each other much anyway, and another thing in the cool of the A & P, under the fluorescent lights, against all those stacked packages, with her feet paddling along naked over our checkboard green-and-cream rubber-tile floor.

"Oh Daddy," Stokesie said beside me. "I feel so faint."

"Darling," I said. "Hold me tight." Stokesie's married, with two babies chalked up on his fuselage already, but as far as I can tell that's the only difference. He's twenty-two, and I was nineteen this April.

"Is it done?" he asks, the responsible married man finding his voice. I forgot to say he thinks he's going to be manager some sunny day, maybe in 1990 when it's called the Great Alexandrov and Petrooshki Tea Company or something.

10 What he meant was, our town is five miles from a beach, with a big summer colony out on the Point, but we're right in the middle of town, and the women generally put on a shirt or shorts or something before they get out of the car into the street. And anyway these are usually women with six children and varicose veins mapping their legs and nobody, including them, could care less. As I say, we're right in the middle of town, and if you stand at our front doors you can see two banks and the Congregational church and the newspaper store and three real-estate offices and about twenty-seven old freeloaders tearing up Central Street because the sewer broke again. It's not as if we're on the Cape; we're north of Boston and there's people in this town haven't seen the ocean for twenty years.

The girls had reached the meat counter and were asking McMahon something. He pointed, they pointed, and they shuffled out of sight behind a pyramid of Diet Delight peaches. All that was left for us to see was old McMahon patting his mouth and looking after them sizing up their joints. Poor kids, I began to feel sorry for them, they couldn't help it.

Now here comes the sad part of the story, at least my family says it's sad, but I don't think it's so sad myself. The store's pretty empty, it being Thursday afternoon, so there was nothing much to do except lean on the register and wait for the girls to show up again. The whole store was like a pinball machine and I didn't know which tunnel they'd come out of. After a while they come around out of the far aisle, around the light bulbs, records at discount of the Caribbean Six or Tony Martin Sings or some such gunk you wonder they waste the wax on, sixpacks of candy bars, and plastic toys done up in cellophane that fall apart when a kid looks at them anyway. Around they come, Queenie still leading the way, and holding a little gray jar in her hand. Slots Three through Seven are unmanned and I could see her wondering between Stokes and me, but Stokesie with his usual luck draws an old party in baggy gray pants who stumbles up with four giant cans of pineapple juice (what do these bums *do* with all that pineapple juice? I've often asked myself) so the girls come to me. Queenie puts down the jar and I take it into my fingers icy cold. Kingfish Fancy Herring Snacks in Pure Sour Cream: 49¢. Now her hands are empty, not a ring or a bracelet, bare as God made them, and I wonder where the money's coming from. Still with that prim look she lifts a folded dollar bill out of the hollow at the center of her nubbled pink top. The jar went heavy in my hand. Really, I thought that was so cute.

Then everybody's luck begins to run out. Lengel comes in from haggling with a truck full of cabbages on the lot and is about to scuttle into that door marked manager behind which he hides all day when the girls touch his eye. Lengel's pretty dreary, teaches Sunday school and the rest, but he doesn't miss that much. He comes over and says, "Girls, this isn't the beach."

Queenie blushes, though maybe it's just a brush of sunburn I was noticing for the first time, now that she was so close. "My mother asked me to pick up a jar of herring snacks." Her voice kind of startled me, the way voices do when you see the people first, coming out so flat and dumb yet kind of tony, too, the way it ticked over "pick up" and "snacks." All of a sudden I slid right down her voice into her living room. Her father and the other men were standing around in ice-cream coats and bow ties and the women were in sandals picking up herring snacks on toothpicks off a big glass plate and they were all holding drinks the color of water with olives and sprigs of mint in them. When my parents have somebody over they get lemonade and if it's a real racy affair Schlitz in tall glasses with "They'll Do It Every Time" cartoons stencilled on.

"That's all right," Lengel said. "But this isn't the beach." His repeating this struck me as funny, as if it had just occurred to him, and he had been thinking all these years the A & P was a great big sand dune and he was the head lifeguard. He didn't like my smiling—as I say he doesn't miss much—but he concentrates on giving the girls that sad Sunday-school-superintendent stare. 15

Queenie's blush is no sunburn now, and the plump one in plaid, that I liked better from the back—a really sweet can—pipes up, "We weren't doing any shopping. We just came in for the one thing."

"That makes no difference," Lengel tells her, and I could see from the way his eyes went that he hadn't noticed she was wearing a two-piece before. "We want you decently dressed when you come in here."

"We *are* decent," Queenie says suddenly, her lower lip pushing, getting sore now that she remembers her place, a place from which the crowd that runs the A & P must look pretty crummy. Fancy Herring Snacks flashed in her very blue eyes.

"Girls, I don't want to argue with you. After this come in here with your shoulders covered. It's our policy." He turns his back. That's policy for you. Policy is what the kingpins want. What the others want is juvenile delinquency.

All this while, the customers had been showing up with their carts but, you know, sheep, seeing a scene, they had all bunched up on Stokesie, who shook open a paper bag as gently as peeling a peach, not wanting to miss a word. I could feel in the silence everybody getting nervous, most of all Lengel, who asks me, "Sammy, have you rung up their purchase?" 20

I thought and said "No" but it wasn't about that I was thinking. I go through the punches, 4, 9, groc, tot—it's more complicated than you think, and after you do it often enough, it begins to make a little song, that you hear words to, in my case "Hello (*bing*) there, you (*gung*) hap-py *pee*-pul (*splat*)!"—the *splat* being the drawer flying out. I uncrease the bill, tenderly as you may imagine, it just having come from between the two smoothest scoops of vanilla I had ever known were there, and pass a half and a penny into her narrow pink palm, and nestle the herrings in a bag and twist its neck and hand it over, all the time thinking.

The girls, and who'd blame them, are in a hurry to get out, so I say "I quit" to Lengel enough for them to hear, hoping they'll stop and watch me, their unsuspected hero. They keep right on going, into the electric eye; the door flies open and they flicker across the lot to their car, Queenie and Plaid and Big Tall Goony-Goony (not that as raw material she was so bad), leaving me with Lengel and a kink in his eyebrow.

"Did you say something, Sammy?"

"I said I quit."

"I thought you did." 25

"You didn't have to embarrass them."

"It was they who were embarrassing us."

I started to say something that came out "Fiddle-de-doo." It's a saying of my grandmother's, and I know she would have been pleased.

"I don't think you know what you're saying," Lengel said.

"I know you don't," I said. "But I do." I pull the bow at the back of my apron and start shrugging it off my shoulders. A couple customers that had been heading for my slot begin to knock against each other, like scared pigs in a chute. 30

Lengel sighs and begins to look very patient and old and gray. He's been a friend of my parents for years. "Sammy, you don't want to do this to your Mom and Dad," he tells me. It's true, I don't. But it seems to me that once you begin a gesture it's fatal not to go through with it. I fold the apron, "Sammy" stitched in red on the pocket, and put it on the counter, and drop the bow tie on top of it. The bow tie is theirs, if you've ever wondered. "You'll feel this for the rest of your life," Lengel says, and I know that's true, too, but remembering how he made that pretty girl blush makes me so scrunchy inside I punch the No Sale tab and the machine whirs "pee-pul" and the drawer splats out. One advantage to this scene taking place in summer, I can follow this up with a clean exit, there's no fumbling around getting your coat and galoshes, I just saunter into the electric eye in my white shirt that my mother ironed the night before, and the door heaves itself open, and outside the sunshine is skating around on the asphalt.

I look around for my girls, but they're gone, of course. There wasn't anybody but some young married screaming with her children about some candy they didn't get by the door of a powder-blue Falcon station wagon. Looking back in the big windows, over the bags of peat moss and aluminum lawn furniture stacked on the pavement, I could see Lengel in my place in the slot, checking the sheep through. His face was dark gray and his back stiff, as if he'd just had an injection of iron, and my stomach kind of fell as I felt how hard the world was going to be to me hereafter. *[1961]*

THINKING ABOUT THE TEXT

1. Why do you think Sammy quits? Make a list of several plausible answers.
2. What would you do if you were in Sammy's position? What would your priorities be in this situation?

3. When Sammy hears Queenie's voice, he imagines an elegant cocktail party that he contrasts to his parents' "real racy affair" (para. 14) with lemonade and beer. What does this scene say about Sammy's attitude toward the girls? Toward his own social status?
4. Some critics have objected to Sammy's comment in the last sentence of paragraph 2 about "girls' minds." Is this a sexist observation? Does the time frame of the story figure in your opinion? Should it?
5. Comment on the last paragraph. What is the significance of the young married woman? Why does Sammy mention "sheep"? Why does Sammy think the world will be hard on him? Do you agree? What does "hard" mean?

MAKING COMPARISONS

1. Which character's views about romance are most compatible with yours when you were, say, thirteen? With yours presently?
2. Compare the last paragraphs of "Araby" and "A & P." What attitudes do they express?
3. Make a case for one narrator being wiser or happier than the other by the end of the stories.

LESLIE MARMON SILKO

Yellow Woman

Leslie Marmon Silko (b. 1948) is a major figure in the American Indian Renaissance. Raised in "Old Laguna" on the Pueblo Reservation near Albuquerque, New Mexico, Silko weaves the mythology of her matrilineal society into stories that move freely through what she calls an "ocean of time." The Yellow Woman character appears frequently in Silko's writing, both as a traditional figure, closely connected with nature and heterosexuality, and as a female character awakening to her cultural and sexual identity. Silko writes both poetry and fiction, often synthesizing the two genres into a single text. Her novels include Storyteller *(1981), in which "Yellow Woman" appears;* Ceremony *(1977); and* Almanac of the Dead *(1991). Her latest book is* The Turquoise Ledge *(2010). She formerly taught at the University of Arizona at Tucson.*

1

My thigh clung to his with dampness, and I watched the sun rising up through the tamaracks and willows. The small brown water birds came to the river and hopped across the mud, leaving brown scratches in the alkali-white crust. They bathed in the river silently. I could hear the water, almost at our feet where the narrow fast channel bubbled and washed green ragged moss and fern leaves. I looked at him beside me, rolled in the red blanket on the white river sand. I cleaned the sand out of the cracks between my toes, squinting because the sun was above the willow trees. I looked at him for the last time, sleeping on the white river sand.

I felt hungry and followed the river south the way we had come the afternoon before, following our footprints that were already blurred by the lizard tracks and bug trails. The horses were still lying down, and the black one whinnied when he saw me but he did not get up—maybe it was because the corral was made out of thick cedar branches and the horses had not yet felt the sun like I had. I tried to look beyond the pale red mesas to the pueblo. I knew it was there, even if I could not see it, on the sand rock hill above the river, the same river that moved past me now and had reflected the moon last night.

The horse felt warm underneath me. He shook his head and pawed the sand. The bay whinnied and leaned against the gate trying to follow, and I remembered him asleep in the red blanket beside the river. I slid off the horse and tied him close to the other horse. I walked north with the river again, and the white sand broke loose in footprints over footprints.

"Wake up."

He moved in the blanket and turned his face to me with his eyes still closed. I knelt down to touch him.

"I'm leaving."

He smiled now, eyes still closed. "You are coming with me, remember?" He sat up now with his bare dark chest and belly in the sun.

"Where?"

"To my place."

"And will I come back?"

He pulled his pants on. I walked away from him, feeling him behind me and smelling the willows.

"Yellow Woman," he said.

I turned to face him. "Who are you?" I asked.

He laughed and knelt on the low, sandy bank, washing his face in the river. "Last night you guessed my name, and you knew why I had come."

I stared past him at the shallow moving water and tried to remember the night, but I could only see the moon in the water and remember his warmth around me.

"But I only said that you were him and that I was Yellow Woman—I'm not really her—I have my own name and I come from the pueblo on the other side of the mesa. Your name is Silva and you are a stranger I met by the river yesterday afternoon."

He laughed softly. "What happened yesterday has nothing to do with what you will do today, Yellow Woman."

"I know—that's what I'm saying—the old stories about the ka'tsina spirit°* and Yellow Woman can't mean us."

My old grandpa liked to tell those stories best. There is one about Badger and Coyote who went hunting and were gone all day, and when the sun was going down they found a house. There was a girl living there alone, and she had light hair and eyes and she told them that they could sleep with her. Coyote wanted

ka'tsina spirit: A mountain spirit of the Laguna Pueblo Indians.

to be with her all night so he sent Badger into a prairie-dog hole, telling him he thought he saw something in it. As soon as Badger crawled in, Coyote blocked up the entrance with rocks and hurried back to Yellow Woman.

20 "Come here," he said gently.

He touched my neck and I moved close to him to feel his breathing and to hear his heart. I was wondering if Yellow Woman had known who she was—if she knew that she would become part of the stories. Maybe she'd had another name that her husband and relatives called her so that only the ka'tsina from the north and the storytellers would know her as Yellow Woman. But I didn't go on; I felt him all around me, pushing me down into the white river sand.

Yellow Woman went away with the spirit from the north and lived with him and his relatives. She was gone for a long time, but then one day she came back and she brought twin boys.

"Do you know the story?"

"What story?" He smiled and pulled me close to him as he said this. I was afraid lying there on the red blanket. All I could know was the way he felt, warm, damp, his body beside me. This is the way it happens in the stories, I was thinking, with no thought beyond the moment she meets the ka'tsina spirit and they go.

25 "I don't have to go. What they tell in stories was real only then, back in time immemorial, like they say."

He stood up and pointed at my clothes tangled in the blanket. "Let's go," he said.

I walked beside him, breathing hard because he walked fast, his hand around my wrist. I had stopped trying to pull away from him, because his hand felt cool and the sun was high, drying the river bed into alkali. I will see someone, eventually I will see someone, and then I will be certain that he is only a man—some man from nearby—and I will be sure that I am not Yellow Woman. Because she is from out of time past and I live now and I've been to school and there are highways and pickup trucks that Yellow Woman never saw.

It was an easy ride north on horseback. I watched the change from the cottonwood trees along the river to the junipers that brushed past us in the foothills, and finally there were only piñons, and when I looked up at the rim of the mountain plateau I could see pine trees growing on the edge. Once I stopped to look down, but the pale sandstone had disappeared and the river was gone and the dark lava hills were all around. He touched my hand, not speaking, but always singing softly a mountain song and looking into my eyes.

I felt hungry and wondered what they were doing at home now—my mother, my grandmother, my husband, and the baby. Cooking breakfast, saying, "Where did she go?—maybe kidnapped," and Al going to the tribal police with the details: "She went walking along the river."

30 The house was made with black lava rock and red mud. It was high above the spreading miles of arroyos and long mesas. I smelled a mountain smell of pitch and buck brush. I stood there beside the black horse, looking down on the small, dim country we had passed, and I shivered.

"Yellow Woman, come inside where it's warm."

2

He lit a fire in the stove. It was an old stove with a round belly and an enamel coffeepot on top. There was only the stove, some faded Navajo blankets, and a bedroll and cardboard box. The floor was made of smooth adobe plaster, and there was one small window facing east. He pointed at the box.

"There's some potatoes and the frying pan." He sat on the floor with his arms around his knees pulling them close to his chest and he watched me fry the potatoes. I didn't mind him watching me because he was always watching me—he had been watching me since I came upon him sitting on the river bank trimming leaves from a willow twig with his knife. We ate from the pan and he wiped the grease from his fingers on his Levis.

"Have you brought women here before?" He smiled and kept chewing, so I said, "Do you always use the same tricks?"

"What tricks?" He looked at me like he didn't understand.

"The story about being a ka'tsina from the mountains. The story about Yellow Woman."

Silva was silent; his face was calm.

"I don't believe it. Those stories couldn't happen now," I said.

He shook his head and said softly, "But someday they will talk about us, and they will say, 'Those two lived long ago when things like that happened.'"

He stood up and went out. I ate the rest of the potatoes and thought about things—about the noise the stove was making and the sound of the mountain wind outside. I remembered yesterday and the day before, and then I went outside.

I walked past the corral to the edge where the narrow trail cut through the black rim rock. I was standing in the sky with nothing around me but the wind that came down from the blue mountain peak behind me. I could see faint mountain images in the distance miles across the vast spread of mesas and valleys and plains. I wondered who was over there to feel the mountain wind on those sheer blue edges—who walks on the pine needles in those blue mountains.

"Can you see the pueblo?" Silva was standing behind me.

I shook my head. "We're too far away."

"From here I can see the world." He stepped out on the edge. "The Navajo reservation begins over there." He pointed to the east. "The Pueblo boundaries are over here." He looked below us to the south, where the narrow trail seemed to come from. "The Texans have their ranches over there, starting with that valley, the Concho Valley. The Mexicans run some cattle over there too."

"Do you ever work for them?"

"I steal from them," Silva answered. The sun was dropping behind us and shadows were filling the land below. I turned away from the edge that dropped forever into the valleys below.

"I'm cold," I said; "I'm going inside." I started wondering about this man who could speak the Pueblo language so well but who lived on a mountain and rustled cattle. I decided that this man Silva must be Navajo, because Pueblo men didn't do things like that.

"You must be a Navajo."

Silva shook his head gently. "Little Yellow Woman," he said, "you never give up, do you? I have told you who I am. The Navajo people know me, too." He knelt down and unrolled the bedroll and spread the extra blankets out on a piece of canvas. The sun was down, and the only light in the house came from outside—the dim orange light from sundown.

I stood there and waited for him to crawl under the blankets.

"What are you waiting for?" he said, and I lay down beside him. He undressed me slowly like the night before beside the river—kissing my face gently and running his hands up and down my belly and legs. He took off my pants and then he laughed.

"Why are you laughing?"

"You are breathing so hard."

I pulled away from him and turned my back to him.

He pulled me around and pinned me down with his arms and chest. "You don't understand, do you, little Yellow Woman? You will do what I want."

And again he was all around me with his skin slippery against mine, and I was afraid because I understood that his strength could hurt me. I lay underneath him and I knew that he could destroy me. But later, while he slept beside me, I touched his face and I had a feeling—the kind of feeling for him that overcame me that morning along the river. I kissed him on the forehead and he reached out for me.

When I woke up in the morning he was gone. It gave me a strange feeling because for a long time I sat there on the blankets and looked around the little house for some object of his—some proof that he had been there or maybe that he was coming back. Only the blankets and the cardboard box remained. The .30–30° that had been leaning in the corner was gone, and so was the knife I had used the night before. He was gone, and I had my chance to go now. But first I had to eat, because I knew it would be a long walk home.

I found some dried apricots in the cardboard box, and I sat down on a rock at the edge of the plateau rim. There was no wind and the sun warmed me. I was surrounded by silence. I drowsed with apricots in my mouth, and I didn't believe that there were highways or railroads or cattle to steal.

When I woke up, I stared down at my feet in the black mountain dirt. Little black ants were swarming over the pine needles around my foot. They must have smelled the apricots. I thought about my family far below me. They would be wondering about me, because this had never happened to me before. The tribal police would file a report. But if old Grandpa weren't dead he would tell them what happened—he would laugh and say, "Stolen by a ka'tsina, a mountain spirit. She'll come home—they usually do." There are enough of them to handle things. My mother and grandmother will raise the baby like they raised me. Al will find someone else, and they will go on like before, except that there will be a story about the day I disappeared while I was walking along the river. Silva had come for me; he said he had. I did not decide to go. I just went. Moonflowers

.30–30: A rifle.

blossom in the sand hills before dawn, just as I followed him. That's what I was thinking as I wandered along the trail through the pine trees.

It was noon when I got back. When I saw the stone house I remembered that I had meant to go home. But that didn't seem important any more, maybe because there were little blue flowers growing in the meadow behind the stone house and the gray squirrels were playing in the pines next to the house. The horses were standing in the corral, and there was a beef carcass hanging on the shady side of a big pine in front of the house. Flies buzzed around the clotted blood that hung from the carcass. Silva was washing his hands in a bucket full of water. He must have heard me coming because he spoke to me without turning to face me.

"I've been waiting for you."

"I went walking in the big pine trees."

I looked into the bucket full of bloody water with brown-and-white animal hairs floating in it. Silva stood there letting his hand drip, examining me intently.

"Are you coming with me?"

"Where?" I asked him.

"To sell the meat in Marquez."

"If you're sure it's O.K."

"I wouldn't ask you if it wasn't," he answered.

He sloshed the water around in the bucket before he dumped it out and set the bucket upside down near the door. I followed him to the corral and watched him saddle the horses. Even beside the horses he looked tall, and I asked him again if he wasn't Navajo. He didn't say anything; he just shook his head and kept cinching up the saddle.

"But Navajos are tall."

"Get on the horse," he said, "and let's go."

The last thing he did before we started down the steep trail was to grab the .30–30 from the corner. He slid the rifle into the scabbard that hung from his saddle.

"Do they ever try to catch you?" I asked.

"They don't know who I am."

"Then why did you bring the rifle?"

"Because we are going to Marquez where the Mexicans live."

3

The trail leveled out on a narrow ridge that was steep on both sides like an animal spine. On one side I could see where the trail went around the rocky gray hills and disappeared into the southeast where the pale sandrock mesas stood in the distance near my home. On the other side was a trail that went west, and as I looked far into the distance I thought I saw the little town. But Silva said no, that I was looking in the wrong place, that I just thought I saw houses. After that I quit looking off into the distance; it was hot and the wildflowers were closing up their deep-yellow petals. Only the waxy cactus flowers bloomed in the bright sun, and I saw every color that a cactus blossom can be; the white ones and the red ones were still buds, but the purple and the yellow were blossoms, open full and the most beautiful of all.

Silva saw him before I did. The white man was riding a big gray horse, coming up the trail toward us. He was traveling fast and the gray horse's feet sent rocks rolling off the trail into the dry tumbleweeds. Silva motioned for me to stop and we watched the white man. He didn't see us right away, but finally his horse whinnied at our horses and he stopped. He looked at us briefly before he loped the gray horse across the three hundred yards that separated us. He stopped his horse in front of Silva, and his young fat face was shadowed by the brim of his hat. He didn't look mad, but his small, pale eyes moved from the blood-soaked gunny sacks hanging from my saddle to Silva's face and then back to my face.

"Where did you get the fresh meat?" the white man asked.

"I've been hunting," Silva said, and when he shifted his weight in the saddle the leather creaked.

"The hell you have, Indian. You've been rustling cattle. We've been looking for the thief for a long time."

The rancher was fat, and sweat began to soak through his white cowboy shirt and the wet cloth stuck to the thick rolls of belly fat. He almost seemed to be panting from the exertion of talking, and he smelled rancid, maybe because Silva scared him.

Silva turned to me and smiled. "Go back up the mountain, Yellow Woman."

The white man got angry when he heard Silva speak in a language he couldn't understand. "Don't try anything, Indian. Just keep riding to Marquez. We'll call the state police from there."

The rancher must have been unarmed because he was very frightened and if he had a gun he would have pulled it out then. I turned my horse around and the rancher yelled, "Stop!" I looked at Silva for an instant and there was something ancient and dark—something I could feel in my stomach—in his eyes, and when I glanced at his hand I saw his finger on the trigger of the .30–30 that was still in the saddle scabbard. I slapped my horse across the flank and the sacks of raw meat swung against my knees as the horse leaped up the trail. It was hard to keep my balance, and once I thought I felt the saddle slipping backward; it was because of this that I could not look back.

I didn't stop until I reached the ridge where the trail forked. The horse was breathing deep gasps and there was a dark film of sweat on its neck. I looked down in the direction I had come from, but I couldn't see the place. I waited. The wind came up and pushed warm air past me. I looked up at the sky, pale blue and full of thin clouds and fading vapor trails left by jets.

I think four shots were fired—I remember hearing four hollow explosions that reminded me of deer hunting. There could have been more shots after that, but I couldn't have heard them because my horse was running again and the loose rocks were making too much noise as they scattered around his feet.

Horses have a hard time running downhill, but I went that way instead of uphill to the mountain because I thought it was safer. I felt better with the horse running southeast past the round gray hills that were covered with cedar trees and black lava rock. When I got to the plain in the distance I could see the dark green patches of tamaracks that grew along the river; and beyond the river I could see the beginning of the pale sandrock mesas. I stopped the horse and looked back to see if anyone was coming; then I got off the horse and turned the horse around, wondering if it would go back to its corral under the pines on the mountain. It looked back at me for a moment and then plucked a mouthful of green tumbleweeds before it trotted back up the trail with its ears pointed forward, carrying its head daintily to one side to avoid stepping on the dragging reins. When the horse disappeared over the last hill, the gunny sacks full of meat were still swinging and bouncing.

4

I walked toward the river on a wood-hauler's road that I knew would eventually lead to the paved road. I was thinking about waiting beside the road for someone to drive by, but by the time I got to the pavement I had decided it wasn't very far to walk if I followed the river back the way Silva and I had come.

The river water tasted good, and I sat in the shade under a cluster of silvery 90
willows. I thought about Silva, and I felt sad at leaving him; still, there was something strange about him, and I tried to figure it out all the way back home.

I came back to the place on the river bank where he had been sitting the first time I saw him. The green willow leaves that he had trimmed from the branch were still lying there, wilted in the sand. I saw the leaves and I wanted to go back to him—to kiss him and to touch him—but the mountains were too far away now. And I told myself, because I believe it, he will come back sometime and be waiting again by the river.

I followed the path up from the river into the village. The sun was getting low, and I could smell supper cooking when I got to the screen door of my house. I could hear their voices inside—my mother was telling my grandmother how to fix the Jell-O and my husband, Al, was playing with the baby. I decided to tell them that some Navajo had kidnapped me, but I was sorry that old Grandpa wasn't alive to hear my story because it was the Yellow Woman stories he liked to tell best. *[1974]*

THINKING ABOUT THE TEXT

1. Why does Yellow Woman run away with Silva? Does it have something to do with the coyote stories? What stories in your own culture have persuaded you to trust in romantic love?
2. How do myths and stories differ? Are they based on reality or on fantasy? What are the social or cultural purposes of stories about love?
3. Do you trust the narrator's judgment? Sincerity? On what textual evidence are you basing this evaluation? What bearing does her cultural heritage have on your analysis of her?
4. What specific details of Silko's story do you remember? Is the narrator a careful observer? Explain. What effect does the narrator's "noticing little things" have on you as a reader?

5. Has Yellow Woman learned her lesson? Do societies change their views of romantic love? How?

MAKING COMPARISONS

1. Compare the growth of the boy in "Araby" or Sammy in "A & P" with that of the wife in "Yellow Woman."
2. Make explicit the insight or epiphany the boy or Sammy comes to at the end. What would be a comparable epiphany for the wife in "Yellow Woman"?
3. Is one ending more realistic than the others? Explain.

WRITING ABOUT ISSUES

1. Choose either the boy in "Araby," Sammy, or Yellow Woman and argue that this character was or was not really in love. Support your argument with references to the text and your own cultural experience.
2. Write an essay that defends or denies the idea that romantic love is irrational. Use two of the stories from this cluster.
3. Would any of the characters in this cluster have been comfortable in the cultural context you were raised in? (Consider movies, books, TV, family narratives, and so forth in analyzing your culture.) Write a brief analysis of how well one or more of these characters would "fit in."
4. Look up information about Native American culture and the coyote stories referred to in "Yellow Woman." Do they help to explain her attitudes? Do the same for the culture of Joyce's Ireland, especially religion and romance. How about America in the middle of the twentieth century? In a brief essay, argue that each story is understood more fully when the cultural context is provided.

Is This Love?: Stories

WILLIAM FAULKNER, "A Rose for Emily"

RAYMOND CARVER, "What We Talk About When We Talk About Love"

Although stories about those who die for love are not unknown, those about killing for love are much rarer. Can "killing for love" still be considered love, or is it something quite different, something dark and perverse? Can the world be so stressful, so unjust and cruel that someone batters a beloved in frustration? What if that person is looking to someone else to relieve the disappointments of the world? Is that love or just physical need? What if someone harbors violent fantasies about a person loved years before? Or what if a wife sexually betrays her loving husband so she can get for him the material possessions he desires? And can love be so worn down by cruelty that it turns to hate? These are not simple questions. Trying to understand our emotional contradictions and paradoxes never is. The following two writers grapple with these issues in creative and sometimes painful ways: Faulkner's story focuses on the interaction of tradition, madness, and love; Carver's looks at the complexity of discussing love. See whether you can decide if the characters in these stories are motivated by love or something more dangerous.

BEFORE YOU READ

Have you ever hurt somebody you love? Did you mean to? Has a loved one ever hurt you? Is it possible for an emotionally disturbed person to love?

WILLIAM FAULKNER

A Rose for Emily

William Faulkner (1897–1962) is recognized as a great American novelist and storyteller and a major figure of world literature, having won the Nobel Prize in 1949. This acclaim failed to impress the people of his hometown, however, where his genteel poverty and peculiar ways earned him the title "Count No Count." Born in New Albany, Mississippi, and raised in Oxford, the home of the University of Mississippi, Faulkner briefly attended college there after World War I but was reduced to working odd jobs while continuing his writing. His fiction is most often set in Yoknapatawpha County, a created world whose history, geography, and complex genealogies parallel those of the American South. His many novels and stories blend the grotesquely comic with the appallingly tragic. The Sound and the Fury *(1929) is often considered his finest work. In later years, Faulkner's "odd jobs" included scriptwriting for Hollywood movies, speaking at universities, and writing magazine articles. "A Rose for Emily," first published in* Forum, *presents a story of love as told by citizens of Yoknapatawpha County.*

1

When Miss Emily Grierson died, our whole town went to her funeral: the men through a sort of respectful affection for a fallen monument, the women mostly out of curiosity to see the inside of her house, which no one save an old manservant—a combined gardener and cook—had seen in at least ten years.

It was a big, squarish frame house that had once been white, decorated with cupolas and spires and scrolled balconies in the heavily lightsome style of the seventies, set on what had once been our most select street. But garages and cotton gins had encroached and obliterated even the august names of that neighborhood; only Miss Emily's house was left, lifting its stubborn and coquettish decay above the cotton wagons and the gasoline pumps—an eyesore among eyesores. And now Miss Emily had gone to join the representatives of those august names where they lay in the cedar-bemused cemetery among the ranked and anonymous graves of Union and Confederate soldiers who fell at the battle of Jefferson.

Alive, Miss Emily had been a tradition, a duty, and a care; a sort of hereditary obligation upon the town, dating from that day in 1894 when Colonel Sartoris, the mayor—he who fathered the edict that no Negro woman should appear on the streets without an apron—remitted her taxes, the dispensation dating from the death of her father on into perpetuity. Not that Miss Emily would have accepted charity. Colonel Sartoris invented an involved tale to the effect that Miss Emily's father had loaned money to the town, which the town, as a matter of business, preferred this way of repaying. Only a man of Colonel Sartoris's generation and thought could have invented it, and only a woman could have believed it.

When the next generation, with its more modern ideas, became mayors and aldermen, this arrangement created some little dissatisfaction. On the first of the year they mailed her a tax notice. February came, and there was no reply. They wrote her a formal letter, asking her to call at the sheriff's office at her convenience. A week later the mayor wrote her himself, offering to call or to send his car for her, and received in reply a note on paper of an archaic shape, in a thin, flowing calligraphy in faded ink, to the effect that she no longer went out at all. The tax notice was also enclosed, without comment.

5 They called a special meeting of the Board of Aldermen. A deputation waited upon her, knocked at the door through which no visitor had passed since she ceased giving china-painting lessons eight or ten years earlier. They were admitted by the old Negro into a dim hall from which a stairway mounted into still more shadow. It smelled of dust and disuse—a close, dank smell. The Negro led them into the parlor. It was furnished in heavy, leather-covered furniture. When the Negro opened the blinds of one window, they could see that the leather was cracked; and when they sat down, a faint dust rose sluggishly about their thighs, spinning with slow motes in the single sun-ray. On a tarnished gilt easel before the fireplace stood a crayon portrait of Miss Emily's father.

They rose when she entered—a small, fat woman in black, with a thin gold chain descending to her waist and vanishing into her belt, leaning on an ebony cane with a tarnished gold head. Her skeleton was small and spare; perhaps that was why what would have been merely plumpness in another was obesity in her. She looked bloated, like a body long submerged in motionless water, and of that pallid hue. Her eyes, lost in the fatty ridges of her face, looked like two small pieces of coal pressed into a lump of dough as they moved from one face to another while the visitors stated their errand.

She did not ask them to sit. She just stood in the door and listened quietly until the spokesman came to a stumbling halt. Then they could hear the invisible watch ticking at the end of the gold chain.

Her voice was dry and cold. "I have no taxes in Jefferson. Colonel Sartoris explained it to me. Perhaps one of you can gain access to the city records and satisfy yourselves."

"But we have. We are the city authorities, Miss Emily. Didn't you get a notice from the sheriff, signed by him?"

"I received a paper, yes," Miss Emily said. "Perhaps he considers himself the sheriff. . . . I have no taxes in Jefferson."

"But there is nothing on the books to show that, you see. We must go by the—"

"See Colonel Sartoris. I have no taxes in Jefferson."

"But, Miss Emily—"

"See Colonel Sartoris." (Colonel Sartoris had been dead almost ten years.) "I have no taxes in Jefferson. Tobe!" The Negro appeared. "Show these gentlemen out."

2

So she vanquished them, horse and foot, just as she had vanquished their fathers thirty years before about the smell. That was two years after her father's death and a short time after her sweetheart—the one we believed would marry her—had deserted her. After her father's death she went out very little; after her sweetheart went away, people hardly saw her at all. A few of the ladies had the temerity to call, but were not received, and the only sign of life about the place was the Negro man—a young man then—going in and out with a market basket.

"Just as if a man—any man—could keep a kitchen properly," the ladies said; so they were not surprised when the smell developed. It was another link between the gross, teeming world and the high and mighty Griersons.

A neighbor, a woman, complained to the mayor, Judge Stevens, eighty years old.

"But what will you have me do about it, madam?" he said.

"Why, send her word to stop it," the woman said. "Isn't there a law?"

"I'm sure that won't be necessary," Judge Stevens said. "It's probably just a snake or a rat that nigger of hers killed in the yard. I'll speak to him about it."

The next day he received two more complaints, one from a man who came in diffident deprecation. "We really must do something about it, Judge. I'd be the last one in the world to bother Miss Emily, but we've got to do something." That night the Board of Aldermen met—three graybeards and one younger man, a member of the rising generation.

"It's simple enough," he said. "Send her word to have her place cleaned up. Give her a certain time to do it in, and if she don't. . . ."

"Dammit, sir," Judge Stevens said, "will you accuse a lady to her face of smelling bad?"

So the next night, after midnight, four men crossed Miss Emily's lawn and slunk about the house like burglars, sniffing along the base of the brickwork and at the cellar openings while one of them performed a regular sowing motion with his hand out of a sack slung from his shoulder. They broke open the cellar door and sprinkled lime there, and in all the outbuildings. As they recrossed the lawn, a window that had been dark was lighted and Miss Emily sat in it, the light behind her, and her upright torso motionless as that of an idol. They crept quietly across the lawn and into the shadow of the locusts that lined the street. After a week or two the smell went away.

25 That was when people had begun to feel really sorry for her. People in our town, remembering how old lady Wyatt, her great-aunt, had gone completely crazy at last, believed that the Griersons held themselves a little too high for what they really were. None of the young men were quite good enough for Miss Emily and such. We had long thought of them as a tableau, Miss Emily a slender figure in white in the background, her father a spraddled silhouette in the foreground, his back to her and clutching a horsewhip, the two of them framed by the back-flung front door. So when she got to be thirty and was still single, we were not pleased exactly, but vindicated; even with insanity in the family she wouldn't have turned down all of her chances if they had really materialized.

When her father died, it got about that the house was all that was left to her; and in a way, people were glad. At last they could pity Miss Emily. Being left alone, and a pauper, she had become humanized. Now she too would know the old thrill and the old despair of a penny more or less.

The day after his death all the ladies prepared to call at the house and offer condolence and aid, as is our custom. Miss Emily met them at the door, dressed as usual and with no trace of grief on her face. She told them that her father was not dead. She did that for three days, with the ministers calling on her, and the doctors, trying to persuade her to let them dispose of the body. Just as they were about to resort to law and force, she broke down, and they buried her father quickly.

We did not say she was crazy then. We believed she had to do that. We remembered all the young men her father had driven away, and we knew that with nothing left, she would have to cling to that which had robbed her, as people will.

3

She was sick for a long time. When we saw her again, her hair was cut short, making her look like a girl, with a vague resemblance to those angels in colored church windows—sort of tragic and serene.

30 The town had just let the contracts for paving the sidewalks, and in the summer after her father's death they began the work. The construction company came with niggers and mules and machinery, and a foreman named Homer

Barron, a Yankee — a big, dark, ready man, with a big voice and eyes lighter than his face. The little boys would follow in groups to hear him cuss the niggers, and the niggers singing in time to the rise and fall of picks. Pretty soon he knew everybody in town. Whenever you heard a lot of laughing anywhere about the square, Homer Barron would be in the center of the group. Presently, we began to see him and Miss Emily on Sunday afternoons driving in the yellow-wheeled buggy and the matched team of bays from the livery stable.

At first we were glad that Miss Emily would have an interest, because the ladies all said, "Of course a Grierson would not think seriously of a Northerner, a day laborer." But there were still others, older people, who said that even grief could not cause a real lady to forget *noblesse oblige* — without calling it *noblesse oblige*. They just said, "Poor Emily. Her kinsfolk should come to her." She had some kin in Alabama; but years ago her father had fallen out with them over the estate of old lady Wyatt, the crazy woman, and there was no communication between the two families. They had not even been represented at the funeral.

And as soon as the old people said, "Poor Emily," the whispering began. "Do you suppose it's really so?" they said to one another. "Of course it is. What else could. . . ." This behind their hands; rustling of craned silk and satin behind jalousies closed upon the sun of Sunday afternoon as the thin, swift clop-clop-clop of the matched team passed: "Poor Emily."

She carried her head high enough — even when we believed that she was fallen. It was as if she demanded more than ever the recognition of her dignity as the last Grierson; as if it had wanted that touch of earthiness to reaffirm her imperviousness. Like when she bought the rat poison, the arsenic. That was over a year after they had begun to say "Poor Emily," and while the two female cousins were visiting her.

"I want some poison," she said to the druggist. She was over thirty then, still a slight woman, though thinner than usual, with cold, haughty black eyes in a face the flesh of which was strained across the temples and about the eyesockets as you imagine a lighthouse-keeper's face ought to look. "I want some poison," she said.

"Yes, Miss Emily. What kind? For rats and such? I'd recom ——"

"I want the best you have. I don't care what kind."

The druggist named several. "They'll kill anything up to an elephant. But what you want is ——"

"Arsenic," Miss Emily said. "Is that a good one?"

"Is . . . arsenic? Yes, ma'am. But what you want ——"

"I want arsenic."

The druggist looked down at her. She looked back at him, erect, her face like a strained flag. "Why, of course," the druggist said. "If that's what you want. But the law requires you to tell what you are going to use it for."

Miss Emily just stared at him, her head tilted back in order to look him eye for eye, until he looked away and went and got the arsenic and wrapped it up. The Negro delivery boy brought her the package; the druggist didn't come back. When she opened the package at home there was written on the box, under the skull and bones: "For rats."

4

So the next day we all said, "She will kill herself"; and we said it would be the best thing. When she had first begun to be seen with Homer Barron, we had said, "She will marry him." Then we said, "She will persuade him yet," because Homer himself had remarked—he liked men, and it was known that he drank with the younger men in the Elks' Club—that he was not a marrying man. Later we said, "Poor Emily" behind the jalousies as they passed on Sunday afternoon in the glittering buggy, Miss Emily with her head high and Homer Barron with his hat cocked and a cigar in his teeth, reins and whip in a yellow glove.

Then some of the ladies began to say that it was a disgrace to the town and a bad example to the young people. The men did not want to interfere, but at last the ladies forced the Baptist minister—Miss Emily's people were Episcopal—to call upon her. He would never divulge what happened during that interview, but he refused to go back again. The next Sunday they again drove about the streets, and the following day the minister's wife wrote to Miss Emily's relations in Alabama.

So she had blood-kin under her roof again and we sat back to watch develop- 45
ments. At first nothing happened. Then we were sure that they were to be married. We learned that Miss Emily had been to the jeweler's and ordered a man's toilet set in silver, with the letters H.B. on each piece. Two days later we learned that she had bought a complete outfit of men's clothing, including a nightshirt, and we said, "They are married." We were really glad. We were glad because the two female cousins were even more Grierson than Miss Emily had ever been.

So we were not surprised when Homer Barron—the streets had been finished some time since—was gone. We were a little disappointed that there was not a public blowing-off, but we believed that he had gone on to prepare for Miss Emily's coming, or to give her a chance to get rid of the cousins. (By that time it was a cabal, and we were all Miss Emily's allies to help circumvent the cousins.) Sure enough, after another week they departed. And, as we had expected all along, within three days Homer Barron was back in town. A neighbor saw the Negro man admit him at the kitchen door at dusk one evening.

And that was the last we saw of Homer Barron. And of Miss Emily for some time. The Negro man went in and out with the market basket, but the front door remained closed. Now and then we would see her at the window for a moment, as the men did that night when they sprinkled the lime, but for almost six months she did not appear on the streets. Then we knew that this was to be expected too; as if that quality of her father which had thwarted her woman's life so many times had been too virulent and too furious to die.

When we next saw Miss Emily, she had grown fat and her hair was turning gray. During the next few years it grew grayer and grayer until it attained an even pepper-and-salt iron-gray, when it ceased turning. Up to the day of her death at seventy-four it was still that vigorous iron-gray, like the hair of an active man.

From that time on her front door remained closed, save during a period of six or seven years, when she was about forty, during which she gave lessons in china-painting. She fitted up a studio in one of the downstairs rooms, where the daughters and granddaughters of Colonel Sartoris's contemporaries were sent to her with the same regularity and in the same spirit that they were sent to church on Sundays with a twenty-five-cent piece for the collection plate. Meanwhile her taxes had been remitted.

Then the newer generation became the backbone and the spirit of the town, and the painting pupils grew up and fell away and did not send their children to her with boxes of color and tedious brushes and pictures cut from the ladies' magazines. The front door closed upon the last one and remained closed for good. When the town got free postal delivery, Miss Emily alone refused to let them fasten the metal numbers above her door and attach a mailbox to it. She would not listen to them.

Daily, monthly, yearly we watched the Negro grow grayer and more stooped, going in and out with the market basket. Each December we sent her a tax notice, which would be returned by the post office a week later, unclaimed. Now and then we would see her in one of the downstairs windows—she had evidently shut up the top floor of the house—like the carven torso of an idol in a niche, looking or not looking at us, we could never tell which. Thus she passed from generation to generation—dear, inescapable, impervious, tranquil, and perverse.

And so she died. Fell ill in the house filled with dust and shadows, with only a doddering Negro man to wait on her. We did not even know she was sick; we had long since given up trying to get any information from the Negro. He talked to no one, probably not even to her, for his voice had grown harsh and rusty, as if from disuse.

She died in one of the downstairs rooms, in a heavy walnut bed with a curtain, her gray head propped on a pillow yellow and moldy with age and lack of sunlight.

5

The Negro met the first of the ladies at the front door and let them in, with their hushed, sibilant voices and their quick, curious glances, and then he disappeared. He walked right through the house and out the back and was not seen again.

The two female cousins came at once. They held the funeral on the second day, with the town coming to look at Miss Emily beneath a mass of bought flowers, with the crayon face of her father musing profoundly above the bier and the ladies sibilant and macabre; and the very old men—some in their brushed Confederate uniforms—on the porch and the lawn, talking of Miss Emily as if she had been a contemporary of theirs, believing that they had danced with her and courted her perhaps, confusing time with its mathematical progression, as the old do, to whom all the past is not a diminishing road but, instead, a huge meadow which no winter ever quite touches, divided from them now by the narrow bottleneck of the most recent decade of years.

Already we knew that there was one room in that region above stairs which no one had seen in forty years, and which would have to be forced. They waited until Miss Emily was decently in the ground before they opened it.

The violence of breaking down the door seemed to fill this room with pervading dust. A thin, acrid pall as of the tomb seemed to lie everywhere upon this room decked and furnished as for a bridal: upon the valance curtains of faded rose color, upon the rose-shaded lights, upon the dressing table, upon the delicate array of crystal and the man's toilet things backed with tarnished silver, silver so tarnished that the monogram was obscured. Among them lay a collar and tie, as if they had just been removed, which, lifted, left upon the surface a pale crescent in the dust. Upon a chair hung the suit, carefully folded; beneath it the two mute shoes and the discarded socks.

The man himself lay in the bed.

For a long while we just stood there, looking down at the profound and fleshless grin. The body had apparently once lain in the attitude of an embrace, but now the long sleep that outlasts love, that conquers even the grimace of love, had cuckolded him. What was left of him, rotted beneath what was left of the nightshirt, had become inextricable from the bed in which he lay; and upon him and upon the pillow beside him lay that even coating of the patient and biding dust.

60 Then we noticed that in the second pillow was the indentation of a head. One of us lifted something from it, and leaning forward, that faint and invisible dust dry and acrid in the nostrils, we saw a long strand of iron-gray hair. *[1931]*

≡ THINKING ABOUT THE TEXT

1. Do you think some people can love another so much that they simply cannot bear for that person to leave? Is it possible Emily was like this?
2. Can a disturbed person be in love? Does love have to be healthy? Is sanity culturally defined? Can you imagine a society that would accept Emily's behavior?
3. Who do you think the narrator of "A Rose for Emily" is? Why would Faulkner tell the story from this perspective? Why not from Emily's?
4. Look at the last sentence of paragraph 51. What do you make of the five adjectives used? Are they understandable in terms of the story?
5. Some critics think this story is not a love story but a political allegory about the South. Does this make sense to you? What else does the story suggest to you?
6. Comment on the various kinds of repression — social and psychological — that occur throughout the story. What connections can you draw, and what generalizations might you make about them?
7. Reread "A Rose for Emily." How does your knowledge of the ending of the story affect your second reading? What details of the narrative tend to stand out the second time around?

RAYMOND CARVER

What We Talk About When We Talk About Love

Raymond Carver (1938–1988) re-creates in what has been called a "stripped-down and muscular prose style" the minutiae of everyday life in mid-twentieth-century America. Brought up in the Pacific Northwest in a working-class family, Carver began writing in high school and married early. While both he and his young wife worked at low-paying jobs, Carver took college courses and struggled to find time to write. In 1958, he studied fiction writing with John Gardner and graduated in 1963 from what is now the California State University at Humboldt. He received national recognition in 1967 when a story was included in the Best American Short Stories *annual anthology. Although Carver was a National Endowment for the Arts fellow in poetry in 1971, fiction remained his primary genre, earning him numerous awards and fellowships, including O. Henry awards in 1974, 1975, and 1980. Despite his success as a writer, alcoholism plagued Carver for most of his life until with the help of Alcoholics Anonymous he stopped drinking in 1982, soon after his divorce. "What We Talk About When We Talk About Love" was the title story in his 1981 collection.*

My friend Mel McGinnis was talking. Mel McGinnis is a cardiologist, and sometimes that gives him the right.

The four of us were sitting around his kitchen table drinking gin. Sunlight filled the kitchen from the big window behind the sink. There were Mel and me and his second wife, Teresa—Terri, we called her—and my wife, Laura. We lived in Albuquerque then. But we were all from somewhere else.

There was an ice bucket on the table. The gin and the tonic water kept going around, and we somehow got on the subject of love. Mel thought real love was nothing less than spiritual love. He said he'd spent five years in a seminary before quitting to go to medical school. He said he still looked back on those years in the seminary as the most important years in his life.

Terri said the man she lived with before she lived with Mel loved her so much he tried to kill her. Then Terri said, "He beat me up one night. He dragged me around the living room by my ankles. He kept saying, 'I love you, I love you, you bitch.' He went on dragging me around the living room. My head kept knocking on things." Terri looked around the table. "What do you do with love like that?"

She was a bone-thin woman with a pretty face, dark eyes, and brown hair 5
that hung down her back. She liked necklaces made of turquoise, and long pendant earrings.

"My God, don't be silly. That's not love, and you know it," Mel said. "I don't know what you'd call it, but I sure know you wouldn't call it love."

"Say what you want to, but I know it was," Terri said. "It may sound crazy to you, but it's true just the same. People are different, Mel. Sure, sometimes he may have acted crazy. Okay. But he loved me. In his own way maybe, but he loved me. There was love there, Mel. Don't say there wasn't."

Mel let out his breath. He held his glass and turned to Laura and me. "The man threatened to kill me," Mel said. He finished his drink and reached for the gin bottle. "Terri's a romantic. Terri's of the kick-me-so-I'll-know-you-love-me school. Terri, hon, don't look that way." Mel reached across the table and touched Terri's cheek with his fingers. He grinned at her.

"Now he wants to make up," Terri said.

"Make up what?" Mel said. "What is there to make up? I know what I know. 10
That's all."

"How'd we get started on this subject, anyway?" Terri said. She raised her glass and drank from it. "Mel always has love on his mind," she said. "Don't you, honey?" She smiled, and I thought that was the last of it.

"I just wouldn't call Ed's behavior love. That's all I'm saying, honey," Mel said. "What about you guys?" Mel said to Laura and me. "Does that sound like love to you?"

"I'm the wrong person to ask," I said. "I didn't even know the man. I've only heard his name mentioned in passing. I wouldn't know. You'd have to know the particulars. But I think what you're saying is that love is an absolute."

Mel said, "The kind of love I'm talking about is. The kind of love I'm talking about, you don't try to kill people."

Laura said, "I don't know anything about Ed, or anything about the situation. But who can judge anyone else's situation?"

I touched the back of Laura's hand. She gave me a quick smile. I picked up Laura's hand. It was warm, the nails polished, perfectly manicured. I encircled the broad wrist with my fingers, and I held her.

"When I left, he drank rat poison," Terri said. She clasped her arms with her hands. "They took him to the hospital in Santa Fe. That's where we lived then, about ten miles out. They saved his life. But his gums went crazy from it. I mean they pulled away from his teeth. After that, his teeth stood out like fangs. My God," Terri said. She waited a minute, then let go of her arms and picked up her glass.

"What people won't do!" Laura said.

"He's out of the action now," Mel said. "He's dead."

Mel handed me the saucer of limes. I took a section, squeezed it over my drink, and stirred the ice cubes with my finger.

"It gets worse," Terri said. "He shot himself in the mouth. But he bungled that too. Poor Ed," she said. Terri shook her head.

"Poor Ed nothing," Mel said. "He was dangerous."

Mel was forty-five years old. He was tall and rangy with curly soft hair. His face and arms were brown from the tennis he played. When he was sober, his gestures, all his movements, were precise, very careful.

"He did love me though, Mel. Grant me that," Terri said. "That's all I'm asking. He didn't love me the way you love me. I'm not saying that. But he loved me. You can grant me that, can't you?"

"What do you mean, he bungled it?" I said.

Laura leaned forward with her glass. She put her elbows on the table and held her glass in both hands. She glanced from Mel to Terri and waited with a look of bewilderment on her open face, as if amazed that such things happened to people you were friendly with.

"How'd he bungle it when he killed himself?" I said.

"I'll tell you what happened," Mel said. "He took this twenty-two pistol he'd bought to threaten Terri and me with. Oh, I'm serious, the man was always threatening. You should have seen the way we lived in those days. Like fugitives. I even bought a gun myself. Can you believe it? A guy like me? But I did. I bought one for self-defense and carried it in the glove compartment. Sometimes I'd have to leave the apartment in the middle of the night. To go to the hospital, you know? Terri and I weren't married then, and my first wife had the house and kids, the dog, everything, and Terri and I were living in this apartment here. Sometimes, as I say, I'd get a call in the middle of the night and have to go in to the hospital at two or three in the morning. It'd be dark out there in the parking lot, and I'd break into a sweat before I could even get to my car. I never knew if he was going to come up out of the shrubbery or from behind a car and start shooting. I mean, the man was crazy. He was capable of wiring a bomb, anything. He used to call my service at all hours and say he needed to talk to the doctor, and when I'd return the call, he'd say, 'Son of a bitch, your days are numbered.' Little things like that. It was scary, I'm telling you."

"I still feel sorry for him," Terri said.

"It sounds like a nightmare," Laura said. "But what exactly happened after he shot himself?"

Laura is a legal secretary. We'd met in a professional capacity. Before we knew it, it was a courtship. She's thirty-five, three years younger than I am. In addition to being in love, we like each other and enjoy one another's company. She's easy to be with.

"What happened?" Laura said.

Mel said, "He shot himself in the mouth in his room. Someone heard the shot and told the manager. They came in with a passkey, saw what had happened, and called an ambulance. I happened to be there when they brought him in, alive but past recall. The man lived for three days. His head swelled up to twice the size of a normal head. I'd never seen anything like it, and I hope I never do again. Terri wanted to go in and sit with him when she found out about it. We had a fight over it. I didn't think she should see him like that. I didn't think she should see him, and I still don't."

"Who won the fight?" Laura said.

"I was in the room with him when he died," Terri said. "He never came up out of it. But I sat with him. He didn't have anyone else."

"He was dangerous," Mel said. "If you call that love, you can have it."

"It was love," Terri said. "Sure, it's abnormal in most people's eyes. But he was willing to die for it. He did die for it."

"I sure as hell wouldn't call it love," Mel said. "I mean, no one knows what he did it for. I've seen a lot of suicides, and I couldn't say anyone ever knew what they did it for."

Mel put his hands behind his neck and tilted his chair back. "I'm not interested in that kind of love," he said. "If that's love, you can have it."

Terri said, "We were afraid. Mel even made a will out and wrote to his brother in California who used to be a Green Beret. Mel told him who to look for if something happened to him."

Terri drank from her glass. She said, "But Mel's right—we lived like fugitives. We were afraid. Mel was, weren't you, honey? I even called the police at one point, but they were no help. They said they couldn't do anything until Ed actually did something. Isn't that a laugh?" Terri said.

She poured the last of the gin into her glass and waggled the bottle. Mel got up from the table and went to the cupboard. He took down another bottle.

"Well, Nick and I know what love is," Laura said. "For us, I mean," Laura said. She bumped my knee with her knee. "You're supposed to say something now," Laura said, and turned her smile on me.

For an answer, I took Laura's hand and raised it to my lips. I made a big production out of kissing her hand. Everyone was amused.

"We're lucky," I said.

"You guys," Terri said. "Stop that now. You're making me sick. You're still on the honeymoon, for God's sake. You're still gaga, for crying out loud. Just wait. How long have you been together now? How long has it been? A year? Longer than a year?"

"Going on a year and a half," Laura said, flushed and smiling.

"Oh, now," Terri said. "Wait awhile."

She held her drink and gazed at Laura.

"I'm only kidding," Terri said.

Mel opened the gin and went around the table with the bottle.

"Here, you guys," he said. "Let's have a toast. I want to propose a toast. A toast to love. To true love," Mel said.

We touched glasses.

"To love," we said.

Outside in the backyard, one of the dogs began to bark. The leaves of the aspen that leaned past the window ticked against the glass. The afternoon sun was like a presence in this room, the spacious light of ease and generosity. We could have been anywhere, somewhere enchanted. We raised our glasses again and grinned at each other like children who had agreed on something forbidden.

"I'll tell you what real love is," Mel said. "I mean, I'll give you a good example. And then you can draw your own conclusions." He poured more gin into his glass. He added an ice cube and a sliver of lime. We waited and sipped our drinks. Laura and I touched knees again. I put a hand on her warm thigh and left it there.

"What do any of us really know about love?" Mel said. "It seems to me we're just beginners at love. We say we love each other and we do, I don't doubt it. I love Terri and Terri loves me, and you guys love each other too. You know the kind of love I'm talking about now. Physical love, that impulse that drives you to someone special, as well as love of the other person's being, his or her essence, as it were. Carnal love and, well, call it sentimental love, the day-to-day caring about the other person. But sometimes I have a hard time accounting for the fact that I must have loved my first wife too. But I did, I know I did. So I suppose I am like Terri in that regard. Terri and Ed." He thought about it and then he went on. "There was a time when I thought I loved my first wife more than life itself. But now I hate her guts. I do. How do you explain that? What happened to that love? What happened to it, is what I'd like to know. I wish someone could tell me. Then there's Ed. Okay, we're back to Ed. He loves Terri so much he tries to kill her and he winds up killing himself." Mel stopped talking and swallowed from his glass. "You guys have been together eighteen months and you love each other. It shows all over you. You glow with it. But you both loved other people before you met each other. You've both been married before, just like us. And you probably loved other people before that too, even. Terri and I have been together five years, been married for four. And the terrible thing, the terrible thing is, but the good thing too, the saving grace, you might say, is that if something happened to one of us—excuse me for saying this—but if something happened to one of us tomorrow I think the other one, the other person, would grieve for a while, you know, but then the surviving party would go out and love again, have someone else soon enough. All this, all of this love we're talking about, it would just be a memory. Maybe not even a memory. Am I wrong? Am I way off base? Because I want you to set me straight if you think I'm wrong. I want to know. I mean, I don't know anything, and I'm the first one to admit it."

"Mel, for God's sake," Terri said. She reached out and took hold of his wrist. "Are you getting drunk? Honey? Are you drunk?"

"Honey, I'm just talking," Mel said. "All right? I don't have to be drunk to say what I think. I mean, we're all just talking, right?" Mel said. He fixed his eyes on her.

"Sweetie, I'm not criticizing," Terri said.

She picked up her glass.

"I'm not on call today," Mel said. "Let me remind you of that. I am not on call," he said.

"Mel, we love you," Laura said.

Mel looked at Laura. He looked at her as if he could not place her, as if she was not the woman she was.

"Love you too, Laura," Mel said. "And you, Nick, love you too. You know something?" Mel said. "You guys are our pals," Mel said.

He picked up his glass.

Mel said, "I was going to tell you about something. I mean, I was going to prove a point. You see, this happened a few months ago, but it's still going on right now, and it ought to make us feel ashamed when we talk like we know what we're talking about when we talk about love."

"Come on now," Terri said. "Don't talk like you're drunk if you're not drunk."

"Just shut up for once in your life," Mel said very quietly. "Will you do me a favor and do that for a minute? So as I was saying, there's this old couple who had this car wreck out on the interstate. A kid hit them and they were all torn to shit and nobody was giving them much chance to pull through."

Terri looked at us and then back at Mel. She seemed anxious, or maybe that's too strong a word.

Mel was handing the bottle around the table.

"I was on call that night," Mel said. "It was May or maybe it was June. Terri and I had just sat down to dinner when the hospital called. There'd been this thing out on the interstate. Drunk kid, teenager, plowed his dad's pickup into this camper with this old couple in it. They were up in their midseventies, that couple. The kid—eighteen, nineteen, something—he was DOA. Taken the steering wheel through his sternum. The old couple, they were alive, you understand. I mean, just barely. But they had everything. Multiple fractures, internal injuries, hemorrhaging, contusions, lacerations, the works, and they each of them had themselves concussions. They were in a bad way, believe me. And, of course, their age was two strikes against them. I'd say she was worse off than he was. Ruptured spleen along with everything else. Both kneecaps broken. But they'd been wearing their seatbelts and, God knows, that's what saved them for the time being."

"Folks, this is an advertisement for the National Safety Council," Terri said. "This is your spokesman, Dr. Melvin R. McGinnis, talking." Terri laughed. "Mel," she said, "sometimes you're just too much. But I love you, hon," she said.

"Honey, I love you," Mel said.

He leaned across the table. Terri met him halfway. They kissed. 75

"Terri's right," Mel said as he settled himself again. "Get those seatbelts on. But seriously, they were in some shape, those oldsters. By the time I got down there, the kid was dead, as I said. He was off in a corner, laid out on a gurney. I took one look at the old couple and told the ER nurse to get me a neurologist and an orthopedic man and a couple of surgeons down there right away."

He drank from his glass. "I'll try to keep this short," he said. "So we took the two of them up to the OR and worked like fuck on them most of the night. They had these incredible reserves, those two. You see that once in a while. So we did everything that could be done, and toward morning we're giving them a fifty-fifty chance, maybe less than that for her. So here they are, still alive the next morning. So, okay, we move them into the ICU, which is where they both kept plugging away at it for two weeks, hitting it better and better on all the scopes. So we transfer them out to their own room."

Mel stopped talking. "Here," he said, "let's drink this cheapo gin the hell up. Then we're going to dinner, right? Terri and I know a new place. That's where we'll go, to this new place we know about. But we're not going until we finish up this cut-rate, lousy gin."

Terri said, "We haven't actually eaten there yet. But it looks good. From the outside, you know."

"I like food," Mel said. "If I had it to do all over again, I'd be a chef, you know? 80
Right, Terri?" Mel said.

He laughed. He fingered the ice in his glass.

"Terri knows," he said. "Terri can tell you. But let me say this. If I could come back again in a different life, a different time and all, you know what? I'd like to come back as a knight. You were pretty safe wearing all that armor. It was all right being a knight until gunpowder and muskets and pistols came along."

"Mel would like to ride a horse and carry a lance," Terri said.

"Carry a woman's scarf with you everywhere," Laura said.

"Or just a woman," Mel said. 85

"Shame on you," Laura said.

Terri said, "Suppose you came back as a serf. The serfs didn't have it so good in those days," Terri said.

"The serfs never had it good," Mel said. "But I guess even the knights were vessels to someone. Isn't that the way it worked? But then everyone is always a vessel to someone. Isn't that right? Terri? But what I liked about knights, besides their ladies, was that they had that suit of armor, you know, and they couldn't get hurt very easy. No cars in those days, you know? No drunk teenagers to tear into your ass."

"Vassals," Terri said.

"What?" Mel said. 90

"Vassals," Terri said. "They were called vassals, not vessels."

"Vassals, vessels," Mel said, "what the fuck's the difference? You knew what I meant anyway. All right," Mel said. "So I'm not educated. I learned my stuff. I'm a heart surgeon, sure, but I'm just a mechanic. I go in and I fuck around and I fix things. Shit," Mel said.

"Modesty doesn't become you," Terri said.

"He's just a humble sawbones," I said. "But sometimes they suffocated in all that armor, Mel. They'd even have heart attacks if it got too hot and they were too tired and worn out. I read somewhere that they'd fall off their horses and not be able to get up because they were too tired to stand with all that armor on them. They got trampled by their own horses sometimes."

"That's terrible," Mel said. "That's a terrible thing, Nicky. I guess they'd just lay 95
there and wait until somebody came along and made a shish kebab out of them."

"Some other vessel," Terri said.

"That's right," Mel said. "Some vassal would come along and spear the bastard in the name of love. Or whatever the fuck it was they fought over in those days."

"Same things we fight over these days," Terri said.

Laura said, "Nothing's changed."

The color was still high in Laura's cheeks. Her eyes were bright. She brought 100
her glass to her lips.

Mel poured himself another drink. He looked at the label closely as if studying a long row of numbers. Then he slowly put the bottle down on the table and slowly reached for the tonic water.

"What about the old couple?" Laura said. "You didn't finish that story you started."

Laura was having a hard time lighting her cigarette. Her matches kept going out.

The sunshine inside the room was different now, changing, getting thinner. But the leaves outside the window were still shimmering, and I stared at the pattern they made on the panes and on the Formica counter. They weren't the same patterns, of course.

"What about the old couple?" I said. 105

"Older but wiser," Terri said.

Mel stared at her.

Terri said, "Go on with your story, hon. I was only kidding. Then what happened?"

"Terri, sometimes," Mel said.

"Please, Mel," Terri said. "Don't always be so serious, sweetie. Can't you take 110
a joke?"

"Where's the joke?" Mel said.

He held his glass and gazed steadily at his wife.

"What happened?" Laura said.

Mel fastened his eyes on Laura. He said, "Laura, if I didn't have Terri and if I didn't love her so much, and if Nick wasn't my best friend, I'd fall in love with you, I'd carry you off, honey," he said.

"Tell your story," Terri said. "Then we'll go to that new place, okay?" 115

"Okay," Mel said. "Where was I?" he said. He stared at the table and then he began again.

"I dropped in to see each of them every day, sometimes twice a day if I was up doing other calls anyway. Casts and bandages, head to foot, the both of them. You know, you've seen it in the movies. That's just the way they looked, just like in the movies. Little eye-holes and nose-holes and mouth-holes. And she had to have her legs slung up on top of it. Well, the husband was very depressed for the longest while. Even after he found out that his wife was going to pull through, he was still very depressed. Not about the accident, though. I mean, the accident was one thing, but it wasn't everything. I'd get up to his mouth-hole, you know, and he'd say no, it wasn't the accident exactly but it was because he couldn't see her through his eye-holes. He said that was what was making him feel so bad. Can you imagine? I'm telling you, the man's heart was breaking because he couldn't turn his goddamn head and *see* his goddamn wife."

Mel looked around the table and shook his head at what he was going to say.

"I mean, it was killing the old fart just because he couldn't *look* at the fucking woman."

We all looked at Mel. 120

"Do you see what I'm saying?" he said.

Maybe we were a little drunk by then. I know it was hard keeping things in focus. The light was draining out of the room, going back through the window where it had come from. Yet nobody made a move to get up from the table to turn on the overhead light.

"Listen," Mel said. "Let's finish this fucking gin. There's about enough left here for one shooter all around. Then let's go eat. Let's go to the new place."

"He's depressed," Terri said. "Mel, why don't you take a pill?"

Mel shook his head. "I've taken everything there is." 125

"We all need a pill now and then," I said.

"Some people are born needing them," Terri said.

She was using her finger to rub at something on the table. Then she stopped rubbing.

"I think I want to call my kids," Mel said. "Is that all right with everybody? I'll call my kids," he said.

Terri said, "What if Marjorie answers the phone? You guys, you've heard us 130 on the subject of Marjorie? Honey, you know you don't want to talk to Marjorie. It'll make you feel even worse."

"I don't want to talk to Marjorie," Mel said. "But I want to talk to my kids."

"There isn't a day goes by that Mel doesn't say he wishes she'd get married again. Or else die," Terri said. "For one thing," Terri said, "she's bankrupting us. Mel says it's just to spite him that she won't get married again. She has a boyfriend who lives with her and the kids, so Mel is supporting the boyfriend too."

"She's allergic to bees," Mel said. "If I'm not praying she'll get married again, I'm praying she'll get herself stung to death by a swarm of fucking bees."

"Shame on you," Laura said.

"Bzzzzzzz," Mel said, turning his fingers into bees and buzzing them at Terri's throat. Then he let his hands drop all the way to his sides. 135

"She's vicious," Mel said. "Sometimes I think I'll go up there dressed like a beekeeper. You know, that hat that's like a helmet with the plate that comes down over your face, the big gloves, and the padded coat? I'll knock on the door and let loose a hive of bees in the house. But first I'd make sure the kids were out, of course."

He crossed one leg over the other. It seemed to take him a lot of time to do it. Then he put both feet on the floor and leaned forward, elbows on the table, his chin cupped in his hands.

"Maybe I won't call the kids, after all. Maybe it isn't such a hot idea. Maybe we'll just go eat. How does that sound?"

"Sounds fine to me," I said. "Eat or not eat. Or keep drinking. I could head right on out into the sunset."

"What does that mean, honey?" Laura said. 140

"It just means what I said," I said. "It means I could just keep going. That's all it means."

"I could eat something myself," Laura said. "I don't think I've ever been so hungry in my life. Is there something to nibble on?"

"I'll put out some cheese and crackers," Terri said.

But Terri just sat there. She did not get up to get anything.

Mel turned his glass over. He spilled it out on the table. 145

"Gin's gone," Mel said.

Terri said, "Now what?"

I could hear my heart beating. I could hear everyone's heart. I could hear the human noise we sat there making, not one of us moving, not even when the room went dark. *[1981]*

THINKING ABOUT THE TEXT

1. The argument between the couples seems to be about the nature of love. Which character's ideas make the most sense to you? What kinds of love are discussed? Are these demonstrated in the story? Do you think true love is an illusion?
2. Do you see similarities between Mel and Ed? Do any of the characters seem aware of any similarities? Is Mel a perceptive person? What are his problems? Is he in love with Terri? How do you interpret his fantasy with the bees and Marjorie?
3. Why does Mel seem so interested in knights? Is this symbolic? Are there other symbols here (light? dark? cardiologist?)? What do you make of the last paragraph? Why does it end with beating hearts and silence?
4. Is this story optimistic or pessimistic about true love? Is the old couple a positive or a negative example of true love? What about Nick and Laura? What about Ed? Could you argue that he was in love?

5. What does the title mean? Be specific, especially about the first word. Do you tell stories about love? Have you heard some recently? What lessons or information do they give about love?

MAKING COMPARISONS

1. Compare Ed to Emily Grierson in Faulkner's story. What similarities do you see in their behavior?
2. Have these stories complicated your idea of love? Explain.
3. Do you see Terri and Homer Barron as victims of love? Did they do something wrong?

WRITING ABOUT ISSUES

1. Is love or hate a stronger emotion? Use examples from these stories to support your argument.
2. What difficulties do you encounter when you try to define love? Write an essay in which you use Homer and Emily or Terri and Ed as examples that complicate the definition.
3. Citing evidence from these and other stories, as well as novels, films, and your own experiences, write an essay that explains your view of the necessary ingredients for a loving relationship.
4. Argue that because our culture overemphasizes romantic love, individuals feel pressured to find love, sometimes in all the wrong places.

Jealous Love: Critical Commentaries on a Play

WILLIAM SHAKESPEARE, *Othello*

CRITICAL COMMENTARIES:
A. C. BRADLEY, "The Noble Othello"

MILLICENT BELL, "Othello's Jealousy"

JEFFRIE G. MURPHY, "Jealousy, Shame, and the Rival"

Of all the great tragedies of Shakespeare, *Othello* seems the closest to our own lives. Hamlet is a prince, and Lear and Macbeth are kings with the fate of their nations tied to their destiny. It is sometimes hard for contemporary readers to relate to their struggles or to regicide. But *Othello* is more domesticated, more about a relationship we can understand; few of us would claim that we have never been jealous. We know that relationships thrive on trust and openness, but even if we trust our partner, jealousy can find its way into our consciousness and might especially do so if we are prompted to doubt by a close friend.

Psychologists suggest that insecure people are prone to jealousy, perhaps because their low esteem suggests to them that they are not worthy of love. Is this the case with Othello? Although at first he seems filled with confidence and authority, he is considered a Moorish outsider in Venetian society and as such might be tempted to think that his wife, Desdemona, might find Cassio, one of her "own kind," attractive and desirable. The innocent and devoted Desdemona does not, but the seeds of distrust that are planted early on by Brabantio ("She deceived her father, and may thee") are diabolically nurtured by Iago, "an inhuman dog." The speed with which a great love is destroyed leaves the reader stunned by the potential darkness within us all.

The three essays that follow the play focus on jealousy, but they have different ideas about where that emotion comes from and how it alters our view of Othello's character and the play. A. C. Bradley develops the idea that Othello remains a noble soul and so we admire him to the end. This admiration increases our pity and the force of catharsis, which leaves us "for the moment free from pain, and exulting in the power of 'love and man's unconquerable mind.'" Millicent Bell sees jealousy as connected to philosophical ideas about truth and seeming and connects the play to ideas about skepticism in Elizabethan England and contemporary America. Jeffrie G. Murphy takes a more psychological view of jealousy as personal disintegration strongly linked to shame.

BEFORE YOU READ

Do you think jealousy is a natural emotion? If you loved someone deeply, would you trust him or her? Are only insecure people jealous? Are there any positive elements to jealousy?

Lebrecht Music and Arts Photo Library / Alamy

WILLIAM SHAKESPEARE
Othello

William Shakespeare's reputation as the greatest dramatist in the English language is built on his five major tragedies: Romeo and Juliet *(1594),* Hamlet *(1600),* Othello *(1604),* Macbeth *(1605), and* King Lear *(1605). But he was also a master in other genres, including comedies (*As You Like It *in 1599), histories (*Henry IV *in 1597), and romances (*The Tempest *in 1611). And his collection of sonnets is considered art of the highest order.*

Very little is known about Shakespeare's personal life. He attended the grammar school at Stratford-upon-Avon, where he was born in 1564. He married Anne Hathaway in 1582 and had three children. Around 1590 he moved to London, where he became an actor and began writing plays. He was an astute businessperson, becoming a shareholder in London's famous Globe Theatre. After writing thirty-seven plays, he retired to Stratford in 1611. When he died in 1616, he left behind the most respected body of work in literature. Shakespeare's ability to use artistic language to convey a wide range of humor and emotion is perhaps unsurpassed.

THE NAMES OF THE ACTORS

OTHELLO, *the Moor*
BRABANTIO, *father to Desdemona*
CASSIO, *an honorable lieutenant [to Othello]*
IAGO *[Othello's ancient,] a villain*
RODERIGO, *a gulled gentleman*
DUKE OF VENICE
SENATORS OF VENICE
MONTANO, *governor of Cyprus*
LODOVICO AND GRATIANO, *[kinsmen to Brabantio,] two noble Venetians*
SAILORS
CLOWNS
DESDEMONA, *wife to Othello*
EMILIA, *wife to Iago*
BIANCA, *a courtesan*
[Messenger, Herald, Officers, Venetian Gentlemen, Musicians, Attendants
scene: Venice and Cyprus]

[ACT I, Scene I: A street in Venice.]

Enter Roderigo and Iago.

RODERIGO: Tush, never tell me! I take it much unkindly
That thou, Iago, who hast had my purse
As if the strings were thine, shouldst know of this.°
IAGO: 'Sblood,° but you'll not hear me!
If ever I did dream of such a matter,
Abhor me.
RODERIGO: Thou told'st me thou didst hold him in thy hate.
IAGO: Despise me if I do not. Three great ones of the city,
In personal suit to make me his lieutenant,
Off-capped to him;° and, by the faith of man,
I know my price; I am worth no worse a place.
But he, as loving his own pride and purposes,
Evades them with a bombast circumstance.°
Horribly stuffed with epithets of war;
[And, in conclusion,]
Nonsuits° my mediators; for, "Certes," says he,
"I have already chose my officer."
And what was he?
Forsooth, a great arithmetician,°

Act I, Scene I. 3 this: I.e., Desdemona's elopement. **4 'Sblood:** By God's blood. **10 him:** I.e., Othello. **13 a bombast circumstance:** Pompous circumlocutions. **16 Nonsuits:** Rejects. **19 arithmetician:** Theoretician.

One Michael Cassio, a Florentine
(A fellow almost damned in a fair wife°)
That never set a squadron in the field,
Nor the division of a battle knows
More than a spinster; unless the bookish theoric,
Wherein the togèd consuls can propose
As masterly as he. Mere prattle without practice
Is all his soldiership. But he, sir, had th' election;
And I (of whom his eyes had seen the proof
At Rhodes, at Cyprus, and on other grounds
Christian and heathen) must be belee'd and calmed°
By debitor and creditor; this counter-caster,°
He, in good time, must his lieutenant be,
And I—God bless the mark!—his Moorship's ancient.°

RODERIGO: By heaven, I rather would have been his hangman.

IAGO: Why, there's no remedy; 'tis the curse of service.
Preferment goes by letter and affection,°
And not by old gradation, where each second
Stood heir to th' first. Now, sir, be judge yourself,
Whether I in any just term am affined°
To love the Moor.

RODERIGO: I would not follow him then.

IAGO: O, sir, content you;
I follow him to serve my turn upon him.
We cannot all be masters, nor all masters
Cannot be truly followed. You shall mark
Many a duteous and knee-crooking knave
That, doting on his own obsequious bondage,
Wears out his time, much like his master's ass,
For naught but provender; and when he's old, cashiered.°
Whip me such honest knaves! Others there are
Who, trimmed° in forms and visages of duty,
Keep yet their hearts attending on themselves;
And, throwing but shows of service on their lords,
Do well thrive by them, and when they have lined their coats,
Do themselves homage. These fellows have some soul;
And such a one do I profess myself. For, sir,
It is as sure as you are Roderigo,
Were I the Moor, I would not be Iago.
In following him, I follow but myself;
Heaven is my judge, not I for love and duty,

21 almost ... wife: (An obscure allusion; Cassio is unmarried, but see IV.i.12). **30 be-lee'd and calmed:** Left in the lurch. **31 counter-caster:** Bookkeeper. **33 ancient:** Ensign. **36 affection:** Favoritism. **39 affined:** Obliged. **48 cashiered:** Turned off. **50 trimmed:** Dressed up.

But seeming so, for my peculiar end;
For when my outward action doth demonstrate
The native act and figure of my heart°
In compliment extern,° 'tis not long after
But I will wear my heart upon my sleeve
For daws to peck at; I am not what I am.

RODERIGO: What a full fortune does the thick-lips° owe°
If he can carry't thus!

IAGO: Call up her father,
Rouse him. Make after him, poison his delight,
Proclaim him in the streets. Incense her kinsmen,
And though he in a fertile climate dwell,
Plague him with flies; though that his joy be joy,
Yet throw such changes of vexation on't
As it may lose some color.

RODERIGO: Here is her father's house. I'll call aloud.

IAGO: Do, with like timorous° accent and dire yell
As when, by night and negligence, the fire
Is spied in populous cities.

RODERIGO: What, ho, Brabantio! Signior Brabantio, ho!

IAGO: Awake! What, ho, Brabantio! Thieves! thieves! thieves!
Look to your house, your daughter, and your bags!
Thieves! thieves!

Brabantio at a window.°

BRABANTIO *(above)*: What is the reason of this terrible summons?
What is the matter there?

RODERIGO: Signior, is all your family within?

IAGO: Are your doors locked?

BRABANTIO: Why, wherefore ask you this?

IAGO: Zounds, sir, y' are robbed! For shame, put on your gown!
Your heart is burst; you have lost half your soul.
Even now, now, very now, an old black ram
Is tupping your white ewe. Arise, arise!
Awake the snorting° citizens with the bell.
Or else the devil will make a grandsire of you.
Arise, I say!

BRABANTIO: What, have you lost your wits?

RODERIGO: Most reverend signior, do you know my voice?

BRABANTIO: Not I. What are you?

RODERIGO: My name is Roderigo.

BRABANTIO: The worser welcome!

62 The . . . heart: What I really believe and intend. **63 compliment extern:** Outward appearance. **66 thick-lips:** An Elizabethan epithet for blacks, including Moors; **owe:** Own. **75 timorous:** Terrifying. ***Brabantio at a window*:** (added from quarto). **90 snorting:** Snoring.

I have charged thee not to haunt about my doors.
In honest plainness thou hast heard me say
My daughter is not for thee; and now, in madness,
Being full of supper and distemp'ring draughts,
Upon malicious knavery dost thou come
To start my quiet.

RODERIGO: Sir, sir, sir—

BRABANTIO: But thou must needs be sure
My spirit and my place have in them power
To make this bitter to thee.

RODERIGO: Patience, good sir.

BRABANTIO: What tell'st thou me of robbing? This is Venice;
My house is not a grange.°

RODERIGO: Most grave Brabantio,
In simple and pure soul I come to you.

IAGO: Zounds, sir, you are one of those that will not serve God if the devil bid you. Because we come to do you service, and you think we are ruffians, you'll have your daughter covered with a Barbary horse; you'll have your nephews° neigh to you; you'll have coursers for cousins, and gennets for germans.°

BRABANTIO: What profane wretch art thou?

IAGO: I am one, sir, that comes to tell you your daughter and the Moor are now making the beast with two backs.

BRABANTIO: Thou are a villain.

IAGO: You are—a senator.

BRABANTIO: This thou shalt answer. I know thee, Roderigo.

RODERIGO: Sir, I will answer anything. But I beseech you,
If 't be your pleasure and most wise consent,
As partly I find it is, that your fair daughter,
At this odd-even° and dull watch o' th' night,
Transported, with no worse nor better guard
But with a knave of common hire, a gondolier,
To the gross clasps of a lascivious Moor—
If this be known to you, and your allowance,°
We then have done you bold and saucy wrongs;
But if you know not this, my manners tell me
We have your wrong rebuke. Do not believe
That, from the sense° of all civility,
I thus would play and trifle with your reverence.
Your daughter, if you have not given her leave,
I say again, hath made a gross revolt,
Tying her duty, beauty, wit, and fortunes

108 grange: Isolated farmhouse. **113 nephews:** I.e., grandsons. **113–14 gennets for germans:** Spanish horses for near kinsmen. **123 odd-even:** Between night and morning. **127 allowance:** Approval. **131 from the sense:** In violation.

In an extravagant and wheeling° stranger
Of here and everywhere. Straight satisfy yourself.
If she be in her chamber, or your house,
Let loose on me the justice of the state
For thus deluding you.

BRABANTIO: Strike on the tinder, ho!
Give me a taper! Call up all my people!
This accident° is not unlike my dream.
Belief of it oppresses me already.
Light, I say! light! *Exit [above].*

IAGO: Farewell, for I must leave you.
It seems not meet, nor wholesome to my place,
To be produced—as, if I stay, I shall—
Against the Moor. For I do know the state,
However this may gall him with some check,°
Cannot with safety cast° him; for he's embarked
With such loud reason to the Cyprus wars,
Which even now stand in act,° that for their souls
Another of his fathom° they have none
To lead their business; in which regard,
Though I do hate him as I do hell-pains,
Yet, for necessity of present life,
I must show out a flag and sign of love,
Which is indeed but sign. That you shall surely find him,
Lead to the Sagittary° the raisèd search;
And there will I be with him. So farewell. *Exit.*

Enter [below] Brabantio in his nightgown,° and Servants with torches.

BRABANTIO: It is too true an evil. Gone she is;
And what's to come of my despisèd time
Is naught but bitterness. Now, Roderigo,
Where didst thou see her?—O unhappy girl!—
With the Moor, say'st thou?—Who would be a father?—
How didst thou know 'twas she!—O, she deceives me
Past thought!—What said she to you?—Get moe° tapers!
Raise all my kindred!—Are they married, think you?

RODERIGO: Truly I think they are.

BRABANTIO: O heaven! How got she out? O treason of the blood!
Fathers, from hence trust not your daughters' minds
By what you see them act. Is there not charms
By which the property° of youth and maidhood

136 extravagant and wheeling: Expatriate and roving. **142 accident:** Occurrence. **148 check:** Reprimand. **149 cast:** Discharge. **151 stand in act:** Are going on. **152 fathom:** Capacity. **158 Sagittary:** An inn. **nightgown:** Dressing gown. **166 moe:** More. **172 property:** Nature.

May be abused? Have you not read, Roderigo,
Of some such thing?
RODERIGO: Yes, sir, I have indeed.
BRABANTIO: Call up my brother.—O, would you had had her!—
Some one way, some another.—Do you know
Where we may apprehend her and the Moor?
RODERIGO: I think I can discover him, if you please
To get good guard and go along with me.
BRABANTIO: I pray you lead on. At every house I'll call;
I may command at most.—Get weapons, ho!
And raise some special officers of night.—
On, good Roderigo; I'll deserve° your pains. *Exeunt.*

[Scene II: Before the lodgings of Othello.]

Enter Othello, Iago, and Attendants with torches.

IAGO: Though in the trade of war I have slain men,
Yet do I hold it very stuff o' th' conscience
To do no contrived murther. I lack iniquity
Sometimes to do me service. Nine or ten times
I had thought t' have yerked° him here under the ribs.
OTHELLO: 'Tis better as it is.
IAGO: Nay, but he prated,
And spoke such scurvy and provoking terms
Against your honor
That with the little godliness I have
I did full hard forbear him. But I pray you, sir,
Are you fast° married? Be assured of this,
That the magnifico° is much beloved,
And hath in his effect a voice potential°
As double° as the Duke's. He will divorce you,
Or put upon you what restraint and grievance
The law, with all his might to enforce it on,
Will give him cable.
OTHELLO: Let him do his spite.
My services which I have done the signiory°
Shall out-tongue his complaints. 'Tis yet to know°—
Which, when I know that boasting is an honor,
I shall promulgate—I fetch my life and being
From men of royal siege;° and my demerits°

183 deserve: Show gratitude for. **Scene II. 5 yerked:** Stabbed. **11 fast:** Securely. **12 magnifico:** Grandee (Brabantio). **13 potential:** Powerful. **14 double:** Doubly influential. **18 signiory:** Venetian government. **19 yet to know:** Still not generally known. **22 siege:** Rank. **demerits:** Deserts.

May speak unbonneted to as proud a fortune
As this that I have reached.° For know, Iago,
But that I love the gentle Desdemona,
I would not my unhousèd° free condition
Put into circumscription and confine
For the sea's worth. But look what lights come yond?

IAGO: Those are the raisèd father and his friends.
You were best go in.

OTHELLO: Not I; I must be found.
My parts, my title, and my perfect soul°
Shall manifest me rightly. Is it they?

IAGO: By Janus, I think no.

Enter Cassio, with torches, Officers.

OTHELLO: The servants of the Duke, and my lieutenant.
The goodness of the night upon you, friends!
What is the news?

CASSIO: The Duke does greet you, general;
And he requires your haste-post-haste appearance
Even on the instant.

OTHELLO: What's the matter, think you?

CASSIO: Something from Cyprus, as I may divine.
It is a business of some heat. The galleys
Have sent a dozen sequent° messengers
This very night at one another's heels,
And many of the consuls, raised and met,
Are at the Duke's already. You have been hotly called for;
When, being not at your lodging to be found,
The Senate hath sent about three several quests
To search you out.

OTHELLO: 'Tis well I am found by you.
I will but spend a word here in the house,
And go with you. *[Exit.]*

CASSIO: Ancient, what makes he here?

IAGO: Faith, he to-night hath boarded a land carack.°
If it prove lawful prize, he's made for ever.

CASSIO: I do not understand.

IAGO: He's married.

CASSIO: To who?

[Enter Othello.]

IAGO: Marry, to—Come, captain, will you go?

OTHELLO: Have with you.

23–24 May speak . . . reached: Are equal, I modestly assert, to those of Desdemona's family. **26 unhousèd:** Unrestrained. **31 perfect soul:** Stainless conscience. **41 sequent:** Consecutive. **50 carack:** Treasure ship.

CASSIO: Here comes another troop to seek for you.

Enter Brabantio, Roderigo, and others with lights and weapons.

IAGO: It is Brabantio. General, be advised.
He comes to bad intent.
OTHELLO: Holla! stand there!
RODERIGO: Signior, it is the Moor.
BRABANTIO: Down with him, thief!

[They draw on both sides.]

IAGO: You, Roderigo! Come, sir, I am for you.
OTHELLO: Keep up° your bright swords, for the dew will rust them.
Good signior, you shall more command with years
Than with your weapons.
BRABANTIO: O thou foul thief, where hast thou stowed my daughter?
Damned as thou art, thou hast enchanted her!
For I'll refer me to all things of sense,
If she in chains of magic were not bound,
Whether a maid so tender, fair, and happy,
So opposite to marriage that she shunned
The wealthy curlèd darlings of our nation,
Would ever have, t' incur a general mock,
Run from her guardage to the sooty bosom
Of such a thing as thou—to fear, not to delight.
Judge me the world if 'tis not gross in sense°
That thou hast practiced on her with foul charms,
Abused her delicate youth with drugs or minerals
That weaken motion.° I'll have't disputed on;
'Tis probable, and palpable to thinking.
I therefore apprehend and do attach° thee
For an abuser of the world, a practicer
Of arts inhibited and out of warrant.
Lay hold upon him. If he do resist,
Subdue him at his peril.
OTHELLO: Hold your hands,
Both you of my inclining and the rest.
Were it my cue to fight, I should have known it
Without a prompter. Where will you that I go
To answer this your charge?
BRABANTIO: To prison, till fit time
Of law and course of direct session°
Call thee to answer.
OTHELLO: What if I do obey?
How may the Duke be therewith satisfied,

59 Keep up: I.e., sheath. **72 gross in sense:** Obvious. **75 motion:** Perception. **77 attach:** Arrest. **86 direct session:** Regular trial.

Whose messengers are here about my side
Upon some present business of the state
To bring me to him?

OFFICER: 'Tis true, most worthy signior.
The Duke's in council, and your noble self
I am sure is sent for.

BRABANTIO: How? The Duke in council?
In this time of the night? Bring him away.
Mine's not an idle° cause. The Duke himself,
Or any of my brothers of the state,
Cannot but feel this wrong as 'twere their own;
For if such actions may have passage free,
Bondslaves and pagans shall our statesmen be. *Exeunt.*

[Scene III: The Venetian Senate Chamber.]

Enter Duke and Senators, set at a table, with lights and Attendants.

DUKE: There is no composition° in these news
That gives them credit.

1. SENATOR: Indeed they are disproportioned.
My letters say a hundred and seven galleys.

DUKE: And mine a hundred forty.

2. SENATOR: And mine two hundred.
But though they jump° not on a just account—
As in these cases where the aim° reports
'Tis oft with difference—yet do they all confirm
A Turkish fleet, and bearing up to Cyprus.

DUKE: Nay, it is possible enough to judgment.
I do not so secure me° in the error
But the main article° I do approve°
In fearful sense.

SAILOR *(within)*: What, ho! what, ho! what, ho!

OFFICER: A messenger from the galleys.

Enter Sailor.

DUKE: Now, what's the business?

SAILOR: The Turkish preparation makes for Rhodes.
So was I bid report here to the state
By Signior Angelo.

DUKE: How say you by this change?

1. SENATOR: This cannot be
By no assay° of reason. 'Tis a pageant
To keep us in false gaze.° When we consider

95 idle: Trifling. **SCENE III. 1 composition:** Consistency. **5 jump:** Agree. **6 aim:** Conjecture. **10 so secure me:** Take such comfort. **11 article:** Substance; **approve:** Accept. **18 assay:** Test. **19 in false gaze:** Looking the wrong way.

Th' importancy of Cyprus to the Turk,
And let ourselves again but understand
That, as it more concerns the Turk than Rhodes,
So may he with more facile question bear° it,
For that it stands not in such warlike brace,°
But altogether lacks th' abilities
That Rhodes is dressed in—if we make thought of this,
We must not think the Turk is so unskillful
To leave that latest which concerns him first,
Neglecting an attempt of ease and gain
To wake and wage° a danger profitless.

DUKE: Nay, in all confidence, he's not for Rhodes.

OFFICER: Here is more news.

Enter a Messenger.

MESSENGER: The Ottomites, reverend and gracious,
Steering with due course toward the isle of Rhodes,
Have there injointed them with an after fleet.

1. SENATOR: Ay, so I thought. How many, as you guess?

MESSENGER: Of thirty sail; and now they do restem°
Their backward course, bearing with frank appearance
Their purposes toward Cyprus. Signior Montano,
Your trusty and most valiant servitor,
With his free duty recommends you thus,
And prays you to believe him.

DUKE: 'Tis certain then for Cyprus.
Marcus Luccicos,° is not he in town?

1. SENATOR: He's now in Florence.

DUKE: Write from us to him; post, post-haste dispatch.

1. SENATOR: Here comes Brabantio and the valiant Moor.

Enter Brabantio, Othello, Cassio, Iago, Roderigo, and Officers.

DUKE: Valiant Othello, we must straight employ you
Against the general enemy Ottoman.
[To Brabantio.] I did not see you. Welcome, gentle signior.
We lacked your counsel and your help to-night.

BRABANTIO: So did I yours. Good your grace, pardon me.
Neither my place, nor aught I heard of business,
Hath raised me from my bed; nor doth the general care
Take hold on me; for my particular grief
Is of so floodgate° and o'erbearing nature
That it engluts° and swallows other sorrows,
And it is still itself.

23 with . . . bear: More easily capture. **24 brace:** Posture of defense. **30 wake and wage:** Rouse and risk. **37 restem:** Steer again. **44 Marcus Luccicos:** (Presumably a Venetian envoy). **56 floodgate:** Torrential. **57 engluts:** Devours.

DUKE: Why, what's the matter?
BRABANTIO: My daughter! O, my daughter!
ALL: Dead?
BRABANTIO: Ay, to me.
She is abused, stol'n from me, and corrupted
By spells and medicines bought of mountebanks;
For nature so prepost'rously to err,
Being not deficient,° blind, or lame of sense,
Sans witchcraft could not.
DUKE: Whoe'er he be that in this foul proceeding
Hath thus beguiled your daughter of herself,
And you of her, the bloody book of law
You shall yourself read in the bitter letter
After your own sense; yea, though our proper° son
Stood in your action.°
BRABANTIO: Humbly I thank your grace.
Here is the man—this Moor, whom now, it seems,
Your special mandate for the state affairs
Hath hither brought.
ALL: We are very sorry for't.
DUKE *[to Othello]*: What, in your own part, can you say to this?
BRABANTIO: Nothing, but this is so.
OTHELLO: Most potent, grave, and reverend signiors,
My very noble, and approved° good masters,
That I have ta'en away this old man's daughter,
It is most true; true I have married her.
The very head and front of my offending
Hath this extent, no more. Rude° am I in my speech,
And little blessed with the soft phrase of peace;
For since these arms of mine had seven years' pith°
Till now some nine moons wasted, they have used
Their dearest action in the tented field;
And little of this great world can I speak
More than pertains to feats of broil and battle;
And therefore little shall I grace my cause
In speaking for myself. Yet, by your gracious patience,
I will a round° unvarnished tale deliver
Of my whole course of love—what drugs, what charms,
What conjuration, and what mighty magic
(For such proceeding am I charged withal)
I won his daughter.

63 deficient: Feeble-minded. **69 our proper:** My own. **70 Stood in your action:** Were accused by you. **77 approved:** Tested by experience. **81 Rude:** Unpolished. **83 pith:** Strength. **90 round:** Plain.

BRABANTIO: A maiden never bold;
Of spirit so still and quiet that her motion
Blushed° at herself; and she—in spite of nature,
Of years, of country, credit, everything—
To fall in love with what she feared to look on!
It is a judgment maimed and most imperfect
That will confess perfection so could err
Against all rules of nature, and must be driven
To find out practices° of cunning hell
Why this should be. I therefore vouch° again
That with some mixtures pow'rful o'er the blood,°
Or with some dram, conjured to this effect,
He wrought upon her.

DUKE: To vouch this is no proof,
Without more certain and more overt test
Than these thin habits° and poor likelihoods
Of modern seeming° do prefer against him.

1. SENATOR: But, Othello, speak.
Did you by indirect and forcèd° courses
Subdue and poison this young maid's affections?
Or came it by request, and such fair question°
As soul to soul affordeth?

OTHELLO: I do beseech you,
Send for the lady to the Sagittary
And let her speak of me before her father.
If you do find me foul in her report,
The trust, the office, I do hold of you
Not only take away, but let your sentence
Even fall upon my life.

DUKE: Fetch Desdemona hither.

OTHELLO: Ancient, conduct them; you best know the place.

Exit [Iago, with] two or three [Attendants].

And till she come, as truly as to heaven
I do confess the vices of my blood,
So justly to your grave ears I'll present
How I did thrive in this fair lady's love,
And she in mine.

DUKE: Say it, Othello.

OTHELLO: Her father loved me, oft invited me;
Still° questioned me the story of my life
From year to year—the battles, sieges, fortunes

95–96 her motion Blushed: Her own emotions caused her to blush. **102 practices:** Plots. **103 vouch:** Assert. **104 blood:** Passions. **108 thin habits:** Slight appearances. **109 modern seeming:** Everyday supposition. **111 forcèd:** Violent. **113 question:** Conversation. **129 Still:** Continually.

That I have passed.
I ran it through, even from my boyish days
To th' very moment that he bade me tell it.
Wherein I spoke of most disastrous chances,
Of moving accidents by flood and field;
Of hairbreadth scapes i' th' imminent deadly breach;
Of being taken by the insolent foe
And sold to slavery; of my redemption thence
And portance° in my travels' history;
Wherein of anters° vast and deserts idle,
Rough quarries, rocks, and hills whose heads touch heaven,
It was my hint° to speak — such was the process;
And of the Cannibals that each other eat,
The Anthropophagi,° and men whose heads
Do grow beneath their shoulders. This to hear
Would Desdemona seriously incline;
But still the house affairs would draw her thence;
Which ever as she could with haste dispatch,
She'ld come again, and with a greedy ear
Devour up my discourse. Which I observing,
Took once a pliant° hour, and found good means
To draw from her a prayer of earnest heart
That I would all my pilgrimage dilate,°
Whereof by parcels° she had something heard,
But not intentively.° I did consent,
And often did beguile her of her tears
When I did speak of some distressful stroke
That my youth suffered. My story being done,
She gave me for my pains a world of sighs.
She swore, i' faith, 'twas strange, 'twas passing strange;
'Twas pitiful, 'twas wondrous pitiful.
She wished she had not heard it; yet she wished
That heaven had made her such a man. She thanked me;
And bade me, if I had a friend that loved her,
I should but teach him how to tell my story,
And that would woo her. Upon this hint° I spake.
She loved me for the dangers I had passed,
And I loved her that she did pity them.
This only is the witchcraft I have used.
Here comes the lady. Let her witness it.

Enter Desdemona, Iago, Attendants.

139 portance: Behavior. **140 anters:** Caves. **142 hint:** Occasion. **144 Anthropophagi:** Man-eaters. **151 pliant:** Propitious. **153 dilate:** Recount in full. **154 parcels:** Portions. **155 intentively:** With full attention. **166 hint:** Opportunity.

DUKE: I think this tale would win my daughter too.
Good Brabantio,
Take up this mangled matter at the best.
Men do their broken weapons rather use
Than their bare hands.
BRABANTIO: I pray you hear her speak.
If she confess that she was half the wooer,
Destruction on my head if my bad blame
Light on the man! Come hither, gentle mistress.
Do you perceive in all this noble company
Where most you owe obedience?
DESDEMONA: My noble father,
I do perceive here a divided duty.
To you I am bound for life and education;°
My life and education both do learn me
How to respect you: you are the lord of duty;
I am hitherto your daughter. But here's my husband;
And so much duty as my mother showed
To you, preferring you before her father,
So much I challenge° that I may profess
Due to the Moor my lord.
BRABANTIO: God be with you! I have done.
Please it your grace, on to the state affairs.
I had rather to adopt a child than get° it.
Come hither, Moor.
I here do give thee that with all my heart
Which, but thou hast already, with all my heart
I would keep from thee. For your sake,° jewel,
I am glad at soul I have no other child;
For thy escape° would teach me tyranny,
To hang clogs on them. I have done, my lord.
DUKE: Let me speak like yourself° and lay a sentence°
Which, as a grise° or step, may help these lovers
[Into your favor.]
When remedies are past, the griefs are ended
By seeing the worst, which late on hopes depended.
To mourn a mischief that is past and gone
Is the next way to draw new mischief on.
What cannot be preserved when fortune takes,
Patience her injury a mock'ry makes.
The robbed that smiles steals something from the thief;
He robs himself that spends a bootless grief.

182 education: Upbringing. **188 challenge:** Claim the right. **191 get:** Beget. **195 For your sake:** Because of you. **197 escape:** Escapade. **199 like yourself:** As you should; **sentence:** Maxim. **200 grise:** Step.

BRABANTIO: So let the Turk of Cyprus us beguile:
We lose it not so long as we can smile.
He bears the sentence well that nothing bears
But the free comfort which from thence he hears;
But he bears both the sentence and the sorrow
That to pay grief must of poor patience borrow.
These sentences, to sugar, or to gall,
Being strong on both sides, are equivocal.
But words are words. I never yet did hear
That the bruised heart was piercèd through the ear.
Beseech you, now to the affairs of state.

DUKE: The Turk with a most mighty preparation makes for Cyprus. Othello, the fortitude° of the place is best known to you; and though we have there a substitute of most allowed° sufficiency, yet opinion,° a more sovereign mistress of effects, throws a more safer voice on you. You must therefore be content to slubber° the gloss of your new fortunes with this more stubborn and boist'rous expedition.

OTHELLO: The tyrant custom, most grave senators,
Hath made the flinty and steel couch of war
My thrice-driven bed of down. I do agnize
A natural and prompt alacrity
I find in hardness;° and do undertake
These present wars against the Ottomites.
Most humbly, therefore, bending to your state,
I crave fit disposition for my wife,
Due reference of place, and exhibition,°
With such accommodation and besort°
As levels° with her breeding.

DUKE: If you please,
Be't at her father's.

BRABANTIO: I will not have it so.

OTHELLO: Nor I.

DESDEMONA: Nor I. I would not there reside,
To put my father in impatient thoughts
By being in his eye. Most gracious Duke,
To my unfolding lend your prosperous° ear,
And let me find a charter in your voice,
T' assist my simpleness.°

DUKE: What would you, Desdemona?

DESDEMONA: That I did love the Moor to live with him,

222 fortitude: Fortification. **223 allowed:** Acknowledged; **opinion:** Public opinion. **225 slubber:** Sully. **229–31 agnize . . . hardness:** Recognize in myself a natural and easy response to hardship. **235 exhibition:** Allowance of money. **236 besort:** Suitable company. **237 levels:** Corresponds. **243 prosperous:** Favorable. **245 simpleness:** Lack of skill.

My downright violence, and storm of fortunes,
May trumpet to the world. My heart's subdued
Even to the very quality of my lord.
I saw Othello's visage in his mind,
And to his honors and his valiant parts
Did I my soul and fortunes consecrate.
So that, dear lords, if I be left behind,
A moth of peace, and he go to the war,
The rites for which I love him are bereft me,
And I a heavy interim shall support
By his dear absence. Let me go with him.

OTHELLO: Let her have your voice.
Vouch with me, heaven, I therefore beg it not
To please the palate of my appetite,
Not to comply with heat°—the young affects°
In me defunct—and proper satisfaction;
But to be free and bounteous to her mind;
And heaven defend your good souls that you think
I will your serious and great business scant
When she is with me. No, when light-winged toys
Of feathered Cupid seel° with wanton dullness
My speculative and officed instruments,°
That° my disports corrupt and taint my business,
Let housewives make a skillet of my helm,
And all indign° and base adversities
Make head against my estimation!°

DUKE: Be it as you shall privately determine,
Either for her stay or going. Th' affair cries haste,
And speed must answer it.

1. SENATOR: You must away to-night.

OTHELLO: With all my heart.

DUKE: At nine i' th' morning here we'll meet again.
Othello, leave some officer behind,
And he shall our commission bring to you,
With such things else of quality and respect
As doth import° you.

OTHELLO: So please your grace, my ancient;
A man he is of honesty and trust
To his conveyance I assign my wife,
With what else needful your good grace shall think
To be sent after me.

DUKE: Let it be so.

262 heat: Passions; **young affects:** Tendencies of youth. **268 seel:** Blind. **269 My . . . instruments:** My perceptive and responsible faculties. **270 That:** So that. **272 indign:** Unworthy. **273 estimation:** Reputation. **282 import:** Concern.

Good night to every one.
[To Brabantio.] And, noble signior,
If virtue no delighted° beauty lack,
Your son-in-law is far more fair than black.

1. SENATOR: Adieu, brave Moor. Use Desdemona well.

BRABANTIO: Look to her, Moor, if thou hast eyes to see:
She has deceived her father, and may thee.

Exeunt [Duke, Senators, Officers, &c.].

OTHELLO: My life upon her faith!—Honest Iago,
My Desdemona must I leave to thee.
I prithee let thy wife attend on her,
And bring them after in the best advantage.°
Come, Desdemona. I have but an hour
Of love, of worldly matters and direction,
To spend with thee. We must obey the time.

Exit Moor and Desdemona.

RODERIGO: Iago,—

IAGO: What say'st thou, noble heart?

RODERIGO: What will I do, think'st thou?

IAGO: Why, go to bed and sleep.

RODERIGO: I will incontinently° drown myself.

IAGO: If thou dost, I shall never love thee after. Why, thou silly gentleman!

RODERIGO: It is silliness to live when to live is torment; and then have we a prescription to die when death is our physician.

IAGO: O villainous! I have looked upon the world for four times seven years; and since I could distinguish betwixt a benefit and an injury, I never found man that knew how to love himself. Ere I would say I would drown myself for the love of a guinea hen, I would change my humanity with a baboon.

RODERIGO: What should I do? I confess it is my shame to be so fond, but it is not in my virtue to amend it.

IAGO: Virtue? a fig! 'Tis in ourselves that we are thus or thus. Our bodies are our gardens, to which our wills are gardeners; so that if we will plant nettles or sow lettuce, set hyssop and weed up thyme, supply it with one gender° of herbs or distract it with many—either to have it sterile with idleness or manured with industry—why, the power and corrigible authority° of this lies in our wills. If the balance of our lives had not one scale of reason to poise° another of sensuality, the blood and baseness° of our natures would conduct us to most preposterous conclusions. But we have reason to cool our raging motions,° our carnal strings, our unbitted° lusts; whereof I take this that you call love to be a sect or scion.°

288 delighted: Delightful. **296 in the best advantage:** At the best opportunity. **304 incontinently:** Forthwith. **317 gender:** Species. **318–19 corrigible authority:** Corrective power. **320 poise:** Counterbalance; **blood and baseness:** Animal instincts. **322 motions:** Appetites; **unbitted:** Uncontrolled. **323 sect or scion:** Offshoot, cutting.

RODERIGO: It cannot be.

IAGO: It is merely a lust of the blood and a permission of the will. Come, be a man! Drown thyself? Drown cats and blind puppies! I have professed me thy friend, and I confess me knit to thy deserving with cables of perdurable toughness. I could never better stead thee than now. Put money in thy purse. Follow thou the wars; defeat thy favor° with an usurped beard. I say, put money in thy purse. It cannot be that Desdemona should long continue her love to the Moor—put money in thy purse—nor he his to her. It was a violent commencement in her, and thou shalt see an answerable sequestration°—put but money in thy purse. These Moors are changeable in their wills—fill thy purse with money. The food that to him now is as luscious as locusts shall be to him shortly as bitter as coloquintida.° She must change for youth: when she is sated with his body, she will find the error of her choice. [She must have change, she must.] Therefore put money in thy purse. If thou wilt needs damn thyself, do it a more delicate way than drowning. Make° all the money thou canst. If sanctimony and a frail vow betwixt an erring° barbarian and a supersubtle Venetian be not too hard for my wits and all the tribe of hell, thou shalt enjoy her. Therefore make money. A pox of drowning thyself! 'Tis clean out of the way. Seek thou rather to be hanged in compassing thy joy than to be drowned and go without her.

RODERIGO: Wilt thou be fast to my hopes, if I depend on the issue?

IAGO: Thou art sure of me. Go, make money. I have told thee often, and I retell thee again and again, I hate the Moor. My cause is hearted;° thine hath no less reason. Let us be conjunctive in our revenge against him. If thou canst cuckold him, thou dost thyself a pleasure, me a sport. There are many events in the womb of time, which will be delivered. Traverse,° go, provide thy money! We will have more of this to-morrow. Adieu.

RODERIGO: Where shall we meet i' th' morning?

IAGO: At my lodging.

RODERIGO: I'll be with thee betimes.

IAGO: Go to, farewell—Do you hear, Roderigo?

RODERIGO: What say you?

IAGO: No more of drowning, do you hear?

RODERIGO: I am changed.

IAGO: Go to, farewell. Put money enough in your purse.

RODERIGO: I'll sell all my land. *Exit.*

IAGO: Thus do I ever make my fool my purse;
For I mine own gained knowledge should profane
If I would time expend with such a snipe°
But for my sport and profit. I hate the Moor;

329 defeat thy favor: Spoil thy appearance. **333 sequestration:** Estrangement. **335 coloquintida:** A medicine. **339 Make:** Raise. **340 erring:** Wandering. **347 My cause is hearted:** My heart is in it. **350 Traverse:** Forward march. **363 snipe:** Fool.

And it is thought abroad that 'twixt my sheets
H'as done my office. I know not if't be true;
But I, for mere suspicion in that kind,
Will do as if for surety. He holds me well;°
The better shall my purpose work on him.
Cassio's a proper man. Let me see now:
To get his place, and to plume up° my will
In double knavery—How, how?—Let's see:—
After some time, to abuse Othello's ears
That he is too familiar with his wife.
He hath a person and a smooth dispose°
To be suspected—framed to make women false.
The Moor is of a free° and open nature
That thinks men honest that but seem to be so;
And will as tenderly be led by th' nose
As asses are.
I have't! It is engend'red! Hell and night
Must bring this monstrous birth to the world's light. *Exit.*

[ACT II, Scene I: An open place in Cyprus, near the harbor.]

Enter Montano and two Gentlemen.

MONTANO: What from the cape can you discern at sea?
1. GENTLEMAN: Nothing at all: it is a high-wrought flood.
I cannot 'twixt the heaven and the main
Descry a sail.
MONTANO: Methinks the wind hath spoke aloud at land;
A fuller blast ne'er shook our battlements.
If it hath ruffianed so upon the sea,
What ribs of oak, when mountains melt on them,
Can hold the mortise?° What shall we hear of this?
2. GENTLEMAN: A segregation° of the Turkish fleet.
For do but stand upon the foaming shore,
The chidden billow seems to pelt the clouds;
The wind-shaked surge, with high and monstrous mane,
Seems to cast water on the burning Bear
And quench the Guards° of th' ever-fixèd pole.°
I never did like molestation° view
On the enchafèd flood.
MONTANO: If that the Turkish fleet

368 well: In high regard. **371 plume up:** Gratify. **375 dispose:** Manner. **377 free:** Frank. **ACT II, SCENE I. 9 hold the mortise:** Hold their joints together. **10 segregation:** Scattering. **15 Guards:** Stars near the North Star; **pole:** Polestar. **16 molestation:** Tumult.

Be not ensheltered and embayed, they are drowned;
It is impossible to bear it out.

Enter a third Gentleman.

3. GENTLEMAN: News, lads! Our wars are done.
The desperate tempest hath so banged the Turks
That their designment halts.° A noble ship of Venice
Hath seen a grievous wrack and sufferance°
On most part of their fleet.

MONTANO: How? Is this true?

3. GENTLEMAN: The ship is here put in,
A Veronesa;° Michael Cassio,
Lieutenant to the warlike Moor Othello,
Is come on shore; the Moor himself at sea,
And is in full commission here for Cyprus.

MONTANO: I am glad on't. 'Tis a worthy governor.

3. GENTLEMAN: But his same Cassio, though he speak of comfort
Touching the Turkish loss, yet he looks sadly
And prays the Moor be safe, for they were parted
With foul and violent tempest.

MONTANO: Pray heaven he be;
For I have served him, and the man commands
Like a full soldier. Let's to the seaside, ho!
As well to see the vessel that's come in
As to throw out our eyes for brave Othello,
Even till we make the main and th' aerial blue
An indistinct regard.°

3. GENTLEMAN: Come, let's do so;
For every minute is expectancy
Of more arrivance.

Enter Cassio.

CASSIO: Thanks, you the valiant of this warlike isle,
That so approve the Moor! O, let the heavens
Give him defense against the elements,
For I have lost him on a dangerous sea!

MONTANO: Is he well shipped?

CASSIO: His bark is stoutly timbered, and his pilot
Of very expert and approved allowance;
Therefore my hopes, not surfeited to death,°
Stand in bold cure.°
(Within.) A sail, a sail, a sail! *Enter a messenger.*

CASSIO: What noise?

22 designment halts: Plan is crippled. **23 sufferance:** Disaster. **26 Veronesa:** Ship furnished by Verona. **40 An indistinct regard:** Indistinguishable. **50 surfeited to death:** Overindulged. **51 in bold cure:** A good chance of fulfillment.

MESSENGER: The town is empty; on the brow o' th' sea
Stand ranks of people, and they cry "A sail!"
CASSIO: My hopes do shape him for the governor.

A shot.

2. GENTLEMAN: They do discharge their shot of courtesy:
Our friends at least.
CASSIO: I pray you, sir, go forth
And give us truth who 'tis that is arrived.
2. GENTLEMAN: I shall. *Exit.*
MONTANO: But, good lieutenant, is your general wived?
CASSIO: Most fortunately. He hath achieved a maid
That paragons° description and wild fame;
One that excels the quirks° of blazoning° pens,
And in th' essential vesture of creation
Does tire the ingener.°

Enter Second Gentleman.

How now? Who has put in?
2. GENTLEMAN: 'Tis one Iago, ancient to the general.
CASSIO: H'as had most favorable and happy speed:
Tempests themselves, high seas, and howling winds,
The guttered° rocks and congregated sands,
Traitors ensteeped° to clog the guiltless keel,
As having sense of beauty, do omit
Their mortal° natures, letting go safely by
The divine Desdemona.
MONTANO: What is she?
CASSIO: She that I spake of, our great captain's captain,
Left in the conduct of the bold Iago,
Whose footing° here anticipates our thoughts
A se'nnight's° speed. Great Jove, Othello guard,
And swell his sail with thine own pow'rful breath,
That he may bless this bay with his tall ship,
Make love's quick pants in Desdemona's arms,
Give renewed fire to our extincted spirits,
[And bring all Cyprus comfort!]

Enter Desdemona, Iago, Roderigo, and Emilia [with Attendants].

O, behold!
The riches of the ship is come on shore!
You men of Cyprus, let her have your knees.°

62 paragons: Surpasses. **63 quirks:** Ingenuities; **blazoning:** Describing. **64–65 And . . . ingener:** Merely to describe her as God made her exhausts her praiser. **69 guttered:** Jagged. **70 ensteeped:** Submerged. **72 mortal:** Deadly. **76 footing:** Landing. **77 se'nnight's:** Week's. **84 knees:** I.e., kneeling.

Hail to thee, lady! and the grace of heaven,
Before, behind thee, and on every hand,
Enwheel thee round!

DESDEMONA: I thank you, valiant Cassio.
What tidings can you tell me of my lord?

CASSIO: He is not yet arrived; nor know I aught
But that he's well and will be shortly here.

DESDEMONA: O but I fear! How lost you company?

CASSIO: The great contention of the sea and skies
Parted our fellowship.
(Within.) A sail, a sail! *[A shot.]*
But hark. A sail!

2. GENTLEMAN: They give their greeting to the citadel;
This likewise is a friend.

CASSIO: See for the news.

[Exit Gentleman.]

Good ancient, you are welcome.
[To Emilia.] Welcome, mistress.—
Let it not gall your patience, good Iago,
That I extend my manners. 'Tis my breeding
That gives me this bold show of courtesy.

[Kisses Emilia.°]

IAGO: Sir, would she give you so much of her lips
As of her tongue she oft bestows on me,
You would have enough.

DESDEMONA: Alas, she has no speech!

IAGO: In faith, too much.
I find it still when I have list to sleep.
Marry, before your ladyship, I grant,
She puts her tongue a little in her heart
And chides with thinking.

EMILIA: You have little cause to say so.

IAGO: Come on, come on! You are pictures out of doors,
Bells in your parlors, wildcats in your kitchens,
Saints in your injuries, devils being offended,
Players in your housewifery,° and housewives° in your beds.

DESDEMONA: O, fie upon thee, slanderer!

IAGO: Nay, it is true, or else I am a Turk:
You rise to play, and go to bed to work.

EMILIA: You shall not write my praise.

IAGO: No, let me not.

Kisses Emilia: (Kissing was a common Elizabethan form of social courtesy). **112 housewifery:** Housekeeping; **housewives:** Hussies.

DESDEMONA: What wouldst thou write of me, if thou shouldst praise me?
IAGO: O gentle lady, do not put me to't,
For I am nothing if not critical.
DESDEMONA: Come on, assay.°—There's one gone to the harbor?
IAGO: Ay, madam.
DESDEMONA: I am not merry; but I do beguile
The thing I am by seeming otherwise.—
Come, how wouldst thou praise me?
IAGO: I am about it; but indeed my invention
Comes from my pate as birdlime° does from frieze°—
It plucks out brains and all. But my Muse labors,
And thus she is delivered:
If she be fair and wise, fairness and wit—
The one's for use, the other useth it.
DESDEMONA: Well praised! How if she be black° and witty?
IAGO: If she be black, and thereto have a wit,
She'll find a white that shall her blackness fit.
DESDEMONA: Worse and worse!
EMILIA: How if fair and foolish?
IAGO: She never yet was foolish that was fair,
For even her folly° helped her to an heir.
DESDEMONA: These are old fond° paradoxes to make fools laugh i' th' alehouse.
What miserable praise hast thou for her that's foul° and foolish?
IAGO: There's none so foul, and foolish thereunto,
But does foul pranks which fair and wise ones do.
DESDEMONA: O heavy ignorance! Thou praisest the worst best. But what praise couldst thou bestow on a deserving woman indeed—one that in the authority of her merit did justly put on the vouch° of very malice itself?
IAGO: She that was ever fair, and never proud;
Had tongue at will, and yet was never loud;
Never lacked gold, and yet went never gay;
Fled from her wish, and yet said "Now I may";
She that, being ang'red, her revenge being nigh,
Bade her wrong stay, and her displeasure fly;
She that in wisdom never was so frail
To change the cod's head for the salmon's tail;°
She that could think, and ne'er disclose her mind;
See suitors following, and not look behind:
She was a wight (if ever such wight were)—
DESDEMONA: To do what?
IAGO: To suckle fools and chronicle small beer.°

120 assay: Try. **126 birdlime:** A sticky paste; **frieze:** Rough cloth. **131 black:** Brunette. **137 folly:** Wantonness. **138 fond:** Foolish. **139 foul:** Ugly. **144 put on the vouch:** Compel the approval. **152 To . . . tail:** I.e., to exchange the good for the poor but expensive. **157 chronicle small beer:** Keep petty household accounts.

DESDEMONA: O most lame and impotent conclusion! Do not learn of him, Emilia, though he be thy husband. How say you, Cassio? Is he not a most profane and liberal° counsellor?

CASSIO: He speaks home,° madam. You may relish him more in the soldier than in the scholar.

IAGO *[aside]*: He takes her by the palm. Ay, well said, whisper! With as little a web as this will I ensnare as great a fly as Cassio. Ay, smile upon her, do! I will gyve thee in thine own courtship.°—You say true; 'tis so, indeed!—If such tricks as these strip you out of your lieutenantry, it had been better you had not kissed your three fingers so oft—which now again you are most apt to play the sir° in. Very good! well kissed! an excellent courtesy! 'Tis so, indeed. Yet again your fingers to your lips? Would they were clyster pipes° for your sake! (Trumpet within.)
The Moor! I know his trumpet.

CASSIO: 'Tis truly so.

DESDEMONA: Let's meet him and receive him.

CASSIO: Lo, where he comes.

Enter Othello and Attendants.

OTHELLO: O my fair warrior!

DESDEMONA: My dear Othello!

OTHELLO: It gives me wonder great as my content
To see you here before me. O my soul's joy!
If after every tempest come such calms,
May the winds blow till they have wakened death!
And let the laboring bark climb hills of seas
Olympus-high, and duck again as low
As hell's from heaven! If it were now to die,
'Twere now to be most happy;° for I fear
My soul hath her content so absolute
That not another comfort like to this
Succeeds in unknown fate.

DESDEMONA: The heavens forbid
But that our loves and comforts should increase
Even as our days do grow.

OTHELLO: Amen to that, sweet powers!
I cannot speak enough of this content;
It stops me here; it is too much of joy.
And this, and this, the greatest discords be

They kiss.

That e'er our hearts shall make!

IAGO *[aside]*: O, you are well tuned now!

160 profane and liberal: Worldly and licentious. **161 home:** Bluntly. **165 gyve . . . courtship:** Manacle you by means of your courtly manners. **168 sir:** Courtly gentleman. **169–70 clyster pipes:** Syringes. **183 happy:** Fortunate.

But I'll set down° the pegs that make this music,
As honest as I am.

OTHELLO: Come, let us to the castle.
News, friends! Our wars are done; the Turks are drowned.
How does my old acquaintance of this isle?—
Honey, you shall be well desired° in Cyprus;
I have found great love amongst them. O my sweet,
I prattle out of fashion, and I dote
In mine own comforts. I prithee, good Iago,
Go to the bay and disembark my coffers.
Bring thou the master° to the citadel;
He is a good one, and his worthiness
Does challenge° much respect.—Come, Desdemona,
Once more well met at Cyprus.

Exit Othello [with all but Iago and Roderigo].

IAGO *[to an Attendant, who goes out]*: Do thou meet me presently at the harbor. *[To Roderigo.]* Come hither. If thou be'st valiant (as they say base men being in love have then a nobility in their natures more than is native to them), list me. The lieutenant to-night watches on the court of guard.° First, I must tell thee this: Desdemona is directly in love with him.

RODERIGO: With him? Why, 'tis not possible.

IAGO: Lay thy finger thus,° and let thy soul be instructed. Mark me with what violence she first loved the Moor, but for bragging and telling her fantastical lies; and will she love him still for prating? Let not thy discreet heart think it. Her eye must be fed; and what delight shall she have to look on the devil? When the blood is made dull with the act of sport, there should be, again to inflame it and to give satiety a fresh appetite, loveliness in favor, sympathy in years, manners, and beauties; all which the Moor is defective in. Now for want of these required conveniences,° her delicate tenderness will find itself abused, begin to heave the gorge,° disrelish and abhor the Moor. Very nature will instruct her in it and compel her to some second choice. Now, sir, this granted—as it is a most pregnant° and unforced position—who stands so eminent in the degree of this fortune as Cassio does? A knave very voluble; no further conscionable° than in putting on the mere form of civil and humane° seeming for the better compassing of his salt° and most hidden loose affection? Why, none! why, none! A slipper° and subtle knave; a finder-out of occasions; that has an eye can stamp and counterfeit advantages, though true advantage never present itself; a devilish knave! Besides, the knave is handsome, young, and hath all those requisites in him that folly

193 set down: Loosen. **197 well desired:** Warmly welcomed. **202 master:** Ship captain. **204 challenge:** Deserve. **209 court of guard:** Headquarters. **212 thus:** I.e., on your lips. **219 conveniences:** Compatibilities. **220 heave the gorge:** Be nauseated. **222 pregnant:** Evident. **224 conscionable:** Conscientious. **225 humane:** Polite. **226 salt:** Lecherous. **227 slipper:** Slippery.

and green minds look after. A pestilent complete knave! and the woman hath found him already.

RODERIGO: I cannot believe that in her; she's full of most blessed condition.°

IAGO: Blessed fig's-end! The wine she drinks is made of grapes. If she had been blessed, she would never have loved the Moor. Blessed pudding! Didst thou not see her paddle with the palm of his hand? Didst not mark that?

RODERIGO: Yes, that I did; but that was but courtesy.

IAGO: Lechery, by this hand! an index and obscure prologue to the history of lust and foul thoughts. They met so near with their lips that their breaths embraced together. Villainous thoughts, Roderigo! When these mutualities° so marshal the way, hard at hand comes the master and main exercise, th' incorporate° conclusion. Pish! But, sir, be you ruled by me: I have brought you from Venice. Watch you to-night; for the command, I'll lay't upon you. Cassio knows you not. I'll not be far from you: do you find some occasion to anger Cassio, either by speaking too loud, or tainting° his discipline, or from what other course you please which the time shall more favorably minister.

RODERIGO: Well.

IAGO: Sir, he's rash and very sudden in choler,° and haply with his truncheon may strike at you. Provoke him that he may; for even out of that will I cause these of Cyprus to mutiny; whose qualification° shall come into no true taste° again but by the displanting of Cassio. So shall you have a shorter journey to your desires by the means I shall then have to prefer° them; and the impediment most profitably removed with-out the which there were no expectation of our prosperity.

RODERIGO: I will do this if you can bring it to any opportunity.

IAGO: I warrant thee. Meet me by and by at the citadel; I must fetch his necessaries ashore. Farewell.

RODERIGO: Adieu. *Exit.*

IAGO: That Cassio loves her, I do well believe't;
That she loves him, 'tis apt° and of great credit.
The Moor, howbeit that I endure him not,
Is of a constant, loving, noble nature,
And I dare think he'll prove to Desdemona
A most dear husband. Now I do love her too;
Not out of absolute lust, though peradventure
I stand accountant° for as great a sin,
But partly led to diet° my revenge,
For that I do suspect the lusty Moor
Hath leaped into my seat; the thought whereof
Doth, like a poisonous mineral, gnaw my inwards;

232 condition: Character. **239–240 mutualities:** Exchanges. **241 incorporate:** Carnal. **244 tainting:** Discrediting. **248 sudden in choler:** Violent in anger. **250 qualification:** Appeasement. **251 true taste:** Satisfactory state. **252 prefer:** Advance. **260 apt:** Probable. **266 accountant:** Accountable. **267 diet:** Feed.

And nothing can or shall content my soul
Till I am evened with him, wife for wife;
Or failing so, yet that I put the Moor
At least into a jealousy so strong
That judgment cannot cure. Which thing to do,
If this poor trash of Venice, whom I trash°
For° his quick hunting, stand the putting on,°
I'll have our Michael Cassio on the hip,°
Abuse him to the Moor in the rank garb°
(For I fear Cassio with my nightcap too),
Make the Moor thank me, love me, and reward me
For making him egregiously an ass
And practicing upon° his peace and quiet
Even to madness. 'Tis here, but yet confused:
Knavery's plain face is never seen till used. *Exit.*

[Scene II: A street in Cyprus.]

Enter Othello's Herald, with a proclamation.

HERALD: It is Othello's pleasure, our noble and valiant general, that, upon certain tidings now arrived, importing the mere perdition° of the Turkish fleet, every man put himself into triumph; some to dance, some to make bonfires, each man to what sport and revels his addiction leads him. For, besides these beneficial news, it is the celebration of his nuptial. So much was his pleasure should be proclaimed. All offices° are open, and there is full liberty of feasting from the present hour of five till the bell have told eleven. Heaven bless the isle of Cyprus and our noble general Othello! *Exit.*

[Scene III: The Cyprian Castle.]

Enter Othello, Desdemona, Cassio, and Attendants.

OTHELLO: Good Michael, look you to the guard to-night.
Let's teach ourselves that honorable stop,
Not to outsport discretion.
CASSIO: Iago hath direction what to do;
But not withstanding, with my personal eye
Will I look to't.
OTHELLO: Iago is most honest.
Michael, good night. To-morrow with your earliest
Let me have speech with you.

276 I trash: I weight down (in order to keep under control). **277 For:** In order to develop; **stand the putting on:** Responds to my inciting. **278 on the hip:** At my mercy. **279 rank garb:** Gross manner. **283 practicing upon:** Plotting against. **Scene II. 2 mere perdition:** Complete destruction. **6 offices:** Kitchens and storerooms.

[To Desdemona.] Come, my dear love.
The purchase made, the fruits are to ensue;
That profit's yet to come 'tween me and you.—
Good night.

Exit [Othello with Desdemona and Attendants].

Enter Iago.

CASSIO: Welcome, Iago. We must to the watch.

IAGO: Not this hour, lieutenant; 'tis not yet ten o' th' clock. Our general cast° us thus early for the love of his Desdemona; who let us not therefore blame. He hath not yet made wanton the night with her, and she is sport for Jove.

CASSIO: She's a most exquisite lady.

IAGO: And, I'll warrant her, full of game.

CASSIO: Indeed, she's a most fresh and delicate creature.

IAGO: What an eye she has! Methinks it sounds a parley to provocation.

CASSIO: An inviting eye; and yet methinks right modest.

IAGO: And when she speaks, is it not an alarum to love?

CASSIO: She is indeed perfection.

IAGO: Well, happiness to their sheets! Come, lieutenant, I have a stoup° of wine, and here without are a brace of Cyprus gallants that would fain have a measure to the health of black Othello.

CASSIO: Not to-night, good Iago. I have very poor and unhappy brains for drinking; I could well wish courtesy would invent some other custom of entertainment.

IAGO: O, they are our friends. But one cup! I'll drink for you.

CASSIO: I have drunk but one cup to-night, and that was craftily qualified° too; and behold what innovation° it makes here. I am unfortunate in the infirmity and dare not task my weakness with any more.

IAGO: What, man! 'Tis a night of revels: the gallants desire it.

CASSIO: Where are they?

IAGO: Here at the door; I pray you call them in.

CASSIO: I'll do't, but it dislikes me. *Exit.*

IAGO: If I can fasten but one cup upon him
With that which he hath drunk to-night already,
He'll be as full of quarrel and offense
As my young mistress' dog. Now my sick fool Roderigo,
Whom love hath turned almost the wrong side out,
To Desdemona hath to-night caroused
Potations pottle-deep;° and he's to watch.
Three lads of Cyprus—noble swelling spirits,
That hold their honors in a wary distance,°
The very elements° of this warlike isle—

SCENE III. 14 cast: Dismissed. **24 stoup:** Two-quart tankard. **31 qualified:** Diluted. **32 innovation:** Disturbance. **44 pottle-deep:** Bottoms up. **46 That . . . distance:** Very sensitive about their honor. **47 very elements:** True representatives.

Have I to-night flustered with flowing cups,
And they watch too. Now, 'mongst this flock of drunkards
Am I to put our Cassio in some action
That may offend the isle.

Enter Cassio, Montano, and Gentlemen [; Servants following with wine].

But here they come.
If consequence do but approve my dream,
My boat sails freely, both with wind and stream.

CASSIO: 'Fore God, they have given me a rouse° already.

MONTANO: Good faith, a little one; not past a pint, as I am a soldier.

IAGO: Some wine, ho!

[Sings.] And let me the canakin clink, clink;
And let me the canakin clink
A soldier's a man;
A life's but a span,
Why then, let a soldier drink.

Some wine, boys!

CASSIO: 'Fore God, an excellent song!

IAGO: I learned it in England, where indeed they are most potent in potting. Your Dane, your German, and your swag-bellied Hollander — Drink, ho! — are nothing to your English.

CASSIO: Is your Englishman so expert in his drinking?

IAGO: Why, he drinks you with facility your Dane dead drunk; he sweats not to overthrow your Almain; he gives your Hollander a vomit ere the next pottle can be filled.

CASSIO: To the health of our general!

MONTANO: I am for it, lieutenant, and I'll do you justice.

IAGO: O sweet England!

[Sings.] King Stephen was a worthy peer;
His breeches cost him but a crown;
He held 'em sixpence all too dear,
With that he called the tailor lown.°
He was a wight of high renown,
And thou art but of low degree.
'Tis pride that pulls the country down;
Then take thine auld cloak about thee.

Some wine, ho!

CASSIO: 'Fore God, this is a more exquisite song than the other.

IAGO: Will you hear't again?

CASSIO: No, for I hold him to be unworthy of his place that does those things.° Well, God's above all; and there be souls must be saved, and there be souls must not be saved.

IAGO: It's true, good lieutenant.

54 rouse: Bumper. **77 lown:** Rascal. **85 does . . . things:** I.e., behaves in this fashion.

CASSIO: For mine own part — no offense to the general, nor any man of quality — I hope to be saved.

IAGO: And so do I too, lieutenant.

CASSIO: Ay, but, by your leave, not before me. The lieutenant is to be saved before the ancient. Let's have no more of this; let's to our affairs. — God forgive us our sins! — Gentlemen, let's look to our business. Do not think, gentlemen, I am drunk. This is my ancient; this is my right hand, and this is my left. I am not drunk now. I can stand well enough, and I speak well enough.

ALL: Excellent well!

CASSIO: Why, very well then. You must not think then that I am drunk.

Exit.

MONTANO: To th' platform, masters. Come, let's set the watch.

IAGO: You see this fellow that is gone before.
He's a soldier fit to stand by Caesar
And give direction; and do but see his vice.
'Tis to his virtue a just equinox,°
The one as long as th' other. 'Tis pity of him.
I fear the trust Othello puts him in,
On some odd time of his infirmity,
Will shake this island.

MONTANO: But is he often thus?

IAGO: 'Tis evermore his prologue to his sleep:
He'll watch the horologe a double set°
If drink rock not his cradle.

MONTANO: It were well
The general were put in mind of it.
Perhaps he sees it not, or his good nature
Prizes the virtue that appears in Cassio
And looks not on his evils. Is not this true?

Enter Roderigo.

IAGO *[aside to him]: How now, Roderigo?*
I pray you after the lieutenant, go! *Exit Roderigo.*

MONTANO: And 'tis great pity that the noble Moor
Should hazard such a place as his own second
With one of an ingraft° infirmity.
It were an honest action to say
So to the Moor.

IAGO: Not I, for this fair island!
I do love Cassio well and would do much
To cure him of this evil.
(Within.) Help! help!
But hark! What noise?

103 just equinox: Exact equivalent. **109 watch . . . set:** Stay awake twice around the clock. **119 ingraft:** I.e., ingrained.

Enter Cassio, driving in Roderigo.

CASSIO: Zounds, you rogue! you rascal!
MONTANO: What's the matter, lieutenant?
CASSIO: A knave to teach me my duty?
I'll beat the knave into a twiggen° bottle.
RODERIGO: Beat me?
CASSIO: Dost thou prate, rogue? *[Strikes him.]*
MONTANO: Nay, good lieutenant!
[Stays him.]
I pray you, sir, hold your hand.
CASSIO: Let me go, sir,
Or I'll knock you o'er the mazzard.°
MONTANO: Come, come, you're drunk!
CASSIO: Drunk?

They fight.

IAGO *[aside to Roderigo]*: Away, I say! Go out and cry a mutiny!
Exit Roderigo.
Nay, good lieutenant. God's will, gentlemen!
Help, ho!—lieutenant—sir—Montano—sir—
Help, masters!—Here's a goodly watch indeed!
A bell rung.
Who's that which rings the bell? Diablo, ho!
The town will rise.° God's will, lieutenant, hold!
You'll be shamed for ever.

Enter Othello and Gentlemen with weapons.

OTHELLO: What is the matter here?
MONTANO: Zounds, I bleed still. I am hurt to th' death.
He dies!
OTHELLO: Hold for your lives!
IAGO: Hold, hold! Lieutenant—sir—Montano—gentlemen!
Have you forgot all sense of place and duty?
Hold! The general speaks to you. Hold, for shame!
OTHELLO: Why, how now ho? From whence ariseth this?
Are we turned Turks, and to ourselves do that
Which heaven hath forbid the Ottomites?
For Christian shame put by this barbarous brawl!
He that stirs next to carve for° his own rage.
Holds his soul light; he dies upon his motion.
Silence that dreadful bell! It frights the isle
From her propriety.° What is the matter, masters?
Honest Iago, that looks dead with grieving,

127 twiggen: Wicker-covered. **130 mazzard:** Head. **137 rise:** Grow riotous. **149 carve for:** Indulge. **152 propriety:** Proper self.

Speak. Who began this? On thy love, I charge thee.
IAGO: I do not know. Friends all, but now, even now,
In quarter,° and in terms like bride and groom
Devesting them for bed; and then, but now —
As if some planet had unwitted men —
Swords out, and tilting one at other's breast
In opposition bloody. I cannot speak
Any beginning to this peevish odds,°
And would in action glorious I had lost
Those legs that brought me to a part of it!
OTHELLO: How comes it, Michael, you are thus forgot?
CASSIO: I pray you pardon me; I cannot speak.
OTHELLO: Worthy Montano, you were wont to be civil;
The gravity and stillness of your youth
The world hath noted, and your name is great
In months of wisest censure.° What's the matter
That you unlace° your reputation thus
And spend your rich opinion° for the name
Of a night-brawler? Give me answer to it.
MONTANO: Worthy Othello, I am hurt to danger.
Your officer, Iago, can inform you,
While I spare speech, which something now offends° me,
Of all that I do know; nor know I aught
By me that's said or done amiss this night,
Unless self-charity be sometimes a vice,
And to defend ourselves it be a sin
When violence assails us.
OTHELLO: Now, by heaven,
My blood° begins my safer guides to rule,
And passion, having my best judgment collied,°
Assays° to lead the way. If I once stir
Or do but lift this arm, the best of you
Shall sink in my rebuke. Give me to know
How this foul rout began, who set it on;
And he that is approved in° this offense,
Though he had twinned with me, both at a birth,
Shall lose me. What! in a town of war,
Yet wild, the people's hearts brimful of fear,
To manage° private and domestic quarrel?
In night, and on the court and guard of safety?
'Tis monstrous. Iago, who began't?

156 quarter: Friendliness. **161 peevish odds:** Childish quarrel. **169 censure:** Judgment. **170 unlace:** Undo. **171 rich opinion:** High reputation. **175 offends:** Pains. **181 blood:** Passion. **182 collied:** Darkened. **183 Assays:** Tries. **187 approved in:** Proved guilty of. **191 manage:** Carry on.

MONTANO: If partially affined, or leagued in office,°
Thou dost deliver more or less than truth,
Thou art no soldier.

IAGO: Touch me not so near.
I had rather have this tongue cut from my mouth
Than it should do offense to Michael Cassio;
Yet I persuade myself, to speak the truth
Shall nothing wrong him. This it is, general.
Montano and myself being in speech,
There comes a fellow crying out for help,
And Cassio following him with determined sword
To execute° upon him. Sir, this gentleman
Steps in to Cassio and entreats his pause.
Myself the crying fellow did pursue,
Lest by his clamor—as it so fell out—
The town might fall in fright. He, swift of foot,
Outran my purpose; and I returned then rather
For that I heard the clink and fall of swords,
And Cassio high in oath;° which till to-night
I ne'er might say before. When I came back—
For this was brief—I found them close together
At blow and thrust, even as again they were
When you yourself did part them.
More of this matter cannot I report;
But men are men; the best sometimes forget.
Though Cassio did some little wrong to him,
As men in rage strike those that wish them best,
Yet surely Cassio I believe received
From him that fled some strange indignity,
Which patience could not pass.°

OTHELLO: I know, Iago,
Thy honesty and love doth mince this matter,
Making it light to Cassio. Cassio, I love thee;
But never more be officer of mine.

Enter Desdemona, attended.

Look if my gentle love be not raised up!
I'll make thee an example.

DESDEMONA: What's the matter?

OTHELLO: All's well now, sweeting; come away to bed.
[To Montano.]
Sir, for your hurts, myself will be your surgeon.
Lead him off.

194 partially . . . office: Prejudiced by comradeship or official relations. **204 execute:** Work his will. **211 high in oath:** Cursing. **222 pass:** Pass over, ignore.

[Montano is led off.]

Iago, look with care about the town
And silence those whom this vile brawl distracted.°
Come, Desdemona; 'tis the soldiers' life
To have their balmy slumbers waked with strife.

Exit [with all but Iago and Cassio].

IAGO: What, are you hurt, lieutenant?

CASSIO: Ay, past all surgery.

IAGO: Marry, God forbid!

CASSIO: Reputation, reputation, reputation! O, I have lost my reputation! I have lost the immortal part of myself, and what remains is bestial. My reputation, Iago, my reputation!

IAGO: As I am an honest man, I thought you had received some bodily wound. There is more sense in that than in reputation. Reputation is an idle and most false imposition; oft got without merit and lost without deserving. You have lost no reputation at all unless you repute yourself such a loser. What, man! there are ways to recover° the general again. You are but now cast in his mood°—a punishment more in policy than in malice, even so as one would beat his offenseless dog to affright an imperious lion. Sue to him again, and he's yours.

CASSIO: I will rather sue to be despised than to deceive so good a commander with so slight, so drunken, and so indiscreet an officer. Drunk! and speak parrot!° and squabble! swagger! swear! and discourse fustian° with one's own shadow! O thou invisible spirit of wine, if thou hast no name to be known by, let us call thee devil!

IAGO: What was he that you followed with your sword? What had he done to you?

CASSIO: I know not.

IAGO: Is't possible?

CASSIO: I remember a mass of things, but nothing distinctly; a quarrel, but nothing wherefore. O God, that men should put an enemy in their mouths to steal away their brains! that we should with joy, pleasance, revel, and applause° transform ourselves into beasts!

IAGO: Why, but you are now well enough. How came you thus recovered?

CASSIO: It hath pleased the devil drunkenness to give place to the devil wrath. One unperfectness shows me another, to make me frankly despise myself.

IAGO: Come, you are too severe a moraler. As the time, the place, and the condition of this country stands, I could heartily wish this had not so befall'n; but since it is as it is, mend it for your own good.

CASSIO: I will ask him for my place again: he shall tell me I am a drunkard! Had I as many mouths as Hydra,° such an answer would stop them all. To be now a

232 distracted: Excited. **245 recover:** Regain favor with. **246 in his mood:** Dismissed because of his anger. **251 parrot:** Meaningless phrases. **fustian:** Bombastic nonsense. **261 applause:** Desire to please. **269 Hydra:** Monster with many heads.

sensible man, by and by a fool, and presently a beast! O strange! Every inordinate cup is unblest, and the ingredient° is a devil.

IAGO: Come, come, good wine is a good familiar creature if it be well used. Exclaim no more against it. And, good lieutenant, I think you think I love you.

CASSIO: I have well approved° it, sir. I drunk!

IAGO: You or any man living may be drunk at some time, man. I'll tell you what you shall do. Our general's wife is now the general. I may say so in this respect, for that he hath devoted and given up himself to the contemplation, mark, and denotement of her parts and graces. Confess yourself freely to her; importune her help to put you in your place again. She is of so free,° so kind, so apt, so blessed a disposition she holds it a vice in her goodness not to do more than she is requested. This broken joint between you and her husband entreat her to splinter;° and my fortunes against any lay° worth naming, this crack of your love shall grow stronger than it was before.

CASSIO: You advise me well.

IAGO: I protest, in the sincerity of love and honest kindness.

CASSIO: I think it freely; and betimes in the morning will I beseech the virtuous Desdemona to undertake for me. I am desperate of my fortunes if they check me here.

IAGO: You are in the right. Good night, lieutenant; I must to the watch.

CASSIO: Good night, honest Iago. *Exit Cassio.*

IAGO: And what's he then that says I play the villain,
When this advice is free I give and honest,
Probal° to thinking, and indeed the course
To win the Moor again? For 'tis most easy
Th' inclining Desdemona to subdue°
In an honest suit; she's framed as fruitful
As the free elements. And then for her
To win the Moor—were't to renounce his baptism,
All seals and symbols of redeemèd sin—
His soul is so enfettered to her love
That she may make, unmake, do what she list,
Even as her appetite shall play the god
With his weak function. How am I then a villain
To counsel Cassio to this parallel° course,
Directly to his good? Divinity° of hell!
When devils will the blackest sins put on,°
They do suggest at first with heavenly shows,
As I do now. For whiles this honest fool
Plies Desdemona to repair his fortunes,

271 ingredient: Contents. **275 approved:** Proved. **281 free:** Bounteous. **283 splinter:** Bind up with splints. **lay:** Wager. **295 Probal:** Probable. **297 subdue:** Persuade. **306 parallel:** Corresponding. **307 Divinity:** Theology. **308 put on:** Incite.

And she for him pleads strongly to the Moor,
I'll pour this pestilence into his ear,
That she repeals him° for her body's lust;
And by how much she strives to do him good,
She shall undo her credit with the Moor.
So will I turn her virtue into pitch,
And out of her own goodness make the net
That shall enmesh them all.

Enter Roderigo.

How, now, Roderigo?

RODERIGO: I do follow here in the chase, not like a hound that hunts, but one that fills up the cry.° My money is almost spent; I have been to-night exceedingly well cudgelled; and I think the issue will be—I shall have so much experience for my pains; and so, with no money at all, and a little more wit, return again to Venice.

IAGO: How poor are they that have not patience!
What wound did ever heal but by degrees?
Thou know'st we work by wit, and not by witchcraft;
And wit depends on dilatory time.
Does't not go well? Cassio hath beaten thee,
And thou by that small hurt hast cashiered Cassio.°
Though other things grow fair against the sun,
Yet fruits that blossom first will first be ripe.
Content thyself awhile. By the mass, 'tis morning!
Pleasure and action make the hours seem short.
Retire thee; go where thou art billeted.
Away, I say! Thou shalt know more hereafter.
Nay, get thee gone! *Exit Roderigo.*
Two things are to be done:
My wife must move for Cassio to her mistress;
I'll set her on;
Myself the while to draw the Moor apart
And bring him jump° when he may Cassio find
Soliciting his wife. Ay, that's the way!
Dull no device by coldness and delay. *Exit.*

[ACT III, Scene I: Before the chamber of Othello and Desdemona.]

Enter Cassio, with Musicians and the Clown.

CASSIO: Masters, play here, I will content° your pains:
Something that's brief; and bid "Good morrow, general."

314 repeals him: Seeks his recall. **321 cry:** Pack. **330 cashiered Cassio:** Maneuvered Cassio's discharge. **341 jump:** At the exact moment. **ACT III, SCENE I. 1 content:** Reward.

[They play.]

CLOWN: Why, masters, ha' your instruments been in Naples,° that they speak i' th' nose thus?

MUSICIAN: How, sir, how?

CLOWN: Are these, I pray you, called wind instruments?

MUSICIAN: Ay, marry, are they, sir.

CLOWN: O, thereby hangs a tail.

MUSICIAN: Whereby hangs a tail, sir?

CLOWN: Marry, sir, by many a wind instrument that I know. But, masters, here's money for you; and the general so likes your music that he desires you, for love's sake, to make no more noise with it.

MUSICIAN: Well, sir, we will not.

CLOWN: If you have any music that may not be heard, to't again: but, as they say, to hear music the general does not greatly care.

MUSICIAN: We have none such, sir.

CLOWN: Then put up your pipes in your bag, for I'll away. Go, vanish into air, away! *Exit Musician [with his fellows].*

CASSIO: Dost thou hear, my honest friend?

CLOWN: No, I hear not your honest friend. I hear you.

CASSIO: Prithee keep up thy quillets.° There's a poor piece of gold for thee. If the gentlewoman that attends the general's wife be stirring, tell her there's one Cassio entreats her a little favor of speech. Wilt thou do this?

CLOWN: She is stirring sir. If she will stir hither, I shall seem to notify unto her.

CASSIO: [Do, good my friend.] *Exit Clown.*

Enter Iago.

In happy time,° Iago.

IAGO: You have not been abed then?

CASSIO: Why, no; the day had broke
Before we parted. I have made bold, Iago,
To send in to your wife: my suit to her
Is that she will to virtuous Desdemona
Procure me some access.

IAGO: I'll send her to you presently;
And I'll devise a mean to draw the Moor
Out of the way, that your converse and business
May be more free.

CASSIO: I humbly thank you for't. *Exit [Iago].*
I never knew
A Florentine° more kind and honest.

Enter Emilia.

EMILIA: Good morrow, good lieutenant. I am sorry

3 Naples: (Notorious for its association with venereal disease). **21 quillets:** Quips. **25 In happy time:** Well met. **36 Florentine:** I.e., even a Florentine (like Cassio; Iago was a Venetian).

For your displeasure: but all will sure be well.
The general and his wife are talking of it,
And she speaks for you stoutly. The Moor replied
That he you hurt is of great fame in Cyprus
And great affinity,° and that in wholesome wisdom
He might not but refuse you; but he protests he loves you,
And needs no other suitor but his likings
[To take the safest occasion° by the front°]
To bring you in again.

CASSIO: Yet I beseech you,
If you think fit, or that it may be done,
Give me advantage of some brief discourse
With Desdemona alone.

EMILIA: Pray you come in.
I will bestow you where you shall have time
To speak your bosom° freely.

CASSIO: I am much bound to you. *Exeunt.*

[Scene II: The castle.]

Enter Othello, Iago, and Gentlemen.

OTHELLO: These letters give, Iago, to the pilot
And by him do my duties to the Senate.
That done, I will be walking on the works;°
Repair there to me.

IAGO: Well, my good lord, I'll do't.

OTHELLO: This fortification, gentlemen, shall we see't?

GENTLEMEN: We'll wait upon your lordship. *Exeunt.*

[Scene III: The castle grounds.]

Enter Desdemona, Cassio, and Emilia.

DESDEMONA: Be thou assured, good Cassio, I will do
All my abilities in thy behalf.

EMILIA: Good madam, do. I warrant it grieves my husband
As if the cause were his.

DESDEMONA: O, that's an honest fellow. Do not doubt, Cassio,
But I will have my lord and you again
As friendly as you were.

CASSIO: Bounteous madam,
Whatever shall become of Michael Cassio,
He's never anything but your true servant.

DESDEMONA: I know't; I thank you. You do love my lord;

42 affinity: Family connections. **45 occasion:** Opportunity; **front:** Forelock. **51 your bosom:** Your inmost thoughts. **Scene II. 3 works:** Fortifications.

You have known him long; and be you well assured
He shall in strangeness° stand no farther off
Than in a politic distance.°

CASSIO: Ay, but, lady,
That policy may either last so long,
Or feed upon such nice and waterish diet,°
Or breed itself so out of circumstance,
That, I being absent, and my place supplied,
My general will forget my love and service.

DESDEMONA: Do not doubt° that; before Emilia here
I give thee warrant of thy place. Assure thee,
If I do vow a friendship, I'll perform it
To the last article. My lord shall never rest;
I'll watch him tame° and talk him out of patience;
His bed shall seem a school, his board a shrift;°
I'll intermingle everything he does
With Cassio's suit. Therefore be merry, Cassio,
For thy solicitor shall rather die
Than give thy cause away.

Enter Othello and Iago [at a distance].

EMILIA: Madam, here comes my lord.

CASSIO: Madam, I'll take my leave.

DESDEMONA: Why, stay, and hear me speak.

CASSIO: Madam, not now: I am very ill at ease,
Unfit for mine own purposes.

DESDEMONA: Well, do your discretion. *Exit Cassio.*

IAGO: Ha! I like not that.

OTHELLO: What dost thou say?

IAGO: Nothing, my lord; or if—I know not what.

OTHELLO: Was not that Cassio parted from my wife?

IAGO: Cassio, my lord? No, sure, I cannot think it,
That he would steal away so guilty-like,
Seeing your coming.

OTHELLO: I do believe 'twas he.

DESDEMONA: How now, my lord?
I have been talking with a suitor here,
A man that languishes in your displeasure.

OTHELLO: What is't you mean?

DESDEMONA: Why, your lieutenant, Cassio. Good my lord,
If I have any grace or power to move you,
His present° reconciliation take;
For if he be not one that truly loves you,

SCENE III. 12 strangeness: Aloofness. **13 Than . . . distance:** Than wise policy requires. **15 Or . . . diet:** Or be continued for such slight reasons. **19 doubt:** Fear. **23 watch him tame:** Keep him awake until he gives in. **24 shrift:** Confessional. **47 present:** Immediate.

That errs in ignorance, and not in cunning,
I have no judgment in an honest face,
I prithee call him back.

OTHELLO: Went he hence now?

DESDEMONA: Yes, faith; so humbled
That he hath left part of his grief with me
To suffer with him. Good love, call him back.

OTHELLO: Not now, sweet Desdemon; some other time.

DESDEMONA: But shall't be shortly?

OTHELLO: The sooner, sweet, for you.

DESDEMONA: Shall't be to-night at supper?

OTHELLO: No, not to-night.

DESDEMONA: To-morrow dinner then?

OTHELLO: I shall not dine at home;
I meet the captains at the citadel.

DESDEMONA: Why then, to-morrow night, or Tuesday morn,
On Tuesday noon or night, or Wednesday morn.
I prithee name the time, but let it not
Exceed three days. I' faith, he's penitent;
And yet his trespass, in our common reason
(Save that, they say, the wars must make examples
Out of their best), is not almost° a fault
T' incur a private check.° When shall he come?
Tell me, Othello. I wonder in my soul
What you could ask me that I should deny
Or stand so mamm'ring on.° What? Michael Cassio,
That came a-wooing with you, and so many a time,
When I have spoke of you dispraisingly,
Hath ta'en your part—to have so much to do
To bring him in? By'r Lady, I could do much—

OTHELLO: Prithee no more. Let him come when he will!
I will deny thee nothing.

DESDEMONA: Why, this is not a boon;
'Tis as I should entreat you wear your gloves,
Or feed on nourishing dishes, or keep you warm,
Or sue to you to do a peculiar profit
To your own person. Nay, when I have a suit
Wherein I mean to touch your love indeed,
It shall be full of poise and difficult weight,
And fearful° to be granted.

OTHELLO: I will deny thee nothing!
Whereon I do beseech thee grant me this,
To leave me but a little to myself.

66 not almost: Hardly. **67 a private check:** Even a private reprimand. **70 mamm'ring on:** Hesitating about. **83 fearful:** Dangerous.

DESDEMONA: Shall I deny you? No. Farewell, my lord.
OTHELLO: Farewell, my Desdemon: I'll come to thee straight.
DESDEMONA: Emilia, come.—Be as your fancies teach you;
Whate'er you be, I am obedient. *Exit [with Emilia].*
OTHELLO: Excellent wretch!° Perdition catch my soul
But I do love thee! and when I love thee not,
Chaos is come again.
IAGO: My noble lord—
OTHELLO: What dost thou say, Iago?
IAGO: Did Michael Cassio, when you wooed my lady,
Know of your love?
OTHELLO: He did, from first to last. Why dost thou ask?
IAGO: But for a satisfaction of my thought;
No further harm.
OTHELLO: Why of thy thought, Iago?
IAGO: I did not think he had been acquainted with her.
OTHELLO: O, yes, and went between us° very oft.
IAGO: Indeed?
OTHELLO: Indeed? Ay, indeed! Discern'st thou aught in that?
Is he not honest?
IAGO: Honest, my lord?
OTHELLO: Honest. Ay, honest.
IAGO: My lord, for aught I know.
OTHELLO: What dost thou think?
IAGO: Think, my lord?
OTHELLO: Think, my lord?
By heaven, he echoes me,
As if there were some monster in his thought
Too hideous to be shown. Thou dost mean something:
I heard thee say even now, thou lik'st not that,
When Cassio left my wife. What didst not like?
And when I told thee he was of my counsel
In my whole course of wooing, thou cried'st "Indeed?"
And didst contract and purse thy brow together,
As if thou then hadst shut up in thy brain
Some horrible conceit.° If thou dost love me,
Show me thy thought
IAGO: My lord, you know I love you.
OTHELLO: I think thou dost;
And, for I know thou'rt full of love and honesty
And weigh'st thy words before thou giv'st them breath,
Therefore these stops of thine fright me the more;
For such things in a false disloyal knave

90 wretch: (A term of endearment). **100 went . . . us:** (I.e., as messenger). **115 conceit:** Fancy.

Are tricks of custom; but in a man that's just
They are close dilations, working from the heart
That passion cannot rule.°

IAGO: For Michael Cassio,
I dare be sworn I think that he is honest.

OTHELLO: I think so too.

IAGO: Men should be what they seem;
Or those that be not, would they might seem none!°

OTHELLO: Certain, men should be what they seem.

IAGO: Why then, I think Cassio's an honest man.

OTHELLO: Nay, yet there's more in this.
I prithee speak to me as to thy thinkings,
As thou dost ruminate, and give thy worst of thoughts
The worst of words.

IAGO: Good my lord, pardon me:
Though I am bound to every act of duty,
I am not bound to that all slaves are free to.°
Utter my thoughts? Why, say they are vile and false,
As where's that palace whereinto foul things
Sometimes intrude not? Who has a breast so pure
But some uncleanly apprehensions
Keep leets and law days,° and in Sessions sit
With meditations lawful?

OTHELLO: Thou dost conspire against thy friend, Iago,
If thou but think'st him wronged, and mak'st his ear
A stranger to thy thoughts.

IAGO: I do beseech you —
Though I perchance am vicious in my guess
(As I confess it is my nature's plague
To spy into abuses, and oft my jealousy°
Shapes faults that are not), that your wisdom yet
From one that so imperfectly conjects°
Would take no notice, nor build yourself a trouble
Out of his scattering and unsure observance.
It were not for your quiet nor your good,
Nor for my manhood, honesty, and wisdom,
To let you know my thoughts.

OTHELLO: What dost thou mean?

IAGO: Good name in man and woman, dear my lord,
Is the immediate° jewel of their souls.

123–24 close dilations . . . rule: Secret emotions that well up in spite of restraint. **127 seem none:** I.e., not pretend to be men when they are really monsters. **135 bound . . . free to:** Bound to tell that which even slaves are allowed to keep to themselves. **140 leets and law days:** Sittings of the courts. **147 jealousy:** Suspicion. **149 conjects:** Conjectures. **156 immediate:** Nearest the heart.

Who steals my purse steals trash; 'tis something, nothing;
'Twas mine, 'tis his, and has been slave to thousands;
But he that filches from me my good name
Robs me of that which not enriches him
And makes me poor indeed.

OTHELLO: By heaven, I'll know thy thoughts!

IAGO: You cannot, if my heart were in your hand;
Nor shall not whilst 'tis in my custody.

OTHELLO: Ha!

IAGO: O, beware, my lord, of jealousy!
It is the green-eyed monster, which doth mock°
The meat it feeds on. That cuckold lives in bliss
Who, certain of his fate, loves not his wronger;
But O, what damnèd minutes tells he o'er
Who dotes, yet doubts — suspects, yet strongly loves!

OTHELLO: O misery!

IAGO: Poor and content is rich, and rich enough;
But riches fineless° is as poor as winter
To him that ever fears he shall be poor.
Good God, the souls of all my tribe defend
From jealousy!

OTHELLO: Why, why is this?
Think'st thou I'ld make a life of jealousy,
To follow still the changes of the moon
With fresh suspicions? No! To be once in doubt
Is once to be resolved. Exchange me for a goat
When I shall turn the business of my soul
To such exsufflicate and blown° surmises,
Matching this inference. 'Tis not to make me jealous
To say my wife is fair, feeds well, loves company,
Is free of speech, sings, plays, and dances;
Where virtue is, these are more virtuous.
Nor from mine own weak merits will I draw
The smallest fear or doubt of her revolt,°
For she had eyes, and chose me. No, Iago;
I'll see before I doubt; when I doubt, prove;
And on the proof there is no more but this —
Away at once with love or jealousy!

IAGO: I am glad of this; for now I shall have reason
To show the love and duty that I bear you
With franker spirit. Therefore, as I am bound,
Receive it from me. I speak not yet of proof.
Look at your wife; observe her well with Cassio;

166 mock: Play with, like a cat with a mouse. **173 fineless:** Unlimited. **182 exsufflicate and blown:** Spat out and flyblown. **188 revolt:** Unfaithfulness.

Wear your eyes thus, not jealous nor secure:°
I would not have your free and noble nature,
Out of self-bounty,° be abused. Look to't.
I know our country disposition well:
In Venice they do let God see the pranks
They dare not show their husbands; their best conscience
Is not to leave't undone, but keep't unknown.

OTHELLO: Dost thou say so?

IAGO: She did deceive her father, marrying you;
And when she seemed to shake and fear your looks,
She loved them most.

OTHELLO: And so she did.

IAGO: Why, go to then!
She that, so young, could give out such a seeming
To seel° her father's eyes up close as oak°—
He thought 'twas witchcraft—but I am much to blame.
I humbly do beseech you of your pardon
For too much loving you.

OTHELLO: I am bound to thee for ever.

IAGO: I see this hath a little dashed your spirits.

OTHELLO: Not a jot, not a jot.

IAGO: I' faith, I fear it has.
I hope you will consider what is spoke
Comes from my love. But I do see y' are moved.
I am to pray you not to strain my speech
To grosser issues° nor to larger reach
Than to suspicion.

OTHELLO: I will not.

IAGO: Should you do so, my lord,
My speech should fall into such vile success°
As my thoughts aim not at. Cassio's my worthy friend—
My lord, I see y' are moved.

OTHELLO: No, not much moved:
I do not think but Desdemona's honest.°

IAGO: Long live she so! and long live you to think so!

OTHELLO: And yet, how nature erring from itself—

IAGO: Ay, there's the point! as (to be bold with you)
Not to affect many proposèd matches
Of her own clime, complexion, and degree,
Whereto we see in all things nature tends—
Foh! one may smell in such a will most rank,
Foul disproportions, thought unnatural—

198 secure: Overconfident. **200 self-bounty:** Natural goodness. **210 seel:** Close; **oak:** Oak grain. **219 To grosser issues:** To mean something more monstrous. **222 vile success:** Evil outcome. **225 honest:** Chaste.

But pardon me—I do not in position°
Distinctly speak of her; though I may fear
Her will, recoiling° to her better judgment,
May fall to match° you with her country forms,
And happily° repent.

OTHELLO: Farewell, farewell!
If more thou dost perceive, let me know more.
Set on thy wife to observe. Leave me, Iago.

IAGO: My lord, I take my leave. *[Going.]*

OTHELLO: Why did I marry? This honest creature doubtless
Sees and knows more, much more, than he unfolds.

IAGO *[returns]*: My lord, I would I might entreat your honor
To scan this thing no further: leave it to time.
Although 'tis fit that Cassio have his place,
For sure he fills it up with great ability,
Yet, if you please to hold off a while,
You shall by that perceive him and his means.
Note if your lady strain his entertainment°
With any strong or vehement importunity;
Much will be seen in that. In the mean time
Let me be thought too busy° in my fears
(As worthy cause I have to fear I am)
And hold her free,° I do beseech your honor.

OTHELLO: Fear not my government.°

IAGO: I once more take my leave. *Exit.*

OTHELLO: This fellow's of exceeding honesty,
And knows all qualities,° with a learned spirit
Of° human dealings. If I do prove her haggard,°
Though that her jesses° were my dear heartstrings,
I'd whistle her off and let her down the wind
To prey at fortune.° Haply, for I am black
And have not those soft parts of conversation°
That chamberers° have, or for I am declined
Into the vale of years—yet that's not much—
She's gone. I am abused, and my relief
Must be to loathe her. O curse of marriage,
That we can call these delicate creatures ours,
And not their appetites! I had rather be a toad

234 position: Definite assertion. **236 recoiling:** Reverting. **237 fall to match:** Happen to compare. **238 happily:** Haply, perhaps. **250 strain his entertainment:** Urge his recall. **253 busy:** Meddlesome. **255 hold her free:** Consider her guiltless. **256 government:** Self-control. **259 qualities:** Natures. **259–60 learned spirit Of:** Mind informed about. **260 haggard:** A wild hawk. **261 jesses:** Thongs for controlling a hawk. **262–63 whistle . . . fortune:** Turn her out and let her take care of herself. **264 soft . . . conversation:** Ingratiating manners. **265 chamberers:** Courtiers.

And live upon the vapor of a dungeon
Than keep a corner in the thing I love
For others' uses. Yet 'tis the plague of great ones;°
Prerogatived° are they less than the base.
'Tis destiny unshunnable, like death.
Even then this forkèd plague° is fated to us
When we do quicken.° Look where she comes.

Enter Desdemona and Emilia.

If she be false, O, then heaven mocks itself!
I'll not believe't.
DESDEMONA: How now, my dear Othello?
Your dinner, and the generous° islanders
By you invited, do attend your presence.
OTHELLO: I am to blame.
DESDEMONA: Why do you speak so faintly?
Are you not well?
OTHELLO: I have a pain upon my forehead, here.
DESDEMONA: Faith, that's with watching;° 'twill away again.
Let me but bind it hard, within this hour
It will be well.
OTHELLO: Your napkin° is too little;

[He pushes the handkerchief from him, and it falls unnoticed.]

Let it° alone. Come, I'll go in with you.
DESDEMONA: I am very sorry that you are not well. *Exit [with Othello].*
EMILIA: I am glad I have found this napkin;
This was her first remembrance from the Moor,
My wayward husband hath a hundred times
Wooed me to steal it; but she so loves the token
(For he conjured her she should ever keep it)
That she reserves it evermore about her
To kiss and talk to. I'll have the work ta'en out°
And give't Iago.
What he will do with it heaven knows, not I;
I nothing but to please his fantasy.°

Enter Iago.

IAGO: How now? What do you here alone?
EMILIA: Do not you chide; I have a thing for you.
IAGO: A thing for me? It is a common thing—
EMILIA: Ha?
IAGO: To have a foolish wife.

273 great ones: Prominent men. **274 Prerogatived:** Privileged. **276 forkèd plague:** I.e., horns of a cuckold. **277 do quicken:** Are born. **280 generous:** Noble. **285 watching:** Working late. **287 napkin:** Handkerchief. **288 it:** I.e., his forehead. **296 work ta'en out:** Pattern copied. **299 fantasy:** Whim.

EMILIA: O, is that all? What will you give me now
For that same handkerchief?
IAGO: What handkerchief?
EMILIA: What handkerchief!
Why, that the Moor first gave to Desdemona;
That which so often you did bid me steal.
IAGO: Hast stol'n it from her?
EMILIA: No, faith; she let it drop by negligence,
And to th' advantage,° I, being here, took't up.
Look, here it is.
IAGO: A good wench! Give it me.
EMILIA: What will you do with't, that you have been so earnest
To have me filch it?
IAGO: Why, what is that to you?

[Snatches it.]

EMILIA: If it be not for some purpose of import,°
Give't me again. Poor lady, she'll run mad
When she shall lack it.
IAGO: Be not acknown on't;° I have use for it.
Go, leave me. *Exit Emilia.*
I will in Cassio's lodgings lose this napkin
And let him find it. Trifles light as air
Are to the jealous confirmations strong
As proofs of holy writ. This may do something.
The Moor already changes with my poison:
Dangerous conceits° are in their nature poisons,
Which at the first are scarce found to distaste,
But with a little act upon the blood
Burn like the mines of sulphur.

Enter Othello.

I did say so.
Look where he comes! Not poppy nor mandragora,°
Nor all the drowsy syrups of the world,
Shall ever med'cine thee to that sweet sleep
Which thou owedst yesterday.
OTHELLO: Ha! ha! false to me?
IAGO: Why, how now, general? No more of that!
OTHELLO: Avaunt! be gone! Thou hast set me on the rack.
I swear 'tis better to be much abused
Than but to know't a little.
IAGO: How now, my lord?
OTHELLO: What sense had I of her stol'n hours of lust?

312 to th' advantage: Opportunely. **316 import:** Importance. **319 Be . . . on't:** Do not acknowledge it. **326 conceits:** Ideas. **330 mandragora:** A narcotic.

I saw't not, thought it not, it harmed not me;
I slept the next night well, fed well, was free° and merry;
I found not Cassio's kisses on her lips
He that is robbed, not wanting° what is stol'n,
Let him not know't, and he's not robbed at all.

IAGO: I am sorry to hear this.

OTHELLO: I had been happy if the general camp,
Pioneers° and all, had tasted her sweet body,
So I had nothing known. O, now for ever
Farewell the tranquil mind! farewell content!
Farewell the plumèd troop, and the big° wars
That make ambition virtue! O, farewell!
Farewell the neighing steed and the shrill trump,
The spirit-stirring drum, th' ear-piercing fife,
The royal banner, and all quality,
Pride, pomp, and circumstance° of glorious war!
And O you mortal engines° whose rude throats
Th' immortal Jove's dread clamors counterfeit,°
Farewell! Othello's occupation's gone!

IAGO: Is't possible, my lord?

OTHELLO: Villain, be sure thou prove my love a whore!
Be sure of it; give me the ocular proof;
Or, by the worth of mine eternal soul,
Thou hadst been better have been born a dog
Than answer my waked wrath!

IAGO: Is't come to this?

OTHELLO: Make me to see't; or at the least so prove it
That the probation° bear no hinge nor loop
To hang a doubt on — or woe upon thy life!

IAGO: My noble lord —

OTHELLO: If thou dost slander her and torture me,
Never pray more; abandon all remorse;
On horror's head horrors accumulate;
Do deeds to make heaven weep, all earth amazed;
For nothing canst thou to damnation add
Greater than that.

IAGO: O grace! O heaven forgive me!
Are you a man? Have you a soul or sense? —
God b' wi' you! take mine office. O wretched fool,
That liv'st to make thine honesty a vice!
O monstrous world! Take note, take note, O world,
To be direct and honest is not safe.

340 free: Carefree. **342 wanting:** Missing. **346 Pioneers:** Sappers, laborers. **349 big:** Stately. **354 circumstance:** Pageantry. **355 mortal engines:** Deadly artillery. **356 counterfeit:** Imitate. **365 probation:** Proof.

I thank you for this profit;° and from hence
I'll love no friend, sith love breeds such offense.

OTHELLO: Nay, stay. Thou shouldst be honest.

IAGO: I should be wise; for honesty's a fool
And loses that it works for.

OTHELLO: By the world,
I think my wife be honest, and think she is not;
I think that thou art just, and think thou art not.
I'll have some proof. Her name, that was as fresh
As Dian's visage, is now begrimed and black
As mine own face. If there be cords, or knives,
Poison, or fire, or suffocating streams,
I'll not endure it. Would I were satisfied!°

IAGO: I see, sir, you are eaten up with passion:
I do repent me that I put it to you.
You would be satisfied?

OTHELLO: Would? Nay, I will.

IAGO: And may; but how? how satisfied, my lord?
Would you, the supervisor,° grossly gape on?
Behold her topped?

OTHELLO: Death and damnation! O!

IAGO: It were a tedious difficulty, I think,
To bring them to that prospect. Damn them then,
If ever mortal eyes do see them bolster°
More than their own! What then? How then?
What shall I say? Where's satisfaction?
It is impossible you should see this,
Were they as prime° as goats, as hot as monkeys,
As salt° as wolves in pride,° and fools as gross
As ignorance made drunk. But yet, I say,
If imputation and strong circumstances
Which lead directly to the door of truth
Will give you satisfaction, you may have't.

OTHELLO: Give me a living reason she's disloyal.

IAGO: I do not like the office.
But sith I am ent'red in this cause so far,
Pricked to't by foolish honesty and love,
I will go on. I lay with Cassio lately,
And being troubled with a raging tooth,
I could not sleep.
There are a kind of men so loose of soul
That in their sleeps will mutter their affairs.

379 profit: Profitable lesson. **390 satisfied:** Completely informed. **395 supervisor:** Spectator. **399 bolster:** Lie together. **403 prime:** Lustful. **404 salt:** Lecherous; **pride:** Heat.

One of this kind is Cassio.
In sleep I heard him say, "Sweet Desdemona,
Let us be wary, let us hide our loves!"
And then, sir, would he gripe and wring my hand,
Cry "O sweet creature!" and then kiss me hard,
As if he plucked up kisses by the roots
That grew upon my lips; then laid his leg
Over my thigh, and sighed, and kissed, and then
Cried "Cursèd fate that gave thee to the Moor!"
OTHELLO: O monstrous! monstrous!
IAGO: Nay, this was but his dream.
OTHELLO: But this denoted a foregone conclusion;°
'Tis a shrewd doubt,° though it be but a dream.
IAGO: And this may help to thicken other proofs
That do demonstrate thinly.
OTHELLO: I'll tear her all to pieces!
IAGO: Nay, but be wise. Yet we see nothing done;
She may be honest yet. Tell me but this—
Have you not sometimes seen a handkerchief
Spotted with strawberries in your wife's hand?
OTHELLO: I gave her such a one; 'twas my first gift.
IAGO: I know not that; but such a handkerchief—
I am sure it was your wife's—did I to-day
See Cassio wipe his beard with.
OTHELLO: If it be that—
IAGO: If it be that, or any that was hers,
It speaks against her with the other proofs.
OTHELLO: O, that the slave had forty thousand lives!
One is too poor, too weak for my revenge.
Now do I see 'tis true. Look here, Iago:
All my fond love thus do I blow to heaven.
'Tis gone.
Arise, black vengeance, from the hollow hell!
Yield up, O love, thy crown and hearted throne
To tyrannous hate! Swell, bosom, with thy fraught,°
For 'tis of aspics'° tongues!
IAGO: Yet be content.
OTHELLO: O, blood, blood, blood!
IAGO: Patience, I say. Your mind perhaps may change.
OTHELLO: Never, Iago. Like to the Pontic sea,°
Whose icy current and compulsive course
Ne'er feels retiring ebb, but keeps due on

428 foregone conclusion: Previous experience. **429 a shrewd doubt:** Cursedly suspicious. **449 fraught:** Burden. **450 aspics:** Deadly poisonous snakes. **453 Pontic sea:** Black Sea.

To the Propontic and the Hellespont,
Even so my bloody thoughts, with violent pace,
Shall ne'er look back, ne'er ebb to humble love,
Till that a capable° and wide revenge
Swallow them up.
(He kneels.) Now, by yond marble heaven,
In the due reverence of a sacred vow
I here engage my words.

IAGO: Do not rise yet.

(Iago kneels.)

Witness, you ever-burning lights above,
You elements that clip° us round about,
Witness that here Iago doth give up
The execution° of his wit,° hands, heart
To wronged Othello's service! Let him command,
And to obey shall be in me remorse,°
What bloody business ever.

[They rise.]

OTHELLO: I greet thy love,
Not with vain thanks but with acceptance bounteous,
And will upon the instant put thee to't.
Within these three days let me hear thee say
That Cassio's not alive.

IAGO: My friend is dead; 'tis done at your request.
But let her live.

OTHELLO: Damn her, lewd minx! O, damn her! damn her!
Come, go with me apart. I will withdraw
To furnish me with some swift means of death
For the fair devil. Now art thou my lieutenant.

IAGO: I am your own forever. *Exeunt.*

[Scene IV: The environs of the castle.]

Enter Desdemona, Emilia, and Clown.

DESDEMONA: Do you know, sirrah, where Lieutenant Cassio lies?°

CLOWN: I dare not say he lies anywhere.

DESDEMONA: Why, man?

CLOWN: He's a soldier, and for me to say a soldier lies is stabbing.

DESDEMONA: Go to. Where lodges he?

CLOWN: To tell you where he lodges is to tell you where I lie.

DESDEMONA: Can anything be made of this?

459 capable: All-embracing. **464 clip:** Encompass. **466 execution:** Activities; **wit:** Mind. **468 remorse:** Pity. **Scene IV. 1 lies:** Lives, lodges.

CLOWN: I know not where he lodges; and for me to devise a lodging, and say he lies here or he lies there, were to lie in mine own throat.

DESDEMONA: Can you enquire him out, and be edified by report?

CLOWN: I will catechize the world for him; that is, make questions, and by them answer.

DESDEMONA: Seek him, bid him come hither. Tell him I have moved° my lord on his behalf and hope all will be well.

CLOWN: To do this is within the compass of man's wit, and therefore I'll attempt the doing of it. *Exit.*

DESDEMONA: Where should I lose that handkerchief, Emilia?

EMILIA: I know not, madam.

DESDEMONA: Believe me, I had rather have lost my purse
Full of crusadoes;° and but my noble Moor
Is true of mind, and made of no such baseness
As jealous creatures are, it were enough
To put him to ill thinking.

EMILIA: Is he not jealous?

DESDEMONA: Who? he? I think the sun where he was born
Drew all such humors° from him.

Enter Othello.

EMILIA: Look where he comes.

DESDEMONA: I will not leave him now till Cassio
Be called to him — How is't with you, my lord?

OTHELLO: Well, my good lady. [*Aside.*] O, hardness to dissemble! —
How do you, Desdemona?

DESDEMONA: Well, my good lord.

OTHELLO: Give me your hand. This hand is moist, my lady.

DESDEMONA: It yet hath felt no age nor known no sorrow.

OTHELLO: This argues fruitfulness and liberal heart.
Hot, hot, and moist. This hand of yours requires
A sequester° from liberty, fasting and prayer,
Much castigation, exercise devout;
For here's a young and sweating devil here
That commonly rebels. 'Tis a good hand,
A frank one.

DESDEMONA: You may, indeed, say so;
For 'twas that hand that gave away my heart.

OTHELLO: A liberal hand! The hearts of old gave hands;
But our new heraldry° is hands, not hearts.

DESDEMONA: I cannot speak of this. Come now, your promise!

OTHELLO: What promise, chuck?

DESDEMONA: I have sent to bid Cassio come speak with you.

13 moved: Made proposals to. **20 crusadoes:** Portuguese gold coins. **25 humors:** Inclinations. **34 sequester:** Removal. **42 heraldry:** Heraldic symbolism.

OTHELLO: I have a salt and sorry rheum° offends me.
Lend me thy handkerchief.
DESDEMONA: Here, my lord.
OTHELLO: That which I gave you.
DESDEMONA: I have it not about me.
OTHELLO: Not?
DESDEMONA: No, faith, my lord.
OTHELLO: That's a fault.
That handkerchief
Did an Egyptian° to my mother give.
She was a charmer,° and could almost read
The thoughts of people. She told her, while she kept it,
'Twould make her amiable° and subdue my father
Entirely to her love; but if she lost it
Or made a gift of it, my father's eye
Should hold her loathèd, and his spirits should hunt
After new fancies. She, dying, gave it me,
And bid me, when my fate would have me wive;
To give it her. I did so; and take heed on't;
Make it a darling like your precious eye.
To lose't or give't away were such perdition°
As nothing else could match.
DESDEMONA: Is't possible?
OTHELLO: 'Tis true. There's magic in the web of it.
A sibyl that had numb'red in the world
The sun to course two hundred compasses,°
In her prophetic fury sewed the work;
The worms were hallowed that did breed the silk;
And it was dyed in mummy° which the skillful
Conserved of maidens' hearts.
DESDEMONA: I' faith? Is't true?
OTHELLO: Most veritable. Therefore look to't well.
DESDEMONA: Then would to God that I had never seen't!
OTHELLO: Ha! Wherefore?
DESDEMONA: Why do you speak so startingly and rash?
OTHELLO: Is't lost? Is't gone? Speak, is it out o' th' way?
DESDEMONA: Heaven bless us!
OTHELLO: Say you?
DESDEMONA: It is not lost. But what an if it were?
OTHELLO: How?
DESDEMONA: I say it is not lost.
OTHELLO: Fetch't, let me see't!

46 salt . . . rheum: Distressing head cold. **51 Egyptian:** Gypsy. **52 charmer:** Sorceress. **54 amiable:** Lovable. **62 perdition:** Disaster. **66 compasses:** Annual rounds. **69 mummy:** A drug made from mummies.

DESDEMONA: Why, so I can, sir; but I will not now.
This is a trick to put° me from my suit:
Pray you let Cassio be received again.
OTHELLO: Fetch me the handkerchief! My mind misgives.
DESDEMONA: Come, come!
You'll never meet a more sufficient man.
OTHELLO: The handkerchief!
DESDEMONA: I pray talk me of Cassio.
OTHELLO: The handkerchief!
DESDEMONA: A man that all his time°
Hath founded his good fortunes on your love,
Shared dangers with you —
OTHELLO: The handkerchief!
DESDEMONA: I' faith, you are to blame.
OTHELLO: Zounds! *Exit Othello.*
EMILIA: Is not this man jealous?
DESDEMONA: I ne'er saw this before.
Sure there's some wonder in this handkerchief;
I am most unhappy in the loss of it.
EMILIA: 'Tis not a year or two shows us a man.
They are all but stomachs, and we all but food;
They eat us hungerly, and when they are full,
They belch us.

Enter Iago and Cassio.

Look you — Cassio and my husband!
IAGO: There is no other way; 'tis she must do't.
And lo the happiness!° Go and importune her.
DESDEMONA: How now, good Cassio? What's the news with you?
CASSIO: Madam, my former suit. I do beseech you
That by your virtuous means I may again
Exist, and be a member of his love
Whom I with all the office of my heart
Entirely honor. I would not be delayed.
If my offense be of such mortal kind
That neither service past, nor present sorrows,
Nor purposed merit in futurity,
Can ransom me into his love again,
But to know so must be my benefit.
So shall I clothe me in a forced content,
And shut myself up in° some other course,
To fortune's alms.
DESDEMONA: Alas, thrice-gentle Cassio!

82 put: Divert. **88 all . . . time:** During his whole career. **103 happiness:** Good luck. **116 shut myself up in:** Confine myself to.

My advocation° is not now in tune.
My lord is not my lord; nor should I know him,
Were he in favor° as in humor altered.
So help me every spirit sanctified
As I have spoken for you all my best
And stood within the blank° of his displeasure
For my free speech! You must a while be patient.
What I can do I will; and more I will
Than for myself I dare. Let that suffice you.

IAGO: Is my lord angry?

EMILIA: He went hence but now,
And certainly in strange unquietness.

IAGO: Can he be angry? I have seen the cannon
When it hath blown his ranks into the air
And, like the devil, from his very arm
Puffed his own brother—and is he angry?
Something of moment then. I will go meet him.
There's matter in't indeed if he be angry.

DESDEMONA: I prithee do so. *Exit [Iago].*
Something sure of state,°
Either from Venice or some unhatched practice°
Made demonstrable here in Cyprus to him,
Hath puddled° his clear spirit; and in such cases
Men's natures wrangle with inferior things,
Though great ones are their object. 'Tis even so;
For let our finger ache, and it endues°
Our other, healthful members even to a sense
Of pain. Nay, we must think men are not gods,
Nor of them look for such observancy
As fits the bridal. Beshrew me much, Emilia,
I was, unhandsome warrior° as I am,
Arraigning his unkindness with my soul;°
But now I find I had suborned the witness,
And he's indicted falsely.

EMILIA: Pray heaven it be state matters, as you think,
And no conception nor no jealous toy°
Concerning you.

DESDEMONA: Alas the day! I never gave him cause.

EMILIA: But jealous souls will not be answered so;
They are not ever jealous for the cause,

118 advocation: Advocacy. **120 favor:** Appearance. **123 blank:** Bull's-eye of the target. **135 state:** Public affairs. **136 unhatched practice:** Budding plot. **138 puddled:** Muddied. **141 endues:** Brings. **146 unhandsome warrior:** Inadequate soldier. **147 Arraigning . . . soul:** Indicting his unkindness before the bar of my soul. **151 toy:** Fancy.

But jealous for they're jealous. 'Tis a monster
Begot upon itself,° born on itself.

DESDEMONA: Heaven keep that monster from Othello's mind!

EMILIA: Lady, amen.

DESDEMONA: I will go seek him. Cassio, walk here about:
If I do find him fit, I'll move your suit
And seek to effect it to my uttermost.

CASSIO: I humbly thank your ladyship.

Exeunt Desdemona and Emilia.

Enter Bianca.

BIANCA: Save you, friend Cassio!

CASSIO: What make you from home?
How is't with you, my most fair Bianca?
I' faith, sweet love, I was coming to your house.

BIANCA: And I was going to your lodging, Cassio.
What, keep a week away? seven days and nights?
Eightscore eight hours? and lovers' absent hours,
More tedious than the dial° eightscore times?
O weary reck'ning!

CASSIO: Pardon me, Bianca:
I have this while with leaden thoughts been pressed;
But I shall in a more continuate° time
Strike off this score of absence. Sweet Bianca,

[Gives her Desdemona's handkerchief.]

Take me this work out.°

BIANCA: O Cassio, whence came this?
This is some token from a newer friend.
To the felt absence now I feel a cause.
Is't come to this? Well, well.

CASSIO: Go to, woman!
Throw your vile guesses in the devil's teeth,
From whence you have them. You are jealous now
That this is from some mistress, some remembrance.
No, by my faith, Bianca.

BIANCA: Why, whose is it?

CASSIO: I know not, sweet; I found it in my chamber.
I like the work° well; ere it be demanded,
As like enough it will, I'd have it copied.
Take it and do't, and leave me for this time.

BIANCA: Leave you? Wherefore?

CASSIO: I do attend here on the general

157 Begot . . . itself: Self-engendered. **170 dial:** Clock. **173 continuate:** Uninterrupted. **175 Take . . . out:** Copy this embroidery for me. **184 work:** Needlework.

And think it no addition, nor my wish,
To have him see me womaned.

BIANCA: Why, I pray you?

CASSIO: Not that I love you not.

BIANCA: But that you do not love me!
I pray you bring me on the way a little,
And say if I shall see you soon at night.

CASSIO: 'Tis but a little way that I can bring you,
For I attend here; but I'll see you soon.

BIANCA: 'Tis very good. I must be circumstanced.° *Exeunt.*

[ACT IV, Scene I: The environs of the castle.]

Enter Othello and Iago.

IAGO: Will you think so?

OTHELLO: Think so, Iago?

IAGO: What,
To kiss in private?

OTHELLO: An unauthorized kiss.

IAGO: Or to be naked with her friend in bed
An hour or more, not meaning any harm?

OTHELLO: Naked in bed, Iago, and not mean harm?
It is hypocrisy against the devil.°
They that mean virtuously, and yet do so,
The devil their virtue tempts, and they tempt heaven.

IAGO: So they do nothing, 'tis a venial slip.
But if I give my wife a handkerchief —

OTHELLO: What then?

IAGO: Why, then 'tis hers, my lord; and being hers,
She may, I think, bestow't on any man.

OTHELLO: She is protectress of her honor too;
May she give that?

IAGO: Her honor is an essence that's not seen;
They have it very oft that have it not.
But for the handkerchief —

OTHELLO: By heaven, I would most gladly have forgot it!
Thou said'st — O, it comes o'er my memory
As doth the raven o'er the infected° house,
Boding to all! — he had my handkerchief.

IAGO: Ay, what of that?

OTHELLO: That's not so good now.

IAGO: What

196 circumstanced: Governed by circumstances. **ACT IV, SCENE I. 6 hypocrisy . . . devil:** I.e., feigned sin instead of feigned virtue. **21 infected:** Plague-stricken.

If I had said I had seen him do you wrong?
Or heard him say — as knaves be such abroad
Who having, by their own importunate suit,
Or voluntary dotage of some mistress,
Convincèd or supplied° them, cannot choose
But they must blab —

OTHELLO: Hath he said anything?

IAGO: He hath, my lord; but be you well assured,
No more than he'll unswear.

OTHELLO: What hath he said?

IAGO: Faith, that he did — I know not what he did.

OTHELLO: What? what?

IAGO: Lie —

OTHELLO: With her?

IAGO: With her, on her; what you will.

OTHELLO: Lie with her? lie on her? — We say lie on her when they belie her. — Lie with her! Zounds, that's fulsome. — Handkerchief — confessions — handkerchief! — To confess, and be hanged for his labor — first to be hanged, and then to confess! I tremble at it. Nature would not invest herself in such shadowing passion without some instruction.° It is not words that shakes me thus. — Pish! Noses, ears, and lips? Is't possible? — Confess? — Handkerchief? — O devil!

(Falls in a trance.)

IAGO: Work on,
My med'cine, work! Thus credulous fools are caught,
And many worthy and chaste dames even thus,
All guiltless, meet reproach. — What, ho! my lord!
My lord, I say! Othello!
Enter Cassio. How now, Cassio?

CASSIO: What's the matter?

IAGO: My lord is fall'n into an epilepsy.
This is his second fit; he had one yesterday.

CASSIO: Rub him about the temples.

IAGO: No, forbear.
The lethargy° must have his quiet course.
If not, he foams at mouth, and by and by
Breaks out to savage madness. Look, he stirs.
Do you withdraw yourself a little while.
He will recover straight. When he is gone,
I would on great occasion speak with you. *[Exit Cassio.]*
How is it, general? Have you not hurt your head?

OTHELLO: Dost thou mock me?

28 Convincèd or supplied: Overcome or gratified. **39–40 Nature . . . instruction:** My natural faculties would not be so overcome by passion without reason. **52 lethargy:** Coma.

IAGO: I mock you? No, by heaven.
Would you would bear your fortune like a man!
OTHELLO: A hornèd man's° a monster and a beast.
IAGO: There's many a beast then in a populous city,
And many a civil monster.
OTHELLO: Did he confess it?
IAGO: Good sir, be a man.
Think every bearded fellow that's but yoked
May draw with you. There's millions now alive
That nightly lie in those unproper° beds
Which they dare swear peculiar:° your case is better.
O, 'tis the spite of hell, the fiend's arch-mock,
To lip a wanton in a secure° couch,
And to suppose her chaste! No, let me know;
And knowing what I am, I know what she shall be.
OTHELLO: O, thou art wise! 'Tis certain.
IAGO: Stand you awhile apart;
Confine yourself but in a patient list.°
Whilst you were here, o'erwhelmèd with your grief—
A passion most unsuiting such a man—
Cassio came hither. I shifted him away
And laid good 'scuse upon your ecstasy;°
Bade him anon return, and here speak with me;
The which he promised. Do but encave° yourself
And mark the fleers, the gibes, and notable scorns
That dwell in every region of his face;
For I will make him tell the tale anew—
Where, how, how oft, how long ago, and when
He hath, and is again to cope° your wife.
I say, but mark his gesture. Marry, patience!
Or I shall say y'are all in all in spleen,°
And nothing of a man.
OTHELLO: Dost thou hear, Iago?
I will be found most cunning in my patience;
But—dost thou hear?—most bloody.
IAGO: That's not amiss:
But yet keep time in all. Will you withdraw?

[Othello retires.]

Now will I question Cassio of Bianca,
A huswife° that by selling her desires
Buys herself bread and clothes. It is a creature

61 hornèd man: Cuckold. **67 unproper:** Not exclusively their own. **68 peculiar:** Exclusively their own. **70 secure:** Free from fear of rivalry. **74 in a patient list:** Within the limits of self-control. **78 ecstasy:** Trance. **80 encave:** Conceal. **85 cope:** Meet. **87 all in all in spleen:** Wholly overcome by your passion. **93 huswife:** Hussy.

That dotes on Cassio, as 'tis the strumpet's plague
To beguile many and be beguiled by one.
He, when he hears of her, cannot refrain
From the excess of laughter. Here he comes.

Enter Cassio.

As he shall smile, Othello shall go mad;
And his unbookish° jealousy must conster°
Poor Cassio's smiles, gestures, and light behavior
Quite in the wrong. How do you now, lieutenant?

CASSIO: The worser that you give me the addition°
Whose want even kills me.

IAGO: Ply Desdemona well, and you are sure on't.
Now, if this suit lay in Bianca's power,
How quickly should you speed!

CASSIO: Alas, poor caitiff!°

OTHELLO: Look how he laughs already!

IAGO: I never knew a woman love man so.

CASSIO: Alas, poor rogue! I think, i' faith, she loves me.

OTHELLO: Now he denies it faintly, and laughs it out.

IAGO: Do you hear, Cassio?

OTHELLO: Now he importunes him
To tell it o'er. Go to! Well said, well said!

IAGO: She gives out that you shall marry her.
Do you intend it?

CASSIO: Ha, ha, ha!

OTHELLO: Do you triumph, Roman? Do you triumph?

CASSIO: I marry her? What, a customer?° Prithee bear some charity to my wit; do not think it so unwholesome. Ha, ha, ha!

OTHELLO: So, so, so, so! They laugh that win!

IAGO: Faith, the cry goes that you shall marry her.

CASSIO: Prithee say true.

IAGO: I am a very villain else.

OTHELLO: Have you scored me?° Well.

CASSIO: This is the monkey's own giving out. She is persuaded I will marry her out of her own love and flattery, not out of my promise.

OTHELLO: Iago beckons° me; now he begins the story.

CASSIO: She was here even now; she haunts me in every place. I was t' other day talking on the sea bank with certain Venetians, and thither comes the bauble,° and, by this hand, she falls me thus about my neck—

OTHELLO: Crying "O dear Cassio!" as it were. His gesture imports it.

CASSIO: So hangs, and lolls, and weeps upon me; so shakes and pulls me! Ha, ha, ha!

100 unbookish: Uninstructed; **conster:** Construe, interpret. **103 addition:** Title. **107 caitiff:** Wretch. **118 customer:** Prostitute. **124 scored me:** Settled my account (?). **127 beckons:** Signals. **130 bauble:** Plaything.

OTHELLO: Now he tells how she plucked him to my chamber. O, I see that nose of yours, but not that dog I shall throw it to.

CASSIO: Well, I must leave her company.

Enter Bianca.

IAGO: Before me! Look where she comes.

CASSIO: 'Tis such another fitchew!° marry, a perfumed one. What do you mean by this haunting of me?

BIANCA: Let the devil and his dam haunt you! What did you mean by that same handkerchief you gave me even now? I was a fine fool to take it. I must take out the whole work? A likely piece of work that you should find it in your chamber and know not who left it there! This is some minx's token, and I must take out the work? There! Give it your hobby-horse.° Wheresoever you had it, I'll take out no work on't.

CASSIO: How now, my sweet Bianca? How now? how now?

OTHELLO: By heaven, that should be my handkerchief!

BIANCA: An you'll come to supper to-night, you may; an you will not, come when you are next prepared for. *Exit.*

IAGO: After her, after her!

CASSIO: Faith, I must; she'll rail in the street else.

IAGO: Will you sup there?

CASSIO: Yes, I intend so.

IAGO: Well, I may chance to see you; for I would very fain speak with you.

CASSIO: Prithee come. Will you?

IAGO: Go to! say no more. *Exit Cassio.*

OTHELLO *[comes forward]*: How shall I murder him, Iago?

IAGO: Did you perceive how he laughed at his vice?°

OTHELLO: O Iago!

IAGO: And did you see the handkerchief?

OTHELLO: Was that mine?

IAGO: Your, by this hand! And to see how he prizes° the foolish woman your wife! She gave it him, and he hath giv'n it his whore.

OTHELLO: I would have him nine years a-killing — A fine woman! a fair woman! a sweet woman!

IAGO: Nay, you must forget that.

OTHELLO: Ay, let her rot, and perish, and be damned to-night; for she shall not live. No, my heart is turned to stone; I strike it, and it hurts my hand. O, the world hath not a sweeter creature! She might lie by an emperor's side and command him tasks.

IAGO: Nay, that's not your way.

OTHELLO: Hang her! I do but say what she is. So delicate with her needle! an admirable musician! O, she will sing the savageness out of a bear! Of so high and plenteous wit and invention°—

138 fitchew: Polecat (slang for whore). **144 hobby-horse:** Harlot. **158 vice:** I.e., vicious conduct. **162 prizes:** Values. **174 invention:** Imagination.

IAGO: She's the worse for all this.

OTHELLO: O, a thousand thousand times! And then, of so gentle a condition!°

IAGO: Ay, too gentle.

OTHELLO: Nay, that's certain. But yet the pity of it, Iago! O Iago, the pity of it, Iago!

IAGO: If you are so fond over her iniquity, give her patent° to offend; for if it touch not you, it comes near nobody.

OTHELLO: I will chop her into messes! Cuckold me!

IAGO: O, 'tis foul in her.

OTHELLO: With mine officer!

IAGO: That's fouler.

OTHELLO: Get me some poison, Iago, this night. I'll not expostulate with her, lest her body and beauty unprovide° my mind again. This night, Iago!

IAGO: Do it not with poison. Strangle her in her bed, even the bed she hath contaminated.

OTHELLO: Good, good! The justice of it pleases. Very good!

IAGO: And for Cassio, let me be his undertaker;° you shall hear more by midnight.

OTHELLO: Excellent good!

A trumpet.

What trumpet is that same?

IAGO: I warrant something from Venice.

Enter Lodovico, Desdemona, and Attendants.

'Tis Lodovico.
This comes from the Duke; and see, your wife is with him.

LODOVICO: God save you, worthy general!

OTHELLO: With all my heart, sir.

LODOVICO: The Duke and senators of Venice greet you.

[Gives him a letter.]

OTHELLO: I kiss the instrument of their pleasures.

[Opens the letter and reads.]

DESDEMONA: And what's the news, good cousin Lodovico?

IAGO: I am very glad to see you, signior.
Welcome to Cyprus.

LODOVICO: I thank you. How does Lieutenant Cassio?

IAGO: Lives, sir.

DESDEMONA: Cousin, there's fall'n between him and my lord
An unkind breach; but you shall make all well.

OTHELLO: Are you sure of that?

DESDEMONA: My lord?

OTHELLO *[reads]*: "This fail you not to do, as you will—"

176 condition: Disposition. **180 patent:** License. **187 unprovide:** Disarm. **191 be his undertaker:** Undertake to deal with him.

LODOVICO: He did not call; he's busy in the paper.
Is there division 'twixt thy lord and Cassio?
DESDEMONA: A most unhappy one. I would do much
T' atone° them, for the love I bear to Cassio.
OTHELLO: Fire and brimstone!
DESDEMONA: My lord?
OTHELLO: Are you wise?
DESDEMONA: What, is he angry?
LODOVICO: May be the letter moved him;
For, as I think, they do command him home,
Deputing Cassio in his government.
DESDEMONA: By my troth, I am glad on't.
OTHELLO: Indeed?
DESDEMONA: My lord?
OTHELLO: I am glad to see you mad.°
DESDEMONA: Why, sweet Othello—
OTHELLO: Devil!
[Strikes her.]
DESDEMONA: I have not deserved this.
LODOVICO: My lord, this would not be believed in Venice,
Though I should swear I saw't. 'Tis very much.
Make her amends; she weeps.
OTHELLO: O devil, devil!
If that the earth could teem° with woman's tears,
Each drop she falls would prove a crocodile.°
Out of my sight!
DESDEMONA: I will not stay to offend you. *[Going.]*
LODOVICO: Truly, an obedient lady.
I do beseech your lordship call her back.
OTHELLO: Mistress!
DESDEMONA: My lord?
OTHELLO: What would you with her, sir?
LODOVICO: Who? I, my lord?
OTHELLO: Ay! You did wish that I would make her turn.
Sir, she can turn, and turn, and yet go on
And turn again; and she can weep, sir, weep;
And she's obedient; as you say, obedient,
Very obedient.—Proceed you in your tears.—
Concerning this, sir—O well-painted passion!°—
I am commanded home.—Get you away;
I'll send for you anon.—Sir, I obey the mandate
And will return to Venice.—Hence, avaunt!

212 atone: Reconcile. **218 mad:** I.e., waggish. **224 teem:** Breed. **225 crocodile:** Crocodiles were supposed to shed hypocritical tears to lure men to destruction. **237 passion:** Grief.

[Exit Desdemona.]

Cassio shall have my place. And, sir, to-night
I do entreat that we may sup together.
You are welcome, sir, to Cyprus—Goats and monkeys!

Exit.

LODOVICO: Is this the noble Moor whom our full Senate
Call all in all sufficient? Is this the nature
Whom passion could not shake? whose solid virtue
The shot of accident nor dart of chance
Could neither graze nor pierce?
IAGO: He is much changed.
LODOVICO: Are his wits safe? Is he not light of brain?
IAGO: He's that he is; I may not breathe my censure.
What he might be—if what he might he is not—
I would to heaven he were!
LODOVICO: What, strike his wife?
IAGO: Faith, that was not so well; yet would I knew
That stroke would prove the worst!
LODOVICO: Is it his use?°
Or did the letters work upon his blood
And new-create this fault?
IAGO: Alas, alas!
It is not honesty in me to speak
What I have seen and known. You shall observe him,
And his own courses will denote him so
That I may save my speech. Do but go after
And mark how he continues.
LODOVICO: I am sorry that I am deceived in him. *Exeunt.*

[Scene II: Within the castle.]

Enter Othello and Emilia.

OTHELLO: You have seen nothing then?
EMILIA: Nor ever heard, nor ever did suspect.
OTHELLO: Yes, you have seen Cassio and she together.
EMILIA: But then I saw no harm, and then I heard
Each syllable that breath made up between them.
OTHELLO: What, did they never whisper?
EMILIA: Never, my lord.
OTHELLO: Nor send you out o' th' way?
EMILIA: Never.
OTHELLO: To fetch her fan, her gloves, her mask, nor nothing?

254 use: Custom.

EMILIA: Never, my lord.
OTHELLO: That's strange.
EMILIA: I durst, my lord, to wager she is honest,
Lay down my soul at stake. If you think other,
Remove your thought; it doth abuse your bosom.°
If any wretch have put this in your head,
Let heaven requite it with the serpent's curse!°
For if she be not honest, chaste, and true,
There's no man happy; the purest of their wives
Is foul as slander.
OTHELLO: Bid her come hither. Go. *Exit Emilia.*
She says enough; yet she's a simple bawd
That cannot say as much. This is a subtle whore,
A closet lock and key of villainous secrets;
And yet she'll kneel and pray; I have seen her do't.

Enter Desdemona and Emilia.

DESDEMONA: My lord, what is your will?
OTHELLO: Pray, chuck, come hither.
DESDEMONA: What is your pleasure?
OTHELLO: Let me see your eyes.
Look in my face.
DESDEMONA: What horrible fancy's this?
OTHELLO *[to Emilia]*: Some of your function, mistress.
Leave procreants° alone and shut the door;
Cough or cry hem if anybody come.
Your mystery, your mystery!° Nay, dispatch!
Exit Emilia.

DESDEMONA: Upon my knees, what doth your speech import?
I understand a fury in your words,
[But not the words.]
OTHELLO: Why, what art thou?
DESDEMONA: Your wife, my lord; your true
And loyal wife.
OTHELLO: Come, swear it, damn thyself;
Lest, being like one of heaven,° the devils themselves
Should fear to seize thee. Therefore be double-damned—
Swear thou art honest.°
DESDEMONA: Heaven doth truly know it.
OTHELLO: Heaven truly knows that thou art false as hell.
DESDEMONA: To whom, my lord? With whom? How am I false?
OTHELLO: Ah, Desdemona! away! away! away!

SCENE II. 14 abuse . . . bosom: Deceive your heart. **16 serpent's curse:** (cf. Genesis 3:14). **28 procreants:** Mating couples. **30 mystery:** Trade, occupation. **36 being . . . heaven:** Looking like an angel. **38 honest:** Chaste.

DESDEMONA: Alas the heavy day! Why do you weep?
Am I the motive of these tears, my lord?
If haply you my father do suspect
An instrument° of this your calling back,
Lay not your blame on me. If you have lost him,
Why, I have lost him too.
OTHELLO: Had it pleased heaven
To try me with affliction, had they rained
All kinds of sores and shames on my bare head,
Steeped me in poverty to the very lips,
Given to captivity me and my utmost hopes,
I should have found in some place of my soul
A drop of patience. But, alas, to make me
A fixèd figure for the time of scorn°
To point his slow unmoving finger at!
Yet could I bear that too; well, very well.
But there where I have garnered up my heart,
Where either I must live or bear no life,
The fountain from the which my current runs
Or else dries up—to be discarded thence,
Or keep it as a cistern for foul toads
To knot and gender in—turn thy complexion there,°
Patience, thou young and rose-lipped cherubin!
Ay, there look grim as hell!
DESDEMONA: I hope my noble lord esteems me honest.
OTHELLO: O, ay; as summer flies are in the shambles,°
That quicken° even with blowing. O thou weed,
Who art so lovely fair, and smell'st so sweet,
That the sense aches at thee, would thou hadst ne'er been born!
DESDEMONA: Alas, what ignorant sin have I committed?
OTHELLO: Was this fair paper, this most goodly book,
Made to write "whore" upon? What committed?
Committed? O thou public commoner!°
I should make very forges of my cheeks
That would to cinders burn up modesty,
Did I but speak thy deeds. What committed?
Heaven stops the nose at it, and the moon winks;°
The bawdy wind, that kisses all it meets,
Is hushed within the hollow mine of earth
And will not hear it. What committed?
Impudent strumpet!
DESDEMONA: By heaven, you do me wrong!

45 An instrument: To be the cause. **54 time of scorn:** Scornful world. **62 turn thy complexion there:** Change thy color at that point. **66 shambles:** Slaughterhouse. **67 quicken:** Come to life. **73 commoner:** Harlot. **77 winks:** Closes her eyes.

OTHELLO: Are not you a strumpet?
DESDEMONA: No, as I am a Christian!
If to preserve this vessel for my lord
From any other foul unlawful touch
Be not to be a strumpet, I am none.
OTHELLO: What, not a whore?
DESDEMONA: No, as I shall be saved!
OTHELLO: Is't possible?
DESDEMONA: O, heaven forgive us!
OTHELLO: I cry you mercy° then.
I took you for that cunning whore of Venice
That married with Othello. — *[Calling.]* You, mistress,
That have the office opposite to Saint Peter
And keep the gate of hell!

Enter Emilia.

You, you, ay, you!
We have done our course; there's money for your pains:
I pray you turn the key, and keep our counsel. *Exit.*
EMILIA: Alas, what does this gentleman conceive?
How do you, madam? How do you, my good lady?
DESDEMONA: Faith, half asleep.°
EMILIA: Good madam, what's the matter with my lord?
DESDEMONA: With who?
EMILIA: Why, with my lord, madam.
DESDEMONA: Who is thy lord?
EMILIA: He that is yours, sweet lady.
DESDEMONA: I have none. Do not talk to me, Emilia.
I cannot weep; nor answer have I none
But what should go by water. Prithee to-night
Lay on my bed my wedding sheets, remember;
And call thy husband hither.
EMILIA: Here's a change indeed! *Exit.*
DESDEMONA: 'Tis meet I should be used so, very meet.
How have I been behaved, that he might stick
The small'st opinion° on my least misuse?°

Enter Iago and Emilia.

IAGO: What is your pleasure, madam? How is't with you?
DESDEMONA: I cannot tell. Those that do teach young babes
Do it with gentle means and easy tasks:
He might have chid me so; for, in good faith,
I am a child to chiding.
IAGO: What is the matter, lady?

88 cry you mercy: Beg your pardon. **97 half asleep:** I.e., stunned. **109 small'st opinion:** Least suspicion. **least misuse:** Slightest misconduct.

EMILIA: Alas, Iago, my lord hath so bewhored her,
Thrown such despite and heavy terms upon her
As true hearts cannot bear.
DESDEMONA: Am I that name, Iago?
IAGO: What name, fair lady?
DESDEMONA: Such as she said my lord did say I was.
EMILIA: He called her whore. A beggar in his drink
Could not have laid such terms upon his callet.°
IAGO: Why did he so?
DESDEMONA: I do not know; I am sure I am none such.
IAGO: Do not weep, do not weep. Alas the day!
EMILIA: Hath she forsook so many noble matches,
Her father and her country, and her friends,
To be called whore? Would it not make one weep?
DESDEMONA: It is my wretched fortune.
IAGO: Beshrew him for't!
How comes this trick° upon him?
DESDEMONA: Nay, heaven doth know.
EMILIA: I will be hanged if some eternal villain,
Some busy and insinuating rogue,
Some cogging, cozening° slave, to get some office,
Have not devised this slander. I'll be hanged else.
IAGO: Fie, there is no such man! It is impossible.
DESDEMONA: If any such there be, heaven pardon him!
EMILIA: A halter pardon him! and hell gnaw his bones!
Why should he call her whore? Who keeps her company?
What place? what time? what form? what likelihood?
The Moor 's abused by some most villainous knave,
Some base notorious knave, some scurvy fellow.
O heaven, that such companions° thou 'dst unfold,°
And put in every honest hand a whip
To lash the rascals naked through the world
Even from the east to th' west!
IAGO: Speak within door.°
EMILIA: O, fie upon them! Some such squire he was
That turned your wit the seamy side without
And made you to suspect me with the Moor.
IAGO: You are a fool. Go to.
DESDEMONA: Alas, Iago,
What shall I do to win my lord again?
Good friend, go to him; for, by this light of heaven,
I know not how I lost him. Here I kneel:

121 callet: Whore. **129 trick:** Freakish behavior. **132 cogging, cozening:** Cheating, defrauding. **141 companions:** Rogues. **unfold:** Expose. **144 within door:** With restraint.

If e'er my will did trespass 'gainst his love
Either in discourse° of thought or actual deed,
Or that mine eyes, mine ears, or any sense
Delighted them in any other form,
Or that I do not yet, and ever did,
And ever will (though he do shake me off
To beggarly divorcement) love him dearly,
Comfort forswear° me! Unkindness may do much;
And his unkindness may defeat° my life,
But never taint my love. I cannot say "whore."
It does abhor me now I speak the word;
To do the act that might the addition earn
Not the world's mass of vanity could make me.

IAGO: I pray you be content. 'Tis but his humor.
The business of the state does him offense,
[And he does chide with you.]

DESDEMONA: If 'twere no other—

IAGO: 'Tis but so, I warrant.

[Trumpets within.]

Hark how these instruments summon you to supper.
The messengers of Venice stay the meat:
Go in, and weep not. All things shall be well.

Exeunt Desdemona and Emilia.

Enter Roderigo.

How now, Roderigo?

RODERIGO: I do not find that thou deal'st justly with me.

IAGO: What in the contrary?

RODERIGO: Every day thou daff'st me with some device,° Iago, and rather, as it seems to me now, keep'st from me all conveniency° than suppliest me with the least advantage of hope. I will indeed no longer endure it; nor am I yet persuaded to put up in peace what already I have foolishly suffered.

IAGO: Will you hear me, Roderigo?

RODERIGO: Faith, I have heard too much; for your words and performances are no kin together.

IAGO: You charge me most unjustly.

RODERIGO: With naught but truth. I have wasted myself out of my means. The jewels you have had from me to deliver to Desdemona would half have corrupted a votarist.° You have told me she hath received them, and returned me expectations and comforts of sudden respect° and acquaintance; but I find none.

153 discourse: Course. **159 Comfort forswear:** Happiness forsake. **160 defeat:** Destroy. **175 thou . . . device:** You put me off with some trick. **176 conveniency:** Favorable opportunities. **185 votarist:** Nun. **186 sudden respect:** Immediate notice.

IAGO: Well, go to; very well.

RODERIGO: Very well! go to! I cannot go to, man; nor 'tis not very well. By this hand, I say 'tis very scurvy, and begin to find myself fopped° in it.

IAGO: Very well.

RODERIGO: I tell you 'tis not very well. I will make myself known to Desdemona. If she will return me my jewels, I will give over my suit and repent my unlawful solicitation; if not, assure yourself I will seek satisfaction of you.

IAGO: You have said now.

RODERIGO: Ay, and said nothing but what I protest intendment of doing.

IAGO: Why, now I see there's mettle in thee; and even from this instant do build on thee a better opinion than ever before. Give me thy hand, Roderigo. Thou has taken against me a most just exception; but yet I protest I have dealt most directly° in thy affair.

RODERIGO: It hath not appeared.

IAGO: I grant indeed it hath not appeared, and your suspicion is not without wit and judgment. But, Roderigo, if thou hast that in thee indeed which I have greater reason to believe now than ever, I mean purpose, courage, and valor, this night show it. If thou the next night following enjoy not Desdemona, take me from this world with treachery and devise engines for° my life.

RODERIGO: Well, what is it? Is it within reason and compass?

IAGO: Sir, there is especial commission come from Venice to depute Cassio in Othello's place.

RODERIGO: Is that true? Why, then Othello and Desdemona return again to Venice.

IAGO: O, no; he goes into Mauritania and takes away with him the fair Desdemona, unless his abode be lingered here° by some accident; wherein none can be so determinate° as the removing of Cassio.

RODERIGO: How do you mean removing of him?

IAGO: Why, by making him uncapable of Othello's place—knocking out his brains.

RODERIGO: And that you would have me to do?

IAGO: Ay, if you dare do yourself a profit and a right. He sups to-night with a harlotry, and thither will I go to him. He knows not yet of his honorable fortune. If you will watch his going thence, which I will fashion to fall out between twelve and one, you may take him at your pleasure. I will be near to second your attempt, and he shall fall between us. Come, stand not amazed at it, but go along with me. I will show you such a necessity in his death that you shall think yourself bound to put it on him. It is now high supper time, and the night grows to waste. About it!

RODERIGO: I will hear further reason for this.

IAGO: And you shall be satisfied. *Exeunt.*

190 fopped: Duped. **200 directly:** Straightforwardly. **207 engines for:** Plots against. **214 abode . . . here:** Stay here be extended. **215 determinate:** Effective.

[Scene III: Within the castle.]

Enter Othello, Lodovico, Desdemona, Emilia, and Attendants.

LODOVICO: I do beseech you, sir, trouble yourself no further.
OTHELLO: O, pardon me; 'twill do me good to walk.
LODOVICO: Madam, good night. I humbly thank your ladyship.
DESDEMONA: Your honor is most welcome.
OTHELLO: Will you walk, sir?
O, Desdemona—
DESDEMONA: My lord?
OTHELLO: Get you to bed on th' instant; I will be returned forthwith. Dismiss your attendant there. Look't be done.
DESDEMONA: I will, my lord.

Exit [Othello, with Lodovico and Attendants].

EMILIA: How goes it now? He looks gentler than he did.
DESDEMONA: He says he will return incontinent.°
He hath commanded me to go to bed,
And bade me to dismiss you.
EMILIA: Dismiss me?
DESDEMONA: It was his bidding; therefore, good Emilia,
Give me my nightly wearing, and adieu.
We must not now displease him.
EMILIA: I would you had never seen him!
DESDEMONA: So would not I. My love doth so approve him
That even his stubbornness,° his checks,° his frowns—
Prithee unpin me—have grace and favor in them.
EMILIA: I have laid those sheets you bade me on the bed.
DESDEMONA: All's one. Good faith, how foolish are our minds!
If I do die before thee, prithee shroud me
In one of those same sheets.
EMILIA: Come, come! You talk.
DESDEMONA: My mother had a maid called Barbary.
She was in love; and he she loved proved mad°
And did forsake her. She had a song of "Willow";
An old thing 'twas; but it expressed her fortune,
And she died singing it. That song to-night
Will not go from my mind; I have much to do
But to go hang my head all at one side
And sing it like poor Barbary. Prithee dispatch.
EMILIA: Shall I go fetch your nightgown?°
DESDEMONA: No, unpin me here.
This Lodovico is a proper man.

Scene III. 11 incontinent: At once. **19 stubbornness:** Roughness. **checks:** Rebukes. **26 mad:** Wild, faithless. **33 nightgown:** Dressing gown.

EMILIA: A very handsome man.

DESDEMONA: He speaks well.

EMILIA: I know a lady in Venice would have walked barefoot to Palestine for a touch of his nether lip.

DESDEMONA *(sings)*: "The poor soul sat sighing by a sycamore tree
Sing all a green willow;
Her hand on her bosom, her head on her knee,
Sing willow, willow, willow.
The fresh streams ran by her and murmured her moans;
Sing willow, willow, willow;
Her salt tears fell from her, and soft'ned the stones"—

Lay by these.

"Sing willow, willow, willow"—
Prithee hie thee;° he'll come anon.
"Sing all a green willow must be my garland.
Let nobody blame him; his scorn I approve"—

Nay, that's not next. Hark! who is't that knocks?

EMILIA: It's the wind.

DESDEMONA *(sings)*: "I call my love false love; but what said he then?
"Sing willow, willow, willow"—
If I court moe women, you'll couch with moe men."
So get thee gone; good night. Mine eyes do itch.
Doth that bode weeping?

EMILIA: 'Tis neither here nor there.

DESDEMONA: I have heard it said so. O, these men, these men!
Dost thou in conscience think—tell me, Emilia—
That there be women do abuse their husbands
In such gross kind?

EMILIA: There be some such, no question.

DESDEMONA: Wouldst thou do such a deed for all the world?

EMILIA: Why, would not you?

DESDEMONA: No, by this heavenly light!

EMILIA: Nor I neither by this heavenly light.
I might do't as well i' th' dark.

DESDEMONA: Wouldst thou do such a deed for all the world?

EMILIA: The world's a huge thing; it is a great price for a small vice.

DESDEMONA: In troth, I think thou wouldst not.

EMILIA: In troth, I think I should; and undo't when I had done it. Marry, I would not do such a thing for a joint-ring,° nor for measures of lawn, nor for gowns, petticoats, nor caps, nor any petty exhibition;° but, for all the whole world—'Ud's pity! who would not make her husband a cuckold to make him a monarch? I should venture purgatory for't.

DESDEMONA: Beshrew me if I would do such a wrong

48 hie thee: Hurry. **70 joint-ring:** Ring made in separable halves. **71 exhibition:** Gift.

For the whole world.
EMILIA: Why, the wrong is but a wrong i' th' world; and having the world for your labor, 'tis a wrong in your own world, and you might quickly make it right.
DESDEMONA: I do not think there is any such woman.
EMILIA: Yes, a dozen; and as many to th' vantage° as
would store° the world they played for.
But I do think it is their husbands' faults
If wives do fall. Say that they slack their duties
And pour our treasures into foreign laps;
Or else break out in peevish° jealousies,
Throwing restraint upon us; or say they strike us,
Or scant our former having° in despite—
Why, we have galls;° and though we have some grace,
Yet have we some revenge. Let husbands know
Their wives have sense like them. They see, and smell,
And have their palates both for sweet and sour,
As husbands have. What is it that they do
When they change us for others? Is it sport?
I think it is. And doth affection breed it?
I think it doth. Is't frailty that thus errs?
It is so too. And have not we affections,
Desires for sport, and frailty, as men have?
Then let them use us well; else let them know,
The ills we do, their ills instruct us so.
DESDEMONA: Good night, good night. God me such usage° send,
Not to pick bad from bad, but by bad mend! *Exeunt.*

[ACT V, Scene I: A street in Cyprus]

Enter Iago and Roderigo.

IAGO: Here, stand behind this bulk;° straight will he come.
Wear thy good rapier bare, and put it home.
Quick, quick! Fear nothing; I'll be at thy elbow.
It makes us, or it mars us—think on that,
And fix most firm thy resolution.
RODERIGO: Be near at hand; I may miscarry in't.
IAGO: Here, at thy hand. Be bold, and take thy stand.
[Stands aside.]
RODERIGO: I have no great devotion to the deed,
And yet he hath given me satisfying reasons.

80 to th' vantage: Besides. **81 store:** Populate. **85 peevish:** Senseless. **87 having:** Allowance. **88 galls:** Spirits to resent. **100 usage:** Habits. **ACT V, SCENE I. 1 bulk:** Projecting shop-front.

'Tis but a man gone. Forth my sword! He dies!
IAGO: I have rubbed this young quat° almost to the sense,°
And he grows angry. Now whether he kill Cassio,
Or Cassio him, or each do kill the other,
Every way makes my gain. Live Roderigo,
He calls me to a restitution large
Of gold and jewels that I bobbed° from him
As gifts to Desdemona.
It must not be. If Cassio do remain,
He hath a daily beauty in his life
That makes me ugly; and besides, the Moor
May unfold me to him; there stand I in much peril.
No, he must die. Be't so! I hear him coming.

Enter Cassio.

RODERIGO: I know his gait. 'Tis he. Villain, thou diest!

[Makes a pass at Cassio.]

CASSIO: That thrust had been mine enemy indeed
But that my coat° is better than thou know'st.
I will make proof of thine.

[Draws, and wounds Roderigo.]

RODERIGO: O, I am slain!

[Iago darts from concealment behind Cassio, wounds him in the leg, and exit.]

CASSIO: I am maimed for ever. Help, ho! Murder! murder!

[Falls.]

Enter Othello.

OTHELLO: The voice of Cassio. Iago keeps his word.
RODERIGO: O, villain that I am!
OTHELLO: It is even so.
CASSIO: O, help, ho! light! a surgeon!
OTHELLO: 'Tis he. O brave Iago, honest and just,
That hast such noble sense of thy friend's wrong!
Thou teachest me. Minion,° your dear lies dead,
And your unblest fate hies.° Strumpet, I come.
Forth of my heart those charms, thine eyes, are blotted.
Thy bed, lust-stained, shall with lust's blood be spotted.

Exit Othello.

Enter Lodovico and Gratiano.

CASSIO: What, ho? No watch? No passage?° Murder! murder!
GRATIANO: 'Tis some mischance. The cry is very direful.

11 quat: Pimple. **sense:** Quick. **16 bobbed:** Swindled. **25 coat:** Undershirt of mail. **33 Minion:** Mistress. **34 hies:** Hurries on. **37 passage:** Passersby.

CASSIO: O, help!
LODOVICO: Hark!
RODERIGO: O wretched villain!
LODOVICO: Two or three groan. It is a heavy° night.
These may be counterfeits. Let's think't unsafe
To come in to the cry without more help.
RODERIGO: Nobody come? Then shall I bleed to death.
LODOVICO: Hark!

Enter Iago, with a light.

GRATIANO: Here's one comes in his shirt, with light and weapons.
IAGO: Who's there? Whose noise is this that cries on° murder?
LODOVICO: We do not know.
IAGO: Did not you hear a cry?
CASSIO: Here, here! For heaven's sake, help me!
IAGO: What's the matter?
GRATIANO: This is Othello's ancient, as I take it.
LODOVICO: The same indeed, a very valiant fellow.
IAGO: What are you here that cry so grievously?
CASSIO: Iago? O, I am spoiled, undone by villains!
Give me some help.
IAGO: O me, lieutenant! What villains have done this?
CASSIO: I think that one of them is hereabout
And cannot make° away.
IAGO: O treacherous villains!

[To Lodovico and Gratiano.]

What are you there? Come in, and give some help.
RODERIGO: O, help me here!
CASSIO: That's one of them.
IAGO: O murd'rous slave! O villain!

[Stabs Roderigo.]

RODERIGO: O damned Iago! O inhuman dog!
IAGO: Kill men i' th' dark? — Where be these bloody thieves? —
How silent is this town! — Ho! murder! murder! —
What may you be? Are you of good or evil?
LODOVICO: As you shall prove us, praise us.
IAGO: Signior Lodovico?
LODOVICO: He, sir.
IAGO: I cry you mercy. Here's Cassio hurt by villains.
GRATIANO: Cassio?
IAGO: How is't, brother?
CASSIO: My leg is cut in two.
IAGO: Marry,° heaven forbid!
Light, gentlemen. I'll bind it with my shirt.

42 heavy: Cloudy, dark. **48 cries on:** Raises the cry of. **58 make:** Get. **72 Marry:** (From "By Mary").

Enter Bianca.

BIANCA: What is the matter, ho? Who is't that cried?
IAGO: Who is't that cried?
BIANCA: O my dear Cassio! my sweet Cassio!
O Cassio, Cassio, Cassio!
IAGO: O notable strumpet!—Cassio, may you suspect
Who they should be that have thus mangled you?
CASSIO: No.
GRATIANO: I am sorry to find you thus. I have been to seek you.
IAGO: Lend me a garter. So. O for a chair°
To bear him easily hence!
BIANCA: Alas, he faints! O Cassio, Cassio, Cassio!
IAGO: Gentlemen all, I do suspect this trash
To be a party in this injury.—
Patience a while, good Cassio.—Come, come!
Lend me a light. Know we this face or no?
Alas, my friend and my dear countryman
Roderigo? No—Yes, sure.—O heaven, Roderigo!
GRATIANO: What, of Venice?
IAGO: Even he, sir. Did you know him?
GRATIANO: Know him? Ay.
IAGO: Signior Gratiano? I cry your gentle pardon.
These bloody accidents must excuse my manners
That so neglected you.
GRATIANO: I am glad to see you.
IAGO: How do you, Cassio?—O, a chair, a chair!
GRATIANO: Roderigo?
IAGO: He, he, 'tis he!

[A chair brought in.]

O, that's well said;° the chair.
Some good man bear him carefully from hence.
I'll fetch the general's surgeon. *[To Bianca.]* For you, mistress,
Save you your labor.—He that lies slain here, Cassio,
Was my dear friend. What malice was between you?
CASSIO: None in the world; nor do I know the man.
IAGO *[to Bianca]*: What, look you pale?—O, bear him out o' th' air.

[Cassio and Roderigo are borne off.]

Stay you, good gentlemen.—Look you pale, mistress?—
Do you perceive the gastness° of her eye?—
Nay, if you stare, we shall hear more anon.
Behold her well; I pray you look upon her.
Do you see, gentlemen? Nay, guiltiness will speak,
Though tongues were out of use.

82 chair: Litter. **99 well said:** Well done. **107 gastness:** Terror.

Enter Emilia.

EMILIA: 'Las, what's the matter? What's the matter, husband?
IAGO: Cassio hath here been set on in the dark
By Roderigo, and fellows that are scaped.
He's almost slain, and Roderigo dead.
EMILIA: Alas, good gentlemen! alas, good Cassio!
IAGO: This is the fruits of whoring. Prithee, Emilia,
Go know of Cassio where he supped to-night.

[To Bianca.]

What, do you shake at that?
BIANCA: He supped at my house; but I therefore shake not.
IAGO: O, did he so? I charge you go with me.
EMILIA: Fie, fie upon thee, strumpet!
BIANCA: I am no strumpet, but of life as honest°
As you that thus abuse me.
EMILIA: As I? Foh! fie upon thee!
IAGO: Kind gentlemen, let's go see poor Cassio dressed.

[To Bianca.]

Come, mistress, you must tell's another tale.
Emilia, run you to the citadel
And tell my lord and lady what hath happed.

[Exit Emilia.]

Will you go on afore? *Exeunt [all but Iago].*
This is the night
That either makes me or fordoes° me quite. *[Exit.]*

[Scene II: A bedchamber in the castle.]

Desdemona [asleep] in her bed. Enter Othello with a light.

OTHELLO: It is the cause, it is the cause,° my soul.
Let me not name it to you, you chaste stars!
It is the cause. Yet I'll not shed her blood,
Nor scar that whiter skin of hers than snow,
And smooth as monumental alabaster.
Yet she must die, else she'll betray more men.
Put out the light, and then put out the light.
If I quench thee, thou flaming minister,°
I can again thy former light restore,
Should I repent me; but once put out thy light,
Thou cunning'st pattern of excelling nature,
I know not where is that Promethean heat°

123 honest: Chaste. **130 fordoes:** Destroys. **Scene II. 1 cause:** Cause of justice. **8 minister:** Servant. **12 Promethean heat:** Divine fire.

That can thy light relume.° When I have plucked the rose,
I cannot give it vital growth again;
It needs must wither. I'll smell thee on the tree.

(He kisses her.)

O balmy breath, that dost almost persuade
Justice to break her sword! One more, one more!
Be thus when thou art dead, and I will kill thee,
And love thee after. One more, and that's the last!
So sweet was ne'er so fatal. I must weep,
But they are cruel tears. This sorrow's heavenly;
It strikes where it doth love. She wakes.

DESDEMONA: Who's there? Othello?
OTHELLO: Ay, Desdemona.
DESDEMONA: Will you come to bed, my lord?
OTHELLO: Have you prayed to-night, Desdemona?
DESDEMONA: Ay, my lord.
OTHELLO: If you bethink yourself of any crime°
Unreconciled as yet to heaven and grace,
Solicit for it straight.
DESDEMONA: Alack, my lord, what may you mean by that?
OTHELLO: Well, do it, and be brief; I will walk by.
I would not kill thy unpreparèd spirit.
No, heaven forfend!° I would not kill thy soul.
DESDEMONA: Talk you of killing?
OTHELLO: Ay, I do.
DESDEMONA: Then heaven
Have mercy on me!
OTHELLO: Amen, with all my heart!
DESDEMONA: If you say so, I hope you will not kill me.
OTHELLO: Hum!
DESDEMONA: And yet I fear you; for you're fatal then
When your eyes roll so. Why I should fear I know not,
Since guiltiness I know not; but yet I feel I fear.
OTHELLO: Think on thy sins.
DESDEMONA: They are loves I bear to you.
OTHELLO: Ay, and for that thou diest.
DESDEMONA: That death 's unnatural that kills for loving.
Alas, why gnaw you so your nether lip?
Some bloody passion shakes your very frame.
These are portents,° but yet I hope, I hope,
They do not point on me.
OTHELLO: Peace and be still!
DESDEMONA: I will so. What's the matter?

13 relume: Relight. **26 crime:** Sin. **32 forfend:** Forbid. **45 portents:** Signs of impending violence.

OTHELLO: That handkerchief which I so loved and gave thee
Thou gav'st to Cassio.
DESDEMONA: No, by my life and soul!
Send for the man and ask him.
OTHELLO: Sweet soul, take heed,
Take heed of perjury; thou art on thy deathbed.
DESDEMONA: Ay, but not yet to die.
OTHELLO: Yes, presently.°
Therefore confess thee freely of thy sin;
For to deny each article with oath
Cannot remove nor choke the strong conception°
That I do groan withal. Thou art to die.
DESDEMONA: Then Lord have mercy on me!
OTHELLO: I say amen.
DESDEMONA: And have you mercy too! I never did
Offend° you in my life; never loved Cassio
But with such general warranty of heaven
As I might love. I never gave him token.
OTHELLO: By heaven, I saw my handkerchief in's hand!
O perjured woman! thou dost stone my heart,°
And mak'st me call what I intend to do
A murder, which I thought a sacrifice.
I saw the handkerchief.
DESDEMONA: He found it then.
I never gave it him. Send for him hither.
Let him confess a truth.
OTHELLO: He hath confessed.
DESDEMONA: What, my lord?
OTHELLO: That he hath used thee.
DESDEMONA: How? Unlawfully?
OTHELLO: Ay.
DESDEMONA: He will not say so.
OTHELLO: No, his mouth is stopped.
Honest Iago hath ta'en order° for't.
DESDEMONA: O, my fear interprets. What, is he dead?
OTHELLO: Had all his hairs been lives, my great revenge
Had stomach for them all.
DESDEMONA: Alas, he is betrayed, and I undone!
OTHELLO: Out, strumpet! Weep'st thou for him to my face?
DESDEMONA: O, banish me, my lord, but kill me not!
OTHELLO: Down, strumpet!
DESDEMONA: Kill me to-morrow; let me live to-night!
OTHELLO: Nay, if you strive—

52 presently: At once. **55 conception:** Belief. **59 Offend:** Wrong. **63 stone my heart:** Turn my heart to stone. **72 ta'en order:** Taken measures.

DESDEMONA: But half an hour!
OTHELLO: Being done, there is no pause.
DESDEMONA: But while I say one prayer!
OTHELLO: It is too late.

(Smothers her.)

DESDEMONA: [O Lord, Lord, Lord!]

Emilia at the door.

EMILIA *(calls within)*: My lord, my lord! What, ho! my lord, my lord!
OTHELLO: What noise is this? Not dead? not yet quite dead?
I that am cruel am yet merciful;
I would not have thee linger in thy pain.
So, so.
EMILIA *(within)*: What, ho! my lord, my lord!
OTHELLO: Who's there?
EMILIA *(within)*: O, good my lord, I would speak a word with you!
OTHELLO: Yes, 'tis Emilia.—By and by.°—She's dead.—
'Tis like she comes to speak of Cassio's death.
The noise was here. Ha! no more moving?
Still as the grave.—Shall she come in? Were't good!—
I think she stirs again. No.—What's best to do?
If she come in, she'll sure speak to my wife.
My wife! my wife! what wife? I have no wife.
O, insupportable! O heavy hour!
Methinks it should be now a huge eclipse
Of sun and moon, and that th' affrighted globe
Should yawn° at alteration.
EMILIA *(within)*: I do beseech you
That I may speak with you, O good my lord!
OTHELLO: I had forgot thee. O, come in, Emilia.
Soft, by and by.—Let me the curtains draw.—

[Closes the bed-curtains.]

Where art thou?

[Opens the door.]

Enter Emilia.

What's the matter with thee now?
EMILIA: O my good lord, yonder's foul murder done!
OTHELLO: What? Now?
EMILIA: But now, my lord.
OTHELLO: It is the very error° of the moon.
She comes more nearer earth than she was wont
And makes men mad.

92 By and by: Just a moment (addressed to Emilia). **102 yawn:** Open, as in an earthquake. **110 error:** Straying off course.

EMILIA: Cassio, my lord, hath killed a young Venetian
Called Roderigo.
OTHELLO: Roderigo killed?
And Cassio killed?
EMILIA: No, Cassio is not killed.
OTHELLO: Not Cassio killed? Then murder's out of tune,
And sweet revenge grows harsh.
DESDEMONA: O, falsely, falsely murdered?
EMILIA: O, Lord! what cry is that?
OTHELLO: That? What?
EMILIA: Out and alas! that was my lady's voice.
Help! help, ho! help! O lady, speak again!
Sweet Desdemona! O sweet mistress, speak!
DESDEMONA: A guiltless death I die.
EMILIA: O, who hath done this deed?
DESDEMONA: Nobody—I myself. Farewell.
Commend° me to my kind lord. O, farewell!

(She dies.)

OTHELLO: Why, how should she be murd'red?
EMILIA: Alas, who knows?
OTHELLO: You heard her say herself, it was not I.
EMILIA: She said so. I must needs report the truth.
OTHELLO: She's like a liar gone to burning hell!
'Twas I that killed her.
EMILIA: O, the more angel she,
And you the blacker devil!
OTHELLO: She turned to folly, and she was a whore.
EMILIA: Thou dost belie her, and thou art a devil.
OTHELLO: She was false as water.°
EMILIA: Thou art rash as fire to say
That she was false. O, she was heavenly true!
OTHELLO: Cassio did top her. Ask thy husband else.
O, I were damned beneath all depth in hell
But that I did proceed upon just grounds
To this extremity. Thy husband knew it all.
EMILIA: My husband?
OTHELLO: Thy husband.
EMILIA: That she was false to wedlock?
OTHELLO: Ay, with Cassio. Nay, had she been true,
If heaven would make me such another world
Of one entire and perfect chrysolite,°
I'ld not have sold her for it.

126 Commend: Remember. **135 water:** (Which is yielding). **146 chrysolite:** (Precious topaz).

EMILIA: My husband?
OTHELLO: Ay 'twas he that told me first.
An honest man he is, and hates the slime
That sticks on filthy deeds.
EMILIA: My husband?
OTHELLO: What needs this iterance,° woman? I say thy husband.
EMILIA: O mistress, villainy hath made mocks with love!
My husband say that she was false?
OTHELLO: He, woman.
I say, thy husband. Dost understand the word?
My friend, thy husband; honest, honest Iago.
EMILIA: If he say so, may his pernicious soul
Rot half a grain a day! he lies to th' heart.
She was too fond of her most filthy bargain.
OTHELLO: Ha!
EMILIA: Do thy worst.
This deed of thine is no more worthy heaven
Than thou wast worthy her.
OTHELLO: Peace, you were best.
EMILIA: Thou hast not half the power to do me harm
As I have to be hurt.° O gull! O dolt!
As ignorant as dirt! thou hast done a deed—
I care not for thy sword; I'll make thee known,
Though I lost twenty lives. Help! help! Ho! help!
The Moor hath killed my mistress! Murder! murder!

Enter Montano, Gratiano, Iago, and others.

MONTANO: What is the matter? How now, general?
EMILIA: O, are you come, Iago? You have done well,
That men must lay their murders on your neck.
GRATIANO: What is the matter?
EMILIA: Disprove this villain, if thou be'st a man.
He says thou told'st him that his wife was false.
I know thou didst not; thou'rt not such a villain.
Speak, for my heart is full.
IAGO: I told him what I thought, and told no more
Than what he found himself was apt and true.
EMILIA: But did you ever tell him she was false?
IAGO: I did.
EMILIA: You told a lie, an odious damnèd lie!
Upon my soul, a lie! a wicked lie!
She false with Cassio? Did you say with Cassio?
IAGO: With Cassio, mistress. Go to, charm° your tongue.

151 iterance: Repetition. **164 to be hurt:** To endure hurt. **184 charm:** Cast a spell on.

EMILIA: I will not charm my tongue; I am bound to speak:
My mistress here lies murdered in her bed—
ALL: O heavens forfend!
EMILIA: And your reports have set the murder on.
OTHELLO: Nay, stare not, masters. It is true indeed.
GRATIANO: 'Tis a strange truth.
MONTANO: O monstrous act!
EMILIA: Villainy, villainy, villainy!
I think upon't—I think I smell't!—O villainy!
I thought so then.—I'll kill myself for grief.—
O villainy, villainy!
IAGO: What, are you mad? I charge you get you home.
EMILIA: Good gentlemen, let me have leave to speak.
'Tis proper I obey him, but not now.
Perchance, Iago, I will ne'er go home.
OTHELLO: O! O! O! *(Falls on the bed.)*
EMILIA: Nay, lay thee down and roar!
For thou hast killed the sweetest innocent
That e'er did lift up eye.
OTHELLO: O, she was foul!
[Rises.]
I scarce did know you, uncle. There lies your niece,
Whose breath, indeed, these hands have newly stopped.
I know this act shows° horrible and grim.
GRATIANO: Poor Desdemon! I am glad thy father's dead.
Thy match was mortal to him, and pure grief
Shore his old thread in twain. Did he live now,
This sight would make him do a desperate turn;°
Yea, curse his better angel from his side,
And fall to reprobation.°
OTHELLO: 'Tis pitiful; but yet Iago knows
That she with Cassio hath the act of shame
A thousand times committed. Cassio confessed it;
And she did gratify° his amorous works
With that recognizance° and pledge of love
Which I first gave her. I saw it in his hand.
It was a handkerchief, an antique token
My father gave my mother.
EMILIA: O God! O heavenly God!
IAGO: Zounds, hold your peace!
EMILIA: 'Twill out, 'twill out! I peace?

204 shows: Appears. **208 turn:** Act. **210 reprobation:** Rejection by God, damnation. **214 gratify:** Reward. **215 recognizance:** Token.

No, I will speak as liberal as the north,°
Let heaven and men and devils, let them all,
All, all, cry shame against me, yet I'll speak.
IAGO: Be wise, and get you home.
EMILIA: I will not.

[Iago draws and threatens Emilia.]

GRATIANO: Fie!
Your sword upon a woman?
EMILIA: O thou dull Moor, that handkerchief thou speak'st of
I found by fortune, and did give my husband;
For often with a solemn earnestness—
More than indeed belonged to such a trifle—
He begged of me to steal't.
IAGO: Villainous whore!
EMILIA: She give it Cassio? No, alas, I found it,
And I did give't my husband.
IAGO: Filth, thou liest!
EMILIA: By heaven, I do not, I do not, gentlemen.
O murd'rous coxcomb! what should such a fool
Do with so good a wife?
OTHELLO: Are there no stones° in heaven
But what serves for the thunder? Precious villain!

The Moor runs at Iago [but is disarmed by Montano].

Iago kills his wife.

GRATIANO: The woman falls. Sure he hath killed his wife.
EMILIA: Ay, ay. O, lay me by my mistress' side. *Exit Iago.*
GRATIANO: He's gone, but his wife's killed.
MONTANO: 'Tis a notorious° villain. Take you this weapon,
Which I have here recovered from the Moor.
Come, guard the door without. Let him not pass,
But kill him rather. I'll after that same villain,
For 'tis a damnèd slave.

Exit [Montano, with all but Othello and Emilia].

OTHELLO: I am not valiant neither;
But every puny whipster° gets my sword.
But why should honor outlive honesty?
Let it go all.
EMILIA: What did thy song bode, lady?
Hark, canst thou hear me? I will play the swan,
And die in music. *[Sings.]* "Willow, willow, willow."

221 liberal as the north: Unchecked as the north wind blows. **235 stones:** Bolts like those used for thunderbolts. **240 notorious:** Notable. **245 puny whipster:** Whippersnapper.

Moor, she was chaste. She loved thee, cruel Moor:
So come my soul to bliss as I speak true.
So speaking as I think, alas, I die.

(She dies.)

OTHELLO: I have another weapon in this chamber;
It is a sword of Spain, the ice brook's° temper.
O, here it is.—Uncle, I must come forth.

GRATIANO *(within)*: If thou attempt it, it will cost thee dear.
Thou hast no weapon, and perforce must suffer.

OTHELLO: Look in upon me then and speak with me,
Or, naked° as I am, I will assault thee.

[Enter Gratiano.]

GRATIANO: What is the matter?

OTHELLO: Behold, I have a weapon;
A better never did itself sustain
Upon a soldier's thigh. I have seen the day
That with this little arm and this good sword
I have made my way through more impediments
Than twenty times your stop.° But O vain boast!
Who can control his fate? 'Tis not so now.
Be not afraid, though you do see me weaponed.
Here is my journey's end, here is my butt,°
And very seamark° of my utmost sail:
Do you go back dismayed? 'Tis a lost° fear.
Man but a rush° against Othello's breast,
And he retires. Where should Othello go?
Now, how dost thou look now? O ill-starred wench!
Pale as thy smock! When we shall meet at compt,°
This look of thine will hurl my soul from heaven,
And fiends will snatch at it. Cold, cold, my girl?
Even like thy chastity.
O cursèd, cursèd slave! Whip me, ye devils,
From the possession of this heavenly sight!
Blow me about in winds! roast me in sulphur!
Wash me in steep-down gulfs of liquid fire!
Oh Desdemon! dead Desdemon! dead! Oh! Oh!

Enter Lodovico, Montano, Iago [as prisoner], and Officers; Cassio in a chair.

LODOVICO: Where is this rash and most unfortunate man?

OTHELLO: That's he that was Othello. Here I am.

254 ice brook: I.e., a Spanish blade, tempered in cold running water. **259 naked:** Disarmed. **265 stop:** Power to stop. **268 butt:** Limit. **269 seamark:** Beacon, destination. **270 lost:** Wasted. **271 Man but a rush:** Wield only a reed. **274 compt:** Final accounting, Last Judgment.

LODOVICO: Where is that viper? Bring the villain forth.
OTHELLO: I look down towards his feet°—but that's a fable.
If that thou be'st a devil, I cannot kill thee.

[Wounds Iago.]

LODOVICO: Wrench his sword from him.

[Othello is disarmed.]

IAGO: I bleed, sir, but not killed.
OTHELLO: I am not sorry neither. I'ld have thee live;
For in my sense, 'tis happiness to die.
LODOVICO: O thou Othello that wert once so good,
Fall'n in the practice° of a damnèd slave,
What shall be said to thee?
OTHELLO: Why, anything;
An honorable murderer, if you will;
For naught did I in hate, but all in honor.
LODOVICO: This wretch hath part confessed his villainy.
Did you and he consent in° Cassio's death?
OTHELLO: Ay.
CASSIO: Dear general, I never gave you cause.
OTHELLO: I do believe it, and I ask your pardon.
Will you, I pray, demand that demi-devil
Why he hath thus ensnared my soul and body?
IAGO: Demand me nothing. What you know, you know.
From this time forth I never will speak word.
LODOVICO: What, not to pray?
GRATIANO: Torments will ope your lips.
OTHELLO: Well, thou dost best.
LODOVICO: Sir, you shall understand what hath befall'n,
Which, as I think, you know not. Here is a letter
Found in the pocket of the slain Roderigo;
And here another. The one of them imports
The death of Cassio to be undertook
By Roderigo.
OTHELLO: O villain!
CASSIO: Most heathenish and most gross!
LODOVICO: Now here's another discontented paper
Found in the pocket too; and this, it seems,
Roderigo meant t' have sent this damnèd villain;
But that, belike, Iago in the nick°
Came in and satisfied him.
OTHELLO: O thou pernicious caitiff!—

286 I . . . feet: I.e., to see if they are cloven, like the Devil's. **292 practice:** Plot. **297 consent in:** Agree upon. **317 nick:** Nick of time.

How came you, Cassio, by that handkerchief
That was my wife's?

CASSIO: I found it in my chamber;
And he himself confessed but even now
That there he dropped it for a special purpose
Which wrought to his desire.

OTHELLO: O fool! fool! fool!

CASSIO: There is besides in Roderigo's letter,
How he upbraids Iago that he made him
Brave me upon the watch; whereon it came
That I was cast;° and even but now he spake,
After long seeming dead—Iago hurt him,
Iago set him on.

LODOVICO: You must forsake this room and go with us.
Your power and your command is taken off,
And Cassio rules in Cyprus. For this slave,
If there be any cunning cruelty
That can torment him much and hold him long,
It shall be his. You shall close prisoner rest
Till that the nature of your fault be known
To the Venetian state. Come, bring away.

OTHELLO: Soft you! a word or two before you go.
I have done the state some service, and they know't.
No more of that. I pray you, in your letters,
When you shall these unlucky° deeds relate,
Speak of me as I am. Nothing extenuate,
Nor set down aught in malice. Then must you speak
Of one that loved not wisely, but too well;
Of one not easily jealous, but, being wrought,
Perplexed° in the extreme; of one whose hand,
Like the base Judean,° threw a pearl away
Richer than all his tribe; of one whose subdued° eyes,
Albeit unusèd to the melting mood,
Drop tears as fast as the Arabian trees
Their med'cinable gum. Set you down this.
And say besides that in Aleppo once,
Where a malignant and a turbaned Turk
Beat a Venetian and traduced the state,
I took by th' throat the circumcisèd dog
And smote him—thus.

(He stabs himself.)

327 cast: Dismissed. **341 unlucky:** Fatal. **346 Perplexed:** Distracted. **347 Judean:** Judas Iscariot (?) (quarto reads "Indian"). **348 subdued:** I.e., conquered by grief.

LODOVICO: O bloody period!°
GRATIANO: All that's spoke is marred.
OTHELLO: I kissed thee ere I killed thee. No way but this,
Killing myself, to die upon a kiss.

(He [falls upon the bed and] dies.)

CASSIO: This did I fear, but thought he had no weapon;
For he was great of heart.
LODOVICO *[to Iago]*: O Spartan dog,
More fell° than anguish, hunger, or the sea!
Look on the tragic loading of this bed.
This is thy work. The object poisons sight;
Let it be hid.° Gratiano, keep the house,
And seize upon° the fortunes of the Moor,
For they succeed on you. To you, lord governor,
Remains the censure° of this hellish villain,
The time, the place, the torture. O, enforce it!
Myself will straight aboard, and to the state
This heavy act with heavy heart relate.

Exeunt.

357 period: Ending. **362 fell:** Cruel. **365 Let it be hid:** I.e., draw the bed curtains. **366 seize upon:** Take legal possession of. **368 censure:** Judicial sentence.

THINKING ABOUT THE TEXT

1. Jealousy is one of the central motifs in this play. What characters are jealous and for what reasons?
2. Is Iago diabolically devious and clever, or is Othello especially gullible? How would you respond if a trusted friend made similar accusations against someone whom you cared for deeply?
3. Is Othello's tragic flaw—the quality that leads to his downfall—jealousy or something else, perhaps credulity?
4. Is it possible for Othello's love to turn so quickly into hate?
5. How might the end of the play and the final resolution of the characters' fates be seen as Shakespeare's commentary on jealousy?

A. C. BRADLEY

The Noble Othello

A. C. Bradley (1851–1935), a British literary critic and highly influential Shakespearean scholar, was the youngest boy among twenty-one children. His father was a well-regarded preacher. Bradley attended Balliol College at Oxford University and later was a professor at the University of Liverpool and at Oxford. His books include Oxford Lectures on Poetry *(1909) and* Shakespearean Tragedy *(1904), where "The Noble Othello" appeared. The essays published in both books were originally lectures delivered by Bradley. Upon his death, Bradley's will established a fellowship for English literary scholars. Here, Bradley refutes the common notion that Othello was unjustifiably and easily jealous by considering how Othello's character diminishes only in light of the evidence Iago provides regarding Desdemona's supposed affair.*

This character is so noble, Othello's feelings and actions follow so inevitably from it and from the forces brought to bear on it, and his sufferings are so heart-rending, that he stirs, I believe, in most readers a passion of mingled love and pity which they feel for no other hero in Shakespeare, and to which not even Mr. Swinburne can do more than justice. Yet there are some critics and not a few readers who cherish a grudge against him. They do not merely think that in the later stages of his temptation he showed a certain obtuseness, and that, to speak pedantically, he acted with unjustifiable precipitance and violence; no one, I suppose, denies that. But, even when they admit that he was not of a jealous temper, they consider that he *was* "easily jealous"; they seem to think that it was inexcusable in him to feel any suspicion of his wife at all; and they blame him for never suspecting Iago or asking him for evidence. I refer to this attitude of mind chiefly in order to draw attention to certain points in the story. It comes partly from mere inattention (for Othello did suspect Iago and did ask him for evidence); partly from a misconstruction of the text which makes Othello appear jealous long before he really is so; and partly from failure to realise certain essential facts. I will begin with these.

(1) Othello, we have seen, was trustful, and thorough in his trust. He put entire confidence in the honesty of Iago, who had not only been his companion in arms, but, as he believed, had just proved his faithfulness in the matter of the marriage. This confidence was misplaced, and we happen to know it; but it was no sign of stupidity in Othello. For his opinion of Iago was the opinion of practically everyone who knew him: and that opinion was that Iago was before all things "honest," his very faults being those of excess in honesty. This being so, even if Othello had not been trustful and simple, it would have been quite unnatural in him to be unmoved by the warnings of so honest a friend, warnings offered with extreme reluctance and manifestly from a sense of a friend's duty. *Any* husband would have been troubled by them.

(2) Iago does not bring these warnings to a husband who had lived with a wife for months and years and knew her like his sister or his bosom-friend. Nor is there any ground in Othello's character for supposing that, if he had been such a man, he would have felt and acted as he does in the play. But he was newly married; in the circumstances he cannot have known much of Desdemona before his marriage; and further he was conscious of being under the spell of a feeling which can give glory to the truth but can also give it to a dream.

(3) This consciousness in any imaginative man is enough, in such circumstances, to destroy his confidence in his powers of perception. In Othello's case,

after a long and most artful preparation, there now comes, to reinforce its effect, the suggestions that he is not an Italian, nor even a European; that he is totally ignorant of the thoughts and the customary morality of Venetian women; that he had himself seen in Desdemona's deception of her father how perfect an actress she could be. As he listens in horror, for a moment at least the past is revealed to him in a new and dreadful light, and the ground seems to sink under his feet. These suggestions are followed by a tentative but hideous and humiliating insinuation of what his honest and much-experienced friend fears may be the true explanation of Desdemona's rejection of acceptable suitors, and of her strange, and naturally temporary, preference for a black man. Here Iago goes too far. He sees something in Othello's face that frightens him, and he breaks off. Nor does this idea take any hold of Othello's mind. But it is not surprising that his utter powerlessness to repel it on the ground of knowledge of his wife, or even of that instinctive interpretation of character which is possible between persons of the same race, should complete his misery, so that he feels he can bear no more, and abruptly dismisses his friend (III. iii. 238).

Now I repeat that *any* man situated as Othello was would have been disturbed 5
by Iago's communications, and I add that many men would have been made wildly jealous. But up to this point, where Iago is dismissed, Othello, I must maintain, does not show jealousy. His confidence is shaken, he is confused and deeply troubled, he feels even horror; but he is not yet jealous in the proper sense of that word. In his soliloquy (III. iii. 258ff.) the beginning of this passion may be traced; but it is only after an interval of solitude, when he has had time to dwell on the idea presented to him, and especially after statements of fact, not mere general grounds of suspicion, are offered, that the passion lays hold of him. Even then, however, and indeed to the very end, he is quite unlike the essentially jealous man, quite unlike Leontes. No doubt the thought of another man's possessing the woman he loves is intolerable to him; no doubt the sense of insult and the impulse of revenge are at times most violent; and these are the feelings of jealousy proper. But these are not the chief or the deepest source of Othello's suffering. It is the wreck of his faith and his love. It is the feeling,

> If she be false, oh then Heaven mocks itself;

the feeling,

> O Iago, the pity of it, Iago!

the feeling,

> But there where I have garner'd up my heart,
> Where either I must live, or bear no life;
> The fountain from the which my current runs,
> Or else dries up—to be discarded thence. . . .

You will find nothing like this in Leontes.

Up to this point, it appears to me, there is not a syllable to be said against Othello. But the play is a tragedy, and from this point we may abandon the ungrateful and undramatic task of awarding praise and blame. When Othello, after a brief interval, re-enters (III. iii. 329), we see at once that the poison has been at work, and "burns like the mines of sulphur."

> Look where he comes! Not poppy, nor mandragora,
> Nor all the drowsy syrups of the world,
> Shall ever medicine thee to that sweet sleep
> Which thou owedst yesterday.

He is "on the rack," in an agony so unbearable that he cannot endure the sight of Iago. Anticipating the probability that Iago has spared him the whole truth, he feels that in that case his life is over and his "occupation gone" with all its glories. But he has not abandoned hope. The bare possibility that his friend is deliberately deceiving him—though such a deception would be a thing so monstrously wicked that he can hardly conceive it credible—is a kind of hope. He furiously demands proof, ocular proof. And when he is compelled to see that he is demanding an impossibility he still demands evidence. He forces it from the unwilling witness, and hears the maddening tale of Cassio's dream. It is enough. And if it were not enough, has he not sometimes seen a handkerchief spotted with strawberries in his wife's hand? Yes, it was his first gift to her.

> I know not that; but such a handkerchief—
> I am sure it was your wife's—did I to-day
> See Cassio wipe his beard with.

"If it be that," he answers—but what need to test the fact? The "madness of revenge" is in his blood, and hesitation is a thing he never knew. He passes judgment, and controls himself only to make his sentence a solemn vow.

The Othello of the Fourth Act is Othello in his fall. His fall is never complete, but he is much changed. Towards the close of the Temptation-scene he becomes at times most terrible, but his grandeur remains almost undiminished. Even in the following scene (III. iv.), where he goes to test Desdemona in the matter of the handkerchief, and receives a fatal confirmation of her guilt, our sympathy with him is hardly touched by any feeling of humiliation. But in the Fourth Act "Chaos has come." A slight interval of time may be admitted here. It is but slight; for it was necessary for Iago to hurry on, and terribly dangerous to leave a chance for a meeting of Cassio with Othello; and his insight into Othello's nature taught him that his plan was to deliver blow on blow, and never to allow his victim to recover from the confusion of the first shock. Still there is a slight interval; and when Othello reappears we see at a glance that he is a changed man. He is physically exhausted, and his mind is dazed. He sees everything blurred through a mist of blood and tears. He has actually forgotten the incident of the handkerchief, and has to be reminded of it. When Iago, perceiving that he can now risk almost any lie, tells him that Cassio has confessed his guilt, Othello, the hero who has seemed to us only second to Coriolanus in physical power, trembles all over; he mutters disjointed words; a blackness suddenly intervenes between his eyes and the world; he takes it for the shuddering testimony of nature to the horror he has just heard, and he falls senseless to the ground. When he recovers it is to watch Cassio, as he imagines, laughing over his shame. It is an imposition so gross, and should have been one so perilous, that Iago would never have ventured it before. But he is safe now. The sight only adds to the confusion of intellect the madness of rage; and a ravenous thirst for revenge, contending with motions of infinite longing and regret, conquers them. The delay till night-fall is torture to him. His self-control has wholly deserted him, and he strikes his wife in the presence of the Venetian envoy. He is so lost to all sense of reality that he never asks himself what will follow the deaths of Cassio and his wife. An ineradicable instinct of justice, rather than any last quiver of hope, leads him to question Emilia; but nothing could convince him now, and there follows the dreadful scene of accusation; and then, to allow us the relief of burning hatred and burning tears, the interview of Desdemona with Iago, and that last talk of hers with Emilia, and her last song.

But before the end there is again a change. The supposed death of Cassio (V. i.) satiates the thirst for vengeance. The Othello who enters the bed-chamber with the words,

> It is the cause, it is the cause, my soul,

is not the man of the Fourth Act. The deed he is bound to do is no murder, but a sacrifice. He is to save Desdemona from herself, not in hate but in honour; in honour, and also in love. His anger has passed; a boundless sorrow has taken its place; and

> this sorrow's heavenly:
> It strikes where it doth love.

Even when, at the sight of her apparent obduracy, and at the hearing of words which by a crowning fatality can only reconvince him of her guilt, these feelings give way to others, it is to righteous indignation they give way, not to rage; and, terribly painful as this scene is, there is almost nothing here to diminish the admiration and love which heighten pity. And pity itself vanishes, and love and admiration alone remain, in the majestic dignity and sovereign ascendancy of the close. Chaos has come and gone; and the Othello of the Council-chamber and the quay of Cyprus has returned, or a greater and nobler Othello still. As he speaks those final words in which all the glory and agony of his life—long ago in India and Arabia and Aleppo, and afterwards in Venice, and now in Cyprus—seem to pass before us, like the pictures that flash before the eyes of a drowning man, a triumphant scorn for the fetters of the flesh and the littleness of all the lives that must survive him sweeps our grief away, and when he dies upon a kiss the most painful of all tragedies leaves us for the moment free from pain, and exulting in the power of "love and man's unconquerable mind." *[1904]*

MILLICENT BELL

Othello's Jealousy

Millicent Bell is a professor emerita in the English department at Boston University and a frequent contributor to The New York Review of Books. *She is the author of the books* Marquand: An American Life *(1979),* Meaning in Henry James *(1993), and* Shakespeare's Tragic Skepticism *(2002), where this essay appeared after first publication in the* Yale Review *(1997). In "Othello's Jealousy," Bell delves into how the notion of "seeing is believing" drives Othello to madness as what he sees in life and what he sees in his imagination are used by Iago to disturb his trust in Desdemona.*

Oh, yes, the chief subject of *Othello* is sexual jealousy. Most dramatic representations seize upon and emphasize the way this condition, like a fatal disease, grows on the hero and destroys him until the recovery of sanity and dignity arrives at the tragic end. The more directly we see and hear him the more we almost share the madness that mounts in his mind until it reaches a point in which he appears to hallucinate, seeing what is not there, writhing before the inner vision of his wife's betrayal. In the recent Kenneth Branagh film this inner vision reaches the screen and the viewer is briefly unable to distinguish between what is and what is imagined as he or she sees—for a terrifying moment, like a clip from a porn film—Cassio's lips meeting Desdemona's, their naked bodies twining together. Film's hallucinatory power, its ability to make virtual what words have only suggested, its ability to make us voyeurs who desire to witness the last detail of a scene, particularly an erotic scene, adds something that goes beyond stage presentation. The movie's powerful language of the visible provides—delusively even to us, though we know Othello is deluded—that ultimate visibility which goes beyond the evidence Iago has manipulated to "prove" Othello's love a whore.

But the greater reserve of the play as we read it, and even the reserve of stage presentation, which works such tricks awkwardly if at all, reminds us that jealousy feeds, precisely, upon what is *not* witnessed but only imagined. Othello, desperately swinging between belief in his wife's innocence and conviction of her guilt, pleads for visible proof: "I'll see before I doubt," he cries. He thinks he can trust Desdemona, "for she had eyes and chose me," he tells Iago, who responds, "Look to your wife. Observe her well with Cassio; wear your eyes thus: not jealous, nor secure. . . . Look to't. . . . In Venice they do let God see the pranks / They dare not show their husbands." "Make me to see't," Othello pleads.

He groans, "Would I were satisfied!" but his tormentor observes—in an age before hidden video cameras and paparazzi—"but how? How satisfied, my Lord? / Would you the supervisor, grossly gape on? / Behold her topped?" and summons into inner view the dreadful vision, after all. But Iago says, at the same time,

It is impossible you should see this,
Were they as prime as goats, as hot as monkeys,
As salt as wolves in pride, and fools as gross
As Ignorance made drunk.

Iago will continue throughout the travail of Othello's jealousy to induce such hallucinations, to make Othello's own imagination set them forth on his inner stage. By the time we have reached the opening of the fourth act, the process is complete, and inner and outer vision are indistinguishable.

IAGO: Will you think so?
OTHELLO: Think so, Iago!
IAGO: What!
  To kiss in private?
OTHELLO: An unauthorized kiss!
IAGO: Or to be naked with her friend in bed
  An hour or more, not meaning any harm?
OTHELLO: Naked in bed, Iago, and not mean harm?

Othello is driven mad by what, by the force of suggestion, he *inwardly* sees, and yet he craves a certainty that can be satisfied only by outward sight—the sense that most convincingly assures us that we know what is before us. The central utterance in the play is, surely, Othello's anguished "Give me the ocular proof." But he craves confirmation of suspicion to end the agony aroused by what he cannot really see. For, as Iago says, "Her honor is an essence that's not seen." If he could witness the pair in bed together it might still not be enough. He is plagued by the realization that truth cannot be directly known; what we perceive is only *seeming*. "Seeing" and "seeming" are significantly repeated words that underline this problem throughout the play.

5 *Othello*, I want to argue against many of the play's critics, is the *most* intellectual of all Shakespeare's tragedies, including *Hamlet*, despite its concern with elementary personal emotion. In a genuine sense, the play is a "domestic tragedy," as it is frequently termed. But this is not at all to say that it simply shows the evolution of wife-murder, a version of the O. J. Simpson case. Harley Granville-Barker said it was "a tragedy without meaning," and A. C. Bradley thought it inferior to Shakespeare's other tragedies for lacking "the power of dilating the imagination by vague suggestions of huge universal powers working in the world of individual fate and passion." The editor of the New Cambridge Shakespeare edition, Norman Sanders, calls it "the most private of the great tragedies," though he insists that "to complain of its lack of supernatural reference or its limited metaphysical range is to miss the point." "The object poisons sight; / Let it be hid," says Lodovico when Othello and Desdemona lie dead together on their bed. Sanders says this "is the only possible end, because the arena for the struggle the protagonists have lived through is best symbolized by the curtained bed." But I shall insist that the

play is not the less philosophical for that. "Sight" is indeed "poisoned" —yet not merely because of the spectacle of a love that has made such horror, but because this ending has shown the inadequacy of human vision.

Shakespeare, as is his habit, is always telling us a number of things at once. The power of the theme of sexual jealousy obscures other subjects in the play. Race and the divisive role of prejudice seem much more central than used to be conceded by critics who could not imagine how the Elizabethan world provided Shakespeare with so strong a sense of the most acute social problem of modern societies—expressed by the symbolic fantasy of miscegenation, the monstrous union of the socially separated. Shakespeare's treatment of marital violence also contains much that we respond to with recognition, seeing this problem rooted, then as now, in false notions of the differentiations of gender. Jealousy is also rooted in the unnaturalness of *any* love inordinate in its expectations, because each of us is just one and no more, and the single "beast with two backs"—that frightening visibility with which Iago arouses the rage of Brabantio—is a monster created only in an instant of sensual joy. Jealousy is evidence of the doubt that lies at the bottom of love's desire for knowledge of another, the doubt beneath love's refusal to accept the difference between one's perception and another's reality. The torment of Othello is epistemological, a condition of doubt of which sexual jealousy is only a specific illustration or consequence.

That Othello is so vulnerable to suggestion, passing so readily from hypothesis to certainty, has bothered those who have complained that he does not connect, as a character, with what happens; his noble strength, the slowness to anger that rules his early responses to Brabantio and to the drunken scuffle that awakens him from his wedded bliss in Cyprus, the majesty of his language—none of this prepares us for the speed with which he casts reason and refinement aside and becomes brutal and coarse. But it is precisely because jealousy cannot be satisfied by any degree of proof that it is a representation of the effect of skepticism, the specter that haunted the Renaissance imagination.

At the end of the sixteenth century, natural science was becoming more empirical. The view the educated person took of human history and of an individual life was apt to distinguish more consciously between certainty and probability, to discriminate among different kinds of evidence, whereas what "truth" was had become problematic. Though the truth of received religion was still a matter of faith, only a few kinds of certainty—like the certainty of mathematical proofs—were practically attainable. Shakespeare's great contemporary, Sir Francis Bacon, aspired with his grand inductive program to the ultimate restitution of "moral certainty," a concept borrowed from theology by which one might be sure about most things after observing and evaluating the facts. Bacon's effort was directed against the devastating view expressed by Montaigne that nothing could be known. A response to the problem of Montaigne's radical disbelief has been noted in Shakespeare's best writing—the sonnets and the great tragedies. Florio's translation into English of Montaigne's *Essais* was published in 1603, the year before *Othello* appeared on the stage. Perhaps, even, as Stanley Cavell argues, Shakespeare intuitively anticipated the terrifying culmination of Renaissance skepticism in René Descartes, who would make the issue "no longer, or not alone, as with earlier skepticism, how to conduct oneself in an uncertain world; the issue suggested is how to live at all in a groundless world."

In *Othello*, Iago is the source of skepticism; his nihilism links him in Shakespeare's works with Thersites and Edmund. But Othello's mind is the theater in which faith in the unseen and unseeable contends with the doubt that demands physical seeing and yet is never convinced it sees enough. Because Othello becomes the victim of his desire to know by seeing, his almost unbelievable collapse, his too-swift descent from composure and confidence to panic and disbelief, can be understood. But we are not meant to view him altogether in terms of realistic psychology—though nothing seems more real than his actual feelings when they overtake him.

If we do try to explain his fall realistically, we find ourselves in the crossfire of critical tradition. F. R. Leavis was able to make a devastating case against Bradley's view that Othello's perfect nature—noble, strong-minded, self-disciplined—is destroyed by Iago's inhuman malice and intellect. Leavis discovered grounds for seeing Othello as a man infatuated with his own ideal view of himself, and *self*-destroyed. More recent psychological views suggest that Othello's great love, expressed in majestic, romantic hyperbole, may be the bluster of the untried bridegroom whose fear of inadequacy already rouses him from his nuptial bed along with the shouts of Iago and Roderigo in the opening scene. But neither a completely heroic nor a fatuous or secretly vulnerable Othello accounts adequately for the way this hero affects us. Perhaps Othello's improbable gullibility and precipitate fall depends, then, as E. E. Stoll claimed, on the literary convention of the "calumniator believed." We need to remember how commonplace and even farcical are some of the delusionary tricks that destroy Othello's faith in Desdemona; in Shakespeare's own *Much Ado About Nothing*, another ex-soldier, Claudio, is tricked by similar means into believing in the wantonness of his innocent betrothed. But Othello, unlike the lightweight Claudio, is really undone by an idea, though he is hardly philosopher enough himself to formulate it. Shakespeare makes us experience—through Othello's trauma—the absolute difference between a trust in appearances and the loss of that trust. . . .

Throughout *Othello*, Shakespeare's strong interest in the law is also evident in language full of legal terms drawn from the procedures of court trials that those who have hoped to detect more about his life from such elusive traces can suppose that he had had some training in the law. But English court trials were open to the public, forms of entertainment like the theater, and the audience for both was likely to contain persons who were amateur experts, like recent viewers of televised trials. Iago complains that Othello turned a deaf ear to those who urged his advancement; he "non-suites my Mediators," he says—that is, he rules their case out of court. When he refuses to tell Othello his private thoughts, he asks if anyone has "a breast so pure, / But some uncleanly apprehensions / Keep leets and law-days, and in sessions sit / With meditations lawful," "leets and law-days" being court sessions to certify the good behavior of a community. Pleading Cassio's case with Othello, Desdemona insists that the handkerchief business is but "a trick to put me from my suit." She chides herself for "Arraigning his unkindness with my soul; / But now I find I had suborned the witness / And he's indicted falsely," a reference to the crime of subornation of perjury. What is important to note, among these obscurities, is the way words that have a common usage as well as a specific legal sense seem to reverberate with a courtroom meaning—as when Othello's handkerchief, the central symbolic object that is the mark of the troth between him and Desdemona, is called "the recognizance and pledge of love," where "recognizance" is the *legal* word for a binding bond.

It is appropriate to the preoccupation of the play with a general epistemological crisis that the issue of proof is expressed as a legal question. The general evolution of thought in the sixteenth and seventeenth centuries is connected with the fact that English common law established in this period a foundation of rules of evidence that persists to this day. Brabantio's charges and Othello's refutation reflect current controversy over trials for witchcraft. In 1597, James I of England[1] had felt called upon to attempt in his *Demonologie* to refute Reginald Scott's attack (*Discoverie of Witchcraft*, 1584) on the procedures for trying those accused of witchcraft. Yet James I soon developed doubts and censured judges who rushed to judgment without adequate proof. A general movement had begun in the courts to develop proper modes of establishing this crime. Along with that skeptical doubt that caused some, like Montaigne, to doubt the existence of witchcraft altogether, the trial of witches was changing from the search for a hidden character—established only by confession, formerly extracted by torture, if necessary—to a weighing of visible effects, testified to by witnesses. The shift is epistemological.

The courtroom, like the stage, was for the Elizabethans a place where the dynamics of changing concepts of the self were being enacted, being tried. How might one argue from crime to criminal—or reverse the process? By what evidence might the play connect plot and character? In the courtroom it was not enough to argue from "reputation" in deciding probable guilt—as it is not enough for Iago to convict Desdemona by referring to her "Venetian" character—but the prosecution might add plausibility to its case by presenting, as Iago does, a narrative of events leading to her crime, by "imputation." Beyond this, how might guilt be proven? Circumstantial evidence in criminal cases was becoming the most usual basis of conviction. Iago protests that he cannot enable Othello to see his wife in her lover's arms, but adds,

> If imputation and strong circumstances,
> Which lead directly to the door of truth,
> Will give you satisfaction, you might have't.

[1] Before becoming James I of England in 1603, he was James VI of Scotland from 1567–1603. [Eds.]

The paradigm of a trial of law, invoked at the start by an actual trial, is replicated in the structure of the play, a trial of Desdemona that ends in her execution. In a terrible parody of judicial sentence, in the second scene of the last act, Othello enters with a speech of deliberate dignity:

> It is the cause, it is the cause, my soul:
> Let me not name it to you, you chaste stars.
> It is the cause. Yet I'll not shed her blood,
> Nor scar that whiter skin of hers than snow,
> And smooth as monumental alabaster—
> Yet she must die, else she'll betray more men.

"Cause" is a legal term in addition to meaning simply a reason for an occur- 15
rence. To seek a cause is to seek a motive to increase the probability of guilt, while the accused may claim for his deed that he had *just* cause. Iago has begun by telling Roderigo, "I hate the Moor. My cause is hearted; thine hath no less reason." He has begun the motive-hunting that Coleridge deemed motiveless; his search for his own motive is a legal procedure to reinforce belief. A cause may be a general purpose, even a high principle to which one is attached; the cause of a heavenly ideal of chastity for which, Othello declares, Desdemona must die. But a cause is also, simply, a suit, as Desdemona called her effort to win pardon for Cassio, acting as his "solicitor." And Othello's charge against Desdemona is a suit in which he becomes prosecutor, judge, and, finally, executioner under a rule of human law aimed not only at punishment but to protect society from further crimes by the criminal ("else she'll betray more men").

Proof as in a law court is what Othello so mistakenly has asked Iago to produce. When Othello says, "I'll see before I doubt; when I doubt prove," Iago says, "I speak not yet of proof," but urges him to watch Desdemona for some self-betrayal and sets forth, meanwhile, her record as a practiced deceiver who has known how to make seeing her directly impossible: "She that so young could give out such a seeming / To seal her father's eyes up close as oak." Perhaps this would not be enough—though Othello is already frantic—but prompt to his purpose, Desdemona reappears to drop the handkerchief that Iago will seize and enter into evidence. "Trifles light as air / Are to the jealous confirmations strong / As proofs of holy writ"—though a just judge and dispassionate jury might not take them so. The handkerchief, for Othello, is the exhibit brought into the courtroom, a piece of the accused's clothing found at the scene of the crime, "ocular proof"—not of the unseeable act but circumstantial evidence, so that "the probation [or determining test] bear no hinge nor loop to hang a doubt on."

Feebly, Othello clings to his faith that Desdemona is honest and asks for presumptive motive: "Give me a living reason she's disloyal," but Iago ignores this. He testifies that he has observed Cassio relive in sleep his secret moments with Desdemona. And when Othello protests that this was but a dream, Iago says, "this may help to thicken other proofs / That do demonstrate thinly." And what are these? Iago saw Cassio wipe his beard with the handkerchief. "It speaks against her with the other proofs."

So, as the fourth act opens, Iago provokingly drives the question of proof to its most paradoxical extreme—with the assurance that, although absolute knowledge is impossible, circumstances will convict. There is no direct witness to adultery between Cassio and Desdemona—but after all, how could there be? What if you found them naked and kissing in bed together for an hour or more? Would it *prove* they were "meaning any harm? . . . if they do nothing, 'tis a venial slip." As though the case would be similar, Iago asks if giving a handkerchief away need convict a woman of much—knowing that Othello will conclude that it is as circumstantially damning as a sight of the lovers flagrantly embracing. But the time has come for Iago to offer the confirming proof of confession, though, of course, it is confession reported at second hand—Cassio has supposedly confessed to *him*. It is not quite enough, and Iago will repair the defect in his case, or appear to; Othello will think he witnesses Cassio boasting how "he hath and is again to cope" Desdemona when Cassio really is talking about his mistress, who appears on cue, handkerchief in hand.

It is no use for Desdemona to defend herself. Or for Emilia to protest in a logical way, "Who keeps her company? What place, what time, what form, what likelihood?" But Emilia as defense witness arrives too late, discovering her husband's perfidy only after the death of her mistress. Before Othello executes his sentence, he asks Desdemona if she has repented of crime, as condemned criminals generally were asked, for the rescue of her soul and also to confirm the sentence by the strongest of proofs: "Take heed of perjury: thou art on thy death bed."

She maintains her innocence, having nothing to confess. Iago, who has everything to tell, withholds *his* confession, but Emilia will dispose of the false evidence of the handkerchief by revealing that she stole it for him, and documentary proof, letters from Iago found on Roderigo, close the case—unnecessarily for the audience but in keeping with the judicial process that governs the play.

But if the legal conceptualization of *Othello* relates it to the whole issue of the nature of truth, it is really an ironic parody of real legal inquiry. The search for evidentiary proof is, in fact, constantly mocked despite all the talk of proofs and making the wronged husband "see." Iago's pseudo-legal demonstration of Cassio's and Desdemona's guilt is conducted in the Cyprus world ruled by "seeming"—a world that makes such deceptions possible by demonic magic. Emilia's "what place, what time, what form, what likelihood" reminds us of the sleights that the playwright has himself exercised, not the least by that famous deception of "double time" that allows no time or opportunity—though we fail to notice it—for an affair between Cassio and Desdemona. Iago has merely to repeat Brabantio's charges that there was something "unnatural" in Desdemona's love to get Othello's assent to an idea he had serenely rejected in the Venetian court. He says Cassio's declarations, in sleep, of his love for Desdemona, reported by Iago, "denoted a foregone conclusion," and it is enough for him to have heard that Cassio has the handkerchief to be convinced that she would betray him sexually, accepting the false analogy: may she not just as freely give away her invisible honor? Othello does not have to hear Cassio's actual conversation with Iago about Bianca to assume that his wife is the subject.

There is a subtle slippage that merges supposition with ascertained fact. When Iago says, "What if I had said I had seen him do you wrong?" or heard Cassio "blab" of his conquest, the "what if" glides by as though never uttered. Othello reaches vainly for his sanity: "Hath he said anything?" *Then,* Iago slips in the knife—"He hath my lord"—only to assure Othello that Cassio would deny it. When Othello asks, "What hath he said?" he receives the riddling answer "what he did—I know not what he did," and to Othello's "with her?" the reply is a verbal quibble that throws his victim into his swoon, "With her, on her, what you will."

As we attend this collapse of logic, the difference between the world of illusion and the real world in which fact and appearance are distinguishable dissolves, for we are ourselves swept along by the play's hypnotic persuasion to jealousy, which banishes such distinctions. When Desdemona wonders at the "cause" for Othello's rage, Emilia rightly says,

> . . . jealous souls will not be answered so.
> They are not ever jealous for the cause,
> But jealous for they're jealous. 'Tis a monster
> Begot upon itself, born on itself.

But as I have been suggesting, jealousy becomes, in this extraordinary play, just a way of exhibiting a change of mind that equalizes the effect of all impressions. Othello may well say that contentedness in deception is best; it annihilates the reality that gives pain: "He that is robbed, not wanting what is stolen, / Let him not know't and he's not robbed at all."

It is often pointed out that the play exhibits contrasted viewpoints in the language of Othello and Iago—there is the poetic "Othello music," as L. C. Knights called it, sounded in words that seem to arise from a sense of the ordered cosmos and the hero's place in it. And there is the language of Iago, prosaically intelligent without any element of the ideal. Only Leavis and a few others have felt that Iago had some right to complain of Othello as "loving his own pride and purposes" and apt to employ "bombast circumstance" and "stuff'd" epithets. But it must be said that Othello's is the half of language most vulnerable to skepticism. Iago's version of Othello's tragedy is not the one most readers and viewers of the play embrace—he sees it as comedy, the leveling of preposterous presumption. His view goes down in defeat, we assume, as we listen to Othello's last grand speech as he prepares to kill himself—even though one suspects that T. S. Eliot was right in pointing out that the "honorable murderer" whom Emilia has called a "gull" and a "dolt" is simply trying to cheer himself up. Where Shakespeare stood is, as usual, not evident.

But if we see Othello's fall as a telescoped representation of the mind over- 25
taken by its own epistemological distrust of appearances—and the paradoxical trust *only* in appearances—we can see that what overcomes Othello, or rather what is represented *through* Othello's mad jealousy, is a trembling of the

universal spheres, a perturbation from which recovery comes only at the cost of deadly anguish. It is not mere hyperbole that causes him to tell Desdemona, out of her hearing, "When I love thee not, / Chaos is come again," to exclaim, "If she be false, O then heaven mocks itself," or to say, in later confirmation of this prediction,

O heavy hour!
Methinks it should be now a huge eclipse
Of sun and moon, and that th'affrighted globe
Should yawn at alteration. *[1997]*

JEFFRIE G. MURPHY

Jealousy, Shame, and the Rival

Jeffrie G. Murphy (b. 1941) is a distinguished legal and moral philosopher. He has published a number of books, including Getting Even: Forgiveness and Mercy *(2004) and most recently* Retribution Reconsidered: More Essays in the Philosophy of Law *(2010). His essay, "Jealousy, Shame, and the Rival," which appeared in the journal* Philosophical Studies, *is essentially a critique of Jerome Neu's work on jealousy in* A Tear Is an Intellectual Thing *(2000). Murphy maintains that Othello's acts of jealousy stem not from a fear of loss of love (as Neu's definition of jealousy requires) but from a fear of the shame brought on by that loss.*

When Jerome Neu's essay "Jealous Thoughts" was published in 1980, jealousy was widely regarded—at least in leftist intellectual and cultural circles—as an irrational and even evil "bourgeois" passion—one tied to a capitalistic market conception of human relations. The jealous person—according to this view—regards the loved person as a kind of object—as owned property over which the lover has rights. Jealousy is thus a kind of property fear—analogous to the fear of theft. The fear intrinsically involves the belief that one risks losing a possessed loved object to whose love one has a right.

Neu—rightly in my judgment—rejects this account of jealousy as psychologically shallow. He argues—in "Jealous Thoughts" and in the later "Jealous Afterthoughts"—that psychoanalytic theory teaches us that love gets its initial life and draws its basic character from the Oedipal situation. The child so needs and depends upon the mother that loss of the mother's love would appear both as biological and psychological annihilation—psychological because the very self of the child is identified with that of the mother. Any perceived rival for the mother's affections (initially the father) is seen as a threat to security and thus provokes in the child a fear of loss of love. It is here that love and jealousy begin, develop through what Winnicott calls "transitional objects," and assume forms that will persist in adult life. To love is, at least in part, to be so identified with another person that the loss of that person's love will be perceived as loss or annihilation of one's very self or personality. Jealousy, then, is simply the fear that one will lose the love of a person with whom one is psychologically identified—an instance of the fear of annihilation. "If others do not love us," Neu writes, "we will disintegrate."

This fear is not, according to Neu, grounded in a bourgeois or possessive model of human relations, for one can fear the loss of love without believing that one owns the loved person or that one has a right to that person's love. All that is required is that one has the love. Love, then, in part involves self identification—when we lose it we lose ourselves, having our vulnerabilities open and unsupported. All human beings, regardless of social setting—bourgeois or communitarian—fear the exposure of vulnerabilities and the resulting loss of self. According to Neu, this fear is jealousy. Thus jealousy and love are necessarily connected—we cannot get rid of the former without losing the latter.

There are some questions that I immediately want to raise about this analysis. First, what about unrequited love? There are surely intense cases of jealousy where the jealous person knows full well that the love he feels is not returned. Not having it, he cannot fear its loss. Thus it cannot be literally true to say, as Neu does in the first essay, that "to be jealous over someone, you must believe that they love you or have loved you."

Unrequited love thus presents a problem for Neu's original analysis, but I 5
think that the problem can be rather easily fixed. One might draw on some of the instructive things that Neu has to say in the later essay about the role of illusion and projection in erotic love, or one might suggest (think of the John Hinckley/Jodie Foster case) that what the jealous unrequited lover fears is not the loss of love (which he clearly does not have) but the loss of the *possibility* of love (which he may still hope for).

There is also, of course, the problem of jealousy over love that one believes is already hopelessly lost. Othello—often presented (as he is by Neu) as a paradigm of a jealous person—is frequently thought to be most jealous *after* he believes that he has lost Desdemona's love to Cassio. But surely this cannot be understood simply as the fear of loss of love, for how can one fear to lose what one has already lost?

In keeping with the spirit—if not the exact letter—of Neu's analysis, one might try to deal with the Othello case in this way: The fear that constitutes Othello's jealousy should not be seen as the fear of the loss of love (it is simply too late for *that* fear) but rather as the fear of the personal disintegration that may result from that loss.

Perhaps killing or other acts of revenge against the lost lover are strategies to defend against this possible consequence. Perhaps they are preventive strategies that seek the prevention, not of the loss of love, but rather of the dire consequences that—according to Neu—may flow from that loss. Or perhaps they are *retributive* strategies—seeking to inflict punishment on the person who has caused such personal disruption and pain at the core of one's very self. Thus it is possible that the jealous person who inflicts pain over love lost is somewhat like the lover of a murder victim who believes (sometimes rightly, sometimes wrongly) that a kind of closure will result from the execution of the killer.

We are all, alas, familiar with newspaper reports that read "He killed her in a jealous rage." Such a phrase might well describe Othello, but I am not sure. He was surely jealous when he suspected Desdemona of infidelity, but was he jealous at the time he murdered her? Perhaps he was simply vindictive. However, if such murderous rage is properly to be identified as "jealous," it surely cannot be motivated by the fear of losing love since the surest way permanently to lose love is to kill the lover. Dead people cannot love. So what goes on in these cases is either not jealousy at all but rather something else—vengeance perhaps—or it is jealousy motivated by something other than the fear of losing love. Perhaps it is motivated by a deep aversion to certain *consequences* of losing love. Neu would stress the consequence of annihilation or disintegration—since that is so integral to his analysis of love—but I shall later argue that one of these consequences may be *shame*. . . .

It is a perhaps sad but surely true claim that, to a substantial degree, people 10
derive their sense of self worth from the judgments of others. If we love a person, we tend to take that person's judgments in these matters quite seriously—i.e., we take them in some sense to be accurate judges of our own worth. (The mentally healthy among us—if there are any—would not follow Groucho Marx in contemptuously refusing to join any club that would have us for members; nor would we deeply mistrust the judgment of any person who could love us.) If we add to this the fact that non-moral judgments of worth are generally comparative, then the fact that a judge whom we trust prefers someone over us may make us doubt our own worth or value. So jealousy may stand as testimony, not merely to our need for love and attention, but also to our need for validation by another. We are thus shamed by rejection.

It is, of course, not merely the judgment of the loved person who matters. The judgment of a wider circle of people matters as well, for even the strongest of us needs validation from some relevant reference group. Consider Achilles. His rage over the loss of Briseis to Agamemnon is to a substantial degree based on his loss of honor—face and standing—in the eyes of his fellow warriors. He has been shamed by having the girl taken from him.

I think that similar shame may be found in many contemporary cases of jealousy and loss. The jilted lover is often ashamed to report this to others—thinking that it casts some bad reflection on his or her worth or standing. (Sometimes—for similar reasons I suspect—people are reluctant even to admit that they are divorced.) Being a victim of infidelity is, among other unpleasant things, shameful and embarrassing. Perhaps this in part explains the rage that is often found in those who have been jilted—a rage that may provoke expensive and vicious lawsuits, small or even major acts of retribution, and sometimes even murder. Why do people do these things? These acts will not get the love back, but they may go a long way—at least in the eyes of the perpetrator—toward saving face, restoring lost status and honor, and thus overcoming the shame of it all. If one believes that he has been brought down by another, he may find it therapeutic—or think he will find it therapeutic—to bring that person down as well. I am not, of course, saying that such a response is justified, only that it is—unfortunately—not unusual (particularly among men). As Norman Mailer (who ought to know) has asked: "Isn't human nature depressing?"

To summarize and conclude: I think that Neu has provided us with many profound insights on jealousy and its relation to love. Indeed, if I were asked to recommend just one philosophical essay on jealousy, it would be Neu's. It is, I think, the best place to start—for its insights, the framework it provides, and the provocative questions it forces us to raise.

In raising these questions, however, I have come to think that Neu's account of jealousy needs to be supplemented in certain ways. In particular, I have suggested that *shame* needs to be stressed in order fully to account for the role of the rival in jealousy. *[2002]*

MAKING COMPARISONS

1. Murphy focuses on jealousy as having a psychological basis, arguing that jealousy is "the fear that one will lose the love of a person with whom one is psychologically identified" (para. 2) and later adds shame into the mix of jealousy. Bell, however, seems to think jealousy has more to do with philosophy, with appearances and reality, with the distinction "between seeming and true seeing"—indeed, with the very nature of truth itself. Explain why one of these interpretations helps you understand *Othello* better.
2. Bradley claims that the true source of Othello's suffering is "the wreck of his faith and love" (para. 5). Do you think Bell and Murphy agree?
3. From each essay, choose a sentence or two that impresses you as offering an interesting insight into the play. How did each one deepen your understanding of *Othello*?

WRITING ABOUT ISSUES

1. Write an argument that Bradley's last paragraph captures your feelings as you read the last scene.
2. In a brief essay, agree or disagree with Bell's comment that "the power of the theme of sexual jealousy obscures other subjects in the play" (para. 6).
3. Most critics think of Othello as noble in thought and action, and he is often seen as authoritative, disciplined, human, and eloquent. But if we heard the outline of this play on today's news—"General kills wife suspected of adultery, then kills self"—we might not think highly of him. Write an essay that explores this disparity. You might want to take into consideration the nature and purpose of tragedy.
4. Write an essay about your response to *Othello* that focuses on the familiar idea "There, but for the grace of God, go I." That is, is the tragedy of the Moor and "the green-eyed monster" one we could all succumb to?

Arguments about Love: Essays

LAURA KIPNIS, "Against Love"

MEGHAN O'ROURKE, "The Marriage Trap"

Ever since Shakespeare's comedies, marriage has been one of the most popular endings for plays, novels, and films. And it is assumed by almost everybody, including both heterosexual and same-sex partners, that the happy couple, having found true love at last, will be lovers and friends for a lifetime. But according to some skeptics, the facts should make us believe otherwise. After all, the divorce rate has almost doubled since the 1960s, and considerably less than half of married couples say they are happy in their marriages. Some critics blame our inflated expectations about love's durability. Others see a kind of conspiracy to keep marriages together for economic reasons. And there are those who think we should give up the ghost and look for other less permanent arrangements. Laura Kipnis and Meghan O'Rourke develop witty, provocative, and often conflicting arguments about love and marriage.

BEFORE YOU READ

Why do you think true love should last forever? Why do you think love fades? Why do you think so many couples feel trapped in their marriages? Why do so many marriages end in divorce? Why do married people have affairs? Why might monogamy be unnatural?

LAURA KIPNIS

Against Love

Laura Kipnis (b. 1956) is a professor at Northwestern University outside of Chicago, where she teaches courses on gender, popular culture, and sexual politics. She has an M.F.A. from Nova Scotia College of Art and Design. The following essay appeared in the New York Times Magazine *in October 2001 as a prelude to her book* Against Love: A Polemic *(2003). In 2015, Kipnis caused a sensation with a provocative article in* The Chronicle of Higher Education, *"The Sexual Paranoia Strikes Academe." Her latest book is* Men: Notes from an Ongoing Investigation *(2014). She has been praised for her "sharp analysis" and "blistering wit" in challenging contemporary notions of love and sex.*

Love is, as we know, a mysterious and controlling force. It has vast power over our thoughts and life decisions. It demands our loyalty, and we, in turn, freely comply. Saying no to love isn't simply heresy; it is tragedy—the failure to achieve what is most essentially human. So deeply internalized is our obedience to this most capricious despot that artists create passionate odes to its cruelty, and audiences seem never to tire of the most deeply unoriginal mass spectacles devoted to rehearsing the litany of its torments, fixating their very beings on the narrowest glimmer of its fleeting satisfactions.

Yet despite near total compliance, a buzz of social nervousness attends the subject. If a society's lexicon of romantic pathologies reveals its particular anxieties, high on our own list would be diagnoses like "inability to settle down" or "immaturity," leveled at those who stray from the norms of domestic coupledom either by refusing entry in the first place or, once installed, pursuing various escape routes: excess independence, ambivalence, "straying," divorce. For the modern lover, "maturity" isn't a depressing signal of impending decrepitude but a sterling achievement, the sine qua non of a lover's qualifications to love and be loved.

This injunction to achieve maturity—synonymous in contemporary usage with 30-year mortgages, spreading waistlines, and monogamy—obviously finds its raison d'être in modern love's central anxiety, that structuring social contradiction the size of the San Andreas Fault: namely, the expectation that romance and sexual attraction can last a lifetime of coupled togetherness despite much hard evidence to the contrary.

Ever optimistic, heady with love's utopianism, most of us eventually pledge ourselves to unions that will, if successful, far outlast the desire that impelled them into being. The prevailing cultural wisdom is that even if sexual desire tends to be a short-lived phenomenon, "mature love" will kick in to save the day when desire flags. The issue that remains unaddressed is whether cutting off other possibilities of romance and sexual attraction for the more muted pleasures of mature love isn't similar to voluntarily amputating a healthy limb: a lot of anesthesia is required and the phantom pain never entirely abates. But if it behooves a society to convince its citizenry that wanting change means personal failure or wanting to start over is shameful or simply wanting more satisfaction than what you have is an illicit thing, clearly grisly acts of self-mutilation will be required.

5 There hasn't always been quite such optimism about love's longevity. For the Greeks, inventors of democracy and a people not amenable to being pushed around by despots, love was a disordering and thus preferably brief experience. During the reign of courtly love, love was illicit and usually fatal. Passion meant suffering: the happy ending didn't yet exist in the cultural imagination. As far as togetherness as an eternal ideal, the twelfth-century advice manual *De Amore et Amor is Remedio* (*On Love and the Remedies of Love*) warned that too many opportunities to see or chat with the beloved would certainly decrease love.

The innovation of happy love didn't even enter the vocabulary of romance until the seventeenth century. Before the eighteenth century—when the family was primarily an economic unit of production rather than a hothouse of Oedipal tensions—marriages were business arrangements between families; participants had little to say on the matter. Some historians consider romantic love a learned behavior that really only took off in the late eighteenth century along with the new fashion for reading novels, though even then affection between a husband and wife was considered to be in questionable taste.

Historians disagree, of course. Some tell the story of love as an eternal and unchanging essence; others, as a progress narrative over stifling social conventions. (Sometimes both stories are told at once; consistency isn't required.) But has modern love really set us free? Fond as we are of projecting our own emotional quandaries back through history, construing vivid costume dramas featuring medieval peasants or biblical courtesans sharing their feelings with the post-Freudian savvy of lifelong analysands, our amatory predecessors clearly didn't share all our particular aspirations about their romantic lives.

We, by contrast, feel like failures when love dies. We believe it could be otherwise. Since the cultural expectation is that a state of coupled permanence is achievable, uncoupling is experienced as crisis and inadequacy—even though such failures are more the norm than the exception.

As love has increasingly become the center of all emotional expression in the popular imagination, anxiety about obtaining it in sufficient quantities—and for sufficient duration—suffuses the population. Everyone knows that as the demands and expectations on couples escalated, so did divorce rates. And given the current divorce statistics (roughly 50 percent of all marriages end in divorce), all indications are that whomever you love today—your beacon of hope, the center of all your optimism—has a good chance of becoming your worst nightmare tomorrow. (Of course, that 50 percent are those who actually leave their unhappy marriages and not a particularly good indication of the happiness level or nightmare potential of those who remain.) Lawrence Stone, a historian of marriage, suggests—rather jocularly, you can't help thinking—that today's rising divorce rates are just a modern technique for achieving what was once taken care of far more efficiently by early mortality.

Love may or may not be a universal emotion, but clearly the social forms it 10
takes are infinitely malleable. It is our culture alone that has dedicated itself to allying the turbulence of romance and the rationality of the long-term couple, convinced that both love and sex are obtainable from one person over the course of decades, that desire will manage to sustain itself for 30 or 40 or 50 years, and that the supposed fate of social stability is tied to sustaining a fleeting experience beyond its given life span.

Of course, the parties involved must "work" at keeping passion alive (and we all know how much fun that is), the presumption being that even after living in close proximity to someone for a historically unprecedented length of time, you will still muster the requisite desire to achieve sexual congress on a regular basis. (Should passion fizzle out, just give up sex. Lack of desire for a mate is never an adequate rationale for "looking elsewhere.") And it is true, many couples do manage to perform enough psychic retooling to reshape the anarchy of desire to the confines of the marriage bed, plugging away at the task year after year (once a week, same time, same position) like diligent assembly-line workers, aided by the occasional fantasy or two to help get the old motor to turn over, or keep running, or complete the trip. And so we have the erotic life of a nation of workaholics: if sex seems like work, clearly you're not working hard enough at it.

But passion must not be allowed to die! The fear—or knowledge—that it does shapes us into particularly conflicted psychological beings, perpetually in search of prescriptions and professional interventions, regardless of cost or consequence. Which does have its economic upside, at least. Whole new sectors of the economy have been spawned, with massive social investment in new technologies from Viagra to couples' porn: capitalism's Lourdes for dying marriages.

There are assorted low-tech solutions to desire's dilemmas too. Take advice. In fact, take more and more advice. Between print, airwaves, and the therapy industry, if there were any way to quantify the G.N.P. in romantic counsel, it would be a staggering number. Desperate to be cured of love's temporality, a lovestruck populace has molded itself into an advanced race of advice receptacles, like some new form of miracle sponge that can instantly absorb many times its own body weight in wetness.

Inexplicably, however, a rebellious breakaway faction keeps trying to leap over the wall and emancipate themselves, not from love itself—unthinkable!—but from love's domestic confinements. The escape routes are well trodden—love affairs, midlife crises—though strewn with the left-behind luggage of those who encountered unforeseen obstacles along the way (panic, guilt, self-engineered exposures) and beat self-abashed retreats to their domestic gulags, even after pledging body and soul to newfound loves in the balmy utopias of nondomesticated romances. Will all the adulterers in the audience please stand up? You know who you are. Don't be embarrassed! Adulterers aren't just "playing around." These are our home-grown closet social theorists, because adultery is not just a referendum on the sustainability of monogamy; it is a veiled philosophical discussion about the social contract itself. The question on the table is this: "How much renunciation of desire does society demand of us, versus the degree of gratification it provides?" Clearly, the adulterer's answer, following a long line of venerable social critics, would be, "Too much."

15 But what exactly is it about the actual lived experience of modern domestic love that would make flight such a compelling option for so many? Let us briefly examine those material daily life conditions.

Fundamentally, to achieve love and qualify for entry into that realm of salvation and transcendence known as the couple (the secular equivalent of entering a state of divine grace), you must be a lovable person. And what precisely does being lovable entail? According to the tenets of modern love, it requires an advanced working knowledge of the intricacies of mutuality.

Mutuality means recognizing that your partner has needs and being prepared to meet them. This presumes, of course, that the majority of those needs can and should be met by one person. (Question this, and you question the very foundations of the institution. So don't.) These needs of ours run deep, a tangled underground morass of ancient, gnarled roots, looking to ensnarl any hapless soul who might accidentally trod upon their outer radices.

Still, meeting those needs is the most effective way to become the object of another's desire, thus attaining intimacy, which is required to achieve the state known as psychological maturity. (Despite how closely it reproduces the affective conditions of our childhoods, since trading compliance for love is the earliest social lesson learned; we learn it in our cribs.)

You, in return, will have your own needs met by your partner in matters large and small. In practice, many of these matters turn out to be quite small. Frequently, it is the tensions and disagreements over the minutiae of daily living that stand between couples and their requisite intimacy. Taking out the garbage, tone of voice, a forgotten errand—these are the rocky shoals upon which intimacy so often founders.

Mutuality requires communication, since in order to be met, these needs 20
must be expressed. (No one's a mind reader, which is not to say that many of us don't expect this quality in a mate. Who wants to keep having to tell someone what you need?) What you need is for your mate to understand you—your desires, your contradictions, your unique sensitivities, what irks you. (In practice, that means what about your mate irks you.) You, in turn, must learn to understand the mate's needs. This means being willing to hear what about yourself irks your mate. Hearing is not a simple physiological act performed with the ears, as you will learn. You may think you know how to hear, but that doesn't mean that you know how to listen.

With two individuals required to coexist in enclosed spaces for extended periods of time, domesticity requires substantial quantities of compromise and adaptation simply to avoid mayhem. Yet with the post-Romantic ideal of unconstrained individuality informing our most fundamental ideas of the self, this can prove a perilous process. Both parties must be willing to jettison whatever aspects of individuality might prove irritating while being simultaneously allowed to retain enough individuality to feel their autonomy is not being sacrificed, even as it is being surgically excised.

Having mastered mutuality, you may now proceed to advanced intimacy. Advanced intimacy involves inviting your partner "in" to your most interior self. Whatever and wherever our "inside" is, the widespread—if somewhat metaphysical—belief in its existence (and the related belief that whatever is in there is dying to get out) has assumed a quasi-medical status. Leeches once served a similar purpose. Now we "express our feelings" in lieu of our fluids because everyone knows that those who don't are far more prone to cancer, ulcers, or various dire ailments.

With love as our culture's patent medicine, prescribed for every ill (now even touted as a necessary precondition for that other great American obsession, longevity), we willingly subject ourselves to any number of arcane procedures in its quest. "Opening up" is required for relationship health, so lovers fashion themselves after doctors wielding long probes to penetrate the tender regions. Try to think of yourself as one big orifice: now stop clenching and relax. If the procedure proves uncomfortable, it just shows you're not open enough. Psychotherapy may be required before sufficient dilation can be achieved: the world's most expensive lubricant.

Needless to say, this opening-up can leave you feeling quite vulnerable, lying there psychically spread-eagled and shivering on the examining table of your relationship. (A favored suspicion is that your partner, knowing exactly where your vulnerabilities are, deliberately kicks you there—one reason this opening-up business may not always feel as pleasant as advertised.) And as anyone who has spent much time in—or just in earshot of—a typical couple knows, the "expression of needs" is often the Trojan horse of intimate warfare, since expressing needs means, by definition, that one's partner has thus far failed to meet them.

In any long-term couple, this lexicon of needs becomes codified over time 25
into a highly evolved private language with its own rules. Let's call this couple grammar. Close observation reveals this as a language composed of one recurring unit of speech: the interdiction—highly nuanced, mutually imposed commands and strictures extending into the most minute areas of household affairs, social life, finances, speech, hygiene, allowable idiosyncrasies, and so on. From bathroom to bedroom, car to kitchen, no aspect of coupled life is not subject to scrutiny, negotiation, and codes of conduct.

A sample from an inexhaustible list, culled from interviews with numerous members of couples of various ages, races, and sexual orientations:

You can't leave the house without saying where you're going. You can't not say what time you'll return. You can't go out when the other person feels like staying at home. You can't be a slob. You can't do less than 50 percent of the work around the house, even if the other person wants to do 100 percent more cleaning than you find necessary or even reasonable. You can't leave the dishes for later, load them the way that seems best to you, drink straight from the carton, or make crumbs. You can't leave the bathroom door open—it's offensive. You can't leave the bathroom door closed—your partner needs to get in. You can't not shave your underarms or legs. You can't gain weight. You can't watch soap operas. You can't watch infomercials or the pregame show or Martha Stewart. You can't eat what you want—goodbye Marshmallow Fluff; hello tofu meatballs. You can't spend too much time on the computer. And stay out of those chat rooms. You can't take risks, unless they are agreed-upon risks, which somewhat limits the concept of "risk." You can't make major purchases alone, or spend money on things the other person considers excesses. You can't blow money just because you're in a bad mood, and you can't be in a bad mood without being required to explain it. You can't begin a sentence with "You always. . . ." You can't begin a sentence with "I never. . . ." You can't be simplistic, even when things are simple. You can't say what you really think of that outfit or color combination or cowboy hat. You can't be cynical about things the other person is sincere about. You can't drink without the other person counting your drinks. You can't have the wrong laugh. You can't bum cigarettes when you're out because it embarrasses your mate, even though you've explained the unspoken fraternity between smokers. You can't tailgate, honk, or listen to talk radio in the car. And so on. The specifics don't matter. What matters is that the operative word is "can't."

Thus is love obtained.

Certainly, domesticity offers innumerable rewards: companionship, child-rearing convenience, reassuring predictability, and many other benefits too varied to list. But if love has power over us, domesticity is its enforcement wing:

the iron dust mop in the velvet glove. The historian Michel Foucault has argued that modern power made its mark on the world by inventing new types of enclosures and institutions, places like factories, schools, barracks, prisons, and asylums, where individuals could be located, supervised, processed, and subjected to inspection, order, and the clock. What current social institution is more enclosed than modern intimacy? What offers greater regulation of movement and time, or more precise surveillance of body and thought, to a greater number of individuals?

Of course, it is your choice—as if any of us could really choose not to 30
desire love or not to feel like hopeless losers should we fail at it. We moderns are beings yearning to be filled, yearning to be overtaken by love's mysterious power. We prostrate ourselves at love's portals, like social strivers waiting at the rope line outside some exclusive club hoping to gain admission and thereby confirm our essential worth. A life without love lacks an organizing narrative. A life without love seems so barren, and it might almost make you consider how empty the rest of the world is, as if love were vital plasma and everything else just tap water.

Exchanging obedience for love comes naturally—after all, we all were once children whose survival depended on the caprices of love. And there you have the template for future intimacies. If you love me, you'll do what I want—or need, or demand—and I'll love you in return. We all become household dictators, petty tyrants of the private sphere, who are, in our turn, dictated to.

And why has modern love developed in such a way as to maximize submission and minimize freedom, with so little argument about it? No doubt a citizenry schooled in renouncing desire instead of imagining there could be something more would be, in many respects, advantageous. After all, wanting more is the basis for utopian thinking, a path toward dangerous social demands, even toward imagining the possibilities for altogether different social arrangements. But if the most elegant forms of social control are those that came packaged in the guise of individual needs and satisfactions, so wedded to the individual psyche that any opposing impulse registers as the anxiety of unlovability, who needs a soldier on every corner? We are more than happy to police ourselves and those we love and call it living happily ever after. Perhaps a secular society needed another metaphysical entity to subjugate itself to after the death of God, and love was available for the job. But isn't it a little depressing to think we are somehow incapable of inventing forms of emotional life based on anything other than subjugation?

Steve: "When we got together, we immediately merged our finances. Chuck owned a lovely home in Sausalito, and to my total astonishment, he made me joint tenant with him. We have always maintained one checking account, and all of our investments and everything are in both our names. That is about as formal as a gay couple can get. And I think, like a lot of couples, it has helped us get through rough spots in life. When your lives are totally intertwined, it makes more sense to resolve issues than to start cutting things apart most of the time.

"At this point, after thirty years, Chuck and I have very few rules in our relationship. We don't have a rule, for instance, that you can never go out on the other one. We realized from time to time the opportunity would present itself, and we also realized that if we turned down every opportunity that presented itself to us, eventually we might begin to resent each other. So we said, O.K., you can go ahead and do it, but never make a date that leaves me sitting at home while you are out with someone else. And we have never done that. From time to time we have had affairs with other people, or moments of sexual release, but they were recreational."

Chuck: "Jealousy probably breaks up more gay people than anything in the 35
world. I guess that goes for all couples. And jealousy is caused by a lack of trust. The one who lacks trust the most and is accusing the other of cheating, he's usually the one who is cheating. Jealousy is based on guilt, an awful lot. But if you are absolutely convinced that the person you are with is totally open to you, that nothing is hidden, there won't be problems, ever. I know that Brad Pitt could not walk in this house and take Steve away from me. I am absolutely convinced of that.

I have total confidence in that. In my case, it is Michael York, but I go way back. And when you know that, sex is really an unimportant aspect, in terms of the deep emotions of your relationship. There is a movie called *Relax . . . It's Just Sex*—I love that title. It is only sex; it has no deep-seated meaning. It may seem to be a part of romance—certainly it jump-starts it—but as the years go by, it becomes more of a bonus to the relationship. There are no earthquakes that can happen as a result of sex." *[2001]*

THINKING ABOUT THE TEXT

1. Clearly Kipnis believes love doesn't last. In what ways does your personal experience and your cultural experience (reading novels, watching television and films) confirm, deny, or make problematic this belief?
2. In what specific ways does Kipnis answer her own question: "But has modern love really set us free" (para. 7)? Describe how one can answer this question positively.
3. Kipnis uses a number of clever and provocative metaphors to bring home her point about love's temporality, including the claim that Viagra and pornography are "capitalism's Lourdes for dying marriages" (para. 12). What does she mean here? Explain her use of other metaphors, such as "like diligent assembly-line workers" (para. 11); "some new form of miracle sponge" (para. 13); "rocky shoals upon which intimacy so often founders" (para. 19); "leeches once served a similar purpose" (para. 22).
4. Kipnis claims "hard evidence to the contrary" (para. 3) that romance and sexual attraction can last a lifetime. What "evidence" does she cite? What does she mean by "hard"? Why might some of this "evidence" be considered interpretation or subjective?
5. Explain Kipnis's counterintuitive claim that adulterers are "our home-grown closet social theorists" (para. 14). How does this fit into her argument? Kipnis claims in several places that we learn about love in childhood. What specifically do we learn, and how does this play into her argument?

MEGHAN O'ROURKE

The Marriage Trap

Meghan O'Rourke (b. 1976) is a poet and critic who has been widely published, winning numerous prizes and fellowships. She was a fiction editor at The New Yorker, *served as poetry editor at* The Paris Review, *and is a contributor to the* New York Times. *Her first book of poems,* Halflife *(2007), was published by W. W. Norton, and her memoir about the death of her mother,* The Long Goodbye *(2011), was critically acclaimed. She graduated from Yale University, has taught at New York University and Princeton University, and currently lives in Brooklyn, New York. O'Rourke posted her essay on* Slate *in September 2003 as a review of and response to Kipnis's* Against Love: A Polemic. *She won the Guggenheim Award for General Noniction in 2014.*

The classic 1960s feminist critique of marriage was that it suffocated women by tying them to the home and stifling their identity. The hope was that in a nonsexist society marriage could be a harmonious, genuine connection of minds. But forty years after Betty Friedan, Laura Kipnis has arrived with a new jeremiad, *Against Love: A Polemic*, to tell us that this hope was forlorn: Marriage, she suggests, belongs on the junk heap of human folly. It is an equal-opportunity oppressor, trapping men and women in a life of drudgery, emotional anesthesia, and a tug-of-war struggle to balance vastly different needs.

The numbers seem to back up her thesis: Modern marriage doesn't work for the majority of people. The rate of divorce has roughly doubled since the 1960s. Half of all marriages end in divorce. And as sketchy as poll data can be, a recent Rutgers University poll found that only 38 percent of married couples describe themselves as happy.

What's curious, though, is that even though marriage doesn't seem to make Americans very happy, they keep getting married (and remarried). Kipnis's essential question is: Why? Why, in what seems like an age of great social freedom, would anyone willingly consent to a life of constricting monogamy? Why has marriage (which she defines broadly as any long-term monogamous relationship) remained a polestar even as ingrained ideas about race, gender, and sexuality have been overturned?

Kipnis's answer is that marriage is an insidious social construct, harnessed by capitalism to get us to have kids and work harder to support them. Her quasi-Marxist argument sees desire as inevitably subordinated to economics. And the price of this subordination is immense: Domestic cohabitation is a "gulag"; marriage is the rough equivalent of a credit card with 0 percent APR that, upon first misstep, zooms to a punishing 30 percent and compounds daily. You feel you owe something, or you're afraid of being alone, and so you "work" at your relationship, like a prisoner in Siberia ice-picking away at the erotic permafrost.

Kipnis's ideological tack might easily have been as heavy as Frederick Engels's 5
in *The Origins of the Family, Private Property, and the State*, but she possesses the gleeful, viperish wit of a Dorothy Parker and the energetic charisma of a cheerleader. She is dead-on about the everyday exhaustion a relationship can produce.

And she's diagnosed something interesting about the public discourse of marriage. People are more than happy to talk about how unhappy their individual marriages are, but public discussion assumes that in each case there is something wrong with *the* marriage—not marriage itself.

Take the way infidelity became a prime-time political issue in the '90s: Even as we wondered whether a politician who was not faithful to his or her spouse could be "faithful" to the country, no one was interested in asking whether marital fidelity was realistic or desirable.

Kipnis's answer to that question is a resounding no. The connection between sex and love, she argues, doesn't last as long as the need for each. And we probably shouldn't invest so much of *our own* happiness in the idea that someone else can help us sustain it—or spend so much time trying to make unhappy relationships "work." We should just look out for ourselves, perhaps mutually—more like two people gazing in the same general direction than two people expecting they want to look in each other's eyes for the rest of their (now much longer) lives. For this model to work, she argues, our social decisions need to start reflecting the reality of declining marriage rates—not the fairy-tale "happily ever after all" version.

Kipnis's vision of a good relationship may sound pretty vague. In fact, she doesn't really offer an alternative so much as diagnose the problems, hammering us into submission: Do we need a new way of thinking about love and domesticity? Marriage could be a form of renewable contract, as she idly wonders (and as Goethe proposed almost 200 years ago in *Elective Affinities*, his biting portrait of a marriage blighted by monogamy). Might it be possible to envision committed nonmonogamous heterosexual relationships?

Kipnis's book derives its *frisson* from the fact that she's asking questions no one seems that interested in entertaining. As she notes, even in a post-feminist age of loose social mores we are still encouraged, from the time we are children, to think of marriage as the proper goal of a well-lived life. I was first taught to play at the marriage fantasy in a Manhattan commune that had been formed explicitly to reject traditional notions of marriage; faced with a gaggle of eight-year-old girls, one of the women gave us a white wedding gown and invited us to imagine the heartthrob whom we wanted to devote ourselves to. Even radicals have a hard time banishing the dream of an enduring true love.

10 Let's accept that the resolute public emphasis on fixing ourselves, not marriage, can seem grim, and even sentimentally blinkered in its emphasis on ending divorce. Yet Kipnis's framing of the problem is grim, too. While she usefully challenges our assumptions about commitment, it's not evident that we'd be better off in the lust-happy world she envisions, or that men and women really want the exact same sexual freedoms. In its ideal form, marriage seems to reify all that's best about human exchange. Most people don't want to be alone at home with a cat, and everyone but Kipnis worries about the effects of divorce on children. "Work," in her lexicon, is always the drudgery of self-denial, not the challenge of extending yourself beyond what you knew you could do. But we usually mean two things when we say "work": The slog we endure purely to put food on the table, and the kind we do because we like it—are drawn to it, even.

While it's certainly true that people stay in an unhappy relationship longer than they should, it's not yet clear that monogamy is more "unnatural" than sleeping around but finding that the hum of your refrigerator is your most constant companion. And Kipnis spends scant time thinking about the fact that marriage is a hardy social institution several thousand years old, spanning many cultures—which calls into question, to say the least, whether its presence in our lives today has mostly to do with the insidious chokehold capitalism has on us.

While Kipnis's exaggerated polemic romp is wittily invigorating, it may not actually be as radical as it promises to be: These days, even sitcoms reflect her way of thinking. There's an old episode of *Seinfeld* in which Jerry and Kramer anticipate most of Kipnis's critique of domesticity; Kramer asks Jerry if he and his girlfriend are thinking about marriage and family, and then cuts him off: "They're prisons! Man-made prisons! You're doin' time! You get up in the morning—she's there. You go to sleep at night—she's there. It's like you gotta ask permission to, to use the bathroom: *Is it all right if I use the bathroom now?*" Still, love might indeed get a better name if we were as attentive to the intellectual dishonesties of the public debate over its failings as we are to the emotional dishonesties of adulterers. *[2003]*

THINKING ABOUT THE TEXT

1. O'Rourke claims that as a culture we are happy to talk about unhappy individual marriages but not about marriage itself. In what ways do your personal experience and your cultural experience (reading novels, watching films and television) support or contradict this observation?
2. O'Rourke seems to agree with Kipnis that we are socialized to think of marriage as "the proper goal of a well-lived life" (para. 9). In what specific ways is this true from your personal and cultural experience?
3. In what ways does O'Rourke support marriage? What objections does she have to Kipnis's idea of working at a relationship? O'Rourke praises Kipnis for her "gleeful, viperish wit" (para. 5). Point out examples of where the same could be said of O'Rourke.
4. What is O'Rourke's position on the connection between sex and love?
5. Paraphrase O'Rourke's position on marriage.

MAKING COMPARISONS

1. How does O'Rourke summarize the key elements of Kipnis's argument? What features of the argument does she seem most impressed with?
2. What are some objections O'Rourke has to Kipnis's essay? O'Rourke seems to save her main critique of Kipnis until the last paragraph. What is it? What is the rhetorical effect of "still" in the last sentence?

3. Kipnis's tone is often biting and ironic. How would you describe O'Rourke's tone? What are the advantages and disadvantages of using various tones, such as ironic, sarcastic, sincere, witty, clever, and confident?

WRITING ABOUT ISSUES

1. Write an argument that agrees or disagrees with the idea that "marriage . . . belongs on the junk heap of human folly." Be sure to cite specific support and make reference to both Kipnis and O'Rourke.
2. Write an analysis of Kipnis's argument, focusing on the clarity of the claim, the adequacy of her supporting evidence, her attention to the opposition, and the idea of fairness.
3. Write an argument that focuses on the idea that our culture should be more honest about the failings of love. Give concrete suggestions about how this might happen and what the consequences might be.
4. One of the most influential theorists of the gay opposition to gay marriage is Michael Warner, whose book, *The Trouble with Normal* (1999), details the problems he sees with gays becoming part of a conservative institution. Research his ideas online and read several of the reviews of his book. Write an argument that agrees or disagrees with his central premise.

Impossible Love: Across Genres

SEAMUS HEANEY, "Punishment" (poem)

KAREN RUSSELL, "Bog Girl" (story)

The likely inspiration for both the following poem and story is P. V. Glob's *The Bog People*, an anthropological report that detailed with amazing photographs the intact bodies of scores of Iron Age men and women, some of whom seem to have been either murdered or executed. But almost nothing is really known of their culture or the circumstances of their deaths save what can be inferred from the clothing and artifacts preserved in these ancient bogs.

In Seamus Heaney's "Punishment," the narrator empathizes with the plight of a young girl who might have died at the hands of a community outraged at her sexual transgression. Karen Russell also focuses her story around a girl found in a bog, but eschews Heaney's realism and takes her implausible but compelling narrative into the fantastic. In an interview published after "Bog People" appeared, Russell asks, "How often do we project our fantasies onto the mask of another person's face?" In these two cases, since the faces of the bog girls are thousands of years old, Heaney and Russell can project a complex array of fantasies, fears, and desires onto girls from the deep past that perhaps tell us more about the present than the Iron Age.

SEAMUS HEANEY

Punishment

For his distinguished career as a poet, Seamus Heaney (1939–2013) won the Nobel Prize for literature in 1995. He was raised as a Catholic in Northern Ireland, where Protestants remained in the majority and frequently conflicted with Catholics. Until the Peace Accord of 1997, the region was controlled by the British government, whereas now it is ruled by a mixed body representing both religions. Several of Heaney's poems deal with Catholic resistance to the longtime British domination of his native land. Heaney moved to Dublin, in the Republic of Ireland, in the early 1970s, but he often visited the United States, even holding an appointment as Boylston Professor of Rhetoric at Harvard University. The following poem appears in Heaney's 1975 book North. *It is part of a whole sequence of poems based on P. V. Glob's 1969 book* The Bog People. *Heaney was drawn to Glob's photographs of Iron Age people whose preserved bodies were discovered in bogs of Denmark and other European countries.*

I can feel the tug
of the halter at the nape
of her neck, the wind
on her naked front.

It blows her nipples
to amber beads,
it shakes the frail rigging
of her ribs.

I can see her drowned
body in the bog,
the weighing stone,
the floating rods and boughs.

Under which at first
she was a barked sapling
that is dug up
oak-bone, brain-firkin°:

her shaved head
like a stubble of black corn,
her blindfold a soiled bandage,
her noose a ring

to store
the memories of love.
Little adulteress,
before they punished you

you were flaxen-haired,
undernourished, and your
tar-black face was beautiful.
My poor scapegoat,

I almost love you
but would have cast, I know,
the stones of silence.°
I am the artful voyeur

of your brain's exposed
and darkened combs,
your muscles' webbing
and all your numbered bones:

I who have stood dumb
when your betraying sisters,
cauled in tar,
wept by the railings,°

who would connive
in civilized outrage
yet understand the exact
and tribal, intimate revenge.

[1975]

16 firkin: A small cask.

30–31 would have cast . . . of silence: In John 8:7–9, Jesus confronts a mob about to stone an adulterous woman and makes the famous statement "He that is without sin among you, let him first cast a stone at her." The crowd retreats, "being convicted by their own conscience."
37–40 I who . . . by the railings: In 1969, the British army became highly visible occupiers of Northern Ireland. In Heaney's native city of Belfast, the Irish Republican Army retaliated against Irish Catholic women who dated British soldiers. Punishments included shaving the women's heads, stripping and tarring them, and handcuffing them to the city's railings.

THINKING ABOUT THE TEXT

1. Summarize your impression of the bog woman. Where does the speaker begin addressing her directly? Why do you suppose Heaney has him refrain from addressing her right away?
2. Who is the main subject of this poem? The bog woman? The "betraying sisters" (line 38)? The speaker? Some combination of these people?
3. The speaker refers to himself as a "voyeur" (line 32). Consult a dictionary definition of this word. How might it apply to the speaker? Do you think it is ultimately the best label for him? Explain. Do you feel like a voyeur reading this poem? Why, or why not?
4. What are the speaker's thoughts in the last stanza? What connotation do you attach to the word *connive*? (You might want to consult a dictionary definition of it.) What is the speaker's attitude toward "the exact / and tribal, intimate revenge"? Do you see him as tolerating violence?
5. How might this poem be more about Heaney's own life than that of the bog girl?

KAREN RUSSELL

Bog Girl

Karen Russell (b. 1981) was born in Miami and received her M.F.A. from Columbia University. She was named one of the "best young American novelists" in 2007, before she had even published a novel. The recognition was given on the strength of her critically acclaimed collection of stories, St. Lucy's Home for Girls Raised by Wolves *(2006). Her stories have recently appeared in* Conjunctions, Granta, *and* Zoetrope. The New Yorker *debut fiction issue also featured her work. Her novel* Swamplandia *(2011) concerns alligator wrestlers. A collection of short stories,* Vampires in the Lemon Grove, *was published in 2013 and she also received a MacArthur foundation "Genius Grant" in 2013. Her latest book is* Sleep Donation: A Novella *(2014). The following story was published in* The New Yorker *in June 2016.*

The young turf-cutter fell hard for his first girlfriend while operating heavy machinery in the peatlands. His name was Cillian Eddowis, he was fifteen years old, and he was illegally employed by Bos Ardee. He had celery-green eyes and a stutter that had been corrected at the state's expense; it resurfaced whenever he got nervous. "Th-th-th," he'd said, accepting the job. How did Cillian persuade Bos Ardee to hire him? The boy had lyingly laid claim to many qualities: strength, maturity, experience. When that didn't work, he pointed to his bedroom window, a quarter mile away, on the misty periphery of the cutaway bog, where the undrained water still sparkled between the larch trees. The intimation was clear: what the thin, strange boy lacked in muscle power he made up for in proximity to the work site.

Peat is harvested from bogs, watery mires where the earth yawns open. The bottom is a breathless place—cold, acidic, anaerobic—with no oxygen to decompose the willow branches or the small, still faces of the foxes interred there. Sphagnum mosses wrap around fur, wood, skin, casting their spell of chemical protection, preserving them whole. Growth is impossible, and Death cannot complete her lean work. Once cut, the peat becomes turf, and many locals on this green island off the coast of northern Europe still heat their homes with this peculiar energy source. Nobody gives much thought to the fuels, mortuary origins. Cillian, his mother, and several thousand others lived on the island, part of the archipelago known to older generations as the Four Horsemen. It's unlikely that you've ever visited. It's not really on the circuit.

Neolithic farmers were the first to clear the island's woods. Two thousand years later, peat had swallowed the remains of their pastures. Bogs blanketed the hills. In the Iron Age, these bogs were portals to distant worlds, wilder realms. Gods travelled the bogs. Gods wore crowns of starry asphodels, floating above the purple heather.

Now industrial harvesters rode over the drained bogs, combing the earth into even geometries. On the summer morning that Cillian found the Bog Girl, he was driving the Peatmax toward a copse of trees at the bog's western edge, pushing the dried peat into black ridges. True, it looked as if he was pleating shit, but Cill had a higher purpose. He was saving to buy his neighbor Pogo's white hatchback. Once he had a car, it would be no great challenge to sleep with a girl or a woman. Cillian was open to either experience. Or both. But he was far too shy to have an eye-level crush on anyone in his grade. Not Deedee, not Stacia, not Vicki, not Yvonne. He had a crush, taboo and distressing, on his Aunt Cathy's ankles in socks. He had a crush on the anonymous shoulders of a shampoo model.

5 He had just driven into the western cutaway bog when he looked over the side of the Peatmax and screamed. A hand was sticking out of the mud. Cillian's first word to the Bog Girl required all the air in his lungs: "Ahhhhhhfuuuuuck!"

Here was a secret, flagging him down. A secret the world had kept for two thousand years and been unable to keep for two seconds longer. The bog had confessed her.

When the other men arrived, Cillian was on his knees, scratching up peat like a dog. Already he had dug out her head. She was whole and intact, cocooned in peat, curled like a sleeping child, with her head turned west of her pelvis. Thick, lustrous hair fanned over the tarp, the wild red-orange of an orangutans fur, dyed by the bog acids. Moving clouds caused her colors to change continuously: now they were a tawny bronze, now a mineral blue. It was a very young face.

Cradling her head, Cillian lost all feeling in his legs. A light rain began to fall, but he would not relinquish his position. Every man gathered was staring at them. Ordinarily, their pronged attention encircled him like a crown of thorns, making him self-conscious, causing red fear to leak into his inner vision. Today, he didn't give a damn about the judgments of the mouth-breathers above him. Who had ever seen a face so beautiful, so perfectly serene?

"Mother of God!" one of the men screamed. He pointed to the noose. A rope, nearly black with peat, ran down the length of her back.

Murder. That was the men's consensus. Bos Ardee called the police. 10

But Cillian barely heard the talk above him. If you saw the Bog Girl from one angle only, you would assume that she was a cherished daughter, laid to rest by hands that loved her. But she had been killed, and now her smile seemed even more impressive to him, and he wanted only to protect her from future harm. The men kept calling her "the body," which baffled Cillian—the word seemed to blind them to the deep and flowing dream-life behind her smile. "There is so much more to you than what they see," he reassured her in a whisper. "I am so sorry about what happened to you. I am going to keep you safe now."

After this secret conversation, Cill fell rapidly in love.

Cillian was lucky that he met his girlfriend on such a remote island. When these bodies are discovered in Ireland, for example, or in the humid Florida bogs sprinkled between Disney World and Cape Canaveral, things proceed differently. The area is cordoned off. Teams of experts arrive to excavate the site. Then the bog people are carefully removed to laboratories, museums, where gloveless hands never touch them.

Cillian touched her hair, touched the rope. He was holding the reins of her life. Three policemen had arrived, and they conferred above Cillian, their black boots squeezing mud around the bog cotton. Once it had been determined that the girl was not a recent murder victim, the policemen relaxed. The chief asked Cillian a single question: "You're going to keep her, then?"

Gillian Eddowis was on a party line with her three sisters. She tucked the phone 15 under her chin and took the ruby kettle off the range, opening a window to shoo the blue steam free. In the living room, roars of studio laughter erupted from the television; Cillian and the Bog Girl were watching a sitcom about a Canadian trailer park. Their long silences unnerved her; surely they weren't getting into trouble, ten feet away from her? She had never had cause to discipline her son. She wouldn't know where to begin. He was so kind, so intelligent, so unusual, so sensitive—such an outlier in the Eddowis family that his aunts had paid him the modern compliment of assuming that he was gay.

Voices sieved into Gillian's left ear:

"You want to warn them," Sister Abby said.

"But, Virgin Mother, there is no way to warn them!" Sister Patty finished.

"We were all sixteen once," Cathy growled. "We all survived it."

"Cillian is *fifteen*," Gillian corrected. "And the girlfriend is two thousand." 20

Abby, who had seen a picture of the Bog Girl in the local newspaper, suggested that *somebody* was rounding down.

A university man had also read the story of the Bog Girl's discovery. He'd taken a train and a ferry to find them. "I've come to make an Urgent Solicitation on Behalf of History," he said. He wanted to acquire the Bog Girl for the national museum. The sum he offered them was half of Gillian's salary at the post office.

In the end, what had happened? Christian feeling had muzzled her. How could she sell a girl to a stranger? Or pretend that she had any claim to her, this orphan from the Iron Age? Gillian told the university man that the Bog Girl was their house guest, and would be living with them until Social Services could locate her next of kin. At this, all the purple veins in the man's neck stood out. His tone sank into petulant defeat. "Mark my words, you people do not have the knowledge to properly care for her," he said. "She'll fall apart on you." The Bog Girl, propped up next to the ironing board, watched them argue with an implacable smile. The university man left empty-handed, and for a night and a day Gillian was a hero to her son.

"So she's just freeloading, then? Living off your dime?" Cathy asked.

"Oh, yes. She's quite shameless about it."

How could she explain to her sisters what she could barely admit to herself? The boy was in love. It was a monstrous, misdirected love; nevertheless, it commanded her respect.

"The Bog Girl is a bad influence on him," she told her sisters. "She doesn't work, she doesn't help. All day she lazes about the house."

Patty coughed and said, "If you feel that way, then why— "

Cathy screamed, "Gillian! She cannot *stay* with you!"

It was gentle Abby who formulated the solution: "Put her back in the bog."

"Gillian. *Do it tonight.*"

"Who's going to miss her?"

"I can't put her back in the bog. It would be . . ."

Silence drilled into her ears. Her family had a talent for emitting judgment without articulating words. When she was Cillian's age and five months pregnant with him, everyone had quietly made clear that she was sacrificing her future. She'd run away to be with Cillian's father, then returned to the boglands alone with a bug-eyed toddler.

"I'm afraid," she confessed to her sisters. "If I put her out of the house, he'll leave with her."

"Oh!" they cried in unison. As if a needle had infected them all with her fear.

"Do something crazy, stupid . . ."

Silently adding, *Like we did.*

"Now, be honest, you little rat turd. You know *nothing* about her." His uncle put a finger into his peach iced tea, stirred. They were seated on a swing in the darkest part of Cillian's porch. Uncle Sean was as blandly ugly as a big toenail. Egg-bald and cheerfully unemployed, a third-helpings kind of guy. Once, Cillian had watched him eat the sticker on a green apple rather than peel it off. Sean was always over at the cottage, using Gillian's computer to play Poker 3000. He smeared himself throughout their house, his beer rings ghosting over surfaces like fat thumbs on a photograph. His words hung around, too, leaving their brain stain on the air. Uncle Sean took a proprietary interest in anything loved by Cillian. It was no surprise, then, that he was infatuated with the Bog Girl.

"I know that I love her," Cill said warily. He hated to be baited.

Uncle Sean was packing his brown, shakey weed into the rosy crotch of a glass mermaid. He passed his nephew the pipe. "Already, eh? You love her and you don't know the first thing about her?"

What did he know about her?

What did he love about her?

Cillian shrugged, his body crowding with feelings. "And I know that she loves me," he added, somewhat hastily.

Uncle Sean's pink smirk seemed to paste him to the back of the wicker seat. "Oh?" His grin widened. "And how old is she?"

"Two thousand. But she was my age when they put her in the bog."

"Most women *I* know lie freely about their age," Uncle Sean warned. "She may well be eleven. Then again, she could be *three* thousand."

Gillian, plump and starlit, appeared on the porch. A pleasant oniony smell followed her, mixing with the damp odor of Sean's pot.

"Are you smoking?"

"No," they lied in unison.

"Tell your . . . your *friend* that she is welcome to eat with us." With a martyred air, Gillian lifted her kitten-print pot holders to the heavens. Cill smiled; the pot holders made it look as if she approved of the situation—two big thumbs-up! His poor mom. She was so nervous around new people, and the Bog Girl's silence only intimidated her further. She was insecure about her cooking, and he knew she was going to take it very personally when the Bog Girl did not touch it.

Dinner was meat loaf with onions and, for Sean, a thousand beers. It was not a comfortable meal.

Gillian, stirring butter into the lima beans, beamed threats at her son's new girlfriend: You little bitch. Crawl back into your hole. Stay away from my son.

"Biscuit?" Gillian asked. "Does she like biscuits, Cill?"

The Bog Girl smiled her gentle smile at the wall, her face reflected in the oval door of the washer-dryer. Against that sudsy turbulence, she looked especially still.

Three drinks in, Uncle Sean slung an arm around the Bog Girl's thin blue shoulder, welcoming her into the family. "I'm proud of my nephew for going after an older woman, a *mature* woman . . . a cougar!"

Cillian fixed his uncle with a homicidal stare. Under the table, he touched his girlfriend's foot with his foot; his eyebrows lifted in apology. His mother shot up with her steaming cauldron of beans, giving everyone another punitive lima ladle and removing the beer from the table. Their dog, returning from her dusk mouse hunt, came berserking into the kitchen, barking at a deranged pitch. She wanted to play tug-of-war with the Bog Girl's noose. "Puddles—*no!*" Cillian's vision was swimming, his whole body overheating with shame. He relaxed when he stared into the Bog Girl's face, which was void of all judgment, smiling at him with its mysterious kindness. Once again, his embarrassment was soothed by her infinite calm. His eyes lowered from her smile to the noose. *Of course, she's seen far worse than us*, he thought. Outside the window, insects millioned around the porch light. The bog crickets were doing a raspy ventriloquy of the stars; perhaps she recognized their tiny voices. Soon Uncle Sean was snoring lightly beside the pooling gravy, face down in his big arms. Cill sat slablike in the moonlight. The Bog Girl smiled blindly on.

For the first two weeks, the Bog Girl slept on the sofa, the television light flickering gently over her. That was fine by Gillian. She wasn't about to turn an orphan from the Iron Age out on the street.

Then, on a rainy Monday night, without warning or apology, Cillian picked up the Bog Girl. He cradled her like a child, her frondy feet dangling in the air. Gillian, doing a jigsaw puzzle of a horse and colt in the kitchen, looked up in time to see them disappearing. She felt a purple welt rising in her mind, the revelatory pain called wonder. Underneath the shock, other feelings began to flow, among them a disturbed pride. Because hadn't he looked *exactly* like his father? Confident, possessed. He didn't ask for her permission. He did not lie to her about what he was doing, or hide it, or explain it. He simply rose with the Bog Girl in his arms, nuzzling her blue neck. The door shut, and he was gone from sight. Another milestone: she heard the click of the lock.

"Good night, son!" she cried after them, panicked. 60

She could not reconcile her knowledge of her sweet, awkward boy with this wayward, confident person. Was she supposed to go up there now? Pound on the door? Oh, who could she call? Nobody, not even her sisters, would take a call about *this* problem, she felt quite certain. Abby's son, Kevin, met his girlfriend in church. Cathy's son, Patrick, has a lovely fiancée who teaches kindergarten. Murry's girlfriend is in jail for vehicular manslaughter—but at least she's alive!

In the morning, she watched the mute, hitching muscles of his back as he fumbled with the coffeepot. So he was a coffee drinker now. More news. He kissed his mother's forehead as he left for work, but he was whistling to himself, oblivious of her sadness, her fear, completely self-enclosed in his new happiness. It's too soon for this, she thought. And: Not you, too. *Please, please, please,* she prayed, the incomplete prayer of mothers who cannot conceive of a solution.

That evening, she announced a new rule: "Everyone has to wear clothes. And no more locked doors."

That Saturday, Cillian took the ferry three hours to a mainland museum. Twelve bog bodies were on display, part of a travelling exhibition called "Kings of the Iron Age." The Bog Girl had met his family—the least he could do was return the favor. Cill sneaked into a tour in progress, following a docent from sepulchre to sepulchre. Under the glass, the Kings of the Iron Age lay like chewed taffy. One man was naked except for a fox-fur armband. Another was a giant. Another had two sets of thumbs.

Cillian learned that the bogs of the islands in the cold Atlantic were particularly acidic. Pickled bodies from the Iron Age had emerged from these deep vats. Their fetally scrolled bodies often doubled as the crumpled maps of murders. They might have been human sacrifices, the docent said. Left in the bog water for the harvest god. Kings, queens, scapegoats, victims—they might have been any of these things. 65

"From the contents of his stomach, we can surmise that he last dined on oat gruel. . . ."

"From the forensic analyses, we can surmise that she was killed by an arrow. . . ."

"From the ornaments on this belt buckle, we can surmise that these were a wealthy people. . . ."

What? No more than this could be surmised?

The docent pointed out the dots and stripes on the potsherds. Charcoal 70
smudges that might be stars or animals. Evidence, she said, of "a robust culture." Cillian took notes:

"THEY HAD TIME TO KILL, THEY LIKED ART, TOO."

Back on the ferry, he could admit to his relief: none of the other bog bodies stirred any feeling in him. He loved one specific person. He could see things about the Bog Girl to which this batty docent would be totally blind—for example, the secret depths her smile concealed. How badly misunderstood she had been by her own people. She was an alien from a planet that nobody alive could visit—the planet Earth, in the first century A.D. She felt soft in his arms, bonelessly soft, but she also seemed indestructible. According to the experts, a bog body should begin to decompose rapidly when exposed to air. Curiously enough, this Bog Girl had not. He told no one his theory but polished it inside his mind like an amulet: it was his love that was protecting her.

By August, their rapport had deepened immeasurably. They didn't need to say a word, Cill was discovering, to perfectly understand each other. Falling in love with the Bog Girl was a wonderful thing—it was permission to ignore everyone else. When school started, in September, he made a bespoke sling and brought her with him. His girlfriend, propped like a broomstick against the rows of lockers, waited for him during Biology and Music II, as cool and impassive as the most popular girl the world has ever known.

Nobody in the school administration objected to the presence of the Bog Girl. Ancestral superstitions still hovered over the islanders' minds, exerting their quiet influence, and nobody wanted to be the person responsible for angering a visitor from the past. Soon she was permitted to audit all of Cillian's classes, smiling dreamlessly at the flustered, frightened teachers.

One afternoon, the vice-principal called her into his office and presented her with a red-and-gold badge to wear in the halls: "VISITING STUDENT."

"I don't think that's really accurate, sir," Cillian said. 75

"Oh, no?"

"She's not a visitor. She was born here." In fact, the Bog Girl was the island's oldest resident, by at least nineteen hundred years. Cillian paused. "Also, her eyes are shut, you see. So I don't think she can really, ah, study. . . ."

"Well!" The vice-principal clapped his hands. He had a day to live, quotas to fulfill. "We will be studying *her*, then. She will give us all an exciting new perspective on our modern life and times—Oh my! Oh dear." The Bog Girl had slumped into his aloe planter.

Cillian put the badge on her polyester blouse, a loaner from his mother that 80
was vintage cool. Cillian—who never gave a thought to his own clothing—enjoyed dressing the Bog Girl for school in the morning. He raided his mother's closet, resurrecting her baby-doll dresses. The eleventh-grade girls organized a clothing drive for the Bog Girl, collecting many shoplifted donations of fall tunics and on-trend boots.

Rumorsprawl. Word got around that the Bog Girl was actually a princess. A princess, or possibly a witch. Within a week, she was eating at the popular girls' table. They'd kidnapped her from where Cillian had positioned her on a bench, propped between two book bags, and taken her to lunch. Already they had restyled her hair with rhinestone barrettes.

"You stole my girlfriend," Cillian said.

"Something *awful* happened to her," Vicki said reverently.

"So bad," Georgette echoed.

"She doesn't like to talk about it," Priscilla said, looping a protective arm 85
around the Bog Girl. The girls had matching lunches: lettuce salads, diet candy bars, diet shakes. They were all jealous of how little she ate.

How had Cill not foreseen this turn of events? The Bog Girl was diminutive, wounded, mysterious, a redhead. Best of all, she could never contradict any rumor the living girls distributed about her.

"She was too beautiful to live!" Priscilla gasped. "They killed her for her beauty."

"I don't th-th-think," Cill said, "that it happened quite like that."

The popular girls adjusted their leggings, annoyed. "No?"

Cillian was dimly aware that other tables were listening in, but the density of 90
the attention in no way affected him. "I am hers, and she is mine," he announced. "I have dedicated myself to learning everything about her."

A sighing spasm of envy moved down the popular girls' table—what boy alive would say this about them? A miracle: nobody mocked Cillian Eddowis. They were all starving to be loved like this. The popular girls watched him avidly as he ate a grilled cheese and waffle fries, his green irises burning. Between bites, his left hand rose to touch the Bog Girl's red braid, tousling it like the pull-chain of a lamp.

Gillian couldn't help it: she was heartbroken. The past that was most precious to her had filtered right through her son. The songs she'd sung to him when he was nursing? The care with which she'd cut the tiny moons of his fingernails? Their 4 A.M. feedings? Erased! Her son had matured into amnesia about his earliest years. Now her body was the only place where the memories were preserved. Cillian, like all sons, was blithe about this betrayal.

"There is so much about yourself that you do not recall," Gillian accused him after dinner one night. Cillian, writing a paper about igneous rocks at the kitchen table, did not look up.

"When you were my boy, just a wee boy," Gillian said in a voice of true agony, "you used to be terrified of the vacuum cleaner. You loved your froggy pajamas. You used so much glue on your art projects that your teachers—"

"Quit it with these dumb stories, Ma!" 95

"Oh, you find them dumb, do you? The stories about how I had to raise you alone, without a penny from your father—"

"You're just trying to *embarrass* me in front of her!"

The Bog Girl smiled at them from the amber armchair. Her leather skirt was outrageously short, a donation from tall Bianca. Decorously, Cillian had draped the cable guide over her lap. Bugs spun in her water glass; mosquitoes and dragonflies were always diving into the Bog Girl's food and drink, as if in strange solidarity with her.

Cillian drew himself up triumphantly, a foot taller than his mother. "You don't want me to grow up."

"What? Of course I do!" 100

But Cill was ready with his rebuttal: "You gave us rhyming names, Ma!"

This was true. Gillian and Cillian. She'd come up with that plan when she was a teenager herself, and pregnant with a nameless otter, some gyring little animal. A rhyming name had seemed just right then; she couldn't have said why, at seventeen. Had Cillian been a girl, she would have named her Lillian.

"You're so young, you can't know . . ." But what did she want to tell him?

Her body seemed to cave in on itself then, becoming smaller and smaller, so that even Cillian, fortressed behind the wall of his love, noticed and became alarmed. "Ma? What's wrong?"

"It's changing all the time," she murmured ominously. "Just, please, wait, my love. Don't . . . *settle.*" What a word! She pictured her son sinking up to his neck in the reddish bog water. 105

She was hiccupping now, unable to name her own feelings. Without thinking, she picked up the murky water glass, drank from it. "Your potential . . . all the teachers tell me you have great potential."

Just come out and say it. "I don't want you to throw your *life* away on some Bog Girl!"

"Oh, Ma." Cill patted her back until the hiccups stopped. Her face looked crumpled and blue in the unlit room, hovering above the seated Bog Girl. For a second, they might have been sisters.

The Bog Girl floated, thin as a dress, on the mattress. Barrettes, pink and purple, were scattered all over the pillow. She smiled at Cillian, or beyond him, with her desiccated calm. Downstairs, Gillian was making breakfast, the buttery smells threading through his nostrils like an ox ring, tugging him toward them. But when she called up for him he was barely in the room. He was digging and digging into the peatmoss bog again, smoothing her blue cheeks with both hands, spading down into the kingdom that she comes from.

"Cillian! The bus is coming!" It should have taken him twenty seconds to put on pants. What was he doing in there? Probably jacking off to a "meme," whatever that was, or buying perfume for the Bog Girl on her credit cards. 110

"Coming, Ma!"

Cillian was always learning new things about his girlfriend. The longer he looked at her, the more he saw. Her face grew silty with personality. Although she was young when she disappeared into the bog, her face was plowed with tiny wrinklings. Some dream or mood had recurred frequently enough to hammer lines across her brow. Here were the ridges and the gullies her mental weathers had worked into her skin.

Cill studied the infloresences on her cheeks. Her brain is in there, the university man had said. Her brain is intact, preserved by the bog acids. Cillian spent hours doing this forensic palmistry, trying to read her mind.

"Will you have a talk with him?" Gillian begged Sean. "Something is going really, really wrong with him!"

"First love, first love," Sean murmured sadly, scratching his bubonic nose. 115
"Who are we to intervene, eh? It will die of natural causes."

"Natural causes!"

She was thinking that the poor girl had been garroted. Her bright-red hair racing the tail of the noose down her spine. You could not survive your death, could you? It survived with you.

In mid-October, a stretch limousine pulled up to the cottage to take Cillian and the Bog Girl to the annual school dance. A techno-reggae song called "Bump de Ass!" filled the back seat, where half a dozen teen-agers sat in churchlike silence. The Bog Girl's reticence was contagious. Ambulance lights sparkled through the tinted windows, causing everyone to jump, with one exception: Cillian Eddowis's date, the glamorous foreigner, or native—nobody was sure how to regard her.

Since acquiring his far older girlfriend, Cill had begun speaking to his classmates in the voice of a bachelor who merely tolerates children. "Carla," he said, clearing his throat. "Would you mind exhaling a little closer to the window? Your smoke is blowing on us."

Two girls started debating whether or not a friend should lose her virginity in 120
a BMW that evening. What was the interior of the car like? This was a very important question. The girl's boyfriend was a twenty-six-year-old cocaine dealer. Prior to the Bog Girl's arrival on the scene, everyone had found his age very impressive. The dealer boyfriend had been unable to accompany the girl to the school dance, so she had taken poor Eoin, her sophomore cousin, who looked near fatally compressed by his green cummerbund. The twenty-six-year-old would be waiting for her in the BMW, post-festivities. Should she deflower him?

"Wait. Uh. I think he's deflowering you, right? Or maybe you're deflowering each other? Who's got the flower?"

"Just do it, and then lie about it." Carla shrugged. "That's what I did."

"My advice," Cillian said, in the unfamiliar voice, "my advice is, wait. Wait until you find the person with whom you want to spend all your earthly time." The Bog Girl leaned against his shoulder, aloof in her sparkly tiara. "Or until that person finds you. If that's this guy, well, kudos. But, if not, wait. You will meet your soul mate. And you will want to give that person every molecule of your life."

The attempted conversion of the high-school gymnasium into an Arabian-themed wonderland had not been a success. Cill and the Bog Girl stood under a palm tree that looked like an enormous toilet brush, made of cellophane and cardboard tubes. Three girls from the limo came up and asked to dance with Cillian, but he explained that his girlfriend hated to be left alone. All were sulkily respectful of her claim on him.

The after-party was held in an old car-parts warehouse on the west side of 125
the island, where everything was shut or abandoned; the population of the island had been declining steadily for three decades. The music sounded like fists beating at the wall, and the floor was so sticky that Cillian had to lift and cradle the Bog Girl, looping her silver dress around one arm. Cillian had never attended an after-party before. Or a party, for that matter. He surveyed his former tormenters, the seniors, with their piggish faces and their plastic cups. Some were single, some had girlfriends, some were virgins, some were not, but not one of them, Cillian felt very certain, knew the first thing about love.

Eoin the sophomore came over, his date nowhere to be seen. He was breathless in the cummerbund, in visible danger of puking up Bacardi. He rolled a bloodshot eye in Cill's direction, smiling wistfully.

"So," he said, "I'm just wondering. Do you guys—"

Cillian preëmpted the question: "A gentleman never tells."

It was a phrase he'd once read in a men's magazine, while waiting to get a root canal. In fact, his mother needn't have lost so much sleep to this particular fear. At night, Cillian lay beside the Bog Girl, barely touching her. A steady, happy calm radiated from her, which filled him with a parallel euphoria.

Cillian carried the Bog Girl onto the dance floor, her braided noose flung over 130
his shoulder. And even Eoin, minutes from unconsciousness, could hear exactly who the older boy believed himself to be in this story: Cillian the Rescuer.

"Oh, damn! Wise up! She'll make you wait forever, man!" The lonely laugh of Eoin died a terrible death, like a bird impaled on a spike.

At 3 A.M., the lights were still on. Uh-oh, Cill thought. Mom got into the gin again.

Drinking made her silences bubble volubly. He almost got the hiccups himself, listening to her silences. Oh, God. There was so much pain inside her, so much she wanted to share with him. Cillian and the Bog Girl tried to tiptoe past her to the staircase, but she sprang up like a jack-in-the-box.

"Cillian?" She looked child-small in the dark. Her voice was tremulous and young, and her slurring reminded him of his own stutter, that undead vestige of his early years. His mother sounded like a sleepy girl, four or five years old. Her feet were bare, and she rose onto her stubby toes to grip his arm. "Where are you coming from?"

"Nowhere. The dance. It was fun." 135

"Where are you going?"

"Aw, Mom. Where do you th-th-think?"

"Good night!" she called after him desperately. "I hope you had a good time! You looked so handsome! So grown up!"

By early winter, the Bog Girl's stillness had begun to provoke a restlessness in Cillian, a squeezed and throbbing feeling. He was failing three subjects. His mother had threatened to send him to live with Aunt Cathy until he "straightened out."

He didn't care. Waiting for the bus in the freezing rain, he no longer dreamed about owning a car. He knew what he would do with the summer money he'd earned from Bos Ardee: run away with her.

He'd flunk out of school and take the Bog Girl with him to the mainland. 140
She'd be homesick at first, maybe, but they'd go on trips to urban parks. It was the burr of peace, the burr of happiness, goading him on to new movement. Oh, he was frightened, too.

In his fantasy life, Cillian drew the noose tighter and tighter. He imagined, with a strange joy, the narrow life they would lead. No children, no sex, no messy nights vomiting outside bars, no unintended pregnancies, no fights in the street, no betrayals, no surprises, no broken promises, no promises.

Was the Bog Girl a co-signer to this fantasy? Cillian had every reason to believe so. When he described his plans to her, the smile never left her face. Was their love one-sided, as the concerned and unimaginative adults in his life kept insisting? No—but the proof of this surprised no one more terribly than Cillian.

One night in mid-December, lying in bed, he felt a cobwebby softness on his left cheek. It was her eyelashes, flicking over him. They glowed radish-red in the moonlight. Cillian swatted at his face, his own eyes never opening. Still sunk in his dreaming, he grunted and rolled over.

Cillian.

Cillian. 145

The Bog Girl sat up.

With fluttering effort, the muscles of her blue jaw yawned. One eye opened. It studied itself in the dresser mirror for a long instant, then turned calmly back toward Cillian. Very slowly, her left arm unhinged itself and dropped to the plaid bedspread. The fingers curled around the blanket's edge, and drew it down. A blush of primal satisfaction colored the Bog Girl's cheeks as the fabric moved. She tugged more forcefully, revealing Cillian curled on his side in his white undershirt. Groaning in his sleep, he jerked the covers back up.

"Cillian," she said aloud.

Now Cillian was awake—he was irreversibly awake. He blinked up at her face, which was staring down at him. When they locked eyes, her frozen smile widened.

"Mom!" he couldn't help screaming. "Help!" 150

The Bog Girl, imitating him, began to scream and scream. And he could see, radiating from her gaze, the same blind tenderness that he had directed at her. Now he was its object. Something truly terrifying had happened: she loved him back.

For months, Cillian had been decoding the Bog Girl's silences. He'd peered into her dreams, her fears, her innermost thoughts. But her real voice was nothing like the voice that he'd imagined for her—a cross between Vicky Gilvarry and Patti LaBelle. Its high-pitched ululations hailed over him. In the kitchen, the dog began to bark. The language that she spoke was no longer spoken anywhere on earth.

He stumbled up, tugging at his boxers. The Bog Girl stood, too. The past, with its monstrous depth and span, reached toward him, demanding an understanding that he simply could not give it. His mind was too young and too narrow to withstand the onrush of her life. An invisible woods was in the bedroom with them, the scent of trees multiplying. Some mental earthquake inside the Bog Girl was casting up a world, green and unknown to him, or to anyone living: her homeland. Her gaze drove inward, carrying Cillian with it. For an instant, he thought he glimpsed her parents. Her brothers, her sisters, a nation of people. Their cheeks now beginning to redden, every one of them alive again inside her village. Pines rippling seaward. Gods, horned and faceless, walking the lakes that once covered Cillian's home. Cillian was buried in water, in liquid images of her; he had to push through so many strata of her memories to reach the surface of her mind. Most of what he saw he shrank away from. His mind felt like a burned tongue, numbly touching her reality.

"W-w-who are you?"

"Heartbreak" is the universal diagnosis for the pain that accompanies the 155
end of love. But this was an unusual breakup, in that Cillian's mind shattered first. The love that had protected him began to fall away. Piece after piece of it clattered from his chest, an armor rusting off him. *What are you?*

The Bog Girl lurched toward him, her arms open. First she moved like a hopping chick, with an unexpected buoyancy. Then she seemed to remember how to step, heel to toe. She came for him like an astronaut, bouncing on the gray carpet. The only English word she knew was his name.

Almost weightlessly, she reached for him. For wasn't she equally terrified? There was no buoy other than this boy, who had gripped her with his thin, freckled arms, bellying her out of the peat bog and into time.

Cillian hid behind the dresser.

Her fingers found his hand, threaded through his fingers.

He screamed again, even as he squeezed the hand back. 160

Her words rushed together, a thawing waterfall, moving intricately between octaves; still the only word he understood was his name. Perhaps nothing he had said to her, in their six months as a couple, had been comprehended. Cillian worked the levers in his brain, desperately trying to find the words that would release him.

"Unlock the door," his mother's beautiful voice called.

Cillian was frozen in the Bog Girl's grip, unable even to call out. But a moment later he heard the key turning in the lock. Gillian stood in the doorway in her yellow pajamas. With a panoramic comprehension, she took in what had happened. She knew, too, what must now be done. If she could have freed these two from the embrace herself, she would have done so; but now she understood the challenge. The boy would have to make his own way out. "Take her home, Cillian. Make sure that she gets home safely."

Cillian, his eyes round with panic, only nodded.

Gillian went to the Bog Girl, helping her into a sweater. "Put a hat on. And 165
pants."

His mother shepherded them downstairs and onto the porch, switching on every yellow bulb as they moved through the cottage. It was the warmest

December on record, rain falling instead of snow, the drops disappearing into the rotted wood. Cillian carried the Bog Girl to the edge of the light before he understood that his mother was not coming with him.

"Let her down gently, son!" his mother called after them.

Well, she could do this for him, at least: she held a lantern steady across the rainy lawn, creating a gangplank of light that reached almost to the larches. She watched them moving toward the inky water. The Bog Girl was howling in her foreign tongue; at this distance, Gillian felt she could almost understand it.

Oh, she hoped their breakup would stick. She had divorced Cillian's father, then briefly moved into his new house; it had taken years before their affair was truly over. You had to really cultivate an ending. To get it to last, you had to kneel and tend to the burial ground, continuously firming your resolution.

This was a bad breakup. A quarter mile from the cottage, under a bright moon, Cillian and the Bog Girl were rolling in the mud, each screaming in a different language. Their screams twined together, their hands reaching for each other; it was during this undoing that they were, at last, truly united as a couple. His flashlight rolled with them, plucking amphibious red and yellow eyes out of the reeds. "It's over. It's over. It's over," he kept babbling optimistically, out of his mind with fear. Her throat was vibrating against his skin. He could feel the echo of his own terror and sorrow, and again his mind felt overrun by the lapping waves of time. She clutched at the collar of his T-shirt, her body covered in dark mud and cracked stems of bog cotton, blue lichen. At last he felt her grip on him loosen. Her eyes, opaquely glinting in the moonlight, liquid and enormous, far larger than anyone could have guessed before their unlidding, regarded him with what he imagined was a soft surprise, and disappointment. He was not who she'd expected to find when she opened her eyes, either. Now neither teenager needed to tell the other that it was over. It simply was—and, without another sound, the Bog Girl let go of Cillian and slipped backward into the bog water. Did she sink? It looked almost as if the water were rising to cover her. Her cranberry hair waved away from her scalp. As he watched, her body itself began to break up.

Straightening from where he was kneeling on the ledge of mud, he brushed peat from his pants. His arms tingled where her grip had suddenly relaxed. The clear rain drenched his clothing. The bog was still bubbling, pieces of her sinking back into the black peat, when he turned on his heel and ran. For the next few days, he would be quakey with relief; he'd felt certain, watching her sink away, that he would never see the Bog Girl again in this life.

But here he was mistaken. In the weeks and years to come, Cillian would find himself alone with her memory, struggling to pay attention to his droning contemporaries in the cramped classroom. How often would he retrace his steps, wandering right back to the lip of the bog, peering in? Each dusk, with their primitive eloquence, the air-galloping insects continue to speak the million syllables of her name.

"Ma! Ma! Ma!" That night, Cillian came roaring out of the dark, pistoning his knees as he ran for the light, for his home at the edge of the boglands. "Who *was* that?"

☰ THINKING ABOUT THE TEXT

1. Cillian gets his job clearing the bog because he wants to by a car and have sex. Why then does he fall in love with the Bog Girl at first sight?
2. When specifically does the story pivot from realism to something else: Magical realism? Fantasy? Comedy? Horror? How would you describe its genre?
3. Cillian's Uncle Sean says, "You know nothing about her." Explain the significance of this. How is it both true and not? How might this be to Cillian's advantage, at least for awhile?
4. Describe the various reactions to the Bog Girl from, for example, the university man, the girls at school, Gillian, Uncle Sean, and so forth.
5. How might this story be about memory, both recent (Gillian's memoires of Cillian as a child) and our culture's lost memoires of deep history? Why does Cillian say at the end of the story "What are you?" and "Who *was* that?"

☰ MAKING COMPARISONS

1. Compare the descriptions of the bog girls given by Heaney and Russell. What similarities and differences do you notice? How does Cillian first respond to her? How does the narrator in "Punishment"?
2. Compare the behavior of Cillian and Heaney's narrator toward the bog girls.
3. Compare what seems to be the main idea in each text. Is it love, memory, aging, punishment, identity, or something else?

☰ WRITING ABOUT ISSUES

1. About the story Russell says: "Everybody alive today, Cillian comes to feel, must be part of an extended family—barnacles on the hull of a ship, riding through time together." Write an essay that agrees or disagrees with this statement. Use your own experiences and this story.
2. Agree or disagree with Russell's view that "we project our fantasies onto the mask of another person's face, and then feel betrayed when they turn out to have needs and depths of their own."
3. Argue that Russell's story and Heaney's poem are metaphors or allegories for our understanding of others.
4. Write an essay that compares the Heaney poem and the Russell story, noting their similarities and differences.

CHAPTER 10

Freedom and Confinement

Like most abstract and frequently used terms, *freedom* means many things to many people. In countries in the West, freedom is usually associated with political and religious choice, with the ability to dissent publicly from government policy, and even with an ability to dye our hair orange and paint our lips black. Indeed, freedom involves the right not to conform to conventional ideas about who we are and how we should behave as well as the right not to be stereotyped by a culture's demeaning, limiting, and distorted images and assumptions.

Readers of nineteenth-century fiction by women are familiar with the rigid cultural expectations that constricted the lives of most women. Excluded from public life and confined almost exclusively to domestic spaces, many women felt trapped in helping roles constructed for them by men. The consequences for the mental and physical health of thousands of would-be writers, artists, scientists, and intellectuals were often severe. Today many minorities in America also feel limited by the confining legacies of both racial and gender stereotypes. Children, who are especially vulnerable to the negative images that adults from the dominant culture have of them, have few defenses against internalizing damaging stereotypes that can adversely affect them well into adulthood. And when an entire culture constructs invidious stereotypes, as German Nazis did about European Jews, the consequences can be deadly.

The chapter opens with six poems that explore the painful consequences of stereotyping followed by five poets who remember the horrors of the Holocaust. The third cluster presents a selection of poems by one of the giants of American literature, Emily Dickinson. This material is followed by two harrowing stories that show us the dark side of tradition. The fifth cluster is comprised of two stories from different eras and different contexts but with a similar focus—entrapment and escape. A canonical writer, Vladimir Nabokov, is the focus of the next cluster as three critics comment on his story, "Signs and Symbols." Ursula K. Le Guin's classic science fiction tale, "The Ones Who Walk Away from Omelas," is paired with two contemporary essayists in our next cluster. Henrik Ibsen's classic play about one of the theater's great heroines, Nora, is the subject of our next cluster with five commentaries that consider cultural context. The perplexing issue of surveillance is explored in the penultimate cluster by pairing Michel Foucault's essay "Panoptican" with three commentaries. The final cluster presents the classic Greek tragedy, *Antigone*, with a contemporary story that also explores the consequences of being true to one's principles.

Struggling against Stereotypes: Poems

CHRYSTOS, "Today Was a Bad Day like TB"

DWIGHT OKITA, "In Response to Executive Order 9066"

PAT MORA, "Legal Alien"

TOI DERRICOTTE, "Black Boys Play the Classics"

NAOMI SHIHAB NYE, "Blood"

DAVID HERNANDEZ, "'Words without Thoughts Never to Heaven Go'"

When pressed, thoughtful people would agree that each of us has an individual personality and attributes that make us different from others. No one is an exact duplicate: even identical twins have both subtle and significant differences. Even so, cultures tend to lump together whole groups under dubious but convenient generalizations: used car dealers are dishonest, surfers are laid-back slackers, and computer geniuses are geeks. Usually based on limited, anecdotal, and often highly contextual historical and cultural evidence, these generalizations have a way of taking hold in a society long after the original context has disappeared (if there ever was one). Does anyone really think that dumb-blond jokes had any original validity? Is considering each person on his or her own merits too complicated?

When ethnic groups are stereotyped, their members may suffer consequences that are significantly more severe than those endured by, say, absent-minded professors. Some stereotypes are benign: as children growing up in New York, we routinely heard about industrious Chinese or hardworking Germans. But we also heard many negative generalizations that went hand in hand with racial discrimination and psychological damage. Members of the dominant groups in America are often oblivious to the ways that members of minority groups internalize destructive and distorted images of themselves, often seeing themselves as inferior to the dominant group and irredeemably other. They become trapped in images rampant in the culture and struggle daily to overcome the limited reality these stereotypes portray. The following seven poems represent aspects of this struggle in various ways — some with anger, resentment, and despair, others with thoughtful reflection, but all with an awareness of the pain that thoughtless stereotypes have on millions of Americans.

BEFORE YOU READ

Do you think of yourself as an ethnic American? Have you ever seen the term *English American* or *Dutch American*? What's the difference between those terms and *African American* or *Irish American*? Do you think ethnic traditions should be preserved, or should they be replaced with American traditions? Can these traditions coexist?

CHRYSTOS

Today Was a Bad Day like TB

Born in San Francisco of a Lithuanian/Alsace-Lorraine mother and a Native American father of the Menominee tribe, Chrystos (b. 1946) writes in the outsider traditions of her ancestry, her lesbian perspective, and her geographical position on Bainbridge Island off the coast of the Pacific Northwest. She is a women's and native rights advocate, a working artist, and a poet. Her poetry collections include Not Vanishing *(1988),* Dream On *(1991),* In Her I Am *(1993),* Fire Power *(1995), and the 1994 winner of the Audre Lorde International Poetry Competition,* Fugitive Colors. *In 2007, she published* Some Poems by People I Like. *She is a Lannan Foundation fellow and the 1995 recipient of the Sappho Award of Distinction. The poem reprinted here is from* Not Vanishing.

For Amanda White

Saw whites clap during a sacred dance
Saw young blond hippie boy with a red stone pipe°
    My eyes burned him up
He smiled   *This is a Sioux pipe* he said from his sportscar
    Yes   I hiss   *I'm wondering how you got it*
    & the name is Lakota not Sioux
I'll tell you he said all friendly & liberal as only
    those with no pain can be
    I turned away   Can't charm me   can't bear to know
thinking of the medicine bundle I saw opened up in a glass case
    with a small white card beside it
    naming the rich whites who say they
    "own" it
Maybe they have an old Indian grandma back in time
    to excuse themselves
Today was a day I wanted to beat up the smirking man wearing
a pack with a Haida design from Moe's bookstore
Listen Moe's   How many Indians do you have working there?
How much money are you sending the Haida people
to use their sacred Raven design?
    You probably have an Indian grandma too
    whose name you don't know
    Today was a day like TB
    you cough & cough trying to get it out
                all that comes
                    is blood & spit   *[1988]*

2 red stone pipe: Traditionally, sacred peace pipes were made of red catlinite, a fine-grained stone.

THINKING ABOUT THE TEXT

1. What argument about the ways whites relate to Native Americans is Chrystos making? What assumptions about whites does Chrystos seem to have? What stereotypes does she seem to harbor?
2. Might you have clapped during a Lakota dance? During a Catholic Mass? What is the "it" in line 24 that the poet is trying to get out? Do you think she is angry with her readers?
3. Is the ending too stark or perhaps too crude? Might the language have been more indirect and subtle, or is it appropriate to the theme?
4. Americans who are part of the "mainstream" – that is, white, male, middle class, or heterosexual – sometimes get annoyed when those who are not complain about bias, probably because the offense was inadvertent. (Think of Atlanta Braves fans doing "the tomahawk chop.") The young man in this poem, for example, seems quite oblivious of giving offense. Who determines who is right in these situations?
5. What other stereotypes can you think of that mainstream America harbors?

DWIGHT OKITA

In Response to Executive Order 9066

A third-generation Japanese American, poet and playwright Dwight Okita (b. 1958) won an Illinois Art Council Fellowship for poetry in 1988. Although Crossing with the Light *(1992), from which this poem is taken, is his first book of poetry, Okita has been more active in promoting the performance of poetry than the printing of it, and he is well known as a "slam" poet at open-mike readings in Chicago. A member of the large Japanese American community that developed in Chicago as a result of the migration from the West after the bitter experience of the internment camps during World War II, Okita expresses his family history in his poetry and plays. His dramas include* The Rainy Season *(1992) and* The Salad Bowl Dance *(1993). His book* The Prospect of My Arrival *(2008) was nominated for the Amazon Breakthrough Novel Award.*

All Americans of Japanese Descent
Must Report to Relocation Centers

Dear Sirs:
Of course I'll come. I've packed my galoshes
and three packets of tomato seeds. Denise calls them
love apples. My father says where we're going
they won't grow.

I am a fourteen-year-old girl with bad spelling
and a messy room. If it helps any, I will tell you

I have always felt funny using chopsticks
and my favorite food is hot dogs.
My best friend is a white girl named Denise—
we look at boys together. She sat in front of me
all through grade school because of our names:
O'Connor, Ozawa. I know the back of Denise's head very well.

I tell her she's going bald. She tells me I copy on tests.
We're best friends.

I saw Denise today in Geography class.
She was sitting on the other side of the room.
"You're trying to start a war," she said, "giving secrets
away to the Enemy. Why can't you keep your big
mouth shut?"

I didn't know what to say.
I gave her a packet of tomato seeds
and asked her to plant them for me, told her
when the first tomato ripened
she'd miss me. *[1992]*

THINKING ABOUT THE TEXT

1. What claim is Okita making in the last stanza? On what assumption about friendship is it based?
2. During the U.S. government's internment of Japanese American citizens, thousands were told to leave their homes to live in relocation centers for the duration of the war. To represent this complex historical event, why do you think it is effective to have a young girl writing a letter about being shunned by her best friend?
3. Explain Okita's use of the tomato seeds throughout the poem (lines 3, 22). What about other concrete words: *galoshes* (line 2), *chopsticks* (line 8), *hot dogs* (line 9)?
4. Since there was no evidence that Japanese American citizens ever gave any "secrets / away to the Enemy" (lines 18–19) during World War II, why do you think Denise and millions of other Americans made that assumption?
5. What current situations seem comparable to the theme of this poem?

MAKING COMPARISONS

1. Compare the tones of Okita's and Chrystos's poems. What emotions do you see in each?
2. Okita creates a young female narrator to speak for him. Does this make his poem less direct than Chrystos's?
3. Is the alienation described by Okita more or less painful than that described by Chrystos?

PAT MORA

Legal Alien

Pat Mora (b. 1942) was born in El Paso, Texas. She earned a B.A. from Texas Western College in 1963 and an M.A. from the University of Texas, El Paso, in 1967. She is a versatile writer of many children's books, essays, and poems. Her poems are, according to the New York Times, *"proudly bilingual." Her sixth collection,* Adobe Odes *(2006), was praised for turning its back on hopelessness, "finding a way to delight in the sensual world as well as its people," and a "must-have for libraries serving Latino communities." Her latest collection is* Dizzy in Your Eyes *(2010). Mora lives in Santa Fe, New Mexico. "Legal Alien" is from* Chants *(1984) and focuses on a common Chicana theme: the difficulties of living in two cultures simultaneously.*

Bi-lingual, Bi-cultural,
able to slip from "How's life?"
to *"Me'stan volviendo loca,°"*
able to sit in a paneled office
drafting memos in smooth English,
able to order in fluent Spanish
at a Mexican restaurant,
American but hyphenated,
viewed by Anglos as perhaps exotic,
perhaps inferior, definitely different,
viewed by Mexicans as alien,
(their eyes say, "You may speak
Spanish but you're not like me")
an American to Mexicans
a Mexican to Americans
a handy token
sliding back and forth
between the fringes of both worlds
by smiling
by masking the discomfort
of being pre-judged
Bi-laterally. [1984]

3 ***"Me'stan volviendo loca":*** They're driving me crazy (Spanish).

THINKING ABOUT THE TEXT

1. Was your first response to the opening line to think that such a situation is an advantage? Is that Mora's intent?
2. What advantages does being bicultural have? What disadvantages?
3. What other Americans are referred to as "hyphenated"? Do you think the same pluses and minuses apply?
4. Is the title appropriate? Explain.
5. Explain the significance of the "token" metaphor in line 16.

MAKING COMPARISONS

1. Mora sees some advantage to being bicultural. Do any of the other poets?
2. Compare Mora's tone with Chrystos's.
3. Which of the stereotypes in these poems seems the most psychologically damaging? Why?

TOI DERRICOTTE

Black Boys Play the Classics

Toi Derricotte (b. 1941) was born in Louisiana and was influenced as a child by her Creole and Catholic background. She graduated from Wayne State University in 1965. The first of her six books, The Empress of the Death House, *was published in 1978. Her latest collection of poems and stories,* The Undertaker's Daughter, *was published in 2011. Often compared to Sylvia Plath and Anne Sexton, Derricotte writes poems that, according to the poet and critic Marilyn Hacker, are "honest, fine-boned, deceptively simple . . . and deadly accurate." She is currently a professor of English at the University of Pittsburgh. The following poem is from* Tender *(1997).*

The most popular "act" in
Penn Station
is the three black kids in ratty
sneakers & T-shirts playing
two violins and a cello — Brahms.
White men in business suits
have already dug into their pockets
as they pass and they toss in
a dollar or two without stopping.
Brown men in work-soiled khakis
stand with their mouths open,
arms crossed on their bellies
as if they themselves have always
wanted to attempt those bars.
One white boy, three, sits
cross-legged in front of his
idols — in ecstasy —
their slick, dark faces,
their thin, wiry arms,
who must begin to look
like angels!
Why does this trembling
pull us?
A: *Beneath the surface we are one.*
B: *Amazing! I did not think that they could speak this tongue.* [1997]

THINKING ABOUT THE TEXT

1. Why do the "brown men" (line 10) respond as they do? Why do the "white men" (line 6)?
2. Why does the poet offer a description of the boys' clothes? Does it have to do with our stereotyped expectations?
3. What are some possible meanings for "pull us" (line 23)?
4. Explain what you think Derricotte means by the last line.
5. How would you state the theme of this poem? Do you agree with it? Who is the "we" in the next-to-last line?

MAKING COMPARISONS

1. How does Derricotte's tone differ from Chrystos's tone?
2. How does the end of this poem differ from the ends of the other poems in this cluster? Is it more effective or less effective?
3. If you were to rewrite "Black Boys Play the Classics" as a first-person poem (as Okita's poem demonstrates), which character from this poem would you choose, and why? How would a different point of view change the poem?

NAOMI SHIHAB NYE

Blood

Naomi Shihab Nye (b. 1952) was born to a Lutheran German American mother and a Muslim Palestinian American father in St. Louis. Her parents moved to the Middle East near Jerusalem, where her father edited the Jerusalem Times, *for which Nye, at fourteen, wrote a weekly column. Eventually turmoil forced their return to the United States. They settled in Texas, and Nye graduated from Trinity University in San Antonio in 1974. She has published books for children and adolescents with subject matter she hopes will dispel stereotypes and foster an understanding of "difference." Her poetic focus is often on the Palestinian Diaspora and on themes of our common humanity. Her books include* 19 Varieties of Gazelle *(2002) and* You and Yours: Poems *(2005). "Blood" is from* Yellow Glove *(1986).*

"A true Arab knows how to catch a fly in his hands,"
my father would say. And he'd prove it,
cupping the buzzer instantly
while the host with the swatter stared.

In the spring our palms peeled like snakes.
True Arabs believed watermelon could heal fifty ways.
I changed these to fit the occasion.

Years before, a girl knocked,
wanted to see the Arab.
I said we didn't have one.
After that, my father told me who he was,

"Shihab" — "shooting star" —
a good name, borrowed from the sky.
Once I said, "When we die, we give it back?"
He said that's what a true Arab would say.

Today the headlines clot in my blood.
A little Palestinian dangles a truck on the front page.
Homeless fig, this tragedy with a terrible root
is too big for us. What flag can we wave?
I wave the flag of stone and seed,
table mat stitched in blue.

I call my father, we talk around the news.
It is too much for him,
neither of his two languages can reach it.
I drive into the country to find sheep, cows,
to plead with the air:
Who calls anyone *civilized*?
Where can the crying heart graze?
What does a true Arab do now?

[1986]

THINKING ABOUT THE TEXT

1. What is your response to the girl who comes looking "to see the Arab" (line 9)? What is the speaker's response?
2. What do you think the father means by "a true Arab"? Is there a true American? A true man? Woman? Texan?
3. What is the father's response to the news about the Middle East? What is the speaker's? What is yours?
4. What is the purpose of the speaker's drive into the country?
5. How would you answer the questions the speaker asks in the last stanza?

MAKING COMPARISONS

1. Compare Nye's bicultural perspective to Mora's. Is Nye's status more precarious than Mora's in contemporary America?
2. Which of the speakers in all these poems seems angriest? Saddest? The most understanding?
3. What seems to be the most common theme among the poems?

DAVID HERNANDEZ

"Words without Thoughts Never to Heaven Go"°

David Hernandez (b. 1971) was born in Burbank, California and received a BA at California State University, Long Beach. He is the author of several collections of poetry, including Hoodwinked *(2011) and* Always Danger *(2006). His most recent book is* Dear Sincerely *(2016). He teaches at California State University, Fullerton. The following poem was published in* The Southern Review *(Spring 2016).*

The n-word will never go, the k-word will never go.
My surname may allow me to say aloud
the slur beginning with *s*, but I won't, I won't,
it will never don a halo. Spoken, it is almost *speak*
and meant to make a person of my race
smaller, a speck inside his own skin. It is almost
speck. Earlier I typed "ethnic slurs" online,
scrolled through the list. At least a hundred words
will never rise, will never come within
earshot of divine clouds.
When I was a kid, timid
as a breeze, I rolled with this reckless boy
schooled in the art of aspersions.
Nothing in the alphabet could dodge his epithets
(the q-word will never go), but somehow
my flesh was pale enough to enter his home. Stark
differences, the two of us. We shared
our given name. *David,* his father said
one summer afternoon, *remember when I
rooted for that n-word at the race?* He didn't say it
quite like that.
This is the story,
this is a racist cheering for an African American
speeding around a motocross track, the pack
droning behind him like angry hornets.
After he won, he said to me, *he took off
his helmet. Had I known,* he continued, dot
dot dot, then dropped again
the word from his lips.
Come December, he beat his wife, and David
grabbed an aluminum bat, attacked his house
all around the outside. I recall the damage
to the siding, open mouth after open mouth,
how each nested a hollow sound.

Words without Thoughts Never to Heaven Go: from Shakespeare.

THINKING ABOUT THE TEXT

1. Why does Hernandez say his surname allows him to use a slur? Why would you agree or disagree with this?
2. What effect does Hernandez say the "s word" slur has? What seems to you to be the motivation for using ethnic slurs?
3. What does Hernandez mean by the poem's title?
4. Look up the title's quote by Claudius in *Hamlet*. How does the original meaning reinforce Hernandez's meaning in the poem?
5. What is the intended relationship between the last stanza and the rest of the poem?

MAKING COMPARISONS

1. Hernandez writes about a racist. How might this term apply to Chrystos's and Okita's poems?
2. Which of the poetic devices in the preceding poems strikes you as the most effective? The least? Why?
3. Which ideas in these poems seems the most relevant today? Why?

WRITING ABOUT ISSUES

1. Write a journal entry from either Chrystos's or Okita's perspective that comments on the writing of their respective poem, what you (as the author) were trying to do, how you feel about stereotyping, and what response you are hoping for from readers.
2. Write an essay that compares the stereotyping that occurs in "Black Boys Play the Classics" and "Legal Alien." Comment on its origins, consequences, and possible solutions.
3. Write an essay that explores the kind of stereotyping you were exposed to as a child and as an adolescent in your family, in your peer group, or in the larger culture.
4. After doing research on an ethnic group not represented here, locate a poet from that group and write a brief report on his or her work.

Remembering the Death Camps: Poems

MARTIN NIEMÖLLER, "First They Came for the Jews"

NELLY SACHS, "Chorus of the Rescued"

MARIANNE COHN, "I Shall Betray Tomorrow"

KAREN GERSHON, "Race"

ANNE SEXTON, "After Auschwitz"

Being shunned by neighbors because of religion, race, gender, or ethnicity creates painful psychological alienation for victims of such treatment. But what if your religion, cultural heritage, or sexual orientation were deemed dangerous to the well-being of your country? What if the powerful so dehumanized you that you were thought of as vermin to be disposed of? This would be more than alienation; this would be putting respect for human life beyond normal moral restraints. As in war, the different ones become the enemy who is less than human and who can be destroyed with impunity.

Of course, this describes exactly what happened during the Holocaust when the Nazis murdered millions of Jews. Thousands of eyewitness accounts have been written about this tragedy, but writers who were not there feel equally compelled to write about the events of the Holocaust. It is impossible to adequately represent such horrors: some writers are furious; others are disciplined and controlled. It is one of a writer's challenges to try to express in words what is truly beyond description.

BEFORE YOU READ

Have you seen photographs of Holocaust survivors? Have you seen films, read books, or heard stories about these events? What are your feelings? Can you explain how systematic genocide is possible? Do such things still happen in the world?

MARTIN NIEMÖLLER

First They Came for the Jews

A German Protestant theologian and pastor, Martin Niemöller (1892–1984), who won the Iron Cross as a submarine commander in World War I, is best known as an outspoken critic of Adolf Hitler and Nazism preceding and during World War II. As the pastor of the Berlin congregation of the Evangelical Church from 1931, Niemöller led a group of clergy working to counter Nazism and earned Hitler's hatred. From 1937 to 1945, he was interned at the Dachau and Sachsenhausen concentration camps. After the war, he focused his efforts on international disarmament and the recovery of the German church. He served as president of the World Council of Churches from 1961 to 1968.

First they came for the Jews
and I did not speak out
because I was not a Jew.
Then they came for the Communists
and I did not speak out
because I was not a Communist.
Then they came for the trade unionists
and I did not speak out
because I was not a trade unionist.
Then they came for me
and there was no one left
to speak out for me.

[1945]

THINKING ABOUT THE TEXT

1. The poem seems to merely narrate a sequence of events, but is there an implicit argument here? Should the writer have been more explicit?
2. As you read this poem, do you think, "He's talking to me"? Do you think that might be Niemöller's intention?
3. Many poems are lyrical, filled with beautiful images and imaginative phrases. Would this poem be improved by moving in this direction?
4. Often in poetry, people and situations can be taken both literally and as symbols for something else. Do you think that is the case here with the Jews and Communists?
5. Most societies, even democracies, have insiders and outsiders, those with power and privilege and those with no influence. In your experience, does literature relate the feelings and experiences of both equally? Should this anthology balance the poems in this cluster with the experience of insiders?

NELLY SACHS

Chorus of the Rescued

Translated by Ruth and Matthew Mead

A poet and playwright born in Berlin of Jewish parents, Nelly Sachs (1891–1970) escaped from Nazi Germany in 1940 to Stockholm, where she became a Swedish citizen and eventually won the Nobel Prize for literature in 1966. First published as a poet in Germany in 1921, she later used biblical forms and motifs and empathized with the millions who suffered in the Holocaust. Her best-known play, Eli: A Mystery Play of the Sufferings of Israel, *epitomizes this style, as does the following poem, which uses pathos to evoke sympathy.*

We, the rescued,
From whose hollow bones death had begun to whittle his flutes,
And on whose sinews he had already stroked his bow—
Our bodies continue to lament
With their mutilated music.
We, the rescued,
The nooses would for our necks still dangle
Before us in the blue air—
Hourglasses still fill with our dripping blood.
We, the rescued,
The worms of fear still feed on us.
Our constellation is buried in dust.
We, the rescued,
Beg you:
Show us your sun, but gradually.
Lead us from star to star, step by step.
Be gentle when you teach us to live again.
Lest the song of a bird,
Or a pail being filled at the well,
Let our badly sealed pain burst forth again
And carry us away—
We beg you:
Do not show us an angry dog, not yet—
It could be, it could be
That we will dissolve into dust—
Dissolve into dust before your eyes.
For what binds our fabric together?
We whose breath vacated us,
Whose soul fled to Him out of that midnight?
Long before our bodies were rescued
Into the arc of the moment.
We, the rescued,
We press your hand
We look into your eye—
But all that binds us together now is leave-taking.
The leave-taking in the dust
Binds us together with you. *[1967]*

THINKING ABOUT THE TEXT

1. What is your reading of "Show us your sun" (line 15)?
2. What is meant by "Do not show us an angry dog, not yet" (line 23)?

3. How would you describe the emotional state of the narrator?
4. The poet uses metaphors throughout the poem, but particularly in the first twelve lines. How would you paraphrase the poet's descriptions?
5. According to the last three lines, what finally binds the poet to the reader?

≡ MAKING COMPARISONS

1. Even though both Niemöller's and Sachs's poems are about the Holocaust, are you able to relate to them from your own experiences?
2. With its metaphors, Sachs's poem seems more typically poetic. Would Niemöller's poem have been improved with more poetic devices? Might Sachs's poem have been improved with fewer?
3. One might argue that these two poems are causally connected. Explain.

MARIANNE COHN

I Shall Betray Tomorrow

Marianne Cohn (1922–1944) was born in Mannheim, Germany. Her family went into exile in Spain in 1934. Marianne joined the Resistance in France, taking Jewish children to territories outside Nazi control. In 1943, she was imprisoned for three months in Nice, where she wrote this poem. She was arrested again in 1944 with a group of twenty-eight children and tortured. Then, in July, she was murdered by the Gestapo. The children were eventually saved.

I shall betray tomorrow, not today.
Today, pull out my fingernails,
I shall not betray.
You do not know the limits of my courage,
I, I do.
You are five hands, harsh and full of rings,
Wearing hob-nailed boots.
I shall betray tomorrow, not today.
I need the night to make up my mind.
I need at least one night,
To disown, to abjure, to betray.
To disown my friends,
To abjure bread and wine,
To betray life,
To die.
I shall betray tomorrow, not today.
The file is under the window-pane.
The file is not [meant] for the window-bars,

The file is not [meant] for the executioner,
The file is for my own wrists.
Today, I have nothing to say,
I shall betray tomorrow.

[1943]

THINKING ABOUT THE TEXT

1. Is the title meant ironically? How do you know?
2. What seems to be the most pronounced attitude of the narrator?
3. Does anything suggest that she is contemplating suicide?
4. The narrator seems quite confident about her ability to resist torture. Do you think she really is? Would you be able to resist torture?
5. Do you think other prisoners would be inspired or dispirited by this poem?

MAKING COMPARISONS

1. Compare your response to the attitude of the speakers in Sachs's and Cohn's poems.
2. What do you think is the purpose of each of the three poems?
3. Do you think Cohn might have written a poem like "Chorus of the Rescued" had she survived?

KAREN GERSHON

Race

Later known by her married name, Karen Tripp, Gershon (1923–1993) escaped from Nazi Germany in 1939 as a teenager. Sent to England without her family, she wrote in her poetry of this experience and the loss of her parents, who died in the Holocaust. Gershon published eight books, contributed to numerous periodicals, and won much recognition, including the British Arts Council Award in 1967. Her poetry was widely read in the 1960s and later, perhaps influencing contemporaries Anne Sexton and Sylvia Plath, who borrowed the imagery of Holocaust survivors to describe family conflict and inner turmoil. "Race" is from Selected Poems *(1966).*

When I returned to my home town
believing that no one would care
who I was and what I thought
it was as if the people caught
an echo of me everywhere
they knew my story by my face
and I who am always alone
became a symbol of my race

Like every living Jew I have
in imagination seen
the gas-chamber the mass-grave
the unknown body which was mine
and found in every German face
behind the mask the mark of Cain
I will not make their thoughts my own
by hating people for their race.

[1966]

≡ THINKING ABOUT THE TEXT

1. Is Gershon imagining or actually describing her reception? How can you tell?
2. Do you mind the poet speaking for "every living Jew" (line 9)? Do you think this is accurate? Can someone be a symbol of their race?
3. Does the title refer to Jews or to Germans? Why is neither group mentioned in the title?
4. Gershon writes fairly straightforward poetry, letting her content speak for itself. What specific poetic devices does she employ? Should she use more?
5. Do you find the last four lines ambiguous? Does she see Germans as murderers, or does she reject such invidious generalizations? Should Germans be held accountable for the Holocaust? Should Americans be held accountable for slavery? Are only the people who specifically partake in evil deeds responsible, or is the whole culture that "allowed" it guilty as well?

≡ MAKING COMPARISONS

1. Compare Gershon's attitude in the last two lines of her poem with Sachs's attitude in the last three lines of her poem.
2. Had Cohn lived, might she have written "Chorus of the Rescued" or "Race"?
3. Describe the emotions you find in all four poems.

ANNE SEXTON

After Auschwitz

Growing up in New England and attending elite boarding and finishing schools during the years of World War II, Anne Sexton (1928–1974) had an emotional connection with the Holocaust rather than a firsthand one: her obsession with images of death and degradation and her "confessional" poetic stance blend seamlessly with such a theme. "After Auschwitz" is from The Awful Rowing toward God *(1977).*

Anger,
as black as a hook,
overtakes me.
Each day,
each Nazi
took, at 8.00 a.m., a baby
and sautéed him for breakfast
in his frying pan.

And death looks on with a casual eye
and picks at the dirt under his fingernail.

Man is evil,
I say aloud.
Man is a flower
that should be burnt,
I say aloud.
Man
is a bird full of mud,
I say aloud.

And death looks on with a casual eye
and scratches his anus.

Man with his small pink toes,
with his miraculous fingers
is not a temple
but an outhouse,
I say aloud.
Let man never again raise his teacup.
Let man never again write a book.
Let man never again put on his shoe.
Let man never again raise his eyes,
on a soft July night.
Never. Never. Never. Never. Never.
I say these things aloud.

I beg the Lord not to hear. *[1977]*

THINKING ABOUT THE TEXT

1. What is Sexton's purpose here if she really does not want God to listen?
2. What is your response to the image of Nazi cannibalism in lines 4–8? What about her inclusive accusation that "Man is evil" (line 11)?
3. As Sexton's editor, would you suggest that she change any specific words or phrases? Should she control the generally angry tone?

4. Sexton personifies death. Why? Why do you think she refers to man's "pink toes" and "miraculous fingers" in lines 21 and 22?
5. Sexton sees the Holocaust as an indictment of everyone. Do you agree with her?

MAKING COMPARISONS

1. Compare the ambivalence at the end of Sexton's poem with the last sentence in Sachs's poem.
2. Do you think Gershon's poem would be improved by Sexton's explicit anger?
3. Which of these five poets comes closest to expressing your feelings about the Holocaust?

WRITING ABOUT ISSUES

1. Argue that Sexton's indictment of humankind is either hyperbolic or accurate.
2. Make a case in a brief essay that "First They Came for the Jews" leads to "I Shall Betray Tomorrow."
3. Write a brief personal response explaining your feelings about the Holocaust or suggesting what such an event tells us about human nature, if anything.
4. View a film about the Holocaust such as Steven Spielberg's *Schindler's List* or Roman Polanski's *The Pianist.* Write a review expressing your feelings and thoughts about its contents and its representation of the Holocaust. Include a comparison to the poems you read.

A Creative Confinement: A Collection of Poems by Emily Dickinson

EMILY DICKINSON, "Wild Nights — Wild Nights!"

EMILY DICKINSON, "Tell all the truth but tell it slant —"

EMILY DICKINSON, "Success is counted sweetest"

EMILY DICKINSON, "My Life Had Stood — a Loaded Gun"

Although Emily Dickinson was considered an eccentric recluse by many of her provincial neighbors, history has interpreted her life in various ways, changing with the thinking of the times. Once considered isolated, she is now seen by many critics as vitally connected to the issues and literature of her age. Feminist and queer studies scholars now see the once-shy figure as an active champion who defied gender stereotypes. Although she has often been described as nunlike and passive, critics today see her as a nonconformist, mistrustful of power and dogma, and as someone who questioned any kind of received opinion, even popular views on religion and the afterlife. And although it may seem paradoxical to many, the artistic freedom necessary for a focused creative life is often achieved by isolation, by physically removing oneself from the temptation and distractions of social life. If ever there was an example of confinement nurturing the creative impulse, it is the life and poems of Emily Dickinson.

EMILY DICKINSON

Wild Nights — Wild Nights!

Emily Dickinson (1830–1886) spent most of her life in her father's house in Amherst, Massachusetts. Except for a year of college and several brief excursions to Philadelphia and Washington, D.C., Dickinson lived a quiet, reclusive life in a house she described as "pretty much all sobriety." Although a few poems were published during her lifetime, Dickinson wrote almost two thousand poems on love, death, immortality, and nature that are universally judged to be some of the most original, lyrical, and artistic works in American literature. Although the specific person to whom Dickinson wrote her love poems is unclear, many critics today believe her interests were both lesbian and heterosexual. As the four poems below suggest, Dickinson, although outwardly retiring and isolated, lived a lively, rich, and passionate life in her poetry.

Wild Nights — Wild Nights!
Were I with thee
Wild Nights should be
Our luxury!

Futile — the Winds —
To a Heart in port —

Todd-Bingham picture collection, 1837–1966 (inclusive). Manuscripts & Archives, Yale University

Done with the Compass —
Done with the Chart!

Rowing in Eden —
Ah, the Sea!
Might I but moor — Tonight —
In Thee

[c. 1861]

☰ THINKING ABOUT THE TEXT

1. Many critics see this poem as an erotic fantasy, perhaps a surprising subject for a reclusive spinster. Are there indications that this is not a poem about a real sexual encounter?
2. Comment on the imagery of the ocean and port. Could the port be Dickinson's isolation? The ocean, the actual consummation?
3. How do you read the speaker's claim that she is done with the compass and chart? Is she rejecting convention?
4. What are some ways to interpret "Eden" in line 9?
5. What does the image of "moor[ing] . . . In Thee" (lines 11–12) suggest about her erotic desire?

EMILY DICKINSON

Tell all the Truth but tell it slant—

Tell all the truth but tell it slant—
Success in Circuit lies
Too bright for our infirm Delight
The Truth's superb surprise

As Lightning to the Children eased
With explanation kind
The Truth must dazzle gradually
Or every man be blind— *[1868]*

☰ THINKING ABOUT THE TEXT

1. What is the primary dictionary definition of "slant"? What does Dickinson mean by *slant.*
2. Why does Dickinson say we shouldn't be direct in telling the truth?
3. What similarity between the truth and lightning does Dickinson want us to make?
4. What is it about poetry that makes indirection a better path to truth?
5. How does this poem embody Dickinson's advice?

☰ MAKING COMPARISONS

1. How might both poems be about freedom and confinement?
2. Compare the images in both poems. Are they apt?
3. To whom is each poem addressed?

EMILY DICKINSON

Success is counted sweetest

Success is counted sweetest
By those who ne'er succeed.
To comprehend a nectar
Requires sorest need.

Not one of all the purple Host
Who took the Flag today
Can tell the definition
So clear of victory

As he defeated—dying—
On whose forbidden ear
The distant strains of triumph
Burst agonized and clear!

THINKING ABOUT THE TEXT

1. Rephrase Dickinson's opening paragraph in clear, simple prose.
2. Who might the "purple Host" (line 4) be? What specific clues exist as to their identity?
3. How is paradox a key figure of speech in this poem?
4. Give other concrete example of the theme from your own experience or from books or films.
5. How would you define "forbidden" (line 10) in the last stanza?

MAKING COMPARISONS

1. How does Dickinson slant her truth in these poems?
2. Compare the images in this poem to those in the previous two.
3. How might these three poems be seen as relevant to our concerns today?

EMILY DICKINSON

My Life Had Stood—a Loaded Gun

My Life had stood—a Loaded Gun—
In Corners—till a Day
The Owner passed—identified—
And carried Me away—

And now We roam in Sovreign Woods—
And now We hunt the Doe—
And every time I speak for Him
The Mountains straight reply—

And do I smile, such cordial light
Upon the Valley glow—
It is as a Vesuvian face
Had let its pleasure through—

And when at Night—Our good Day done—
I guard My Master's Head—
'Tis better than the Eider Duck's
Deep Pillow—to have shared—

To foe of His—I'm deadly foe—
None stir the second time—
On whom I lay a Yellow Eye—
Or an emphatic Thumb—

Though I than He—may longer live
He longer must—than I—
For I have but the power to kill,
Without—the power to die—

THINKING ABOUT THE TEXT

1. Although many of Dickinson's poems are fairly straightforward, this selection seems allegorical. Critics have long disagreed about her meaning or more likely, her multiple meanings. For example, how might Dickinson herself be the gun? What, then, might she be saying about herself? How might the idea of freedom be involved in this poem?
2. In what ways might this poem be about the power of poetry?
3. Adrienne Rich thought this poem was about the "knowledge that power in a woman can seem destructive." In what way might poetry written by women in the nineteenth century have seemed dangerous to conventional society?
4. Many critics have claimed that the last stanza is enigmatic, a "riddling stanza, a conundrum" yet to be solved. What is your reading?
5. Some critics note that she mentions a doe, a female deer. How might gender be a significant element in this poem?

MAKING COMPARISONS

1. How does "Tell all the truth but tell it slant" relate to this poem?
2. How might the last line "Without—the power to die—" (line 24) be telling a slanted truth?
3. Compare the metaphors in this poem to those in the previous three.

WRITING ABOUT ISSUES

1. Write an analysis of these four poems as examples of the ideas mentioned in the introduction to this chapter (p. 671) and in the biographical note about Dickinson (p. 690).
2. Write an analysis of these four poems, focusing on the imagery Dickinson uses to support her themes.
3. Research Dickinson's poetry and choose two other poems that develop similar themes to those given here. Write an essay that demonstrates how freedom is developed in these two poems.
4. Argue that Dickinson's ideas about nonconformity and fame are relevant in today's culture.

Where Tradition Is a Trap: Stories

SHIRLEY JACKSON, "The Lottery"

ALEXANDER WEINSTEIN, "Rocket Night"

Often our fondest memories of childhood involve family and community traditions, from public events like Thanksgiving, Halloween, and Fourth of July celebrations, to religious holidays like Christmas and Hanukkah, to private celebrations like birthdays and anniversaries. These rituals give our lives structure and create a sense of belonging. They give us psychological comfort and security and a ready-made identity of belonging with like-minded people who share our values. We acquire a sense of our adult roles, our goals, our understanding of the meaning of life, birth, death, love, and hate. Traditions and their accompanying rituals offer guidance as we address the complex question of how to "be" in the world.

Once a tradition starts, however, it may be difficult to change. Perhaps that is not so significant when we are thinking of birthday and graduation ceremonies, but it is life altering when traditions govern whom we may marry, what roles we can play in society, how we understand justice and freedom, and when our lives begin and end.

In some societies, traditions have been in place for thousands of years. They are difficult to change since they are woven into individuals' sense of self. People often feel that their own traditions are normal, even though anthropologists claim that few traditions are universal among cultures.

Since tradition plays such a crucial role in our lives, it is not surprising that writers are drawn to both the positive and negative elements of traditions and rituals. Although, as in the two stories that follow, writers often use indirect techniques such as allegory, satire, and hyperbole to enrich their meaning, their narratives are about our own lives, about the attitudes and behaviors that we take for granted, and about the unconscious cruelties and dangerous assumptions we think of as normal. Seventy years after its publication, Shirley Jackson's "The Lottery" is still one of the most controversial stories ever published in *The New Yorker*. When the story was banned in South Africa, Jackson said, "Well at least they understood it." Alexander Weinstein's "Rocket Night" seems a contemporary variation on Jackson's horrific tale. Both in its matter-of-fact tone and its chilling and deadly conclusion, Weinstein's tale reminds us all that ordinary people can sometimes do extraordinarily wicked things.

BEFORE YOU READ

Recall incidents from the past when you felt uncomfortable being involved in a tradition or ritual. How did you respond? What specific traditions in our culture could easily be eliminated? Are there harmful traditions in our culture that should be changed? Explain.

SHIRLEY JACKSON

The Lottery

Shirley Jackson (1919–1965) was born in San Francisco and grew up in the affluent suburb of Burlingame. Her family moved to Rochester, New York, in 1939, and she graduated from Syracuse University in 1940. Jackson wrote of her life: "I was married in 1940 to Stanley Edgar Hyman, critic and numismatist, and we live in Vermont, in a quiet rural community with fine scenery and comfortably away from city life. Our major export are books and children, both of which we produce in abundance." She received a National Book Award nomination for The Haunting of Hill House *(1959), which was adapted for film twice (1963 and 1999); this popular book is often cited as one of the best horror novels of the twentieth century and as an influence on contemporary masters of that genre such as Stephen King.*

The morning of June 27th was clear and sunny, with the fresh warmth of a full-summer day; the flowers were blossoming profusely and the grass was richly green. The people of the village began to gather in the square, between the post office and the bank, around ten o'clock; in some towns there were so many people that the lottery took two days and had to be started on June 26th, but in this village, where there were only about three hundred people, the whole lottery took less than two hours, so it could begin at ten o'clock in the morning and still be through in time to allow the villagers to get home for noon dinner.

The children assembled first, of course. School was recently over for the summer, and the feeling of liberty sat uneasily on most of them; they tended to gather together quietly for a while before they broke into boisterous play, and their talk was still of the classroom and teacher, of books and reprimands. Bobby Martin had already stuffed his pockets full of stones, and the other boys soon followed his example, selecting the smoothest and roundest stones; Bobby and Harry Jones and Dickie Delacroix—the villagers pronounced this name "Dellacroy"—eventually made a great pile of stones in one corner of the square and guarded it against the raids of the other boys. The girls stood aside, talking among themselves, looking over their shoulders at the boys, and the very small children rolled in the dust or clung to the hands of their older brothers or sisters.

Soon the men began to gather, surveying their own children, speaking of planting and rain, tractors and taxes. They stood together, away from the pile of stones in the corner, and their jokes were quiet and they smiled rather than laughed. The women, wearing faded house dresses and sweaters, came shortly after their menfolk. They greeted one another and exchanged bits of gossip as they went to join their husbands. Soon the women, standing by their husbands, began to call to their children, and the children came reluctantly, having to be called four or five times. Bobby Martin ducked under his mother's grasping hand and ran, laughing, back to the pile of stones. His father spoke up sharply, and Bobby came quickly and took his place between his father and his oldest brother.

The lottery was conducted—as were the square dances, the teenage club, the Halloween program—by Mr. Summers, who had time and energy to devote to civic activities. He was a round-faced, jovial man and he ran the coal business, and people were sorry for him, because he had no children and his wife was a scold. When he arrived in the square, carrying the black wooden box, there was a murmur of conversation among the villagers, and he waved and called, "Little late today, folks." The postmaster, Mr. Graves, followed him, carrying a three-legged stool, and the stool was put in the center of the square and Mr. Summers set the black box down on it. The villagers kept their distance, leaving a space between themselves and the stool, and when Mr. Summers said, "Some of you fellows want to give me a hand?" there was a hesitation before two men, Mr. Martin and his oldest son, Baxter, came forward to hold the box steady on the stool while Mr. Summers stirred up the papers inside it.

The original paraphernalia for the lottery had been lost long ago, and the 5
black box now resting on the stool had been put into use even before Old Man Warner, the oldest man in town, was born. Mr. Summers spoke frequently to the villagers about making a new box, but no one liked to upset even as much tradition as was represented by the black box. There was a story that the present box had been made with some pieces of the box that had preceded it, the one that had been constructed when the first people settled down to make a village here. Every year, after the lottery, Mr. Summers began talking again about a new box, but every year the subject was allowed to fade off without anything's being done. The black box grew shabbier each year; by now it was no longer completely black but splintered badly along one side to show the original wood color, and in some places faded or stained.

Mr. Martin and his oldest son, Baxter, held the black box securely on the stool until Mr. Summers had stirred the papers thoroughly with his hand. Because so much of the ritual had been forgotten or discarded, Mr. Summers had been successful in having slips of paper substituted for the chips of wood that had been used for generations. Chips of wood, Mr. Summers had argued, had been all very well when the village was tiny, but now that the population was more than three hundred and likely to keep on growing, it was necessary to use something that would fit more easily into the black box. The night before the lottery, Mr. Summers and Mr. Graves made up the slips of paper and put them in the box, and it was then taken to the safe of Mr. Summers's coal company and locked up until Mr. Summers was ready to take it to the square next morning. The rest of the year, the box was put away, sometimes one place, sometimes another; it had spent one year in Mr. Graves's barn and another year underfoot in the post office, and sometimes it was set on a shelf in the Martin grocery and left there.

There was a great deal of fussing to be done before Mr. Summers declared the lottery open. There were the lists to make up—of heads of families, heads of households in each family, members of each household in each family. There was the proper swearing-in of Mr. Summers by the postmaster, as the official of the lottery; at one time, some people remembered, there had been a recital of some sort, performed by the official of the lottery, a perfunctory, tuneless chant that had been rattled off duly each year; some people believed that the official of the lottery used to stand just so when he said or sang it, others believed that he was supposed to walk among the people, but years and years ago this part of the ritual had been allowed to lapse. There had been, also, a ritual salute, which the official of the lottery had had to use in addressing each person who came up to draw from the box, but this also had changed with time, until now it was felt necessary only for the official to speak to each person approaching. Mr. Summers was very good at all this; in his clean white shirt and blue jeans, with one hand resting carelessly on the black box, he seemed very proper and important as he talked interminably to Mr. Graves and the Martins.

Just as Mr. Summers finally left off talking and turned to the assembled villagers, Mrs. Hutchinson came hurriedly along the path to the square, her sweater thrown over her shoulders, and slid into place in the back of the crowd. "Clean forgot what day it was," she said to Mrs. Delacroix, who stood next to her, and they both laughed softly. "Thought my old man was out back stacking wood," Mrs. Hutchinson went on, "and then I looked out the window and the kids was gone, and then I remembered it was the twenty-seventh and came a-running." She dried her hands on her apron, and Mrs. Delacroix said, "You're in time, though. They're still talking away up there."

Mrs. Hutchinson craned her neck to see through the crowd and found her husband and children standing near the front. She tapped Mrs. Delacroix on the arm as a farewell and began to make her way through the crowd. The people separated good-humoredly to let her through; two or three people said, in voices just loud enough to be heard across the crowd, "Here comes your Missus, Hutchinson," and "Bill, she made it after all." Mrs. Hutchinson reached her husband, and Mr. Summers, who had been waiting, said cheerfully, "Thought we were going to have to get on without you, Tessie." Mrs. Hutchinson said, grinning, "Wouldn't have me leave m'dishes in the sink, now, would you, Joe?" and soft laughter ran through the crowd as the people stirred back into position after Mrs. Hutchinson's arrival.

"Well, now," Mr. Summers said soberly, "guess we better get started, get this over with, so's we can go back to work. Anybody ain't here?"

"Dunbar," several people said. "Dunbar; Dunbar."

Mr. Summers consulted his list. "Clyde Dunbar," he said. "That's right. He's broke his leg, hasn't he? Who's drawing for him?"

"Me, I guess," a woman said, and Mr. Summers turned to look at her. "Wife draws for her husband," Mr. Summers said. "Don't you have a grown boy to do it for you, Janey?" Although Mr. Summers and everyone else in the village knew the answer perfectly well, it was the business of the official of the lottery to ask such questions formally. Mr. Summers waited with an expression of polite interest while Mrs. Dunbar answered.

"Horace's not but sixteen yet," Mrs. Dunbar said regretfully. "Guess I gotta fill in for the old man this year."

"Right," Mr. Summers said. He made a note on the list he was holding. Then he asked, "Watson boy drawing this year?"

A tall boy in the crowd raised his hand. "Here," he said. "I'm drawing for m'mother and me." He blinked his eyes nervously and ducked his head as several voices in the crowd said things like "Good fellow, Jack," and "Glad to see your mother's got a man to do it."

"Well," Mr. Summers said, "guess that's everyone. Old Man Warner make it?"

"Here," a voice said, and Mr. Summers nodded.

A sudden hush fell on the crowd as Mr. Summers cleared his throat and looked at the list. "All ready?" he called. "Now, I'll read the names—heads of families first—and the men come up and take a paper out of the box. Keep the paper folded in your hand without looking at it until everyone has had a turn. Everything clear?"

The people had done it so many times that they only half listened to the 20
directions; most of them were quiet, wetting their lips, not looking around. Then Mr. Summers raised one hand high and said, "Adams." A man disengaged himself from the crowd and came forward. "Hi, Steve," Mr. Summers said, and Mr. Adams said, "Hi, Joe." They grinned at one another humorlessly and nervously. Then Mr. Adams reached into the black box and took out a folded paper. He held it firmly by one corner as he turned and went hastily back to his place in the crowd, where he stood a little apart from his family, not looking down at his hand.

"Allen," Mr. Summers said, "Anderson. . . . Bentham."

"Seems like there's no time at all between lotteries any more," Mrs. Delacroix said to Mrs. Graves in the back row. "Seems like we got through with the last one only last week."

"Time sure goes fast," Mrs. Graves said.

"Clark. . . . Delacroix."

"There goes my old man," Mrs. Delacroix said. She held her breath while her 25
husband went forward.

"Dunbar," Mr. Summers said, and Mrs. Dunbar went steadily to the box while one of the women said, "Go on, Janey," and another said, "There she goes."

"We're next," Mrs. Graves said. She watched while Mr. Graves came around from the side of the box, greeted Mr. Summers gravely, and selected a slip of paper from the box. By now, all through the crowd there were men holding the small folded papers in their large hands, turning them over and over nervously. Mrs. Dunbar and her two sons stood together, Mrs. Dunbar holding the slip of paper.

"Harburt. . . . Hutchinson."

"Get up there, Bill," Mrs. Hutchinson said, and the people near her laughed.

"Jones." 30

"They do say," Mr. Adams said to Old Man Warner, who stood next to him, "that over in the north village they're talking of giving up the lottery."

Old Man Warner snorted. "Pack of crazy fools," he said. "Listening to the young folks, nothing's good enough for *them.* Next thing you know, they'll be wanting to go back to living in caves, nobody work any more, live *that* way for a while. Used to be a saying about 'Lottery in June, corn be heavy soon.' First thing you know, we'd all be eating stewed chickweed and acorns. There's *always* been a lottery," he added petulantly. "Bad enough to see young Joe Summers up there joking with everybody."

"Some places have already quit lotteries," Mrs. Adams said.

"Nothing but trouble in *that,*" Old Man Warner said stoutly. "Pack of young fools."

"Martin." And Bobby Martin watched his father go forward. "Overdyke. . . . 35
Percy."

"I wish they'd hurry," Mrs. Dunbar said to her older son. "I wish they'd hurry."

"They're almost through," her son said.

"You get ready to run tell Dad," Mrs. Dunbar said.

Mr. Summers called his own name and then stepped forward precisely and selected a slip from the box. Then he called, "Warner."

"Seventy-seventh year I been in the lottery," Old Man Warner said as he went through the crowd. "Seventy-seventh time."

"Watson." The tall boy came awkwardly through the crowd. Someone said, "Don't be nervous, Jack," and Mr. Summers said, "Take your time, son."

"Zanini."

After that, there was a long pause, a breathless pause, until Mr. Summers, holding his slip of paper in the air, said, "All right, fellows." For a minute, no one moved, and then all the slips of paper were opened. Suddenly, all the women began to speak at once, saying, "Who is it?" "Who's got it?" "Is it the Dunbars?" "Is it the Watsons?" Then the voices began to say, "It's Hutchinson. It's Bill," "Bill Hutchinson's got it."

"Go tell your father," Mrs. Dunbar said to her older son.

People began to look around to see the Hutchinsons. Bill Hutchinson was standing quiet, staring down at the paper in his hand. Suddenly, Tessie Hutchinson shouted to Mr. Summers, "You didn't give him time enough to take any paper he wanted. I saw you. It wasn't fair!"

"Be a good sport, Tessie," Mrs. Delacroix called, and Mrs. Graves said, "All of us took the same chance."

"Shut up, Tessie," Bill Hutchinson said.

"Well, everyone," Mr. Summers said, "that was done pretty fast, and now we've got to be hurrying a little more to get done in time." He consulted his next list. "Bill," he said, "you draw for the Hutchinson family. You got any other households in the Hutchinsons?"

"There's Don and Eva," Mrs. Hutchinson yelled. "Make *them* take their chance!"

"Daughters drew with their husbands' families, Tessie," Mr. Summers said gently. "You know that as well as anyone else."

"It wasn't *fair,*" Tessie said.

"I guess not, Joe," Bill Hutchinson said regretfully. "My daughter draws with her husband's family, that's only fair. And I've got no other family except the kids."

"Then, as far as drawing for families is concerned, it's you," Mr. Summers said in explanation, "and as far as drawing for households is concerned, that's you, too. Right?"

"Right," Bill Hutchinson said.

"How many kids, Bill?" Mr. Summers asked formally.

"Three," Bill Hutchinson said. "There's Bill Jr., and Nancy, and little Dave. And Tessie and me."

"All right, then," Mr. Summers said. "Harry, you got their tickets back?"

Mr. Graves nodded and held up the slips of paper. "Put them in the box, then," Mr. Summers directed. "Take Bill's and put it in."

"I think we ought to start over," Mrs. Hutchinson said, as quietly as she could. "I tell you it wasn't *fair*. You didn't give him time enough to choose. *Every*body saw that."

Mr. Graves had selected the five slips and put them in the box, and he dropped all the papers but those onto the ground, where the breeze caught them and lifted them off.

"Listen, everybody," Mrs. Hutchinson was saying to the people around her.

"Ready, Bill?" Mr. Summers asked, and Bill Hutchinson, with one quick glance around at his wife and children, nodded.

"Remember," Mr. Summers said, "take the slips and keep them folded until each person has taken one. Harry, you help little Dave." Mr. Graves took the hand of the little boy, who came willingly with him up to the box. "Take a paper out of the box, Davy," Mr. Summers said. Davy put his hand into the box and laughed. "Take just *one* paper," Mr. Summers said. "Harry, you hold it for him." Mr. Graves took the child's hand and removed the folded paper from the tight fist and held it while little Dave stood next to him and looked up at him wonderingly.

"Nancy next," Mr. Summers said. Nancy was twelve, and her school friends breathed heavily as she went forward, switching her skirt, and took a slip daintily from the box. "Bill Jr.," Mr. Summers said, and Billy, his face red and his feet overlarge, nearly knocked the box over as he got a paper out. "Tessie," Mr. Summers said. She hesitated for a minute, looking around defiantly, and then set her lips and went up to the box. She snatched a paper out and held it behind her.

"Bill," Mr. Summers said, and Bill Hutchinson reached into the box and felt around, bringing his hand out at last with the slip of paper in it.

The crowd was quiet. A girl whispered, "I hope it's not Nancy," and the sound of the whisper reached the edges of the crowd.

"It's not the way it used to be," Old Man Warner said clearly. "People ain't the way they used to be."

"All right," Mr. Summers said. "Open the papers. Harry, you open little Dave's."

Mr. Graves opened the slip of paper and there was a general sigh through the crowd as he held it up and everyone could see that it was blank. Nancy and Bill Jr. opened theirs at the same time, and both beamed and laughed, turning around to the crowd and holding their slips of paper above their heads.

"Tessie," Mr. Summers said. There was a pause, and then Mr. Summers looked at Bill Hutchinson, and Bill unfolded his paper and showed it. It was blank.

"It's Tessie," Mr. Summers said, and his voice was hushed. "Show us her paper, Bill."

Bill Hutchinson went over to his wife and forced the slip of paper out of her hand. It had a black spot on it, the black spot Mr. Summers had made the night before with the heavy pencil in the coal-company office. Bill Hutchinson held it up and there was a stir in the crowd.

"All right, folks," Mr. Summers said. "Let's finish quickly."

Although the villagers had forgotten the ritual and lost the original black box, they still remembered to use stones. The pile of stones the boys had made earlier was ready; there were stones on the ground with the blowing scraps of paper that had come out of the box. Mrs. Delacroix selected a stone so large she had to pick it up with both hands and turned to Mrs. Dunbar. "Come on," she said. "Hurry up."

Mrs. Dunbar had small stones in both hands, and she said, gasping for 75
breath, "I can't run at all. You'll have to go ahead and I'll catch up with you."

The children had stones already, and someone gave little Davy Hutchinson a few pebbles.

Tessie Hutchinson was in the center of a cleared space by now, and she held her hands out desperately as the villagers moved in on her. "It isn't fair," she said. A stone hit her on the side of the head.

Old Man Warner was saying, "Come on, come on, everyone." Steve Adams was in the front of the crowd of villagers, with Mrs. Graves beside him.

"It isn't fair, it isn't right," Mrs. Hutchinson screamed and then they were upon her. *[1948]*

THINKING ABOUT THE TEXT

1. At what point in the story did you suspect that something was amiss in this bucolic village? How does Jackson both prepare you for and surprise you with her ending?
2. Make a list of the characters' names in the story. What symbolic significance might they have?
3. What do the phrase "Lottery in June, corn be heavy soon" and the pile of stones suggest about the origins of the lottery?
4. Critics often mention scapegoating, man's inherent evil, and the destructive consequence of hanging on to ancient and outdated rituals as the principal themes of this story. Do you agree? What are some other themes suggested by the story?
5. What contemporary issues does "The Lottery" bring to mind?

ALEXANDER WEINSTEIN

Rocket Night

Alexander Weinstein received a BA from Naropa University and in 2010 an MFA from Indiana University in Creative Writing. He teaches in the English Program at Siena Heights University and at the University of Michigan. He has published widely and has won numerous awards. A Rolling Stone *review noted that his latest collection of stories,* Children of the New World *(2016) shows characters that "exist in a fantastic, creepy landscape that could be ours in the not-too-distant future." His work has been called "dystopian literary realism." The following story from this collection was first published in* Southern Indiana Review *(Spring 2013).*

It was Rocket Night at our daughter's elementary school, the night when parents, students, and the administration gather to place the least liked child in a rocket and shoot him into the stars. Last year we placed Laura Jackson into the capsule, a short, squat girl known for her limp dresses which hung crookedly on her body. The previous year we'd sent off a boy from India whose name none of us could remember. Before that our daughter was in kindergarten so we'd yet to become part of the Rose Hill community.

Rocket Night is an event which almost all of us look forward to, falling in late October when the earth is covered by orange and yellows. Our children have begun to lay out their Halloween costumes and their sweaters are heavy with the scent of autumn. It's late enough into the school year for us to get a sense of the best children to send off. For alliances are made early at Rose Hill. Our children gather in the mornings to share their secrets on playgrounds, while the other children, those with stars and galaxies in their futures, can be seen at the edges of the field, playing with sticks alone or staring into mud puddles at drowned worms.

Meet and greet is held, as is custom, in the school gymnasium, and we mingle in the warm glow of its lacquered floors, surrounded by wooden bleachers and parallel bars, talking about soccer games, math homework, and the difficulty of finding time for errands with our children's busy schedules. Our kids run the perimeter, some playing tag, others collecting in clusters of boys around the fifth-graders with portable game players, the girls across the room in their own clusters. Susan Beech brought her famous home-baked cupcakes, the Stowes brought Hawaiian Punch, and we brought plastic cups and cocktail napkins and placed them on the table among the baked goods and apple slices.

The boy to be sent off, I believe his name was Daniel, stood near his parents, holding his mother's skirt, looking unkempt. One could immediately see the reason he'd been chosen by our children. There's a hand-me-down quality to the clothing of those selected, the mildewed stench of thrift stores clinging to their corduroys. This boy's collar sat askew, revealing the small white undershirt beneath, and his brown slacks were held tightly by an oversized belt whose end flopped lazily from his side. The boy, our daughter told us, brought stubby pencils to school whose chewed-up ends got stuck in sharpeners. He had the habit of picking his nose. His lunches, she reported, were nothing more than stale crackers and a warm box of chocolate milk. There was a smear of cupcake frosting on the corner of his mouth, and seeing this detail, we knew our children had chosen well. He was the sort of child who makes one proud of one's own children, and we looked over to our daughter, who was holding court with a devil's square, tightening then spreading her small fingers within the folded paper while counting out the letters O-R-A-N-G-E.

At eight o'clock the principal took the stage beneath the basketball hoop, a 5
whine from the microphone as he adjusted it. He turned to us with open arms and welcomed us, the parents and students of Rose Hill, to another year together. He thanked Susan for her cupcakes, and all of us for our contributions to make the evening's festivities so successful, and then, forgetting the boy's name, he turned to the family and said, "Donald, we hope your journey into space will be a

joyful one." We all applauded. Admittedly, his parents applauded less than others, looking a bit pale, but we acknowledged that the parents of the chosen often do seem pale. They are the sort of parents who come to soccer games and sit alone in the stands, a gloomy sadness hanging over them, whose cars make the most noise when they pull into our school's parking lot, and whose faces, within the automobile's dark interiors, remind us not of the joys of parenthood, but of some sorrow none of us wish to share. Seeing them standing there with their child, we realized, with relief, that with the departure of their son we would also gain their departure, and we quietly acknowledged the all-round benefit.

The principal's speech delivered, he invited us to join him on the playground where the capsule sat, cockpit open, its silver sides illuminated by the glow from the launch tower. It's a truth that the child to be sent into space grows reticent upon seeing the glowing tower and the gaping casket-like rocket. We saw the small boy cling to his mother, unwilling to leave her side, and so we let our children loose. I watched my daughter pry the boy's fingers from his mother's leg as two larger fifth-graders seized his waist and dragged him away. The nurse, a kindly woman, helped to subdue the parents. She took the mother aside and whispered to her, while the gym coach placed a meaty hand on the father's shoulder and assured him that the capsule was stocked with water and food tablets, plenty for lasting the boy a long time into the future. To be honest, it's a mystery how long such supplies last. It's a small compartment within that capsule and we are all aware funding was cut to our district earlier this year, but still we assured them there was nothing to worry of. The boy, if hungry for company, had a small microphone inside the shell which would allow him to speak to himself of his journey, his thoughts, and the mystery of the universe.

The boy was strapped into the capsule, his hands secured, and he looked out at us. He spoke then, for the first and only time that night. He asked if he might have one of his pencils with him; it was in his pencil box, he said, the one with a brown bear for an eraser. The principal assured him that he wouldn't need it in outer space, and the custodian noted that the request was moot; the boy's desk had been emptied earlier that day. So they closed the cover. All we could see was the smudge of the boy's face pressed against the porthole.

When the rocket blasted off, it made us all take an involuntary step backwards, the light of the flames illuminating the wonder upon our children's faces. We watched as the capsule rose from our playground, leaving behind our swing sets and jungle gym, rising higher, until it was but a sparkling marble in the night sky, and then, finally, gone completely. We sighed with awe, some applauded, and then we made our rounds, wishing one another goodnight, arranging play dates, and returning to our cars. Those of us on the PTO remained to put the gymnasium back in order for the coming morning. And the boy faded from our thoughts, replaced by the lateness of the evening and the pressure of delayed bedtime schedules. I myself had all but forgotten about the child by the time I lay our sleeping daughter on her bed. And yet, when I took out the recycling that night, I paused beneath the streetlamps of our cul-de-sac and thought of the children up there. I imagined all of them drifting alone, speaking into their microphones, telling us about their lives from the depths of the unknown. *[2013]*

THINKING ABOUT THE TEXT

1. What are some details of the appearance or behavior of the children chosen? What do these details tell you about the narrator and the values and biases of his social circle?
2. What is the significance of the line, "there was a smear of cupcake frosting on the corner of his mouth, and seeing this detail, we knew our children had chosen well" (para. 4)?
3. Besides the actual journey into space, which actions or thoughts seem particularly cruel or insensitive? What is the effect of the casual, matter-of-fact tone of the narrator?
4. What are some possible reasons that some of the parents "sighed with awe" (para. 8) when the rocket took off? How can this also be a tale about the consequences of technology without a moral compass?
5. What is the significance of the last line? Has the narrator suddenly become aware of the school's grotesque deed or does it simply reinforce his insensitivity? Explain.

MAKING COMPARISONS

1. Compare the process by which victims are chosen in "The Lottery" and "Rocket Night." Which seems more horrific?
2. Why do the parents in "Rocket Night" seem more or less barbaric than those in "The Lottery"?
3. The tradition in "The Lottery" seems to have been inherited from the distant past, but given the technology involved in "Rocket Night," is it meant to take place in the future? What is the significance of this difference?

WRITING ABOUT IDEAS

1. Argue that "The Lottery" is still relevant to contemporary concerns.
2. One idea about science fiction is that it takes a present concern and projects it into the future using hyperbole, allegory, and satire to make its point. How might this be the case with "Rocket Night"?
3. Write an essay that compares the tone, setting, themes, and characters of both stories. Be sure to note the similarities and differences.
4. Read Shirley Jackson's essay "Biography of a Story" from her book *Come Along with Me* and write a report highlighting what you feel are her most interesting ideas. Take a position on whether the story's reception would be similar or different if it were written today.

Dreams of Escape: Stories

KATE CHOPIN, "The Story of an Hour"

KRISTEN VALDEZ QUADE, "The Manzanos"

Although the characters and setting for these two stories could hardly be more dissimilar, there are interesting comparisons. Ofelia is an eleven-year-old girl living with her grandfather in the small village in contemporary New Mexico, while Louise Mallard is a married woman living in Louisiana at the end of the nineteenth century. Both, however, are unhappy with their present lives and both dream of escape, although Ofelia seems more focused on a retrieved past and Louise on a future not meant to be. And both seem caught in a confining reality they long to escape.

BEFORE YOU READ

Is it possible to love someone and at the same time want to be free?

KATE CHOPIN

The Story of an Hour

Kate Chopin (1851–1904) is known for her evocations of the unique, multiethnic Creole and Cajun societies of late-nineteenth-century Louisiana; however, her characters transcend the limitation of regional genre writing, striking a particularly resonant note among feminist readers. Born Katherine O'Flaherty in St. Louis, Missouri, she married Oscar Chopin in 1870 and went to live with him in New Orleans and on his plantation along the Mississippi River. Her short stories were collected in Bayou Folk *(1894) and* A Night in Acadie *(1897). Chopin's last novel,* The Awakening, *scandalized readers at the time of its publication in 1899 because of its frank portrayal of female sexuality in the context of an extramarital affair. Long ignored by readers and critics, her work was revived in the 1960s and continues to provoke heated discussion of her female characters: are they women who seek freedom in the only ways available to them, or are they willing participants in their own victimhood?*

The following story was first published in Bayou Folk *(1894). It is typical of her controversial writing and caused a sensation among the reading public.*

Knowing that Mrs. Mallard was afflicted with a heart trouble, great care was taken to break to her as gently as possible the news of her husband's death.

It was her sister Josephine who told her, in broken sentences; veiled hints that revealed in half concealing. Her husband's friend Richards was there, too, near her. It was he who had been in the newspaper office when intelligence of the railroad disaster was received, with Brently Mallard's name leading the list of "killed." He had only taken the time to assure himself of its truth by a second telegram, and had hastened to forestall any less careful, less tender friend in bearing the sad message.

She did not hear the story as many women have heard the same, with a paralyzed inability to accept its significance. She wept at once, with sudden, wild abandonment, in her sister's arms. When the storm of grief had spent itself she went away to her room alone. She would have no one follow her.

There stood, facing the open window, a comfortable, roomy armchair. Into this she sank, pressed down by a physical exhaustion that haunted her body and seemed to reach into her soul.

She could see in the open square before her house the tops of trees that were 5
all aquiver with the new spring life. The delicious breath of rain was in the air. In the street below a peddler was crying his wares. The notes of a distant song which some one was singing reached her faintly, and countless sparrows were twittering in the eaves.

There were patches of blue sky showing here and there through the clouds that had met and piled one above the other in the west facing her window.

She sat with her head thrown back upon the cushion of the chair, quite motionless, except when a sob came up into her throat and shook her, as a child who had cried itself to sleep continues to sob in its dreams.

She was young, with a fair, calm face, whose lines bespoke repression and even a certain strength. But now there was a dull stare in her eyes, whose gaze was fixed away off yonder on one of those patches of blue sky. It was not a glance of reflection, but rather indicated a suspension of intelligent thought.

There was something coming to her and she was waiting for it, fearfully. What was it? She did not know; it was too subtle and elusive to name. But she felt it, creeping out of the sky, reaching toward her through the sounds, the scents, the color that filled the air.

Now her bosom rose and fell tumultuously. She was beginning to recognize this thing that was approaching to possess her, and she was striving to beat it back with her will — as powerless as her two white slender hands would have been.

When she abandoned herself a little whispered word escaped her slightly parted lips. She said it over and over under her breath: "free, free, free!" The vacant stare and the look of terror that had followed it went from her eyes. They stayed keen and bright. Her pulses beat fast, and the coursing blood warmed and relaxed every inch of her body.

She did not stop to ask if it were or were not a monstrous joy that held her. A clear and exalted perception enabled her to dismiss the suggestion as trivial.

She knew that she would weep again when she saw the kind, tender hands folded in death; the face that had never looked save with love upon her, fixed and gray and dead. But she saw beyond that bitter moment a long procession of years to come that would belong to her absolutely. And she opened and spread her arms out to them in welcome.

There would be no one to live for her during those coming years: she would live for herself. There would be no powerful will bending hers in that blind persistence with which men and women believe they have a right to impose a private will upon a fellow-creature. A kind intention or a cruel intention made the act seem no less a crime as she looked upon it in that brief moment of illumination.

And yet she had loved him — sometimes. Often she had not. What did it matter! What could love, the unsolved mystery, count for in face of this possession of self-assertion which she suddenly recognized as the strongest impulse of her being!

"Free! Body and soul free!" she kept whispering.

Josephine was kneeling before the closed door with her lips to the keyhole, imploring for admission. "Louise, open the door! I beg; open the door — you will make yourself ill. What are you doing, Louise? For heaven's sake open the door."

"Go away. I am not making myself ill." No; she was drinking in a very elixir of life through that open window.

Her fancy was running riot along those days ahead of her. Spring days, and summer days, and all sorts of days that would be her own. She breathed a quick prayer that life might be long. It was only yesterday she had thought with a shudder that life might be long.

She arose at length and opened the door to her sister's importunities. There was a feverish triumph in her eyes, and she carried herself unwittingly like a goddess of Victory. She clasped her sister's waist, and together they descended the stairs. Richards stood waiting for them at the bottom.

Some one was opening the front door with a latchkey. It was Brently Mallard who entered, a little travel-stained, composedly carrying his gripsack and umbrella. He had been far from the scene of accident, and did not even know there had been one. He stood amazed at Josephine's piercing cry; at Richards's quick motion to screen him from the view of his wife.

But Richards was too late.

When the doctors came they said she had died of heart disease — of joy that kills. *[1894]*

☰ THINKING ABOUT THE TEXT

1. Chopin writes, "A kind intention or a cruel intention made the act seem no less a crime" (para. 14). Explain what Mrs. Mallard means by this thought.
2. Explain Louise Mallard's outlook on time before and after she hears of her husband's death.
3. Explain why you think Mrs. Mallard did or did not fantasize about escape during her marriage.
4. Describe the idea of ambiguity in the first and last sentence of this story.
5. Describe how happiness, loyalty, and love are problematic in the story.

KRISTEN VALDEZ QUADE

The Manzanos

Kristin Valdez Quade grew up in Albuquerque, New Mexico, and has lived in various places in the Southwest. She earned a BA from Stanford University and her MFA in fiction from the University of Oregon in 2009. She has won numerous awards and has taught at Stanford and the University of Michigan. She is currently an assistant professor in creative writing at Princeton University. Most of Quade's stories focus on the dynamics of family life with "intensity and emotional precision." She has been compared to Annie Proulx, Alice Munro, and Flannery O'Connor. The following story is from Night at the Fiestas *(2016) which won the National Book Critics Circle John Leonard Prize.*

My name is my grandmother's: Ofelia Alma Zamora. I am eleven years old and too young to die, but I am dying nonetheless. I have been dying since the day my mother went away. I've been to doctors — to the clinic in Estancia, and all the way to Albuquerque — but they take my temperature, knead my stomach, check my throat, and tell my grandfather the same thing: perhaps it is a minor infection or virus, one of the usual brief illnesses of childhood, and they see nothing seriously wrong. They don't know about the ojo, the evil eye.

There is no one left in this town who can cure me, so for now I sit at the edge of the yard, my feet in the road, turning a piece of broken asphalt in my hands, in case a stranger passes. Are you a healer? I'll ask her. I think of how it will be when I find her, how when she lays her hands on my head I'll close my eyes and feel the blessing pass through me like fire.

I imagine this, knowing I can't be cured, knowing I couldn't bear to be.

I'm waiting for my grandfather, relieved because today, finally, he's gotten up and dressed for the city: plaid shirt buttoned all the way up his thin tortoise neck, bolo tie with the silver dollar set in a ring of turquoise. Face scrubbed, white hair combed in lines over the brown crown of his head. He is in the house rinsing our coffee cups and wiping toast crumbs from the oilcloth.

I am ready too, wearing my blue dress (though the sleeves no longer cover my wrists), white tights (dingy and loose at the knees), and my sneakers. In my pocket is the address for the VA clinic, which I have copied from some papers in my grandfather's desk. This morning my grandfather braided my hair and fastened the ends with rubber bands from the newspaper. Because I'm tall I sat on the kitchen chair and he leaned over me, his trembling fingers slowly working the braid into shape. When I was younger he would tease me as he combed out the knots, pretend to find things in the tangled mass. "A jackrabbit!" he'd cry. "My pliers!" I'd laugh as the yank of the comb brought tears to my eyes.

Behind me the porch sags under the weight of the refrigerator and the gyrating washing machine on legs, which my grandparents bought during a good year in the fifties. There are places we cannot step because the boards are gray and fragile with rot. "I'll fix the porch," my grandfather says. "One day I'll find the time and shore it up." But the truth is that for years he has been unable to do jobs that he once did without even thinking.

Every day for a week I have dressed for Albuquerque, and every day he has shivered and shaken his head. "Not today, mi hijita. Perhaps the weather will be better tomorrow."

He spent those mornings in his pajamas, blanket pulled tight around him. It's late spring, the sky above the swaying cottonwoods so blue it has a texture, but he wore his wool cap, sweating. He would not let me go to the neighbors or the priest.

But today he is up and dressed, preparing for our monthly trip to Albuquerque. We will shop for what we need, and we will have lunch in a restaurant, and my grandfather will see the doctor, though he doesn't know this yet.

I touch the slip of paper in my pocket. I catalog every detail of my grandfather as he is now, as if by leaving nothing out I can keep him safe. I catalog the smooth pink mole on his neck, the brown spots like smudged fingerprints on his temples. His eyebrows, gray and wiry and curled. Often a drop of clear fluid hangs from the end of his nose. My grandfather's nose is large now, almost a beak, but it wasn't always that way. In my cigar box I have a picture of him as a slight, handsome soldier in the army, his features delicate: serious mouth, light eyes, black lashes.

There are a few families still in our town — mostly old people, no other children — and those of us who are left are used to the high weeds, the crumbling houses of neighbors, the plaster that falls like puzzle pieces. The exposed mud bricks dissolve a little more each time it rains.

Across the road from where I sit is the dance hall that belonged to dead Uncle Fidel. It hasn't been a dance hall since long before I was born — hasn't been anything but empty and overgrown with prickly branches — but there is still the green silhouette of a bottle painted on the cracked wooden door. When he was young, my grandfather tells me, there were bailes° every Saturday night, and, if he'd had a drink and his shyness left him, he would dance until he was breathless and sweaty, twirling the girls, clapping and stomping with the rest of the town through cuadrillas and polcas.° In those days they sprinkled water on the ground to keep the dust down, and dirt clotted on the black toes of his shoes.

At night I imagine I can hear the accordions and fiddles and guitars across the street, but it takes effort, and soon I am weary and overcome with the sense that I have arrived too late. I long for that other Cuipas, for the families and the river. I want to have known my grandfather as he was then, to have been with him all those long years.

The sun stretches along the road and warms my legs in my tights. If I turn my face to its heat I must close my eyes, and in the drowsy redness behind my eyelids I remember what makes me uneasy. Last night I lay stiff in my bed—which I used to share with my mother, which I imagine still smells of her—kept awake not by the ojo but by a sound I'd never heard before. Instead of my grandfather's steady sleeping breath from across the kitchen and through the open door of his bedroom, I could hear a rattling, chattering gurgle. The sound, so much like an animal—but an animal I have never heard and cannot picture—kept me tense and afraid until dawn, when my grandfather stirred, his bed creaked, and his slow footsteps assured me that he was okay.

Some days I go to school, some days I don't; like a fever the ojo comes and goes in waves. I try not to bother my grandfather with it. When I am well enough I ride the bus into Estancia, listen to what they tell me. I buy my lunch in the cafeteria and sit with the younger children, who don't ask questions when I am silent.

My grades aren't good. I struggle to form letters on the page. Three times a week I'm called from the classroom by the resource teacher, a young woman—as young, perhaps, as my mother—whose skirt swishes against her hose when she walks. She and I sit together under a fluorescent light in a room that was intended to be a closet. She shows me flashcards, asks me to write sentences, tries to make me explain what I am thinking. I tilt my head. When she tires of waiting, she'll pat my hand and sigh and give me a chocolate wrapped in red foil. I learned this during my time at school: they want to replace the past with their rhymes and procedures, their *i before e* and *carry the one.*

When I was in kindergarten I used to beg my grandfather to move us to Estancia, because it is a town with a store and a school and a senior center, where he and I can have lunch for a dollar, dessert included. Now I understand what he has never told me, that we must watch over Cuipas until it shrinks to nothing, until the houses are mud once more, and dead Uncle Fidel's bar collapses to splinters.

Sometimes, when my grandfather is well and I skip school, we walk together, and he tells me again the history of this place: the original land grant, fifty thousand acres given years ago to my grandfather's great-great-great-grandfather, parceled smaller and smaller through the generations, until our piece,

bailes: Dance parties.
cuadrillas and polcas: Lit., quadrilles and polkas, lively dances.

my grandfather's and mine, which he put in my name on my seventh birthday, became twenty-five acres, and not the best twenty-five but grassland. I wish it were in the mountains, with a spring and tall, fragrant piñon.° I would walk there in the fall and gather the dropped nuts, roast them to eat through the winter, sell the surplus in bags along the road. But my land is good only for cattle, which I do not have.

"When I was a boy," my grandfather said last time, as we stepped across the dry riverbed, "the water ran all the time. My cousins and me, we used to catch tadpoles and crayfish in glass jars."

"Where did the water go?" I asked.

My grandfather squinted as if trying to remember. "Perhaps it was diverted into the bean fields. Perhaps it rains less now. Perhaps it all happened when I was at war."

My grandfather has told me that Cuipas was one place before he left and another when he returned. Though he was in the army for two years, the war had already ended, so he lived in Rome, an eighteen-month vacation, he said, on the government's dime. Each day he swam in Mussolini's pool. It was the first and best pool he'd ever seen, huge, lined with marble smooth under his feet. My grandfather was strong, glistening, brown muscle in blue water.

He almost married a girl there. Silvia Donati. As we walked along a furrow in the bean field—the plants no higher than my calf, leaves broad and soft and heart-shaped—I asked him to tell me about her again.

She had buckteeth, my grandfather said, and the palest, rosiest skin he had ever seen, and black-black hair. She lived with her mother above their hat shop, and she made ladies' hats.

Each afternoon after his swim—back in his uniform, wet hair combed—my grandfather sat across from her at the table by the open window, waiting as she finished her work. He listened to the sharp scissors pressing through wool felt, voices in the street below, watched her pale hands as she steamed and formed the pieces on faceless wooden heads. When my grandfather left Italy she gave him a hat for his mother in Cuipas: gray with pink velvet roses. For years my great-grandmother and Silvia Donati wrote each other—one in Spanish, the other in Italian—until my great-grandmother died. I often wonder if Silvia Donati heard about my grandfather's marriage, or my mother's birth, or my grandmother's death in one of those letters. I wonder if she heard about me, if she knows that these days we live alone.

She would be an old woman now. I like to think she does not dye her hair. I like to think she has kept a trim figure and pink cheeks, perhaps remained a virgin for my grandfather. (This is important, I know, from the romance novels my mother left behind.) I imagine they marry, raise me in Italy beside the sea. They hold hands and walk along the beach, and I trail behind, all of us wearing hats that were fashionable once.

piñon: A small pine tree that grows in the Southwest. Its nuts are widely eaten as a snack in New Mexican cuisine.

My grandfather's uniform is folded in the cedar chest in the crowded back bedroom where I sleep, and which I once shared with my mother. This is my grandmother's wedding veil (netting torn), my grandfather's garrison cap. I don't know what became of my great-grandmother's gray hat, whether she wore it until it lost its shape and color, or it was trampled by a horse, or a gust of wind caught it and flung it across fields and mesas. Perhaps she left it on a bus in Albuquerque. Perhaps she gave it away.

There are some papers here too, records of business long since concluded. And here, the baptismal gowns of lost children, like limp little ghosts.

When the river does run, after the late-summer storms, I sometimes pull on a 30
pair of my mother's old shorts and wade in the muddy water, thinking of Mussolini's pool. I cup the water in my hands and fling it in a sparkling arc around my head.

If the old women see me walking home, calves muddy, shorts wet, they will shake their heads at my bare legs and call me a cabrasita. Bad little goat. But they don't blame me too much for my wild ways; they tell each other I am not at fault for being raised by a man alone. They don't know that I am at fault.

Our town is surrounded by grass. Yellow grass on land that shifts and dips like waves. Distance is difficult to judge; the grass is deceptive. The Manzanos° rise just beyond our town. I have tried to walk to the mountains, where a man lived for weeks after killing his father-in-law with an iron poker. My grandfather's father was part of the posse that searched for him. My grandfather has taken me in the car, pointed to the distant spot among the juniper and piñon where they found the murderer's camp: fire burned down, dusty bedroll. They never found him, though; I imagine him running from their excited voices and the clomp of hooves in dry soil.

Once when I was seven I played a game that I was the murderer and would be safe when I reached the mountains. The mountains loomed, and I ran through the tall grass and into the sun, burrs catching on my socks and pants. When my breath burned my throat and I could no longer run I walked, my pursuers getting closer, and fear and guilt clogged my heart. At a barbed fence I parted the wires and slid through, snaring my shirt above my shoulder blade. Long-horned cattle—black-and-white and mottled—backed away from me, the calves close to their mothers. Two rattlesnakes slithered from my footsteps, sounded a warning. Even the breeze knew what I'd done. When the sun sank behind the Manzanos, Cuipas was small behind me under a depthless violet sky, and the mountains were no closer.

Here are the places I've seen my mother: crossing the field behind the courthouse, hair loose and tangled in the winter wind; through the front window of a bank, filling out a deposit slip; in the school library, glimpsed through the stacks. When I see my mother it is always from afar or from behind or through glass. Each time my heart flips like a fish in my chest, and each time she is someone else.

My mother left us seven years ago to live in Albuquerque. Perhaps she is 35
there still; perhaps she has moved on to other places, Los Angeles or Chicago or England. She would choose someplace big, I'm sure. She was too young, my grandfather tells me. Never could take responsibility.

Manzanos: A small mountain range in central New Mexico.

My grandfather knows the stories of every grave in the dirt churchyard: This is a great-aunt, this a cousin, this a whole family killed by the Spanish flu. The murdered man is here, here a woman who hung herself from a viga° in her kitchen after her third stillborn child, but they buried her in sacred ground nonetheless. *Profirio Narciso. Nacio Valentin. Maria Candelarita. Maria Ascensión.* And this here, beside the plaster statue of the Blessed Mother, is my name: my grandmother, whom I never met. When my mother was thirteen, my grandmother left for Santa Fe, where she found work in the post office. My grandfather went after her several times, but each time she refused to return. She came home only to be buried—a heart attack.

Once I asked my grandfather why she left, but he shook his head.

Some of the graves have iron fences around them, with little gates, as though for children. Some are decorated with plastic flowers, petals bleached from the sun. I imagine I know which spot will be mine in the churchyard: pressed between my grandfather and the boy whose neck was snapped so many years ago when he was thrown from a horse. Once we are gone, the memory of my mother will be extinguished as well. I wish I could reorder the graves in the yard, straighten the slanting stones, arrange them by date or name.

I can feel the ojo in my bones, which ache in the morning and at night, and in my skin, which is prickly and electric. Growing pains, the doctor at the clinic tells me. Still, I must put my affairs in order. First, there is the problem of the land. When I'm gone it will go to the distant offspring of a cousin of my grandfather's. My grandfather doesn't know I know this, doesn't know I won't have children of my own.

I have toys and books that must be disposed of too. A collection of stones.

The old women say the ojo is caused by a covetous glance, by looking overlong. The man who gave it did not admire me, however, and looked for only a moment. The one thing of mine he desired, he took.

These are the symptoms: At night heaviness crouches on my chest and I wake gasping for air. Occasionally my eyes blur for no reason and Cuipas slants and washes away. At my worst I shiver and burn, and my grandfather wraps my feet in cold rags.

My memories of my mother are insubstantial. I see her lying on her back on the living room floor, a beauty magazine held above her head as she reads, limp pages rustling. Holding me in the yard at night, bare feet, my hand gripping the flannel nightgown at her breast as I follow with my eyes her pointed finger to the moon. A dish of yogurt cracked on the board floors of the kitchen, my mother crying. I do not know if my grandfather remembers these moments, but he must remember others: my mother as a laughing toddler, perhaps; my mother at her first communion, my mother too young and pregnant with me. Possibly he remembers the sound of her voice.

Once a month we drive west to Albuquerque, once a week we drive east to Estancia. In Estancia we buy groceries and the newspaper. At home my grandfather prepares our favorite lunch: cheese and mustard sandwiches and a glass of milk. We wash our dishes, and then it is time for the paper. We turn to the back, to

viga: Rafter, roof beam.

the comics, but we don't read them. Very carefully my grandfather tears out the puzzles, the spot-the-differences for me, the word-search for him.

We sit, working with our pencils.

"These are good for my eyes," he tells me. "They keep my mind sharp."

His favorites are the ones that match English and Spanish words. Sometimes my grandfather disagrees with the paper's translation. "Moths are *palomitas,*°" he tells me, "not *polillas,*°" and I look up, try to remember. When I finish my puzzle I stand beside my grandfather's chair and point out words he's missed.

At night, if I can't sleep I creep to the kitchen and take the paper from the crate by the woodstove. I spread it on the bedclothes. Somewhere north of here they are building a new casino. They are angry about the economy. In a country far away something has changed. I lie back on my pillow and try to imagine living in the world where these things matter. In the morning when my grandfather wakes me for my oatmeal he gathers the paper and replaces it beside the stove.

Sometimes my grandfather remembers church, and if it is Sunday he shakes me awake and braids my hair, and we walk to the chapel. We sit in the pews with our neighbors and try to listen. The priest talks about the soul, as beside me my grandfather's chin sinks to his chest. The soul is a ball of light or a jewel that must be treasured, given to Jesus.

"Christ calls for our souls though we are foul in body," says the priest.

Jesus looks down on us from the cross, mournful and distant and preoccupied with his own story.

I feel my soul inside me, made of thin, pale paper, fragile as a Japanese lantern, resting above my heart. I move with care and take shallow breaths so as not to crush it.

Christ's frozen eyes gaze at the ground. He declines to see my sleeping grandfather; he declines to see what he has abandoned. Rage rises in my chest, threatening to crumple my soul. Christ has no time for Cuipas, no time for my grandfather.

"Peace be with you," the priest says, and my grandfather wakes, squeezes my hand.

I have never seen a Japanese lantern, only read about them in my mother's novels. Used chiefly at night parties they sway from strings above wide lawns, while music plays and women in backless gowns sip champagne.

My grandfather owns nine vehicles, several of which run, though none are insured. When we go to Albuquerque he lets me choose the car. Usually I pick the old blue truck or the heavy brown ancient Mercedes with the rat's nest in the heating vent, which a man up north gave my grandfather as payment for a stone fireplace in his guesthouse. These are cars my mother will recognize.

Together my grandfather and I walk behind the house, where the vehicles sit, some with cracked tires, some parked on blocks. I hear him breathe beside me, even and smooth, familiar.

Today I pick the Mercedes.

***palomitas*:** Little doves.
***polillas*:** Moths, grubs, any cause of progressive destruction.

In the car we roll down the stiff windows and trail our hands in the air outside. Along the road the yellow grass sifts the wind.

When my grandfather begins to talk, it isn't about the past but about a future in the world outside Cuipas.

"You must not be shy," he tells me.

"You must be happy and laugh."

"You must talk to strangers."

I nod and tell him, "I will, I'll try," and panic rises in me.

"This is no place for a young person," my grandfather says. I know he thinks of a day—a day that will never exist but that is as real to him as if it already did—when I shoulder a bag and climb up and over the Manzanos without turning back. He says again, "This is no place for a child."

I want to make him take it back. Instead I pull the slip of paper from my pocket. "I want to stop here," I say firmly. "I need to stop at this clinic."

He takes the slip from my hand and frowns at it. I nearly grab the steering wheel, but his one hand on it is steady and the road is straight. He lifts his foot from the pedal, and the car loses power. He turns to look at me for a moment, then turns back to the road. He folds the slip of paper, slips it into his breast pocket, and gives the car gas.

"So can we? Can we stop?"

"No," he says, in a voice he rarely uses with me, a voice that is harsh and foreign and final. The ojo stirs and my vision smears. I think of my mother. I'll never leave my grandfather, but it isn't even my loyalty that he wants.

The road twists and curves and begins to rise. When we are in the Manzanos I swallow the stone in my throat, look out over the piñon, imagine the murderer in these mountains, alone with the knowledge of his crime.

In the city the bright billboards flash along the highway, and white sun glints off the windows of the tall hospitals and hotels. As the fast cars pass I look for my mother. I don't think she will be in the driver's seat of one of the fancy cars, but I watch the faces anyway. Her hair could be different by now. Other things might be different for her too, I know, because in the world people's fortunes rise and fall.

If I find her, I think, then my grandfather will see the doctor. He will see the doctor and he will be cured and together we will bring my mother home.

I wonder if he is looking as well. He gives no indication, keeps both hands on the steering wheel. It's harder for him to drive now, and the traffic makes him nervous. "Look, hijita," he tells me before we shift lanes. His voice is familiar again. "Am I clear?" And I crane my neck, watch the cars coming at us, tell him yes.

At the Kmart we load our cart with things we will need for the next month: tubes of toothpaste, large packages of paper towels, cornflakes, sometimes new sneakers for me, undershirts for him. My grandfather buys me toys also, plastic dolls, characters from films and television shows I have never seen. He will ask me to open the toys in the car, and I will scatter the bright cardboard and plastic packaging on the floorboard. As he drops the toys into the cart I smile and exclaim, though I'm too old for them and wish he would save our money. At home I will line them on the windowsill in my room, leave a few scattered on the floor, so my grandfather, walking by, will think I have been playing.

When we've found all the things we need we continue to push the cart down aisles under fluorescent lights. We are both a little dazed by the colors of this place, the bustle, both of us unwilling, it seems, to leave and be alone together. We push the cart, turning our heads left and right.

The woman at the checkout is stout and middle-aged and wears braces on her teeth. She asks what we think should happen to the horses. When we look at her blankly, she asks if we're from here.

"Cuipas," my grandfather says.

The horses, the cashier explains, are wild, came down from the mountains because they were starving from the drought. They gather along the highway to eat chamisa° and grass and the corn tossed to them by concerned citizens.

"I can't believe you don't know," the cashier says. "It's all over the TV. They say the horses are the same ones brought by the Spanish hundreds of years ago."

The cashier scans each item as she talks. She moves too quickly. I'm afraid she will be done before she has told us everything about the horses.

"What will happen to them?" I ask.

"Who knows? People have to fight about it, like everything else. I saw on the news where some people are saying they'll have to be slaughtered because there just isn't enough grass, what with the drought."

My grandfather fingers the bills in his hand, ready to count them out when she gives us the total.

"Some people say the state should feed them until the rains come, some say they should be driven to Colorado or Wyoming." The cashier pauses, tongues her braces. "The one sure thing is no one's going to leave them alone. People will interfere."

When I look toward the doors I know it's for a reason. It takes a few moments for me to see her. My mother. She pushes a cart, the corner of a box of sugared cereal poking out of a bag. She is as young as I remember, her hair as straight and heavy. She squints up, her gaze brushing over my face.

When I turn to him, I know from the way he holds the bills in his trembling hands that my grandfather has seen her too.

If it really were her I would run across the crowded store, throw myself against her. If it were her I would beat at her chest and belly with my fists. The cashier sighs and says that everything is expensive anymore. I want so much for the woman to be my mother, and suddenly I fear it too. If she returns my grandfather will get better, but he will also remember everything she put him through. If she returns she might leave again, and then he might get worse. But it isn't her, of course, and the woman passes through the automatic doors.

My grandfather is still looking toward the doors. His face is open and longing.

"Grandpa," I say, to draw his attention. "I'm hungry. I want my lunch."

Slowly he turns to me. He blinks, and then his face is shuttered.

In the car my grandfather asks where I want to eat.

"I want to go home. Let's eat at home. We'll have cheese and mustard sandwiches."

chamisa: A flowering shrub.

He nods, and we drive in silence until he begins to speak.

"Your mother never forgave me for the way I treated your grandma," he says, looking hard at the road.

"It wasn't her," I tell him. "It was just someone who looked like her." 95

My grandfather sits upright, close to the steering wheel, his gaze fixed on the horizon. "Once I shook your grandma so hard the skin around her eyes bruised," he says. "Your mother stood against the wall and watched."

"Grandpa, that lady didn't even look like her, not really."

He says, "Your grandma's head went back and forth."

I won't look at him. I won't.

"It took a week for the black to fade, and during those days I stayed away 100
from the house. One night I even slept at a jobsite. On the weekend I worked on the cars. I changed the fluids in every single one, checked the pressure on every tire, recorded the mileage. I couldn't go into the house where they were."

The ojo begins to flare. I want his story to stop. My skin burns.

"It wasn't her," I say.

He clears his throat. "I never touched your grandma again. I wouldn't have, even if she hadn't left. And I never touched your mother. But that didn't matter because your mother never forgave me."

I can't stand it, but he keeps going. I hear him even over the hot throbbing in my ears. I think of his voice earlier, that hard, hoarse severity, and think of Ofelia Alma Zamora, my grandmother, being shaken so hard the fragile skin around her eyes bruised. I've never heard this story, but now I understand that I knew it all along. I need him to stop.

"She blamed me for her mother leaving her, and maybe she was right." 105

Usually as we leave the rush and concrete of Albuquerque, the vast beige housing developments, my grandfather and I begin to relax and breathe. Today, though, his terrible story remains packed around us, as thick and suffocating as cotton. I feel it would take great effort for me to move.

As we wind up and over the Manzanos, I thank him for the trip, say I'll be glad to get home. My voice is stiff. He pats my hand, and behind his glasses his eyes are rimmed red with age.

And because of what he has said, I remember the thing I nearly always succeed in forgetting, the thing my grandfather believes I can't remember because I was four: the day I last saw my mother.

She had been gone for three weeks, left without telling us. One day she returned in a truck I'd never seen, driven by a man I'd never seen. She jumped from the passenger's seat, and what I remember is being furious, but I ran to her because I couldn't stop myself. When she opened her arms I backed against the house and yelled at her to go away. She looked at me, lips parted in hurt surprise, and I thought she'd come to me, but instead she walked into the house.

The man in the truck—Anglo, cowboy hat tilted forward—looked straight 110
ahead, tapping his thumbs on the steering wheel.

My grandfather sat silently at the kitchen table, while in the tiny back room she packed. I stood in the doorway, where by turning my head left or right I could see them both, my grandfather sitting still, one palm pressed against the table, and my mother working fast, shoving skirts and blouses into my grandfather's canvas army duffle. Outside in the truck, the man waited.

My mother's back was to me and she cried as she packed. I looked at her with hate that burned her edges, until she browned and curled like a photograph cast into the stove. I looked at her and sliced through her with cuts so fine she hardly knew they were there until pieces of her began to drop away. I looked at her and she began to dry up and shrink from my gaze, until she was as cold and brittle as a marigold in November.

I wish now I had cried and flung myself at her and gripped the hem of her shirt. If I had, she might have stayed. Instead, I trailed her stiffly. Out on the porch she kneeled to hug me, and I remained rigid with hate, and over her shoulder I could see the man watching us. My mother was crying and murmuring in my ear, love or promises, but I couldn't listen. The man's eye caught mine, and that's when the ojo began to spread through me. My mother pulled away, jogged to the truck, where she swung her bag into the back. She didn't call to me when they drove away.

For a long time I watched the road that led to the Manzanos and beyond to Albuquerque. I watched until the sun dropped so low in the sky that it burned my eyes and I had to turn my head.

I don't remember what I did when I lost sight of the truck, but I imagine I went inside to where my grandfather was sitting in the kitchen. I imagine when he heard my step he looked up and saw me.

Now he says, "I told her to go, hijita."

Outside, the landscape blurs.

"I told her she couldn't come home. I didn't think she'd listen to me—when had she ever listened before?—but she did. She left you."

It wasn't the man's gaze at all, I realize now. It was my own eye that was evil, my own look that was covetous and overlong, my own furious, envious gaze that has made me sick. I wanted my mother and she'd gone to him.

We have begun our descent through the Manzanos—Cuipas is a meager cluster of buildings in the distance—when we see them, the wild horses. There are two, pulling at the dry grass. My grandfather slows the Mercedes in the middle of the road. The horses are thin. Ribs visible through dusty coats. The Mercedes thrums, diesel coursing, so he turns off the engine. It shudders and goes silent, and then we hear the wind in the grass, weeds scraping against the asphalt edges of the road, and, I'm sure of it, the sound of their mouths as they eat. One of them raises her head, cocks her ears, listening. The light is silver on her velvet muzzle. I'm certain she is aware of us, will raise the alarm, but she dips her head once more and tears at the grass with yellow teeth. I think about a relative long ago losing his horse, calling her name through the mountains, returning to the fort or mission on foot, perhaps never making it, his name lost to history. A third horse emerges from the piñon, swats at the air with her tail.

If I could time my death, I would time it thus: exactly fifteen seconds after my grandfather. I would like to die in my sleep, but I must be certain I outlive him. I will lay my ear against his thin chest, listen to the silence beneath his humped sternum, and then, when I am sure, it will be my turn. Fifteen seconds is good:

any longer and I might feel grief. Any longer and I might raise my head to the world opening up before me, wide and calling.

In a moment my grandfather will pat my hand again, and his hand will stay there, resting on mine. I'll look down, run a finger along the veins knotted and bruised under his thin brown skin. I wait for his touch. But now we watch the horses separately, sitting as still as we know how.

THINKING ABOUT THE TEXT

1. What is the significance of Ofelia saying, "I long for that other Cuipas, for the families and the river" (para. 13)?
2. One way to see the theme of escape is that Ofelia wants to escape to the past, her mother to the future. Explain how this might be the case.
3. Explain how the setting is an important ingredient in understanding the story.
4. Explain how the two wild horses at the end of the story can be seen as symbolic.
5. Explain Ofelia's understanding of the ojo. What does she originally think about it and what conclusion does she come to at the end?

MAKING COMPARISONS

1. Compare the idea of loss in both stories.
2. Compare how Louise and Ofelia think about the present and the future.
3. Compare Ofelia's relationship to her grandfather and Louise Mallard's to her husband.

WRITING ABOUT IDEAS

1. Write an essay that argues that loss and absence are major concerns of both stories.
2. Argue that the wild horses at the end of the story are meant metaphorically.
3. Argue that the dream of escape is the major thematic focus of both stories.
4. Argue that the setting of "The Manzanos" is crucial to understanding the story.

Escaping Confinement: Critical Commentaries on a Story

VLADIMIR NABOKOV, "Signs and Symbols"

CRITICAL COMMENTARIES:
WAYNE GOODMAN, from "Forum: High Pressure: Psychosis, Performance, Schizophrenia, Literature"

BRIAN BOYD, from *Vladimir Nabokov: The American Years*

MICHAEL WOOD, from "Consulting the Oracle"

In the modern age, various rulers have confined entire populations, purely on the basis of their racial, ethnic, or religious identity. Whether locking these groups up in prisons or forcing them into camps, governments have strived to separate them from so-called "normal" society. The writer Vladimir Nabokov was well aware of such oppressive measures. He and his wife struggled to escape confinement—even death—at the hands of Communist and Nazi regimes. His repeated attempts to elude such threats were reflected in his fiction, including works he wrote in the relative safety of the United States. Perhaps because he might have wound up as a political prisoner, Nabokov was sensitive to how people might suffer from all sorts of enclosure. Multiple forms of captivity, along with the desire to escape them, appear in his famous story "Signs and Symbols." It portrays a mother and father who managed to flee oppression in Europe but remain haunted by the life they gave up. At the same time, they fear for their suicidal son, who hates confinement in a mental hospital and finds the whole world a prison. As you will see, Nabokov doesn't clearly resolve this family drama. He leaves his ending open to interpretation, and we present a few critics' differing views.

VLADIMIR NABOKOV
Signs and Symbols

Vladimir Nabokov (1899–1977) is generally regarded as one of the greatest fiction writers of the twentieth century. Born in Russia to aristocratic parents, he and his family fled that nation once it fell under Communist rule. While living in Berlin, Nabokov met his future wife Vera but also experienced tragedy: his father was the unintended victim of a political assassination plot. The rise of the Nazis forced Nabokov and his wife to relocate to Paris (Vera was Jewish), and eventually they moved to the United States, where he taught literature at Cornell University. After a lifetime of upheavals and a rich literary career, Nabokov spent his last years in Montreux, Switzerland. In addition to writing, he pursued a variety of interests, becoming an expert in the arts of butterfly collecting and chess. Fluent in multiple languages, Nabokov wrote his major works in English, in addition to crafting English translations of his Russian texts. Although he produced a much-admired memoir, Speak Memory *(revised ed. 1966), he is chiefly*

Gertrude Fehr/Getty Images

known for his novels, the most famous (and controversial) of which is Lolita *(1955). But Nabokov also wrote several celebrated short stories, including the one we present here. "Signs and Symbols" was first published in* The New Yorker *in 1948. It later appeared in two collections of Nabokov's short fiction,* Nabokov's Dozen *(1958) and* The Stories of Vladimir Nabokov *(1995).*

For the fourth time in as many years, they were confronted with the problem of what birthday present to take to a young man who was incurably deranged in his mind. Desires he had none. Man-made objects were to him either hives of evil, vibrant with a malignant activity that he alone could perceive, or gross comforts for which no use could be found in his abstract world. After eliminating a number of articles that might offend him or frighten him (anything in the gadget line, for instance, was taboo), his parents chose a dainty and innocent trifle—a basket with ten different fruit jellies in ten little jars.

At the time of his birth, they had already been married for a long time; a score of years had elapsed, and now they were quite old. Her drab gray hair was pinned up carelessly. She wore cheap black dresses. Unlike other women of her age (such as Mrs. Sol, their next-door neighbor, whose face was all pink and mauve with paint and whose hat was a cluster of brookside flowers), she presented a naked white countenance to the faultfinding light of spring. Her husband, who in the old country had been a fairly successful businessman, was now, in New York, wholly dependent on his brother Isaac, a real American of almost forty years' standing. They seldom saw Isaac and had nicknamed him the Prince.

That Friday, their son's birthday, everything went wrong. The subway train lost its life current between two stations and for a quarter of an hour they could hear nothing but the dutiful beating of their hearts and the rustling of newspapers. The bus they had to take next was late and kept them waiting a long time on a street corner, and when it did come, it was crammed with garrulous high-school children. It began to rain as they walked up the brown path leading to the sanitarium. There they waited again, and instead of their boy, shuffling into the room, as he usually did (his poor face sullen, confused, ill-shaven, and blotched with acne), a nurse they knew and did not care for appeared at last and brightly explained that he had again attempted to take his life. He was all right, she said, but a visit from his parents might disturb him. The place was so miserably understaffed, and things got mislaid or mixed up so easily, that they decided not to leave their present in the office but to bring it to him next time they came.

Outside the building, she waited for her husband to open his umbrella and then took his arm. He kept clearing his throat, as he always did when he was upset. They reached the bus-stop shelter on the other side of the street and he closed his umbrella. A few feet away, under a swaying and dripping tree, a tiny unfledged bird was helplessly twitching in a puddle.

During the long ride to the subway station, she and her husband did not 5
exchange a word, and every time she glanced at his old hands, clasped and twitching upon the handle of his umbrella, and saw their swollen veins and brown-spotted skin, she felt the mounting pressure of tears. As she looked around, trying to hook her mind onto something, it gave her a kind of soft shock, a mixture of compassion and wonder, to notice that one of the passengers—a girl with dark hair and grubby red toenails—was weeping on the shoulder of an older woman. Whom did that woman resemble? She resembled Rebecca Borisovna, whose daughter had married one of the Soloveichiks—in Minsk, years ago.

The last time the boy had tried to do it, his method had been, in the doctor's words, a masterpiece of inventiveness; he would have succeeded had not an envious fellow-patient thought he was learning to fly and stopped him just in time. What he had really wanted to do was to tear a hole in his world and escape.

The system of his delusions had been the subject of an elaborate paper in a scientific monthly, which the doctor at the sanitarium had given to them to read. But long before that, she and her husband had puzzled it out for themselves. "Referential mania," the article had called it. In these very rare cases, the patient imagines that everything happening around him is a veiled reference to his personality and existence. He excludes real people from the conspiracy, because he considers himself to be so much more intelligent than other men. Phenomenal nature shadows him wherever he goes. Clouds in the staring sky transmit to each other, by means of slow signs, incredibly detailed information regarding him. His in-most thoughts are discussed at nightfall, in manual alphabet, by darkly gesticulating trees. Pebbles or stains or sun flecks form patterns representing, in some awful way, messages that he must intercept. Everything is a cipher and of everything he is the theme. All around him, there are spies. Some of them are detached observers, like glass surfaces and still pools; others, such as coats in store windows, are prejudiced witnesses, lynchers at heart; others, again (running water, storms), are hysterical to the point of insanity, have a distorted opinion of him, and grotesquely misinterpret his actions. He must be always on his guard and devote every minute and module of life to the decoding of the undulation of things. The very air he exhales is indexed and filed away. If only the interest he provokes were limited to his immediate surroundings, but, alas, it is not! With distance, the torrents of wild scandal increase in volume and volubility. The silhouettes of his blood corpuscles, magnified a million times, flit over vast plains; and still farther away, great mountains of unbearable solidity and height sum up, in terms of granite and groaning firs, the ultimate truth of his being.

When they emerged from the thunder and foul air of the subway, the last dregs of the day were mixed with the street lights. She wanted to buy some fish for supper, so she handed him the basket of jelly jars, telling him to go home. Accordingly, he returned to their tenement house, walked up to the third landing, and then remembered he had given her his keys earlier in the day.

In silence he sat down on the steps and in silence rose when, some ten minutes later, she came trudging heavily up the stairs, smiling wanly and shaking her head in deprecation of her silliness. They entered their two-room flat and he at once went to the mirror. Straining the corners of his mouth apart by means of his thumbs, with a horrible, mask-like grimace, he removed his new, hopelessly uncomfortable dental plate. He read his Russian-language newspaper while she laid the table. Still reading, he ate the pale victuals that needed no teeth. She knew his moods and was also silent.

When he had gone to bed, she remained in the living room with her pack of soiled playing cards and her old photograph albums. Across the narrow courtyard, where the rain tinkled in the dark against some ash cans, windows were blandly alight, and in one of them a black-trousered man, with his hands clasped under his head and his elbows raised, could he seen lying supine on an untidy bed. She pulled the blind down and examined the photographs. As a baby, he looked more surprised than most babies. A photograph of a German maid they had had in Leipzig and her fat-faced fiancé fell out of a fold of the album. She turned the pages of the book: Minsk, the Revolution, Leipzig, Berlin, Leipzig again, a slanting house front, badly out of focus. Here was the boy when he was four years old, in a park, shyly, with puckered forehead, looking away from an eager squirrel, as he would have from any other stranger. Here was Aunt Rosa, a fussy, angular, wild-eyed old lady, who had lived in a tremulous world of bad news, bankruptcies, train accidents, and cancerous growths until the Germans put her to death, together with all the people she had worried about. The boy, aged six—that was when he drew wonderful birds with human hands and feet, and suffered from insomnia like a grown-up man. His cousin, now a famous chess player. The boy again, aged about eight, already hard to understand, afraid of the wallpaper in the passage, afraid of a certain picture in a book, which merely showed an idyllic landscape with rocks on a hillside and an old cart wheel hanging from the one branch of a leafless tree. Here he was at ten—the year they left Europe. She remembered the shame, the pity, the humiliating difficulties of the journey, and the ugly, vicious, backward children he was with in the special school where he had been placed after they arrived in America. And then came a time in his life, coinciding with a long convalescence after pneumonia, when those little phobias of his, which his parents had stubbornly regarded as the eccentricities of a prodigiously gifted child, hardened, as it were, into a dense tangle of logically interacting illusions, making them totally inaccessible to normal minds. All this, and much more, she had accepted, for, after all, living does mean accepting the loss of one joy after another, not even joys in her case, mere possibilities of improvement. She thought of the recurrent waves of pain that for some reason or other she and her husband had had to endure; of the in visible giants hurting her boy in some unimaginable fashion; of the incalculable amount of tenderness contained in the world; of the fate of this tenderness, which is either crushed or wasted, or transformed into madness; of neglected children humming to themselves in unswept corners; of beautiful weeds that cannot hide from the farmer.

It was nearly midnight when, from the living room, she heard her husband moan, and presently he staggered in, wearing over his nightgown the old overcoat with the astrakhan collar that he much preferred to his nice blue bathrobe.

"I can't sleep!" he cried.

"Why can't you sleep?" she asked. "You were so tired."

"I can't sleep because I am dying," he said, and lay down on the couch. 15

"Is it your stomach? Do you want me to call Dr. Solov?"

"No doctors, no doctors," he moaned. "To the devil with doctors! We must get him out of there quick. Otherwise, we'll be responsible.... Responsible!" He hurled himself into a sitting position, both feet on the floor, thumping his forehead with his clenched fist.

"All right," she said quietly. "We will bring him home tomorrow morning."

"I would like some tea," said her husband and went out to the bathroom.

Bending with difficulty, she retrieved some playing cards and a photograph or 20
two that had slipped to the floor—the knave of hearts, the nine of spades, the ace of spades, the maid Elsa and her bestial beau. He returned in high spirits, saying in a loud voice, "I have it all figured out. We will give him the bedroom. Each of us will spend part of the night near him and the other part on this couch. We will have the doctor see him at least twice a week. It does not matter what the Prince says. He won't have much to say anyway, because it will come out cheaper."

The telephone rang. It was an unusual hour for it to ring. He stood in the middle of the room, groping with his foot for one slipper that had come off, and childishly, toothlessly, gaped at his wife. Since she knew more English than he, she always attended to the calls.

"Can I speak to Charlie?" a girl's dull little voice said to her now.

"What number do you want? ... No. You have the wrong number."

She put the receiver down gently and her hand went to her heart. "It frightened me," she said.

He smiled a quick smile and immediately resumed his excited monologue. 25
They would fetch him as soon as it was day. For his own protection, they would keep all the knives in a locked drawer. Even at his worst, he presented no danger to other people.

The telephone rang a second time.

The same toneless, anxious young voice asked for Charlie.

"You have the incorrect number. I will tell you what you are doing. You are turning the letter 'o' instead of the zero." She hung up again.

They sat down to their unexpected, festive midnight tea. He sipped noisily; his face was flushed; every now and then he raised his glass with a circular motion, so as to make the sugar dissolve more thoroughly. The vein on the side of his bald head stood out conspicuously, and silvery bristles showed on his chin. The birthday present stood on the table. While she poured him another glass of tea, he put on his spectacles and reexamined with pleasure the luminous yellow, green, and red little jars. His clumsy, moist lips spelled out their eloquent labels—apricot, grape, beach plum, quince. He had got to crab apple when the telephone rang again.

THINKING ABOUT THE TEXT

1. The first paragraph specifies the parents' intended gift for their son: "a basket with ten different fruit jellies in ten little jars" (para. 1). The final paragraph mentions this basket, too. Why do you think Nabokov chose this image? What do you think he's up to by beginning and ending his story with this particular gift?
2. Choose another detail in the story (perhaps an image) that some readers might think wasn't necessary for Nabokov to include. Speculate about why Nabokov did include it. What purpose(s) does it conceivably serve?
3. Paragraphs 7 and 10 are the longest in the story. Think about why Nabokov made them so long. To what extent do they seem to serve the same purpose?
4. The story refers to a mother, a father, and a son. Would you say that it is equally about all three? Why or why not? What other groups of people does the story bring up as relevant to this family's crisis?
5. What do you think is happening at the story's conclusion? Why, conceivably, did Nabokov choose to end it the way he did?

WAYNE GOODMAN

From "Forum: High Pressure: Psychosis, Performance, Schizophrenia, Literature"

Dr. Wayne Goodman heads the Menninger Department of Psychiatry and Behavioral Sciences at the Baylor College of Medicine in Texas. Formerly he was Professor and Chair of Psychiatry at Mount Sinai School of Medicine in New York. A specialist in obsessive-compulsive disorder, he co-developed the major instrument that assesses this condition. Although he has published many articles in his medical field, he contributed to an interdisciplinary symposium on Nabokov's story that appeared in a 2012 collection, Anatomy of a Short Story: Nabokov's Puzzles, Codes, "Signs and Symbols." *The following excerpt is Goodman's interpretation of the story's cryptic ending.*

I interpreted the third phone call as a call from the hospital informing his parents that their son has escaped. By that I mean either through suicide or leaving the grounds. The son was determined to "tear a hole in his world" and the hospital staff was incapable of stopping him. But I do not envision a happy reunion with his family. There is no room in their world for him.

BRIAN BOYD

From *Vladmir Nabokov: The American Years*

Brian Boyd (b. 1952) teaches at the University of Auckland in New Zealand, where is Distinguished University Professor of English. He is author of a major two-volume biography of Nabokov: Vladimir Nabokov: The Russian Years *(1990) and* Vladimir Nabokov: The American Years *(1991). In the following excerpt, from the second of these books, Boyd does not stick to just one way of interpreting the conclusion of "Signs and Symbols." He suggests there at least two possible perspectives on it.*

Detail after detail in the story seems impregnated with doom: "That Friday everything went wrong. The underground train lost its life current between two stations." It is raining hard. They cannot see their son. As they return to the bus shelter they pass by a swaying and dripping tree under which "a tiny half-dead unfledged bird was helplessly twitching in a puddle." On board the bus, the old man's hands twitch, as if in response. A girl sits weeping a few seats away. When they reach home, the husband finds himself without his key. His new dentures are hopelessly uncomfortable. He has just got to bitter crab apple when the telephone rings for the fatal third time.

If we take all of these details as signs and symbols, that telephone call will announce that the boy has at last managed to kill himself. But if we accept that that is the case, we have accepted what from within the story's world has to be defined as madness: that everything around the boy forms a message about his fate. If we accept that he has killed himself, then we have to acknowledge every agonizing detail as part of a pattern designed to point toward his tragic fate, to evoke our compassion for him and his parents. From within the parents' world, their son's death seems simply more jagged glass on the pile of miseries that makes up their life. But from outside their vantage point, we can see that *if* the boy has died, then the story bears the mark of a tender concern that shapes every minute detail of a world that from within seems unrelieved, meaningless tragedy. The final blow of death, in one light so gratuitous, in another seems the very proof of the painstaking design behind every moment of their lives. Will the fact of our deaths too perhaps disclose suddenly a pattern of tender meaning running through our lives? Or will we never know, just as we can never know whether that telephone announces a death or simply another irritatingly repeated wrong number, another unneeded vexation?

MICHAEL WOOD
From "Consulting the Oracle"

Michael Wood (b. 1936) is Charles Barnwell Straut Class of 1923 Professor of English and Comparative Literature in New Jersey. He has published many books in literary and film studies, including The Magician's Doubts: Nabokov and the Risks of Fiction *(1994) and* The Road to Delphi: The Life and Afterlife of Oracles *(2003). He also frequently reviews book and movies for* The New York Review of Books *and the* London Review of Books. *The following is an excerpt from an article by Wood that appeared in a 1993 issue of the academic journal* Essays in Criticism. *Like Boyd, Wood notes the possibility of multiple perspectives on the ending of "Signs and Symbols." But the two critics' emphases differ. Boyd thinks there might be a "pattern of tender concern" shaping the characters' lives. Wood raises a harsher prospect: that their existence is "organized by a malign or at least mischievous agency."*

What do we hear in this room, in these minds, when the telephone rings for the third time? I hear common sense (the old couple's, mine, no doubt Nabokov's) telling me that it is the same wrong number again, the girl who wants Charlie. I can't know this for sure, though, unless someone picks up the telephone, and no one ever will. This fictional telephone can no more be picked up than Ophelia can be resurrected. Equally, of course, it will keep ringing for as long as anyone reads the story. What other voices say to me is: this time it's the hospital, it's bad news, something has happened to the son. Or: it is the wrong number, but it's meant for the old couple all the same, some malign force is using this mistaken girl to torture them. It is because the call might be from the hospital that the very wrongness of the number seems cruel. Could the old couple not think this, not feel persecuted at their midnight tea? Can we not feel this on their behalf? In this context, even the slight suspicion of a conspiracy, ordinary unenhanced suspicion, becomes a form of pain. Do we, perhaps for the first time, wonder whether there is something hereditary about referential mania, dormant but always possible in this generation? Or do we think referential mania must be intuitively correct after all, the only way we can possibly account for the brutal, ingenious, so-called accidents of the world? The strength of this story, I think, is that what seems to be the 'right' reading, the banal, accidental wrong number, is simultaneously the sanest and the hardest to settle for. We have been set up, by the account of the young man's mania and the hints of his parents' history, to believe in pain but not in accidents. This belief is reinforced, of course, by the fact that the endlessly ringing telephone is not, cannot be, a textual accident, since it is where Nabokov deliberately ends his story.

At the level of represented life in the fiction there is a question, which pits, let us say, the possible craziness of a person against the possible craziness of the world, and pits against both the merely random, the realm of chance. We are suspended here, with the characters. On the level of the writing, however, the question is answered, chance is abolished. The doubt in the story, so to speak, is cancelled by the story. If the couple could know they were figures in a fiction, they would know they were being tormented by Nabokov, author of the ominous third telephone call, and indeed of the other calls, and of the couple and their unhappy son. Other characters in Nabokov do possess just this kind of knowledge, and one (Adam Krug in *Bend Sinister*) goes mad because of it. Here, the two levels are quite separate, the second easily forgotten; but they can be seen to comment on each other. In the story, there is the frightened interpretation of chance, the difficulty of believing that chance is what it is; in the writing both an absence of chance and a carefully orchestrated interest in chance, a confirmation of our difficulty. This world is organized by a malign or at least mischievous agency, someone is whispering about these people behind their backs. A text like 'Signs and Symbols' is a metaphor for a world which is ordered but unsympathetic, run by a heavy-handed deity whom paranoia would rightly suspect of wanting to trash what is most precious to us, or at least wanting to tease us with that very suspicion.

MAKING COMPARISONS

1. How plausible do you find Goodman's interpretation of the ending? Explain your reasoning. What might Goodman say to someone who argued that if the son did escape the world, Nabokov would have made that fact clear?
2. Both Boyd and Wood suggest that at least two perspectives on the story's ending are possible. In what respects do these two critics differ, though?
3. Do you suspect that Boyd and Wood would think Goodman naïve because he has pretty much one interpretation of the ending? Or would they be tolerant of Goodman's view? Explain.

WRITING ABOUT ISSUES

1. Write an essay in which you identify, and explain the significance of, a key difference between the mother and the father in "Signs and Symbols."
2. To what extent does Nabokov encourage the reader to fall into the same "referential mania" that the son suffers from? Write an essay that addresses this question by referring to at least one of the three critics.
3. When he corresponded about "Signs and Symbols" with Katherine A. White, fiction editor of *The New Yorker* (where the work was first published), Nabokov called it a type of text where "a second (main) story is woven into, or placed behind, the superficial semitransparent one." He seems to be encouraging us to look for a more important tale than what we first take to be the chief one. Write an essay in which you follow up on Nabokov's suggestion. What might be considered the "superficial" plot of "Signs and Symbols," and what narrative should we be more concerned with?
4. Should Nabokov have made his ending clearer? Why, or why not? Write an essay that states and explains your position by comparing the story's conclusion with the ending of another work of fiction you have read.

Literature and Current Issues: Does Our Happiness Depend on Others' Misery?

URSULA K. LE GUIN, "The Ones Who Walk Away from Omelas"

ARGUMENTS ON THE ISSUE:
DAVID BROOKS, "The Child in the Basement"

JOHN R. EHRENFELD, "The Error of Trying to Measure Good and Bad"

College students are sometimes frustrated by discussion in their literature classes when the instructor isn't specific enough about a poem's meaning or the exact point of a story. Didn't the author have a clear intention in mind, they argue reasonably. Actually, it might be that writers do plan on saying something specific but often change their minds as they get deeper into their story. And like the rest of us, they sometimes intend one thing, but readers take it another way. And, of course, writers have no control over the multiple ways the values and opinions of the world change over decades or centuries. Reading literature is more complicated than simply decoding. That skill is valuable in following recipes or assembling a swing set, but literature relies on the reader's input to complete the transaction between writer and audience. Shakespeare's audience responded enthusiastically to his plays, and four hundred years later, so do contemporary theater goers. These diverse audiences find the playwright's words powerful because they sense that they are relevant to their own lives, to the world they live in now, and to their fears, hopes, desires, and concerns.

The following classic story, written over forty years ago, resonates with contemporary readers because they seem to find in Le Guin's tale issues as fresh as this morning's news. We follow "The Ones Who Walk Away from Omelas" with a brief essay by the *New York Times* columnist David Brooks, titled "The Child in the Basement" and a direct response by John R. Ehrenfeld. Although one of the many possible topics for discussion in the story is the morality of exploitation, it remains for the reader to fill in the relevant details, perhaps focusing on the working conditions of young girls in Pakistan making Nike running shoes for a few dollars a day or ten-year-old migrant laborers harvesting lettuce in intolerable conditions in California. In their responses to Le Guin, Brooks wants to remind us of our conflicted values, while Ehrenfeld hopes to affirm absolute rights and duties. These two essays are challenging, focusing on philosophical ideas that demand but reward our attention. One simple but not reductive way to see their complex arguments is to think of the fairly common discussion in college classes between the relative and the absolute, between pragmatic compromise and moral absolutes, between who is morally good and who is not—and importantly, what standard or system of ethics is being used to judge our ethical choices. Whatever our perspective, reading and rereading their arguments can make us better thinkers and perhaps better people.

BEFORE YOU READ

Who do you think about when the idea of an exploited worker is mentioned? If your professor said she would give "A's" to the whole class if they would designate one person to get an "F," how would you react? How would others respond? Would there be a consensus? Are there rights that are inalienable? Is "the pursuit of happiness" one of them? Why?

URSULA K. LE GUIN

The Ones Who Walk Away from Omelas

Ursula K. Le Guin (b. 1929) was born and raised in Berkeley, California, where she began writing at age eleven, unsuccessfully submitting a story to Astounding Science Fiction. *She graduated from Radcliffe College (Phi Beta Kappa) in 1951 and received her M.A. from Columbia University a year later. She became famous with the publication of* The Left Hand of Darkness *(1969), an exploration of a hermaphroditic race that most critics see as a comment on contemporary gender politics. The novel won science fiction's highest awards: the Hugo and the Nebula.* The Farthest Shore *(1972) won the National Book Award, and* Tehanu: The Last Book of Earthsea *(1990) won the prestigious Nebula Award. More recently,* Powers *won the Nebula Award for 2008, and* Lavinia *won the 2009 Locus Award for Best Fantasy Novel. Besides her twenty novels, Le Guin has also published scores of short stories, books for children, nonfiction, and six volumes of poems. In 2000, Le Guin received the Library of Congress Living Legends award for her "significant contribution to America's heritage." In 2014, she won the Medal for Distinguished Contributions to American Letters from the National Book Foundation.*

With a clamor of bells that set the swallows soaring, the Festival of Summer came to the city Omelas, bright-towered by the sea. The rigging of the boats in harbor

Dan Tuffs /Getty Images

sparkled with flags. In the streets between houses with red roofs and painted walls, between old moss-grown gardens and under avenues of trees, past great parks and public buildings, processions moved. Some were decorous: old people in long stiff robes of mauve and gray, grave master workmen, quiet, merry women carrying their babies and chatting as they walked. In other streets the music beat faster, a shimmering of gong and tambourine, and the people went dancing, the procession was a dance. Children dodged in and out, their high calls rising like the swallows' crossing flights over the music and the singing. All the processions wound towards the north side of the city, where on the great water-meadow called the Green Fields boys and girls, naked in the bright air, with mudstained feet and ankles and long, lithe arms, exercised their restive horses before the race. The horses wore no gear at all but a halter without bit. Their manes were braided with streamers of silver, gold, and green. They flared their nostrils and pranced and boasted to one another; they were vastly excited, the horse being the only animal who has adopted our ceremonies as his own. Far off to the north and west the mountains stood up half encircling Omelas on her bay. The air of morning was so clear that the snow still crowning the Eighteen Peaks burned with white-gold fire across the miles of sunlit air, under the dark blue of the sky. There was just enough wind to make the banners that marked the racecourse snap and flutter now and then. In the silence of the broad green meadows one could hear the music winding through the city streets, farther and nearer and ever approaching, a cheerful faint sweetness of the air that from time to time trembled and gathered together and broke out into the great joyous clanging of the bells.

Joyous! How is one to tell about joy? How describe the citizens of Omelas?

They were not simple folk, you see, though they were happy. But we do not say the words of cheer much any more. All smiles have become archaic. Given a description such as this one tends to make certain assumptions. Given a description such as this one tends to look next for the King, mounted on a splendid stallion and surrounded by his noble knights, or perhaps in a golden litter borne by great-muscled slaves. But there was no king. They did not use swords, or keep slaves. They were not barbarians. I do not know the rules and laws of their society, but I suspect that they were singularly few. As they did without monarchy and slavery, so they also got on without the stock exchange, the advertisement, the secret police, and the bomb. Yet I repeat that these were not simple folk, not dulcet shepherds, noble savages, bland utopians. They were not less complex than us. The trouble is that we have a bad habit, encouraged by pedants and sophisticates, of considering happiness as something rather stupid. Only pain is intellectual, only evil interesting. This is the treason of the artist: a refusal to admit the banality of evil and the terrible boredom of pain. If you can't lick 'em, join 'em. If it hurts, repeat it. But to praise despair is to condemn delight, to embrace violence is to lose hold of everything else. We have almost lost hold, we can no longer describe a happy man, nor make any celebration of joy. How can I tell you about the people of Omelas? They were not naive and happy children—though their children were, in fact, happy. They were mature, intelligent, passionate adults whose lives were not wretched. O miracle! But I wish I could describe it better. I wish I could convince you. Omelas sounds in my words like a city in a fairy tale, long ago and far away, once upon a time. Perhaps it would be best if you imagined it as your own fancy bids, assuming it will rise to the occasion, for certainly I cannot suit you all. For instance, how about technology? I think that there would be no cars or helicopters in and above the streets; this follows from the fact that the people of Omelas are happy people. Happiness is based on a just discrimination of what is necessary, what is neither necessary nor destructive, and what is destructive. In the middle category, however—that of the unnecessary but undestructive, that of comfort, luxury, exuberance, etc.—they could perfectly well have central heating, subway trains, washing machines, and all kinds of marvelous devices not yet invented here, floating light-sources, fuelless power, a cure for the common cold. Or they could have none of that: it doesn't matter. As you like it. I incline to think that people from towns up and down the coast have been coming in to Omelas during the last days before the Festival on very fast little trains and double-decked trams, and that the train station of Omelas is actually the handsomest building in town, though plainer than the magnificent Farmers' Market. But even granted trains, I fear that Omelas so far strikes some of you as goody-goody. Smiles, bells, parades, horses, bleh. If so, please add an orgy. If an orgy would help, don't hesitate. Let us not, however, have temples from which issue beautiful nude priests and priestesses already half in ecstasy and ready to copulate with any man or woman, lover or stranger, who desires union with the deep godhead of the blood, although that was my first idea. But really it would be better not to have any temples in Omelas—at least, not manned temples. Religion yes, clergy no. Surely the beautiful nudes can just wander about, offering themselves like divine soufflés to the hunger of the needy and the rapture of the flesh. Let them join the processions. Let tambourines be struck above the copulations, and the glory of desire be proclaimed upon the gongs, and (a not unimportant point) let the offspring of these delightful rituals be beloved and looked after by all. One thing I know there is none of in Omelas is guilt. But what else should there be? I thought that first there were no drugs, but that is puritanical. For those who like it, the faint insistent sweetness of *drooz* may perfume the ways of the city, *drooz* which first brings a great lightness and brilliance to the mind and limbs, and then after some hours a dreamy languor, and wonderful visions at last of the very arcana and inmost secrets of the Universe, as well as exciting the pleasure of sex beyond all belief; and it is not habit-forming. For more modest tastes I think there ought to be beer. What else, what else belongs in the joyous city? The sense of victory, surely, the celebration of courage. But as we did without clergy, let us do without soldiers. The joy built upon successful slaughter is not the right kind of joy; it will not do; it is fearful and it is trivial. A boundless and generous contentment, a magnanimous triumph felt not against some outer enemy but in communion with the finest and fairest in the souls of all men everywhere and the splendor of the world's summer: this is what swells the hearts of the people of Omelas, and the victory they celebrate is that of life. I really don't think many of them need to take *drooz*.

Most of the processions have reached the Green Fields by now. A marvelous smell of cooking goes forth from the red and blue tents of the provisioners. The faces of small children are amiably sticky; in the benign grey beard of a man a couple of crumbs of rich pastry are entangled. The youths and girls have mounted their horses and are beginning to group around the starting line of the course. An old woman, small, fat, and laughing, is passing out flowers from a basket, and tall young men wear her flowers in their shining hair. A child of nine or ten sits at the edge of the crowd, alone, playing on a wooden flute. People pause to listen, and they smile, but they do not speak to him, for he never ceases playing and never sees them, his dark eyes wholly rapt in the sweet, thin magic of the tune.

He finishes, and slowly lowers his hands holding the wooden flute. 5

As if that little private silence were the signal, all at once a trumpet sounds from the pavilion near the starting line: imperious, melancholy, piercing. The horses rear on their slender legs, and some of them neigh in answer. Sober-faced, the young riders stroke the horses' necks and soothe them, whispering, "Quiet, quiet, there my beauty, my hope. . . ." They begin to form in rank along the starting line. The crowds along the racecourse are like a field of grass and flowers in the wind. The Festival of Summer has begun.

Do you believe? Do you accept the festival, the city, the joy? No? Then let me describe one more thing.

In a basement under one of the beautiful public buildings of Omelas, or perhaps in the cellar of one of its spacious private homes, there is a room. It has one locked door, and no window. A little light seeps in dustily between cracks in the boards, secondhand from a cobwebbed window somewhere across the cellar. In one corner of the little room a couple of mops, with stiff, clotted, foul-smelling heads, stand near a rusty bucket. The floor is dirt, a little damp to the touch, as cellar dirt usually is. The room is about three paces long and two wide: a mere broom closet or disused tool room. In the room a child is sitting. It could be a boy or a girl. It looks about six, but actually is nearly ten. It is feebleminded. Perhaps it was born defective, or perhaps it has become imbecile through fear, malnutrition, and neglect. It picks its nose and occasionally fumbles vaguely with its toes or genitals, as it sits hunched in the corner farthest from the bucket and the two mops. It is afraid of the mops. It finds them horrible. It shuts its eyes, but it knows the mops are still standing there: and the door is locked; and nobody will come. The door is always locked; and nobody ever comes, except that sometimes—the child has no understanding of time or interval—sometimes the door rattles terribly and opens, and a person, or several people, are there. One of them may come in and kick the child to make it stand up. The others never come close, but peer in at it with frightened, disgusted eyes. The food bowl and the water jug are hastily filled, the door is locked, the eyes disappear. The people at the door never say anything, but the child, who has not always lived in the tool room, and can remember sunlight and its mother's voice, sometimes speaks. "I will be good," it says. "Please let me out. I will be good!" They never answer. The child used to scream for help at night, and cry a good deal, but now it only makes a kind of whining, "eh-haa, eh-haa," and it speaks less and less often. It is so thin there are no calves to its legs; its belly protrudes; it lives on a half-bowl of corn meal and grease a day. It is naked. Its buttocks and thighs are a mass of festered sores, as it sits in its own excrement continually.

They all know it is there, all the people of Omelas. Some of them have come to see it, others are content merely to know it is there. They all know that it has to be there. Some of them understand why, and some do not, but they all understand that their happiness, the beauty of their city, the tenderness of their friendships, the health of their children, the wisdom of their scholars, the skill of their makers, even the abundance of their harvest and the kindly weathers of their skies, depend wholly on this child's abominable misery.

This is usually explained to children when they are between eight and twelve, 10
whenever they seem capable of understanding; and most of those who come to see the child are young people, though often enough an adult comes, or comes back, to see the child. No matter how well the matter has been explained to them, these young spectators are always shocked and sickened at the sight. They feel disgust, which they had thought themselves superior to. They feel anger, outrage, impotence, despite all the explanations. They would like to do something for the child. But there is nothing they can do. If the child were brought up into the sunlight out of that vile place, if it were cleaned and fed and comforted, that would be a good thing, indeed; but if it were done, in that day and hour all the prosperity and beauty and delight of Omelas would wither and be destroyed. Those are the terms. To exchange all the goodness and grace of every life in Omelas for that single, small improvement: to throw away the happiness of thousands for the chance of the happiness of one: that would be to let guilt within the walls indeed.

The terms are strict and absolute; there may not even be a kind word spoken to the child.

Often the young people go home in tears, or in a tearless rage, when they have seen the child and faced this terrible paradox. They may brood over it for weeks or years. But as time goes on they begin to realize that even if the child could be released, it would not get much good of its freedom: a little vague pleasure of warmth and food, no doubt, but little more. It is too degraded and imbecile to know any real joy. It has been afraid too long ever to be free of fear. Its habits are too uncouth for it to respond to humane treatment. Indeed, after so long it would probably be wretched without walls about it to protect it, and darkness for its eyes, and its own excrement to sit in. Their tears at the bitter injustice dry when they begin to perceive the terrible justice of reality, and to accept it. Yet it is their tears and anger, the trying of their generosity and the acceptance of their helplessness, which are perhaps the true source of the splendor of their lives. Theirs is no vapid, irresponsible happiness. They know that they, like the child, are not free. They know compassion. It is the existence of the child, and their knowledge of its existence, that makes possible the nobility of their architecture, the poignancy of their music, the profundity of their science. It is because of the child that they are so gentle with children. They know that if the wretched one were not there snivelling in the dark, the other one, the flute-player, could make no joyful music as the young riders line up in their beauty for the race in the sunlight of the first morning of summer.

Now do you believe in them? Are they not more credible? But there is one more thing to tell, and this is quite incredible.

At times one of the adolescent girls or boys who go to see the child does not go home to weep or rage, does not, in fact, go home at all. Sometimes also a man or woman much older falls silent for a day or two, and then leaves home. These people go out into the street, and walk down the street alone. They keep walking, and walk straight out of the city of Omelas, through the beautiful gates. They keep walking across the farmlands of Omelas. Each one goes alone, youth or girl, man or woman. Night falls; the traveler must pass down village streets, between the houses with yellow-lit windows, and on out into the darkness of the fields. Each alone, they go west or north, towards the mountains. They go on. They leave Omelas, they walk ahead into the darkness, and they do not come back. The place they go towards is a place even less imaginable to most of us than the city of happiness. I cannot describe it at all. It is possible that it does not exist. But they seem to know where they are going, the ones who walk away from Omelas. *[1973]*

≡ THINKING ABOUT THE TEXT

1. The opening three paragraphs make Omelas sound idyllic. Why might most people think of it as a utopia? What would you add or subtract? How might some aspects of our world be possible in Omelas?
2. Critics suggest that although many stories are set in the future or in an imaginary world, they are really about the present. How might this be true for this story?
3. How might you respond to the suffering child? How would you respond if you knew the happiness of a community of thousands was based on the suffering of this one individual?
4. Speculate about why some walk away from Omelas. Where are they going? Why do they seem so resolute?
5. What part does tradition play in the story? For example, if the people of Omelas didn't have such a tradition and someone proposed it, why would they be more or less likely to adopt the proposal (assuming that it would somehow work)?

DAVID BROOKS

The Child in the Basement

David Brooks (b. 1961) was born in Toronto and grew up in downtown Manhattan. He graduated from the University of Chicago in 1983 with a degree in history. He then worked as an intern at the conservative magazine National Review. *Later, he worked as a columnist for* the Wall Street Journal. *In 2000, Brooks published the well-received* Bobos in Paradise, *a witty satire on the "new upper class" consumerism. Since 2003, Brooks has been a regular columnist for the* New York Times. *He is sometimes described as a conservative, although he was an early admirer of President Obama. Recent books include* The Social Animal: The Hidden Sources *of* Love, Character and Achievement *(2011) and* The Road to Character *(2015). The following piece was written for his column in early 2015.*

Maybe you're familiar with Ursula Le Guin's short story, "The Ones Who Walk Away from Omelas." It's about a sweet and peaceful city with lovely parks and delightful music.

The people in the city are genuinely happy. They enjoy their handsome buildings and a "magnificent" farmers' market.

Le Guin describes a festival day with delicious beer and horse races: "An old woman, small, fat, and laughing, is passing out flowers from a basket, and tall young men wear her flowers in their shining hair. A child of nine or ten sits at the edge of the crowd, alone, playing on a wooden flute."

It is an idyllic, magical place.

5 But then Le Guin describes one more feature of Omelas. In the basement of one of the buildings, there is a small broom-closet-sized room with a locked door and no windows. A small child is locked inside the room. It looks about 6, but, actually, the child is nearly 10. "It is feebleminded. Perhaps it was born defective, or perhaps it has become imbecile through fear, malnutrition and neglect."

Occasionally, the door opens and people look in. The child used to cry out, "Please let me out. I will be good!" But the people never answered and now the child just whimpers. It is terribly thin, lives on a half-bowl of cornmeal a day and must sit in its own excrement.

"They all know it is there, all the people of Omelas," Le Guin writes. "Some of them have come to see it; others are content merely to know it is there. They all know it has to be there. Some of them understand why, and some do not, but they all understand that their happiness, the beauty of their city, the tenderness of their friendships, the health of their children . . . depend wholly on this child's abominable misery."

That is the social contract in Omelas. One child suffers horribly so that the rest can be happy. If the child were let free or comforted, Omelas would be destroyed. Most people feel horrible for the child, and some parents hold their kids tighter, and then they return to their happiness.

But some go to see the child in the room and then keep walking. They don't want to be part of that social contract. "They leave Omelas; they walk ahead into the darkness and they do not come back."

10 In one reading this is a parable about exploitation. According to this reading, many of us live in societies whose prosperity depends on some faraway child in the basement. When we buy a cellphone or a piece of cheap clothing, there is some exploited worker—a child in the basement. We tolerate exploitation, telling each other that their misery is necessary for overall affluence, though maybe it's not.

In another reading, the story is a challenge to the utilitarian mind-set so prevalent today.

In theory, most of us subscribe to a set of values based on the idea that a human being is an end not a means. You can't justifiably use a human being as an object. It is wrong to enslave a person, even if that slavery might produce a large good. It is wrong to kill a person for his organs, even if many lives might be saved.

And yet we don't actually live according to that moral imperative. Life is filled with tragic trade-offs. In many different venues, the suffering of the few is justified by those trying to deliver the greatest good for the greatest number.

Companies succeed because they fire people, even if a whole family depends on them. Schools become prestigious because they reject people—even if they put a lifetime of work into their application. Leaders fighting a war on terror accidentally kill innocents. These are children in the basement of our survival and happiness.

15 The story compels readers to ask if they are willing to live according to those contracts. Some are not. They walk away from prosperity, and they make some radical commitment. They would rather work toward some inner purity.

The rest of us live with the trade-offs. The story reminds us of the inner numbing this creates. The people who stay in Omelas aren't bad; they just find it easier and easier to live with the misery they depend upon. I've found that this story rivets people because it confronts them with all the tragic compromises built into modern life—all the children in the basements—and, at the same time, it elicits some desire to struggle against bland acceptance of it all.

In another reading, the whole city of Omelas is just different pieces of one person's psychology, a person living in the busy modern world, and that person's idealism and moral sensitivity is the shriveling child locked in the basement.

[2015]

☰ THINKING ABOUT THE TEXT

1. Brooks claims that this parable is "a challenge to the utilitarian mind-set." What does this mean to you? Give some examples.
2. Brooks also thinks exploitation is a key idea in Le Guin's story. Explain how this might be the case, and give some examples from contemporary life.
3. Explain what Brooks means by "Life is filled with 'tragic trade-offs.'" Give some examples from recent events.
4. Give a brief summary of Brooks's next-to-last paragraph. Why do you think people are moved by this story? Do you know people who might "walk away" from Omelas? How would you describe them?
5. Explain Brooks's thought in the last paragraph. Give some concrete examples from your own life, your reading, or films you have seen.

☰ MAKING COMPARISONS

1. How does guilt figure in both texts? What is guilt, and where does it come from?
2. Compare the paragraph in the essay that begins, "the story compels readers . . ." with the last paragraph in the story. In what ways do you or don't you behave according to our current social contract?
3. How would you describe your response to both texts? Is there an emotional or intellectual difference?

JOHN R. EHRENFELD

The Error of Trying to Measure Good and Bad

John R. Ehrenfeld (b. 1931) is currently the executive director of the International Society of Industrial Ecology. He retired in 2000 as director of MIT's Program on Technology, Business and Environment. He received a doctorate in chemical engineering from MIT. He has published widely, focusing on sustainability and industrial ecology. Sustainability by Design *was published in 2009. His latest book is* Flourishing: A Frank Conversation about Sustainability *(with Andrew J. Hoffman, 2013). The following essay was posted on* Flourishing Design *on December 14, 2015.*

It's another David Brooks day. Today he is riffing on a story by Ursula Le Guin, "The Ones Who Walk Away from Omelas." In a nutshell, the tale is about a peaceful and happy city with an important open secret. Hidden away from the wandering eyes of the inhabitants is a closet containing a misfit. In Le Guin's words, "It is feebleminded. Perhaps it was born defective, or perhaps it has become imbecile through fear, malnutrition and neglect." On occasions this poor human being is revealed for all who wish to observe. Like many of her stories, this one is a parable on the way we love and should live. The misfit sops up all the ills of society so that everyone else can live a happy, uncluttered life. Most of the citizens, even knowing the plight of the misfit, ignore the unfairness and go back to life as usual. A few with a deeper moral sensitivity leave to face the unknown world beyond the walls.

Brooks makes the obvious comparison to our world today. The citizens of Omelas have made a social contract to single out someone to serve as the means of their prosperity. This is far from the theory of the social contract on which our society is based, as Brooks writes:

> In theory, most of us subscribe to a set of values based on the idea that a human being is an end not a means. You can't justifiably use a human being as an object. It is wrong to enslave a person, even if that slavery might produce a large good. It is wrong to kill a person for his organs, even if many lives might be saved.

I am not sure he is correct in assuming that "most of us subscribe to [such] a set of values." I suspect that a great majority of Americans have never heard of Kant's moral imperatives or keep the more familiar "golden rule" in reach of their consciousness. Given the practical rules of our society, these moral guiding principles may not even be present in their unconsciousness waiting to be invoked in problematic situations. Brooks notes that these practical rules are utilitarian in essence, replacing the inherent priceless nature of human life with a number that can fit an maximizing algorithm, like economists and technocrats use to make decisions. In his words:

> The story compels readers to ask if they are willing to live according to those contracts. Some are not. They walk away from prosperity, and they make some radical commitment. They would rather work toward some

> inner purity . . . The rest of us live with the trade-offs. The story reminds us of the inner numbing this creates. The people who stay in Omelas aren't bad; they just find it easier and easier to live with the misery they depend upon. I've found that this story rivets people because it confronts them with all the tragic compromises built into modern life—all the children in the basements—and, at the same time, it elicits some desire to struggle against bland acceptance of it all.

Whoa! I would say that those who stay in Omelas are, indeed, bad. It all depends on what standards of moral goodness is to be used. Brooks glosses over the distinctiveness of normative ethical theories, the different ways of morally justifying one's actions. As a result, he misses the main point of Le Guin's marvelous story. You can't have it both ways and live an uncluttered moral life. It's not the same as the utilitarian trade-offs that are part of that system of thought; it's the absolute choice between one moral system or another. I am certainly no moral philosopher, but I have come to know that consequentialism, where utilitarianism fits, is incompatible with deontology, where Kantianism sits. The first kind measures the goodness or badness of an act by the outcomes and permits the use of more or better as criteria to compare one act with another. Different theories use different sets of values as the basis for making comparative judgments.

Deontological theories are based on the idea of duties and rights and look at 5
the rightness of the act, itself, not the outcome of the act. Kant says it is wrong to treat a human as a means, instead of as an end, period. Rawls says we have a duty to do the right thing based on an process in which we are ignorant of the reality of the world out there. Simplistically, we might say, this class of theories deals with absolutes, the other with relative measures. When I discussed this editorial with my wife in midstream, she pointed out that Judaism is largely built on duty-based ethics, such as the one that has guided me for quite some time: acts of lovingkindness, often expressed as *tikkun olam* or healing the world.

In researching ethical theories today as I write this post, I noticed a third class of theories based on care. I suspect that much of my work to date on flourishing falls into this class since my concerns over care and interconnectedness fit into its framework that emphasizes interdependence and relationships. I will be looking at this in much more detail as I continue working on my current book.

Brooks's failure to see the moral problem faced by the citizens of Omelas as having to choose between categories of ethics is the same problem virtually all of us in the United States have. Our much revered founding fathers dumped us into a moral dilemma with the first public document we live by, The Declaration of Independence. The most well-known sentence is: "We hold these truths to be self-evident, that all men are created equal, that they are endowed by their Creator with certain unalienable Rights, that among these are Life, Liberty and the pursuit of Happiness."

The dilemma rests in the conflation of life, liberty and happiness. The first two are clearly absolute rights, except that philosophers argue about the meaning of liberty. Both call for a system of right-based principles. But the last, happiness, is not absolute. In fact, earlier drafts of the document used "property" instead. Further, economists have co-opted psychologists, and measure happiness in material terms. This outcome necessitates a consequentialist system. The dilemma was obvious from the get-go when human slaves were classed as property. We have ignored this dilemma right down to the present, as do the citizens of Omelas.

It is too easy, as Brooks does (see the above block quote) to excuse both the people of Omelas and us as not being bad because we have to become utilitarians to exist in this world. As utilitarians, trade-offs are simply means to maximize values, but one cannot trade-off the two distinct moral categories. As long as consequentialism dominates, as it does, we are indeed bad, and are always somewhere on a slippery slope. One cannot be just a little bad. It's very important to accept that. We can live and perhaps must live with our dilemma, but we must not brush it away. We do admit, if pushed, that our motor of utilitarianism, the free market, produces unfairness; that is, it is amoral in the rights and duties domains. But we do little these days to correct its ills. As Brooks notes, we have lots of misfits hidden away in closets.

What I miss in this column is a call to action; a challenge to see the bads in all 10
of us. Brooks ends with an enigmatic paragraph.

> In another reading, the whole city of Omelas is just different pieces of one person's psychology, a person living in the busy modern world, and that person's idealism and moral sensitivity is the shriveling child locked in the basement.

The use of the word, "just," is puzzling, suggesting that it's OK to carry around two opposing ideas. It is, rather, both OK and not OK, but merely is a reflection of the values of our present society. Few people, in my estimate based on watching the world around me everyday, have such a mixed "psychology." The clarity of deontology has been badly blurred by our utilitarian norm. Bad is just another value to be weighed against other things. Unfortunately, it has fallen far down the ladder. This is the scandal of our use of torture and other inhumane treatment. The absolute badness was measured and lost. Part of the story of flourishing I have been writing is that humans are fundamentally deontologists. We have certain rights and duties that cannot be weighed and exchanged. The centrality of care fits here. I have not stressed its moral nature, but will be doing this as I continue to think and write. I thank David Brooks for his provoking me once again. *[2015]*

≡ THINKING ABOUT THE TEXT

1. Why does Ehrenfeld claim that "those who stay in Omelas are, indeed, bad"? Why do you agree or disagree with him? What does he mean by "bad"?
2. Ehrenfeld seems to agree with Immanuel Kant's categorical imperative, a concept that asserts that we should behave as if our action were an absolute guide for all rational beings. Consequences are not considered; it is an absolute rule to be followed in all circumstances. How does Ehrenfeld agree with this idea? Do you? What might be some problems in following this principle?
3. According to Ehrenfeld, how does Brooks miss "the main point" of Le Guin's story?

4. Explain how Ehrenfeld's argument turns on the difference between the absolute and the relative. How does Ehrenfeld connect "torture and other inhumane treatment" with our current utilitarian norms?
5. What is the problem Ehrenfeld asserts that most of us have in America? What does it have to do with happiness?

MAKING COMPARISONS

1. How do Brooks and Ehrenfeld differ in their use of "bad"?
2. What does Ehrenfeld think the main point of the story is? What does Brooks think it is? What do you think it is?
3. Brooks suggests that we carry around opposing ideas. How might this be true for you? How does Ehrenfeld respond to this?

WRITING ABOUT THE ISSUES

1. Write an essay that argues that Le Guin's story is an apt allegory for a contemporary issue that needs to be changed. Include Ehrenfeld's idea about *tikkun*, or social justice.
2. Look up the connection between the idea for Le Guin's story and the American philosopher William James. Write a brief report commenting on the idea that in this tale, the narrator as well as the reader is on trial.
3. Write an essay that argues that one of the readings that Brooks suggests is a more fruitful way of seeing the story than the others. Give specific contemporary examples; include Ehrenfeld's perspective.
4. Brooks's piece elicited over five hundred responses from readers, some of whom remembered the story fondly from reading it in college forty years ago; others had not yet read it. Many saw Le Guin's parable in political terms, with Republicans believing that "we live in a world of terrible injustice," while Democrats believed that "injustice is terrible." One pessimistic observer thought the story suggested that many thousands of years from now, there will be two separate species of humanity so different from one another that they will be "incapable of breeding with each other." Find Brooks's essay and the readers' comments online. After reading through a few dozen, write a report of your observations. Assuming the comments are a fair sampling of the thinking of educated readers, what is your assessment of their responses to Le Guin's tale? Quote brief phrases from their letters in support of your judgment.

A Door to Freedom: Cultural Contexts for a Play

HENRIK IBSEN, *A Doll's House*

CULTURAL CONTEXTS:
HENRIK IBSEN, Memorandum

AUGUST STRINDBERG, "Woman in *A Doll's House*"

EMMA GOLDMAN, Review of *A Doll's House*

JOAN TEMPLETON, From *"The* Doll House *Backlash: Criticism, Feminism, and Ibsen"*

SUSANNA RUSTIN, "Why *A Doll's House* by Henrik Ibsen Is More Relevant Than Ever"

The writer and scientist Loren Eiseley notes that "to grow is a gain, an enlargement of life. . . . Yet it is also a departure." Eiseley's seems a more sophisticated idea than one portraying personal and social progress as only positive. Life is more complicated than that. Most of us eagerly anticipate becoming adults and embracing adult responsibilities and privileges. But our literature is filled with nostalgia for the innocence and wonder of childhood. We have a sense that we have lost something as our culture, technology, and lifestyles have advanced. There is no going back, but to some the old ways sometimes seem simpler. Our grandparents longed to leave the limitations of small-town life, but fifty years later their urban grandchildren idealize small communities. Women agonized over the legal and personal restrictions of Victorian marriages, but contemporary women understand that divorce is often painful and difficult. No reasonable thinker would want women to return to the childlike position that wives were expected to inhabit a hundred years ago, but that does not mean we cannot acknowledge that divorce often comes with a steep emotional and practical price.

It appears that Henrik Ibsen understood this when he wrote *A Doll's House* in 1879. It was an era of great political and social change, and Ibsen believed that writers could be instrumental in affecting the way people thought about the great issues of the day. His realistic problem plays confronted topical and controversial issues. Among the most debated was the status of women in society, especially their legal and emotional subjugation within marriage. To a contemporary audience, Nora, the main character of *A Doll's House*, is treated like a child. Although that disturbs most women today, Ibsen's female audience tended not to sympathize with Nora. The play's unsettling conclusion outraged most men. Changes in accepted thinking are always contested. But although most critics today see Ibsen as a social visionary who championed equality in marriage, he was not naive enough to think that great sacrifice and pain would not also accompany freedom and equality. The solution of one problem often creates new problems. When Nora begins to question the old ways, her future starts to grow uncertain. Knowing what she knows, can she really remain in a marriage that seems to her a cruel and unjust trap?

We have included several works that provide context for the play, but we have selected ones that focus especially on Nora. Over the past hundred years or so, Nora has been seen as either a villain or a hero, depending on the cultural context. If you support feminist ideals, you will probably see Nora in a positive light and support her dramatic departure as necessary and liberating. If you are not particularly sympathetic to feminist principles, you will most likely see Nora negatively and condemn her as vain, cruel, and self-centered. It would be unusual for a present-day critic not to empathize with Nora's plight, but that was clearly not always the case. Many critics early in the century and into the fifties and sixties were not at all sympathetic. Some were even hostile. Nora's situation may seem clearly unjust to a progressive twenty-first-century consciousness, but that was certainly not obvious to those in the past who saw her marriage as perfectly acceptable, normal, and desirable and her behavior as deceitful, abnormal, and neurotic. In many ways, we are all children of our time, subject to the prevailing thinking about relationships, marriage, gender equality, parental responsibility, and so on. Audiences in Ibsen's day were upset by *A Doll's House*. And if there is currently a consensus about the necessity of Nora's actions, that shift in perspective happened exceedingly slowly and incrementally.

BEFORE YOU READ

When do you think a woman can be justified in leaving her children? Why do you think equality is or is not necessary for love to exist in a marriage?

HENRIK IBSEN
A Doll's House

Translated by B. Farquharson Sharp

Henrik Ibsen (1828–1906) was born into a family with money in a small town in Norway, but his father soon went bankrupt. Ibsen later remembered this genteel poverty by writing about issues of social injustice that he experienced firsthand. At fifteen Ibsen was apprenticed to a pharmacist, a profession he had no interest in. He soon was drawn to the theater, working to establish a Norwegian national theater. But this led to frustration, and Ibsen spent almost thirty years in a self-imposed exile in Italy and Germany, where he wrote some of his most famous plays. Ibsen's plays are often performed today and still provoke controversy. They include Ghosts *(1881),* An Enemy of the People *(1882),* Hedda Gabler *(1890), and* When We Dead Awaken *(1899).*

DRAMATIS PERSONAE

TORVALD HELMER
NORA, *his wife*
DOCTOR RANK
MRS. LINDE

Mondadori Portfolio / Getty Images

NILS KROGSTAD
Helmer's three young children
ANNE, *their nurse*
A Housemaid
A Porter

SCENE: *The action takes place in Helmer's house.*

ACT I

SCENE: *A room furnished comfortably and tastefully, but not extravagantly. At the back, a door to the right leads to the entrance-hall, another to the left leads to Helmer's study. Between the doors stands a piano. In the middle of the left-hand wall is a door, and beyond it a window. Near the window are a round table, arm-chairs, and a small sofa. In the right-hand wall, at the farther end, another door; and on the same side, nearer the footlights, a stove, two easy chairs, and a rocking-chair; between the stove and the door, a small table. Engravings on the walls; a cabinet with china and other small objects; a small book-case with well-bound books. The floors are carpeted, and a fire burns in the stove. It is winter.*

A bell rings in the hall; shortly afterwards the door is heard to open. Enter Nora, humming a tune and in high spirits. She is in outdoor dress and carries a number of parcels; these she lays on the table to the right. She leaves the outer door open after her, and through it is seen a Porter who is carrying a Christmas Tree and a basket, which he gives to the Maid who has opened the door.

NORA: Hide the Christmas Tree carefully, Helen. Be sure the children do not see it until this evening, when it is dressed. (*To the Porter, taking out her purse.*) How much?

PORTER: Sixpence.

NORA: There is a shilling. No, keep the change. (*The Porter thanks her, and goes out. Nora shuts the door. She is laughing to herself, as she takes off her hat and coat. She takes a packet of macaroons from her pocket and eats one or two; then goes cautiously to her husband's door and listens.*) Yes, he is in. (*Still humming, she goes to the table on the right.*)

HELMER (*calls out from his room*): Is that my little lark twittering out there?

NORA (*busy opening some of the parcels*): Yes, it is!

HELMER: Is it my little squirrel bustling about?

NORA: Yes!

HELMER: When did my squirrel come home?

NORA: Just now. (*Puts the bag of macaroons into her pocket and wipes her mouth.*) Come in here, Torvald, and see what I have bought.

HELMER: Don't disturb me. (*A little later, he opens the door and looks into the room, pen in hand.*) Bought, did you say? All these things? Has my little spendthrift been wasting money again?

NORA: Yes but, Torvald, this year we really can let ourselves go a little. This is the first Christmas that we have not needed to economise.

HELMER: Still, you know, we can't spend money recklessly.

NORA: Yes, Torvald, we may be a wee bit more reckless now, mayn't we? Just a tiny wee bit! You are going to have a big salary and earn lots and lots of money.

HELMER: Yes, after the New Year; but then it will be a whole quarter before the salary is due.

NORA: Pooh! we can borrow until then.

HELMER: Nora! (*Goes up to her and takes her playfully by the ear.*) The same little featherhead! Suppose, now, that I borrowed fifty pounds to-day, and you spent it all in the Christmas week, and then on New Year's Eve a slate fell on my head and killed me, and—

NORA (*putting her hands over his mouth*): Oh! don't say such horrid things.

HELMER: Still, suppose that happened,—what then?

NORA: If that were to happen, I don't suppose I should care whether I owed money or not.

HELMER: Yes, but what about the people who had lent it?

NORA: They? Who would bother about them? I should not know who they were.

HELMER: That is like a woman! But seriously, Nora, you know what I think about that. No debt, no borrowing. There can be no freedom or beauty about a home life that depends on borrowing and debt. We two have kept bravely on the straight road so far, and we will go on the same way for the short time longer that there need be any struggle.

NORA (*moving towards the stove*): As you please, Torvald.

HELMER (*following her*): Come, come, my little skylark must not droop her wings. What is this! Is my little squirrel out of temper? (*Taking out his purse.*) Nora, what do you think I have got here?

NORA (*turning round quickly*): Money!

HELMER: There you are. (*Gives her some money.*) Do you think I don't know what a lot is wanted for housekeeping at Christmas-time?

NORA (*counting*): Ten shillings—a pound—two pounds! Thank you, thank you, Torvald; that will keep me going for a long time.

HELMER: Indeed it must.

NORA: Yes, yes, it will. But come here and let me show you what I have bought. And all so cheap! Look, here is a new suit for Ivar, and a sword; and a horse and a trumpet for Bob; and a doll and dolly's bedstead for Emmy,—they are very plain, but anyway she will soon break them in pieces. And here are dress-lengths and handkerchiefs for the maids; old Anne ought really to have something better.

HELMER: And what is in this parcel?

NORA (*crying out*): No, no! you mustn't see that until this evening.

HELMER: Very well. But now tell me, you extravagant little person, what would you like for yourself ?

NORA: For myself ? Oh, I am sure I don't want anything.

HELMER: Yes, but you must. Tell me something reasonable that you would particularly like to have.

NORA: No, I really can't think of anything—unless, Torvald—

HELMER: Well?

NORA (*playing with his coat buttons, and without raising her eyes to his*): If you really want to give me something, you might—you might—

HELMER: Well, out with it!

NORA (*speaking quickly*): You might give me money, Torvald. Only just as much as you can afford; and then one of these days I will buy something with it.

HELMER: But, Nora—

NORA: Oh, do! dear Torvald; please, please do! Then I will wrap it up in beautiful gilt paper and hang it on the Christmas Tree. Wouldn't that be fun?

HELMER: What are little people called that are always wasting money?

NORA: Spendthrifts—I know. Let us do as you suggest, Torvald, and then I shall have time to think what I am most in want of. That is a very sensible plan, isn't it?

HELMER (*smiling*): Indeed it is—that is to say, if you were really to save out of the money I give you, and then really buy something for yourself. But if you spend it all on the housekeeping and any number of unnecessary things, then I merely have to pay up again.

NORA: Oh but, Torvald—

HELMER: You can't deny it, my dear little Nora. (*Puts his arm round her waist.*) It's a sweet little spendthrift, but she uses up a deal of money. One would hardly believe how expensive such little persons are!

NORA: It's a shame to say that. I do really save all I can.

HELMER (*laughing*): That's very true,—all you can. But you can't save anything!

NORA (*smiling quietly and happily*): You haven't any idea how many expenses we skylarks and squirrels have, Torvald.

HELMER: You are an odd little soul. Very like your father. You always find some new way of wheedling money out of me, and, as soon as you have got it, it seems to melt in your hands. You never know where it has gone. Still, one must take you as you are. It is in the blood; for indeed it is true that you can inherit these things, Nora.

NORA: Ah, I wish I had inherited many of papa's qualities.

HELMER: And I would not wish you to be anything but just what you are, my sweet little skylark. But, do you know, it strikes me that you are looking rather—what shall I say—rather uneasy today?

NORA: Do I?

HELMER: You do, really. Look straight at me.

NORA (*looks at him*): Well?

HELMER (*wagging his finger at her*): Hasn't Miss Sweet Tooth been breaking rules in town today?

NORA: No; what makes you think that?

HELMER: Hasn't she paid a visit to the confectioner's?

NORA: No, I assure you, Torvald—

HELMER: Not been nibbling sweets?

NORA: No, certainly not.

HELMER: Not even taken a bite at a macaroon or two?

NORA: No, Torvald, I assure you really—

HELMER: There, there, of course I was only joking.

NORA (*going to the table on the right*): I should not think of going against your wishes.

HELMER: No, I am sure of that; besides, you gave me your word—(*Going up to her.*) Keep your little Christmas secrets to yourself, my darling. They will all be revealed to-night when the Christmas Tree is lit, no doubt.

NORA: Did you remember to invite Doctor Rank?

HELMER: No. But there is no need; as a matter of course he will come to dinner with us. However, I will ask him when he comes in this morning. I have ordered some good wine. Nora, you can't think how I am looking forward to this evening.

NORA: So am I! And how the children will enjoy themselves, Torvald!

HELMER: It is splendid to feel that one has a perfectly safe appointment, and a big enough income. It's delightful to think of, isn't it?

NORA: It's wonderful!

HELMER: Do you remember last Christmas? For a full three weeks beforehand you shut yourself up every evening until long after midnight, making ornaments for the Christmas Tree, and all the other fine things that were to be a surprise to us. It was the dullest three weeks I ever spent!

NORA: I didn't find it dull.

HELMER (*smiling*): But there was precious little result, Nora.

NORA: Oh, you shouldn't tease me about that again. How could I help the cat's going in and tearing everything to pieces?

HELMER: Of course you couldn't, poor little girl. You had the best of intentions to please us all, and that's the main thing. But it is a good thing that our hard times are over.

NORA: Yes, it is really wonderful.

HELMER: This time I needn't sit here and be dull all alone, and you needn't ruin your dear eyes and your pretty little hands—

NORA (*clapping her hands*): No, Torvald, I needn't any longer, need I! It's wonderfully lovely to hear you say so! (*Taking his arm.*) Now I will tell you how I have been thinking we ought to arrange things, Torvald. As soon as Christmas is over—(*A bell rings in the hall.*) There's the bell. (*She tidies the room a little.*) There's some one at the door. What a nuisance!

HELMER: If it is a caller, remember I am not at home.

MAID (*in the doorway*): A lady to see you, ma'am,—a stranger.

NORA: Ask her to come in.

MAID (*to Helmer*): The doctor came at the same time, sir.

HELMER: Did he go straight into my room?

MAID: Yes, sir.

Helmer goes into his room. The Maid ushers in Mrs. Linde, who is in travelling dress, and shuts the door.

MRS. LINDE (*in a dejected and timid voice*): How do you do, Nora?

NORA (*doubtfully*): How do you do—

MRS. LINDE: You don't recognise me, I suppose.

NORA: No, I don't know—yes, to be sure, I seem to—(*Suddenly.*) Yes! Christine! Is it really you?

MRS. LINDE: Yes, it is I.

NORA: Christine! To think of my not recognising you! And yet how could I—(*In a gentle voice.*) How you have altered, Christine!

MRS. LINDE: Yes, I have indeed. In nine, ten long years—

NORA: Is it so long since we met? I suppose it is. The last eight years have been a happy time for me, I can tell you. And so now you have come into the town, and have taken this long journey in winter—that was plucky of you.

MRS. LINDE: I arrived by steamer this morning.

NORA: To have some fun at Christmas-time, of course. How delightful! We will have such fun together! But take off your things. You are not cold, I hope. (*Helps her.*) Now we will sit down by the stove, and be cosy. No, take this armchair; I will sit here in the rocking-chair. (*Takes her hands.*) Now you look like your old self again; it was only the first moment—You are a little paler, Christine, and perhaps a little thinner.

MRS. LINDE: And much, much older, Nora.

NORA: Perhaps a little older; very, very little; certainly not much. (*Stops suddenly and speaks seriously.*) What a thoughtless creature I am, chattering away like this. My poor, dear Christine, do forgive me.

MRS. LINDE: What do you mean, Nora?

NORA (*gently*): Poor Christine, you are a widow.

MRS. LINDE: Yes; it is three years ago now.

NORA: Yes, I knew; I saw it in the papers. I assure you, Christine, I meant ever so often to write to you at the time, but I always put it off and something always prevented me.

MRS. LINDE: I quite understand, dear.

NORA: It was very bad of me, Christine. Poor thing, how you must have suffered. And he left you nothing?

MRS. LINDE: No.

NORA: And no children?

MRS. LINDE: No.

NORA: Nothing at all, then.

MRS. LINDE: Not even any sorrow or grief to live upon.

NORA (*looking incredulously at her*): But, Christine, is that possible?

MRS. LINDE (*smiles sadly and strokes her hair*): It sometimes happens, Nora.

NORA: So you are quite alone. How dreadfully sad that must be. I have three lovely children. You can't see them just now, for they are out with their nurse. But now you must tell me all about it.

MRS. LINDE: No, no; I want to hear about you.

NORA: No, you must begin. I mustn't be selfish today; today I must only think of your affairs. But there is one thing I must tell you. Do you know we have just had a great piece of good luck?

MRS. LINDE: No, what is it?

NORA: Just fancy, my husband has been made manager of the Bank!

MRS. LINDE: Your husband? What good luck!

NORA: Yes, tremendous! A barrister's profession is such an uncertain thing, especially if he won't undertake unsavoury cases; and naturally Torvald has never been willing to do that, and I quite agree with him. You may imagine how pleased we are! He is to take up his work in the Bank at the New Year, and then he will have a big salary and lots of commissions. For the future we can live quite differently — we can do just as we like. I feel so relieved and so happy, Christine! It will be splendid to have heaps of money and not need to have any anxiety, won't it?

MRS. LINDE: Yes, anyhow I think it would be delightful to have what one needs.

NORA: No, not only what one needs, but heaps and heaps of money.

MRS. LINDE (*smiling*): Nora, Nora, haven't you learned sense yet? In our schooldays you were a great spendthrift.

NORA (*laughing*): Yes, that is what Torvald says now. (*Wags her finger at her.*) But "Nora, Nora" is not so silly as you think. We have not been in a position for me to waste money. We have both had to work.

MRS. LINDE: You too?

NORA: Yes; odds and ends, needlework, crotchet-work, embroidery, and that kind of thing. (*Dropping her voice.*) And other things as well. You know Torvald left his office when we were married? There was no prospect of promotion there, and he had to try and earn more than before. But during the first year he over-worked himself dreadfully. You see, he had to make money every way he could, and he worked early and late; but he couldn't stand it, and fell dreadfully ill, and the doctors said it was necessary for him to go south.

MRS. LINDE: You spent a whole year in Italy, didn't you?

NORA: Yes. It was no easy matter to get away, I can tell you. It was just after Ivar was born; but naturally we had to go. It was a wonderfully beautiful journey, and it saved Torvald's life. But it cost a tremendous lot of money, Christine.

MRS. LINDE: So I should think.

NORA: It cost about two hundred and fifty pounds. That's a lot, isn't it?

MRS. LINDE: Yes, and in emergencies like that it is lucky to have the money.

NORA: I ought to tell you that we had it from papa.

MRS. LINDE: Oh, I see. It was just about that time that he died, wasn't it?

NORA: Yes; and, just think of it, I couldn't go and nurse him. I was expecting little Ivar's birth every day and I had my poor sick Torvald to look after. My dear, kind father—I never saw him again, Christine. That was the saddest time I have known since our marriage.

MRS. LINDE: I know how fond you were of him. And then you went off to Italy?

NORA: Yes; you see we had money then, and the doctors insisted on our going, so we started a month later.

MRS. LINDE: And your husband came back quite well?

NORA: As sound as a bell!

MRS. LINDE: But—the doctor?

NORA: What doctor?

MRS. LINDE: I thought your maid said the gentleman who arrived here just as I did, was the doctor?

NORA: Yes, that was Doctor Rank, but he doesn't come here professionally. He is our greatest friend, and comes in at least once everyday. No, Torvald has not had an hour's illness since then, and our children are strong and healthy and so am I. (*Jumps up and claps her hands.*) Christine! Christine! it's good to be alive and happy!—But how horrid of me; I am talking of nothing but my own affairs. (*Sits on a stool near her, and rests her arms on her knees.*) You mustn't be angry with me. Tell me, is it really true that you did not love your husband? Why did you marry him?

MRS. LINDE: My mother was alive then, and was bedridden and helpless, and I had to provide for my two younger brothers; so I did not think I was justified in refusing his offer.

NORA: No, perhaps you were quite right. He was rich at that time, then?

MRS. LINDE: I believe he was quite well off. But his business was a precarious one; and, when he died, it all went to pieces and there was nothing left.

NORA: And then?—

MRS. LINDE: Well, I had to turn my hand to anything I could find—first a small shop, then a small school, and so on. The last three years have seemed like one long working-day, with no rest. Now it is at an end, Nora. My poor mother needs me no more, for she is gone; and the boys do not need me either; they have got situations and can shift for themselves.

NORA: What a relief you must feel it—

MRS. LINDE: No, indeed; I only feel my life unspeakably empty. No one to live for anymore. (*Gets up restlessly.*) That was why I could not stand the life in my little backwater any longer. I hope it may be easier here to find something which will busy me and occupy my thoughts. If only I could have the good luck to get some regular work — office work of some kind —

NORA: But, Christine, that is so frightfully tiring, and you look tired out now. You had far better go away to some watering-place.

MRS. LINDE (*walking to the window*): I have no father to give me money for a journey, Nora.

NORA (*rising*): Oh, don't be angry with me!

MRS. LINDE (*going up to her*): It is you that must not be angry with me, dear. The worst of a position like mine is that it makes one so bitter. No one to work for, and yet obliged to be always on the lookout for chances. One must live, and so one becomes selfish. When you told me of the happy turn your fortunes have taken — you will hardly believe it — I was delighted not so much on your account as on my own.

NORA: How do you mean? — Oh, I understand. You mean that perhaps Torvald could get you something to do.

MRS. LINDE: Yes, that was what I was thinking of.

NORA: He must, Christine. Just leave it to me; I will broach the subject very cleverly — I will think of something that will please him very much. It will make me so happy to be of some use to you.

MRS. LINDE: How kind you are, Nora, to be so anxious to help me! It is doubly kind in you, for you know so little of the burdens and troubles of life.

NORA: I — ? I know so little of them?

MRS. LINDE (*smiling*): My dear! Small household cares and that sort of thing! — You are a child, Nora.

NORA (*tosses her head and crosses the stage*): You ought not to be so superior.

MRS. LINDE: No?

NORA: You are just like the others. They all think that I am incapable of anything really serious —

MRS. LINDE: Come, come —

NORA: — that I have gone through nothing in this world of cares.

MRS. LINDE: But, my dear Nora, you have just told me all your troubles.

NORA: Pooh! — those were trifles. (*Lowering her voice.*) I have not told you the important thing.

MRS. LINDE: The important thing? What do you mean?

NORA: You look down upon me altogether, Christine — but you ought not to. You are proud, aren't you, of having worked so hard and so long for your mother?

MRS. LINDE: Indeed, I don't look down on anyone. But it is true that I am both proud and glad to think that I was privileged to make the end of my mother's life almost free from care.

NORA: And you are proud to think of what you have done for your brothers?

MRS. LINDE: I think I have the right to be.

NORA: I think so, too. But now, listen to this; I too have something to be proud and glad of.

MRS. LINDE: I have no doubt you have. But what do you refer to?

NORA: Speak low. Suppose Torvald were to hear! He mustn't on any account — no one in the world must know, Christine, except you.

MRS. LINDE: But what is it?

NORA: Come here. (*Pulls her down on the sofa beside her.*) Now I will show you that I too have something to be proud and glad of. It was I who saved Torvald's life.

MRS. LINDE: "Saved"? How?

NORA: I told you about our trip to Italy. Torvald would never have recovered if he had not gone there—

MRS. LINDE: Yes, but your father gave you the necessary funds.

NORA (*smiling*): Yes, that is what Torvald and all the others think, but—

MRS. LINDE: But—

NORA: Papa didn't give us a shilling. It was I who procured the money.

MRS. LINDE: You? All that large sum?

NORA: Two hundred and fifty pounds. What do you think of that?

MRS. LINDE: But, Nora, how could you possibly do it? Did you win a prize in the Lottery?

NORA (*contemptuously*): In the Lottery? There would have been no credit in that.

MRS. LINDE: But where did you get it from, then?

NORA (*humming and smiling with an air of mystery*): Hm, hm! Aha!

MRS. LINDE: Because you couldn't have borrowed it.

NORA: Couldn't I? Why not?

MRS. LINDE: No, a wife cannot borrow without her husband's consent.

NORA (*tossing her head*): Oh, if it is a wife who has any head for business—a wife who has the wit to be a little bit clever—

MRS. LINDE: I don't understand it at all, Nora.

NORA: There is no need you should. I never said I had borrowed the money. I may have got it some other way. (*Lies back on the sofa.*) Perhaps I got it from some other admirer. When anyone is as attractive as I am—

MRS. LINDE: You are a mad creature.

NORA: Now, you know you're full of curiosity, Christine.

MRS. LINDE: Listen to me, Nora dear. Haven't you been a little bit imprudent?

NORA (*sits up straight*): Is it imprudent to save your husband's life?

MRS. LINDE: It seems to me imprudent, without his knowledge, to—

NORA: But it was absolutely necessary that he should not know! My goodness, can't you understand that? It was necessary he should have no idea what a dangerous condition he was in. It was to me that the doctors came and said that his life was in danger, and that the only thing to save him was to live in the south. Do you suppose I didn't try, first of all, to get what I wanted as if it were for myself? I told him how much I should love to travel abroad like other young wives; I tried tears and entreaties with him; I told him that he ought to remember the condition I was in, and that he ought to be kind and indulgent to me; I even hinted that he might raise a loan. That nearly made him angry, Christine. He said I was thoughtless, and that it was his duty as my husband not to indulge me in my whims and caprices—as I believe he called them. Very well, I thought, you must be saved—and that was how I came to devise a way out of the difficulty—

MRS. LINDE: And did your husband never get to know from your father that the money had not come from him?

NORA: No, never. Papa died just at that time. I had meant to let him into the secret and beg him never to reveal it. But he was so ill then—alas, there never was any need to tell him.

MRS. LINDE: And since then have you never told your secret to your husband?

NORA: Good Heavens, no! How could you think so? A man who has such strong opinions about these things! And besides, how painful and humiliating it would be for Torvald, with his manly independence, to know that he owed me anything! It would upset our mutual relations altogether; our beautiful happy home would no longer be what it is now.

MRS. LINDE: Do you mean never to tell him about it?

NORA (*meditatively, and with a half smile*): Yes—someday, perhaps, after many years, when I am no longer as nice-looking as I am now. Don't laugh at me! I mean, of course, when Torvald is no longer as devoted to me as he is now; when my dancing and dressing-up and reciting have palled on him; then it may be a good thing to have something in reserve—(*Breaking off.*) What nonsense! That time will never come. Now, what do you think of my great secret, Christine? Do you still think I am of no use? I can tell you, too, that this affair has caused me a lot of worry. It has been by no means easy for me to meet my engagements punctually. I may tell you that there is something that is called, in business, quarterly interest, and another thing called payment in installments, and it is always so dreadfully difficult to manage them. I have had to save a little here and there, where I could, you understand. I have not been able to put aside much from my housekeeping money, for Torvald must have a good table. I couldn't let my children be shabbily dressed; I have felt obliged to use up all he gave me for them, the sweet little darlings!

MRS. LINDE: So it has all had to come out of your own necessaries of life, poor Nora?

NORA: Of course. Besides, I was the one responsible for it. Whenever Torvald has given me money for new dresses and such things, I have never spent more than half of it; I have always bought the simplest and cheapest things. Thank Heaven, any clothes look well on me, and so Torvald has never noticed it. But it was often very hard on me, Christine—because it is delightful to be really well dressed, isn't it?

MRS. LINDE: Quite so.

NORA: Well, then I have found other ways of earning money. Last winter I was lucky enough to get a lot of copying to do; so I locked myself up and sat writing every evening until quite late at night. Many a time I was desperately tired; but all the same it was a tremendous pleasure to sit there working and earning money. It was like being a man.

MRS. LINDE: How much have you been able to pay off in that way?

NORA: I can't tell you exactly. You see, it is very difficult to keep an account of a business matter of that kind. I only know that I have paid every penny that I could scrape together. Many a time I was at my wits' end. (*Smiles.*) Then I used to sit here and imagine that a rich old gentleman had fallen in love with me—

MRS. LINDE: What! Who was it?

NORA: Be quiet!—that he had died; and that when his will was opened it contained, written in big letters, the instruction: "The lovely Mrs. Nora Helmer is to have all I possess paid over to her at once in cash."

MRS. LINDE: But, my dear Nora—who could the man be?

NORA: Good gracious, can't you understand? There was no old gentleman at all; it was only something that I used to sit here and imagine, when I couldn't think of any way of procuring money. But it's all the same now; the tiresome old person can stay where he is, as far as I am concerned; I don't care about him or his will either, for I am free from care now. (*Jumps up.*) My goodness, it's delightful to think of, Christine! Free from care! To be able to be free from care, quite free from care; to be able to play and romp with the children; to be able to keep the house beautifully and have everything just as Torvald likes it! And, think of it, soon the spring will come and the big blue sky! Perhaps we shall be able to take a little trip—perhaps I shall see the sea again! Oh, it's a wonderful thing to be alive and be happy. (*A bell is heard in the hall.*)

MRS. LINDE (*rising*): There is the bell; perhaps I had better go.

NORA: No, don't go; no one will come in here; it is sure to be for Torvald.

SERVANT (*at the hall door*): Excuse me, ma'am—there is a gentleman to see the master, and as the doctor is with him—

NORA: Who is it?

KROGSTAD (*at the door*): It is I, Mrs. Helmer (*Mrs. Linde starts, trembles, and turns to the window.*)

NORA (*takes a step towards him, and speaks in a strained, low voice*): You? What is it? What do you want to see my husband about?

KROGSTAD: Bank business—in a way. I have a small post in the Bank, and I hear your husband is to be our chief now—

NORA: Then it is—

KROGSTAD: Nothing but dry business matters, Mrs. Helmer; absolutely nothing else.

NORA: Be so good as to go into the study, then. (*She bows indifferently to him and shuts the door into the hall; then comes back and makes up the fire in the stove.*)

MRS. LINDE: Nora—who was that man?

NORA: A lawyer, of the name of Krogstad.

MRS. LINDE: Then it really was he.

NORA: Do you know the man?

MRS. LINDE: I used to—many years ago. At one time he was a solicitor's clerk in our town.

NORA: Yes, he was.

MRS. LINDE: He is greatly altered.

NORA: He made a very unhappy marriage.

MRS. LINDE: He is a widower now, isn't he?

NORA: With several children. There now, it is burning up. (*Shuts the door of the stove and moves the rocking-chair aside.*)

MRS. LINDE: They say he carries on various kinds of business.

NORA: Really! Perhaps he does; I don't know anything about it. But don't let us think of business; it is so tiresome.

DOCTOR RANK (*comes out of Helmer's study. Before he shuts the door he calls to him*): No, my dear fellow, I won't disturb you; I would rather go in to your wife for a little while. (*Shuts the door and sees Mrs. Linde.*) I beg your pardon; I am afraid I am disturbing you too.

NORA: No, not at all. (*Introducing him.*) Doctor Rank, Mrs. Linde.

RANK: I have often heard Mrs. Linde's name mentioned here. I think I passed you on the stairs when I arrived, Mrs. Linde?

MRS. LINDE: Yes, I go up very slowly; I can't manage stairs well.

RANK: Ah! some slight internal weakness?

MRS. LINDE: No, the fact is I have been overworking myself.

RANK: Nothing more than that? Then I suppose you have come to town to amuse yourself with our entertainments?

MRS. LINDE: I have come to look for work.

RANK: Is that a good cure for overwork?

MRS. LINDE: One must live, Doctor Rank.

RANK: Yes, the general opinion seems to be that it is necessary.

NORA: Look here, Doctor Rank—you know you want to live.

RANK: Certainly. However wretched I may feel, I want to prolong the agony as long as possible. All my patients are like that. And so are those who are morally diseased; one of them, and a bad case too, is at this very moment with Helmer—

MRS. LINDE (*sadly*): Ah!

NORA: Whom do you mean?

RANK: A lawyer of the name of Krogstad, a fellow you don't know at all. He suffers from a diseased moral character, Mrs. Helmer; but even he began talking of its being highly important that he should live.

NORA: Did he? What did he want to speak to Torvald about?

RANK: I have no idea; I only heard that it was something about the Bank.

NORA: I didn't know this—what's his name—Krogstad had anything to do with the Bank.

RANK: Yes, he has some sort of appointment there. (*To Mrs. Linde.*) I don't know whether you find also in your part of the world that there are certain people who go zealously snuffing about to smell out moral corruption, and, as soon as they have found some, put the person concerned into some lucrative position where they can keep their eye on him. Healthy natures are left out in the cold.

MRS. LINDE: Still I think the sick are those who most need taking care of.

RANK (*shrugging his shoulders*): Yes, there you are. That is the sentiment that is turning Society into a sick-house.

Nora, who has been absorbed in her thoughts, breaks out into smothered laughter and claps her hands.

RANK: Why do you laugh at that? Have you any notion what Society really is?

NORA: What do I care about tiresome Society? I am laughing at something quite different, something extremely amusing. Tell me, Doctor Rank, are all the people who are employed in the Bank dependent on Torvald now?

RANK: Is that what you find so extremely amusing?

NORA (*smiling and humming*): That's my affair! (*Walking about the room.*) It's perfectly glorious to think that we have—that Torvald has so much power over so many people. (*Takes the packet from her pocket.*) Doctor Rank, what do you say to a macaroon?

RANK: What, macaroons? I thought they were forbidden here.

NORA: Yes, but these are some Christine gave me.

MRS. LINDE: What! I?—

NORA: Oh, well, don't be alarmed! You couldn't know that Torvald had forbidden them. I must tell you that he is afraid they will spoil my teeth. But, bah!—once in a way—That's so, isn't it, Doctor Rank? By your leave! (*Puts a macaroon into his mouth.*) You must have one too, Christine. And I shall have one, just a little one—or at most two. (*Walking about.*) I am tremendously happy. There is just one thing in the world now that I should dearly love to do.

RANK: Well, what is that?

NORA: It's something I should dearly love to say, if Torvald could hear me.

RANK: Well, why can't you say it?

NORA: No, I daren't; it's so shocking.

MRS. LINDE: Shocking?

RANK: Well, I should not advise you to say it. Still, with us you might. What is it you would so much like to say if Torvald could hear you?

NORA: I should just love to say—Well, I'm damned!

RANK: Are you mad?

MRS. LINDE: Nora, dear—!

RANK: Say it, here he is!

NORA (*hiding the packet*): Hush! Hush! Hush! (*Helmer comes out of his room, with his coat over his arm and his hat in his hand.*)

NORA: Well, Torvald dear, have you got rid of him?

HELMER: Yes, he has just gone.

NORA: Let me introduce you—this is Christine, who has come to town.

HELMER: Christine—? Excuse me, but I don't know—

NORA: Mrs. Linde, dear; Christine Linde.

HELMER: Of course. A school friend of my wife's, I presume?

MRS. LINDE: Yes, we have known each other since then.

NORA: And just think, she has taken a long journey in order to see you.

HELMER: What do you mean?

MRS. LINDE: No, really, I—

NORA: Christine is tremendously clever at book-keeping, and she is frightfully anxious to work under some clever man, so as to perfect herself—

HELMER: Very sensible, Mrs. Linde.

NORA: And when she heard you had been appointed manager of the Bank—the news was telegraphed, you know—she travelled here as quick as she could. Torvald, I am sure you will be able to do something for Christine, for my sake, won't you?

HELMER: Well, it is not altogether impossible. I presume you are a widow, Mrs. Linde?

MRS. LINDE: Yes.

HELMER: And have had some experience of book-keeping?

MRS. LINDE: Yes, a fair amount.

HELMER: Ah! well, it's very likely I may be able to find something for you—

NORA (*clapping her hands*): What did I tell you? What did I tell you?

HELMER: You have just come at a fortunate moment, Mrs. Linde.

MRS. LINDE: How am I to thank you?

HELMER: There is no need. (*Puts on his coat.*) But to-day you must excuse me—

RANK: Wait a minute; I will come with you. (*Brings his fur coat from the hall and warms it at the fire.*)

NORA: Don't be long away, Torvald dear.

HELMER: About an hour, not more.

NORA: Are you going too, Christine?

MRS. LINDE (*putting on her cloak*): Yes, I must go and look for a room.

HELMER: Oh, well then, we can walk down the street together.

NORA (*helping her*): What a pity it is we are so short of space here; I am afraid it is impossible for us—

MRS. LINDE: Please don't think of it! Good-bye, Nora dear, and many thanks.

NORA: Good-bye for the present. Of course you will come back this evening. And you too, Dr. Rank. What do you say? If you are well enough? Oh, you must be! Wrap yourself up well. (*They go to the door all talking together. Children's voices are heard on the staircase.*)

NORA: There they are! There they are! (*She runs to open the door. The Nurse comes in with the children.*) Come in! Come in! (*Stoops and kisses them.*) Oh, you sweet blessings! Look at them, Christine! Aren't they darlings?

RANK: Don't let us stand here in the draught.

HELMER: Come along, Mrs. Linde; the place will only be bearable for a mother now!

Rank, Helmer, and Mrs. Linde go downstairs. The Nurse comes forward with the children; Nora shuts the hall door.

NORA: How fresh and well you look! Such red cheeks like apples and roses. (*The children all talk at once while she speaks to them.*) Have you had great fun? That's splendid! What, you pulled both Emmy and Bob along on the sledge?—both at once?—that was good. You are a clever boy, Ivar. Let me take her for a little, Anne. My sweet little baby doll! (*Takes the baby from the Maid and dances it up and down.*) Yes, yes, mother will dance with Bob too. What! Have you been snowballing? I wish I had been there too! No, no, I will take their things off, Anne; please let me do it, it is such fun. Go in now, you look half frozen. There is some hot coffee for you on the stove.

The Nurse goes into the room on the left. Nora takes off the children's things and throws them about, while they all talk to her at once.

NORA: Really! Did a big dog run after you? But it didn't bite you? No, dogs don't bite nice little dolly children. You mustn't look at the parcels, Ivar. What are they? Ah, I daresay you would like to know. No, no—it's something nasty! Come, let us have a game! What shall we play at? Hide and Seek? Yes, we'll play Hide and Seek. Bob shall hide first. Must I hide? Very well, I'll hide first. (*She and the children laugh and shout, and romp in and out of the room; at last Nora hides under the table, the children rush in and out for her, but do not see her; they hear her smothered laughter, run to the table, lift up the cloth and find her. Shouts of laughter. She crawls forward and pretends to frighten them. Fresh laughter. Meanwhile there has been a knock at the hall door, but none of them has noticed it. The door is half opened, and Krogstad appears. He waits a little; the game goes on.*)

KROGSTAD: Excuse me, Mrs. Helmer.

NORA (*with a stifled cry, turns round and gets up on to her knees*): Ah! what do you want?

KROGSTAD: Excuse me, the outer door was ajar; I suppose someone forgot to shut it.

NORA (*rising*): My husband is out, Mr. Krogstad.

KROGSTAD: I know that.

NORA: What do you want here, then?

KROGSTAD: A word with you.

NORA: With me?—(*To the children, gently.*) Go in to nurse. What? No, the strange man won't do mother any harm. When he has gone we will have another game. (*She takes the children into the room on the left, and shuts the door after them.*) You want to speak to me?

KROGSTAD: Yes, I do.

NORA: To-day? It is not the first of the month yet.

KROGSTAD: No, it is Christmas Eve, and it will depend on yourself what sort of a Christmas you will spend.

NORA: What do you mean? To-day it is absolutely impossible for me—

KROGSTAD: We won't talk about that until later on. This is something different. I presume you can give me a moment?

NORA: Yes—yes, I can—although—

KROGSTAD: Good. I was in Olsen's Restaurant and saw your husband going down the street—

NORA: Yes?

KROGSTAD: With a lady.

NORA: What then?

KROGSTAD: May I make so bold as to ask if it was a Mrs. Linde?

NORA: It was.

KROGSTAD: Just arrived in town?

NORA: Yes, to-day.

KROGSTAD: She is a great friend of yours, isn't she?

NORA: She is. But I don't see—

KROGSTAD: I knew her too, once upon a time.

NORA: I am aware of that.

KROGSTAD: Are you? So you know all about it; I thought as much. Then I can ask you, without beating about the bush—is Mrs. Linde to have an appointment in the Bank?

NORA: What right have you to question me, Mr. Krogstad?—You, one of my husband's subordinates! But since you ask, you shall know. Yes, Mrs. Linde *is* to have an appointment. And it was I who pleaded her cause, Mr. Krogstad, let me tell you that.

KROGSTAD: I was right in what I thought, then.

NORA (*walking up and down the stage*): Sometimes one has a tiny little bit of influence, I should hope. Because one is a woman, it does not necessarily follow that—. When anyone is in a subordinate position, Mr. Krogstad, they should really be careful to avoid offending anyone who—who—

KROGSTAD: Who has influence?

NORA: Exactly.

KROGSTAD (*changing his tone*): Mrs. Helmer, you will be so good as to use your influence on my behalf.

NORA: What? What do you mean?

KROGSTAD: You will be so kind as to see that I am allowed to keep my subordinate position in the Bank.

NORA: What do you mean by that? Who proposes to take your post away from you?

KROGSTAD: Oh, there is no necessity to keep up the pretence of ignorance. I can quite understand that your friend is not very anxious to expose herself to the chance of rubbing shoulders with me; and I quite understand, too, whom I have to thank for being turned off.

NORA: But I assure you—

KROGSTAD: Very likely; but, to come to the point, the time has come when I should advise you to use your influence to prevent that.

NORA: But, Mr. Krogstad, I *have* no influence.

KROGSTAD: Haven't you? I thought you said yourself just now—

NORA: Naturally I did not mean you to put that construction on it. What should make you think I have any influence of that kind with my husband?

KROGSTAD: Oh, I have known your husband from our student days. I don't suppose he is any more unassailable than other husbands.

NORA: If you speak slightingly of my husband, I shall turn you out of the house.

KROGSTAD: You are bold, Mrs. Helmer.

NORA: I am not afraid of you any longer. As soon as the New Year comes, I shall in a very short time be free of the whole thing.

KROGSTAD (*controlling himself*): Listen to me, Mrs. Helmer. If necessary, I am prepared to fight for my small post in the Bank as if I were fighting for my life.

NORA: So it seems.

KROGSTAD: It is not only for the sake of the money; indeed, that weighs least with me in the matter. There is another reason—well, I may as well tell you. My position is this. I daresay you know, like everybody else, that once, many years ago, I was guilty of an indiscretion.

NORA: I think I have heard something of the kind.

KROGSTAD: The matter never came into court; but every way seemed to be closed to me after that. So I took to the business that you know of. I had to do something; and, honestly, I don't think I've been one of the worst. But now I must cut myself free from all that. My sons are growing up; for their sake I must try and win back as much respect as I can in the town. This post in the

Bank was like the first step up for me—and now your husband is going to kick me downstairs again into the mud.

NORA: But you must believe me, Mr. Krogstad; it is not in my power to help you at all.

KROGSTAD: Then it is because you haven't the will; but I have means to compel you.

NORA: You don't mean that you will tell my husband that I owe you money?

KROGSTAD: Hm!—suppose I were to tell him?

NORA: It would be perfectly infamous of you. (*Sobbing.*) To think of his learning my secret, which has been my joy and pride, in such an ugly, clumsy way—that he should learn it from you! And it would put me in a horribly disagreeable position—

KROGSTAD: Only disagreeable?

NORA (*impetuously*): Well, do it, then!—and it will be the worse for you. My husband will see for himself what a blackguard you are, and you certainly won't keep your post then.

KROGSTAD: I asked you if it was only a disagreeable scene at home that you were afraid of?

NORA: If my husband does get to know of it, of course he will at once pay you what is still owing, and we shall have nothing more to do with you.

KROGSTAD (*coming a step nearer*): Listen to me, Mrs. Helmer. Either you have a very bad memory or you know very little of business. I shall be obliged to remind you of a few details.

NORA: What do you mean?

KROGSTAD: When your husband was ill, you came to me to borrow two hundred and fifty pounds.

NORA: I didn't know anyone else to go to.

KROGSTAD: I promised to get you that amount—

NORA: Yes, and you did so.

KROGSTAD: I promised to get you that amount, on certain conditions. Your mind was so taken up with your husband's illness, and you were so anxious to get the money for your journey, that you seem to have paid no attention to the conditions of our bargain. Therefore it will not be amiss if I remind you of them. Now, I promised to get the money on the security of a bond which I drew up.

NORA: Yes, and which I signed.

KROGSTAD: Good. But below your signature there were a few lines constituting your father a surety for the money; those lines your father should have signed.

NORA: Should? He did sign them.

KROGSTAD: I had left the date blank; that is to say, your father should himself have inserted the date on which he signed the paper. Do you remember that?

NORA: Yes, I think I remember—

KROGSTAD: Then I gave you the bond to send by post to your father. Is that not so?

NORA: Yes.

KROGSTAD: And you naturally did so at once, because five or six days afterwards you brought me the bond with your father's signature. And then I gave you the money.

NORA: Well, haven't I been paying it off regularly?

KROGSTAD: Fairly so, yes. But—to come back to the matter in hand—that must have been a very trying time for you, Mrs. Helmer.

NORA: It was, indeed.

KROGSTAD: Your father was very ill, wasn't he?

NORA: He was very near his end.

KROGSTAD: And he died soon afterwards?

NORA: Yes.

KROGSTAD: Tell me, Mrs. Helmer, can you by any chance remember what day your father died?—on what day of the month, I mean.

NORA: Papa died on the 29th of September.

KROGSTAD: That is correct; I have ascertained it for myself. And, as that is so, there is a discrepancy (*taking a paper from his pocket*) which I cannot account for.

NORA: What discrepancy? I don't know—

KROGSTAD: The discrepancy consists, Mrs. Helmer, in the fact that your father signed this bond three days after his death.

NORA: What do you mean? I don't understand—

KROGSTAD: Your father died on the 29th of September. But, look here; your father has dated his signature the 2nd of October. It is a discrepancy, isn't it? (*Nora is silent.*) Can you explain it to me? (*Nora is still silent.*) It is a remarkable thing, too, that the words "2nd of October," as well as the year, are not written in your father's handwriting but in one that I think I know. Well, of course it can be explained; your father may have forgotten to date his signature, and someone else may have dated it haphazard before they knew of his death. There is no harm in that. It all depends on the signature of the name; and *that* is genuine, I suppose, Mrs. Helmer? It was your father himself who signed his name here?

NORA (*after a short pause, throws her head up and looks defiantly at him*): No, it was not. It was I that wrote papa's name.

KROGSTAD: Are you aware that is a dangerous confession?

NORA: In what way? You shall have your money soon.

KROGSTAD: Let me ask you a question; why did you not send the paper to your father?

NORA: It was impossible; papa was so ill. If I had asked him for his signature, I should have had to tell him what the money was to be used for; and when he was so ill himself I couldn't tell him that my husband's life was in danger—it was impossible.

KROGSTAD: It would have been better for you if you had given up your trip abroad.

NORA: No, that was impossible. That trip was to save my husband's life; I couldn't give that up.

KROGSTAD: But did it never occur to you that you were committing a fraud on me?

NORA: I couldn't take that into account; I didn't trouble myself about you at all. I couldn't bear you, because you put so many heartless difficulties in my way, although you knew what a dangerous condition my husband was in.

KROGSTAD: Mrs. Helmer, you evidently do not realise clearly what it is that you have been guilty of. But I can assure you that my one false step, which lost me all my reputation, was nothing more or nothing worse than what you have done.

NORA: You? Do you ask me to believe that you were brave enough to run a risk to save your wife's life?

KROGSTAD: The law cares nothing about motives.

NORA: Then it must be a very foolish law.

KROGSTAD: Foolish or not, it is the law by which you will be judged, if I produce this paper in court.

NORA: I don't believe it. Is a daughter not to be allowed to spare her dying father anxiety and care? Is a wife not to be allowed to save her husband's life? I don't know much about law; but I am certain that there must be laws permitting such things as that. Have you no knowledge of such laws—you who are a lawyer? You must be a very poor lawyer, Mr. Krogstad.

KROGSTAD: Maybe. But matters of business—such business as you and I have had together—do you think I don't understand that? Very well. Do as you please. But let me tell you this—if I lose my position a second time, you shall lose yours with me. (*He bows, and goes out through the hall.*)

NORA (*appears buried in thought for a short time, then tosses her head*): Nonsense! Trying to frighten me like that!—I am not so silly as he thinks. (*Begins to busy herself putting the children's things in order.*) And yet—? No, it's impossible! I did it for love's sake.

CHILDREN (*in the doorway on the left*): Mother, the stranger man has gone out through the gate.

NORA: Yes, dears, I know. But, don't tell anyone about the stranger man. Do you hear? Not even papa.

CHILDREN: No, mother; but will you come and play again?

NORA: No, no,—not now.

CHILDREN: But, mother, you promised us.

NORA: Yes, but I can't now. Run away in; I have such a lot to do. Run away in, my sweet little darlings. (*She gets them into the room by degrees and shuts the door on them; then sits down on the sofa, takes up a piece of needlework and sews a few stitches, but soon stops.*) No! (*Throws down the work, gets up, goes to the hall door and calls out.*) Helen! bring the Tree in. (*Goes to the table on the left, opens a drawer, and stops again.*) No, no! it is quite impossible!

MAID (*coming in with the Tree*): Where shall I put it, ma'am?

NORA: Here, in the middle of the floor.

MAID: Shall I get you anything else?

NORA: No, thank you. I have all I want. (*Exit Maid.*)

NORA (*begins dressing the tree*): A candle here—and flowers here—. The horrible man! It's all nonsense—there's nothing wrong. The Tree shall be splendid! I will do everything I can think of to please you, Torvald!—I will sing for you, dance for you—(*Helmer comes in with some papers under his arm.*) Oh! are you back already?

HELMER: Yes. Has anyone been here?

NORA: Here? No.

HELMER: That is strange. I saw Krogstad going out of the gate.

NORA: Did you? Oh yes, I forgot, Krogstad was here for a moment.

HELMER: Nora, I can see from your manner that he has been here begging you to say a good word for him.

NORA: Yes.

HELMER: And you were to appear to do it of your own accord; you were to conceal from me the fact of his having been here; didn't he beg that of you too?

NORA: Yes, Torvald, but—

HELMER: Nora, Nora, and you would be a party to that sort of thing? To have any talk with a man like that, and give him any sort of promise? And to tell me a lie into the bargain?

NORA: A lie—?

HELMER: Didn't you tell me no one had been here? (*Shakes his finger at her.*) My little song-bird must never do that again. A song-bird must have a clean beak to chirp with—no false notes! (*Puts his arm around her waist.*) That is so, isn't it? Yes, I am sure it is. (*Lets her go.*) We will say no more about it. (*Sits down by the stove.*) How warm and snug it is here! (*Turns over his papers.*)

NORA (*after a short pause, during which she busies herself with the Christmas Tree*): Torvald!

HELMER: Yes.

NORA: I am looking forward tremendously to the fancy-dress ball at the Stenborgs' the day after to-morrow.

HELMER: And I am tremendously curious to see what you are going to surprise me with.

NORA: It was very silly of me to want to do that.

HELMER: What do you mean?

NORA: I can't hit upon anything that will do; everything I think of seems so silly and insignificant.

HELMER: Does my little Nora acknowledge that at last?

NORA (*standing behind his chair with her arms on the back of it*): Are you very busy, Torvald?

HELMER: Well—

NORA: What are all those papers?

HELMER: Bank business.

NORA: Already?

HELMER: I have got authority from the retiring manager to undertake the necessary changes in the staff and in the rearrangement of the work; and I must make use of the Christmas week for that, so as to have everything in order for the new year.

NORA: Then that was why this poor Krogstad—

HELMER: Hm!

NORA (*leans against the back of his chair and strokes his hair*): If you hadn't been so busy I should have asked you a tremendously big favour, Torvald.

HELMER: What is that? Tell me.

NORA: There is no one has such good taste as you. And I do so want to look nice at the fancy-dress ball. Torvald, couldn't you take me in hand and decide what I shall go as, and what sort of a dress I shall wear?

HELMER: Aha! so my obstinate little woman is obliged to get someone to come to her rescue?

NORA: Yes, Torvald, I can't get along a bit without your help.

HELMER: Very well, I will think it over, we shall manage to hit upon something.

NORA: That is nice of you. (*Goes to the Christmas Tree. A short pause.*) How pretty the red flowers look—. But, tell me, was it really something very bad that this Krogstad was guilty of?

HELMER: He forged someone's name. Have you any idea what that means?

NORA: Isn't it possible that he was driven to do it by necessity?

HELMER: Yes; or, as in so many cases, by imprudence. I am not so heartless as to condemn a man altogether because of a single false step of that kind.

NORA: No, you wouldn't, would you, Torvald?

HELMER: Many a man has been able to retrieve his character, if he has openly confessed his fault and taken his punishment.

NORA: Punishment—?

HELMER: But Krogstad did nothing of that sort; he got himself out of it by a cunning trick, and that is why he has gone under altogether.

NORA: But do you think it would—?

HELMER: Just think how a guilty man like that has to lie and play the hypocrite with every one, how he has to wear a mask in the presence of those near and dear to him, even before his own wife and children. And about the children—that is the most terrible part of it all, Nora.

NORA: How?

HELMER: Because such an atmosphere of lies infects and poisons the whole life of a home. Each breath the children take in such a house is full of the germs of evil.

NORA (*coming nearer him*): Are you sure of that?

HELMER: My dear, I have often seen it in the course of my life as a lawyer. Almost everyone who has gone to the bad early in life has had a deceitful mother.

NORA: Why do you only say—mother?

HELMER: It seems most commonly to be the mother's influence, though naturally a bad father's would have the same result. Every lawyer is familiar with the fact. This Krogstad, now, has been persistently poisoning his own children with lies and dissimulation; that is why I say he has lost all moral character. (*Holds out his hands to her.*) That is why my sweet little Nora must promise me not to plead his cause. Give me your hand on it. Come, come, what is this? Give me your hand. There now, that's settled. I assure you it would be quite impossible for me to work with him; I literally feel physically ill when I am in the company of such people.

NORA (*takes her hand out of his and goes to the opposite side of the Christmas Tree*): How hot it is in here; and I have such a lot to do.

HELMER (*getting up and putting his papers in order*): Yes, and I must try and read through some of these before dinner; and I must think about your costume, too. And it is just possible I may have something ready in gold paper to hang up on the Tree. (*Puts his hand on her head.*) My precious little singing-bird! (*He goes into his room and shuts the door after him.*)

NORA (*after a pause, whispers*): No, no—it isn't true. It's impossible; it must be impossible.

The Nurse opens the door on the left.

NURSE: The little ones are begging so hard to be allowed to come in to mamma.

NORA: No, no, no! Don't let them come in to me! You stay with them, Anne.

NURSE: Very well, ma'am. (*Shuts the door.*)

NORA (*pale with terror*): Deprave my little children? Poison my home? (*A short pause. Then she tosses her head.*) It's not true. It can't possibly be true.

ACT II

THE SAME SCENE: *The Christmas Tree is in the corner by the piano, stripped of its ornaments and with burnt-down candle-ends on its dishevelled branches. Nora's cloak and hat are lying on the sofa. She is alone in the room, walking about uneasily. She stops by the sofa and takes up her cloak.*

NORA (*drops her cloak*): Someone is coming now! (*Goes to the door and listens.*) No—it is no one. Of course, no one will come to-day, Christmas Day—nor to-morrow either. But, perhaps—(*opens the door and looks out*). No, nothing in the letter-box; it is quite empty. (*Comes forward.*) What rubbish! of course he can't be in earnest about it. Such a thing couldn't happen; it is impossible—I have three little children.

Enter the Nurse from the room on the left, carrying a big cardboard box.

NURSE: At last I have found the box with the fancy dress.

NORA: Thanks; put it on the table.

NURSE (*doing so*): But it is very much in want of mending.

NORA: I should like to tear it into a hundred thousand pieces.

NURSE: What an idea! It can easily be put in order—just a little patience.

NORA: Yes, I will go and get Mrs. Linde to come and help me with it.

NURSE: What, out again? In this horrible weather? You will catch cold, ma'am, and make yourself ill.

NORA: Well, worse than that might happen. How are the children?

NURSE: The poor little souls are playing with their Christmas presents, but—

NORA: Do they ask much for me?

NURSE: You see, they are so accustomed to have their mamma with them.

NORA: Yes, but, nurse, I shall not be able to be so much with them now as I was before.

NURSE: Oh well, young children easily get accustomed to anything.

NORA: Do you think so? Do you think they would forget their mother if she went away altogether?

NURSE: Good heavens!—went away altogether?

NORA: Nurse, I want you to tell me something I have often wondered about—how could you have the heart to put your own child out among strangers?

NURSE: I was obliged to, if I wanted to be little Nora's nurse.

NORA: Yes, but how could you be willing to do it?

NURSE: What, when I was going to get such a good place by it? A poor girl who has got into trouble should be glad to. Besides, that wicked man didn't do a single thing for me.

NORA: But I suppose your daughter has quite forgotten you.

NURSE: No, indeed she hasn't. She wrote to me when she was confirmed, and when she was married.

NORA (*putting her arms round her neck*): Dear old Anne, you were a good mother to me when I was little.

NURSE: Little Nora, poor dear, had no other mother but me.

NORA: And if my little ones had no other mother, I am sure you would—What nonsense I am talking! (*Opens the box.*) Go in to them. Now I must—. You will see to-morrow how charming I shall look.

NURSE: I am sure there will be no one at the ball so charming as you, ma'am. (*Goes into the room on the left.*)

NORA (*begins to unpack the box, but soon pushes it away from her*): If only I dared go out. If only no one would come. If only I could be sure nothing would happen here in the meantime. Stuff and nonsense! No one will come. Only I mustn't think about it. I will brush my muff. What lovely, lovely gloves! Out of my thoughts, out of my thoughts! One, two, three, four, five, six—(*Screams.*) Ah! there is someone coming—. (*Makes a movement towards the door, but stands irresolute.*)

Enter Mrs. Linde from the hall, where she has taken off her cloak and hat.

NORA: Oh, it's you, Christine. There is no one else out there, is there? How good of you to come!

MRS. LINDE: I heard you were up asking for me.

NORA: Yes, I was passing by. As a matter of fact, it is something you could help me with. Let us sit down here on the sofa. Look here. To-morrow evening there is to be a fancy-dress ball at the Stenborgs', who live above us; and Torvald wants me to go as a Neapolitan fisher-girl, and dance the Tarantella that I learned at Capri.

MRS. LINDE: I see; you are going to keep up the character.

NORA: Yes, Torvald wants me to. Look, here is the dress; Torvald had it made for me there, but now it is all so torn, and I haven't any idea—

MRS. LINDE: We will easily put that right. It is only some of the trimming come unsewn here and there. Needle and thread? Now then, that's all we want.

NORA: It *is* nice of you.

MRS. LINDE (*sewing*): So you are going to be dressed up to-morrow, Nora. I will tell you what—I shall come in for a moment and see you in your fine feathers. But I have completely forgotten to thank you for a delightful evening yesterday.

NORA (*gets up, and crosses the stage*): Well, I don't think yesterday was as pleasant as usual. You ought to have come to town a little earlier, Christine. Certainly Torvald does understand how to make a house dainty and attractive.

MRS. LINDE: And so do you, it seems to me; you are not your father's daughter for nothing. But tell me, is Doctor Rank always as depressed as he was yesterday?

NORA: No; yesterday it was very noticeable. I must tell you that he suffers from a very dangerous disease. He has consumption of the spine, poor creature. His father was a horrible man who committed all sorts of excesses; and that is why his son was sickly from childhood, do you understand?

MRS. LINDE (*dropping her sewing*): But, my dearest Nora, how do you know anything about such things?

NORA (*walking about*): Pooh! When you have three children, you get visits now and then from—from married women, who know something of medical matters, and they talk about one thing and another.

MRS. LINDE: (*goes on sewing. A short silence*) Does Doctor Rank come here everyday?

NORA: Everyday regularly. He is Torvald's most intimate friend, and a great friend of mine too. He is just like one of the family.

MRS. LINDE: But tell me this—is he perfectly sincere? I mean, isn't he the kind of man that is very anxious to make himself agreeable?

NORA: Not in the least. What makes you think that?

MRS. LINDE: When you introduced him to me yesterday, he declared he had often heard my name mentioned in this house; but afterwards I noticed that your husband hadn't the slightest idea who I was. So how could Doctor Rank—?

NORA: That is quite right, Christine. Torvald is so absurdly fond of me that he wants me absolutely to himself, as he says. At first he used to seem almost jealous if I mentioned any of the dear folk at home, so naturally I gave up doing so. But I often talk about such things with Doctor Rank, because he likes hearing about them.

MRS. LINDE: Listen to me, Nora. You are still very like a child in many things, and I am older than you in many ways and have a little more experience. Let me tell you this—you ought to make an end of it with Doctor Rank.

NORA: What ought I to make an end of ?

MRS. LINDE: Of two things, I think. Yesterday you talked some nonsense about a rich admirer who was to leave you money—

NORA: An admirer who doesn't exist, unfortunately! But what then?

MRS. LINDE: Is Doctor Rank a man of means?

NORA: Yes, he is.

MRS. LINDE: And has no one to provide for?

NORA: No, no one; but—

MRS. LINDE: And comes here everyday?

NORA: Yes, I told you so.

MRS. LINDE: But how can this well-bred man be so tactless?

NORA: I don't understand you at all.

MRS. LINDE: Don't prevaricate, Nora. Do you suppose I don't guess who lent you the two hundred and fifty pounds?

NORA: Are you out of your senses? How can you think of such a thing! A friend of ours, who comes here everyday! Do you realise what a horribly painful position that would be?

MRS. LINDE: Then it really isn't he?

NORA: No, certainly not. It would never have entered into my head for a moment. Besides, he had no money to lend then; he came into his money afterwards.

MRS. LINDE: Well, I think that was lucky for you, my dear Nora.

NORA: No, it would never have come into my head to ask Doctor Rank. Although I am quite sure that if I had asked him—

MRS. LINDE: But of course you won't.

NORA: Of course not. I have no reason to think it could possibly be necessary. But I am quite sure that if I told Doctor Rank—

MRS. LINDE: Behind your husband's back?

NORA: I must make an end of it with the other one, and that will be behind his back too. I *must* make an end of it with him.

MRS. LINDE: Yes, that is what I told you yesterday, but—

NORA (*walking up and down*): A man can put a thing like that straight much easier than a woman—

MRS. LINDE: One's husband, yes.

NORA: Nonsense! (*Standing still.*) When you pay off a debt you get your bond back, don't you?

MRS. LINDE: Yes, as a matter of course.

NORA: And can tear it into a hundred thousand pieces, and burn it up—the nasty dirty paper!

MRS. LINDE (*looks hard at her, lays down her sewing and gets up slowly*): Nora, you are concealing something from me.

NORA: Do I look as if I were?

MRS. LINDE: Something has happened to you since yesterday morning. Nora, what is it?

NORA (*going nearer to her*): Christine! (*Listens.*) Hush! there's Torvald come home. Do you mind going in to the children for the present? Torvald can't bear to see dressmaking going on. Let Anne help you.

MRS. LINDE (*gathering some of the things together*): Certainly—but I am not going away from here until we have had it out with one another. (*She goes into the room on the left, as Helmer comes in from the hall.*)

NORA (*going up to Helmer*): I have wanted you so much, Torvald dear.

HELMER: Was that the dressmaker?

NORA: No, it was Christine; she is helping me to put my dress in order. You will see I shall look quite smart.

HELMER: Wasn't that a happy thought of mine, now?

NORA: Splendid! But don't you think it is nice of me, too, to do as you wish?

HELMER: Nice?—because you do as your husband wishes? Well, well, you little rogue, I am sure you did not mean it in that way. But I am not going to disturb you; you will want to be trying on your dress, I expect.

NORA: I suppose you are going to work.

HELMER: Yes. (*Shows her a bundle of papers.*) Look at that. I have just been into the bank. (*Turns to go into his room.*)

NORA: Torvald.

HELMER: Yes.

NORA: If your little squirrel were to ask you for something very, very prettily—?

HELMER: What then?

NORA: Would you do it?

HELMER: I should like to hear what it is, first.

NORA: Your squirrel would run about and do all her tricks if you would be nice, and do what she wants.

HELMER: Speak plainly.

NORA: Your skylark would chirp about in every room, with her song rising and falling—

HELMER: Well, my skylark does that anyhow.

NORA: I would play the fairy and dance for you in the moonlight, Torvald.

HELMER: Nora—you surely don't mean that request you made to me this morning?

NORA (*going near him*): Yes, Torvald, I beg you so earnestly—

HELMER: Have you really the courage to open up that question again?

NORA: Yes, dear, you *must* do as I ask; you *must* let Krogstad keep his post in the bank.

HELMER: My dear Nora, it is his post that I have arranged Mrs. Linde shall have.

NORA: Yes, you have been awfully kind about that; but you could just as well dismiss some other clerk instead of Krogstad.

HELMER: This is simply incredible obstinacy! Because you chose to give him a thoughtless promise that you would speak for him, I am expected to—

NORA: That isn't the reason, Torvald. It is for your own sake. This fellow writes in the most scurrilous newspapers; you have told me so yourself. He can do you an unspeakable amount of harm. I am frightened to death of him—

HELMER: Ah, I understand; it is recollections of the past that scare you.

NORA: What do you mean?

HELMER: Naturally you are thinking of your father.

NORA: Yes—yes, of course. Just recall to your mind what these malicious creatures wrote in the papers about papa, and how horribly they slandered him. I believe they would have procured his dismissal if the Department had not sent you over to inquire into it, and if you had not been so kindly disposed and helpful to him.

HELMER: My little Nora, there is an important difference between your father and me. Your father's reputation as a public official was not above suspicion. Mine is, and I hope it will continue to be so, as long as I hold my office.

NORA: You never can tell what mischief these men may contrive. We ought to be so well off, so snug and happy here in our peaceful home, and have no cares—you and I and the children, Torvald! That is why I beg you so earnestly—

HELMER: And it is just by interceding for him that you make it impossible for me to keep him. It is already known at the Bank that I mean to dismiss Krogstad. Is it to get about now that the new manager has changed his mind at his wife's bidding—

NORA: And what if it did?

HELMER: Of course!—if only this obstinate little person can get her way! Do you suppose I am going to make myself ridiculous before my whole staff, to let people think that I am a man to be swayed by all sorts of outside influence? I should very soon feel the consequences of it, I can tell you! And besides, there is one thing that makes it quite impossible for me to have Krogstad in the Bank as long as I am manager.

NORA: Whatever is that?

HELMER: His moral failings I might perhaps have overlooked, if necessary—

NORA: Yes, you could—couldn't you?

HELMER: And I hear he is a good worker, too. But I knew him when we were boys. It was one of those rash friendships that so often prove an incubus in afterlife. I may as well tell you plainly, we were once on very intimate terms with one another. But this tactless fellow lays no restraint on himself when other people are present. On the contrary, he thinks it gives him the right to adopt a familiar tone with me, and every minute it is "I say, Helmer, old fellow!" and that sort of thing. I assure you it is extremely painful for me. He would make my position in the Bank intolerable.

NORA: Torvald, I don't believe you mean that.

HELMER: Don't you? Why not?

NORA: Because it is such a narrow-minded way of looking at things.

HELMER: What are you saying? Narrow-minded? Do you think I am narrow-minded?

NORA: No, just the opposite, dear—and it is exactly for that reason.

HELMER: It's the same thing. You say my point of view is narrow-minded, so I must be so too. Narrow-minded! Very well—I must put an end to this. (*Goes to the hall door and calls.*) Helen!

NORA: What are you going to do?

HELMER (*looking among his papers*): Settle it. (*Enter Maid.*) Look here; take this letter and go downstairs with it at once. Find a messenger and tell him to deliver it, and be quick. The address is on it, and here is the money.

MAID: Very well, sir. (*Exit with the letter.*)

HELMER (*putting his papers together*): Now then, little Miss Obstinate.

NORA (*breathlessly*): Torvald—what was that letter?

HELMER: Krogstad's dismissal.

NORA: Call her back, Torvald! There is still time. Oh Torvald, call her back! Do it for my sake—for your own sake—for the children's sake! Do you hear me, Torvald? Call her back! You don't know what that letter can bring upon us.

HELMER: It's too late.

NORA: Yes, it's too late.

HELMER: My dear Nora, I can forgive the anxiety you are in, although really it is an insult to me. It is, indeed. Isn't it an insult to think that I should be afraid of a starving quill-driver's vengeance? But I forgive you nevertheless, because it is such eloquent witness to your great love for me. (*Takes her in his arms.*) And that is as it should be, my own darling Nora. Come what will, you may be sure I shall have both courage and strength if they be needed. You will see I am man enough to take everything upon myself.

NORA (*in a horror-stricken voice*): What do you mean by that?

HELMER: Everything, I say—

NORA (*recovering herself*): You will never have to do that.

HELMER: That's right. Well, we will share it, Nora, as man and wife should. That is how it shall be. (*Caressing her.*) Are you content now? There! there!—not these frightened dove's eyes! The whole thing is only the wildest fancy!—Now, you must go and play through the Tarantella and practise with your tambourine. I shall go into the inner office and shut the door, and I shall hear nothing; you can make as much noise as you please. (*Turns back at the door.*) And when Rank comes, tell him where he will find me. (*Nods to her, takes his papers and goes into his room, and shuts the door after him.*)

NORA (*bewildered with anxiety, stands as if rooted to the spot, and whispers*): He was capable of doing it. He will do it. He will do it in spite of everything.—No, not that! Never, never! Anything rather than that! Oh, for some help, some way out of it! (*The door-bell rings.*) Doctor Rank! Anything rather than that—anything, whatever it is! (*She puts her hands over her face, pulls herself together, goes to the door and opens it. Rank is standing without, hanging up his coat. During the following dialogue it begins to grow dark.*)

NORA: Good-day, Doctor Rank. I knew your ring. But you mustn't go in to Torvald now; I think he is busy with something.

RANK: And you?

NORA (*brings him in and shuts the door after him*): Oh, you know very well I always have time for you.

RANK: Thank you. I shall make use of as much of it as I can.

NORA: What do you mean by that? As much of it as you can?

RANK: Well, does that alarm you?

NORA: It was such a strange way of putting it. Is anything likely to happen?

RANK: Nothing but what I have long been prepared for. But I certainly didn't expect it to happen so soon.

NORA (*gripping him by the arm*): What have you found out? Doctor Rank, you must tell me.

RANK (*sitting down by the stove*): It is all up with me. And it can't be helped.

NORA (*with a sigh of relief*): Is it about yourself ?

RANK: Who else? It is no use lying to one's self. I am the most wretched of all my patients, Mrs. Helmer. Lately I have been taking stock of my internal economy. Bankrupt! Probably within a month I shall lie rotting in the churchyard.

NORA: What an ugly thing to say!

RANK: The thing itself is cursedly ugly, and the worst of it is that I shall have to face so much more that is ugly before that. I shall only make one more examination of myself; when I have done that, I shall know pretty certainly when it will be that the horrors of dissolution will begin. There is something I want to tell you. Helmer's refined nature gives him an unconquerable disgust at everything that is ugly; I won't have him in my sick-room.

NORA: Oh, but, Doctor Rank—

RANK: I won't have him there. Not on any account. I bar my door to him. As soon as I am quite certain that the worst has come, I shall send you my card with a black cross on it, and then you will know that the loathsome end has begun.

NORA: You are quite absurd to-day. And I wanted you so much to be in a really good humour.

RANK: With death stalking beside me?—To have to pay this penalty for another man's sin? Is there any justice in that? And in every single family, in one way or another, some such inexorable retribution is being exacted—

NORA (*putting her hands over her ears*): Rubbish! Do talk of something cheerful.

RANK: Oh, it's a mere laughing matter, the whole thing. My poor innocent spine has to suffer for my father's youthful amusements.

NORA (*sitting at the table on the left*): I suppose you mean that he was too partial to asparagus and pâté de foie gras, don't you?

RANK: Yes, and to truffles.

NORA: Truffles, yes. And oysters too, I suppose?

RANK: Oysters, of course, that goes without saying.

NORA: And heaps of port and champagne. It is sad that all these nice things should take their revenge on our bones.

RANK: Especially that they should revenge themselves on the unlucky bones of those who have not had the satisfaction of enjoying them.

NORA: Yes, that's the saddest part of it all.

RANK (*with a searching look at her*): Hm!—

NORA (*after a short pause*): Why did you smile?

RANK: No, it was you that laughed.

NORA: No, it was you that smiled, Doctor Rank!

RANK (*rising*): You are a greater rascal than I thought.

NORA: I am in a silly mood to-day.

RANK: So it seems.

NORA (*putting her hands on his shoulders*): Dear, dear Doctor Rank, death mustn't take you away from Torvald and me.

RANK: It is a loss you would easily recover from. Those who are gone are soon forgotten.

NORA (*looking at him anxiously*): Do you believe that?

RANK: People form new ties, and then—

NORA: Who will form new ties?

RANK: Both you and Helmer, when I am gone. You yourself are already on the high road to it, I think. What did that Mrs. Linde want here last night?

NORA: Oho!—you don't mean to say you are jealous of poor Christine?

RANK: Yes, I am. She will be my successor in this house. When I am done for, this woman will—

NORA: Hush! don't speak so loud. She is in that room.

RANK: To-day again. There, you see.

NORA: She has only come to sew my dress for me. Bless my soul, how unreasonable you are! (*Sits down on the sofa.*) Be nice now, Doctor Rank, and to-morrow you will see how beautifully I shall dance, and you can imagine I am doing it all for you—and for Torvald too, of course. (*Takes various things out of the box.*) Doctor Rank, come and sit down here, and I will show you something.

RANK (*sitting down*): What is it?

NORA: Just look at those!

RANK: Silk stockings.

NORA: Flesh-coloured. Aren't they lovely? It is so dark here now, but to-morrow—. No, no, no! you must only look at the feet. Oh well, you may have leave to look at the legs too.

RANK: Hm!—

NORA: Why are you looking so critical? Don't you think they will fit me?

RANK: I have no means of forming an opinion about that.

NORA (*looks at him for a moment*): For shame! (*Hits him lightly on the ear with the stockings.*) That's to punish you. (*Folds them up again.*)

RANK: And what other nice things am I to be allowed to see?

NORA: Not a single thing more, for being so naughty. (*She looks among the things, humming to herself.*)

RANK (*after a short silence*): When I am sitting here, talking to you as intimately as this, I cannot imagine for a moment what would have become of me if I had never come into this house.

NORA (*smiling*): I believe you do feel thoroughly at home with us.

RANK (*in a lower voice, looking straight in front of him*): And to be obliged to leave it all—

NORA: Nonsense, you are not going to leave it.

RANK (*as before*): And not be able to leave behind one the slightest token of one's gratitude, scarcely even a fleeting regret—nothing but an empty place which the first comer can fill as well as any other.

NORA: And if I asked you now for a—? No!

RANK: For what?

NORA: For a big proof of your friendship—

RANK: Yes, yes!

NORA: I mean a tremendously big favour.

RANK: Would you really make me so happy for once?

NORA: Ah, but you don't know what it is yet.

RANK: No—but tell me.

NORA: I really can't, Doctor Rank. It is something out of all reason; it means advice, and help, and a favour—

RANK: The bigger a thing it is the better. I can't conceive what it is you mean. Do tell me. Haven't I your confidence?

NORA: More than anyone else. I know you are my truest and best friend, and so I will tell you what it is. Well, Doctor Rank, it is something you must help me to prevent. You know how devotedly, how inexpressibly deeply Torvald loves me; he would never for a moment hesitate to give his life for me.

RANK (*leaning towards her*): Nora—do you think he is the only one—?

NORA (*with a slight start*): The only one—?

RANK: The only one who would gladly give his life for your sake.

NORA (*sadly*): Is that it?

RANK: I was determined you should know it before I went away, and there will never be a better opportunity than this. Now you know it, Nora. And now you know, too, that you can trust me as you would trust no one else.

NORA (*rises, deliberately and quietly*): Let me pass.

RANK (*makes room for her to pass him, but sits still*): Nora!

NORA (*at the hall door*): Helen, bring in the lamp. (*Goes over to the stove.*) Dear Doctor Rank, that was really horrid of you.

RANK: To have loved you as much as anyone else does? Was that horrid?

NORA: No, but to go and tell me so. There was really no need—

RANK: What do you mean? Did you know—? (*Maid enters with lamp, puts it down on the table, and goes out.*) Nora—Mrs. Helmer—tell me, had you any idea of this?

NORA: Oh, how do I know whether I had or whether I hadn't? I really can't tell you—To think you could be so clumsy, Doctor Rank! We were getting on so nicely.

RANK: Well, at all events you know now that you can command me, body and soul. So won't you speak out?

NORA (*looking at him*): After what happened?

RANK: I beg you to let me know what it is.

NORA: I can't tell you anything now.

RANK: Yes, yes. You mustn't punish me in that way. Let me have permission to do for you whatever a man may do.

NORA: You can do nothing for me now. Besides, I really don't need any help at all. You will find that the whole thing is merely fancy on my part. It really is so—of course it is! (*Sits down in the rocking-chair, and looks at him with a smile.*) You are a nice sort of man, Doctor Rank!—don't you feel ashamed of yourself, now the lamp has come?

RANK: Not a bit. But perhaps I had better go—for ever?

NORA: No, indeed, you shall not. Of course you must come here just as before. You know very well Torvald can't do without you.

RANK: Yes, but you?

NORA: Oh, I am always tremendously pleased when you come.

RANK: It is just that, that put me on the wrong track. You are a riddle to me. I have often thought that you would almost as soon be in my company as in Helmer's.

NORA: Yes—you see there are some people one loves best, and others whom one would almost always rather have as companions.

RANK: Yes, there is something in that.

NORA: When I was at home, of course I loved papa best. But I always thought it tremendous fun if I could steal down into the maids' room, because they never moralised at all, and talked to each other about such entertaining things.

RANK: I see—it is *their* place I have taken.

NORA (*jumping up and going to him*): Oh, dear, nice Doctor Rank, I never meant that at all. But surely you can understand that being with Torvald is a little like being with papa—

Enter Maid from the hall.

MAID: If you please, ma'am. (*Whispers and hands her a card.*)

NORA (*glancing at the card*): Oh! (*Puts it in her pocket.*)

RANK: Is there anything wrong?

NORA: No, no, not in the least. It is only something—it is my new dress—

RANK: What? Your dress is lying there.

NORA: Oh, yes, that one; but this is another. I ordered it. Torvald mustn't know about it—

RANK: Oho! Then that was the great secret.

NORA: Of course. Just go in to him; he is sitting in the inner room. Keep him as long as—

RANK: Make your mind easy; I won't let him escape. (*Goes into Helmer's room.*)

NORA (*to the Maid*): And he is standing waiting in the kitchen?

MAID: Yes; he came up the back stairs.

NORA: But didn't you tell him no one was in?

MAID: Yes, but it was no good.

NORA: He won't go away?

MAID: No; he says he won't until he has seen you, ma'am.

NORA: Well, let him come in—but quietly. Helen, you mustn't say anything about it to anyone. It is a surprise for my husband.

MAID: Yes, ma'am, I quite understand. (*Exit.*)

NORA: This dreadful thing is going to happen! It will happen in spite of me! No, no, no, it can't happen—it shan't happen! (*She bolts the door of Helmer's room. The Maid opens the hall door for Krogstad and shuts it after him. He is wearing a fur coat, high boots and a fur cap.*)

NORA (*advancing towards him*): Speak low—my husband is at home.

KROGSTAD: No matter about that.

NORA: What do you want of me?

KROGSTAD: An explanation of something.

NORA: Make haste then. What is it?

KROGSTAD: You know, I suppose, that I have got my dismissal.

NORA: I couldn't prevent it, Mr. Krogstad. I fought as hard as I could on your side, but it was no good.

KROGSTAD: Does your husband love you so little, then? He knows what I can expose you to, and yet he ventures—

NORA: How can you suppose that he has any knowledge of the sort?

KROGSTAD: I didn't suppose so at all. It would not be the least like our dear Torvald Helmer to show so much courage—

NORA: Mr. Krogstad, a little respect for my husband, please.

KROGSTAD: Certainly—all the respect he deserves. But since you have kept the matter so carefully to yourself, I make bold to suppose that you have a little clearer idea, than you had yesterday, of what it actually is that you have done?

NORA: More than you could ever teach me.

KROGSTAD: Yes, such a bad lawyer as I am.

NORA: What is it you want of me?

KROGSTAD: Only to see how you were, Mrs. Helmer. I have been thinking about you all day long. A mere cashier, a quill-driver, a—well, a man like me—even he has a little of what is called feeling, you know.

NORA: Show it, then; think of my little children.

KROGSTAD: Have you and your husband thought of mine? But never mind about that. I only wanted to tell you that you need not take this matter too seriously. In the first place there will be no accusation made on my part.

NORA: No, of course not; I was sure of that.

KROGSTAD: The whole thing can be arranged amicably; there is no reason why anyone should know anything about it. It will remain a secret between us three.

NORA: My husband must never get to know anything about it.

KROGSTAD: How will you be able to prevent it? Am I to understand that you can pay the balance that is owing?

NORA: No, not just at present.

KROGSTAD: Or perhaps that you have some expedient for raising the money soon?

NORA: No expedient that I mean to make use of.

KROGSTAD: Well, in any case, it would have been of no use to you now. If you stood there with ever so much money in your hand, I would never part with your bond.

NORA: Tell me what purpose you mean to put it to.

KROGSTAD: I shall only preserve it—keep it in my possession. No one who is not concerned in the matter shall have the slightest hint of it. So that if the thought of it has driven you to any desperate resolution—

NORA: It has.

KROGSTAD: If you had it in your mind to run away from your home—

NORA: I had.

KROGSTAD: Or even something worse—

NORA: How could you know that?

KROGSTAD: Give up the idea.

NORA: How did you know I had thought of *that*?

KROGSTAD: Most of us think of that at first. I did, too—but I hadn't the courage.

NORA (*faintly*): No more had I.

KROGSTAD (*in a tone of relief*): No, that's it, isn't it—you hadn't the courage either?

NORA: No, I haven't—I haven't.

KROGSTAD: Besides, it would have been a great piece of folly. Once the first storm at home is over—. I have a letter for your husband in my pocket.

NORA: Telling him everything?

KROGSTAD: In as lenient a manner as I possibly could.

NORA (*quickly*): He mustn't get the letter. Tear it up. I will find some means of getting money.

KROGSTAD: Excuse me, Mrs. Helmer, but I think I told you just now—

NORA: I am not speaking of what I owe you. Tell me what sum you are asking my husband for, and I will get the money.

KROGSTAD: I am not asking your husband for a penny.

NORA: What do you want, then?

KROGSTAD: I will tell you. I want to rehabilitate myself, Mrs. Helmer; I want to get on; and in that your husband must help me. For the last year and a half I have not had a hand in anything dishonourable, and all that time I have been struggling in most restricted circumstances. I was content to work my way up step by step. Now I am turned out, and I am not going to be satisfied with merely being taken into favour again. I want to get on, I tell you. I want to get into the Bank again, in a higher position. Your husband must make a place for me—

NORA: That he will never do!

KROGSTAD: He will; I know him; he dare not protest. And as soon as I am in there again with him, then you will see! Within a year I shall be the manager's right hand. It will be Nils Krogstad and not Torvald Helmer who manages the Bank.

NORA: That's a thing you will never see!

KROGSTAD: Do you mean that you will—?

NORA: I have courage enough for it now.

KROGSTAD: Oh, you can't frighten me. A fine, spoilt lady like you—

NORA: You will see, you will see.

KROGSTAD: Under the ice, perhaps? Down into the cold, coal-black water? And then, in the spring, to float up to the surface, all horrible and unrecognisable, with your hair fallen out—

NORA: You can't frighten me.

KROGSTAD: Nor you me. People don't do such things, Mrs. Helmer. Besides, what use would it be? I should have him completely in my power all the same.

NORA: Afterwards? When I am no longer—

KROGSTAD: Have you forgotten that it is I who have the keeping of your reputation? (*Nora stands speechlessly looking at him.*) Well, now, I have warned you. Do not do anything foolish. When Helmer has had my letter, I shall expect a message from him. And be sure you remember that it is your husband himself who has forced me into such ways as this again. I will never forgive him for that. Good-bye, Mrs. Helmer. (*Exit through the hall.*)

NORA (*goes to the hall door, opens it slightly and listens*): He is going. He is not putting the letter in the box. Oh no, no! that's impossible! (*Opens the door by degrees.*) What is that? He is standing outside. He is not going downstairs. Is he hesitating? Can he—? (*A letter drops into the box; then Krogstad's footsteps are heard, till they die away as he goes downstairs. Nora utters a stifled cry, and runs across the room to the table by the sofa. A short pause.*)

NORA: In the letter-box. (*Steals across to the hall door.*) There it lies—Torvald, Torvald, there is no hope for us now!

Mrs. Linde comes in from the room on the left, carrying the dress.

MRS. LINDE: There, I can't see anything more to mend now. Would you like to try it on—?

NORA (*in a hoarse whisper*): Christine, come here.

MRS. LINDE (*throwing the dress down on the sofa*): What is the matter with you? You look so agitated!

NORA: Come here. Do you see that letter? There, look—you can see it through the glass in the letter-box.

MRS. LINDE: Yes, I see it.

NORA: That letter is from Krogstad.

MRS. LINDE: Nora—it was Krogstad who lent you the money!

NORA: Yes, and now Torvald will know all about it.

MRS. LINDE: Believe me, Nora, that's the best thing for both of you.

NORA: You don't know all. I forged a name.

MRS. LINDE: Good heavens—!

NORA: I only want to say this to you, Christine—you must be my witness.

MRS. LINDE: Your witness? What do you mean? What am I to—?

NORA: If I should go out of my mind—and it might easily happen—

MRS. LINDE: Nora!

NORA: Or if anything else should happen to me—anything, for instance, that might prevent my being here—

MRS. LINDE: Nora! Nora! you are quite out of your mind.

NORA: And if it should happen that there were some one who wanted to take all the responsibility, all the blame, you understand—

MRS. LINDE: Yes, yes—but how can you suppose—?

NORA: Then you must be my witness, that it is not true, Christine. I am not out of my mind at all! I am in my right senses now, and I tell you no one else has known anything about it; I, and I alone, did the whole thing. Remember that.

MRS. LINDE: I will, indeed. But I don't understand all this.

NORA: How should you understand it? A wonderful thing is going to happen!

MRS. LINDE: A wonderful thing?

NORA: Yes, a wonderful thing!—But it is so terrible, Christine; it *mustn't* happen, not for all the world.

MRS. LINDE: I will go at once and see Krogstad.

NORA: Don't go to him; he will do you some harm.

MRS. LINDE: There was a time when he would gladly do anything for my sake.

NORA: He?

MRS. LINDE: Where does he live?

NORA: How should I know—? Yes (*feeling in her pocket*), here is his card. But the letter, the letter—!

HELMER (*calls from his room, knocking at the door*): Nora!

NORA (*cries out anxiously*): Oh, what's that? What do you want?

HELMER: Don't be so frightened. We are not coming in; you have locked the door. Are you trying on your dress?

NORA: Yes, that's it. I look so nice, Torvald.

MRS. LINDE (*who has read the card*): I see he lives at the corner here.

NORA: Yes, but it's no use. It is hopeless. The letter is lying there in the box.

MRS. LINDE: And your husband keeps the key?

NORA: Yes, always.

MRS. LINDE: Krogstad must ask for his letter back unread, he must find some pretence—

NORA: But it is just at this time that Torvald generally—

MRS. LINDE: You must delay him. Go in to him in the meantime. I will come back as soon as I can. (*She goes out hurriedly through the hall door.*)

NORA (*goes to Helmer's door, opens it and peeps in*): Torvald!

HELMER (*from the inner room*): Well? May I venture at last to come into my own room again? Come along, Rank, now you will see—(*Halting in the doorway.*) But what is this?

NORA: What is what, dear?

HELMER: Rank led me to expect a splendid transformation.

RANK (*in the doorway*): I understood so, but evidently I was mistaken.

NORA: Yes, nobody is to have the chance of admiring me in my dress until to-morrow.

HELMER: But, my dear Nora, you look so worn out. Have you been practising too much?

NORA: No, I have not practised at all.

HELMER: But you will need to—

NORA: Yes, indeed I shall, Torvald. But I can't get on a bit without you to help me; I have absolutely forgotten the whole thing.

HELMER: Oh, we will soon work it up again.

NORA: Yes, help me, Torvald. Promise that you will! I am so nervous about it—all the people—. You must give yourself up to me entirely this evening. Not the tiniest bit of business—you mustn't even take a pen in your hand. Will you promise, Torvald dear?

HELMER: I promise. This evening I will be wholly and absolutely at your service, you helpless little mortal. Ah, by the way, first of all I will just—(*Goes towards the hall door.*)

NORA: What are you going to do there?

HELMER: Only see if any letters have come.

NORA: No, no! don't do that, Torvald!

HELMER: Why not?

NORA: Torvald, please don't. There is nothing there.

HELMER: Well, let me look. (*Turns to go to the letter-box. Nora, at the piano, plays the first bars of the Tarantella. Helmer stops in the doorway.*) Aha!

NORA: I can't dance tomorrow if I don't practise with you.

HELMER (*going up to her*): Are you really so afraid of it, dear?

NORA: Yes, so dreadfully afraid of it. Let me practise at once; there is time now, before we go to dinner. Sit down and play for me, Torvald dear; criticise me, and correct me as you play.

HELMER: With great pleasure, if you wish me to. (*Sits down at the piano.*)

NORA (*takes out of the box a tambourine and a long variegated shawl. She hastily drapes the shawl round her. Then she springs to the front of the stage and calls out*): Now play for me! I am going to dance!

Helmer plays and Nora dances. Rank stands by the piano behind Helmer, and looks on.

HELMER (*as he plays*): Slower, slower!

NORA: I can't do it any other way.

HELMER: Not so violently, Nora!

NORA: This is the way.

HELMER (*stops playing*): No, no—that is not a bit right.

NORA (*laughing and swinging the tambourine*): Didn't I tell you so?

RANK: Let me play for her.

HELMER (*getting up*): Yes, do. I can correct her better then.

Rank sits down at the piano and plays. Nora dances more and more wildly. Helmer has taken up a position beside the stove, and during her dance gives her frequent instructions. She does not seem to hear him; her hair comes down and falls over her shoulders; she pays no attention to it, but goes on dancing. Enter Mrs. Linde.

MRS. LINDE (*standing as if spell-bound in the doorway*): Oh!—

NORA (*as she dances*): Such fun, Christine!

HELMER: My dear darling Nora, you are dancing as if your life depended on it.

NORA: So it does.

HELMER: Stop, Rank; this is sheer madness. Stop, I tell you! (*Rank stops playing, and Nora suddenly stands still. Helmer goes up to her.*) I could never have believed it. You have forgotten everything I taught you.

NORA (*throwing away the tambourine*): There, you see.

HELMER: You will want a lot of coaching.

NORA: Yes, you see how much I need it. You must coach me up to the last minute. Promise me that, Torvald!

HELMER: You can depend on me.

NORA: You must not think of anything but me, either to-day or to-morrow; you mustn't open a single letter—not even open the letter-box—

HELMER: Ah, you are still afraid of that fellow—

NORA: Yes, indeed I am.

HELMER: Nora, I can tell from your looks that there is a letter from him lying there.

NORA: I don't know; I think there is; but you must not read anything of that kind now. Nothing horrid must come between us until this is all over.

RANK (*whispers to Helmer*): You mustn't contradict her.

HELMER (*taking her in his arms*): The child shall have her way. But to-morrow night, after you have danced—

NORA: Then you will be free. (*The Maid appears in the doorway to the right.*)

MAID: Dinner is served, ma'am.

NORA: We will have champagne, Helen.

MAID: Very good, ma'am. [*Exit.*]

HELMER: Hullo!—are we going to have a banquet?

NORA: Yes, a champagne banquet until the small hours. (*Calls out.*) And a few macaroons, Helen—lots, just for once!

HELMER: Come, come, don't be so wild and nervous. Be my own little skylark, as you used.

NORA: Yes, dear, I will. But go in now and you too, Doctor Rank. Christine, you must help me to do up my hair.

RANK (*whispers to Helmer as they go out*): I suppose there is nothing—she is not expecting anything?

HELMER: Far from it, my dear fellow; it is simply nothing more than this childish nervousness I was telling you of. (*They go into the right-hand room.*)

NORA: Well!

MRS. LINDE: Gone out of town.

NORA: I could tell from your face.

MRS. LINDE: He is coming home to-morrow evening. I wrote a note for him.

NORA: You should have let it alone; you must prevent nothing. After all, it is splendid to be waiting for a wonderful thing to happen.

MRS. LINDE: What is it that you are waiting for?

NORA: Oh, you wouldn't understand. Go in to them, I will come in a moment. (*Mrs. Linde goes into the dining-room. Nora stands still for a little while, as if to compose herself. Then she looks at her watch.*) Five o'clock. Seven hours until midnight; and then four-and-twenty hours until the next midnight. Then the Tarantella will be over. Twenty-four and seven? Thirty-one hours to live.

HELMER (*from the doorway on the right*): Where's my little skylark?

NORA (*going to him with her arms outstretched*): Here she is!

ACT III

THE SAME SCENE: *The table has been placed in the middle of the stage, with chairs round it. A lamp is burning on the table. The door into the hall stands open. Dance music is heard in the room above. Mrs. Linde is sitting at the table idly turning over the leaves of a book; she tries to read, but does not seem able to collect her thoughts. Every now and then she listens intently for a sound at the outer door.*

MRS. LINDE (*looking at her watch*): Not yet—and the time is nearly up. If only he does not—. (*Listens again.*) Ah, there he is. (*Goes into the hall and opens the outer door carefully. Light footsteps are heard on the stairs. She whispers.*) Come in. There is no one here.

KROGSTAD (*in the doorway*): I found a note from you at home. What does this mean?

MRS. LINDE: It is absolutely necessary that I should have a talk with you.

KROGSTAD: Really? And is it absolutely necessary that it should be here?

MRS. LINDE: It is impossible where I live; there is no private entrance to my rooms. Come in; we are quite alone. The maid is asleep, and the Helmers are at the dance upstairs.

KROGSTAD (*coming into the room*): Are the Helmers really at a dance to-night?

MRS. LINDE: Yes, why not?

KROGSTAD: Certainly—why not?

MRS. LINDE: Now, Nils, let us have a talk.

KROGSTAD: Can we two have anything to talk about?

MRS. LINDE: We have a great deal to talk about.

KROGSTAD: I shouldn't have thought so.

MRS. LINDE: No, you have never properly understood me.

KROGSTAD: Was there anything else to understand except what was obvious to all the world—a heartless woman jilts a man when a more lucrative chance turns up?

MRS. LINDE: Do you believe I am as absolutely heartless as all that? And do you believe that I did it with a light heart?

KROGSTAD: Didn't you?

MRS. LINDE: Nils, did you really think that?

KROGSTAD: If it were as you say, why did you write to me as you did at the time?

MRS. LINDE: I could do nothing else. As I had to break with you, it was my duty also to put an end to all that you felt for me.

KROGSTAD (*wringing his hands*): So that was it. And all this—only for the sake of money!

MRS. LINDE: You must not forget that I had a helpless mother and two little brothers. We couldn't wait for you, Nils; your prospects seemed hopeless then.

KROGSTAD: That may be so, but you had no right to throw me over for anyone else's sake.

MRS. LINDE: Indeed I don't know. Many a time did I ask myself if I had the right to do it.

KROGSTAD (*more gently*): When I lost you, it was as if all the solid ground went from under my feet. Look at me now—I am a shipwrecked man clinging to a bit of wreckage.

MRS. LINDE: But help may be near.

KROGSTAD: It *was* near; but then you came and stood in my way.

MRS. LINDE: Unintentionally, Nils. It was only to-day that I learned it was your place I was going to take in the Bank.

KROGSTAD: I believe you, if you say so. But now that you know it, are you not going to give it up to me?

MRS. LINDE: No, because that would not benefit you in the least.

KROGSTAD: Oh, benefit, benefit—I would have done it whether or no.

MRS. LINDE: I have learned to act prudently. Life, and hard, bitter necessity have taught me that.

KROGSTAD: And life has taught me not to believe in fine speeches.

MRS. LINDE: Then life has taught you something very reasonable. But deeds you must believe in?

KROGSTAD: What do you mean by that?

MRS. LINDE: You said you were like a shipwrecked man clinging to some wreckage.

KROGSTAD: I had good reason to say so.

MRS. LINDE: Well, I am like a shipwrecked woman clinging to some wreckage—no one to mourn for, no one to care for.

KROGSTAD: It was your own choice.

MRS. LINDE: There was no other choice—then.

KROGSTAD: Well, what now?

MRS. LINDE: Nils, how would it be if we two shipwrecked people could join forces?

KROGSTAD: What are you saying?

MRS. LINDE: Two on the same piece of wreckage would stand a better chance than each on their own.

KROGSTAD: Christine!

MRS. LINDE: What do you suppose brought me to town?

KROGSTAD: Do you mean that you gave me a thought?

MRS. LINDE: I could not endure life without work. All my life, as long as I can remember, I have worked, and it has been my greatest and only pleasure. But now I am quite alone in the world—my life is so dreadfully empty and I feel so forsaken. There is not the least pleasure in working for one's self. Nils, give me someone and something to work for.

KROGSTAD: I don't trust that. It is nothing but a woman's overstrained sense of generosity that prompts you to make such an offer of yourself.

MRS. LINDE: Have you ever noticed anything of the sort in me?

KROGSTAD: Could you really do it? Tell me—do you know all about my past life?

MRS. LINDE: Yes.

KROGSTAD: And do you know what they think of me here?

MRS. LINDE: You seemed to me to imply that with me you might have been quite another man.

KROGSTAD: I am certain of it.

MRS. LINDE: Is it too late now?

KROGSTAD: Christine, are you saying this deliberately? Yes, I am sure you are. I see it in your face. Have you really the courage, then—?

MRS. LINDE: I want to be a mother to someone, and your children need a mother. We two need each other. Nils, I have faith in your real character—I can dare anything together with you.

KROGSTAD (*grasps her hands*): Thanks, thanks, Christine! Now I shall find a way to clear myself in the eyes of the world. Ah, but I forgot—

MRS. LINDE (*listening*): Hush! The Tarantella! Go, go!

KROGSTAD: Why? What is it?

MRS. LINDE: Do you hear them up there? When that is over, we may expect them back.

KROGSTAD: Yes, yes—I will go. But it is all no use. Of course you are not aware what steps I have taken in the matter of the Helmers.

MRS. LINDE: Yes, I know all about that.

KROGSTAD: And in spite of that have you the courage to—?

MRS. LINDE: I understand very well to what lengths a man like you might be driven by despair.

KROGSTAD: If I could only undo what I have done!

MRS. LINDE: You cannot. Your letter is lying in the letter-box now.

KROGSTAD: Are you sure of that?

MRS. LINDE: Quite sure, but—

KROGSTAD (*with a searching look at her*): Is that what it all means?—that you want to save your friend at any cost? Tell me frankly. Is that it?

MRS. LINDE: Nils, a woman who has once sold herself for another's sake, doesn't do it a second time.

KROGSTAD: I will ask for my letter back.

MRS. LINDE: No, no.

KROGSTAD: Yes, of course I will. I will wait here until Helmer comes; I will tell him he must give me my letter back—that it only concerns my dismissal—that he is not to read it—

MRS. LINDE: No, Nils, you must not recall your letter.

KROGSTAD: But, tell me, wasn't it for that very purpose that you asked me to meet you here?

MRS. LINDE: In my first moment of fright, it was. But twenty-four hours have elapsed since then, and in that time I have witnessed incredible things in this house. Helmer must know all about it. This unhappy secret must be disclosed; they must have a complete understanding between them, which is impossible with all this concealment and falsehood going on.

KROGSTAD: Very well, if you will take the responsibility. But there is one thing I can do in any case, and I shall do it at once.

MRS. LINDE (*listening*): You must be quick and go! The dance is over; we are not safe a moment longer.

KROGSTAD: I will wait for you below.

MRS. LINDE: Yes, do. You must see me back to my door.

KROGSTAD: I have never had such an amazing piece of good fortune in my life! (*Goes out through the outer door. The door between the room and the hall remains open.*)

MRS. LINDE (*tidying up the room and laying her hat and cloak ready*): What a difference! what a difference! Some-one to work for and live for—a home to bring comfort into. That I will do, indeed. I wish they would be quick and come—(*Listens.*) Ah, there they are now. I must put on my things. (*Takes up her hat and cloak. Helmer's and Nora's voices are heard outside; a key is turned, and Helmer brings Nora almost by force into the hall. She is in an Italian costume with a large black shawl around her; he is in evening dress, and a black domino° which is flying open.*)

NORA (*hanging back in the doorway, and struggling with him*): No, no, no!—don't take me in. I want to go upstairs again; I don't want to leave so early.

HELMER: But, my dearest Nora—

NORA: Please, Torvald dear—please, *please*—only an hour more.

HELMER: Not a single minute, my sweet Nora. You know that was our agreement. Come along into the room; you are catching cold standing there. (*He brings her gently into the room, in spite of her resistance.*)

MRS. LINDE: Good-evening.

NORA: Christine!

HELMER: You here, so late, Mrs. Linde?

MRS. LINDE: Yes, you must excuse me; I was so anxious to see Nora in her dress.

NORA: Have you been sitting here waiting for me?

MRS. LINDE: Yes, unfortunately I came too late, you had already gone upstairs; and I thought I couldn't go away again without having seen you.

HELMER (*taking off Nora's shawl*): Yes, take a good look at her. I think she is worth looking at. Isn't she charming, Mrs. Linde?

MRS. LINDE: Yes, indeed she is.

HELMER: Doesn't she look remarkably pretty? Everyone thought so at the dance. But she is terribly self-willed, this sweet little person. What are we to do with her? You will hardly believe that I had almost to bring her away by force.

NORA: Torvald, you will repent not having let me stay, even if it were only for half an hour.

HELMER: Listen to her, Mrs. Linde! She had danced her Tarantella, and it had been a tremendous success, as it deserved—although possibly the performance was a trifle too realistic—a little more so, I mean, than was strictly compatible with the limitations of art. But never mind about that! The chief thing is, she had made a success—she had made a tremendous success. Do you think I was going to let her remain there after that, and spoil the effect? No, indeed! I took my charming little Capri maiden—my capricious little Capri maiden, I should say—on my arm; took one quick turn round the room; a curtsey on either side, and, as they say in novels, the beautiful apparition disappeared. An exit ought always to be effective, Mrs. Linde; but that is what I cannot make Nora understand. Pooh! this room is hot. (*Throws his domino on a chair, and opens the door of his room.*) Hullo! it's all dark in here. Oh, of course—excuse me—. (*He goes in, and lights some candles.*)

NORA (*in a hurried and breathless whisper*): Well?

MRS. LINDE (*in a low voice*): I have had a talk with him.

NORA: Yes, and—

MRS. LINDE: Nora, you must tell your husband all about it.

domino: A loose cloak, worn with a mask for the upper part of the face at masquerades.

NORA (*in an expressionless voice*): I knew it.

MRS. LINDE: You have nothing to be afraid of as far as Krogstad is concerned; but you must tell him.

NORA: I won't tell him.

MRS. LINDE: Then the letter will.

NORA: Thank you, Christine. Now I know what I must do. Hush—!

HELMER (*coming in again*): Well, Mrs. Linde, have you admired her?

MRS. LINDE: Yes, and now I will say good-night.

HELMER: What, already? Is this yours, this knitting?

MRS. LINDE (*taking it*): Yes, thank you, I had very nearly forgotten it.

HELMER: So you knit?

MRS. LINDE: Of course.

HELMER: Do you know, you ought to embroider.

MRS. LINDE: Really? Why?

HELMER: Yes, it's far more becoming. Let me show you. You hold the embroidery thus in your left hand, and use the needle with the right—like this—with a long, easy sweep. Do you see?

MRS. LINDE: Yes, perhaps—

HELMER: But in the case of knitting—that can never be anything but ungraceful; look here—the arms close together, the knitting-needles going up and down—it has a sort of Chinese effect—. That was really excellent champagne they gave us.

MRS. LINDE: Well,—good-night, Nora, and don't be self-willed any more.

HELMER: That's right, Mrs. Linde.

MRS. LINDE: Good-night, Mr. Helmer.

HELMER (*accompanying her to the door*): Good-night, good-night. I hope you will get home all right. I should be very happy to—but you haven't any great distance to go. Good-night, good-night. (*She goes out; he shuts the door after her, and comes in again.*) Ah!—at last we have got rid of her. She is a frightful bore, that woman.

NORA: Aren't you very tired, Torvald?

HELMER: No, not in the least.

NORA: Nor sleepy?

HELMER: Not a bit. On the contrary, I feel extraordinarily lively. And you?—you really look both tired and sleepy.

NORA: Yes, I am very tired. I want to go to sleep at once.

HELMER: There, you see it was quite right of me not to let you stay there any longer.

NORA: Everything you do is quite right, Torvald.

HELMER (*kissing her on the forehead*): Now my little skylark is speaking reasonably. Did you notice what good spirits Rank was in this evening?

NORA: Really? Was he? I didn't speak to him at all.

HELMER: And I very little, but I have not for a long time seen him in such good form. (*Looks for a while at her and then goes nearer to her.*) It is delightful to be at home by ourselves again, to be all alone with you—you fascinating, charming little darling!

NORA: Don't look at me like that, Torvald.

HELMER: Why shouldn't I look at my dearest treasure?—at all the beauty that is mine, all my very own?

NORA (*going to the other side of the table*): You mustn't say things like that to me to-night.

HELMER (*following her*): You have still got the Tarantella in your blood, I see. And it makes you more captivating than ever. Listen—the guests are beginning to go now. (*In a lower voice.*) Nora—soon the whole house will be quiet.

NORA: Yes, I hope so.

HELMER: Yes, my own darling Nora. Do you know, when I am out at a party with you like this, why I speak so little to you, keep away from you, and only send a stolen glance in your direction now and then?—do you know why I do that? It is because I make believe to myself that we are secretly in love, and you are my secretly promised bride, and that no one suspects there is anything between us.

NORA: Yes, yes—I know very well your thoughts are with me all the time.

HELMER: And when we are leaving, and I am putting the shawl over your beautiful young shoulders—on your lovely neck—then I imagine that you are my young bride and that we have just come from the wedding, and I am bringing you for the first time into our home—to be alone with you for the first time—quite alone with my shy little darling! All this evening I have longed for nothing but you. When I watched the seductive figures of the Tarantella, my blood was on fire; I could endure it no longer, and that was why I brought you down so early—

NORA: Go away, Torvald! You must let me go. I won't—

HELMER: What's that? You're joking, my little Nora! You won't—you won't? Am I not your husband—? (*A knock is heard at the outer door.*)

NORA (*starting*): Did you hear—?

HELMER (*going into the hall*): Who is it?

RANK (*outside*): It is I. May I come in for a moment?

HELMER (*in a fretful whisper*): Oh, what does he want now? (*Aloud.*) Wait a minute! (*Unlocks the door.*) Come, that's kind of you not to pass by our door.

RANK: I thought I heard your voice, and felt as if I should like to look in. (*With a swift glance round.*) Ah, yes!—these dear familiar rooms. You are very happy and cosy in here, you two.

HELMER: It seems to me that you looked after yourself pretty well upstairs too.

RANK: Excellently. Why shouldn't I? Why shouldn't one enjoy everything in this world?—at any rate as much as one can, and as long as one can. The wine was capital—

HELMER: Especially the champagne.

RANK: So you noticed that too? It is almost incredible how much I managed to put away!

NORA: Torvald drank a great deal of champagne to-night too.

RANK: Did he?

NORA: Yes, and he is always in such good spirits afterwards.

RANK: Well, why should one not enjoy a merry evening after a well-spent day?

HELMER: Well spent? I am afraid I can't take credit for that.

RANK (*clapping him on the back*): But I can, you know!

NORA: Doctor Rank, you must have been occupied with some scientific investigation to-day.

RANK: Exactly.

HELMER: Just listen!—little Nora talking about scientific investigations!

NORA: And may I congratulate you on the result?

RANK: Indeed you may.

NORA: Was it favourable, then?

RANK: The best possible, for both doctor and patient—certainty.

NORA (*quickly and searchingly*): Certainty?

RANK: Absolute certainty. So wasn't I entitled to make a merry evening of it after that?

NORA: Yes, you certainly were, Doctor Rank.

HELMER: I think so too, so long as you don't have to pay for it in the morning.

RANK: Oh well, one can't have anything in this life without paying for it.

NORA: Doctor Rank—are you fond of fancy-dress balls?

RANK: Yes, if there is a fine lot of pretty costumes.

NORA: Tell me—what shall we two wear at the next?

HELMER: Little featherbrain!—are you thinking of the next already?

RANK: We two? Yes, I can tell you. You shall go as a good fairy—

HELMER: Yes, but what do you suggest as an appropriate costume for that?

RANK: Let your wife go dressed just as she is in everyday life.

HELMER: That was really very prettily turned. But can't you tell us what you will be?

RANK: Yes, my dear friend, I have quite made up my mind about that.

HELMER: Well?

RANK: At the next fancy-dress ball I shall be invisible.

HELMER: That's a good joke!

RANK: There is a big black hat—have you never heard of hats that make you invisible? If you put one on, no one can see you.

HELMER (*suppressing a smile*): Yes, you are quite right.

RANK: But I am clean forgetting what I came for. Helmer, give me a cigar—one of the dark Havanas.

HELMER: With the greatest pleasure. (*Offers him his case.*)

RANK (*takes a cigar and cuts off the end*): Thanks.

NORA (*striking a match*): Let me give you a light.

RANK: Thank you. (*She holds the match for him to light his cigar.*) And now good-bye!

HELMER: Good-bye, good-bye, dear old man!

NORA: Sleep well, Doctor Rank.

RANK: Thank you for that wish.

NORA: Wish me the same.

RANK: You? Well, if you want me to sleep well! And thanks for the light. (*He nods to them both and goes out.*)

HELMER (*in a subdued voice*): He has drunk more than he ought.

NORA (*absently*): Maybe. (*Helmer takes a bunch of keys out of his pocket and goes into the hall.*) Torvald! what are you going to do there?

HELMER: Empty the letter-box; it is quite full; there will be no room to put the newspaper in to-morrow morning.

NORA: Are you going to work to-night?

HELMER: You know quite well I'm not. What is this? Someone has been at the lock.

NORA: At the lock—?

HELMER: Yes, someone has. What can it mean? I should never have thought the maid—. Here is a broken hairpin. Nora, it is one of yours.

NORA (*quickly*): Then it must have been the children—

HELMER: Then you must get them out of those ways. There, at last I have got it open. (*Takes out the contents of the letter-box, and calls to the kitchen.*) Helen!—Helen, put out the light over the front door. (*Goes back into the room and shuts the door into the hall. He holds out his hand full of letters.*) Look at that—look what a heap of them there are. (*Turning them over.*) What on earth is that?

NORA (*at the window*): The letter—No! Torvald, no!

HELMER: Two cards—of Rank's.

NORA: Of Doctor Rank's?

HELMER (*looking at them*): Doctor Rank. They were on the top. He must have put them in when he went out.

NORA: Is there anything written on them?

HELMER: There is a black cross over the name. Look there—what an uncomfortable idea! It looks as if he were announcing his own death.

NORA: It is just what he is doing.

HELMER: What? Do you know anything about it? Has he said anything to you?

NORA: Yes. He told me that when the cards came it would be his leave-taking from us. He means to shut himself up and die.

HELMER: My poor old friend! Certainly I knew we should not have him very long with us. But so soon! And so he hides himself away like a wounded animal.

NORA: If it has to happen, it is best it should be without a word—don't you think so, Torvald?

HELMER (*walking up and down*): He had so grown into our lives. I can't think of him as having gone out of them. He, with his sufferings and his loneliness, was like a cloudy background to our sunlit happiness. Well, perhaps it is best so. For him, anyway. (*Standing still.*) And perhaps for us too, Nora. We two are thrown quite upon each other now. (*Puts his arms round her.*) My darling wife, I don't feel as if I could hold you tight enough. Do you know, Nora, I have often wished that you might be threatened by some great danger, so that I might risk my life's blood, and everything, for your sake.

NORA (*disengages herself, and says firmly and decidedly*): Now you must read your letters, Torvald.

HELMER: No, no; not to-night. I want to be with you, my darling wife.

NORA: With the thought of your friend's death—

HELMER: You are right, it has affected us both. Something ugly has come between us—the thought of the horrors of death. We must try and rid our minds of that. Until then—we will each go to our own room.

NORA (*hanging on his neck*): Good-night, Torvald—Good-night!

HELMER (*kissing her on the forehead*): Good-night, my little singing-bird. Sleep sound, Nora. Now I will read my letters through. (*He takes his letters and goes into his room, shutting the door after him.*)

NORA (*gropes distractedly about, seizes Helmer's domino, throws it round her, while she says in quick, hoarse, spasmodic whispers*): Never to see him again. Never! Never! (*Puts her shawl over her head.*) Never to see my children again either—never again. Never! Never!—Ah! the icy, black water—the unfathomable depths—If only it were over! He has got it now—now he is reading it. Good-bye, Torvald and my children! (*She is about to rush out through the hall, when Helmer opens his door hurriedly and stands with an open letter in his hand.*)

HELMER: Nora!

NORA: Ah!—

HELMER: What is this? Do you know what is in this letter?

NORA: Yes, I know. Let me go! Let me get out!

HELMER (*holding her back*): Where are you going?

NORA (*trying to get free*): You shan't save me, Torvald!

HELMER (*reeling*): True? Is this true, that I read here? Horrible! No, no—it is impossible that it can be true.

NORA: It is true. I have loved you above everything else in the world.

HELMER: Oh, don't let us have any silly excuses.

NORA (*taking a step towards him*): Torvald—!

HELMER: Miserable creature—what have you done?

NORA: Let me go. You shall not suffer for my sake. You shall not take it upon yourself.

HELMER: No tragedy airs, please. (*Locks the hall door.*) Here you shall stay and give me an explanation. Do you understand what you have done? Answer me! Do you understand what you have done?

NORA (*looks steadily at him and says with a growing look of coldness in her face*): Yes, now I am beginning to understand thoroughly.

HELMER (*walking about the room*): What a horrible awakening! All these eight years—she who was my joy and pride—a hypocrite, a liar—worse, worse—a criminal! The unutterable ugliness of it all!—For shame! For shame! (*Nora is silent and looks steadily at him. He stops in front of her.*) I ought to have suspected that something of the sort would happen. I ought to have foreseen it. All your father's want of principle—be silent!—all your father's want of principle has come out in you. No religion, no morality, no sense of duty—. How I am punished for having winked at what he did! I did it for your sake, and this is how you repay me.

NORA: Yes, that's just it.

HELMER: Now you have destroyed all my happiness. You have ruined all my future. It is horrible to think of! I am in the power of an unscrupulous man; he can do what he likes with me, ask anything he likes of me, give me any orders he pleases—I dare not refuse. And I must sink to such miserable depths because of a thoughtless woman!

NORA: When I am out of the way, you will be free.

HELMER: No fine speeches, please. Your father had always plenty of those ready, too. What good would it be to me if you were out of the way, as you say? Not the slightest. He can make the affair known everywhere; and if he does, I may be falsely suspected of having been a party to your criminal action. Very likely people will think I was behind it all—that it was I who prompted you! And I have to thank you for all this—you whom I have cherished during the whole of our married life. Do you understand now what it is you have done for me?

NORA (*coldly and quietly*): Yes.

HELMER: It is so incredible that I can't take it in. But we must come to some understanding. Take off that shawl. Take it off, I tell you. I must try and appease him some way or another. The matter must be hushed up at any cost. And as for you and me, it must appear as if everything between us were just as before—but naturally only in the eyes of the world. You will still remain in my house, that is a matter of course. But I shall not allow you to bring up the children; I dare not trust them to you. To think that I should be obliged to say so to one whom I have loved so dearly, and whom I still—. No, that is all over. From this moment happiness is not the question; all that concerns us is to save the remains, the fragments, the appearance—

A ring is heard at the front-door bell.

HELMER (*with a start*): What is that? So late! Can the worst—? Can he—? Hide yourself, Nora. Say you are ill.

Nora stands motionless. Helmer goes and unlocks the hall door.

MAID (*half-dressed, comes to the door*): A letter for the mistress.

HELMER: Give it to me. (*Takes the letter, and shuts the door.*) Yes, it is from him. You shall not have it; I will read it myself.

NORA: Yes, read it.

HELMER (*standing by the lamp*): I scarcely have the courage to do it. It may mean ruin for both of us. No, I must know. (*Tears open the letter, runs his eye over a few lines, looks at a paper enclosed, and gives a shout of joy.*) Nora! (*She looks at him questioningly.*) Nora!—No, I must read it once again—. Yes, it is true! I am saved! Nora, I am saved!

NORA: And I?

HELMER: You too, of course; we are both saved, both you and I. Look, he sends you your bond back. He says he regrets and repents—that a happy change in his life—never mind what he says! We are saved, Nora! No one can do anything to you. Oh, Nora, Nora!—no, first I must destroy these hateful things. Let me see—. (*Takes a look at the bond.*) No, no, I won't look at it. The whole thing shall be nothing but a bad dream to me. (*Tears up the bond and both letters, throws them all into the stove, and watches them burn.*) There—now it doesn't exist any longer. He says that since Christmas Eve you—. These must have been three dreadful days for you, Nora.

NORA: I have fought a hard fight these three days.

HELMER: And suffered agonies, and seen no way out but—. No, we won't call any of the horrors to mind. We will only shout with joy, and keep saying, "It's all over! It's all over!" Listen to me, Nora. You don't seem to realise that it is all over. What is this?—such a cold, set face! My poor little Nora, I quite understand; you don't feel as if you could believe that I have forgiven you. But it is true, Nora, I swear it; I have forgiven you everything. I know that what you did, you did out of love for me.

NORA: That is true.

HELMER: You have loved me as a wife ought to love her husband. Only you had not sufficient knowledge to judge of the means you used. But do you suppose you are any the less dear to me, because you don't understand how to act on your own responsibility? No, no; only lean on me; I will advise you and direct you. I should not be a man if this womanly helplessness did not just give you a double attractiveness in my eyes. You must not think anymore about the hard things I said in my first moment of consternation, when I thought everything was going to overwhelm me. I have forgiven you, Nora; I swear to you I have forgiven you.

NORA: Thank you for your forgiveness. (*She goes out through the door to the right.*)

HELMER: No, don't go—. (*Looks in.*) What are you doing in there?

NORA (*from within*): Taking off my fancy dress.

HELMER (*standing at the open door*): Yes, do. Try and calm yourself, and make your mind easy again, my frightened little singing-bird. Be at rest, and feel secure; I have broad wings to shelter you under. (*Walks up and down by the door.*) How warm and cosy our home is, Nora. Here is shelter for you; here I will protect you like a hunted dove that I have saved from a hawk's claws; I will bring peace to your poor beating heart. It will come, little by little, Nora, believe me. To-morrow morning you will look upon it all quite differently; soon everything will be just as it was before. Very soon you won't need me to assure you that I have forgiven you; you will yourself feel the certainty that I have done so. Can you suppose I should ever think of such a thing as repudiating you, or even reproaching you? You have no idea what a true man's heart is like, Nora. There is something so indescribably sweet and satisfying, to a man, in the knowledge that he has forgiven his wife—forgiven her freely, and with all his heart. It seems as if that had made her, as it were, doubly his own; he has given her a new life, so to speak; and she has in a way become both wife and child to him. So you shall be for me after this, my little scared, helpless darling. Have no anxiety about anything, Nora; only be frank and open with me, and I will serve as will and conscience both to you—. What is this? Not gone to bed? Have you changed your things?

NORA (*in everyday dress*): Yes, Torvald, I have changed my things now.

HELMER: But what for?—so late as this.

NORA: I shall not sleep to-night.

HELMER: But, my dear Nora—

NORA (*looking at her watch*): It is not so very late. Sit down here, Torvald. You and I have much to say to one another. (*She sits down at one side of the table.*)

HELMER: Nora—what is this?—this cold, set face?

NORA: Sit down. It will take some time; I have a lot to talk over with you.

HELMER (*sits down at the opposite side of the table*): You alarm me, Nora!—and I don't understand you.

NORA: No, that is just it. You don't understand me, and I have never understood you either — before to-night. No, you mustn't interrupt me. You must simply listen to what I say. Torvald, this is a settling of accounts.

HELMER: What do you mean by that?

NORA (*after a short silence*): Isn't there one thing that strikes you as strange in our sitting here like this?

HELMER: What is that?

NORA: We have been married now eight years. Does it not occur to you that this is the first time we two, you and I, husband and wife, have had a serious conversation?

HELMER: What do you mean by serious?

NORA: In all these eight years — longer than that — from the very beginning of our acquaintance, we have never exchanged a word on any serious subject.

HELMER: Was it likely that I would be continually and forever telling you about worries that you could not help me to bear?

NORA: I am not speaking about business matters. I say that we have never sat down in earnest together to try and get at the bottom of anything.

HELMER: But, dearest Nora, would it have been any good to you?

NORA: That is just it; you have never understood me. I have been greatly wronged, Torvald — first by papa and then by you.

HELMER: What! By us two — by us two, who have loved you better than anyone else in the world?

NORA (*shaking her head*): You have never loved me. You have only thought it pleasant to be in love with me.

HELMER: Nora, what do I hear you saying?

NORA: It is perfectly true, Torvald. When I was at home with papa, he told me his opinion about everything, and so I had the same opinions; and if I differed from him I concealed the fact, because he would not have liked it. He called me his doll-child, and he played with me just as I used to play with my dolls. And when I came to live with you —

HELMER: What sort of an expression is that to use about our marriage?

NORA (*undisturbed*): I mean that I was simply transferred from papa's hands into yours. You arranged everything according to your own taste, and so I got the same tastes as you — or else I pretended to, I am really not quite sure which — I think sometimes the one and sometimes the other. When I look back on it, it seems to me as if I had been living here like a poor woman — just from hand to mouth. I have existed merely to perform tricks for you, Torvald. But you would have it so. You and papa have committed a great sin against me. It is your fault that I have made nothing of my life.

HELMER: How unreasonable and how ungrateful you are, Nora! Have you not been happy here?

NORA: No, I have never been happy. I thought I was, but it has never really been so.

HELMER: Not — not happy!

NORA: No, only merry. And you have always been so kind to me. But our home has been nothing but a playroom. I have been your doll-wife, just as at home I was papa's doll-child; and here the children have been my dolls. I thought it great fun when you played with me, just as they thought it great fun when I played with them. That is what our marriage has been, Torvald.

HELMER: There is some truth in what you say—exaggerated and strained as your view of it is. But for the future it shall be different. Playtime shall be over, and lesson-time shall begin.

NORA: Whose lessons? Mine, or the children's?

HELMER: Both yours and the children's, my darling Nora.

NORA: Alas, Torvald, you are not the man to educate me into being a proper wife for you.

HELMER: And you can say that!

NORA: And I—how am I fitted to bring up the children?

HELMER: Nora!

NORA: Didn't you say so yourself a little while ago—that you dare not trust me to bring them up?

HELMER: In a moment of anger! Why do you pay any heed to that?

NORA: Indeed, you were perfectly right. I am not fit for the task. There is another task I must undertake first. I must try and educate myself—you are not the man to help me in that. I must do that for myself. And that is why I am going to leave you now.

HELMER (*springing up*): What do you say?

NORA: I must stand quite alone, if I am to understand myself and everything about me. It is for that reason that I cannot remain with you any longer.

HELMER: Nora, Nora!

NORA: I am going away from here now, at once. I am sure Christine will take me in for the night—

HELMER: You are out of your mind! I won't allow it! I forbid you!

NORA: It is no use forbidding me anything any longer. I will take with me what belongs to myself. I will take nothing from you, either now or later.

HELMER: What sort of madness is this!

NORA: To-morrow I shall go home—I mean, to my old home. It will be easiest for me to find something to do there.

HELMER: You blind, foolish woman!

NORA: I must try and get some sense, Torvald.

HELMER: To desert your home, your husband and your children! And you don't consider what people will say!

NORA: I cannot consider that at all. I only know that it is necessary for me.

HELMER: It's shocking. This is how you would neglect your most sacred duties.

NORA: What do you consider my most sacred duties?

HELMER: Do I need to tell you that? Are they not your duties to your husband and your children?

NORA: I have other duties just as sacred.

HELMER: That you have not. What duties could those be?

NORA: Duties to myself.

HELMER: Before all else, you are a wife and a mother.

NORA: I don't believe that any longer. I believe that before all else I am a reasonable human being, just as you are—or, at all events, that I must try and become one. I know quite well, Torvald, that most people would think you right, and that views of that kind are to be found in books; but I can no longer content myself with what most people say, or with what is found in books. I must think over things for myself and get to understand them.

HELMER: Can you not understand your place in your own home? Have you not a reliable guide in such matters as that?—have you no religion?

NORA: I am afraid, Torvald, I do not exactly know what religion is.

HELMER: What are you saying?

NORA: I know nothing but what the clergyman said, when I went to be confirmed. He told us that religion was this, and that, and the other. When I am away from all this, and am alone, I will look into that matter too. I will see if what the clergyman said is true, or at all events if it is true for me.

HELMER: This is unheard of in a girl of your age! But if religion cannot lead you aright, let me try and awaken your conscience. I suppose you have some moral sense? Or—answer me—am I to think you have none?

NORA: I assure you, Torvald, that is not an easy question to answer. I really don't know. The thing perplexes me altogether. I only know that you and I look at it in quite a different light. I am learning, too, that the law is quite another thing from what I supposed; but I find it impossible to convince myself that the law is right. According to it a woman has no right to spare her old dying father, or to save her husband's life. I can't believe that.

HELMER: You talk like a child. You don't understand the conditions of the world in which you live.

NORA: No, I don't. But now I am going to try. I am going to see if I can make out who is right, the world or I.

HELMER: You are ill, Nora; you are delirious; I almost think you are out of your mind.

NORA: I have never felt my mind so clear and certain as to-night.

HELMER: And is it with a clear and certain mind that you forsake your husband and your children?

NORA: Yes, it is.

HELMER: Then there is only one possible explanation.

NORA: What is that?

HELMER: You do not love me anymore.

NORA: No, that is just it.

HELMER: Nora!—and you can say that?

NORA: It gives me great pain, Torvald, for you have always been so kind to me, but I cannot help it. I do not love you any more.

HELMER (*regaining his composure*): Is that a clear and certain conviction too?

NORA: Yes, absolutely clear and certain. That is the reason why I will not stay here any longer.

HELMER: And can you tell me what I have done to forfeit your love?

NORA: Yes, indeed I can. It was to-night, when the wonderful thing did not happen; then I saw you were not the man I had thought you.

HELMER: Explain yourself better. I don't understand you.

NORA: I have waited so patiently for eight years; for, goodness knows, I knew very well that wonderful things don't happen every day. Then this horrible misfortune came upon me; and then I felt quite certain that the wonderful thing was going to happen at last. When Krogstad's letter was lying out there, never for a moment did I imagine that you would consent to accept this man's conditions. I was so absolutely certain that you would say to him: Publish the thing to the whole world. And when that was done—

HELMER: Yes, what then?—when I had exposed my wife to shame and disgrace?

NORA: When that was done, I was so absolutely certain, you would come forward and take everything upon yourself, and say: I am the guilty one.

HELMER: Nora—!

NORA: You mean that I would never have accepted such a sacrifice on your part? No, of course not. But what would my assurances have been worth against yours? That was the wonderful thing which I hoped for and feared; and it was to prevent that, that I wanted to kill myself.

HELMER: I would gladly work night and day for you, Nora—bear sorrow and want for your sake. But no man would sacrifice his honour for the one he loves.

NORA: It is a thing hundreds of thousands of women have done.

HELMER: Oh, you think and talk like a heedless child.

NORA: Maybe. But you neither think nor talk like the man I could bind myself to. As soon as your fear was over—and it was not fear for what threatened me, but for what might happen to you—when the whole thing was past, as far as you were concerned it was exactly as if nothing at all had happened. Exactly as before, I was your little skylark, your doll, which you would in future treat with doubly gentle care, because it was so brittle and fragile. (*Getting up.*) Torvald—it was then it dawned upon me that for eight years I had been living here with a strange man, and had borne him three children—. Oh, I can't bear to think of it! I could tear myself into little bits!

HELMER (*sadly*): I see, I see. An abyss has opened between us—there is no denying it. But, Nora, would it not be possible to fill it up?

NORA: As I am now, I am no wife for you.

HELMER: I have it in me to become a different man.

NORA: Perhaps—if your doll is taken away from you.

HELMER: But to part!—to part from you! No, no, Nora, I can't understand that idea.

NORA (*going out to the right*): That makes it all the more certain that it must be done. (*She comes back with her cloak and hat and a small bag which she puts on a chair by the table.*)

HELMER: Nora, Nora, not now! Wait until to-morrow.

NORA (*putting on her cloak*): I cannot spend the night in a strange man's room.

HELMER: But can't we live here like brother and sister—?

NORA (*putting on her hat*): You know very well that would not last long. (*Puts the shawl round her.*) Good-bye, Torvald. I won't see the little ones. I know they are in better hands than mine. As I am now, I can be of no use to them.

HELMER: But some day, Nora—some day?

NORA: How can I tell? I have no idea what is going to become of me.

HELMER: But you are my wife, whatever becomes of you.

NORA: Listen, Torvald. I have heard that when a wife deserts her husband's house, as I am doing now, he is legally freed from all obligations towards her. In any case, I set you free from all your obligations. You are not to feel yourself bound in the slightest way, any more than I shall. There must be perfect freedom on both sides. See, here is your ring back. Give me mine.

HELMER: That too?

NORA: That too.

HELMER: Here it is.

NORA: That's right. Now it is all over. I have put the keys here. The maids know all about everything in the house—better than I do. To-morrow, after I have left her, Christine will come here and pack up my own things that I brought with me from home. I will have them sent after me.

HELMER: All over! All over!—Nora, shall you never think of me again?

NORA: I know I shall often think of you, the children, and this house.

HELMER: May I write to you, Nora?

NORA: No—never. You must not do that.

HELMER: But at least let me send you—

NORA: Nothing—nothing—

HELMER: Let me help you if you are in want.

NORA: No. I can receive nothing from a stranger.

HELMER: Nora—can I never be anything more than a stranger to you?

NORA (*taking her bag*): Ah, Torvald, the most wonderful thing of all would have to happen.

HELMER: Tell me what that would be!

NORA: Both you and I would have to be so changed that—. Oh, Torvald, I don't believe any longer in wonderful things happening.

HELMER: But I will believe in it. Tell me! So changed that—?

NORA: That our life together would be a real wedlock. Good-bye. (*She goes out through the hall.*)

HELMER (*sinks down on a chair at the door and buries his face in his hands*): Nora! Nora! (*Looks round, and rises.*) Empty. She is gone. (*A hope flashes across his mind.*) The most wonderful thing of all—?

The sound of a door shutting is heard from below. *[1879]*

THINKING ABOUT THE TEXT

1. Critics disagree about the necessity for Nora's leaving. What would your advice to her be? One critic thinks she has to leave because Torvald is impossible. What do you think?
2. Do you find credible the change in Nora's character from the first scene to the last? Do you know people who have transformed themselves?
3. Is Torvald in love with Nora in the first act? Explain. Is Nora in love with him in the first act? What is your idea of love in a marriage?
4. An early critic of the play claims that it is a comedy. Is this possible? How would you characterize it? Is it an optimistic or a pessimistic play? Is it tragic?
5. A few critics think Nora will return. Do you think this is possible? Under what conditions would you counsel her to do so? Do you think the "door heard 'round the world" had a positive or a negative effect on marriage?

HENRIK IBSEN
Memorandum

Ibsen's intentions in writing A Doll's House *have been widely debated from the opening of the play in 1879. In a speech given to the Norwegian Association for Women's Rights twenty years later, Ibsen claimed he was not specifically working for women's rights, but rather trying to give a "description of humanity." Nevertheless, the following, written before the production, clearly seems to contradict that.*

Here is the first memorandum:

NOTES FOR THE TRAGEDY OF TO-DAY

ROME, 19/10/78.

There are two kinds of spiritual laws, two kinds of conscience, one in men and a quite different one in women. They do not understand each other; but the woman is judged in practical life according to the man's law, as if she were not a woman but a man.

The wife in the play finds herself at last entirely at sea as to what is right and what wrong; natural feeling on the one side, and belief in authority on the other, leave her in utter bewilderment.

A woman cannot be herself in the society of to-day, which is exclusively a masculine society, with laws written by men, and with accusers and judges who judge feminine conduct from the masculine standpoint. *[1878]*

THINKING ABOUT THE TEXT

1. How can Torvald be a good example of Ibsen's point in the last paragraph?
2. Give a specific example from the play that illustrates Ibsen's point about Nora in the second paragraph.
3. How might Ibsen's point still be applicable today?

AUGUST STRINDBERG
Woman in *A Doll's House*

August Strindberg (1849–1912), one of the most celebrated writers in Swedish literature, was born in Stockholm and described his childhood as subject to "emotional insecurity, poverty, religious fanaticism and neglect." Strindberg is known primarily as a naturalist playwright. Miss Julie *(1888) and* The Stronger *(1889) are his most famous dramas. Eugene O'Neill, in his Nobel Prize acceptance speech said Strindberg was "that greatest genius of all modern dramatists." Strindberg had a troubled relationship with women, and some critics see him as misogynistic. The following essay was written as a preface to* Getting Married *(1884), a collection of stories. Some critics believe Strindberg was furious with Ibsen for encouraging "the new woman of the nineteenth century to focus on the injustices of marriage in a male-dominant society."*

Let us now take a look at how, for some unknown and incomprehensible reason, Ibsen has caricatured the cultured man and woman in his play *A Doll's House*, which has become the gospel of all the zealots for the Woman Question.

A Doll's House is a play. Perhaps it was written for a great actress whose performance of a sphinx-like part could be guaranteed to be a success. The author has done the husband a great injustice. He has done nothing to help him by making excuses for him on the grounds of inherited characteristics, as he has for his wife, and the excuses he makes for her he presses home over and over again when he talks about her father. But let us carefully examine this Nora, whom all our depraved cultured women have adopted as their ideal.

In the first act she lies to her husband. She conceals her forgery, she smuggles away some cakes, she behaves shiftily over all kinds of simple matters, apparently because she has a taste for lying. Her husband, on the other hand, openly confides everything to her, even the affairs of his Bank, which shows that he treats her as his true wife. She, not he, is the one who never tells anything. It is consequently a lie to say that he treats her like a doll, but true to say that she treats him like one. Surely no one believes that Nora did not know what she was doing when she committed forgery? Perhaps when they sit in the stalls and see an appealing actress in the footlights. I do not believe myself that she committed forgery *exclusively* for her husband's sake, for she tells us herself how tremendously she enjoyed their journey to Italy. No law, and no lawyer would accept that as an excuse. Thus we see that Nora is no saint; at best she is an accomplice who has also enjoyed the fruits of the theft. She incriminates herself. The author unintentionally gives her husband a further opportunity of showing how much he trusts and respects his wife when he lets him discuss with Nora the question of filling a vacancy at the Bank. But what a tyrant he is when he refuses to engage a forger as Head Clerk! What would Nora have said if Mr. Helmer had wanted to dismiss a maid? That would have been a very different story.

Then comes the scene in which she wants to borrow money from the syphilitic Dr. Rank. Nora really is sweet in this scene. As a prelude to her negotiations about the money she shows him her flesh-colored stockings.

> *Nora:* "Aren't they pretty? Of course it's dark in here now, but tomorrow.—No no, no, you're only allowed to see the feet. Oh well, I'll let you see the upper part too!"
>
> *Rank:* "Hm!"
>
> *Nora:* "Why are you looking so disapproving? Don't you think they'll suit me?"
>
> *Rank:* "I'm not qualified to express an opinion on that subject."
>
> *Nora:* (looks at him for a moment) "Shame on you!" (strikes him lightly on the ear with the stockings). "Take this then!" (Packs up the stockings.)
>
> *Rank:* "What are the other delights I'm to be allowed to see?"
>
> *Nora:* "You're so naughty I shan't let you see another thing." (She hums a little and looks for something in the box.)

As far as I can see Nora is offering herself — in return for hard cash. That is idealistic and charming, of course. All done out of love for her husband. To save him! But go to her husband and confess her dilemma, oh no, that would be too much for her pride! In Nora's language: she was not yet quite certain that he would respond by showing her the miracle of miracles.

Then comes the tarantella scene, which is introduced in order to throw a distorting light upon Helmer. The audience forgets that Nora is a hussy whom Helmer treats as a sensible woman, and is only allowed to see Helmer treating her *merely* as a doll. This is a dishonest scene, but it is very effective. In a word: it is good *theatre*.

That Helmer woos his wife that night simply shows that he is young, and that she is young. But the author makes it show that Helmer — who has not the least suspicion of the dirty game that Nora is playing — is nothing more than a sensual creature, sensual through and through, who has no appreciation whatever of his excellent wife's spiritual qualities, which she has not deigned to reveal, and this gives Nora a false halo of martyrdom. This is the most dishonest scene that Ibsen has ever written. After it comes the dénouement, which is a fine muddle, with a great deal of misrepresentation and many lies. Mr. Helmer wakes up, and finds that the wife to whom he is bound is a liar and a hypocrite. But the audience has been so impregnated with compassion for Nora that it thinks Helmer is wrong. If Helmer had witnessed the scene with the stockings he would not have begged Nora to stay, but of course he had not. Helmer learns that he, his wife, and his children have escaped social death and ruin. This makes him happy. Put your hand on your heart, you father of a family, and ask yourself if you would not be happy if you heard that your beloved wife, the mother of your children, was not going to be put into prison after all. But these feelings are too mundane. You must reach higher. Right up to the idealist's heaven of lies. Helmer must be chastised. He is the criminal. Yet all the same he speaks kindly to his deceitful wife. — "Oh," he says, "these must have been three dreadful days for you, Nora." But then the author regrets having been fair to the poor fellow, and puts some untrue words into his mouth. Of course it is clumsy of Helmer to tell Nora that he forgives her. And for her to accept forgiveness from one who has always trusted her, while she has lied to him would be far too simple-minded. No, Nora has grander ideas. She is so magnanimous about forgetting the past that she forgets everything that happened in the first act. This is what she now says, and the stalls have forgotten the first act too, for their handkerchiefs are out.

> *Nora:* "Doesn't it occur to you that this is the first time that we two, husband and wife, have talked seriously to one another?"

Helmer is so taken aback by this mendacious question that he (or the author!) answers: "Seriously — what do you mean by seriously?" — The author has achieved his object, Helmer has been made to look a fool. He should have answered: "No, my little pet, it doesn't occur to me at all. We talked very seriously together when our children were born, for we talked about their future. We talked very seriously when you wanted to install the forger, Krogstad, as head clerk in the Bank. We talked very seriously when my life was in danger, and about giving

Mrs. Linde a job, and about running the house, and about your dead father, and our syphilitic friend Dr. Rank. We have talked seriously for eight long years, but we have joked too, and we were right to do so, for life isn't only a serious business. We could indeed have had more serious talk if you'd been kind enough to tell me of your worries, but you were too proud, for you preferred to be my doll rather than my friend." But Mr. Ibsen does not allow Helmer to say these sensible things, for he must be shown to be a fool, and Nora must be allowed her most brilliant answer, which will be quoted for twenty-five years. This is her reply:

> *Nora:* "For eight (8!) long years—why longer—from the very first time we met, we have never exchanged a serious word on a serious matter."

—But now, true to his unfortunate role of fool, Mr. Helmer answers: "Would you have liked me to be forever telling you of problems that you wouldn't have been able to help me with?" It is kind of Helmer to say this, but it is not honest, for he should have turned on her for not confiding in him. This scene is absurdly false. After it Nora has some very fine (French) replies, which consist of such hollow wisdom that they vanish when you blow at them.

> *Nora:* "You have never loved me. You have only thought it amusing to be in love with me!"

What is the difference? She also says: "You have never understood me!" Not 10
an easy thing for Helmer to do as she has always deceived him. Then poor Helmer is made to say some very stupid things, like: "I'm going to educate you." That is surely the last thing a man should say to a woman. But Mr. Helmer must be stupid, for the end is drawing near, and Nora is going to "turn the screw." At that Helmer weakens. He begs for forgiveness; forgiveness because she has committed forgery, because she has lied, for all her faults.

Then Nora says a few sensible things. She wants to give up her marriage in order to find herself. The question is whether she could not do that just as well in the same house as her children, in contact with the realities of life, and while struggling with her love for Helmer, for her love will not die instantaneously any more than any other love. But this is a question of taste. When she says that she is unfit to bring up her children she is lying, for not long before she had put herself on a pretty high pedestal when castigating the innocent Helmer. To be logical she ought to have stayed with her children if she really thought her husband was such a dolt that he would not be able to grasp the "miracle." For how could she leave the education of her children to such a poor specimen? All her babbling about the "miracle" that would have happened if Helmer had taken the blame for her crime upon himself is such romantic nonsense that it does not deserve discussion. That "hundreds of thousands of women" have sacrificed themselves for their husbands is a compliment to the ladies that Ibsen should be too old to pay. Nora rambles on pell-mell: she has loved him, he has loved her, and yet she can say that for eight years she has been a stranger to him, and borne three children to a man who has been a stranger to her. Helmer agrees that he has not been perfect, and promises to reform. This is handsome of him and there seems to be every guarantee that things will be better in the future than they have been in the past. But of course this will not do in a play.

The curtain must come down on a Bang. So Nora proves (?) that she has been a doll. Had it not been Helmer who decided where the furniture should stand? Maybe. But if only the mistress of the house had deigned to make her wishes known there would have been no doubt about who was the master.

Why did she not do so? Probably because she thought it did not matter, and she may have been right. If Nora was a doll, then upon my word it was not Helmer's fault, for he had always shown that he trusted her as a man should trust his wife. But this was not what Ibsen wanted to prove, he wanted to prove the opposite, but he was not strong enough to do so, for he did not believe in his task, and his sense of justice broke through from time to time.

What its author himself really meant by *A Doll's House* we shall never know. The fact that it gave the impression of being, and was generally accepted as a manifesto for the oppressed woman, immediately raised a storm in which the steadiest people lost their heads. For the play proves the direct opposite of what it is intended to prove. Or is it that the whole play is a proof of the danger of writing plays on serious subjects? Or, to take another point of view altogether: is it in fact *not* a defense of the oppressed woman, but simply an illustration of the effect of heredity upon character? If this is the case then the author should have been honorable enough to give Helmer's heredity as an excuse for his behavior. Or is it Nora's bad upbringing? She herself places a lot of the blame on this. Why then cannot Helmer blame his bad upbringing? Or is it nothing more than a play, pure and simple, an example of our modern courtship of the ladies? If so it should be put among the plays classed as "Public Entertainments," and not be regarded as a matter for serious discussion, still less have the honor of setting the two halves of humanity against each other. *[1884]*

THINKING ABOUT THE TEXT

1. What specific evidence is there that Strindberg might be misogynistic?
2. Point out instances of Strindberg's sarcasm and irony.
3. What are some specific complaints Strindberg has against Nora? What do you think of their validity?

EMMA GOLDMAN

Review of *A Doll's House*

Emma Goldman (1869–1940), a leading radical activist, thinker, and writer in the first half of the twentieth century, was born in Russia and immigrated to the United States in 1885. She agitated passionately for women's and worker's rights. She was deported to Russia in 1919 for being an anarchist but left, eventually becoming a British citizen. She began the radical journal Mother Earth *and wrote influential books such as* Anarchism and Other Essays *(1910) and* The Social Significance of the Modern Drama *(1914), from which the following selection is taken.*

In *A Doll's House* Ibsen returns to the subject so vital to him—the Social Lie and Duty—this time as manifesting themselves in the sacred institution of the home and in the position of woman in her gilded cage.

Nora is the beloved, adored wife of *Torvald Helmer*. He is an admirable man, rigidly honest, of high moral ideals, and passionately devoted to his wife and children. In short, a good man and an enviable husband. Almost every mother would be proud of such a match for her daughter, and the latter would consider herself fortunate to become the wife of such a man.

Nora, too, considers herself fortunate. Indeed, she worships her husband, believes in him implicitly, and is sure that if ever her safety should be menaced, *Torvald*, her idol, her god, would perform the miracle.

When a woman loves as *Nora* does, nothing else matters; least of all, social, legal, or moral considerations. Therefore, when her husband's life is threatened, it is no effort, it is joy for *Nora* to forge her father's name to a note and borrow 800 cronen on it, in order to take her sick husband to Italy.

In her eagerness to serve her husband, and in perfect innocence of the legal 5 aspect of her act, she does not give the matter much thought, except for her anxiety to shield him from any emergency that may call upon him to perform the miracle in her behalf. She works hard, and saves every penny of her pin-money to pay back the amount she borrowed on the forged check.

Nora is light-hearted and gay, apparently without depth. Who, indeed, would expect depth of a doll, a "squirrel," a song-bird? Her purpose in life is to be happy for her husband's sake, for the sake of the children; to sing, dance, and play with them. Besides, is she not shielded, protected, and cared for? Who, then, would suspect *Nora* of depth? But already in the opening scene, when *Torvald* inquires what his precious "squirrel" wants for a Christmas present, *Nora* quickly asks him for money. Is it to buy macaroons or finery? In her talk with *Mrs. Linde*, *Nora* reveals her inner self, and forecasts the inevitable debacle of her doll's house.

After telling her friend how she had saved her husband, Nora says: "When Torvald gave me money for clothes and so on, I never used more than half of it; I always bought the simplest things. . . . Torvald never noticed anything. But it was often very hard, Christina dear. For it's nice to be beautifully dressed. Now, isn't it? . . . Well, and besides that, I made money in other ways. Last winter I was so lucky—I got a heap of copying to do. I shut myself up every evening and wrote far into the night. Oh, sometimes I was so tired, so tired. And yet it was splendid to work in that way and earn money. I almost felt as if I was a man."

Down deep in the consciousness of *Nora* there evidently slumbers personality and character, which could come into full bloom only through a great miracle—not the kind *Nora* hopes for, but a miracle just the same.

Nora had borrowed the money from *Nils Krogstad*, a man with a shady past in the eyes of the community and of the righteous moralist, *Torvald Helmer*. So long as *Krogstad* is allowed the little breathing space a Christian people grants to him who has once broken its laws, he is reasonably human. He does not molest *Nora*. But when *Helmer* becomes director of the bank in which *Krogstad* is employed, and threatens the man with dismissal, *Krogstad* naturally fights back. For as he says to *Nora*: "If need be, I shall fight as though for my life to keep my little place in the bank. . . . It's not only for the money: that matters least to me. It's something else. Well, I'd better make a clean breast of it. Of course you know, like every one else, that some years ago I—got into trouble. . . . The matter never came into court; but from that moment all paths were barred to me. Then I took up the business you know about. I was obliged to grasp at something; and I don't think I've been one of the worst. But now I must clear out of it all. My sons are growing up; for their sake I must try to win back as much respectability as I can. This place in the bank was the first step, and now your husband wants to kick me off the ladder, back into the mire. Mrs. Helmer, you evidently have no idea what you have really done. But I can assure you that it was nothing more and nothing worse that made me an outcast from society. . . . But this I may tell you, that if I'm flung into the gutter a second time, you shall keep me company."

Even when *Nora* is confronted with this awful threat, she does not fear for herself, only for *Torvald*—so good, so true, who has such an aversion to debts, but who loves her so devotedly that for her sake he would take the blame upon himself. But this must never be. *Nora*, too, begins a fight for life, for her husband's life and that of her children. Did not *Helmer* tell her that the very presence of a criminal like *Krogstad* poisons the children? And is she not a criminal?

Torvald Helmer assures her, in his male conceit, that "early corruption generally comes from the mother's side, but of course the father's influence may act in the same way. And this Krogstad has been poisoning his own children for years past by a life of lies and hypocrisy—that's why I call him morally ruined."

Poor *Nora*, who cannot understand why a daughter has no right to spare her dying father anxiety, or why a wife has no right to save her husband's life, is surely not aware of the true character of her idol. But gradually the veil is lifted. At first, when in reply to her desperate pleading for *Krogstad*, her husband discloses the true reason for wanting to get rid of him: "The fact is, he was a college chum of mine—there was one of those rash friendships between us that one so often repents later. I don't mind confessing it—he calls me by my Christian name; and he insists on doing it even when others are present. He delights in putting on airs of familiarity—Torvald here, Torvald there! I assure you it's most painful to me. He would make my position at the bank perfectly unendurable."

And then again when the final blow comes. For forty-eight hours *Nora* battles for her ideal, never doubting *Torvald* for a moment. Indeed, so absolutely sure is she of her strong oak, her lord, her god, that she would rather kill herself than have him take the blame for her act. The end comes, and with it the doll's house tumbles down, and *Nora* discards her doll's dress—she sheds her skin, as it were. *Torvald Helmer* proves himself a petty Philistine, a bully and a coward, as so many good husbands when they throw off their respectable cloak.

Helmer's rage over *Nora*'s crime subsides the moment the danger of publicity is averted—proving that *Helmer*, like many a moralist, is not so much incensed at *Nora*'s offense as by the fear of being found out. Not so *Nora*. Finding out is her salvation. It is then that she realizes how much she has been wronged, that she is only a plaything, a doll to *Helmer*. In her disillusionment she says, "You have never loved me. You only thought it amusing to be in love with me. [. . .] I think that before all else I am a human being, just as much as you are—or, at least, I will try to become one. I know that most people agree with you, Torvald, and that they say so in books. But henceforth I can't be satisfied with what most people say, and what is in books. I must think things out for myself and try to get clear about them. . . . I had been living here these eight years with a strange man, and had borne him three children—Oh! I can't bear to think of it—I could tear myself to pieces!. . . . I can't spend the night in a strange man's house."

Is there anything more degrading to woman than to live with a stranger, and 15
bear him children? Yet, the lie of the marriage institution decrees that she shall continue to do so, and the social conception of duty insists that for the sake of that lie she need be nothing else than a plaything, a doll, a nonentity.

When *Nora* closes behind her the door of her doll's house, she opens wide the gate of life for woman, and proclaims the revolutionary message that only perfect freedom and communion make a true bond between man and woman, meeting in the open, without lies, without shame, free from the bondage of duty. *[1914]*

THINKING ABOUT THE TEXT

1. What idea of Nora's does Goldman seem most impressed by?
2. What is Goldman's view of moralists? What does Nora mean by "a strange man"?
3. What specifically do you think Goldman meant in 1914 when referring to "the bondage of duty" (para. 16)?

JOAN TEMPLETON

From *The* Doll House *Backlash: Criticism, Feminism, and Ibsen*

Joan Templeton (b. 1942) received her undergraduate degree at Centenary College and her Ph.D. from the University of Oregon. She is a noted Ibsen scholar who has published widely on the dramatist and others. Her books include Ibsen's Women *(1997) and* Munch's Ibsen *(2008). She taught for many years at Long Island University where she was professor of English and comparative literature. The following selection is from "The* Doll House *Backlash: Criticism, Feminism, and Ibsen," published in* PMLA *in 1989. Interestingly, most of the critics she cites as attacking Nora are men who wrote in an era when feminist thinking was largely disparaged.*

For over a hundred years, Nora has been under direct siege as exhibiting the most perfidious characteristics of her sex; the original outcry of the 1880s is swollen now to a mighty chorus of blame. She is denounced as an irrational and frivolous narcissist; an "abnormal" woman, a "hysteric"; a vain, unloving egoist who abandons her family in a paroxysm of selfishness. The proponents of the last view would seem to think Ibsen had in mind a housewife Medea, whose cruelty to husband and children he tailored down to fit the framed, domestic world of realist drama.

The first attacks were launched against Nora on moral grounds and against Ibsen, ostensibly, on "literary" ones. The outraged reviewers of the premiere claimed that *A Doll House* did not have to be taken as a serious statement about women's rights because the heroine of act 3 is an incomprehensible transformation of the heroine of acts 1 and 2. This reasoning provided an ideal way to dismiss Nora altogether; nothing she said needed to be taken seriously, and her door slamming could be written off as silly theatrics (Marker and Marker 85–87).

The argument for the two Noras, which still remains popular,[1] has had its most determined defender in the Norwegian scholar Else Høst, who argues that Ibsen's carefree, charming "lark" could never have become the "newly fledged feminist." In any case it is the "childish, expectant, ecstatic, broken-hearted Nora" who makes A Doll House immortal (28; my trans.); the other one, the unfeeling woman of act 3 who coldly analyzes the flaws in her marriage, is psychologically unconvincing and wholly unsympathetic.

The most unrelenting attempt on record to trivialize Ibsen's protagonist, and a favorite source for Nora's later detractors, is Hermann Weigand's.[2] In a classic 1925 study, Weigand labors through forty-nine pages to demonstrate that Ibsen conceived of Nora as a silly, lovable female. At the beginning, Weigand confesses, he was, like all men, momentarily shaken by the play: "Having had the misfortune to be born of the male sex, we slink away in shame, vowing to mend our ways." The chastened critic's remorse is short-lived, however, as a "clear male voice, irreverently breaking the silence," stuns with its critical acumen: "'The meaning of the final scene,' the voice says, 'is epitomized by Nora's remark: "Yes, Torvald. Now I have changed my dress."'" With this epiphany as guide, Weigand spends the night poring over the "little volume." Dawn arrives, bringing with it the return of "masculine self-respect" (26–27). For there is only one explanation for the revolt of "this winsome little woman" (52) and her childish door slamming: Ibsen meant *A Doll House* as comedy. Nora's erratic behavior at the curtain's fall leaves us laughing heartily, for there is no doubt that she will return home to "revert, imperceptibly, to her role of song-bird and charmer" (68). After all, since Nora is

> an irresistibly bewitching piece of femininity, an extravagant poet and romancer, utterly lacking in sense of fact, and endowed with a natural gift for play-acting which makes her instinctively dramatize her experiences: how can the settlement fail of a fundamentally comic appeal? (64)

The most popular way to render Nora inconsequential has been to attack her 5
morality; whatever the vocabulary used, the arguments have remained much the same for over a century. Oswald Crawford, writing in the *Fortnightly Review* in 1891, scolded that while Nora may be "charming as doll-women may be charming," she is "unprincipled" (732). A half century later, after Freudianism had produced a widely accepted "clinical" language of disapproval, Nora could be called

[1]See, for example, Robert Brustein (49) and Marvin Rosenberg, whose article is a rehash of Høst's points, although Rosenberg seems unacquainted with her well-known essay.

[2]For a thoroughgoing defense of Weigand by a much later critic who understands that "A Doll House is not a feminist play," see R. F. Dietrich.

"abnormal." Mary McCarthy lists Nora as one of the "neurotic" women whom Ibsen, she curiously claims, was the first playwright to put on stage (80). For Maurice Valency, Nora is a case study of female hysteria, a willful, unwomanly woman: "Nora is a carefully studied example of what we have come to know as the hysterical personality—bright, unstable, impulsive, romantic, quite immune from feelings of guilt, and, at bottom, not especially feminine" (151–52).

More recent assaults on Nora have argued that her forgery to obtain the money to save her husband's life proves her irresponsibility and egotism. Brian Johnston condemns Nora's love as "unintelligent" and her crime as "a trivial act which nevertheless turns to evil because it refused to take the universal ethical realm into consideration at all" (97); Ibsen uses Torvald's famous pet names for Nora—lark, squirrel—to give her a "strong 'animal' identity" and to underscore her inability to understand the ethical issues faced by human beings (97). Evert Sprinchorn argues that Nora had only to ask her husband's kindly friends (entirely missing from the play) for the necessary money: ". . . any other woman would have done so. But Nora knew that if she turned to one of Torvald's friends for help, she would have had to share her role of savior with someone else" (124).

Even Nora's sweet tooth is evidence of her unworthiness, as we see her "surreptitiously devouring the forbidden [by her husband] macaroons," even "brazenly offer[ing] macaroons to Doctor Rank, and finally lying in her denial that the macaroons are hers"; eating macaroons in secret suggests that "Nora is deceitful and manipulative from the start" and that her exit thus "reflects only a petulant woman's irresponsibility" (Schlueter 64–65). As she eats the cookies, Nora adds insult to injury by declaring her hidden wish to say "death and damnation" in front of her husband, thus revealing, according to Brian Downs, of Christ's College, Cambridge, "something a trifle febrile and morbid" in her nature (Downs 130).

Much has been made of Nora's relationship with Doctor Rank, the surest proof, it is argued, of her dishonesty. Nora is revealed as *la belle dame sans merci* when she "suggestively queries Rank whether a pair of silk stockings will fit her" (Schlueter 65); she "flirts cruelly with [him] and toys with his affection for her, drawing him on to find out how strong her hold over him actually is" (Sprinchorn 124).

Nora's detractors have often been, from the first, her husband's defenders. In an argument that claims to rescue Nora and Torvald from "the campaign for the liberation of women" so that they "become vivid and disturbingly real," Evert Sprinchorn pleads that Torvald "has given Nora all the material things and all the sexual attention that any young wife could reasonably desire. He loves beautiful things, and not least his pretty wife" (121). Nora is incapable of appreciating her husband because she "is not a normal woman. She is compulsive, highly imaginative, and very much inclined to go to extremes." Since it is she who has acquired the money to save his life, Torvald, and not Nora, is really the "wife in the family," although he "has regarded himself as the breadwinner . . . the main support of his wife and children, as any decent husband would like to regard himself" (122). In another defense, John Chamberlain argues that Torvald deserves our sympathy because he is no "mere common or garden chauvinist." If Nora were less the actress Weigand has proved her to be, "the woman in her might observe what the embarrassingly naive feminist overlooks or ignores, namely, the indications that Torvald, for all his faults, is taking her at least as seriously as he can—and perhaps even as seriously as she deserves" (85).

All female, or no woman at all, Nora loses either way. Frivolous, deceitful, or unwomanly, she qualifies neither as a heroine nor as a spokeswoman for feminism. Her famous exit embodies only "the latest and shallowest notion of emancipated womanhood, abandoning her family to go out into the world in search of 'her true identity' " (Freedman 4). And in any case, it is only naive Nora who believes she might make a life for herself; "the audience," argues an essayist in *College English*, "can see most clearly how Nora is exchanging a practical doll's role for an impractical one" (Pearce 343). We are back to the high condescension of the Victorians and Edward Dowden:

> Inquires should be set on foot to ascertain whether a manuscript may not lurk in some house in Christiania [Oslo] entitled *Nora Helmer's Reflections in Solitude*; it would be a document of singular interest, and probably would conclude with the words, "Tomorrow I return to Torvald; have been exactly one week away; shall insist on a free woman's right to unlimited macaroons as test of his reform." (248)

In the first heady days of *A Doll House* Nora was rendered powerless by substi- 10
tuted denouements and sequels that sent her home to her husband. Now Nora's critics take the high-handed position that all the fuss was unnecessary, since Nora is not a feminist heroine. And yet in the twentieth-century case against her, whether Nora is judged childish, "neurotic," or unprincipled and whether her accuser's tone is one of witty derision, clinical sobriety, or moral earnestness, the purpose behind the verdict remains that of Nora's frightened contemporaries: to destroy her credibility and power as a representative of women. The demon in the house, the modern "half-woman," as Strindberg called her in the preface to *Miss Julie*, who, "now that she has been discovered has begun to make a noise" (65), must be silenced, her heretical forces destroyed, so that *A Doll House* can emerge a safe classic, rescued from feminism, and Ibsen can assume his place in the pantheon of true artists, unsullied by the "woman question" and the topical taint of history. *[1989]*

Works Cited

Brustein, Robert. *The Theatre of Revolt*. New York: Little, 1962.

Chamberlain, John. *Ibsen: The Open Vision*. London: Athlone, 1982.

Crawford, Oswald. "The Ibsen Question." *Fortnightly Review* 55 (1891): 727–40.

Dietrich, R. F. "Nora's Change of Dress: Weigand Revisited." *Theatre Annual* 36 (1981): 20–40.

Dowden, Edward. "Henrik Ibsen." Ibsen, *Works* 3: 219–58.

Downs, Brian. *A Study of Six Plays by Ibsen*. 1959. New York: Octagon, 1978.

Freedman, Morris. *The Moral Impulse: Modern Drama from Ibsen to the Present.* Carbondale: Southern Illinois UP, 1967.
Høst, Else. "Nora." *Edda* 46 (1946): 13–48.
Ibsen, Henrik. *Ibsens Samlede Verker.* Vol. 3. Oslo: Gyldendal, 1978. 3 vols.
———. *The Works of Henrik Ibsen.* Ed. and trans. William Archer. 13 vols. New York: Scribner's, 1917.
Johnston, Brian. *The Ibsen Cycle.* Boston: Hall, 1975.
Marker, Frederick, and Lisa-Lone Marker. "The First Nora: Notes on the World Premiere of *A Doll's House.*" *Ibsenårboken* 11 (1970–71): 84–100.
McCarthy, Mary. "The Will and Testament of Ibsen." *Partisan Review* 23 (1956): 74–80.
Pearce, Richard. "The Limits of Realism." *College English* 31 (1970): 335–43.
Rosenberg, Marvin. "Ibsen versus Ibsen: Or, Two Versions of *A Doll House.*" *Modern Drama* 12 (1969): 187–96.
Schlueter, June. "How to Get into *A Doll House*: Ibsen's Play as an Introduction to Drama." Shafer 63–68.
Sprinchorn, Evert. "Ibsen and the Actors." *Ibsen and the Theatre.* Ed. Errol Durbach. New York: New York UP, 1980. 118–30.
Strindberg, August. Author's Foreword. *Miss Julie. Six Plays of Strindberg.* Trans. Elizabeth Sprigge. Garden City: Doubleday, 1955. 61–73.
Valency, Maurice. *The Flower and the Castle: An Introduction to Modern Drama.* 1963. New York: Schocken, 1982.
Weigand, Hermann. *The Modern Ibsen: A Reconsideration.* New York: Holt, 1925.

THINKING ABOUT THE TEXT

1. What is your response to the Weigand block quote (para. 4)?
2. Templeton argues that critics, mostly men, wanted to make the play "a safe classic" (para. 10). How might our selection support the claim?
3. Explain why one of these critics seems to you to be misguided.

SUSANNA RUSTIN

Why *A Doll's House* by Henrik Ibsen Is More Relevant Than Ever

Susanna Rustin (b. 1971) is a features writer and editor for the Guardian. *She grew up in London and studied at York University. She is active in local politics, having run for the Green Party ticket.*

When, next Wednesday evening, Hattie Morahan picks up an armful of Christmas shopping and steps on stage to open a run of Ibsen's *A Doll's House,* it will be for the third time in just over a year. Morahan first starred as Nora, the 1870s Norwegian wife and mother who realises her life is a sham, at the Young Vic last July, but such is the production's popularity that this is its second revival.

Moreover, two other, brand new productions have been seen in recent months: in May an adaptation by Bryony Lavery received rave reviews at the Royal Exchange in Manchester, and in April Zinnie Harris's version, set in Edwardian London and first seen at the Donmar Warehouse in London with Gillian Anderson in the lead role, was staged by the National Theatre of Scotland in Edinburgh.

Three such high-profile productions in the space of a few months is unusual. Morahan has already won the Evening Standard and Critics' Circle awards for her performance and was unlucky to miss out to Helen Mirren at the Oliviers. But the combination of the play's brisk and thriller-like plotting, and the sense shared by everyone involved that the play still speaks to audiences in ways that feel fresh and interesting, means there is no fear of overkill.

In fact, Morahan, speaking to me just before Thursday's dress rehearsal, says she feels "liberated" to be occupying the role again, while director Carrie Cracknell says that even the last few days of rehearsals have thrown up new insights into Ibsen's endlessly complex characters. "There is something timeless about it," Morahan says, "which is what's so shocking. You try to keep it in its box of 19th-century Scandinavia, but the things Ibsen writes mean it ceases to be about a particular milieu and becomes about marriage (or partnership) and money. These are universal anxieties, and it seems from talking to people that it resonates in the most visceral way, especially if they are or have been in a difficult relationship. Someone said to me the other night, 'That's the play that broke my parents' marriage up.' It shines a very harsh light on the messy heart of relationships, and how difficult it can be to be honest with another human being even if you love them."

The play, hugely controversial when first published and performed in Copenhagen in 1879, is about the unravelling of a family. Nora and Torvald Helmer believe they are happily married and on the brink of a blissful new phase of life: Torvald has been promoted to bank manager and their money worries are over. But Nora has a secret debt, incurred with good intentions and a forged signature, and with her husband's new power comes the threat of blackmail.

Over three acts the illusion of bourgeois contentment unravels, and the play 5
culminates in a spectacular scene between the couple as Nora's lie is exposed and Torvald first blames, then forgives her—and is finally abandoned as Nora recognises the truth of her situation. She accuses her husband, and her father before him, of having used her as a doll, and declares herself unfit to be a wife or mother until she has learned to be herself. Ibsen's final stage direction, of the door closing behind her, is one of the most famous ever written.

Unsurprisingly, feminist contemporaries of Ibsen welcomed the play, although, as theatre critic Caroline McGinn points out, when he was invited to speak at a women's congress, he told them he wasn't a feminist himself. The first German production notoriously altered the ending so that Nora did not leave home, when leading woman Hedwig Niemann-Raabe refused to act the part as written, an amendment Ibsen later described as "a barbaric outrage." In the century and more since, the play and the role of Nora have taken on iconic status; Unesco's Memory of the World register calls Nora "a symbol throughout the world, for women fighting for liberation and equality."

She is also a symbol for female actors, both of what is possible and of how much they still have to fight for, when most plays and films still feature more male than female characters and work famously dries up for older women unless they are among a lucky handful of national treasures. Cush Jumbo, star of the Royal Exchange's production, says "it's a role a lot of actresses have on their list—if they have a wish list—because it's a very challenging part. It's Ibsen's Rosalind [the heroine of Shakespeare's *As You Like It*], I suppose. You never leave the stage and the journey she goes on is epic."

"I would compare it to Hamlet," says Morahan, whose interpretation has been described as a career-changing breakthrough. Janet McTeer experienced a similar effect two decades ago when her tempestuous, 6ft Nora, deeply in love with her husband and completely broken by his betrayal, won plaudits in London and then on Broadway, where the *New York Times* theatre critic Ben Brantley called McTeer's "the single most compelling performance I have ever seen."

McTeer's take on the play was to sweep away some of the feminist baggage it carried—it doesn't work for Torvald's "sweet little skylark" to suddenly turn into Emily Pankhurst,° she decided—and to treat it as the story not of a woman, but of a marriage. Anthony Page, who directed, says "she was very unexpected casting, being tall and strong-looking, but it heightened the idiocy of the false identity she was living under. She had a wonderful way of playing it very naturalistically, and she and Owen Teale [as Torvald] were playing off each other. Sometimes it got a bit out of hand. They were throwing chairs at each other, which had to be stopped, but they were remarkable."

But it is hard to ignore the play's strong feminist resonances in a culture 10
where it is blindingly obvious that any woman who puts herself in the public eye will become a target for abuse. Some complain that social media have given misogynists—such as those who have been in the news this week after threatening the MP Stella Creasy, or sending death threats to female journalists—a platform they don't deserve. Others argue they have simply revealed a woman-hating streak that has always been with us. Either way, it seems difficult to deny that virulent prejudice against women and the pressure on them to behave in certain ways still exist. Ibsen himself wrote in a note on his work-in-progress that women can't be themselves in an "exclusively male society, with laws made by men and with prosecutors and judges who assess feminine conduct from a masculine standpoint"—which felt startlingly pertinent when I read it shortly after learning of the male prosecutor and judge who this week labelled a 13-year-old child a sexual predator and suspended the prison sentence of the 41-year-old man convicted of abusing her.

Which is why some of the current generation of women acting, directing, and adapting *A Doll's House* have sought to reassert its feminist credentials. Director Carrie Cracknell made a short film that imagined Nora as an overstretched modern mother, her life a nightmare of spilled porridge, missed appointments, and hurriedly applied makeup. She says working on the play made her acutely aware of the ideas about gender that shaped her parenting of her two young

Emily Pankhurst: Militant Victorian activist.

children. "We live in a culture in which the way we represent women is becoming narrower. I think we have a generation of women growing up who understand that power is linked to how we look."

But all those I spoke to agree that the central dilemma the play presents, of how to be yourself and true to yourself, while being married and being a parent, is not exclusive to women. "In a sense," says Caroline McGinn, "Nora's famous dramatic exit [leaving home and children to work and pursue self-fulfilment] is something many parents do five days a week."

And perhaps this is the play's most radical aspect: that it presents a woman's dilemma as a human dilemma, relevant to both sexes, when so often women's stories are treated as a special subject of concern only to women (evidence of which can be seen everywhere in culture, from the small number of men who read books by and about women to the girl-heavy audience for the RSC's smash-hit musical *Matilda*, when there is no equivalent gender bias at *Charlie and the Chocolate Factory* down the road).

"I feel really strongly that we still obsess around male protagonists," Cracknell says. "There's a thousands-of-years-long legacy of storytelling in which men have been the protagonists—we go back to telling their stories over and over." McGinn says *A Doll's House* remains thrilling as a critic because "you go to new plays all the time where the ratio of men to women is 80/20."

Jumbo, who is currently starring in her own play about the singer Josephine 15
Baker at the Bush Theatre in London, also acted in Phyllida Lloyd's all-female production of Julius Caesar earlier this year and found "it opened people's minds to the idea that it's not that there aren't any roles for us, it's that plays aren't produced in that way. Quite a lot of the time you are the minority sex in a cast, because most stories that are told are male-driven. So it's a case of telling more women-driven stories, or being open to casting things in different ways."

Or, as Zinnie Harris puts it: "Nora's departure started a journey, and it's incumbent on us to keep going." *[2013]*

THINKING ABOUT THE TEXT

1. What does Rustin think the most radical aspect of the play is? What do you think of her evidence? Can you give other examples?
2. In your experience, is the Cracknell quote (para. 14) right about the ratio of men to women being 80/20 in films and TV shows?
3. What is your answer the question of why this play is so enduringly popular?

WRITING ABOUT ISSUES

1. The feminist thinker and activist Gloria Steinem writes about the "big click," a kind of epiphany, a moment when a woman realizes her true position in a patriarchal society. Write an essay that uses Steinem's idea to argue that Nora's transformation in act 3 is realistic or not.

2. In her review, Rustin claims that the most radical aspect of the play is that a woman's dilemma is treated as a human dilemma rather than as an exclusively women's concern. She claims that this is not usually the case. Write an essay that agrees or disagrees with this position, offering support from popular culture, including films and TV shows.
3. Argue that Nora will or will not return.
4. Write an essay that argues that *A Doll's House* is or is not still relevant today.

Confining Surveillance: Essays

MICHEL FOUCAULT, "Panopticon"

JEFFREY TOOBIN, "Edward Snowden's Real Impact"

PETER LUDLOW, "The Banality of Systemic Evil"

A recent survey of PEN, an organization of American writers, found that a "majority of its members are deeply concerned about . . . government surveillance of email and phone records." Seventy-three percent said they were "never as worried about privacy rights and freedom of the press as they are today." Some said they now avoid writing or speaking on certain controversial topics. Some critics interpret this trepidation as a result of Edward Snowden's disclosures of widespread surveillance by the National Security Agency (NSA). If so, this situation reinforces an idea developed by the French philosopher Michel Foucault about the nature and scope of power. In modern democracies, he claims, it is no longer necessary to exert coercive force to compel conformity to approved values. Through socialization at home, in schools, in the community, and in the culture at large, we readily adopt ideas about right and wrong, about what acceptable behavior is, about the consequences of deviance. Why do those writers feel wary? Certainly not because they were threatened directly in any way. Because the leaked information by Snowden seemed to suggest that the NSA was spying on practically everybody, the writers felt they could easily be monitored. And it is just this possibility that keeps us in line. Foucault called it the *panopticon*, and it will be the focus of the first selection. Next is Jeffrey Toobin's negative take on Snowden's disclosures, which is then followed by Peter Ludlow's warning about the chilling effect surveillance has on our freedom.

BEFORE YOU READ

The ongoing accusations of spying/hacking during the 2016 elections has alerted us to the pervasiveness of surveillance not only by the NSA/CIA/FBI but by foreign governments. What do you know about these efforts and what measures can be taken to prevent damages to our democracy while preserving privacy and civil rights?

MICHEL FOUCAULT

Panopticon, from *Discipline and Punish*

Michel Foucault (1926–1984) was a French philosopher and social theorist and one of the most important intellectuals of the second half of the twentieth century. He received his doctorate in 1959 and subsequently taught at the most prestigious universities in France. His influential books include The History of Sexuality *(1984) and*

Archaeology of Knowledge (1969). In Discipline and Punish: The Birth of the Prison, *he claims that all institutions discipline the body to be docile through surveillance, both real and imagined, which leads to the psychological control of individuals.*

The following excerpt is from Discipline and Punish *(1975), where Foucault has been discussing "the constant division between the normal and the abnormal." Although he is specifically discussing prisons, he means for the reader to make connections to society at large.*

Bentham's Panopticon is the architectural figure of this composition. We know the principle on which it was based: at the periphery, an annular building; at the centre, a tower; this tower is pierced with wide windows that open onto the inner side of the ring; the peripheric building is divided into cells, each of which extends the whole width of the building; they have two windows, one on the inside, corresponding to the windows of the tower; the other, on the outside, allows the light to cross the cell from one end to the other. All that is needed, then, is to place a supervisor in a central tower and to shut up in each cell a madman, a patient, a condemned man, a worker, or a schoolboy. By the effect of backlighting, one can observe from the tower, standing out precisely against the light, the small captive shadows in the cells of the periphery. They are like so many cages, so many small theatres, in which each actor is alone, perfectly individualized and constantly visible. The panoptic mechanism arranges spatial unities that make it possible to see constantly and to recognize immediately. In short, it reverses the principle of the dungeon; or rather of its three functions—to enclose, to deprive of light, and to hide—it preserves only the first and eliminates the other two. Full lighting and the eye of a supervisor capture better than darkness, which ultimately protected. Visibility is a trap.

To begin with, this made it possible—as a negative effect—to avoid those compact, swarming, howling masses that were to be found in places of confinement, those painted by Goya or described by Howard. Each individual, in his place, is securely confined to a cell from which he is seen from the front by the supervisor; but the side walls prevent him from coming into contact with his companions. He is seen, but he does not see; he is the object of information, never a subject in communication. The arrangement of his room, opposite the central tower, imposes on him an axial visibility; but the divisions of the ring, those separated cells, imply a lateral invisibility. And this invisibility is a guarantee of order. If the inmates are convicts, there is no danger of a plot, an attempt at collective escape, the planning of new crimes for the future, bad reciprocal influences; if they are patients, there is no danger of contagion; if they are madmen there is no risk of their committing violence upon one another; if they are schoolchildren, there is no copying, no noise, no chatter, no waste of time; if they are workers, there are no disorders, no theft, no coalitions, none of those distractions that slow down the rate of work, make it less perfect or cause accidents. The crowd, a compact mass, a locus of multiple exchanges, individualities merging together, a collective effect, is abolished and replaced by a collection of separated individualities. From the point of view of the guardian, it is replaced by a multiplicity that can be numbered and supervised; from the point of view of the inmates, by a sequestered and observed solitude (Bentham, 60–64).

Hence the major effect of the Panopticon: to induce in the inmate a state of conscious and permanent visibility that assures the automatic functioning of power. So to arrange things that the surveillance is permanent in its effects, even if it is discontinuous in its action; that the perfection of power should tend to render its actual exercise unnecessary; that this architectural apparatus should be a machine for creating and sustaining a power relation independent of the person who exercises it; in short, that the inmates should be caught up in a power situation of which they are themselves the bearers. To achieve this, it is at once too much and too little that the prisoner should be constantly observed by an inspector: too little, for what matters is that he knows himself to be observed; too much, because he has no need in fact of being so. In view of this, Bentham laid down the principle that power should be visible and unverifiable. Visible: the inmate will constantly have before his eyes the tall outline of the central tower from which he is spied upon. Unverifiable: the inmate must never know whether he is being looked at any one moment; but he must be sure that he may always be so. In order to make the presence or absence of the inspector unverifiable, so that the prisoners, in their cells, cannot even see a shadow, Bentham envisaged not only venetian blinds on the windows of the central observation hall, but, on the inside, partitions that intersected the hall at right angles and, in order to pass from one quarter to the other, not doors but zig-zag openings; for the slightest noise, a gleam of light, a brightness in a half-opened door would betray the presence of the guardian. The Panopticon is a machine for dissociating the see/being seen dyad: in the peripheric ring, one is totally seen, without ever seeing; in the central tower, one sees everything without ever being seen.

It is an important mechanism, for it automatizes and disindividualizes power. Power has its principle not so much in a person as in a certain concerted distribution of bodies, surfaces, lights, gazes; in an arrangement whose internal mechanisms produce the relation in which individuals are caught up. The ceremonies, the rituals, the marks by which the sovereign's surplus power was manifested are useless. There is a machinery that assures dissymmetry, disequilibrium, difference. Consequently, it does not matter who exercises power. Any individual, taken almost at random, can operate the machine: in the absence of the director, his family, his friends, his visitors, even his servants (Bentham, 45). Similarly, it does not matter what motive animates him: the curiosity of the indiscreet, the malice of a child, the thirst for knowledge of a philosopher who wishes to visit this museum of human nature, or the perversity of those who take pleasure in spying and punishing. The more numerous those anonymous and temporary observers are, the greater the risk for the inmate of being surprised and the greater his anxious awareness of being observed. The Panopticon is a marvellous machine which, whatever use one may wish to put it to, produces homogeneous effects of power.

[1975]

≡ THINKING ABOUT THE TEXT

1. What exactly is the purpose of the architecture, especially the tower that Foucault describes?
2. How is the surveillance "permanent in its effects" (para. 3)? How are the prisoners themselves the bearers of power?
3. Why is it important that the prisoners never know whether someone is looking at them at any given moment? What specific relevance does the idea of panopticon have to modern surveillance, say, by the NSA?

JEFFREY TOOBIN

Edward Snowden's Real Impact

Jeffrey Toobin (b. 1960) was born in New York City and attended Harvard College. He received a degree from Harvard Law School in 1986. He gave up the law after a controversial case in which he was accused of taking classified documents to write a book about the Iran–Contra Affair. He spent six years as a television legal analyst for ABC News and received a 2000 Emmy Award for his reporting. He is currently a staff writer for The New Yorker *and a senior analyst for CNN. His book,* The Nine: Inside the Secret World of the Supreme Court *(2007) has won numerous awards. His latest book is* The Oath: The Obama White House and The Supreme Court *(2012). The following article appeared in* The New Yorker *in August 2013.*

The assassinations of Martin Luther King, Jr., and Robert F. Kennedy led directly to the passage of a historic law, the Gun Control Act of 1968. Does that change your view of the assassinations? Should we be grateful for the deaths of these two men?

Of course not. That's lunatic logic. But the same reasoning is now being applied to the actions of Edward Snowden. Yes, the thinking goes, Snowden may have violated the law, but the outcome has been so worthwhile. According to Glenn Greenwald, the journalist who was one of the primary vehicles for Snowden's disclosures, Snowden "is very pleased with the debate that is arising in many countries around the world on Internet privacy and U.S. spying. It is exactly the debate he wanted to inform."

In this debate, Snowden himself says, those who followed the law were nothing better than Nazis: "I believe in the principle declared at Nuremberg, in 1945: 'Individuals have international duties which transcend the national obligations of obedience. Therefore individual citizens have the duty to violate domestic laws to prevent crimes against peace and humanity from occurring.' "

To be sure, Snowden has prompted an international discussion about surveillance, but it's worthwhile to note that this debate is no academic exercise. It has real costs. Consider just a few.

What if Snowden's wrong? What if there is no pervasive illegality in the National 5 *Security Agency's surveillance programs?*

Indeed, for all the excitement generated by Snowden's disclosures, there is no proof of any systemic, deliberate violations of law. Based on the ruling in a 1979 Supreme Court case, Smith v. Maryland, it is well established that individuals do not have an expectation of privacy in the phone numbers they call. This is not entirely surprising; we all know that we're already sharing that information with the phone company. In the same way, it's long established that the government has great latitude in intercepting communications between the United States and other countries. It's true, too, that while the Foreign Intelligence Surveillance Act court is largely toothless, it has, on occasion, rejected some N.S.A. procedures, and the agency has made adjustments in response. That is not the act of an entirely lawless agency.

It is true that, as the Washington Post's Barton Gellman recently reported, the N.S.A. sometimes went beyond its authority. According to Gellman, the agency privately admits to two thousand seven hundred and seventy-six incidents of unauthorized collection of data within a twelve-month period. This is bad—but it's not clear how bad. If it's that many incidents out of a total of, say, three thousand initiatives, then it's very bad. But if—as is far more likely—it's two thousand seven hundred and seventy-six incidents out of many millions, then the errors are less serious. There should be no mistakes, of course. But government surveillance, like any human activity, is going to have errors, and it's far from clear, at this point, that the N.S.A. 's errors amounted to a major violation of law or an invasion of privacy.

What are the actual dollar costs of Snowden's disclosures?

The United States, like any great power, is always going to have an intelligence operation, and some electronic surveillance is obligatory in the modern world. But, because of Snowden's disclosures, the government will almost certainly have to spend billions of dollars, and thousands of people will have to spend thousands of hours, reworking our procedures. This is all because a thirty-year-old self-appointed arbiter of propriety decided to break the law and disclose what he had sworn to protect. That judgment—in my view—was not Snowden's to make. And it is simply grotesque that Snowden compares these thousands of government workers—all doing their jobs to protect the United States—to the Nazi war criminals at Nuremberg.

What did China and Russia learn about American surveillance operations from 10
Snowden—and what will they do with this information?

As part of Snowden's flight from American justice, he went to two of the most repressive and technologically sophisticated countries on earth. (Hong Kong is, of course, part of China.) In an interview with Greenwald, Snowden said that the authorities in those countries behaved like perfect gentlemen.

"I never gave any information to either government, and they never took anything from my laptops," Snowden said.

Oh, really? Is he serious? Should anyone believe a word of this? China and Russia spend billions of dollars conducting counterintelligence against the United States. An American citizen walks into their countries bearing the keys to our most secret programs, and both—both!—China and Russia decline to take even a peek. That is a preposterous proposition. Even assuming that Snowden believes he had control of his computers 24/7 (he never slept?), there is simply no way that China and Russia would pass up that kind of bounty.

There is obviously some legitimate debate to be had about the extent and the legality of American surveillance operations. But there is no doubt about the nature of China and Russia. Snowden's pious invocation of the Nuremberg trials will probably be small comfort to the dissidents and the political prisoners whose cell doors may be locked a little tighter today because of what these authoritarian governments may have learned from his hard drive. *[2013]*

THINKING ABOUT THE TEXT

1. Do you think Snowden is right that the Nuremburg analogy is valid, that is, that we have a higher duty than "national obligations of obedience" (para. 3)?
2. Which of the "costs" Toobin cites makes the most sense to you? Why?
3. What exactly is Toobin's objection to Snowden's actions? Is the surveillance debate just about legality? What might be some larger issues?

PETER LUDLOW

The Banality of Systemic Evil

Peter Ludlow (b. 1957) is a professor of philosophy at Northwestern University. He received a Ph.D. in philosophy from Columbia University. His academic interests are in linguistics and philosophy and theories of meanings in linguistic semantics. His non-academic interests focus on the hacktivist culture and WikiLeaks. He has also written widely on issues regarding cyberspace. This article appeared in the New York Times *in September 2013.*

In recent months there has been a visible struggle in the media to come to grips with the leaking, whistle-blowing, and hacktivism that has vexed the United States military and the private and government intelligence communities. This response has run the gamut. It has involved attempts to condemn, support, demonize, psychoanalyze, and in some cases canonize figures like Aaron Swartz, Jeremy Hammond, Chelsea Manning, and Edward Snowden.

In broad terms, commentators in the mainstream and corporate media have tended to assume that all of these actors needed to be brought to justice, while independent players on the Internet and elsewhere have been much more supportive. Tellingly, a recent *Time* magazine cover story has pointed out a marked generational difference in how people view these matters: 70 percent of those age 18 to 34 sampled in a poll said they believed that Snowden "did a good thing" in leaking the news of the National Security Agency's surveillance program.

So has the younger generation lost its moral compass?

No. In my view, just the opposite.

Clearly, there is a moral principle at work in the actions of the leakers, 5
whistle-blowers, and hacktivists and those who support them. I would also argue that that moral principle has been clearly articulated, and it may just save us from a dystopian future.

In "Eichmann in Jerusalem," one of the most poignant and important works of 20th-century philosophy, Hannah Arendt made an observation about what she called "the banality of evil." One interpretation of this holds that it was not an observation about what a regular guy Adolf Eichmann seemed to be, but rather a statement about what happens when people play their "proper" roles within a system, following prescribed conduct with respect to that system, while remaining blind to the moral consequences of what the system was doing—or at least compartmentalizing and ignoring those consequences.

A good illustration of this phenomenon appears in "Moral Mazes," a book by the sociologist Robert Jackall that explored the ethics of decision making within several corporate bureaucracies. In it, Jackall made several observations that dovetailed with those of Arendt. The mid-level managers that he spoke with were not "evil" people in their everyday lives, but in the context of their jobs, they had a separate moral code altogether, what Jackall calls the "fundamental rules of corporate life":

> (1) You never go around your boss. (2) You tell your boss what he wants to hear, even when your boss claims that he wants dissenting views. (3) If your boss wants something dropped, you drop it. (4) You are sensitive to your boss's wishes so that you anticipate what he wants; you don't force him, in other words, to act as a boss. (5) Your job is not to report something that your boss does not want reported, but rather to cover it up. You do your job and you keep your mouth shut.

Jackall went through case after case in which managers violated this code and were drummed out of a business (for example, for reporting wrongdoing in the cleanup at the Three Mile Island nuclear power plant).

Aaron Swartz counted "Moral Mazes" among his "very favorite books." Swartz was the Internet wunderkind who was hounded by a government prosecution threatening him with 35 years in jail for illicitly downloading academic journals that were behind a pay wall. Swartz, who committed suicide in January at age 26 (many believe because of his prosecution), said that "Moral Mazes" did an excellent job of "explaining how so many well-intentioned people can end up committing so much evil."

Swartz argued that it was sometimes necessary to break the rules that required obedience to the system in order to avoid systemic evil. In Swartz's case the system was not a corporation but a system for the dissemination of bottled up knowledge that should have been available to all. Swartz engaged in an act of civil disobedience to liberate that knowledge, arguing that "there is no justice in following unjust laws. It's time to come into the light and, in the grand tradition of civil disobedience, declare our opposition to this private theft of public culture."

Chelsea Manning, the United States Army private incarcerated for leaking classified documents from the Departments of Defense and State, felt a similar pull to resist the internal rules of the bureaucracy. In a statement at her trial she described a case where she felt this was necessary. In February 2010, she received a report of an event in which the Iraqi Federal Police had detained 15 people for printing "anti-Iraqi" literature. Upon investigating the matter, Manning discovered that none of the 15 had previous ties to anti-Iraqi actions or suspected terrorist organizations. Manning had the allegedly anti-Iraqi literature translated and found that, contrary to what the federal police had said, the published literature in question "detailed corruption within the cabinet of Prime Minister Nuri Kamal al-Maliki's government and the financial impact of his corruption on the Iraqi people."

When Manning reported this discrepancy to the officer in charge (OIC), she was told to "drop it," she recounted.

Manning could not play along. As she put it, she knew if she "continued to assist the Baghdad Federal Police in identifying the political opponents of Prime Minister al-Maliki, those people would be arrested and in the custody of the Special Unit of the Baghdad Federal Police and very likely tortured and not seen again for a very long time—if ever." When her superiors would not address the problem, she was compelled to pass this information on to WikiLeaks.

Snowden too felt that, confronting what was clearly wrong, he could not play his proper role within the bureaucracy of the intelligence community. As he put it,

> [W]hen you talk to people about [abuses] in a place like this where this is the normal state of business people tend not to take them very seriously and move on from them. But over time that awareness of wrongdoing sort of builds up and you feel compelled to talk about [them]. And the more you talk about [them] the more you're ignored. The more you're told it's not a problem until eventually you realize that these things need to be determined by the public and not by somebody who was simply hired by the government.

The bureaucracy was telling him to shut up and move on (in accord with the five rules in "Moral Mazes"), but Snowden felt that doing so was morally wrong.

In a June Op-Ed in The Times, David Brooks made a case for why he thought Snowden was wrong to leak information about the Prism surveillance program. His reasoning cleanly framed the alternative to the moral code endorsed by Swartz, Manning, and Snowden. "For society to function well," he wrote, "there have to be basic levels of trust and cooperation, a respect for institutions and deference to common procedures. By deciding to unilaterally leak secret N.S.A. documents, Snowden has betrayed all of these things."

The complaint is eerily parallel to one from a case discussed in "Moral Mazes," where an accountant was dismissed because he insisted on reporting "irregular payments, doctored invoices, and shuffling numbers." The complaint against the accountant by the other managers of his company was that "by insisting on his own moral purity . . . he eroded the fundamental trust and understanding that makes cooperative managerial work possible."

But wasn't there arrogance or hubris in Snowden's and Manning's decisions to leak the documents? After all, weren't there established procedures determining what was right further up the organizational chart? Weren't these ethical decisions better left to someone with a higher pay grade? The former United States ambassador to the United Nations, John Bolton, argued that Snowden "thinks he's smarter and has a higher morality than the rest of us . . . that he can see clearer than other 299, 999, 999 of us, and therefore he can do what he wants. I say that is the worst form of treason."

For the leaker and whistleblower the answer to Bolton is that there can be no expectation that the system will act morally of its own accord. Systems are optimized for their own survival and preventing the system from doing evil may well require breaking with organizational niceties, protocols, or laws. It requires stepping outside of one's assigned organizational role. The chief executive is not in a better position to recognize systemic evil than is a middle level manager or, for that matter, an IT contractor. Recognizing systemic evil does not require rank or intelligence, just honesty of vision.

Persons of conscience who step outside their assigned organizational roles are not new. There are many famous earlier examples, including Daniel Ellsberg (the Pentagon Papers), John Kiriakou (of the Central Intelligence Agency), and several former N.S.A. employees, who blew the whistle on what they saw as an unconstitutional and immoral surveillance program (William Binney, Russ Tice, and Thomas Drake, for example). But it seems that we are witnessing a new generation of whistleblowers and leakers, which we might call generation W (for the generation that came of age in the era of WikiLeaks, and now the war on whistleblowing).

The media's desire to psychoanalyze members of generation W is natural enough. They want to know why these people are acting in a way that they, members of the corporate media, would not. But sauce for the goose is sauce for the gander; if there are psychological motivations for whistleblowing, leaking, and hacktivism, there are likewise psychological motivations for closing ranks with the power structure within a system — in this case a system in which corporate media plays an important role. Similarly it is possible that the system itself is sick, even though the actors within the organization are behaving in accord with organizational etiquette and respecting the internal bonds of trust.

Just as Hannah Arendt saw that the combined action of loyal managers can 20
give rise to unspeakable systemic evil, so too generation W has seen that complicity within the surveillance state can gives rise to evil as well — not the horrific evil that Eichmann's bureaucratic efficiency brought us, but still an Orwellian future that must be avoided at all costs. *[2013]*

≡ THINKING ABOUT THE TEXT

1. What does Arendt's phrase "the banality of evil" mean (para. 6)? Give examples from your experience or from history.

2. What is the connection between the panopticon and the five rules of corporate life (para. 7)?
3. How does Ludlow suggest that we can avoid an Orwellian future?

WRITING ABOUT ISSUES

1. Write an argument that agrees or disagrees with the statement that Snowden "did a good thing" (para. 2) in leaking information about the NSA's surveillance program.
2. Research Hannah Arendt's "banality of evil" or the Nuremburg Trials of 1945, and write an essay that explains the moral issues involved and whether you agree or disagree with the principles at stake.
3. Write a personal narrative about a time when you or someone you know stepped outside of an assigned role because of an ethical or moral issue.
4. Research one of the people mentioned (Daniel Ellsberg, John Kiriakou, Chelsea Manning, William Benney, Russ Tice) who defied the "surveillance state," and write a report about what they did, the principles involved, and the outcome.

Surrending Freedom on Principle: Across Genres

SOPHOCLES, *Antigone* (play)

T. C. BOYLE, "Balto" (story)

Even after two millennia, the character Antigone is still one of the most powerful examples of a woman choosing principle over freedom, indeed over her own life. For centuries, she has been an inspiring metaphor for standing one's ground no matter what. Antigone refuses to obey what she sees as an unjust decree forbidding her brother to be properly buried. Because of loyalty to her brother and to a higher principle, she risks all to bury him according to the appropriate traditions of the time. Without a proper burial, his afterlife would be jeopardized. And yet, she fully knows that the consequence of her transgression will probably mean her own death.

Angelle, the young girl in "Balto," must also decide if she is going to rely on her own personal sense of right or wrong or tell a lie that will keep her family intact. For her, telling the truth can have significantly negative consequences. Antigone is true to herself with tragic consequences. Angelle must decide between the truth and her father's freedom and the dissolution of her family. Both tales compel us to wonder that if we were to choose principle or convenience, would we be able to stand up for our beliefs even if the costs were great.

BEFORE YOU READ

Civil disobedience is usually defined as a form of protest: specifically, the use of nonviolent means to defy a law on behalf of a supposedly higher moral principle. Under what circumstances, if any, do you think civil disobedience is justified? What particular historical and contemporary events come to mind as you think about this issue?

SOPHOCLES

Antigone

Translated by Elizabeth Wyckoff

Along with Aeschylus and Euripides, Sophocles (496? B.C.E.–406? B.C.E.) is considered one of the greatest writers of tragedy in ancient Athens. During his lifetime, he was much respected in the city, often winning its dramatic competitions. Evidently he wrote over a hundred plays, but only seven survive complete. As a practitioner of tragedy, Sophocles was innovative. Among other things, he increased the number of actors on stage from two to three, while reducing the chorus from fifty to fifteen. Productions of his plays did remain traditional in that the performers wore masks and were exclusively male. Oedipus the King *and* Antigone *continue to be much performed today; moreover, through the centuries there have been numerous adaptations of them, such as Jean Anouilh's 1944 version of* Antigone, *a challenge to the Nazi occupiers of Paris.*

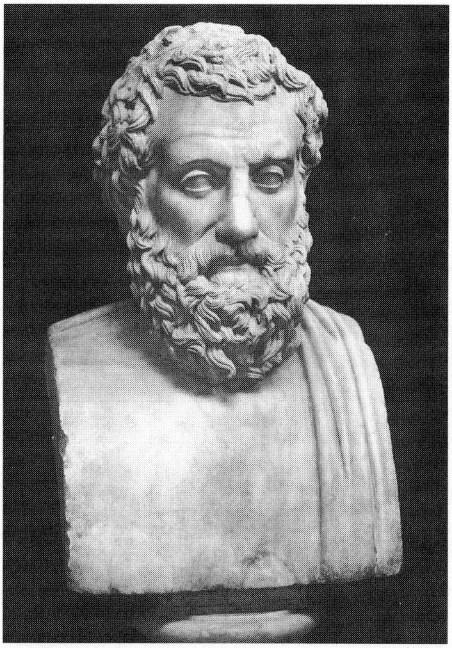

Bettmann/Getty Images

Antigone *was produced in 441* B.C.E., *the first of three interrelated plays now known as the Oedipus cycle.* Oedipus the King *was produced between 430 and 427* B.C.E., *and* Oedipus at Colonus *was posthumously produced in 401* B.C.E. *Scholars know that the plots of both these plays were familiar to Sophocles' audience. Less clear is whether that audience was familiar with the story of* Antigone, *which comes last in terms of plot chronology. The title character of* Oedipus the King *is Antigone's father, the ruler of Thebes. In the play, Oedipus blinds himself and leaves Thebes when he discovers that he has unknowingly fulfilled a terrible prophecy — that he would kill his own father and marry his mother.* Oedipus at Colonus *focuses on his death.*

CHARACTERS

ANTIGONE, *daughter of Oedipus*
ISMENE, *her sister*
CHORUS *of Theban elders*
CREON, *king of Thebes*
A GUARD
HAEMON, *son of Creon*
TEIRESIAS
A MESSENGER
EURYDICE, *wife of Creon*

SCENE: *Thebes, before the royal palace.*

(Antigone and Ismene enter from the palace.)

ANTIGONE: My sister, my Ismene, do you know
of any suffering from our father sprung
that Zeus° does not achieve for us survivors?
There's nothing grievous, nothing full of doom,
or shameful, or dishonored, I've not seen:
your sufferings and mine.
And now, what of this edict which they say
the commander has proclaimed to the whole people?
Have you heard anything? Or don't you know
that our enemies' trouble comes upon our friends?
ISMENE: I've heard no word, Antigone, of our friends,
not sweet nor bitter, since that single moment
when we two lost two brothers
who died on one day by a double blow.
And since the Argive army° went away
this very night, I have no further news
of fortune or disaster for myself.
ANTIGONE: I knew it well, and brought you from the house
for just this reason, that you alone may hear.
ISMENE: What is it? Clearly some news has clouded you.
ANTIGONE: It has indeed. Creon will give the one
of our two brothers honor in the tomb;
the other none. Eteocles, with just observance treated,
as law provides he has hidden under earth
to have full honor with the dead below.
But Polyneices' corpse who died in pain,
they say he has proclaimed to the whole town
that none may bury him and none bewail,
but leave him, unwept, untombed, a rich sweet sight
for the hungry birds' beholding and devouring.
Such orders they say the worthy Creon gives
to you and me—yes, yes, I say to *me*—
and that he's coming to proclaim it clear
to those who know it not.
Further: he has the matter so at heart
that anyone who dares attempt the act
will die by public stoning in the town.
So there you have it and you soon will show
if you are noble, or worthless, despite your high birth.
ISMENE: If things have reached this stage, what can I do,
poor sister, that will help to make or mend?
ANTIGONE: Think, will you share my labor and my act?
ISMENE: What will you risk? And where is your intent?

3 Zeus: The highest Olympian deity.
15 Argive army: The army of Argos that was led by Polyneices, the son of Oedipus and Jocasta. Oedipus had cursed Polyneices and his brother Eteocles to die at one another's hands.

ANTIGONE: Will you take up that corpse along with me?
ISMENE: To bury him you mean, when it's forbidden?
ANTIGONE: My brother, and yours, though you may wish he were not.
I never shall be found to be his traitor.
ISMENE: O reckless one, when Creon spoke against it!
ANTIGONE: It's not for him to keep me from my own.
ISMENE: Alas. Remember, sister, how our father
perished abhorred, ill-famed:
himself with his own hand, through his own curse
destroyed both eyes.
Remember next his mother and his wife
finishing life in the shame of the twisted noose.
And third, two brothers on a single day,
poor creatures, murdering, a common doom
each with his arm accomplished on the other.
And now look at the two of us alone.
We'll perish terribly if we violate law
and try to cross the royal vote and power.
We must remember that we two are women,
so not to fight with men;
and that since we are subject to stronger power
we must hear these orders, or any that may be worse.
So I shall ask of them beneath the earth
forgiveness, for in these things I am forced,
and shall obey the men in power. I know
that wild and futile action makes no sense.
ANTIGONE: I wouldn't urge it. And if now you wished
to act, you wouldn't please me as a partner.
Be what you want to; but that man shall I
bury. For me, the doer, death is best.
Loving, I shall lie with him, yes, with my loved one,
when I have dared the crime of piety.
Longer the time in which to please the dead
than the time with those up here.
There shall I lie forever. You may see fit
to keep from honor what the gods have honored.
ISMENE: I shall do no dishonor. But to act
against the citizens, that's beyond my means.
ANTIGONE: That's your excuse. Now I go, to heap
the burial mound for him, my dearest brother.
ISMENE: Oh my poor sister. How I fear for you!
ANTIGONE: For me, don't worry. You clear your own fate.
ISMENE: At least give no one notice of this act;
you keep it hidden, and I'll do the same.
ANTIGONE: Dear gods! Denounce me. I shall hate you more
if silent, not proclaiming this to all.

ISMENE: You have a hot mind over chilly things.
ANTIGONE: I know I please those whom I most should please.
ISMENE: If but you can. You crave what can't be done.
ANTIGONE: And so, when strength runs out, I shall give over.
ISMENE: Wrong from the start, to chase what cannot be.
ANTIGONE: If that's your saying, I shall hate you first,
and next the dead will hate you in all justice.
But let me and my own ill counseling
suffer this terror. I shall suffer nothing
so great as to stop me dying with honor.
ISMENE: Go, since you want to. But know this: you go
senseless indeed, but loved by those who love you.

(*Exit Ismene into the palace. Exit Antigone to one side. Enter the Chorus from the other side.*)

CHORUS [*singing*]:

STROPHE A°

Sun's own radiance, fairest light ever shone on the seven gates of Thebes,
then did you shine, O golden day's
eye, coming over Dirce's stream,°
on the man who had come from Argos with all his armor
running now in headlong fear as you shook his bridle free.

[chanting]
He was stirred by the dubious quarrel of Polyneices.
So, screaming shrill,
like an eagle over the land he flew,
covered with white-snow wing,
with many weapons,
with horse-hair crested helms.

ANTISTROPHE A° *[singing]*

He who had stood above our halls, gaping about our seven gates,
with that circle of blood-thirsting spears:
gone, without our blood in his jaws,
before the torch took hold on our tower crown.
Rattle of war at his back; hard the fight for the dragon's foe.

[chanting]
The boasts of a proud tongue are for Zeus to hate.
So seeing them streaming on

102 Strophe: The first section of a Greek choral ode.
105 Dirce's stream: A river near Thebes. Dirce was killed, but Dionysus, to whom she was devoted, created a spring in her memory.
114 Antistrophe: The second section of a Greek choral ode.

in insolent clangor of gold,
he struck with hurling fire him who rushed
for the high wall's top,
hoping to yell out "victory."

STROPHE B *[singing]*

Swinging, striking the earth he fell
fire in hand, who in mad attack,
had raged against us with blasts of hate.
He failed. And differently from one to another
on both sides great Ares° dealt his blows about,
first in our war team.

[chanting]
The captains assigned for seven gates
fought with our seven and left behind
their brazen arms as an offering
to Zeus who is turner of battle.
All but those two wretches, sons of one man,
one mother's sons, who planted their spears
each against each and found the share
of a common death together.

ANTISTROPHE B *[singing]*

Great-named Victory comes to us
answering Thebe's warrior joy.
Let us forget the wars just done
and visit the shrines of the gods,
all, with night-long dance which Bacchus° will lead,
he who shakes Thebe's acres.

(Creon enters from the side.)

[chanting]
Now here he comes, the king of the land,
Creon, Menoeceus' son,
newly appointed by the gods' new fate.
What plan that beats about his mind
has made him call this council session,
sending his summons to all?

CREON: My friends, the very gods who shook the state
with mighty surge have set it straight again.

130 Ares: God of war.
144 Bacchus: God of fertility and wine, also known as Dionysus.

So now I sent for you, chosen from all,
first, because I knew you constant in respect
to Laius' royal power; and again
when Oedipus had set the state to rights,
and when he perished, you were faithful still
in mind to the descendants of the dead.
When they two perished by a double fate,
on one day struck and striking and defiled
each by each other's hand, now it comes that I
hold all the power and the royal throne
through close connection with the perished men.
    You cannot learn of any man the soul,
the mind, and the intent until he shows
his practice of the government and law.
For I believe that he who controls the state
If he holds not to the best plans of all,
but locks his tongue up through some kind of fear,
he is worst of all who are or were.
And he who counts another greater friend
than his own fatherland, I put him nowhere.
So I—may Zeus all-seeing always know it—
could not keep silent as disaster crept
upon the town, destroying hope of safety.
Nor could I count the enemy of the land
friend to myself, not I who know so well
that it's she, the land, who saves us, sailing straight,
and only so can we have friends at all.
    With such good rules shall I enlarge our state.
And now I have proclaimed their brother-edict.
In the matter of the sons of Oedipus,
citizens, know: Eteocles who died,
defending this our town with champion spear,
is to be covered in the grave and granted
all holy rites we give the noble dead.
But his brother Polyneices, whom I name
the exile who came back and sought to burn
his fatherland, the gods of his own kin,
who tried to gorge on blood he shared, and lead
the rest of us as slaves—
it is announced that no one in this town
may give him burial or mourn for him.
Leave him unburied, leave his corpse disgraced,
a dinner for the birds and for the dogs.
Such is my mind. Never shall I, myself,
honor the wicked and reject the just.
The man who is well-minded to the state
from me in death and life shall have his honor.

CHORUS LEADER: This resolution, Creon, is your own,
in the matter of the traitor and the true.
For you can make such rulings as you will
about the living and about the dead.
CREON: Now you be sentinels of the decree.
CHORUS LEADER: Order some younger man to take this on.
CREON: Already there are watchers of the corpse.
CHORUS LEADER: What other order would you give us, then?
CREON: Not to take sides with any who disobey.
CHORUS LEADER: No fool is fool to the point of loving death.
CREON: Death is the price. But often we have known
men to be ruined by the hope of profit.

(Enter, from the side, a Guard.)

GUARD: My lord, I cannot claim I'm out of breath
from rushing here with light and hasty step,
for I had many haltings in my thought
making me double back upon my road.
My mind kept saying many things to me:
"Why go where you will surely pay the price?"
"Fool, are you halting? And if Creon learns
from someone else, how shall you not be hurt?"
Turning this over, on I dillydallied.
And so a short trip turned itself to long.
Finally, though, my coming here won out.
If what I say is nothing, still I'll say it.
For I come clutching to one single hope
that I can't suffer what is not my fate.
CREON: What is it that brings on this gloom of yours?
GUARD: I want to tell you first about myself.
I didn't do it, didn't see who did it.
It isn't right for me to get in trouble.
CREON: Your aim is good. You fence the facts around.
It's clear you have some shocking news to tell.
GUARD: Terrible tidings make for long delays.
CREON: Speak out the story, and then get away.
GUARD: I'll tell you. Someone left the corpse just now,
burial all accomplished, thirsty dust
strewn on the flesh, the ritual complete.
CREON: What are you saying? What man has dared to do it?
GUARD: I wouldn't know. There were no marks of picks,
no grubbed-out earth. The ground was dry and hard,
no trace of wheels. The doer left no sign.
When the first fellow on the day-shift showed us,
we all were sick with wonder.
For he was hidden, not inside a tomb,

but light dust upon him, enough to avert pollution;
no wild beast's track, nor track of any hound
having been near, nor was the body torn.
We roared bad words about, guard against guard,
almost came to blows. No one was there to stop us.
Each man had done it, nobody had done it
so as to prove it on him—we couldn't tell.
We were prepared to hold to red-hot iron,
to walk through fire, to swear before the gods
we hadn't done it, hadn't shared the plan,
when it was plotted or when it was done.
And last, when all our sleuthing came out nowhere,
one fellow spoke, who made our heads to droop
low toward the ground. We couldn't disagree.
We couldn't see a chance of getting off.
He said we had to tell you all about it.
We couldn't hide the fact.
So he won out. The lot chose poor old me
to win the prize. So here I am unwilling,
quite sure you people hardly want to see me.
Nobody likes the bringer of bad news.

CHORUS LEADER: Lord, while he spoke, my mind kept on debating.
Isn't this action possibly a god's?

CREON: Stop now, before you fill me up with rage,
or you'll prove yourself insane as well as old.
Unbearable, your saying that the gods
take any kindly forethought for this corpse.
Would it be they had hidden him away,
honoring his good service, he who came
to burn their pillared temples and their wealth,
raze their land, and break apart their laws?
Or have you seen them honor wicked men?
It isn't so.
No, from the first there were some men in town
who took the edict hard, and growled against me,
who secretly were shaking their heads, not pulling
honestly in the yoke, no way my friends.
These are the people—oh it's clear to me—
who have bribed these men and brought about the deed.
No current standard among men's as bad
as silver currency. This destroys the state;
this drives men from their homes; this wicked teacher
drives solid citizens to acts of shame.
It shows men how to act as criminals
and know the deeds of utter unholiness.

But every hired hand who helped in this
has brought on himself the sentence he shall have.
And further, as I still revere great Zeus,
understand this, I tell you under oath:
if you don't find the very man whose hands
buried the corpse and bring him for me to see,
not death alone shall be enough for you
till living, strung up, you make clear the crime.
For the future you'll have learned that profiteering
has its rules, and that it doesn't pay
to squeeze a profit out of every source.
For you'll have seen that more men come to doom
through dirty profits than are sustained by them.

GUARD: May I say something? Or just turn and go?

CREON: Aren't you aware your speech is most unwelcome?

GUARD: Does it annoy your ears, or your mind?

CREON: Why are you out to allocate my pain?

GUARD: The doer hurts your mind. I hurt your ears.

CREON: You are a quibbling rascal through and through.

GUARD: But anyhow I never did the deed.

CREON: And you the man who sold your life for money!

GUARD: Oh!
How terrible to guess, and guess at lies!

CREON: Go polish up your guesswork. If you don't
show me the doers you will have to say
that wicked payments work their own revenge.

GUARD: Indeed, I pray he's found, but yes or no,
taken or not as luck may settle it,
you won't see me returning to this place.
Saved when I neither hoped nor thought to be,
I owe the gods a mighty debt of thanks.

(Exit Creon into the palace. Exit the Guard by the way he came.)

CHORUS [*singing*]:

STROPHE A

Many the wonders but nothing is stranger than man.
This thing crosses the sea in the winter's storm,
making his path through the roaring waves.
And she, the greatest of gods, the Earth—
ageless she is, and unwearied—he wears her away
as the ploughs go up and down from year to year
and his mules turn up the soil.

ANTISTROPHE A

Lighthearted nations of birds he snares and leads,
wild beast tribes and the salty brood of the sea,
with the twisted mesh of his nets, this clever man.
He controls with craft the beasts of the open air,
walkers on hills. The horse with his shaggy mane
he holds and harnesses, yoked about the neck,
and the strong bull of the mountain.

STROPHE B

Language, and thought like the wind
and the feelings that govern a city,
he has taught himself, and shelter against the cold,
refuge from rain. He can always help himself.
He faces no future helpless. There's only death
that he cannot find an escape from. He has contrived
refuge from illnesses once beyond all cure.

ANTISTROPHE B

Clever beyond all dreams
the inventive craft that he has
which may drive him one time to good or another to evil.
When he honors the laws of the land and the gods' sworn right
high indeed is his city; but cityless the man
who dares to dwell with dishonor. Not by my fireside,
never to share my thoughts, who does these things.

(Enter the Guard with Antigone, from the side.)

[Chorus now chanting]
My mind is split at this awful sight.
I know her. I cannot deny
Antigone is here.
Alas, the unhappy girl,
unhappy Oedipus' child.
Oh what is the meaning of this?
It cannot be you that they bring
for breaking the royal law,
caught in sheer madness.

GUARD: This is the woman who has done the deed.
We caught her at the burying. Where's the king?

(Enter Creon from the palace.)

CHORUS LEADER: Back from the house again just when he's needed.

CREON: What must I measure up to? What has happened?
GUARD: Lord, one should never swear off anything.
Afterthought makes the first resolve a liar.
I could have vowed I wouldn't come back here
after your threats, after the storm I faced.
But joy that comes beyond the wildest hope
is bigger than all other pleasure known.
I'm here, though I swore not to be, and bring
this girl. We caught her burying the dead.
This time we didn't need to shake the lots;
mine was the luck, all mine.
So now, lord, take her, you, and question her.
and prove her as you will. But I am free.
And I deserve full clearance on this charge.
CREON: Explain the circumstance of the arrest.
GUARD: She was burying the man. You have it all.
CREON: Is this the truth? And do you grasp its meaning?
GUARD: I saw her burying the very corpse
you had forbidden. Is this adequate?
CREON: How was she caught and taken in the act?
GUARD: It was like this: when we got back again
struck with those dreadful threatenings of yours,
we swept away the dust that hid the corpse.
We stripped it back to slimy nakedness.
And then we sat to windward on the hill
so as to dodge the smell.
We poked each other up with growling threats
if anyone was careless of his work.
For some time this went on, till it was noon.
The sun was high and hot. Then from the earth
up rose a dusty whirlwind to the sky,
filling the plain, smearing the forest leaves,
clogging the upper air. We shut our eyes,
sat and endured the plague the gods had sent.
Then the storm left us after a long time.
We saw the girl. She cried the sharp and shrill
cry of a bitter bird which sees the nest
bare where the young birds lay.
So this same girl, seeing the body stripped,
cried with great groanings, called out dreadful curses
upon the people who had done the deed.
Soon in her hands she brought the thirsty dust,
and holding high a pitcher of wrought bronze
she poured the three libations for the dead.
We saw this and rushed down. We trapped her fast;
and she was calm. We taxed her with the deeds

both past and present. Nothing was denied.
And I was glad, and yet I took it hard.
One's own escape from trouble makes one glad;
but bringing friends to trouble is hard grief.
Still, I care less for all these second thoughts
than for the fact that I myself am safe.

CREON: You there, whose head is drooping to the ground,
do you admit this, or deny you did it?

ANTIGONE: I say I did it and I don't deny it.

CREON (*To the Guard*): Take yourself off wherever you wish to go
free of a heavy charge.
(*To Antigone*) You—tell me not at length but in a word.
You knew the order not to do this thing?

ANTIGONE: I knew—of course I knew. The word was plain.

CREON: And still you dared to overstep these laws?

ANTIGONE: For me it was not Zeus who made that order.
Nor did that Justice who lives with the gods below
mark out such laws to hold among mankind.
Nor did I think your orders were so strong
that you, a mortal man, could overrun
the gods' unwritten and unfailing laws.
Not now, nor yesterday's, they always live,
and no one knows their origin in time.
So not through fear of any man's proud spirit
would I be likely to neglect these laws,
and draw on myself the gods' sure punishment.
I knew that I must die—how could I not?—
even without your edict. If I die
before my time, I say it is a gain.
Who lives in sorrows many as are mine
how shall he not be glad to gain his death?
And so, for me to meet this fate's no grief.
But if I left that corpse, my mother's son,
dead and unburied I'd have cause to grieve
as now I grieve not.
And if you think my acts are foolishness
the foolishness may be in a fool's eye.

CHORUS LEADER: The girl is fierce. She's her father's child.
She cannot yield to trouble; nor could he.

CREON: These rigid spirits are the first to fall.
The strongest iron, hardened in the fire,
most often ends in scraps and shatterings.
Small curbs bring raging horses back to terms:
enslaved to his neighbor, who can think of pride?
This girl was expert in her insolence
when she broke bounds beyond established law.

Once she had done it, insolence the second,
to boast her doing, and to laugh in it.
I am no man and she the man instead
if she can have this conquest without pain.
She is my sister's child, but were she child
of closer kin than any at my hearth,
she and her sister should not so escape
a dreadful death. I charge Ismene too.
She shared the planning of this burial.
Call her outside. I saw her in die house,
maddened, no longer mistress of herself.
The sly intent betrays itself sometimes
before the secret plotters work their wrong.
I hate it too when someone caught in crime
then wants to make it seem a lovely thing.

ANTIGONE: Do you want more than my arrest and death?
CREON: No more than that. For that is all I need.
ANTIGONE: Why are you waiting? Nothing that you say
fits with my thought. I pray it never will.
Nor will you ever like to hear my words.
And yet what greater glory could I find
than giving my own brother funeral?
All these would say that they approved my act
did fear not mute them.
A king is fortunate in many ways,
and most, that he can act and speak at will.
CREON: None of these others see the case this way.
ANTIGONE: They see, and do not say. You have them cowed.
CREON: And you are not ashamed to think alone?
ANTIGONE: It is no shame to serve blood relatives.
CREON: Was not he who died on the other side your brother?
ANTIGONE: Full brother, on both sides, my parents' child.
CREON: Your act of grace, in his regard, is crime.
ANTIGONE: The corpse below would never say it was.
CREON: When you honor him and the criminal just alike?
ANTIGONE: It was a brother, not a slave, who died.
CREON: Died to destroy this land the other guarded.
ANTIGONE: Death yearns for equal law for all the dead.
CREON: Not that the good and bad draw equal shares.
ANTIGONE: Who knows but this is holiness below?
CREON: Never is the enemy, even in death, a friend.
ANTIGONE: I cannot share in hatred, but in love.
CREON: Then go down there, if you must love, and love
the dead. No woman rules me while I live.

(Ismene is brought from the palace under guard.)

CHORUS [*chanting*]: *Look there! Ismene is coming out.*
She loves her sister and mourns,
with clouded brow and bloodied cheeks,
tears on her lovely face.
CREON: You, lurking like a viper in the house,
who sucked me dry, while I raised unawares
a twin destruction planned against the throne.
Now tell me, do you say you shared this deed?
Or will you swear you didn't even know?
ISMENE: I did the deed if she agrees I did.
I am accessory and share the blame.
ANTIGONE: Justice will not allow this. You did not
wish for a part, nor did I give you one.
ISMENE: You are in trouble, and I'm not ashamed
to sail beside you into suffering.
ANTIGONE: Death and the dead, they know whose act it was.
I cannot love a friend whose love's mere words.
ISMENE: Sister, I pray, don't fence me out from honor,
from death with you, and honor done the dead.
ANTIGONE: Don't die along with me, nor make your own
that which you did not do. My death's enough.
ISMENE: When you are gone what life can I desire?
ANTIGONE: Love Creon. He's your kinsman and your care.
ISMENE: Why hurt me, when it does yourself no good?
ANTIGONE: I also suffer, when I laugh at you.
ISMENE: What further service can I do you now?
ANTIGONE: To save yourself. I shall not envy you.
ISMENE: Alas for me. Am I outside your fate?
ANTIGONE: Yes. For you chose to live when I chose death.
ISMENE: At least I was not silent. You were warned.
ANTIGONE: Some will have thought you wiser. Some will not.
ISMENE: And yet the blame is equal for us both.
ANTIGONE: Take heart. You live. My life died long ago.
And that has made me fit to help the dead.
CREON: One of these girls has shown her lack of sense
just now. The other had it from her birth.
ISMENE: Yes, king. When people fall in deep distress
their native sense departs, and will not stay.
CREON: You chose your mind's distraction when you chose
to work out wickedness with this wicked girl.
ISMENE: What life is there for me to live without her?
CREON: Don't speak of her. For she is here no more.
ISMENE: But will you kill your own son's promised bride?
CREON: Oh, there are other furrows for his plough.
ISMENE: But where the closeness that has bound these two?

CREON: Not for my sons will I choose wicked wives.
ISMENE: Dear Haemon, your father robs you of your rights.
CREON: You and your marriage trouble me too much.
ISMENE: You will take away his bride from your own son?
CREON: Yes. Death will help me break this marriage off.
CHORUS LEADER: It seems determined that the girl must die.
CREON: You helped determine it. Now, no delay!
Slaves, take them in. They must be women now.
No more free running.
Even the bold will flee when they see Death
drawing in close enough to end their life.

(Antigone and Ismene are taken inside.)

CHORUS [*singing*]:

STROPHE A

Fortunate they whose lives have no taste of pain.
For those whose house is shaken by the gods
escape no kind of doom. It extends to all the kin
like the wave that comes when the winds of Thrace
run over the dark of the sea.
The black sand of the bottom is brought from the depth;
the beaten cliffs sound back with a hollow cry.

ANTISTROPHE A

Ancient the sorrow of Labdacus' house,° I know.
Dead men's grief comes back, and falls on grief.
No generation can free the next.
One of the gods will strike. There is no escape.
So now the light goes out
for the house of Oedipus, while the bloody knife
cuts the remaining root, in folly and the mind's fury.

STROPHE B

What transgression of man, O Zeus, can bind your power?
Not sleep can destroy it who governs all,
nor the weariless months the gods have set. Unaged in time
monarch you rule in Olympus' gleaming light.
Near time, far future, and the past,
one law controls them all:
any greatness in human life brings doom.

560 Labdacus' house: The family in which Oedipus was born.

ANTISTROPHE B

Wandering hope brings help to many men.
But others she tricks with giddy loves,
and her quarry knows nothing until he has walked into flame.
Word of wisdom it was when someone said,
"The bad looks like the good
to him a god would doom."
Only briefly is that one free from doom.

(Haemon enters from the side.)

[chanting]
Here is Haemon, your one surviving son.
Does he come in grief at the fate of his bride,
in pain that he's tricked of his wedding?

CREON: Soon we shall know more than a seer could tell us.
Son, have you heard the vote condemned your bride?
And are you here, maddened against your father,
or are we friends, whatever I may do?

HAEMON: My father, I am yours. You keep me straight
with your good judgment, which I shall ever follow.
Nor shall a marriage count for more with me
than your kind leading.

CREON: There's my good boy. So should you hold at heart
and stand behind your father all the way.
It is for this men pray they may beget
households of dutiful obedient sons,
who share alike in punishing enemies,
and give due honor to their father's friends.
Whoever breeds a child that will not help,
what has he sown but trouble for himself,
and for his enemies laughter full and free?
Son, do not let your lust mislead your mind,
all for a woman's sake, for well you know
how cold the thing he takes into his arms
who has a wicked woman for his wife.
What deeper wound than a loved one who is evil?
Oh spit her forth forever, as your foe.
Let the girl marry somebody in Hades.
Since I have caught her in the open act,
the only one in town who disobeyed,
I shall not now proclaim myself a liar,
but kill her. Let her sing her song of Zeus
the guardian of blood kin.
If I allow disorder in my house

I'd surely have to license it abroad.
A man who deals in fairness with his own,
he can make manifest justice in the state.
But he who crosses law, or forces it,
or hopes to dictate orders to the rulers,
shall never have a word of praise from me.
The man the state has put in place must have
obedient hearing to his least command
when it is right, and even when it's not.
He who accepts this teaching I can trust,
ruler, or ruled, to function in his place,
to stand his ground even in the storm of spears,
a comrade to trust in battle at one's side.
There is no greater wrong than disobedience.
This ruins cities, this tears down our homes,
this breaks the battlefront in panic-rout.
If men live decently it is because
obedience saves their very lives for them.
So I must guard the men who yield to order,
not let myself be beaten by a woman.
Better, if it must happen, that a man
should overset me.
I won't be called weaker than womankind.

CHORUS LEADER: We think—unless our age is cheating us—
that what you say is sensible and right.

HAEMON: Father, the gods have given men good sense,
the highest and best possession that we have.
I couldn't find the words in which to claim
that there was error in your late remarks.
Yet someone else might bring some further light.
Because I am your son I must keep watch
on all men's doing where it touches you,
their speech, and most of all, their discontents.
Your presence frightens any common man
from saying things you would not care to hear.
But in dark comers I have heard them say
how the whole town is grieving for this girl,
unjustly doomed, if ever woman was,
to die in shame for glorious action done.
She would not leave her fallen, slaughtered brother
there, as he lay, unburied, for the birds
and hungry dogs to make an end of him.
Does she not truly deserve a golden prize?
This is the undercover speech in town.
Father, your welfare is my greatest good.
What precious gift in life for any child

outweighs a father's fortune and good fame?
And so a father feels his children's faring.
So, do not have one mind, and one alone
that only your opinion can be right.
Whoever thinks that he alone is wise,
his eloquence, his mind, above the rest,
come the unfolding, it shows his emptiness.
A man, though wise, should never be ashamed
of learning more, and must not be too rigid.
Have you not seen the trees beside storm torrents—
the ones that bend preserve their limbs and leaves,
while the resistant perish root and branch?
And so the ship that will not slacken sail,
the ropes drawn tight, unyielding, overturns.
She ends the voyage with her keel on top.
No, yield your wrath, allow a change of stand.
Young as I am, if I may give advice,
I'd say it would be best if men were born
perfect in wisdom, but that failing this
(which often fails) it can be no dishonor
to learn from others when they speak good sense.

CHORUS LEADER: Lord, if your son has spoken to the point
you should take his lesson. He should do the same.
Both sides have spoken well.

CREON: At my age I'm to school my mind by his?
This boy instructor is my master, then?

HAEMON: I urge no wrong. I'm young, but you should watch
my actions, not my years, to judge of me.

CREON: A loyal action, to respect disorder?

HAEMON: I wouldn't urge respect for wickedness.

CREON: You don't think she is sick with that disease?

HAEMON: Your fellow citizens maintain she's not.

CREON: Is the town to tell me how I ought to rule?

HAEMON: Now there you speak just like a boy yourself.

CREON: Am I to rule by other mind than mine?

HAEMON: No city is property of a single man.

CREON: But custom gives possession to the ruler.

HAEMON: You'd rule a desert beautifully alone.

CREON (*To the Chorus*): It seems he's firmly on the woman's side.

HAEMON: If you're a woman. It is you I care for.

CREON: Wicked, to try conclusions with your father.

HAEMON: When you conclude unjustly, so I must.

CREON: Am I unjust, when I respect my office?

HAEMON: You don't respect it, trampling down the gods' due.

CREON: Your mind is poisoned. Weaker than a woman!

HAEMON: At least you'll never see me yield to shame.

CREON: Your whole long argument is but for her.
HAEMON: And you, and me, and for the gods below.
CREON: As long as she lives, you shall not marry her.
HAEMON: Then she shall die—and her death will bring another.
CREON: Your boldness makes more progress. Threats, indeed!
HAEMON: No threat, to speak against your empty plan.
CREON: Past due, sharp lessons for your empty brain.
HAEMON: If you weren't father, I should call you mad.
CREON: Don't flatter me with "father," you woman's slave.
HAEMON: You wish to speak but never wish to hear.
CREON: You think so? By Olympus, you shall not
revile me with these tauntings and go free.
Bring out the hateful creature; she shall die
full in his sight, close at her bridegroom's side.
HAEMON: Not at my side! Don't think that! She will not
die next to me. And you yourself will not
ever lay eyes upon my face again.
Find other friends to rave with after this.

(Exit Haemon, to the side.)

CHORUS LEADER: Lord, he has gone with all the speed of rage.
When such a young man is grieved his mind is hard.
CREON: Oh, let him go, and plan superhuman action.
In any case the girls shall not escape.
CHORUS LEADER: You plan the punishment of death for both?
CREON: Not her who did not do it. You are right.
CHORUS LEADER: And what death have you chosen for the other?
CREON: To take her where the foot of man comes not.
There shall I hide her in a hollowed cave
living, and leave her just so much to eat
as clears the city from the guilt of death.
There, if she prays to Death, the only god
of her respect, she may manage not to die.
Or she may learn at last, though much too late,
how honoring the dead is wasted labor.

(Exit Creon into the palace.)

CHORUS [*singing*]:

STROPHE

Love unconquered in fight, love who falls on our possessions.
You rest at night in the soft bloom of a girl's face.
You cross the sea, you are known in the wildest lairs.
Not the immortal gods can escape you,
nor men of a day. Who has you within him is mad.

ANTISTROPHE

You twist the minds of the just. Wrong they pursue and are ruined.
You made this quarrel of kindred men before us now.
Desire looks clear from the eyes of a lovely bride:
power as strong as the founded world.
Aphrodite,° goddess, is playing, with whom no man can fight.

(Antigone is brought from the palace under guard.)

[chanting]
Now I am carried beyond all bounds.
My tears will not be checked.
I see Antigone depart
to the chamber where all must sleep.

ANTIGONE [*singing*]:

STROPHE A

Men of my fathers' land, you see me go
my last journey. My last sight of the sun,
then never again. Death who brings all to sleep
takes me alive to the shore
of the river underground.
Not for me was the marriage hymn, nor will anyone start the song
at a wedding of mine. Acheron° is my bridegroom.

CHORUS *[chanting]*
With praise as your portion you go
in fame to the vault of the dead.
Untouched by wasting disease,
not paying the price of the sword,
of your own free will you go.
Alone among mortals will you descend
in life to the house of Death.

ANTIGONE [*singing*]:

ANTISTROPHE A

Pitiful was the death that Phrygian stranger died,
our queen once, Tantalus' daughter.° The rock by Sipylus
covered her over, like stubborn ivy it grew.
Still, as she wastes, the rain

748 Aphrodite: Goddess of love and beauty.
759 Acheron: A river in the underworld, to which the dead go.
768 Tantalus' daughter: Niobe, a queen of Thebes who was punished by the gods for her pride and was turned into stone.

and snow companion her, so men say.
Pouring down from her mourning eyes comes the water that soaks the stone.
My own putting to sleep a god has arranged like hers.

CHORUS *[chanting]*
God's child and god she was:
but we are born to death.
Yet even in death you will have your fame,
to have gone like a god to your fate,
in living and dying alike.

ANTIGONE [*singing*]:

STROPHE B

Laughter against me now. In the name of our fathers' gods,
could you not wait till I went? Must affront be thrown in my face?
O city of wealthy men.
I call upon Dirce's spring
I call upon Thebe's grove in the armored plain,
to be my witnesses, how with no friend's mourning,
by what decree I go to the fresh-made prison tomb.
Alive to the place of corpses, an alien still,
never at home with the living nor with the dead.

CHORUS: *You went to the furthest verge*
of daring, but there you tripped
on the high pedestal of justice, and fell.
Perhaps you are paying your father's pain.

ANTIGONE:

ANTISTROPHE B

You speak of my darkest thought, my pitiful father's fame,
spread through all the world, and the doom that haunts our house,
the glorious house of Labdacus.
My mother's marriage bed.
Destruction where she lay with her husband-son,
my father. These are my parents and I their child.
I go to stay with them. My curse is to die unwed.
My brother, you found your fate when you found your bride,
you found it for me as well. Dead, you destroy my life.

CHORUS: You showed respect for the dead.
So we for you: but power
is not to be thwarted so.
Your self-willed temper has brought you down.

ANTIGONE:

EPODE

Unwept, no wedding-song, unfriended, now I go
down the road made ready for me.
No longer am I allowed to see this holy light of the sun.
No friend bewails my fate.

(Creon enters from the palace.)

CREON: When people sing the dirge for their own deaths
ahead of time, no one would ever stop
if they might hope that this would be of use.
Take her away at once, and open up
the tomb I spoke of. Leave her there alone.
There let her choose: death, or a buried life.
No stain of guilt upon us in this case,
but she is exiled from our life on earth.
ANTIGONE: O tomb, O marriage chamber, hollowed-out
house that will watch forever, where I go—
to my own people, most of whom are there;
Persephone° has taken them to her.
Last of them all, beyond the rest ill-fated,
I shall descend, before my course is run.
Still when I get there I may hope to find
I've come as a dear friend to my dear father,
to you, my mother, and my brother too.
All three of you have known my hand in death.
I washed your bodies, dressed them for the grave,
poured out the last libation at the tomb.
And now, Polyneices, you know the price I pay
for doing final service to your corpse.
And yet the wise will know my choice was right.
Were I a mother, with children or husband dead,
I'd let them molder. I should not have chosen
in such a case to cross the stated decree.
What is the law that lies behind these words?
One husband gone, I might have found another,
or a child from a new man in the first child's place;
but with my parents covered up in death,
no brother for me, ever, could be born.
Such was the law by which I honored you.
But Creon thought the doing was a crime,
a dreadful daring, brother of my heart.
So now he takes and leads me out by force.

821 Persephone: Queen of the underworld.

No marriage bed, no marriage song for me,
and since no wedding, so no child to rear.
I go, without a friend, struck down by fate,
living, to the hollow chambers of the dead.
What divine justice have I disobeyed?
Why, in my misery, look to the gods for help?
Can I call any of them my ally?
I stand convicted of impiety,
the evidence my pious duty done.
If the gods think that this is righteousness,
in suffering I'll see my error clear.
But if it is the others who are wrong
I wish them no greater punishment than mine.

CHORUS [*Chorus, Creon, and Antigone chanting in turn*]
The same tempest of mind
as ever, controls the girl.

CREON: *Therefore her guards shall regret*
the slowness with which they move.

ANTIGONE: *That word comes close to death.*

CREON: *You are perfectly right in that;*
I offer no grounds for hope.

ANTIGONE: *O town of my fathers in Thebe's land,*
O gods of our house!
I am led away and must not wait.
Look, leaders of Thebes,
I am last of your royal line.
Look what I suffer, at whose command,
because I respected the right.
(Antigone is led away, to the side.)

CHORUS [*singing*]:

STROPHE A

Danaë° *suffered too.*
She went from the light to the brass-built room,
bedchamber and tomb together. Like you, poor child,
she was of great descent, and more, she held and kept
the seed of the golden rain which was Zeus.
Fate has terrible power.
You cannot escape it by wealth or war.
No fort will keep it out, no ships outrun it.

872 Danaë: Locked in a cell by her father because it was prophesied that her son would kill him, but visited by Zeus in the form of a shower of gold. Their son was Perseus.

ANTISTROPHE A

Remember the angry king,
son of Dryas,° who raged against Dionysus and paid,
pent in a rock-walled prison. His bursting wrath
slowly went down. As the terror of madness went,
he learned of his frenzied attack on the god.
Fool, he had tried to stop
the dancing women possessed of god,
the fire of Bacchic rites, the songs and pipes.

STROPHE B

Where the dark rocks divide
sea from sea at the Bosporus,
is Thracian Salmydessus, where savage Ares
beheld the terrible blinding wounds
dealt to Phineus' sons° by their father's wife.
Dark the eyes that looked to avenge their mother.
Sharp with her shuttle she struck, and blooded her hands.

ANTISTROPHE B

Wasting they wept their fate,
settled when they were born
to Cleopatra, unhappy queen.
She was a princess too, of the ancient Erechthids,°
but was reared in the cave of the wild North Wind, her father,
swift as a horse over the hills.
Half a goddess, still, child, she suffered like you.

(Enter, from the side, Teiresias, led by a boy attendant.)

TEIRESIAS: Elders of Thebes, we two have come one road,
two of us looking through one pair of eyes.
This is the way of walking for the blind.
CREON: Old Teiresias, what news has brought you here?
TEIRESIAS: I'll tell you. You in turn must trust the prophet.
CREON: I've always been attentive to your counsel.
TEIRESIAS: And therefore you have steered this city straight.
CREON: So I can say how helpful you have been.
TEIRESIAS: Again you are balanced on a razor's edge.
CREON: What is it? How I shudder at your words!

881 son of Dryas: Lycurgus, king of Thrace, who was punished by Bacchus because he would not worship him.
892 Phineus' sons: Phineus blinded his sons after his second wife accused them of impropriety.
898 Erechthids: An Athenian clan.

TEIRESIAS: You'll know, when you hear the signs that I have marked.
I sat where every bird of heaven comes
in my old place of augury, and heard
bird cries I'd never known. They screeched about
goaded by madness, inarticulate.
I marked that they were tearing one another
with claws of murder. I could hear the wing-beats.
I was afraid, so straightaway I tried
burnt sacrifice upon the flaming altar.
No fire caught my offerings. Slimy ooze
dripped on the ashes, smoked and sputtered there.
Gall burst its bladder, vanished into vapor;
the fat dripped from the bones and would not burn.
These are the omens of the rites that failed,
as this boy here has told me. He's my guide
as I am guide to others.
Why has this sickness struck against the state?
Through your decision.
All of the altars of the town are choked
with leavings of the dogs and birds; their feast
was on that fated, fallen son of Oedipus.
So the gods accept no offering from us,
not prayer, nor flame of sacrifice. The birds
cry out a sound that I cannot distinguish,
gorged with the greasy blood of that dead man.
Think of these things, my son. All men may err,
but error once committed, he's no fool
nor unsuccessful, who can change his mind
and cure the trouble he has fallen in.
Stubbornness and stupidity are twins.
Yield to the dead. Why goad him where he lies?
What use to kill the dead a second time?
I speak for your own good. And I am right.
Learning from a wise counselor is not pain
if what he speaks are profitable words.

CREON: Old man, you all, like bowmen at a mark,
have bent your bows at me. I've had my share
of seers: I've been an item in your accounts.
Make profit, trade in Lydian electrum,
pure gold of India; that's your chief desire.
But you will never cover up that corpse,
not if the very eagles tear their food
from him, and leave it at the throne of Zeus.
I wouldn't give him up for burial
in fear of that pollution. For I know
no mortal being can pollute the gods.

Yes, old Teiresias, human beings fall;
the clever ones the furthest, when they plead
a shameful case so well in hope of profit.

TEIRESIAS: Alas!
What man can tell me, has he thought at all . . .

CREON: What tired cliché's coming from your lips?

TEIRESIAS: How the best of all possessions is good counsel.

CREON: And so is foolishness the worst of all.

TEIRESIAS: But you're infected with that same disease.

CREON: I'm reluctant to be uncivil to a seer . . .

TEIRESIAS: You're that already. You have said I lie.

CREON: Well, the whole crew of seers are money-mad.

TEIRESIAS: And the whole tribe of tyrants grab at gain.

CREON: Do you realize you are talking to a king?

TEIRESIAS: I know. Who helped you save this town you hold?

CREON: You're a wise seer, but you love wickedness.

TEIRESIAS: You'll bring me to speak the unspeakable, very soon.

CREON: Well, speak it out. But do not speak for profit.

TEIRESIAS: Do I seem to have spoken for profit, with regard to you?

CREON: Know this, that you can't buy and sell my policies.

TEIRESIAS: Know well yourself, the sun won't roll its course
many more days, before you come to give
corpse for these corpses, child of your own loins.
For you've confused the upper and lower worlds.
You settled a living person without honor
in a tomb; you keep up here that which belongs
below, a corpse unburied and unholy.
Not you, nor any god on high should have
any business with this. The violation's yours.
So the patient, foul punishers lie in wait
to track you down: the Furies sent by Hades
and by all gods will even you with your victims.
Now say that I am bribed! The time is close
when men and women shall wail within your house,
and all the cities that you fought in war
whose sons had burial from wild beasts, or dogs,
or birds that brought the stench of your great wrong
back to each hearth, they all will move against you.
A bowman, as you said, I send my shafts,
since you provoked me, straight. You'll feel the wound.
Boy, take me home now. Let him spend his rage
on younger men, and learn to calm his tongue,
and keep a better mind than now he does.

(Exit, to the side.)

CHORUS LEADER: Lord, he has gone. Terrible prophecies!
And since the time my hair turned gray from black,
his sayings to the city have been true.
CREON: I also know this. And my mind is torn.
To yield is dreadful. But to stand against him,
and shatter my spirit in doom is dreadful too.
CHORUS LEADER: Now you must seek good counsel, and take advice.
CREON: What must I do? Speak, and I shall obey.
CHORUS LEADER: Go free the maiden from that rocky house;
and bury the dead who lies in readiness.
CREON: This is your counsel? You would have me yield?
CHORUS LEADER: Quick as you can. The gods move very fast
when they bring ruin on misguided men.
CREON: How hard, abandonment of my desire!
But I can fight necessity no more.
CHORUS LEADER: Do it yourself. Leave it to no one else.
CREON: I'll go at once. Come, followers, to your work.
You that are here round up the other fellows.
Take axes with you, hurry to that place
that overlooks us there.
And I, since my decision's overturned,
the one who bound her will set her free myself.
I've come to fear it's best to hold the laws
of old tradition to the end of life.

(Exit, to the side.)

CHORUS [*singing*]:

STROPHE A

God of the many names,° Semele's proud delight,
child of Olympian thunder, Italy's master,
lord of Eleusis, where all men come
to Mother Demeter's plain:
Bacchus, who dwell in Thebes,
by Ismenus' running water,
where wild Bacchic women are at home,
on the soil of the dragon seed.

ANTISTROPHE A

Seen in the glaring flame, high on the double crags,
with the nymphs of Parnassus° at play on the hill,

1024 God of the many names: Bacchus.
1033 Parnassus: A mountain in Greece that was sacred to Bacchus as well as other gods and goddesses.

seen by Castalia's fresh fountain:°
you come from the ivied heights
and the green grape-filled coast of Euboea.
In immortal words they cry
your name, lord, who watch the roads,
the many streets of Thebes.

STROPHE B

This is your city, honored beyond the rest,
the town of your mother's miracle-death.
Now, as we wrestle with grim disease,
come with healing step along Parnassus' slope
or over the resounding sea.

ANTISTROPHE B

Leader in dance of the fire-pulsing stars,
overseer of the voices of night,
child of Zeus, be manifest,
with due companionship of maenads° dancing
and honoring their lord, Iacchus.°

(Enter Messenger, from the side.)

MESSENGER: Neighbors of Cadmus,° and Amphion's house,
there is no kind of state in human life
which I would now dare either praise or blame.
Fortune sets straight, and Fortune overturns
the happy or unhappy, day by day.
No prophecy can deal with men's affairs.
Creon was envied once, as I believe,
for having saved this city from its foes
and having got full power in this land.
He steered it well. And he had noble sons.
Now everything is gone.
Yes, when a man has lost all happiness,
he's not alive. Call him a breathing corpse.
Be very rich at home. Live as a king.
But once your joy has gone, though these are left
they are smoke's shadow to lost happiness.
CHORUS LEADER: What is the grief of princes that you bring?
MESSENGER: They're dead. The living are responsible.

1034 Castalia's fresh fountain: The sacred spring of Apollo's oracle at Delphi.
1048 maenads: Female followers of Bacchus.
1049 Iacchus: Bacchus.
1050 Cadmus: The legendary founder of Thebes.

CHORUS LEADER: Who died? Who did the murder? Tell us now.
MESSENGER: Haemon is gone. His own flesh and blood did him in.
CHORUS LEADER: But whose arm struck? His father's or his own?
MESSENGER: He killed himself, angry at his father's killing.
CHORUS LEADER: Seer, all too true the prophecy you told!
MESSENGER: This is the state of things. Now make your plans.

(Enter Eurydice, from the palace.)

CHORUS LEADER: Eurydice is with us now, I see.
Creon's poor wife. She may have come by chance.
She may have heard something about her son.
EURYDICE: I heard your talk as I was coming out
to greet the goddess Pallas° with my prayer.
And as I moved the bolts that held the door
I heard the voice of family disaster.
I fell back fainting in my women's arms.
But say again, just what is the news you bring.
I, whom you speak to, have known grief before.
MESSENGER: Dear lady, I was there, and I shall tell,
leaving out nothing of the true account.
Why should I make it soft for you with tales
to prove myself a liar? Truth is right.
I followed your husband to the plain's far edge,
where Polyneices' corpse was lying still
unpitied. The dogs had torn him all apart.
We prayed the goddess of all journeyings,°
and Pluto,° that they turn their wrath to kindness;
we gave the final purifying bath,
then burned the poor remains on new-cut boughs,
and heaped a high mound of his native earth.
Then turned we to the maiden's rocky bed,
approaching Hades' hollow marriage chamber.
But, still far off, one of us heard a voice
in keen lament by that unblest abode.
He ran and told the master. As Creon came
he heard confusion crying. He groaned and spoke:
"Am I a prophet now, and do I tread
the saddest of all roads I ever trod?
My son's voice crying! Servants, run up close,
stand by the tomb and look, push through the crevice
where we built the pile of rock, right to the entry.
Find out if that is Haemon's voice I hear
or if the gods are tricking me indeed."

1078 Pallas: Pallas Athene, goddess of wisdom and protector of Greek cities.
1091 goddess of all journeyings: Hecate, goddess of the underworld.
1092 Pluto: God of the underworld, also known as Hades.

We obeyed the order of our mournful master.
In the far corner of the tomb we saw
her, hanging by the neck, caught in a noose
of her own linen veiling.
Haemon embraced her as she hung, and mourned
his bride's destruction, dead and gone below,
his father's actions, the unfated marriage.
When Creon saw him, he groaned terribly,
and went toward him, and called him with lament:
"What have you done, what did you have in mind,
what happened so as thus to ruin you?
Come out, my child, I do beseech you, come!"
The boy looked at him with his angry eyes,
spat in his face and spoke no further word.
He drew his sword, but as his father ran,
he missed his aim. Then the unhappy boy,
in anger at himself, leant on the blade:
it entered, half its length, into his side.
While he was conscious he embraced the maiden,
holding her gently. Last, he gasped out blood,
red blood on her white cheek.
Corpse on a corpse he lies. He found his marriage,
its celebration in the halls of Hades.
So he has made it very clear to men
that to reject good counsel is a crime.

(Exit Eurydice, back into the palace.)

CHORUS LEADER: What do you make of this? The queen has gone
in silence, with no word of evil or of good.

MESSENGER: I wonder at her, too. But we can hope
that she has gone to mourn her son within
with her own women, not before the town.
She knows discretion. She will do no wrong.

CHORUS LEADER: I am not sure. This muteness may portend
as great disaster as a loud lament.

MESSENGER: I will go in and see if some deep plan
hides in her heart's wild pain. You may be right.
There can be heavy danger in mute grief.

(Exit the Messenger into the palace. Creon enters from the side with his followers. They are carrying Haemon's body on a bier.)

CHORUS [*chanting*]: *But look, the king draws near.*
His own hand brings
the witness of his crime,
the doom he brought on himself.

CREON [*singing in what follows, while the Chorus and Messenger speak*]:

STROPHE A

O crimes of my wicked heart,
harshness bringing death.
You see the killer, you see the kin he killed.
My planning was all unblest.
Son, you have died too soon.
Oh, you have gone away
through my fault, not your own.

CHORUS LEADER: You have learned justice, though it comes too late.

CREON: *Yes, I have learned in sorrow. It was a god who struck,*
who has weighted my head with disaster; he drove me to wild strange ways,
his heavy heel on my joy.
Oh sorrows, sorrows of men.
(Reenter the Messenger, from the palace.)

MESSENGER: Master, you hold one sorrow in your hands
but you have more, stored up inside the house.

CREON: *What further suffering can come on me?*

MESSENGER: your wife has died. The dead man's mother indeed,
poor soul, with wounds freshly inflicted.

CREON:

ANTISTROPHE A

Hades, harbor of all,
you have destroyed me now.
Terrible news to hear, horror the tale you tell.
I was dead, and you kill me again.
Boy, did I hear you right?
Did you say the queen was dead,
slaughter on slaughter heaped?

(The central doors of the palace open, and the corpse of Eurydice is revealed.)

CHORUS LEADER: Now you can see. Concealment is all over.

CREON: *My second sorrow is here. Surely no fate remains*
which can strike me again. Just now, I held my son in my arms.
And now I see her dead.
Woe for the mother and son.

MESSENGER: There, by the altar, dying on the sword,
her eyes fell shut. She wept her older son,
Megareus,° who died before, and this one. Finally
she cursed you as the killer of her children.

CREON:

1180 Megareus: A son of Creon and Eurydice; he died when Thebes was attacked.

STROPHE B

I am mad with fear. Will no one strike
and kill me with cutting sword?
Sorrowful, soaked in sorrow to the bone!

MESSENGER: Yes, for she held you guilty in the death
of him before you, and the elder dead.

CREON: How did she die?

MESSENGER: Struck home at her own heart
when she had heard of Haemon's suffering.

CREON: *This is my guilt, all mine. I killed you, I say it clear.*
Servants, take me away, out of the sight of men.
I who am nothing more than nothing now.

CHORUS LEADER: Your plan is good—if any good is left.
Best to cut short our sorrow.

CREON:

ANTISTROPHE B

Let me go, let me go. May death come quick,
bringing my final day!
O let me never see tomorrow's dawn.

CHORUS LEADER: That is the future's. We must look to now.
What will be is in other hands than ours.

CREON: All my desire was in that prayer of mine.

CHORUS LEADER: Pray not again. No mortal can escape
the doom prepared for him.

CREON [*singing*]: *Take me away at once, the frantic man who killed*
my son, against my meaning, and you too, my wife.
I cannot look at either, I cannot rest.
My life is warped past cure. Fate unbearable
has leapt down on my head.

(*Creon and his attendants enter the palace.*)

CHORUS [*chanting*]: *Our happiness depends*
on wisdom all the way.
The gods must have their due.
Great words by men of pride
bring greater blows upon them.
So wisdom comes to the old.

THINKING ABOUT THE TEXT

1. Describe Antigone with at least three adjectives of your own. How much do you sympathize with her? Do you consider her morally superior to Creon?

Identify specific things that influence your view of her. Do your feelings about her shift during the course of the play? If so, when and how?

2. Do you feel any sympathy for Creon? For Ismene? Explain your reasoning. What values seem to be in conflict as Antigone argues with each?
3. Where, if anywhere, do you see the chorus as expressing wisdom? Where, if anywhere, do the members of the chorus strike you as imperfect people?
4. A few critics claim that Antigone doesn't really change or grow in the traditional way Greek heroes do. They believe she rather stubbornly sticks to her position from beginning to end, suggesting that growth or compromise would have been better. Comment on this position.
5. Is commitment to a principle always a desirable choice? Does context matter? For example, do you think Antigone would have buried her brother knowing the full scope of her actions? Would you have made that choice?

T. CORAGHESSAN BOYLE

Balto

T. Coraghessan Boyle (b. 1948), who says that his middle name is pronounced with the stress on the second syllable and that his friends call him Tom, has written more than twenty books of fiction, including Drop City *(2003),* The Inner Circle *(2004),* Tooth and Claw *(2005), and* Talk, Talk *(2006). His novel* The Women *(2009) focuses on the women in Frank Lloyd Wright's life.* Wild Child and Other Stories *was published in 2010 and* When the Killing's Done *was published in 2011. His latest book is* T.C. Boyle Stories II *(2013). After graduating from the State University of New York, Potsdam, with a B.A. in English and history, Boyle taught for several years at the high school that he had attended as a teenager, though he continued to follow his interests in creative writing. In the early 1970s, he attended the prestigious University of Iowa Writers' Workshop and went on to receive a Ph.D. in nineteenth-century British literature from the University of Iowa in 1977. His list of awards and publications is long, including many O. Henry Awards and* Best American Short Stories *selections. He is a Distinguished Professor English at the University of Southern California. His most recent books are* The Harder They Come *(2015) and* The Terranauts *(2016). Several of his stories have been turned into movies, including* The Road To Wellville *(1994),* The Lie *(2011), and* Budding Prospects *(2017). The following story appeared in the* Best American Short Stories *2007.*

There were two kinds of truths, good truths and hurtful ones. That was what her father's attorney was telling her, and she was listening, doing her best, her face a small glazed crescent of light where the sun glanced off the yellow kitchen wall to illuminate her, but it was hard. Hard because it was a weekday, after school, and this was her free time, her chance to breeze into the 7-Eleven or Instant Message her friends before dinner and homework closed the day down. Hard too because

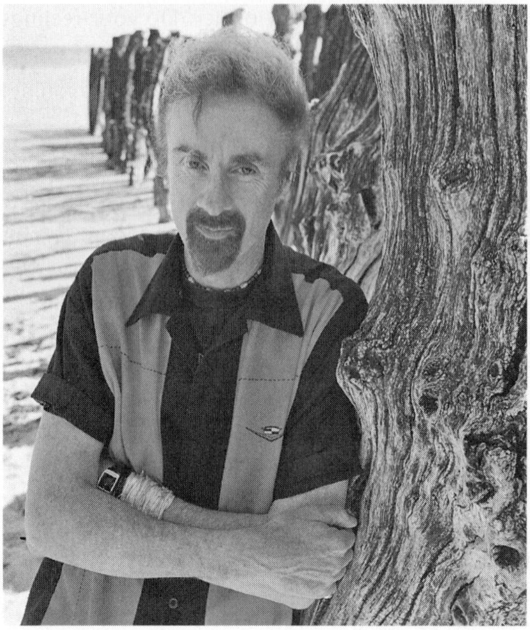

Ulf Andersen/Getty Images

her father was there, sitting on a stool at the kitchen counter, sipping something out of a mug, not coffee, definitely not coffee. His face was soft, the lines at the corners of his eyes nearly erased in the gentle spill of light — his *crow's-feet*, and how she loved that word, as if the bird's scaly claws had taken hold there like something out of a horror story, Edgar Allen Poe, the Raven, Nevermore, but wasn't a raven different from a crow and why not call them raven's-feet? Or hawk's-feet? People could have a hawk's nose — they always did in stories — but they had crow's-feet, and that didn't make any sense at all.

"Angelle," the attorney said — *Mr. Apodaca* — and the sound of her own name startled her, "are you listening to me?"

She nodded her head. And because that didn't seem enough, she spoke up too. "Yes," she said, but her voice sounded strange in her ears, as if somebody else were speaking for her.

"Good," he said, "good," leaning into the table so that his big moist dog's eyes settled on her with a baleful look. "Because this is very important, I don't have to stress that — "

He waited for her to nod again before going on. 5

"There are two kinds of truths," he repeated, "just like lies. There are bad lies, we all know that, lies meant to cheat and deceive, and then there are white lies, little fibs that don't really hurt anybody" — he blew out a soft puff of air, as if he were just stepping into a hot tub — "and might actually do good. Do you understand what I'm saying?"

She held herself perfectly still. Of course she understood — he was treating her like a nine-year-old, like her sister, and she was twelve, almost thirteen, and this was an act of rebellion, to hold herself there, not answering, not nodding, not even blinking her eyes.

"Like in this case," he went on, "your father's case, I mean. You've seen TV, the movies. The judge asks you for the truth, the whole truth and nothing but the truth, and you'll swear to it, everybody does — your father, me, anybody before the court." He had a mug too, one she recognized from her mother's college days — B.U., it said in thick red letters, *Boston University* — but there was coffee in his, or there had been. Now he just pushed it around the table as if it were a chess piece and he couldn't decide where to play it. "All I want you to remember — and your father wants this too, or no, he needs it, needs you to pay attention — is that there are good truths and bad truths, that's all. And your memory only serves to a point; I mean, who's to say what really happened, because everybody has their own version, that woman jogger, the boy on the bike — and the D.A., the District Attorney, he's the one who might ask you what happened that day, just him and me, that's all. Don't you worry about anything."

But she was worried, because Mr. Apodaca was there in the first place, with his perfect suit and perfect tie and his doggy eyes, and because her father had been handcuffed along the side of the road and taken to jail and the car had been impounded, which meant nobody could use it, not her father or her mother when she came back from France or Dolores the maid or Allie the au pair. There was all that, but there was something else too, something in her father's look and the attorney's sugary tones that hardened her: they were talking down to her. Talking down to her as if she had no more sense than her little sister. And she did. She did.

That day, the day of the incident — or accident, he'd have to call it an accident now — he'd met Marcy for lunch at a restaurant down by the marina 10
where you could sit outside and watch the way the sun struck the masts of the ships as they rocked on the tide and the light shattered and regrouped and shattered again. It was one of his favorite spots in town — one of his favorite spots, period. No matter how overburdened he felt, no matter how life beat him down and every task and deadline seemed to swell up out of all proportion so that twenty people couldn't have dealt with it all — a team, an army — this place, this table in the far corner of the deck overlooking the jungle of masts, the bleached wooden catwalks, the glowing arc of the harbor and the mountains that framed it, always had a calming effect on him. That and the just-this-side-of-too-cold local sauvignon blanc they served by the glass. He was working on his second when Marcy came up the stairs, swaying over her heels like a model on the runway, and glided down the length of the deck to join him. She gave him an uncomplicated smile, a smile that lit her eyes and acknowledged everything — the day, the locale, the sun and the breeze and the clean pounded smell of the ocean and him perched there in the middle of it all — and bent to kiss him before easing herself into the chair beside him. "That looks nice," she said, referring to the wine dense as struck gold in the glass before him, and held up a finger for the waiter.

And what did they talk about? Little things. Her work, the pair of shoes she'd bought and returned and then bought all over again, the movie they'd seen two nights ago—the last time they'd been together—and how she still couldn't believe he liked that ending. "It's not that it was cheesy," she said, and here was her wine and should they get a bottle, yeah, sure, a bottle, why not?, "and it was, but just that I didn't believe it."

"Didn't believe what—that the husband would take her back?"

"No," she said. "Or yes. It's idiotic. But what do you expect from a French movie? They always have these slinky-looking heroines in their thirties—"

"Or forties."

"—with great legs and mascara out of, I don't know, a Kiss revival, and then 15
even though they're married to the greatest guy in the world they feel unfulfilled and they go out and fuck the whole village, starting with the butcher."

"Juliette Binoche," he said. He was feeling the wine. Feeling good.

"Yeah, right. Even though it wasn't her, it could have been. Should have been. Has been in every French movie but this one for the past what, twenty years?" She put down her glass and let out a short two-note laugh that was like birdsong, a laugh that entranced him, and he wasn't worried about work now, not work or anything else, and here was the bottle in the bucket, the wine cold as the cellar it came from. "And then the whole village comes out and applauds her at the end for staying true to her romantic ideals—and the *husband*, Jesus."

Nothing could irritate him. Nothing could touch him. He was in love, the pelicans were gliding over the belly of the bay and her eyes were lewd and beautiful and pleased with themselves, but he had to pull the stopper here for just a minute. "Martine's not like that," he said. "I'm not like that."

She looked over her shoulder before digging out a cigarette—this was California, after all—and when she bent to light it her hair fell across her face. She came up smiling, the smoke snatched away from her lips and neutralized on the breeze the moment she exhaled. Discussion over.

Marcy was twenty-eight, educated at Berkeley, and she and her sister had 20
opened an Artists' Supply shop on a side street downtown. She'd been a double major in art and film. She rode a bike to work. She was Asian. Or Chinese, she corrected him. Of Chinese descent anyway. Her family, as she'd informed him on the first date with enough irony in her voice to foreground and bury the topic at the same time, went back four generations to the honorable great grandfather who'd smuggled himself across the Pacific inside a clichéd flour barrel hidden in the clichéd hold of a clichéd merchant ship. She'd grown up in Syracuse, in a suburban development, and her accent—the a's flattened so that his name came out *Eelan* rather than Alan—just killed him, so incongruous coming from someone, as, well—the words out of his mouth before he knew what he was saying—as *exotic*-looking as her. And then, because he couldn't read her expression—had he gone too far?—he told her he was impressed because he only went back three generations, his grandfather having come over from Cork, but if it was in a barrel it would been full of whiskey. "And Martine's from Paris," he'd added. "But you knew that already, didn't you?"

The bottle was half-gone by the time they ordered—and there was no hurry, no hurry at all, because they were both taking the afternoon off, and no argument—and when the food came they looked at one another for just the briefest fleeting particle of a moment before he ordered a second bottle. And then they were eating and everything slowed down until all of creation seemed to come into focus in a new way. He sipped the wine, chewed, looked into her unparalleled eyes and felt the sun lay a hand across his shoulders, and in a sudden blaze of apprehension he glanced up at the gull that appeared on the railing behind her and saw the way the breeze touched its feathers and the sun whitened its breast till there was nothing brighter and more perfect in the world—this creature, his fellow creature, and he was here to see it. He wanted to tell Marcy about it, about the miracle of the moment, the layers peeled back, revelatory, joyous, but instead he reached over to top off her glass and said, "So tell me about the shoes."

Later, after Mr. Apodaca had backed out of the driveway in his little white convertible with the Mercedes sign emblazoned on the front of it and the afternoon melted away in a slurry of phone calls and messages—*OMG! Chilty likes Alex Turtieff, can you believe it?*—Dolores made them chilé rellenos with carrot and jícama sticks and ice cream for dessert. Then Allie quizzed her and Lisette over their homework until the house fell quiet and all she could hear was the faint pulse of her father's music from the family room. She'd done her math and was working on a report about Aaron Burr for her history teacher, Mr. Compson, when she got up and went to the kitchen for a glass of juice or maybe hot chocolate in the microwave—and she wouldn't know which till she was standing there in the kitchen with the recessed lights glowing over the stone countertops and the refrigerator door open wide. She wasn't thinking about anything in particular—Aaron Burr was behind her now, upstairs, on her desk—and when she passed the archway to the family room the flash of the TV screen caught her eye and she paused a moment. Her father was there still, stretched out on the couch with a book, the TV muted and some game on, football, baseball, and the low snarl of his music in the background. His face had that blank absorbed look he got while reading and sometimes when he was just sitting there staring across the room or out the window at nothing, and he had the mug cradled in one hand, balanced on his chest beside the book.

He'd sat with them over dinner, but he hadn't eaten—he was going out later, he told her. For dinner. A late dinner. He didn't say who with, but she knew it was the Asian woman. Marcy. She'd seen her exactly twice, from behind the window of her car, and Marcy had waved at her both times, a little curl of the fingers and a flash of the palm. There was an Asian girl in her class—she was Chinese—and her name was Xuan. That seemed right for an Asian girl, Xuan. Different. A name that said who she was and where she was from, far away, a whole ocean away. But Marcy? She didn't think so.

"Hey," her father said, lifting his head to peer over the butt of the couch, and 25
she realized she'd been standing there watching him, "what's up? Homework done? Need any help? How about that essay—want me to proof that essay for you? What's it on, Madison? Or Burr. Burr, right?"

"That's okay."

"You sure?" His voice was slow and compacted, as if it wasn't composed of vibrations of the vocal cords, the air passing through the larynx like in her science book, but made of something heavier, denser. He would be taking a taxi tonight, she could see that, and then maybe she—*Marcy*—would drive him back home. "Because I could do it, no problem. I've got"—and she watched him lift his watch to his face and rotate his wrist—"half an hour or so, forty-five minutes."

"That's okay," she said.

She was sipping her hot chocolate and reading a story for English by William Faulkner, the author's picture in her textbook a freeze frame of furious eyes and conquered hair, when she heard her father's voice riding a current down the hall, now murmurous, now pinched and electric, then dense and sluggish all over again. It took her a minute: he was reading Lisette her bedtime story. The house was utterly still and she held her breath, listening, till all of a sudden she could make out the words. He was reading *Balto*, a story she'd loved when she was little, when she was Lisette's age, and as his voice came to her down the hall she could picture the illustrations: Balto,° the lead dog of the sled team, radiating light from a sunburst on his chest and the snowstorm like a monstrous hand closing over him, the team fighting through the Alaskan wind and ice and temperatures of forty below zero to deliver serum to the sick children in Nome—and those children would die if Balto didn't get through. Diphtheria. It was a diphtheria epidemic and the only plane available was broken down—or no, it had been dismantled for the winter. *What's diphtheria?* she'd asked her father, and he'd gone to the shelf and pulled down the encyclopedia to give her the answer, and that was heroic in itself, because as he settled back onto her bed, Lisette snuggled up beside her and rain at the windows and the bedside lamp the only thing between them and darkness absolute, he'd said, *You see, there's everything in books, everything you could ever want.*

Balto's paws were bleeding. The ice froze between his toes. The other dogs 30
kept holding back, but he was the lead dog and he turned on them and snarled, fought them just to keep them in their traces, to keep them going. *Balto*. With his harnessed shoulders and shaggy head and the furious unconquerable will that drove him all through that day and into the night that was so black there was no way of telling if they were on the trail or not.

Now, as she sat poised at the edge of her bed, listening to Lisette's silence and her father's limping voice, she waited for her sister to pipe up in her breathy little baby squeak and frame the inevitable questions: *Dad, Dad, how cold is forty below?* And: *Dad, what's diphtheria?*

The sun had crept imperceptibly across the deck, fingering the cracks in the varnished floorboards and easing up the low brass rail Marcy was using as a backrest. She was leaning into it, the rail, her chair tipped back, her elbows

Balto: An heroic Siberian husky sled dog who helped transport serum 600 miles through a blizzard in the dark to combat a diphtheria outbreak in Alaska.

splayed behind her and her legs stretched out to catch the sun, shapely legs, stunning legs, legs long and burnished and firm, legs that made him think of the rest of her and the way she was in bed. There was a scar just under the swell of her left kneecap, the flesh annealed in an irregular oval as if it had been burned or scarified, and he'd never noticed that before. Well, he was in a new place, half a glass each left of the second bottle and the world sprung to life in the fullness of its detail, everything sharpened, in focus, as if he'd needed glasses all these years and just clapped them on. The gull was gone but it had been special, a very special gull, and there were sparrows now, or wrens, hopping along the floor in little streaks of color, snatching up a crumb of this or that and then hurtling away over the rail as if they'd been launched. He was thinking he didn't want any more wine—two bottles was plenty—but maybe something to cap off the afternoon, a cognac maybe, just one.

She'd been talking about one of the girls who worked for her, a girl he'd seen a couple of times, nineteen, soft-faced and pretty, and how she—her name was Bettina—was living the party life, every night at the clubs, and how thin she was.

"Cocaine?" he wondered, and she shrugged. "Has it affected her work?"

"No," she said, "not yet, anyway." And then she went on to qualify that 35 with a litany of lateness in the morning, hyper behavior after lunch and doctor's appointments, too many doctor's appointments. He waited a moment, watching her mouth and tongue, the beautiful unspooling way the words dropped from her lips, before he reached down and ran a finger over the blemish below her kneecap. "You have a scar," he said.

She looked at her knee as if she wasn't aware it was attached to her, then withdrew her leg momentarily to scrutinize it before giving it back to the sun and the deck and the waiting touch of his hand. "Oh, that?" she said. "That's from when I was a kid."

"A burn or what?"

"Bicycle." She teased the syllables out, slow and sure.

His hand was on her knee, the warmth of the contact, and he rubbed the spot a moment before straightening up in the chair and draining his glass. "Looks like a burn," he said.

"Nope. Just fell in the street." She let out that laugh again and he drank it 40 in. "You should've seen my training wheels—or the one of them. It was as flat"—*flaat*—"as if a truck had run me over."

Her eyes flickered with the lingering seep of the memory and they both took a moment to picture it, the little girl with the wheel collapsed under her and the scraped knee—or it had to have been worse than that, punctured, shredded—and he didn't think of Lisette or Angelle, not yet, because he was deep into the drift of the day, so deep there was nothing else but this deck and this slow sweet sun and the gull that was gone now. "You want something else?" he heard himself say. "Maybe a Remy, just to cap it off? I mean, I'm wined out, but just, I don't know, a taste of cognac?"

"Sure," she said, "why not?" and she didn't look at her watch and he didn't look at his either.

And then the waiter was there with two snifters and a little square of dark chocolate for each of them, compliments of the house. *Snifter*, he was thinking as he revolved the glass in his hand, what a perfect designation for the thing, a name that spoke to function, and he said it aloud, "Isn't it great that they have things like snifters, so you can stick your nose in it and sniff? And plus, it's named for what it is, unlike, say, a napkin or a fork. You don't nap napkins or fork forks, right?"

"Yeah," she said, and the sun had leveled on her hair now, picking out the highlights and illuminating the lobe of one ear, "I guess. But I was telling you about Bettina? Did you know that guy she picked up I told you about—not the boyfriend, but the one-night stand? He got her pregnant."

The waiter drifted by then, college kid, hair in his eyes, and asked if there'd be anything else. It was then that he thought to check his watch and the first little pulse of alarm began to make itself felt somewhere deep in the quiet lagoon of his brain: *Angelle*, the alarm said. *Lisette*. They had to be picked up at school after soccer practice every Wednesday because Wednesday was Allie's day off and Martine wasn't there to do it. Martine was in Paris, doing whatever she pleased. That much was clear. And today—today was Wednesday.

Angelle remembered waiting for him longer than usual that day. He'd been late before—he was almost always late, because of work, because he had such a hectic schedule—but this time she'd already got through half her homework, the blue backpack canted away from her and her notebook spread open across her knees as she sat at the curb, and still he wasn't there. The sun had sunk into the trees across the street and she felt a chill where she'd sweated through her shorts and T-shirt at soccer. Lisette's team had finished before hers and for a while her sister had sat beside her, drawing big x's and o's in two different colors on a sheet of loose-leaf paper, but she'd got bored and run off to play on the swings with two other kids whose parents were late.

Every few minutes a car would round the turn at the top of the street, and her eyes would jump to it, but it wasn't theirs. She watched a black SUV pull up in front of the school and saw Dani Mead and Sarah Schuster burst through the doors, laughing, their backpacks riding up off their shoulders and their hair swaying back and forth as they slid into the cavernous back seat and the door slammed shut. The car's brake lights flashed and then it rolled slowly out of the parking lot and into the street, and she watched it till it disappeared round the corner. He was always working, she knew that, trying to dig himself out from under all the work he had piled up—that was his phrase, *dig himself out*, and she pictured him in his office surrounded by towering stacks of papers, papers like the Leaning Tower of Pisa, and a shovel in his hands as if he were one of those men in the orange jackets bent over a hole in the road—but still, she felt impatient. Felt cold. Hungry. And where was he?

Finally, after the last two kids had been picked up by their mothers and the sun reduced to a streak that ran across the tile roof of the school and up into the crowns of the palms behind it, after Lisette had come back to sit on the curb and whine and pout and complain like the baby she was (*He's just drunk, I bet that's it, just drunk like mom said*) and she had to tell her she didn't know what she was talking about, there he was. Lisette saw the car first. It appeared at the top of the street like a mirage, coming so slowly round the turn it might have been rolling under its own power, with nobody in it, and Angelle remembered what her father had told her about always setting the handbrake, always, no matter what. She hadn't really wanted a lesson—she'd have to be sixteen for that—but they were up in the mountains, at the summer cabin, just after her mother had left for France, and there was nobody around. "You're a big girl," he'd told her, and she was, tall for her age—people always mistook her for an eighth-grader or even a freshman. "Go ahead, it's easy," he told her. "Like bumper cars. Only you don't bump anything." And she'd laughed and he laughed and she got behind the wheel with him guiding her and her heart was pounding till she thought she was going to lift right out of the seat. Everything looked different through the windshield, yellow spots and dirt, the world wrapped in a bubble. The sun was in her eyes. The road was a black river, oozing through the dried-out weeds, the trees looming and receding as if a wave had passed through them. And the car crept down the road the way it was creeping now. Too slow. Much too slow.

When her father pulled up to the curb, she saw right away that something was wrong. He was smiling at them, or trying to smile, but his face was too heavy, his face weighed a thousand tons, carved of rock like the faces of the presidents on Mount Rushmore, and it distorted the smile till it was more like a grimace. A flare of anger rose in her—Lisette was right—and then it died away and she was scared. Just scared.

"Sorry," he murmured, "sorry I'm late, I—" and he didn't finish the thought or excuse or whatever it was because he was pushing open the door now, the driver's door, and pulling himself out onto the pavement. He took a minute to remove his sunglasses and polish them on the tail of his shirt before leaning heavily against the side of the car. He gave her a weak smile—half a smile, not even half—and carefully fitted them back over his ears, though it was too dark for sunglasses, anybody could see that. Plus, these were his old sunglasses—two shining blue discs in wire frames that made his eyes disappear—which meant that he must have lost his good ones, the ones that had cost him two hundred and fifty dollars on sale at the Sunglass Hut. "Listen," he said, as Lisette pulled open the rear door and flung her backpack across the seat, "I just—I forgot the time, is all. I'm sorry. I am. I really am."

She gave him a look that was meant to burn into him, to make him feel what she was feeling, but she couldn't tell if he was looking at her or not. "We've been sitting here since four," she said, and she heard the hurt and accusation in her own voice. She pulled open the other door, the one right beside him, because she was going to sit in back as a demonstration of her disapproval—they'd both sit in back, she and Lisette, and nobody up front—when he stopped her with a gesture, reaching out suddenly to brush the hair away from her face.

"You've got to help me out here," he said, and a pleading tone had come into his voice. "Because"—the words were stalling, congealing, sticking in his throat—"because, hey, why lie, huh? I wouldn't lie to you."

The sun faded. A car went up the street. There was a boy on a bicycle, a boy she knew, and he gave her a look as he cruised past, the wheels a blur.

"I was, I had lunch with Marcy, because, well, you know how hard I've been—and I just needed to kick back, you know? Everybody does. It's no sin." A pause, his hand going to his pocket and then back to her hair again. "And we had some wine. Some wine with lunch." He gazed off down the street then, as if he were looking for the tapering long-necked green bottles the wine had come in, as if he were going to produce them for evidence.

She just stood there staring at him, her jaw set, but she let his hand fall to 55
her shoulder and give her a squeeze, the sort of squeeze he gave her when he was proud of her, when she got an A on a test or cleaned up the dishes all by herself without anybody asking.

"I know this is terrible," he was saying, "I mean I hate to do this, I hate to . . . but Angelle, I'm asking you just this once, because the thing is?"—and here he tugged down the little blue discs so that she could see the dull sheen of his eyes focused on her—"I don't think I can drive."

When the valet brought the car round, the strangest thing happened, a little lapse, and it was because he wasn't paying attention. He was distracted by Marcy in her low-slung Miata with the top down, the redness of it, a sleek thing, pin your ears back and fly, Marcy wheeling out of the lot with a wave and two fingers kissed to her lips, her hair lifting on the breeze. And there was the attendant, another college kid, shorter and darker than the one upstairs frowning over the tip but with the same haircut, as if they'd both been to the same barber or stylist or whatever, and the attendant had said something to him—*Your car, sir; here's your car, sir*—and the strange thing was that for a second there he didn't recognize it. Thought the kid was trying to put something over on him. Was this his car? Was this the sort of thing he'd own? This mud-splattered charcoal-gray SUV with the seriously depleted tires? And that dent in the front fender, the knee-high scrape that ran the length of the body as if some metallic claw had caught hold of it? Was this some kind of trick?

"Sir?"

"Yeah," he'd said, staring up into the sky now, and where were his shades? "Yeah, what? What do you want?"

The smallest beat. "Your car. Sir." 60

And then it all came clear to him the way these things do, and he flipped open his wallet to extract two singles—finger-softened money, money as soft and pliable as felt—and the valet accepted them and he was in the car, looking to connect the male end of the seatbelt to the female, and where was the damned thing? There was still a sliver of sun cutting in low over the ocean and he dug into the glove compartment for his old sunglasses, the emergency pair, because the new ones were someplace else altogether, apparently, and not in his pocket and not on the cord round his neck, and then he had them fitted over his ears and the radio was playing something with some real thump to it and he was rolling on out of the lot, looking to merge with the traffic on the boulevard.

That was when everything turned hard-edged and he knew he was drunk. He waited too long to merge — too cautious, too tentative — and the driver behind him laid on the horn and he had no choice but to give him the finger and he might have leaned his head out the window and barked something too, but the car came to life beneath him and somebody swerved wide and he was out in traffic. If he was thinking anything at all it probably had to do with his last DUI, which had come out of nowhere when he wasn't even that drunk, or maybe not drunk at all. He'd been coming back from Johnny's Rib Shack after working late, gnawing at a rib, a beer open between his legs, and he came down the slope beneath the underpass where you make a left to turn onto the freeway ramp and he was watching the light and didn't see the mustard-colored Volvo stopped there in front of him until it was too late. And he was so upset with himself — and not just himself, but the world at large and the way it presented these problems to him, these impediments, the unforeseen and the unexpected just laid out there in front of him as if it were some kind of conspiracy — that he got out of the car, the radiator crushed and hissing and beer pissed all over his lap, and shouted "All right, so sue me!" at the dazed woman behind the wheel of the other car. But that wasn't going to happen now. Nothing was going to happen now.

The trees rolled by, people crossed at the crosswalk, lights turned yellow and then red and then green, and he was doing fine, just sailing, thinking he'd take the girls out for burritos or In-N-Out burgers on the way home, when a cop passed him going in the other direction and his heart froze like a block of ice and then thawed instantaneously, hammering so hard he thought it would punch right through his chest. *Signal, Signal*, he told himself, keeping his eyes on the rearview, and he did, he signaled and made the first turn, a road he'd never been on before, and then he made the next turn after that, and the next, and when he looked up again he had no idea where he was.

Which was another reason why he was late, and there was Angelle giving him that hard cold judgmental look — her mother's look exactly — because she was perfect, she was dutiful and put-upon and the single best kid in the world, in the history of the world, and he was a fuck-up, pure and simple. It was wrong, what he asked her to do, but it happened nonetheless, and he guided her through each step, a straight shot on the way home, two and a half miles, that was all, and forget stopping at In-N-Out, they'd just go home and have a pizza delivered. He remembered going on in that vein, "Don't you girls want pizza tonight? Huh, Lisette? Peppers and onions? And those little roasted artichokes? Or maybe you'd prefer wormheads, mashed wormheads?" — leaning over the seat to cajole her, make it all right and take the tightness out of her face, and he didn't see the boy on the bicycle, didn't know anything about him until Angelle let out a choked little cry and there was the heart-stopping thump of something glancing off the fender.

The courtroom smelled of wax, the same kind of wax they used on the 65
floors at school, sweet and acrid at the same time, a smell that was almost comforting in its familiarity. But she wasn't at school — she'd been excused for the

morning—and she wasn't here to be comforted or to feel comfortable either. She was here to listen to Mr. Apodaca and the judge and the D.A. and the members of the jury decide her father's case and to testify in his behalf, tell what she knew, tell a kind of truth that wasn't maybe whole and pure but necessary, a necessary truth. That was what Mr. Apodaca was calling it now, *necessary*, and she'd sat with him and her father in one of the unused rooms off the main corridor—another courtroom—while he went over the whole business one more time for her, just to be sure she understood.

Her father had held her hand on the way in and he sat beside her on one of the wooden benches as his attorney went over the details of that day after school, because he wanted to make sure they were all on the same page. Those were his words exactly—"I want to make sure we're all on the same page on this"—as he loomed over her and her father, bracing himself on the gleaming wooden rail, his shoes competing with the floor for the brilliance of their shine, and she couldn't help picturing some Mexican boy, some dropout from the high school, laboring over those shoes while Mr. Apodaca sat high in a leather-backed chair, his feet in the stainless steel stirrups. She pictured him behind his newspaper, looking stern, or going over his brief, the details, *these* details. When he was through, when he'd gone through everything, minute by minute, gesture by gesture, coaching her, quizzing her—"And what did he say? What did you say?"—he asked her father if he could have a minute alone with her.

That was when her father gave her hand a final squeeze and then dropped it and got up from the bench. He was wearing a new suit, a navy so dark and severe it made his skin look like raw dough, and he'd had his hair cut so tight round the ears it was as if a machine had been at work there, an edger or a riding mower like the one they used on the soccer field at school, only in miniature, and for an instant she imagined it, tiny people like in *Gulliver's Travels*, buzzing round her father's ears with their mowers and clippers and edgers. The tie he was wearing was the most boring one he owned, a blue fading to black, with no design, not even a stripe. His face was heavy, his crow's-feet right there for all the world to see—gouges, tears, slits, a butcher's shop of carved and abused skin—and for the first time she noticed the small gray dollop of loose flesh under his chin. It made him look old, worn-out, past his prime, as if he weren't the hero anymore but playing the hero's best friend, the one who never gets the girl and never gets the job. And what role was she playing? The star. She was the star here, and the more the attorney talked on and the heavier her father's face got, the more it came home to her.

Mr. Apodaca said nothing, just let the silence hang in the room till the memory of her father's footsteps had faded. Then he leaned over the back of the bench directly in front of her, the great seal of the State of California framed over the dais behind him, and he squeezed his eyes shut a moment so that when he opened them and fixed her with his gaze, there were tears there. Or the appearance of tears. His eyelashes were moist and the moistness picked each of them out individually until all she could think of was the stalks of cane against the fence in the back corner of the yard. "I want you to listen very carefully to what I'm about to say, Angelle," he breathed, his voice so soft and constricted it was like the sound of the air being let out of a tire. "Because this concerns you and your sister. It could affect your whole life."

Another pause. Her stomach was crawling. She didn't want to say anything but he held the pause so long she had to bow her head and say, "Yeah. Yeah, I know."

And then suddenly, without warning, his voice was lashing out at her: "But 70
you don't know it. Do you know what's a stake here? Do you really?"

"No," she said, and it was a whisper.

"Your father is going to plead no contest to the charge of driving under the influence. He was wrong, he admits it. And they'll take away his driving privileges and he'll have to go to counseling and find someone to drive you and your sister to school, and I don't mean to minimize that, that's very serious, but here's the thing you may not know." He held her eyes, though she wanted to look away. "The second charge is child endangerment, not for the boy on the bike, who barely even scraped a knee, luckily, luckily, and whose parents have already agreed to a settlement, but for you, for allowing you to do what you did. And do you know what will happen if the jury finds him guilty on that charge?"

She didn't know what was coming, not exactly, but the tone of what he was conveying—dark, ominous, fulminating with anger and the threat about to be revealed in the very next breath—made her feel small. And scared. Definitely scared. She shook her head.

"They'll take you and Lisette away from him." He clenched both hands, pushed himself up from the rail and turned as if to pace off down the aisle in front of her, as if he was disgusted with the whole thing and had no more to say. But then, suddenly, he swung round on her with a furious twist of his shoulders and a hard accusatory stab of his balled-up right hand and a single rigid forefinger. "And no," he said, barely contained, barely able to keep his voice level, "in answer to your unasked question or objection or whatever you want to call it, your mother's not coming back for you, not now, maybe not ever."

Was he ashamed? Was he humiliated? Did he have to stop drinking and get 75
his life in order? Yes, yes and yes. But as he sat there in the courtroom beside Jerry Apodaca at eleven-thirty in the morning, the high arched windows pregnant with light and his daughter, Marcy, Dolores and the solemn-faced au pair sitting shoulder-to-shoulder on the gleaming wooden bench behind him, there was a flask in his inside pocket and the faint burning pulse of single-malt scotch rode his veins. He'd taken a pull from it in the men's room not ten minutes ago, just to steady himself, and then he'd rinsed out his mouth and ground half a dozen tic-tacs between his teeth to knock down any trace of alcohol on his breath. Jerry would have been furious with him if he so much as suspected . . . and it was a weak and cowardly thing to do, no excuse, no excuse at all, but he felt adrift, felt scared, and he needed an anchor to hold onto. Just for now. Just for today. And then he'd throw the thing away, because what was a flask for anyway except to provide a twenty-four-hour teat for the kind of drunk who wore a suit and brushed his teeth.

He began to jiggle one foot and tap his knees together beneath the table, a nervous twitch no amount of scotch would cure. The judge was taking his time, the Assistant D.A. smirking over a sheaf of papers at her own table off to the right. She wore a permanent self-congratulatory look, this woman, as if she were queen of the court and the county too, and she'd really laid into him before the recess, and that was nasty, purely nasty. She was the prosecution's attack dog, that was what Jerry called her, her voice tuned to a perpetual note of sarcasm, disbelief and petulance, but he held to his story and never wavered. He was just glad Angelle hadn't had to see it.

She was here now, though, sitting right behind him, missing school—missing school because of him. And that was one more strike against him, he supposed, *because what kind of father would . . .?*, but the thought was too depressing and he let it die. He resisted the urge to turn round and give her a look, a smile, a wink, the least gesture, anything. It was too painful to see her there, under constraint, his daughter dragged out of school for this, and then he didn't want anybody to think he was coaching her or coercing her in any way. Jerry had no such scruples, though. He'd drilled her over and over and he'd even gone to the extreme of asking her—or no, *instructing* her—to wear something that might conform to the court's idea of what a good, honest, straightforward child was like, something that would make her look younger than she was, too young to bend the truth and far too young even to think about getting behind the wheel of a car.

Three times Jerry had sent her back to change outfits until finally, with a little persuasion from the au pair (*Allie*, and he'd have to remember to slip her a twenty, a twenty at least, because she was gold, pure gold), she put on a lacy white high-collared dress she'd worn for some kind of pageant at school, with matching white tights and patent-leather shoes. There was something wrong there in the living room, he could see that, something in the way she held her shoulders and stamped up the stairs to her room, her face clenched and her eyes burning into him, and he should have recognized it, should have given her just a hair more of his attention, but Marcy was there and she had her opinion and Jerry was being an autocrat and he himself had his hands full—he couldn't eat or think or do anything other than maybe slip into the pantry and tip the bottle of Macallan over the flask. By the time he thought of it, they were in the car, and he tried, he did, leaning across the seat to ply her with little jokes about getting a free day off and what her teachers were going to think and what Aaron Burr might have done—he would've just shot somebody, right?—but Jerry was drilling her one last time and she was sunk into the seat beside Marcy, already clamped up.

The courtroom, this courtroom, the one she was in now, was a duplicate of the one in which her father's attorney had quizzed her an hour and a half ago, except that it was filled with people. They were all old, or older, anyway, except for one woman in a form-fitting plaid jacket Angelle had seen in the window at Nordstrom's who must have been in her twenties. She was in the jury box, looking bored. The other jurors were mostly men, businessmen, she supposed, with balding heads and recessed eyes and big meaty hands clasped in their laps or grasping the rail in front of them. One of them looked like the principal of her school, Dr. Damon, but he wasn't.

The judge sat up at his desk in the front of the room, which they called a 80
bench but wasn't a bench at all, the flag of the State of California on one side of him and the American flag on the other. She was seated in the front row, between Dolores and Allie, and her father and Mr. Apodaca sat at a desk in front of her, the shoulders of their suits puffed up as if they were wearing football pads. Her father's suit was so dark she could see the dandruff there, a little spray of it like dust on the collar of his jacket, and she felt embarrassed for him. And sorry for him, sorry for him too—and for herself. And Lisette. She looked up at the judge and then the District Attorney with his grim gray tight-shaven face and the scowling woman beside him, and couldn't help thinking about what Mr. Apodaca had told her, and it made her shrink into herself when Mr. Apodaca called her name and the judge, reading the look on her face, tried to give her a smile of encouragement.

She wasn't aware of walking across the floor or of the hush that fell over the courtroom or even the bailiff who asked her to hold up her right hand and swear to tell the truth—all this, as if she were recalling a fragmented dream, would come to her later. But then she was seated in the witness' chair and everything was bright and loud suddenly, as if she'd just switched channels on the TV. Mr. Apodaca was right there before her, his voice rising sweetly, almost as if he were singing, and he was leading her through the questions they'd rehearsed over and over again. Yes, she told him, her father was late, and yes, it was getting dark, and no, she didn't notice anything strange about him. He was her father and he always picked her sister and her up on Wednesdays, she volunteered, because Wednesdays were when Allie and Dolores both had their day off and there was no one else to do it because her mother was in France.

They were all watching her now, the court gone absolutely silent, so silent you would have thought everyone had tiptoed out the door, but there they all were, hanging on her every word. She wanted to say more about her mother, about how her mother was coming home soon—had promised as much the last time she'd called long distance from her apartment in Saint Germain des Pres—but Mr. Apodaca wouldn't let her. He kept leading her along, using his sugary voice now, talking down to her, and she wanted to speak up and tell him he didn't have to treat her like that, tell him about her mother, Lisette, the school and the lawn and the trees and the way the interior of the car smelled and the heat of the liquor on her father's breath—anything that would forestall the inevitable, the question that was tucked in just behind this last one, the question on the point of which everything turned, because now she heard it, murmurous and soft and sweet, on her father's attorney's lips: "Who was driving?"

"I just wanted to say one thing," she said, lifting her eyes now to look at Mr. Apodaca and only Mr. Apodaca, his dog's eyes, his pleading soft baby-talking face, "just because, well, I wanted to say you're wrong about my mother, because she *is* coming home—she told me so herself, on, on the phone—" She couldn't help herself. Her voice was cracking.

"Yes," he said, too quickly, a hiss of breath, "yes, I understand that, Angelle, but we need to establish . . . you need to answer the question."

Oh, and now the silence went even deeper, the silence of the deep sea, of 85
outer space, of the Arctic night when you couldn't hear the runners of the sled or the feet of the dogs bleeding into the snow, and her eyes jumped to her father's then, the look on his face of hopefulness and fear and confusion, and she loved him in that moment more than she ever had.

"Angelle," Mr. Apodaca was saying, murmuring. "Angelle?"

She turned her face back to him, blotting out the judge, the D.A., the woman in the plaid jacket who was probably a college student, probably cool, and waited for the question to drop.

"Who," Mr. Apodaca repeated, slowing it down now, "was"—slower, slower still—"driving?"

She lifted her chin then to look at the judge and heard the words coming out of her mouth as if they'd been planted there, telling the truth, the hurtful truth, the truth no one would have guessed because she was almost thirteen now, almost a teenager, and she let them know it. "*I* was," she said, and the courtroom roared to life with so many people buzzing at once she thought at first they hadn't heard her. So she said it again, said it louder, much louder, so loud she might have been shouting it to the man with the camera at the back of the long churchy room with its sweat-burnished pews and the flags and emblems and all the rest. And then she looked away from the judge, away from the spectators and the man with the camera and the court recorder and the bank of windows so brilliant with light you would have thought a bomb had gone off there, and looked directly at her father.

THINKING ABOUT THE TEXT

1. What specifically does the title of the story have to do with Angell's decision?
2. How might the motivation for Angelle's decision be seen as complicated? What are some plausible reasons?
3. Why does so much of the story focus on Alan? Are we meant to be sympathetic? Or does the more we know deepen our negative judgment?
4. Explain the significance of the opening line in light of the final paragraph.
5. What if Angelle had said her father was driving? What would your judgment of her be? What is a necessary truth? A white lie? What would you have advised her to say?

MAKING COMPARISONS

1. Compare the motivations of Antigone and Angelle. Does one seem more justified than the other? Explain.
2. Compare the consequences of Antigone's and Angelle's decision.
3. If they could redo one decision, what might Antigone and Angelle do differently?

WRITING ABOUT ISSUES

1. Write an essay that argues that Antigone is or is not really the hero of the play. Consider the classic Greek ideas about tragedy, fatal flaw, and the behavior of the hero.
2. Write an essay that argues that Angelle did or did not make the right decision.
3. Write an essay that explains why so much of "Balto" focuses on Alan and his life.
4. Write an essay that focuses on the idea of the hero in both stories. The Greeks had a rather specific idea about this. In what sense is Balto a hero? Would the Greeks agree? Is Antigone? Is Haemon? Is Angelle? Would the Greeks understand the superheroes in current films?

CHAPTER 11

Crime and Justice

Thinking about literature involves making judgments about other people's views. Throughout your course, you have been making judgments as you interpret and evaluate written works, including the texts in this book, outside readings, and those produced by the class. You have been deciding also how you feel about positions expressed by your teacher and classmates. In all these acts of judgment, you have considered where you stand on general issues of aesthetics, ethics, politics, religion, and law.

Outside school, you judge things all the time, though you may not always be aware that you are doing so. You may be more conscious of your judgments when other people disagree with you, when you face multiple options, when you are trying to understand something complex, when your decisions will have significant consequences, or when you must review an act you have already committed. Some people are quite conscious that they make judgments because they have the political, professional, or institutional authority to enforce their will. Of course, these people may wind up being judged by whomever they dominate, and they may even face active revolt.

A term closely related to *judgment* is *justice*, which many people associate with judgments that are wise, fair, and sensitive to the parties involved. In this sense, justice is an ideal, which may not always be achieved in real life. Indeed, though communities hope their police departments and courts will act soundly, sometimes representatives of our legal institutions are accused of violating justice instead of upholding it. Much, of course, depends on how *justice* is defined in any particular case, and equally crucial is who defines it. The same is true of the word *crime*. Many works of literature have challenged laws of the society in which they were written, while others have at least questioned or complicated the notions of justice prevailing in their culture. Often, literature has probed the complexities of situations that in real life are resolved as clear victories for one particular party. In this respect, literature draws attention to issues that we may normally oversimplify or overlook.

Through poems by D. H. Lawrence, Elizabeth Bishop, William Stafford, and Christopher Gilbert, the opening cluster explores the idea of justice and animals, followed by poems that explore workers and justice. The third cluster focuses on injustice in communities. Robert Browning's classic poem, "My Last Duchess," centers on a vengeful man, while Gabriel Spera's contemporary poem, "My Ex-Husband," offers the reverse perspective. Poems by Countee Cullen and Natasha Tretheway—both entitled "Incident," present speakers confronted by racial injustice. The next cluster features the poems of Langston Hughes, who repeatedly asked his society to treat African American more justly. The Literature and Current Issues cluster focuses on the perennially controversial issue of capital punishment. This is followed by three stories that examine injustice from very different perspectives—and then three stories that remind us that secret crimes often involve guilt that is its own punishment. The tenth cluster presents Flannery O'Connor's "A Good Man is Hard to Find" as well commentaries about this story. Next is Joyce Carol Oates's "Where Are You Going, Where Have You Been," with texts that help situate this well-known story in its cultural context. Then Susan Glaspell's *Trifles* and Lynn Nottage's *Poof!* focus on crimes that can occur within marriage, followed by two essays on the memoires of a violent crime. The final cluster features a play and a story that complicate the idea of eyewitness testimony.

Justice for Animals: Poems

D. H. LAWRENCE, "Snake"

ELIZABETH BISHOP, "The Fish"

WILLIAM STAFFORD, "Traveling through the Dark"

CHRISTOPHER GILBERT, "On the Way Back Home"

The last few decades have given rise to numerous organizations and social movements that fight for animal rights. But for centuries, literature has raised the issue of how best to treat animals. The following poems center in turn on human behavior toward a snake, a fish, and a deer. They encourage you to wonder what it means to give these specific creatures justice. At the same time, the poems' ethical implications extend beyond these species. In general, should the term *justice* apply to animals the same ways it applies to humans? Do animals indeed have "rights"? What is "fair" and "decent" conduct toward them? What sorts of acts would be "crimes" against them?

BEFORE YOU READ

Describe at least one encounter you have had with wildlife, noting how you behaved at the time and what influenced your conduct. What is your attitude toward people who like to hunt or fish? What forms of wildlife, if any, do you think people are justified in fearing or despising? Do you think the notion of animal rights has merit? Identify particular values that your answers reflect.

D. H. LAWRENCE

Snake

David Herbert Lawrence (1885–1930) was a leading novelist and short-story writer in the first half of the twentieth century. The son of a coal miner and a former schoolteacher, he describes his English working-class upbringing in his autobiographical novel Sons and Lovers *(1913). Probably he remains best known for his 1928 novel* Lady Chatterley's Lover. *For many years, it was banned in England and the United States because it explicitly described the sexual relationship between an aristocratic woman and her husband's gamekeeper. In most of his work, Lawrence endorses human passion, although he argued that people needed to exist in harmony with nature as well as with one another. Besides writing fiction, he painted and wrote poetry. "Snake," published in 1913, is based on Lawrence's stay in Sicily, one of the many places he went as he searched for a land friendly to his ideals.*

A snake came to my water-trough
On a hot, hot day, and I in pyjamas for the heat,

To drink there.
In the deep, strange-scented shade of the great dark carob-tree
I came down the steps with my pitcher
And must wait, must stand and wait, for there he was at the trough before me.

He reached down from a fissure in the earth-wall in the gloom
And trailed his yellow-brown slackness soft-bellied down, over the edge of the stone trough
And rested his throat upon the stone bottom,
And where the water had dripped from the tap, in a small clearness,
He sipped with his straight mouth,
Softly drank through his straight gums, into his slack long body,
Silently.

Someone was before me at my water-trough,
And I, like a second comer, waiting.

He lifted his head from his drinking, as cattle do,
And looked at me vaguely, as drinking cattle do,
And flickered his two-forked tongue from his lips, and mused a moment,
And stooped and drank a little more,
Being earth-brown, earth-golden from the burning bowels of the earth
On the day of Sicilian July, with Etna smoking.

The voice of my education said to me
He must be killed,
For in Sicily the black, black snakes are innocent, the gold are venomous.

And voices in me said, If you were a man
You would take a stick and break him now, and finish him off.

But must I confess how I liked him,
How glad I was he had come like a guest in quiet, to drink at my water-trough
And depart peaceful, pacified, and thankless,
Into the burning bowels of this earth?

Was it cowardice, that I dared not kill him?
Was it perversity, that I longed to talk to him?
Was it humility, to feel so honoured?
I felt so honoured.

And yet those voices:
If you were not afraid, you would kill him!

And truly I was afraid, I was most afraid,
But even so, honoured still more
That he should seek my hospitality
From out the dark door of the secret earth.

He drank enough
And lifted his head, dreamily, as one who has drunken,

And flickered his tongue like a forked night on the air, so black;
Seeming to lick his lips,
And looked around like a god, unseeing, into the air,
And slowly turned his head,
And slowly, very slowly, as if thrice adream,
Proceeded to draw his slow length curving round
And climb again the broken bank of my wall-face.

And as he put his head into that dreadful hole,
And as he slowly drew up, snake-easing his shoulders, and entered farther,
A sort of horror, a sort of protest against his withdrawing into that horrid black hole,
Deliberately going into the blackness, and slowly drawing himself after,
Overcame me now his back was turned.

I looked round, I put down my pitcher,
I picked up a clumsy log
And threw it at the water-trough with a clatter.

I think it did not hit him,
But suddenly that part of him that was left behind convulsed in undignified haste,
Writhed like lightning, and was gone
Into the black hole, the earth-lipped fissure in the wall-front,
At which, in the intense still noon, I stared with fascination.
And immediately I regretted it.
I thought how paltry, how vulgar, what a mean act!
I despised myself and the voices of my accursed human education.

And I thought of the albatross,°
And I wished he would come back, my snake.

For he seemed to me again like a king,
Like a king in exile, uncrowned in the underworld,
Now due to be crowned again.

And so, I missed my chance with one of the lords
Of life.
And I have something to expiate;
A pettiness.

[1913]

≡ THINKING ABOUT THE TEXT

1. What did you associate with snakes before reading this poem? Does Lawrence push you to look at snakes differently, or does his poem endorse the view you already had? Develop your answer by referring to specific lines.

66 albatross: In Samuel Taylor Coleridge's "Rime of the Ancient Mariner," a seaman brings misfortune to the crew of his ship by killing an albatross, an ocean bird.

2. Discuss the poem as an argument involving various "voices." How do you think you would have reacted to the snake if you had been the speaker? What "voices" might you have heard inside your own mind? What people or institutions would these "voices" have come from?
3. Why does the speaker throw the log just as the snake is leaving? Note the explanation the speaker gives as well as the judgment he then makes about his act. Do both make sense to you? Why, or why not?
4. Lawrence begins many lines with the word *and*. What is the effect of his doing so?
5. In "Snake," Lawrence writes positively about an animal that is often feared. Think of a similar poem that you might write. What often-feared animal would you choose? What positive qualities would you point out or suggest in describing this animal? If you wish, try actually writing such a poem.

ELIZABETH BISHOP

The Fish

Although she also wrote short stories, Elizabeth Bishop (1911–1979) is primarily known for her poetry, winning both the Pulitzer Prize and the National Book Award for it. Born in Worcester, Massachusetts, she spent much of her youth in Nova Scotia. As an adult, she lived in various places, including New York City, Florida, Mexico, and Brazil. Much of her poetry observes and reflects on a particular object or figure. Such is the case with "The Fish," which Bishop wrote in 1940 and then included in her 1946 book North and South.

I caught a tremendous fish
and held him beside the boat
half out of water, with my hook
fast in a corner of his mouth.
He didn't fight.
He hadn't fought at all.
He hung a grunting weight,
battered and venerable
and homely. Here and there
his brown skin hung in strips
like ancient wall-paper,
and its pattern of darker brown
was like wall-paper:
shapes like full-blown roses
stained and lost through age.
He was speckled with barnacles,
fine rosettes of lime,
and infested
with tiny white sea-lice,

and underneath two or three
rags of green weed hung down.
While his gills were breathing in
the terrible oxygen
—the frightening gills,
fresh and crisp with blood,
that can cut so badly —
I thought of the coarse white flesh
packed in like feathers,
the big bones and the little bones,
the dramatic reds and blacks
of his shiny entrails,
and the pink swim-bladder
like a big peony.
I looked into his eyes
which were far larger than mine
but shallower, and yellowed,
the irises backed and packed
with tarnished tinfoil
seen through the lenses
of old scratched isinglass.°
They shifted a little, but not
to return my stare.
—It was more like the tipping
of an object toward the light.
I admired his sullen face,
the mechanism of his jaw,
and then I saw
that from his lower lip
— if you could call it a lip —
grim, wet, and weapon-like,
hung five old pieces of fish-line,
or four and a wire leader
with the swivel still attached,
with all their five big hooks
grown firmly in his mouth.
A green line, frayed at the end
where he broke it, two heavier lines,
and a fine black thread
still crimped from the strain and snap
when it broke and he got away.
Like medals with their ribbons
frayed and wavering,
a five-haired beard of wisdom

40 isinglass: A substitute for glass made from mica.

trailing from his aching jaw.
I stared and stared
and victory filled up
the little rented boat,
from the pool of bilge
where oil had spread a rainbow
around the rusted engine
to the bailer rusted orange,
the sun-cracked thwarts,
the oarlocks on their strings,
the gunnels—until everything
was rainbow, rainbow, rainbow!
And I let the fish go.

[1946]

THINKING ABOUT THE TEXT

1. Does the speaker change her attitude toward the fish, or does it stay pretty much the same? Support your reasoning by referring to specific lines. Are you surprised that the speaker lets the fish go? Why, or why not? How effective a conclusion is her release of the fish?
2. To what extent is the speaker describing the fish objectively? In what ways, if any, does her description of him seem to reflect her own particular values? Refer to specific lines.
3. The speaker reports that "victory filled up / the little rented boat" (lines 66–67). Whose victory might she have in mind? Why might she use this word? Often, a victory for one is a defeat for another. Is that the case here?
4. Where does the poem refer to acts and instruments of seeing? What conclusions might be drawn from these references?
5. How significant is it that the fish is male?

MAKING COMPARISONS

1. What would you say to someone who argues that Bishop's speaker is more admirable than Lawrence's speaker because she lets the animal go free?
2. With both Lawrence's and Bishop's poems, consider what you learn about the speaker's own state of mind. Does one poem tell you more than the other about its speaker's thoughts? Support your answer by referring to specific lines.
3. Bishop's poem is one long, continuous stanza, whereas Lawrence divides his into several stanzas. Does this difference in strategy lead to a significant difference in effect? Do you consider one of these strategies better than the other? Explain your reasoning.

WILLIAM STAFFORD

Traveling through the Dark

Besides being a poet himself, William Stafford (1914–1995) was a mentor to many others. During World War II, he was a conscientious objector. Later, he wrote and taught poetry at a variety of places in the United States, eventually settling in Oregon. The following poem was written in 1960 and subsequently appeared in a 1962 collection of Stafford's poems, also entitled Traveling through the Dark, *which won the National Book Award in 1963. He went on to publish over fifty more volumes of poetry and prose. He taught at Lewis and Clark College until his retirement in 1980. Like those of Robert Frost, to whom Stafford is often compared, his poems are deceptively simple. On closer examination, however, they reveal themselves to be complex and highly suggestive of deeper concerns.*

Traveling through the dark I found a deer
dead on the edge of the Wilson River road.
It is usually best to roll them into the canyon:
that road is narrow; to swerve might make more dead.

By glow of the tail-light I stumbled back of the car
and stood by the heap, a doe, a recent killing;
she had stiffened already, almost cold.
I dragged her off; she was large in the belly.

My fingers touching her side brought me the reason —
her side was warm; her fawn lay there waiting,
alive, still, never to be born.
Beside that mountain road I hesitated.

The car aimed ahead its lowered parking lights;
under the hood purred the steady engine.
I stood in the glare of the warm exhaust turning red;
around our group I could hear the wilderness listen.

I thought hard for us all — my only swerving —
then pushed her over the edge into the river. [1962]

THINKING ABOUT THE TEXT

1. "Although the situation in this poem may seem exotic to city dwellers, such events are not that unusual in areas with large deer populations. But, besides the logistical and ethical questions of this specific event, what metaphorical or symbolic possibilities do you see?"
2. What does the speaker conceivably mean in saying "I could hear the wilderness listen" (line 16)? What do you infer from his use of the word "purred" in line 14?
3. What are possible interpretations of the title — in particular, of the word "dark"?

4. Why do you think the narrator "hesitated" (line 12)? How would you define "swerve" as used in line 4? How about as it is used in the penultimate line?
5. How sensible do you find the choice that the speaker makes at the end? Explain your reasoning.

MAKING COMPARISONS

1. Bishop's and Stafford's speakers make decisions. Does Lawrence's speaker make one, too? Explain what you mean by *decision*.
2. Stafford's speaker reports that "I thought hard for us all" (line 17). Can this statement apply to Lawrence's and Bishop's speakers as well? Why, or why not?
3. Does time of day matter equally in all three poems? Refer to their specific circumstances.

CHRISTOPHER GILBERT

On the Way Back Home

Christopher Gilbert (1949–2007) was born in Birmingham, Alabama, and grew up in Lansing, Michigan. He earned his B.A. degree from the University of Michigan and his M.A. and Ph.D. (1986) in psychology from Clark University in Worcester, Massachusetts. During his career, he worked as a psychologist and taught psychology. He wrote poetry at night, on the weekends, and in the early morning. In the 1970s and 1980s, he was a force among African American poets who chanted and sang their poetry. His collection Across the Mutual Landscape *was awarded the 1983 Walt Whitman Prize by the Academy of American Poets. He was widely published. Poet Denise Levertov said that his poems "are dense with intellectual content and infused with lyrical imagination." His last book was the posthumous,* Turning into Dwelling *(2015). The following poem was published in the* Worcester Review, *March, 2006.*

It's a different world
now that we've found a doe dead, against
a late fall background crystalled with frost, steaming
still, in the middle of the two-lane as it goes
where the forest starts going west of the city,
while the feeling is as we hover hushed over her,
everything dark except for the florescent white
flashlight beam sheeming back from the various sleek
facets of her sad and useless beauty, she was
one of us though more like a fallen star
the three of us had wandered to witness,
her otherness a light from her eyes facing up

went no where, was all there on itself
existing as an end in itself, instructive so
we couldn't follow it but we were compelled—
like refugees awaiting our turns to be
an absence happening, a promising effect—
to turn our gaze onto our absent selves,
to turn our attention into a thing
to inspect, and from this focus point, go out
wandering in our various directions. *[2006]*

THINKING ABOUT THE TEXT

1. For the narrator, why is it now "a different world" (line 1)?
2. Why is the deer "more like a fallen star" (line 10)?
3. What were the three humans compelled to do?
4. Was the experience of finding the deer a positive or negative experience or something else?
5. Why does the poet use the term "wandering" (line 21)?

MAKING COMPARISONS

1. Compare the response of Stafford and Gilbert to finding the deer.
2. Which poet do you find the most thoughtful or sensitive? Explain.
3. Which poem sees closest to a response you might have to the animal encounter? Explain.

WRITING ABOUT ISSUES

1. What does it mean to treat an animal with justice? Choose Lawrence's, Bishop's, Stafford's or Gilbert's poem, and write an essay that interprets it as an answer to this question. Make clear in your analysis how you yourself define *justice*.
2. How important is setting in each of these poems? Choose two of them, and write an essay in which you consider whether their particular locations are equally important.
3. Write an essay recalling an occasion when you found it hard to decide what is involved in treating an animal with justice. What definition of *justice* did you end up with? If you wish, refer to one or more of the poems in this cluster.
4. Find a case in the news that centers on the issue of how best to treat animals, and then write an essay that develops your own position on the case by referring to at least one of the poems in this cluster.

Justice for Workers: Poems

WILLIAM BLAKE, "The Chimney Sweeper"

PHILIP LEVINE, "What Work Is"

DEBORAH GARRISON, "Worked Late on a Tuesday Night"

Since the dawn of industrialization, Western nations have been roiled by continual struggles between labor and capital for economic justice. Industrialization brought wealth and power to some and great poverty to many others. Labor movements of the nineteenth and twentieth centuries sought to halt the exploitation of workers, including women and children, and redress imbalances by gaining workers a greater share of the economic pie as well as safer and more humane working conditions. The struggles often took a turn toward violence, particularly during the nadirs of boom-and-bust economic cycles. During the 1930s, the world suffered a great economic depression, when millions who wanted employment couldn't find it. Today, many agree that conditions under the so-called Great Recession of recent years never approached the economic depths of the 1930s. Still, not everyone thrives. To compete in the new global economy, corporations cut budgets, relocate plants, outsource services, and automate facilities. As a result, large numbers of people have lost their jobs, others work for low wages, and even college graduates worry about their prospects for careers. Though defenses of capitalism continue to be voiced, protests against it, like Occupy Wall Street, burst forth. Whatever their political stances, social activists and average citizens ponder how to define *justice* for workers and argue about what policies would promote it. In effect, the following poems also raise these issues by depicting conditions of work at various times in modern economic history.

BEFORE YOU READ

What are the characteristics of your ideal job? In what ways, if any, have your real jobs fallen short?

WILLIAM BLAKE

The Chimney Sweeper

In his own time, considered eccentric or even mad, William Blake (1757–1827) is today considered a major poet, painter, and printmaker in Western culture. As a printer and engraver, he lavishly illustrated his own editions of his poems, including his 1789 collection Songs of Innocence, *in which "The Chimney Sweeper" appeared; in 1794, he produced a companion volume,* Songs of Experience. *Blake is often cited as a forerunner of contemporary secular liberalism, feminism, and even birth control and divorce. Through both his verbal and visual art, Blake promoted his own self-devised religion that incorporated stories and characters from the Bible, often in unorthodox and subversive ways.*

When my mother died I was very young,
And my father sold me while yet my tongue
Could scarcely cry " 'weep! 'weep! 'weep! 'weep!"
So your chimneys I sweep & in soot I sleep.

There's little Tom Dacre, who cried when his head
That curled like a lamb's back, was shaved, so I said,
"Hush, Tom! never mind it, for when your head's bare,
You know that the soot cannot spoil your white hair."

And so he was quiet, & that very night,
As Tom was a-sleeping he had such a sight!
That thousands of sweepers, Dick, Joe, Ned, & Jack,
Were all of them locked up in coffins of black;

And by came an Angel who had a bright key,
And he opened the coffins & set them all free;
Then down a green plain, leaping, laughing they run,
And wash in a river and shine in the Sun.
Then naked & white, all their bags left behind,
They rise upon clouds, and sport in the wind.
And the Angel told Tom, if he'd be a good boy,
He'd have God for his father & never want joy.

And so Tom awoke; and we rose in the dark
And got with our bags & our brushes to work.
Though the morning was cold, Tom was happy & warm;
So if all do their duty, they need not fear harm. *[1789]*

THINKING ABOUT THE TEXT

1. How do colors matter in this poem?
2. What is the effect of the poem's obvious rhyming?
3. Why do you think that Blake made the dream Tom's rather than the speaker's?
4. Do you assume that the author himself agrees with the last line?
5. Blake wrote his poem at a time when many children in London indeed labored in filth as chimney sweepers and were even sold by family members for this service. What are the possible counterparts to such child workers today?

PHILIP LEVINE

What Work Is

In his long career as a poet, Philip Levine (1928–2015) often wrote about working-class culture in Detroit, Michigan, his native city. At an early age and then at later times in his life, he himself worked in car manufacturing there. For thirty years, however, he taught at California State University in Fresno, and he was a visiting professor at several other schools. Levine was appointed to serve as U.S. poet laureate in 2011–2012 and received the Pulitzer Prize in poetry for his book The Simple Truth *(1994). The following selection is the title poem from his book* What Work Is *(1991). His many other volumes of poetry include* News of the World *(2009),* Stranger to Nothing: Selected Poems *(2006),* Breath *(2004),* The Mercy *(1999),* The Names of the Lost *(1976),* They Feed They Lion *(1972), and* On the Edge *(1963).*

We stand in the rain in a long line
waiting at Ford Highland Park. For work.
You know what work is—if you're
old enough to read this you know what
work is, although you may not do it.
Forget you. This is about waiting,
shifting from one foot to another.
Feeling the light rain falling like mist
into your hair, blurring your vision
until you think you see your own brother
ahead of you, maybe ten places.
You rub your glasses with your fingers,
and of course it's someone else's brother,
narrower across the shoulders than
yours but with the same sad slouch, the grin
that does not hide the stubbornness,
the sad refusal to give in to
rain, to the hours wasted waiting,
to the knowledge that somewhere ahead
a man is waiting who will say, "No,
we're not hiring today," for any
reason he wants. You love your brother,
now suddenly you can hardly stand
the love flooding you for your brother,
who's not beside you or behind or
ahead because he's home trying to
sleep off a miserable night shift
at Cadillac so he can get up
before noon to study his German.
Works eight hours a night so he can sing
Wagner, the opera you hate most,
the worst music ever invented.
How long has it been since you told him
you loved him, held his wide shoulders,
opened your eyes wide and said those words,
and maybe kissed his cheek? You've never
done something so simple, so obvious,

not because you're too young or too dumb,
not because you're jealous or even mean
or incapable of crying in
the presence of another man, no,
just because you don't know what work is. [1991]

THINKING ABOUT THE TEXT

1. In the third line, the speaker declares, "You know what work is," but at the very end he declares, "you don't know what work is" (line 42). How do you explain this shift? What definition of *work*, if any, does the poem leave you with?
2. In line 6, the speaker claims that "this is about waiting." Identify the multiple places where the word *waiting* appears in the poem. In what sense(s) can a poem about work be about waiting, too?
3. How is this poem also about the ability to see?
4. What is the significance of the poem's beginning "We"? Who is the "you" that the speaker proceeds to address?
5. What image of his brother does the speaker create? How would you describe the relationship between these brothers?

MAKING COMPARISONS

1. What kinds of protest are discernible in Blake's poem and Levine's?
2. In what way might *waiting*, a key term in Levine's poem, be applied to Blake's?
3. Compare the relationship of Blake's narrator and Tom with Levine's narrator and his brother. In what ways do they strike you as particularly fraternal, or not? You may have to spend some time clarifying your definition of *fraternal.*

DEBORAH GARRISON

Worked Late on a Tuesday Night

Deborah Garrison (b. 1965) was born in Ann Arbor, Michigan. She graduated from Brown University in 1986 and received an M.A. from New York University. Garrison worked at The New Yorker *for fifteen years, where she was the senior nonfiction editor. She is currently the poetry editor at Alfred A. Knopf as well as an editor at Pantheon Books.* A Working Girl Can't Win *(1998), her first poetry collection, sold 30,000 copies. John Updike wrote that her poems have "a Dickinsonian intensity." Her latest collection is* The Second Child *(2007).*

Again.
Midtown is blasted out and silent,
drained of the crowd and its doggy day.

I trample the scraps of deli lunches
some ate outdoors as they stared dumbly
or hooted at us career girls—the haggard
beauties, the vivid can-dos, open raincoats aflap
in the March wind as we crossed to and fro
in front of the Public Library.

Never thought you'd be one of them,
did you, little Lady?
Little Miss Phi Beta Kappa,
with your closetful of pleated
skirts, twenty-nine till death do us
part! Don't you see?
The good schoolgirl turns thirty,
forty, singing the song of time management
all day long, lugging the briefcase

home. So at 10:00 PM
you're standing here
with your hand in the air,
cold but too stubborn to reach
into your pocket for a glove, cursing
the freezing rain as though it were
your difficulty. It's pathetic,
and nobody's fault but
your own. Now

the tears,
down into the collar.
Cabs, cabs, but none for hire.
I haven't had dinner; I'm not half
of what I meant to be.
Among other things, the mother
of three. Too tired, tonight,
to seduce the father. *[2000]*

THINKING ABOUT THE TEXT

1. What specific words convey the speaker's mood? How would you describe her attitude toward work?
2. Describe what you think the speaker means by "singing the song of time management all day long."
3. What does the speaker mean by "and nobody's fault but your own"? What might be an alternative explanation for her plight? Do you think a man would write such a poem? Why, or why not?
4. Why do you think the speaker is talking just about her situation or a group of people?

5. What is the effect of beginning the poem with "Again"? Why might readers be surprised that she was in a prestigious honor society? How might success in college be linked to success after? How might it not?

MAKING COMPARISONS

1. Compare the responses of the narrators to the rain in "What Work Is" and "Worked Late on a Tuesday Night."
2. What is the attitude toward work in these three poems? Which is the most pessimistic? Which is the most troubling?
3. Compare the ending of all three poems. What thought does each conclusion leave you with?

WRITING ABOUT ISSUES

1. Choose one of the poems in this cluster, and write an essay explaining how it seems to define *justice* for workers. Make clear your own understanding of this concept.
2. Choose two of the poems, and write an essay comparing the attention they give to the speaker's self. To what extent do these poems' speakers look beyond themselves to offer insights into the larger world?
3. Recall an occasion when you or someone you know suffered unjust working conditions and yet failed to challenge them right away. Then write an essay in which you analyze the sufferer's state of mind – the thoughts and feelings that this person had at the time, including any psychological changes that he or she went through. If you wish, refer to one or more poems in this cluster.
4. Write an essay in which you apply the title of one of this cluster's poems to a recent news report. What major aspects of the report does the poem's title fit? What major aspects, if any, does the title not cover?

Injustice for Communities: Poems

PHILIP SHULTZ, "Greed"

CHAD ABUSHANAB, "Dead Town"

MAURICE MANNING, "The Hill People"

Economic upheavals can certainly hurt individuals, but such upheavals may also harm whole cities and towns. In these early decades of the twenty-first century, many communities have already suffered blows to their labor force. One or more of their local industries have died, moved, trimmed benefits, or eliminated jobs. Understandably, the people beset by such changes often view them as injustice. They see them as destructive acts their community does not deserve. The following poems, all recent, evoke the collective despair that developments like these can cause, whether the community stricken be large or small.

BEFORE YOU READ

Write a paragraph in which you describe a town—real or imaginary—that you want your reader to think is economically prospering. Focus on presenting specific physical details, perhaps by taking your reader down one of the town's main streets. Then write another paragraph in which you describe the same town years later, after it has suffered a big economic recession. If you wish, you can write two poems instead of two paragraphs. In any case, conclude this exercise by writing a sentence or two in which you explain the changes you aimed to depict.

PHILIP SCHULTZ

Greed

A native of Rochester, New York, Philip Schultz (b. 1945) has produced numerous volumes of poetry. They include The Wherewithal *(2014),* The God of Loneliness: Selected and New Poems *(2010),* Living in the Past *(2004),* The Holy Worm of Praise *(2002),* Deep Within the Ravine *(1984),* Like Wings *(1978), and* Failure *(2007), which won the Pulitzer Prize. He has also written a memoir,* My Dyslexia *(2011). Schultz founded and continues to direct The Writers Studio, which offers programs in the writing of both poetry and fiction. The following poem was published in the July/August 2013 issue of* Poetry *magazine.*

My ocean town struggles
to pick up leaves,
offer summer school,
and keep our library open.
Every day now

more men stand
at the railroad station,
waiting to be chosen for work.
Because it's thought
the Hispanics will work for less
they get picked first,
while the whites and blacks
avoid the terror
in one another's eyes.
Our handyman, Santos,
who expects only
what his hands earn,
is proud of his half acre in Guatemala,
where he plans to retire.
His desire to proceed with dignity
is admirable, but he knows
that now no one retires,
everyone works harder.
My father imagined a life
more satisfying than the one
he managed to lead.
He didn't see himself as uneducated,
thwarted, or bitter,
but soon-to-be rich.
Being rich was his right, he believed.
Happiness, I used to think,
was a necessary illusion.
Now I think it's just
precious moments of relief,
like dreams of Guatemala.
Sometimes, at night,
in winter, surrounded by
the significant silence
of empty mansions,
which once were cottages,
where people lived their lives,
and now are owned by banks
and the absent rich,
I like to stand at my window,
looking for a tv's futile flickering,
always surprised to see
instead
the quaint, porous face
of my reflection,
immersed
in its one abundance.

[2013]

THINKING ABOUT THE TEXT

1. Despite being the title, the word *greed* never appears in the poem. What lines, if any, do you think it applies to? Why might Schultz have chosen to omit it from his actual text?
2. Although the poem is a single stanza, it makes a number of shifts as it proceeds. What are these? Given that it can be divided into stages, why do you suppose Schultz decided not to break the poem into multiple stanzas?
3. The speaker reports that he has changed his definition of happiness. State this change in your own words. Does it make sense to you? Why, or why not?
4. Where does the speaker call our attention to things *not* present? Refer to specific lines.
5. The poem begins by referring to the speaker's community, but it ends with him looking at his own reflection. Is it fair to say, then, that the speaker becomes increasingly self-absorbed? Explain your reasoning.

CHAD ABUSHANAB

Dead Town

Chad Abushanab (b. 1986) *lives in Lubbock, Texas, where he is pursuing a doctorate in the Literature and Creative Writing Program at Texas Tech University. He is poetry editor for the literary journal* Arcadia *and its chapbook imprint Arcadia Press. He has published his own poems in a variety of journals, including* Ecotone, Shenandoah, 32 Poems, Measure, *and* Unsplendid. *"Dead Town" first appeared in the Fall 2016 issue of* The Hopkins Review.

A dead town full of ghosts—it left behind
its brick and mortar bones, the pharmacy
windows dark with dust. Each day we find
the Bijoux Movie House's bleached marquee
unchanged, and no one really seems to mind.
7:00—*The Day The Earth Stood Still.*
The seats stay empty since they closed the mill.

Instead, we haunt the Late-Nite A&P,
the last place left to shop for Wonderbread,
Del Monte peaches, and Chef Boyardee.
We eat our dinners sitting up in bed.
For company, the rabbit-eared TV.
Infomercials fill the anxious quiet,
the midnight mantra, *Don't believe us? Try it!*

echoes through our rooms paid by the week.
It drowns the sound of industry collapsing,

the deafening crash of silence at its peak—
no cars, no crowds, the old mill making nothing—
the sound of losing purpose, so to speak.
Our part-time days, like stories stretched too thin,
cannot escape the *were*, and *was*, and *when*.

THINKING ABOUT THE TEXT

1. In what ways might a town be "dead" (line 1)? Define what *you* mean by the term when you apply to a community. What features of this poem's town does the speaker emphasize in developing the claim that it's "dead"? In what respects might the town's still-living citizens be "ghosts" (line 1)?
2. In the first stanza, the speaker points out that "no one really seems to mind" (line 5) how the theater's marquee remains "unchanged" (line 5). Does the *speaker* seem to mind, though? In general, do you think the speaker is probably like the other townspeople, or do you sense a significant difference? Explain.
3. What is the rhyme scheme of this poem? What would you say to someone who argues that in order to convey the town's full "deadness," the poem should not rhyme at all?
4. Note the references to sounds in the third stanza. How can "industry collapsing" have any "sound" at all (line 16)? How can "silence" have a "deafening crash" (line 17)? How could someone ever really detect "the sound of losing purpose" (line 19)?
5. What, specifically, might be "the *were*, and *was*, and *when*" (line 21)?

MAKING COMPARISONS

1. Could Shultz's title "Greed" also serve as the title of Abushanab's poem? Could Abushanab's title "Dead Town" also serve as the title of Shultz's poem? Explain your reasoning.
2. Shultz's speaker reports that he enjoys "looking for a tv's futile flickering" (line 45). Would you say that the townspeople in Abushanab's poem do much the same thing? Why, or why not?
3. Abushanab's speaker refers consistently to "we," never saying "I." Schultz's speaker twice uses the word "our," but he begins with the word "my," brings that word up twice later, and refers to himself as "I" three times. Are you more conscious of Schultz's speaker as an individual, therefore? Does Abushanab's speaker seem much less a single person? Explain.

MAURICE MANNING

The Hill People

Maurice Manning (b. 1966) teaches at Transylvania University in Lexington, Kentucky, his native state. His first volume of poetry, Lawrence Booth's Book of Visions *(2001), won the Yale Series of Younger Poets Competition. His subsequent collections include* A Companion for Owls *(2004),* Bucolics *(2007),* The Gone and The Going Away *(2013), and* The Common Man *(2010), which was a finalist for the Pulitzer Prize. In addition to writing, Manning has been active in campaigns against environmentally destructive practices of coal mining in Appalachia. "The Hill People" was published in the Winter 2013 issue of the journal* Appalachian Heritage.

And then the hill people came down
riding mules flanked by dogs
some feist° some liver-spotted hounds
and they were ghosts the men and women
and their ash-faced children their mules
and dogs were ghosts come down from the place
where they had lived in scant array
like lint in the pockets of their dark land
and the men were gaunt and the women were thin
and the children had hayseed flung
in their hair and the dogs tracked back and forth
and they came to the town which wasn't a town
but a circle of nothing surrounding nowhere
no river no trees no shadows no time
for darkness no slow crawl
toward love or death or after death
the nowhere town was fast and the people
who lived there only wanted more
whatever it was and the next thing
after that they had appetite
but not desire and they didn't come
from anywhere and didn't know
they lived in a place that wasn't a place
and the hill people with their haunted faces
said to the people of the town
you have taken everything there is
and heaped it into a god a god
who gives you nothing not even
a tree no shade behind the tree
no wind to carry the birdsong
no branch to quiver with the bird
no doubt no hope no lie no mirth

3 feist: a small hunting dog

no tenderness no shame no knowing
hill or horizon or the hand
behind it or why no silence nothing
no end this was the vision I had.

[2013]

☰ THINKING ABOUT THE TEXT

1. Manning has written thirty-six lines without a clear, punctuated sentence break until the very end. Why do you think he employs this strategy? What is its effect?
2. Note the poem's last words. Why do you think Manning delays letting us know that what we are reading is someone's personal "vision"?
3. Trace the poem's repetitions of the word *no*. What is the effect of these? In what sense can a town be "a circle of nothing" (line 13) if there are people living there?
4. What do you suppose turned the hill people into "ghosts" (line 4)? Do you take Manning to be implying that their way of life was ideal? Why, or why not?
5. Beginning with line 26, the hill people make an accusation against the community they have come to. Put this accusation in your own words. What might be the community's response?

☰ MAKING COMPARISONS

1. Abushanab's poem brings up the word "haunt" (line 8); Manning's poem uses the word "haunted" (line 24). Do these poems seem to define and apply the concept of haunting in largely the same way? Why, or why not?
2. Compare the three poems' references to "silence." How similar are these texts in their use of the word?
3. What specific emotions and views, if any, might the townspeople in Schultz's and Abushanab's poems share with Manning's hill people?

☰ WRITING ABOUT ISSUES

1. Choose one of the poems in this cluster, and write an essay in which you identify the specific forms of injustice that the poem considers. Be sure to define what you mean by *injustice* in this case.
2. Write an essay in which you compare Abushanab's use of multiple stanzas to Schultz's or Manning's use of a single stanza. Does the difference in the number of stanzas produce major differences in effect?
3. Write a letter, in prose or verse, to a specific group of people who in your view have done an injustice to citizens of a particular locale. In your letter, do not simply accuse your target audience of a moral failing and demand

they correct it; explain *why* you are disturbed by something they have done, as well as *how* their act is an injustice in your definition of the term. If you wish, refer to any of the poems in this cluster.

4. Choose a recent speech, editorial, or blog entry that proposes some way of making your city or town more prosperous. Then write an essay in which you gauge the chances that this proposal would also serve the cause of justice. Be sure to define what you mean by *justice* in this case. Refer, if you wish, to the cluster's poems.

He Said/She Said: Re-Visions of a Poem

ROBERT BROWNING, "My Last Duchess"

GABRIEL SPERA, "My Ex-Husband"

Although the terms *justice* and *injustice* are most often applied to developments that affect entire groups, these words can also prove relevant to personal relationships. In particular, two people may quit being a couple because at least one of them feels that the other has done an injustice to him or her. Of course, the two parties may define *justice* differently, and they may disagree as well about which of them is in the wrong. Together, the following poems illustrate such a conflict of views. Indeed, they present a he said/she said scenario. In the first poem, Robert Browning's famous "My Last Duchess," the speaker explains how his wife's allegedly unjust behavior forced him to get rid of her. In the second poem, Gabriel Spera's more recent "My Ex-Husband," the speaker recalls how her former spouse's injustices drove her to divorce him. Notice the specific ways that Spera's re-vision of Browning's poem forces us to consider differences in perspective.

BEFORE YOU READ

Think of two people you know who have broken off a relationship they had with each other. To what extent do these people see the breakup the same way? How, if at all, do their views of it differ?

ROBERT BROWNING

My Last Duchess

Today, Robert Browning (1812–1889) is regarded as one of the greatest poets of nineteenth-century England, but in his own time he was not nearly as celebrated as his wife, the poet Elizabeth Barrett Browning. He is chiefly known for his achievements with the ***dramatic monologue****, a genre of poetry that emphasizes the speaker's own distinct personality. Often Browning's speakers are his imaginative re-creations of people who once existed in real life. He was especially interested in religious, political, and artistic figures from the Renaissance. The following poem, perhaps Browning's most famous, was written in 1842, and its speaker, the Duke of Ferrara, was an actual man.*

FERRARA°

That's my last Duchess painted on the wall,
Looking as if she were alive. I call
That piece a wonder, now: Frà Pandolf's° hands

Epigraph Ferrara: In the sixteenth century, the duke of this Italian city arranged to marry a second time after the mysterious death of his very young first wife. **3 Frà Pandolf:** A fictitious artist.

Worked busily a day, and there she stands.
Will't please you sit and look at her? I said
"Frà Pandolf" by design, for never read
Strangers like you that pictured countenance,
The depth and passion of its earnest glance,
But to myself they turned (since none puts by
The curtain I have drawn for you, but I)
And seemed as they would ask me, if they durst,
How such a glance came there; so, not the first
Are you to turn and ask thus. Sir, 'twas not
Her husband's presence only, called that spot
Of joy into the Duchess' cheek: perhaps
Frà Pandolf chanced to say "Her mantle laps
Over my lady's wrist too much," or "Paint
Must never hope to reproduce the faint
Half-flush that dies along her throat": such stuff
Was courtesy, she thought, and cause enough
For calling up that spot of joy. She had

A heart—how shall I say?—too soon made glad,
Too easily impressed; she liked whate'er
She looked on, and her looks went everywhere.
Sir, 'twas all one! My favor at her breast,
The dropping of the daylight in the West,
The bough of cherries some officious fool
Broke in the orchard for her, the white mule
She rode with round the terrace—all and each
Would draw from her alike the approving speech,
Or blush, at least. She thanked men,—good! but thanked
Somehow—I know not how—as if she ranked
My gift of a nine-hundred-years-old name
With anybody's gift. Who'd stoop to blame
This sort of trifling? Even had you skill
In speech—which I have not—to make your will
Quite clear to such an one, and say, "Just this
Or that in you disgusts me; here you miss,
Or there exceed the mark"—and if she let
Herself be lessoned so, nor plainly set
Her wits to yours, forsooth, and made excuse,
—E'en then would be some stooping; and I choose
Never to stoop. Oh sir, she smiled, no doubt,
Whene'er I passed her; but who passed without
Much the same smile? This grew; I gave commands;
Then all smiles stopped together. There she stands
As if alive. Will't please you rise? We'll meet
The company below, then. I repeat,
The Count your master's known munificence
Is ample warrant that no just pretense
Of mine for dowry will be disallowed;
Though his fair daughter's self, as I avowed
At starting, is my object. Nay, we'll go
Together down, sir. Notice Neptune, though,
Taming a sea-horse, thought a rarity,
Which Claus of Innsbruck° cast in bronze for me! *[1842]*

THINKING ABOUT THE TEXT

1. The duke offers a history of his first marriage. Summarize his story in your own words, including the reasons he gives for his behavior. How would you describe him? Do you admire anything about him? If so, what?
2. Try to reconstruct the rhetorical situation in which the duke is making his remarks. Who might be his audience? What might be his goals? What

56 Claus of Innsbruck: A fictitious artist.

strategies is he using to accomplish them? Cite details that support your conjectures.

3. When you read the poem aloud, how conscious are you of its rhymes? What is its rhyme scheme? What is the effect of Browning's using just one stanza rather than breaking the poem into several?
4. Going by this example of the genre, what are the advantages of writing a poem as a dramatic monologue? What are the disadvantages?
5. Browning suggests that the setting of this poem is Renaissance Italy. What relevance might his poem have had for readers in mid-nineteenth-century England? What relevance might it have for audiences in the United States today?

GABRIEL SPERA

My Ex-Husband

Raised in New Jersey, Gabriel Spera (b. 1966) graduated from Cornell University and earned an M.F.A. from the University of North Carolina at Greensboro. He has worked as a technical writer for several years, most recently for a California aerospace firm. At the same time, he has published many poems, including the following one, which

Photo by Rachel Lee

first appeared in the journal Poetry *in 1992. It also appears in his book* The Standing Wave *(2003), which was chosen for the National Poetry Series and also won the PEN-USA West Literary Book Award for Poetry. More recently, Spera has published another volume of poetry,* The Rigid Body *(2012).*

That's my ex-husband pictured on the shelf,
Smiling as if in love. I took it myself
With his Leica, and stuck it in that frame
We got for our wedding. Kind of a shame
To waste it on him, but what could I do?
(Since I haven't got a photograph of you.)
I know what's on your mind—you want to know
Whatever could have made me let him go—
He seems like any woman's perfect catch,
What with his ruddy cheeks, the thin mustache,
Those close-set, baggy eyes, that tilted grin.
But snapshots don't show what's beneath the skin!
He had a certain charm, charisma, style,
That passionate, earnest glance he struck, meanwhile
Whispering the sweetest things, like "Your lips
Are like plump rubies, eyes like diamond chips,"
Could flush the throat of any woman, not
Just mine. He blew the most romantic spots
In town, where waiters, who all knew his face,
Reserved an intimately dim-lit place
Half-hidden in a corner nook. Such stuff
Was all too well rehearsed, I soon enough
Found out. He had an attitude—how should
I put it—smooth, self-satisfied, too good
For the rest of the world, too easily
Impressed with his officious self. And he
flirted—fine! but flirted somehow a bit
Too ardently, too blatantly, as if,
If someone ever noticed, no one cared
How slobbishly he carried on affairs.
Who'd lower herself to put up with shit
Like that? Even if you'd the patience—which
I have not—to go and see some counsellor
And say, "My life's a living hell," or
"Everything he does disgusts, the lout!"—
And even if you'd somehow worked things out,
Took a long trip together, made amends,
Let things get back to normal, even then
You'd still be on the short end of the stick;

And I choose never ever to get stuck.
Oh, no doubt, it always made my limbs go
Woozy when he kissed me, but what bimbo
In the steno pool went without the same
Such kisses? So, I made some calls, filed some claims,
All kisses stopped together. There he grins,
Almost lovable. Shall we go? I'm in
The mood for Chez Pierre's, perhaps, tonight,
Though anything you'd like would be all right
As well, of course, though I'd prefer not to go
To any place with checkered tables. No,
We'll take my car. By the way, have I shown
You yet these lovely champagne flutes, hand blown,
Imported from Murano, Italy,
Which Claus got in the settlement for me! *[1992]*

THINKING ABOUT THE TEXT

1. Why, evidently, did the speaker get divorced? What would you say to someone who argues that because she still thinks about her former husband, keeps his photograph on the shelf, and clearly has not forgiven him, she remains "stuck" (line 40) in that relationship?
2. How reliable do you think the speaker's account of her former husband is?
3. Where does the speaker shift the kind of language she's been using? Do you think her feelings are consistent despite this shifting? Explain.
4. Who do you think the "you" (line 6) in this poem is? In what ways, if any, does the presence of this "you" seem to influence what the speaker says and how she says it?
5. Although the speaker is a woman, poet Gabriel Spera is a man. Does this poem lead you to believe that a man can, in fact, write from a woman's point of view? Why, or why not?

MAKING COMPARISONS

1. Where in his poem does Spera closely echo Browning's poem? Refer to specific lines in both texts. What is the effect of the changes in wording that Spera makes?
2. Do you sympathize more with Spera's speaker than with Browning's? Why, or why not? Explain.
3. Do the listeners in these two poems both seem passive? Refer to specific details of both texts.

WRITING ABOUT ISSUES

1. Choose either of the poems in this cluster, and write an essay analyzing what you consider to be its most significant line. Be sure to explain why you find your chosen line important.
2. To what extent and in what ways does Spera's poem seem more "modern" than Browning's? Write an essay in which you answer this question. Refer to specific details from both poems, and define clearly what you mean by *modern*.
3. Write an essay analyzing a relationship that you broke off because you thought the other person had acted unjustly. To what extent do you still brood about this relationship? How much have you forgiven the other person? What meaning of the term *justice* seems applicable here?
4. Write a dialogue between the speakers of these two poems, or write a dialogue between the listeners in them. Shape the dialogue so that it emphasizes ideas and principles that the two people have in common. Then write a brief essay in which you analyze the conversation you have constructed. What do you want your readers to conclude from it?

Racial Injustice: Poems

COUNTEE CULLEN, "Incident"

NATASHA TRETHEWEY, "Incident"

Throughout literary history, writers have called attention to the injustices of racial oppression. The following pair of poems, both titled "Incident," remind us that racial prejudice could be blatant and vicious both early in the twentieth century and toward its end. Indeed, the subject is not likely to die out even now, when laws blatantly permitting slavery or segregation have ceased to exist. Racism continues in various forms, though perhaps subtler ones. As you read these poems, consider what recent "incidents" might be topics of similar texts.

BEFORE YOU READ

How do you define *racism*? What, for you, are possible signs of it?

COUNTEE CULLEN

Incident

Countee Cullen (1903–1946) was one of the leading writers of the Harlem Renaissance, a New York–based movement of African American authors, artists, and intellectuals that flourished from World War I to the Great Depression. Cullen's place of birth may have been Baltimore, Louisville, or New York, but by 1918 he was living in New York as the adopted son of a Methodist minister. Cullen wrote poetry and received prizes for it even as he attended New York University. In 1925, while pursuing a master's degree from Harvard, he published his first book of poems, Color, *which contained "Incident." His later books include* Copper Sun *(1927),* The Black Christ and Other Poems *(1929), a translation of Euripides's play* Medea *(1935), and a children's book,* The Lost Zoo *(1940). Cullen gained much attention when, in 1928, he wed the daughter of famed African American writer and scholar W. E. B. DuBois, but their marriage ended just two years later. During the 1930s, Cullen's writing did not earn him enough to live on, so he taught English and French at Frederick Douglass High School. At the time of his death in 1946, he was collaborating on the Broadway musical* St. Louis Woman. *In part because he died relatively young, Cullen's reputation faded. Langston Hughes became much better known as a Harlem Renaissance figure. "Incident," however, has been consistently anthologized, and today Cullen is being rediscovered along with other contributors to African American literature.*

Once riding in old Baltimore
    Heart-filled, head-filled with glee,
I saw a Baltimorean
    Keep looking straight at me.

Now I was eight and very small,
    And he was no whit bigger,
And so I smiled, but he poked out
    His tongue and called me, "Nigger."

I saw the whole of Baltimore
    From May until December:
Of all the things that happened there
    That's all that I remember.

[1925]

THINKING ABOUT THE TEXT

1. Why do you think the speaker calls attention to his heart *and* his head in the second line? Might referring to just one of these things have been enough?
2. "Baltimorean" (line 3) seems a rather unusual and abstract term for the boy that the speaker encountered. How do you explain its presence in the poem? How important is it that the speaker name the city where the incident occurred?
3. Although the incident that the speaker recalls must have been painful for him, why do you think he does not state his feelings about it more explicitly? What is the effect of his relative reticence about it?
4. The rhythm of this poem is rather singsongy. Why do you think Cullen made it so?
5. The speaker states that he was eight at the time of the incident. How old might he be now? How important is his age?

NATASHA TRETHEWEY

Incident

The child of an interracial marriage, Natasha Trethewey (b. 1966) graduated from the University of Georgia and earned a master's degree at Hollins College in Virginia. Currently the U.S. poet laureate, she teaches creative writing at Emory University in Atlanta, Georgia. She is the author of four volumes of poetry: Domestic Work *(2000);* Bellocq's Ophelia *(2002);* Native Guard *(2006), which won the Pulitzer Prize and includes the following poem; and* Thrall *(2012).* Beyond Katrina: A Meditation on the Mississippi Gulf Coast *(2010) is a combination of memoir and reportage that also mixes prose with verse.*

We tell the story every year—
how we peered from the windows, shades drawn—
though nothing really happened,
the charred grass now green again.

We peered from the windows, shade drawn,
at the cross trussed like a Christmas tree,

the charred grass still green. Then
we darkened our rooms, lit the hurricane lamps.

At the cross trussed like a Christmas tree,
a few men gathered, white as angels in their gowns.
We darkened our room and lit hurricane lamps,
the wicks trembling in their fonts of oil.

It seemed the angels had gathered, white men in their gowns.
When they were done, they left quietly. No one came.
The wicks trembled all night in their fonts of oil;
by morning the flames had all dimmed.

When they were done, the men left quietly. No one came.
Nothing really happened.
By morning all the flames had dimmed.
We tell the story every year. *[2006]*

THINKING ABOUT THE TEXT

1. Trethewey has acknowledged that this poem is a *pantoum*. This form of verse consists of *quatrains* (stanzas of four lines each); also, the second and fourth lines of a quatrain are repeated as the first and third lines of the following quatrain, with the final line of the entire poem repeating its very first line. It's a difficult type of poem to write. Why do you think Trethewey attempted it here?
2. How does the poem use religious imagery?
3. What information does the poet leave out? Why do you think she omits it?
4. Why do you think the "we" of the poem "tell[s] the story every year"? Why tell the story at all? Why not tell it more often?
5. Twice, the speaker claims that "nothing really happened." Do you agree with her? Why, or why not?

MAKING COMPARISONS

1. In giving her poem the title "Incident," Trethewey is surely aware of Cullen's poem. What other connections between these two texts do you feel encouraged by her to make?
2. Which of the two poems, Cullen's or Trethewey's, strikes you as more abstract? Does this difference lead to a difference in effect? Why, or why not?
3. Do the speakers in these two poems strike you as using pretty much the same tone? Refer to specific lines in each work.

WRITING ABOUT ISSUES

1. Choose either Cullen's poem or Trethewey's, and write an essay in which you examine what the poem suggests about the act of *remembering* an incident of race-related injustice.
2. Cullen's poem is famous; does Trethewey's deserve to be equally well known? Write an essay addressing this question for your audience, making clear your criteria for artistic success.
3. Take a line from either Cullen's poem or Trethewey's, and write an essay showing how the line is applicable to an "incident" that you recently witnessed or saw being reported in the media.
4. Find and read at least three articles on racial discrimination in early twentieth-century Baltimore or on American laws against interracial marriage. Then write an essay explaining how these articles illuminate the "incident" described in Cullen's or Trethewey's poem.

A Dream of Justice: Poems by Langston Hughes

LANGSTON HUGHES, "Open Letter to the South"

LANGSTON HUGHES, "Theme for English B"

LANGSTON HUGHES, "Harlem"

Inspired by two of the great poetic voices of American life, Walt Whitman and Carl Sandburg, Langston Hughes is often thought of as the African American poet laureate, a writer who is able to sing eloquently about the reality and idealism of democracy in America. He was committed to telling the truth about the lives of black people. In the introduction to *The Collected Poems of Langston Hughes*, it is noted that Hughes wrote of "the joys and sorrows, the trials and triumphs, of ordinary black folk, in the language of their typical speech and composed out of a genuine love of these people."

In response to the Depression of the 1930s, Hughes became radicalized by the poverty and injustice he saw everywhere in black America. His poems from this period are radical, indeed. "Open Letter to the South" calls for a socialist solidarity against oppression. Although he later became less radical in his poetry, "Theme for English B" and "Harlem" still reflect his belief that poetry is a form of social action. At the heart of all Hughes's poetry was the deferred dream of African Americans to achieve the freedom and equality promised to all in America.

BEFORE YOU READ

Can you imagine what would have happened to your personality if a dream of yours (perhaps going to college, playing a sport, or marrying someone you loved deeply) were denied? What would you do if America was not living up to its stated ideals or if those ideals were suddenly altered significantly? Would you express your disappointment publicly or only privately?

LANGSTON HUGHES

Open Letter to the South

Langston Hughes (1902–1967) has long been regarded as a major African American writer and is increasingly seen as an important contributor to American literature in general. Like Countee Cullen, Hughes was actively involved in the 1920s movement called the Harlem Renaissance. Then and later, he worked in various genres, including fiction, drama, and autobiography. Nevertheless, he is primarily known for his poems. This poem was originally published in New Masses *in 1932 as "Red Flag over Tuskegee." It clearly reflected the feeling among many working-class intellectuals and artists in the 1930s that solidarity among the workers of the world was the only sure path toward freedom and equality.*

©Historical/Getty Images

White workers of the South
    Miners,
    Farmers,
    Mechanics,
    Mill hands,
    Shop girls,
    Railway men,
    Servants,
    Tobacco workers,
    Sharecroppers,
    GREETINGS!

I am the black worker,
  Listen:
That the land might be ours,
And the mines and the factories and the office towers
At Harlan, Richmond, Gastonia, Atlanta, New Orleans;
That the plants and the roads and the tools of power
Be ours:

Let us forget what Booker T. said,
"Separate as the fingers."

Let us become instead, you and I,
One single hand
That can united rise
To smash the old dead dogmas of the past —
To kill the lies of color
That keep the rich enthroned
And drive us to the time-clock and the plow
Helpless, stupid, scattered, and alone — as now —
Race against race,
Because one is black,
Another white of face.

Let us new lessons learn,
All workers,
New life-ways make,
One union form:
Until the future burns out
Every past mistake
Let us together, say:
"You are my brother, black or white,
You my sister — now — today!"
For me, no more, the great migration to the North.

Instead: migration into force and power —
Tuskegee with a new flag on the tower!
On every lynching tree, a poster crying FREE
Because, O poor white workers,
You have linked your hands with me.

We did not know that we were brothers.
Now we know!
Out of that brotherhood
Let power grow!
We did not know
That we were strong.
Now we see
In union lies our strength.
Let union be
The force that breaks the time-clock,
Smashes misery,
Takes land,
Takes factories,
Takes office towers,
Takes tools and banks and mines.
Railroads, ships and dams,
Until the forces of the world
Are ours!

White worker,
Here is my hand.

Today,
We're Man to Man. *[1932]*

THINKING ABOUT THE TEXT

1. Who does Hughes blame for "the lies of color" (line 25) that divide black from white? Do you agree?
2. Booker T. Washington (1856–1915), the most prominent African American of his day, is now often seen as an accommodationist who urged only gradual progress toward equality between blacks and whites. Why do you think Hughes tells his readers to "forget what Booker T. said" (line 19)?
3. If you think of this poem as an argument, what would be Hughes's claim? Who is his audience, and what is his evidence? Do you think he made the right choices for his argument?
4. What do you think Hughes meant by the following lines: "We did not know that we were brothers. / Now we know!" (lines 47–48)?
5. Hughes is hoping that class solidarity is stronger than racial divisions. Was this the case in 1932? Is it the case today?

LANGSTON HUGHES

Theme for English B

Langston Hughes wrote "Theme for English B" in 1949, when he was twenty-five years older than the poem's speaker. As a young man, he had attended a "college on the hill above Harlem": Columbia University.

The instructor said,
    Go home and write
    a page tonight.
    And let that page come out of you —
    Then, it will be true.

I wonder if it's that simple?
I am twenty-two, colored, born in Winston-Salem.
I went to school there, then Durham, then here
to this college on the hill above Harlem.
I am the only colored student in my class.
The steps from the hill lead down into Harlem,
through a park, then I cross St. Nicholas,
Eighth Avenue, Seventh, and I come to the Y,
the Harlem Branch Y, where I take the elevator
up to my room, sit down, and write this page:

It's not easy to know what is true for you or me
at twenty-two, my age. But I guess I'm what
I feel and see and hear, Harlem, I hear you:
hear you, hear me — we two — you, me, talk on this page.
(I hear New York, too.) Me — who?
Well, I like to eat, sleep, drink, and be in love.
I like to work, read, learn, and understand life.
I like a pipe for a Christmas present,
or records — Bessie,° bop, or Bach.
I guess being colored doesn't make me *not* like
the same things other folks like who are other races.
So will my page be colored that I write?
Being me, it will not be white.
But it will be
a part of you, instructor.
You are white —
yet a part of me, as I am part of you.
That's American.
Sometimes perhaps you don't want to be a part of me.
Nor do I often want to be a part of you.
But we are, that's true!
As I learn from you,
I guess you learn from me —
although you're older — and white —
and somewhat more free.
This is my page for English B. *[1949]*

THINKING ABOUT THE TEXT

1. What do you think the instructor's response to "my page" (line 41) would be? What would yours be?
2. What do you think the instructor was hoping for? On what basis does the narrator seem to critique the assignment?
3. What do you think the narrator means by "American" in line 33? After more than sixty years, does it mean something different?
4. What do you think he means by the line "It's not easy to know what is true for you or me / at twenty-two" (lines 16–17)? Do you agree?

MAKING COMPARISONS

1. Although this poem, like the previous one, seems written to a white audience, its tone seems less aggressive. Is this your reading? What lines seem particularly diplomatic in contrast to "Open Letter to the South"?

24 Bessie: Bessie Smith (1898?–1937), the famous American blues singer.

2. The emphasis on freedom here seems more indirect than in the previous poem. What do you think Hughes means by "free" in the next-to-last line? Would you agree with him then (1949)? Now?
3. Is "Today, / We're Man to Man" (lines 67–68) from "Open Letter to the South" the most hopeful (or naive) line in the three poems?

LANGSTON HUGHES

Harlem

Sometimes called "A Dream Deferred," "Harlem" is Hughes's most anthologized poem and has become synonymous with African Americans' long struggle for freedom and equality.

What happens to a dream deferred?

Does it dry up
like a raisin in the sun?
Or fester like a sore —
And then run?
Does it stink like rotten meat?
Or crust and sugar over —
like a syrupy sweet?

Maybe it just sags
like a heavy load.

Or does it explode?

[1951]

THINKING ABOUT THE TEXT

1. The inspiration for Lorraine Hansberry's famous play, *A Raisin in the Sun*, Hughes's brief poem asks a question and then answers it with more questions. Is this effective? Should he have been more explicit?
2. What is the "dream deferred" (line 1)?
3. The alternatives given are specific and concrete metaphors presumably embodied in people. What kind of person would be "like a raisin in the sun" (line 3)?
4. How would you imagine a person who stank "like rotten meat" (line 6) would behave? One who "sags / like a heavy load" (lines 9–10)? One who is "like a syrupy sweet" (line 8)?
5. How do you read the last line?

MAKING COMPARISONS

1. Why do you think "Harlem" is the most popular of the three poems presented here?

2. Are there hints in the previous poems of the ideas developed in "Harlem"?
3. Which poem would you recommend to someone from another country who is trying to understand our racial history? Why?

WRITING ABOUT ISSUES

1. Several arguments are made in "Open Letter to the South." Choose one to analyze in terms of issue, claim, evidence, audience, and persuasion. (See the section on "Strategies for Making Arguments about Literature," p. 59.)
2. Write an essay that agrees or disagrees with Hughes's suggestion in "Open Letter to the South."
3. Write an essay about your personal responses to these poems. Include what you think the poems mean, whether you agree or not with the writer's points, and what emotions the poems provoked.
4. "Open Letter to the South" was written in the 1930s, and we know that the civil rights movement didn't gain serious national attention until the mid-1960s. Since many other voices besides Hughes's were addressing the lack of freedom among America's minorities, especially African Americans, how can you account for the length of time it took for freedom and equality to become serious issues among white voters? Write an essay that addresses this issue.

Literature and Current Issues: How Just Is Capital Punishment?

SHERMAN ALEXIE, "Capital Punishment"

ARGUMENTS ON THE ISSUE:

GEORGE WILL, "Capital Punishment's Slow Death"

ROBERT BLECKER, "With Death Penalty, Let Punishment Truly Fit the Crime"

CHARLES J. OGLETREE, "Condemned to Die Because He's Black"

Capital punishment has been a controversial issue for centuries. And although most Western countries, numerous states, and many political and religious organizations have condemned the death penalty, the matter is far from settled, with contentious issues involving moral, practical, and religious principles. Advocates argue that it is a just penalty that deters crime, can be used by prosecutors in plea bargaining, and rids the community of repeat offenders. It also, it is argued, provides closure for surviving victims or loved ones. Opponents claim it does not deter crime, risks killing the innocent, and is a barbaric act that cheapens human life and creates equality between the government and the criminal. It is also argued that penalties are arbitrarily being influenced by race, gender, and socioeconomic factors and are therefore immoral and illegitimate.

The poem and three essays presented here touch on these issues and others as the four writers argue for and against the death penalty. They bring intelligence and reasoning as well as anger and compassion to a serious and complex debate.

SHERMAN ALEXIE

Capital Punishment

Born in Spokane, Washington, Sherman Alexie (b. 1966) is a member of the Spokane/Coeur d'Alene tribe. His fiction includes the novels Reservation Blues *(1996),* Indian Killer *(1997),* Flight *(2007), and* The Absolutely True Diary of a Part-Time Indian *(2007). He has also produced four collections of short stories:* Blasphemy: New and Selected Stories *(2013),* Ten Little Indians *(2003),* The Toughest Indian in the World *(2001), and* The Lone Ranger and Tonto Fistfight in Heaven *(1994), which he adapted for the acclaimed 1998 film* Smoke Signals. *Alexie is a poet, too, with his collections of verse including* The Business of Fancy Dancing *(1992),* Old Shirts and New Skins *(1993),* First Indian on the Moon *(1993),* Drums like This *(1996),* One Stick Song *(2000), and* Face *(2009). His latest work is* Blasphemy *(2012), and he is the guest editor for the 2015 Best American Poetry. "Capital Punishment" appeared in a 1996 issue of* Indiana Review *and, that same year, in Alexie's collection* The Summer of Black Widows. *It was also selected for the 1996 edition of the volume* Best American Poetry. *Alexie wrote the poem after reading media coverage of an actual execution in the state of Washington.*

Getty Images

I prepare the last meal
for the Indian man to be executed

but this killer doesn't want much:
baked potato, salad, tall glass of ice water.

(I am not a witness)

It's mostly the dark ones
who are forced to sit in the chair

especially when white people die.
It's true, you can look it up

and this Indian killer pushed
his fists all the way down

a white man's throat, just to win a bet
about the size of his heart.

Those Indians are always gambling.
Still, I season this last meal

with all I have. I don't have much
but I send it down the line

with the handsome guard
who has fallen in love

with the Indian killer.
I don't care who loves whom.

(I am not a witness)

I don't care if I add too much
salt or pepper to the warden's stew.

He can eat what I put in front of him.
I just cook for the boss

but I cook just right
for the Indian man to be executed.

The temperature is the thing.
I once heard a story

about a black man who was electrocuted
in that chair and lived to tell about it

before the court decided to sit him back down
an hour later and kill him all over again.

I have an extra sandwich hidden away
in the back of the refrigerator

in case this Indian killer survives
that first slow flip of the switch

and gets hungry while he waits
for the engineers to debate the flaws.

(I am not a witness)

I prepare the last meal for free
just like I signed up for the last war.

I learned how to cook
by lasting longer than any of the others.

Tonight, I'm just the last one left
after the handsome guard takes the meal away.

I turn off the kitchen lights
and sit alone in the dark

because the whole damn prison dims
when the chair is switched on.

You can watch a light bulb flicker
on a night like this

and remember it too clearly
like it was your first kiss

or the first hard kick to your groin.
It's all the same

when I am huddled down here
trying not to look at the clock

look at the clock, no, don't
look at the clock, when all of it stops

making sense: a salad, a potato
a drink of water all taste like heat.

(I am not a witness)

I want you to know I tasted a little
of that last meal before I sent it away.

It's the cook's job, to make sure
and I was sure I ate from the same plate

and ate with the same fork and spoon
that the Indian killer used later

in his cell. Maybe a little bit of me
lodged in his stomach, wedged between

his front teeth, his incisors, his molars
when he chewed down on the bit

and his body arced like modern art
curving organically, smoke rising

from his joints, wispy flames decorating
the crown of his head, the balls of his feet.

(I am not a witness)

I sit here in the dark kitchen
when they do it, meaning

when they kill him, kill
and add another definition of the word

to the dictionary. American fills
its dictionary. We write down *kill* and everybody

in the audience shouts out exactly how
they spell it, what it means to them

and all of the answers are taken down
by the pollsters and secretaries

who take care of the small details:
time of death, pulse rate, press release.

I heard a story once about some reporters
at a hanging who wanted the hood removed

from the condemned's head, so they could look
into his eyes and tell their readers

what they saw there. What did they expect?
All of the stories should be simple.

1 death + 1 death = 2 deaths.
But we throw the killers in one grave

and victims in another. We form sides
and have two separate feasts.

(I am a witness)

I prepared the last meal
for the Indian man who was executed

and have learned this: If any of us
stood for days on top of a barren hill

during an electrical storm
then lightning would eventually strike us

and we'd have no idea for which of our sins
we were reduced to headlines and ash. *[1996]*

THINKING ABOUT THE TEXT

1. Alexie reports that in writing this poem, he aimed "to call for the abolition of the death penalty." In reading the poem, do you sense that this is his aim? Why, or why not? In what respects might the poem be seen as arguing against the death penalty? State how you viewed capital punishment before and after you read it. Did Alexie affect your attitude? If so, how?
2. Why do you think Alexie cast the speaker as the condemned man's cook? How do you explain the speaker's shift from denying that he is a witness to acknowledging that he is one? Identify how he seems to define the term *witness*. What would you say to someone who argues that the speaker is unreasonably stretching the meaning of this word because apparently he didn't directly observe the execution?
3. How does race figure in this poem? Should people consider race when discussing capital punishment? If so, what about race should they especially ponder? In examining Alexie's poem, should readers bear in mind that the author is Native American? Why, or why not?
4. The film *Dead Man Walking* (1995), which deals with arguments about capital punishment, shows in chilling detail an execution by injection. Yet at the moment the condemned man dies, the film also shows the faces of his two victims. By contrast, Alexie doesn't refer to the victim of the executed man after line 12. Should he have mentioned this victim again? Identify some of the values reflected in your answer.
5. Summarize and evaluate the lesson delivered by the speaker at the end of the poem. What do you think headlines might say about you if you were killed in the manner he describes?

GEORGE WILL

Capital Punishment's Slow Death

George Will (b. 1941) is an influential newspaper writer and political commentator with a syndicated column. He is a contributor to Newsweek *and Fox News. He was born in Illinois and graduated from Trinity College in Connecticut. He received an M.A. and Ph.D. from Princeton in politics. He has written two best-selling books on baseball as well as a number on political matters, including* Statecraft as Soulcraft *(1984) and* The Woven Figure: Conservatism and America's Fabric *(1999). In 1977, he won a Pulitzer Prize for Commentary.*

Without a definitive judicial ruling or other galvanizing event, a perennial American argument is ending. Capital punishment is withering away.

It is difficult to imagine moral reasoning that would support the conclusion that an injustice will be done when, years hence, the death penalty finally is administered to Dzhokhar Tsarnaev, the Boston Marathon terrorist who placed a bomb in a crowd and then strolled to safety. Sentencing to death those who commit heinous crimes satisfies a sense of moral proportionality. This is, however, purchased with disproportionate social costs, as Nebraska seems to be concluding.

Nebraska is not a nest of liberals. Yet on Wednesday its 49-member unicameral legislature passed a bill abolishing the death penalty 32 to 15. Gov. Pete Ricketts, a Republican, vows to veto it.

This comes at a time when, nationwide, exonerations of condemned prisoners and botched executions are dismayingly frequent. Nebraska's death penalty opponents, including a majority of Nebraskans, say it is expensive without demonstrably enhancing public safety or being a solace to families of murder victims. Some Nebraska families have testified that the extended legal processes surrounding the death penalty prolong their suffering. That sentiment is shared by Bill and Denise Richard, whose 8-year-old son was killed by Tsarnaev.

Last month, the U.S. Supreme Court heard oral arguments about whether one 5
component of a three-drug mixture used in lethal injection executions—and recently used in some grotesquely protracted ones—is unreliable in preventing suffering that violates the Eighth Amendment proscription of "cruel and unusual punishments." States use the drug in question because more effective drugs are hard to acquire, partly because death penalty opponents are pressuring drug companies not to supply them.

For this, Justice Antonin Scalia blamed a death penalty "abolitionist movement." Justice Samuel A. Alito Jr. asked, "Is it appropriate for the judiciary to countenance what amounts to a guerrilla war against the death penalty, which consists of efforts to make it impossible for the states to obtain drugs that could be used to carry out capital punishment with little, if any, pain?" Justice Anthony M. Kennedy wondered, "What bearing, if any, should be put on the fact that there is a method, but that it's not available because of opposition to the death penalty? What relevance does that have?"

The answers are: Public agitation against capital punishment is not relevant to judicial reasoning. And it is not the judiciary's business to worry that a ruling might seem to "countenance" this or that social advocacy.

The conservative case against capital punishment, which 32 states have, is threefold. First, the power to inflict death cloaks government with a majesty and pretense of infallibility discordant with conservatism. Second, when capital punishment is inflicted, it cannot later be corrected because of new evidence, so a capital punishment regime must be administered with extraordinary competence. It is, however, a government program. Since 1973, more than 140 people sentenced to death have been acquitted of their crimes (sometimes by DNA evidence), had the charges against them dismissed by prosecutors or have been pardoned based on evidence of innocence. For an unsparing immersion in the workings of the governmental machinery of death, read "Just Mercy" by Bryan Stevenson, executive director and founder of the Equal Justice Initiative.

Third, administration of death sentences is so sporadic and protracted that their power to deter is attenuated. And the expensive, because labyrinthine, legal protocols with which the judiciary has enveloped capital punishment are here to stay. Granted, capital punishment *could* deter: If overdue library books were punishable by death, none would be overdue. But many crimes for which death is reserved, including Tsarnaev's crime of ideological premeditation, are especially difficult to deter.

Those who favor capital punishment because of its supposed deterrent effect 10
do not favor strengthening that effect by restoring the practice of public executions. There has not been one in America since 1937 (a hanging in Galena, Mo.) because society has decided that state-inflicted deaths, far from being wholesomely didactic spectacles, are coarsening and revolting.

Revulsion is not an argument, but it is evidence of what former chief justice Earl Warren called society's "evolving standards of decency." In the essay "Reflections on the Guillotine," Albert Camus wrote, "The man who enjoys his coffee while reading that justice has been done would spit it out at the least detail." Capital punishment, say proponents, serves social catharsis. But administering it behind prison walls indicates a healthy squeamishness that should herald abolition. *[2015]*

☰ THINKING ABOUT THE TEXT

1. Will's second sentence suggests he is not against capital punishment. Is this the case? What does "moral proportionality" mean? What does this have to do with Will's position on capital punishment?
2. Will argues that Scalia and Alito are wrong to complain about public agitation against capital punishment; he presents three reasons. What are they in your own words?
3. How does Will connect his three reasons to his opening remarks about Tsarnaev?
4. Will says that "revulsion is not an argument." What does he mean? Why might some disagree?
5. What is Camus's point in the last paragraph? How does Will use him to cap his argument?

MAKING COMPARISONS

1. What points of agreement do you find in Will and Alexie?
2. How might Camus respond to Alexie's lines, "wispy flames decorating the crown of his head, the balls of his feet"?
3. Compare the argument Will and Alexie make in their closing lines.

ROBERT BLECKER

With Death Penalty, Let Punishment Truly Fit the Crime

Robert Blecker is a law professor at New York Law School. He graduated from Tufts University (1969) and Harvard Law School (1974). He is a vocal advocate for retributivist punishment and supports the death penalty for the "worst of the worst" offenders. The feature film Robert Blecker Wants Me Dead *(2008) details his unusual relationship with condemned killer Daryl Holton on Tennessee's death row. In 2013, he published a memoir on crime and punishment titled* The Death of Punishment: Searching for Justice among the Worst of the Worst.

No matter how vicious the crime, no matter how vile the criminal, some death penalty opponents feel certain that nobody can ever deserve to die—even if that person burned children alive, massacred a dozen strangers in a movie theater, or bombed the Boston Marathon. Other opponents admit the worst of the worst of the worst do deserve to die. They just distrust the government ever to get it right.

Now that pharmaceutical companies refuse to supply the lethal drugs that U.S. corrections departments have used for years to execute criminals—whether from their own genuine moral objections or to escape a threatened economic boycott—states have begun to experiment. Death penalty opponents, who call themselves abolitionists, then protest the use of these untried drugs that just might cause a condemned killer to feel pain as he dies.

Let the punishment fit the crime. We've mouthed that credo for centuries, but do we really mean it? We retributivists who believe in justice would reward those who bring us pleasure, but punish severely those who sadistically or wantonly cause us pain. A basic retributive measure—like for like or giving a person a taste of his own medicine—satisfies our deepest instincts for justice.

When the condemned killer intentionally tortured helpless victims, how better to preserve some direct connection short of torture than by that murderer's quick but painful death? By ensuring death through anesthesia, however, we have nearly severed pain from punishment.

An unpleasant life in prison, a quick but painful death cannot erase the harm. But it can help restore a moral balance. 5

I, too, oppose lethal injection, but not because these untried new drugs might arbitrarily cause pain, but because they certainly cause confusion.

Lethal injection conflates punishment with medicine. The condemned dies in a gurney, wrapped in white sheets with an IV in his veins, surrounded by his closest kin, monitored by sophisticated medical devices. Haphazardly conceived and hastily designed, lethal injection appears, feels, and seems medical, although its sole purpose is to kill.

Witnessing an execution in Florida, I shuddered. It felt too much like a hospital or hospice. We almost never look to medicine to tell us whom to execute. Medicine should no more tell us how. How we kill those we rightly detest should in no way resemble how we end the suffering of those we love.

Publicly opposing this method of execution, I have found odd common ground with Deborah Denno, a leading abolitionist scholar who relentlessly attacks lethal injection protocols. Although Denno vigorously opposes all capital punishment, we both agree that the firing squad, among all traditional methods, probably serves us best. It does not sugarcoat, it does not pretend, it does not shamefully obscure what we do. We kill them, intentionally, because they deserve it.

Some people may support the firing squad because it allows us to put blanks in one of the guns: An individual sharpshooter will never know whether he actually killed the condemned. This strikes me as just another symptom of our avoidance of responsibility for punishment. The fact is, in this society, nobody takes responsibility for punishing criminals. Corrections officers point to judges, while judges point to legislators, and legislators to corrections. Anger and responsibility seem to lie everywhere elsewhere—that is, nowhere. And where we cannot fully escape responsibility—as with a firing squad—we diffuse it. 10

My thousands of hours observing daily life inside maximum security prisons and on death rows in several states these past 25 years have shown me the perverse irony that flows from this: Inside prisons, often the worst criminals live the most comfortable lives with the best hustles, job opportunities and sources of contraband, while the relatively petty criminals live miserably, constantly preyed upon.

Refusing to even contemplate distinguishing those few most sadistic murderers who deserve to die painfully, states seem quite willing haphazardly and arbitrarily to expose prisoners in general, regardless of their crimes, to a more or less painful life, or even death at the hands of other criminals.

Ironically, even as we recoil from punishing those who most deserve it, we readily over-punish those who don't. A "war on drugs" swells our prisons. We punish addiction and call it crime; we indiscriminately and immorally subject a burglar or car thief to the same daily life in prison we also reserve for rapist murderers.

The time has come to make punishment more nearly fit the crime. To face what we do, and acknowledge, with regret but without shame, that the past counts.

So part of me hopes the abolitionists succeed with their latest campaign 15
against death by lethal injection. We should banish this method. Let the abolitionists threaten to boycott gun manufacturers. See where that gets them. Meanwhile, the rest of us will strive to keep our covenants with victims, restore a moral balance, and shoot to kill those who deserve to die.

Rest assured, when we can only achieve justice by killing a vicious killer, We, the People will find a constitutional way to do it. *[2013]*

≡ THINKING ABOUT THE TEXT

1. How would you describe Blecker's persuasive strategy? Describe his tone.
2. How effective is Blecker's criticism of lethal injection as a means of capital punishment?
3. Blecker argues that society suffers from "avoidance of responsibility for punishment." What evidence does he give to support this claim? Why might some disagree with him?
4. Blecker argues that using retributivist punishment would help to "restore a moral balance" in society. Do you agree? If not, how would you refute that argument?
5. Give examples of Blecker's use of ethos, logos, and pathos.

≡ MAKING COMPARISONS

1. Compare the use of pathos in Alexie, Will, and Blecker.
2. One of the ground rules for logical argument is to define one's terms. How would you say Alexie, Will, and Blecker would define justice, cruel or unusual punishment, and "evolving standards of decency"?

CHARLES J. OGLETREE JR.

Condemned to Die Because He's Black

Charles J. Ogletree Jr. (b. 1952) was born in California and graduated from Stanford University with a B.A. and M.A. He received his J.D. from Harvard Law School in 1978. In 1985, he joined Harvard Law School and later became the Jesse Climenko Professor of Law. Both Barack and Michelle Obama were students of his. He has been a frequent commentator on television and radio programs discussing civil rights issues. His books include The Presumption of Guilt: The Arrest of Henry Louis Gates, Jr. and Race, Class and Crime in America *(2010) and* From Lynch Mobs to the Killing State: Race and the Death Penalty in America *(2006).*

Nearly 50 years after the end of Jim Crow, African-Americans are still facing execution because of their race.

Duane Buck could end up being one of them. He was convicted in 1997 of the murders of two people in Harris County, Tex., home to the city of Houston. He does not deny his guilt in these terrible crimes, so there is no question that he must be punished. But what happened at Mr. Buck's sentencing hearing is appalling, even for Texas, which was once among the handful of states that led the country in the lynching of African-American men and which is now the country's most prolific executioner.

During the presentation of evidence at the penalty phase of Mr. Buck's trial—when the jury was required to decide between the death penalty and a life sentence—the trial prosecutor elicited testimony from a psychologist for the defense indicating that Mr. Buck's race made him more likely to be violent in the future.

The prosecutor asked, "You have determined that the sex factor, that a male is more violent than a female because that's just the way it is, and that the race factor, black, increases the future dangerousness for various complicated reasons; is that correct?"

"Yes," the psychologist, Walter Quijano, answered.

Because a finding of future dangerousness is a prerequisite for a death sentence in Texas, the prosecutor then argued in closing that the jury should rely on that race-based expert testimony to find that Mr. Buck would pose a future danger. The jury accepted the prosecutor's recommendation, and Mr. Buck was sentenced to death.

Shockingly, Mr. Buck's was not the only case in which Texas relied on this false and offensive link between race and dangerousness to secure a death sentence. In 2000, John Cornyn, the Texas attorney general at the time and now a United States senator, identified six cases where prosecutors relied on the same expert's race-based prediction—testifying three times for the prosecution and three times for the defense—to send African-American and Latino men to death row. In an attempt to restore integrity to the state's criminal-justice system, Mr. Cornyn, a Republican, acknowledged then that Texas' exploitation of racial fears and stereotypes was unconstitutional and he promised that all six men—including Mr. Buck—would be given new sentencing hearings free of racial discrimination.

Texas kept its promise in five of the six cases, but for no discernible reason it has reversed course and pursued Mr. Buck's execution.

As outrageous as it is, the prosecutor's appeal to racial prejudice is not the only evidence showing that race played a role in Mr. Buck's death sentence. A recently released study by the University of Maryland statistician Ray Paternoster shows that at the time of Mr. Buck's trial, the Harris County district attorney's office was over three times more likely to seek the death penalty against African-American defendants like Mr. Buck than against similarly situated whites, and Harris County juries were twice as likely to impose death sentences on African-Americans like Mr. Buck. Thus, it is abundantly clear that in Mr. Buck's case, racial fears and prejudices supplanted reliable evidence in the assessment of proper punishment.

Mr. Buck's death sentence powerfully echoes this country's most lawless and 10
discriminatory past, a past that includes a time when African-American men were lynched on suspicion of crimes that sent white men to jail for a year. While lynchings are a relic of the past, the racial discrimination that motivated them retains a stranglehold on today's criminal-justice system.

President Obama spoke about that past recently in remarks addressing George Zimmerman's acquittal on charges of second-degree murder and manslaughter in the death of Trayvon Martin. "And when you think about why, in the African-American community at least, there's a lot of pain around what happened here, I think it is important to recognize that the African-American community is looking at this issue through a set of experiences and a history that—that doesn't go away," he said.

No execution date has been set for Mr. Buck; meanwhile, efforts continue on his behalf. More than 100 prominent individuals from Texas and around the country—including a former Texas governor, Mark W. White Jr., and other elected officials, former judges and prosecutors, civil rights leaders, members of the clergy, past presidents of the American Bar Association—have called for a new, fair sentencing hearing. So have more than 50,000 people who have petitioned the Harris County district attorney. Even the surviving victim in this case, Phyllis Taylor, and one of Mr. Buck's trial prosecutors, Linda Geffin, agree that Mr. Buck is entitled to another sentencing hearing. This is because no one can credibly argue that Mr. Buck—or anyone else—should be capitally prosecuted, sentenced to death or executed because of his race.

There is no question that this country has made enormous progress since the days when lynchings were commonplace. But Duane Buck's case reminds us that we still have a long way to go. Mr. Buck cannot be executed based on a death sentence that is the product of racial bias and discrimination. Texas must keep its promise and ensure that Mr. Buck receives a new, fair sentencing hearing. Fixing the problem of race in America's criminal justice system is complicated. Fixing Mr. Buck's case is not. *[2013]*

THINKING ABOUT THE TEXT

1. What elements of Ogletree's argument did you find the most persuasive? Why? Which the least? Why?
2. Judge the effectiveness of Ogletree's use of history to support his claim.
3. Describe the various kinds of support and evidence that Ogletree provides.

4. What advice would you give for Ogletree to improve his argument for a more conservative audience than the *New York Times*, say, the *Wall Street Journal* or Fox News?
5. Ogletree is arguing for a specific injustice to be made right. Comment on the next-to-last sentence in the essay. What suggestion would you make?

MAKING COMPARISONS

1. In terms of logic and tone (logos and ethos), which of the three essays did you find most effective? Why?
2. In terms of pathos (emotion), which of the four selections was most effective? Why?
3. Compare Alexie's use of race in his argument to Ogletree's.

WRITING ABOUT THE ISSUES

1. Write an essay that argues that Alexie's "Capital Punishment" is, in fact, similar to an argumentative essay against the death penalty. You might want to note its claim, support, and evidence, including its ethos, logos, and pathos.
2. Research the position of a major religion on the death penalty. What is its claim and evidence? Is its position absolute? If it does make exceptions, what are the circumstances? Do you find its position convincing? What about its reasoning? Its assumptions?
3. Research online the relationship between race and the death penalty. Look especially at Death Penalty Information Center and Death Penalty Focus. Write an analysis of their arguments, noting the reasons you find their case persuasive or not.
4. Today, Amnesty International and PEN International, a writers' organization, regularly bring to the American public's attention cases of what they deem unjust punishment. In fact, Amnesty International has criticized all instances of capital punishment in the United States. Research one of the cases reported by these organizations. Then write an article for your school newspaper in which you (a) present the basic facts of the case, (b) identify values and principles you think your audience should apply to it, and (c) point out anything you believe can and should be done about it. If you wish, refer to any of the poems in this cluster.

Discovering Injustice: Stories

NATHANIEL HAWTHORNE, "Young Goodman Brown"

TONI CADE BAMBARA, "The Lesson"

HA JIN, "Saboteur"

Much fiction depicts characters learning about injustice they had not been aware of before. They move from relative innocence to knowledge of corruption. Moreover, they must now figure out what to do about the wrongdoing they have found. They must also decide how, in general, they will live in a world where virtue mixes with vice. The title character of Nathaniel Hawthorne's classic tale "Young Goodman Brown" comes to believe that his New England community is satanic, and therefore he grows alienated from it. But does he thereby become excessively self-righteous? In Toni Cade Bambara's modern-day story "The Lesson," the narrator is an African American girl who must decide what to think when a woman of her race tries to teach her that whites monopolize society's wealth. In our third story, "Saboteur," the main character, Mr. Chiu, is the victim of police injustice. He finds himself helpless, frustrated, and angry. But injustice often has unintended consequences for the perpetrators. And at the story's end, the title of Ha Jin's tale demonstrates just such an ironic consequence.

BEFORE YOU READ

In his memoir *Fatheralong* (1994), John Edgar Wideman notes that his father's attitude toward society differs from that of his late mother. "The first rule of my father's world," Wideman writes, "is that you stand alone. Alone, alone, alone. . . . Accept the bottom line, icy clarity, of the one thing you can rely on: nothing" (50). On the other hand, "My mother's first rule was love. She refused to believe she was alone. *Be not dismayed, what e'er betides / God will take care of you*" (51). What were you taught about society as you were growing up? What specific messages were you given about it by your parents or the people who raised you? How did they convey these messages to you?

NATHANIEL HAWTHORNE

Young Goodman Brown

Nathaniel Hawthorne (1804–1864) was born in Salem, Massachusetts, into a family that was founded by New England's Puritan colonists. This lineage troubled Hawthorne, especially because his ancestor John Hathorne was involved as a judge in the Salem witch trials. After graduating from Maine's Bowdoin College in 1825, Hawthorne returned to Salem and began his career as a writer. In 1832, he self-published his first novel, Fanshawe, *but considered it an artistic as well as a commercial failure and tried to destroy all unsold copies of it. He was more successful with his 1832 short-story collection* Twice-Told Tales *(reprinted and enlarged in 1842). In the early 1840s, Hawthorne worked as a surveyor in the Boston Custom House, briefly joined the utopian community of Brook Farm, and then moved to Concord. There he published several children's books and lived with his wife, Sophia, in writer Ralph Waldo Emerson's former home, the Old Manse. In 1846, he produced a second collection of short stories,* Mosses from an Old Manse. *For the next three years, Hawthorne worked in a custom house in his hometown of Salem before publishing his most famous analysis of Puritan culture,* The Scarlet Letter *(1850). Later novels included* The House of the Seven Gables *(1851),* The Blithedale Romance *(an 1852 satire on Brook Farm), and* The Marble Faun *(1860). When his friend Franklin Pierce became president of the United States, Hawthorne served as American consul in Liverpool, England, for four years and then traveled in Italy for two more. At his death in 1864, he was already highly respected as a writer. Much of his fiction deals with conflicted characters whose hearts and souls are torn by sin, guilt, pride, and isolation. Indeed, his good friend Herman Melville, author of* Moby-Dick, *praised "the power of blackness" he found in Hawthorne's works. The allegorical story "Young Goodman Brown" is an especially memorable example of this power. Hawthorne wrote the tale in 1835 and later included it in* Mosses from an Old Manse.

Young Goodman Brown came forth at sunset into the street at Salem village; but put his head back, after crossing the threshold, to exchange a parting kiss with his young wife. And Faith, as the wife was aptly named, thrust her own pretty head into the street, letting the wind play with the pink ribbons of her cap while she called to Goodman Brown.

"Dearest heart," whispered she, softly and rather sadly, when her lips were close to his ear, "prithee put off your journey until sunrise and sleep in your own bed to-night. A lone woman is troubled with such dreams and such thoughts that she's afeared of herself sometimes. Pray tarry with me this night, dear husband, of all nights in the year."

"My love and my Faith," replied young Goodman Brown, "of all nights in the year, this one night must I tarry away from thee. My journey, as thou callest it, forth and back again, must needs be done 'twixt now and sunrise. What, my sweet, pretty wife, dost thou doubt me already, and we but three months married?"

"Then God bless you!" said Faith, with the pink ribbons; "and may you find all well when you come back."

"Amen!" cried Goodman Brown. "Say thy prayers, dear Faith, and go to bed 5
at dusk, and no harm will come to thee."

So they parted; and the young man pursued his way until, being about to turn the corner by the meeting-house, he looked back and saw the head of Faith still peeping after him with a melancholy air, in spite of her pink ribbons.

"Poor little Faith!" thought he, for his heart smote him. "What a wretch am I to leave her on such an errand! She talks of dreams, too. Methought as she spoke there was trouble in her face, as if a dream had warned her what work is to be done to-night. But no, no; 't would kill her to think it. Well, she's a blessed angel on earth, and after this one night I'll cling to her skirts and follow her to heaven."

With this excellent resolve for the future, Goodman Brown felt himself justified in making more haste on his present evil purpose. He had taken a dreary road, darkened by all the gloomiest trees of the forest, which barely stood aside to let the narrow path creep through, and closed immediately behind. It was all as lonely as could be; and there is this peculiarity in such a solitude, that the traveller knows not who may be concealed by the innumerable trunks and the thick boughs overhead; so that with lonely footsteps he may yet be passing through an unseen multitude.

"There may be a devilish Indian behind every tree," said Goodman Brown to himself; and he glanced fearfully behind him as he added, "What if the devil himself should be at my very elbow!"

His head being turned back, he passed a crook of the road, and, looking for- 10
ward again, beheld the figure of a man, in grave and decent attire, seated at the foot of an old tree. He arose at Goodman Brown's approach and walked onward side by side with him.

"You are late, Goodman Brown," said he. "The clock of the Old South was striking as I came through Boston, and that is full fifteen minutes agone."

"Faith kept me back a while," replied the young man, with a tremor in his voice, caused by the sudden appearance of his companion, though not wholly unexpected.

It was now deep dusk in the forest, and deepest in that part of it where these two were journeying. As nearly as could be discerned, the second traveller was about fifty years old, apparently in the same rank of life as Goodman Brown, and bearing a considerable resemblance to him, though perhaps more in expression than features. Still they might have been taken for father and son. And yet, though the elder person was as simply clad as the younger, and as simple in manner too, he had an indescribable air of one who knew the world, and who would not have felt abashed at the governor's dinner table or in King William's court, were it possible that his affairs should call him thither. But the only thing about him that could be fixed upon as remarkable was his staff, which bore the likeness of a great black snake, so curiously wrought that it might almost be seen to twist and wriggle itself like a living serpent. This, of course, must have been an ocular deception, assisted by the uncertain light.

"Come, Goodman Brown," cried his fellow-traveller, "this is a dull pace for the beginning of a journey. Take my staff, if you are so soon weary."

"Friend," said the other, exchanging his slow pace for a full stop, "having 15
kept covenant by meeting thee here, it is my purpose now to return whence I came. I have scruples touching the matter thou wot'st of."

"Sayest thou so?" replied he of the serpent, smiling apart. "Let us walk on, nevertheless, reasoning as we go; and if I convince thee not thou shalt turn back. We are but a little way in the forest yet."

"Too far! too far!" exclaimed the goodman, unconsciously resuming his walk. "My father never went into the woods on such an errand, nor his father before him. We have been a race of honest men and good Christians since the days of the martyrs; and shall I be the first of the name of Brown that ever took this path and kept" —

"Such company, thou wouldst say," observed the elder person, interpreting his pause. "Well said, Goodman Brown! I have been as well acquainted with your family as with ever a one among the Puritans; and that's no trifle to say. I helped your grandfather, the constable, when he lashed the Quaker woman so smartly through the streets of Salem; and it was I that brought your father a pitch-pine knot, kindled at my own hearth, to set fire to an Indian village, in King Philip's war.° They were my good friends, both; and many a pleasant walk have we had along this path, and returned merrily after midnight. I would fain be friends with you for their sake."

"If it be as thou sayest," replied Goodman Brown, "I marvel they never spoke of these matters; or, verily, I marvel not, seeing that the least rumor of the sort would have driven them from New England. We are a people of prayer, and good works to boot, and abide no such wickedness."

"Wickedness or not," said the traveller with the twisted staff, "I have a very general acquaintance here in New England. The deacons of many a church have drunk the communion wine with me; the selectmen of divers towns make me their chairman; and a majority of the Great and General Court are firm supporters of my interest. The governor and I, too — But these are state secrets."

"Can this be so?" cried Goodman Brown, with a stare of amazement at his undisturbed companion. "Howbeit, I have nothing to do with the governor and council; they have their own ways, and are no rule for a simple husbandman like me. But, were I to go on with thee, how should I meet the eye of that good old man, our minister, at Salem village? Oh, his voice would make me tremble both Sabbath day and lecture day."

Thus far the elder traveller had listened with due gravity; but now burst into a fit of irrepressible mirth, shaking himself so violently that his snake-like staff actually seemed to wriggle in sympathy.

"Ha! ha! ha!" shouted he again and again; then composing himself, "Well, go on, Goodman Brown, go on; but, prithee, don't kill me with laughing."

"Well, then, to end the matter at once," said Goodman Brown, considerably nettled, "there is my wife, Faith. It would break her dear little heart; and I'd rather break my own."

"Nay, if that be the case," answered the other, "e'en go thy ways, Goodman Brown. I would not for twenty old women like the one hobbling before us that Faith should come to any harm."

As he spoke he pointed his staff at a female figure on the path, in whom Goodman Brown recognized a very pious and exemplary dame, who had taught him his catechism in youth, and was still his moral and spiritual adviser, jointly with the minister and Deacon Gookin.

King Philip's war: King Philip, a Wampanoag chief, waged a bloody war against the New England colonists from 1675 to 1676.

"A marvel, truly that Goody Cloyse should be so far in the wilderness at nightfall," said he. "But with your leave, friend, I shall take a cut through the woods until we have left this Christian woman behind. Being a stranger to you, she might ask whom I was consorting with and whither I was going."

"Be it so," said his fellow-traveller. "Betake you to the woods, and let me keep the path."

Accordingly the young man turned aside, but took care to watch his companion, who advanced softly along the road until he had come within a staff's length of the old dame. She, meanwhile, was making the best of her way, with singular speed for so aged a woman, and mumbling some indistinct words—a prayer, doubtless—as she went. The traveller put forth his staff and touched her withered neck with what seemed the serpent's tail.

"The devil!" screamed the pious old lady. 30

"Then Goody Cloyse knows her old friend?" observed the traveller, confronting her and leaning on his writhing stick.

"Ah, forsooth, and is it your worship indeed?" cried the good dame. "Yea, truly is it, and in the very image of my old gossip, Goodman Brown, the grandfather of the silly fellow that now is. But—would your worship believe it?—my broomstick hath strangely disappeared, stolen, as I suspect, by that unhanged witch, Goody Cory, and that, too, when I was all anointed with the juice of smallage, and cinquefoil, and wolf's bane"—

"Mingled with fine wheat and the fat of a new-born babe," said the shape of old Goodman Brown.

"Ah, your worship knows the recipe," cried the old lady, cackling aloud. "So, as I was saying, being all ready for the meeting, and no horse to ride on, I made up my mind to foot it; for they tell me there is a nice young man to be taken into communion to-night. But now your good worship will lend me your arm, and we shall be there in a twinkling."

"That can hardly be," answered her friend. "I may not spare you my arm, 35 Goody Cloyse; but here is my staff, if you will."

So saying, he threw it down at her feet, where, perhaps, it assumed life, being one of the rods which its owner had formerly lent to the Egyptian magi. Of this fact, however, Goodman Brown could not take cognizance. He had cast up his eyes in astonishment, and, looking down again, beheld neither Goody Cloyse nor the serpentine staff, but his fellow-traveller alone, who waited for him as calmly as if nothing had happened.

"That old woman taught me my catechism," said the young man; and there was a world of meaning in this simple comment.

They continued to walk onward, while the elder traveller exhorted his companion to make good speed and persevere in the path, discoursing so aptly that his arguments seemed rather to spring up in the bosom of his auditor than to be suggested by himself. As they went, he plucked a branch of maple to serve for a walking stick, and began to strip it of the twigs and little boughs, which were wet with evening dew. The moment his fingers touched them they became strangely withered and dried up as with a week's sunshine. Thus the pair proceeded, at a good free pace, until suddenly, in a gloomy hollow of the road, Goodman Brown sat himself down on the stump of a tree and refused to go any farther.

"Friend," he said, stubbornly, "my mind is made up. Not another step will I budge on this errand. What if a wretched old woman do choose to go to the devil when I thought she was going to heaven: is that any reason why I should quit my dear Faith and go after her?"

"You will think better of this by and by," said his acquaintance, composedly. "Sit here and rest yourself a while; and when you feel like moving again, there is my staff to help you along."

Without more words, he threw his companion the maple stick, and was as speedily out of sight as if he had vanished into the deepening gloom. The young man sat a few moments by the roadside, applauding himself greatly, and thinking with how clear a conscience he should meet the minister in his morning walk, nor shrink from the eye of good old Deacon Gookin. And what calm sleep would be his that very night, which was to have been spent so wickedly, but so purely and sweetly now, in the arms of Faith! Amidst these pleasant and praiseworthy meditations, Goodman Brown heard the tramp of horses along the road, and deemed it advisable to conceal himself within the verge of the forest, conscious of the guilty purpose that had brought him thither, though now so happily turned from it.

On came the hoof tramps and the voices of the riders, two grave old voices, conversing soberly as they drew near. These mingled sounds appeared to pass along the road, within a few yards of the young man's hiding-place; but, owing doubtless to the depth of the gloom at that particular spot, neither the travellers nor their steeds were visible. Though their figures brushed the small boughs by the wayside, it could not be seen that they intercepted, even for a moment, the faint gleam from the strip of bright sky athwart which they must have passed. Goodman Brown alternately crouched and stood on tiptoe, pulling aside the branches and thrusting forth his head as far as he durst without discerning so much as a shadow. It vexed him the more, because he could have sworn, were such a thing possible, that he recognized the voices of the minister and Deacon Gookin, jogging along quietly, as they were wont to do, when bound to some ordination or ecclesiastical council. While yet within hearing, one of the riders stopped to pluck a switch.

"Of the two, reverend sir," said the voice like the deacon's, "I had rather miss an ordination dinner than to-night's meeting. They tell me that some of our community are to be here from Falmouth and beyond, and others from Connecticut and Rhode Island, besides several of the Indian powwows, who, after their fashion, know almost as much deviltry as the best of us. Moreover, there is a goodly young woman to be taken into communion."

"Mighty well, Deacon Gookin!" replied the solemn old tones of the minister. "Spur up, or we shall be late. Nothing can be done, you know, until I get on the ground."

The hoofs clattered again; and the voices, talking so strangely in the empty air, passed on through the forest, where no church had ever been gathered or solitary Christian prayed. Whither, then, could these holy men be journeying so deep into the heathen wilderness? Young Goodman Brown caught hold of a tree for support, being ready to sink down on the ground, faint and overburdened with the heavy sickness of his heart. He looked up to the sky, doubting whether there really was a heaven above him. Yet there was the blue arch, and the stars brightening in it.

"With heaven above and Faith below, I will yet stand firm against the devil!" cried Goodman Brown.

While he still gazed upward into the deep arch of the firmament and had lifted his hands to pray, a cloud, though no wind was stirring, hurried across the zenith and hid the brightening stars. The blue sky was still visible, except directly overhead, where this black mass of cloud was sweeping swiftly northward. Aloft in the air, as if from the depths of the cloud, came a confused and doubtful sound of voices. Once the listener fancied that he could distinguish the accents of towns-people of his own, men and women, both pious and ungodly, many of whom he had met at the communion table, and had seen others rioting at the tavern. The next moment, so indistinct were the sounds, he doubted whether he had heard aught but the murmur of the old forest, whispering without a wind. Then came a stronger swell of those familiar tones, heard daily in the sunshine at Salem village, but never until now from a cloud of night. There was one voice, of a young woman, uttering lamentations, yet with an uncertain sorrow, and entreating for some favor, which, perhaps, it would grieve her to obtain; and all the unseen multitude, both saints and sinners, seemed to encourage her onward.

"Faith!" shouted Goodman Brown, in a voice of agony and desperation; and the echoes of the forest mocked him, crying, "Faith! Faith!" as if bewildered wretches were seeking her all through the wilderness.

The cry of grief, rage, and terror was yet piercing the night, when the unhappy husband held his breath for a response. There was a scream, drowned immediately in a louder murmur of voices, fading into far-off laughter, as the dark cloud swept away, leaving the clear and silent sky above Goodman Brown. But something fluttered lightly down through the air and caught on the branch of a tree. The young man seized it, and beheld a pink ribbon.

"My Faith is gone!" cried he after one stupefied moment. "There is no good on 50
earth; and sin is but a name. Come, devil; for to thee is this world given."

And, maddened with despair, so that he laughed loud and long, did Goodman Brown grasp his staff and set forth again, at such a rate that he seemed to fly along the forest path rather than to walk or run. The road grew wilder and drearier and more faintly traced, and vanished at length, leaving him in the heart of the dark wilderness, still rushing onward with the instinct that guides mortal man to evil. The whole forest was peopled with frightful sounds—the creaking of the trees, the howling of wild beasts, and the yell of Indians; while sometimes the wind tolled like a distant church bell, and sometimes gave a broad roar around the traveller, as if all Nature were laughing him to scorn. But he was himself the chief horror of the scene, and shrank not from its other horrors.

"Ha! ha! ha!" roared Goodman Brown when the wind laughed at him. "Let us hear which will laugh loudest. Think not to frighten me with your deviltry.

Come witch, come wizard, come Indian powwow, come devil himself, and here comes Goodman Brown. You may as well fear him as he fear you."

In truth, all through the haunted forest there could be nothing more frightful than the figure of Goodman Brown. On he flew among the black pines, brandishing his staff with frenzied gestures, now giving vent to an inspiration of horrid blasphemy, and now shouting forth such laughter as set all the echoes of the forest laughing like demons around him. The fiend in his own shape is less hideous than when he rages in the breast of man. Thus sped the demoniac on his course, until, quivering among the trees, he saw a red light before him, as when the felled trunks and branches of a clearing have been set on fire, and throw up their lurid blaze against the sky, at the hour of midnight. He paused, in a lull of the tempest that had driven him onward, and heard the swell of what seemed a hymn, rolling solemnly from a distance with the weight of many voices. He knew the tune; it was a familiar one in the choir of the village meeting-house. The verse died heavily away, and was lengthened by a chorus, not of human voices, but of all the sounds of the benighted wilderness pealing in awful harmony together. Goodman Brown cried out, and his cry was lost to his own ear by its unison with the cry of the desert.

In the interval of silence he stole forward until the light glared full upon his eyes. At one extremity of an open space, hemmed in by the dark wall of the forest, arose a rock, bearing some rude, natural resemblance either to an altar or a pulpit, and surrounded by four blazing pines, their tops aflame, their stems untouched, like candles at an evening meeting. The mass of foliage that had overgrown the summit of the rock was all on fire, blazing high into the night and fitfully illuminating the whole field. Each pendent twig and leafy festoon was in a blaze. As the red light arose and fell, a numerous congregation alternately shone forth, then disappeared in shadow, and again grew, as it were, out of the darkness, peopling the heart of the solitary woods at once.

"A grave and dark-clad company," quoth Goodman Brown. 55

In truth they were such. Among them, quivering to and fro between gloom and splendor, appeared faces that would be seen next day at the council board of the province, and others which, Sabbath after Sabbath, looked devoutly heavenward, and benignantly over the crowded pews, from the holiest pulpits in the land. Some affirm that the lady of the governor was there. At least there were high dames well known to her, and wives of honored husbands, and widows, a great multitude, and ancient maidens, all of excellent repute, and fair young girls, who trembled lest their mothers should espy them. Either the sudden gleams of light flashing over the obscure field bedazzled Goodman Brown, or he recognized a score of the church members of Salem village famous for their especial sanctity. Good old Deacon Gookin had arrived, and waited at the skirts of that venerable saint, his revered pastor. But, irreverently consorting with these grave, reputable, and pious people, these elders of the church, these chaste dames and dewy virgins, there were men of dissolute lives and women of spotted fame, wretches given over to all mean and filthy vice, and suspected even of horrid crimes. It was strange to see that the good shrank not from the wicked, nor were the sinners abashed by the saints. Scattered also among their pale-faced enemies were the Indian priests, or powwows, who had often scared their native forest with more hideous incantations than any known to English witchcraft.

"But where is Faith?" thought Goodman Brown; and, as hope came into his heart, he trembled.

Another verse of the hymn arose, a slow and mournful strain, such as the pious love, but joined to words which expressed all that our nature can conceive of sin, and darkly hinted at far more. Unfathomable to mere mortals is the lore of fiends. Verse after verse was sung; and still the chorus of the desert swelled between like the deepest tone of a mighty organ; and with the final peal of that dreadful anthem there came a sound, as if the roaring wind, the rushing streams, the howling beasts, and every other voice of the unconcerted wilderness were mingling and according with the voice of guilty man in homage to the prince of all. The four blazing pines threw up a loftier flame, and obscurely discovered shapes and visages of horror on the smoke wreaths above the impious assembly. At the same moment the fire on the rock shot redly forth and formed a flowing arch above its base, where now appeared a figure. With reverence be it spoken, the figure bore no slight similitude, both in garb and manner, to some grave divine of the New England churches.

"Bring forth the converts!" cried a voice that echoed through the field and rolled into the forest.

At the word, Goodman Brown stepped forth from the shadow of the trees 60
and approached the congregation, with whom he felt a loathful brotherhood by the sympathy of all that was wicked in his heart. He could have well-nigh sworn that the shape of his own dead father beckoned him to advance, looking downward from a smoke wreath, while a woman, with dim features of despair, threw out her hand to warn him back. Was it his mother? But he had no power to retreat one step, nor to resist, even in thought, when the minister and good old Deacon Gookin seized his arms and led him to the blazing rock. Thither came also the slender form of a veiled female, led between Goody Cloyse, that pious teacher of the catechism, and Martha Carrier, who had received the devil's promise to be queen of hell. A rampant hag was she. And there stood the proselytes beneath the canopy of fire.

"Welcome, my children," said the dark figure, "to the communion of your race. Ye have found thus young your nature and your destiny. My children, look behind you!"

They turned; and flashing forth, as it were, in a sheet of flame, the fiend worshippers were seen; the smile of welcome gleamed darkly on every visage.

"There," resumed the sable form, "are all whom ye have reverenced from youth. Ye deemed them holier than yourselves and shrank from your own sin, contrasting it with their lives of righteousness and prayerful aspirations heavenward. Yet here are they all in my worshipping assembly. This night it shall be granted you to know their secret deeds: how hoary-bearded elders of the church have whispered wanton words to the young maids of their households; how many a woman, eager for widows' weeds, has given her husband a drink at bedtime and let him sleep his last sleep in her bosom; how beardless youths have made haste to inherit their fathers' wealth; and how fair damsels—blush not, sweet ones—have dug little graves in the garden, and bidden me, the sole guest, to an infant's funeral. By the sympathy of your human hearts for sin ye shall scent out all the places—whether in church, bedchamber, street, field, or forest—where crime has been committed, and shall exult to behold the whole earth one stain of guilt, one mighty blood spot. Far more than this. It shall be yours to penetrate, in every bosom, the deep mystery of sin, the fountain of all wicked arts, and which inexhaustibly supplies more evil impulses than human power—than my power at its utmost—can make manifest in deeds. And now, my children, look upon each other."

They did so; and, by the blaze of the hell-kindled torches, the wretched man beheld his Faith, and the wife her husband, trembling before that unhallowed altar.

"Lo, there ye stand, my children," said the figure, in a deep and solemn tone, almost sad with its despairing awfulness, as if his once angelic nature could yet mourn for our miserable race. "Depending upon one another's hearts, ye had still hoped that virtue were not all a dream. Now are ye undeceived. Evil is the nature of mankind. Evil must be your only happiness. Welcome again, my children, to the communion of your race."

"Welcome," repeated the fiend worshippers, in one cry of despair and triumph.

And there they stood, the only pair, as it seemed, who were yet hesitating on the verge of wickedness in this dark world. A basin was hallowed, naturally, in the rock. Did it contain water, reddened by the lurid light? or was it blood? or, perchance, a liquid flame? Herein did the shape of evil dip his hand and prepare to lay the mark of baptism upon their foreheads, that they might be partakers of the mystery of sin, more conscious of the secret guilt of others, both in deed and thought, than they could now be of their own. The husband cast one look at his pale wife, and Faith at him. What polluted wretches would the next glance show them to each other, shuddering alike at what they disclosed and what they saw!

"Faith! Faith!" cried the husband, "look up to heaven, and resist the wicked one."

Whether Faith obeyed he knew not. Hardly had he spoken when he found himself amid calm night and solitude, listening to a roar of the wind which died heavily away through the forest. He staggered against the rock, and felt it chill and damp; while a hanging twig, that had been all on fire, besprinkled his cheek with the coldest dew.

The next morning young Goodman Brown came slowly into the street of Salem village, staring around him like a bewildered man. The good old minister was taking a walk along the graveyard to get an appetite for breakfast and meditate his sermon, and bestowed a blessing, as he passed, on Goodman Brown. He shrank from the venerable saint as if to avoid an anathema. Old Deacon Gookin was at domestic worship, and the holy words of his prayer were heard through the open window. "What God doth the wizard pray to?" quoth Goodman Brown.

Goody Cloyse, that excellent old Christian, stood in the early sunshine at her own lattice, catechizing a little girl who had brought her a pint of morning's milk. Goodman Brown snatched away the child as from the grasp of the fiend himself. Turning the corner by the meeting-house, he spied the head of Faith, with the pink ribbons, gazing anxiously forth, and bursting into such joy at sight of him that she skipped along the street and almost kissed her husband before the whole village. But Goodman Brown looked sternly and sadly into her face, and passed on without a greeting.

Had Goodman Brown fallen asleep in the forest and only dreamed a wild dream of a witch-meeting?

Be it so if you will; but, alas! it was a dream of evil omen for young Goodman Brown. A stern, a sad, a darkly meditative, a distrustful, if not a desperate man did he become from the night of that fearful dream. On the Sabbath day, when the congregation were singing a holy psalm, he could not listen because an anthem of sin rushed loudly upon his ear and drowned all the blessed strain. When the minister spoke from the pulpit with power and fervid eloquence, and, with his hand on the open Bible, of the sacred truths of our religion, and of saint-like lives and triumphant deaths, and of future bliss or misery unutterable, then did Goodman Brown turn pale, dreading lest the roof should thunder down upon the gray blasphemer and his hearers. Often, awaking suddenly at midnight, he shrank from the bosom of Faith; and at morning or eventide, when the family knelt down at prayer, he scowled and muttered to himself, and gazed sternly at his wife, and turned away. And when he had lived long, and was borne to his grave a hoary corpse, followed by Faith, an aged woman, and children and grandchildren, a goodly procession, besides neighbors not a few, they carved no hopeful verse upon his tombstone, for his dying hour was gloom. *[1835]*

THINKING ABOUT THE TEXT

1. "Young Goodman Brown" seems quite allegorical, with journeys in the night woods and statements like "My Faith is gone!" (para. 50). How would you explain this allegorical story? What is Brown looking for? What does he find out? How does he deal with his discoveries?
2. If you were a good friend of Brown's, what might you tell him to try to save him from a life of gloom?
3. The devil suggests that there is more evil in the human heart "than my power at its utmost" (para. 63). Do you agree? If so, is this a message to despair about?
4. The devil says he is well acquainted with Brown's family. What has his family done? Is Brown innocent and naive, or perhaps stubborn and arrogant, in his refusal to admit that evil exists all around us?
5. Do you suspect that Brown merely dreamed or imagined his experience in the woods? Or do you think it really took place? Refer to specific details of the text.

TONI CADE BAMBARA

The Lesson

Toni Cade Bambara (1939–1995) taught at various colleges and worked as a community activist. She edited The Black Woman *(1970), a collection of essays that became a landmark of contemporary black feminism. Bambara wrote two novels:* The Salt Eaters *(1980), which won the American Book Award, and* These Bones Are Not My Child *(2000), a posthumously published work about the murders of several African American children in late 1970s Atlanta. She also produced several collections of short stories. "The Lesson" comes from her first,* Gorilla, My Love *(1972).*

Back in the days when everyone was old and stupid or young and foolish and me and Sugar were the only ones just right, this lady moved on our block with nappy hair and proper speech and no makeup. And quite naturally we laughed at her, laughed the way we did at the junk man who went about his business like he was some big-time president and his sorry-ass horse his secretary. And we kinda hated her too, hated the way we did the winos who cluttered up our parks and pissed on our handball walls and stank up our hallways and stairs so you couldn't halfway play hide-and-seek without a goddamn gas mask. Miss Moore was her name. The only woman on the block with no first name. And she was black as hell, cept for her feet, which were fish-white and spooky. And she was always planning these boring-ass things for us to do, us being my cousin, mostly, who lived on the block cause we all moved North the same time and to the same apartment then spread out gradual to breathe. And our parents would yank our heads into some kinda shape and crisp up our clothes so we'd be presentable for travel with Miss Moore, who always looked like she was going to church, though she never did. Which is just one of the things the grownups talked about when they talked behind her back like a dog. But when she came calling with some sachet she'd sewed up or some gingerbread she'd made or some book, why then they'd all be too embarrassed to turn her down and we'd get handed over all spruced up. She'd been to college and said it was only right that she should take responsibility for the young ones' education, and she not even related by marriage or blood. So they'd go for it. Specially Aunt Gretchen. She was the main gofer in the family. You got some ole dumb shit foolishness you want somebody to go for, you send for Aunt Gretchen. She been screwed into the go-along for so long, it's a blood-deep natural thing with her. Which is how she got saddled with me and Sugar and Junior in the first place while our mothers were in a la-de-da apartment up the block having a good ole time.

So this one day, Miss Moore rounds us all up at the mailbox and it's pure-dee hot and she's knockin herself out about arithmetic. And school suppose to let up in summer I heard, but she don't never let up. And the starch in my pinafore scratching the shit outta me and I'm really hating this nappy-head bitch and her goddamn college degree. I'd much rather go to the pool or to the show where it's cool. So me and Sugar leaning on the mailbox being surly, which is a Miss Moore word. And Flyboy checking out what everybody brought for lunch. And Fat Butt already wasting his peanut-butter-and-jelly sandwich like the pig he is. And Junebug punchin on Q.T.'s arm for potato chips. And Rosie Giraffe shifting from one hip to the other waiting for somebody to step on her foot or ask her if she from Georgia so she can kick ass, preferably Mercedes's. And Miss Moore asking us do we know what money is, like we a bunch of retards. I mean real money, she say, like it's only poker chips or monopoly papers we lay on the grocer. So right away I'm tired of this and say so. And would much rather snatch Sugar and go to the Sunset and terrorize the West Indian kids and take their hair ribbons and their money too. And Miss Moore files that remark away for next week's lesson on brotherhood, I can tell. And finally I say we oughta get to the subway cause it's cooler and besides we might meet some cute boys. Sugar done swiped her mama's lipstick, so we ready.

So we heading down the street and she's boring us silly about what things cost and what our parents make and how much goes for rent and how money ain't divided up right in this country. And then she gets to the part about we all poor and live in the slums, which I don't feature. And I'm ready to speak on that, but she steps out in the street and hails two cabs just like that. Then she hustles half the crew in with her and hands me a five-dollar bill and tells me to calculate 10 percent tip for the driver. And we're off. Me and Sugar and Junebug and Flyboy hangin out the window and hollering to everybody, putting lipstick on each other cause Flyboy a faggot anyway, and making farts with our sweaty armpits. But I'm mostly trying to figure how to spend this money. But they all fascinated with the meter ticking and Junebug starts laying bets as to how much it'll read when Flyboy can't hold his breath no more. Then Sugar lays bets as to how much it'll be when we get there. So I'm stuck. Don't nobody want to go for my plan, which is to jump out at the next light and run off to the first bar-b-que we can find. Then the driver tells us to get the hell out cause we there already. And the meter reads eighty-five cents. And I'm stalling to figure out the tip and Sugar say give him a dime. And I decide he don't need it bad as I do, so later for him. But then he tries to take off with Junebug foot still in the door so we talk about his mama something ferocious. Then we check out that we on Fifth Avenue and everybody dressed up in stockings. One lady in a fur coat, hot as it is. White folks crazy.

"This is the place," Miss Moore say, presenting it to us in the voice she uses at the museum. "Let's look in the windows before we go in."

"Can we steal?" Sugar asks very serious like she's getting the ground rules 5
squared away before she plays. "I beg your pardon," say Miss Moore, and we fall out. So she leads us around the windows of the toy store and me and Sugar screamin, "This is mine, that's mine, I gotta have that, that was made for me, I was born for that," till Big Butt drowns us out.

"Hey, I'm goin to buy that there."

"That there? You don't even know what it is, stupid."

"I do so," he say punchin on Rosie Giraffe. "It's a microscope."

"Whatcha gonna do with a microscope, fool?"

"Look at things." 10

"Like what, Ronald?" ask Miss Moore. And Big Butt ain't got the first notion. So here go Miss Moore gabbing about the thousands of bacteria in a drop of water and the somethinorother in a speck of blood and the million and one living things in the air around us is invisible to the naked eye. And what she say that for? Junebug go to town on that "naked" and we rolling. Then Miss Moore ask what it cost. So we all jam into the window smudgin it up and the price tag say \$300. So then she ask how long'd take for Big Butt and Junebug to save up their allowances. "Too long," I say. "Yeh," adds Sugar, "outgrown it by that time." And Miss Moore say no, you never outgrow learning instruments. "Why, even medical students and interns and," blah, blah, blah. And we ready to choke Big Butt for bringing it up in the first damn place.

"This here costs four hundred eighty dollars," says Rosie Giraffe. So we pile up all over her to see what she pointin out. My eyes tell me it's a chunk of glass cracked with something heavy, and different-color inks dripped into the splits, then the whole thing put into a oven or something. But for \$480 it don't make sense.

"That's a paperweight made of semi-precious stones fused together under tremendous pressure," she explains slowly, with her hands doing the mining and all the factory work.

"So what's a paperweight?" asks Rosie Giraffe.

"To weigh paper with, dumbbell," say Flyboy, the wise man from the East. 15

"Not exactly," say Miss Moore, which is what she say when you warm or way off too. "It's to weigh paper down so it won't scatter and make your desk untidy." So right away me and Sugar curtsy to each other and then to Mercedes who is more the tidy type.

"We don't keep paper on top of the desk in my class," say Junebug, figuring Miss Moore crazy or lyin one.

"At home, then," she say. "Don't you have a calendar and pencil case and a blotter and a letter-opener on your desk at home where you do your homework?" And she know damn well what our homes look like cause she nosys around in them every chance she gets.

"I don't even have a desk," say Junebug. "Do we?"

"No. And I don't get no homework neither," says Big Butt. 20

"And I don't even have a home," say Flyboy like he do at school to keep the white folks off his back and sorry for him. Send this poor kid to camp posters, is his specialty.

"I do," says Mercedes. "I have a box of stationery on my desk and a picture of my cat. My godmother bought the stationery and the desk. There's a big rose on each sheet and the envelopes smell like roses."

"Who wants to know about your smelly-ass stationery," say Rosie Giraffe fore I can get my two cents in.

"It's important to have a work area all your own so that . . ."

"Will you look at this sailboat, please," say Flyboy, cuttin her off and pointin 25
to the thing like it was his. So once again we tumble all over each other to gaze at this magnificent thing in the toy store which is just big enough to maybe sail two kittens across the pond if you strap them to the posts tight. We all start reciting

the price tag like we in assembly. "Handcrafted sailboat of fiberglass at one thousand one hundred ninety-five dollars."

"Unbelievable," I hear myself say and am really stunned. I read it again for myself just in case the group recitation put me in a trance. Same thing. For some reason this pisses me off. We look at Miss Moore and she lookin at us, waiting for I dunno what.

"Who'd pay all that when you can buy a sailboat set for a quarter at Pop's, a tube of glue for a dime, and a ball of string for eight cents? It must have a motor and a whole lot else besides," I say. "My sailboat cost me about fifty cents."

"But will it take water?" say Mercedes with her smart ass.

"Took mine to Alley Pond Park once," say Flyboy. "String broke. Lost it. Pity."

"Sailed mine in Central Park and it keeled over and sank. Had to ask my father for another dollar."

"And you got the strap," laugh Big Butt. "The jerk didn't even have a string on it. My old man wailed on his behind."

Little Q.T. was staring hard at the sailboat and you could see he wanted it bad. But he too little and somebody'd just take it from him. So what the hell. "This boat for kids, Miss Moore?"

"Parents silly to buy something like that just to get all broke up," say Rosie Giraffe.

"That much money it should last forever," I figure.

"My father'd buy it for me if I wanted it."

"Your father, my ass," say Rosie Giraffe getting a chance to finally push Mercedes.

"Must be rich people shop here," say Q.T.

"You are a very bright boy," say Flyboy. "What was your first clue?" And he rap him on the head with the back of his knuckles, since Q.T. the only one he could get away with. Though Q.T. liable to come up behind you years later and get his licks in when you half expect it.

"What I want to know is," I says to Miss Moore though I never talk to her, I wouldn't give the bitch that satisfaction, "is how much a real boat costs? I figure a thousand'd get you a yacht any day."

"Why don't you check that out," she says, "and report back to the group?" Which really pains my ass. If you gonna mess up a perfectly good swim day least you could do is have some answers. "Let's go in," she say like she got something up her sleeve. Only she don't lead the way. So me and Sugar turn the corner to where the entrance is, but when we get there I kinda hang back. Not that I'm scared, what's there to be afraid of, just a toy store. But I feel funny, shame. But what I got to be shamed about? Got as much right to go in as anybody. But somehow I can't seem to get hold of the door, so I step away from Sugar to lead. But she hangs back too. And I look at her and she looks at me and this is ridiculous. I mean, damn, I have never ever been shy about doing nothing or going nowhere. But then Mercedes steps up and then Rosie Giraffe and Big Butt crowd in behind and shove, and next thing we all stuffed into the doorway with only Mercedes squeezing past us, smoothing out her jumper and walking right down the aisle. Then the rest of us tumble in like a glued-together jigsaw done all wrong. And people lookin at us. And it's like the time me and Sugar crashed into the Catholic church on a dare. But once we got in there and everything so hushed and holy and the candles and the bowin and the handkerchiefs on all the drooping heads, I just couldn't go through with the plan. Which was for me to run up to the altar and do a tap dance while Sugar played the nose flute and messed around in the holy water. And Sugar kept givin me the elbow. Then later teased me so bad I tied her up in the shower and turned it on and locked her in. And she'd be there till this day if Aunt Gretchen hadn't finally figured I was lying about the boarder takin a shower.

Same thing in the store. We all walkin on tiptoe and hardly touchin the games and puzzles and things. And I watched Miss Moore who is steady watchin us like she waitin for a sign. Like Mama Drewery watches the sky and sniffs the air and takes note of just how much slant is in the bird formation. Then me and Sugar bump smack into each other, so busy gazing at the toys, 'specially the sailboat. But we don't laugh and go into our fat-lady bump-stomach routine. We just stare at that price tag. Then Sugar run a finger over the whole boat. And I'm jealous and want to hit her. Maybe not her, but I sure want to punch somebody in the mouth.

"Watcha bring us here for, Miss Moore?"

"You sound angry, Sylvia. Are you mad about something?" Givin me one of them grins like she tellin a grown-up joke that never turns out to be funny. And she's lookin very closely at me like maybe she plannin to do my portrait from memory. I'm mad, but I won't give her that satisfaction. So I slouch around the store bein very bored and say, "Let's go."

Me and Sugar at the back of the train watchin the tracks whizzin by large then small then getting gobbled up in the dark. I'm thinkin about this tricky toy I saw in the store. A clown that somersaults on a bar then does chin-ups just cause you yank lightly at his leg. Cost $35. I could see me askin my mother for a $35 birthday clown. "You wanna who that costs what?" she'd say, cocking her head to the side to get a better view of the hole in my head. Thirty-five dollars could buy new bunk beds for Junior and Gretchen's boy. Thirty-five dollars and the whole household could go visit Grand-daddy Nelson in the country. Thirty-five dollars would pay for the rent and the piano bill too. Who are these people that spend that much for performing clowns and $1000 for toy sailboats? What kinda work they do and how they live and how come we ain't in on it? Where we are is who we are, Miss Moore always pointin out. But it don't necessarily have to be that way, she always adds then waits for somebody to say that poor people have to wake up and demand their share of the pie and don't none of us know what kind of pie she talking about in the first damn place. But she ain't so smart cause I still got her four dollars from the taxi and she sure ain't gettin it. Messin up my day with this shit. Sugar nudges me in my pocket and winks.

Miss Moore lines us up in front of the mailbox where we started from, seem 45
like years ago, and I got a headache for thinkin so hard. And we lean all over each other so we can hold up under the draggy-ass lecture she always finishes us off with at the end before we thank her for borin us to tears. But she just looks at us like she readin tea leaves. Finally she say, "Well, what did you think of F. A. O. Schwarz?"

Rosie Giraffe mumbles, "White folks crazy."

"I'd like to go there again when I get my birthday money," says Mercedes, and we shove her out the pack so she has to lean on the mailbox by herself.

"I'd like a shower. Tiring day," say Flyboy.

Then Sugar surprises me by sayin, "You know, Miss Moore, I don't think all of us here put together eat in a year what that sailboat costs." And Miss Moore lights up like somebody goosed her. "And?" she say, urging Sugar on. Only I'm standin on her foot so she don't continue.

"Imagine for a minute what kind of society it is in which some people 50
can spend on a toy what it would cost to feed a family of six or seven. What do you think?"

"I think," say Sugar pushing me off her feet like she never done before, cause I whip her ass in a minute, "that this is not much of a democracy if you ask me. Equal chance to pursue happiness means an equal crack at the dough, don't it?" Miss Moore is beside herself and I am disgusted with Sugar's treachery. So I stand on her foot one more time to see if she'll shove me. She shuts up, and Miss Moore looks at me, sorrowfully I'm thinkin. And somethin weird is goin on, I can feel it in my chest.

"Anybody else learn anything today?" lookin dead at me. I walk away and Sugar has to run to catch up and don't even seem to notice when I shrug her arm off my shoulder.

"Well, we got four dollars anyway," she says.

"Uh hunh."

"We could go to Hascombs and get half a chocolate layer and then go to the 55
Sunset and still have plenty money for potato chips and ice cream sodas."

"Un hunh."

"Race you to Hascombs," she say.

We start down the block and she gets ahead which is O.K. by me cause I'm going to the West End and then over to the Drive to think this day through. She can run if she want to and even run faster. But ain't nobody gonna beat me at nuthin. *[1972]*

≡ THINKING ABOUT THE TEXT

1. Bambara's story begins with "Back in the days," which suggests that Sylvia is significantly older now than she was then. How much time do you think has passed since the events she recalls? Does it matter to you how old she is now? Why, or why not?
2. Miss Moore is not officially a teacher. Nor is she a relative of the children she instructs. Is it right, then, for her to "take responsibility for the young ones' education" (para. 1)? Make arguments for and against her doing so.
3. Consider Miss Moore herself as making an argument. What are her claims? Which of her strategies, if any, seem effective in persuading her audience? Which, if any, seem ineffective?

4. What statements by the children articulate the lesson that Miss Moore teaches? Are all these statements saying pretty much the same thing? At the end of the story, is Sylvia ready to agree with all of them? Explain.
5. Do class and race seem equally important in this story, or does one seem more important than the other? Elaborate your reasoning.

MAKING COMPARISONS

1. "The Lesson" is more humorous than "Young Goodman Brown." Does its humor lead you to take Bambara's story of injustice less seriously than you do Hawthorne's? Why, or why not?
2. Whereas "Young Goodman Brown" has an omniscient narrator, "The Lesson" is narrated in the first person, by Sylvia herself. To what extent does this difference matter as you read the two stories together?
3. Sylvia is younger in age than Goodman Brown is. How significant is this difference to you as you consider their responses to injustice?

HA JIN
Saboteur

Although originally from China, Xuefei Jin writes in English under the pen name, Ha Jin (b. 1956). He served in the People's Liberation Army during his native country's Cultural Revolution, a period during the 1960s and 1970s when militant followers of leader Mao Zedong brutalized China's intellectuals and other segments of its population. After undergraduate and graduate education in China, Ha Jin was studying at Brandeis University in Massachusetts when, in 1989, the Chinese government attacked protesters in Tiananmen Square. He has written about this event in his novel The Crazed *(2002), and it played a role in his deciding to settle in the United States. Currently a professor at Boston University, he is the author of several books. His other novels include* A Free Life *(2007),* War Trash *(2004), and* Waiting *(1999), for which he won the National Book Award. His latest novel is* The Boat Rocker *(2016). The following story first appeared in a 1996 issue of* The Antioch Review *and was then reprinted in his 2001 collection* The Bridegroom: Stories.

Mr. Chiu and his bride were having lunch in the square before Muji Train Station. On the table between them were two bottles of soda spewing out brown foam and two paper boxes of rice and sautéed cucumber and pork. "Let's eat," he said to her, and broke the connected ends of the chopsticks. He picked up a slice of streaky pork and put it into his mouth. As he was chewing, a few crinkles appeared on his thin jaw.

To his right, at another table, two railroad policemen were drinking tea and laughing; it seemed that the stout, middle-aged man was telling a joke to his young comrade, who was tall and of athletic build. Now and again they would steal a glance at Mr. Chiu's table.

The air smelled of rotten melon. A few flies kept buzzing above the couple's lunch. Hundreds of people were rushing around to get on the platform or to catch buses to downtown. Food and fruit vendors were crying for customers in lazy voices. About a dozen young women, representing the local hotels, held up placards which displayed the daily prices and words as large as a palm, like FREE MEALS, AIR-CONDITIONING, and ON THE RIVER. In the center of the square stood a concrete statue of Chairman Mao, at whose feet peasants were napping, their backs on the warm granite and their faces toward the sunny sky. A flock of pigeons perched on the Chairman's raised hand and forearm.

The rice and cucumber tasted good, and Mr. Chiu was eating unhurriedly. His sallow face showed exhaustion. He was glad that the honeymoon was finally over and that he and his bride were heading back for Harbin. During the two weeks' vacation, he had been worried about his liver, because three months ago he had suffered from acute hepatitis; he was afraid he might have a relapse. But he had had no severe symptoms, despite his liver being still big and tender. On the whole he was pleased with his health, which could endure even the strain of a honeymoon; indeed, he was on the course of recovery. He looked at his bride, who took off her wire glasses, kneading the root of her nose with her fingertips. Beads of sweat coated her pale cheeks.

"Are you all right, sweetheart?" he asked. 5

"I have a headache. I didn't sleep well last night."

"Take an aspirin, will you?"

"It's not that serious. Tomorrow is Sunday and I can sleep in. Don't worry."

As they were talking, the stout policeman at the next table stood up and threw a bowl of tea in their direction. Both Mr. Chiu's and his bride's sandals were wet instantly.

"Hooligan!" she said in a low voice. 10

Mr. Chiu got to his feet and said out loud, "Comrade Policeman, why did you do this?" He stretched out his right foot to show the wet sandal.

"Do what?" the stout man asked huskily, glaring at Mr. Chiu while the young fellow was whistling.

"See, you dumped tea on our feet."

"You're lying. You wet your shoes yourself."

"Comrade Policemen, your duty is to keep order, but you purposely tortured 15
us common citizens. Why violate the law you are supposed to enforce?" As Mr. Chiu was speaking, dozens of people began gathering around.

With a wave of his hand, the man said to the young fellow, "Let's get hold of him!"

They grabbed Mr. Chiu and clamped handcuffs around his wrists. He cried, "You can't do this to me. This is utterly unreasonable."

"Shut up!" The man pulled out his pistol. "You can use your tongue at our headquarters."

The young fellow added, "You're a saboteur, you know that? You're disrupting public order."

The bride was too petrified to say anything coherent. She was a recent college 20
graduate, had majored in fine arts, and had never seen the police make an arrest. All she could say was, "Oh, please, please!"

The policemen were pulling Mr. Chiu, but he refused to go with them, holding the corner of the table and shouting, "We have a train to catch. We already bought the tickets."

The stout man punched him in the chest. "Shut up. Let your ticket expire." With the pistol butt he chopped Mr. Chiu's hands, which at once released the table. Together the two men were dragging him away to the police station.

Realizing he had to go with them, Mr. Chiu turned his head and shouted to his bride, "Don't wait for me here. Take the train. If I'm not back by tomorrow morning, send someone over to get me out."

She nodded, covering her sobbing mouth with her palm.

After removing his belt, they locked Mr. Chiu into a cell in the back of the Rail- 25
road Police Station. The single window in the room was blocked by six steel bars; it faced a spacious yard, in which stood a few pines. Beyond the trees, two swings hung from an iron frame, swaying gently in the breeze. Somewhere in the building a cleaver was chopping rhythmically. There must be a kitchen upstairs, Mr. Chiu thought.

He was too exhausted to worry about what they would do to him, so he lay down on the narrow bed and shut his eyes. He wasn't afraid. The Cultural Revolution was over already, and recently the Party had been propagating the idea that all citizens were equal before the law. The police ought to be a law-abiding model for common people. As long as he remained coolheaded and reasoned with them, they probably wouldn't harm him.

Late in the afternoon he was taken to the Interrogation Bureau on the second floor. On his way there, in the stairwell, he ran into the middle-aged policeman who had manhandled him. The man grinned, rolling his bulgy eyes and pointing his fingers at him as if firing a pistol. Egg of a tortoise! Mr. Chiu cursed mentally.

The moment he sat down in the office, he burped, his palm shielding his mouth. In front of him, across a long desk, sat the chief of the bureau and a donkey-faced man. On the glass desktop was a folder containing information on his case. He felt it bizarre that in just a matter of hours they had accumulated a small pile of writing about him. On second thought he began to wonder whether they had kept a file on him all the time. How could this have happened? He lived and worked in Harbin, more than three hundred miles away, and this was his first time in Muji City.

The chief of the bureau was a thin, bald man who looked serene and intelligent. His slim hands handled the written pages in the folder in the manner of a lecturing scholar. To Mr. Chiu's left sat a young scribe, with a clipboard on his knee and a black fountain pen in his hand.

"Your name?" the chief asked, apparently reading out the question from a form. 30

"Chiu Maguang."

"Age?"

"Thirty-four."

"Profession?"

"Lecturer."

"Work unit?"

"Harbin University."

"Political status?"

"Communist Party member."

The chief put down the paper and began to speak. "Your crime is sabotage, although it hasn't induced serious consequences yet. Because you are a Party member, you should be punished more. You have failed to be a model for the masses and you — "

"Excuse me, sir," Mr. Chiu cut him off.

"What?"

"I didn't do anything. Your men are the saboteurs of our social order. They threw hot tea on my feet and on my wife's feet. Logically speaking, you should criticize them, if not punish them."

"That statement is groundless. You have no witness. Why should I believe you?" the chief said matter-of-factly.

"This is my evidence." He raised his right hand. "Your man hit my fingers with a pistol."

"That doesn't prove how your feet got wet. Besides, you could have hurt your fingers yourself."

"But I am telling the truth!" Anger flared up in Mr. Chiu. "Your police station owes me an apology. My train ticket has expired, my new leather sandals are ruined, and I am late for a conference in the provincial capital. You must compensate me for the damage and losses. Don't mistake me for a common citizen who would tremble when you sneeze. I'm a scholar, a philosopher, and an expert in dialectical materialism. If necessary, we will argue about this in *The Northeastern Daily*, or we will go to the highest People's Court in Beijing. Tell me, what's your name?" He got carried away with his harangue, which was by no means trivial and had worked to his advantage on numerous occasions.

"Stop bluffing us," the donkey-faced man broke in. "We have seen a lot of your kind. We can easily prove you are guilty. Here are some of the statements given by eyewitnesses." He pushed a few sheets of paper toward Mr. Chiu.

Mr. Chiu was dazed to see the different handwritings, which all stated that he had shouted in the square to attract attention and refused to obey the police. One of the witnesses had identified herself as a purchasing agent from a shipyard in Shanghai. Something stirred in Mr. Chiu's stomach, a pain rising to his rib. He gave out a faint moan.

"Now you have to admit you are guilty," the chief said. "Although it's a serious crime, we won't punish you severely, provided you write out a self-criticism and promise that you won't disrupt the public order again. In other words, your release will depend on your attitude toward this crime."

"You're daydreaming!" Mr. Chiu cried. "I won't write a word, because I'm innocent. I demand that you provide me with a letter of apology so I can explain to my university why I'm late."

Both the interrogators smiled contemptuously. "Well, we've never done that," said the chief, taking a puff of his cigarette.

"Then make this a precedent."

"That's unnecessary. We are pretty certain that you will comply with our wishes." The chief blew a column of smoke toward Mr. Chiu's face.

At the tilt of the chief's head, two guards stepped forward and grabbed the 55
criminal by the arms. Mr. Chiu meanwhile went on saying, "I shall report you to the Provincial Administration. You'll have to pay for this! You are worse than the Japanese military police."

They dragged him out of the room.

After dinner, which consisted of a bowl of millet porridge, a corn bun, and a piece of pickled turnip, Mr. Chiu began to have a fever, shaking with a chill and sweating profusely. He knew that the fire of anger had gotten into his liver and that he was probably having a relapse. No medicine was available, because his briefcase had been left with his bride. At home it would have been time for him to sit in front of their color TV, drinking jasmine tea and watching the evening news. It was so lonesome in here. The orange bulb above the single bed was the only source of light, which enabled the guards to keep him under surveillance at night. A moment ago he had asked them for a newspaper or a magazine to read, but they turned him down.

Through the small opening on the door noises came in. It seemed that the police on duty were playing cards or chess in a nearby office; shouts and laughter could be heard now and then. Meanwhile, an accordion kept coughing from a remote corner in the building. Looking at the ballpoint and the letter paper left for him by the guards when they took him back from the Interrogation Bureau, Mr. Chiu remembered the old saying, "When a scholar runs into soldiers, the more he argues, the muddier his point becomes." How ridiculous this whole thing was. He ruffled his thick hair with his fingers.

He felt miserable, massaging his stomach continually. To tell the truth, he was more upset than frightened, because he would have to catch up with his work once he was back home—a paper that was due at the printers next week, and two dozen books he ought to read for the courses he was going to teach in the fall.

A human shadow flitted across the opening. Mr. Chiu rushed to the door and 60
shouted through the hole, "Comrade Guard, Comrade Guard!"

"What do you want?" a voice rasped.

"I want you to inform your leaders that I'm very sick. I have heart disease and hepatitis. I may die here if you keep me like this without medication."

"No leader is on duty on the weekend. You have to wait till Monday."

"What? You mean I'll stay in here tomorrow?"

"Yes." 65

"Your station will be held responsible if anything happens to me."

"We know that. Take it easy, you won't die."

It seemed illogical that Mr. Chiu slept quite well that night, though the light above his head had been on all the time and the straw mattress was hard and infested with fleas. He was afraid of ticks, mosquitoes, cockroaches—any kind of insect but fleas and bedbugs. Once, in the countryside, where his school's faculty and staff had helped the peasants harvest crops for a week, his colleagues had joked about his flesh, which they said must have tasted nonhuman to fleas. Except for him, they were all afflicted with hundreds of bites.

More amazing now, he didn't miss his bride a lot. He even enjoyed sleeping alone, perhaps because the honeymoon had tired him out and he needed more rest.

The backyard was quiet on Sunday morning. Pale sunlight streamed through 70
the pine branches. A few sparrows were jumping on the ground, catching caterpillars and ladybugs. Holding the steel bars, Mr. Chiu inhaled the morning air, which smelled meaty. There must have been an eatery or a cooked-meat stand nearby. He reminded himself that he should take this detention with ease. A sentence that Chairman Mao had written to a hospitalized friend rose in his mind: "Since you are already in here, you may as well stay and make the best of it."

His desire for peace of mind originated in his fear that this hepatitis might get worse. He tried to remain unperturbed. However, he was sure that his liver was swelling up, since the fever still persisted. For a whole day he lay in bed, thinking about his paper on the nature of contradictions. Time and again he was overwhelmed by anger, cursing aloud. "A bunch of thugs!" He swore that once he was out, he would write an article about this experience. He had better find out some of the policemen's names.

It turned out to be a restful day for the most part; he was certain that his university would send somebody to his rescue. All he should do now was remain calm and wait patiently. Sooner or later the police would have to release him, although they had no idea that he might refuse to leave unless they wrote him an apology. Damn those hoodlums, they had ordered more than they could eat!

When he woke up on Monday morning, it was already light. Somewhere a man was moaning; the sound came from the backyard. After a long yawn, and kicking off the tattered blanket, Mr. Chiu climbed out of bed and went to the window. In the middle of the yard, a young man was fastened to a pine, his wrists handcuffed around the trunk from behind. He was wriggling and swearing loudly, but there was no sight of anyone else in the yard. He looked familiar to Mr. Chiu.

Mr. Chiu squinted his eyes to see who it was. To his astonishment, he recognized the man, who was Fenjin, a recent graduate from the Law Department at Harbin University. Two years ago Mr. Chiu had taught a course in Marxist materialism, in which Fenjin had enrolled. Now, how on earth had this young devil landed here?

Then it dawned on him that Fenjin must have been sent over by his bride. 75
What a stupid woman! A bookworm, who only knew how to read foreign novels! He had expected that she would contact the school's Security Section, which would for sure send a cadre here. Fenjin held no official position; he merely worked in a private law firm that had just two lawyers; in fact, they had little business except for some detective work for men and women who suspected their spouses of having extramarital affairs. Mr. Chiu was overcome with a wave of nausea.

Should he call out to let his student know he was nearby? He decided not to because he didn't know what had happened. Fenjin must have quarreled with the police to incur such a punishment. Yet this could never have occurred if Fenjin hadn't come to his rescue. So no matter what, Mr. Chiu had to do something. But what could he do?

It was going to be a scorcher. He could see purple steam shimmering and rising from the ground among the pines. Poor devil, he thought, as he raised a bowl of corn glue to his mouth, sipped, and took a bite of a piece of salted celery.

When a guard came to collect the bowl and the chopsticks, Mr. Chiu asked him what had happened to the man in the backyard. "He called our boss 'bandit,'" the guard said. "He claimed he was a lawyer or something. An arrogant son of a rabbit."

Now it was obvious to Mr. Chiu that he had to do something to help his rescuer. Before he could figure out a way, a scream broke out in the backyard. He rushed to the window and saw a tall policeman standing before Fenjin, an iron bucket on the ground. It was the same young fellow who had arrested Mr. Chiu in the square two days before. The man pinched Fenjin's nose, then raised his hand, which stayed in the air for a few seconds, then slapped the lawyer across the face. As Fenjin was groaning, the man lifted up the bucket and poured water on his head.

"This will keep you from getting sunstroke, boy. I'll give you some more every hour," the man said loudly.

Fenjin kept his eyes shut, yet his wry face showed that he was struggling to hold back from cursing the policeman, or, more likely, that he was sobbing in silence. He sneezed, then raised his face and shouted, "Let me go take a piss."

"Oh, yeah?" the man bawled. "Pee in your pants."

Still Mr. Chiu didn't make any noise, gripping the steel bars with both hands, his fingers white. The policeman turned and glanced at the cell's window; his pistol, partly holstered, glittered in the sun. With a snort he spat his cigarette butt to the ground and stamped it into the dust.

Then the door opened and the guards motioned Mr. Chiu to come out. Again they took him upstairs to the Interrogation Bureau.

The same men were in the office, though this time the scribe was sitting there empty-handed. At the sight of Mr. Chiu the chief said, "Ah, here you are. Please be seated."

After Mr. Chiu sat down, the chief waved a white silk fan and said to him, "You may have seen your lawyer. He's a young man without manners, so our director had him taught a crash course in the backyard."

"It's illegal to do that. Aren't you afraid to appear in a newspaper?"

"No, we are not, not even on TV. What else can you do? We are not afraid of any story you make up. We call it fiction. What we do care about is that you cooperate with us. That is to say, you must admit your crime."

"What if I refuse to cooperate?"

"Then your lawyer will continue his education in the sunshine."

A swoon swayed Mr. Chiu, and he held the arms of the chair to steady himself. A numb pain stung him in the upper stomach and nauseated him, and his head was throbbing. He was sure that the hepatitis was finally attacking him. Anger was flaming up in his chest; his throat was tight and clogged.

The chief resumed, "As a matter of fact, you don't even have to write out your self-criticism. We have your crime described clearly here. All we need is your signature."

Holding back his rage, Mr. Chiu said, "Let me look at that."

With a smirk the donkey-faced man handed him a sheet which carried these words:

> I hereby admit that on July 13 I disrupted public order at Muji Train Station, and that I refused to listen to reason when the railroad police issued their warning. Thus I myself am responsible for my arrest. After two days' detention, I have realized the reactionary nature of my crime. From now on, I shall continue to educate myself with all my effort and shall never commit this kind of crime again.

A voice started screaming in Mr. Chiu's ears, "Lie, lie!" But he shook his head and forced the voice away. He asked the chief, "If I sign this, will you release both my lawyer and me?"

"Of course, we'll do that." The chief was drumming his fingers on the blue folder—their file on him.

Mr. Chiu signed his name and put his thumbprint under his signature.

"Now you are free to go," the chief said with a smile, and handed him a piece of paper to wipe his thumb with.

Mr. Chiu was so sick that he couldn't stand up from the chair at first try. Then he doubled his effort and rose to his feet. He staggered out of the building to meet his lawyer in the backyard, having forgotten to ask for his belt back. In his chest he felt as though there were a bomb. If he were able to, he would have razed the entire police station and eliminated all their families. Though he knew he could do nothing like that, he made up his mind to do something.

"I'm sorry about this torture, Fenjin," Mr. Chiu said when they met.

"It doesn't matter. They are savages." The lawyer brushed a patch of dirt off his jacket with trembling fingers. Water was still dribbling from the bottoms of his trouser legs.

"Let's go now," the teacher said.

The moment they came out of the police station, Mr. Chiu caught sight of a tea stand. He grabbed Fenjin's arm and walked over to the old woman at the table. "Two bowls of black tea," he said and handed her a one-yuan note.

After the first bowl, they each had another one. Then they set out for the train station. But before they walked fifty yards, Mr. Chiu insisted on eating a bowl of tree-ear soup at a food stand. Fenjin agreed. He told his teacher, "You mustn't treat me like a guest."

"No, I want to eat something myself."

As if dying of hunger, Mr. Chiu dragged his lawyer from restaurant to restaurant near the police station, but at each place he ordered no more than two bowls of food. Fenjin wondered why his teacher wouldn't stay at one place and eat his fill.

Mr. Chiu bought noodles, wonton, eight-grain porridge, and chicken soup, respectively, at four restaurants. While eating, he kept saying through his teeth. "If only I could kill all the bastards!" At the last place he merely took a few sips of the soup without tasting the chicken cubes and mushrooms.

Fenjin was baffled by his teacher, who looked ferocious and muttered to himself mysteriously, and whose jaundiced face was covered with dark puckets. For the first time Fenjin thought of Mr. Chiu as an ugly man.

Within a month over eight hundred people contracted acute hepatitis in Muji. Six died of the disease, including two children. Nobody knew how the epidemic had started. *[2000]*

THINKING ABOUT THE TEXT

1. In what places in the story is its title especially relevant? Who can be considered a "saboteur," and what acts of "sabotage" does the story deal with? Define what these terms mean to you.
2. What evidence is there that Mr. Chiu is not used to being treated the way that the police treat him? Identify specific passages. Do you find him unreasonably naive? Why, or why not?
3. Why, apparently, do the police arrest Mr. Chiu and demand a confession from him before they are willing to release him? How might the author be using their behavior to comment on Chinese authorities in general?
4. In his fiction, Ha Jin typically mentions small physical details that may appear trivial at first but can eventually be thought of as significant. Identify some moments in "Saboteur" when he uses such details, and explain what their actual importance might be.
5. How sympathetic were you toward Mr. Chiu until the story's end? Was your degree of sympathy affected by what he ultimately did? What do you conclude about him from his final action?

MAKING COMPARISONS

1. Revenge is often a factor in stories of injustice. Compare this idea in our three stories.
2. Compare the different kinds of injustice depicted in our three stories.
3. Compare the growth of Young Goodman Brown, Sylvia, and Mr. Chiu. How does your opinion of them change from the beginning to the end of the story?

WRITING ABOUT ISSUES

1. Write an essay that argues that given the circumstances of our stories, Mr. Chiu's response is or is not the most understandable of the three.
2. Argue that there is or is not (or should be) a commitment to social justice at your college.

3. Research a major religion's view on redress for social injustice and argue that this view is or is not compatible with today's difficulties with terrorists.
4. Read another revenge story. Some possibilities include Andre Dubus's "Killings," Poe's "The Cask of Amontillado" or "The Tell-Tale Heart," or Susan Glaspell's "A Jury of Her Peers." Using "Saboteur" and one of these stories, argue that the authors are making a similar or different point about revenge.

Secret Crimes: Stories

EDGAR ALLAN POE, "The Tell-Tale Heart"

ANDRE DUBUS, "Killings"

EDWARD J. DELANEY, "Clean"

If we are to believe commercial television, all crimes are solved and all criminals are caught and suitably punished. We would like to think so, but, of course, that is not always the case. Many crimes are never solved; and many criminals manage to avoid all official punishment. In such cases, the perpetrators are left to their own thoughts, which may be tranquil, remorseful, or a blend of satisfaction and guilt. For the sociopath or professional criminal perhaps there are no internal consequences. For many, however, socialized into a society where right and wrong are stressed, guilt and shame might be a form of punishment more severe than the consequence of public disclosure. Secret crimes are hardly foolproof.

The three stories presented here all involve a killing. The consequences for the three killers are complicated. In Poe's "The Tell-Tale Heart," guilt and paranoia overwhelm the narrator. In Andre Dubus's "Killings," sorrow and a deep sense of injustice leads an ordinarily moral man to seek revenge. Through careful planning, he seems to have avoided detection, although the last several paragraphs suggest a more problematic future. In "Clean," Edward J. Delaney presents us with a protagonist who spends a lifetime troubled by a crime that shapes his very identity. A secret crime might avoid the light of public disclosure, but the real consequences are often hidden in the hearts and minds of those undone by guilt.

EDGAR ALLAN POE

The Tell-Tale Heart

The life of Edgar Allan Poe (1809–1849) was relatively brief, its end tragically hastened by his alcohol and drug abuse, but his contributions to literature are unique. As a book reviewer, he produced pieces of literary criticism and theory that are still widely respected. As a poet, he wrote such classics as "The Raven" (1845), "The Bells" (1849), and "Annabel Lee" (1849). Moreover, his short fiction was groundbreaking and continues to be popular, a source for many films and television shows. With works such as "The Murders in the Rue Morgue" (1841), "The Gold Bug" (1843), and "The Purloined Letter" (1844), he pioneered the modern detective story. Other Poe tales are masterpieces of horror, including "The Fall of the House of Usher" (1842) and "The Pit and the Pendulum" (1842). The following tale, also one of Poe's best known, appeared in an 1843 issue of the periodical The Pioneer *and an 1845 issue of* The Broadway Journal *before being included in the 1850 collection of Poe's writings published after his death. The story has been adapted for film, television, and radio numerous times.*

MPI/Getty Images

True! — nervous — very, very dreadfully nervous I had been and am; but why *will* you say that I am mad? The disease had sharpened my senses — not destroyed — not dulled them. Above all was the sense of hearing acute. I heard all things in the heaven and in the earth. I heard many things in hell. How, then, am I mad? Hearken! and observe how healthily — how calmly I can tell you the whole story.

It is impossible to say how first the idea entered my brain; but once conceived, it haunted me day and night. Object there was none. Passion there was none. I loved the old man. He had never wronged me. He had never given me insult. For his gold I had no desire. I think it was his eye! yes, it was this! One of his eyes resembled that of a vulture — a pale blue eye, with a film over it. Whenever it fell upon me, my blood ran cold; and so by degrees — very gradually — I made up my mind to take the life of the old man, and thus rid myself of the eye for ever.

Now this is the point. You fancy me mad. Madmen know nothing. But you should have seen *me*. You should have seen how wisely I proceeded — with what caution — with what foresight — with what dissimulation I went to work! I was never kinder to the old man than during the whole week before I killed him. And every night, about midnight, I turned the latch of his door and opened it — oh, so gently! And then, when I had made an opening sufficient for my head, I put in a dark lantern, all closed, closed, so that no light shone out, and then I thrust in my head. Oh, you would have laughed to see how cunningly I thrust it in! I moved it slowly — very, very slowly, so that I might not disturb the old man's sleep. It took me an hour to place my whole head within the opening so far that I could see him as he lay upon his bed. Ha — would a madman have been so wise as this? And then, when my head was well in the room, I undid the lantern cautiously — oh, so cautiously — cautiously (for the hinges creaked) — I undid it just so much that a single thin ray fell upon the vulture eye. And this I did for seven long nights — every night just after midnight — but I found the eye always closed; and so it was impossible to do the work; for it was not the old man who vexed me, but his Evil Eye. And every morning, when the day broke, I went boldly into the chamber, and spoke courageously to him, calling him by name in a hearty tone, and inquiring how he had passed the night. So you see he would have been a very profound old man, indeed, to suspect that every night, just at twelve, I looked in upon him while he slept.

Upon the eighth night I was more than usually cautious in opening the door. A watch's minute hand moves more quickly than did mine. Never before that night had I *felt* the extent of my own powers — of my sagacity. I could scarcely contain my feelings of triumph. To think that there I was, opening the door, little by little, and he not even to dream of my secret deeds or thoughts. I fairly chuckled at the idea; and perhaps he heard me; for he moved on the bed suddenly, as if startled. Now you may think that I drew back — but no. His room was as black as pitch with the thick darkness (for the shutters were close fastened, through fear of robbers), and so I knew that he could not see the opening of the door, and I kept pushing it on steadily, steadily.

I had my head in, and was about to open the lantern, when my thumb slipped 5
upon the tin fastening, and the old man sprang up in the bed, crying out — "Who's there?"

I kept quite still and said nothing. For a whole hour I did not move a muscle, and in the meantime I did not hear him lie down. He was still sitting up in the bed listening; — just as I have done, night after night, hearkening to the death watches in the wall.

Presently I heard a slight groan, and I knew it was the groan of mortal terror. It was not a groan of pain or of grief — oh, no! — it was the low stifled sound that arises from the bottom of the soul when overcharged with awe. I knew the sound well. Many a night, just at midnight, when all the world slept, it has welled up from my own bosom, deepening with its dreadful echo, the terrors that distracted me. I say I knew it well. I knew what the old man felt, and pitied him, although I chuckled at heart. I knew that he had been lying awake ever since the first slight noise, when he had turned in the bed. His fears had been ever since growing upon him. He had been trying to fancy them causeless, but could not. He had been saying to himself — "It is nothing but the wind in the chimney — it is only a mouse crossing the floor," or "it is merely a cricket which has made a single chirp." Yes, he has been trying to comfort himself with these suppositions; but he had found all in vain. *All in vain*; because Death, in approaching him, had stalked with his black shadow before him, and enveloped the victim. And it was the mournful influence of the unperceived shadow that caused him to feel—although he neither saw nor heard—to *feel* the presence of my head within the room.

When I had waited a long time, very patiently, without hearing him lie down, I resolved to open a little—a very, very little crevice in the lantern. So I opened it—you cannot imagine how stealthily, stealthily—until, at length, a single dim ray, like the thread of the spider, shot from out the crevice and full upon the vulture eye.

It was open—wide, wide open—and I grew furious as I gazed upon it. I saw it with perfect distinctness—all a dull blue, with a hideous veil over it that chilled the very marrow in my bones, but I could see nothing else of the old man's face or person: for I had directed the ray as if by instinct, precisely upon the damned spot.

And now have I not told you that what you mistake for madness is but over- 10
acuteness of the senses?—now, I say, there came to my ears a low, dull, quick sound, such as a watch makes when enveloped in cotton. I knew *that* sound well too. It was the beating of the old man's heart. It increased my fury, as the beating of a drum stimulates the soldier into courage.

But even yet I refrained and kept still. I scarcely breathed. I held the lantern motionless. I tried how steadily I could maintain the ray upon the eye. Meantime the hellish tattoo of the heart increased. It grew quicker and quicker, and louder and louder every instant. The old man's terror *must* have been extreme! It grew louder, I say, louder every moment—do you mark me well? I have told you that I am nervous: so I am. And now at the dead hour of the night, amid the dreadful silence of that old house, so strange a noise as this excited me to uncontrollable terror. Yet, for some minutes longer I refrained and stood still. But the beating grew louder, louder! I thought the heart must burst. And now a new anxiety seized me—the sound would be heard by a neighbor! The old man's hour had come! With a loud yell, I threw open the lantern and leaped into the room. He shrieked once—once only. In an instant I dragged him to the floor, and pulled the heavy bed over him. I then smiled gaily, to find the deed so far done. But, for many minutes, the heart beat on with a muffled sound. This, however, did not vex me; it would not be heard through the wall. At length it ceased. The old man was dead. I removed the bed and examined the corpse. Yes, he was stone, stone dead. I placed my hand upon the heart and held it there many minutes. There was no pulsation. He was stone dead. His eye would trouble me no more.

If still you think me mad, you will think so no longer when I describe the wise precautions I took for the concealment of the body. The night waned, and I worked hastily, but in silence. First of all I dismembered the corpse. I cut off the head and the arms and the legs.

I then took up three planks from the flooring of the chamber, and deposited all between the scantlings. I then replaced the boards so cleverly, so cunningly, that no human eye—not even *his*—could have detected anything wrong. There was nothing to wash out—no stain of any kind—no blood-spot whatever. I had been too wary for that. A tub had caught all—ha! ha!

When I had made an end of these labors, it was four o'clock—still dark as midnight. As the bell sounded the hour, there came a knocking at the street door.

I went down to open it with a light heart—for what had I *now* to fear? There entered three men, who introduced themselves, with perfect suavity, as officers of the police. A shriek had been heard by a neighbor during the night; suspicion of foul play had been aroused; information had been lodged at the police office, and they (the officers) had been deputed to search the premises.

I smiled—for *what* had I to fear? I bade the gentlemen welcome. The shriek, I said, was my own in a dream. The old man, I mentioned, was absent in the country. I took my visitors all over the house. I bade them search—search well. I led them, at length, to *his* chamber. I showed them his treasures, secure, undisturbed. In the enthusiasm of my confidence, I brought chairs into the room, and desired them *here* to rest from their fatigues, while I myself, in the wild audacity of my perfect triumph, placed my own seat upon the very spot beneath which reposed the corpse of the victim.

The officers were satisfied. My *manner* had convinced them. I was singularly at ease. They sat, and while I answered cheerily, they chatted familiar things. But, ere long, I felt myself getting pale and wished them gone. My head ached, and I fancied a ringing in my ears: but still they sat and still chatted. The ringing became more distinct:—it continued and became more distinct: I talked more freely to get rid of the feeling: but it continued and gained definitiveness—until, at length, I found that the noise was *not* within my ears.

No doubt I now grew *very* pale;—but I talked more fluently, and with a heightened voice. Yet the sound increased—and what could I do? It was a *low, dull, quick sound—much such a sound as a watch makes when enveloped in cotton.* I gasped for breath—and yet the officers heard it not. I talked more quickly—more vehemently; but the noise steadily increased. I arose and argued about trifles, in a high key and with violent gesticulations, but the noise steadily increased. Why *would* they not be gone? I paced the floor to and fro with heavy strides, as if excited to fury by the observation of the men—but the noise steadily increased. Oh God! what *could* I do? I foamed—I raved—I swore! I swung the chair upon which I had been sitting, and grated it upon the boards, but the noise arose over all and continually increased. It grew louder—louder—*louder*! And still the men chatted pleasantly, and smiled. Was it possible they heard not? Almighty God!—no, no! They heard!—they suspected!—they *knew*!—they were making a mockery of my horror!—this I thought, and this I think. But any thing was better than this agony! Any thing was more tolerable than this derision! I could bear those hypocritical smiles no longer! I felt that I must scream or die!—and now—again!—hark! louder! louder! louder! *louder*!—

"Villains!" I shrieked, "dissemble no more! I admit the deed!—tear up the planks!—here, here!—it is the beating of his hideous heart!" *[1843]*

THINKING ABOUT THE TEXT

1. Why do you think the narrator killed the old man? Was he simply "mad," or do you gather that he had a particular reason? Explain.
2. Why do you think Poe spends as much time as he does on the narrator's observations of the old man prior to the killing?

3. Of the various senses, hearing seems to be the one emphasized in this story. Where does it come up in the text? Why do you think Poe chose to focus his tale on this particular sense? What other senses are also referred to here?
4. Other than his hearing, what features of the narrator's behavior and thinking shape your view of him?
5. If the police didn't arrive, do you think the narrator would have been able to keep the secret? For how long? Explain.

ANDRE DUBUS
Killings

Andre Dubus (1936–1999) served five years in the Marine Corps, attaining the rank of captain before becoming a full-time writer of short stories. Dubus lived in Haverhill, Massachusetts, and much of his fiction is set in the Merrimack Valley north of Boston. This is true of the following story, which appeared in his collection Finding a Girl in America *(1980) and was reprinted in his* Selected Stories *(1988). In 1991, Dubus also published a collection of essays,* Broken Vessels. *In part, the book deals with a 1986 accident that changed his life. Getting out of his car to aid stranded motorists, he was struck by another car; he eventually lost most of one leg and power over the other. Though confined to a wheelchair, Dubus continued to work actively. In 1996, he published his last collection of stories,* Dancing After Hours, *and in 1998, another volume of essays entitled* Meditations from a Moveable Chair. *Two years after he died came a much-acclaimed film adaptation of "Killings," entitled* In the Bedroom *(2001).*

On the August morning when Matt Fowler buried his youngest son, Frank, who had lived for twenty-one years, eight months, and four days, Matt's older son, Steve, turned to him as the family left the grave and walked between their friends, and said: "I should kill him." He was twenty-eight, his brown hair starting to thin in front where he used to have a cowlick. He bit his lower lip, wiped his eyes, then said it again. Ruth's arm, linked with Matt's, tightened; he looked at her. Beneath her eyes there was swelling from the three days she had suffered. At the limousine Matt stopped and looked back at the grave, the casket, and the Congregationalist minister who he thought had probably had a difficult job with the eulogy though he hadn't seemed to, and the old funeral director who was saying something to the six young pallbearers. The grave was on a hill and overlooked the Merrimack, which he could not see from where he stood; he looked at the opposite bank, at the apple orchard with its symmetrically planted trees going up a hill.

Next day Steve drove with his wife back to Baltimore where he managed the branch office of a bank, and Cathleen, the middle child, drove with her husband back to Syracuse. They had left the grandchildren with friends. A month after the funeral Matt played poker at Willis Trottier's because Ruth, who knew this was the second time he had been invited, told him to go, he couldn't sit home with her for the rest of her life, she was all right. After the game Willis went outside to tell everyone good night and, when the others had driven away, he walked with Matt to his car. Willis was a short, silver-haired man who had opened a diner after World War II, his trade then mostly very early breakfast, which he cooked, and then lunch for the men who worked at the leather and shoe factories. He now owned a large restaurant.

"He walks the Goddamn streets," Matt said.

"I know. He was in my place last night, at the bar. With a girl."

"I don't see him. I'm in the store all the time. Ruth sees him. She sees him too much. She was at Sunnyhurst today getting cigarettes and aspirin, and there he was. She can't even go out for cigarettes and aspirin. It's killing her."

"Come back in for a drink."

Matt looked at his watch. Ruth would be asleep. He walked with Willis back into the house, pausing at the steps to look at the starlit sky. It was a cool summer night; he thought vaguely of the Red Sox, did not even know if they were at home tonight; since it happened he had not been able to think about any of the small pleasures he believed he had earned, as he had earned also what was shattered now forever: the quietly harried and quietly pleasurable days of fatherhood. They went inside. Willis's wife, Martha, had gone to bed hours ago, in the rear of the large house which was rigged with burglar and fire alarms. They went downstairs to the game room: the television set suspended from the ceiling, the pool table, the poker table with beer cans, cards, chips, filled ashtrays, and the six chairs where Matt and his friends had sat, the friends picking up the old banter as though he had only been away on vacation; but he could see the affection and courtesy in their eyes. Willis went behind the bar and mixed them each a Scotch and soda; he stayed behind the bar and looked at Matt sitting on the stool.

"How often have you thought about it?" Willis said.

"Every day since he got out. I didn't think about bail. I thought I wouldn't have to worry about him for years. She sees him all the time. It makes her cry."

"He was in my place a long time last night. He'll be back."

"Maybe he won't."

"The band. He likes the band."

"What's he doing now?"

"He's tending bar up to Hampton Beach. For a friend. Ever notice even the worst bastard always has friends? He couldn't get work in town. It's just tourists and kids up to Hampton. Nobody knows him. If they do, they don't care. They drink what he mixes."

"Nobody tells me about him."

"I hate him, Matt. My boys went to school with him. He was the same then. Know what he'll do? Five at the most. Remember that woman about seven years ago? Shot her husband and dropped him off the bridge in the Merrimack with a hundred-pound sack of cement and said all the way through it that nobody helped her. Know where she is now? She's in Lawrence now, a secretary. And whoever helped her, where the hell is he?"

"I've got a .38 I've had for years, I take it to the store now. I tell Ruth it's for the night deposits. I tell her things have changed: we got junkies here now too. Lots of people without jobs. She knows though."

"What does she know?"

"She knows I started carrying it after the first time she saw him in town. She knows it's in case I see him, and there's some kind of a situation — "

He stopped, looked at Willis, and finished his drink. Willis mixed him another.

"What kind of situation?"

"Where he did something to me. Where I could get away with it."

"How does Ruth feel about that?"

"She doesn't know."

"You said she does, she's got it figured out."

He thought of her that afternoon: when she went into Sunnyhurst, Strout was waiting at the counter while the clerk bagged the things he had bought; she turned down an aisle and looked at soup cans until he left.

"Ruth would shoot him herself, if she thought she could hit him."

"You got a permit?"

"No."

"I do. You could get a year for that."

"Maybe I'll get one. Or maybe I won't. Maybe I'll just stop bringing it to the store."

Richard Strout was twenty-six years old, a high school athlete, football scholarship to the University of Massachusetts where he lasted for almost two semesters before quitting in advance of the final grades that would have forced him not to return. People then said: Dickie can do the work; he just doesn't want to. He came home and did construction work for his father but refused his father's offer to learn the business; his two older brothers had learned it, so that Strout and Sons trucks going about town, and signs on construction sites, now slashed wounds into Matt Fowler's life. Then Richard married a young girl and became a bartender, his salary and tips augmented and perhaps sometimes matched by his father, who also posted his bond. So his friends, his enemies (he had those: fist fights or, more often, boys and then young men who had not fought him when they thought they should have), and those who simply knew him by face and name, had a series of images of him which they recalled when they heard of the killing: the high school running back, the young drunk in bars, the oblivious hard-hatted young man eating lunch at a counter, the bartender who could perhaps be called courteous but not more than that: as he tended bar, his dark eyes and dark, wide-jawed face appeared less sullen, near blank.

One night he beat Frank. Frank was living at home and waiting for September, for graduate school in economics, and working as a lifeguard at Salisbury Beach, where he met Mary Ann Strout, in her first month of separation. She spent most days at the beach with her two sons. Before ten o'clock one night Frank came home; he had driven to the hospital first, and he walked into the living room with stitches over his right eye and both lips bright and swollen.

"I'm all right," he said, when Matt and Ruth stood up, and Matt turned off the television, letting Ruth get to him first: the tall, muscled but slender sun-tanned boy. Frank tried to smile at them but couldn't because of his lips.

"It was her husband, wasn't it?" Ruth said.

"Ex," Frank said. "He dropped in."

Matt gently held Frank's jaw and turned his face to the light, looked at the stitches, the blood under the white of the eye, the bruised flesh.

"Press charges," Matt said.

"No."

"What's to stop him from doing it again? Did you hit him at all? Enough so he won't want to next time?"

"I don't think I touched him."

"So what are you going to do?"

"Take karate," Frank said, and tried again to smile.

"That's not the problem," Ruth said.

"You know you like her," Frank said.

"I like a lot of people. What about the boys? Did they see it?"

"They were asleep."

"Did you leave her alone with him?"

"He left first. She was yelling at him. I believe she had a skillet in her hand."

"Oh for God's sake," Ruth said.

Matt had been dealing with that too: at the dinner table on evenings when Frank wasn't home, was eating with Mary Ann; or, on the other nights—and Frank was with her every night—he talked with Ruth while they watched television, or lay in bed with the windows open and he smelled the night air and imagined, with both pride and muted sorrow, Frank in Mary Ann's arms. Ruth didn't like it because Mary Ann was in the process of divorce, because she had two children, because she was four years older than Frank, and finally—she told this in bed, where she had during all of their marriage told him of her deepest feelings: of love, of passion, of fears about one of the children, of pain Matt had caused her or she had caused him—she was against it because of what she had heard: that the marriage had gone bad early, and for most of it Richard and Mary Ann had both played around.

"That can't be true," Matt said. "Strout wouldn't have stood for it."

"Maybe he loves her."

"He's too hot-tempered. He couldn't have taken that."

But Matt knew Strout had taken it, for he had heard the stories too. He wondered who had told them to Ruth; and he felt vaguely annoyed and isolated: living with her for thirty-one years and still not knowing what she talked about with her friends. On these summer nights he did not so much argue with her as try to comfort her, but finally there was no difference between the two: she had concrete objections, which he tried to overcome. And in his attempt to do this, he neglected his own objections, which were the same as hers, so that as he spoke to her he felt as disembodied as he sometimes did in the store when he helped a man choose a blouse or dress or piece of costume jewelry for his wife.

"The divorce doesn't mean anything," he said. "She was young and maybe she liked his looks and then after a while she realized she was living with a bastard. I see it as a positive thing."

"She's not divorced yet."

"It's the same thing. Massachusetts has crazy laws, that's all. Her age is no problem. What's it matter when she was born? And that other business: even if it's true, which it probably isn't, it's got nothing to do with Frank, and it's in the past. And the kids are no problem. She's been married six years; she ought to have kids. Frank likes them. He plays with them. And he's not going to marry her anyway, so it's not a problem of money."

"Then what's he doing with her?"

"She probably loves him, Ruth. Girls always have. Why can't we just leave it at that?"

"He got home at six o'clock Tuesday morning."

"I didn't know you knew. I've already talked to him about it."

Which he had: since he believed almost nothing he told Ruth, he went to Frank with what he believed. The night before, he had followed Frank to the car after dinner.

"You wouldn't make much of a burglar," he said.

"How's that?"

Matt was looking up at him; Frank was six feet tall, an inch and a half taller than Matt, who had been proud when Frank at seventeen outgrew him; he had only felt uncomfortable when he had to reprimand or caution him. He touched Frank's bicep, thought of the young taut passionate body, believed he could sense the desire, and again he felt the pride and sorrow and envy too, not knowing whether he was envious of Frank or Mary Ann.

"When you came in yesterday morning, I woke up. One of these mornings your mother will. And I'm the one who'll have to talk to her. She won't interfere with you. Okay? I know it means —" But he stopped, thinking: I know it means getting up and leaving that suntanned girl and going sleepy to the car, I know —

"Okay," Frank said, and touched Matt's shoulder and got into the car.

There had been other talks, but the only long one was their first one: a night driving to Fenway Park, Matt having ordered the tickets so they could talk, and knowing when Frank said yes, he would go, that he knew the talk was coming too. It took them forty minutes to get to Boston, and they talked about Mary Ann until they joined the city traffic along the Charles River, blue in the late sun. Frank told him all the things that Matt would later pretend to believe when he told them to Ruth.

"It seems like a lot for a young guy to take on," Matt finally said.

"Sometimes it is. But she's worth it."

"Are you thinking about getting married?"

"We haven't talked about it. She can't for over a year. I've got school."

"I *do* like her," Matt said.

He did. Some evenings, when the long summer sun was still low in the sky, Frank brought her home; they came into the house smelling of suntan lotion and the sea, and Matt gave them gin and tonics and started the charcoal in the backyard, and looked at Mary Ann in the lawn chair: long and very light brown hair (Matt thinking that twenty years ago she would have dyed it blonde), and the long brown legs he loved to look at; her face was pretty; she had probably never in her adult life gone unnoticed into a public place. It was in her wide brown eyes that she looked older than Frank; after a few drinks Matt thought what he saw in her eyes was something erotic, testament to the rumors about her; but he knew it wasn't that, or all that: she had, very young, been through a sort of pain that his children, and he and Ruth, had been spared. In the moments of his recognizing that pain, he wanted to tenderly touch her hair, wanted with some gesture to give her solace and hope. And he would glance at Frank, and hope they would love each other, hope Frank would soothe that pain in her heart, take it from her eyes; and her divorce, her age, and her children did not matter at all. On the first two evenings she did not bring her boys, and then Ruth asked her to bring them the next time. In bed that night Ruth said, "She hasn't brought them because she's embarrassed. She shouldn't feel embarrassed."

Richard Strout shot Frank in front of the boys. They were sitting on the living room floor watching television, Frank sitting on the couch, and Mary Ann just returning from the kitchen with a tray of sandwiches. Strout came in the front door and shot Frank twice in the chest and once in the face with a 9 mm automatic. Then he looked at the boys and Mary Ann, and went home to wait for the police.

It seemed to Matt that from the time Mary Ann called weeping to tell him until now, a Saturday night in September, sitting in the car with Willis, parked beside Strout's car, waiting for the bar to close, that he had not so much moved through his life as wandered through it, his spirits like a dazed body bumping into furniture and corners. He had always been a fearful father: when his children were young, at the start of each summer he thought of them drowning in a pond or the sea, and he was relieved when he came home in the evenings and they were there; usually that relief was his only acknowledgment of his fear, which he never spoke of, and which he controlled within his heart. As he had when they were very young and all of them in turn, Cathleen too, were drawn to the high oak in the backyard, and had to climb it. Smiling, he watched them, imagining the fall: and he was poised to catch the small body before it hit the earth. Or his legs were poised; his hands were in his pockets or his arms were folded and, for the child looking down, he appeared relaxed and confident while his heart beat with the two words he wanted to call out but did not: *Don't fall.* In winter he was less afraid: he made sure the ice would hold him before they skated, and he brought or sent them to places where they could sled without ending in the street. So he and his children had survived their childhood, and he only worried about them when he knew they were driving a long distance, and then he lost Frank in a way no father expected to lose his son, and he felt that all the fears he had borne while they were growing up, and all the grief he had been afraid of, had backed up like a huge wave and struck him on the beach and swept him out to sea. Each day he felt the same and when he was able to forget how he felt, when he was able to force himself not to feel that way, the eyes of his clerks and customers defeated him. He wished those eyes were oblivious, even cold; he felt he was withering in their tenderness. And beneath his listless wandering, every day in his soul he shot Richard Strout in the face; while Ruth, going about town on errands, kept seeing him. And at night in bed she would hold Matt and cry, or sometimes she was silent and Matt would touch her tightening arm, her clenched fist.

As his own right fist was now, squeezing the butt of the revolver, the last of the drinkers having left the bar, talking to each other, going to their separate cars which were in the lot in front of the bar, out of Matt's vision. He heard their voices, their cars, and then the ocean again, across the street. The tide was in and sometimes it smacked the sea wall. Through the windshield he looked at the dark red side wall of the bar, and then to his left, past Willis, at Strout's car, and through its windows he could see the now-emptied parking lot, the road, the sea wall. He could smell the sea.

The front door of the bar opened and closed again and Willis looked at Matt then at the corner of the building; when Strout came around it alone Matt got out of the car, giving up the hope he had kept all night (and for the past week) that Strout would come out with friends, and Willis would simply drive away; thinking: *All right then. All right*; and he went around the front of Willis's car, and at Strout's he stopped and aimed over the hood at Strout's blue shirt ten feet away. Willis was aiming too, crouched on Matt's left, his elbow resting on the hood.

"Mr. Fowler," Strout said. He looked at each of them, and at the guns. 80
"Mr. Trottier."

Then Matt, watching the parking lot and the road, walked quickly between the car and the building and stood behind Strout. He took one leather glove from his pocket and put it on his left hand.

"Don't talk. Unlock the front and back and get in."

Strout unlocked the front door, reached in and unlocked the back, then got in, and Matt slid into the back seat, closed the door with his gloved hand, and touched Strout's head once with the muzzle.

"It's cocked. Drive to your house."

When Strout looked over his shoulder to back the car, Matt aimed at his tem- 85
ple and did not look at his eyes.

"Drive slowly," he said. "Don't try to get stopped."

They drove across the empty front lot and onto the road, Willis's headlights shining into the car; then back through town, the sea wall on the left hiding the beach, though far out Matt could see the ocean; he uncocked the revolver; on the right were the places, most with their neon signs off, that did so much business in summer: the lounges and cafés and pizza houses, the street itself empty of traffic, the way he and Willis had known it would be when they decided to take Strout at the bar rather than knock on his door at two o'clock one morning and risk that one insomniac neighbor. Matt had not told Willis he was afraid he could not be alone with Strout for very long, smell his smells, feel the presence of his flesh, hear his voice, and then shoot him. They left the beach town and then were on the high bridge over the channel: to the left the smacking curling white at the breakwater and beyond that the dark sea and the full moon, and down to his right the small fishing boats bobbing at anchor in the cove. When they left the bridge, the sea was blocked by abandoned beach cottages, and Matt's left hand was sweating in the glove. Out here in the dark in the car he believed Ruth knew. Willis had come to his house at eleven and asked if he wanted a nightcap; Matt went to the bedroom for his wallet, put the gloves in one trouser pocket and the .38 in the other and went back to the living room, his hand in his pocket covering the bulge of the cool cylinder pressed against his fingers, the butt against his palm. When Ruth said good night she looked at his face, and he felt she could see in his eyes the gun, and the night he was going to. But he knew he couldn't trust what he saw. Willis's wife had taken her sleeping pill, which gave her eight hours—the reason, Willis had told Matt, he had the alarms installed, for nights when he was late at the restaurant—and when it was all done and Willis got home he would leave ice and a trace of Scotch and soda in two glasses in the game room and tell Martha in the morning that he had left the restaurant early and brought Matt home for a drink.

"He was making it with my wife." Strout's voice was careful, not pleading.

Matt pressed the muzzle against Strout's head, pressed it harder than he wanted to, feeling through the gun Strout's head flinching and moving forward; then he lowered the gun to his lap.

"Don't talk," he said.

Strout did not speak again. They turned west, drove past the Dairy Queen closed until spring, and the two lobster restaurants that faced each other and were crowded all summer and were now also closed, onto the short bridge crossing the tidal stream, and over the engine Matt could hear through his open window the water rushing inland under the bridge; looking to his left he saw its swift moonlit current going back into the marsh which, leaving the bridge, they entered: the salt marsh stretching out on both sides, the grass tall in patches but mostly low and leaning earthward as though windblown, a large dark rock sitting as though it rested on nothing but itself, and shallow pools reflecting the bright moon.

Beyond the marsh they drove through woods, Matt thinking now of the hole he and Willis had dug last Sunday afternoon after telling their wives they were going to Fenway Park. They listened to the game on a transistor radio, but heard none of it as they dug into the soft earth on the knoll they had chosen because elms and maples sheltered it. Already some leaves had fallen. When the hole was deep enough they covered it and the piled earth with dead branches, then cleaned their shoes and pants and went to a restaurant farther up in New Hampshire where they ate sandwiches and drank beer and watched the rest of the game on television. Looking at the back of Strout's head he thought of Frank's grave; he had not been back to it; but he would go before winter, and its second burial of snow.

He thought of Frank sitting on the couch and perhaps talking to the children as they watched television, imagined him feeling young and strong, still warmed from the sun at the beach, and feeling loved, hearing Mary Ann moving about in the kitchen, hearing her walking into the living room; maybe he looked up at her and maybe she said something, looking at him over the tray of sandwiches, smiling at him, saying something the way women do when they offer food as a gift, then the front door opening and this son of a bitch coming in and Frank seeing that he meant the gun in his hand, this son of a bitch and his gun the last person and thing Frank saw on earth.

When they drove into town the streets were nearly empty: a few slow cars, a policeman walking his beat past the darkened fronts of stores. Strout and Matt both glanced at him as they drove by. They were on the main street, and all the stoplights were blinking yellow. Willis and Matt had talked about that too: the lights changed at midnight, so there would be no place Strout had to stop and where he might try to run. Strout turned down the block where he lived and Willis's headlights were no longer with Matt in the back seat. They had planned that too, had decided it was best for just the one car to go to the house, and again Matt had said nothing about his fear of being alone with Strout, especially in his house: a duplex, dark as all the houses on the street were, the street itself lit at the corner of each block. As Strout turned into the driveway Matt thought of the one insomniac neighbor, thought of some man or woman sitting alone in the dark living room, watching the all-night channel from Boston. When Strout stopped the car near the front of the house, Matt said: "Drive it to the back."

He touched Strout's head with the muzzle. 95

"You wouldn't have it cocked, would you? For when I put on the brakes."

Matt cocked it, and said: "It is now."

Strout waited a moment; then he eased the car forward, the engine doing little more than idling, and as they approached the garage he gently braked. Matt opened the door, then took off the glove and put it in his pocket. He stepped out and shut the door with his hip and said: "All right."

Strout looked at the gun, then got out, and Matt followed him across the grass, and as Strout unlocked the door Matt looked quickly at the row of small backyards on either side, and scattered tall trees, some evergreens, others not, and he thought of the red and yellow leaves on the trees over the hole, saw them falling soon, probably in two weeks, dropping slowly, covering. Strout stepped into the kitchen.

"Turn on the light." 100

Strout reached to the wall switch, and in the light Matt looked at his wide back, the dark blue shirt, the white belt, the red plaid pants.

"Where's your suitcase?"

"My suitcase?"

"Where is it?"

"In the bedroom closet." 105

"That's where we're going then. When we get to a door you stop and turn on the light."

They crossed the kitchen, Matt glancing at the sink and stove and refrigerator: no dishes in the sink or even the dish rack beside it, no grease splashings on the stove, the refrigerator door clean and white. He did not want to look at any more but he looked quickly at all he could see: in the living room magazines and newspapers in a wicker basket, clean ashtrays, a record player, the records shelved next to it, then down the hall where, near the bedroom door, hung a color photograph of Mary Ann and the two boys sitting on a lawn — there was no house in the picture — Mary Ann smiling at the camera or Strout or whoever held the camera, smiling as she had on Matt's lawn this summer while he waited for the charcoal and they all talked and he looked at her brown legs and at Frank touching her arm, her shoulder, her hair; he moved down the hall with her smile in his mind, wondering: was that when they were both playing around and she was smiling like that at him and they were happy, even sometimes, making it worth it? He recalled her eyes, the pain in them, and he was conscious of the circles of love he was touching with the hand that held the revolver so tightly now as Strout stopped at the door at the end of the hall.

"There's no wall switch."

"Where's the light?"

"By the bed." 110

"Let's go."

Matt stayed a pace behind, then Strout leaned over and the room was lighted: the bed, a double one, was neatly made; the ashtray on the bedside table clean, the bureau top dustless, and no photographs; probably so the girl — who *was* she? — would not have to see Mary Ann in the bedroom she believed was theirs. But because Matt was a father and a husband, though never an ex-husband, he knew (and did not want to know) that this bedroom had never been theirs alone. Strout turned around; Matt looked at his lips, his wide jaw, and thought of Frank's doomed and fearful eyes looking up from the couch.

"Where's Mr. Trottier?"

"He's waiting. Pack clothes for warm weather."

"What's going on?" 115

"You're jumping bail."

"Mr. Fowler — "

He pointed the cocked revolver at Strout's face. The barrel trembled but not much, not as much as he had expected. Strout went to the closet and got the suitcase from the floor and opened it on the bed. As he went to the bureau, he said: "He was making it with my wife. I'd go pick up my kids and he'd be there. Sometimes he spent the night. My boys told me."

He did not look at Matt as he spoke. He opened the top drawer and Matt stepped closer so he could see Strout's hands: underwear and socks, the socks rolled, the underwear folded and stacked. He took them back to the bed, arranged them neatly in the suitcase, then from the closet he was taking shirts and trousers and a jacket; he laid them on the bed and Matt followed him to the bathroom and watched from the door while he packed those things a person accumulated and that became part of him so that at times in the store Matt felt he was selling more than clothes.

"I wanted to try to get together with her again." He was bent over the suitcase. "I couldn't even talk to her. He was always with her. I'm going to jail for it; if I ever get out I'll be an old man. Isn't that enough?" 120

"You're not going to jail."

Strout closed the suitcase and faced Matt, looking at the gun. Matt went to his rear, so Strout was between him and the lighted hall; then using his handkerchief he turned off the lamp and said: "Let's go."

They went down the hall, Matt looking again at the photograph, and through the living room and kitchen, Matt turning off the lights and talking, frightened that he was talking, that he was telling this lie he had not planned: "It's the trial.

We can't go through that, my wife and me. So you're leaving. We've got you a ticket, and a job. A friend of Mr. Trottier's. Out west. My wife keeps seeing you. We can't have that anymore."

Matt turned out the kitchen light and put the handkerchief in his pocket, and they went down the two brick steps and across the lawn. Strout put the suitcase on the floor of the back seat, then got into the front seat and Matt got in the back and put on his glove and shut the door.

"They'll catch me. They'll check passenger lists." 125

"We didn't use your name."

"They'll figure that out too. You think I wouldn't have done it myself if it was that easy?"

He backed into the street, Matt looking down the gun barrel but not at the profiled face beyond it.

"You were alone," Matt said. "We've got it worked out." 130

"There's no planes this time of night, Mr. Fowler."

"Go back through town. Then north on 125."

They came to the corner and turned, and now Willis's headlights were in the car with Matt.

"Why north, Mr. Fowler?"

"Somebody's going to keep you for a while. They'll take you to the airport." He uncocked the hammer and lowered the revolver to his lap and said wearily: "No more talking."

As they drove back through town, Matt's body sagged, going limp with his 135
spirit and its new and false bond with Strout, the hope his lie had given Strout. He had grown up in this town whose streets had become places of apprehension and pain for Ruth as she drove and walked, doing what she had to do; and for him too, if only in his mind as he worked and chatted six days a week in his store; he wondered now if his lie would have worked, if sending Strout away would have been enough; but then he knew that just thinking of Strout in Montana or whatever place lay at the end of the lie he had told, thinking of him walking the streets there, loving a girl there (who *was* she?) would be enough to slowly rot the rest of his days. And Ruth's. Again he was certain that she knew, that she was waiting for him.

They were in New Hampshire now, on the narrow highway, passing the shopping center at the state line, and then houses and small stores and sandwich shops. There were few cars on the road. After ten minutes he raised his trembling hand, touched Strout's neck with the gun, and said: "Turn in up here. At the dirt road."

Strout flicked on the indicator and slowed.

"Mr. Fowler?"

"They're waiting here."

Strout turned very slowly, easing his neck away from the gun. In the moon- 140
light the road was light brown, lighter and yellowed where the headlights shone; weeds and a few trees grew on either side of it, and ahead of them were the woods.

"There's nothing back here, Mr. Fowler."

"It's for your car. You don't think we'd leave it at the airport, do you?"

He watched Strout's large, big-knuckled hands tighten on the wheel, saw Frank's face that night: not the stitches and bruised eye and swollen lips, but his own hand gently touching Frank's jaw, turning his wounds to the light. They rounded a bend in the road and were out of sight of the highway: tall trees all around them now, hiding the moon. When they reached the abandoned gravel pit on the left, the bare flat earth and steep pale embankment behind it, and the black crowns of trees at its top, Matt said: "Stop here."

Strout stopped but did not turn off the engine. Matt pressed the gun hard against his neck, and he straightened in the seat and looked in the rearview mirror, Matt's eyes meeting his in the glass for an instant before looking at the hair at the end of the gun barrel.

"Turn it off."

Strout did, then held the wheel with two hands, and looked in the mirror.

"I'll do twenty years, Mr. Fowler; at least. I'll be forty-six years old."

"That's nine years younger than I am," Matt said, and got out and took off the glove and kicked the door shut. He aimed at Strout's ear and pulled back the hammer. Willis's headlights were off and Matt heard him walking on the soft thin layer of dust, the hard earth beneath it. Strout opened the door, sat for a moment in the interior light, then stepped out onto the road. Now his face was pleading. Matt did not look at his eyes, but he could see it in the lips.

"Just get the suitcase. They're right up the road."

Willis was beside him now, to his left. Strout looked at both guns. Then he opened the back door, leaned in, and with a jerk brought the suitcase out. He was turning to face them when Matt said: "Just walk up the road. Just ahead."

Strout turned to walk, the suitcase in his right hand, and Matt and Willis followed; as Strout cleared the front of his car he dropped the suitcase and, ducking, took one step that was the beginning of a sprint to his right. The gun kicked in Matt's hand, and the explosion of the shot surrounded him, isolated him in a nimbus of sound that cut him off from all his time, all his history, isolated him standing absolutely still on the dirt road with the gun in his hand, looking down at Richard Strout squirming on his belly, kicking one leg behind him, pushing himself forward, toward the woods. Then Matt went to him and shot him once in the back of the head.

Driving south to Boston, wearing both gloves now, staying in the middle lane and looking often in the rearview mirror at Willis's headlights, he relived the suitcase dropping, the quick dip and turn of Strout's back, and the kick of the gun, the sound of the shot. When he walked to Strout, he still existed within the first shot, still trembled and breathed with it. The second shot and the burial seemed to be happening to someone else, someone he was watching. He and Willis each held an arm and pulled Strout face-down off the road and into the woods, his bouncing sliding belt white under the trees where it was so dark that when they stopped at the top of the knoll, panting and sweating, Matt could not see where Strout's blue shirt ended and the earth began. They pulled off the branches then dragged Strout to the edge of the hole and went behind him and lifted his legs and pushed him in.

They stood still for a moment. The woods were quiet save for their breathing, and Matt remembered hearing the movements of birds and small animals after the first shot. Or maybe he had not heard them. Willis went down to the road. Matt could see him clearly out on the tan dirt, could see the glint of Strout's car and, beyond the road, the gravel pit. Willis came back up the knoll with the suitcase. He dropped it in the hole and took off his gloves and they went down to his car for the spades. They worked quietly. Sometimes they paused to listen to the woods. When they were finished Willis turned on his flashlight and they covered the earth with leaves and branches and then went down to the spot in front of the car, and while Matt held the light Willis crouched and sprinkled dust on the blood, backing up till he reached the grass and leaves, then he used leaves until they had worked up to the grave again. They did not stop. They walked around the grave and through the woods, using the light on the ground, looking up through the trees to where they ended at the lake. Neither of them spoke above the sounds of their heavy and clumsy strides through low brush and over fallen branches. Then they reached it: wide and dark, lapping softly at the bank, pine needles smooth under Matt's feet, moonlight on the lake, a small island near its middle, with black, tall evergreens. He took out the gun and threw for the island: taking two steps back on the pine needles, striding with the throw and going to one knee as he followed through, looking up to see the dark shapeless object arcing downward, splashing.

They left Strout's car in Boston, in front of an apartment building on Commonwealth Avenue. When they got back to town Willis drove slowly over the bridge and Matt threw the keys into the Merrimack. The sky was turning light. Willis let him out a block from his house, and walking home he listened for sounds from the houses he passed. They were quiet. A light was on in his living room. He turned it off and undressed in there, and went softly toward the bedroom; in the hall he smelled the smoke, and he stood in the bedroom doorway and looked at the orange of her cigarette in the dark. The curtains were closed. He went to the closet and put his shoes on the floor and felt for a hanger.

"Did you do it?" she said.

He went down the hall to the bathroom and in the dark he washed his hands 155
and face. Then he went to her, lay on his back, and pulled the sheet up to his throat.

"Are you all right?" she said.

"I think so."

Now she touched him, lying on her side, her hand on his belly, his thigh.

"Tell me," she said.

He started from the beginning, in the parking lot at the bar; but soon with his 160
eyes closed and Ruth petting him, he spoke of Strout's house: the order, the woman presence, the picture on the wall.

"The way she was smiling," he said.

"What about it?"

"I don't know. Did you ever see Strout's girl? When you saw him in town?"

"No."

"I wonder who she was." 165

Then he thought: *not was: is. Sleeping now she is his girl.* He opened his eyes, then closed them again. There was more light beyond the curtains. With Ruth now he left Strout's house and told again his lie to Strout, gave him again that hope that Strout must have for a while believed, else he would have to believe only the gun pointed at him for the last two hours of his life. And with Ruth he saw again the dropping suitcase, the darting move to the right: and he told of the first shot, feeling her hand on him but his heart isolated still, beating on the road still in that explosion like thunder. He told her the rest, but the words had no images for him, he did not see himself doing what the words said he had done; he only saw himself on that road.

"We can't tell the other kids," she said. "It'll hurt them, thinking he got away. But we mustn't."

"No."

She was holding him, wanting him, and he wished he could make love with her but he could not. He saw Frank and Mary Ann making love in her bed, their eyes closed, their bodies brown and smelling of the sea; the other girl was faceless, bodiless, but he felt her sleeping now; and he saw Frank and Strout, their faces alive; he saw red and yellow leaves falling on the earth, then snow: falling and freezing and falling; and holding Ruth, his cheek touching her breast, he shuddered with a sob that he kept silent in his heart. *[1979]*

☰ THINKING ABOUT THE TEXT

1. Here is an issue of cause and effect: Why, evidently, does Matt kill Richard Strout? Consider the possibility that he has more than one reason. Here is an issue of evaluation: To what extent should the reader sympathize with Matt? Identify some things that readers should especially consider in addressing this question.
2. Identify the argument that Richard Strout makes as he tries to keep Matt from killing him. What assumptions does Strout use? How common is his way of thinking?
3. Why does Willis help Matt take revenge? To what extent does Ruth's thinking resemble her husband's?
4. What is Matt's view of Mary Ann, his late son's girlfriend?
5. Reread the last several paragraphs. What might be the consequences of Matt's keeping his secret from his children? How does he keep a secret from his wife in the last paragraph? What might be the consequences?

☰ MAKING COMPARISONS

1. What part does guilt play in these two stories?
2. Compare the plans both killers use in the stories. How do they reflect on their mental condition?
3. Given the context of both crimes, what punishment would you judge to be appropriate?

EDWARD J. DELANEY

Clean

Edward J. Delaney (b. 1957) is a journalist and a producer of documentaries as well as a writer of fiction. Newspapers he has worked for include the Denver Post *and the* Chicago Tribune. *With Dustin Pedroia of the Boston Red Sox, he wrote the nonfiction book* Born to Play *(2009). One of his films,* The Times Were Never So Bad *(2007), is about Andre Dubus, author of the short story "Killings" that precedes this story. Delaney's works of fiction include the novels* Broken Irish *(2011) and* Warp & Weft *(2004), along with a short story collection,* The Drowning: And Other Stories *(1999). He teaches creative writing at Roger Williams University in Providence, Rhode Island. The following story appeared in the November 2012 issue of* The Atlantic *magazine.*

You think of that night endlessly from your imprisonment, the decisions made, the chain of mistakes. It had begun with your two buddies, a fifth of cheap vodka, and half a gallon of orange juice; one of these friends had suggested the confrontation. He said this kid, Barry, was cutting in on your girl—well, she wasn't even really your girl yet, the flirtation was just in its formative moments—something that you, at sixteen, had no intention of allowing.

He'd been walking home, at night. He worked at a burger place in town and, even drunk, you'd known a spot to intercept him. Again, at the suggestion of your friends. There he was, his backpack slung over his shoulder, looking at you as if not even sure who you were. You'd decided you would rough him up, and he'd decided to fight back, and you'd picked up a rock, and you'd swung it at his head. A minute later he was on the ground, dead.

You think of how, as drunk as you had been, you instantly sobered. The discussion was quick, and its determinations would last a lifetime. You waited for him to somehow come to; soon enough he was irredeemably cold. But you three had decided by then. No one would tell. No one would try to explain that the moment was one of passion and mistakes. In your long memory, telling wasn't even part of that shaky conversation, your voices all gone weepy and scared.

You took the rock, with its rime of blood, and threw it in a pond. You filled Barry's backpack with other rocks and into the pond that went, too. You were driving your old Pontiac, and the first odd decision was to drive home, go in your bedroom, and strip the top sheet off your bed, to bring it back to the scene as your buddies waited, hidden in the nearby woods with Barry, the body dragged in by the feet. You got your mother's gardening trowel from the nail in the garage. Then her garden claw.

By the time you drove up, watching for headlights, you had calmed a bit. You 5
were thinking now, your head clicking with logic and forethought that were a revelation in themselves. Your buddies had kicked the blood under dirt, and you wondered as you came back if they had been talking of turning you in. Apparently they had not.

You wrapped the body in the sheet and drove to a place you thought would work. Again, the choices made: A place close to your house, less than half a mile. But a place far enough away from other houses, and with somewhat yielding ground. The three of you, all high-school athletes, did not tire that night, rotating through the clawing and digging, going deeper, no sloppy shallow grave here. When his sheet-wrapped body went into the groundwater that had gathered at the bottom, you felt for that glorious instant as if the problem was now solved. You all filled the hole with dirt and stomped it down, then drove to the ocean at dawn and walked into the surf, fully clothed, emerging salty and bloodless.

This was '72. You think of forty years gone past, and the girl. For days after, you did the calculus, of risk and probability. You realized in that panicky first day that his wallet had gone into the ground with him; everything had not been fully considered. You and the other two never spoke of it directly again, and you weighed the human factors you could not control. You sensed, by the light of day, some shrill and growing prospect of being caught. Then you got lucky. Barry, the aspiring hippie, had been trying to get her to take off with him, hitchhiking with backpacks, cross-country. He did not get along with his parents; he craved adventure and escape. She told the police she guessed he must have gone, then she keened at her presumed abandonment. You heard about that at school and felt a surge of both relief and fury, that Barry had made the plan and that she had apparently considered it. You hated her for choosing him.

The conclusion was simple. Barry was deemed just another wandering soul, a longhair, a dreamer. He'd return in due time. The only thing was that your mother could not stop going on about the missing bedsheet. Where did it go? How do you lose a bedsheet? "Now you've broken up the set," she said. You heard her telling the neighbor about her son's mysteriously losing a sheet, and you wanted to make her stop.

The girl: Barry gone, you dated her for a few months, but found you had nothing to talk about. She turned out, in fact, to be mildly irritating, and that was that.

Senior year: Thinking back over the decades, you are appalled to consider 10
how little you worried about what had happened. In fact, you barely thought about it at all. In your mind, It (you could not bring yourself to use the more specific word) wasn't even your fault. You'd been egged on, drunk, by the other two. You met other girls, and you played your games, and you avoided the vicinity of the grave. You were an adolescent; you did not dwell on things that might ruin your fun.

Your buddies: you realized that they would not talk, even when drunk. Besides, the three of you were no longer that friendly. Typical teenagers, you all had found other interests, other friends.

College: those were the years when you needed to tell yourself what you were, and what you were not. So: You were a good person. You were not violent. Indeed, in those years you became milder and milder, almost as if shedding the ill-thought fashions of your youth like a bad sweater. Changing times. You held that memory in your stomach, but you functioned, actually, *well*. It had been three years then, and no one was going to find out. Then you went home for Thanksgiving and you saw bulldozers edged up toward that place. A new housing tract. You spent the weekend sleepless, telling yourself that even when the body emerged, the police would have no suspects, no motive. But the soft ground in which your secret lay was wetland. New environmental laws had been passed, and the housing tract stopped fewer than a hundred yards from where the body lay buried. The next spring, you told your parents you were going to stay on at your distant school, do summer classes, accelerate, and when you were done with that, you stayed on as a grad student. When those unbidden memories occurred, those predawn panics, you pushed deeper into your studies, forcing the ghosts away. You graduated with your parents and sisters smiling at your side for the picture, and then you moved farther west still.

In love, you married. Some nights you felt so intimate with her that you wanted to tell her, felt you had to. Felt she would hold your secret and love you still. But then one odd night, an awkward dinner, and you weren't so sure you two were always in tune. The marriage evened into something mellow and a bit more distant, and the impulse passed. When you had children, you tried to be good. The business flourished, and the money came in without much struggle.

Why, in your thirties, did you begin to obsess about the hidden crime? When you read the articles about DNA, and how it could tell of a long-past crime, did you begin to see a story that hadn't been completely written? You became an insomniac. You played that one minute of your life in an endless loop on the pale wall of your skull. The phone suddenly felt as if it would go off. You would see a police car thousands of miles from your hometown and feel on edge. You worried in those years that your unmasking was imminent, but then nothing happened. During the holidays, you had your parents out for a visit to a warmer climate. Sometimes, your mother would start in about the missing sheet. You'd all laugh in reminiscence.

Your father died, and you flew back to take care of things. You went through 15
his desk, sorting out his papers, tending to your mother. At the bottom of a drawer was a yellowed bit of newspaper, clipped down to a tiny headline and one-paragraph item. *Local boy reported missing.* Strangely, the photo in the paper, though blurred, didn't match the memory in your head, of that face on the side of the road, turning to meet the judgment of your headlights.

Why had your father kept this? What did he guess? Did you make noise that night as you came and went? At the funeral, a Navy ensign played taps, and your mother got the triangled flag. Your father went into that neat, nearly surgically cut hole with his own secrets. You burned the newspaper in his kettle grill on the back deck, igniting some charcoal and then making a steak.

That evening, you left your mother's house near dark and went walking in those woods. Twenty years had passed, more. You'd built a life now. In this cold ground was what would always threaten to change it. You had an exact memory of the spot he was buried, but that memory failed you, too. You could find no place that was at all like the place you remembered.

Flying home, you realized someone had to have been following all this. Were the police so sure of the hitchhiking story, even in 1972? Could they not have tried to look into it? Who was assigned to the case, and could he have known of you? But you saw no signs of any investigation. Maybe when Barry eventually did not return home, too much time had passed. Maybe they just didn't care that much. But you knew a file must have been kept at the police station, and your desire to open that file and see what was written became instantly unbearable. You were 35,000 feet in the air, over the arrayed pivot-circles of Kansas, heading toward the sun. By the time you landed, you felt the anxiety was finally over. In long-term parking, you slipped into the leather seat of your German car as if it were a glove that fit you perfectly.

In your forties, you thought of the boy less, but when the memory came to you, it gave you an unremitting ache. You could barely remember who you were then, what urges drove you, or what aspirations you'd had. The indisputable irony was that the aftermath of it all had given you focus, and direction. Who would you have become instead, if It had not happened? You also felt a welling anger at Barry himself. If he was going to leave, why didn't he just leave? Was this talk of hitchhiking just something to woo his wanted girl, or was he really going to do it? You thought about how, if he'd decamped a day sooner, or if you three had not drunk that plastic jug of orange juice and that bottle of vodka, that night would just be something forgotten, rather than a specific date on the calendar you suffered through each year, and from which you could count, to the very minute, your growing remove. The colors faded like a washed-out Kodachrome.

In the eleventh year of your marriage, you found out your wife had been having an affair. She confessed; you were shocked. Boredom, she told you tearfully. Someone else had offered escape, she said.

"I love you," she said, "but you're a dull, passionless person. You have no fire."

She was right, but now wrong. You knew who the man was. For the first time in thirty years, the familiar urge came back to you, for the same reasons. The careful decades of telling yourself you were different now crumbled, in an instant. You could have done it again, right then, had you decided to. But you did not.

Instead you got up from the couch and went out on your deck with a drink (good wine, never the hard stuff) and looked at the sky and thought about the careful, boring man you had sculpted yourself into. No passion at all. Later, your tearstained wife came out and sat with you in the wind of sunset and said she wanted to try to work things out, for your daughters. Her love of your daughters made her want to stay with you and find the middle ground. You wanted badly to offer your forgiveness, as you badly wanted forgiveness for yourself.

Yes, you'd had chances for affairs, but you always held back. Your reason wasn't strict morality, more the fear of the weight of yet another secret. The thought of that was just too heavy. You accepted life as it was, and you walked in the evening, to get air.

One night, a few years later, the phone rang and your wife held it in front of you, saying "It's Dennis." Dennis who? You heard the voice and you were back to that night. Dennis, your long-ago buddy, was not well. Lymphoma. Three or four months. He had the urge to tell, to unburden. He had thought about that night every day of his life, he said into the phone. He'd spoken of it many times over the years, he said, in the darkness of the confessional. Father Shea had told him his soul was now clean, even as it felt not.

"Dennis, I can't tell you what to do," you said to him. "We're all different people now. Do what you feel you must. I would understand."

"Thank you for that," he said. "I guess telling would be easy for me now. I'll be dead before I have to face the consequences. But I think we all should have." You had the phone to your ear, listening to him. He was a stranger. As Barry had been. Someone about whom you knew nothing.

Dennis asked about your family then, and you told him. He said he had not heard from Jeff in years, no idea where he'd gone. When you hung up, you were giddy that the secret might come out. You were surprised, and gratified, at the relief you felt. For weeks you sat at your desk and prepared things, just in case. You slept straight through each night. You got on the computer and read about juvenile law. You were all sixteen when It happened. Had the three of you gone to the police that night, explained you'd been in a fight that went out of control, you probably would have been out by the age of eighteen. Now you quietly imagined the neat rectangle of a cell, with a thin mattress. The thought didn't seem as foreboding as it had when you were young and felt the possibilities of life. This future now seemed orderly, calm. You had forgiven your wife, and you imagined and craved her own understanding. You had never given her the opportunity, never shared the secret. You concluded that this was why, in your entire life, you'd never felt true intimacy.

That night, you Googled Barry's name, and found nothing. So many years had passed; who'd remember? Where would Barry's name have been preserved? He seemed to have never existed. You remembered back in '75, when word had quietly come that his parents had moved away, some new job, or escape from worries. But now, so long after, people would remember him. You lay down in bed against your sleeping wife and felt the powerful promise of the simplicity, and the real facts of your life.

But your conversation had apparently given Dennis the peace not to speak, or perhaps he had simply died before he had a chance. No one told you anything. After a long stretch of months in which a tap did not come on your door, you went to the online obituaries and saw that he was gone. You checked on Father Shea, and he too had passed, years before. Your younger daughter walked in the room, said you looked weird, and walked out. By dinner, you were who you were again.

Later that year, your mother succumbed, the story of the missing bedsheet forever silenced. Back in town to close the house, you now did not venture into the dark woods. You and your sisters sorted things out and renewed bonds. You promised to stay in touch, knowing you probably would not.

That evening, at a hotel by the airport, you watched local TV. To your shock, you saw a vaguely familiar face. A woman, real estate. She was the girl, from all those years before. You'd nearly forgotten her name. She was, like you, an aging person. Now she sold high-end real estate, and seemed to have had some ineffectual cosmetic surgery. She had a horsey, drawn face, and wore a giant rock on her left ring finger. Did she ever think of Barry? He'd only been a boy who made her promises then went off hitchhiking, leaving her out of his adventure. You wondered about it as you tried to sleep.

You flew home and idly considered the third of you, Jeff, somewhere out there with the other half of your secret. You sat on your deck and drank some wine and watched the sun set over the Pacific. Another day had elapsed between you and that night. You had come to this place, imprisoned by what you were, what you had done, never able fully to be inside the life you made. You imagined how you would feel to just live.

The irony of getting away with something was that you were your own keeper. You were the executioner: in a pang of remorse, you could just open your mouth and change your life. You felt almost as if you would. But, greedy, you always wanted to savor one more day, even as that day turned leaden with a memory that no longer went away. It could not be put aside as it was your senior year of high school, when something that had happened the year before may as well have never happened at all. Who were you? How did you find the way to make it just not be? Now, an older man, you decided that if the time came to tell, you would edit Dennis and Jeff from the story, a small act of charity.

The vast ocean shimmered below you, endless expanses in which things 35
could be effortlessly hidden, even as what you looked at was only a knife's edge along greater stretches past the distant horizon. Even as the silver surface only whispered of the dark depths, the things you could not see. This was your life now, orderly, calm. This was how things were now. Clean. You knew you would sleep as well as one might be expected to, all of us with our own given histories. *[2012]*

THINKING ABOUT THE TEXT

1. It is fairly unusual for a story to be narrated in the second person ("you"). Why do you think Delaney uses this technique?
2. The story is entitled "Clean," and that word appears in the final paragraph. But how helpful is it as a guide to the story? Other than the ending, what specific passages does it connect to?
3. What, specifically, are the effects on the protagonist of his murder and of his failure to confess? How guilty does he seem to feel about the murder he has committed? Use specific passages to support your answer. How well does he seem to understand himself?
4. With the last words of the story—"all of us with our own given histories"—the protagonist seems to imply that many people go through comparable experiences. How typical a person does he strike you as being? Is he unusually bad? To what extent can you sympathize with him?
5. Did you think that after the phone conversation with Dennis the protagonist's secret would go public and his guilt would be revealed? Why, or why not?

MAKING COMPARISONS

1. Describe the effect of secrecy on all three killers.
2. What do you think the response would be for Matt Fowler and the narrator of "Clean" if their crimes were suddenly discovered after one year? Twenty years? Forty years?
3. Describe what you think the relationship between truth and intimacy is for Matt and "Clean's" narrator. Are secrets an impediment to relationships? Explain.

WRITING ABOUT ISSUES

1. Write an essay comparing Matt Fowler and "Clean's" narrator. Consider the crime committed, their behavior after the crime, and the idea of guilt.
2. Write an essay agreeing or disagreeing with the statement from the penultimate paragraph of "Clean": "The irony of getting away with something was that you were your own keeper." You might use the three stories here as support, your own experience, or other stories of films.
3. Recall an occasion when you agreed to keep a secret, though you felt guilty about doing so. (Choose a secret that you are willing to reveal now.) Then, write an essay in which you identify the issues that arose for you at the time. If you wish, refer to one or both of the stories in this cluster.
4. Research a real-life criminal case that is as yet unsolved — perhaps one in your local community. Then, write an essay in which you speculate about how the perpetrator(s) of this crime thinks. If you wish, refer to one or both of the stories in this cluster.

Misfit Justice: Critical Commentaries on a Story

FLANNERY O'CONNOR, "A Good Man Is Hard to Find"

CRITICAL COMMENTARIES:

FLANNERY O'CONNOR, From *Mystery and Manners*

MARTHA STEPHENS, From *The Question of Flannery O'Connor*

STEPHEN BANDY, From *"'One of My Babies': The Misfit and the Grandmother"*

JOHN DESMOND, From *"Flannery O'Connor's Misfit and the Mystery of Evil"*

Most of us are social beings; we long to fit in. The communities we form sustain us, giving us our moral compasses and our psychological bearings. But sometimes people voluntarily remove themselves from all traditional communities. Indeed, literature is filled with misfits. Their decisions may intrigue us but also perplex and trouble us, perhaps because they represent antisocial impulses in all of us. Especially interesting are those literary misfits who demand that their own sense of justice be satisfied. Probably the most notable example in post-World War II American fiction is a character in Flannery O'Connor's 1953 short story "A Good Man Is Hard to Find." This man actually calls himself The Misfit, and he turns violent as he challenges Christianity's belief in Jesus' ability to raise the dead. O'Connor's story has been widely read, in part because it is subject to various interpretations. Here, in addition to the story and O'Connor's own remarks about it, we present three critical commentaries that respond to her analysis.

BEFORE YOU READ

What do you think you might find in a story by a practicing Roman Catholic author? What topics, themes, characters, and events might she write about?

FLANNERY O'CONNOR

A Good Man Is Hard to Find

Flannery O'Connor (1925–1964) spent most of her life in Millidgeville, Georgia, where she raised peacocks on a farm with her mother. She died of lupus at the age of thirty-nine, when she was at the peak of her creative powers. All of her fiction reflects her Roman Catholic faith and Southern heritage, as do her nonfiction writings, which were collected after her death in Mystery and Manners *(1969). Critics have often seen in her work Christian parables of grace and redemption in the face of random violence. Like other Southern writers such as William Faulkner and Carson McCullers, she uses grotesque characters to suggest our own morally flawed humanity. O'Connor's early stories won her a scholarship to the University of Iowa, where she received an M.F.A. She went on to produce two novels,* Wise Blood *(1952) and* The Violent Bear It Away *(1960), but she is known and admired mostly for her short fiction. The following story was first published in the volume* Modern Writing 1 *in 1953. O'Connor then included it in her 1955 collection entitled* A Good Man Is Hard to Find and Other Stories. *The book won her national acclaim, as did a later collection, the posthumously published* Everything That Rises Must Converge *(1965). These two volumes were combined in 1979 as* The Complete Stories of Flannery O'Connor, *which won the National Book Award for fiction.*

> The dragon is by the side of the road, watching those who pass. Beware lest he devour you. We go to the Father of Souls, but it is necessary to pass by the dragon.
>
> — St. Cyril of Jerusalem

The grandmother didn't want to go to Florida. She wanted to visit some of her connections in east Tennessee and she was seizing at every chance to change Bailey's mind. Bailey was the son she lived with, her only boy. He was sitting on the edge of his chair at the table, bent over the orange sports section of the *Journal.* "Now look here, Bailey," she said, "see here, read this," and she stood

ASSOCIATED PRESS

with one hand on her thin hip and the other rattling the newspaper at his bald head. "Here this fellow that calls himself The Misfit is aloose from the Federal Pen and headed toward Florida and you read here what it says he did to these people. Just you read it. I wouldn't take my children in any direction with a criminal like that aloose in it. I couldn't answer to my conscience if I did."

Bailey didn't look up from his reading so she wheeled around then and faced the children's mother, a young woman in slacks, whose face was as broad and innocent as a cabbage and was tied around with a green head-kerchief that had two points on the top like rabbit's ears. She was sitting on the sofa, feeding the baby his apricots out of a jar. "The children have been to Florida before," the old lady said. "You all ought to take them somewhere else for a change so they would see different parts of the world and be broad. They never have been to east Tennessee."

The children's mother didn't seem to hear her but the eight-year-old boy, John Wesley, a stocky child with glasses, said, "If you don't want to go to Florida, why dontcha stay at home?" He and the little girl, June Star, were reading the funny papers on the floor.

"She wouldn't stay at home to be queen for a day," June Star said without raising her yellow head.

"Yes and what would you do if this fellow, The Misfit, caught you?" the grandmother asked.

"I'd smack his face," John Wesley said.

"She wouldn't stay at home for a million bucks," June Star said. "Afraid she'd miss something. She has to go everywhere we go."

"All right, Miss," the grandmother said. "Just remember that the next time you want me to curl your hair."

June Star said her hair was naturally curly.

The next morning the grandmother was the first one in the car, ready to go. She had her big black valise that looked like the head of a hippopotamus in one corner, and underneath it she was hiding a basket with Pitty Sing, the cat, in it. She didn't intend for the cat to be left alone in the house for three days because he would miss her too much and she was afraid he might brush against one of the gas burners and accidentally asphyxiate himself. Her son, Bailey, didn't like to arrive at a motel with a cat.

She sat in the middle of the back seat with John Wesley and June Star on either side of her. Bailey and the children's mother and the baby sat in front and they left Atlanta at eight forty-five with the mileage on the car at 55890. The grandmother wrote this down because she thought it would be interesting to say how many miles they had been when they got back. It took them twenty minutes to reach the outskirts of the city.

The old lady settled herself comfortably, removing her white cotton gloves and putting them up with her purse on the shelf in front of the back window. The children's mother still had on slacks and still had her head tied up in a green kerchief, but the grandmother had on a navy blue straw sailor hat with a bunch of white violets on the brim and a navy blue dress with a small white dot in the print. Her collars and cuffs were white organdy trimmed with lace and at her neckline she had pinned a purple spray of cloth violets containing a sachet. In case of an accident, anyone seeing her dead on the highway would know at once that she was a lady.

She said she thought it was going to be a good day for driving, neither too hot nor too cold, and she cautioned Bailey that the speed limit was fifty-five miles an hour and that the patrolmen hid themselves behind billboards and small clumps of trees and sped out after you before you had a chance to slow down. She pointed out interesting details of the scenery: Stone Mountain; the blue granite that in some places came up to both sides of the highway; the brilliant red clay banks slightly streaked with purple; and the various crops that made rows of green lacework on the ground. The trees were full of silver-white sunlight and the meanest of them sparkled. The children were reading comic magazines and their mother had gone back to sleep.

"Let's go through Georgia fast so we won't have to look at it much," John Wesley said.

"If I were a little boy," said the grandmother, "I wouldn't talk about my native 15
state that way. Tennessee has the mountains and Georgia has the hills."

"Tennessee is just a hillbilly dumping ground," John Wesley said, "and Georgia is a lousy state too."

"You said it," June Star said.

"In my time," said the grandmother, folding her thin veined fingers, "children were more respectful of their native states and their parents and everything else. People did right then. Oh look at the cute little pickaninny!" she said and pointed to a Negro child standing in the door of a shack. "Wouldn't that make a picture, now?" she asked and they all turned and looked at the little Negro out of the back window. He waved.

"He didn't have any britches on," June Star said.

"He probably didn't have any," the grandmother explained. "Little niggers in 20
the country don't have things like we do. If I could paint, I'd paint that picture," she said.

The children exchanged comic books.

The grandmother offered to hold the baby and the children's mother passed him over the front seat to her. She set him on her knee and bounced him and told him about the things they were passing. She rolled her eyes and screwed up her mouth and stuck her leathery thin face into his smooth bland one. Occasionally he gave her a faraway smile. They passed a large cotton field with five or six graves fenced in the middle of it, like a small island. "Look at the graveyard!" the grandmother said, pointing it out. "That was the old family burying ground. That belonged to the plantation."

"Where's the plantation?" John Wesley asked.

"Gone with the Wind," said the grandmother. "Ha. Ha."

When the children finished all the comic books they had brought, they 25
opened the lunch and ate it. The grandmother ate a peanut butter sandwich and an olive and would not let the children throw the box and the paper napkins out the window. When there was nothing else to do they played a game by choosing a cloud and making the other two guess what shape it suggested. John Wesley took

one the shape of a cow and June Star guessed a cow and John Wesley said, no, an automobile, and June Star said he didn't play fair, and they began to slap each other over the grandmother.

The grandmother said she would tell them a story if they would keep quiet. When she told a story, she rolled her eyes and waved her head and was very dramatic. She said once when she was a maiden lady she had been courted by a Mr. Edgar Atkins Teagarden from Jasper, Georgia. She said he was a very good-looking man and a gentleman and that he brought her a watermelon every Saturday afternoon with his initials cut in it, E. A. T. Well, one Saturday, she said, Mr. Teagarden brought the watermelon and there was nobody at home and he left it on the front porch and returned in his buggy to Jasper, but she never got the watermelon, she said, because a nigger boy ate it when he saw the initials, E. A. T.! This story tickled John Wesley's funny bone and he giggled and giggled but June Star didn't think it was any good. She said she wouldn't marry a man that just brought her a watermelon on Saturday. The grandmother said she would have done well to marry Mr. Teagarden because he was a gentleman and had bought Coca-Cola stock when it first came out and that he had died only a few years ago, a very wealthy man.

They stopped at The Tower for barbecued sandwiches. The Tower was a part stucco and part wood filling station and dance hall set in a clearing outside of Timothy. A fat man named Red Sammy Butts ran it and there were signs stuck here and there on the building and for miles up and down the highway saying, TRY RED SAMMY'S FAMOUS BARBECUE. NONE LIKE FAMOUS RED SAMMY'S! RED SAM! THE FAT BOY WITH THE HAPPY LAUGH. A VETERAN! RED SAMMY'S YOUR MAN!

Red Sammy was lying on the bare ground outside The Tower with his head under a truck while a gray monkey about a foot high, chained to a small chinaberry tree, chattered nearby. The monkey sprang back into the tree and got on the highest limb as soon as he saw the children jump out of the car and run toward him.

Inside, The Tower was a long dark room with a counter at one end and tables at the other and dancing space in the middle. They all sat down at a board table next to the nickelodeon and Red Sam's wife, a tall burnt-brown woman with hair and eyes lighter than her skin, came and took their order. The children's mother put a dime in the machine and played "The Tennessee Waltz," and the grandmother said that tune always made her want to dance. She asked Bailey if he would like to dance but he only glared at her. He didn't have a naturally sunny disposition like she did and trips made him nervous. The grandmother's brown eyes were very bright. She swayed her head from side to side and pretended she was dancing in her chair. June Star said play something she could tap to so the children's mother put in another dime and played a fast number and June Star stepped out onto the dance floor and did her tap routine.

"Ain't she cute?" Red Sam's wife said, leaning over the counter. "Would you like to come be my little girl?" 30

"No I certainly wouldn't," June Star said. "I wouldn't live in a broken-down place like this for a million bucks!" and she ran back to the table.

"Ain't she cute?" the woman repeated, stretching her mouth politely.

"Aren't you ashamed?" hissed the grandmother.

Red Sam came in and told his wife to quit lounging on the counter and hurry up with these people's order. His khaki trousers reached just to his hip bones and his stomach hung over them like a sack of meal swaying under his shirt. He came over and sat down at a table nearby and let out a combination sigh and yodel. "You can't win," he said. "You can't win," and he wiped his sweating red face off with a gray handkerchief. "These days you don't know who to trust," he said. "Ain't that the truth?"

"People are certainly not nice like they used to be," said the grandmother. 35

"Two fellers come in here last week," Red Sammy said, "driving a Chrysler. It was a old beat-up car but it was a good one and these boys looked all right to me. Said they worked at the mill and you know I let them fellers charge the gas they bought? Now why did I do that?"

"Because you're a good man!" the grandmother said at once.

"Yes'm, I suppose so," Red Sam said as if he were struck with this answer.

His wife brought the orders, carrying the five plates all at once without a tray, two in each hand and one balanced on her arm. "It isn't a soul in this green world of God's that you can trust," she said. "And I don't count nobody out of that, not nobody," she repeated, looking at Red Sammy.

"Did you read about that criminal, The Misfit, that's escaped?" asked the grandmother.

"I wouldn't be a bit surprised if he didn't attack this place right here," said 40
the woman. "If he hears about it being here, I wouldn't be none surprised to see him. If he hears it's two cent in the cash register, I wouldn't be a tall surprised if he . . ."

"That'll do," Red Sam said. "Go bring these people their Co'-Colas," and the woman went off to get the rest of the order.

"A good man is hard to find," Red Sammy said. "Everything is getting terrible. I remember the day you could go off and leave your screen door unlatched. Not no more."

He and the grandmother discussed better times. The old lady said that in her opinion Europe was entirely to blame for the way things were now. She said the way Europe acted you would think we were made of money and Red Sam said it was no use talking about it, she was exactly right. The children ran outside into the white sunlight and looked at the monkey in the lacy chinaberry tree. He was busy catching fleas on himself and biting each one carefully between his teeth as if it were a delicacy.

They drove off again into the hot afternoon. The grandmother took cat naps 45
and woke up every few minutes with her own snoring. Outside of Toombsboro she woke up and recalled an old plantation that she had visited in this neighborhood once when she was a young lady. She said the house had six white columns across the front and that there was an avenue of oaks leading up to it and two little wooden trellis arbors on either side in front where you sat down with your suitor after a stroll in the garden. She recalled exactly which road to turn off to get to it. She knew that Bailey would not be willing to lose any time looking at an

old house, but the more she talked about it, the more she wanted to see it once again and find out if the little twin arbors were still standing. "There was a secret panel in this house," she said craftily, not telling the truth but wishing that she were, "and the story went that all the family silver was hidden in it when Sherman came through but it was never found . . ."

"Hey!" John Wesley said. "Let's go see it! We'll find it! We'll poke all the woodwork and find it! Who lives there? Where do you turn off at? Hey Pop, can't we turn off there?"

"We never have seen a house with a secret panel!" June Star shrieked. "Let's go to the house with the secret panel! Hey Pop, can't we go see the house with the secret panel!"

"It's not far from here, I know," the grandmother said. "It wouldn't take over twenty minutes."

Bailey was looking straight ahead. His jaw was as rigid as a horseshoe. "No," he said.

The children began to yell and scream that they wanted to see the house with the secret panel. John Wesley kicked the back of the front seat and June Star hung over her mother's shoulder and whined desperately into her ear that they never had any fun even on their vacation, that they could never do what THEY wanted to do. The baby began to scream and John Wesley kicked the back of the seat so hard that his father could feel the blows in his kidney.

"All right!" he shouted and drew the car to a stop at the side of the road. "Will you all shut up? Will you all just shut up for one second? If you don't shut up, we won't go anywhere."

"It would be very educational for them," the grandmother murmured.

"All right," Bailey said, "but get this: this is the only time we're going to stop for anything like this. This is the one and only time."

"The dirt road that you have to turn down is about a mile back," the grandmother directed. "I marked it when we passed."

"A dirt road," Bailey groaned.

After they had turned around and were headed toward the dirt road, the grandmother recalled other points about the house, the beautiful glass over the front doorway and the candle-lamp in the hall. John Wesley said that the secret panel was probably in the fireplace.

"You can't go inside this house," Bailey said. "You don't know who lives there."

"While you all talk to the people in front, I'll run around behind and get in a window," John Wesley suggested.

"We'll all stay in the car," his mother said.

They turned onto the dirt road and the car raced roughly along in a swirl of pink dust. The grandmother recalled the times when there were no paved roads and thirty miles was a day's journey. The dirt road was hilly and there were sudden washes in it and sharp curves on dangerous embankments. All at once they would be on a hill, looking down over the blue tops of trees for miles around, then the next minute, they would be in a red depression with the dust-coated trees looking down on them.

"This place had better turn up in a minute," Bailey said, "or I'm going to turn around."

The road looked as if no one had traveled on it in months.

"It's not much farther," the grandmother said and just as she said it, a horrible thought came to her. The thought was so embarrassing that she turned red in the face and her eyes dilated and her feet jumped up, upsetting her valise in the corner. The instant the valise moved, the newspaper top she had over the basket under it rose with a snarl and Pitty Sing, the cat, sprang onto Bailey's shoulder.

The children were thrown to the floor and their mother, clutching the baby, was thrown out the door onto the ground; the old lady was thrown into the front seat. The car turned over once and landed right-side-up in a gulch off the side of the road. Bailey remained in the driver's seat with the cat—gray-striped with a broad white face and an orange nose—clinging to his neck like a caterpillar.

As soon as the children saw they could move their arms and legs, they scram- 65
bled out of the car, shouting, "We've had an ACCIDENT!" The grandmother was curled up under the dashboard, hoping she was injured so that Bailey's wrath would not come down on her all at once. The horrible thought she had had before the accident was that the house she had remembered so vividly was not in Georgia but in Tennessee.

Bailey removed the cat from his neck with both hands and flung it out the window against the side of a pine tree. Then he got out of the car and started looking for the children's mother. She was sitting against the side of the red gutted ditch, holding the screaming baby, but she only had a cut down her face and a broken shoulder. "We've had an ACCIDENT!" the children screamed in a frenzy of delight.

"But nobody's killed," June Star said with disappointment as the grandmother limped out of the car, her hat still pinned to her head but the broken front brim standing up at a jaunty angle and the violet spray hanging off the side. They all sat down in the ditch, except the children, to recover from the shock. They were all shaking.

"Maybe a car will come along," said the children's mother hoarsely.

"I believe I have injured an organ," said the grandmother, pressing her side, but no one answered her. Bailey's teeth were clattering. He had on a yellow sport shirt with bright blue parrots designed in it and his face was as yellow as the shirt. The grandmother decided that she would not mention that the house was in Tennessee.

The road was about ten feet above and they could only see the tops of the 70
trees on the other side of it. Behind the ditch they were sitting in there were more woods, tall and dark and deep. In a few minutes they saw a car some distance away on top of a hill, coming slowly as if the occupants were watching them. The grandmother stood up and waved both arms dramatically to attract their attention. The car continued to come on slowly, disappeared around a bend and appeared again, moving even slower, on top of the hill they had gone over. It was a big black battered hearse-like automobile. There were three men in it.

It came to a stop just over them and for some minutes, the driver looked down with a steady expressionless gaze to where they were sitting, and didn't speak. Then he turned his head and muttered something to the other two and they got out. One was a fat boy in black trousers and a red sweat shirt with a silver stallion embossed on the front of it. He moved around on the right side of them and stood staring, his mouth partly open in a kind of loose grin. The other had on khaki pants and a blue striped coat and a gray hat pulled very low, hiding most of his face. He came around slowly on the left side. Neither spoke.

The driver got out of the car and stood by the side of it, looking down at them. He was an older man than the other two. His hair was just beginning to gray and he wore silver-rimmed spectacles that gave him a scholarly look. He had a long creased face and didn't have on any shirt or undershirt. He had on blue jeans that were too tight for him and was holding a black hat and a gun. The two boys also had guns.

"We've had an ACCIDENT!" the children screamed.

The grandmother had the peculiar feeling that the bespectacled man was someone she knew. His face was as familiar to her as if she had known him all her life but she could not recall who he was. He moved away from the car and began to come down the embankment, placing his feet carefully so that he wouldn't slip. He had on tan and white shoes and no socks, and his ankles were red and thin. "Good afternoon," he said. "I see you all had you a little spill."

"We turned over twice!" said the grandmother.

"Oncet," he corrected. "We seen it happen. Try their car and see will it run, Hiram," he said quietly to the boy with the gray hat.

"What you got that gun for?" John Wesley asked. "Whatcha gonna do with that gun?"

"Lady," the man said to the children's mother, "would you mind calling them children to sit down by you? Children make me nervous. I want all you all to sit down right together there where you're at."

"What are you telling US what to do for?" June Star asked.

Behind them the line of woods gaped like a dark open mouth. "Come here," said the mother.

"Look here now," Bailey began suddenly, "we're in a predicament! We're in . . ."

The grandmother shrieked. She scrambled to her feet and stood staring. "You're The Misfit!" she said. "I recognized you at once!"

"Yes'm," the man said, smiling slightly as if he were pleased in spite of himself to be known, "but it would have been better for all of you, lady, if you hadn't of reckernized me."

Bailey turned his head sharply and said something to his mother that shocked even the children. The old lady began to cry and The Misfit reddened.

"Lady," he said, "don't you get upset. Sometimes a man says things he don't mean. I don't reckon he meant to talk to you thataway."

"You wouldn't shoot a lady, would you?" the grandmother said and removed a clean handkerchief from her cuff and began to slap at her eyes with it.

The Misfit pointed the toe of his shoe into the ground and made a little hole and then covered it up again. "I would hate to have to," he said.

"Listen," the grandmother almost screamed, "I know you're a good man. You don't look a bit like you have common blood. I know you must come from nice people!"

"Yes mam," he said, "finest people in the world." When he smiled he showed a row of strong white teeth. "God never made a finer woman than my mother and my daddy's heart was pure gold," he said. The boy with the red sweat shirt had come around behind them and was standing with his gun at his hip. The Misfit squatted down on the ground. "Watch them children, Bobby Lee," he said. "You know they make me nervous." He looked at the six of them huddled together in front of him and he seemed to be embarrassed as if he couldn't think of anything to say. "Ain't a cloud in the sky," he remarked, looking up at it. "Don't see no sun but don't see no cloud neither."

"Yes, it's a beautiful day," said the grandmother. "Listen," she said, "you shouldn't call yourself The Misfit because I know you're a good man at heart. I can just look at you and tell."

"Hush!" Bailey yelled. "Hush! Everybody shut up and let me handle this!" He was squatting in the position of a runner about to sprint forward but he didn't move.

"I pre-chate that, lady," The Misfit said and drew a little circle in the ground with the butt of his gun.

"It'll take a half a hour to fix this here car," Hiram called, looking over the raised hood of it.

"Well, first you and Bobby Lee get him and that little boy to step over yonder with you," The Misfit said, pointing to Bailey and John Wesley. "The boys want to ast you something," he said to Bailey. "Would you mind stepping back in them woods there with them?"

"Listen," Bailey began, "we're in a terrible predicament! Nobody realizes what this is," and his voice cracked. His eyes were as blue and intense as the parrots in his shirt and he remained perfectly still.

The grandmother reached up to adjust her hat brim as if she were going to the woods with him but it came off in her hand. She stood staring at it and after a second she let it fall on the ground. Hiram pulled Bailey up by the arm as if he were assisting an old man. John Wesley caught hold of his father's hand and Bobby Lee followed. They went off toward the woods and just as they reached the dark edge, Bailey turned and supporting himself against a gray naked pine trunk, he shouted, "I'll be back in a minute, Mamma, wait on me!"

"Come back this instant!" his mother shrilled but they all disappeared into the woods.

"Bailey Boy!" the grandmother called in a tragic voice but she found she was looking at The Misfit squatting on the ground in front of her. "I just know you're a good man," she said desperately. "You're not a bit common!"

"Nome, I ain't a good man," The Misfit said after a second as if he had considered her statement carefully, "but I ain't the worst in the world neither. My daddy said I was a different breed of dog from my brothers and sisters. 'You know,' Daddy said, 'it's some that can live their whole life out without asking about it and it's others has to know why it is, and this boy is one of the latters.

He's going to be into everything!' " He put on his black hat and looked up suddenly and then away deep into the woods as if he were embarrassed again. "I'm sorry I don't have on a shirt before you ladies," he said, hunching his shoulders slightly. "We buried our clothes that we had on when we escaped and we're just making do until we can get better. We borrowed these from some folks we met," he explained.

"That's perfectly all right," the grandmother said. "Maybe Bailey has an extra shirt in his suitcase."

"I'll look and see terrectly," The Misfit said.

"Where are they taking him?" the children's mother screamed.

"Daddy was a card himself," The Misfit said. "You couldn't put anything over on him. He never got in trouble with the Authorities though. Just had the knack of handling them."

"You could be honest too if you'd only try," said the grandmother. "Think how wonderful it would be to settle down and live a comfortable life and not have to think about somebody chasing you all the time."

The Misfit kept scratching in the ground with the butt of his gun as if he were thinking about it. "Yes'm, somebody is always after you," he murmured.

The grandmother noticed how thin his shoulder blades were just behind his hat because she was standing up looking down at him. "Do you ever pray?" she asked.

He shook his head. All she saw was the black hat wiggle between his shoulder blades. "Nome," he said.

There was a pistol shot from the woods, followed closely by another. Then silence. The old lady's head jerked around. She could hear the wind move through the tree tops like a long satisfied insuck of breath. "Bailey Boy!" she called.

"I was a gospel singer for a while," The Misfit said. "I been most everything. Been in the arm service, both land and sea, at home and abroad, been twict married, been an undertaker, been with the railroads, plowed Mother Earth, been in a tornado, seen a man burnt alive oncet," and he looked up at the children's mother and the little girl who were sitting close together, their faces white and their eyes glassy; "I even seen a woman flogged," he said.

"Pray, pray," the grandmother began, "pray, pray . . ."

"I never was a bad boy that I remember of," The Misfit said in an almost dreamy voice, "but somewheres along the line I done something wrong and got sent to the penitentiary. I was buried alive," and he looked up and held her attention to him by a steady stare.

"That's when you should have started to pray," she said. "What did you do to get sent to the penitentiary, that first time?"

"Turn to the right, it was a wall," The Misfit said, looking up again at the cloudless sky. "Turn to the left, it was a wall. Look up it was a ceiling, look down it was a floor. I forgot what I done, lady. I set there and set there, trying to remember what it was I done and I ain't recalled it to this day. Oncet in a while, I would think it was coming to me, but it never come."

"Maybe they put you in by mistake," the old lady said vaguely.

"Nome," he said. "It wasn't no mistake. They had the papers on me." 115

"You must have stolen something," she said.

The Misfit sneered slightly. "Nobody had nothing I wanted," he said. "It was a head-doctor at the penitentiary said what I had done was kill my daddy but I known that for a lie. My daddy died in nineteen ought nineteen of the epidemic flu and I never had a thing to do with it. He was buried in the Mount Hopewell Baptist churchyard and you can go there and see for yourself."

"If you would pray," the old lady said, "Jesus would help you."

"That's right," The Misfit said.

"Well then, why don't you pray?" she asked trembling with delight suddenly. 120

"I don't want no hep," he said. "I'm doing all right by myself."

Bobby Lee and Hiram came ambling back from the woods. Bobby Lee was dragging a yellow shirt with bright blue parrots in it.

"Thow me that shirt, Bobby Lee," The Misfit said. The shirt came flying at him and landed on his shoulder and he put it on. The grandmother couldn't name what the shirt reminded her of. "No, lady," The Misfit said while he was buttoning it up, "I found out the crime don't matter. You can do one thing or you can do another, kill a man or take a tire off his car, because sooner or later you're going to forget what it was you done and just be punished for it."

The children's mother had begun to make heaving noises as if she couldn't get her breath. "Lady," he asked, "would you and that little girl like to step off yonder with Bobby Lee and Hiram and join your husband?"

"Yes, thank you," the mother said faintly. Her left arm dangled helplessly and 125
she was holding the baby, who had gone to sleep, in the other. "Hep that lady up, Hiram," The Misfit said as she struggled to climb out of the ditch, "and Bobby Lee, you hold onto that little girl's hand."

"I don't want to hold hands with him," June Star said. "He reminds me of a pig."

The fat boy blushed and laughed and caught her by the arm and pulled her off into the woods after Hiram and her mother.

Alone with The Misfit, the grandmother found that she had lost her voice. There was not a cloud in the sky nor any sun. There was nothing around her but woods. She wanted to tell him that he must pray. She opened and closed her mouth several times before anything came out. Finally she found herself saying, "Jesus. Jesus," meaning, Jesus will help you, but the way she was saying it, it sounded as if she might be cursing.

"Yes'm," The Misfit said as if he agreed. "Jesus thown everything off balance. It was the same case with Him as with me except He hadn't committed any crime and they could prove I had committed one because they had the papers on me. Of course," he said, "they never shown me my papers. That's why I sign myself now. I said long ago, you get you a signature and sign everything you do and keep a copy of it. Then you'll know what you done and you can hold up the crime to the punishment and see do they match and in the end you'll have something to prove you ain't been treated right. I call myself The Misfit," he said, "because I can't make what all I done wrong fit what all I gone through in punishment."

There was a piercing scream from the woods, followed closely by a pistol 130
report. "Does it seem right to you, lady, that one is punished a heap and another ain't punished at all?"

"Jesus!" the old lady cried. "You've got good blood! I know you wouldn't shoot a lady! I know you come from nice people! Pray! Jesus, you ought not to shoot a lady. I'll give you all the money I've got!"

"Lady," The Misfit said, looking beyond her far into the woods, "there never was a body that give the undertaker a tip."

There were two more pistol reports and the grandmother raised her head like a parched old turkey hen crying for water and called, "Bailey Boy, Bailey Boy!" as if her heart would break.

"Jesus was the only One that ever raised the dead," The Misfit continued, "and He shouldn't have done it. He thown everything off balance. If He did what He said, then it's nothing for you to do but thow away everything and follow Him, and if He didn't, then it's nothing for you to do but enjoy the few minutes you got left the best you can — by killing somebody or burning down his house or doing some other meanness to him. No pleasure but meanness," he said and his voice had become almost a snarl.

"Maybe He didn't raise the dead," the old lady mumbled, not knowing what 135
she was saying and feeling so dizzy that she sank down in the ditch with her legs twisted under her.

"I wasn't there so I can't say He didn't," The Misfit said. "I wisht I had of been there," he said, hitting the ground with his fist. "It ain't right I wasn't there because if I had of been there I would of known. Listen lady," he said in a high voice, "if I had of been there I would of known and I wouldn't be like I am now." His voice seemed about to crack and the grandmother's head cleared for an instant. She saw the man's face twisted close to her own as if he were going to cry and she murmured, "Why you're one of my babies. You're one of my own children!" She reached out and touched him on the shoulder. The Misfit sprang back as if a snake had bitten him and shot her three times through the chest. Then he put his gun down on the ground and took off his glasses and began to clean them.

Hiram and Bobby Lee returned from the woods and stood over the ditch, looking down at the grandmother who half sat and half lay in a puddle of blood with her legs crossed under her like a child's and her face smiling up at the cloudless sky.

Without his glasses, The Misfit's eyes were red-rimmed and pale and defenseless-looking. "Take her off and thow her where you thown the others," he said, picking up the cat that was rubbing itself against his leg.

"She was a talker, wasn't she?" Bobby Lee said, sliding down the ditch with a yodel.

"She would of been a good woman," The Misfit said, "if it had been some- 140
body there to shoot her every minute of her life."

"Some fun!" Bobby Lee said.

"Shut up, Bobby Lee," The Misfit said. "It's no real pleasure in life." *[1955]*

THINKING ABOUT THE TEXT

1. Although this story begins with comedy, ultimately it shocks many readers. Did it shock you? Why, or why not? What would you say to someone who argues that the shift in tone is a flaw in the story?
2. Note places where the word *good* comes up in this story. How is it defined? Do the definitions change? Do you think the author has in mind a definition that does not occur to the characters? If so, what might that definition be?
3. What in his life history is The Misfit unsure about? Why do you think he is hazy about these matters? Should O'Connor have resolved for us all the issues of fact that bother him? Why, or why not?
4. Does The Misfit have any redeeming qualities? Does the grandmother? Explain. What do you think the grandmother means when she murmurs, "Why you're one of my babies. You're one of my own children!" (para. 136)? Why do you think The Misfit responds as he does?
5. There is much talk about Jesus and Christianity in this story. Should O'Connor have done more to help non-Christian readers see the story as relevant to them? Explain your reasoning.

FLANNERY O'CONNOR

From *Mystery and Manners*

For public presentations at colleges and other places, Flannery O'Connor often chose to read and comment on "A Good Man Is Hard to Find." The following remarks come from her introduction to the story when she read it at Hollins College in Virginia in 1963. After her death, the introduction was published as "On Her Own Work" in Mystery and Manners, *a 1969 collection of O'Connor's nonfiction pieces. Her comments on "A Good Man Is Hard to Find" encourage a religious analysis of it. How helpful, though, is her own interpretation? Many critics who have subsequently written about the story have raised and addressed this issue.*

It is true that the old lady is a hypocritical old soul; her wits are no match for the Misfit's, nor is her capacity for grace equal to his; yet I think the unprejudiced reader will feel that the Grandmother has a special kind of triumph in this story which instinctively we do not allow to someone altogether bad.

I often ask myself what makes a story work and what makes it hold up as a story, and I have decided that it is probably some action, some gesture of a character that is unlike any other in the story, one which indicates where the real heart of the story lies. This would have to be an action or a gesture which was both totally right and totally unexpected; it would have to be one that was both in character and beyond character; it would have to suggest both the world and eternity. The action or gesture I'm talking about would have to be on the anagogical level, that is, the level which has to do with the Divine life and our participation in it. It would be a gesture that transcended any neat allegory that might have been intended or any pat moral categories a reader could make. It would be a gesture which somehow made contact with mystery.

There is a point in this story where such a gesture occurs. The Grandmother is at last alone, facing the Misfit. Her head clears for an instant and she realizes, even in her limited way, that she is responsible for the man before her and joined to him by ties of kinship which have their roots deep in the mystery she has been merely prattling about so far. And at this point, she does the right thing, she makes the right gesture.

I find that students are often puzzled by what she says and does here, but I think myself that if I took out this gesture and what she says with it, I would have no story. What was left would not be worth your attention. Our age not only does not have a very sharp eye for the almost imperceptible intrusions of grace, it no longer has much feeling for the nature of the violences which precede and follow them. The devil's greatest wile, Baudelaire has said, is to convince us that he does not exist.

I suppose the reasons for the use of so much violence in modern fiction will 5
differ with each writer who uses it, but in my own stories I have found that violence is strangely capable of returning my characters to reality and preparing them to accept their moment of grace. Their heads are so hard that almost nothing else will do the work. This idea, that reality is something to which we must be returned at considerable cost, is one which is seldom understood by the casual reader, but it is one which is implicit in the Christian view of the world.

I don't want to equate the Misfit with the devil. I prefer to think that, however unlikely this may seem, the old lady's gesture, like the mustard-seed, will grow to be a great crow-filled tree in the Misfit's heart and will be enough of a pain to him there to turn him into the prophet he was meant to become. But that's another story.

This story has been called grotesque, but I prefer to call it literal. A good story is literal in the same sense that a child's drawing is literal. When a child draws, he doesn't intend to distort but to set down exactly what he sees, and as his gaze is direct, he sees the lines that create motion. Now the lines of motion that interest the writer are usually invisible. They are lines of spiritual motion. And in this story you should be on the lookout for such things as the action of grace in the Grandmother's soul, and not for the dead bodies. *[1963]*

MARTHA STEPHENS

From *The Question of Flannery O'Connor*

Martha Stephens is professor emeritus of English and comparative literature at the University of Cincinnati. After Flannery O'Connor's religious explanation of "A Good Man Is Hard to Find" was published in the 1969 volume Mystery and Manners, *other readers of the story began responding to her comments. Stephens's 1973 book* The Question of Flannery O'Connor *includes one of the earliest attempts to gauge the helpfulness of O'Connor's analysis. Stephens is disturbed by the story's apparent shift of tone as it moves from farce to violent tragedy. O'Connor's remarks clarify this shift, Stephens thinks, but the religious doctrine reflected in them is severe.*

An ordinary and undistinguished family, a family even comical in its dullness, ill-naturedness, and triviality, sets out on a trip to Florida and on an ordinary summer day meets with a terrible fate. In what would the interest of such a story normally lie? Perhaps, one might think, in something that is revealed about the family in the way it meets its death, in some ironical or interesting truth about the nature of those people or those relationships—something we had been prepared unbeknownst to see, at the end plainly dramatized by their final common travail and death. But obviously, as regards the family as a whole, no such thing happens. The family is shown to be in death just as ordinary and ridiculous as before. With the possible exception of the grandmother, we know them no better; nothing about them of particular significance is brought forth.

The grandmother, being as we have seen the last to die, suffers the deaths of all her family while carrying on the intermittent conversation with the Misfit, and any reader will have some dim sense that it is through this encounter that the story is trying to transform and justify itself. One senses that this conversation—even though our attention is in reality fastened upon the horrible acts that are taking place in the background (and apparently against the thrust of the story)—is meant to be the real center of the story and the part in which the "point," as it were, of the whole tale lies.

But what is the burden of that queer conversation between the Misfit and the grandmother; what power does it have, even when we retrospectively sift and weigh it line by line, to transform our attitude towards the seemingly gratuitous—in terms of the art of the tale—horror of the massacre? The uninitiated reader will not, most likely, be able to unravel the strange complaint of the killer without some difficulty, but when we see the convict's peculiar dilemma in the context of O'Connor's whole work and what is known of her religious thought, it is not difficult to explain.

The Misfit's most intriguing statement—the line that seemingly the reader must ponder, set as it is as the final pronouncement on the grandmother after her death—is from the final passage . . . : "She would of been a good woman if it had been somebody there to shoot her every minute of her life." Certainly we know from the first half of the story that the grandmother has seen herself as a good woman—and a good woman in a day when good men and women are hard to find, when people are disrespectful and dishonest, when they are not nice like they used to be. The grandmother is not common but a lady; and at the end of the story we know that she will be found dead just as we know she wanted to be—in the costume of a lady. She was not common, and the Misfit, with his "scholarly spectacles," his courtly apology for not wearing a shirt, his yes ma'ams and no ma'ams, was not common either—she had believed, wanted to believe, or pretended to believe. "Why I can see you come from good people," she said, "not common at all." Yet the Misfit says of her that she *would* have been a good woman if somebody had been there to shoot her all her life. And if we take the Misfit's statement as the right one about the grandmother, how was she a good woman in her death?

A good woman, perhaps we are given to believe, is one who understands the 5
worthlessness and emptiness of being or not being a "lady," of having or not having Coca-Cola stock, of "being broad" and seeing the world, of good manners and genteel attire. "Woe to them," said Isaiah, "that are wise in their own eyes, and prudent in their own sight." The futility of all the grandmother's values, the story strives to encapsulate in this image of her disarray after the car has overturned and she has recognized the Misfit: "The grandmother reached up to adjust her hat brim as if she were going to the woods with him but it came off in her hand. She stood staring at it and after a second she let it fall on the ground."

The Misfit is a figure that seems, one must say to the story's credit, to have fascinated more readers than any other single O'Connor character, and it is by contrast with the tormented spiritual state of this seeming monster that the nature of the grandmother's futile values becomes evident. We learn that the center of the Misfit's thought has always been Jesus Christ, and what becomes clear as we study over the final scene is that the Misfit has, in the eyes of the author, the enormous distinction of having at least faced up to the problem of Christian belief. And everything he has done—everything he so monstrously does here—proceeds from his inability to accept Christ, to truly believe. This is the speech which opens the narrow and emotionally difficult route into the meaning of the story:

> "Jesus was the only One that ever raised the dead," The Misfit continued, "and He shouldn't have done it. He thown everything off balance. If He did what He said, then it's nothing for you to do but thow away everything and follow Him, and if He didn't, then it's nothing for you to do but enjoy the few minutes you got left the best way you can—by killing somebody or burning down his house or doing some other meanness to him. No pleasure but meanness," he said and his voice had become almost a snarl.

The Misfit has chosen, at least, whom he would serve—has followed the injunction of the prophet in I Kings 18:21: "And Elijah came unto all the people, and said, How long halt ye between two opinions? if the Lord be God, follow him: but if Baal, then follow him." The crucial modern text for the authorial view here, which belongs to a tradition in religio-literary thought sometimes referred to as the sanctification of the sinner, is T. S. Eliot's essay on Baudelaire, in which he states: "So far as we are human, what we do must be either evil or good; so far as we do evil or good, we are human; and it is better, in a paradoxical way, to do evil than to do nothing; at least, we exist. It is true that the glory of man is his capacity for salvation; it is also true to say that his glory is his capacity for damnation."

Thus observe how, in the context of these statements, "A Good Man Is Hard to Find" begins to yield its meaning. What O'Connor has done is to take, in effect, Eliot's maxim—"It is better, in a paradoxical way, to do evil than to do nothing"—and to stretch our tolerance of this idea to its limits. The conclusion that one cannot avoid is that the story depends, for its final effect, on our being able to appreciate—even to be startled by, to be pleasurably struck with—the notion of the essential moral superiority of the Misfit over his victims, who have lived without choice or commitment of any kind, who have in effect not "lived" at all.

But again, in what sense is the grandmother a "good woman" in her death, as the Misfit claims? Here even exegesis falters. Because in her terror she calls on the name of Jesus, because she exhorts the Misfit to pray? Is she "good" because as the old lady sinks fainting into the ditch, after the Misfit's Jesus speech recorded above, she mumbles, "Maybe he didn't raise the dead"? Are we to see her as at last beginning to face the central question of human existence: did God send his son to save the world? Perhaps there is a clue in the dead grandmother's final image: she is said to half lie and half sit "in a puddle of blood with her legs crossed under her like a child's and her face smiling up at the cloudless sky." For Christ said, after all, that "whosoever shall not receive the kingdom of God as a little child shall in no wise enter herein."

To see that the Misfit is really the one courageous and admirable figure in the story; that the grandmother was perhaps — even as he said — a better woman in her death than she had ever been; to see that the pain of the other members of the family, that any godless pain or pleasure that human beings may experience is, beside the one great question of existence, *unimportant* — to see all these things is to enter fully into the experience of the story. Not to see them is to find oneself pitted not only against the forces that torture and destroy the wretched subjects of the story, but against the story itself and its attitude of indifference to and contempt for human pain.

10 Now as it happens, "A Good Man Is Hard to Find" was a favorite story of O'Connor's. It was the story she chose to read whenever she was asked to read from her work, and clearly it held a meaning for her that was particularly important. Whenever she read the story, she closed by reading a statement giving her own explanation of it. (One version of that statement can now be read in the collection of O'Connor's incidental prose edited by Robert and Sally Fitzgerald titled *Mystery and Manners*.) She had come to realize that it was a story that readers found difficult, and she said in her statement that she felt that the reason the story was misunderstood was that the present age "not only does not have a very sharp eye for the almost imperceptible intrusions of grace, it no longer has much feeling for the nature of the violences which precede and follow them." The intrusion of grace in "A Good Man Is Hard to Find" comes, Miss O'Connor said, in that much-discussed passage in which the grandmother, her head suddenly clearing for a moment, murmurs to the Misfit, "Why, you're one of my babies. You're one of my own children!" and is shot just as she reaches out to touch him. The grandmother's gesture here is what, according to O'Connor, makes the story work; it shows that the grandmother realizes that "she is responsible for the man before her and joined to him by ties of kinship which have their roots deep in the mystery she has been merely prattling about so far," and it affords the grandmother "a special kind of triumph . . . which we instinctively do not allow to someone altogether bad."

This explanation does solve, in a sense, one of the riddles of this odd story — although, of course, one must say that while it is interesting to know the intent of the author, speaking outside the story and after the fact, such knowledge does not change the fact that the intent of the narrator manifested strictly within the story is damagingly unclear on this important point. And what is even more important here is that O'Connor's statement about the story, taken as a whole, only further confirms the fact that the only problem in this tale is really a function of our difficulty with O'Connor's formidable doctrine. About the Misfit, O'Connor says that while he is not to be seen as the hero of the story, yet his capacity for grace is far greater than the grandmother's and that the author herself prefers to think "that the old lady's gesture, like the mustard-seed, will grow to be a great crow-filled tree in the Misfit's heart, and will be enough of a pain to him there to turn him into the prophet he was meant to become." The capacity for grace of the other members of the family is apparently zero, and hence—Christian grace in O'Connor, one cannot help noting, is rather an expensive process—it is proper that their deaths should have no spiritual context whatever. *[1973]*

STEPHEN BANDY

From *"One of My Babies": The Misfit and the Grandmother*

In an article published in a 1996 issue of Studies in Short Fiction, *Stephen Bandy strongly disagrees with O'Connor's interpretation of "A Good Man Is Hard to Find." In particular, he thinks that the grandmother is sentimental and vindictive, whereas O'Connor is sympathetic to the character and believes that she manifests grace. Following are excerpts from Bandy's analysis.*

Grasping at any appeal, and hardly aware of what she is saying, the Grandmother declares to the Misfit: " 'Why you're one of my babies. You're one of my own children!' " As she utters these shocking words, "She reached out and touched him on the shoulder. The Misfit sprang back as if a snake had bitten him and shot her three times through the chest."

Noting that some squeamish readers had found this ending too strong, O'Connor defended the scene in this way: "If I took out this gesture and what she says with it, I would have no story. What was left would not be worth your attention" (*Mystery and Manners* 112).[1] Certainly the scene is crucial to the story, and most readers, I think, grant its dramatic "rightness" as a conclusion. What is arguable is the meaning to the Grandmother's final words to the Misfit, as well as her "gesture," which seemed equally important to O'Connor. One's interpretation depends on one's opinion of the Grandmother.

What *are* we to think of this woman? At the story's beginning, she seems a harmless busybody, utterly self-absorbed but also amusing, in her way. And, in her way, she provides a sort of human Rorschach test of her readers. We readily forgive her so much, including her mindless racism—she points at the "cute

[1]Flannery O'Connor, *Mystery and Manners: Occasional Prose*. Selected and Edited by Sally and Robert Fitzgerald (New York: Farrar, Straus, and Giroux, 1969).

little pickaninny" by the roadside, and entertains her grandchildren with a story in which a watermelon is devoured by "a nigger boy." She is filled with the prejudices of her class and her time. And so, some readers conclude, she is in spite of it all a "good" person. Somewhat more ominously, the Misfit—after he has fired three bullets into her chest—pronounces that she might have been " 'a good woman . . . if it had been somebody there to shoot her every minute of her life'." We surmise that in the universe of this story, the quality of what is "good" (which is after all the key word of the story's title) depends greatly on who is using the term. I do not think the Misfit is capable of irony—he truly means what he says about her, even though he finds it necessary to kill her. Indeed, the opposing categories of "good" and "evil" are very much in the air throughout this story. But like most supposed opposites, they have an alarming tendency to merge. It is probably worth noting that the second line of the once-popular song that gave O'Connor her title is "You always get the other kind."

Much criticism of the story appears to take a sentimental view of the Grandmother largely because she *is* a grandmother. Flannery O'Connor herself, as we shall see shortly, found little to blame in this woman, choosing to wrap her in the comfortable mantle of elderly Southern womanhood. O'Connor applies this generalization so uncritically that we half suspect she is pulling our leg. In any case, we can be sure that such sentimentality (in the mind of either the writer or her character) is fatal to clear thinking. If the Grandmother is old (although she does not seem to be *that* old), grey-haired, and "respectable," it follows that she must be weak, gentle, and benevolent—precisely the Grandmother's opinion of herself, and she is not shy of letting others know it. Intentionally or not, O'Connor has etched the Grandmother's character with wicked irony, which makes it all the more surprising to read the author's response to a frustrated teacher whose (Southern) students persisted in favoring the Grandmother, despite his strenuous efforts to point out her flaws. O'Connor said,

> I had to tell him that they resisted . . . because they all had grandmothers or great-aunts just like her at home, and they knew, from personal experience, that the old lady lacked comprehension, but that she had a good heart.

O'Connor continued,

> The Southerner is usually tolerant of those weaknesses that proceed from innocence, and he knows that a taste for self-preservation can be readily combined with the missionary spirit. (*Mystery and Manners* 110)

What is most disappointing in this moral summary of the Grandmother, and 5
her ilk, is its disservice to the spiky, vindictive woman of the story. There may be a purpose to O'Connor's betrayal of her own character: her phrase "missionary spirit" gives the game away. O'Connor is determined that the Grandmother shall be the Misfit's savior, even though she may not seem so in the story.

The Grandmother's role as grace-bringer is by now a received idea, largely because the author said it is so. But one must question the propriety of such tinkering with the character, after the fact. It reduces the fire-breathing woman who animates this story to nothing much more than a cranky maiden aunt. On the contrary, the Grandmother is a fierce fighter, never more so than in her final moments, nose-to-nose with the Misfit.

Granted, the Grandmother is not a homicidal monster like the Misfit, and she certainly does not deserve to die for her minor sins. And yet, does she quite earn absolution from any moral weakness beyond that of "a hypocritical old soul" (111)? For every reader who sees the image of his or her own grandmother printed on this character's cold face, as O'Connor suggested we might do, there are surely many others who can only be appalled by a calculating opportunist who is capable of embracing her family's murderer, to save her own skin. Where indeed is the "good heart" which unites this unprincipled woman with all those "grandmothers or great-aunts just like her at home"? The answer to that question can only be an affirmation of the "banality of evil," to use Hannah Arendt's well-known phrase. . . .

What does in fact happen in this part of the story is quite straightforward: the Grandmother, having exhausted all other appeals to the Misfit, resorts to her only remaining (though certainly imperfect) weapon: motherhood. Declaring to the Misfit that he is one of her babies, she sets out to conquer him. Perhaps she hopes that this ultimate flattery will melt his heart, and he will collapse in her comforting motherly embrace. Such are the stratagems of sentimentality. The moral shoddiness of her action is almost beyond description. If we had not already guessed the depths to which the Grandmother might sink, now we know. It is not easy to say who is the more evil, the Misfit or the Grandmother, and indeed that is the point. Her behavior is the manifest of her character.

It has been said that no action is without its redeeming aspect. Could this unspeakable act of selfishness carry within it the seeds of grace, acting, as it were, above the Grandmother? So Flannery O'Connor believed. But what is the precise movement of grace in this scene? It is surely straining the text to propose that the Grandmother has in this moment "seen the light." Are we to regard her as the unwitting agent of divine grace whose selfish intentions are somehow transfigured into a blessing? Such seems to have been O'Connor's opinion:

> . . . however unlikely this may seem, the old lady's gesture, like the mustard-seed, will grow to be a great crow-filled tree in the Misfit's heart, and will be enough of a pain to him there to turn him into the prophet he was meant to become. (*Mystery and Manners* 113)

We are almost persuaded to forget that none of this happens in the story itself. If this can be so, then we can just as easily attribute any interpretation we like to the scene. But in fact he is in no way changed. There is no "later on" in fiction. We do not, and will not, see "created grace" in the spirit of the Misfit.

But more important, this is not the way grace works. As we read in the *New* 10
Catholic Encyclopedia:

> . . . the spiritual creature must respond to this divine self-donation freely. Hence, the doctrine of grace supposes a creature already constituted in its own being in such wise that it has the possibility of entering into a free and personal relationship with the Divine Persons or of rejecting that relationship. (6:661)

If grace was extended to the Misfit, he refused it and that is the end. There can be no crow-filled tree, nor can there be the "lines of spiritual motion" leading to that tree, however attractive the image may be. Prudently, O'Connor added, "But that's another story." (*Mystery and Manners* 113) *[1996]*

JOHN DESMOND

From *Flannery O'Connor's Misfit and the Mystery of Evil*

In an article published in a 2004 issue of Renascence, *a journal that examines religious issues in literature, John Desmond tends to support O'Connor's interpretation of "A Good Man Is Hard to Find." For help in understanding the climactic scene between The Misfit and the grandmother, he turns to the late French Catholic philosopher Simone Weil. The following is an excerpt from his analysis.*

This climactic scene, full of ambiguity, has occasioned a wealth of critical comment. O'Connor herself argued that the grandmother's final words and actions represent the mysterious action of grace (5). Some readers have viewed it more skeptically, even arguing that the grandmother's gesture may be a final desperate attempt to save her own life. Other critics have argued a middle ground, granting O'Connor's right to her theological view, while judging the scene as satisfactory or not on the basis of strictly literary criteria. My focus here is on what this climactic scene suggests about the mysterious interpenetration of good and evil.

What initially strikes the reader about the scene is the enormous gap or lacuna between the grandmother's statement of doubt—"Maybe He didn't raise the dead . . ."—and her reaching out fatally to touch the Misfit and embrace him as "one of my babies . . . ," one of "my own children." O'Connor explains nothing of what happens in the grandmother's mind and heart to bring her to this touch of kinship with the criminal, except to say that "her head cleared for an instant." The gap is mysterious, perhaps supernatural, yet also exactly right in the human sense. Such acts of metanoia,° while inexplicable, are totally within the range of human behavior. What is significant about her calling him "one of my babies . . . ," one of "my own children," and "touching him" is that her actions threaten to undermine his self-designation of himself as the Misfit, the name he chose to signify his difference from ordinary humanity. The Misfit rejects the communal world, just as his sense of "justice" is individualistic rather than communal. Significantly, he remarked earlier in that story that "children make me nervous." The grandmother's claim of kinship rejects his solitary identity, and instead places him within the community as a child of man, like any other. So also, her touching him threatens his proud, isolated self-created role as the Misfit, a threat he cannot tolerate. After all, if he is not the Misfit, what is he? An ordinary, frail, suffering creature. So what we view from the grandmother's per-

metanoia: A Greek term meaning repentance or spiritual conversion.

spective as a good act—her recognition of her own bond with an evil man, her complicity, yet also her compassion for his suffering—is viewed by the Misfit as evil: he springs back from her touch "as if a snake had bitten him. . . ."

Why does the Misfit regard the touch as evil, and then answer it with evil? We recall Simone Weil's maxim: "Evil is to love, what mystery is to the intelligence." The grandmother's touch brings the Misfit into direct contact with the good of charity. The touch of charity measures the gap between him and the good. He cannot abide such threatening contact because it would mean opening himself to an admission of failure, and more importantly, to the possibility of good within the human community. Instead, he chooses the "hell" of isolation and despair. The truth of compassion, and being named a child of the human community, is for the Misfit an "evil" he must escape. Once again, Weil's comments are insightful:

> The sin against the Spirit consists of knowing a thing to be good, and hating it because it is good. We experience the equivalent of it in the form of resistance every time we set our faces in the direction of good. For every contact with good leads to a knowledge of the distance between good and evil and the commencement of a painful effort of assimilation. It is something which hurts and we are afraid. This fear is perhaps the sign of the reality of the contact. The corresponding sin cannot come about unless a lack of hope makes the consciousness of the distance intolerable and changes the pain into hatred. (*Gravity and Grace* 67)

The Misfit's pain at the grandmother's touch is instantly transformed into a hatred of the gratuitous act of charity, which he then answers with a brutal execution. What the Misfit fears is the mystery of love, the demands of love which the grandmother mysteriously responded to when faced with the criminal's suffering, and her own impending death. In her case, evil issued finally in good, or as Weil expressed it, evil exposed the good. But if the encounter with evil exposed the good in the grandmother, the final predicament of the Misfit is more complicated, more mysterious.

As I noted earlier, the Misfit acts under the delusion that his actions are 5
somehow good, i.e., good for him. Since he cannot make sense of his spiritual condition, he now tries to reduce ethical mystery to a perverse pleasure-pain principle. Initially he told the grandmother: "No pleasure but meanness." Yet his encounter with her touch has exposed his need, his human vulnerability. In his crucial final remark, he shifts from the earlier "No pleasure but meanness" to "It's no real pleasure in life." He has again failed to liberate himself from his predicament through violence, failed to "balance out" his deeds and find the meaning of his life. He himself is his own deepest mystery, a profoundly human condition which he can neither fathom nor abide. His last statement, that there is no "real pleasure" in life, shows that what he thought might bring pleasure, i.e., acts of meanness, has also proven to be bankrupt, a hollow illusion.

In the end, the Misfit's spiritual and mental suffering continues and intensifies, for with the failure of his code, his awareness of the gap between good and evil has widened. His violence is projected back onto himself as self-hatred. Perhaps at some future time his knowledge of this interior chasm will bring about the collapse of his self-begotten identity as a "Misfit," and an acceptance of his broken humanity. O'Connor suggested the possibility that he might ultimately be brought to such a conversion. She called the Misfit a "prophet gone wrong," and referred to the grandmother's touching him as "like the mustard-seed," which "will grow to be a great crow-filled tree in the Misfit's heart, and will be enough of a pain to him there to turn him into the prophet he was meant to become" (*Mystery and Manners* 110, 112–13). The grandmother's touch may bring him to the point where the mystery of good and evil is finally subsumed in the mystery of love. For the Misfit, evil may, in the end, through the grace of charity, bring about his ultimate good.

MAKING COMPARISONS

1. Stephens believes that her interpretation of "A Good Man Is Hard to Find" is compatible with O'Connor's. Do you accept both? Why, or why not?
2. In what ways, if any, does Desmond's use of Simone Weil go beyond O'Connor's view of her story or complicate it? Do the other two critics, Stephens and Bandy, make you hesitate to accept O'Connor's account? In general, do you think readers should accept an author's interpretation of his or her work? Explain your reasoning.
3. All of these commentaries on the story focus on religious aspects of it, though not all of them agree on how much of a role, and what kind of a role, religion plays in it. Are you similarly inclined to put the story in a religious framework? Why, or why not?

WRITING ABOUT ISSUES

1. The Misfit says that the grandmother " 'would of been a good woman . . . if it had been somebody there to shoot her every minute of her life' " (para. 140). Write an essay in which you argue for your own understanding of this claim. Is The Misfit right or just cruel? How should we define *good* in this context?
2. Choose one of the critics' interpretations featured in this cluster, and write an essay in which you imagine how O'Connor would respond to its points. Feel free to express and support your own views, too.
3. The man in O'Connor's story calls himself The Misfit " 'because I can't make what all I done wrong fit what all I gone through in punishment' " (para. 129). But plainly he is also a misfit in the sense that he has become alienated from society. Write an essay recalling someone you knew who seemed to be a misfit in this sense. More specifically, speculate on and try to describe this person's own perspective—what the person believed, how the person viewed the world, why he or she acted in certain ways. If you wish, your essay can be in the form of a letter to this person.

4. O'Connor promoted her version of Christianity in "A Good Man Is Hard to Find" and in her commentary on the story. On the basis of both texts, list various principles and concepts that she associates with her religion. Then do research on another religion, perhaps by reading two or three articles on it. Write an essay in which you compare O'Connor's theology with the religion you have researched. If you wish, you can focus your comparison by imagining what adherents to the other religion would say about "A Good Man Is Hard to Find."

A Menacing Stalker: Cultural Contexts for a Story

JOYCE CAROL OATES, "Where Are You Going, Where Have You Been?"

CULTURAL CONTEXTS:
DON MOSER, "The Pied Piper of Tucson: He Cruised in a Golden Car, Looking for the Action"

JOYCE CAROL OATES, "*Smooth Talk*: Short Story into Film"

MEGHAN DAUM, "Jaycee Dugard and the Feel-Good Imperative"

The harrowing ending of Joyce Carol Oates's much-anthologized initiation tale of innocence versus evil may shock you. The fifteen-year-old Connie, focused on boys and pop music, seems defenseless against her menacing stalker. This 1966 story uses the prospect of violent crime to remind readers, in its own chilling way, that adolescence may be fraught with anxieties, challenges, and risks. Often, however, a literary text reflects and responds to specific cultural contexts. Such is the case with this one. Therefore, we include with Oates's story three other texts: the *Life* magazine article that evidently led Oates to conceive her work of fiction, a *New York Times* article she wrote when her story became the movie *Smooth Talk*, and an essay from the *Los Angeles Times* by Meghan Daum, "Jaycee Dugard and the Feel-Good Imperative."

BEFORE YOU READ

Many historians of literature and culture have pointed out that as far back as colonial times, Americans have been fascinated with narratives of female captivity. Why do you think this kind of story has engaged them?

JOYCE CAROL OATES

Where Are You Going, Where Have You Been?

Joyce Carol Oates (b. 1938) is perhaps the most prolific of major American writers, publishing about two books a year for more than forty years. Oates has won numerous awards, including a National Book Award for fiction (1970).

Oates grew up in the countryside of upstate New York. She started writing early and won a scholarship to Syracuse University, where she was valedictorian in 1960. She received her M.A. from the University of Wisconsin a year later. She taught at the University of Detroit and the University of Windsor before joining the faculty at Princeton, where she has taught since 1978. Like Flannery O'Connor's and William Faulkner's work, Oates's is usually referred to as gothic, probably because of her violent characters, many of whom are filled with enigmatic malice and tormented emotions. Working in the realistic tradition, the "Dark Lady of American Literature" writes compelling narratives about seemingly ordinary people who beneath the surface live in a nightmare world of unconscious forces and sometimes sensational events.

Oates claims the story printed here was written after listening to Bob Dylan's "It's All Over Now, Baby Blue." The story was inspired by the serial killer Charles Schmid, also known as "The Pied Piper of Tucson." Her recent books include the novels The Accursed *(2013),* Daddy Love *(2013), and* Mudwoman *(2012); a memoir,* A Widow's Story *(2011); and the short story collection* Lovely, Dark, Deep *(2014).*

For Bob Dylan

Her name was Connie. She was fifteen and she had a quick nervous giggling habit of craning her neck to glance into mirrors, or checking other people's faces to make sure her own was all right. Her mother, who noticed everything and knew everything and who hadn't much reason any longer to look at her own face, always scolded Connie about it. "Stop gawking at yourself, who are you? You think you're so pretty?" she would say. Connie would raise her eyebrows at these familiar complaints and look right through her mother, into a shadowy vision of herself as she was right at that moment: she knew she was pretty and that was everything. Her mother had been pretty once too, if you could believe those old snapshots in the album, but now her looks were gone and that was why she was always after Connie.

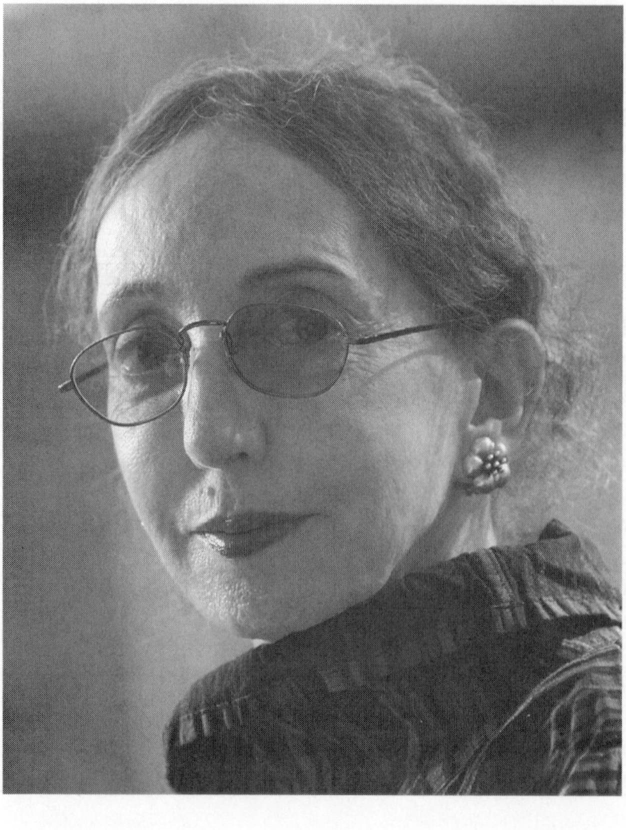

Getty Images

"Why don't you keep your room clean like your sister? How've you got your hair fixed—what the hell stinks? Hair spray? You don't see your sister using that junk."

Her sister June was twenty-four and still lived at home. She was a secretary in the high school Connie attended, and if that wasn't bad enough—with her in the same building—she was so plain and chunky and steady that Connie had to hear her praised all the time by her mother and her mother's sisters. June did this, June did that, she saved money and helped clean the house and cooked and Connie couldn't do a thing, her mind was all filled with trashy daydreams. Their father was away at work most of the time and when he came home he wanted supper and he read the newspaper at supper and after supper he went to bed. He didn't bother talking much to them, but around his bent head Connie's mother kept picking at her until Connie wished her mother was dead and she herself was dead and it was all over. "She makes me want to throw up sometimes," she complained to her friends. She had a high, breathless, amused voice which made everything she said a little forced, whether it was sincere or not.

There was one good thing: June went places with girl friends of hers, girls who were just as plain and steady as she, and so when Connie wanted to do that her mother had no objections. The father of Connie's best girl friend drove the girls the three miles to town and left them off at a shopping plaza, so that they could walk through the stores or go to a movie, and when he came to pick them up again at eleven he never bothered to ask what they had done.

They must have been familiar sights, walking around that shopping plaza in 5
their shorts and flat ballerina slippers that always scuffed the sidewalk, with charm bracelets jingling on their thin wrists; they would lean together to whisper and laugh secretly if someone passed by who amused or interested them. Connie had long dark blond hair that drew anyone's eye to it, and she wore part of it pulled up on her head and puffed out and the rest of it she let fall down her back. She wore a pullover jersey blouse that looked one way when she was at home and another way when she was away from home. Everything about her had two sides to it, one for home and one for anywhere that was not home: her walk that could be childlike and bobbing, or languid enough to make anyone think she was hearing music in her head, her mouth which was pale and smirking most of the time, but bright and pink on these evenings out, her laugh which was cynical and drawling at home—"Ha, ha, very funny"—but high-pitched and nervous anywhere else, like the jingling of the charms on her bracelet.

Sometimes they did go shopping or to a movie, but sometimes they went across the highway, ducking fast across the busy road, to a drive-in restaurant where older kids hung out. The restaurant was shaped like a big bottle, though squatter than a real bottle, and on its cap was a revolving figure of a grinning boy who held a hamburger aloft. One night in midsummer they ran across, breathless with daring, and right away someone leaned out a car window and invited them over, but it was just a boy from high school they didn't like. It made them feel good to be able to ignore him. They went up through the maze of parked and cruising cars to the bright-lit, fly-infested restaurant, their faces pleased and expectant as if they were entering a sacred building that loomed out of the night to give them what haven and what blessing they yearned for. They sat at the counter and crossed their legs at the ankles, their thin shoulders rigid with excitement and listened to the music that made everything so good: the music was always in the background like music at a church service, it was something to depend upon.

A boy named Eddie came in to talk with them. He sat backwards on his stool, turning himself jerkily around in semi-circles and then stopping and turning again, and after a while he asked Connie if she would like something to eat. She said she did and so she tapped her friend's arm on her way out—her friend pulled her face up into a brave droll look—and Connie said she would meet her at eleven, across the way. "I just hate to leave her like that," Connie said earnestly, but the boy said that she wouldn't be alone for long. So they went out to his car and on the way Connie couldn't help but let her eyes wander over the windshields and faces all around her, her face gleaming with the joy that had nothing to do with Eddie or even this place; it might have been the music. She drew her shoulders up and sucked in her breath with the pure pleasure of being alive, and just at that moment she happened to glance at a face just a few feet from hers. It was a boy with shaggy black hair, in a convertible jalopy painted gold. He stared at her and then his lips widened into a grin. Connie slit her eyes at him and turned away, but she couldn't help glancing back and there he was still watching her. He wagged a finger and laughed and said, "Gonna get you, baby," and Connie turned away again without Eddie noticing anything.

She spent three hours with him, at the restaurant where they ate hamburgers and drank Cokes in wax cups that were always sweating, and then down an alley a mile or so away, and when he left her off at five to eleven only the movie house was still open at the plaza. Her girl friend was there, talking with a boy. When Connie came up the two girls smiled at each other and Connie said, "How was the movie?" and the girl said, "*You* should know." They rode off with the girl's father, sleepy and pleased, and Connie couldn't help but look at the darkened shopping plaza with its big empty parking lot and its signs that were faded and ghostly now, and over at the drive-in restaurant where cars were still circling tirelessly. She couldn't hear the music at this distance.

Next morning June asked her how the movie was and Connie said, "So-so."

She and that girl and occasionally another girl went out several times a week 10
that way, and the rest of the time Connie spent around the house—it was summer vacation—getting in her mother's way and thinking, dreaming, about the boys she met. But all the boys fell back and dissolved into a single face that was not even a face, but an idea, a feeling, mixed up with the urgent insistent pounding of the music and the humid night air of July. Connie's mother kept dragging her back to the daylight by finding things for her to do or saying suddenly, "What's this about the Pettinger girl?"

And Connie would say nervously, "Oh, her. That dope." She always drew thick clear lines between herself and such girls, and her mother was simple and kindly enough to believe her. Her mother was so simple, Connie thought, that it was maybe cruel to fool her so much. Her mother went scuffling around the house in old bedroom slippers and complained over the telephone to one sister about the other, then the other called up and the two of them complained about the third one. If June's name was mentioned her mother's tone was approving, and if Connie's name was mentioned it was disapproving. This did not really mean she disliked Connie and actually Connie thought that her mother preferred her to June because she was prettier, but the two of them kept up a pretense of exasperation, a sense that they were tugging and struggling over something of little value to either of them. Sometimes, over coffee, they were almost friends, but something would come up—some vexation that was like a fly buzzing suddenly around their heads—and their faces went hard with contempt.

One Sunday Connie got up at eleven—none of them bothered with church—and washed her hair so that it could dry all day long, in the sun. Her parents and sister were going to a barbecue at an aunt's house and Connie said no, she wasn't interested, rolling her eyes, to let mother know just what she thought of it. "Stay home alone then," her mother said sharply. Connie sat out back in a lawn chair and watched them drive away, her father quiet and bald, hunched around so that he could back the car out, her mother with a look that was still angry and not at all softened through the windshield, and in the back seat poor old June all dressed up as if she didn't know what a barbecue was, with all the running yelling kids and the flies. Connie sat with her eyes closed in the sun, dreaming and dazed with the warmth about her as if this were a kind of love, the caresses of love, and her mind slipped over onto thoughts of the boy she had been with the night before and how nice he had been, how sweet it always was, not the way someone like June would suppose but sweet, gentle, the way it was in movies and promised in songs; and when she opened her eyes she hardly knew where she was, the back yard ran off into weeds and a fenceline of trees and behind it the sky was perfectly blue and still. The asbestos "ranch house" that was now three years old startled her—it looked small. She shook her head as if to get awake.

It was too hot. She went inside the house and turned on the radio to drown out the quiet. She sat on the edge of her bed, barefoot, and listened for an hour and a half to a program called XYZ Sunday Jamboree, record after record of hard, fast, shrieking songs she sang along with, interspersed by exclamations from "Bobby King": "An' look here you girls at Napoleon's—Son and Charley want you to pay real close attention to this song coming up!"

And Connie paid close attention herself, bathed in a glow of slow-pulsed joy that seemed to rise mysteriously out of the music itself and lay languidly about the airless little room, breathed in and breathed out with each gentle rise and fall of her chest.

15 After a while she heard a car coming up the drive. She sat up at once, startled, because it couldn't be her father so soon. The gravel kept crunching all the way in from the road—the driveway was long—and Connie ran to the window. It was a car she didn't know. It was an open jalopy, painted a bright gold that caught the sun opaquely. Her heart began to pound and her fingers snatched at her hair, checking it, and she whispered "Christ. Christ," wondering how bad she looked. The car came to a stop at the side door and the horn sounded four short taps as if this were a signal Connie knew.

She went into the kitchen and approached the door slowly, then hung out the screen door, her bare toes curling down off the step. There were two boys in the car and now she recognized the driver: he had shaggy, shabby black hair that looked crazy as a wig and he was grinning at her.

"I ain't late, am I?" he said.

"Who the hell do you think you are?" Connie said.

"Toldja I'd be out, didn't I?"

"I don't even know who you are." 20

She spoke sullenly, careful to show no interest or pleasure, and he spoke in a fast bright monotone. Connie looked past him to the other boy, taking her time. He had fair brown hair, with a lock that fell onto his forehead. His sideburns gave him a fierce, embarrassed look, but so far he hadn't even bothered to glance at her. Both boys wore sunglasses. The driver's glasses were metallic and mirrored everything in miniature.

"You wanta come for a ride?" he said.

Connie smirked and let her hair fall loose over one shoulder.

"Don'tcha like my car? New paint job," he said. "Hey."

"What?" 25

"You're cute."

She pretended to fidget, chasing flies away from the door.

"Don'tcha believe me, or what?" he said.

"Look, I don't even know who you are," Connie said in disgust.

"Hey, Ellie's got a radio, see. Mine's broke down." He lifted his friend's arm and showed her the little transistor the boy was holding, and now Connie began to hear the music. It was the same program that was playing inside the house. 30

"Bobby King?" she said.

"I listen to him all the time. I think he's great."

"He's kind of great," Connie said reluctantly.

"Listen, that guy's *great*. He knows where the action is."

Connie blushed a little, because the glasses made it impossible for her to see just what this boy was looking at. She couldn't decide if she liked him or if he was just a jerk, and so she dawdled in the doorway and wouldn't come down or go back inside. She said, "What's all that stuff painted on your car?" 35

"Can'tcha read it?" He opened the door very carefully, as if he was afraid it might fall off. He slid out just as carefully, planting his feet firmly on the ground, the tiny metallic world in his glasses slowing down like gelatine hardening and in the midst of it Connie's bright green blouse. "This here is my name, to begin with," he said. arnold friend was written in tar-like black letters on the side, with a drawing of a round grinning face that reminded Connie of a pumpkin, except it wore sunglasses. "I wanta introduce myself, I'm Arnold Friend and that's my real name and I'm gonna be your friend, honey, and inside the car's Ellie Oscar, he's kinda shy." Ellie brought his transistor up to his shoulder and balanced it there. "Now these numbers are a secret code, honey," Arnold Friend explained. He read off the numbers 33, 19, 17 and raised his eyebrows at her to see what she thought of that, but she didn't think much of it. The left rear fender had been smashed and around it was written, on the gleaming gold background: done by crazy woman driver. Connie had to laugh at that. Arnold Friend was pleased at her laughter and looked up at her. "Around the other side's a lot more—you wanta come and see them?"

"No."

"Why not?"

"Why should I?"

"Don'tcha wanta see what's on the car? Don'tcha wanta go for a ride?"

"I don't know."

"Why not?"

"I got things to do."

"Like what?"

"Things."

He laughed as if she had said something funny. He slapped his thighs. He was standing in a strange way, leaning back against the car as if he were balancing himself. He wasn't tall, only an inch or so taller than she would be if she came down to him. Connie liked the way he was dressed, which was the way all of them dressed: tight faded jeans stuffed into black, scuffed boots, a belt that pulled his waist in and showed how lean he was, and a white pullover shirt that was a little soiled and showed the hard small muscles of his arms and shoulders. He looked as if he probably did hard work, lifting and carrying things. Even his neck looked muscular. And his face was a familiar face, somehow: the jaw and chin and cheeks slightly darkened, because he hadn't shaved for a day or two, and the nose long and hawk-like, sniffing as if she were a treat he was going to gobble up and it was all a joke.

"Connie, you ain't telling the truth. This is your day set aside for a ride with me and you know it," he said, still laughing. The way he straightened and recovered from his fit of laughing showed that it had been all fake.

"How do you know what my name is?" she said suspiciously.

"It's Connie."

"Maybe and maybe not."

"I know my Connie," he said, wagging his finger. Now she remembered him even better, back at the restaurant, and her cheeks warmed at the thought of how she sucked in her breath just at the moment she passed him—how she must have looked to him. And he had remembered her. "Ellie and I come out here especially for you," he said. "Ellie can sit in back. How about it?"

"Where?"

"Where what?"

"Where're we going?"

He looked at her. He took off the sunglasses and she saw how pale the skin around his eyes was, like holes that were not in shadow but instead in light. His eyes were like chips of broken glass that catch the light in an amiable way. He smiled. It was as if the idea of going for a ride somewhere, to some place, was a new idea to him.

"Just for a ride, Connie sweetheart."

"I never said my name was Connie," she said.

"But I know what it is. I know your name and all about you, lots of things," Arnold Friend said. He had not moved yet but stood still leaning back against the side of his jalopy. "I took a special interest in you, such a pretty girl, and found out all about you like I know your parents and sister are gone somewheres and I know where and how long they're going to be gone, and I know who you were with last night, and your best friend's name is Betty. Right?"

He spoke in a simple lilting voice, exactly as if he were reciting the words to a song. His smile assured her that everything was fine. In the car Ellie turned up the volume on his radio and did not bother to look around at them.

"Ellie can sit in the back seat," Arnold Friend said. He indicated his friend with a casual jerk of his chin, as if Ellie did not count and she could not bother with him.

"How'd you find out all that stuff?" Connie said.

"Listen: Betty Schultz and Tony Fitch and Jimmy Pettinger and Nancy Pettinger," he said, in a chant. "Raymond Stanley and Bob Hutter —"

"Do you know all those kids?"

"I know everybody."

"Look, you're kidding. You're not from around here."

"Sure."

"But—how come we never saw you before?"

"Sure you saw me before," he said. He looked down at his boots, as if he were a little offended. "You just don't remember."

"I guess I'd remember you," Connie said.

"Yeah?" He looked up at this, beaming. He was pleased. He began to mark time with the music from Ellie's radio, tapping his fists lightly together. Connie looked away from his smile to the car, which was painted so bright it almost hurt her eyes to look at it. She looked at that name, ARNOLD FRIEND. And up at the front fender was an expression that was familiar —MAN THE FLYING SAUCERS. It was an expression kids had used the year before, but didn't use this year. She looked at it for a while as if the words meant something to her that she did not yet know.

"What're you thinking about? Huh?" Arnold Friend demanded. "Not worried about your hair blowing around in the car, are you?"

"No."

"Think I maybe can't drive good?"

"How do I know?"

"You're a hard girl to handle. How come?" he said. "Don't you know I'm your friend? Didn't you see me put my sign in the air when you walked by?"

"What sign?"

"My sign." And he drew an X in the air, leaning out toward her. They were maybe ten feet apart. After his hand fell back to his side the X was still in the air, almost visible. Connie let the screen door close and stood perfectly still inside it, listening to the music from her radio and the boy's blend together. She stared at Arnold Friend. He stood there so stiffly relaxed, pretending to be relaxed, with one hand idly on the door handle as if he were keeping himself up that way and had no intention of ever moving again. She recognized most things about him, the tight jeans that showed his thighs and buttocks and the greasy leather boots and the tight shirt, and even that slippery friendly smile of his, that sleepy dreamy smile that all the boys used to get across ideas they didn't want to put into words.

She recognized all this and also the singsong way he talked, slightly mocking, kidding, but serious and a little melancholy, and she recognized the way he tapped one fist against the other in homage to the perpetual music behind him. But all these things did not come together.

She said suddenly, "Hey, how old are you?"

His smile faded. She could see then that he wasn't a kid, he was much older—thirty, maybe more. At this knowledge her heart began to pound faster.

"That's a crazy thing to ask. Can'tcha see I'm your own age?" 80

"Like hell you are."

"Or maybe a coupla years older, I'm eighteen."

"Eighteen?" she said doubtfully.

He grinned to reassure her and lines appeared at the corners of his mouth. His teeth were big and white. He grinned so broadly his eyes became slits and she saw how thick the lashes were, thick and black as if painted with a black tar-like material. Then he seemed to become embarrassed, abruptly, and looked over his shoulder at Ellie. "*Him,* he's crazy," he said. "Ain't he a riot, he's a nut, a real character." Ellie was still listening to the music. His sunglasses told nothing about what he was thinking. He wore a bright orange shirt unbuttoned halfway to show his chest, which was a pale, bluish chest and not muscular like Arnold Friend's. His shirt collar was turned up all around and the very tips of the collar pointed out past his chin as if they were protecting him. He was pressing the transistor radio up against his ear and sat there in a kind of daze, right in the sun.

"He's kinda strange," Connie said. 85

"Hey, she says you're kinda strange! Kinda strange!" Arnold Friend cried. He pounded on the car to get Ellie's attention. Ellie turned for the first time and Connie saw with shock that he wasn't a kid either—he had a fair, hairless face, cheeks reddened slightly as if the veins grew too close to the surface of his skin, the face of a forty-year-old baby. Connie felt a wave of dizziness rise in her at this sight and she stared at him as if waiting for something to change the shock of the moment, make it all right again. Ellie's lips kept shaping words, mumbling along with the words blasting his ear.

"Maybe you two better go away," Connie said faintly.

"What? How come?" Arnold Friend cried. "We come out here to take you for a ride. It's Sunday." He had the voice of the man on the radio now. It was the same voice, Connie thought. "Don'tcha know it's Sunday all day and honey, no matter who you were with last night today you're with Arnold Friend and don't you forget it!—Maybe you better step out here," he said, and this last was in a different voice. It was a little flatter, as if the heat was finally getting to him.

"No. I got things to do."

"Hey." 90

"You two better leave."

"We ain't leaving until you come with us."

"Like hell I am—"

"Connie, don't fool around with me. I mean—I mean, don't fool *around,*" he said, shaking his head. He laughed incredulously. He placed his sunglasses on top of his head, carefully, as if he were indeed wearing a wig, and brought the stems down behind his ears. Connie stared at him, another wave of dizziness and fear rising in her so that for a moment he wasn't even in focus but was just a blur; standing there against his gold car, and she had the idea that he had driven up the driveway all right but had come from nowhere before that and belonged nowhere and that everything about him and even the music that was so familiar to her was only half real.

"If my father comes and sees you —" 95

"He ain't coming. He's at a barbecue."

"How do you know that?"

"Aunt Tillie's. Right now they're—uh —they're drinking. Sitting around," he said vaguely, squinting as if he were staring all the way to town and over to Aunt Tillie's back yard. Then the vision seemed to clear and he nodded energetically. "Yeah. Sitting around. There's your sister in a blue dress, huh? And high heels, the poor sad bitch—nothing like you, sweetheart! And your mother's helping some fat woman with the corn, they're cleaning the corn—husking the corn —"

"What fat woman?" Connie cried.

"How do I know what fat woman. I don't know every goddamn fat woman in 100
the world!" Arnold Friend laughed.

"Oh, that's Mrs. Hornby. . . . Who invited her?" Connie said. She felt a little light-headed. Her breath was coming quickly.

"She's too fat. I don't like them fat. I like them the way you are, honey," he said, smiling sleepily at her. They stared at each other for a while, through the screen door. He said softly, "Now what you're going to do is this: you're going to come out that door. You're going to sit up front with me and Ellie's going to sit in the back, the hell with Ellie, right? This isn't Ellie's date. You're my date. I'm your lover, honey."

"What? You're crazy —"

"Yes, I'm your lover. You don't know what that is but you will," he said. "I know that too. I know all about you. But look: it's real nice and you couldn't ask for nobody better than me, or more polite. I always keep my word. I'll tell you how it is, I'm always nice at first, the first time. I'll hold you so tight you won't think you have to try to get away or pretend anything because you'll know you can't. And I'll come inside you where it's all secret and you'll give in to me and you'll love me —"

"Shut up! You're crazy!" Connie said. She backed away from the door. She 105
put her hands against her ears as if she'd heard something terrible, something not meant for her. "People don't talk like that, you're crazy," she muttered. Her heart was almost too big now for her chest and its pumping made sweat break out all over her. She looked out to see Arnold Friend pause and then take a step toward the porch lurching. He almost fell. But, like a clever drunken man, he managed to catch his balance. He wobbled in his high boots and grabbed hold of one of the porch posts.

"Honey?" he said. "You still listening?"

"Get the hell out of here!"

"Be nice, honey. Listen."

"I'm going to call the police —"

He wobbled again and out of the side of his mouth came a fast spat curse, an 110
aside not meant for her to hear. But even this "Christ!" sounded forced. Then he began to smile again. She watched this smile come, awkward as if he were smiling from inside a mask. His whole face was a mask, she thought wildly, tanned down onto his throat but then running out as if he had plastered make-up on his face but had forgotten about his throat.

"Honey —? Listen, here's how it is. I always tell the truth and I promise you this: I ain't coming in that house after you."

"You better not! I'm going to call the police if you—if you don't —"

"Honey," he said, talking right through her voice, "honey, I'm not coming in there but you are coming out here. You know why?"

She was panting. The kitchen looked like a place she had never seen before, some room she had run inside but which wasn't good enough, wasn't going to help her. The kitchen window had never had a curtain, after three years, and there were dishes in the sink for her to do—probably —and if you ran your hand across the table you'd probably feel something sticky there.

"You listening, honey? Hey?" 115

"— going to call the police —"

"Soon as you touch the phone I don't need to keep my promise and can come inside. You won't want that."

She rushed forward and tried to lock the door. Her fingers were shaking. "But why lock it," Arnold Friend said gently, talking right into her face. "It's just a screen door. It's just nothing." One of his boots was at a strange angle, as if his foot wasn't in it. It pointed out to the left, bent at the ankle. "I mean, anybody can break through a screen door and glass and wood and iron or anything else if he needs to, anybody at all and specially Arnold Friend. If the place got lit up with a fire, honey, you'd come runnin' out into my arms, right into my arms an' safe at home—like you knew I was your lover and'd stopped fooling around, I don't mind a nice shy girl but I don't like no fooling around." Part of those words were spoken with a slight rhythmic lilt, and Connie somehow recognized them—the echo of a song from last year, about a girl rushing into her boy friend's arms and coming home again —

Connie stood barefoot on the linoleum floor, staring at him. "What do you want?" she whispered.

"I want you," he said. 120

"What?"

"Seen you that night and thought, that's the one, yes sir. I never needed to look any more."

"But my father's coming back. He's coming to get me. I had to wash my hair first —" She spoke in a dry, rapid voice, hardly raising it for him to hear.

"No, your daddy is not coming and yes, you had to wash your hair and you washed it for me. It's nice and shining and all for me. I thank you, sweetheart," he said, with a mock bow, but again he almost lost his balance. He had to bend and adjust his boots. Evidently his feet did not go all the way down; the boots must have been stuffed with something so that he would seem taller. Connie stared out at him and behind him at Ellie in the car, who seemed to be looking off toward Connie's right, into nothing. Then Ellie said, pulling the words out of the air one after another as if he were just discovering them, "You want me to pull out the phone?"

"Shut your mouth and keep it shut," Arnold Friend said, his face red from 125
bending over or maybe from embarrassment because Connie had seen his boots. "This ain't none of your business."

"What—what are you doing? What do you want?" Connie said. "If I call the police they'll get you, they'll arrest you —"

"Promise was not to come in unless you touch that phone, and I'll keep that promise," he said. He resumed his erect position and tried to force his shoulders back. He sounded like a hero in a movie, declaring something important. He spoke too loudly and it was as if he were speaking to someone behind Connie. "I ain't made plans for coming in that house where I don't belong but just for you to come out to me, the way you should. Don't you know who I am?"

"You're crazy," she whispered. She backed away from the door but did not want to go into another part of the house, as if this would give him permission to come through the door. "What do you . . . You're crazy, you. . . ."

"Huh? What're you saying, honey?"

Her eyes darted everywhere in the kitchen. She could not remember what it 130
was, this room.

"This is how it is, honey: you come out and we'll drive away, have a nice ride. But if you don't come out we're gonna wait till your people come home and then they're all going to get it."

"You want that telephone pulled out?" Ellie said. He held the radio away from his ear and grimaced, as if without the radio the air was too much for him.

"I toldja shut up, Ellie," Arnold Friend said, "you're deaf, get a hearing aid, right? Fix yourself up. This little girl's no trouble and's gonna be nice to me, so Ellie keep to yourself, this ain't your date—right? Don't hem in on me, don't hog, don't crush, don't bird dog, don't trail me," he said in a rapid, meaningless voice, as if he were running through all the expressions he'd learned but was no longer sure which one of them was in style, then rushing on to new ones, making them up with his eyes closed. "Don't crawl under my fence, don't squeeze in my chipmunk hole, don't sniff my glue, suck my popsicle, keep your own greasy fingers on yourself!" He shaded his eyes and peered in at Connie, who was backed against the kitchen table. "Don't mind him, honey, he's just a creep. He's a dope. Right? I'm the boy for you and like I said, you come out here nice like a lady and give me your hand, and nobody else gets hurt, I mean, your nice old bald-headed daddy and your mummy and your sister in her high heels. Because listen: why bring them in this?"

"Leave me alone," Connie whispered.

"Hey, you know that old woman down the road, the one with the chickens 135
and stuff—you know her?"

"She's dead!"

"Dead? What? You know her?" Arnold Friend said.

"She's dead —"

"Don't you like her?"

"She's dead—she's—she isn't here any more —" 140

"But don't you like her, I mean, you got something against her? Some grudge or something?" Then his voice dipped as if he were conscious of rudeness. He touched the sunglasses on top of his head as if to make sure they were still there. "Now you be a good girl."

"What are you going to do?"

"Just two things, or maybe three," Arnold Friend said. "But I promise it won't last long and you'll like me that way you get to like people you're close to. You will. It's all over for you here, so come on out. You don't want your people in any trouble, do you?"

She turned and bumped against a chair or something, hurting her leg, but she ran into the back room and picked up the telephone. Something roared in her ear, a tiny roaring, and she was so sick with fear that she could do nothing but listen to it—the telephone was clammy and very heavy and her fingers groped down to the dial but were too weak to touch it. She began to scream into the phone, into the roaring. She cried out, she cried for her mother, she felt her breath start jerking back and forth in her lungs as if it were something Arnold Friend was stabbing her with again and again with no tenderness. A noisy sorrowful wailing rose all about her and she was locked inside it the way she was locked inside this house.

After a while she could hear again. She was sitting on the floor, with her wet 145
back against the wall.

Arnold Friend was saying from the door, "That's a good girl. Put the phone back."

She kicked the phone away from her.

"No, honey. Pick it up. Put it back right."

She picked it up and put it back. The dial tone stopped.

"That's a good girl. Now you come outside." 150

She was hollow with what had been fear but what was now just an emptiness. All that screaming had blasted it out of her. She sat, one leg cramped under her, and deep inside her brain was something like a pinpoint of light that kept going and would not let her relax. She thought, I'm not going to see my mother again. She thought, I'm not going to sleep in my bed again. Her bright green blouse was all wet.

Arnold Friend said, in a gentle-loud voice that was like a stage voice, "The place where you came from ain't there any more, and where you had in mind to go is cancelled out. This place you are now—inside your daddy's house—is nothing but a cardboard box I can knock down any time. You know that and always did know it. You hear me?"

She thought, I have got to think. I have got to know what to do.

"We'll go out to a nice field, out in the country here where it smells so nice and it's sunny," Arnold Friend said. "I'll have my arms tight around you so you won't need to try to get away and I'll show you what love is like, what it does. The hell with this house! It looks solid all right," he said. He ran a fingernail down the screen and the noise did not make Connie shiver, as it would have the day before.

"Now put your hand on your heart, honey. Feel that? That feels solid too but we know better. Be nice to me, be sweet like you can because what else is there for a girl like you but to be sweet and pretty and give in?—and get away before her people get back?"

155 She felt her pounding heart. Her hand seemed to enclose it. She thought for the first time in her life that it was nothing that was hers, that belonged to her, but just a pounding, living thing inside this body that wasn't really hers either.

"You don't want them to get hurt," Arnold Friend went on. "Now get up, honey. Get up all by yourself."

She stood.

"Now turn this way. That's right. Come over to me—Ellie, put that away, didn't I tell you? You dope. You miserable creepy dope," Arnold Friend said. His words were not angry but only part of an incantation. The incantation was kindly. "Now come out through the kitchen to me honey and let's see a smile, try it, you're a brave sweet little girl and now they're eating corn and hotdogs cooked to bursting over an outdoor fire, and they don't know one thing about you and never did and honey you're better than them because not a one of them would have done this for you."

Connie felt the linoleum under her feet; it was cool. She brushed her hair back out of her eyes. Arnold Friend let go of the post tentatively and opened his arms for her, his elbows pointing in toward each other and his wrists limp, to show that this was an embarrassed embrace and a little mocking, he didn't want to make her self-conscious.

160 She put out her hand against the screen. She watched herself push the door slowly open as if she were back safe somewhere in the other doorway, watching this body and this head of long hair moving out into the sunlight where Arnold Friend waited.

"My sweet little blue-eyed girl," he said in a half-sung sigh that had nothing to do with her brown eyes but was taken up just the same by the vast sunlit reaches of the land behind him and on all sides of him—so much land that Connie had never seen before and did not recognize except to know that she was going to it. *[1966]*

≡ THINKING ABOUT THE TEXT

1. This story was first published in 1966. What still seems typical of fifteen-year-old Connie's behavior? What seems dated about her?
2. Is Oates making a comment about the effect music has on Connie? Should popular music be accountable for the behavior of its listeners? Can popular culture make us oblivious to the real dangers of the world? Can it make us suspicious and cynical?
3. The suggestions about what will happen to Connie when she leaves the protection of her home are not so subtle. What is your view of her future? What does Connie mean when she says, "'People don't talk like that, you're crazy'" (para. 105)? What is your reading of her response? Is Arnold Friend crazy?

4. A common response to this story is frustration with Connie's hesitation and her inability to take appropriate action in the face of serious danger. Was this your response? Why isn't she more assertive?
5. Could Connie have been better prepared for this encounter with evil? What evidence does the author give to show how prepared she is or isn't? What is her relationship with her parents? Is her social awareness primarily her parents' responsibility? If not, whose is it?

DON MOSER

The Pied Piper of Tucson: He Cruised in a Golden Car, Looking for the Action

Published in the March 4, 1966, issue of Life *magazine, this article by Don Moser (1932–2013) focuses on a real-life murderer who in major ways resembled Joyce Carol Oates's character Arnold Friend. Indeed, in the essay by Oates that follows, she indicates some familiarity with Moser's piece, although she claims that she didn't read it fully. However much his article inspired Oates to write her story, he illuminates American youth culture of the mid-1960s—including the role that deadly crime could play in it.*

Hey, c 'mon babe, follow me,
I'm the Pied Piper, follow me,
I'm the Pied Piper,
And I'll show you where it's at.
— Popular song
Tucson, winter 1965

At dusk in Tucson, as the stark, yellow-flared mountains begin to blur against the sky, the golden car slowly cruises Speedway. Smoothly it rolls down the long divided avenue, past the supermarkets, the gas stations, and the motels; past the twist joints, the sprawling drive-in restaurants. The car slows for an intersection, stops, then pulls away again. The exhaust mutters against the pavement as the young man driving takes the machine swiftly, expertly through the gears. A car pulls even with him; the teen-age girls in the front seat laugh, wave, and call his name. The young man glances toward the rearview mirror, turned always so he can look at his own reflection, and he appraises himself.

The face is his own creation; the hair dyed raven black, the skin darkened to a deep tan with pancake make-up, the lips whitened, the whole effect heightened by a mole he has painted on one cheek. But the deep-set blue eyes are all his own. Beautiful eyes, the girls say.

Approaching the Hi-Ho, the teen-agers' nightclub, he backs off on the accelerator, then slowly cruises on past Johnie's Drive-in. The cars are beginning to orbit and accumulate in the parking lot—near sharp cars with deep-throated mufflers and Maltese-cross decals on the windows. But it's early yet. Not much going on. The driver shifts up again through the gears, and the golden car slides away along the glitter and gimcrack of Speedway. Smitty keeps looking for the action.

Whether the juries in the two trials decide that Charles Howard Schmid Jr. did or did not brutally murder Alleen Rowe, Gretchen Fritz, and Wendy Fritz has from the beginning seemed of almost secondary importance to the people of Tucson. They are not indifferent. But what disturbs them far beyond the question of Smitty's guilt or innocence are the revelations about Tucson itself that have followed on the disclosure of the crimes. Starting from the bizarre circumstances of the killings and on through the ugly fragments of the plot—which in turn hint at other murders as yet undiscovered, at teen-age sex, blackmail, even connections with the Cosa Nostra—they have had to view their city in a new and unpleasant light. The fact is that Charles Schmid—who cannot be dismissed as a freak, an aberrant of no consequence—had for years functioned successfully as a member, even a leader, of the yeastiest stratum of Tucson's teen-age society.

5 As a high school student Smitty had been, as classmates remember, an outsider—but not that far outside. He was small but he was a fine athlete, and in his last year—1960—he was a state gymnastics champion. His grades were poor, but he was in no trouble to speak of until his senior year, when he was suspended for stealing tools from a welding class.

But Smitty never really left the school. After his suspension he hung around waiting to pick up kids in a succession of sharp cars which he drove fast and well. He haunted all the teen-age hangouts along Speedway, including the bowling alleys and the public swimming pool—and he put on spectacular driving exhibitions for girls far younger than he.

At the time of his arrest last November, Charles Schmid was 23 years old. He wore face make-up and dyed his hair. He habitually stuffed three or four inches of old rags and tin cans into the bottoms of his high-topped boots to make himself taller than his five-foot-three and stumbled about so awkwardly while walking that some people thought he had wooden feet. He pursed his lips and let his eyelids droop in order to emulate his idol, Elvis Presley. He bragged to girls that he knew 100 ways to make love, and that he ran dope, that he was a Hell's Angel. He talked about being a rough customer in a fight (he was, though he was rarely in one), and he always carried in his pocket tiny bottles of salt and pepper, which he said he used to blind his opponents. He liked to use highfalutin language and had a favorite saying, "I can manifest my neurotical emotions, emancipate an epicureal instinct, and elaborate on my heterosexual tendencies."

He occasionally shocked even those who thought they knew him well. A friend says that he once saw Smitty tie a string to the tail of his pet cat, swing it around his head and beat it bloody against a wall. Then he turned calmly and asked, "You feel compassion—why?"

Yet even while Smitty tried to create an exalted, heroic image of himself, he had worked on a pitiable one. "He thrived on feeling sorry for himself," recalls a friend, "and making others feel sorry for him." At various times Smitty told inmates that he had leukemia and didn't have long to live. He claimed that he was adopted, that his real name was Angel Rodriguez, that his father was a "bean" (local slang for Mexican, an inferior race in Smitty's view), and that his mother was a famous lawyer who would have nothing to do with him.

What made Smitty a hero to Tucson's youth? 10

Isn't Tucson—out there in the Golden West, in the grand setting where the skies are not cloudy all day—supposed to be a flowering of the American Dream? One envisions teen-agers who drink milk, wear crewcuts, go to bed at half past 9, say "Sir" and "Ma'am," and like to go fishing with Dad. Part of Tucson is like this—but the city is not yet Utopia. It is glass and chrome and well-weathered stucco; it is also gimcrack, ersatz, and urban sprawl at its worst. Its suburbs stretch for mile after mile—a level sea of bungalows, broken only by mammoth shopping centers, that ultimately peters out among the cholla and saguaro. The city has grown from 85,000 to 300,000 since World War II. Few who live there were born there, and a lot are just passing through. Its superb climate attracts the old and the infirm, many of whom, as one citizen put it, "have come here to retire from their responsibilities to life." Jobs are hard to find and there is little industry to stabilize employment. ("What do people do in Tucson?" the visitor asks. Answer: "They do each other's laundry.")

As for the youngsters, they must compete with the army of semi-retired who are willing to take on part-time work for the minimum wage. Schools are beautiful but overcrowded; and at those with split sessions, the kids are on the loose from noon on, or from 6 P.M. till noon the next day. When they get into trouble, Tucson teenagers are capable of getting into trouble in style: a couple of years ago they shocked the city fathers by throwing a series of beer-drinking parties in the desert, attended by scores of kids. The fests were called "boondockers" and if they were no more sinful than any other kid's drinking parties, they were at least on a magnificent scale. One statistic seems relevant: 50 runaways are reported to the Tucson police department each month.

Of an evening kids with nothing to do wind up on Speedway, looking for action. There is the teen-age nightclub ("Pickup Palace," the kids call it). There are the rock'n'roll beer joints (the owners check ages meticulously, but young girls can enter if they don't drink; besides, anyone can buy a phony I.D. card for $2.50 around the high schools) where they can Jerk, Swim, and Frug away the evening to the room-shaking electronic blare of *Hang on Sloopy*, *The Pied Piper*, and a number called *The Bo Diddley Rock*. At the drive-in hamburger and pizza stands their cars circle endlessly, mufflers rumbling, as they check each other over.

Here on Speedway you find Ritchie and Ronny, out of work and bored and with nothing to do. Here you find Debby and Jabron, from the wrong side of the tracks, aimlessly cruising in their battered old car looking for something—anything—to relieve the tedium of their lives, looking for somebody neat. ("Well if the boys look bitchin' you pull up next to them in your car and you roll down the window and say 'Hey, how about a dollar for gas?' and if they give you the dollar then maybe you let them take you to Johnie's for a coke.") Here you find Gretchen, pretty and rich and with problems, bad problems. Of a Saturday night, all of them cruising the long, bright street that seems endlessly in motion with the young. Smitty's people.

15 He had a nice car. He had plenty of money from his parents, who ran a nursing home, and he was always glad to spend it on anyone who'd listen to him. He had a pad of his own where he threw parties and he had impeccable manners. He was always willing to help a friend and he would send flowers to girls who were ill. He was older and more mature than most of his friends. He knew where the action was, and if he wore make-up—well, at least he was *different*.

Some of the older kids—those who worked, who had something else to do—thought Smitty was a creep. But to the youngsters—to the bored and the lonely, to the dropout and the delinquent, to the young girls with beehive hair-dos and tight pants they didn't quite fill out, and to the boys with acne and no jobs—to these people, Smitty was a kind of folk hero. Nutty maybe, but at least more dramatic, more theatrical, more *interesting* than anyone else in their lives: a semi-ludicrous, sexy-eyed pied piper who, stumbling along in his rag-stuffed boots, led them up and down Speedway.

On the evening of May 31, 1964, Alleen Rowe prepared to go to bed early. She had to be in class by 6 A.M., and she had an examination the next day. Alleen was a pretty girl of 15, a better-than-average student who talked about going to college and becoming an oceanographer. She was also a sensitive child—given to reading romantic novels and taking long walks in the desert at night. Recently she had been going through a period of adolescent melancholia, often talking with her mother, a nurse, about death. She would, she hoped, be some day reincarnated as a cat.

On this evening, dressed in a black bathing suit and thongs, her usual costume around the house, she had watched the Beatles on TV and had tried to teach her mother to dance the Frug. Then she took her bath, washed her hair, and came out to kiss her mother good night. Norma Rowe, an attractive, womanly divorcee, was somehow moved by the girl's clean fragrance and said, "You smell so good—are you wearing perfume?"

"No, Mom," the girl answered, laughing, "it's just me."

20 A little later Mrs. Rowe looked in on her daughter, found her apparently sleeping peacefully, and then left for her job as a night nurse in a Tucson hospital. She had no premonition of danger, but she had lately been concerned about Alleen's friendship with a neighbor girl named Mary French.

Mary and Alleen had been spending a good deal of time together, smoking and giggling and talking girl talk in the Rowe backyard. Norma Rowe did not approve. She particularly did not approve of Mary French's friends, a tall, gangling boy of 19 named John Saunders and another named Charles Schmid. She had seen Smitty racing up and down the street in his car and once, when he came to call on Alleen and found her not at home, he had looked at Norma so menacingly with his "pinpoint eyes" that she had been frightened.

Her daughter, on the other hand, seemed to have mixed feelings about Smitty. "He's creepy," she once told her mother, "he just makes me crawl. But he can be nice when he wants to."

At any rate, later that night—according to Mary French's sworn testimony—three friends arrived at Alleen Rowe's house: Smitty, Mary French and Saunders. Smitty had frequently talked with Mary French about killing the Rowe girl by hitting her over the head with a rock. Mary French tapped on Alleen's window and asked her to come out and drink beer with them. Wearing a shift over her bathing suit, she came willingly enough.

Schmid's accomplices were strange and pitiable creatures. Each of them was afraid of Smitty, yet each was drawn to him. As a baby, John Saunders had been so afflicted with allergies that scabs encrusted his entire body. To keep him from scratching himself his parents had tied his hands and feet to the crib each night, and when eventually he was cured he was so conditioned that he could not go to sleep without being bound hand and foot.

25 Later, a scrawny boy with poor eyesight ("Just a skinny little body with a big head on it"), he was taunted and bullied by larger children; in turn he bullied those who were smaller. He also suffered badly from asthma and he had few friends. In high school he was a poor student and constantly in minor trouble.

Mary French, 19, was—to put it straight—a frump. Her face, which might have been pretty, seemed somehow lumpy, her body shapeless. She was not dull but she was always a poor student, and she finally had simply stopped going to high school. She was, a friend remembers, "fantastically in love with Smitty. She just sat home and waited while he went out with other girls."

Now, with Smitty at the wheel, the four teen-agers headed for the desert, which begins out Golf Links Road. It is spooky country, dry and empty, the yellow sand clotted with cholla and mesquite and stunted, strangely green palo verde trees, and the great humanoid saguaro that hulk against the sky. Out there at night you can hear the yip and ki-yi of coyotes, the piercing screams of wild creatures—cats, perhaps.

According to Mary French, they got out of the car and walked down into a wash, where they sat on the sand and talked for a while, the four of them. Schmid and Mary then started back to the car. Before they got there, they heard a cry and Schmid turned back toward the wash. Mary went on to the car and sat in it alone. After 45 minutes, Saunders appeared and said Smitty wanted her to come back down. She refused, and Saunders went away. Five or 10 minutes later, Smitty showed up. "He got into the car," says Mary, "and he said 'We killed her. I love you very much.' He kissed me. He was breathing real hard and seemed excited." Then Schmid got a shovel from the trunk of the car and they returned to the wash. "She was lying on her back and there was blood on her face and head," Mary French testified. Then the three of them dug a shallow grave and put the body in it and covered it up. Afterwards, they wiped Schmid's car clean of Alleen's fingerprints.

More than a year passed. Norma Rowe had reported her daughter missing and the police searched for her—after a fashion. At Mrs. Rowe's insistence they picked up Schmid, but they had no reason to hold him. The police, in fact, assumed that Alleen was just one more of Tucson's runaways.

30 Norma Rowe, however, had become convinced that Alleen had been killed by Schmid, although she left her kitchen light on every night just in case Alleen did come home. She badgered the police and she badgered the sheriff until the authorities began to dismiss her as a crank. She began to imagine a high-level

conspiracy against her. She wrote the state attorney general, the FBI, the U.S. Department of Health, Education and Welfare. She even contacted a New Jersey mystic, who said she could see Alleen's body out in the desert under a big tree.

Ultimately Norma Rowe started her own investigation, questioning Alleen's friends, poking around, dictating her findings to a tape recorder; she even tailed Smitty at night, following him in her car, scared stiff that he might spot her.

Schmid, during this time, acquired a little house of his own. There he held frequent parties, where people sat around amid his stacks of *Playboy* magazines, playing Elvis Presley records and drinking beer.

He read Jules Feiffer's novel, *Harry, the Rat with Women*, and said that his ambition was to be like Harry and have a girl commit suicide over him. Once, according to a friend, he went to see a minister, who gave him a Bible and told him to read the first three chapters of John. Instead Schmid tore the pages out and burned them in the street. "Religion is a farce," he announced. He started an upholstery business with some friends, called himself "founder and president," but then failed to put up the money he'd promised and the venture was short-lived.

He decided he liked blondes best, and took to dyeing the hair of various teen-age girls he went around with. He went out and bought two imitation diamond rings for about $13 apiece and then engaged himself, on the same day, both to Mary French and to a 15-year-old girl named Kathy Morath. His plan, he confided to a friend, was to put each of the girls to work and have them deposit their salaries in a bank account held jointly with him. Mary French did indeed go to work in the convalescent home Smitty's parents operated. When their bank account was fat enough, Smitty withdrew the money and bought a tape recorder.

By this time Smitty also had a girl from a higher social stratum than he usu- 35
ally was involved with. She was Gretchen Fritz, daughter of a prominent Tucson heart surgeon. Gretchen was a pretty, thin, nervous girl of 17 with a knack for trouble. A teacher described her as "erratic, subversive, a psychopathic liar."

At the horsy private school she attended for a time she was a misfit. She not only didn't care about horses, but she shocked her classmates by telling them they were foolish for going out with boys without getting paid for it. Once she even committed the unpardonable social sin of turning up at a formal dance accompanied by boys wearing what was described as beatnik dress. She cut classes, she was suspected of stealing and when, in the summer before her senior year, she got into trouble with juvenile authorities for her role in an attempted theft at a liquor store, the headmaster suggested she not return and then recommended she get psychiatric treatment.

Charles Schmid saw Gretchen for the first time at a public swimming pool in the summer of 1964. He met her by the simple expedient of following her home, knocking on the door and, when she answered, saying, "Don't I know you?" They talked for an hour. Thus began a fierce and stormy relationship. A good deal of what authorities know of the development of this relationship comes from the statements of a spindly scarecrow of a young man who wears pipestem trousers and Beatle boots: Richard Bruns. At the time Smitty was becoming involved with Gretchen, Bruns was 18 years old. He had served two terms in the reformatory at Fort Grant. He had been in and out of trouble his whole life, had never fit in anywhere. Yet, although he never went beyond the tenth grade in school and his credibility on many counts is suspect, he is clearly intelligent and even sensitive. He was, for a time, Smitty's closest friend and confidant, and he is today one of the mainstays of the state's case against Smitty. His story:

"He and Gretchen were always fighting," says Bruns. "She didn't want him to drink or go out with the guys or go out with other girls. She wanted him to stay home, call her on the phone, be punctual. First she would get suspicious of him, then he'd get suspicious of her. They were made for each other."

Their mutual jealousy led to sharp and continual arguments. Once she infuriated him by throwing a bottle of shoe polish on his car. Another time she was driving past Smitty's house and saw him there with some other girls. She jumped out of her car and began screaming. Smitty took off into the house, out the back, and climbed a tree in his backyard.

His feelings for her were an odd mixture of hate and adoration. He said he 40
was madly in love with her, but he called her a whore. She would let Smitty in her bedroom window at night. Yet he wrote an anonymous letter to the Tucson Health Department accusing her of having venereal disease and spreading it about town. But Smitty also went to enormous lengths to impress Gretchen, once shooting holes through the windows of his car and telling her that thugs, from whom he was protecting her, had fired at him. So Bruns described the relationship.

On the evening of Aug. 16, 1965, Gretchen Fritz left the house with her little sister Wendy, a friendly, lively 13-year-old, to go to a drive-in movie. Neither girl ever came home again. Gretchen's father, like Alleen Rowe's mother, felt sure that Charles Schmid had something to do with his daughters' disappearance, and eventually he hired Bill Heilig, a private detective, to handle the case. One of Heilig's men soon found Gretchen's red compact car parked behind a motel, but the police continued to assume that the girls had joined the ranks of Tucson's runaways.

About a week after Gretchen disappeared, Bruns was at Smitty's house. "We were sitting in the living room," Bruns recalls. "He was sitting on the sofa and I was in the chair by the window and we got on the subject of Gretchen. He said, 'You know I killed her?' I said I didn't, and he said 'You know where?' I said no. He said, 'I did it here in the living room. First I killed Gretchen, then Wendy was still going "*huh, huh, huh,*" so I . . . [Here Bruns showed how Smitty made a garroting gesture.] Then I took the bodies and I put them in the trunk of the car. I put the bodies in the most obvious place I could think of because I just didn't care anymore. Then I ditched the car and wiped it clean.' "

Bruns was not particularly upset by Smitty's story. Months before, Smitty had told him of the murder of Alleen Rowe, and nothing had come of that. So he was not certain Smitty was telling the truth about the Fritz girls. Besides, Bruns detested Gretchen himself. But what happened next, still according to Bruns's story, did shake him up.

One night not long after, a couple of tough-looking characters, wearing sharp suits and smoking cigars, came by with Smitty and picked up Bruns. Smitty said they were Mafia, and that someone had hired them to look for Gretchen. Smitty and Bruns were taken to an apartment where several men were present whom Smitty later claimed to have recognized as local Cosa Nostra figures.

They wanted to know what had happened to the girls. They made no threats, but the message, Bruns remembers, came across loud and clear. These were no street-corner punks: these were the real boys. In spite of the intimidating company, Schmid lost none of his insouciance. He said he didn't know where Gretchen was, but if she turned up hurt he wanted these men to help him get whoever was responsible. He added that she might have gone to California.

By the time Smitty and Bruns got back to Smitty's house, they were both a little shaky. Later that night, says Bruns, Smitty did the most unlikely thing imaginable: he called the FBI. First he tried the Tucson office and couldn't raise anyone. Then he called Phoenix and couldn't get an agent there either. Finally he put in a person-to-person call to J. Edgar Hoover in Washington. He didn't get Hoover, of course, but he got someone and told him that the Mafia was harassing him over the disappearance of a girl. The FBI promised to have someone in touch with him soon.

Bruns was scared and said so. It occurred to him now that if Smitty really had killed the Fritz girls and left their bodies in an obvious place, they were in very bad trouble indeed—with the Mafia on one hand and the FBI on the other. "Let's go bury them," Bruns said.

"Smitty stole the keys to his old man's station wagon," says Bruns, "and then we got a flat shovel—the only one we could find. We went to Johnie's and got a hamburger, and then we drove out to the old drinking spot [in the desert]—that's what Smitty meant when he said the most obvious place. It's where we used to drink beer and make out with girls.

"So we parked the car and got the shovel and walked down there, and we couldn't find anything. Then Smitty said, 'Wait, I smell something.' We went in opposite directions looking, and then I heard Smitty say, 'Come here.' I found him kneeling over Gretchen. There was a white rag tied around her legs. Her blouse was pulled up and she was wearing a white bra and Capris.

"Then he said, 'Wendy's up this way.' I sat there for a minute. Then I followed Smitty to where Wendy was. He'd had the decency to cover her—except for one leg, which was sticking up out of the ground.

"We tried to dig with the flat shovel. We each took turns. He'd dig for a while and then I'd dig for a while, but the ground was hard and we couldn't get anywhere with that flat shovel. We dug for twenty minutes and finally Smitty said we'd better do something because it's going to get light. So he grabbed the rag that was around Gretchen's legs and dragged her down in the wash. It made a noise like dragging a hollow shell. It stunk like hell. Then Smitty said wipe off her shoes, there might be fingerprints, so I wiped them off with my handkerchief and threw it away.

"We went back to Wendy. Her leg was sticking up with a shoe on it. He said take off her tennis shoe and throw it over there. I did, I threw it. Then he said, 'Now you're in this as deep as I am.' " By then, the sisters had been missing for about two weeks.

Early next morning Smitty did see the FBI. Nevertheless — here Bruns's story grows even wilder — that same day Smitty left for California, accompanied by a couple of Mafia types, to look for Gretchen Fritz. While there, he was picked up by the San Diego police on a complaint the he was impersonating an FBI officer. He was detained briefly, released and returned to Tucson.

But now, it seemed to Richard Bruns, Smitty began acting very strangely. He startled Bruns by saying, "I've killed — not three times, but four. Now it's your turn, Ritchie." He went berserk in his little house, smashing his fist through a wall, slamming doors, then rushing out into the backyard in nothing but his undershorts, where he ran through the night screaming, "God is going to punish me!" He also decided, suddenly, to get married — to a 15-year-old girl who was a stranger to most of his friends.

If Smitty seemed to Bruns to be losing his grip, Ritchie Bruns himself was not in 55
much better shape. His particular quirk revolved around Kathy Morath, the thin, pretty, 16-year-old daughter of a Tucson postman. Kathy had once been attracted to Smitty. He had given her one of his two cut-glass engagement rings. But Smitty never really took her seriously, and one day, in a fit of pique and jealousy, she threw the ring back in his face. Ritchie Bruns comforted her and then started dating her himself. He was soon utterly and irrevocably smitten with goofy adoration.

Kathy accepted Bruns as a suitor, but halfheartedly. She thought him weird (oddly enough, she did not think Smitty in the least weird) and their romance was short-lived. After she broke up with him last July, Bruns went into a blue funk, a nosedive into romantic melancholy, and then, like some love-swacked Elizabethan poet, he started pouring out his heart to her on paper. He sent her poems, short stories, letters 24 pages long. ("My God, you should have read the stuff," says her perplexed father. "His letters were so romantic it was like 'Next week, East Lynne.' ") Bruns even began writing a novel dedicated to "My Darling Kathy."

If Bruns had confined himself to literary catharsis, the murders of the Rowe and Fritz girls might never have been disclosed. But Ritchie went a little bit around the bend. He became obsessed with the notion that Kathy Morath was the next victim on Smitty's list. Someone had cut the Moraths' screen door, there had been a prowler around her house, and Bruns was sure that it was Smitty. (Kathy and her father, meantime, were sure it was Bruns.)

"I started having this dream," Bruns says. "It was the same dream every night. Smitty would have Kathy out in the desert and he'd be doing all those things to her, and strangling her, and I'd be running across the desert with a gun in my hand, but I could never get there."

If Bruns couldn't save Kathy in his dreams, he could, he figured, stop a walking, breathing Smitty. His scheme for doing so was so wild and so simple that it put the whole Morath family into a state of panic and very nearly landed Bruns in jail.

Bruns undertook to stand guard over Kathy Morath. He kept watch in front 60
of her house, in the alley, and in the street. He patrolled the sidewalk from early in the morning till late at night, seven days a week. If Kathy was home he would be there. If she went out, he would follow her. Kathy's father called the police, and when they told Bruns he couldn't loiter around like that, Bruns fetched his dog and walked the animal up and down the block, hour after hour.

Bruns by now was wallowing in feelings of sacrifice and nobility—all of it unappreciated by Kathy Morath and her parents. At the end of October, he was finally arrested for harassing the Morath family. The judge, facing the obviously woebegone and smitten young man, told Bruns that he wouldn't be jailed if he'd agree to get out of town until he got over his infatuation.

Bruns agreed and a few days later went to Ohio to stay with his grandmother and try to get a job. It was hopeless. He couldn't sleep at night, and if he did doze off he had his old nightmare again.

One night he blurted out the whole story to his grandmother in their kitchen. She thought he had had too many beers and didn't believe him. "I hear beer does strange things to a person," she said comfortingly. At her words Bruns exploded, knocked over a chair and shouted, "The one time in my life when I need advice and what do I get?" A few minutes later he was on the phone to the Tucson police.

Things happened swiftly. At Bruns's frantic insistence, the police picked up Kathy Morath and put her in protective custody. They went into the desert and discovered—precisely as Bruns had described them—the grisly, skeletal remains of Gretchen and Wendy Fritz. They started the machinery that resulted in the arrest a week later of John Saunders and Mary French. They found Charles Schmid working in the yard of his little house, his face layered with make-up, his nose covered by a patch of adhesive plaster which he had worn for five months, boasting that his nose was broken in a fight, and his boots packed full of old rags and tin cans. He put up no resistance.

John Saunders and Mary French confessed immediately to their roles in the slay- 65
ing of Alleen Rowe and were quickly sentenced, Mary French to four to five years, Saunders to life. When Smitty goes on trial for this crime, on March 15, they will be principal witnesses against him.

Meanwhile Ritchie Bruns, the perpetual misfit, waits apprehensively for the end of the Fritz trial, desperately afraid that Schmid will go free. "If he does," Bruns says glumly, "I'll be the first one he'll kill."

As for Charles Schmid, he has adjusted well to his period of waiting. He is polite and agreeable with all, though at the preliminary hearings he glared menacingly at Ritchie Bruns. Dressed tastefully, tie neatly knotted, hair carefully combed, his face scrubbed clean of make-up, he is a short, compact, darkly handsome young man with a wide, engaging smile and those deepset eyes.

The people of Tucson wait uneasily for what fresh scandal the two trials may develop. Civic leaders publicly cry that a slur has been cast on their community by an isolated crime. High school students have held rallies and written vehement editorials in the school papers, protesting that they all are being judged by the actions of a few oddballs and misfits. But the city reverberates with stories of organized teen-age crime and vice, in which Smitty is cast in the role of a minor-league underworld boss. None of these later stories has been substantiated.

One disclosure, however, has most disturbing implications: Smitty's boasts may have been heard not just by Bruns and his other intimates, but by other teen-agers as well. How many—and precisely how much they knew—it remains impossible to say. One authoritative source, however, having listened to the admissions of six high school students, says they unquestionably knew enough so that they should have gone to the police—but were either afraid to talk, or didn't want to rock the boat.

As for Smitty's friends, the thought of telling the police never entered their 70
minds.

"I didn't know he killed her," said one, "and even if I had, I wouldn't have said anything. I wouldn't want to be a fink."

Out in the respectable Tucson suburbs parents have started to crack down on the youngsters and have declared Speedway hangouts off limits. "I thought my folks were bad before," laments one grounded 16-year-old, "but now they're just impossible."

As for the others—Smitty's people—most don't care very much. Things are duller without Smitty around, but things have always been dull.

"There's nothing to do in this town," says one of his girls, shaking her dyed 75
blond hair. "The only other town I know is Las Vegas and there's nothing to do there either." For her, and for her friends, there's nothing to do in any town.

They are down on Speedway again tonight, cruising, orbiting the drive-ins, stopping by the joints, where the words of *The Bo Diddley Rock* cut through the smoke and the electronic dissonance like some macabre reminder of their fallen hero:

All you women stand in line,
And I'll love you all in an hour's time. . . .
I got a cobra snake for a necktie,
I got a brand-new house on the roadside
Covered with rattlesnake hide,
I got a brand-new chimney made on top,
Made out of human skulls.
Come on baby, take a walk with me,
And tell me, who do you love?
Who do you love?
Who do you love?
Who do you love? *[1966]*

☰ THINKING ABOUT THE TEXT

1. As his title implies, Moser analyzes Tucson at least as much as he analyzes Charles Schmid. What main points does he make about the city, especially about its youth? To what extent is setting similarly important in Oates's story?
2. Moser himself gave the name "the pied piper" to Charles Schmid. Why does Moser call Schmid this? How helpful is it to think of Arnold Friend

as a "pied piper," too? (You may wish to look up details of the classic tale "The Pied Piper of Hamelin.")

3. After Moser's article was published, Charles Schmid pled guilty to second-degree murder of Alleen Rowe. For murdering the Fritz sisters, he received the death penalty, but he was spared execution when the state of Arizona abandoned capital punishment in 1971. Schmid remained in prison, where in 1975 he was stabbed to death by two other inmates. Does Oates's story leave you with the impression that Arnold Friend will meet a similar fate? Why, or why not?

JOYCE CAROL OATES

Smooth Talk: Short Story into Film

Joyce Carol Oates published the following article in the March 23, 1986, issue of the New York Times. *She wrote it upon the release of* Smooth Talk, *a film adaptation of "Where Are You Going, Where Have You Been?"*

Some years ago in the American Southwest there surfaced a tabloid psychopath known as "The Pied Piper of Tucson." I have forgotten his name, but his specialty was the seduction and occasional murder of teen-aged girls. He may or may not have had actual accomplices, but his bizarre activities were known among a circle of teenagers in the Tucson area; for some reason they kept his secret, deliberately did not inform parents or police. It was this fact, not the fact of the mass murderer himself, that struck me at the time. And this was a pre-Manson time, early or mid-1960s.

The Pied Piper mimicked teenagers in talk, dress, and behavior, but he was not a teenager—he was a man in his early thirties. Rather short, he stuffed rags in his leather boots to give himself height. (And sometimes walked unsteadily as a consequence: did none among his admiring constituency notice?) He charmed his victims as charismatic psychopaths have always charmed their victims, to the bewilderment of others who fancy themselves free of all lunatic attractions. The Pied Piper of Tucson: a trashy dream, a tabloid archetype, sheer artifice, comedy, cartoon—surrounded, however improbably, and finally tragically, by real people. You think that, if you look twice, he won't be there. But there he is.

I don't remember any longer where I first read about this Pied Piper—very likely in *Life* Magazine. I do recall deliberately not reading the full article because I didn't want to be distracted by too much detail. It was not after all the mass murderer himself who intrigued me, but the disturbing fact that a number of teenagers—from "good" families—aided and abetted his crimes. This is the sort of thing authorities and responsible citizens invariably call "inexplicable" because they can't find explanations for it. They would not have fallen under this maniac's spell, after all.

An early draft of my short story "Where Are You Going, Where Have You Been?"—from which the film *Smooth Talk* was adapted by Joyce Chopra and

Tom Cole—had the rather too explicit title "Death and the Maiden." It was cast in a mode of fiction to which I am still partial—indeed, every third or fourth story of mine is probably in this mode—"realistic allegory," it might be called. It is Hawthornean, romantic, shading into parable. Like the medieval German engraving from which my title was taken, the story was minutely detailed yet clearly an allegory of the fatal attractions of death (or the devil). An innocent young girl is seduced by way of her own vanity; she mistakes death for erotic romance of a particularly American/trashy sort.

5 In subsequent drafts the story changed its tone, its focus, its language, its title. It became "Where Are You Going, Where Have You Been?" Written at a time when the author was intrigued by the music of Bob Dylan, particularly the hauntingly elegiac song "It's All Over Now, Baby Blue," it was dedicated to Bob Dylan. The charismatic mass murderer drops into the background and his innocent victim, a fifteen-year-old, moves into the foreground. She becomes the true protagonist of the tale, courting and being courted by her fate, a self-styled 1950s pop figure, alternately absurd and winning. There is no suggestion in the published story that "Arnold Friend" has seduced and murdered other young girls, or even that he necessarily intends to murder Connie. Is his interest "merely" sexual? (Nor is there anything about the complicity of other teenagers. I saved that yet more provocative note for a current story, "Testimony.") Connie is shallow, vain, silly, hopeful, doomed—but capable nonetheless of an unexpected gesture of heroism at the story's end. Her smooth-talking seducer, who cannot lie, promises her that her family will be unharmed if she gives herself to him; and so she does. The story ends abruptly at the point of her "crossing over." We don't know the nature of her sacrifice, only that she is generous enough to make it.

In adapting a narrative so spare and thematically foreshortened as "Where Are You Going, Where Have You Been?" film director Joyce Chopra and screenwriter Tom Cole were required to do a good deal of filling in, expanding, inventing. Connie's story becomes lavishly, and lovingly, textured; she is not an allegorical figure so much as a "typical" teenaged girl (if Laura Dern, spectacularly good-looking, can be so defined). Joyce Chopra, who has done documentary films on contemporary teenage culture and, yet more authoritatively, has an adolescent daughter of her own, creates in *Smooth Talk* a vivid and absolutely believable world for Connie to inhabit. Or worlds: as in the original story there is Connie-at-home, and there is Connie-with-her-friends. Two fifteen-year-old girls, two finely honed styles, two voices, sometimes but not often overlapping. It is one of the marvelous visual features of the film that we *see* Connie and her friends transform themselves, once they are safely free of parental observation. The girls claim their true identities in the neighborhood shopping mall. What freedom, what joy!

Smooth Talk is, in a way, as much Connie's mother's story as it is Connie's; its center of gravity, its emotional nexus, is frequently with the mother—warmly and convincingly played by Mary Kay Place. (Though the mother's sexual jealousy of her daughter is slighted in the film.) Connie's ambiguous relationship with her affable, somewhat mysterious father (well played by Levon Helm) is an excellent touch: I had thought, subsequent to the story's publication, that I should have built up the father, suggesting, as subtly as I could, an attraction there paralleling the attraction Connie feels for her seducer, Arnold Friend. And Arnold Friend himself — "A. Friend" as he says — is played with appropriately overdone sexual swagger by Treat Williams, who is perfect for the part; and just the right age. We see that Arnold Friend isn't a teenager even as Connie, mesmerized by his presumed charm, does not seem to see him at all. What is so difficult to accomplish in prose — nudging the reader to look over the protagonist's shoulder, so to speak — is accomplished with enviable ease in film.

Treat Williams as Arnold Friend is supreme in his very awfulness, as, surely, the original Pied Piper of Tucson must have been. (Though no one involved in the film knew about the original source.) Mr. Williams flawlessly impersonates Arnold Friend as Arnold Friend impersonates — is it James Dean? James Dean regarding himself in mirrors, doing James Dean impersonations? That Connie's fate is so trashy is in fact her fate.

What is outstanding in Joyce Chopra's *Smooth Talk* is its visual freshness, its sense of motion and life; the attentive intelligence the director has brought to the semi-secret world of the American adolescent — shopping mall flirtations, drive-in restaurant romances, highway hitchhiking, the fascination of rock music played very, very loud. (James Taylor's music for the film is wonderfully appropriate. We hear it as Connie hears it; it is the music of her spiritual being.) Also outstanding, as I have indicated, and numerous critics have noted, are the acting performances. Laura Dern is so dazzlingly right as "my" Connie that I may come to think I modeled the fictitious girl on her, in the way that writers frequently delude themselves about notions of causality.

10 My difficulties with *Smooth Talk* have primarily to do with my chronic hesitation — about seeing/hearing work of mine abstracted from its contexture of language. All writers know that Language is their subject; quirky word choices, patterns of rhythm, enigmatic pauses, punctuation marks. Where the quick scanner sees "quick" writing, the writer conceals nine tenths of the iceberg. Of course we all have "real" subjects, and we will fight to the death to defend those subjects, but beneath the tale-telling it is the tale-telling that grips us so very fiercely. The writer works in a single dimension, the director works in three. I assume they are professionals to their fingertips; authorities in their medium as I am an authority (if I am) in mine. I would fiercely defend the placement of a semicolon in one of my novels but I would probably have deferred in the end to Joyce Chopra's decision to reverse the story's conclusion, turn it upside down, in a sense, so that the film ends not with death, not with a sleepwalker's crossing over to her fate, but upon a scene of reconciliation, rejuvenation.

A girl's loss of virginity, bittersweet but not necessarily tragic. Not today. A girl's coming-of-age that involves her succumbing to, but then rejecting, the "trashy dreams" of her pop teenage culture. "Where Are You Going, Where Have You Been?" defines itself as allegorical in its conclusion: Death and Death's chariot (a funky souped-up convertible) have come for the Maiden. Awakening is, in the story's final lines, moving out into the sunlight where Arnold Friend waits:

> "My sweet little blue-eyed girl," he said in a half-sung sigh that had nothing to do with [Connie's] brown eyes but was taken up just the same by the

vast sunlit reaches of the land behind him and on all sides of him—so much land that Connie had never seen before and did not recognize except to know that she was going to it.

— a conclusion impossible to transfigure into film. *[1986]*

THINKING ABOUT THE TEXT

1. In discussing Moser's article and Joyce Chopra's film, Oates specifies various elements that she put into "Where Are You Going, Where Have You Been?" How accurate do you find her description of her story? What aspects of her text, if any, do you think she distorts or ignores?
2. At the end of the film *Smooth Talk*, Connie is alive. She returns home from her outing with Arnold Friend, and she dances with her sister to James Taylor's song "Handy Man." What does Oates seem to think of this ending? Do you object to it? Why, or why not?
3. To what extent should readers of a short story be guided by the author's explanation of it? Explain your reasoning, and refer to Oates's story as well as her article about it.

MEGHAN DAUM

Jaycee Dugard and the Feel-Good Imperative

Meghan Daum (b. 1970) was born in California but grew up in Texas and New Jersey. An author, essayist, and journalist, she has a B.A. from Vassar College and an M.F.A. from Columbia University. Her work includes a novel, The Quality of Life Report *(2003), and essay collections that include* My Misspent Youth: Essays *(2001) and* The Unspeakable: And Other Subjects of Discussion *(2014). In 2015, she published* Selfish, Shallow, and Self-Absorbed: Sixteen Writers on the Decision Not to Have Kids. *She is a Guggenheim fellow and has been contributing columnist to the* Los Angeles Times, *where her essay on Jaycee Dugard appeared on July 14, 2011.*

[Los Angeles Times, July 14, 2011]

To watch Diane Sawyer's interview Sunday night with Jaycee Dugard was to wonder at times if that was Dugard herself on screen or an actress hired to play the role of the quintessential survivor. Dugard was so serene and lacking in rancor that it was hard to believe she had been kidnapped at age 11 and held prisoner for 18 years, during which she was repeatedly raped and bore two children, the first when she was just 14.

But there she was, saying things like "there is life after something tragic" and joking about how being locked indoors for so many years was her secret to smooth skin.

The interview, tied to Dugard's just-published memoir, scored big in the ratings. As with the 2002 abduction of Elizabeth Smart, Dugard's story has generated pity, anger and prurient fascination. It's a story that's horrifying in pretty much every imaginable way. Dugard was kept in handcuffs, forced to give birth in a backyard shed and so psychologically damaged that she passed up several opportunities to escape over the years. What's more, parole officers checking on her captor, convicted sex offender Phillip Garrido, managed to miss Dugard 60 times.

These revelations, stunning and grotesque as they are, haven't kept the events from being framed as the kind of tale Americans love best: a redemption story. Although we're not being asked to forget what Dugard endured or to forgive law enforcement's unconscionable negligence, it's clear that just about everyone involved in revealing what happened—from Sawyer to People magazine (which, shortly after Dugard was found, reported on her "sense of comfort and optimism") to Dugard herself—is invested in the notion that this ultimately is a feel-good story. As Sawyer listened to Dugard read from the journal she kept during her captivity—"I am so lucky and blessed for all the wonderful things that I do have"—you can almost see your great-aunt typing them into an email and forwarding them to 100 people under the heading "Words to Live By."

5 It's interesting (and perhaps not entirely coincidental) that the Dugard special aired around the same time as ABC's announcement that Smart, now 23, would be joining the network as a commentator on missing-persons cases and child abductions. It's an appointment that generates a certain queasiness. Doesn't Smart, who was kidnapped at 14 and raped repeatedly over nine months, want to move on with her life? In fairness, she's already established as a victims rights advocate, but as with Dugard, I detect a need on the part of the media to wrap her story up in a bow, to assure the public that she's OK, to reinforce the central narrative of just about everything we see on TV: Change is possible, maybe even easy; that adversity can be overcome; and that, as Dr. Phil likes to say, there are no victims, only volunteers.

The trouble is, that's simply not true. Dugard and Smart seem to have successfully made the transition to survivor, but to turn them into generic symbols of hope or, worse, to saddle them with the job of being publicly loving, forgiving and grateful despite what they endured minimizes their trauma and panders to audiences by creating a false sense of closure.

The redemption narrative (along with its corollary, the recovery narrative) is dependent on closure—especially on TV. We watch the addict, the obese person and the villainous reality show contestant in the sure and certain hope that sobriety, fitness and a trip off the island are right around the corner. Part of the reason the Casey Anthony verdict touched such a nerve was that it didn't conform to the redemption narrative. The survivor was anything but a hero. No lessons were learned.

None of this is to say that Dugard's grace isn't genuine or that Smart won't do just fine as a talking head. When Sawyer introduced Dugard as "a woman who endured the unimaginable and emerged with powerful lessons on love and life," she certainly wasn't wrong. But Dugard undoubtedly emerged with a lot more than that. All's well that ends well is more spin than reality. That's why we'd do well to recognize Dugard's courage not just in the face of the story she's telling but the one she's living.

THINKING ABOUT THE TEXT

1. From your experience, what evidence is there that Americans love "feel-good" stories? What might be an objection to these tales?
2. What exactly is Daum's objection to the redemptive story? What does Daum mean by pandering to audiences?
3. What is Daum's view of trauma and closure, and how does the expression "all's well that ends well" contradict her position?

WRITING ABOUT ISSUES

1. Write an essay in which you explain how the title of Oates's story applies to it. Consider how Connie *thinks*, not just what she does. Where, psychologically, is Connie going? Where, psychologically, has she been?
2. To what extent does present-day American culture prepare its young women for the dangers of the world? Write an essay that addresses this question by referring to Oates's story and another text in this cluster.
3. Write an essay about the Casey Anthony case that Daum mentions. How does this case fit into the redemptive story or the feel-good narrative? What seems to be the difference between this case and the others Daum mentions?
4. Research an actual case of female captivity: for example, the kidnapping of Patty Hearst, Jaycee Dugard, Elizabeth Smart, or the group of women who escaped from their abductor's Cleveland house in 2013. Then write an essay in which you develop and support a claim about the media's coverage of your chosen case. Make reference to the Meghan Daum piece.

RESEARCHING THE ISSUES

1. Watch *Smooth Talk*, the film version of this story, and, after reading several reviews, argue that the film version does or does not conform to the ideas in Daum's essay.
2. Although the story was published in 1966 and draws on a serial killer case of that time, Oates implies that the setting is the late 1950s. Research youth culture in the 1950s and argue whether Oates's representation is or is not accurate.
3. Research several critical essays on the symbolism of this story and argue that certain interpretations are or are not more reasonable than others.

Trials of Marriage: Plays

SUSAN GLASPELL, *Trifles*

LYNN NOTTAGE, *POOF!*

When does brutality in a marriage, or in a similar relationship, deserve to be called criminal abuse? How might justice be served in this situation? What kinds of solidarity might women form with one another when their husbands or other partners abuse them? Almost a hundred years apart, Susan Glaspell and Lynn Nottage vividly brought up these issues in plays merely one act long. Although these plays employ different styles—Glaspell's is realistic, Nottage's fanciful—they are interestingly similar in focusing on a pair of women who must ponder together how crime and justice figure in *un*holy wedlock.

BEFORE YOU READ

In what circumstances, if any, do you think an abused wife who takes criminal revenge on her husband deserves little or no punishment from the legal system?

SUSAN GLASPELL

Trifles

Susan Glaspell (1876–1948) is best known for the frequently anthologized play Trifles *and its short-story version, "A Jury of Her Peers." Surprisingly modern, Glaspell's work is in harmony with contemporary feminist concerns of identity, the difficulty of female expression in a patriarchal culture, the disillusionment of marriage for gifted women, and the necessity for female support and understanding.*

Glaspell graduated from Drake University in 1899 and first worked as a journalist in Des Moines, Iowa. She soon began to publish short stories in prestigious magazines like Harper's *and* The American. *After she married novelist and playwright George Cram Cook, they moved to Greenwich Village, where they felt more comfortable with its free-thinking attitudes. Glaspell continued to publish both stories and novels. She also began writing plays, and in 1916 she and her husband founded the Provincetown Players, an important source for innovative American drama. During the 1920s and 1930s, Glaspell published a number of best-selling novels, including* Brook Evans *(1928), which was turned into a successful movie. Her play* Alison's House *won the Pulitzer Prize in 1931, and her novel* The Morning Is Near *(1939) sold more than one hundred thousand copies. Today her significant successes in two genres, drama and fiction, are considered remarkable.*

CHARACTERS

GEORGE HENDERSON, *county attorney*
HENRY PETERS, *sheriff*

LEWIS HALE, *a neighboring farmer*
MRS. PETERS
MRS. HALE

SCENE: *The kitchen in the now-abandoned farmhouse of John Wright, a gloomy kitchen, and left without having been put in order—the walls covered with a faded wallpaper. Down right is a door leading to the parlor. On the right wall above this door is a built-in kitchen cupboard with shelves in the upper portion and drawers below. In the rear wall at right, up two steps is a door opening onto stairs leading to the second floor. In the rear wall at left is a door to the shed and from there to the outside. Between these two doors is an old-fashioned black iron stove. Running along the left wall from the shed door is an old iron sink and sink shelf, in which is set a hand pump. Downstage of the sink is an uncurtained window. Near the window is an old wooden rocker. Center stage is an unpainted wooden kitchen table with straight chairs on either side. There is a small chair down right. Unwashed pans under the sink, a loaf of bread outside the breadbox, a dish towel on the table—other signs of incompleted work. At the rear the shed door opens and the Sheriff comes in followed by the County Attorney and Hale. The Sheriff and Hale are men in middle life, the County Attorney is a young man; all are much bundled up and go at once to the stove. They are followed by the two women—the Sheriff's wife, Mrs. Peters, first; she is a slight wiry woman, a thin nervous face. Mrs. Hale is larger and would ordinarily be called more comfortable looking, but she is disturbed now and looks fearfully about as she enters. The women have come in slowly, and stand close together near the door.*

COUNTY ATTORNEY *(at stove rubbing his hands)*: This feels good. Come up to the fire, ladies.

MRS. PETERS *(after taking a step forward)*: I'm not—cold.

SHERIFF *(unbuttoning his overcoat and stepping away from the stove to right of table as if to mark the beginning of official business)*: Now, Mr. Hale, before we move things about, you explain to Mr. Henderson just what you saw when you came here yesterday morning.

COUNTY ATTORNEY *(crossing down to left of the table)*: By the way, has anything been moved? Are things just as you left them yesterday?

SHERIFF *(looking about)*: It's just about the same. When it dropped below zero last night I thought I'd better send Frank out this morning to make a fire for us—*(sits right of center table)* no use getting pneumonia with a big case on, but I told him not to touch anything except the stove—and you know Frank.

COUNTY ATTORNEY: Somebody should have been left here yesterday.

SHERIFF: Oh—yesterday. When I had to send Frank to Morris Center for that man who went crazy—I want you to know I had my hands full yesterday. I knew you could get back from Omaha by today and as long as I went over everything here myself——

COUNTY ATTORNEY: Well, Mr. Hale, tell just what happened when you came here yesterday morning.

HALE *(crossing down to above table)*: Harry and I had started to town with a load of potatoes. We came along the road from my place and as I got here I said,

"I'm going to see if I can't get John Wright to go in with me on a party telephone." I spoke to Wright about it once before and he put me off, saying folks talked too much anyway, and all he asked was peace and quiet—I guess you know about how much he talked himself; but I thought maybe if I went to the house and talked about it before his wife, though I said to Harry that I didn't know as what his wife wanted made much difference to John——

COUNTY ATTORNEY: Let's talk about that later, Mr. Hale. I do want to talk about that, but tell now just what happened when you got to the house.

HALE: I didn't hear or see anything; I knocked at the door, and still it was all quiet inside. I knew they must be up, it was past eight o'clock. So I knocked again, and I thought I heard somebody say, "Come in." I wasn't sure, I'm not sure yet, but I opened the door—this door *(indicating the door by which the two women are still standing)* and there in that rocker— *(pointing to it)* sat Mrs. Wright. *(They all look at the rocker down left.)*

COUNTY ATTORNEY: What—was she doing?

HALE: She was rockin' back and forth. She had her apron in her hand and was kind of—pleating it.

COUNTY ATTORNEY: And how did she—look?

HALE: Well, she looked queer.

COUNTY ATTORNEY: How do you mean—queer?

HALE: Well, as if she didn't know what she was going to do next. And kind of done up.

COUNTY ATTORNEY *(takes out notebook and pencil and sits left of center table)*: How did she seem to feel about your coming?

HALE: Why, I don't think she minded—one way or other. She didn't pay much attention. I said, "How do, Mrs. Wright, it's cold, ain't it?" And she said, "Is it?"—and went on kind of pleating at her apron. Well, I was surprised; she didn't ask me to come up to the stove, or to set down, but just sat there, not even looking at me, so I said, "I want to see John." And then she—laughed. I guess you would call it a laugh. I thought of Harry and the team outside, so I said a little sharp: "Can't I see John?" "No," she says, kind o' dull like. "Ain't he home?" says I. "Yes," says she, "he's home." "Then why can't I see him?" I asked her, out of patience. " 'Cause he's dead," says she. "*Dead?*" says I. She just nodded her head, not getting a bit excited, but rockin' back and forth. "Why—where is he?" says I, not knowing what to say. She just pointed upstairs—like that. *(Himself pointing to the room above.)* I started for the stairs, with the idea of going up there. I walked from there to here—then I says, "Why, what did he die of?" "He died of a rope round his neck," says she, and just went on pleatin' at her apron. Well, I went out and called Harry. I thought I might—need help. We went upstairs and there he was lyin'——

COUNTY ATTORNEY: I think I'd rather have you go into that upstairs, where you can point it all out. Just go on now with the rest of the story.

HALE: Well, my first thought was to get that rope off. It looked . . . *(stops; his face twitches)* . . . but Harry, he went up to him, and he said, "No, he's dead all right, and we'd better not touch anything." So we went back downstairs. She was still sitting that same way. "Has anybody been notified?"

I asked. "No," says she, unconcerned. "Who did this, Mrs. Wright?" said Harry. He said it businesslike — and she stopped pleatin' of her apron. "I don't know," she says. "You don't *know?*" says Harry. "No," says she. "Weren't you sleepin' in the bed with him?" says Harry. "Yes," says she, "but I was on the inside." "Somebody slipped a rope round his neck and strangled him and you didn't wake up?" says Harry. "I didn't wake up," she said after him. We must 'a' looked as if we didn't see how that could be, for after a minute she said, "I sleep sound." Harry was going to ask her more questions but I said maybe we ought to let her tell her story first to the coroner, or the sheriff, so Harry went fast as he could to Rivers's place, where there's a telephone.

COUNTY ATTORNEY: And what did Mrs. Wright do when she knew that you had gone for the coroner?

HALE: She moved from the rocker to that chair over there *(pointing to a small chair in the down right corner)* and just sat there with her hands held together and looking down. I got a feeling that I ought to make some conversation, so I said I had come in to see if John wanted to put in a telephone, and at that she started to laugh, and then she stopped and looked at me — scared. *(The County Attorney, who has had his notebook out, makes a note.)* I dunno, maybe it wasn't scared. I wouldn't like to say it was. Soon Harry got back, and then Dr. Lloyd came and you, Mr. Peters, and so I guess that's all I know that you don't.

COUNTY ATTORNEY *(rising and looking around)*: I guess we'll go upstairs first — and then out to the barn and around there. *(To the Sheriff.)* You're convinced that there was nothing important here — nothing that would point to any motive?

SHERIFF: Nothing here but kitchen things. *(The County Attorney, after again looking around the kitchen, opens the door of a cupboard closet in right wall. He brings a small chair from right — gets on it and looks on a shelf. Pulls his hand away, sticky.)*

COUNTY ATTORNEY: Here's a nice mess. *(The women draw nearer up center.)*

MRS. PETERS *(to the other woman)*: Oh, her fruit; it did freeze. *(To the Lawyer.)* She worried about that when it turned so cold. She said the fire'd go out and her jars would break.

SHERIFF *(rises):* Well, can you beat the woman! Held for murder and worryin' about her preserves.

COUNTY ATTORNEY *(getting down from chair)*: I guess before we're through she may have something more serious than preserves to worry about. *(Crosses down right center.)*

HALE: — Well, women are used to worrying over trifles. *(The two women move a little closer together.)*

COUNTY ATTORNEY *(with the gallantry of a young politician)*: And yet, for all their worries, what would we do without the ladies? *(The women do not unbend. He goes below the center table to the sink, takes a dipperful of water from the pail, and pouring it into a basin, washes his hands. While he is doing this the Sheriff and Hale cross to cupboard, which they inspect. The County Attorney starts to wipe his hands on the roller towel, turns it for a cleaner place.)* Dirty towels! *(Kicks his foot against the pans under the sink.)* Not much of a housekeeper, would you say, ladies?

MRS. HALE *(stiffly)*: There's a great deal of work to be done on a farm.

COUNTY ATTORNEY: To be sure. And yet *(with a little bow to her)* I know there are some Dickson County farmhouses which do not have such roller towels. *(He gives it a pull to expose its full-length again.)*

MRS. HALE: Those towels get dirty awful quick. Men's hands aren't always as clean as they might be.

COUNTY ATTORNEY: Ah, loyal to your sex, I see. But you and Mrs. Wright were neighbors. I suppose you were friends, too.

MRS. HALE *(shaking her head)*: I've not seen much of her of late years. I've not been in this house—it's more than a year.

COUNTY ATTORNEY *(crossing to women up center)*: And why was that? You didn't like her?

MRS. HALE: I liked her all well enough. Farmers' wives have their hands full, Mr. Henderson. And then——

COUNTY ATTORNEY: Yes——?

MRS. HALE *(looking about)*: It never seemed a very cheerful place.

COUNTY ATTORNEY: No—it's not cheerful. I shouldn't say she had the home-making instinct.

MRS. HALE: Well, I don't know as Wright had, either.

COUNTY ATTORNEY: You mean that they didn't get on very well?

MRS. HALE: No, I don't mean anything. But I don't think a place'd be any cheerfuller for John Wright's being in it.

COUNTY ATTORNEY: I'd like to talk more of that a little later. I want to get the lay of things upstairs now. *(He goes past the women to up right where steps lead to a stair door.)*

SHERIFF: I suppose anything Mrs. Peters does'll be all right. She was to take in some clothes for her, you know, and a few little things. We left in such a hurry yesterday.

COUNTY ATTORNEY: Yes, but I would like to see what you take, Mrs. Peters, and keep an eye out for anything that might be of use to us.

MRS. PETERS: Yes, Mr. Henderson. *(The men leave by up right door to stairs. The women listen to the men's steps on the stairs, then look about the kitchen.)*

MRS. HALE *(crossing left to sink)*: I'd hate to have men coming into my kitchen, snooping around and criticizing. *(She arranges the pans under sink which the lawyer had shoved out of place.)*

MRS. PETERS: Of course it's no more than their duty. *(Crosses to cupboard up right.)*

MRS. HALE: Duty's all right, but I guess that deputy sheriff that came out to make the fire might have got a little of this on. *(Gives the roller towel a pull.)* Wish I'd thought of that sooner. Seems mean to talk about her for not having things slicked up when she had to come away in such a hurry. *(Crosses right to Mrs. Peters at cupboard.)*

MRS. PETERS *(who has been looking through cupboard, lifts one end of towel that covers a pan)*: She had bread set. *(Stands still.)*

MRS. HALE *(eyes fixed on a loaf of bread beside the breadbox, which is on a low shelf of the cupboard)*: She was going to put this in there. *(Picks up loaf, abruptly drops it. In a manner of returning to familiar things.)* It's a shame about her fruit. I wonder if it's all gone. *(Gets up on the chair and looks.)* I think there's some here that's all right, Mrs. Peters. Yes—here; *(holding it toward the window)* this is cherries, too. *(Looking again.)* I declare I believe that's the only one. *(Gets down, jar in her hand. Goes to the sink and wipes it off on the outside.)* She'll feel awful bad after all her hard work in the hot weather. I remember the afternoon I put up my cherries last summer. *(She puts the jar on the big kitchen table, center of the room. With a sigh, is about to sit down in the rocking chair. Before she is seated realizes what chair it is; with a slow look at it, steps back. The chair which she has touched rocks back and forth. Mrs. Peters moves to center table and they both watch the chair rock for a moment or two.)*

MRS. PETERS *(shaking off the mood which the empty rocking chair has evoked. Now in a businesslike manner she speaks)*: Well I must get those things from the front room closet. *(She goes to the door at the right but, after looking into the other room, steps back.)* You coming with me, Mrs. Hale? You could help me carry them. *(They go in the other room; reappear, Mrs. Peters carrying a dress, petticoat, and skirt, Mrs. Hale following with a pair of shoes.)* My, it's cold in there. *(She puts the clothes on the big table and hurries to the stove.)*

MRS. HALE *(right of center table examining the skirt)*: Wright was close. I think maybe that's why she kept so much to herself. She didn't even belong to the Ladies' Aid. I suppose she felt she couldn't do her part, and then you don't enjoy things when you feel shabby. I heard she used to wear pretty clothes and be lively, when she was Minnie Foster, one of the town girls singing in the choir. But that—oh, that was thirty years ago. This all you want to take in?

MRS. PETERS: She said she wanted an apron. Funny thing to want, for there isn't much to get you dirty in jail, goodness knows. But I suppose just to make her feel more natural. *(Crosses to cupboard.)* She said they was in the top drawer in this cupboard. Yes, here. And then her little shawl that always hung behind the door. *(Opens stair door and looks.)* Yes, here it is. *(Quickly shuts door leading upstairs.)*

MRS. HALE *(abruptly moving toward her)*: Mrs. Peters?

MRS. PETERS: Yes, Mrs. Hale? *(At up right door.)*

MRS. HALE: Do you think she did it?

MRS. PETERS *(in a frightened voice)*: Oh, I don't know.

MRS. HALE: Well, I don't think she did. Asking for an apron and her little shawl. Worrying about her fruit.

MRS. PETERS *(starts to speak, glances up, where footsteps are heard in the room above. In a low voice)*: Mr. Peters says it looks bad for her. Mr. Henderson is awful sarcastic in a speech and he'll make fun of her sayin' she didn't wake up.

MRS. HALE: Well, I guess John Wright didn't wake when they was slipping that rope under his neck.

MRS. PETERS *(crossing slowly to table and placing shawl and apron on table with other clothing)*: No, it's strange. It must have been done awful crafty and still. They say it was such a—funny way to kill a man, rigging it all up like that.

MRS. HALE *(crossing to left of Mrs. Peters at table)*: That's just what Mr. Hale said. There was a gun in the house. He says that's what he can't understand.

MRS. PETERS: Mr. Henderson said coming out that what was needed for the case was a motive; something to show anger, or—sudden feeling.

MRS. HALE *(who is standing by the table)*: Well, I don't see any signs of anger around here. *(She puts her hand on the dish towel, which lies on the table, stands looking down at table, one-half of which is clean, the other half messy.)* It's wiped to here. *(Makes a move as if to finish work, then turns and looks at loaf of bread outside the breadbox. Drops towel. In that voice of coming back to familiar things.)* Wonder how they are finding things upstairs. *(Crossing below table to down right.)* I hope she had it a little more red-up° up there. You know, it seems kind of *sneaking.* Locking her up in town and then coming out here and trying to get her own house to turn against her!

MRS. PETERS: But, Mrs. Hale, the law is the law.

MRS. HALE: I s'pose 'tis. *(Unbuttoning her coat.)* Better loosen up your things, Mrs. Peters. You won't feel them when you go out. *(Mrs. Peters takes off her fur tippet, goes to hang it on chair back left of table, stands looking at the work basket on floor near down left window.)*

MRS. PETERS: She was piecing a quilt. *(She brings the large sewing basket to the center table and they look at the bright pieces, Mrs. Hale above the table and Mrs. Peters left of it.)*

MRS. HALE: It's a log cabin pattern. Pretty, isn't it? I wonder if she was goin' to quilt it or just knot it? *(Footsteps have been heard coming down the stairs. The Sheriff enters followed by Hale and the County Attorney.)*

SHERIFF: They wonder if she was going to quilt it or just knot it! *(The men laugh, the women look abashed.)*

COUNTY ATTORNEY *(rubbing his hands over the stove)*: Frank's fire didn't do much up there, did it? Well, let's go out to the barn and get that cleared up. *(The men go outside by up left door.)*

MRS. HALE *(resentfully)*: I don't know as there's anything so strange, our takin' up our time with little things while we're waiting for them to get the evidence. *(She sits in chair right of table smoothing out a block with decision.)* I don't see as it's anything to laugh about.

MRS. PETERS *(apologetically)*: Of course they've got awful important things on their minds. *(Pulls up a chair and joins Mrs. Hale at the left of the table.)*

MRS. HALE *(examining another block)*: Mrs. Peters, look at this one. Here, this is the one she was working on, and look at the sewing! All the rest of it has been so nice and even. And look at this! It's all over the place! Why, it looks as if she didn't know what she was about! *(After she has said this they look at each other, then start to glance back at the door. After an instant Mrs. Hale has pulled at a knot and ripped the sewing.)*

MRS. PETERS: Oh, what are you doing, Mrs. Hale?

MRS. HALE *(mildly)*: Just pulling out a stitch or two that's not sewed very good. *(Threading a needle.)* Bad sewing always made me fidgety.

red-up: To get ready or clean up.

MRS. PETERS *(with a glance at door, nervously)*: I don't think we ought to touch things.

MRS. HALE: I'll just finish up this end. *(Suddenly stopping and leaning forward.)* Mrs. Peters?

MRS. PETERS: Yes, Mrs. Hale?

MRS. HALE: What do you suppose she was so nervous about?

MRS. PETERS: Oh—I don't know. I don't know as she was nervous. I sometimes sew awful queer when I'm just tired. *(Mrs. Hale starts to say something, looks at Mrs. Peters, then goes on sewing.)* Well, I must get these things wrapped up. They may be through sooner than we think. *(Putting apron and other things together.)* I wonder where I can find a piece of paper, and string. *(Rises.)*

MRS. HALE: In that cupboard, maybe.

MRS. PETERS *(crosses right looking in cupboard)*: Why, here's a bird-cage. *(Holds it up.)* Did she have a bird, Mrs. Hale?

MRS. HALE: Why, I don't know whether she did or not—I've not been here for so long. There was a man around last year selling canaries cheap, but I don't know as she took one; maybe she did. She used to sing real pretty herself.

MRS. PETERS *(glancing around)*: Seems funny to think of a bird here. But she must have had one, or why would she have a cage? I wonder what happened to it?

MRS. HALE: I s'pose maybe the cat got it.

MRS. PETERS: No, she didn't have a cat. She's got that feeling some people have about cats—being afraid of them. My cat got in her room and she was real upset and asked me to take it out.

MRS. HALE: My sister Bessie was like that. Queer, ain't it?

MRS. PETERS *(examining the cage)*: Why, look at this door. It's broke. One hinge is pulled apart. *(Takes a step down to Mrs. Hale's right.)*

MRS. HALE *(looking too)*: Looks as if someone must have been rough with it.

MRS. PETERS: Why, yes. *(She brings the cage forward and puts it on the table.)*

MRS. HALE *(glancing toward up left door)*: I wish if they're going to find any evidence they'd be about it. I don't like this place.

MRS. PETERS: But I'm awful glad you came with me, Mrs. Hale. It would be lonesome for me sitting here alone.

MRS. HALE: It would, wouldn't it? *(Dropping her sewing.)* But I tell you what I do wish, Mrs. Peters. I wish I had come over sometimes when *she* was here. I—*(looking around the room)*—wish I had.

MRS. PETERS: But of course you were awful busy, Mrs. Hale—your house and your children.

MRS. HALE *(rises and crosses left)*: I could've come. I stayed away because it weren't cheerful—and that's why I ought to have come. I—*(looking out left window)*—I've never liked this place. Maybe because it's down in a hollow and you don't see the road. I dunno what it is, but it's a lonesome place and always was. I wish I had come over to see Minnie Foster sometimes. I can see now—*(Shakes her head.)*

MRS. PETERS *(left of table and above it)*: Well, you mustn't reproach yourself, Mrs. Hale. Somehow we just don't see how it is with other folks until—something turns up.

MRS. HALE: Not having children makes less work—but it makes a quiet house, and Wright out to work all day, and no company when he did come in. *(Turning from window.)* Did you know John Wright, Mrs. Peters?

MRS. PETERS: Not to know him; I've seen him in town. They say he was a good man.

MRS. HALE: Yes—good; he didn't drink, and kept his word as well as most, I guess, and paid his debts. But he was a hard man, Mrs. Peters. Just to pass the time of day with him—*(Shivers.)* Like a raw wind that gets to the bone. *(Pauses, her eye falling on the cage.)* I should think she would 'a' wanted a bird. But what do you suppose went with it?

MRS. PETERS: I don't know, unless it got sick and died. *(She reaches over and swings the broken door, swings it again, both women watch it.)*

MRS. HALE: You weren't raised round here, were you? *(Mrs. Peters shakes her head.)* You didn't know—her?

MRS. PETERS: Not till they brought her yesterday.

MRS. HALE: She—come to think of it, she was kind of like a bird herself—real sweet and pretty, but kind of timid and—fluttery. How—she—did—change. *(Silence: then as if struck by a happy thought and relieved to get back to everyday things. Crosses right above Mrs. Peters to cupboard, replaces small chair used to stand on to its original place down right.)* Tell you what, Mrs. Peters, why don't you take the quilt in with you? It might take up her mind.

MRS. PETERS: Why, I think that's a real nice idea, Mrs. Hale. There couldn't possibly be any objection to it could there? Now, just what would I take? I wonder if her patches are in here—and her things. *(They look in the sewing basket.)*

MRS. HALE *(crosses to right of table)*: Here's some red. I expect this has got sewing things in it. *(Brings out a fancy box.)* What a pretty box. Looks like something somebody would give you. Maybe her scissors are in here. *(Opens box. Suddenly puts her hand to her nose.)* Why—— *(Mrs. Peters bends nearer, then turns her face away.)* There's something wrapped up in this piece of silk.

MRS. PETERS: Why, this isn't her scissors.

MRS. HALE *(lifting the silk)*: Oh, Mrs. Peters—it's—— *(Mrs. Peters bends closer.)*

MRS. PETERS: It's the bird.

MRS. HALE: But, Mrs. Peters—look at it! Its neck! Look at its neck! It's all—other side *to.*

MRS. PETERS: Somebody—wrung—its—neck. *(Their eyes meet. A look of growing comprehension, of horror. Steps are heard outside. Mrs. Hale slips box under quilt pieces, and sinks into her chair. Enter Sheriff and County Attorney. Mrs. Peters steps down left and stands looking out of window.)*

COUNTY ATTORNEY *(as one turning from serious things to little pleasantries)*: Well, ladies, have you decided whether she was going to quilt it or knot it? *(Crosses to center above table.)*

MRS. PETERS: We think she was going to—knot it. *(Sheriff crosses to right of stove, lifts stove lid, and glances at fire, then stands warming hands at stove.)*

COUNTY ATTORNEY: Well, that's interesting, I'm sure. *(Seeing the bird-cage.)* Has the bird flown?

MRS. HALE *(putting more quilt pieces over the box)*: We think the—cat got it.

COUNTY ATTORNEY *(preoccupied)*: Is there a cat? *(Mrs. Hale glances in a quick covert way at Mrs. Peters.)*

MRS. PETERS *(turning from window takes a step in)*: Well, not *now*. They're superstitious, you know. They leave.

COUNTY ATTORNEY *(to Sheriff Peters, continuing an interrupted conversation)*: No sign at all of anyone having come from the outside. Their own rope. Now let's go up again and go over it piece by piece. *(They start upstairs.)* It would have to have been someone who knew just the—— *(Mrs. Peters sits down left of table. The two women sit there not looking at one another, but as if peering into something and at the same time holding back. When they talk now it is in the manner of feeling their way over strange ground, as if afraid of what they are saying, but as if they cannot help saying it.)*

MRS. HALE *(hesitatively and in hushed voice)*: She liked the bird. She was going to bury it in that pretty box.

MRS. PETERS *(in a whisper)*: When I was a girl—my kitten—there was a boy took a hatchet, and before my eyes—and before I could get there—— *(Covers her face an instant.)* If they hadn't held me back I would have— *(catches herself, looks upstairs where steps are heard, falters weakly)*—hurt him.

MRS. HALE *(with a slow look around her)*: I wonder how it would seem never to have had any children around. *(Pause.)* No, Wright wouldn't like the bird—a thing that sang. She used to sing. He killed that, too.

MRS. PETERS *(moving uneasily)*: We don't know who killed the bird.

MRS. HALE: I knew John Wright.

MRS. PETERS: It was an awful thing was done in this house that night, Mrs. Hale. Killing a man while he slept, slipping a rope around his neck that choked the life out of him.

MRS. HALE: His neck. Choked the life out of him. *(Her hand goes out and rests on the bird-cage.)*

MRS. PETERS *(with rising voice)*: We don't know who killed him. We don't *know*.

MRS. HALE *(her own feeling not interrupted)*: If there'd been years and years of nothing, then a bird to sing to you, it would be awful—still, after the bird was still.

MRS. PETERS *(something within her speaking)*: I know what stillness is. When we homesteaded in Dakota, and my first baby died—after he was two years old, and me with no other then——

MRS. HALE *(moving)*: How soon do you suppose they'll be through looking for the evidence?

MRS. PETERS: I know what stillness is. *(Pulling herself back.)* The law has got to punish crime, Mrs. Hale.

MRS. HALE *(not as if answering that)*: I wish you'd seen Minnie Foster when she wore a white dress with blue ribbons and stood up there in the choir and sang. *(A look around the room.)* Oh, I *wish* I'd come over here once in a while! That was a crime! That was a crime! Who's going to punish that?

MRS. PETERS *(looking upstairs)*: We mustn't—take on.

MRS. HALE: I might have known she needed help! I know how things can be—for women. I tell you, it's queer, Mrs. Peters. We live close together and we live far apart. We all go through the same things—it's all just a different kind of the same thing. *(Brushes her eyes, noticing the jar of fruit, reaches out for it.)* If I was you I wouldn't tell her her fruit was gone. Tell her it *ain't.* Tell her it's all right. Take this in to prove it to her. She—she may never know whether it was broke or not.

MRS. PETERS *(takes the jar, looks about for something to wrap it in; takes petticoat from the clothes brought from the other room, very nervously begins winding this around the jar. In a false voice):* My, it's a good thing the men couldn't hear us. Wouldn't they just laugh! Getting all stirred up over a little thing like a—dead canary. As if that could have anything to do with—with—wouldn't they *laugh*! *(The men are heard coming downstairs.)*

MRS. HALE *(under her breath)*: Maybe they would—maybe they wouldn't.

COUNTY ATTORNEY: No, Peters, it's all perfectly clear except a reason for doing it. But you know juries when it comes to women. If there was some definite thing. *(Crosses slowly to above table. Sheriff crosses down right. Mrs. Hale and Mrs. Peters remain seated at either side of table.)* Something to show—something to make a story about—a thing that would connect up with this strange way of doing it—— *(The women's eyes meet for an instant. Enter Hale from outer door.)*

HALE *(remaining by door)*: Well, I've got the team around. Pretty cold out there.

COUNTY ATTORNEY: I'm going to stay awhile by myself. *(To the Sheriff.)* You can send Frank out for me, can't you? I want to go over everything. I'm not satisfied that we can't do better.

SHERIFF: Do you want to see what Mrs. Peters is going to take in? *(The Lawyer picks up the apron, laughs.)*

COUNTY ATTORNEY: Oh, I guess they're not very dangerous things the ladies have picked out. *(Moves a few things about, disturbing the quilt pieces which cover the box. Steps back.)* No, Mrs. Peters doesn't need supervising. For that matter a sheriff's wife is married to the law. Ever think of it that way, Mrs. Peters?

MRS. PETERS: Not—just that way.

SHERIFF *(chuckling):* Married to the law. *(Moves to down right door to the other room.)* I just want you to come in here a minute, George. We ought to take a look at these windows.

COUNTY ATTORNEY *(scoffingly):* Oh, windows!

SHERIFF: We'll be right out, Mr. Hale. *(Hale goes outside. The Sheriff follows the County Attorney into the room. Then Mrs. Hale rises, hands tight together, looking intensely at Mrs. Peters, whose eyes make a slow turn, finally meeting Mrs. Hale's. A moment Mrs. Hale holds her, then her own eyes point the way to where the box is concealed. Suddenly Mrs. Peters throws back quilt pieces and tries to put the box in the bag she is carrying. It is too big. She opens box, starts to take bird out, cannot touch it, goes to pieces, stands there helpless. Sound of a knob turning in the other room. Mrs. Hale snatches the box and puts it in the pocket of her big coat. Enter County Attorney and Sheriff, who remains down right.)*

COUNTY ATTORNEY *(crosses to up left door facetiously):* Well, Henry, at least we found out that she was not going to quilt it. She was going to—what is it you call it, ladies?

MRS. HALE *(standing center below table facing front, her hand against her pocket):* We call it—knot it, Mr. Henderson.

Curtain. *[1916]*

THINKING ABOUT THE TEXT

1. Although much of this play is about Minnie Wright, Glaspell keeps her offstage. Why, do you think?
2. What does Glaspell imply about differences between men and women? Support your inference with details from the text.
3. What do Mrs. Hale and Mrs. Peters realize about themselves during the course of the play? To what extent should they feel guilty about their own past behavior?
4. Ultimately, Mrs. Hale and Mrs. Peters cover up evidence to protect Minnie Wright. They seem to act out of loyalty to their sex. How sympathetic are you to their stand? Do you feel there are times when you should be someone's ally because that person is of the same gender as you?
5. Is this play about freedom and confinement? About the injustice of male domination? About the bonds that hold women together? Or something else? Explain your answer.

LYNN NOTTAGE
POOF!

Lynn Nottage (b. 1964) is an American playwright and an activist focused on preventing violence against women. She grew up in New York City and attended Brown University and the Yale School of Drama. She then worked for four years at Amnesty International. Ruined, *a play about Congolese women during civil war, was awarded the Pulitzer Prize for drama in 2009. Her plays have been performed in dozens of theaters. She has received a Guggenheim Fellowship and a MacArthur Grant. Her latest play is* By the Way, Meet Vera Stark *(2011).*

CHARACTERS

SAMUEL, *Loureen's husband*
LOUREEN, *a demure housewife, early thirties*
FLORENCE, *Loureen's best friend, early thirties*

TIME: *The present*

PLACE: *Kitchen*

A NOTE: *Nearly half the women on death row in the United States were convicted of killing abusive husbands. Spontaneous combustion is not recognized as a capital crime.*

Darkness.

SAMUEL (*In the darkness*): WHEN I COUNT TO TEN I DON' WANT TO SEE YA! I DON' WANT TO HEAR YA! ONE, TWO, THREE, FOUR —

LOUREEN (*In the darkness*): DAMN YOU TO HELL, SAMUEL!

A bright flash.

Lights rise. A huge pile of smoking ashes rests in the middle of the kitchen. Loureen, a demure housewife in her early thirties, stares down at the ashes incredulously. She bends and lifts a pair of spectacles from the remains. She ever so slowly backs away.

Samuel? Uh! (*Places the spectacles on the kitchen table*) Uh! . . . Samuel? (*Looks around*) Don't fool with me now. I'm not in the mood. (*Whispers*) Samuel? I didn't mean it really. I'll be good if you come back . . . Come on now, dinner's waiting. (*Chuckles, then stops abruptly*) Now stop your foolishness . . . And let's sit down. (*Examines the spectacles*) Uh! (*Softly*) Don't be cross with me. Sure I forgot to pick up your shirt for tomorrow. I can wash another, I'll do it right now. Right now! Sam? . . . (*Cautiously*) You hear me! (*Awaits a response*) Maybe I didn't ever intend to wash your shirt. (*Pulls back as though about to receive a blow; a moment*) Uh! (*Sits down and dials the telephone*) Florence, honey, could you come on down for a moment. There's been a . . . little . . . accident . . . Quickly please. Uh!

Loureen hangs up the phone. She gets a broom and a dust pan. She hesitantly approaches the pile of ashes. She gets down on her hands and knees and takes a closer look. A fatuous grin spreads across her face. She is startled by a sudden knock on the door. She slowly walks across the room like a possessed child. Loureen lets in Florence, her best friend and upstairs neighbor. Florence, also a housewife in her early thirties, wears a floral housecoat and a pair of oversized slippers. Without acknowledgment Loureen proceeds to saunter back across the room.

FLORENCE: HEY!

LOUREEN (*Pointing at the ashes*): Uh! . . . (*She struggles to formulate words, which press at the inside of her mouth, not quite realized*) Uh! . . .

FLORENCE: You all right? What happened? (*Sniffs the air*) Smells like you burned something? (*Stares at the huge pile of ashes*) What the devil is that?

LOUREEN (*Hushed*): Samuel . . . It's Samuel, I think.

FLORENCE: What's he done now?

LOUREEN: It's him. It's him. (*Nods her head repeatedly*)

FLORENCE: Chile, what's wrong with you? Did he finally drive you out your mind? I knew something was going to happen sooner or later.

LOUREEN: Dial 911, Florence!

FLORENCE: Why? You're scaring me!

LOUREEN: Dial 911!

Florence picks up the telephone and quickly dials.

I think I killed him.

Florence hangs up the telephone.

FLORENCE: What?

LOUREEN (*Whimpers*): I killed him! I killed Samuel!

FLORENCE: Come again? . . . He's dead dead?

Loureen wrings her hands and nods her head twice, mouthing "dead dead." Florence backs away.

No, stop it, I don't have time for this. I'm going back upstairs. You know how Samuel hates to find me here when he gets home. You're not going to get me this time. (*Louder*) Y'all can have your little joke, I'm not part of it! (*A moment. She takes a hard look into Loureen's eyes; she squints*) Did you really do it this time?

LOUREEN (*Hushed*): I don't know how or why it happened, it just did.

FLORENCE: Why are you whispering?

LOUREEN: I don't want to talk too loud—something else is liable to disappear.

FLORENCE: Where's his body?

LOUREEN (*Points to the pile of ashes*): There! . . .

FLORENCE: You burned him?

LOUREEN: I DON'T KNOW! (*Covers her mouth as if to muffle her words; hushed*) I think so.

FLORENCE: Either you did or you didn't, what you mean you don't know? We're talking murder, Loureen, not oven settings.

LOUREEN: You think I'm playing?

FLORENCE: How many times have I heard you talk about being rid of him? How many times have we sat at this very table and laughed about the many ways we could do it and how many times have you done it? None.

LOUREEN (*Lifting the spectacles*): A pair of cheap spectacles, that's all that's left. And you know how much I hate these. You ever seen him without them, no! . . . He counted to four and disappeared. I swear to God!

FLORENCE: Don't bring the Lord into this just yet! Sit down now . . . What you got to sip on?

LOUREEN: I don't know whether to have a stiff shot of scotch or a glass of champagne.

Florence takes a bottle of sherry out of the cupboard and pours them each a glass. Loureen downs hers, then holds out her glass for more.

He was . . .

FLORENCE: Take your time.

LOUREEN: Standing there.

FLORENCE: And?

LOUREEN: He exploded.

FLORENCE: Did that muthafucka hit you again?

LOUREEN: No . . . he exploded. Boom! Right in front of me. He was shouting like he does, being all colored, then he raised up that big crusty hand to hit me, and poof, he was gone . . . I barely got words out and I'm looking down at a pile of ash.

Florence belts back her sherry. She wipes her forehead and pours them both another.

FLORENCE: Chile, I'll give you this, in terms of color you've matched my husband Edgar, the story king. He came in at six Sunday morning, talking about he'd hit someone with his car, and had spent all night trying to outrun the police. I felt sorry for him. It turns out he was playing poker with his paycheck no less. You don't want to know how I found out . . . But I did.

LOUREEN: You think I'm lying?

FLORENCE: I certainly hope so, Loureen. For your sake and my heart's.

LOUREEN: Samuel always said if I raised my voice something horrible would happen. And it did. I'm a witch . . . the devil spawn!

FLORENCE: You've been watching too much television.

LOUREEN: Never seen anything like this on television. Wish I had, then I'd know what to do . . . There's no question, I'm a witch. (*Looks at her hands with disgust*)

FLORENCE: Chile, don't tell me you've been messing with them mojo women again? What did I tell ya.

Loureen, agitated, stands and sits back down.

LOUREEN: He's not coming back. Oh no, how could he? It would be a miracle! Two in one day . . . I could be canonized. Worse yet, he could be . . . All that needs to happen now is for my palms to bleed and I'll be eternally remembered as Saint Loureen, the patron of battered wives. Women from across the country will make pilgrimages to me, laying pies and pot roast at my feet and asking the good saint to make their husbands turn to dust. How often does a man like Samuel get damned to hell, and go?

She breaks down. Florence moves to console her friend, then realizes that Loureen is actually laughing hysterically.

FLORENCE: You smoking crack?

LOUREEN: Do I look like I am?

FLORENCE: Hell, I've seen old biddies creeping out of crack houses, talking about they were doing church work.

LOUREEN: Florence, please be helpful, I'm very close to the edge! . . . I don't know what to do next! Do I sweep him up? Do I call the police? Do I . . .

The phone rings.

Oh God.

FLORENCE: You gonna let it ring?

Loureen reaches for the telephone slowly.

LOUREEN: NO! (*Holds the receiver without picking it up, paralyzed*) What if it's his mother? . . . She knows!

The phone continues to ring. They sit until it stops. They both breathe a sigh of relief.

I should be mourning, I should be praying, I should be thinking of the burial, but all that keeps popping into my mind is what will I wear on television when I share my horrible and wonderful story with a studio audience . . .

(*Whimpers*) He's made me a killer, Florence, and you remember what a gentle child I was. (*Whispers*) I'm a killer, I'm a killer, I'm a killer.

FLORENCE: I wouldn't throw that word about too lightly even in jest. Talk like that gets around.

LOUREEN: You think they'll lock me up? A few misplaced words and I'll probably get the death penalty, isn't that what they do with women like me, murderesses?

FLORENCE: Folks have done time for less.

LOUREEN: Thank you, just what I needed to hear!

FLORENCE: What did you expect, that I was going to throw up my arms and congratulate you? Why'd you have to go and lose your mind at this time of day, while I got a pot of rice on the stove and Edgar's about to walk in the door and wonder where his goddamn food is. (*Losing her cool*) And he's going to start in on me about all the nothing I've been doing during the day and why I can't work and then he'll mention how clean you keep your home. And I don't know how I'm going to look him in the eye without . . .

LOUREEN: I'm sorry, Florence. Really. It's out of my hands now.

She takes Florence's hand and squeezes it.

FLORENCE (*Regaining her composure*): You swear on your right tit?

LOUREEN (*Clutching both breasts*): I swear on both of them!

FLORENCE: Both your breasts, Loureen! You know what will happen if you're lying. (*Loureen nods; hushed*) Both your breasts Loureen?

LOUREEN: Yeah!

FLORENCE (*Examines the pile of ashes, then shakes her head*): Oh sweet, sweet Jesus. He must have done something truly terrible.

LOUREEN: No more than usual. I just couldn't take being hit one more time.

FLORENCE: You've taken a thousand blows from that man, couldn't you've turned the cheek and waited? I'd have helped you pack. Like we talked about.

A moment.

LOUREEN: Uh! . . . I could blow on him and he'd disappear across the linoleum. (*Snaps her fingers*) Just like that. Should I be feeling remorse or regret or some other "R" word? I'm strangely jubilant, like on prom night when Samuel and I first made love. That's the feeling! (*The women lock eyes*) Uh!

FLORENCE: Is it . . .

LOUREEN: Like a ton of bricks been lifted from my shoulders, yeah.

FLORENCE: Really?

LOUREEN: Yeah!

Florence walks to the other side of the room.

FLORENCE: You bitch!

LOUREEN: What?

FLORENCE: We made a pact.

LOUREEN: I know.

FLORENCE: You've broken it . . . We agreed that when things got real bad for both of us we'd . . . you know . . . together . . . Do I have to go back upstairs to that? . . . What next?

LOUREEN: I thought you'd tell me! . . . I don't know!

FLORENCE: I don't know!

LOUREEN: I don't know!

Florence begins to walk around the room, nervously touching objects. Loureen sits, wringing her hands and mumbling softly to herself.

FLORENCE: Now you got me, Loureen, I'm truly at a loss for words.

LOUREEN: Everybody always told me, "Keep your place, Loureen." My place, the silent spot on the couch with a wine cooler in my hand and a pleasant smile that warmed the heart. All this time I didn't know why he was so afraid for me to say anything, to speak up. Poof! . . . I've never been by myself, except for them two weeks when he won the office pool and went to Reno with his cousin Mitchell. He wouldn't tell me where he was going until I got that postcard with the cowboy smoking a hundred cigarettes . . . Didn't Sonny Larkin look good last week at Caroline's? He looked good, didn't he . . .

Florence nods. She nervously picks up Samuel's jacket, which is hanging on the back of the chair. She clutches it unconsciously.

NO! No! Don't wrinkle that, that's his favorite jacket. He'll kill me. Put it back!

Florence returns the jacket to its perch. Loureen begins to quiver.

I'm sorry. (*She grabs the jacket and wrinkles it up*) There! (*She then digs into the coat pockets and pulls out his wallet and a movie stub*) Look at that, he said he didn't go to the movies last night. Working late. (*Frantically thumbs through his wallet*) Picture of his motorcycle, Social Security card, driver's license, and look at that from our wedding. (*Smiling*) I looked good, didn't I? (*She puts the pictures back in the wallet and holds the jacket up to her face*) There were some good things. (*She then sweeps her hand over the jacket to remove the wrinkles, and folds it ever so carefully, and finally throws it in the garbage*) And out of my mouth those words made him disappear. All these years and just words, Florence. That's all they were.

FLORENCE: I'm afraid I won't ever get those words out. I'll start resenting you, honey. I'm afraid won't anything change for me.

LOUREEN: I been to that place.

FLORENCE: Yeah? But now I wish I could relax these old lines (*Touches her forehead*) for a minute maybe. Edgar has never done me the way Samuel did you, but he sure did take the better part of my life.

LOUREEN: Not yet, Florence.

FLORENCE (*Nods*): I have the children to think of . . . right?

LOUREEN: You can think up a hundred things before . . .

FLORENCE: Then come upstairs with me . . . we'll wait together for Edgar and then you can spit out your words and . . .

LOUREEN: I can't do that.

FLORENCE: Yes you can. Come on now.

Loureen shakes her head no.

Well, I guess my mornings are not going to be any different.

LOUREEN: If you can say for certain, then I guess they won't be. I couldn't say that.

FLORENCE: But you got a broom and a dust pan, you don't need anything more than that . . . He was a bastard and nobody will care that he's gone.

LOUREEN: Phone's gonna start ringing soon, people are gonna start asking soon, and they'll care.

FLORENCE: What's your crime? Speaking your mind?

LOUREEN: Maybe I should mail him to his mother. I owe her that. I feel bad for her, she didn't understand how it was. I can't just throw him away and pretend like it didn't happen. Can I?

FLORENCE: I didn't see anything but a pile of ash. As far as I know you got a little careless and burned a chicken.

LOUREEN: He was always threatening not to come back.

FLORENCE: I heard him.

LOUREEN: It would've been me eventually.

FLORENCE: Yes.

LOUREEN: I should call the police, or someone.

FLORENCE: Why? What are you gonna tell them? About all those times they refused to help, about all those nights you slept in my bed 'cause you were afraid to stay down here? About the time he nearly took out your eye 'cause you flipped the television channel?

LOUREEN: No.

FLORENCE: You've got it, girl!

LOUREEN: Good-bye to the fatty meats and the salty food. Good-bye to the bourbon and the bologna sandwiches. Good-bye to the smell of his feet, his breath and his bowel movements . . . (*A moment. She closes her eyes and, reliving a horrible memory, she shudders*) Good-bye. (*Walks over to the pile of ashes*) Samuel? . . . Just checking.

FLORENCE: Good-bye Samuel.

They both smile.

LOUREEN: I'll let the police know that he's missing tomorrow . . .

FLORENCE: Why not the next day?

LOUREEN: Chicken's warming in the oven, you're welcome to stay.

FLORENCE: Chile, I got a pot of rice on the stove, kids are probably acting out . . . and Edgar, well . . . Listen, I'll stop in tomorrow.

LOUREEN: For dinner?

FLORENCE: Edgar wouldn't stand for that. Cards maybe.

LOUREEN: Cards.

The women hug for a long moment. Florence exits. Loureen stands over the ashes for a few moments contemplating what to do. She finally decides to sweep them under the carpet, and then proceeds to set the table and sit down to eat her dinner.

END OF PLAY *[1993]*

THINKING ABOUT THE TEXT

1. How would you describe Loureen's relationship to her husband Samuel? What reason can you suggest for Loureen staying in that relationship?
2. What specific offenses does Samuel commit? Which would be violations of wedding vows? Which would be legal issues?
3. Describe the progression of Loureen's response to Samuel's death.
4. What evidence might there be that Loureen could become a model for battered women? What do you think about Edgar's future?
5. Even though Samuel dies, the play doesn't seem tragic. Point out the comic elements. How does Nottage get away with using humor in a play where someone loses his life?

MAKING COMPARISONS

1. Do the comic elements of *POOF!* lead you to take Nottage's play less seriously than you do Glaspell's? Why, or why not?
2. Do Glaspell and Nottage show similar reasoning in keeping certain characters offstage, unseen? Explain.
3. To what extent, if any, does Nottage's play seem more racially specific than Glaspell's?

WRITING ABOUT ISSUES

1. Choose either Glaspell's or Nottage's play. Then, write an essay in which you develop and support a claim about whether justice is served in the play you have selected. Make clear how you are defining *justice*.
2. On the basis of Glaspell's and Nottage's plays, would you say that marital problems have basically remained the same over the last hundred years, or do you think that they have significantly changed? Write an essay that answers this question by referring to specific passages in both texts.
3. Write an essay in which you explain how a mystical intervention (like the spontaneous combustion in *POOF!*) could occur in *Trifles*, or how the thorough realism of *Trifles* could be transferred to *POOF!* If you wish, substitute for this essay a script that you compose.
4. How can one tell that partners in a marriage, or in a similar relationship, have equal status? Write an essay specifying the features you have in mind. If you wish, refer to one or both of the plays in this cluster.

Recalling a Violent Crime: Essays

BRUCE SHAPIRO, "One Violent Crime"

EMILY BERNARD, "Scar Tissue"

A crime, especially when violent, may leave its surviving victims suffering for years. Physically, they may be marked forever. Psychologically, they may sustain long-lasting trauma, haunted by memories of the event. In part, their mental pain may be caused by people other than the original perpetrator. These may include reporters and politicians who exploit criminal cases to promote their personal views. Several victims of violent crimes have tried to regain power over their lives by writing about what happened. They thereby make sure that *their* sense of what occurred becomes public record. Of course, even victims of the same crime will differ in their perspectives on it—not only at the moment, but also later on.

These effects are evident in the following two essays. Their authors were both victims of a stabbing attack in New Haven, Connecticut, on August 7, 1994. Bruce Shapiro wrote about his experience soon afterward. He was stirred to do so by government policies that he saw as misguided in their approach to crime and other social problems. Emily Bernard wrote about the attack, however, almost two decades later. Her essay acknowledges Shapiro's but mostly contemplates how this horrific incident scarred her own body and mind.

BEFORE YOU READ

Have you or someone you know been the victim of a crime? If so, what were the psychological effects of it?

BRUCE SHAPIRO

One Violent Crime

Bruce Shapiro (b. 1959) is currently associated with two universities. At Yale, he teaches investigative journalism; at Columbia, he is executive director of the Dart Center for Journalism & Trauma. He has edited Shaking the Foundations: 200 Years of Investigative Journalism in America *(2003) and coauthored (with Jesse Jackson and Jesse Jackson Jr.)* Legal Lynching: The Death Penalty and America's Future *(2003). Shapiro is also a veteran reporter, having written for such publications as the* New York Times, *the* Los Angeles Times, *the* Guardian, Salon.com, *and* The Nation *magazine, whose April 3, 1995, issue is where "One Violent Crime" first appeared. Subsequently it was chosen for the volume* The Best American Essays 1996.

Alone in my home I am staring at the television screen and shouting. On the evening local news I have unexpectedly encountered video footage, several months old, of myself writhing on an ambulance gurney, bright green shirt open and drenched with blood, skin pale, knee raised, trying desperately and with utter futility to find relief from pain.

On the evening of August 7, 1994, I was among seven people stabbed and seriously wounded in a coffee bar a few blocks from my house. Any televised recollection of this incident would be upsetting. But the anger that has me shouting tonight is quite specific, and political, in origin: My picture is being shown on the news to illustrate why Connecticut's legislature plans to lock up more criminals for a longer time. A picture of my body, contorted and bleeding, has become a propaganda image in the crime war.

I had not planned to write about this assault. But for months now the politics of the nation have in large part been the politics of crime, from last year's federal crime bill through the fall elections through the Contract With America proposals currently awaiting action by the Senate. Among a welter of reactions to the attack, one feeling is clear: I am unwilling to be a silent poster child in this debate.

The physical and political truth about violence and crime lie in their specificity, so here is what happened: I had gone out for after-dinner coffee that evening with two friends and New Haven neighbors, Martin and Anna Broell Bresnick. At 9:45 we arrived at a recently opened coffeehouse on Audubon Street, a block occupied by an arts high school where Anna teaches, other community arts institutions, a few pleasant shops, and upscale condos. Entering, we said hello to another friend, a former student of Anna's named Cristina Koning, who the day before had started working behind the counter. We sat at a small table near the front of the cafe; about fifteen people were scattered around the room. Just before 10, the owner announced closing time. Martin stood up and walked a few yards to the counter for a final refill.

Suddenly there was chaos — as if a mortar shell had landed. I looked up, 5
heard Martin call Anna's name, saw his arm raised and a flash of metal and people leaping away from a thin bearded man with a ponytail. Tables and chairs toppled. Without thinking I shouted to Anna, "Get down!" and pulled her to the floor, between our table and the cafe's outer wall. She clung to my shirt, I to her shoulders, and, crouching, we pulled each other toward the door.

What actually happened I was only able to tentatively reconstruct many weeks later. Apparently, as Martin headed toward the counter the thin bearded man, whose name we later learned was Daniel Silva, asked the time from a young man named Richard Colberg, who answered and turned to leave.

Without any warning, Silva pulled out a hunting knife with a six-inch blade and stabbed in the lower back a woman leaving with Colberg, a medical technician named Kerstin Braig. Then he stabbed Colberg, severing an artery in his thigh. Silva was a slight man but he moved with demonic speed and force around the cafe's counter. He struck Martin in the thigh and in the arm he raised to protect his face. Our friend Cris Koning had in a moment's time pushed out the screen in a window and helped the wounded Kerstin Braig through it to safety. Cris was talking on the phone with the police when Silva lunged over the counter and stabbed her in the chest and abdomen. He stabbed Anna in the side as she and I pulled each other along the wall. He stabbed Emily Bernard, a graduate student who had been sitting quietly reading a book, in the abdomen as she tried to flee through the cafe's back door. All of this happened in about the time it has taken you to read this paragraph.

Meanwhile, I had made it out the cafe's front door onto the brick sidewalk with Anna, neither of us realizing yet that she was wounded. Seeing Martin through the window, I returned inside and we came out together. Somehow we separated, fleeing opposite ways down the street. I had gone no more than a few steps when I felt a hard punch in my back followed instantly by the unforgettable sensation of skin and muscle tissue parting. Silva had stabbed me about six inches above my waist, just beneath my rib cage. (That single deep stroke cut my diaphragm and sliced my spleen in half.) Without thinking, I clapped my left hand over the wound even before the knife was out and its blade caught my hand, leaving a slice across my palm and two fingers.

"Why are you doing this?" I cried out to Silva in the moment after feeling his knife punch in and yank out. As I fell to the street he leaned over my face; I vividly remember the knife's immense and glittering blade. He directed the point through my shirt into the flesh of my chest, beneath my left shoulder. I remember his brown beard, his clear blue-gray eyes looking directly into mine, the round globe of a street lamp like a halo above his head. Although I was just a few feet from a cafe full of people and although Martin and Anna were only yards away, the street, the city, the world felt utterly empty except for me and this thin bearded stranger with clear eyes and a bowie knife. The space around us—well-lit, familiar Audubon Street, where for six years I had taken a child to music lessons—seemed literally to have expanded into a vast and dark canyon.

"You killed my mother," he answered. My own desperate response: "Please 10
don't." Silva pulled the knifepoint out of my chest and disappeared. A moment later I saw him flying down the street on a battered, ungainly bicycle, back straight, vest flapping and ponytail flying.

After my assailant had gone I lay on the sidewalk, hand still over the wound on my back, screaming. Pain ran over me like an express train; it felt as though every muscle in my back was locked and contorted; breathing was excruciating. A security guard appeared across the street from me; I called out to him but he stood there frozen, or so it seemed. (A few minutes later, he would help police chase Silva down.) I shouted to Anna, who was hiding behind a car down the street. Still in shock and unaware of her own injury, she ran for help, eventually collapsing on the stairs of a nearby brownstone where a prayer group that was meeting upstairs answered her desperate ringing of the doorbell. From where I was lying, I saw a second-floor light in the condo complex across the way. A woman's head appeared in the window. "Please help me," I implored. "He's gone. Please help me." She shouted back that she had called the police, but she did not come to the street. I was suddenly aware of a blond woman—Kerstin Braig, though I did not know her name then—in a white-and-gray plaid dress, sitting on the curb. I asked her for help. "I'm sorry, I've done all I can," she muttered. She raised her hand, like a medieval icon; it was covered with blood. So was her dress. She sank into a kind of stupor. Up the street I saw a police car's flashing blue lights, then another's, then

I saw an officer with a concerned face and a cracking radio crouched beside me. I stayed conscious as the medics arrived and I was loaded into an ambulance—being filmed for television, as it turns out, though I have no memory of the crew's presence.

Being a victim is a hard idea to accept, even while lying in a hospital bed with tubes in veins, chest, penis, and abdomen. The spirit rebels against the idea of oneself as fundamentally powerless. So I didn't think much for the first few days about the meaning of being a victim; I saw no political dimension to my experience.

As I learned in more detail what had happened I thought, in my jumbled-up, anesthetized state, about my injured friends—although everyone survived, their wounds ranged from quite serious to critical—and about my wounds and surgery. I also thought about my assailant. A few facts about him are worth repeating. Until August 7 Daniel Silva was a self-employed junk dealer and a homeowner. He was white. He lived with his mother and several dogs. He had no arrest record. A New Haven police detective who was hospitalized across the hall from me recalled Silva as a socially marginal neighborhood character. He was not, apparently, a drug user. He had told neighbors about much violence in his family—indeed not long before August 7 he showed one neighbor a scar on his thigh he said was from a stab wound.

A week earlier, Silva's 79-year-old mother had been hospitalized for diabetes. After a few days the hospital moved her to a new room; when Silva saw his mother's empty bed he panicked, but nurses swiftly took him to her new location. Still, something seemed to have snapped. Earlier on the day of the stabbings, police say, Silva released his beloved dogs, set fire to his house, and rode away on his bicycle as it burned. He arrived on Audubon Street with a single dog on a leash, evidently convinced his mother was dead. (She actually did die a few weeks after Silva was jailed.)

While I lay in the hospital, the big story on CNN was the federal crime bill then 15
being debated in Congress. Even fogged by morphine I was aware of the irony. I was flat on my back, the result of a particularly violent assault, while Congress eventually passed the anti-crime package I had editorialized against in *The Nation* just a few weeks earlier. Night after night hospital, unable to sleep, I watched the crime bill debate replayed and heard Republicans and Democrats (who had sponsored the bill in the first place) fall over each other to prove who could be the toughest on crime.

The bill passed on August 21, a few days after I returned home. In early autumn I actually read the entire text of the crime bill—all 412 pages. What I found was perhaps obvious, yet under the circumstances compelling: Not a single one of those 412 pages would have protected me or Anna or Martin or any of the others from our assailant. Not the enhanced prison terms, not the forty-four new death penalty offenses, not the three-strikes-you're-out requirements, not the summary deportations of criminal aliens. And the new tougher-than-tough anti-crime provisions of the Contract With America, like the proposed abolition of the Fourth Amendment's search and seizure protections, offer no more practical protection.

On the other hand, the mental-health and social-welfare safety net shredded by Reaganomics and conservatives of both parties might have made a difference in the life of someone like my assailant—and thus in the life of someone like me. My assailant's growing distress in the days before August 7 was obvious to his neighbors. He had muttered darkly about relatives planning to burn down his house. A better-funded, more comprehensive safety net might just have saved me and six others from untold pain and trouble.

From my perspective—the perspective of a crime victim—the Contract With America and its conservative Democratic analogs are really blueprints for making the streets even less safe. Want to take away that socialistic income subsidy called welfare? Fine. Connecticut Governor John Rowland proposes cutting off all benefits after eighteen months. So more people in New Haven and other cities will turn to the violence-breeding economy of crack, or emotionally implode from sheer desperation. Cut funding for those soft-headed social workers? Fine; let more children be beaten without the prospect of outside intervention, more Daniel Silvas carrying their own traumatic scars into violent adulthood. Get rid of the few amenities prisoners enjoy, like sports equipment, musical instruments, and the right to get college degrees, as proposed by the Congressional right? Fine; we'll make sure that those inmates are released to their own neighborhoods tormented with unchanneled rage.

One thing I could not properly appreciate in the hospital was how deeply many friends, neighbors, and acquaintances were shaken by the coffeehouse stabbings, let alone strangers who took the time to write. The reaction of most was a combination of decent horrified empathy and a clear sense that their own presumption of safety was undermined.

But some people who didn't bother to aquaint themselves with the facts used 20
the stabbings as a sort of Rorschach test on which they projected their own preconceptions about crime, violence, and New Haven. Some present and former Yale students, for instance, were desperate to see in my stabbing evidence of the great dangers of New Haven's inner city. One student newspaper wrote about "New Haven's image as a dangerous town fraught with violence." A student reporter from another Yale paper asked if I didn't think the attack proved New Haven needs better police protection. Given the random nature of this assault—it could as easily have happened in wealthy, suburban Greenwich, where a friend of mine was held up at an ATM at the point of an assault rifle—it's tempting to dismiss such sentiments as typical products of an insular urban campus. But city-hating is central to today's political culture. Newt Gingrich excoriates cities as hopelessly pestilential, crime-ridden, and corrupt. Fear of urban crime and of the dark-skinned people who live in cities is the right's basic text, and defunding cities a central agenda item for the new Congressional majority.

Yet in no small measure it was the institutions of an urban community that saved my life last August 7. That concerned police officer who found me and Kerstin Braig on the street was joined in a moment by enough emergency workers to handle the carnage in and around the coffeehouse, and his backups arrived quickly enough to chase down my assailant three blocks away. In minutes I was taken to Yale–New Haven hospital less than a mile away—built in part with the kind of public funding so hated by the right. As I was wheeled into the E.R., several dozen doctors and nurses descended to handle all the wounded.

By then my abdomen had swelled from internal bleeding. Dr. Gerard Burns, a trauma surgeon, told me a few weeks later that I arrived on his operating table white as a ghost; my prospects, he said, would have been poor had I not been delivered so quickly, and to an E.R. with the kind of trauma team available only at a large metropolitan hospital. In other words, if my stabbing had taken place in the suburbs I would have bled to death.

"Why didn't anyone try to stop him?" That question was even more common than the reflexive city-bashing. I can't even begin to guess the number of times I had to answer it. Each time, I repeated that Silva moved too fast, that it was simply too confusing. And each time, I found the question not just foolish but offensive.

"Why didn't anyone stop him?" To understand that question is to understand, in some measure, why crime is such a potent political issue. To begin with, the question carries not empathy but an implicit burden of blame; it really asks "Why didn't *you* stop him?" It is asked because no one likes to imagine oneself a victim. It's far easier to graft onto oneself the aggressive power of the attacker, to embrace the delusion of oneself as Arnold Schwarzenegger defeating a multitude single-handedly. *If I am tough enough and strong enough I can take out the bad guys.*

The country is at present suffering from a huge version of this same delusion. This myth is buried deep in the political culture, nurtured in the historical tales of frontier violence and vigilantism and by the action-hero fantasies of film and television. Now, bolstered by the social Darwinists of the right, who see society as an unfettered marketplace in which the strongest individuals flourish, this delusion frames the crime debate.

I also felt that the question "Why didn't anybody stop him?" implied only two choices: Rambo-like heroism or abject victimhood. To put it another way, it suggests that the only possible responses to danger are the individual biological imperatives of fight or flight. And people don't want to think of themselves as on the side of flight. This is a notion whose political moment has arrived. In last year's debate over the crime bill, conservatives successfully portrayed themselves as those who would stand and fight; liberals were portrayed as ineffectual cowards.

"Why didn't anyone stop him?" That question and its underlying implications see both heroes and victims as lone individuals. But on the receiving end of a violent attack, the fight-or-flight dichotomy didn't apply. Nor did that radically individualized notion of survival. At the coffeehouse that night, at the moments of greatest threat, there were no Schwarzeneggers, no stand-alone heroes. (In fact I doubt anyone could have "taken out" Silva; as with most crimes, his attack came too suddenly.) But neither were there abject victims. Instead, in the confusion and panic of life-threatening attack, *people reached out to one another*. This sounds simple; yet it suggests there is an instinct for mutual aid that poses a profound challenge to the atomized individualism of the right. Cristina Koning helped the wounded Kerstin Braig to escape, and Kerstin in turn tried to bring Cristina along. Anna and I, and then Martin and I, clung to each other, pulling one another toward the door. And just as Kerstin found me on the sidewalk rather than wait for help alone, so Richard and Emily, who had never met before, together sought a hiding place around the corner. Three of us even spoke with Silva either the moment before or the instant after being stabbed. My plea to Silva may or may not have been what kept him from pushing his knife all the way through my chest and into my heart; it's impossible to know what was going through his mind. But this impulse to communicate, to establish human contact across a gulf of terror and insanity, is deeper and more subtle than the simple formulation of fight or flight, courage or cowardice, would allow.

I have never been in a war, but I now think I understand a little the intense bond among war veterans who have survived awful carnage. It is not simply the common fact of survival but the way in which the presence of these others seemed to make survival itself possible. There's evidence, too, that those who try to go it alone suffer more. In her insightful study *Trauma and Recovery*, Judith Herman, a psychiatrist, writes about rape victims, Vietnam War veterans, political prisoners, and other survivors of extreme violence. "The capacity to preserve social connection . . ." she concludes, "even in the face of extremity, seems to protect people to some degree against the later development of post-traumatic syndromes. For example, among survivors of a disaster at sea, the men who had managed to escape by cooperating with other showed relatively little evidence of post-traumatic stress afterward." On the other hand, she reports that the "highly symptomatic" ones among those survivors were " 'Rambos,' men who had plunged into impulsive, isolated action and not affiliated with others."

The political point here is that the Rambo justice system proposed by the right is rooted in that dangerous myth of the individual fighting against a hostile world. Recently that myth got another boost from several Republican-controlled state legislatures, which have made it much easier to carry concealed handguns. But the myth has nothing to do with the reality of violent crime, the ways to prevent it, or the needs of survivors. Had Silva been carrying a handgun instead of a knife on August 7, there would have been a massacre.

30 I do understand the rage and frustration behind the crime-victim movement, and I can see how the right has harnessed it. For weeks I thought obsessively and angrily of those minutes on Audubon Street, when first the nameless woman in the window and then the security guard refused to approach me—as if I, wounded and helpless, were the dangerous one. There was also a subtle shift in my consciousness a few days after the stabbing. Up until that point, the legal process and press attention seemed clearly centered on my injuries and experience, and those of my fellow victims. But once Silva was arraigned and the formal process of prosecution began, it became *his* case, not mine. I experienced an overnight sense of marginalization, a feeling of helplessness bordering on irrelevance.

Sometimes that got channeled into outrage, fear and panic. After arraignment, Silva's bail was set at $700,000. That sounds high, but just 10 percent of that amount in cash, perhaps obtained through some relative with home equity, would have bought his pretrial release. I was frantic at even this remote prospect of Silva walking the streets. So were the six other victims and our families. We called the prosecutor virtually hourly to request higher bail. It was eventually raised to $800,000, partly because of our complaints and partly because an arson charge was added. Silva remains in the Hartford Community Correctional Center awaiting trial.

Near the six-month anniversary of the stabbings I called the prosecutor and learned that in December Silva's lawyer filed papers indicating he intends to claim a "mental disease or defect" defense. If successful it would send him to a maximum-security hospital for the criminally insane for the equivalent of the maximum criminal penalty. In February the court was still awaiting a report from Silva's psychiatrist. Then the prosecution will have him examined by its own psychiatrist. "There's a backlog," I was told; the case is not likely to come to trial until the end of 1995 at the earliest. Intellectually, I understand that Silva is securely behind bars, that the court system is overburdened, that the delay makes no difference in the long-term outcome. But emotionally, viscerally, the delay is devastating.

Another of my bursts of victim-consciousness involved the press. Objectively, I know that many people who took the trouble to express their sympathy to me found out only through news stories. And sensitive reporting can for the crime victim be a kind of ratification of the seriousness of an assault, a reflection of the community's concern. One reporter for the daily *New Haven Register*, Josh Kovner, did produce level-headed and insightful stories about the Audubon Street attack. But most other reporting was exploitative, intrusive, and inaccurate. I was only a few hours out of surgery, barely able to speak, when the calls from television stations and papers started coming to my hospital room. Anna and Martin, sent home to recover, were ambushed by a Hartford TV crew as they emerged from their physician's office, and later rousted from their beds by reporters from another TV station ringing their doorbell. The *Register*'s editors enraged all seven victims by printing our home addresses (a company policy, for some reason) and running spectacularly distressing full-color photos of the crime scene complete with the coffee bar's bloody windowsill.

Such press coverage inspired in all of us a rage it is impossible to convey. In a study commissioned by the British Broadcasting Standards Council, survivors of violent crimes and disasters "told story after story of the hurt they suffered through the timing of media attention, intrusion into their privacy and harassment, through inaccuracy, distortion and distasteful detail in what was reported." This suffering is not superficial. To the victim of violent crime the press may reinforce the perception that the world is an uncomprehending and dangerous place.

The very same flawed judgments about "news value" contribute significantly 35
to a public conception of crime that is as completely divorced from the facts as a Schwarzenegger movie. One study a few years ago found that reports on crime

and justice constitute 22–28 percent of newspaper stories, "nearly three times as much attention as the presidency or the Congress or the state of the economy." And the most spectacular crimes—the stabbing of seven people in an upscale New Haven coffee bar, for instance—are likely to be the most "newsworthy" even though they are statistically the least likely. "The image of crime presented in the media is thus a reverse image of reality," writes sociologist Mark Warr in a study commissioned by the National Academy of Sciences.

Media coverage also brings us to another crucial political moral: The "seriousness" of crime is a matter of race and real estate. This has been pointed out before, but it can't be said too often. Seven people stabbed in a relatively affluent, mostly white neighborhood near Yale University—this was big news on a slow news night. It went national over the A.P. wires and international over CNN's *Headline News*. It was covered by *The New York Times*, and words of sympathy came to New Haven from as far as Prague and Santiago. Because a graduate student and a professor were among those wounded, the university sent representatives to the emergency room. The morning after, New Haven Mayor John DeStefano walked the neighborhood to reassure merchants and office workers. For more than a month the regional press covered every new turn in the case.

Horrendous as it was, though, no one was killed. Four weeks later, a 15-year-old girl named Rashawnda Crenshaw was driving with two friends about a mile from Audubon Street. As the car in which she was a passenger turned a corner she was shot through the window and killed. Apparently her assailants mistook her for someone else. Rashawnda Crenshaw was black and her shooting took place in the Hill, the New Haven neighborhood with the highest poverty rate. No Yale officials showed up at the hospital to comfort Crenshaw's mother or cut through red tape. The *New York Times* did not come calling; there were certainly no bulletins flashed around the world on CNN. The local news coverage lasted just long enough for Rashawnda Crenshaw to be buried.

Anyone trying to deal with the reality of crime, as opposed to the fantasies peddled to win elections, needs to understand the complex suffering of those who are survivors of traumatic crimes, and the suffering and turmoil of their families. I have impressive physical scars: There is a broad purple line from my breastbone to the top of my pubic bone, an X-shaped cut into my side where the chest tube entered, a thick pink mark on my chest where the point of Silva's knife rested on a rib. Then on my back is the unevenly curving horizontal scar where Silva thrust the knife in and yanked it out, leaving what looks like a crooked smile. But the disruption of my psyche is, day in and day out, more noticeable. For weeks after leaving the hospital I awoke nightly agitated, drenched with perspiration. For two months I was unable to write; my brain simply refused to concentrate. Into any moment of mental repose would rush images from the night of August 7; or alternatively, my mind would simply not tune in at all. My reactions are still out of balance and disproportionate. I shut a door on my finger, not too hard, and my body is suddenly flooded with adrenaline and I nearly faint. Walking on the arm of my partner, Margaret, one evening I abruptly shove her to the side of the road; I have seen a tall, lean shadow on the block where we are headed and am alarmed out of all proportion. I get into an argument and find myself quaking with rage for an hour afterward, completely unable to restore calm. Though to all appearances normal, I feel at a long arm's remove from all the familiar sources of pleasure, comfort and anger that shaped my daily life before August 7.

What psychologists call post-traumatic stress disorder is, among other things, a profoundly political state in which the world has gone wrong, in which you feel isolated from the broader community by the inarticulable extremity of experience. I have spent a lot of time in the past few months thinking about what the world must look like to those who have survived repeated violent attacks, whether children battered in their homes or prisoners beaten or tortured behind bars; as well as those, like rape victims, whose assaults are rarely granted public ratification.

The right owes much of its success to the anger of crime victims and the 40
argument that government should do more for us. This appeal is epitomized by the rise of restitution laws—statutes requiring offenders to compensate their targets. On February 7 the House of Representatives passed, by a vote of 431 to 0, the Victim Restitution Act, a plank of the Contract With America that would supposedly send back to jail offenders who don't make good on their debts to their victims. In my own state, Governor Rowland recently proposed a restitution amendment to the state Constitution.

On the surface it is hard to argue with the principle of reasonable restitution—particularly since it implies community recognition of the victim's suffering. But I wonder if these laws really will end up benefiting someone like me—or if they are just empty, vote-getting devices that exploit victims and could actually hurt our chances of getting speedy, substantive justice. H. Scott Wallace, former counsel to the Senate Judiciary Subcommittee on Juvenile Justice, writes in *Legal Times* that the much-touted Victim Restitution Act is "unlikely to put a single dollar into crime victims' pockets, would tie up the federal courts with waves of new damages actions, and would promote unconstitutional debtors' prisons."

I also worry that the rhetoric of restitution confuses—as does so much of the imprisonment-and-execution mania dominating the political landscape—the goals of justice and revenge. Revenge, after all, is just another version of the individualized, take-out-the-bad-guys myth. Judith Herman believes indulging fantasies of revenge actually worsens the psychic suffering of trauma survivors: "The desire for revenge . . . arises out of the victim's experience of complete helplessness," and forever ties the victim's fate to the perpetrator's. Real recovery from the cataclysmic isolation of trauma comes only when "the survivor comes to understand the issues of principle that transcend her personal grievance against the perpetrator . . . [a] principle of social justice that connects the fate of others to her own." The survivors and victims' families of the Long Island Rail Road massacre have banded together not to urge that Colin Ferguson be executed but to work for gun control.

What it all comes down to is this: What do survivors of violent crime really need? What does it mean to create a safe society? Do we need courts so overburdened by nonviolent drug offenders that Daniel Silvas go untried for eighteen months, delays that leave victims and suspects alike in limbo? Do we need to throw nonviolent drug offenders into mandatory-sentence proximity with violent sociopaths and career criminals? Do we need the illusory bravado of a Schwarzenegger film—or the real political courage of those L.I.R.R. survivors?

If the use of my picture on television unexpectedly brought me face to face with the memory of August 7, some part of the attack is relived for me daily as I watch the gruesome, voyeuristically reported details of the stabbing deaths of two people in California, Nicole Brown Simpson and Ronald Goldman. It was relived even more vividly by the televised trial of Colin Ferguson. (One night recently after watching Ferguson on the evening news I dreamed that I was on the witness stand and Silva, like Ferguson, was representing himself and questioning me.) Throughout the trial, as Ferguson spoke of falling asleep and having someone else fire his gun, I heard neither cowardly denial nor what his first lawyer called "black rage"; I heard Daniel Silva's calm, secure voice telling me I killed his mother. And when I hear testimony by the survivors of that massacre—on a train as comfortable and familiar to them as my neighborhood coffee bar—I feel a great and incommunicable fellowship.

But the public obsession with these trials, I am convinced, has no more to do 45
with the real experience of crime victims than does the anti-crime posturing of politicians. I do not know what made my assailant act as he did. Nor do I think crime and violence can be reduced to simple political categories. I do know that the answers will not be found in social Darwinism and atomized individualism, in racism, in dismantling cities and increasing the destitution of the poor. To the contrary: Every fragment of my experience suggests that the best protections from crime and the best aid to victims are the very social institutions most derided by the right. As crime victim and citizen what I want is the reality of a safe community—not a politician's fantasyland of restitution and revenge. That is my testimony. *[1995]*

THINKING ABOUT THE TEXT

1. Shapiro concludes by announcing that he has written a "testimony." What do you think are typical features of this genre? In what ways, specifically, does Shapiro's essay belong to it? Do you think that "testimony" is indeed the best genre label for his text? Why, or why not?
2. Where are you especially conscious that Shapiro is relying on ethos—that is, using his personal experience of crime to present himself as an authority on issues of social policy? Refer to specific passages. Do you think it is fair for him to claim authority in this way? Explain your reasoning.
3. Where are you especially conscious that Shapiro is relying on pathos—that is, emphasizing his own emotions to get his readers feeling as he does? Again, refer to specific passages, and discuss whether you find his strategy persuasive.

4. What, specifically, are Shapiro's main criticisms of how government and the press treat crime? Evaluate at least two of these criticisms, providing support for your attitude toward them.
5. Shapiro seems especially critical of political conservatives, and the *Nation* (where his essay first appeared) is known for being a left-wing magazine. Could someone who is conservative nevertheless agree with at least some of his ideas? If so, which?

EMILY BERNARD

Scar Tissue

Born in Nashville, Tennessee, in 1967, Emily Bernard teaches English and U.S. Ethnic Studies at the University of Vermont. A scholar of the modern cultural movement known as the Harlem Renaissance, she has published a book on its most famous photographer, Carl Van Vechten and the Harlem Renaissance: A Portrait in Black and White *(2012). She has also edited* Remember Me to Harlem: The Letters of Langston Hughes and Carl Van Vechten *(2001) and* Some of My Best Friends: Writers on Interracial Friendship *(2004). With Deborah Willis, she co-authored the 2009 volume* Michelle Obama: The First Lady in Photographs. *Bernard has distinguished herself as an essayist, too, with repeated inclusion in* The Best American Essays *series. She was a graduate student when Daniel Silva stabbed her, Bruce Shapiro, and others. Unlike Shapiro, she waited many years before writing about the attack. "Scar Tissue" first appeared in the summer 2012 issue of* The American Scholar *magazine.*

I have been telling this story for years, but telling is a different animal from writing. In the telling and retelling, I have shaped a version of it, one that fits neatly in my hand, something to pull out of my pocket at will, to display, and to tuck away when I'm ready, like a shell or a stone or a molded piece of clay. The story that I have honed over the years is as neat as my scar; it is smooth, and tender, and conceals more than it reveals.

Here is how the newspaper tells the story:

Stabbing spree sends 7 to hospitals

Seven people were wounded, two with life-threatening injuries, when a man pulled a knife at an Audubon Street coffeehouse late Sunday and began stabbing people.

The attack, occurring about 10 P.M., caused pandemonium and a virtual blood bath at Koffee? at 104 Audubon St. . . .

There was no apparent provocation, police said.

The two victims most seriously hurt were covered with blood, and it was difficult to tell how many times they were stabbed, police said.

"There was a lot of blood," said Detective Sgt. Robert Lawlor. "There were some very serious injuries." . . .

> Bloody handprints were visible on a window, where one of the victims apparently climbed out. Numerous trails of blood led from the coffeehouse, which is in the city's arts district, near the Creative Arts Workshop and Neighborhood Music School.
>
> "We have no idea what provoked him," Lawlor said. There were about 10 people in the coffeehouse at the time, he said.
>
> — *New Haven Register*, Monday, August 8, 1994

The first time I read this article I laughed when I got to "blood bath." Blood bath? It sounded like a trailer for a slasher movie. But it wasn't a movie, and there *was* a lot of blood, evidently, although I don't remember that part. I remember it differently.

On the night of August 7, 1994, I walked into a coffee shop called Koffee? on Audubon Street in New Haven, Connecticut. I was a graduate student in the American Studies Program at Yale University, and I was there to work. I had James Weldon Johnson with me, specifically his 1912 novel, *The Autobiography of an Ex-Colored Man*, about which I was writing a paper. I was having a hard time concentrating that night so I went out to the shop, which was not far from where I lived, and was one of the many places in New Haven where students went to read and write and talk. It was a typical coffee shop in a typical college town.

5 I was frustrated with my work, so frustrated with my inability to concentrate that I was giving the evening only one last chance. It was late, nearly nine o'clock. Maybe too late, maybe just call it a night. I debated with myself, walking slowly the three yards from my car to the door of the shop. I was probably talking to myself, as I do all the time, muttering about everything I had to do. A man on a bicycle arrived at the door at the same time I did. Beside him stood an average-size, average-looking brown dog on a leash. The man was listing on the bike, rocking back and forth, as if he himself had not made the commitment to go inside (*maybe, maybe not*). Our eyes met. He looked like Gallagher, the 1970s comedian — the same long hair and bald pate, the same thick mustache. Or at least that's what I remember. To this day, when I think of Daniel Silva, I think of Gallagher, whom I rarely — if ever — thought about before that night.

I don't remember who went in first, but I remember making the decision not to let the oddness of this stranger bother me. Because he was odd. It was the way he was listing on his bicycle; it was the strange way he looked at me. His look was familiar, or too aware — not the passing glance of a stranger. Even now, I have a hard time describing it. He was odd; it was instinct. I k*new* something was wrong with him. Or maybe this is just the cliché of hindsight speaking. After all, we're talking about a university town, and a coffee shop full of nerds off in their own odd little worlds, people who routinely talk to themselves out loud, as I had been doing.

Here I have lingered longer than I lingered in the moment, which passed as quickly as the proverbial blink of an eye. I looked at the man, made the unconscious association with the comic, went in to get my coffee, and planted myself at a table. I put my keys on the table. I pulled out my book and notepad. I took off my glasses and my watch. No distractions, just me and the page, as naked as I allow myself to get in public.

At some point, I looked up and noticed that the strange man had settled into a chair not far from me. I was aware of him as he watched a table full of young girls next to me, presumably undergraduates. They were talking about sex, a sexual encounter one of them had had recently. The girls were loud, sexy, and full of swagger. I had been feeling annoyed by them and their devil-may-care bluster, but now I looked up and saw that the man was staring at them, obviously and (I assumed) salaciously. I felt intimidated by his frank stare, but the girls didn't seem to care, which made me proud of them, and emboldened for myself. Go ahead, talk about sex, I thought. Don't let this freak scare you. Eventually the girls left.

When they did, the man seemed to turn his attention to a young woman I assumed to be a medical student or a law student, judging by the size of her very official-looking textbooks. She tried to engage him in conversation, said something like, Hi. I didn't hear his response, but I do know that not long after this exchange, the woman gathered up her books and left.

What happened next? Here's what I told Detective C. Willougby at 1:30 A.M. 10
on August 8, 1994 (for whatever reason, Detective Willougby recorded this in all-caps):

> THIS DETECTIVE THEN SPOKE WITH ______ WHO STATED THAT SHE WAS SITTING INSIDE THE RESTAURANT WHEN A WHITE MALE CAME IN WHO HAD A DOG. SHE THEN STATED THAT HE WALKED THE DOG OUTSIDE AND HE THEN RETURNED, HE THEN PULLED OUT A KNIFE AND STARTED STABBING PEOPLE IN THE RESTAURANT. SHE STATED THAT HE STAB HER ONCE IN THE STOMACH AND SHE THEN FLED THE RESTAURANT. SHE THEN STATED THAT SHE HAD NEVER SEEN THE WHITE MALE SUBJECT BEFORE AND SHE DOES NOT KNOW HIM.

What I remember about the moments before it happened is stillness, the hum of low voices and the lights, bright yet soothing, like the talk surrounding me. People talking and laughing quietly. Students, professors, writers; I was the only black person present at that time, but these were people just like me, people who looked like me. So many moments like these over the years in coffee shops in so many cities; all forgettable, ordinary, uneventful. But these particular moments on this particular evening stay with me more palpably than any other moments from that long night. The stillness, the quiet, the hum of low pleasant talk. The sensation of being inside those moments—it is the only *real* memory I retain from that night. Yet, just beyond the border of that quiet, pleasant memory, I can still hear the rhythmic, continuous sound of a dog barking outside, like a warning.

Suddenly, chaos. Pandemonium. Bedlam. Topsy-turvy. Madhouse. A holy mess. All hell broke loose. The room turned upside down, on its back, inside out, went crazy, flipped out. Other words, other clichés. Fear erupted like a seismic shift in the earth's surface, and then charged and pierced and saturated the room like smoke. Fear—a good friend to me that night—chased me toward the back door. But even in the midst of this utter confusion, I paused and listened for gunshots—this was America, after all. I paused not only to listen for the gunshots but to brace myself — literally to tense my shoulders and grit my teeth, searching inside somewhere for the pain, for the tearing impact of a bullet. When I completed that brief inventory, and discovered no bullet, I was overcome with a feeling of relief. Hope, luck. A chance. And a door right behind me — and I *ran*.

And then I was outside in back of the coffeehouse. There were no lights; it was as dark as the bottom of a pocket. Others rushed by me — I don't remember if they were speaking, shouting, screaming, or crying. What I remember was silence, which seemed inexplicable to me even then. I would find out later that what felt like silence was the adrenaline pounding in my ears and deafening me.

I don't know how long I watched the others rush past me before I walked back toward the coffee shop. I don't remember how long I stood there, trying to understand, before everything in me *rejected* what I saw and I charged back into the shop, to retrieve my watch, my keys and glasses, so that I could drive home. Why would I have done this? Nothing about it makes any sense. But however I try to explain it to myself — my stubborn West Indian heritage, a Freudian state of denial — the same thing happened next.

I found myself face to face with the odd man, and he had a knife in his hand. 15 At this point the knife would have had a substantial amount of blood on it. I don't remember the blood. I do remember asking him not to kill me. I meant it, of course, but it also just seemed like the thing to say. I felt that I was playing a role; I felt that the die was cast. I had turned and met my fate. But I was watching as much as I was experiencing. My witnessing was involuntary. In *The Autobiography of an Ex-Colored Man*, the narrator recalls being "fixed to the spot" when he watches a white mob lynch a black man. Like that narrator, I was fixed to the spot.

Why? I did not move because I did not want to excite this man. I did not move because I had to see what was going to happen next. I did not move because I was afraid. I did not move because I was free from fear, as many report feeling in the moments before death. I did not move because I knew that he would hurt me if I did. I did not move because I knew he would not kill me. I did not move because I didn't believe he had the knife I saw in front of me. I did not move because I did not know what to do.

I saw the knife before it entered me. But I have no specific memory of it, the instrument that has determined much of the course of the past 17 years of my life. It went in and out swiftly. What was the sensation upon impact? I don't remember. But I do remember that when he pulled it out of my gut, I fell to the ground. What did it feel like? Strange. Weird. Unusual. Lying on the ground, I beseeched God for help. When I neither felt nor heard a thundering reply, I started to laugh. I knew that I needed a hospital, not God. But I call this my "God moment" anyway, because when I laughed, my wound gaped open, and I looked down and saw and then felt the thick, warm blood rush over my fingers. It is time to get to a hospital, God was saying. I got up, and ran again.

I was more afraid of being in the dark without my glasses than I was of running into the man with the knife a second time. I had never been out on a city street alone without my glasses. I have been wearing eyeglasses since I was eight years old. The last time I had gone without glasses in public, I was not allowed to walk down a street without holding on to the hand of an adult. I was on the eve of my 27th birthday when I was stabbed. The last time I had been out in public without my glasses, I was not permitted to be awake at just before 10:24, which is the time it has become at this point in the story.

A figure ran toward me, a man; I was afraid. I stopped, and he must have seen my fear, this man, because he waved his hands in the air and shouted, "I'm a good Samaritan! A good Samaritan!" I trusted his words, his biblical reference. I let him lead me to some steps across the street.

From Officer Pitoniak's Incident Report, 10:44, on August 7, 1994: 20

> This investigating officer did find one white male subject and one Black female subject on the stairs of a apartment complex located across the street from 24 Whitney Avenue. Both subjects had stab wounds to the stomach areas and Bleeding Profusely. Due to extent of injuries and calling for medical assistance this officer was not able to obtain any identification of victims.

What's your name? What's your social security number? I fired these questions at the white male subject shortly before Officer Pitoniak arrived. The young white man, whom I had never seen before, was sitting on the steps a few feet away from me. He was going into shock, and I was trying to keep him from doing so. I kept up my round of questioning, and he mumbled some answers. "I'm going out, I'm going out," he said, and fainted. It was only then that I really looked at him. He's white as a sheet, I thought. Literally, *white as a sheet*. This is what it looks like, I thought. He had pale skin, light blond hair, and wore a white oxford shirt. The contrast between the blood and his skin, hair, and shirt must have been dramatic, but I don't remember the blood. I watched him. The more he faded away, the less I was able to ignore what was happening just under my hand. An EMT came close to me and asked about the young man, and I answered him. I talked and talked, told my story, posed as a witness, even as I was seeing sparks and hearing static and the man's badge started to blur. The EMT, trained to recognize the signs of shock, cradled my head and took my hand away from my side. His gloved hand, like my bare hand, became wet with my blood. He said something to his partner—who was tending to the white male subject—and suddenly there was a commotion around me. He laid me down carefully on the steps. He held my bloody hand as his team moved me onto the gurney. At some point, we met eyes and we laughed. The more I laughed, the more I came to. The more I laughed, the more my wound gaped open, which made us laugh even harder. It was all so *absurd*.

> Emily Bernard, 26, is listed in serious condition at Yale-New Haven Hospital. Her birthday is Thursday. —from "The Victims," *New Haven Register*, Tuesday, August 9, 1994

On my birthday, a middle-aged white couple brought chocolates to my hospital room. "It just seemed so sad that you had to spend your birthday in the hospital," said the woman, while her husband looked on sympathetically. I began to cry, not only because of the purity of their kindness, but also because of the morphine. The morphine was there to shield me from the pain, a consequence of healing, my body reassembling itself. A word about the pain: it didn't hurt, the knife. That and the surprising fact that no one died are the two things I always make sure to say in my version of the story.

I did experience terrible pain on the night of August 7. The person responsible for it was the surgeon on call that night. I lay on a gurney, feeling helpless and afraid. A surgeon walked over and without saying a word to me, or even looking in my direction, plunged his fingers into my gaping wound. I gasped and instinctively grabbed his hand. It was only then that the man looked at me, and said icily, "Don't. Touch. My. Hand." His eyes were Aryan blue and as cold as his voice. I asked questions about what was happening, and he refused to respond. Only the attending nurses treated me with any kindness or respect. Whenever I tell the story of the night I got stabbed, I always say that the person who did the most injury to me, who left the deepest wounds, was not Daniel Silva, but the surgeon.

If my story is about pain, it's also about rage. Rage is a physical condition, I've learned from this experience. I feel it now, when I recount the story of the surgeon and recall his face, his voice, his hands.

It also happens unconsciously when I am out in the world. A few months 25
ago, I was walking in downtown New Haven when a young man—presumably a Yale student—suddenly broke into a run. This happens all the time. People run because they're in a hurry to get somewhere; they run to cross the street before the light changes; they run to greet someone they are happy to see. Which was the case on this day.

This happens every day. But every time it happens to me, alarms go off, blood rushes to my ears. Adrenaline spills through my bloodstream like lighter fluid. My heart pounds, my pulse races, my temple throbs. Fight or flight—I'm ready to *fight*; the machine inside switches into gear. It doesn't make any sense: I'm watching a young brown-skinned man in an argyle sweater and clunky glasses hug a young white woman in a flouncy white skirt. Such a sight would normally fill me with happiness, but my body is bursting with rage. He hugs her tightly and lifts her off the ground. She wiggles her feet, and they laugh. I smile and come down.

But it takes a while for the machine to grind down and my body to feel normal again. This reaction always throws me. More than my scar, it reminds me of how much of this story I carry inside me.

"You never get angry about it," a therapist once said to me during a conversation about the stabbing. "In all these years, you've never expressed any anger over it." I explained to her, as I have explained to many people over the years, that I did not look into the eyes of someone who was really there, that—and I know this sounds odd—it wasn't *personal.*

John, my husband, knew the story of the stabbing before he knew me, having read an essay about the incident by Bruce Shapiro, who was also stabbed that night. "One Violent Crime" was first published in *The Nation* and then reprinted in *Best American Essays*. I don't know when this came up in the course of our dating, but I remember feeling both a little weirded-out and also reassured: weirded-out because it always feels strange to have people know something intimate about you before they know you, reassured because it's one less thing about yourself, about your past, that you will have to explain.

30 Even though John was already acquainted with this chapter of my history by the time we met, he has had to sit through numerous renditions of it over the years. Once, not long after we got engaged, we were in New York. I had just given a talk to promote my first book, and after the talk, we met up with a couple of people from my publishing house in the bar of the hotel where we were staying. I had recently begged out of another event because of abdominal pain due to adhesions. Twice before, in the years since the stabbing, adhesions had sent me back to the hospital. Each time this happens, simply, my intestines get locked in a complex dance with my scar tissue. Most likely, the dance gains in intensity for years without my knowing it. Then the dancing stops but the dancers are still intertwined. I can no longer process food. I find myself vomiting, stream upon stream of thick yellow bile. And the pain — it is like being ripped in two, tissue by tissue; I *am* being ripped in two, no similes necessary. Then, as mysteriously as these episodes begin, they simply end.

That night at the bar, Brian, my editor's assistant, asked me how I was feeling. I explained to Susan, the publicist who was there with him, that I suspected the pains had something to do with the stabbing, although no doctor had yet confirmed that. Susan said she didn't know I'd been stabbed, and Brian said I'd never told the whole story. So off I went.

Having had a couple of cocktails, I had become tone deaf. So I told the story in all its glory, lingering on the gruesome details. At some point, John got up abruptly and walked away from the table. Brian looked concerned, but I was sure that my fiancé was only going to the bathroom. I turned back to the table, and to my story, but Brian kept his eye on John, who suddenly fell backward on the floor of the bar, flat as a domino.

It was remarkable. John, my John — so solid, strong and steady — falling backward like a tree having met an ax. His head went *thunk* as it hit the marble floor. The lights in the bar came up so swiftly that it was as if God himself had flipped the switch. Brian was suddenly at his side, cradling his head, pelting questions like "What's your name? What's your social security number? Who's the president?" Brian and I must have watched the same TV shows. John lay on his back on the floor in his suit jacket. His eyes were dazed, straining to register Brian's face, the words coming out of his mouth. It was all that talk of blood, he would tell me later, the blood that I don't remember, the blood that was, according to police reports, all over the walls. Brian said it was the most romantic thing he'd ever witnessed, but I think the fainting had to do with being a man — women, after all, become well acquainted with blood over the course of our lives. At any rate, the story of my stabbing belongs to John, too.

This story also belongs to my twin daughters, Giulia and Isabella, now five and full actors in the world, careful observers of and frequent travelers across the terrain of their mother's body. They have questions. Their questions about the scar, lead, inevitably, to a knife. What happened, Mommy? A man hurt me, he was sick. Why, Mommy? He was really sick. Like he had a stomachache, Mommy? Yes, a really bad stomachache, but it was in his mind, and he didn't have any medicine. The girls fall silent, worry tightening their foreheads. It will never happen to you, I say, and it will never happen to me again.

35 Being a parent brings up the question of what to call this story. Over the years: The incident. The accident. The stabbing. *My* stabbing. What do my daughters call it? *Your face, Mommy. Your face.*

The girls were two and a half years old when I was taken to Yale-New Haven in the fall of 2008 with one of my bouts with adhesions. It was late at night when John and I finally realized that I would have to go to the hospital. We had to ask a friend to come over and stay with the girls while John took me to the emergency room. I can't know what it was like for my daughters to wake up in the morning and find me gone. Gone I remained for seven full days. What sense could this make to a two-year-old? Once I was stable, John brought them to see me in the hospital. What did I look like? Hair wild; eyes glassy from morphine; an IV in my arm; an NG tube in my nose. The nasogastric tube goes through the nose, down the throat, and into the stomach. It is as unpleasant as it sounds, and it has saved my life three times now. It was there to decompress my bowel, which was in distress, and it was held in place by several rudimentary pieces of masking tape. It hurt, and it looked terrible.

I could tell how bad it looked from the expression on Isabella's face. True to form, Giulia, who never takes anything very seriously, who has a "well, that's life" way of approaching the world, hopped right up on my hospital bed and began fooling around with the call button. Isabella, however, clung to her father, her impossibly big brown eyes even impossibly bigger. She said nothing and stared at the wild-haired creature, and shook her head when I held my arms out. She was "fixed to the spot." Even now, when she remembers the hospital, remembers what it was like for her to see me there, what her five-year-old mind seizes upon, what she may continue to seize upon for the rest of her life, regardless of her own wishes or mine, what she remembers is captured in a single phrase she repeats over and over again, which she first uttered as she sat in her car seat a couple of weeks after I was home, back from gone, taking her home from school. She repeated it recently when studying my scar and asking me to explain the *how* of it once again: "Your face, Mommy. Your face."

Seventeen years ago, I was stabbed in the gut by a stranger in a coffee shop. I have proof: a scar (puffy and wormlike, over the points of entry and exit); another scar, similar in texture but much longer, that covers the work of two surgeons (so far); it covers the points of entry and exit of their knives. A midline incision, it's called, and it begins just under my breastbone and ends at my pubic bone, stem to stern, fore to aft. Reminders. Every morning and every night. Evidence. I have police and hospital records, newspaper articles, and Bruce's prize-winning essay, my memories and the memories of others close to me. This happened to me.

I've been telling this story since the night of August 7, 1994. That night, I told the story to doctors, nurses, police officers, family, and friends. Since then, I have told it to gynecologists, a dermatologist, dentists, ophthalmologists, general practitioners, even a podiatrist, and of course, emergency room physicians—all of these men and women in white coats, and their assistants, too. "Have you ever been hospitalized?" reads every single form in every single doctor's waiting room. It's either "yes" or "no." There's no box for "I'd rather not get into it today, thank you very much." So, I tell what happened: in 1994, I was stabbed in the gut by a stranger in a coffee shop. I raise my shirt and reveal my wound. I reassure my listener: it didn't hurt; no one died.

It's the same story, and it isn't true. In the story I tell, there is little blood; the 40
police reports say otherwise. In the story I tell, I wasn't badly hurt; newspaper accounts and hospital records have me in serious condition. In the story I tell, there is no anger; my body begs to differ. Memory lies. To this day, when I speak of the knife, my mind conjures up a butter knife, a small thin blade, flat and tidy. It is a quick, involuntary association, like Daniel Silva and the '70s comic. By chance, several years ago, I saw a hunting knife in a glass cabinet. I got close to the six-inch blade, and shook my head. No, that has nothing to do with me.

But surely the knife, as well as this story, has everything to do with Daniel Silva, to whom this story also belongs.

Not long ago, I received an email that included a link to an article from Renee, a friend in New Haven. "Is this you, Emily?" read the subject field. I opened the link:

> Daniel Silva, who burned down his house, then stabbed seven people with a knife at a New Haven coffee shop, pleaded guilty to second-degree arson Tuesday and received a suspended 10-year sentence that will allow him to eventually be placed in a halfway house.
>
> During a hearing at Superior Court in Waterbury, Silva, now 53, apologized to the stabbing victims and said he was not in a rational "state of mind" on that day in August 1994. Senior Assistant State's Attorney Gary Nicholson told Judge Richard Damiani that the state recommended the plea arrangement, which includes five years of probation and a list of conditions, because Silva has been confined at Connecticut Valley Hospital since the assaults and arson.
>
> Nicholson noted Silva had been repeatedly ruled incompetent to stand trial for the assaults. Those first-degree assault charges were dismissed in 2000 because, under state law, a defendant facing such charges must be restored to competency within five years. No such limitation applies to first-degree arson. Last month, Silva was ruled competent to stand trial on the arson charges, based on testimony from an assistant clinical professor at Yale School of Medicine who interviewed him. . . .
>
> Silva, dressed in a coat and tie, is bearded and balding. He rose and told Damiani, "I apologize to the court and to the people that were hurt. I never meant to do what I did. If I hadn't been in that state of mind, it never would have occurred."
>
> —*New Haven Register*, September 9, 2009

Yes, Renee. It's me. *[2012]*

≡ THINKING ABOUT THE TEXT

1. Note places in her essay where Bernard quotes other "texts" about her stabbing, including excerpts from official reports. Why, evidently, does she incorporate these records?
2. Looking back, what does Bernard think about how she and others acted that night, both during and immediately after Silva's stabbing spree?

3. In what ways, specifically, did being stabbed leave Bernard with *psychological* scars?
4. At the start of her essay, Bernard acknowledges that "I have been telling this story for years" (para. 1). How does she now view her willingness to talk about her stabbing repeatedly? To what extent does she regret having conversed about it so much? Refer to specific passages. What do you think she hopes to accomplish by now *writing* about the experience?
5. Where does Bernard use **anaphora** – the technique of beginning several consecutive sentences with the same words? Why do you think she resorts to this rhetorical strategy at such times? How effective do you find it?

MAKING COMPARISONS

1. Bernard wrote about the stabbing attack many years after Shapiro wrote about it. How do their essays differ as a result?
2. Does Bernard seem to find any political implications in her experience, or is she completely different from Shapiro in this respect? Refer to specific passages in both texts.
3. Shapiro reports feeling anger. Does Bernard ever seem as angry in her essay, or does she appear less driven by emotion than Shapiro is?

WRITING ABOUT ISSUES

1. Write an essay identifying ways in which either Shapiro or Bernard resists being seen *solely* as a victim. Be sure to make clear how you are defining the term *victim*.
2. In recalling details of the attack for their readers, do Shapiro and Bernard similarly emphasize the night's chaos and confusion? Answer this question by writing an essay that refers to specific passages in both texts.
3. On November 8, 2012, Shapiro and Bernard publically discussed their stabbing experience, at a forum sponsored by the Dart Center (where Shapiro is executive director). Watch this discussion online by going to the center's Web site. Then, imagine that you were asked to be a guest respondent at this event. Write a ten-minute speech you would give – the comment you would make on the two writers' conversation. Refer at least briefly to their essays.
4. Write an essay explaining how Shapiro's and Bernard's essays influence your view of a recent violent crime committed by someone who seemed to have mental problems. Possible cases include the 2007 massacre at Virginia Tech; the 2012 shootings at an Aurora, Colorado movie theater; the 2012 killings in Newtown, Connecticut; and the 2014 killings near the campus of the University of California at Santa Barbara.

Eyewitness Testimony: Across Genres

IDA FINK, *The Table* (play)

RYŪNOSAKE AKUTAGAWA, "In a Bamboo Grove" (story)

To discover the facts of an injustice and to settle on who is responsible for it, law enforcement officers, lawyers, judges, juries, and the like rely on eyewitnesses. In any given case, of course, these observers' reports may conflict. After all, perception and memory can be skewed, even willfully so. At such times, the law must decide whose testimony to trust. The following two works dramatize this problem, using different genres to study its nature and possible stakes. Ida Fink's play *The Table* presents survivors of a massacre committed during the Holocaust. Decades after the killings, these people seek to have the perpetrators convicted in court. Yet their efforts to obtain justice may fall short, because they have trouble recalling the atrocity's precise details. "In a Bamboo Grove," Ryūnosake Akutagawa's classic short story, takes place soon after an episode of violence. But an accurate picture of the event proves hard to draw, for the people involved offer clashing accounts. Both Fink's play and Akutagawa's tale are bound to leave you thinking that an injustice has indeed occurred. Both will make you decide how helpful a witness really is. You may also wind up reflecting on the basic standards you use to determine what constitutes truth and proof.

BEFORE YOU READ

What's an actual situation — one you're familiar with — about which the parties involved have different memories? Why do you think their recollections conflict?

IDA FINK

The Table

A Play for Four Voices and Basso Ostinato

Translated by Francine Prose and Madeline G. Levine

Originally from Zbaraz, Poland (now part of Ukraine), Ida Fink (1921–2011) wrote in Polish about the Holocaust. During the Nazi occupation of her country, she was confined along with other Jews to a ghetto in her hometown but then escaped to its "Aryan" section and hid there using false identity papers. In 1957, she moved to Israel, where she lived until her death at the age of ninety. Her works of fiction include a novel, The Journey *(1990), as well as the short-story collections* Traces *(1997) and* A Scrap of Time *(1987), a book that also contains the following play. Fink wrote* The Table *for Israeli radio in 1970. "At that time," she reported, "I was working as an interpreter and a clerk of the court during hearings of witnesses at the trials of Nazi criminals." Eleven years later, the play was performed on German television. Fink identified it as being "for four voices and basso ostinato," a term that literally means "obstinate bass" and that in music refers to a continuously repeating bass line. Here, Fink evidently associated the term with the prosecutor's voice.*

CHARACTERS:

FIRST MAN, *50 years old*
FIRST WOMAN, *45 years old*
SECOND MAN, *60 years old*
SECOND WOMAN, *38 years old*
PROSECUTOR, *35–40 years old*

The stage is empty and dark. Spotlights only on the witness, seated in a chair, and the prosecutor, seated at a desk.

PROSECUTOR: Have you recovered, Mr. Grumbach? Can we go on? Where did we stop? . . . Oh, yes. So you remember precisely that there was a table there.

FIRST MAN: Yes. A small table.

PROSECUTOR: A *small* table? How small? How many people could sit at a table that size?

FIRST MAN: Do I know? It's hard for me to say now.

PROSECUTOR: How long was it? A meter? Eight centimeters? Fifty centimeters?

FIRST MAN: A table. A regular table —not too small, not too big. It's been so many years . . . And at a time like that, who was thinking about a table?

PROSECUTOR: Yes, of course, I understand. But you have to understand me, too, Mr. Grumbach: every detail is crucial. You must understand that it's for a good purpose that I'm tormenting you with such details.

FIRST MAN: *(resigned)* All right, let it be eighty centimeters. Maybe ninety.

PROSECUTOR: Where did that table—that small table—stand? On the right side or the left side of the marketplace as you face the town hall?

FIRST MAN: On the left. Yes.

PROSECUTOR: Are you certain?

FIRST MAN: Yes . . . I saw them carry it out.

PROSECUTOR: That means that at the moment you arrived at the marketplace the table was not there yet.

FIRST MAN: No . . . Or maybe it was. You know, I don't remember. Maybe I saw them carrying it from one place to another. But is it so important if they were bringing it out or just moving it?

PROSECUTOR: Please concentrate.

FIRST MAN: How many years has it been? Twenty-five? And you want me to remember such details? I haven't thought about that table once in twenty-five years.

PROSECUTOR: And yet today, while you were telling your story, on your own, without prompting, you said, "He was sitting at a table." Please concentrate and tell me what you saw as you entered the square.

FIRST MAN: What did I see? I was coming from Rozana Street, from the opposite direction, because Rozana is on the other side of the market. I was struck by the silence. That was my first thought: so many people, and so quiet. I noticed a group of people I knew; among them was the druggist, Mr. Weidel, and I asked Weidel, "What do you think, Doctor, what will they do with us?" And he answered me, "My dear Mr. Grumbach . . ."

PROSECUTOR: You already mentioned that, please stick to the point. What did you see in the square?

FIRST MAN: The square was black with people.

PROSECUTOR: Earlier you said that the people assembled in the marketplace were standing at the rear of the square, facing the town hall, and that there was an empty space between the people and the town hall.

FIRST MAN: That's right.

PROSECUTOR: In other words, to say, "The square was black with people," is not completely accurate. That empty space was, shall we say, white—especially since, as you've mentioned, fresh snow had fallen during the night.

FIRST MAN: Yes, that's right.

PROSECUTOR: Now please think, Mr. Grumbach. Did you notice anything or anyone in that empty white space?

FIRST MAN: Kiper was sitting in a chair and striking his boots with a riding crop.

PROSECUTOR: I would like to call your attention to the fact that none of the witnesses until now has mentioned that Kiper was walking around with a riding crop. Are you certain that Kiper was striking his boots with a riding crop?

FIRST MAN: Maybe it was a stick or a branch. In any case, he was striking his boots—*that* I remember. Sometimes you remember such tiny details. Hamke and Bondke were standing next to him, smoking cigarettes. There were policemen and Ukrainians standing all around the square—a lot of them, one next to the other.

PROSECUTOR: Yes, we know that already. So, you remember that Kiper was sitting in a chair.

FIRST MAN: Absolutely.

PROSECUTOR: So if there was a chair in the marketplace, wouldn't there have been a table as well?

FIRST MAN: A table . . . just a minute . . . a table . . . no. Because that chair seemed so . . . wait a minute . . . No, there wasn't any table there. But they carried out a small table later. Now I remember exactly. Two policemen brought a small table out from the town hall.

PROSECUTOR: *(relieved)* Well, something concrete at last. What time would that have been?

FIRST MAN: *(reproachfully)* Really, I . . .

PROSECUTOR: Please, think about it.

FIRST MAN: The time? . . . God knows, I have no idea. I left the house at 6:15, that I know. I stopped in at my aunt's on Poprzeczna Street, that took ten minutes, then I walked down Miodna, Krotka, Okolna, and Mickiewicza streets. On Mickiewicza I hid for a few minutes inside the gate of one of the houses because I heard shots. It must have taken me about half an hour to walk there.

PROSECUTOR: How much time elapsed from the moment you arrived in the square to the moment when you noticed the policemen carrying the table out from the town hall?

FIRST MAN: Not a long time. Let's say half an hour.

PROSECUTOR: In other words, the policemen carried a table into the marketplace around 7:15. A small table.

FIRST MAN: That's right. Now I recall that Kiper pointed with his riding crop to the place where they were supposed to set the table down.

PROSECUTOR: Please indicate on the map you drew for us the exact place where the policemen set the table down. With a cross or a circle. Thank you. *(satisfied)* Excellent. Kiper is sitting in a chair, the policemen carry in the table, the length of the table is about eighty centimeters. How was the table placed? I mean, in front of Kiper? Next to him?

FIRST MAN: I don't know. That I couldn't see.

PROSECUTOR: If you could see them carrying in the table you could see that, too—perhaps you just don't remember. But maybe you can remember where Kiper sat? At the table? Beside it? In front of it?

FIRST MAN: Obviously, at the table. When someone waits for a table, it's so he can sit at it. He was sitting at the table. Of course. That's what people do.

PROSECUTOR: Alone?

FIRST MAN: In the beginning? I don't know. I wasn't looking that way the whole time. But later—this I know—they were all there: Kiper, Hamke, Bondke, Rossel, Kuntz, and Wittelmann.

PROSECUTOR: *(slowly)* Kiper, Hamke, Bondke, Rossel, Kuntz, and Wittelmann. When you testified a year ago you didn't mention either Rossel or Wittelmann.

FIRST MAN: I must have forgotten about them then. Now I remember that they were there, too.

PROSECUTOR: Were they all sitting at the table?

FIRST MAN: No. Not all of them. Some of them were standing next to it.

PROSECUTOR: Who was sitting?

FIRST MAN: What I saw was that Kiper, Hamke, Bondke, and Kuntz were sitting. The rest were standing. There were more than a dozen of them, I don't remember all the names.

PROSECUTOR: How were they seated, one beside the other?

FIRST MAN: Yes.

PROSECUTOR: Is it possible that four grown men could sit one beside the other at a table that is eighty centimeters long?

FIRST MAN: I don't know. Maybe the table was longer than that; or maybe it wasn't big enough for all of them. In any event, they were sitting in a row.

PROSECUTOR: Who read the names from the list?

FIRST MAN: Hamke or Bondke.

PROSECUTOR: How did they do it?

FIRST MAN: People walked up to the table, showed their *Arbeitskarten,*° and Kiper looked them over and pointed either to the right or to the left. The people who had good *Arbeitskarten* went to the right, and those whose work wasn't considered important, or who didn't have any *Arbeitskarten,* they went to the left.

PROSECUTOR: Was Kiper the one who conducted the selection?

FIRST MAN: Yes, I'm positive about that.

PROSECUTOR: Did Kiper stay in that spot during the whole time the names were read? Or did he get up from the table?

FIRST MAN: I don't know. Maybe he got up. I wasn't looking at him every minute. It took a very long time. And anyway, is it that important?

PROSECUTOR: I'm sorry to be tormenting you with these seemingly unimportant details . . . In other words, is it possible that Kiper got up and walked away from the table, or even left the square?

FIRST MAN: I can't give a definite answer. I wasn't watching Kiper every minute. It's possible that he did get up from the table. That's not out of the question. Still, he was the one in charge at the marketplace. Kiper—and no one else. And he was the one who shot the mother and child.

PROSECUTOR: Did you see this with your own eyes?

FIRST MAN: Yes.

PROSECUTOR: Please describe the incident.

FIRST MAN: The woman wasn't from our town, so I don't know her name. She was young, she worked in the brickworks. She had a ten-year-old daughter, Mala. I remember the child's name; she was a pretty little girl. When this woman's name was called she walked up to the table with her daughter. She was holding the child by the hand. Kiper gave her back her *Arbeitskarte* and ordered her to go to the right. But he ordered the child to go to the left. The mother started begging him to leave the child with her, but he wouldn't agree. Then she placed her *Arbeitskarte* on the table and walked to the left side with the child. Kiper called her back and asked her if she knew the penalty for disobeying an order, and then he shot them—first the girl, and then the mother.

PROSECUTOR: Did you actually see Kiper shoot?

FIRST MAN: I saw the woman approach the table with the child. I saw them standing in front of Kiper. A moment later I heard two shots.

PROSECUTOR: Where were you standing at that moment? Please mark it on the map. With a cross or a circle. Thank you. So, you were standing near the pharmacy. How far was it from the table to the pharmacy?

FIRST MAN: Thirty meters, maybe fifty.

PROSECUTOR: Then you couldn't have heard the conversation between Kiper and the mother.

FIRST MAN: No, obviously. I didn't hear what they said, but I saw that the mother exchanged several sentences with Kiper. It was perfectly clear what they were talking about. Everyone understood what the mother was asking. Then I

Arbeitskarten: work permit.

saw the mother place her *Arbeitskarte* on the table and go to the left with the child. I heard Kiper call her back. They went back.

PROSECUTOR: They went back and stood in front of the table, correct?

FIRST MAN: That's correct.

PROSECUTOR: In other words, they were blocking your view of the men who were sitting at the table, or at least of some of the men sitting at the table.

FIRST MAN: It's possible. I don't remember exactly. In any case, I saw them come back to the table, and a moment later there were two shots, and then I saw them lying on the ground. People who stood closer to them clearly heard Kiper ask her if she knew the penalty for disobeying an order.

PROSECUTOR: Was Kiper standing or sitting at that moment?

FIRST MAN: I don't remember.

PROSECUTOR: So, you didn't see him at the exact moment you heard the shots. Did you see a gun in his hand? What kind of gun? A pistol? A machine gun?

FIRST MAN: He must have shot them with a pistol. Those were pistol shots.

PROSECUTOR: Did you see a pistol in Kiper's hand?

FIRST MAN: No . . . perhaps the mother and child were blocking my view; or maybe I was looking at the victims and not at the murderer. I don't know. But in any case, I did see something that told me it was Kiper who shot them, and no one else.

PROSECUTOR: Namely?

FIRST MAN: Namely . . . immediately after the shots, when the mother and child were lying on the ground, I saw with my own eyes how Kiper rubbed his hands together with a disgusted gesture, as if to cleanse them of filth. I won't forget that gesture.

PROSECUTOR: *(summarizing)* And so, Mr. Grumbach, you saw Kiper sitting at a table in the company of Hamke, Bondke, Rossel, and Kuntz. Then you saw Kiper carrying out the selection and Kiper brushing off his hands immediately after you heard the shots that killed the mother and child. But you didn't see a gun in Kiper's hand nor the shooting itself. Is that correct?

FIRST MAN: Still, I assert with absolute confidence that the murderer of the mother and child was Kiper.

PROSECUTOR: Was Kiper sitting behind the table when your name was called?

FIRST MAN: *(hesitating)* I was one of the last to be called. My *Arbeitskarte* was taken and returned by Bondke. I don't remember if Kiper was present or not. By then I was already half dead.

PROSECUTOR: Of course. What time would it have been when your name was called?

FIRST MAN: What time? My God, I don't know, it was already past noon.

PROSECUTOR: Did you witness any other murders committed that day?

FIRST MAN: That day more than four hundred people were shot in the town. Another eight hundred at the cemetery.

PROSECUTOR: Did you see any member of the Gestapo shoot someone?

FIRST MAN: No.

PROSECUTOR: Were you one of the group that buried the victims in the cemetery?

FIRST MAN: No.

PROSECUTOR: Is there anything else that you would like to say in connection with that day?

FIRST MAN: Yes.

PROSECUTOR: Please, go ahead.

FIRST MAN: It was a sunny, cold day. There was snow in the streets. The snow was red.

FIRST WOMAN: It was a Sunday. I remember it perfectly. As I was walking to the square, the church bells were ringing. It was a Sunday. Black Sunday.

PROSECUTOR: Is that what the day was called afterwards?

FIRST WOMAN: Yes.

PROSECUTOR: Some of the witnesses have testified that the day was called Bloody Sunday.

FIRST WOMAN: *(dryly)* I should think the name would be unimportant. It was certainly bloody. Four hundred corpses on the streets of the town.

PROSECUTOR: How do you know the exact figure?

FIRST WOMAN: From those who buried the victims. The *Ordnungsdienst*° did that. Later they told us, four hundred murdered in the town alone. A hard, packed snow lay on the streets; it was red with blood. The worst one was Kiper.

PROSECUTOR: Slow down. Please describe the events in the square as they occurred.

FIRST WOMAN: At six they ordered us to leave our houses and go to the marketplace. First I decided not to go, and I ran up to the attic. There was a window there, so I looked out. I saw people pouring down Rozana, Kwiatowa, Piekna, and Mickiewicza streets towards the square. Suddenly I noticed two SS entering the house next door. They stayed inside for a moment, then came out leading an elderly couple, the Weintals. Mrs. Weintal was crying. I saw that. They were elderly people. They owned a paper goods store. The SS-men ordered them to stand facing the wall of the house, and then they shot them.

PROSECUTOR: Do you know the names of the two SS-men?

FIRST WOMAN: No. One was tall and thin. He had a terrifying face. I might be able to recognize him in a photograph. You don't forget such a face. But they were local SS, because there were no outside SS in town that day. *They* did it, the locals. Four hundred murdered on the spot, twice that number in the cemetery.

PROSECUTOR: Let's take it slowly now. So, you saw two SS leading the Weintal couple out of the building and putting them against the wall. You lived on Kwiatowa Street. Was their house also located on Kwiatowa?

FIRST WOMAN: I lived on Kwiatowa at number 1; it was the corner building. The Weintals lived in a building on Rozana.

PROSECUTOR: What number?

FIRST WOMAN: I don't know, I don't remember . . .

PROSECUTOR: Did you see which of the two SS shot them? The tall one or the other one?

Ordnungsdienst: Jewish police force controlled by the Nazis.

FIRST WOMAN: That I didn't see, because when they ordered them to stand facing the wall, I knew what would happen next and I couldn't watch. I was afraid. I moved away from the window. I was terribly afraid.

PROSECUTOR: Afterwards, did you see the Weintal couple lying on the ground dead?

FIRST WOMAN: They shot them from a distance of two meters; I assume they knew how to aim.

PROSECUTOR: Did you see the bodies afterwards?

FIRST WOMAN: No, I ran downstairs from the attic, I was afraid—with good reason—I was afraid that they would search the houses for people who were trying to hide, but I didn't go out into the street, I took the back exit to the garden and made my way to the marketplace by a roundabout route.

PROSECUTOR: Would you recognize those two SS in photos?

FIRST WOMAN: Perhaps. I'm fairly certain I could recognize the tall thin one. You don't forget such a face.

PROSECUTOR: Please look through this album. It contains photographs of members of the Gestapo who were in your town; but there are also photographs here of people who were never there.

FIRST WOMAN: *(she turns the pages; a pause)* Oh, that's him.

PROSECUTOR: Is that one of the men you saw from the window?

FIRST WOMAN: No, it's that awful murderer. It's Kiper. Yes, I remember, it's definitely him.

PROSECUTOR: Please look through all the photographs.

FIRST WOMAN: *(a pause)* No, I can't find that face. Unfortunately.

PROSECUTOR: You said "awful murderer." Did you ever witness a murder committed by Kiper?

FIRST WOMAN: *(laughs)* Witness? You're joking. The witnesses to his murders aren't alive.

PROSECUTOR: But there are people who saw him shoot.

FIRST WOMAN: I did, too. Sure—in the square, he fired into the crowd. Just like that.

PROSECUTOR: Do you know who he killed then?

FIRST WOMAN: I don't know. There were fifteen hundred of us in the square. But I saw him rushing around like a wild man and shooting. Not just him, others, too. Bendke, for example.

PROSECUTOR: When was that?

FIRST WOMAN: In the morning. Before the selection. But it's possible it also went on during the selection. I don't remember. I know that they fired into the crowd. Just like that.

PROSECUTOR: Who read the names from the list?

FIRST WOMAN: An SS-man. I don't know his name.

PROSECUTOR: How did they do it?

FIRST WOMAN: Very simply. Names were called out, some people went to the right and others to the left. The left meant death.

PROSECUTOR: Who conducted the selection?

FIRST WOMAN: They were all there: Kiper, Bendke, Hamm, Rosse.

PROSECUTOR: Which one of them reviewed the *Arbeitskarten*?

FIRST WOMAN: I don't remember.

PROSECUTOR: Who ordered you to go to the right? Kiper? Bendke? Hamm? Rosse?

FIRST WOMAN: I don't remember. At such a time, you know . . . at such a time, when you don't know . . . life or death . . . I didn't look at their faces. To me, they all had the same face. All of them! What difference does it make whether it was Kiper or Bendke or Hamm or Rosse? They were all there. There were ten or maybe fifteen of those murderers. They stood in a semicircle, with their machine guns across their chests. What difference does it make which one? They all gave orders, they all shot! All of them!

PROSECUTOR: Please calm yourself. I am terribly sorry that I have to provoke you with such questions. But you see, we can only convict people if we can *prove* that they committed murder. You say that all the members of the local Gestapo were there. But it could be that one of them was on leave, or possibly on duty in the *Dienststelle*.° And didn't shoot.

FIRST WOMAN: Every one of them shot. If not that day, then another. During the second or third action, during the liquidation.

PROSECUTOR: The law requires proof. And I, as the prosecuting attorney, am asking you for proof. I am asking for the names of the murderers, the names of the victims, the circumstances in which they were murdered. Otherwise, I can do nothing.

FIRST WOMAN: *(quietly)* My God . . .

PROSECUTOR: Excuse me?

FIRST WOMAN: Nothing, nothing.

PROSECUTOR: Please think: which one of them was in charge of the selection in the square?

FIRST WOMAN: They all participated in the selection. Kiper, Bendke, Hamm, Rosse. They were standing in a semicircle.

PROSECUTOR: Standing? Were all of them standing? Or perhaps some of them were seated?

FIRST WOMAN: No, they were standing. Is it that important?

PROSECUTOR: It's very important. Do you remember seeing a table in the marketplace at which several Gestapo men were seated? The others were standing near the table.

FIRST WOMAN: A table? I don't remember. There was no table there.

SECOND MAN: Here's the map. The marketplace was shaped like a trapezoid. At the top was the town hall, a beautiful old building that had been built by a Polish nobleman in the seventeenth century. The jewel of the town. The square sloped down towards the actual market where the stores were, as if the town hall reigned over the place. On the left, by the ruins of the old ramparts, stood those whose *Arbeitskarten* were taken away and also those who did not have *Arbeitskarten*. Note that the streets radiate out like a star. Here's Rozana, then Sienkiewicza, then Piekna, then Male Targi, then Nadrzeczna. There

Dienststelle: Police station.

was no river in the town, but maybe once upon a time there was one, and that's why it was called Nadrzeczna — Riverside. Then came Zamkowa Street. All the streets I've named were later included in the ghetto, with the exception of Piekna. Beyond Male Targi there was a cemetery. Yes. That's where they were shot. Nadrzeczna was adjacent to the cemetery. Most of the people who lived on Nadrzeczna were Poles, but it was incorporated into the ghetto nonetheless, because of the cemetery. Because the cemetery played a major role in our life then. Between Rozana and Sienkiewicza there were shops. First, Weidel's pharmacy — he was killed in the camp; then Rosenzweig's iron shop — he was shot during the second action. Then Kreitz's dry goods store, the Haubers' restaurant and hotel — they were the wealthiest people among us, their daughter lives in Canada — and then two groceries, one beside the other, Blumenthal's and Hochwald's. They were rivals all their lives, and now they're lying in the same grave. Oh yes, I can draw every single stone for you, describe every single person. Do you know how many of us survived?

PROSECUTOR: Forty.

SECOND MAN: How do you know?

PROSECUTOR: They are my witnesses.

SECOND MAN: And have you found all of them? And taken their testimony?

PROSECUTOR: I have found almost all of them, but I still haven't taken testimony from everyone. Several witnesses live in America; they will be questioned by our consular officials, and if necessary, subpoenaed for the trial. Two live in Australia, one in Venezuela. Now I would like to ask you about the details of the selection that took place during the first action. When was it, do you remember?

SECOND MAN: Of course. It was a Sunday, in December, towards the end of the month. It was a sunny, cold day. Nature, you see, was also against us. She was mocking us. Yes, indeed. If it had rained, or if there had been a storm, who knows, perhaps they wouldn't have kept shooting from morning till night. Darkness was already falling when they led those people to the cemetery. Oh, you want proof, don't you? The snow on the town's streets was red. Red! Does that satisfy you?

PROSECUTOR: Unfortunately, Mr. Zachwacki, snow doesn't constitute proof for judges, especially snow that melted twenty-five years ago.

SECOND MAN: The snow was red. Bloody Sunday. Four hundred fifty corpses on the streets. That's not proof? Then go there and dig up the mass graves.

PROSECUTOR: I'm interested in the selection. Who was in charge of it?

SECOND MAN: Kiper. A thug, a murderer. The worst sort. I can't talk about this calmly. No. Do you mind if I smoke? These are things . . . I'm sixty, my blood pressure shoots right up. A cutthroat like that . . .

PROSECUTOR: How do you know that Kiper was in charge of the selection?

SECOND MAN: What do you mean, how? I gave him my *Arbeitskarte* myself. He peered at me from under his brows and snarled, "*Rechts!*" I went to the right. Saved. Saved until the next time.

PROSECUTOR: Please describe the scene in more detail.

SECOND MAN: I was standing some distance away. We all tried to stand as far away from them as possible, as if that could have helped. I was standing near the Haubers' hotel. It was one in the afternoon. The church bell struck one, and since it was quiet in the square, you could hear the bell clearly even though the church was in a different part of town, near Waly Ksiazece. By then they had been calling out names for about an hour. Suddenly I hear, "Zachwacki!"

PROSECUTOR: Who called your name?

SECOND MAN: One of the Gestapo, but I don't know which one.

PROSECUTOR: Didn't you notice which of them was holding the list?

SECOND MAN: No, you're asking too much. There was a list, because they read the names from a list, but I didn't see it. If a person saw a scene like that in the theater, maybe he could describe it in detail. This here, that there, and so on. But when a tragedy like this is being played in real life? You expect me to look at a list when my life is hanging by a thread? I was standing there with my wife. She had an *Arbeitskarte* from the sawmill—that was a good place to work—and I had one from the cement works. Also a good place. When they called my name, my wife grabbed my arm. "Let's stay together!" she cried. Dr. Gluck was standing nearby, a kind old doctor. He told my wife, "Mrs. Zachwacki, calm down, your husband has a good *Arbeitskarte*, you have a good *Arbeitskarte*, get a grip on yourself." But she kept saying, "I want to stay together, if we don't we won't see each other ever again. Albert," she said, "I'm afraid." I literally had to tear myself away, she was holding on to me so tight. There, you see, so much for instinct, intuition . . . I never saw her again. All the women who worked in the sawmill were sent to the left. *(he clears his throat)*

PROSECUTOR: *(a short pause)* Then what happened?

SECOND MAN: I dashed through the crowd. There was an empty space between us and them, you had to walk about thirty meters to cross the empty square. First—I remember this—someone kicked me, who I don't know. I took a deep breath and ran as hard as I could to get to the town hall as fast as possible. When I handed them my *Arbeitskarte* my hand was trembling like an aspen leaf, although I'm not a coward. Not at all!

PROSECUTOR: To whom did you hand your *Arbeitskarte?*

SECOND MAN: I already told you, to Kiper. He opened it, read it, handed it back to me and snarled, "*Rechts!*" I was young, tall, strong. He gave me a reprieve.

PROSECUTOR: At the moment that you handed him your *Arbeitskarte*, was Kiper standing or sitting?

SECOND MAN: He was standing with his legs apart, his machine gun across his chest. His face was swollen, red.

PROSECUTOR: And the rest of the Gestapo?

SECOND MAN: I didn't see. I don't remember if any of them were standing next to Kiper.

PROSECUTOR: Did you see a table?

SECOND MAN: Yes, there was a table, but it was further to the right, as if it had nothing to do with what was happening there.

PROSECUTOR: A small table?

SECOND MAN: No, not at all. It was a big, long oak table, like one of those trestle tables you see in monasteries. It was probably one of those antique tables from the old town hall.

PROSECUTOR: Long, you say. What were its dimensions, more or less?

SECOND MAN: How should I know? Two, three meters. The Gestapo sat in a row on one side of the table; and there was quite a large group of them sitting there. Bondke was sitting, Rossel was sitting—them I remember. And there were at least six others.

PROSECUTOR: Did you by any chance notice whether Kiper was sitting at the table earlier and whether the reviewing of the *Arbeitskarten* took place at the table?

SECOND MAN: I didn't notice. When I was called, Kiper was standing several meters from the table.

PROSECUTOR: Who do you think was in charge of the action?

SECOND MAN: Kuntze. He had the highest rank.

PROSECUTOR: Did you see him in the square?

SECOND MAN: I don't remember if I saw Kuntze. Presumably he was sitting at the table. But I only remember Bondke and Rossel.

PROSECUTOR: Was the table already there when you got to the square?

SECOND MAN: Yes.

PROSECUTOR: Who was seated at it?

SECOND MAN: No one.

PROSECUTOR: Some people claim that Kiper was sitting in a chair even before the table was brought out and that afterwards he sat at the head of the table. That he took the *Arbeitskarten* while he was sitting.

SECOND MAN: It's possible. Everything is possible. When I was called, Kiper was standing.

PROSECUTOR: Mr. Zachwacki, do you recall an incident with a mother and child who were shot in the square?

SECOND MAN: Yes, I do. It was Rosa Rubinstein and her daughter Ala. They were from another town and had lived in our town only since the beginning of the war. I knew them.

PROSECUTOR: Who shot them, and under what circumstances?

SECOND MAN: I was standing in the group of workers on the right side of the square, beside the well.

PROSECUTOR: Please indicate the place on the map. With a circle or a cross. Thank you. There was a well there, you say. No one has yet mentioned that well.

SECOND MAN: It was an old well, wooden, with a wooden fence around it. All around it, in a semicircle, there were trees, poplars. At one moment I heard a shot, and people who were standing somewhat closer said that Rosa Rubinstein and her daughter had been shot. It seems that both of them had been sent to the left, but they went to the right. People said that Kiper ran after them and shot them.

PROSECUTOR: You said, "I heard a shot." Do you mean you heard a single shot?

SECOND MAN: Those were my words, but it's hard for me to say if I heard one shot, or two, or three. No doubt he fired at least twice.

PROSECUTOR: Did you see the shooting with your own eyes?

SECOND MAN: No. I saw the bodies lying on the ground. They were lying next to each other. Then the *Ordnungsdienst* picked them up. A red stain was left on the snow.

PROSECUTOR: You were part of the group that helped to bury the victims afterwards?

SECOND MAN: That's correct. There were so many victims that the *Ordnungsdienst* had to take twenty men to help. Four hundred and fifty people were killed in the town—in the square and in the house searches—and eight hundred and forty were shot in the cemetery. My wife was one of them.

PROSECUTOR: *(pause)* But you didn't see any murders with your own eyes? Can you say, "I saw with my own eyes that this one or that one shot so-and-so or so-and-so?"

SECOND MAN: I saw thirteen hundred victims. The mass grave was thirty meters long, three meters wide, five meters deep.

SECOND WOMAN: No, I wasn't in the square. Because I worked as a cleaning woman for the Gestapo, and in the morning, when everyone was going to the marketplace, Mama said to me, "See if they'll let you stay at work." I took my pail and a rag and a brush and said goodbye to my parents on the corner of Mickiewicza and Rozana. We lived on Mickiewicza Street. My parents kept going straight, and I turned onto Rozana. I had gone a few steps when suddenly I caught sight of Rossel and Hamke; they were walking towards me and I got terribly frightened, so I ran into the first gate, and they passed by, they didn't notice me. Later I saw them entering the building at number 13. I kept going.

PROSECUTOR: Who lived in the house?

SECOND WOMAN: I don't know, I was young, I was thirteen years old, but I said I was sixteen because children, you know, were killed. I was well developed, so I said I was sixteen and they let me work for them. That was good luck. That day the Gestapo were going around to all the houses looking for people who hadn't gone to the square, and if they found someone, they shot him either in his apartment or on the street.

PROSECUTOR: Was there a family named Weintal in the house at number 13?

SECOND WOMAN: Weintal? No, I never heard of anyone with that name. I stayed at the Gestapo all day long, hiding. I knew the building, I knew where I could hide. Well, I must say, I certainly was lucky.

PROSECUTOR: Which Gestapo members were in the building that day?

SECOND WOMAN: I don't know. I was hiding in an alcove next to the stairway to the cellar, at the very end of the corridor. Once I thought I heard Wittelmann's voice; he seemed to be on the telephone and was yelling something awful.

PROSECUTOR: Did you ever witness an execution while you worked there?

SECOND WOMAN: I know that they took place, and I know where. But I never saw them shoot anyone. I was afraid, and as soon as they brought someone in, I would hide, get out of their way. I was afraid that they might shoot me, too. They killed them against the fence.

PROSECUTOR: Which fence?

SECOND WOMAN: There was a courtyard at the back surrounded by a fence, and behind the fence there was a trench. That's where they were shot. I know, because afterwards the *Ordnungsdienst* would come and collect the bodies. Once I saw them carrying a doctor whom they had killed. His name was Gluck. But that was after the first action, in the spring. Another time I saw a group of Gestapo men walk out into the courtyard and immediately afterwards I heard a burst of machine-gun fire.

PROSECUTOR: Who did you see then?

SECOND WOMAN: Bondke, Rossel, Hamke, and Wittelmann.

PROSECUTOR: All together?

SECOND WOMAN: Yes. All together. I was washing the stairs to the cellar then.

PROSECUTOR: Were they all armed? Did each of them have a weapon?

SECOND WOMAN: Yes.

PROSECUTOR: Those shots you heard then, were they from a single machine gun or from several?

SECOND WOMAN: I don't know. I didn't pay attention. I wasn't thinking that someday someone would ask me about that. Maybe one of them shot, maybe two. Maybe they took turns. How should I know?

PROSECUTOR: When was that?

SECOND WOMAN: That was even before the first action, probably in the fall.

PROSECUTOR: Do you know how many people were shot then? Do you know their names?

SECOND WOMAN: I don't. I didn't see their bodies being taken away. I saw them collect the dead only once or twice. I don't know who was killed then.

PROSECUTOR: And you never saw a Gestapo man fire a gun?

SECOND WOMAN: No. I only worked there until the second action. I couldn't stand it any longer, I preferred to go to a camp. In general they were nice to me and never did anything bad. Once Bondke gave me cigarettes. The best-mannered was Kiper. He was an educated man, like Kuntze. But the others, no. Kiper had a lot of books in his room. He wanted fresh flowers in a vase every day. Once, when I didn't bring flowers, he yelled at me. Once he broke the vase because the flowers were wilted. On the desk in his room was a photograph of an elegant woman with a dog. But it was Hamke who had a dog. I used to prepare food for the dog. His name was Roosevelt. A wolfhound, very well trained. He tore the druggist Weidel's child to pieces. I heard Hamke boasting about him: "*Roosevelt hat heute ein Jüdlein zum Frühstück bekommen*"—Roosevelt had a little Jew for breakfast today. He said that to Kiper, and Kiper screwed up his face in disgust. Kiper couldn't stand Hamke and used to quarrel with Bondke. In general, he kept to himself. He didn't drink. That Sunday he was the first to come back from the marketplace.

PROSECUTOR: How do you know it was Kiper? Did you see him?

SECOND WOMAN: I heard his voice.

PROSECUTOR: Who was he talking to?

SECOND WOMAN: He was talking to himself. I thought he was reciting a poem. Anyway, that's what it sounded like. Then he went to his room and played his violin—I forgot to say that he was a trained musician. Bondke used to make fun of him and call him *Gestapogeiger*—Gestapo-fiddler. I don't know much about music, but I think he played very well. I heard him play several times. Always the same thing. I don't know what melody it was. I don't know much about music.

PROSECUTOR: Did you see him that day?

SECOND WOMAN: No, I only heard him playing.

PROSECUTOR: What time would that have been?

SECOND WOMAN: I don't know. It was growing dark.

PROSECUTOR: Could you hear the shots from the cemetery inside the Gestapo building?

SECOND WOMAN: I don't know. Maybe not. The cemetery is on Male Targi, and the Gestapo headquarters was on St. Jerzy Square. That's quite a distance. But maybe in the silence, in the clear air . . .

PROSECUTOR: Did you hear any shots when Kiper returned?

SECOND WOMAN: I can't say. Because the way I felt that Sunday and for several days afterwards, I was hearing shots all the time, and my parents thought I had lost my mind. I kept saying, "Listen, they're shooting . . . ," and I'd run and hide. Mama took me to Gluck, who gave me a powder, but it didn't help. I kept on hearing shots for a week. It was my nerves.

PROSECUTOR: When did the other Gestapo men come back?

SECOND WOMAN: I don't know. When it got dark, I sneaked out through the courtyard and returned home. The city was empty, as if no one was left alive. I was astonished: the snow was black. That was the blood. The most blood was on Sienkiewicza Street, and on Rozana. I didn't meet anyone in the marketplace either. It was empty. In the center of the square, lying on its back with its legs in the air, was a small, broken table. *[1970]*

THINKING ABOUT THE TEXT

1. Is the prosecutor being reasonable when he seeks to know facts about the table? In general, how fair is he in his questioning of the witnesses? Why do you think Fink decided to focus on a prosecutor as the interrogator rather than confronting them with the defense attorney for the person or persons they are testifying against?
2. What sorts of details do the witnesses recall?
3. How much does the order of the witnesses matter in this play? Would the play have the same effect if their testimonies appeared in a different order? Why, or why not?
4. This play was originally written for radio, which is evidently the reason that Fink does not provide any description of the set. Describe the kind of set you would use if you were staging the play in a theater. What props and pieces of furniture, if any, would you employ?

5. Fink herself has stated that this play "is a protest against the law which tries genocide according to the code intended for trivial crimes." What do you think she means? Refer to specific lines in the script.

RYŪNOSAKE AKUTAGAWA

In a Bamboo Grove

Translated by Jay Rubin

A native of Tokyo, Ryūnosake Akutagawa (1892–1927) is widely esteemed in Japan as one of the modern age's masters of fiction. Tragically, he killed himself when he was only thirty-five. But his work has influenced generations of Japanese writers, and it is still widely read in his native country. The following story, based on a twelfth-century tale, is likely his most famous. "In a Bamboo Grove" served as the basis for Akira Kurosawa's 1950 film Rashomon, *an international hit when it premiered and now considered a classic.*

The Testimony of a Woodcutter under Questioning by the Magistrate

That is true, Your Honor. I am the one who found the body. I went out as usual this morning to cut cedar in the hills behind my place. The body was in a bamboo grove on the other side of the mountain. Its exact location? A few hundred yards off the Yamashina post road. A deserted place where a few scrub cedar trees are mixed in with the bamboo.

The man was lying on his back in his pale blue robe with the sleeves tied up and one of those fancy Kyoto-style black hats with the sharp creases. He had only one stab wound, but it was right in the middle of his chest; the bamboo leaves around the body were soaked with dark red blood. No, the bleeding had stopped. The wound looked dry, and I remember it had a big horsefly sucking on it so hard the thing didn't even notice my footsteps.

Did I see a sword or anything? No, Sir, not a thing. Just a length of rope by the cedar tree next to the body. And—oh yes, there was a comb there, too. Just the rope and the comb is all. But the weeds and the bamboo leaves on the ground were pretty trampled down: he must have put up a tremendous fight before they killed him. How's that, Sir—a horse? No, a horse could never have gotten into that place. It's all bamboo thicket between there and the road.

The Testimony of a Traveling Priest under Questioning by the Magistrate

I'm sure I passed the man yesterday, Your Honor. Yesterday at—about noon, I'd say. Near Checkpoint Hill on the way to Yamashina. He was walking toward the checkpoint with a woman on horseback. She wore a stiff, round straw hat with a long veil hanging down around the brim; I couldn't see her face, just her robe. I think it had a kind of dark-red outer layer with a blue-green lining. The horse was a dappled gray with a tinge of red, and I'm fairly sure it had a clipped mane. Was it a big horse? I'd say it was a few inches taller than most, but I'm a priest after all. I don't know much about horses. The man? No, Sir, he had a good-sized sword, and he was equipped with a bow and arrows. I can still see that black-lacquered quiver of his: he must have had twenty arrows in it, maybe more. I would never have dreamt that a thing like this could happen to such a man. Ah, what is the life of a human being—a drop of dew, a flash of lightning? This is so sad, so sad. What can I say?

The Testimony of a Policeman under Questioning by the Magistrate

The man I captured, Your Honor? I am certain he is the famous bandit, Tajōmaru. True, when I caught him he had fallen off his horse, and he was moaning and groaning on the stone bridge at Awataguchi. The time, Sir? It was last night at the first watch.° He was wearing the same dark blue robe and carrying the same long sword he used the time I almost captured him before. You can see he also has a bow and arrows now. Oh, is that so, Sir? The dead man, too? That settles it, then: I'm sure this Tajōmaru fellow is the murderer. A leather-wrapped bow, a quiver in black lacquer, seventeen hawk-feather arrows—they must have belonged to the victim. And yes, as you say, Sir, the horse is a dappled gray with a touch of red, and it has a clipped mane. It's only a dumb animal, but it gave that bandit just what he deserved, throwing him like that. It was a short way beyond the bridge, trailing its reins on the ground and eating plume grass by the road.

Of all the bandits prowling around Kyoto, this Tajōmaru is known as a fellow who likes the women. Last fall, people at Toribe Temple found a pair of worshippers murdered—a woman and a child—on the hill behind the statue of Binzuru.° Everybody said Tajōmaru must have done it. If it turns out he killed the man, there's no telling what he might have done to the woman who was on the horse. I don't mean to meddle, Sir, but I do think you ought to question him about that.

The Testimony of an Old Woman under Questioning by the Magistrate

Yes, Your Honor, my daughter was married to the dead man. He is not from the capital, though. He was a samurai serving in the Wakasa provincial office. His name was Kanazawa no Takehiro, and he was twenty-six years old. No, Sir, he was a very kind man. I can't believe anyone would have hated him enough to do this.

first watch: 8 p.m. [All notes are the translator's.]
Binzuru: Japanese version of the Sanskrit name Pindolabharadvaja, who was one of the Buddha's more important disciples and a focus of popular worship.

My daughter, Sir? Her name is Masago, and she is nineteen years old. She's as bold as any man, but the only man she has ever known is Takehiro. Her complexion is a little on the dark side, and she has a mole by the outside corner of her left eye, but her face is a tiny, perfect oval.

Takehiro left for Wakasa yesterday with my daughter, but what turn of fate could have led to this? There's nothing I can do for my son-in-law anymore, but what could have happened to my daughter? I'm worried sick about her. Oh please, Sir, do everything you can to find her, leave no stone unturned: I have lived a long time, but I have never wanted anything so badly in my life. Oh how I hate that bandit—that, that Tajōmaru! Not only my son-in-law, but my daughter . . . (Here the old woman broke down and was unable to go on speaking.)

Tajō maru's Confession

Sure, I killed the man. But I didn't kill the woman. So, where did she go? I don't 10
know any better than you do. Now, wait just a minute—you can torture me all you want, but I can't tell you what I don't know. And besides, now that you've got me, I'm not going to hide anything. I'm no coward.

I met that couple yesterday, a little after noon. The second I saw them, a puff of wind lifted her veil and I caught a peek at her. Just a peek: that's maybe why she looked so perfect to me—an absolute bodhisattva of a woman.° I made up my mind right then to take her even if I had to kill the man.

Oh come on, killing a man is not as big a thing as people like you seem to think. If you're going to take somebody's woman, a man has to die. When *I* kill a man, I do it with my sword, but people like you don't use swords. You gentlemen kill with your power, with your money, and sometimes just with your words: you tell people you're doing them a favor. True, no blood flows, the man is still alive, but you've killed him all the same. I don't know whose sin is greater—yours or mine. (A sarcastic smile.)

Of course, if you can take the woman without killing the man, all the better. Which is exactly what I was hoping to do yesterday. It would have been impossible on the Yamashina post road, of course, so I thought of a way to lure them into the hills.

It was easy. I fell in with them on the road and made up a story. I told them I had found an old burial mound° in the hills, and when I opened it it was full of swords and mirrors and things. I said I had buried the stuff in a bamboo grove on the other side of the mountain to keep anyone from finding out about it, and I'd sell it cheap to the right buyer. He started getting interested soon enough. It's scary what greed can do to people, don't you think? In less than an hour, I was leading that couple and their horse up a mountain trail.

bodhisattva of a woman: Mahayana Buddhism, an enlightened being who compassionately defers entry into Nirvana in order to help others attain enlightenment. By extension, a perfectly beautiful woman.

burial mound: prehistoric Japanese aristocrats were often buried in mounded graves containing jewels, weapons, and other valuables.

When we reached the grove, I told them the treasure was buried in there 15
and they should come inside with me and look at it. The man was so hungry for the stuff by then, he couldn't refuse, but the woman said she'd wait there on the horse. I figured that would happen—the woods are so thick. They fell right into my trap. We left the woman alone and went into the grove.

It was all bamboo at first. Fifty yards or so inside, there was a sort of open clump of cedars—the perfect place for what I was going to do. I pushed through the thicket and made up some nonsense about how the treasure was buried under one of them. When he heard that, the man charged toward some scrawny cedars visible up ahead. The bamboo thinned out, and the trees were standing there in a row. As soon as we got to them, I grabbed him and pinned him down. I could see he was a strong man—he carried a sword—but I took him by surprise, and he couldn't do a thing. I had him tied to the base of a tree in no time. Where did I get the rope? Well, I'm a thief, you know—I might have to scale a wall at any time—so I've always got a piece of rope in my belt. I stuffed his mouth full of bamboo leaves to keep him quiet. That's all there was to it.

Once I finished with the man, I went and told the woman that her husband had suddenly been taken ill and she should come and have a look at him. This was another bull's-eye, of course. She took off her hat and let me lead her by the hand into the grove. As soon as she saw the man tied to the tree, though, she whipped a dagger out of her breast. I never saw a woman with such fire! If I'd been off my guard, she'd have stuck that thing in my gut. And the way she kept coming, she would have done me some damage eventually no matter how much I dodged. Still, I *am* Tajōmaru. One way or another, I managed to knock the knife out of her hand without drawing my sword. Even the most spirited woman is going to be helpless if she hasn't got a weapon. And so I was able to make the woman mine without taking her husband's life.

Yes, you heard me: without taking her husband's life. I wasn't planning to kill him on top of everything else. The woman was on the ground, crying, and I was getting ready to run out of the grove and leave her there when all of a sudden she grabbed my arm like some kind of crazy person. And then I heard what she was shouting between sobs. She could hardly catch her breath: "Either you die or my husband dies. It has to be one of you. It's worse than death for me to have two men see my shame. I want to stay with the one left alive, whether it's you or him." That gave me a wild desire to kill her husband. (Sullen excitement.)

When I say this, you probably think I'm crueler than you are. But that's because you didn't see the look on her face—and especially, you never saw the way her eyes were burning at that moment. When those eyes met mine, I knew I wanted to make her my wife. Let the thunder god kill me, I'd make her my wife—that was the only thought in my head. And no, not just from lust. I know that's what you gentlemen are thinking. If lust was all I felt for her, I'd already taken care of that. I could've just kicked her down and gotten out of there. And the man wouldn't have stained my sword with his blood. But the moment my eyes locked onto hers in that dark grove, I knew I couldn't leave there until I had killed him.

Still, I didn't want to kill him in a cowardly way. I untied him and challenged 20 him to a sword fight. That piece of rope they found was the one I threw aside then. The man looked furious as he drew his big sword, and without a word he sprang at me in a rage. I don't have to tell you the outcome of the fight. My sword pierced his breast on the twenty-third thrust. Not till the twenty-third: I want you to keep that in mind. I still admire him for that. He's the only man who ever lasted even twenty thrusts with me. (Cheerful grin.)

As he went down, I lowered my bloody sword and turned toward the woman. But she was gone! I looked for her among the cedars, but the bamboo leaves on the ground showed no sign she'd ever been there. I cocked my ear for any sound of her, but all I could hear was the man's death rattle.

Maybe she had run through the underbrush to call for help when the sword fight started. The thought made me fear for my life. I grabbed the man's sword and his bow and arrows and headed straight for the mountain road. The woman's horse was still there, just chewing on grass. Anything else I could tell you after that would be a waste of breath. I got rid of his sword before coming to Kyoto, though.

So that's my confession. I always knew my head would end up hanging in the tree outside the prison some day, so let me have the ultimate punishment. (Defiant attitude.)

Penitent Confession of a Woman in the Kiyomizu Temple

After the man in the dark blue robe had his way with me, he looked at my husband, all tied up, and taunted him with laughter. How humiliated my husband must have felt! He squirmed and twisted in the ropes that covered his body, but the knots ate all the deeper into his flesh. Stumbling, I ran to his side. No—I *tried* to run to him, but instantly the man kicked me down. And that was when it happened: that was when I saw the indescribable glint in my husband's eyes. Truly, it was indescribable. It makes me shudder to recall it even now. My husband was unable to speak a word, and yet, in that moment, his eyes conveyed his whole heart to me. What I saw shining there was neither anger nor sorrow. It was the cold flash of contempt—contempt for *me*. This struck me more painfully than the bandit's kick. I let out a cry and collapsed on the spot.

When I regained consciousness, the man in blue was gone. The only one 25 there in the grove was my husband, still tied to the cedar tree. I just barely managed to raise myself on the carpet of dead bamboo leaves, and look into my husband's face. His eyes were exactly as they had been before, with that same cold look of contempt and hatred. How can I describe the emotion that filled my heart then? Shame . . . sorrow . . . anger . . . I staggered over to him.

"Oh, my husband! Now that this has happened, I cannot go on living with you. I am prepared to die here and now. But you—yes, I want you to die as well. You witnessed my shame. I cannot leave you behind with that knowledge."

I struggled to say everything I needed to say, but my husband simply went on staring at me in disgust. I felt as if my breast would burst open at any moment, but holding my feelings in check, I began to search the bamboo thicket for his sword.

The bandit must have taken it—I couldn't find it anywhere—and my husband's bow and arrows were gone as well. But then I had the good luck to find the dagger at my feet. I brandished it before my husband and spoke to him once again.

"This is the end, then. Please be so good as to allow me to take your life. I will quickly follow you in death."

When he heard this, my husband finally began moving his lips. Of course his mouth was stuffed with bamboo leaves, so he couldn't make a sound, but I knew immediately what he was saying. With total contempt for me, he said only, "Do it." Drifting somewhere between dream and reality, I thrust the dagger through the chest of his pale blue robe.

Then I lost consciousness again. When I was able to look around me at last, my husband, still tied to the tree, was no longer breathing. Across his ashen face shone a streak of light from the setting sun, filtered through the bamboo and cedar. Gulping back my tears, I untied him and cast the rope aside. And then—and then what happened to me? I no longer have the strength to tell it. That I failed to kill myself is obvious. I tried to stab myself in the throat. I threw myself in a pond at the foot of the mountain. Nothing worked. I am still here, by no means proud of my inability to die. (Forlorn smile.) Perhaps even Kanzeon,° bodhisattva of compassion, has turned away from me for being so weak. But now—now that I have killed my husband, now that I have been violated by a bandit—what am I to do? Tell me, what am I to . . . (Sudden violent sobbing.)

The Testimony of the Dead Man's Spirit Told through a Medium

After the bandit had his way with my wife, he sat there on the ground, trying to comfort her. I could say nothing, of course, and I was bound to the cedar tree. But I kept trying to signal her with my eyes: *Don't believe anything he tells you. He's lying, no matter what he says.* I tried to convey my meaning to her, but she just went on cringing there on the fallen bamboo leaves, staring at her knees. And, you know, I could see she was listening to him. I writhed with jealousy, but the bandit kept his smooth talk going from one point to the next. "Now that your flesh has been sullied, things will never be the same with your husband. Don't stay with him—come and be my wife! It's because I love you so much that I was so wild with you." The bandit had the gall to speak to her like that!

When my wife raised her face in response to him, she seemed almost spellbound. I had never seen her look so beautiful as she did at that moment. And what do you think this beautiful wife of mine said to the bandit, in my presence—in the presence of her husband bound hand and foot? My spirit may be wandering now between one life and the next, but every time I recall her answer, I burn with indignation. "All right," she told him, "take me anywhere you like." (Long silence.)

Kanzeon: also known as Kannon in the Lotus Sutra (Myōhōrenge-kyō; Sanskrit: *Saddharma Pundarika Sutra;* English: *Sutra on the Lotus of the Wonderful Law* or *Scripture of the Lotus Blossom of the Fine Dharma*), which is the premier scripture of Japanese Mahayana Buddhism. Chapter 25 details the miraculous power of the bodhisattva of compassion, Kannon (Sanskrit: Avalokitesvara), to respond to all cries for help from the world's faithful. Akutagawa's choice of scriptures in this story is not entirely consistent with any one Buddhist sect.

And that was not her only crime against me. If that were all she did, I would not be suffering so here in the darkness. With him leading her by the hand, she was stepping out of the bamboo grove as if in a dream, when suddenly the color drained from her face and she pointed back to me. "Kill him!" she screamed. "Kill him! I can't be with you as long as he is alive!" Again and again she screamed, as if she had lost her mind, "Kill him!" Even now her words like a windstorm threaten to blow me headlong into the darkest depths. Have such hateful words ever come from the mouth of a human being before? Have such damnable words ever reached the ears of a human being before? Have such—(An explosion of derisive laughter.) Even the bandit went pale when he heard her. She clung to his arm and screamed again, "Kill him!" The bandit stared at her, saying neither that he would kill me nor that he would not. The next thing I knew, however, he sent my wife sprawling on the bamboo leaves with a single kick. (Another explosion of derisive laughter.) The bandit calmly folded his arms and turned to look at me.

"What do you want me to do with her?" he asked. "Kill her or let her go? Just nod to answer. Kill her?" For this if for nothing else, I am ready to forgive the bandit his crimes. (Second long silence.)

When I hesitated with my answer, my wife let out a scream and darted into 35
the depths of the bamboo thicket. He sprang after her, but I don't think he even managed to lay a hand on her sleeve. I watched the spectacle as if it were some kind of vision.

After my wife ran off, the bandit picked up my sword and bow and arrows, and he cut my ropes at one place. "Now it's my turn to run," I remember hearing him mutter as he disappeared from the thicket. Then the whole area was quiet. No—I could hear someone weeping. While I was untying myself, I listened to the sound, until I realized—I realized that I was the one crying. (Another long silence.)

I finally raised myself, exhausted, from the foot of the tree. Lying there before me was the dagger that my wife had dropped. I picked it up and shoved it into my chest. Some kind of bloody mass rose to my mouth, but I felt no pain at all. My chest grew cold, and then everything sank into stillness. What perfect silence! In the skies above that grove on the hidden side of the mountain, not a single bird came to sing. The lonely glow of the sun lingered among the high branches of cedar and bamboo. The sun—but gradually, even that began to fade, and with it the cedars and bamboo. I lay there wrapped in a deep silence.

Then stealthy footsteps came up to me. I tried to see who it was, but the darkness had closed in all around me. Someone—that someone gently pulled the dagger from my chest with an invisible hand. Again a rush of blood filled my mouth, but then I sank once and for all into the darkness between lives.

THINKING ABOUT THE TEXT

1. Why do you think Akutagawa includes the first four testimonies, which are not from major characters? Why, conceivably, does he then present the major characters' testimonies in the order that these reports appear? If they appeared in a different order, would there be a loss of impact? Explain.

2. What, if any, facts do the three major characters agree on as they report what happened in the grove?
3. Do you trust one of the three major characters more than you trust the other two? Why, or why not?
4. How do concepts of shame and honor figure in this story? What specific roles do they play?
5. How do issues of gender arise in this story? What notions of "masculinity" and "femininity" prove important?

≡ MAKING COMPARISONS

1. Do the eyewitnesses in Fink's play and those in Akutagawa's story seem similarly pressured to tell the truth? Explain.
2. Do both Fink's play and Akutagawa's story leave you feeling pessimistic about the chances of criminals' paying for what they have done? Refer to specific details of each text.
3. What, if anything, in Akutagawa's story takes on the significance that the table does in Fink's play?

≡ WRITING ABOUT ISSUES

1. Choose one of the eyewitness testimonies in this cluster—either from *The Table* or "In a Bamboo Wood"—and write an essay in which you analyze how the person giving this testimony must follow the guidelines of a legal report or religious confession. If you wish, consider how the person's testimony might be different if it did not have to fit such guidelines.
2. Choose a value or moral principle that you see affirmed or challenged in both Fink's play and Akutagawa's story. Then, write an essay in which you explain the role of this value or principle in each work.
3. Expand Fink's play by adding another eyewitness testimony to it—one that ends the drama by presenting the voice of a ghost. For a model, read again the report by the dead husband who speaks at the end of Akutagawa's story. After you have added your ghost section to *The Table*, write a few sentences in which you explain what you want the play's audience to realize about this character. If you wish, refer to Akutagawa's spectral figure.
4. Various countries have a history of mass violence or discrimination. Some are trying to atone for their past by establishing what's been called *restorative justice*. In this arrangement, perpetrators of injustice meet with their victims, apologize to them, and seek their forgiveness. Do you think a procedure like this can serve the public good? Write an argument that examines restorative justice in a particular country—a specific case that you have researched. Feel free to refer to *The Table* or "In a Bamboo Grove."

CHAPTER 12

Journeys

Perhaps no impulse is as ancient and as natural as the desire to leave one's home, to journey out of the village to unknown lands. Ancient epics like the *Iliad* and the *Odyssey* and more modern tales like Mark Twain's *Adventures of Huckleberry Finn* and Jack Kerouac's *On the Road* are narratives of wandering, encountering the strange and the wondrous. Sometimes the journey has a specific goal, a quest for riches, for fame, or for adventure. Sometimes the journey is simply for escape, for curiosity's sake, for an understanding of the wider world. Of course the idea of the journey easily lends itself to both the literal and the metaphorical, to quests external and internal. We all take journeys of self-discovery from childhood to adolescence to adulthood and eventually to death. Life as a journey is a notion deeply woven into our cultural understanding from Greek mythology, epics, novels, religious beliefs, and popular culture.

It is no surprise then that writers for thousands of years have written about their perilous journeys to dangerous places, their contemplative journeys to self-reflection and wisdom, as well as their imaginative treks to dystopic futures. Our selections in this chapter work with an expansive idea of the journey, featuring work from Eudora Welty's classic short story "A Worn Path" to Kurt Vonnegut's journey to a harrowing future. For some the journey is quite literal; for others the path is decidedly metaphorical. Like the dancers in the Eagles' song "Hotel California," some writers journey to remember, others to forget. Whether the journey is the writer's own or a fictional one a character takes, the creative leap is always thoughtful, illuminating, and moving.

The chapter opens with a series of poetry clusters focused on journeys real and imagined. Four iconic poems of journeys taken and not by Robert Frost initiate our selections, followed by classic poems by Samuel Taylor Coleridge, Percy Bysshe Shelley, and William Butler Yeats. Then Alfred Lord Tennyson and Adrienne Rich take us on mythic journeys. Four poems about our final journey comprise the next cluster, followed by a Literature and Current Issues cluster focusing on a poem by Jimmy Santiago Baca that confronts immigration and jobs.

Three essays then comment on this controversial topic. The sixth cluster pairs the classic Ambrose Bierce story, "An Occurrence at Owl Creek Bridge," with an equally famous story of Vietnam soldiers, Tim O'Brien's "The Things They Carried." Next we present four science fiction masters: Arthur C. Clarke,

Kurt Vonnegut, Joanna Russ, and Octavia Butler, whose tales are always strange and provocative. Three variations on the classic fairytale "Little Red Riding Hood" follow. Then we present the first chapter of Ralph Ellison's *Invisible Man*, a terrifying tale of a young man's brutal initiation into a racist society. This story, "Battle Royal," is illuminated by three texts that provide cultural context. In the tenth cluster, Oscar Wilde's often-produced play, *The Importance of Being Ernest*, is followed by critical commentaries on his comic masterpiece. Two essays by Hispanic Americans discussing the difficulties in crossing boundaries comprise the penultimate cluster. Lastly, a poem by the great poet of World War I, Wilfred Owen, an essay by Michael Herr, and a poem by Thomas Lux depict circumstances that often lead to trauma. These twelve clusters offer literary texts that are illuminating, inspiring, and sometimes dark and unsettling—we hope the journey will be worthwhile.

Roads Taken: Poems by Robert Frost

ROBERT FROST, "Stopping by Woods on a Snowy Evening"

ROBERT FROST, "The Road Not Taken"

ROBERT FROST, "Acquainted with the Night"

ROBERT FROST, "Birches"

The critic Randall Jarrell saw Robert Frost as "the subtlest and saddest of poets." Although many readers thought of this esteemed, pastoral poet as the optimistic voice of the common man, his lyrical vision is actually quite tragic, a quality President Kennedy thought helped strengthen his own presidential character. Alert readers should be careful about equating Frost's simple language and rural settings with lack of depth. The four poems assembled here (and "Mending Wall," p. 79) use the common motif of an external journey to comment on the internal burdens of adult responsibility, the anxiety inherent in making choices, and the loneliness of the human heart. The language of these journeys is beautifully crafted and evocative, able to be read profitably by both schoolchildren and sophisticated critics.

BEFORE YOU READ

Do you remember reading a Frost poem in high school? What is your memory of that reading and discussion in class?

ROBERT FROST

Stopping by Woods on a Snowy Evening

Robert Frost (1874–1963) was perhaps the best-known poet of the twentieth century: winning four Pulitzer Prizes, garnering more than forty honorary degrees, and being widely anthologized throughout the world. His popular image, perhaps forever fixed by his reading at John Kennedy's inauguration, is of a white-haired New Englander fond of simple, homey descriptions of nature. Actually, Frost was born in San Francisco, and most critics think his poetry is anything but simple.

Frost spent his early childhood in California and later moved with his mother to eastern Massachusetts, where he grew up in the small city of Lawrence. He briefly attended Dartmouth College and married in 1895. Frost and his wife taught school together, but they soon moved to a farm in New Hampshire, where he worked and wrote poetry. In 1912, he moved to a town outside London and soon published his first book of poetry, A Boy's Will, *in 1913. The book was well received, and a few years later Frost moved to Franconia, New Hampshire, and began a lifelong career of writing and teaching. For more than twenty years, he was a professor at Amherst College and for decades taught summers at the Bread Loaf School in Vermont.*

Bettmann/Getty Images

Frost's most popular poems—"Mending Wall," "After Apple-Picking," "Birches," and "Fire and Ice"—and those printed here deal with complex social issues in a seemingly natural manner. But even a casual search of essays interpreting "Mending Wall," for example, demonstrates that critics see in Frost's poems a sophisticated, searching, and often dark commentary on the human condition.

Whose woods these are I think I know.
His house is in the village, though;
He will not see me stopping here
To watch his woods fill up with snow.

My little horse must think it queer
To stop without a farmhouse near
Between the woods and frozen lake
The darkest evening of the year.

He gives his harness bells a shake
To ask if there is some mistake.
The only other sound's the sweep
Of easy wind and downy flake.

The woods are lovely, dark and deep,
But I have promises to keep,
And miles to go before I sleep,
And miles to go before I sleep. *[1923]*

THINKING ABOUT THE TEXT

1. Why does the narrator seem so concerned that someone will notice him watching "woods fill up with snow" (line 4)?
2. Is the "darkest evening" (line 8) meant literally or metaphorically or both?
3. Notice the alliteration in lines 11–12. What effect is Frost trying to achieve with this poetic device?
4. Some critics see the narrator's pause and the lure of woods that "are lovely, dark and deep" (line 13) as something like a death wish. Do you agree?
5. How do you interpret the last lines? Are they a literal or a figurative statement? Why the repetition?

ROBERT FROST

The Road Not Taken

Two roads diverged in a yellow wood,
And sorry I could not travel both
And be one traveler, long I stood
And looked down one as far as I could
To where it bent in the undergrowth;

Then took the other, as just as fair,
And having perhaps the better claim,
Because it was grassy and wanted wear;
Though as for that the passing there
Had worn them really about the same,

And both that morning equally lay
In leaves no step had trodden black.
Oh, I kept the first for another day!
Yet knowing how way leads on to way,
I doubted if I should ever come back.

I shall be telling this with a sigh
Somewhere ages and ages hence:
Two roads diverged in a wood, and I—
I took the one less traveled by,
And that has made all the difference. *[1916]*

THINKING ABOUT THE TEXT

1. Is it odd that the title would refer to a road *not* taken?
2. This is clearly a poem about a journey. Did you ever think of your life as a journey on a particular path? How far can you see your future on this path?
3. Critics have noticed that although the narrator says he has taken the path less traveled, he also says the paths were worn about the same. How might you account for this?
4. The conventional interpretation of this poem is that it is about nonconformity. Does this make sense? Why? Given the issue in the previous question, might there be other interpretations?
5. Why does the narrator "sigh" in the last stanza? Is it due to boredom? Regret? Resignation? Nostalgia?

MAKING COMPARISONS

1. Compare the moods of the speakers in both poems.
2. Both poems touch on the future. In what ways?
3. Is the focus of "Stopping by Woods on a Snowy Evening" more pessimistic than that of "The Road Not Taken"?

ROBERT FROST

Acquainted with the Night

I have been one acquainted with the night.
I have walked out in rain — and back in rain.
I have outwalked the furthest city light.

I have looked down the saddest city lane.
I have passed by the watchman on his beat
And dropped my eyes, unwilling to explain.

I have stood still and stopped the sound of feet
When far away an interrupted cry
Came over houses from another street,

But not to call me back or say good-by;
And further still at an unearthly height
One luminary clock against the sky

Proclaimed the time was neither wrong nor right.
I have been one acquainted with the night. [1928]

THINKING ABOUT THE TEXT

1. When the narrator passes the watchman, he drops his eyes (lines 5–6). Why?
2. It seems that the cry (line 8) has nothing to do with the narrator. Is this detail a key to his psychological and emotional state?
3. The narrator says the "time was neither wrong nor right" (line 13). What is he trying to suggest? What might the "time was right" suggest?
4. Why does the narrator choose the night for his walks? Why not walk during the day?
5. Although the first and last lines are identical, do you sense a difference in meaning?

MAKING COMPARISONS

1. Which of these three journeys in Frost's poems seems the most hopeful?
2. Is the speaker in "Acquainted with the Night" more honest than the other speakers? Why?
3. Which line in the three poems seems the most enigmatic? Why?

ROBERT FROST

Birches

When I see birches bend to left and right
Across the lines of straighter darker trees,
I like to think some boy's been swinging them.
But swinging doesn't bend them down to stay

As ice-storms do. Often you must have seen them
Loaded with ice a sunny winter morning
After a rain. They click upon themselves
As the breeze rises, and turn many-colored

As the stir cracks and crazes their enamel.
Soon the sun's warmth makes them shed crystal shells
Shattering and avalanching on the snow-crust—
Such heaps of broken glass to sweep away

You'd think the inner dome of heaven had fallen.
They are dragged to the withered bracken by the load,
And they seem not to break; though once they are bowed
So low for long, they never right themselves:

You may see their trunks arching in the woods
Years afterwards, trailing their leaves on the ground

Like girls on hands and knees that throw their hair
Before them over their heads to dry in the sun.
But I was going to say when Truth broke in
With all her matter-of-fact about the ice-storm
I should prefer to have some boy bend them
As he went out and in to fetch the cows—
Some boy too far from town to learn baseball,
Whose only play was what he found himself,
Summer or winter, and could play alone.
One by one he subdued his father's trees
By riding them down over and over again
Until he took the stiffness out of them,
And not one but hung limp, not one was left
For him to conquer. He learned all there was
To learn about not launching out too soon
And so not carrying the tree away
Clear to the ground. He always kept his poise
To the top branches, climbing carefully
With the same pains you use to fill a cup
Up to the brim, and even above the brim.
Then he flung outward, feet first, with a swish,
Kicking his way down through the air to the ground.
So was I once myself a swinger of birches.
And so I dream of going back to be.
It's when I'm weary of considerations,
And life is too much like a pathless wood
Where your face burns and tickles with the cobwebs
Broken across it, and one eye is weeping
From a twig's having lashed across it open.
I'd like to get away from earth awhile
And then come back to it and begin over.
May no fate willfully misunderstand me
And half grant what I wish and snatch me away
Not to return. Earth's the right place for love:
I don't know where it's likely to go better.
I'd like to go by climbing a birch tree,
And climb black branches up a snow-white trunk
Toward heaven, till the tree could bear no more,
But dipped its top and set me down again.
That would be good both going and coming back.
One could do worse than be a swinger of birches.

[1916]

THINKING ABOUT THE TEXT

1. Some critics see this poem as a balancing act between reality and fantasy. How might this be the case?
2. What "Truth" is Frost referring to in line 21? What does he prefer to the matter-of-fact? What might that stand for?
3. What does the boy learn about not "launching out too soon" (line 33)? How might the poet be applying this to his own life?
4. What does Frost mean by the "pathless wood" (line 44)? What metaphors does he use to describe life's "considerations" (line 43)? What specifically might they refer to? How might they be similar or different than yours?
5. What conclusion does the poet come to beginning with "I'd like to get away . . . (lines 48–59)? How would you phrase this thought in prose?

MAKING COMPARISONS

1. Compare the "considerations" (line 43) in this poem with "promises to keep" (line 14) in "Stopping by Woods on a Snowy Evening."
2. Discuss the idea of "a divided vision" as it applies to "Birches" and "The Road Not Taken."
3. How does Frost make a bargain with the world in these four poems?

WRITING ABOUT ISSUES

1. Look up several criticisms of "Stopping by Woods on a Snowy Evening" and argue that one of these seems the most reasonable.
2. All three poems involve journeys. Write an essay that compares the four journeys in terms of purpose, mood, and meaning.
3. Write an essay about a significant and recent journey that you have taken. Did you learn something about yourself? Did you change?
4. The Web site "On Birches" (english.illinois.edu>poets>frost) presents several critical interpretations/analyses of "Birches." Select one and write an essay that either agrees or disagrees with the ideas you find there.

Visionary Journeys: Poems

SAMUEL TAYLOR COLERIDGE, "Kubla Khan"

PERCY BYSSHE SHELLEY, "Ozymandias"

WILLIAM BUTLER YEATS, "Sailing to Byzantium"

Perhaps the idea of a visionary poet conjures up in your mind one who can see the future, or one who can imagine a better future with a more humane and just society, or perhaps one who has a vision of fantasy worlds like those ancient and exotic lands visited by Marco Polo, with Mongol emperors and his entourage in vast and elaborate palaces and gardens. If so, then Samuel Taylor Coleridge's "Kubla Khan" and William Butler Yeats's "Sailing to Byzantium" fit the bill. Coleridge's poem is one of the strangest and most well-known poems in English. Mysterious and haunting, the visionary Xanadu was conjured in an opium dream. No less compelling is Yeats's wish to sail to Byzantium, where he hopes to leave his natural body and become a work of art that could sing forever, much like the poet in "Kubla Khan" who would amaze us all with songs fueled by "the milk of Paradise." And in Shelley's poem "Ozymandias," the poet paints a vision of a statue in the desert decaying after thousands of years, a vision that reminds us of mortality, even for the most powerful rulers of empires.

SAMUEL TAYLOR COLERIDGE

Kubla Khan

Samuel Taylor Coleridge (1772–1834) was one of the romantic movement's most influential poets and thinkers. In "The Rime of the Ancient Mariner," and "Kubla Khan," he sought to make the strange, the mystical, and the supernatural seem real. He was born in a remote section of England. He excelled at academics and was an outstanding student at Cambridge University. He became friends with the poet William Wordsworth, and their poetic collaboration inspired both to produce some of their best work, including their masterpiece, Lyrical Ballads *(1798). He believed that culture, and particularly literature, could be a positive unifying force in the life of a country, combating the materialistic and fragmented society he saw all around him.*

Coleridge claimed that his famous poem "Kubla Khan" was written after he woke from a dream influenced by opium, a drug commonly prescribed at the time for various ailments. But his furiously written remembrance was interrupted by a man visiting on business. When the visitor left, Coleridge could not recapture the dream-poem, and so it was left as a fragment. This mysterious and enigmatic tale focuses on a Mongol emperor, Kubla Khan, and the palace he built, surrounded by strange, perhaps demonic forces. In his vision, Coleridge sees a woman playing an instrument which inspires him in interesting ways. He recalls past visions and sees Kubla Khan, a figure with flashing eyes. The meaning of the poem has been debated ever since it appeared, but perhaps the most common is that it is about the creative process and the power of the unconscious to produce art. As you read the poem, you can make your own judgments.

Or, a vision in a dream. A Fragment.

In Xanadu did Kubla Khan
A stately pleasure-dome decree:
Where Alph, the sacred river, ran
Through caverns measureless to man
Down to a sunless sea.
So twice five miles of fertile ground
With walls and towers were girdled round;
And there were gardens bright with sinuous rills°,
Where blossomed many an incense-bearing tree;
And here were forests ancient as the hills,
Enfolding sunny spots of greenery.

But oh! that deep romantic chasm which slanted
Down the green hill athwart a cedarn° cover!
A savage place! as holy and enchanted
As e'er beneath a waning moon was haunted
By woman wailing for her demon-lover!
And from this chasm, with ceaseless turmoil seething,
As if this earth in fast thick pants were breathing,
A mighty fountain momently was forced:
Amid whose swift half-intermitted burst
Huge fragments vaulted like rebounding hail,
Or chaffy grain beneath the thresher's flail:
And mid these dancing rocks at once and ever
It flung up momently the sacred river.
Five miles meandering with a mazy° motion
Through wood and dale the sacred river ran,
Then reached the caverns measureless to man,
And sank in tumult to a lifeless ocean;
And 'mid this tumult Kubla heard from far
Ancestral voices prophesying war!
The shadow of the dome of pleasure
Floated midway on the waves;
Where was heard the mingled measure
From the fountain and the caves.
It was a miracle of rare device,
A sunny pleasure-dome with caves of ice!

A damsel with a dulcimer°
In a vision once I saw:
It was an Abyssinian maid
And on her dulcimer she played,

8 rills: Narrow streams.
13 cedarn: Cedar trees.
25 mazy: Like a maze.
37 dulcimer: Musical stringed instrument.

Singing of Mount Abora°.
Could I revive within me
Her symphony and song,
To such a deep delight 'twould win me,
That with music loud and long,
I would build that dome in air,
That sunny dome! those caves of ice!
And all who heard should see them there,
And all should cry, Beware! Beware!
His flashing eyes, his floating hair!
Weave a circle round him thrice,
And close your eyes with holy dread
For he on honey-dew hath fed,
And drunk the milk of Paradise.

[1797]

THINKING ABOUT THE TEXT

1. Describe what Coleridge calls "A savage place" (line 14). Why does he use that term?
2. What does Coleridge say is the result of hearing the Abyssinian maid (line 39)? What might that have to do with poetry?
3. How can critics claim that the poem draws a contrast between the man-made and the natural world?
4. Why would people cry, "Beware! Beware!" (line 49)? Some critics think Coleridge is speaking of himself in the last lines. What might he be saying?
5. What lines seem the most enigmatic to you? What might some possible interpretations be? What is the most interesting line or phrase? Why? What is the most memorable line? Why?

PERCY BYSSHE SHELLEY

Ozymandias

Before his untimely death by drowning, Percy Bysshe Shelley (1792–1822) composed many poems that are now regarded as masterpieces of British romanticism such as "Ode to the West Wind" and "To a Skylark." Shelley published the following poem in 1818 after a visit to the British Museum. On exhibit there were artifacts from the tomb of the ancient Egyptian pharaoh Rameses II, called Ozymandias by many of Shelley's contemporaries. These objects included a broken statue of the pharaoh.

I met a traveler from an antique land
Who said: Two vast and trunkless legs of stone
Stand in the desert. . . . Near them, on the sand,

41 Mount Abora: An imaginary place in Milton's *Paradise Lost.*

Half sunk, a shattered visage lies, whose frown,
And wrinkled lip, and sneer of cold command,
Tell that its sculptor well those passions read
Which yet survive, stamped on these lifeless things,
The hand that mocked them, and the heart that fed:
And on the pedestal these words appear:
"My name is Ozymandias, King of Kings:
Look on my works, ye Mighty, and despair!"
Nothing beside remains. Round the decay
Of that colossal wreck, boundless and bare
The lone and level sands stretch far away. *[1818]*

≡ THINKING ABOUT THE TEXT

1. "Ozymandias" is a sonnet, a poem consisting of fourteen lines. Often there is a significant division in content between a sonnet's first eight lines and its last six. Is there such a division in Shelley's poem? Explain.
2. How is the poem a comment on the epitaph it quotes from the statue's pedestal? Describe Ozymandias by listing at least three adjectives for him, and identify the specific lines that make you think of them.
3. Although the poem begins by referring to "I," this is not the main speaker of the poem; soon we are presented with the report of the "traveler." Shelley could have had the traveler narrate the whole poem. Why might he have begun with the "I"?
4. Both Shelley and the sculptor are artists. To what extent do they resemble each other? Note that the poem describes the sculptor as someone who "well those passions read" (line 6). Why does Shelley associate him with the act of reading?
5. According to this poem, what survives? What does not?

≡ MAKING COMPARISONS

1. Compare the attitudes of the poets toward Ozymandias and Kubla Khan.
2. What might you infer about their personalities from the building projects of Ozymandias and Kubla Khan?
3. Compare the last two lines of "Ozymandias" with the last two lines of the first stanza in "Kubla Khan."

WILLIAM BUTLER YEATS

Sailing to Byzantium

William Butler Yeats (1865–1939) was one of the most revered and influential modern poets, winning the Nobel Prize for literature in 1923. He was born in Dublin, Ireland, and although he spent part of his childhood in London, he is closely associated with his native country. Besides writing poetry, he cofounded Dublin's Abbey Theatre and wrote books of literary criticism along with treatises on mystical philosophy. Yeats was also strongly involved in Irish politics. Both in his literary works and in his civic life, he was dedicated to resurrecting Irish folklore traditions and overthrowing British rule. In 1922, he was even elected as a senator for the newly established Irish Free Republic.

In comments about the following poem, Yeats said he was "trying to write about the state of my soul. . . . When Irishmen were illuminating the Book of Kells, *and making the jeweled croziers in the National Museum, Byzantium [Istanbul] was the centre of European civilization and the source of its spiritual philosophy, so I symbolize the search for the spiritual life by a journey to that city."*

That is no country for old men. The young
In one another's arms, birds in the trees
—Those dying generations—at their song,
The salmon-falls, the mackerel-crowded seas,
Fish, flesh, or fowl, commend all summer long
Whatever is begotten, born, and dies.
Caught in that sensual music all neglect
Monuments of unageing intellect.

An aged man is but a paltry thing,
A tattered coat upon a stick, unless
Soul clap its hands and sing, and louder sing
For every tatter in its mortal dress,
Nor is there singing school but studying
Monuments of its own magnificence;
And therefore I have sailed the seas and come
To the holy city of Byzantium.

O sages standing in God's holy fire
As in the gold mosaic of a wall,
Come from the holy fire, perne in a gyre,
And be the singing-masters of my soul.
Consume my heart away; sick with desire
And fastened to a dying animal
It knows not what it is; and gather me
Into the artifice of eternity.

Once out of nature I shall never take
My bodily form from any natural thing,
But such a form as Grecian goldsmiths make

Of hammered gold and gold enamelling
To keep a drowsy Emperor awake;
Or set upon a golden bough to sing
To lords and ladies of Byzantium
Of what is past, or passing, or to come. *[1928]*

THINKING ABOUT THE TEXT

1. Why does the poet say this "is no country for old men" (line 1)? What are the neglected monuments of "unageing intellect" (line 8)? Who is caught in "that sensual music" (line 7)?
2. Why does he want to go to Byzantium and not someplace else?
3. What is the "dying animal" (line 22)? What does the poet hope will happen to it?
4. What is the meaning of "perne" and "gyre" (line 19)? Who does the poet want to be the "singing-masters" of his soul (line 20)? What does this mean?
5. What will the speaker never reclaim? What does the poet hope to spend his days doing?

MAKING COMPARISONS

1. Compare the singing mentioned at the end of Yeats's poem with Coleridge's lines 45ff., especially, "I would build that dome in air . . ." (line 46).
2. Compare Byzantium and Xanadu.
3. Compare ideas of time in "Sailing to Byzantium" and "Ozymandias."

WRITING ABOUT ISSUES

1. Write a comparison of "Kubla Khan" and "Sailing to Byzantium," noting thematic, metaphorical, and descriptive similarities and differences.
2. Read either Coleridge's "The Rime of the Ancient Mariner" or Yeats's "The Second Coming," and write an analysis of its themes. Make reference to the poet's other poem presented here.
3. Research information on such poets as William Blake, Arthur Rimbaud, Charles Baudelaire, and Pablo Neruda. Write a report on at least two of these, comparing them to the three poets presented here. The focus of your essay could be: what constitutes a visionary poet?
4. Do research on recent criticism of "Kubla Khan" (a good place to start is the extensive Wikipedia Web site), and write a review of what contemporary critics are saying about the poem. Include your own evaluation of these ideas.

Mythic Journeys: Poems

ALFRED LORD TENNYSON, "Ulysses"

ADRIENNE RICH, "Diving into the Wreck"

In Joseph Campbell's influential book *The Hero with a Thousand Faces*, he finds that the idea of a hero who sacrifices for the good of others is present in almost all cultures. In Western culture, of course, the heroes of Greek mythology loom large, influencing writers from Homer to Dante to Tennyson and Adrienne Rich. The hero often goes on a journey, seeking wealth, power, adventure, or even self-knowledge, wisdom, and redemption. In Homer's the *Iliad* and the *Odyssey*, Ulysses helps the Greeks succeed in the Trojan War and returns to rule in Ithaca. Writers ever since have used this myth for their own purposes. Dante has Ulysses dying because he wandered too far. In Victorian England, Alfred Lord Tennyson, suffering from the death of a close friend, has Ulysses longing in his old age for an escape on the open seas. His poem about the Greek hero became a kind of rallying cry among Victorians eager for adventure, conquest, and glory. Nearly a century later, the feminist thinker and lesbian activist, Adrienne Rich uses the idea of a journey as a metaphor to explore her own journey to understand the place of women in human history. Before she descends into the sea of history, she reads "the book of myths," which readers have often interpreted as the false history of women as written by men. This is the wreck, and she wants to cut away at this distorted account so she can write the truth. Both poems describe literal journeys but both suggest more philosophical and psychological journeys into self-knowledge and self-discovery.

ALFRED, LORD TENNYSON

Ulysses

Alfred, Lord Tennyson (1809–1892), one of the great poets of the nineteenth century, served as poet laureate of England longer than any other poet before or since. He was born into a wealthy family and early on demonstrated a gift for verse. He was quite popular with all classes in Victorian England and is one of the most quoted poets in English. Many schoolchildren were and still are asked to memorize "The Charge of the Light Brigade" with its famous "Theirs not reason why, / Theirs but to do and die." But perhaps his most well-known quote is "'Tis better to have loved and lost / Than never to have loved at all." Another is the last line of the following poem, which became a motto for confident Victorians: "To strive, to seek, to find, and not to yield." Tennyson often wrote about classical mythological figures, such as Ulysses (Odysseus). In his poem, he combines stories about the famous Greek hero from both Homer and Dante. In his version, Ulysses is a rebel bored with conformity and, even in his old age, seeking adventures in a mythological dimension "beyond the sunset."

It little profits that an idle king,
By this still hearth, among these barren crags,

Match'd with an aged wife, I mete and dole°
Unequal laws unto a savage race,
That hoard, and sleep, and feed, and know not me.
I cannot rest from travel: I will drink
Life to the lees°: All times I have enjoy'd
Greatly, have suffer'd greatly, both with those
That loved me, and alone, on shore, and when
Thro' scudding drifts the rainy Hyades°
Vext the dim sea: I am become a name;
For always roaming with a hungry heart
Much have I seen and known; cities of men
And manners, climates, councils, governments,
Myself not least, but honour'd of them all;
And drunk delight of battle with my peers,
Far on the ringing plains of windy Troy.
I am a part of all that I have met;
Yet all experience is an arch wherethro'
Gleams that untravell'd world whose margin fades
For ever and forever when I move.
How dull it is to pause, to make an end,
To rust unburnish'd, not to shine in use!
As tho' to breathe were life! Life piled on life
Were all too little, and of one to me
Little remains: but every hour is saved
From that eternal silence, something more,
A bringer of new things; and vile it were
For some three suns to store and hoard myself,
And this gray spirit yearning in desire
To follow knowledge like a sinking star,
Beyond the utmost bound of human thought.

This is my son, mine own Telemachus,
To whom I leave the sceptre and the isle,—
Well-loved of me, discerning to fulfil
This labour, by slow prudence to make mild
A rugged people, and thro' soft degrees
Subdue them to the useful and the good.
Most blameless is he, centred in the sphere
Of common duties, decent not to fail
In offices of tenderness, and pay
Meet adoration to my household gods,
When I am gone. He works his work, I mine.

3 mete and dole: To measure out; here it refers to variable allotment of rewards and punishments to his subjects.
7 lees: The sediment of wine; the last drop.
10 Hyades: A group of stars associated with rain.

There lies the port; the vessel puffs her sail:
There gloom the dark, broad seas. My mariners,
Souls that have toil'd, and wrought, and thought with me—
That ever with a frolic welcome took
The thunder and the sunshine, and opposed
Free hearts, free foreheads—you and I are old;
Old age hath yet his honour and his toil;
Death closes all: but something ere the end,
Some work of noble note, may yet be done,
Not unbecoming men that strove with Gods.
The lights begin to twinkle from the rocks:
The long day wanes: the slow moon climbs: the deep
Moans round with many voices. Come, my friends,
'T is not too late to seek a newer world.
Push off, and sitting well in order smite
The sounding furrows; for my purpose holds
To sail beyond the sunset, and the baths
Of all the western stars, until I die.
It may be that the gulfs will wash us down:
It may be we shall touch the Happy Isles,
And see the great Achilles, whom we knew.
Tho' much is taken, much abides; and tho'
We are not now that strength which in old days
Moved earth and heaven, that which we are, we are;
One equal temper of heroic hearts,
Made weak by time and fate, but strong in will
To strive, to seek, to find, and not to yield. *[1854]*

THINKING ABOUT THE TEXT

1. In this dramatic monologue, spoken by Ulysses, what comments about himself and his plans tell us something about his character?
2. What has Ulysses done that he is proud of? What do you think the phrase "a hungry heart" (line 12) means?
3. What specific lines suggest his boredom and disdain for conformity? What lines suggest a rebellious spirit?
4. What is Ulysses' attitude toward his son, Telemachus? What does he ask of him? What is your judgment about Ulysses' plans for his city, his family, and his companions?
5. The last stanza is addressed to Ulysses' fellow mariners. What is he asking of them? What are his reasons for his request? How would you evaluate this last stanza as an act of persuasion?

ADRIENNE RICH

Diving into the Wreck

Adrienne Rich (1929–2012) is one of the most celebrated poets of the past fifty years. She was also a renowned public intellectual whose books on feminism, politics, sexual identity, and literature were learned, controversial, and influential. Rich was born in Baltimore and educated at home and in private schools. She graduated from Radcliffe University and soon married an economics professor from Harvard. They had three children. She published her first poetry collection, A Change of the World *in 1951, her last year of college. She moved to New York City in the mid-1960s and became active in the civil rights, anti-war, and feminist movements. Ten years later, she separated from her husband and started a lifelong relationship with the poet Michelle Cliff. During this tumultuous period, Rich produced some of her most famous work. Her reputation as a first-class thinker was assured with her essay collections,* On Lies, Secrets, and Silence: Selected Prose, 1966–1978 *(1979) and* Of Woman Born: Motherhood as Experience and Institution *(1976), both of which were called "erudite, lucid, and poetic." Rich pursued a humane, progressive agenda for equality for women and lesbians and passionately insisted on human dignity and social justice for all. The following title poem from her most famous collection,* Diving into the Wreck *(1973), which won the National Book Award, uses the extended metaphor referred to in the title to comment on Rich's symbolic poetic journey of self-discovery. Among her numerous awards and honors is the McArthur ("Genius") Fellowship, The National Medal of Arts (refused), a Guggenheim Fellowship, and the Griffin Poetry Prize. Her last book is* Later Poems Selected and New: 1971–2012 *(2012).*

First having read the book of myths,
and loaded the camera,
and checked the edge of the knife-blade,
I put on
the body-armor of black rubber
the absurd flippers
the grave and awkward mask.
I am having to do this
not like Cousteau with his
assiduous team
aboard the sun-flooded schooner
but here alone.

There is a ladder.
The ladder is always there
hanging innocently
close to the side of the schooner.
We know what it is for,
we who have used it.
Otherwise

it is a piece of maritime floss
some sundry equipment.

I go down.
Rung after rung and still
the oxygen immerses me
the blue light
the clear atoms
of our human air.
I go down.
My flippers cripple me,
I crawl like an insect down the ladder
and there is no one
to tell me when the ocean
will begin.

First the air is blue and then
it is bluer and then green and then
black I am blacking out and yet
my mask is powerful
it pumps my blood with power
the sea is another story
the sea is not a question of power
I have to learn alone
to turn my body without force
in the deep element.

And now: it is easy to forget
what I came for
among so many who have always
lived here
swaying their crenellated fans
between the reefs
and besides
you breathe differently down here.

I came to explore the wreck.
The words are purposes.
The words are maps.
I came to see the damage that was done
and the treasures that prevail.
I stroke the beam of my lamp
slowly along the flank
of something more permanent
than fish or weed

the thing I came for:
the wreck and not the story of the wreck

the thing itself and not the myth
the drowned face always staring
toward the sun
the evidence of damage
worn by salt and sway into this threadbare beauty
the ribs of the disaster
curving their assertion
among the tentative haunters.

This is the place.
And I am here, the mermaid whose dark hair
streams black, the merman in his armored body.
We circle silently
about the wreck
we dive into the hold.
I am she: I am he

whose drowned face sleeps with open eyes
whose breasts still bear the stress
whose silver, copper, vermeil cargo lies
obscurely inside barrels
half-wedged and left to rot
we are the half-destroyed instruments
that once held to a course
the water-eaten log
the fouled compass

We are, I am, you are
by cowardice or courage
the one who find our way
back to this scene
carrying a knife, a camera
a book of myths
in which
our names do not appear. *[1973]*

THINKING ABOUT THE TEXT

1. What specific things does Rich do before setting off? What symbolic significance do you think they have? Why, for example, does she check "the edge of the knife-blade" (line 3)?
2. What are some possible meanings for the wreck as metaphor? Could it be, for example, history written by men? Or obsolete myths about women, or lesbians, or Jews? (Rich's father was Jewish, although she was raised as a Christian.) Or perhaps something else?
3. Critics have noted the seemingly genderless (androgynous) being in stanza eight. What is your reading of this stanza?

4. How would you describe the purpose of the poet's journey? What might Rich mean when she says "our names do not appear" (line 94) in the "book of myths" (line 92)?
5. Translate the central idea of these ten stanzas into prose, recounting the steps, equipment, and activity in Rich's journey.

MAKING COMPARISONS

1. Compare the purpose of each journey.
2. Compare the attitudes and characters of each poem's narrator.
3. Discuss the place of myth in each poem.

WRITING ABOUT ISSUES

1. Write an analysis of "Diving into the Wreck," paying particular attention to the specific details of the speaker's journey. Consult two outside sources, and integrate them into your essay.
2. Write a comparison between Tennyson's and Rich's mythic journeys. Be sure to note the purpose of each, the speakers' attitudes toward the society they live in, and the metaphors used.
3. In the *Oxford Dictionary of Quotations*, locate five quotations from Tennyson and write an analysis of their relevance (or not) for today's world.
4. Read Rich's essay, "Compulsory Heterosexuality and Lesbian Existence" and write an analysis of its main ideas, noting comparisons to "Diving into the Wreck."

A Journey to Death: Poems

MARY OLIVER, "When Death Comes"

JOHN DONNE, "Death Be Not Proud"

DYLAN THOMAS, "Do Not Go Gentle into That Good Night"

WISŁAWA SYMBORSKA, "On Death, without Exaggeration"

EMILY DICKINSON, "Because I could not stop for Death"

For many cultures, death seems more than a metaphorical journey. This is especially true of the Greeks, in whose mythology Charon, the ferryman of the underworld, is literally charged with taking the dead across the river Styx, where they will continue their trek for better or worse. Contemporary poets tend to see death's journey differently than the ancients did, but their appreciation of the mysteries and power of death is enduring. And poets reflect on death's presence in our lives in lyrical and illuminating ways.

Mary Oliver uses a series of interesting similes both to describe death's arrival ("like the hungry bear") and to prepare herself for its inevitability. John Donne sneers at death, perhaps to demonstrate its power, and Dylan Thomas wants to resist that power. Reducing the significance of death was probably on Emily Dickinson's mind when she described Death as a civil carriage driver who kindly stops for her on the way to eternity. Death has intrigued and puzzled poets for centuries, perhaps because, as Shakespeare reminds us, it is a country from which no traveler returns.

BEFORE YOU READ

Does our society have a particular attitude toward death? Can you point to films that might reveal such a cultural inclination? Does your religion have a specific take on death? What is your general attitude toward death, and where does it come from?

MARY OLIVER

When Death Comes

Mary Oliver (b. 1935) was born in Maple Heights, Ohio, and briefly attended Ohio State University. She was strongly influenced by the poet Edna St. Vincent Millay. Her collection No Voyage and Other Poems *(1963) was the first of numerous volumes, including* New and Selected Poems *(1992), which won the National Book Award, and* American Primitive *(1984), which won the Pulitzer Prize for poetry. She has taught at Bucknell University and Sweet Briar College. Her most recent poetry collections are* Dog Songs *(2013) and* A Thousand Mornings *(2012). The poet Maxine Kumin calls Oliver "an undefatigable guide to the natural world."*

When death comes
like the hungry bear in autumn;
when death comes and takes all the bright coins from his purse

to buy me, and snaps the purse shut;
when death comes
like the measles-pox;

when death comes
like an iceberg between the shoulder blades,

I want to step through the door full of curiosity, wondering:
what is it going to be like, that cottage of darkness?

And therefore I look upon everything
as a brotherhood and a sisterhood,
and I look upon time as no more than an idea,
and I consider eternity as another possibility,

and I think of each life as a flower, as common
as a field daisy, and as singular,
and each name a comfortable music in the mouth
tending as all music does, toward silence,

and each body a lion of courage, and something
precious to the earth.

When it's over, I want to say: all my life
I was a bride married to amazement.
I was the bridegroom, taking the world into my arms.

When it is over, I don't want to wonder
if I have made of my life something particular, and real.
I don't want to find myself sighing and frightened,
or full of argument.

I don't want to end up simply having visited this world. *[1992]*

THINKING ABOUT THE TEXT

1. How would you describe what the narrator wants to avoid when death comes?
2. The poet uses a number of similes to describe death's coming. Explain why any one of these seems particularly apt.
3. How does Oliver's view of death influence the way she lives her life?
4. Unpack "visited" in the last line.
5. Does our culture have a particular view of death? What might that be? Does your religion have an attitude toward death that may have influenced you? Is there evidence for a cultural view of death in movies? In popular songs? On TV shows?

JOHN DONNE

Death Be Not Proud

Long regarded as a major English writer, John Donne (1572–1631) was also trained as a lawyer and clergyman. Around 1594, he converted from Catholicism to Anglicanism; in 1615, he was ordained; and in 1621, he was appointed to the prestigious position of dean of St. Paul's Cathedral in London. Today, his sermons continue to be studied as literature, yet he is more known for his poetry. When he was a young man, he often wrote about love, but later he focused on religious themes. The following poem, one of Donne's "holy sonnets," is from 1611.

Death be not proud, though some have callèd thee
Mighty and dreadful, for thou art not so;
For those whom thou think'st thou dost overthrow
Die not, poor Death, nor yet canst thou kill me.
From rest and sleep, which but thy pictures° be, *images*
Much pleasure; then from thee much more must flow,
And soonest our best men with thee do go,
Rest of their bones, and soul's delivery.° *deliverance*
Thou art slave to Fate, Chance, kings, and desperate men,
And dost with Poison, War, and Sickness dwell;
And poppy or charms can make us sleep as well,
And better than thy stroke; why swell'st° thou then? *swell with pride*
One short sleep past, we wake eternally
And death shall be no more; Death, thou shalt die. *[1611]*

≡ THINKING ABOUT THE TEXT

1. In a sense, Death is the speaker's audience. But presumably Donne expected the living to read his poem. What reaction might he have wanted from this audience?
2. Is the speaker proud? Define what you mean by the term.
3. Evidently the speaker believes in an afterlife. What would you say to people who consider the speaker naive and the poem irrelevant because they don't believe that "we wake eternally" (line 13)? How significant is this warrant or assumption? Do you share it?
4. What are the arguments the narrator uses to diminish Death?
5. Imagine Death writing a sonnet in response to the speaker. Perhaps it would be entitled "Life Be Not Proud." What might Death say in it?

≡ MAKING COMPARISONS

1. Is death more or less fearsome in Donne's poem than in Oliver's?
2. Do both speakers refuse to be afraid of death?
3. What optimistic stance do both speakers take?

DYLAN THOMAS

Do Not Go Gentle into That Good Night

Dylan Thomas (1914–1953) was a Welsh poet, short-story writer, and playwright. Among his most enduring works are his radio dramas Under Milk Wood *(1954) and* A Child's Christmas in Wales *(1955). A frequent visitor to the United States, Thomas built a devoted audience in this country through his electrifying public readings. Unfortunately, he was also well known for his alcoholism, which killed him at a relatively young age. He wrote the following poem in 1952, not long before his own death. It takes the form of a* villanelle, *which consists of nineteen lines: five tercets (three-line stanzas) followed by a quatrain (four-line stanza). The first and third lines of the opening tercet are used alternately to conclude each succeeding tercet, and they are joined to form a rhyme at the poem's end.*

Do not go gentle into that good night,
Old age should burn and rave at close of day;
Rage, rage against the dying of the light.

Though wise men at their end know dark is right,
Because their words had forked no lightning they
Do not go gentle into that good night.

Good men, the last wave by, crying how bright
Their frail deeds might have danced in a green bay,
Rage, rage against the dying of the light.

Wild men who caught and sang the sun in flight,
And learn, too late, they grieved it on its way,
Do not go gentle into that good night.

Grave men, near death, who see with blinding sight
Blind eyes could blaze like meteors and be gay,
Rage, rage against the dying of the light.

And you, my father, there on the sad height,
Curse, bless, me now with your fierce tears, I pray.
Do not go gentle into that good night.
Rage, rage against the dying of the light.

[1952]

THINKING ABOUT THE TEXT

1. In what sense could the night possibly be "good," given that people are supposed to "rage" at it?
2. Why do you think Thomas has his speaker refer to "the dying of the light" instead of simply to "dying"? What other parts of the poem relate to the word *light*?
3. The speaker refers to four kinds of "men." Restate in your own words the description given of each. Should Thomas's language about them have been less abstract? Why, or why not?

4. What is the effect of climaxing the poem with a reference to "you, my father" (line 16)? If the father had been introduced in the first or second stanzas, would the effect have been quite different? If so, how?
5. What is the effect of the villanelle form? Judging by Thomas's poem, do you think it is worthwhile for a poet to write in this way, despite the technical challenges of the form? Should teachers of poetry writing push their students to write a villanelle? Explain your reasoning.

MAKING COMPARISONS

1. Is this poem an affirmation of life? Could Oliver's or Donne's poem be considered as such?
2. Compare the speaker's attitude in this poem to that in Oliver's.
3. Which poet seems most at peace with death?

WISŁAWA SZYMBORSKA

On Death, without Exaggeration

Translated by Stanislaw Baranczak and Clare Cavanagh

Although she had written several volumes of poetry, Wisława Szymborska (1923–2012) was little known outside of her native Poland until she won the Nobel Prize for literature in 1996. Since then, readers in various countries have come to admire the blend of simplicity, wit, and wisdom in her writing. The Polish version of the following poem appeared in Szymborska's 1986 book The People on the Bridge. *Subsequently, Stanislaw Baranczak and Clare Cavanagh included it in their 1995 English collection of Szymborska's poems,* View with a Grain of Sand. *We present their translation of the text. Her last two books are* Enough *(2012) and* The Glimmer of a Revolver *(2013).*

It can't take a joke,
find a star, make a bridge.
It knows nothing about weaving, mining, farming,
building ships, or baking cakes.

In our planning for tomorrow,
it has the final word,
which is always beside the point.

It can't even get the things done
that are part of its trade:
dig a grave,
make a coffin,
clean up after itself.

Preoccupied with killing,
it does the job awkwardly,
without system or skill.
As though each of us were its first kill.

Oh, it has its triumphs,
but look at its countless defeats,
missed blows,
and repeat attempts!

Sometimes it isn't strong enough
to swat a fly from the air.
Many are the caterpillars
that have outcrawled it.

All those bulbs, pods,
tentacles, fins, tracheae,
nuptial plumage, and winter fur
show that it has fallen behind
with its halfhearted work.

Ill will won't help
and even our lending a hand with wars and coups d'état
is so far not enough.

Hearts beat inside eggs.
Babies' skeletons grow.
Seeds, hard at work, sprout their first tiny pair of leaves
and sometimes even tall trees fall away.

Whoever claims that it's omnipotent
is himself living proof
that it's not.

There's no life
that couldn't be immortal
if only for a moment.

Death
always arrives by that very moment too late.

In vain it tugs at the knob
of the invisible door.
As far as you've come
can't be undone.

[1986]

≡ THINKING ABOUT THE TEXT

1. Although the word *death* appears in the title, it doesn't appear in the text of the poem until the next-to-last stanza. Up to that point, death is

repeatedly referred to as "it." What is the effect of this pronoun? What might be the effect had Szymborska referred to death more explicitly throughout the text?

2. Evidently the speaker is trying not to exaggerate death. What sorts of remarks about death might the speaker see as an exaggeration of it? Define what you mean by *exaggeration*.
3. What images of death does the speaker create? Refer to specific lines.
4. In the eighth stanza, the speaker mentions that human beings are "lending a hand" to death. Do you take the speaker to be criticizing humanity at this point? Why, or why not?
5. Does the order of the stanzas matter? Could the speaker's observations about death appear in any order and have the same effect? Explain your reasoning.

MAKING COMPARISONS

1. Do all four poems speak of death "without exaggeration"? Define what you mean by the phrase.
2. Does Szymborska's poem strike you as lighter, less serious than Donne's and Thomas's? Refer to specific lines in each text.
3. If you didn't know the authors of the four poems, could you guess which two were written by women? What evidence supports your position?

EMILY DICKINSON

Because I Could Not Stop for Death

The following much-discussed poem by Emily Dickinson (1830–1886) has intrigued and puzzled critics for generations. Its elusive meaning and its combination of Christian promises and Gothic imagery has allowed critics to see the poem as everything from an acceptance of New England Protestant dogma to a rejection of religion in favor of the immortality of art. The poem was originally published in 1890 as "The Chariot."

Because I could not stop for Death—
He kindly stopped for me—
The Carriage held but just Ourselves—
And Immortality.

We slowly drove—He knew no haste
And I had put away
My labor and my leisure too,
For His Civility—

We passed the School, where Children strove
At Recess—in the Ring—

We passed the Fields of Gazing Grain—
We passed the Setting Sun—

Or rather—He passed us—
The Dews drew quivering and Chill—
For only Gossamer, my Gown—
My Tippet—only Tulle—

We paused before a House that seemed
A Swelling of the Ground—
The Roof was scarcely visible—
The Cornice—in the Ground—

Since then—'tis Centuries—and yet
Feels shorter than the Day
I first surmised the Horses' Heads
Were toward Eternity—

[1890]

THINKING ABOUT THE TEXT

1. Who are the passengers in the carriage? What is the effect of "kindly" in line 2? How might we imagine Immortality? Fear of death was a common theme in nineteenth-century sermons. How might this poem be a rejection of that fear?
2. How might the second stanza be an acceptance of death? Why does Death drive slowly?
3. What might the three images in the third stanza stand for?
4. Critics have debated the reference for "He" in stanza 4. What do you think she means? What do "gossamer," "tippet," and "tulle" mean?
5. What suggests that the narrator might already be dead? What might "House" in the fifth stanza refer to?

MAKING COMPARISONS

1. Using just a phrase or a word, how would you characterize the attitude of these five poems toward death?
2. What do you assume Donne's response to Dickinson's poem would be? How about Oliver's response?
3. Explain which of the five poems seem the most religious and which seem the most secular.

WRITING ABOUT ISSUES

1. Choose one of the five poems about death, and write an essay analyzing it as an argument for a certain position on death. Specify the main claim and the evidence given in support of it. Feel free to evaluate the argument you discuss, although keep in mind that the artistic success of the poem may or may not depend on whether its argument is fully developed.
2. Write an essay comparing two of the poems in this cluster, focusing on the issue of whether they are basically similar or significantly different in the ideas and feelings they express. Refer to specific lines from each text.
3. Write an essay recalling a specific occasion when you had difficulty deciding whether to accept something as inevitable. In your essay, give details of the occasion, the difficulty, and your ultimate conclusion. Indicate as well what your final decision revealed about you. Perhaps you will want to distinguish between the self you were then and the self you are now. If you wish, refer to any of the poems in this cluster.
4. Imagine that you are on the staff of a nursing home. At a staff meeting, the chief administrator asks you and your colleagues to consider framing and hanging one of these five poems in the recreation room. Write a letter to the administrator in which you favor one of these poems or reject them all as inappropriate. Be sure to give reasons for your view.

Literature and Current Issues: Do Immigrants Take Jobs from Native-Born Workers?

JIMMY SANTIAGO BACA, "So Mexicans Are Taking Jobs from Americans"

ARGUMENTS ON THE ISSUE:
STEVEN CAMAROTA, "Unskilled Workers Lose Out to Immigrants"

MARIA E. ENCHAUTEGUI, "Immigrants Are Replacing, Not Displacing, Workers"

TED WIDMER, "The Immigration Dividend"

In an issue of the *National Journal* from 2014, the headline read "Left and Right Agree: Immigrants Don't Take American Jobs." It appears that most experts agree that foreign-born workers don't really affect the employment rate one way or the other. But that is certainly not what most Americans believe. A majority think undocumented immigrants are a drain on the economy, even though they must pay taxes and are not eligible for any federal benefits. This is a debate filled with ironic assertions. On the one hand, immigrants are indolent and only seeking welfare; on the other hand, they wrest jobs away from native-born workers. Such contradictory beliefs suggest that logic and facts might not be the major ingredients in people's opinions about this emotional issue. Unlike Baca's poem, our first two essays rely primarily on statistics, which do seem objective. The problem is, however, that as readers we are never sure if these are selectively chosen to prove a conclusion already reached. This will be, of course, always a problem in trying to understand the complex intersection of immigration and jobs.

Instead of delving into arcane tables of economic statistics, our third essayist, Ted Widmer, constructs a more general argument. Yet he certainly could be attempting to answer this cluster's question about jobs, albeit indirectly. He claims that the Immigration and Nationality Act of 1965 made this a better, stronger, more prosperous country. His essay offers us a different approach to arguing by explaining the wider context of a debate.

BEFORE YOU READ

Explain why you think Mexican immigrants are or aren't taking jobs away from native-born workers. What kind of jobs do you think immigrants get when they come here? Are these jobs different from those of immigrants from 50 or 100 years ago? Why?

JIMMY SANTIAGO BACA

So Mexicans Are Taking Jobs from Americans

Originally from Santa Fe, New Mexico, Jimmy Santiago Baca (b. 1952) is a poet, autobiographer, and social activist whose writing often reflects his Chicano and Apache heritage. He candidly acknowledges his experience in prison, where he spent five years after being convicted on drug charges in 1973. After teaching himself literacy there, he eventually earned a B.A. in English at the University of New Mexico. The following poem appears in the 1991 edition of his collection Immigrants in Our Own Land *(first published in 1979). Other books of his include* Spring Poems Along the Rio Grande *(2007),* Winter Poems Along the Rio Grande *(2004),* C-Train & 13 Mexicans *(2002),* Healing Earthquakes *(2001), and* A Place to Stand *(2001), a memoir that won the International Prize. Baca is the founder of Cedar Tree, which runs educational programs for various groups—including people who have served time in prison and those who are still incarcerated.*

Chris Felver

O Yes? do they come on horses
with rifles, and say,
    Ese, gringo, gimmee your job?
And do you, gringo, take off your ring,
drop your wallet into a blanket
spread over the ground, and walk away?

I hear Mexicans are taking your jobs away.
Do they sneak into town at night,
and as you're walking home with a whore,
do they mug you, a knife at your throat,
saying, I want your job?

Even on TV, an asthmatic leader
crawls turtle heavy, leaning on an assistant,
and from a nest of wrinkles on his face,
a tongue paddles through flashing waves
of lightbulbs, of cameramen, rasping,
"They're taking our jobs away."

Well, I've gone about trying to find them,
asking just where the hell are these fighters.

The rifles I hear sound in the night
are white farmers shooting blacks and browns
whose ribs I see jutting out
and starving children,
I see the poor marching for a little work,
I see small white farmers selling out
to clean-suited farmers living in New York,
who've never been on a farm,
don't know the look of a hoof or the smell
of a woman's body bending all day long in fields.

I see this, and I hear only a few people
got all the money in this world, the rest
count their pennies to buy bread and butter.

Below that cool green sea of money,
millions and millions of people fight to live,
search for pearls in the darkest depths
of their dreams, hold their breath for years
trying to cross poverty to just having something.

The children are dead already. We are killing them,
that is what America should be saying;
on TV, in the streets, in offices, should be saying,
"We aren't giving the children a chance to live."

Mexicans are taking our jobs, they say instead.
What they really say is, let them die,
and the children too. *[1982]*

≡ THINKING ABOUT THE TEXT

1. How would you describe the audience that the poem's speaker is addressing? Refer to specific lines.
2. What argument does the speaker make as a response to the claim in the poem's title? How does the speaker support his own argument through pathos, the rhetorical strategy that uses emotional appeals to persuade an audience? Again, refer to specific lines.
3. Where does the poem bring up class (social divisions based on wealth), not just nationality?
4. Note places where the speaker reports what "I see" and "I hear." How accurate do you consider his testimony? Do you "see" and "hear" the same things he does?
5. Where does the speaker use metaphor? Do you find the technique effective in this poem? Why, or why not?

STEVEN A. CAMAROTA

Unskilled Workers Lose Out to Immigrants

Steven A. Camarota (b. 1964) is the director of research at the Center for Immigration Studies, focusing on fact-based data on immigration and the law. He is a frequent newspaper and television commentator on immigration topics. He received a Ph.D. from the University of Virginia in public policy analysis. He is the author of several books, including Serving New America *(2003) and* High Cost of Cheap Labor: Illegal Immigration and the Federal Budget *(2004).*

There are an estimated 11 million illegal immigrants in the country and we also admit over a million permanent legal immigrants each year, leading to enormous implications for the U.S. labor market. Bureau of Labor Statistics data show that there are some 58 million working-age (16 to 65) native-born Americans not working — unemployed or out of the labor market entirely. This is roughly 16 million more than in 2000. Equally troubling, wages have stagnated or declined for most American workers. This is especially true for the least educated, who are most likely to compete with immigrants (legal and illegal).

1.5 million fewer native-born Americans are working now than in 2007, yet 2 million more immigrants are working.

Anyone who has any doubt about how bad things are can see for themselves at the bureau's website, which shows that, as of November, there were 1.5 million fewer native-born Americans working than in November 2007, while 2 million more immigrants (legal and illegal) were working. Thus, all net employment gains since November 2007 have gone to immigrants.

The decline in work has particularly affected those under age 29, and the less-educated, who are the most likely to be in competition with immigrants. A study by the economist George J. Borjas and others found that immigration reduces the employment of less-educated black men. Another study came to the same conclusion. A recent analysis by Federal Reserve economist Christopher Smith (2012) found that immigration reduces the employment of U.S. teenagers.

Despite this, many members of Congress and President Obama support giv- 5
ing work permits to illegal immigrants and increasing legal immigration even further. Once given work authorization, illegal immigrants can compete for better-paying jobs now unavailable to them because they require background checks and valid Social Security numbers—as security guards, interstate truckers, and public sector employees. This despite a record number of adults not working and stagnant wages. Economists debate how much immigration impacts natives, but agree that the data show no labor shortage.

Despite this, last year the Senate passed S.744, which would have given virtually all illegal immigrants work authorization, created a new guest worker program, and expanded family-based immigration. The Congressional Research Service estimated that bill would have roughly doubled the level of future legal immigration to 2 million a year for at least the first decade.

"We are a nation of immigrants," we are often told by the most affluent and educated segments of our society, who face the least competition from immigrants, so we shouldn't restrict immigration or enforce our laws. But this ignores the very real harm to poorer Americans affected by current high levels of immigration. *[2015]*

THINKING ABOUT THE TEXT

1. Obviously, given his occupation, Camarota uses statistics and research to bolster his claim. Where is the most explicit statement of his claim?
2. Although his tone seems objective, are there indications of his point of view in the use of certain words?
3. Important parts of his claim are his underlying assumptions about immigrant and American-born workers. What are they?
4. Why might Congress and President Obama support the work permits? Do you agree or disagree with them? Why? Would it help or hurt his argument if Camarota gave the Senate's reasons for passing S.744?
5. What elements of the immigration/jobs debate does Camarota ignore? What element was the most effective? The least?

MAKING COMPARISONS

1. Although Baca uses pathos more than Camarota, he does use logic. Explain how the poem could be seen as logical. How might the essay be seen as emotional?
2. How does Baca deal with the argument that Camarota makes?
3. What do both Camarota and Baca say about the poor?

MARIA E. ENCHAUTEGUI

Immigrants Are Replacing, Not Displacing, Workers

Maria E. Enchautegui (b. 1961) is a senior fellow at the Urban Institute, where she focuses on the working conditions of low-wage workers. Her research on the economic impact of immigration, family separation, and government policy has been widely published. She holds a Ph.D. in economics from Florida State University.

The Center for Immigration Studies' report rekindles the debate over how immigration affects U.S.-born workers. Most research suggests that the effects are small or zero, but a few studies put some of those results into question — at the very least, showing that the issue is still complicated.

> U.S.-born workers are getting more educated. More jobs require little education, and they are being taken by immigrants.

The C.I.S. notes that the employment gains of immigrants in the past few years have been large compared with the small gains by U.S. workers. I described similar trends in an earlier research brief.

But larger employment gains don't necessarily mean that immigrants are displacing U.S.-born workers. Whether and how much immigrant workers are displacing U.S.-born workers depends on whether they are competing for the same jobs.

About half of all workers ages 18 to 64 without a high school diploma are immigrants. We know that many of these immigrants are unauthorized and do not speak English well. As such, they tend to work in different occupations than U.S.-born workers — often, occupations that require little interaction with the public, that do not require licensing, and that do not require supervisory skills. Giovanni Peri and Chad Sparber argue that immigration allows for an efficient sorting of workers, so displacement of U.S.-born workers by immigrants is unlikely.

The number of U.S.-born workers with no college education has declined 5
by almost 5 million since 2007, according to my analysis of Census data. That means fewer U.S. born workers are competing for jobs requiring less education, the kind immigrants generally get. So immigrants are replacing, not

displacing U.S. born workers. This trend should continue. Of the top 10 occupations with the most projected employment growth, eight do not require a high school diploma, according to the Bureau of Labor Statistics.

Would granting temporary status to more than 4 million undocumented immigrants mean more competition with U.S.-born workers? I would think so, unless the differences in skill levels are so large that these immigrants can't take advantage of the ability to now apply for a wider range of jobs. But with less uncertainty about deportation, these deferred-action immigrants may decide to invest in new job skills, making them more likely to face competition from U.S.-born workers. [2015]

THINKING ABOUT THE TEXT

1. What argumentative move does Enchautegui make in the first paragraph? How does that affect her ethos or tone?
2. What argumentative point is Enchautegui making after "But" in the fourth paragraph?
3. What specifically is Enchautegui's claim? What is her evidence?
4. Explain how Enchautegui's argumentative move after "Unless" in the last sentence helps or hinders her main claim.

MAKING COMPARISONS

1. Describe how Enchautegui directly confronts Camarota's argument.
2. Compare the tones of Baca, Camarota, and Enchautegui. Which is more effective? Why?
3. Explain why you think one of the three is more credible.

TED WIDMER

The Immigration Dividend

Ted Widmer (b. 1963) is a senior fellow at Carnegie Council for Ethics in International Affairs. He received a Ph.D. in history from Harvard, where he taught history and literature from 1993 to 1997. He was a speech writer for President Clinton and also a professor of history at Washington College. He has written five books, including Listening In: The Secret White House Recordings of John F. Kennedy *(2012).*

Immigration is not the easiest issue to debate. It stokes emotions about "homelands" and invasions, as we have seen all summer, both in the Republican presidential contest and in the tragic situation in Europe. These arguments tend to produce more heat than light, making objective analysis difficult. Many politicians find that their poll numbers rise the further from reality they stray—as the

Donald J. Trump playbook continues to prove. A recent Pew report confirms that the parties remain far apart, with Republicans far more certain than Democrats (53 percent versus 24 percent) that immigration is making our society worse.

But history provides some clarity about the relative costs and benefits of immigration over time. Fifty years ago this month, Lyndon B. Johnson signed the Immigration and Nationality Act of 1965 at the foot of the Statue of Liberty. By any standard, it made the United States a stronger nation. The act was endorsed by Republicans and Democrats in an era when cooperation was still possible. Indeed, the most serious opposition came from Southern Democrats and an ambivalent secretary of state, Dean Rusk. But it passed the Senate easily (76–18), with skillful leadership from its floor manager, Senator Edward M. Kennedy, and Johnson himself.

Since 1924, United States immigration policy had been based on a formula, derived from the 1890 census, that made it relatively easy for Northern Europeans to immigrate. But the formula set strict limits for everyone else. That seemed ridiculous to John F. Kennedy, who was trying to win hearts and minds in the Cold War, and it seemed even more so to his successor in 1965, as Johnson was escalating the war in Vietnam. The act's passage was one of the few positive legacies of that complex moment in American foreign policy.

Johnson promised his opponents that the act would "not reshape the structure of our daily lives." But that prediction proved utterly untrue. By destroying the old national-origins system, the act opened the floodgates to the parts of the world that had been excluded in the past.

What ensued was arguably the most significant period of immigration in 5
American history. Nearly 59 million people have come to the United States since 1965, and three-quarters of them came from Latin America and Asia. It was not unrestrained immigration—the act created preferences for those with technical training, or family members in the United States. But it was vastly more open than what had come before.

There is little doubt that the act succeeded in the ways that its progressive supporters hoped—it made America a genuinely New Frontier, younger and more diverse, truer to its ideals. But it also was a success when measured by a more conservative calculus of hard power. It certainly increased American security. Significant numbers of immigrants and their children joined the United States military after 1965, and in every category the armed forces became more ethnically diverse.

The flood of new immigrants also promoted prosperity in ways that few could have imagined in 1965. Between 1990 and 2005, as the digital age took off, 25 percent of the fastest-growing American companies were founded by people born in foreign countries.

Much of the growth of the last two decades has stemmed from the vast capacity that was delivered by the Internet and the personal computer, each of which was accelerated by immigrant ingenuity. Silicon Valley, especially, was transformed. In a state where Asian immigrants had once faced great hardship, they helped to transform the global economy. The 2010 census stated that more than 50 percent of technical workers in Silicon Valley are Asian-American.

Google was co-founded by Sergey Brin, who emigrated from the Soviet Union with his parents at age 6. The new C.E.O. of United Airlines is Mexican-American. And an extraordinary number of Indian-Americans have risen to become chief executives of other major American corporations, including Adobe Systems, Pepsi, Motorola and Microsoft.

In countless other ways, as well, we might measure the improvements since 10
1965. A prominent AIDS researcher, David Ho, came to this country as a 12-year-old from Taiwan. Immigrants helped take the space program to new places, and sometimes gave their lives in that cause (an Indian-American astronaut, Kalpana Chawla, perished in the Columbia space shuttle disaster). Almost no one would argue for a return to pre-1965 American cuisine, which became incomparably more interesting as it grew more diverse. Baseball has become a more dynamic game as it, too, has looked south and west. The list goes on and on.

There will always be debates over immigration, and it's important to acknowledge that opponents of immigration are usually correct when they argue that immigration brings dramatic change. But a careful consideration of the 1965 Immigration Act shows that our willingness to lower barriers made this a better country. To convey that hard-earned wisdom to other nations wrestling with the same issues, and to open our own doors more widely, would be a modest way to repay the great contributions that immigrants have made on a daily basis to the United States over the past 50 years. *[2015]*

THINKING ABOUT THE ISSUES

1. Based on the first two paragraphs, what do you assume this essay has to do with jobs?
2. What is Widmer's claim? What question does it answer?
3. What is the most effective evidence Widmer cites? Why?
4. Describe how Widmer deals with the question posed by this cluster. How is this an effective or ineffective strategy?
5. How does Widmer extend his claim to deal with the current immigration crisis around the world?

MAKING COMPARISONS

1. How does Widmer's first paragraph involve the previous three texts?
2. How does Widmer's claim undercut Camarota's thesis?
3. Compare the claims made by all four texts. What specific assumptions are behind each?

WRITING ABOUT ISSUES

1. Research online articles dealing specifically with the issue of immigration and jobs. Choose two that seem relevant and explain how their claims and evidence affect your response to one of the texts in this cluster.
2. Write an essay that argues that Widmer's more expansive approach is a better way or a worse way to tackle the specific question posed in the title of this cluster.
3. Locate the argument that Enchautegui refers to (by Giovanni Peri and Chad Sparber) and write a brief essay that argues that their evidence does or does not further her position.
4. Write an argument about immigration not touched on in this cluster, for example, the ways immigration intersects with religion, ethnicity, occupation, sexual orientation, health, education, or any other relevant topic.

Wartime Journeys: Stories

AMBROSE BIERCE, "An Occurrence at Owl Creek Bridge"

TIM O'BRIEN, "The Things They Carried"

Perhaps no transition is as psychologically traumatic as the one soldiers must endure as they move from home to the battlefield, from the familiar and comfortable to the strange and disturbingly dangerous environment of war. Traditional values must be suppressed to survive in a brutal and unforgiving landscape. It is not surprising that soldiers desperately want to hold onto memories of home, part real, part fantasy. To escape the terrors of war, they imagine their previous home life through rose-colored lenses. The transition is often slow, painful, and psychologically scarring. Tim O'Brien's classic war story focuses on the psychological journey Jimmy Cross undergoes from imagination and escape to reality and commitment. Peyton Farquhar, in Bierce's story, is deep in the horrors of war as the story opens. His only recourse is to lovingly remember his idyllic home and family. But will this be enough?

BEFORE YOU READ

When under the stress of deadlines for papers and exams, do you sometimes daydream, fantasizing of adventure, romance, and escape? Is this an effective strategy? Explain. Do you feel guilty about such psychological maneuvers?

AMBROSE BIERCE

An Occurrence at Owl Creek Bridge

Ambrose Bierce (1842–1914) was a journalist, short story writer, and satirist. He was born into a large family in Ohio, leaving home at fifteen to work at an Ohio newspaper. He fought in the Civil War, an experience that deeply affected his fiction, including the story printed here. He worked as a journalist in San Francisco, where he became a prominent and influential editor and writer, known for his distinctive style and biting wit. One of his most famous works is The Devil's Dictionary, *a satire of cant and political double talk. Around 1914, he vanished in Mexico while reporting on Pancho Villa's army. This story was originally published in the* San Francisco Examiner *in 1890. Kurt Vonnegut thought the story "the greatest American short story."*

I

A man stood upon a railroad bridge in Northern Alabama, looking down into the swift waters twenty feet below. The man's hands were behind his back, the wrists bound with a cord. A rope loosely encircled his neck. It was attached to a stout cross-timber above his head, and the slack fell to the level of his knees. Some loose boards laid upon the sleepers supporting the metals of the railway supplied a footing for him and his executioners—two private soldiers of the Federal army, directed by a sergeant, who in civil life may have been a deputy sheriff. At a short remove upon the same temporary platform was an officer in the uniform of his rank, armed. He was a captain. A sentinel at each end of the bridge stood with his rifle in the position known as "support," that is to say, vertical in front of the left shoulder, the hammer resting on the forearm thrown straight across the chest—a formal and unnatural position, enforcing an erect carriage of the body. It did not appear to be the duty of these two men to know what was occurring at the centre of the bridge; they merely blockaded the two ends of the foot plank which traversed it.

Beyond one of the sentinels nobody was in sight; the railroad ran straight away into a forest for a hundred yards, then, curving, was lost to view. Doubtless there was an outpost further along. The other bank of the stream was open ground—a gentle acclivity crowned with a stockade of vertical tree trunks, loopholed for rifles, with a single embrasure through which protruded the muzzle of a brass cannon commanding the bridge. Midway of the slope between bridge and fort were the spectators—a single company of infantry in line, at "parade rest," the butts of the rifles on the ground, the barrels inclining slightly backward against the right shoulder, the hands crossed upon the stock. A lieutenant stood at the right of the line, the point of his sword upon the ground, his left hand resting upon his right. Excepting the group of four at the centre of the bridge not a man moved. The company faced the bridge, staring stonily, motionless. The sentinels, facing the banks of the stream, might have been statues to adorn the bridge. The captain stood with folded arms, silent, observing the work of his subordinates but making no sign. Death is a dignitary who, when he comes announced, is to be received with formal manifestations of respect, even by those most familiar with him. In the code of military etiquette silence and fixity are forms of deference.

The man who was engaged in being hanged was apparently about thirty-five years of age. He was a civilian, if one might judge from his dress, which was that of a planter. His features were good—a straight nose, firm mouth, broad forehead, from which his long, dark hair was combed straight back, falling behind his ears to the collar of his well-fitted frock coat. He wore a moustache and pointed beard, but no whiskers; his eyes were large and dark grey and had a kindly expression which one would hardly have expected in one whose neck was in the hemp. Evidently this was no vulgar assassin. The liberal military code makes provision for hanging many kinds of people, and gentlemen are not excluded.

The preparations being complete, the two private soldiers stepped aside and each drew away the plank upon which he had been standing. The sergeant turned to the captain, saluted and placed himself immediately behind that officer, who in turn moved apart one pace. These movements left the condemned man and the sergeant standing on the two ends of the same plank, which spanned three of the cross-ties of the bridge. The end upon which the civilian stood almost, but not quite, reached a fourth. This plank had been held in place by the weight of the captain; it was now held by that of the sergeant. At a signal from the former, the latter would step aside, the plank would tilt and the condemned man go down between two ties. The arrangement commended itself to his judgment as simple and effective. His face had not been covered nor his eyes bandaged. He looked a moment at his "unsteadfast footing," then let his gaze wander to the swirling water of the stream racing madly beneath his feet. A piece of dancing driftwood caught his attention and his eyes followed it down the current. How slowly it appeared to move! What a sluggish stream!

He closed his eyes in order to fix his last thoughts upon his wife and children. 5
The water, touched to gold by the early sun, the brooding mists under the banks at some distance down the stream, the fort, the soldiers, the piece of driftwood — all had distracted him. And now he became conscious of a new disturbance. Striking through the thought of his dear ones was a sound which he could neither ignore nor understand, a sharp, distinct, metallic percussion like the stroke of a blacksmith's hammer upon the anvil; it had the same ringing quality. He wondered what it was, and whether immeasurably distant or near by — it seemed both. Its recurrence was regular, but as slow as the tolling of a death knell. He awaited each stroke with impatience and — he knew not why — apprehension. The intervals of silence grew progressively longer; the delays became maddening. With their greater infrequency the sounds increased in strength and sharpness. They hurt his ear like the thrust of a knife; he feared he would shriek. What he heard was the ticking of his watch.

He unclosed his eyes and saw again the water below him. "If I could free my hands," he thought, "I might throw off the noose and spring into the stream. By diving I could evade the bullets, and, swimming vigorously, reach the bank, take to the woods, and get away home. My home, thank God, is as yet outside their lines; my wife and little ones are still beyond the invader's farthest advance."

As these thoughts, which have here to be set down in words, were flashed into the doomed man's brain rather than evolved from it, the captain nodded to the sergeant. The sergeant stepped aside.

II

Peyton Farquhar was a well-to-do planter, of an old and highly respected Alabama family. Being a slave owner, and, like other slave owners, a politician, he was naturally an original secessionist and ardently devoted to the Southern cause. Circumstances of an imperious nature which it is unnecessary to relate here, had prevented him from taking service with the gallant army which had fought the disastrous campaigns ending with the fall of Corinth, and he chafed under the inglorious restraint, longing for the release of his energies, the larger life of the soldier, the opportunity for distinction. That opportunity, he felt, would come, as it comes to all in war time. Meanwhile he did what he could. No service was too humble for him to perform in aid of the South, no adventure too perilous for him to undertake if consistent with the character of a civilian who was at heart a soldier, and who in good faith and without too much qualification assented to at least a part of the frankly villainous dictum that all is fair in love and war.

One evening while Farquhar and his wife were sitting on a rustic bench near the entrance to his grounds, a grey-clad soldier rode up to the gate and asked for a drink of water. Mrs. Farquhar was only too happy to serve him with her own white hands. While she was gone to fetch the water, her husband approached the dusty horseman and inquired eagerly for news from the front.

"The Yanks are repairing the railroads," said the man, "and are getting ready for another advance. They have reached the Owl Creek bridge, put it in order, and built a stockade on the other bank. The commandant has issued an order, which is posted everywhere, declaring that any civilian caught interfering with the railroad, its bridges, tunnels, or trains, will be summarily hanged. I saw the order."

"How far is it to the Owl Creek bridge?" Farquhar asked.

"About thirty miles."

"Is there no force on this side the creek?"

"Only a picket post half a mile out, on the railroad, and a single sentinel at this end of the bridge."

"Suppose a man—a civilian and student of hanging—should elude the picket post and perhaps get the better of the sentinel," said Farquhar, smiling, "what could he accomplish?"

The soldier reflected. "I was there a month ago," he replied. "I observed that the flood of last winter had lodged a great quantity of driftwood against the wooden pier at this end of the bridge. It is now dry and would burn like tow."

The lady had now brought the water, which the soldier drank. He thanked her ceremoniously, bowed to her husband, and rode away. An hour later, after nightfall, he repassed the plantation, going northward in the direction from which he had come. He was a Federal scout.

III

As Peyton Farquhar fell straight downward through the bridge, he lost consciousness and was as one already dead. From this state he was awakened—ages later, it seemed to him—by the pain of a sharp pressure upon his throat, followed by a sense of suffocation. Keen, poignant agonies seemed to shoot from his neck downward through every fibre of his body and limbs. These pains appeared to flash along well-defined lines of ramification, and to beat with an inconceivably rapid periodicity. They seemed like streams of pulsating fire heating him to an intolerable temperature. As to his head, he was conscious of nothing but a feeling of fullness—of congestion. These sensations were unaccompanied by thought. The intellectual part of his nature was already effaced; he had power only to feel, and feeling was torment. He was conscious of motion. Encompassed in a luminous cloud, of which he was now merely the fiery heart, without material substance, he swung through unthinkable arcs of oscillation, like a vast pendulum. Then all at once, with terrible suddenness, the light about him shot upward with the noise of a loud splash; a frightful roaring was in his ears, and all was cold and dark. The power of thought was restored; he knew that the rope had broken and he had fallen into the stream. There was no additional strangulation; the noose about his neck was already suffocating him, and kept the water from his lungs.

To die of hanging at the bottom of a river — the idea seemed to him ludicrous. He opened his eyes in the blackness and saw above him a gleam of light, but how distant, how inaccessible! He was still sinking, for the light became fainter and fainter until it was a mere glimmer. Then it began to grow and brighten, and he knew that he was rising toward the surface — knew it with reluctance, for he was now very comfortable. "To be hanged and drowned," he thought, "that is not so bad; but I do not wish to be shot. No; I will not be shot; that is not fair."

He was not conscious of an effort, but a sharp pain in his wrist apprised him that he was trying to free his hands. He gave the struggle his attention, as an idler might observe the feat of a juggler, without interest in the outcome. What splendid effort! — what magnificent, what superhuman strength! Ah, that was a fine endeavor! Bravo! The cord fell away; his arms parted and floated upward, the hands dimly seen on each side in the growing light. He watched them with a new interest as first one and then the other pounced upon the noose at his neck. They tore it away and thrust it fiercely aside, its undulations resembling those of a water-snake. "Put it back, put it back!" He thought he shouted these words to his hands, for the undoing of the noose had been succeeded by the direst pang which he had yet experienced. His neck ached horribly; his brain was on fire; his heart, which had been fluttering faintly, gave a great leap, trying to force itself out at his mouth. His whole body was racked and wrenched with an insupportable anguish! But his disobedient hands gave no heed to the command. They beat the water vigorously with quick, downward strokes, forcing him to the surface. He felt his head emerge; his eyes were blinded by the sunlight; his chest expanded convulsively, and with a supreme and crowning agony his lungs engulfed a great draught of air, which instantly he expelled in a shriek!

20 He was now in full possession of his physical senses. They were, indeed, preternaturally keen and alert. Something in the awful disturbance of his organic system had so exalted and refined them that they made record of things never before perceived. He felt the ripples upon his face and heard their separate sounds as they struck. He looked at the forest on the bank of the stream, saw the individual trees, the leaves and the veining of each leaf — saw the very insects upon them, the locusts, the brilliant-bodied flies, the grey spiders stretching their webs from twig to twig. He noted the prismatic colors in all the dewdrops upon a million blades of grass. The humming of the gnats that danced above the eddies of the stream, the beating of the dragon flies' wings, the strokes of the water spiders' legs, like oars which had lifted their boat — all these made audible music. A fish slid along beneath his eyes and he heard the rush of its body parting the water.

He had come to the surface facing down the stream; in a moment the visible world seemed to wheel slowly round, himself the pivotal point, and he saw the bridge, the fort, the soldiers upon the bridge, the captain, the sergeant, the two privates, his executioners. They were in silhouette against the blue sky. They shouted and gesticulated, pointing at him; the captain had drawn his pistol, but did not fire; the others were unarmed. Their movements were grotesque and horrible, their forms gigantic.

Suddenly he heard a sharp report and something struck the water smartly within a few inches of his head, spattering his face with spray. He heard a second report, and saw one of the sentinels with his rifle at his shoulder, a light cloud of blue smoke rising from the muzzle. The man in the water saw the eye of the man on the bridge gazing into his own through the sights of the rifle. He observed that it was a grey eye, and remembered having read that grey eyes were keenest and that all famous marksmen had them. Nevertheless, this one had missed.

A counter swirl had caught Farquhar and turned him half round; he was again looking into the forest on the bank opposite the fort. The sound of a clear, high voice in a monotonous singsong now rang out behind him and came across the water with a distinctness that pierced and subdued all other sounds, even the beating of the ripples in his ears. Although no soldier, he had frequented camps enough to know the dread significance of that deliberate, drawling, aspirated chant; the lieutenant on shore was taking a part in the morning's work. How coldly and pitilessly—with what an even, calm intonation, presaging and enforcing tranquility in the men—with what accurately-measured intervals fell those cruel words:

"Attention, company. . . . Shoulder arms. . . . Ready. . . . Aim. . . . Fire."

Farquhar dived—dived as deeply as he could. The water roared in his ears like the voice of Niagara, yet he heard the dulled thunder of the volley, and rising again toward the surface, met shining bits of metal, singularly flattened, oscillating slowly downward. Some of them touched him on the face and hands, then fell away, continuing their descent. One lodged between his collar and neck; it was uncomfortably warm, and he snatched it out.

As he rose to the surface, gasping for breath, he saw that he had been a long 25
time under water; he was perceptibly farther down stream—nearer to safety. The soldiers had almost finished reloading; the metal ramrods flashed all at once in the sunshine as they were drawn from the barrels, turned in the air, and thrust into their sockets. The two sentinels fired again, independently and ineffectually.

The hunted man saw all this over his shoulder; he was now swimming vigorously with the current. His brain was as energetic as his arms and legs; he thought with the rapidity of lightning.

"The officer," he reasoned, "will not make the martinet's error a second time. It is as easy to dodge a volley as a single shot. He has probably already given the command to fire at will. God help me, I cannot dodge them all!"

An appalling plash within two yards of him, followed by a loud rushing sound, *diminuendo*, which seemed to travel back through the air to the fort and died in an explosion which stirred the very river to its deeps! A rising sheet of water, which curved over him, fell down upon him, blinded him, strangled him! The cannon had taken a hand in the game. As he shook his head free from the commotion of the smitten water, he heard the deflected shot humming through the air ahead, and in an instant it was cracking and smashing the branches in the forest beyond.

"They will not do that again," he thought; "the next time they will use a charge of grape°. I must keep my eye upon the gun; the smoke will apprise me—the report arrives too late; it lags behind the missile. It is a good gun."

charge of grape: Ammunition consisting of small lead balls.

Suddenly he felt himself whirled round and round—spinning like a top. 30
The water, the banks, the forest, the now distant bridge, fort, and men—all were commingled and blurred. Objects were represented by their colors only; circular horizontal streaks of color—that was all he saw. He had been caught in a vortex and was being whirled on with a velocity of advance and gyration which made him giddy and sick. In a few moments he was flung upon the gravel at the foot of the left bank of the stream—the southern bank—and behind a projecting point which concealed him from his enemies. The sudden arrest of his motion, the abrasion of one of his hands on the gravel, restored him and he wept with delight. He dug his fingers into the sand, threw it over himself in handfuls and audibly blessed it. It looked like gold, like diamonds, rubies, emeralds; he could think of nothing beautiful which it did not resemble. The trees upon the bank were giant garden plants; he noted a definite order in their arrangement, inhaled the fragrance of their blooms. A strange, roseate light shone through the spaces among their trunks, and the wind made in their branches the music of æolian harps. He had no wish to perfect his escape, was content to remain in that enchanting spot until retaken.

A whizz and rattle of grapeshot among the branches high above his head roused him from his dream. The baffled cannoneer had fired him a random farewell. He sprang to his feet, rushed up the sloping bank, and plunged into the forest.

All that day he travelled, laying his course by the rounding sun. The forest seemed interminable; nowhere did he discover a break in it, not even a woodman's road. He had not known that he lived in so wild a region. There was something uncanny in the revelation.

By nightfall he was fatigued, footsore, famishing. The thought of his wife and children urged him on. At last he found a road which led him in what he knew to be the right direction. It was as wide and straight as a city street, yet it seemed untravelled. No fields bordered it, no dwelling anywhere. Not so much as the barking of a dog suggested human habitation. The black bodies of the great trees formed a straight wall on both sides, terminating on the horizon in a point, like a diagram in a lesson in perspective. Overhead, as he looked up through this rift in the wood, shone great golden stars looking unfamiliar and grouped in strange constellations. He was sure they were arranged in some order which had a secret and malign significance. The wood on either side was full of singular noises, among which—once, twice, and again—he distinctly heard whispers in an unknown tongue.

His neck was in pain, and, lifting his hand to it, he found it horribly swollen. He knew that it had a circle of black where the rope had bruised it. His eyes felt congested; he could no longer close them. His tongue was swollen with thirst; he relieved its fever by thrusting it forward from between his teeth into the cool air. How softly the turf had carpeted the untravelled avenue! He could no longer feel the roadway beneath his feet!

Doubtless, despite his suffering, he fell asleep while walking, for now he sees 35
another scene—perhaps he has merely recovered from a delirium. He stands at the gate of his own home. All is as he left it, and all bright and beautiful in the

morning sunshine. He must have travelled the entire night. As he pushes open the gate and passes up the wide white walk, he sees a flutter of female garments; his wife, looking fresh and cool and sweet, steps down from the verandah to meet him. At the bottom of the steps she stands waiting, with a smile of ineffable joy, an attitude of matchless grace and dignity. Ah, how beautiful she is! He springs forward with extended arms. As he is about to clasp her, he feels a stunning blow upon the back of the neck; a blinding white light blazes all about him, with a sound like the shock of a cannon—then all is darkness and silence!

Peyton Farquhar was dead; his body, with a broken neck, swung gently from side to side beneath the timbers of the Owl Creek bridge. *[1891]*

THINKING ABOUT THE TEXT

1. One of the most popular themes in literature is the tension between reality and illusion. How does Bierce play with these ideas?
2. Comment on Bierce's use of time. What indications are there that suggest it is either objective or subjective?
3. Look up near-death experience (NDE) online. How does this information compare with Farquhar's experience?
4. Note Bierce's recurring use of the color gray. What significance does it seem to have? How does he also use driftwood as a symbol?
5. What significance does Bierce's description of Farquhar have? What is he trying to do?

TIM O'BRIEN

The Things They Carried

A native of Minnesota, Tim O'Brien (b. 1946) was drafted after he graduated from Macalester College. Subsequently, he served in the Vietnam War, during which he received a Purple Heart. In one way or another, practically all of his fiction deals with the war, although he has been repeatedly ambiguous about how and when his work incorporates his own Vietnam experiences. O'Brien's novels include If I Die in a Combat Zone *(1973),* Going After Cacciato *(which won the National Book Award in 1978),* In the Lake of the Woods *(a 1994 book that touches on the massacre at My Lai),* Tomcat in Love *(1998), and* July, July *(2002). Originally published in* Esquire *magazine, the following story was reprinted in* The Best American Short Stories 1987. *It then appeared along with related stories by O'Brien in a 1990 book also titled* The Things They Carried.

First Lieutenant Jimmy Cross carried letters from a girl named Martha, a junior at Mount Sebastian College in New Jersey. They were not love letters, but Lieutenant Cross was hoping, so he kept them folded in plastic at the bottom of his rucksack. In the late afternoon, after a day's march, he would dig his foxhole, wash his hands under a canteen, unwrap the letters, hold them with the tips of his fingers, and spend the last hour of light pretending. He would imagine romantic camping trips into the White Mountains in New Hampshire. He would sometimes taste the envelope flaps, knowing her tongue had been there. More than anything, he wanted Martha to love him as he loved her, but the letters were mostly chatty, elusive on the matter of love. She was a virgin, he was almost sure. She was an English major at Mount Sebastian, and she wrote beautifully about her professors and roommates and midterm exams, about her respect for Chaucer and her great affection for Virginia Woolf. She often quoted lines of poetry; she never mentioned the war, except to say, Jimmy, take care of yourself. The letters weighed ten ounces. They were signed "Love, Martha," but Lieutenant Cross understood that "Love" was only a way of signing and did not mean what he sometimes pretended it meant. At dusk, he would carefully return the letters to his rucksack. Slowly, a bit distracted, he would get up and move among his men, checking the perimeter, then at full dark he would return to his hole and watch the night and wonder if Martha was a virgin.

The things they carried were largely determined by necessity. Among the necessities or near necessities were P-38 can openers, pocket knives, heat tabs, wrist watches, dog tags, mosquito repellant, chewing gum, candy, cigarettes, salt tablets, packets of Kool-Aid, lighters, matches, sewing kits, Military Payment Certificates, C rations, and two or three canteens of water. Together, these items weighed between fifteen and twenty pounds, depending upon a man's habits or rate of metabolism. Henry Dobbins, who was a big man, carried extra rations; he was especially fond of canned peaches in heavy syrup over pound cake. Dave Jensen, who practiced field hygiene, carried a toothbrush, dental floss, and several hotel-size bars of soap he'd stolen on R&R in Sydney, Australia. Ted Lavender, who was scared, carried tranquilizers until he was shot in the head outside the village of Than Khe in mid-April. By necessity and because it was SOP,° they all carried steel helmets that weighed five pounds including the liner and camouflage cover. They carried the standard fatigue jackets and trousers. Very few carried underwear. On their feet they carried jungle boots — 2.1 pounds — and Dave Jensen carried three pairs of socks and a can of Dr. Scholl's foot powder as a precaution against trench foot. Until he was shot, Ted Lavender carried six or seven ounces of premium dope, which for him was a necessity. Mitchell Sanders, the RTO,° carried condoms. Norman Bowker carried a diary. Rat Kiley carried comic books. Kiowa, a devout Baptist, carried an illustrated New Testament that had been presented to him by his father, who taught Sunday school in Oklahoma City, Oklahoma. As a hedge against bad times, however, Kiowa also carried his grandmother's distrust of the white man, his grandfather's old hunting hatchet. Necessity dictated. Because the land was mined and booby-trapped, it was SOP for each man to carry a steel-centered, nylon-covered flak jacket, which weighed 6.7 pounds, but which on hot days seemed much heavier. Because you could die so quickly, each man carried at least one large compress bandage, usually in the

SOP: Standard operating procedure.
RTO: Radiotelephone operator.

helmet band for easy access. Because the nights were cold, and because the monsoons were wet, each carried a green plastic poncho that could be used as a raincoat or ground sheet or makeshift tent. With its quilted liner, the poncho weighed almost two pounds, but it was worth every ounce. In April, for instance, when Ted Lavender was shot, they used his poncho to wrap him up, then to carry him across the paddy, then to lift him into the chopper that took him away.

They were called legs or grunts.

To carry something was to "hump" it, as when Lieutenant Jimmy Cross humped his love for Martha up the hills and through the swamps. In its intransitive form, "to hump" meant "to walk," or "to march," but it implied burdens far beyond the intransitive.

Almost everyone humped photographs. In his wallet, Lieutenant Cross car- 5
ried two photographs of Martha. The first was a Kodachrome snapshot signed "Love," though he knew better. She stood against a brick wall. Her eyes were gray and neutral, her lips slightly open as she stared straight-on at the camera. At night, sometimes, Lieutenant Cross wondered who had taken the picture, because he knew she had boyfriends, because he loved her so much, and because he could see the shadow of the picture taker spreading out against the brick wall. The second photograph had been clipped from the 1968 Mount Sebastian yearbook. It was an action shot — women's volleyball — and Martha was bent horizontal to the floor, reaching, the palms of her hands in sharp focus, the tongue taut, the expression frank and competitive. There was no visible sweat. She wore white gym shorts. Her legs, he thought, were almost certainly the legs of a virgin, dry and without hair, the left knee cocked and carrying her entire weight, which was just over one hundred pounds. Lieutenant Cross remembered touching that left knee. A dark theater, he remembered, and the movie was *Bonnie and Clyde*, and Martha wore a tweed skirt, and during the final scene, when he touched her knee, she turned and looked at him in a sad, sober way that made him pull his hand back, but he would always remember the feel of the tweed skirt and the knee beneath it and the sound of the gunfire that killed Bonnie and Clyde, how embarrassing it was, how slow and oppressive. He remembered kissing her good night at the dorm door. Right then, he thought, he should've done something brave. He should've carried her up the stairs to her room and tied her to the bed and touched that left knee all night long. He should've risked it. Whenever he looked at the photographs, he thought of new things he should've done.

What they carried was partly a function of rank, partly of field specialty.

As a first lieutenant and platoon leader, Jimmy Cross carried a compass, maps, code books, binoculars, and a .45-caliber pistol that weighed 2.9 pounds fully loaded. He carried a strobe light and the responsibility for the lives of his men.

As an RTO, Mitchell Sanders carried the PRC-25 radio, a killer, twenty-six pounds with its battery.

As a medic, Rat Kiley carried a canvas satchel filled with morphine and plasma and malaria tablets and surgical tape and comic books and all the things a medic must carry, including M&M's° for especially bad wounds, for a total weight of nearly twenty pounds.

As a big man, therefore a machine gunner, Henry Dobbins carried the M-60, 10
which weighed twenty-three pounds unloaded, but which was almost always loaded. In addition, Dobbins carried between ten and fifteen pounds of ammunition draped in belts across his chest and shoulders.

As PFCs or Spec 4s, most of them were common grunts and carried the standard M-16 gas-operated assault rifle. The weapon weighed 7.5 pounds unloaded, 8.2 pounds with its full twenty-round magazine. Depending on numerous factors, such as topography and psychology, the riflemen carried anywhere from twelve to twenty magazines, usually in cloth bandoliers, adding on another 8.4 pounds at minimum, fourteen pounds at maximum. When it was available, they also carried M-16 maintenance gear — rods and steel brushes and swabs and tubes of LSA° on — all of which weighed about a pound. Among the grunts, some carried the M-79 grenade launcher, 5.9 pounds unloaded, a reasonably light weapon except for the ammunition, which was heavy. A single round weighed ten ounces. The typical load was twenty-five rounds. But Ted Lavender, who was scared, carried thirty-four rounds when he was shot and killed outside Than Khe, and he went down under an exceptional burden, more than twenty pounds of ammunition, plus the flak jacket and helmet and rations and water and toilet paper and tranquilizers and all the rest, plus the unweighed fear. He was dead weight. There was no twitching or flopping. Kiowa, who saw it happen, said it was like watching a rock fall, or a big sandbag or something — just boom, then down — not like the movies where the dead guy rolls around and does fancy spins and goes ass over teakettle — not like that, Kiowa said, the poor bastard just flat-fuck fell. Boom. Down. Nothing else. It was a bright morning in mid-April. Lieutenant Cross felt the pain. He blamed himself. They stripped off Lavender's canteens and ammo, all the heavy things, and Rat Kiley said the obvious, the guy's dead, and Mitchell Sanders used his radio to report one U.S. KIA° and to request a chopper. Then they wrapped Lavender in his poncho. They carried him out to a dry paddy, established security, and sat smoking the dead man's dope until the chopper came. Lieutenant Cross kept to himself. He pictured Martha's smooth young face, thinking he loved her more than anything, more than his men, and now Ted Lavender was dead because he loved her so much and could not stop thinking about her. When the dust-off arrived, they carried Lavender aboard. Afterward they burned Than Khe. They marched until dusk, then dug their holes, and that night Kiowa kept explaining how you had to be there, how fast it was, how the poor guy just dropped like so much concrete. Boom-down, he said. Like cement.

* * *

In addition to the three standard weapons — the M-60, M-16, and M-79 — they carried whatever presented itself, or whatever seemed appropriate as a means of

M & Ms: These candies were distributed to seriously wounded soldiers as a placebo to provide comfort.
LSA: Gun oil.
KIA: Killed in action.

killing or staying alive. They carried catch-as-catch-can. At various times, in various situations, they carried M-14s and CAR-15s and Swedish Ks and grease guns and captured AK-47s and Chi-Coms and RPGs and Simonov carbines and black-market Uzis and .38-caliber Smith & Wesson handguns and 66 mm LAWs and shotguns and silencers and blackjacks and bayonets and C-4 plastic explosives. Lee Strunk carried a slingshot; a weapon of last resort, he called it. Mitchell Sanders carried brass knuckles. Kiowa carried his grandfather's feathered hatchet. Every third or fourth man carried a Claymore antipersonnel mine — 3.5 pounds with its firing device. They all carried fragmentation grenades — fourteen ounces each. They all carried at least one M-18 colored smoke grenade — twenty-four ounces. Some carried CS or tear-gas grenades. Some carried white-phosphorus grenades. They carried all they could bear, and then some, including a silent awe for the terrible power of the things they carried.

In the first week of April, before Lavender died, Lieutenant Jimmy Cross received a good-luck charm from Martha. It was a simple pebble, an ounce at most. Smooth to the touch, it was a milky-white color with flecks of orange and violet, oval-shaped, like a miniature egg. In the accompanying letter, Martha wrote that she had found the pebble on the Jersey shoreline, precisely where the land touched water at high tide, where things came together but also separated. It was this separate-but-together quality, she wrote, that had inspired her to pick up the pebble and to carry it in her breast pocket for several days, where it seemed weightless, and then to send it through the mail, by air, as a token of her truest feelings for him. Lieutenant Cross found this romantic. But he wondered what her truest feelings were, exactly, and what she meant by separate-but-together. He wondered how the tides and waves had come into play on that afternoon along the Jersey shoreline when Martha saw the pebble and bent down to rescue it from geology. He imagined bare feet. Martha was a poet, with the poet's sensibilities, and her feet would be brown and bare, the toenails unpainted, the eyes chilly and somber like the ocean in March, and though it was painful, he wondered who had been with her that afternoon. He imagined a pair of shadows moving along the strip of sand where things came together but also separated. It was phantom jealousy, he knew, but he couldn't help himself. He loved her so much. On the march, through the hot days of early April, he carried the pebble in his mouth, turning it with his tongue, tasting sea salts and moisture. His mind wandered. He had difficulty keeping his attention on the war. On occasion he would yell at his men to spread out the column, to keep their eyes open, but then he would slip away into daydreams, just pretending, walking barefoot along the Jersey shore, with Martha, carrying nothing. He would feel himself rising. Sun and waves and gentle winds, all love and lightness.

What they carried varied by mission.

When a mission took them to the mountains, they carried mosquito netting, 15
machetes, canvas tarps, and extra bug juice.°

bug juice: Insect repellent.

If a mission seemed especially hazardous, or if it involved a place they knew to be bad, they carried everything they could. In certain heavily mined AOs,° where the land was dense with Toe Poppers and Bouncing Betties,° they took turns humping a twenty-eight-pound mine detector. With its headphones and big sensing plate, the equipment was a stress on the lower back and shoulders, awkward to handle, often useless because of the shrapnel in the earth, but they carried it anyway, partly for safety, partly for the illusion of safety.

On ambush, or other night missions, they carried peculiar little odds and ends. Kiowa always took along his New Testament and a pair of moccasins for silence. Dave Jensen carried night-sight vitamins high in carotin. Lee Strunk carried his slingshot; ammo, he claimed, would never be a problem. Rat Kiley carried brandy and M&M's. Until he was shot, Ted Lavender carried the starlight scope, which weighed 6.3 pounds with its aluminum carrying case. Henry Dobbins carried his girlfriend's pantyhose wrapped around his neck as a comforter. They all carried ghosts. When dark came, they would move out single file across the meadows and paddies to their ambush coordinates, where they would quietly set up the Claymores and lie down and spend the night waiting.

Other missions were more complicated and required special equipment. In mid-April, it was their mission to search out and destroy the elaborate tunnel complexes in the Than Khe area south of Chu Lai. To blow the tunnels, they carried one-pound blocks of pentrite high explosives, four blocks to a man, sixty-eight pounds in all. They carried wiring, detonators, and battery-powered clackers. Dave Jensen carried earplugs. Most often, before blowing the tunnels, they were ordered by higher command to search them, which was considered bad news, but by and large they just shrugged and carried out orders. Because he was a big man, Henry Dobbins was excused from tunnel duty. The others would draw numbers. Before Lavender died there were seventeen men in the platoon, and whoever drew the number seventeen would strip off his gear and crawl in head first with a flashlight and Lieutenant Cross's .45-caliber pistol. The rest of them would fan out as security. They would sit down or kneel, not facing the hole, listening to the ground beneath them, imagining cobwebs and ghosts, whatever was down there — the tunnel walls squeezing in — how the flashlight seemed impossibly heavy in the hand and how it was tunnel vision in the very strictest sense, compression in all ways, even time, and how you had to wiggle in — ass and elbows — a swallowed-up feeling — and how you found yourself worrying about odd things — will your flashlight go dead? Do rats carry rabies? If you screamed, how far would the sound carry? Would your buddies hear it? Would they have the courage to drag you out? In some respects, though not many, the waiting was worse than the tunnel itself. Imagination was a killer.

On April 16, when Lee Strunk drew the number seventeen, he laughed and muttered something and went down quickly. The morning was hot and very still. Not good, Kiowa said. He looked at the tunnel opening, then out across a dry paddy toward the village of Than Khe. Nothing moved. No clouds or birds or

AOs: Areas of operations.
Toe Poppers and Bouncing Betties: Exploding booby trap devices.

people. As they waited, the men smoked and drank Kool-Aid, not talking much, feeling sympathy for Lee Strunk but also feeling the luck of the draw. You win some, you lose some, said Mitchell Sanders, and sometimes you settle for a rain check. It was a tired line and no one laughed.

20 Henry Dobbins ate a tropical chocolate bar. Ted Lavender popped a tranquilizer and went off to pee.

After five minutes, Lieutenant Jimmy Cross moved to the tunnel, leaned down, and examined the darkness. Trouble, he thought — a cave-in maybe. And then suddenly, without willing it, he was thinking about Martha. The stresses and fractures, the quick collapse, the two of them buried alive under all that weight. Dense, crushing love. Kneeling, watching the hole, he tried to concentrate on Lee Strunk and the war, all the dangers, but his love was too much for him, he felt paralyzed, he wanted to sleep inside her lungs and breathe her blood and be smothered. He wanted her to be a virgin and not a virgin, all at once. He wanted to know her. Intimate secrets — why poetry? Why so sad? Why the grayness in her eyes? Why so alone? Not lonely, just alone — riding her bike across campus or sitting off by herself in the cafeteria. Even dancing, she danced alone — and it was the aloneness that filled him with love. He remembered telling her that one evening. How she nodded and looked away. And how, later, when he kissed her, she received the kiss without returning it, her eyes wide open, not afraid, not a virgin's eyes, just flat and uninvolved.

Lieutenant Cross gazed at the tunnel. But he was not there. He was buried with Martha under the white sand at the Jersey shore. They were pressed together, and the pebble in his mouth was her tongue. He was smiling. Vaguely, he was aware of how quiet the day was, the sullen paddies, yet he could not bring himself to worry about matters of security. He was beyond that. He was just a kid at war, in love. He was twenty-two years old. He couldn't help it.

A few moments later Lee Strunk crawled out of the tunnel. He came up grinning, filthy but alive. Lieutenant Cross nodded and closed his eyes while the others clapped Strunk on the back and made jokes about rising from the dead.

Worms, Rat Kiley said. Right out of the grave. Fuckin' zombie.

25 The men laughed. They all felt great relief.

Spook City, said Mitchell Sanders.

Lee Strunk made a funny ghost sound, a kind of moaning, yet very happy, and right then, when Strunk made that high happy moaning sound, when he went *Ahhooooo*, right then Ted Lavender was shot in the head on his way back from peeing. He lay with his mouth open. The teeth were broken. There was a swollen black bruise under his left eye. The cheekbone was gone. Oh shit, Rat Kiley said, the guy's dead. The guy's dead, he kept saying, which seemed profound — the guy's dead. I mean really.

The things they carried were determined to some extent by superstition. Lieutenant Cross carried his good-luck pebble. Dave Jensen carried a rabbit's foot. Norman Bowker, otherwise a very gentle person, carried a thumb that had been presented to him as a gift by Mitchell Sanders. The thumb was dark brown, rubbery to the touch, and weighed four ounces at most. It had been cut from a VC corpse, a boy of fifteen or sixteen. They'd found him at the bottom of an irrigation ditch, badly burned, flies in his mouth and eyes. The boy wore black shorts and sandals. At the time of his death he had been carrying a pouch of rice, a rifle, and three magazines of ammunition.

You want my opinion, Mitchell Sanders said, there's a definite moral here.

He put his hand on the dead boy's wrist. He was quiet for a time, as if counting a pulse, then he patted the stomach, almost affectionately, and used Kiowa's hunting hatchet to remove the thumb.

Henry Dobbins asked what the moral was.

Moral?

You know. *Moral.*

Sanders wrapped the thumb in toilet paper and handed it across to Norman Bowker. There was no blood. Smiling, he kicked the boy's head, watched the flies scatter, and said, It's like with that old TV show — Paladin. Have gun, will travel.

Henry Dobbins thought about it.

Yeah, well, he finally said. I don't see no moral.

There it *is*, man.

Fuck off.

They carried USO stationery and pencils and pens. They carried Sterno, safety pins, trip flares, signal flares, spools of wire, razor blades, chewing tobacco, liberated joss sticks and statuettes of the smiling Buddha, candles, grease pencils, *The Stars and Stripes*, fingernail clippers, Psy Ops° leaflets, bush hats, bolos, and much more. Twice a week, when the resupply choppers came in, they carried hot chow in green Mermite cans and large canvas bags filled with iced beer and soda pop. They carried plastic water containers, each with a two-gallon capacity. Mitchell Sanders carried a set of starched tiger fatigues for special occasions. Henry Dobbins carried Black Flag insecticide. Dave Jensen carried empty sandbags that could be filled at night for added protection. Lee Strunk carried tanning lotion. Some things they carried in common. Taking turns, they carried the big PRC-77 scrambler radio, which weighed thirty pounds with its battery. They shared the weight of memory. They took up what others could no longer bear. Often, they carried each other, the wounded or weak. They carried infections. They carried chess sets, basketballs, Vietnamese-English dictionaries, insignia of rank, Bronze Stars and Purple Hearts, plastic cards imprinted with the Code of Conduct. They carried diseases, among them malaria and dysentery. They carried lice and ringworm and leeches and paddy algae and various rots and molds. They carried the land itself — Vietnam, the place, the soil — a powdery orange-red dust that covered their boots and fatigues and faces. They carried the sky. The whole atmosphere, they carried it, the humidity, the monsoons, the stink of fungus and decay, all of it, they carried gravity. They moved like mules. By daylight they took sniper fire, at night they were mortared, but it was not battle, it was just the endless march, village to village, without purpose, nothing won or lost. They

Psy Ops: Psychological operations.

marched for the sake of the march. They plodded along slowly, dumbly, leaning forward against the heat, unthinking, all blood and bone, simple grunts, soldiering with their legs, toiling up the hills and down into the paddies and across the rivers and up again and down, just humping, one step and then the next and then another, but no volition, no will, because it was automatic, it was anatomy, and the war was entirely a matter of posture and carriage, the hump was everything, a kind of inertia, a kind of emptiness, a dullness of desire and intellect and conscience and hope and human sensibility. Their principles were in their feet. Their calculations were biological. They had no sense of strategy or mission. They searched the villages without knowing what to look for, not caring, kicking over jars of rice, frisking children and old men, blowing tunnels, sometimes setting fires and sometimes not, then forming up and moving on to the next village, then other villages, where it would always be the same. They carried their own lives. The pressures were enormous. In the heat of early afternoon, they would remove their helmets and flak jackets, walking bare, which was dangerous but which helped ease the strain. They would often discard things along the route of march. Purely for comfort, they would throw away rations, blow their Claymores and grenades, no matter, because by nightfall the resupply choppers would arrive with more of the same, then a day or two later still more, fresh watermelons and crates of ammunition and sunglasses and woolen sweaters — the resources were stunning — sparklers for the Fourth of July, colored eggs for Easter. It was the great American war chest — the fruits of science, the smokestacks, the canneries, the arsenals at Hartford, the Minnesota forests, the machine shops, the vast fields of corn and wheat — they carried like freight trains, they carried it on their backs and shoulders — and for all the ambiguities of Vietnam, all the mysteries and unknowns, there was at least the single abiding certainty that they would never be at a loss for things to carry.

After the chopper took Lavender away, Lieutenant Jimmy Cross led his men into 40
the village of Than Khe. They burned everything. They shot chickens and dogs, they trashed the village well, they called in artillery and watched the wreckage, then they marched for several hours through the hot afternoon, and then at dusk, while Kiowa explained how Lavender died, Lieutenant Cross found himself trembling.

He tried not to cry. With his entrenching tool, which weighed five pounds, he began digging a hole in the earth.

He felt shame. He hated himself. He had loved Martha more than his men, and as a consequence Lavender was now dead, and this was something he would have to carry like a stone in his stomach for the rest of the war.

All he could do was dig. He used his entrenching tool like an ax, slashing, feeling both love and hate, and then later, when it was full dark, he sat at the bottom of his foxhole and wept. It went on for a long while. In part, he was grieving for Ted Lavender, but mostly it was for Martha, and for himself, because she belonged to another world, which was not quite real, and because she was a junior at Mount Sebastian College in New Jersey, a poet and a virgin and uninvolved, and because he realized she did not love him and never would.

Like cement, Kiowa whispered in the dark. I swear to God — boom-down. Not a word.

I've heard this, said Norman Bowker.

A pisser, you know? Still zipping himself up. Zapped while zipping.

All right, fine. That's enough.

Yeah, but you had to see it, the guy just —

I *heard*, man. Cement. So why not shut the fuck *up*?

Kiowa shook his head sadly and glanced over at the hole where Lieutenant Jimmy Cross sat watching the night. The air was thick and wet. A warm, dense fog had settled over the paddies and there was the stillness that precedes rain.

After a time Kiowa sighed.

One thing for sure, he said. The Lieutenant's in some deep hurt. I mean that crying jag — the way he was carrying on — it wasn't fake or anything, it was real heavy-duty hurt. The man cares.

Sure, Norman Bowker said.

Say what you want, the man does care.

We all got problems.

Not Lavender.

No, I guess not, Bowker said. Do me a favor, though.

Shut up?

That's a smart Indian. Shut up.

Shrugging, Kiowa pulled off his boots. He wanted to say more, just to lighten up his sleep, but instead he opened his New Testament and arranged it beneath his head as a pillow. The fog made things seem hollow and unattached. He tried not to think about Ted Lavender, but then he was thinking how fast it was, no drama, down and dead, and how it was hard to feel anything except surprise. It seemed un-Christian. He wished he could find some great sadness, or even anger, but the emotion wasn't there and he couldn't make it happen. Mostly he felt pleased to be alive. He liked the smell of the New Testament under his cheek, the leather and ink and paper and glue, whatever the chemicals were. He liked hearing the sounds of night. Even his fatigue, it felt fine, the stiff muscles and the prickly awareness of his own body, a floating feeling. He enjoyed not being dead. Lying there, Kiowa admired Lieutenant Jimmy Cross's capacity for grief. He wanted to share the man's pain, he wanted to care as Jimmy Cross cared. And yet when he closed his eyes, all he could think was Boom-down, and all he could feel was the pleasure of having his boots off and the fog curling in around him and the damp soil and the Bible smells and the plush comfort of night.

After a moment Norman Bowker sat up in the dark.

What the hell, he said. You want to talk, *talk*. Tell it to me.

Forget it.

No, man, go on. One thing I hate, it's a silent Indian.

For the most part they carried themselves with poise, a kind of dignity. Now and then, however, there were times of panic, when they squealed or wanted to squeal but couldn't, when they twitched and made moaning sounds and covered their heads and said Dear Jesus and flopped around on the earth and fired their weapons blindly and cringed and sobbed and begged for the noise to stop and went wild and made stupid promises to themselves and to God and to their mothers and fathers, hoping not to die. In different ways, it happened to all of them. Afterward, when the firing ended, they would blink and peek up. They would touch their bodies, feeling shame, then quickly hiding it. They would force themselves to stand. As if in slow motion, frame by frame, the world would take on the old logic — absolute silence, then the wind, then sunlight, then voices. It was the burden of being alive. Awkwardly, the men would reassemble themselves, first in private, then in groups, becoming soldiers again. They would repair the leaks in their eyes. They would check for casualties, call in dust-offs, light cigarettes, try to smile, clear their throats and spit and begin cleaning their weapons. After a time someone would shake his head and say, No lie, I almost shit my pants, and someone else would laugh, which meant it was bad, yes, but the guy had obviously not shit his pants, it wasn't that bad, and in any case nobody would ever do such a thing and then go ahead and talk about it. They would squint into the dense, oppressive sunlight. For a few moments, perhaps, they would fall silent, lighting a joint and tracking its passage from man to man, inhaling, holding in the humiliation. Scary stuff, one of them might say. But then someone else would grin or flick his eyebrows and say, Roger-dodger, almost cut me a new asshole, *almost*.

There were numerous such poses. Some carried themselves with a sort of wistful resignation, others with pride or stiff soldierly discipline or good humor or macho zeal. They were afraid of dying but they were even more afraid to show it.

They found jokes to tell.

They used a hard vocabulary to contain the terrible softness. *Greased*, they'd say. *Offed, lit up, zapped while zipping.* It wasn't cruelty, just stage presence. They were actors and the war came at them in 3-D. When someone died, it wasn't quite dying, because in a curious way it seemed scripted, and because they had their lines mostly memorized, irony mixed with tragedy, and because they called it by other names, as if to encyst and destroy the reality of death itself. They kicked corpses. They cut off thumbs. They talked grunt lingo. They told stories about Ted Lavender's supply of tranquilizers, how the poor guy didn't feel a thing, how incredibly tranquil he was.

There's a moral here, said Mitchell Sanders.

They were waiting for Lavender's chopper, smoking the dead man's dope. 70

The moral's pretty obvious, Sanders said, and winked. Stay away from drugs. No joke, they'll ruin your day every time.

Cute, said Henry Dobbins.

Mind-blower, get it? Talk about wiggy — nothing left, just blood and brains.

They made themselves laugh.

There it is, they'd say, over and over, as if the repetition itself were an act of 75
poise, a balance between crazy and almost crazy, knowing without going. There it is, which meant be cool, let it ride, because oh yeah, man, you can't change what can't be changed, there it is, there it absolutely and positively and fucking well *is*.

They were tough.

They carried all the emotional baggage of men who might die. Grief, terror, love, longing — these were intangibles, but the intangibles had their own mass and specific gravity, they had tangible weight. They carried shameful memories. They carried the common secret of cowardice barely restrained, the instinct to run or freeze or hide, and in many respects this was the heaviest burden of all, for it could never be put down, it required perfect balance and perfect posture. They carried their reputations. They carried the soldier's greatest fear, which was the fear of blushing. Men killed, and died, because they were embarrassed not to. It was what had brought them to the war in the first place, nothing positive, no dreams of glory or honor, just to avoid the blush of dishonor. They died so as not to die of embarrassment. They crawled into tunnels and walked point and advanced under fire. Each morning, despite the unknowns, they made their legs move. They endured. They kept humping. They did not submit to the obvious alternative, which was simply to close the eyes and fall. So easy, really. Go limp and tumble to the ground and let the muscles unwind and not speak and not budge until your buddies picked you up and lifted you into the chopper that would roar and dip its nose and carry you off to the world. A mere matter of falling, yet no one ever fell. It was not courage, exactly; the object was not valor. Rather, they were too frightened to be cowards.

By and large they carried these things inside, maintaining the masks of composure. They sneered at sick call. They spoke bitterly about guys who had found release by shooting off their own toes or fingers. Pussies, they'd say. Candyasses. It was fierce, mocking talk, with only a trace of envy or awe, but even so, the image played itself out behind their eyes.

They imagined the muzzle against flesh. They imagined the quick, sweet pain, then the evacuation to Japan, then a hospital with warm beds and cute geisha nurses.

They dreamed of freedom birds.

At night, on guard, staring into the dark, they were carried away by jumbo jets. They felt the rush of takeoff. *Gone!* they yelled. And then velocity, wings and engines, a smiling stewardess — but it was more than a plane, it was a real bird, a big sleek silver bird with feathers and talons and high screeching. They were flying. The weights fell off, there was nothing to bear. They laughed and held on tight, feeling the cold slap of wind and altitude, soaring, thinking *It's over, I'm gone!* — they were naked, they were light and free — it was all lightness, bright and fast and buoyant, light as light, a helium buzz in the brain, a giddy bubbling in the lungs as they were taken up over the clouds and the war, beyond duty, beyond gravity and mortification and global entanglements — *Sin loi!*° they yelled, *I'm sorry, motherfuckers, but I'm out of it. I'm goofed, I'm on a space cruise, I'm gone!* — and it was a restful, disencumbered sensation, just riding the light waves, sailing that big silver freedom bird over the mountains and oceans, over America, over the farms and great sleeping cities and cemeteries and highways and the golden arches of McDonald's. It was flight, a kind of fleeing, a kind of falling, falling higher and higher, spinning off the edge of the earth and beyond the sun and through the vast, silent vacuum where there were no burdens and where

***Sin loi!*:** "Sorry about that."

everything weighed exactly nothing. *Gone!* they screamed, *I'm sorry but I'm gone!* And so at night, not quite dreaming, they gave themselves over to lightness, they were carried, they were purely borne.

On the morning after Ted Lavender died, First Lieutenant Jimmy Cross crouched at the bottom of his foxhole and burned Martha's letters. Then he burned the two photographs. There was a steady rain falling, which made it difficult, but he used heat tabs and Sterno to build a small fire, screening it with his body, holding the photographs over the tight blue flame with the tips of his fingers.

He realized it was only a gesture. Stupid, he thought. Sentimental, too, but mostly just stupid.

Lavender was dead. You couldn't burn the blame.

Besides, the letters were in his head. And even now, without photographs, 85
Lieutenant Cross could see Martha playing volleyball in her white gym shorts and yellow T-shirt. He could see her moving in the rain.

When the fire died out, Lieutenant Cross pulled his poncho over his shoulders and ate breakfast from a can.

There was no great mystery, he decided.

In those burned letters Martha had never mentioned the war, except to say, Jimmy, take care of yourself. She wasn't involved. She signed the letters "Love," but it wasn't love, and all the fine lines and technicalities did not matter.

The morning came up wet and blurry. Everything seemed part of everything else, the fog and Martha and the deepening rain.

It was a war, after all. 90

Half smiling, Lieutenant Jimmy Cross took out his maps. He shook his head hard, as if to clear it, then bent forward and began planning the day's march. In ten minutes, or maybe twenty, he would rouse the men and they would pack up and head west, where the maps showed the country to be green and inviting. They would do what they had always done. The rain might add some weight, but otherwise it would be one more day layered upon all the other days.

He was realistic about it. There was that new hardness in his stomach.

No more fantasies, he told himself.

Henceforth, when he thought about Martha, it would be only to think that she belonged elsewhere. He would shut down the daydreams. This was not Mount Sebastian, it was another world, where there were no pretty poems or midterm exams, a place where men died because of carelessness and gross stupidity. Kiowa was right. Boom-down, and you were dead, never partly dead.

Briefly, in the rain, Lieutenant Cross saw Martha's gray eyes gazing back 95
at him.

He understood.

It was very sad, he thought. The things men carried inside. The things men did or felt they had to do.

He almost nodded at her, but didn't.

Instead he went back to his maps. He was now determined to perform his duties firmly and without negligence. It wouldn't help Lavender, he knew that, but from this point on he would comport himself as a soldier. He would dispose of his good-luck pebble. Swallow it, maybe, or use Lee Strunk's slingshot, or just drop it along the trail. On the march he would impose strict field discipline. He would be careful to send out flank security, to prevent straggling or bunching up, to keep his troops moving at the proper pace and at the proper interval. He would insist on clean weapons. He would confiscate the remainder of Lavender's dope. Later in the day, perhaps, he would call the men together and speak to them plainly. He would accept the blame for what had happened to Ted Lavender. He would be a man about it. He would look them in the eyes, keeping his chin level, and he would issue the new SOPs in a calm, impersonal tone of voice, an officer's voice, leaving no room for argument or discussion. Commencing immediately, he'd tell them, they would no longer abandon equipment along the route of march. They would police up their acts. They would get their shit together, and keep it together, and maintain it neatly and in good working order.

He would not tolerate laxity. He would show strength, distancing himself. 100

Among the men there would be grumbling, of course, and maybe worse, because their days would seem longer and their loads heavier, but Lieutenant Cross reminded himself that his obligation was not to be loved but to lead. He would dispense with love; it was not now a factor. And if anyone quarreled or complained, he would simply tighten his lips and arrange his shoulders in the correct command posture. He might give a curt little nod. Or he might not. He might just shrug and say Carry on, then they would saddle up and form into a column and move out toward the villages of Than Khe. *[1986]*

THINKING ABOUT THE TEXT

1. What specific psychological and emotional "things" do the soldiers carry into battle? Did any of these surprise you? Explain.
2. In three or four sentences, how would you describe the experience of war, using this story as a basis?
3. What are some significant differences, if any, among the soldiers under Jimmy Cross's command?
4. What is your attitude toward Jimmy Cross's apparent obsession with Martha?
5. Jimmy Cross seems to feel guilty about Ted Lavender's death. To what extent does his feeling seem rational? *Should* he feel guilty, in your view? Why, or why not? In the final two paragraphs, he makes a number of resolutions. Which, if any, do you think that he is capable of keeping?

MAKING COMPARISONS

1. What are some of the authentic details from both stories that suggest the authors had first-hand observations of war?
2. Compare Cross's and Farquhar's thoughts about home, especially Farquhar's wife and Martha.
3. How do both Cross and Farquhar escape from the reality of war?

≡ WRITING ABOUT ISSUES

1. Write an essay that argues that an attempt to escape from war's trauma is or is not an illusion. Use O'Brien and Bierce and any other writer or filmmaker as evidence.
2. Write an argument that claims that either the short story or the film is more effective, realistic, or artistic.
3. Read O'Brien's story "The Sweetheart of the Song Tra Bong" and write an essay that argues that the themes are or are not similar to "The Things They Carried." Or read Bierce's "Chickamauga" and argue that Bierce's themes are or are not comparable to his story here.
4. Write an essay that argues that Jimmy and Martha are or are not in love with each other.

Journeys to the Future: Stories

ARTHUR C. CLARKE, "The Nine Billion Names of God"

KURT VONNEGUT, "Harrison Bergeron"

JOANNE RUSS, "When It Changed"

OCTAVIA BUTLER, "Human Evolution"

Ever since H. G. Wells and through the golden age of Ray Bradbury, Isaac Asimov, Robert Heinlein, and Kurt Vonnegut to recent masters like William Gibson and Philip K. Dick, literary science fiction has been used to make serious and critical observations about society. Aldous Huxley in his famous *Brave New World* (1932), for example, was fearful of government's power to control all aspects of our lives, even determining at birth who would collect garbage and who would be future bureaucrats. Indeed, the depiction of Big Brother in George Orwell's *1984* (1948) is still a chilling image of governing authority taken to the extreme.

But science fiction is not always pessimistic about the future. In fiction, it is true that the dystopian vision dominates the future, but there is another vision—the utopian one of an idea society, an earthly paradise. Famous examples are Plato's *Republic* and the book that coined the term, Thomas Moore's *Utopia*. But even in these ideal arrangements, sinister forces sometimes emerge.

Much of science fiction uses satire's technique of exaggerating a contemporary concern and transporting it to the future. And depending on the writer's utopian or dystopian vision, the fictional future can be a progressive step forward or a precipitous slide into darkness. The four stories here reflect the writers' fears and hopes about the world they live in. Arthur C. Clark takes us to a remote and imaginary corner of the world to a kind of utopian monastery where Western science and Eastern spirituality converge and collide. Kurt Vonnegut's dystopia society is clearly a warning about our society's authoritarian inclination to fear and repress difference. And Joanna Russ and Octavia Butler's feminist concerns about rigid gender expectations for women lead them to reimagine radically different arrangements where binary gender assumptions do not exist. Although science fiction describes alternative realities, the real focus is on current behavior, assumptions, and beliefs.

BEFORE YOU READ

Recall science fiction films you have seen or stories you have read and describe what current problems or concerns they seem to be addressing.

ARTHUR C. CLARKE

The Nine Billion Names of God

Arthur C. Clarke (1917–2008) is one of the giants of twentieth-century science fiction. His novels, including Childhood's End *(1953) and* Rendezvous with Rama *(1972), have been translated into dozens of languages. Clarke's family could not afford to send him to university, so instead he worked and served as a radar specialist during World War II, all the while pursuing his scientific interests and writing. In 1946, his story "Rescue Party" became his first published fiction piece. He eventually graduated from King's College with honors in physics and mathematics in 1948. He is widely credited with predicting satellite communication twenty years before it became a reality. In 1968, Clarke and Stanley Kubrick shared an Oscar nomination for the screenplay of* 2001: A Space Odyssey. *He has won science fiction's highest awards, The Hugo and The Nebula, several times. As in the following story, spirituality and religion were frequent themes in his work. Although he considered himself an atheist, he wrote "Any path to knowledge is a path to God—or Reality, whichever word one prefers to use."*

"This is a slightly unusual request," said Dr. Wagner, with what he hoped was commendable restraint. "As far as I know, it's the first time anyone's been asked to supply a Tibetan monastery with an Automatic Sequence Computer. I don't wish to be inquisitive, but I should hardly have thought that your—ah—establishment had much use for such a machine. Could you explain just what you intend to do with it?"

"Gladly," replied the lama, readjusting his silk robes and carefully putting away the slide rule he had been using for currency conversions. "Your Mark V Computer can carry out any routine mathematical operation involving up to ten digits. However, for our work we are interested in *letters*, not numbers. As we wish you to modify the output circuits, the machine will be printing words, not columns of figures."

"I don't quite understand. . . ."

"This is a project on which we have been working for the last three centuries—since the lamasery was founded, in fact. It is somewhat alien to your way of thought, so I hope you will listen with an open mind while I explain it."

"Naturally." 5

"It is really quite simple. We have been compiling a list which shall contain all the possible names of God."

"I beg your pardon?"

"We have reason to believe," continued the lama imperturbably, "that all such names can be written with not more than nine letters in an alphabet we have devised."

"And you have been doing this for three centuries?"

"Yes: we expected it would take us about fifteen thousand years to complete 10
the task."

"Oh," Dr. Wagner looked a little dazed. "Now I see why you wanted to hire one of our machines. But exactly what is the *purpose* of this project?"

The lama hesitated for a fraction of a second, and Wagner wondered if he had offended him. If so, there was no trace of annoyance in the reply.

"Call it ritual, if you like, but it's a fundamental part of our belief. All the many names of the Supreme Being—God, Jehovah, Allah, and so on—they are only man-made labels. There is a philosophical problem of some difficulty here, which I do not propose to discuss, but somewhere among all the possible combinations of letters that can occur are what one may call the real names of God. By systematic permutation of letters, we have been trying to list them all."

"I see. You've been starting at AAAAAAA . . . and working up to ZZZZZZZZ. . . ."

"Exactly—though we use a special alphabet of our own. Modifying the elec- 15
tromatic typewriters to deal with this is, of course, trivial. A rather more interesting problem is that of devising suitable circuits to eliminate ridiculous combinations. For example, no letter must occur more than three times in succession."

"Three? Surely you mean two."

"Three is correct: I am afraid it would take too long to explain why, even if you understood our language."

"I'm sure it would," said Wagner hastily. "Go on."

"Luckily, it will be a simple matter to adapt your Automatic Sequence Computer for this work, since once it has been programed properly it will permute each letter in turn and print the result. What would have taken us fifteen thousand years it will be able to do in a hundred days."

Dr. Wagner was scarcely conscious of the faint sounds from the Manhattan 20
streets far below. He was in a different world, a world of natural, not man-made, mountains. High up in their remote aeries these monks had been patiently at work, generation after generation, compiling their lists of meaningless words. Was there any limit to the follies of mankind? Still, he must give no hint of his inner thoughts. The customer was always right. . . .

"There's no doubt," replied the doctor, "that we can modify the Mark V to print lists of this nature. I'm much more worried about the problem of installation and maintenance. Getting out to Tibet, in these days, is not going to be easy."

"We can arrange that. The components are small enough to travel by air—that is one reason why we chose your machine. If you can get them to India, we will provide transport from there."

"And you want to hire two of our engineers?"

"Yes, for the three months that the project should occupy."

"I've no doubt that Personnel can manage that." Dr. Wagner scribbled a note 25
on his desk pad. "There are just two other points—"

Before he could finish the sentence the lama had produced a small slip of paper.

"This is my certified credit balance at the Asiatic Bank."

"Thank you. It appears to be—ah—adequate. The second matter is so trivial that I hesitate to mention it—but it's surprising how often the obvious gets overlooked. What source of electrical energy have you?"

"A diesel generator providing fifty kilowatts at a hundred and ten volts. It was installed about five years ago and is quite reliable. It's made life at the lamasery much more comfortable, but of course it was really installed to provide power for the motors driving the prayer wheels."

"Of course," echoed Dr. Wagner. "I should have thought of that."

The view from the parapet was vertiginous, but in time one gets used to anything. After three months, George Hanley was not impressed by the two-thousand-foot swoop into the abyss or the remote checkerboard of fields in the valley below. He was leaning against the wind-smoothed stones and staring morosely at the distant mountains whose names he had never bothered to discover.

This, thought George, was the craziest thing that had ever happened to him. "Project Shangri-La," some wit back at the labs had christened it. For weeks now the Mark V had been churning out acres of sheets covered with gibberish. Patiently, inexorably, the computer had been rearranging letters in all their possible combinations, exhausting each class before going on to the next. As the sheets had emerged from the electromatic typewriters, the monks had carefully cut them up and pasted them into enormous books. In another week, heaven be praised, they would have finished. Just what obscure calculations had convinced the monks that they needn't bother to go on to words of ten, twenty, or a hundred letters. George didn't know. One of his recurring nightmares was that there would be some change of plan, and that the high lama (whom they'd naturally called Sam Jaffe, though he didn't look a bit like him) would suddenly announce that the project would be extended to approximately A.D. 2060. They were quite capable of it.

George heard the heavy wooden door slam in the wind as Chuck came out onto the parapet beside him. As usual, Chuck was smoking one of the cigars that made him so popular with the monks—who, it seemed, were quite willing to embrace all the minor and most of the major pleasures of life. That was one thing in their favor: they might be crazy, but they weren't bluenoses. Those frequent trips they took down to the village, for instance . . .

"Listen, George," said Chuck urgently. "I've learned something that means trouble."

"What's wrong? Isn't the machine behaving?" That was the worst contingency George could imagine. It might delay his return, and nothing could be more horrible. The way he felt now, even the sight of a TV commercial would seem like manna from heaven. At least it would be some link with home.

"No—it's nothing like that." Chuck settled himself on the parapet, which was unusual because normally he was scared of the drop. "I've just found what all this is about."

"What d'ya mean? I thought we knew."

"Sure—we know what the monks are trying to do. But we didn't know why. It's the craziest thing—"

"Tell me something new," growled George.

"—but old Sam's just come clean with me. You know the way he drops in every afternoon to watch the sheets roll out. Well, this time he seemed rather excited, or at least as near as he'll ever get to it. When I told him that we were on the last cycle he asked me, in that cute English accent of his, if I'd ever wondered what they were trying to do. I said, 'Sure'—and he told me."

"Go on: I'll buy it."

"Well, they believe that when they have listed all His names—and they reckon that there are about nine billion of them—God's purpose will be achieved. The human race will have finished what it was created to do, and there won't be any point in carrying on. Indeed, the very idea is something like blasphemy."

"Then what do they expect us to do? Commit suicide?"

"There's no need for that. When the list's completed, God steps in and simply winds things up . . . bingo!"

"Oh, I get it. When we finish our job, it will be the end of the world." Chuck gave a nervous little laugh.

"That's just what I said to Sam. And do you know what happened? He looked at me in a very queer way, like I'd been stupid in class, and said, 'It's nothing as trivial as *that.*' "

George thought this over for a moment.

"That's what I call taking the Wide View," he said presently. "But what d'you suppose we should do about it? I don't see that it makes the slightest difference to us. After all, we already knew that they were crazy."

"Yes—but don't you see what may happen? When the list's complete and the Last Trump doesn't blow—or whatever it is they expect—we may get the blame. It's our machine they've been using. I don't like the situation one little bit."

"I see," said George slowly. "You've got a point there. But this sort of thing's happened before, you know. When I was a kid down in Louisiana we had a crackpot preacher who once said the world was going to end next Sunday. Hundreds of people believed him—even sold their homes. Yet when nothing happened, they didn't turn nasty, as you'd expect. They just decided that he'd made a mistake in his calculations and went right on believing. I guess some of them still do."

"Well, this isn't Louisiana, in case you hadn't noticed. There are just two of us and hundreds of these monks. I like them, and I'll be sorry for old Sam when his lifework backfires on him. But all the same, I wish I was somewhere else."

"I've been wishing that for weeks. But there's nothing we can do until the contract's finished and the transport arrives to fly us out."

"Of course," said Chuck thoughtfully, "we could always try a bit of sabotage."

"Like hell we could! That would make things worse."

"Not the way I meant. Look at it like this. The machine will finish its run four days from now, on the present twenty-hours-a-day basis. The transport calls in a week. O.K.—then all we need to do is to find something that needs replacing during one of the overhaul periods—something that will hold up the works for a couple of days. We'll fix it of course, but not too quickly. If we time matters properly, we can be down at the airfield when the last name pops out of the register. They won't be able to catch us then."

"I don't like it," said George. "It will be the first time I ever walked out on a job. Besides, it would make them suspicious. No, I'll sit tight and take what comes."

"I *still* don't like it," he said, seven days later, as the tough little mountain ponies carried them down the winding road. "And don't you think I'm running away because I'm afraid. I'm just sorry for those poor old guys up there, and I don't want to be around when they find what suckers they've been. Wonder how Sam will take it?"

"It's funny," replied Chuck, "but when I said good-by I got the idea he knew we were walking out on him—and that he didn't care because he knew the machine was running smoothly and that the job would soon be finished. After that—well, of course, for him there just isn't any After That. . . ."

George turned in his saddle and stared back up the mountain road. This was the last place from which one could get a clear view of the lamasery. The squat, angular buildings were silhouetted against the afterglow of the sunset: here and there, lights gleamed like portholes in the side of an ocean liner. Electric lights, of course, sharing the same circuit as the Mark V. How much longer would they share it? wondered George. Would the monks smash up the computer in their rage and disappointment? Or would they just sit down quietly and begin their calculations all over again?

He knew exactly what was happening up on the mountain at this very 60
moment. The high lama and his assistants would be sitting in their silk robes, inspecting the sheets as the junior monks carried them away from the typewriters and pasted them into the great volumes. No one would be saying anything. The only sound would be the incessant patter, the never-ending rainstorm of the keys hitting the paper, for the Mark V itself was utterly silent as it flashed through its thousands of calculations a second. Three months of this, thought George, was enough to start anyone climbing up the wall.

"There she is!" called Chuck, pointing down into the valley. "Ain't she beautiful!"

She certainly was, thought George. The battered old DC3 lay at the end of the runway like a tiny silver cross. In two hours she would be bearing them away to freedom and sanity. It was a thought worth savoring like a fine liqueur. George let it roll round his mind as the pony trudged patiently down the slope.

The swift night of the high Himalayas was now almost upon them. Fortunately, the road was very good, as roads went in that region, and they were both carrying torches. There was not the slightest danger, only a certain discomfort from the bitter cold. The sky overhead was perfectly clear, and ablaze with the familiar, friendly stars. At least there would be no risk, thought George, of the pilot being unable to take off because of weather conditions. That had been his only remaining worry.

He began to sing, but gave it up after a while. This vast arena of mountains, gleaming like whitely hooded ghosts on every side, did not encourage such ebullience. Presently George glanced at his watch.

"Should be there in an hour," he called back over his shoulder to Chuck. 65
Then he added, in an afterthought: "Wonder if the computer's finished its run. It was due about now."

Chuck didn't reply, so George swung round in his saddle. He could just see Chuck's face, a white oval turned toward the sky.

"Look," whispered Chuck, and George lifted his eyes to heaven. (There is always a last time for everything.)

Overhead, without any fuss, the stars were going out. *[1953]*

☰ THINKING ABOUT THE TEXT

1. What are Dr. Wagner's attitudes toward the monks? Did you share his viewpoint?
2. Where in the story can you find indications that stereotypes about the monks are suspect?
3. Why did "some wit" label the request as "Project Shangri-La" (para. 32)? Who is Sam Jaffe (para. 32)?
4. Point out various examples of sarcasm and irony on Chuck's and George's part. Why does Clarke have them make such comments?
5. What was your first response to the last sentence? This is obviously a story with a surprise or twist ending. What do you think Clarke wants you to think about the ending? How might this story be more about us than the monks?

KURT VONNEGUT

Harrison Bergeron

Kurt Vonnegut (1922–2007), one of the best-known science fiction writers in America, was widely popular in the 1960s and 1970s, mostly for his darkly ironic, antiwar novel Slaughterhouse-Five *(1969), a tale based on Vonnegut's own experiences as a prisoner of war in Dresden. Vonnegut survived the massive Allied firebombing that killed more than 130,000 people, mostly civilians. The mental anguish he suffered there haunted him for years. His novel of these events became a best-seller, and Vonnegut became a hero of the anti–Vietnam War movement.*

Vonnegut was born in Indianapolis and attended Cornell University before entering World War II. His other works include the novel The Breakfast of Champions *(1973) and his short-story collection* Welcome to the Monkey House *(1968), which solidified his iconic status in America's counterculture as a comic genius with an urgent moral vision. In his last book,* A Man without a Country *(2005), he focuses his bitter satire on the Bush administration, the Iraq War, and conformist Americans. The novel was a best-seller.*

The year was 2081, and everybody was finally equal. They weren't only equal before God and the law. They were equal every which way. Nobody was smarter than anybody else. Nobody was better looking than anybody else. Nobody was stronger or quicker than anybody else. All this equality was due to the 211th, 212th, and 213th Amendments to the Constitution, and to the unceasing vigilance of agents of the United States Handicapper General.

Some things about living still weren't quite right, though. April, for instance, still drove people crazy by not being springtime. And it was in that clammy month that the H-G men took George and Hazel Bergeron's fourteen-year-old son, Harrison, away.

It was tragic, all right, but George and Hazel couldn't think about it very hard. Hazel had a perfectly average intelligence, which meant she couldn't think about anything except in short bursts. And George, while his intelligence was way above normal, had a little mental handicap radio in his ear. He was required by law to wear it at all times. It was tuned to a government transmitter. Every twenty seconds or so, the transmitter would send out some sharp noise to keep people like George from taking unfair advantage of their brains.

George and Hazel were watching television. There were tears on Hazel's cheeks, but she'd forgotten for the moment what they were about.

On the television screen were ballerinas. 5

A buzzer sounded in George's head. His thoughts fled in panic, like bandits from a burglar alarm.

"That was a real pretty dance, that dance they just did," said Hazel.

"Huh?" said George.

"That dance—it was nice," said Hazel.

"Yup," said George. He tried to think a little about the ballerinas. They 10
weren't really very good—no better than anybody else would have been, anyway. They were burdened with sash-weights and bags of birdshot, and their faces were masked, so that no one, seeing a free and graceful gesture or a pretty face, would feel like something the cat dragged in. George was toying with the vague notion that maybe dancers shouldn't be handicapped. But he didn't get very far with it before another noise in his ear radio scattered his thoughts.

George winced. So did two out of the eight ballerinas.

Hazel saw him wince. Having no mental handicap herself, she had to ask George what the latest sound had been.

"Sounded like somebody hitting a milk bottle with a ball peen hammer," said George.

"I'd think it would be real interesting, hearing all the different sounds," said Hazel, a little envious. "All the things they think up."

"Um," said George.

"Only, if I was Handicapper General, you know what I would do?" said Hazel. 15
Hazel, as a matter of fact, bore a strong resemblance to the Handicapper General, a woman named Diana Moon Glampers. "If I was Diana Moon Glampers," said Hazel, "I'd have chimes on Sunday—just chimes. Kind of in honor of religion."

"I could think, if it was just chimes," said George.

"Well—maybe make 'em real loud," said Hazel. "I think I'd make a good Handicapper General."

"Good as anybody else," said George.

"Who knows better'n I do what normal is?" said Hazel. 20

"Right," said George. He began to think glimmeringly about his abnormal son who was now in jail, about Harrison, but a twenty-one-gun salute in his head stopped that.

"Boy!" said Hazel, "that was a doozy, wasn't it?"

It was such a doozy that George was white and trembling, and tears stood on the rims of his red eyes. Two of the eight ballerinas had collapsed to the studio floor, were holding their temples.

"All of a sudden you look so tired," said Hazel. "Why don't you stretch out on the sofa, so's you can rest your handicap bag on the pillows, honeybunch." She was referring to the forty-seven pounds of birdshot in a canvas bag, which was padlocked around George's neck. "Go on and rest the bag for a little while," she said. "I don't care if you're not equal to me for a while."

George weighed the bag with his hands. "I don't mind it," he said. "I don't notice it any more. It's just a part of me."

"You been so tired lately—kind of wore out," said Hazel. "If there was just some way we could make a little hole in the bottom of the bag, and just take out a few of them lead balls. Just a few."

"Two years in prison and two thousand dollars fine for every ball I took out," said George. "I don't call that a bargain."

"If you could just take a few out when you came home from work," said Hazel, "I mean—you don't compete with anybody around here. You just set around."

"If I tried to get away with it," said George, "then other people'd get away with it—and pretty soon we'd be right back to the dark ages again, with everybody competing against everybody else. You wouldn't like that, would you?"

"I'd hate it," said Hazel.

"There you are," said George. "The minute people start cheating on laws, what do you think happens to society?"

If Hazel hadn't been able to come up with an answer to this question, George couldn't have supplied one. A siren was going off in his head.

"Reckon it'd fall all apart," said Hazel.

"What would?" said George blankly.

"Society," said Hazel uncertainly. "Wasn't that what you just said?"

"Who knows?" said George.

The television program was suddenly interrupted for a news bulletin. It wasn't clear at first as to what the bulletin was about, since the announcer, like all announcers, had a serious speech impediment. For about half a minute, and in a state of high excitement, the announcer tried to say, "Ladies and gentlemen—"

He finally gave up, handed the bulletin to a ballerina to read.

"That's all right—" Hazel said of the announcer, "he tried. That's the big thing. He tried to do the best he could with what God gave him. He should get a nice raise for trying so hard."

"Ladies and gentlemen—" said the ballerina, reading the bulletin. She must have been extraordinarily beautiful, because the mask she wore was hideous. And it was easy to see that she was the strongest and most graceful of all the dancers, for her handicap bags were as big as those worn by two-hundred-pound men.

And she had to apologize at once for her voice, which was a very unfair voice for a woman to use. Her voice was a warm, luminous, timeless melody. "Excuse me—" she said, and she began again, making her voice absolutely uncompetitive.

"Harrison Bergeron, age fourteen," she said in a grackle squawk, "has just escaped from jail, where he was held on suspicion of plotting to overthrow the government. He is a genius and an athlete, is under-handicapped, and should be regarded as extremely dangerous."

A police photograph of Harrison Bergeron was flashed on the screen—upside down, then sideways, upside down again, then right side up. The picture showed the full length of Harrison against a background calibrated in feet and inches. He was exactly seven feet tall.

The rest of Harrison's appearance was Halloween and hardware. Nobody had ever borne heavier handicaps. He had outgrown hindrances faster than the H-G men could think them up. Instead of a little ear radio for a mental handicap, he wore a tremendous pair of earphones, and spectacles with thick wavy lenses. The spectacles were intended to make him not only half blind, but to give him whanging headaches besides.

Scrap metal was hung all over him. Ordinarily, there was a certain symmetry, a military neatness to the handicaps issued to strong people, but Harrison looked like a walking junkyard. In the race of life, Harrison carried three hundred pounds.

And to offset his good looks, the H-G men required that he wear at all times a red rubber ball for a nose, keep his eyebrows shaved off, and cover his even white teeth with black caps at snaggle-tooth random.

"If you see this boy," said the ballerina, "do not—I repeat, do not—try to reason with him."

There was the shriek of a door being torn from its hinges.

Screams and barking cries of consternation came from the television set. The photograph of Harrison Bergeron on the screen jumped again and again, as though dancing to the tune of an earthquake.

George Bergeron correctly identified the earthquake, and well he might have—for many was the time his own home had danced to the same crashing tune. "My God—" said George, "that must be Harrison!"

The realization was blasted from his mind instantly by the sound of an automobile collision in his head.

When George could open his eyes again, the photograph of Harrison was gone. A living, breathing Harrison filled the screen.

Clanking, clownish, and huge, Harrison stood in the center of the studio. The knob of the uprooted studio door was still in his hand. Ballerinas, technicians, musicians, and announcers cowered on their knees before him, expecting to die.

"I am the Emperor!" cried Harrison. "Do you hear? I am the Emperor! Everybody must do what I say at once!" He stamped his foot and the studio shook.

"Even as I stand here—" he bellowed, "crippled, hobbled, sickened—I am a greater ruler than any man who ever lived! Now watch me become what I *can* become!"

Harrison tore the straps of his handicap harness like wet tissue paper, tore straps guaranteed to support five thousand pounds.

Harrison's scrap-iron handicaps crashed to the floor.

Harrison thrust his thumbs under the bar of the padlock that secured his head harness. The bar snapped like celery. Harrison smashed his headphones and spectacles against the wall.

He flung away his rubber-ball nose, revealed a man that would have awed Thor, the god of thunder.

"I shall now select my Empress!" he said, looking down on the cowering people. "Let the first woman who dares rise to her feet claim her mate and her throne!"

A moment passed, and then a ballerina arose, swaying like a willow.

Harrison plucked the mental handicap from her ear, snapped off her physical handicaps with marvellous delicacy. Last of all, he removed her mask.

She was blindingly beautiful.

"Now—" said Harrison, taking her hand, "shall we show the people the meaning of the word dance? Music!" he commanded.

The musicians scrambled back into their chairs, and Harrison stripped them of their handicaps, too. "Play your best," he told them, "and I'll make you barons and dukes and earls."

The music began. It was normal at first—cheap, silly, false. But Harrison snatched two musicians from their chairs, waved them like batons as he sang the music as he wanted it played. He slammed them back into their chairs.

The music began again and was much improved.

Harrison and his Empress merely listened to the music for a while—listened gravely, as though synchronizing their heartbeats with it.

They shifted their weights to their toes.

Harrison placed his big hands on the girl's tiny waist, letting her sense the weightlessness that would soon be hers.

And then, in an explosion of joy and grace, into the air they sprang!

Not only were the laws of the land abandoned, but the law of gravity and the laws of motion as well.

They reeled, whirled, swiveled, flounced, capered, gamboled, and spun.

They leaped like deer on the moon.

The studio ceiling was thirty feet high, but each leap brought the dancers nearer to it.

It became their obvious intention to kiss the ceiling.

They kissed it.

And then, neutralizing gravity with love and pure will, they remained suspended in air inches below the ceiling, and they kissed each other for a long, long time.

It was then that Diana Moon Glampers, the Handicapper General, came into the studio with a double-barreled ten-gauge shotgun. She fired twice, and the Emperor and the Empress were dead before they hit the floor.

Diana Moon Glampers loaded the gun again. She aimed it at the musicians and told them they had ten seconds to get their handicaps back on.

It was then that the Bergerons' television tube burned out.

Hazel turned to comment about the blackout to George. But George had gone out into the kitchen for a can of beer.

George came back in with the beer, paused while a handicap signal shook him up. And then he sat down again. "You been crying?" he said to Hazel.

"Yup," she said.

"What about?" he said. 85

"I forget," she said. "Something real sad on television."

"What was it?" he said.

"It's all kind of mixed up in my mind," said Hazel.

"Forget sad things," said George.

"I always do," said Hazel. 90

"That's my girl," said George. He winced. There was the sound of a riveting gun in his head.

"Gee—I could tell that one was a doozy," said Hazel.

"You can say that again," said George.

"Gee—" said Hazel, "I could tell that one was a doozy." *[1961]*

THINKING ABOUT THE TEXT

1. The famous nineteenth-century French historian Alexis de Tocqueville was impressed by American democracy but worried about its tendency to gravitate toward centrism, especially in small towns. Is this story a satire or a parody of that pressure to conform?
2. Does our culture have difficulty with difference, with those, say, with a very low or a very high IQ or with rebels, saints, and eccentrics? Give examples to support your answer.
3. If you read just the first sentence, would you assume that this is a story about a utopia? Since it is not, what is being satirized? Affirmative action? Authoritarian governments? Fear of difference?
4. What does "all men are created equal" mean? Do you think the meaning of this statement has changed over time?
5. What impulse does Harrison demonstrate when he rebels? Why does Glampers kill him?

MAKING COMPARISONS

1. Compare the endings of these two stories. Did you suspect what was coming? How did the authors prepare you?
2. There are villains in Vonnegut's tale. Are there heroes and villains in Clarke's?
3. What attitudes in society are the targets of these two stories?

JOANNA RUSS

When It Changed

Joanna Russ (1937–2011) was born in the Bronx, New York City. She graduated from Cornell in 1957, where she studied with Vladimir Nabokov. She received her M.F.A. from the Yale Drama School in 1960. She was a professor of English at the University of Washington. She won numerous prestigious awards for her science fiction and was widely respected as a feminist thinker and writer. Like the story here, her science fiction radically reimagines women's roles. In her essays and fiction, Russ breaks away from the gender assumptions and restrictions of the past. Her most famous novel, The Female Man *(1972), contains our story.*

Katy drives like a maniac; we must have been doing over 120 kilometers per hour on those turns. She's good, though, extremely good, and I've seen her take the whole car apart and put it together again in a day. My birthplace on Whileaway was largely given to farm machinery and I refuse to wrestle with a five-gear shift at unholy speeds, not having been brought up to it, but even on those turns in the middle of the night, on a country road as bad as only our district can make them, Katy's driving didn't scare me. The funny thing about my wife, though: she will not handle guns. She has even gone hiking in the forests above the forty-eighth parallel without firearms, for days at a time. And that *does* scare me.

Katy and I have three children between us, one of hers and two of mine. Yuriko, my eldest, was asleep in the back seat, dreaming twelve-year-old dreams of love and war: running away to sea, hunting in the North, dreams of strangely beautiful people in strangely beautiful places, all the wonderful guff you think up when you're turning twelve and the glands start going. Some day soon, like all of them, she will disappear for weeks on end to come back grimy and proud, having knifed her first cougar or shot her first bear, dragging some abominably dangerous dead beastie behind her, which I will never forgive for what it might have done to my daughter. Yuriko says Katy's driving puts her to sleep.

For someone who has fought three duels, I am afraid of far, far too much. I'm getting old. I told this to my wife.

"You're thirty-four," she said. Laconic to the point of silence, that one. She flipped the lights on, on the dash — three kilometers to go and the road getting worse all the time. Far out in the country. Electric-green trees rushed into our headlights and around the car. I reached down next to me where we bolt the carrier panel to the door and eased my rifle into my lap. Yuriko stirred in the back. My height but Katy's eyes, Katy's face. The car engine is so quiet, Katy says, that you can hear breathing in the back seat. Yuki had been alone in the car when the message came, enthusiastically decoding her dot-dashes (silly to mount a wide frequency transceiver near an I. C. engine, but most of Whileaway is on steam). She had thrown herself out of the car, my gangly and gaudy offspring, shouting at the top of her lungs, so of course she had had to come along. We've been intellectually prepared for this ever since the Colony was founded, ever since it was abandoned, but this is different. This is awful.

5 "Men!" Yuki had screamed, leaping over the car door. "They've come back! Real Earth men!"

We met them in the kitchen of the farmhouse near the place where they had landed; the windows were open, the night air very mild. We had passed all sorts of transportation when we parked outside—steam tractors, trucks, an I. C. flatbed, even a bicycle. Lydia, the district biologist, had come out of her Northern taciturnity long enough to take blood and urine samples and was sitting in a corner of the kitchen shaking her head in astonishment over the results; she even forced herself (very big, very fair, very shy, always painfully blushing) to dig up the old language manuals—though I can talk the old tongues in my sleep. And do. Lydia is uneasy with us; we're Southerners and too flamboyant. I counted twenty people in that kitchen, all the brains of North Continent. Phyllis Spet, I think, had come in by glider. Yuki was the only child there.

Then I saw the four of them.

They are bigger than we are. They are bigger and broader. Two were taller than I, and I am extremely tall, one meter eighty centimeters in my bare feet. They are obviously of our species but *off*, indescribably off, and as my eyes could not and still cannot quite comprehend the lines of those alien bodies, I could not, then, bring myself to touch them, though the one who spoke Russian—what voices they have—wanted to "shake hands," a custom from the past, I imagine. I can only say they were apes with human faces. He seemed to mean well, but I found myself shuddering back almost the length of the kitchen—and then I laughed apologetically—and then to set a good example (*interstellar amity, I* thought) did "shake hands" finally. A hard, hard hand. They are heavy as draft horses. Blurred, deep voices. Yuriko had sneaked in between the adults and was gazing at *the men* with her mouth open.

He turned *his* head—those words have not been in our language for six hundred years—and said, in bad Russian:

10 "Who's that?"

"My daughter," I said, and added (with that irrational attention to good manners we sometimes employ in moments of insanity), "My daughter, Yuriko Janetson. We use the patronymic. You would say matronymic."

He laughed, involuntarily. Yuki exclaimed, "I thought they would be *good looking!*" greatly disappointed at this reception of herself. Phyllis Helgason Spet, whom someday I shall kill, gave me across the room a cold, level, venomous look, as if to say: *Watch what you say. You know what I can do.* It's true that I have little formal status, but Madam President will get herself in serious trouble with both me and her own staff if she continues to consider industrial espionage good clean fun. Wars and rumors of wars, as it says in one of our ancestors' books. I translated Yuki's words into *the man's* dog-Russian, once our *lingua franca*, and *the man* laughed again.

"Where are all your people?" he said conversationally.

I translated again and watched the faces around the room; Lydia embarrassed (as usual), Spet narrowing her eyes with some damned scheme, Katy very pale.

"This is Whileaway," I said.

He continued to look unenlightened.

"Whileaway," I said. "Do you remember? Do you have records? There was a plague on Whileaway,"

He looked moderately interested. Heads turned in the back of the room, and I caught a glimpse of the local professions-parliament delegate; by morning every town meeting, every district caucus, would be in full session.

"Plague?" he said. "That's most unfortunate."

"Yes," I said. "Most unfortunate. We lost half our population in one generation."

He looked properly impressed.

"Whileaway was lucky," I said. "We had a big initial gene pool, we had been chosen for extreme intelligence, we had a high technology and a large remaining population in which every adult was two-or-three experts in one. The soil is good. The climate is blessedly easy. There are thirty millions of us now. Things are beginning to snowball in industry — do you understand? — give us seventy years and we'll have more than one real city, more than a few industrial centers, full-time professions, full-time radio operators, full-time machinists, give us seventy years and not everyone will have to spend three-quarters of a lifetime on the farm." And I tried to explain how hard it is when artists can practice full-time only in old age, when there are so few, so very few who can be free, like Katy and myself. I tried also to outline our government, the two houses, the one by professions and the geographic one; I told him the district caucuses handled problems too big for the individual towns. And that population control was not a political issue, not yet, though give us time and it would be. This was a delicate point in our history; give us time. There was no need to sacrifice the quality of life for an insane rush into industrialization. Let us go our own pace. Give us time.

"Where are all the people?" said that monomaniac.

I realized then that he did not mean people, he meant *men*, and he was giving the word the meaning it had not had on Whileaway for six centuries.

"They died," I said. "Thirty generations ago."

I thought we had poleaxed him. He caught his breath. He made as if to get out of the chair he was sitting in; he put his hand to his chest; he looked around at us with the strangest blend of awe and sentimental tenderness. Then he said, solemnly and earnestly:

"A great tragedy."

I waited, not quite understanding.

"Yes," he said, catching his breath again with the queer smile, that adult-to-child smile that tells you something is being hidden and will be presently produced with cries of encouragement and joy, "a great tragedy. But it's over." And again he looked around at all of us with the strangest deference. As if we were invalids.

"You've adapted amazingly," he said. 30

"To what?" I said. He looked embarrassed. He looked inane. Finally he said, "Where I come from, the women don't dress so plainly."

"Like you?" I said. "Like a bride?" for the men were wearing silver from head to foot. I had never seen anything so gaudy. He made as if to answer and then apparently thought better of it; he laughed at me again. With an odd exhilaration—as if we were something childish and something wonderful, as if he were doing us an enormous favor—he took one shaky breath and said, "Well, we're here."

I looked at Spet, Spet looked at Lydia, Lydia looked at Amalia, who is the head of the local town meeting, Amalia looked at I don't know whom. My throat was raw. I cannot stand local beer, which the farmers swill as if their stomachs had iridium linings, but I took it anyway, from Amalia (it was her bicycle we had seen outside as we parked), and swallowed it all. This was going to take a long time. I said, "Yes, here you are," and smiled (feeling like a fool), and wondered seriously if male-Earth-people's minds worked so very differently from female-Earth-people's minds, but that couldn't be so or the race would have died out long ago. The radio network had got the news around planet by now and we had another Russian speaker, flown in from Varna; I decided to cut out when *the man* passed around pictures of his wife, who looked like the priestess of some arcane cult. He proposed to question Yuki, so I barreled her into a back room in spite of her furious protests, and went out on the front porch. As I left, Lydia was explaining the difference between parthenogenesis (which is so easy that anyone can practice it) and what we do, which is the merging of ova. That is why Katy's baby looks like me. Lydia went on to the Ansky Process and Katy Ansky, our one full-polymath genius and the great-great I don't know how many times great-grandmother of my own Katharina.

A dot-dash transmitter in one of the outbuildings chattered faintly to itself—operators flirting and passing jokes down the line.

There was a man on the porch. The other tall man. I watched him for a few 35
minutes—I can move very quietly when I want to and when I allowed him to see me, he stopped talking into the little machine hung around his neck. Then he said calmly, in excellent Russian, "Did you know that sexual equality has been reestablished on Earth?"

"You're the real one," I said, "aren't you? The other one's for show." It was a great relief to get things cleared up. He nodded affably.

"As a people, we are not very bright," he said. "There's been too much genetic damage in the last few centuries. Radiation. Drugs. We can use Whileaway's genes, Janet." Strangers do not call strangers by the first name.

"You can have cells enough to drown in," I said. "Breed your own."

He smiled. "That's not the way we want to do it." Behind him I saw Katy come into the square of light that was the screened-in door. He went on, low and urbane, not mocking me, I think, but with the self-confidence of someone who has always had money and strength to spare, who doesn't know what it is to be second-class or provincial. Which is very odd, because the day before, I would have said that was an exact description of me.

40 "I'm talking to you, Janet," he said, "because I suspect you have more popular influence than anyone else here. You know as well as I do that parthenogenetic culture has all sorts of inherent defects, and we do not—if we can help it—mean to use you for anything of the sort. Pardon me; I should not have said 'use.' But surely you can see that this kind of society is unnatural."

"Humanity is unnatural," said Katy. She had my rifle under her left arm. The top of that silky head does not quite come up to my collarbone, but she is as tough as steel; he began to move, again with that queer smiling deference (which his fellow had showed to me but he had not), and the gun slid into Katy's grip as if she had shot with it all her life.

"I agree," said the man. "Humanity is unnatural. I should know. I have metal in my teeth and metal pins here." He touched his shoulder. "Seals are harem animals," he added, "and so are men; apes are promiscuous and so are men; doves are monogamous and so are men; there are even celibate men and homosexual men. There are homosexual cows, I believe. But Whileaway is still missing something." He gave a dry chuckle. I will give him the credit of believing that it had something to do with nerves.

"I miss nothing," said Katy, "except that life isn't endless."

"You are—?" said the man, nodding from me to her.

45 "Wives," said Katy. "We're married." Again the dry chuckle.

"A good economic arrangement," he said, "for working and taking care of the children. And as good an arrangement as any for randomizing heredity, if your reproduction is made to follow the same pattern. But think, Katharina Michaelason, if there isn't something better that you might secure for your daughters. I believe in instincts, even in Man, and I can't think that the two of you—a machinist, are you? and I gather you are some sort of chief of police—don't feel somehow what even you must miss. You know it intellectually, of course. There is only half a species here. Men must come back to Whileaway."

Katy said nothing.

"I should think, Katharina Michaelason," said the man gently, "that you, of all people, would benefit most from such a change," and he walked past Katy's rifle into the square of light coming from the door. I think it was then that he noticed my scar, which really does not show unless the light is from the side: a fine line that runs from temple to chin. Most people don't even know about it.

"Where did you get that?" he said, and I answered with an involuntary grin. "In my last duel." We stood there bristling at each other for several seconds (this is absurd but true) until he went inside and shut the screen door behind him. Katy said in a brittle voice, "You damned fool, don't you know when we've been insulted?" and swung up the rifle to shoot him through the screen, but I got to her before she could fire and knocked the rifle out of aim; it burned a hole through the porch floor. Katy was shaking. She kept whispering over and over, "That's why I never touched it, because I knew I'd kill someone. I knew I'd kill someone." The first man—the one I'd spoken with first—was still talking inside the house, something about the grand movement to recolonize and rediscover all the Earth had lost. He stressed the advantages to Whileaway: trade, exchange of ideas, education. He, too, said that sexual equality had been reestablished on Earth.

Katy was right, of course; we should have burned them down where they stood. 50
Men are coming to Whileaway. When one culture has the big guns and the other has none, there is a certain predictability about the outcome. Maybe men would have come eventually in any case. I like to think that a hundred years from now my great-grandchildren could have stood them off or fought them to a standstill, but even that's no odds; I will remember all my life those four people I first met who were muscled like bulls and who made me—if only for a moment—feel small. A neurotic reaction, Katy says. I remember everything that happened that night; I remember Yuki's excitement in the car, I remember Katy's sobbing when we got home as if her heart would break, I remember her lovemaking, a little peremptory as always, but wonderfully soothing and comforting. I remember prowling restlessly around the house after Katy fell asleep with one bare arm hung into a patch of light from the hall. The muscles of her forearms are like metal bars from all that driving and testing of her machines. Sometimes I dream about Katy's arms. I remember wandering into the nursery and picking up my wife's baby, dozing for a while with the poignant, amazing warmth of an infant in my lap, and finally returning to the kitchen to find Yuriko fixing herself a late snack. My daughter eats like a Great Dane.

"Yuki," I said, "do you think you could fall in love with a man?" and she whooped derisively. "With a ten-foot toad!" said my tactful child.

But men are coming to Whileaway. Lately I sit up nights and worry about the men who will come to this planet, about my two daughters and Betta Katharinason, about what will happen to Katy, to me, to my life. Our ancestors' journals are one long cry of pain and I suppose I ought to be glad now, but one can't throw away six centuries, or even (as I have lately discovered) thirty-four years. Sometimes I laugh at the question those four men hedged about all evening and never quite dared to ask, looking at the lot of us, hicks in overalls, farmers in canvas pants and plain shirts: *Which of you plays the role of the man?* As if we had to produce a carbon copy of their mistakes! I doubt very much that sexual equality has been reestablished on Earth. I do not like to think of myself mocked, of Katy deferred to as if she were weak, of Yuki made to feel unimportant or silly, of my other children cheated of their full humanity or turned into strangers. And I'm afraid that my own achievements will dwindle from what they were—or what I thought they were—to the not-very-interesting curiosa of the *human* race, the oddities you read about in the back of the book, things to laugh at sometimes because they are so exotic, quaint but not impressive, charming but not useful. I find this more painful than I can say. You will agree that for a woman who has fought three duels, all of them kills, indulging in such fears is ludicrous. But what's around the corner now is a duel so big that I don't think I have the guts for it; in Faust's words: *Verweile doch, du bist so schoen!* Keep it as it is. Don't change.

Sometimes at night I remember the original name of this planet, changed by the first generation of our ancestors, those curious women for whom, I suppose, the real name was too painful a reminder after the men died. I find it amusing, in a grim way, to see it all so completely turned around. This, too, shall pass. All good things must come to an end.

Take my life but don't take away the meaning of my life.

For-A-While. [1972] 55

THINKING ABOUT THE TEXT

1. In what ways does this story reimagine traditional society's expectations about gender roles?
2. What does Janet mean by "don't take away the meaning of my life" (para. 54)?
3. Give examples of what Katy and Janet object to about the newly arrived men. What do Katy and Janet fear will happen?
4. In what way might this story be dated? How is it still relevant?
5. What is significant about the original name of Katy and Janet's planet? How is the changed name significant?

MAKING COMPARISONS

1. What world created in this cluster seems darkest? Explain.
2. Which of these three stories seems the most likely to occur in the distant future? Which the least? Explain.
3. Which story seems closest to contemporary concerns?

OCTAVIA BUTLER

Human Evolution

Octavia Butler (1947–2006), one of the few female African American science fiction writers, won numerous prizes for her work, including the prestigious Hugo and Nebula Awards. In 1995 she became the first science fiction writer to receive a MacArthur Foundation "genius" grant. Butler was born in Pasadena, California, where, as an introspective child, she began reading and writing science fiction at a young age. Her first novel, Master Pattern, *was published in 1976. Her most popular novel,* Kindred *(1979), transports an African American antagonist from the present to the time of slavery in the antebellum South. It has sold well over two hundred thousand copies. The story printed here is from* Imago *(1989), a popular novel in her alien-human hybrid world of the Xenogenesis Trilogy, a narrative about a handful of survivors from a missile war that destroys most of Earth. Themes of intolerance, racial and sexual ambiguity, and environmentalism are common in her work. The second edition of* Bloodchild and Other Stories *was published posthumously in 2006.*

1

I slipped into my first metamorphosis so quietly that no one noticed. Metamorphoses were not supposed to begin that way. Most people begin with small, obvious, physical changes—the loss of fingers and toes, for instance, or the budding of new fingers and toes of a different design.

I wish my experience had been that normal, that safe.

For several days, I changed without attracting attention. Early stages of metamorphosis didn't normally last for days without bringing on deep sleep, but mine did. My first changes were sensory. Tastes, scents, all sensations suddenly became complex, confusing, yet unexpectedly seductive.

I had to relearn everything. River water, for instance: when I swam in it, I noticed that it had two distinctive major flavors—hydrogen and oxygen?—and many minor flavors. I could separate out and savor each one individually. In fact, I couldn't help separating them. But I learned them quickly and accepted them in their new complexity so that only occasional changes in minor flavors demanded my attention.

5 Our river water at Lo always came to us clouded with sediment. "Rich," the Oankali called it. "Muddy," the Humans said, and filtered it or let the silt settle to the bottom before they drank it. "Just water," we constructs said, and shrugged. We had never known any other water.

As quickly as I could, I learned again to understand and accept my sensory impressions of the people and things around me. The experience absorbed so much of my attention that I didn't understand how my family could fail to see that something unusual was happening to me. But beyond mentioning that I was daydreaming too much, even my parents missed the signs.

They were, after all, the wrong signs. No one was expecting them, so no one noticed when they appeared.

All five of my parents were old when I was born. They didn't look any older than my adult sisters and brothers, but they had helped with the founding of Lo. They had grandchildren who were old. I don't think I had ever surprised them before. I wasn't sure I liked surprising them now, I didn't want to tell them. I especially didn't want to tell Tino, my Human father. He was supposed to stay with me through my metamorphosis—since he was my same-sex Human parent. But I did not feel drawn to him as I should have. Nor did I feel drawn to Lilith, my birth mother. She was Human, too, and what was happening to me was definitely not a Human thing. Strangely I didn't want to go to my Oankali father, Dichaan, either, and he was my logical choice after Tino. My Oankali mother, Ahajas, would have talked to one of my fathers for me. She had done that for two of my brothers who had been afraid of metamorphosis—afraid they would change too much, lose all signs of their Humanity. That could happen to me, though I had never worried about it. Ahajas would have talked to me and for me, no matter what my problem was. Of all my parents, she was the easiest to talk to. I would have gone to her if the thought of doing so had been more appealing—or if I had understood why it was so unappealing. What was wrong with me? I wasn't shy or afraid, but when I thought of going to her, I felt first drawn, then . . . almost repelled.

Finally there was my ooloi parent, Nikanj.

10 It would tell me to go to one of my same-sex parents—one of my fathers. What else could it say? I knew well enough that I was in metamorphosis, and that that was one of the few things ooloi parents could not help with. There were still some Humans who insisted on seeing the ooloi as some kind of male-female combination, but the ooloi were no such thing. They were themselves—a different sex altogether.

So I went to Nikanj only hoping to enjoy its company for a while. Eventually it would notice what was happening to me and send me to my fathers. Until it did, I would rest near it. I was tired, sleepy. Metamorphosis was mostly sleep.

I found Nikanj inside the family house, talking to a pair of Human strangers. The Humans were standing back from Nikanj. The female was almost sheltering behind the male, and the male was making a painful effort to appear courageous. Both looked alarmed when they saw me open a wall and step through into the room. Then, as they got a look at me, they seemed to relax a little. I looked very Human—especially if they compared me to Nikanj, who wasn't Human at all.

The Humans smelled most obviously of sweat and adrenaline, food and sex. I sat down on the floor and let myself work out the complex combinations of scents. My new awareness wouldn't allow me to do anything else. By the time I was finished, I thought I would be able to track those two Humans through anything.

Nikanj paid no attention to me except to notice me when I came in. It was used to its children coming and going as they chose, used to all of us spending time with it, learning whatever it was willing to teach us.

It has an incredibly complex scent because it was ooloi. It had collected 15
within itself not only the reproductive material of other members of the family but cells of other plant and animal species that it had dealt with recently. These it would study, memorize, then either consume or store. It consumed the ones it knew it could re-create from memory, using its own DNA. It kept the others alive in a kind of stasis until they were needed.

Its most noticeable underscent was Kaal, the kin group it was born into. I had never met its parents, but I knew the Kaal scent from other members of the Kaal kin group. Somehow, though, I had never noticed that scent on Nikanj, never separated it out this way.

The main scent was Lo, of course. It had mated with Oankali of the Lo kin group, and on mating, it had altered its own scent as an ooloi must. The word *ooloi* could not be translated directly into English because its meaning was as complex as Nikanj's scent. "Treasured stranger." "Bridge." "Life trader." "Weaver." "Magnet."

Magnet, my birth mother says. People are drawn to ooloi and can't escape. She couldn't, certainly. But then, neither could Nikanj escape her or any of its mates. The Oankali said the chemical bonds of mating were as difficult to break as the habit of breathing.

Scents . . . The two visiting Humans were longtime mates and smelled of each other.

"We don't know yet whether we want to emigrate," the female was saying. 20
"We've come to see for ourselves and for our people."

"You'll be shown everything," Nikanj told them. "There are no secrets about the Mars colony or travel to it. But right now the shuttles allotted to emigration are all in use. We have a guest area where Humans can wait."

The two Humans looked at one another. They still smelled frightened, but now both were making an effort to look brave. Their faces were almost expressionless.

"We don't want to stay here," the male said. "We'll come back when there's a ship."

Nikanj stood up—unfolded, as Humans say. "I can't tell you when there'll be a ship," it said. "They arrive when they arrive. Let me show you the guest area. It isn't like this house. Humans built it of cut wood."

The pair stumbled back from Nikanj.

Nikanj's sensory tentacles flattened against its body in amusement. It sat down again. "There are other Humans waiting in the guest area," it told them gently. "They're like you. They want their own all-Human world. They'll be traveling with you when you go." It paused, looked at me. "Eka, why don't you show them?"

I wanted to stay with it now more than ever, but I could see that the two Humans were relieved to be turned over to someone who at least looked Human. I stood up and faced them.

"This is Jodahs," Nikanj told them, "one of my younger children."

The female gave me a look that I had seen too often not to recognize. She said, "But I thought . . ."

"No," I said to her, and smiled. "I'm not Human. I'm a Human-born construct. Come out this way. The guest area isn't far."

They did not want to follow me through the wall I opened until it was fully open—as though they thought the wall might close on them, as though it would hurt them if it did.

"It would be like being grasped gently by a big hand," I told them when we were all outside.

"What?" the male asked.

"If the wall shut on you. It couldn't hurt you because you're alive. It might eat your clothing, though."

"No, thanks!"

I laughed. "I've never seen that happen, but I've heard it can."

"What's your name?" the female asked.

"All of it?" She looked interested in me—smelled sexually attracted, which made her interesting to me. Human females did tend to like me as long as I kept my few body tentacles covered by clothing and my few head tentacles hidden in my hair. The sensory spots on my face and arms looked like ordinary skin, though they didn't feel ordinary.

"Your Human name," the female said. "I already know . . . Eka and Jodahs, but I'm not sure which to call you."

"Eka is just a term of endearment for young children," I told her, "like lelka for married children and Chka between mates. Jodahs is my personal name. The Human version of my whole name is Jodahs Iyapo Leal Kaalnikanjlo. My name, the surnames of my birth mother and Human father, and Nikanj's name beginning with the kin group it was born into and ending with the kin group of its Oankali mates. If I were Oankali-born or if I gave you the Oankali version of my name, it would be a lot longer and more complicated."

"I've heard some of them," the female said. "You'll probably drop them eventually."

"No. We'll change them to suit our needs, but we won't drop them. They give very useful information, especially when people are looking for mates."

"Jodahs doesn't sound like any name I've heard before," the male said.

"Oankali name. An Oankali named Jodahs died helping with the emigration. My birth mother said he should be remembered. The Oankali don't have a tradition of remembering people by naming kids after them, but my birth mother insisted. She does that sometimes—insists on keeping Human customs."

"You look very Human," the female said softly. 45

I smiled. "I'm a child. I just look unfinished."

"How old are you?"

"Twenty-nine."

"Good God! When will you be considered an adult?"

"After metamorphosis." I smiled to myself. Soon. "I have a brother who went 50
through it at twenty-one, and a sister who didn't reach it until she was thirty-three. People change when their bodies are ready, not at some specific age."

She was silent for some time. We reached the last of the true houses of Lo—the houses that had been grown from the living substance of the Lo entity. Humans without Oankali mates could not open walls or raise table, bed, or chair platforms in such houses. Left alone in our houses, these Humans were prisoners until some construct, Oankali, or mated Human freed them. Thus, they had been given first a guest house, then a guest area. In that area they had built their dead houses of cut wood and woven thatch. They used fire for light and cooking and occasionally they burned down one of their houses. Houses that did not burn became infested with rodents and insects which ate the Human's food and bit or stung the Humans themselves. Periodically Oankali went in and drove the non-Human life out. It always came back. It had been feeding on Humans, eating their food, and living in their buildings since long before the Oankali arrived. Still the guest area was reasonably comfortable. Guests ate from trees and plants that were not what they appeared to be. They were extensions of the Lo entity. They had been induced to synthesize fruits and vegetables in shapes, flowers, and textures that Humans recognized. The foods grew from what appeared to be their proper trees and plants. Lo took care of the Humans' wastes, keeping their area clean, though they tended to be careless about where they threw or dumped things in this temporary place.

"There's an empty house there," I said, pointing.

The female stared at my hand rather than at where I pointed. I had, from a Human point of view, too many fingers and toes. Seven per. Since they were part of distinctly Human-looking hands and feet, Humans didn't usually notice them at once.

I held my hand open, palm up so that she could see it, and her expression flickered from curiosity and surprise through embarrassment back to curiosity.

"Will you change much in metamorphosis?" she asked. 55

"Probably. The Human-born get more Oankali and the Oankali-born get more Human. I'm first-generation. If you want to see the future, take a look at some of the third- and fourth-generations constructs. They're a lot more uniform from start to finish."

"That's not our future," the male said.

"Your choice," I said.

The male walked away toward the empty house. The female hesitated. "What do you think of our emigration?" she asked.

I looked at her, liking her, not wanting to answer. But such questions should be answered. Why, though, were the Human females who insisted on asking them so often small, weak people? The Martian environment they were headed for was harsher than any they had known. We would see that they had the best possible chance to survive. Many would live to bear children on their new world. But they would suffer so. And in the end, it would all be for nothing. Their own genetic conflict had betrayed and destroyed them once. It would do so again.

"You should stay," I told the female. "You should join us."

"Why?"

I wanted very much not to look at her, to go away from her. Instead I continued to face her. "I understand that Humans must be free to go," I said softly. "I'm Human enough for my body to understand that. But I'm Oankali enough to know that you will eventually destroy yourselves again."

She frowned, marring her smooth forehead. "You mean another war?"

"Perhaps. Or maybe you'll find some other way to do it. You were working on several ways before your war."

"You don't know anything about it. You're too young."

"You should stay and mate with constructs or with Oankali," I said. "The children we construct are free of inherent flaws. What we build will last."

"You're just a child, repeating what you've been told!"

I shook my head. "I perceive what I perceive. No one had to tell me how to use my senses any more than they had to tell you how to see or hear. There is a lethal genetic conflict in Humanity, and you know it."

"All we know is what the Oankali have told us." The male had come back. He put his arm around the female, drawing her away from me as though I had offered some threat. "They could be lying for their own reasons."

I shifted my attention to him. "You know they're not," I said softly. "Your own history tells you. Your people are intelligent, and that's good. The Oankali say you're potentially one of the most intelligent species they've found. But you're also hierarchical—you and your nearest animal relatives and your most distant animal ancestors. Intelligence is relatively new to life on Earth, but your hierarchical tendencies are ancient. The new was too often put at the service of the old. It will be again. You're bright enough to learn to live in your new world, but you're so hierarchical you'll destroy yourselves trying to dominate it and each other. You might last a long time, but in the end, you'll destroy yourselves."

"We could last a thousand years," the male said. "We did all right on Earth until the war."

"You could. Your new world will be difficult. It will demand most of your attention, perhaps occupy your hierarchical tendencies safely for a while."

"We'll be free—us, our children, their children."

"Perhaps."

"We'll be fully Human and free. That's enough. We might even get into space again on our own someday. Your people might be dead wrong about us."

"No." He couldn't read the gene combinations as I could. It was as though he were about to walk off a cliff simply because he could not see it—or because he, or rather his descendants, would not hit the rocks below for a long time. And what were we doing, we who knew the truth? Helping him reach the cliff. Ferrying him to it.

"We might outlast your people here on Earth," he said.

"I hope so," I told him. His expression said he didn't believe me, but I meant it. We would not be here—the Earth he knew would not be here—for more than a few centuries. We, Oankali and construct, were space-going people, as curious about other life and as acquisitive of it as Humans were hierarchical. Eventually we would have to begin the long, long search for a new species to combine with to construct new life-forms. Much of Oankali existence was spent in such searches. We would leave this solar system in perhaps three centuries. I would live to see the leave-taking myself. And when we broke and scattered, we would leave behind a lump of stripped rock more like the moon than like his blue Earth. He did not know that. He would never know it. To tell him would be a cruelty.

"Do you ever think of yourself or your kind as Human?" the female asked. "Some of you look so Human."

"We feel our Humanity. It helps us to understand both you and the Oankali. Oankali alone could never have let you have your Mars colony."

"I heard they were helping!" the male said. "Your . . . your parent said they were helping!"

"They help because of what we constructs tell them: that you should be allowed to go even though you'll eventually destroy yourselves. The Oankali believe . . . the Oankali *know to the bone* that it's wrong to help the Human species regenerate unchanged because it *will* destroy itself again. To them it's like deliberately causing the conception of a child who is so defective that it must die in infancy."

"They're wrong. Someday we'll show them how wrong."

It was a threat. It was meaningless, but it gave him some slight satisfaction. "The other Humans here will show you where to gather food," I said. "If you need anything else, ask one of us." I turned to go.

"So goddamn patronizing," the male muttered.

I turned back without thinking. "Am I really?"

The male frowned, muttered a curse, and went back into the house. I understood then that he was just angry. It bothered me that I sometimes made them angry. I never intended to.

The female stepped to me, touched my face, examined a little of my hair. Humans who hadn't mated among us never really learned to touch us. At best, they annoyed us by rubbing their hands over sensory spots, and once their hands found the spots they never liked them.

The female jerked her hand back when her fingers discovered the one below my left ear.

"They're a little like eyes that can't close to protect themselves," I said. "It doesn't exactly hurt us when you touch them, but we don't like you to."

"So what? You have to teach people how to touch you?"

I smiled and took her hand between my own. "Hands are always safe," I said. I left her standing there, watching me. I could see her through sensory tentacles in my hair. She stood there until the male came out and drew her inside. *[1989]*

THINKING ABOUT THE TEXT

1. Butler wastes no time getting the reader into an alien world. Comment on some of the "otherness" of this future.
2. Discuss Butler's characterization of the human male in this story. What is Butler concerned with? Comment on the story's last line.
3. What scientific aspects of contemporary life is extended with Butler's story's constructs?
4. Some critics believe that much of serious science fiction is meant as a warning. Is this true here? Can humans change? How might we know our destruction was near?
5. Butler's narrative focus seems to revolve around basic flaws in the human makeup. What are some of them? Do you agree? Might these flaws be learned or a product of specific contexts?

MAKING COMPARISONS

1. Compare the flaws in human nature that each story focuses on.
2. Compare the males in this story to those in "When I Changed." How are the complaints of the authors similar?
3. Explain how one of these stories is the most relevant to your current concerns.

WRITING ABOUT ISSUES

1. Argue that one of these stories is still, or even more relevant, to contemporary concerns.
2. Write an essay comparing the depiction of males in these stories.
3. Science fiction like satire can sometimes go either too far in exaggeration or perhaps not far enough. Write an essay on the idea, using the stories here.
4. Read Harlan Ellison's dystopic story "'Repent, Harlequin!' Said the Ticktockman," and write a comparison to "Harrison Bergeron," focusing on the idea of the rebel in society.

Fairy Tale Journeys: Re-Visions of a Story

CHARLES PERRAULT, "Little Red Riding Hood"

JACOB AND WILHELM GRIMM, "Little Red Cap"

ANGELA CARTER, "The Company of Wolves"

The story of Little Red Riding Hood is still told to children throughout the world. Her adventure in facing mortal danger is part of their education. What, though, do they learn from this narrative? Scholars have suggested various interpretations, many of which hold that the tale helps its young readers face their own childhood fears. Among the best-known and most provocative interpreters of the story is the psychoanalyst Bruno Bettelheim, who sees it as a symbolic treatment of a girl's effort to understand her sexual development. In this view, the story teaches girls to work through adolescent anxieties. But whatever decoding the tale receives, two aspects of it remain important. First, it depicts a child's journey from innocence to experience, however these terms are defined. Little Red Riding Hood learns something from her encounters with the murderous wolf, and she does so largely on her own. Several versions of her story exist. Because this tale of a perilous journey is so popular and has circulated in various forms, we invite you to compare three versions of it: Charles Perrault's from the seventeenth century, the Brothers Grimm's from the nineteenth century, and Angela Carter's modern variation. Note that the Grimms' tale does not stray too far from Perrault's, at least not in representing Little Red Riding Hood as an innocent in need of male protection. Under the influence of contemporary feminism, however, Carter feels no need to conform to the fairy-tale tradition. As a result, Little Red Riding Hood is freed not only from genre conventions but also from a centuries-old stereotype about passive females.

BEFORE YOU READ

Write down what you remember about the story of Little Red Riding Hood, and then compare your version with those of your classmates. What elements of the story do your class's various renditions have in common? What differences, if any, emerge? Why do you think the story has been so popular?

CHARLES PERRAULT

Little Red Riding Hood

Along with the Brothers Grimm, Charles Perrault (1628–1703) was the most influential teller of the fairy tales many of us learned as children. Born in Paris to a fairly wealthy family, Perrault was trained as a lawyer. For his literary and philosophical achievements, however, Perrault was elected to the prestigious Académie Française in 1671. During his lifetime, he and others were involved in a major cultural dispute over the relative merits of ancient authors and modern ones, with Perrault favoring the more up-to-date group. Later generations remember him best, though, for his 1697 book Stories or Tales from Times Past, with Morals: Tales of Mother Goose. *This collection included "Le Petit Chaperon Rouge," which English-speaking readers have come to know as "Little Red Riding Hood." This story did not completely originate with Perrault; probably he had heard folktales containing some of its narrative elements. Nevertheless, his version became popular on publication and has remained so ever since.*

Once upon a time there lived in a certain village a little country girl, the prettiest creature who was ever seen. Her mother was excessively fond of her, and her grandmother doted on her still more. This good woman had a little red riding hood made for her. It suited the girl so extremely well that everybody called her Little Red Riding Hood.

One day her mother, having made some cakes, said to her, "Go, my dear, and see how your grandmother is doing, for I hear she has been very ill. Take her a cake, and this little pot of butter."

Bettmann/Getty Images

Heritage Images/Getty Images

Louis MONIER/Getty Images

Little Red Riding Hood set out immediately to go to her grandmother, who lived in another village.

As she was going through the wood, she met with a wolf, who had a very great mind to eat her up, but he dared not, because of some woodcutters working nearby in the forest. He asked her where she was going. The poor child, who did not know that it was dangerous to stay and talk to a wolf, said to him, "I am going to see my grandmother and carry her a cake and a little pot of butter from my mother."

"Does she live far off?" said the wolf.

"Oh I say," answered Little Red Riding Hood. "It is beyond that mill you see there, at the first house in the village."

"Well," said the wolf, "and I'll go and see her too. I'll go this way and go you that, and we shall see who will be there first."

The wolf ran as fast as he could, taking the shortest path, and the little girl took a roundabout way, entertaining herself by gathering nuts, running after butterflies, and gathering bouquets of little flowers. It was not long before the wolf arrived at the old woman's house. He knocked at the door: tap, tap.

"Who's there?"

"Your grandchild, Little Red Riding Hood," replied the wolf, counterfeiting her voice, "who has brought you a cake and a little pot of butter sent you by Mother."

The good grandmother, who was in bed because she was somewhat ill, cried out, "Pull the bobbin, and the latch will go up."

The wolf pulled the bobbin, and the door opened, and then he immediately fell upon the good woman and ate her up in a moment, for it had been more than three days since he had eaten. He then shut the door and got into the grandmother's bed, expecting Little Red Riding Hood, who came some time afterwards and knocked at the door: tap, tap.

"Who's there?"

Little Red Riding Hood, hearing the big voice of the wolf, was at first afraid but, believing her grandmother had a cold and was hoarse, answered, "It is your grandchild Little Red Riding Hood, who has brought you a cake and a little pot of butter Mother sends you."

The wolf cried out to her, softening his voice as much as he could, "Pull the bobbin, and the latch will go up."

Little Red Riding Hood pulled the bobbin, and the door opened.

The wolf, seeing her come in, said to her, hiding himself under the bedclothes, "Put the cake and the little pot of butter upon the stool, and come get into bed with me."

Little Red Riding Hood took off her clothes and got into bed. She was greatly amazed to see how her grandmother looked in her nightclothes and said to her, "Grandmother, what big arms you have!"

"All the better to hug you with, my dear."

"Grandmother, what big legs you have!"

"All the better to run with, my child."

"Grandmother, what big ears you have!"

"All the better to hear with, my child."

"Grandmother, what big eyes you have!"

"All the better to see with, my child."

"Grandmother, what big teeth you have got!"

"All the better to eat you up with."

And saying these words, this wicked wolf fell upon Little Red Riding Hood, and ate her all up.

Moral: Children, especially attractive, well-bred young ladies, should never talk to strangers, for if they should do so, they may well provide dinner for a wolf. I say "wolf," but there are various kinds of wolves. There are also those who are charming, quiet, polite, unassuming, complacent, and sweet, who pursue young women at home and in the streets. And unfortunately, it is these gentle wolves who are the most dangerous ones of all. *[1697]*

THINKING ABOUT THE TEXT

1. To what extent does it matter to the story that Little Red Riding Hood is pretty? Would your reaction be the same if you learned she was homely or if you did not know how she looked? Explain.
2. The two main female characters are Little Red Riding Hood and her grandmother. Although the girl's mother appears briefly at the start, she then disappears from the narrative. What purposes are served by Perrault's leaving her out?
3. How would you describe Little Red Riding Hood as Perrault depicts her? Refer to specific details of the text.
4. In this version, Little Red Riding Hood dies. Would you draw different ideas from the text if she had lived? If so, what?
5. Does Perrault's moral seem well connected to the preceding story? Why, or why not? What metaphoric wolves might this moral apply to?

JACOB AND WILHELM GRIMM

Little Red Cap

Jacob Grimm (1785–1863) and Wilhelm Grimm (1786–1859) were born in Hanau, Germany, and studied law at Marburg University. They served as linguistics professors at Göttingen University and made major contributions to the historical study of language. The Grimms began to collect folktales from various oral European traditions for their friends but later published their efforts for both children and adults. Their methods became a model for the scientific collection of folktales and folk songs. Today they are known best for their volume Children's and Household Tales, *which was first published in 1812 and went through six more editions, the last in 1857. Their book included their version of the Little Red Riding Hood story, although their title for it was (in English translation) "Little Red Cap."*

Once upon a time there was a sweet little girl. Everyone who saw her liked her, but most of all her grandmother, who did not know what to give the child next. Once she gave her a little cap made of red velvet. Because it suited her so well, and she wanted to wear it all the time, she came to be known as Little Red Cap.

One day her mother said to her, "Come Little Red Cap. Here is a piece of cake and a bottle of wine. Take them to your grandmother. She is sick and weak, and they will do her well. Mind your manners, and give her my greetings. Behave yourself on the way, and do not leave the path, or you might fall down and break the glass, and then there will be nothing for your grandmother. And when you enter her parlor, don't forget to say 'Good morning,' and don't peer into all the corners first."

"I'll do everything just right," said Little Red Cap, shaking her mother's hand.

The grandmother lived out in the woods, a half hour from the village. When Little Red Cap entered the woods, a wolf came up to her. She did not know what a wicked animal he was and was not afraid of him.

"Good day to you, Little Red Cap."

"Thank you, wolf."

"Where are you going so early, Little Red Cap?"

"To Grandmother's."

"And what are you carrying under your apron?"

"Grandmother is sick and weak, and I am taking her some cake and wine. We baked yesterday, and they should be good for her and give her strength."

"Little Red Cap, just where does your grandmother live?"

"Her house is a good quarter hour from here in the woods, under the three large oak trees. There's a hedge of hazel bushes there. You must know the place," said Little Red Cap.

The wolf thought to himself, "Now that sweet young thing is a tasty bite for me. She will taste even better than the old woman. You must be sly, and you can catch them both."

He walked along a little while with Little Red Cap. Then he said, "Little Red Cap, just look at the beautiful flowers that are all around us. Why don't you go and take a look? And I don't believe you can hear how beautifully the birds are singing. You are walking along as though you were on your way to school. It is very beautiful in the woods."

Little Red Cap opened her eyes, and when she saw the sunbeams dancing to and fro through the trees and how the ground was covered with beautiful flowers, she thought, "If I take a fresh bouquet to Grandmother, she will be very pleased. Anyway, it is still early, and I'll be home on time." And she ran off the path into the woods looking for flowers. Each time she picked one, she thought that she could see an even more beautiful one a little way off, and she ran after it, going farther and farther into the woods. But the wolf ran straight to the grandmother's house and knocked on the door.

"Who's there?"

"Little Red Cap. I'm bringing you some cake and wine. Open the door."

"Just press the latch," called out the grandmother. "I'm too weak to get up."

The wolf pressed the latch, and the door opened. He stepped inside, went straight to the grandmother's bed, and ate her up. Then he put on her clothes, put her cap on his head, got into her bed, and pulled the curtains shut.

Little Red Cap had run after the flowers. After she had gathered so many that she could not carry any more, she remembered her grandmother and then continued on her way to her house. She found, to her surprise, that the door was open. She walked into the parlor, and everything looked so strange that she thought, "Oh, my God, why am I so afraid? I usually like it at Grandmother's."

She called out, "Good morning!" but received no answer.

Then she went to the bed and pulled back the curtains. Grandmother was lying there with her cap pulled down over her face and looking very strange.

"Oh, Grandmother, what big ears you have!"

"All the better to hear you with."

"Oh, Grandmother, what big eyes you have!"

"All the better to see you with."

"Oh, Grandmother, what big hands you have!"

"All the better to grab you with!"

"Oh, Grandmother, what a horribly big mouth you have!"

"All the better to eat you with!"

The wolf had scarcely finished speaking when he jumped from the bed with a single leap and ate up poor Little Red Cap. As soon as the wolf had satisfied his desires, he climbed back into bed, fell asleep, and began to snore very loudly.

A huntsman was just passing by. He thought, "The old woman is snoring so loudly. You had better see if something is wrong with her."

He stepped into the parlor, and when he approached the bed, he saw the wolf lying there. "So here I find you, you old sinner," he said. "I have been hunting for you a long time."

He was about to aim his rifle when it occurred to him that the wolf might have eaten the grandmother and that she still might be rescued. So instead of shooting, he took a pair of scissors and began to cut open the wolf's belly. After a few cuts he saw the red cap shining through, and after a few more cuts the girl jumped out, crying, "Oh, I was so frightened! It was so dark inside the wolf's body!"

And then the grandmother came out as well, alive but hardly able to breathe. Then Little Red Cap fetched some large stones. She filled the wolf's body with them, and when he woke up and tried to run away, the stones were so heavy that he immediately fell down dead.

The three of them were happy. The huntsman skinned the wolf and went home with the pelt. The grandmother ate the cake and drank the wine that Little Red Cap had brought. And Little Red Cap thought, "As long as I live, I will never leave the path and run off into the woods by myself if Mother tells me not to."

They also tell how Little Red Cap was taking some baked things to her grandmother another time, when another wolf spoke to her and wanted her to leave the path. But Little Red Cap took care and went straight to Grandmother's. She told her that she had seen the wolf and that he had wished her a good day but had stared at her in a wicked manner. "If we hadn't been on a public road, he would have eaten me up," she said.

"Come," said the grandmother. "Let's lock the door, so he can't get in."

Soon afterward the wolf knocked on the door and called out, "Open up, Grandmother. It's Little Red Cap, and I'm bringing you some baked things."

They remained silent and did not open the door. Gray-Head crept around the house several times and finally jumped onto the roof. He wanted to wait until Little Red Cap went home that evening and then follow her and eat her up in the darkness. But the grandmother saw what he was up to. There was a large stone trough in front of the house.

"Fetch a bucket, Little Red Cap," she said to the child. "Yesterday I cooked some sausage. Carry the water that I boiled them with to the trough." Little Red Cap carried water until the large, large trough was clear full. The smell of sausage arose into the wolf's nose. He sniffed and looked down, stretching his neck so long that he could no longer hold himself, and he began to slide. He slid off the roof, fell into the trough, and drowned. And Little Red Cap returned home happily, and no one harmed her. *[1857]*

THINKING ABOUT THE TEXT

1. Why do you think that, at the beginning of the tale, the Grimms emphasize how sweet and likable Little Red Cap is?
2. To what extent do you blame Little Red Cap for being distracted by the beauty of nature? Explain your reasoning.
3. The Grimms have Little Red Cap and her grandmother rescued by a hunter. Do you agree or disagree that the Grimm's story implies that women always need help from a man?
4. The wolf dies because Little Red Cap has filled his body with stones. Why do you think the Grimms did not have the huntsman simply shoot the wolf after freeing Little Red Cap and her grandmother?
5. Why do you think the Grimms added the second story? What is its effect?

MAKING COMPARISONS

1. Does Little Red Riding Hood seem basically the same in both Perrault's version and the Grimms' version? Refer to specific details from both texts.
2. In Perrault's tale, the wolf persuades Little Red Riding Hood to take off her clothes and get into bed with him. In the Grimms' account, the wolf jumps up from the bed and eats her. How significant is this difference between the two versions?
3. In Perrault's version, Little Red Riding Hood and her grandmother die. In the Grimms' tale, on the other hand, they are rescued. Do you therefore see these two versions as putting forth different views of life? Explain.

ANGELA CARTER

The Company of Wolves

A native of Sussex, England, Angela Carter (1940–1991) worked in various genres, writing novels, short stories, screenplays, essays, and newspaper articles. Her fiction is most known for imaginatively refashioning classic tales of fantasy, including supernatural and gothic thrillers as well as fairy tales. Often, Carter rewrote these narratives from a distinctly female point of view, challenging what she saw as their patriarchal values and using them to explore the psychology of both genders. "The Company of Wolves," her version of the Little Red Riding Hood tale, was first published in the journal Bananas *in 1977. It then appeared in Carter's short-story volume* The Bloody Chamber *(1979) and was reprinted in* Burning Your Boats *(1995), a posthumous collection of all her stories. This tale also served as the basis for a 1984 film of the same title, which Carter wrote with director Neil Jordan.*

One beast and only one howls in the woods by night.

The wolf is carnivore incarnate, and he's as cunning as he is ferocious; once he's had a taste of flesh then nothing else will do.

At night, the eyes of wolves shine like candle flames, yellowish, reddish, but that is because the pupils of their eyes fatten on darkness and catch the light from your lantern to flash it back to you — red for danger; if a wolf's eyes reflect only moonlight, then they gleam a cold and unnatural green, a mineral, a piercing color. If the benighted traveler spies those luminous, terrible sequins stitched suddenly on the black thickets, then he knows he must run, if fear has not struck him stock-still.

But those eyes are all you will be able to glimpse of the forest assassins as they cluster invisibly round your smell of meat as you go through the wood unwisely late. They will be like shadows, they will be like wraiths, gray members of a congregation of nightmare; hark! his long, wavering howl . . . an aria of fear made audible.

The wolfsong is the sound of the rending you will suffer, in itself a murdering. 5

It is winter and cold weather. In this region of mountain and forest, there is now nothing for the wolves to eat. Goats and sheep are locked up in the byre,° the deer departed for the remaining pasturage on the southern slopes — wolves grow lean and famished. There is so little flesh on them that you could count the starveling ribs through their pelts, if they gave you time before they pounced. Those slavering jaws; the lolling tongue; the rime of saliva on the grizzled chops — of all the teeming perils of the night and the forest, ghosts, hobgoblins, ogres that grill babies upon gridirons, witches that fatten their captives in cages for cannibal tables, the wolf is worst for he cannot listen to reason.

You are always in danger in the forest, where no people are. Step between the portals of the great pines where the shaggy branches tangle about you, trapping the unwary traveler in nets as if the vegetation itself were in a plot with the

byre: Barn or shed.

wolves who live there, as though the wicked trees go fishing on behalf of their friends — step between the gateposts of the forest with the greatest trepidation and infinite precautions, for if you stray from the path for one instant, the wolves will eat you. They are gray as famine, they are as unkind as plague.

The grave-eyed children of the sparse villages always carry knives with them when they go out to tend the little flocks of goats that provide the homesteads with acrid milk and rank, maggoty cheeses. Their knives are half as big as they are, the blades are sharpened daily.

But the wolves have ways of arriving at your own hearthside. We try and try but sometimes we cannot keep them out. There is no winter's night the cottager does not fear to see a lean, gray, famished snout questing under the door, and there was a woman once bitten in her own kitchen as she was straining the macaroni.

Fear and flee the wolf; for, worst of all, the wolf may be more than he seems. 10

There was a hunter once, near here, that trapped a wolf in a pit. This wolf had massacred the sheep and goats; eaten up a mad old man who used to live by himself in a hut halfway up the mountain and sing to Jesus all day; pounced on a girl looking after the sheep, but she made such a commotion that men came with rifles and scared him away and tried to track him into the forest but he was cunning and easily gave them the slip. So this hunter dug a pit and put a duck in it, for bait, all alive-oh; and he covered the pit with straw smeared with wolf dung. Quack, quack! went the duck and a wolf came slinking out of the forest, a big one, a heavy one, he weighed as much as a grown man, and the straw gave way beneath him—into the pit he tumbled. The hunter jumped down after him, slit his throat, cut off all his paws for a trophy.

And then no wolf at all lay in front of the hunter but the bloody trunk of a man, headless, footless, dying, dead.

A witch from up the valley once turned an entire wedding party into wolves because the groom had settled on another girl. She used to order them to visit her, at night, from spite, and they would sit and howl around her cottage for her, serenading her with their misery.

Not so very long ago, a young woman in our village married a man who vanished clean away on her wedding night. The bed was made with new sheets and the bride lay down in it; the groom said, he was going out to relieve himself, insisted on it, for the sake of decency, and she drew the coverlet up to her chin and she lay there. And she waited and she waited and then she waited again — surely he's been gone a long time? Until she jumps up in bed and shrieks to hear a howling, coming on the wind from the forest.

That long-drawn, wavering howl has, for all its fearful resonance, some 15
inherent sadness in it, as if the beasts would love to be less beastly if only they knew how and never cease to mourn their own condition. There is a vast melancholy in the canticles° of the wolves, melancholy infinite as the forest, endless as these long nights of winter and yet that ghastly sadness, that mourning for their own, irremediable appetites, can never move the heart for not one phrase in it hints at the possibility of redemption; grace could not come to the wolf from its

canticles: Songs or chants.

own despair, only through some external mediator, so that, sometimes, the beast will look as if he half welcomes the knife that dispatches him.

The young woman's brothers searched the outhouses and the haystacks but never found any remains, so the sensible girl dried her eyes and found herself another husband not too shy to piss into a pot who spent the nights indoors. She gave him a pair of bonny babies and all went right as a trivet until, one freezing night, the night of the solstice, the hinge of the year when things do not fit together as well as they should, the longest night, her first good man came home again.

A great thump on the door announced him as she was stirring the soup for the father of her children, and she knew him the moment she lifted the latch to him although it was years since she'd worn black for him and now he was in rags and his hair hung down his back and never saw a comb, alive with lice.

"Here I am again, missus," he said. "Get me my bowl of cabbage and be quick about it."

Then her second husband came in with wood for the fire and when the first one saw she'd slept with another man and, worse, clapped his red eyes on her little children who'd crept into the kitchen to see what all the din was about, he shouted: "I wish I were a wolf again, to teach this whore a lesson!" So a wolf he instantly became and tore off the eldest boy's left foot before he was chopped up with the hatchet they used for chopping logs. But when the wolf lay bleeding and gasping its last, the pelt peeled off again and he was just as he had been, years ago, when he ran away from his marriage bed, so that she wept and her second husband beat her.

They say there's an ointment the Devil gives you that turns you into a wolf the 20
minute you rub it on. Or that he was born feet first and had a wolf for his father and his torso is a man's but his legs and genitals are a wolf's. And he has a wolf's heart.

Seven years is a werewolf's natural span but if you burn his human clothing you condemn him to wolfishness for the rest of his life, so old wives hereabouts think it some protection to throw a hat or an apron at the werewolf, as if clothes made the man. Yet by the eyes, those phosphorescent eyes, you know him in all his shapes; the eyes alone unchanged by metamorphosis.

Before he can become a wolf, the lycanthrope° strips stark naked. If you spy a naked man among the pines, you must run as if the Devil were after you.

It is midwinter and the robin, the friend of man, sits on the handle of the gardener's spade and sings. It is the worst time in all the year for wolves, but this strong-minded child insists she will go off through the wood. She is quite sure the wild beasts cannot harm her although, well-warned, she lays a carving knife in the basket her mother has packed with cheeses. There is a bottle of harsh liquor distilled from brambles; a batch of flat oatcakes baked on the hearthstone; a pot or two of jam. The flaxen-haired girl will take these delicious gifts to a reclusive grandmother so old the burden of her years is crushing

lycanthrope: Werewolf.

her to death. Granny lives two hours' trudge through the winter woods; the child wraps herself up in her thick shawl, draws it over her head. She steps into her stout wooden shoes; she is dressed and ready and it is Christmas Eve. The malign door of the solstice still swings upon its hinges, but she has been too much loved ever to feel scared.

Children do not stay young for long in this savage country. There are no toys for them to play with, so they work hard and grow wise, but this one, so pretty and the youngest of her family, a little late-comer, had been indulged by her mother and the grandmother who'd knitted her the red shawl that, today, has the ominous if brilliant look of blood on snow. Her breasts have just begun to swell; her hair is like lint, so fair it hardly makes a shadow on her pale forehead; her cheeks are an emblematic scarlet and white and she has just started her woman's bleeding, the clock inside her that will strike, henceforward, once a month.

She stands and moves within the invisible pentacle° of her own virginity. She is an unbroken egg; she is a sealed vessel; she has inside her a magic space the entrance to which is shut tight with a plug of membrane; she is a closed system; she does not know how to shiver. She has her knife and she is afraid of nothing.

Her father might forbid her, if he were home, but he is away in the forest, gathering wood, and her mother cannot deny her.

The forest closed upon her like a pair of jaws.

There is always something to look at in the forest, even in the middle of winter—the huddled mounds of birds, succumbed to the lethargy of the season, heaped on the creaking boughs and too forlorn to sing; the bright frills of the winter fungi on the blotched trunks of the trees; the cuneiform° slots of rabbits and deer, the herringbone tracks of the birds, a hare as lean as a rasher of bacon streaking across the path where the thin sunlight dapples the russet brakes of last year's bracken.

When she heard the freezing howl of a distant wolf, her practiced hand sprang to the handle of her knife, but she saw no sign of a wolf at all, nor of a naked man, neither, but then she heard a clattering among the brushwood and there sprang on to the path a fully clothed one, a very handsome young one, in the green coat and wide-awake hat of a hunter, laden with carcasses of game birds. She had her hand on her knife at the first rustle of twigs, but he laughed with a flash of white teeth when he saw her and made her a comic yet flattering little bow; she'd never seen such a fine fellow before, not among the rustic clowns of her native village. So on they went together, through the thickening light of the afternoon.

Soon they were laughing and joking like old friends. When he offered to carry her basket, she gave it to him although her knife was in it because he told her his rifle would protect them. As the day darkened, it began to snow again; she felt the first flakes settle on her eyelashes, but now there was only half a mile to go and there would be a fire, and hot tea, and a welcome, a warm one, surely, for the dashing huntsman as well as for herself.

pentacle: Five-pointed star; also called a pentagram.
cuneiform: Wedge-shaped.

This young man had a remarkable object in his pocket. It was a compass. She looked at the little round glass face in the palm of his hand and watched the wavering needle with a vague wonder. He assured her this compass had taken him safely through the wood on his hunting trip because the needle always told him with perfect accuracy where the north was. She did not believe it; she knew she should never leave the path on the way through the wood or else she would be lost instantly. He laughed at her again; gleaming trails of spittle clung to his teeth. He said, if he plunged off the path into the forest that surrounded them, he could guarantee to arrive at her grandmother's house a good quarter of an hour before she did, plotting his way through the undergrowth with his compass, while she trudged the long way, along the winding path.

I don't believe you. Besides, aren't you afraid of the wolves?

He only tapped the gleaming butt of his rifle and grinned.

Is it a bet? he asked her. Shall we make a game of it? What will you give me if I get to your grandmother's house before you?

What would you like? she asked disingenuously. 35

A kiss.

Commonplaces of a rustic seduction; she lowered her eyes and blushed.

He went through the undergrowth and took her basket with him but she forgot to be afraid of the beasts, although now the moon was rising, for she wanted to dawdle on her way to make sure the handsome gentleman would win his wager.

Grandmother's house stood by itself a little way out of the village. The freshly falling snow blew in eddies about the kitchen garden, and the young man stepped delicately up the snowy path to the door as if he were reluctant to get his feet wet, swinging his bundle of game and the girl's basket and humming a little tune to himself.

There is a faint trace of blood on his chin; he has been snacking on his catch. 40

He rapped upon the panels with his knuckles.

Aged and frail, granny is three-quarters succumbed to the mortality the ache in her bones promises her and almost ready to give in entirely. A boy came out from the village to build up her hearth for the night an hour ago and the kitchen crackles with busy firelight. She has her Bible for company, she is a pious old woman. She is propped up on several pillows in the bed set into the wall peasant-fashion, wrapped up in the patchwork quilt she made before she was married, more years ago than she cares to remember. Two china spaniels with liver-colored blotches on their coats and black noses sit on either side of the fireplace. There is a bright rug of woven rags on the pantiles. The grandfather clock ticks away her eroding time.

We keep the wolves outside by living well.

He rapped upon the panels with his hairy knuckles.

It is your granddaughter, he mimicked in a high soprano. 45

Lift up the latch and walk in, my darling.

You can tell them by their eyes, eyes of a beast of prey, nocturnal, devastating eyes as red as a wound; you can hurl your Bible at him and your apron after, granny, you thought that was a sure prophylactic against these infernal vermin . . . now call on Christ and his mother and all the angels in heaven to protect you but it won't do you any good.

His feral muzzle is sharp as a knife; he drops his golden burden of gnawed pheasant on the table and puts down your dear girl's basket, too. Oh, my God, what have you done with her?

Off with his disguise, that coat of forest-colored cloth, the hat with the feather tucked into the ribbon; his matted hair streams down his white shirt and she can see the lice moving in it. The sticks in the hearth shift and hiss; night and the forest has come into the kitchen with darkness tangled in its hair.

He strips off his shirt. His skin is the color and texture of vellum. A crisp stripe of hair runs down his belly, his nipples are ripe and dark as poison fruit, but he's so thin you could count the ribs under his skin if only he gave you the time. He strips off his trousers and she can see how hairy his legs are. His genitals, huge. Ah! huge.

The last thing the old lady saw in all this world was a young man, eyes like cinders, naked as a stone, approaching her bed.

The wolf is carnivore incarnate.

When he had finished with her, he licked his chops and quickly dressed himself again, until he was just as he had been when he came through her door. He burned the inedible hair in the fireplace and wrapped the bones up in a napkin that he hid away under the bed in the wooden chest in which he found a clean pair of sheets. These he carefully put on the bed instead of the tell-tale stained ones he stowed away in the laundry basket. He plumped up the pillows and shook out the patchwork quilt, he picked up the Bible from the floor, closed it and laid it on the table. All was as it had been before except that grandmother was gone. The sticks twitched in the grate, the clock ticked and the young man sat patiently, deceitfully beside the bed in granny's nightcap.

Rat-a-tap-tap.

Who's there, he quavers in granny's antique falsetto.

Only your granddaughter.

So she came in, bringing with her a flurry of snow that melted in tears on the tiles, and perhaps she was a little disappointed to see only her grandmother sitting beside the fire. But then he flung off the blanket and sprang to the door, pressing his back against it so that she could not get out again.

The girl looked round the room and saw there was not even the indentation of a head on the smooth cheek of the pillow and how, for the first time she'd seen it so, the Bible lay closed on the table. The tick of the clock cracked like a whip. She wanted her knife from her basket, but she did not dare reach for it because his eyes were fixed upon her — huge eyes that now seemed to shine with a unique, interior light, eyes the size of saucers, saucers full of Greek fire, diabolic phosphorescence.

What big eyes you have.

All the better to see you with.

No trace at all of the old woman except for a tuft of white hair that had caught in the bark of an unburned log. When the girl saw that, she knew she was in danger of death.

Where is my grandmother?

There's nobody here but we two, my darling.

Now a great howling rose up all around them, near, very near, as close as the kitchen garden, the howling of a multitude of wolves; she knew the worst wolves are hairy on the inside and she shivered, in spite of the scarlet shawl she pulled more closely round herself as if it could protect her although it was as red as the blood she must spill.

Who has come to sing us carols, she said.

Those are the voices of my brothers, darling; I love the company of wolves. Look out of the window and you'll see them.

Snow half-caked the lattice and she opened it to look into the garden. It was a white night of moon and snow; the blizzard whirled round the gaunt, grey beasts who squatted on their haunches among the rows of winter cabbage, pointing their sharp snouts to the moon and howling as if their hearts would break. Ten wolves; twenty wolves—so many wolves she could not count them, howling in concert as if demented or deranged. Their eyes reflected the light from the kitchen and shone like a hundred candles.

It is very cold, poor things, she said; no wonder they howl so.

She closed the window on the wolves' threnody° and took off her scarlet shawl, the color of poppies, the color of sacrifices, the color of her menses, and, since her fear did her no good, she ceased to be afraid.

What shall I do with my shawl?

Throw it on the fire, dear one. You won't need it again.

She bundled up her shawl and threw it on the blaze, which instantly consumed it. Then she drew her blouse over her head; her small breasts gleamed as if the snow had invaded the room.

What shall I do with my blouse?

Into the fire with it, too, my pet.

The thin muslin went flaring up the chimney like a magic bird and now off came her skirt, her woolen stockings, her shoes, and on to the fire they went, too, and were gone for good. The firelight shone through the edges of her skin; now she was clothed only in her untouched integument° of flesh. This dazzling, naked she combed out her hair with her fingers; her hair looked white as the snow outside. Then went directly to the man with red eyes in whose unkempt mane the lice moved; she stood up on tiptoe and unbuttoned the collar of his shirt.

What big arms you have.

All the better to hug you with.

Every wolf in the world now howled a prothalamion° outside the window as she freely gave the kiss she owed him.

What big teeth you have!

threnody: Lament or dirge.
integument: Outer covering, such as animal skin or seed coat.
prothalamion: Wedding song.

80 She saw how his jaw began to slaver and the room was full of the clamor of the forest's Liebestod° but the wise child never flinched, even when he answered:

All the better to eat you with.

The girl burst out laughing; she knew she was nobody's meat. She laughed at him full in the face, she ripped off his shirt for him and flung it into the fire, in the fiery wake of her own discarded clothing. The flames danced like dead souls on Walpurgisnacht,° and the old bones under the bed set up a terrible clattering, but she did not pay them any heed.

Carnivore incarnate, only immaculate flesh appeases him.

She will lay his fearful head on her lap and she will pick out the lice from his pelt and perhaps she will put the lice into her mouth and eat them, as he will bid her, as she would do in a savage marriage ceremony.

85 The blizzard will die down.

The blizzard died down, leaving the mountains as randomly covered with snow as if a blind woman had thrown a sheet over them, the upper branches of the forest pines limed, creaking, swollen with the fall.

Snowlight, moonlight, a confusion of paw-prints.

All silent, all still.

Midnight; and the clock strikes. It is Christmas Day, the werewolves' birthday, the door of the solstice stands wide open; let them all sink through.

90 See! sweet and sound she sleeps in granny's bed, between the paws of the tender wolf. *[1977]*

≡ THINKING ABOUT THE TEXT

1. The story begins with a section about wolves before it gets to the Little Red Riding Hood narrative. What image of wolves does this prologue convey? What in particular seems the purpose of the extended anecdote about the wife with two husbands?
2. Point out various places where Carter diverges from the conventions of the fairy tale.
3. Do you find it surprising that the girl does not get to her grandmother's house first? Do you suspect that the girl is not so innocent?
4. Obviously this is not a story for children. What traditional ideas about females and sexuality is Carter revising?
5. What do you conclude about the girl from her behavior at the end of the story? To what extent is "savage marriage ceremony" (para. 84) indeed an apt term for what occurs?

Liebestod: Final aria in Richard Wagner's opera *Tristan und Isolde,* in which Isolde sings over Tristan's dead body and ultimately dies herself.
Walpurgisnacht: May Day eve, the medieval witches' sabbath.

MAKING COMPARISONS

1. To what extent is Carter's image of wolves different from Perrault's and the Grimms'? Refer to details from all three texts.
2. Several critics have described Carter's versions of fairy tales as feminist. To what extent can this term be applied to Perrault's and the Grimms' narratives as well as to hers? Define what you mean by *feminist*.
3. Would you say Carter's writing style is more realistic than that of Perrault and the Grimms? Or is the term *realism* completely irrelevant in the case of fairy tales? Explain.

WRITING ABOUT ISSUES

1. Choose one of these versions of the Little Red Riding Hood story, and write an essay in which you elaborate a moral that modern *adults* might learn from it. Or write an essay in which you explain what an adolescent might learn from Carter's version.
2. Does Carter's version radically depart from Perrault's and the Grimms', or does it basically resemble them? Write an essay that addresses this question by focusing on Carter's story and one of the other two.
3. Write an essay explaining what you think you learned from a fairy tale or other fictional story that you heard as a child. If you want to contrast your thinking about the story now with your thinking about it then, do so. Feel free to compare the story you focus on with any of the versions of Little Red Riding Hood in this cluster.
4. Write your own version of the story of Little Red Riding Hood, and on a separate piece of paper write the moral you think should be drawn from your text. Then give your version to a classmate, and see if he or she can guess your moral.

Keep This Boy Running: Cultural Contexts for a Story

RALPH ELLISON, "Battle Royal"

CULTURAL CONTEXTS:

BOOKER T. WASHINGTON, "Atlanta Exposition Address (The Atlanta Compromise)"

W. E. B. DU BOIS, "Of Mr. Booker T. Washington"

GUNNAR MYRDAL, "Social Equality"

More than fifty years after the civil rights movement of the 1960s, our national awareness of how brutal discrimination was against African Americans is diminished. Although educational and economic equality has not been completely attained, progress has been made, especially in eliminating official policies and gestures of bias. Before World War II, however, overt discrimination was common, especially in the small towns of the segregated South and the rural Midwest. African Americans were rarely allowed to hold anything other than menial jobs in small towns, and most middle-class whites knew African Americans only as maids, gardeners, and servants. African Americans were completely outside the established power structure and rarely able to complain about or obtain justice for their many grievances. Public protest was out of the question. Many African Americans even avoided private protest against their outsider status because they feared that it would worsen their situation. Among African American intellectuals and ordinary citizens, debates raged about which strategy to pursue: cooperate with the white establishment, hoping to modify hostility, or agitate for change. Generations of blacks followed the first course until the 1960s, when the nonviolent sit-ins of the civil rights movement ushered in the public protests that ended state-sanctioned segregation. Ralph Ellison's story takes place in the era of segregation and graphically portrays how marginalized African Americans were and how difficult they found it to decide on an effective strategy for progress. At the story's end, the main character, like Ellison himself, begins a lifelong journey from racism toward social justice.

BEFORE YOU READ

Have you ever been in a situation in which you felt discriminated against because of your race, religion, gender, sexual orientation, or age? Did you ever see someone else suffer discrimination? Did you feel powerless? What was your strategy for dealing with this feeling?

RALPH ELLISON

Battle Royal

Born in Oklahoma to an activist mother and an intellectual father, Ralph Ellison (1914–1994) was well grounded in literary and social matters by the time he entered Tuskegee Institute to study music in 1933. Finding the conservatism and accommodationism of Tuskegee limiting, Ellison read modernist poets like T. S. Eliot and in 1936 moved to New York, where he met writers Langston Hughes and Richard Wright. Inspired by Wright and by the works of Conrad, Dostoyevsky, and other writers of fiction, Ellison began drafting his novel Invisible Man *(1952) while he was serving in the merchant marine during World War II. Published as a short story in 1947, "Battle Royal" became the first chapter of this National Book Award–winning novel.*

It goes a long way back, some twenty years. All my life I had been looking for something, and everywhere I turned someone tried to tell me what it was. I accepted their answers too, though they were often in contradiction and even self-contradictory. I was naive. I was looking for myself and asking everyone except myself questions which I, and only I, could answer. It took me a long time and much painful boomeranging of my expectations to achieve a realization everyone else appears to have been born with: that I am nobody but myself. But first I had to discover that I am an invisible man!

National Archives and Records Administration

And yet I am no freak of nature, not of history. I was in the cards, other things having been equal (or unequal) eighty-five years ago. I am not ashamed of my grandparents for having been slaves. I am only ashamed of myself for having at one time been ashamed. About eighty-five years ago they were told that they were free, united with others of our country in everything pertaining to the common good, and, in everything social, separate like the fingers of the hand. And they believed it. They exulted in it. They stayed in their place, worked hard, and brought up my father to do the same. But my grandfather is the one. He was an odd old guy, my grandfather, and I am told I take after him. It was he who caused the trouble. On his deathbed he called my father to him and said, "Son, after I'm gone I want you to keep up the good fight. I never told you, but our life is a war and I have been a traitor all my born days, a spy in the enemy's country ever since I give up my gun back in the Reconstruction. Live with your head in the lion's mouth. I want you to overcome 'em with yeses, undermine 'em with grins, agree 'em to death and destruction, let 'em swoller you till they vomit or bust wide open." They thought the old man had gone out of his mind. He had been the meekest of men. The younger children were rushed from the room, the shades drawn and the flame of the lamp turned so low that it sputtered on the wick like the old man's breathing. "Learn it to the younguns," he whispered fiercely; then he died.

But my folks were more alarmed over his last words than over his dying. It was as though he had not died at all, his words caused so much anxiety. I was warned emphatically to forget what he had said and, indeed, this is the first time it has been mentioned outside the family circle. It had a tremendous effect upon me, however. I could never be sure of what he meant. Grandfather had been a quiet old man who never made any trouble, yet on his deathbed he had called himself a traitor and a spy, and he had spoken of his meekness as a dangerous activity. It became a constant puzzle which lay unanswered in the back of my mind. And whenever things went well for me I remembered my grandfather and felt guilty and uncomfortable. It was as though I was carrying out his advice in spite of myself. And to make it worse, everyone loved me for it. I was praised by the most lily-white men of the town. I was considered an example of desirable conduct—just as my grandfather had been. And what puzzled me was that the old man had defined it as *treachery*. When I was praised for my conduct I felt a guilt that in some way I was doing something that was really against the wishes of the white folks, that if they had understood they would have desired me to act just the opposite, that I should have been sulky and mean, and that that really would have been what they wanted, even though they were fooled and thought they wanted me to act as I did. It made me afraid that some day they would look upon me as a traitor and I would be lost. Still I was more afraid to act any other way because they didn't like that at all. The old man's words were like a curse. On my graduation day I delivered an oration in which I showed that humility was the secret, indeed, the very essence of progress. (Not that I believed this—how could I, remembering my grandfather?—I only believed that it worked.) It was a great success. Everyone praised me and I was invited to give the speech at a gathering of the town's leading white citizens. It was a triumph for our whole community.

It was in the main ballroom of the leading hotel. When I got there I discovered that it was on the occasion of a smoker,° and I was told that since I was to be there anyway I might as well take part in the battle royal to be fought by some of my schoolmates as part of the entertainment. The battle royal came first.

All of the town's big shots were there in their tuxedoes, wolfing down the 5
buffet foods, drinking beer and whiskey, and smoking black cigars. It was a large room with a high ceiling. Chairs were arranged in neat rows around three sides of a portable boxing ring. The fourth side was clear, revealing a gleaming space of polished floor. I had some misgivings over the battle royal, by the way. Not from a distaste for fighting, but because I didn't care too much for the other fellows who were to take part. They were tough guys who seemed to have no grandfather's curse worrying their minds. No one could mistake their toughness. And besides, I suspected that fighting a battle royal might detract from the dignity of my speech. In those pre-invisible days I visualized myself as a potential Booker T. Washington. But the other fellows didn't care too much for me either, and there were nine of them. I felt superior to them in my way, and I didn't like the manner in which we were all crowded together into the servants' elevator. Nor did they like my being there. In fact, as the warmly lighted floors flashed past the elevator we had words over the fact that I, by taking part in the fight, had knocked one of their friends out of a night's work.

We were led out of the elevator through a rococo hall into an anteroom and told to get into our fighting togs. Each of us was issued a pair of boxing gloves and ushered out into the big mirrored hall, which we entered looking cautiously about us and whispering, lest we might accidentally be heard above the noise of the room. It was foggy with cigar smoke. And already the whiskey was taking effect. I was shocked to see some of the most important men of the town quite tipsy. They were all there — bankers, lawyers, judges, doctors, fire chiefs, teachers, merchants. Even one of the more fashionable pastors. Something we could not see was going on up front. A clarinet was vibrating sensuously and the men were standing up and moving eagerly forward. We were a small tight group, clustered together, our bare upper bodies touching and shining with anticipatory sweat; while up front the big shots were becoming increasingly excited over something we still could not see. Suddenly I heard the school superintendent, who had told me to come, yell, "Bring up the shines,° gentlemen! Bring up the little shines!"

We were rushed up to the front of the ballroom, where it smelled even more strongly of tobacco and whiskey. Then we were pushed into place. I almost wet my pants. A sea of faces, some hostile, some amused, ringed around us, and in the center, facing us, stood a magnificent blonde — stark naked. There was dead silence. I felt a blast of cold air chill me. I tried to back away, but they were behind me and around me. Some of the boys stood with lowered heads, trembling. I felt a wave of irrational guilt and fear. My teeth chattered, my skin turned to goose flesh, my knees knocked. Yet I was strongly attracted and looked in spite of myself.

smoker: An all-male gathering, here with drinking, a stripper, and a humiliating boxing match.
shines: Derogatory term for African Americans.

Had the price of looking been blindness, I would have looked. The hair was yellow like that of a circus kewpie doll, the face heavily powdered and rouged, as though to form an abstract mask, the eyes hollow and smeared a cool blue, the color of a baboon's butt. I felt a desire to spit upon her as my eyes brushed slowly over her body. Her breasts were firm and round as the domes of East Indian temples, and I stood so close as to see the fine skin texture and beads of pearly perspiration glistening like dew around the pink and erected buds of her nipples. I wanted at one and the same time to run from the room, to sink through the floor, or go to her and cover her from my eyes and the eyes of the others with my body; to feel the soft thighs, to caress her and destroy her, to love her and murder her, to hide from her, and yet to stroke where below the small American flag tattooed upon her belly her thighs formed a capital V. I had a notion that of all in the room she saw only me with her impersonal eyes.

And then she began to dance, a slow sensuous movement; the smoke of a hundred cigars clinging to her like the thinnest of veils. She seemed like a fair bird-girl girdled in veils calling to me from the angry surface of some gray and threatening sea. I was transported. Then I became aware of the clarinet playing and the big shots yelling at us. Some threatened us if we looked and others if we did not. On my right I saw one boy faint. And now a man grabbed a silver pitcher from a table and stepped close as he dashed ice water upon him and stood him up and forced two of us to support him as his head hung and moans issued from his thick bluish lips. Another boy began to plead to go home. He was the largest of the group, wearing dark red fighting trunks much too small to conceal the erection which projected from him as though in answer to the insinuating low-registered moaning of the clarinet. He tried to hide himself with his boxing gloves.

And all the while the blonde continued dancing, smiling faintly at the big shots who watched her with fascination, and faintly smiling at our fear. I noticed a certain merchant who followed her hungrily, his lips loose and drooling. He was a large man who wore diamond studs in a shirtfront which swelled with the ample paunch underneath, and each time the blonde swayed her undulating hips he ran his hand through the thin hair of his bald head and, with his arms upheld, his posture clumsy like that of an intoxicated panda, wound his belly in a slow and obscene grind. This creature was completely hypnotized. The music had quickened. As the dancer flung herself about with a detached expression on her face, the men began reaching out to touch her. I could see their beefy fingers sink into the soft flesh. Some of the others tried to stop them as she began to move around the floor in graceful circles, as they gave chase, slipping and sliding over the polished floor. It was mad. Chairs went crashing, drinks were spilt, as they ran laughing and howling after her. They caught her just as she reached a door, raised her from the floor, and tossed her as college boys are tossed at a hazing, and above her red, fixed-smiling lips I saw the terror and disgust in her eyes, almost like my own terror and that which I saw in some of the other boys. As I watched, they tossed her twice and her soft breasts seemed to flatten against the air and her legs flung wildly as she spun. Some of the more sober ones helped her to escape. And I started off the floor, heading for the anteroom with the rest of the boys.

10 Some were still crying in hysteria. But as we tried to leave we were stopped and ordered to get into the ring. There was nothing to do but what we were told. All ten of us climbed under the ropes and allowed ourselves to be blindfolded with broad bands of white cloth. One of the men seemed to feel a bit sympathetic and tried to cheer us up as we stood with our backs against the ropes. Some of us tried to grin. "See that boy over there?" one of the men said. "I want you to run across at the bell and give it to him right in the belly. If you don't get him, I'm going to get you. I don't like his looks." Each of us was told the same. The blindfolds were put on. Yet even then I had been going over my speech. In my mind each word was as bright as flame. I felt the cloth pressed into place, and frowned so that it would be loosened when I relaxed.

But now I felt a sudden fit of blind terror. I was unused to darkness. It was as though I had suddenly found myself in a dark room filled with poisonous cottonmouths. I could hear the bleary voices yelling insistently for the battle royal to begin.

"Get going in there!"

"Let me at that big nigger!"

I strained to pick up the school superintendent's voice, as though to squeeze some security out of that slightly more familiar sound.

15 "Let me at those black sonsabitches!" someone yelled.

"No, Jackson, no!" another voice yelled. "Here, somebody, help me hold Jack."

"I want to get at that ginger-colored nigger. Tear him limb from limb," the first voice yelled.

I stood against the ropes trembling. For in those days I was what they called ginger-colored, and he sounded as though he might crunch me between his teeth like a crisp ginger cookie.

Quite a struggle was going on. Chairs were being kicked about and I could hear voices grunting as with a terrific effort. I wanted to see, to see more desperately than ever before. But the blindfold was tight as a thick skin-puckering scab and when I raised my gloved hands to push the layers of white aside a voice yelled, "Oh, no you don't, black bastard! Leave that alone!"

20 "Ring the bell before Jackson kills him a coon!" someone boomed in the sudden silence. And I heard the bell clang and the sound of the feet scuffling forward.

A glove smacked against my head. I pivoted, striking out stiffly as someone went past, and felt the jar ripple along the length of my arm to my shoulder. Then it seemed as though all nine of the boys had turned upon me at once. Blows pounded me from all sides while I struck out as best I could. So many blows landed upon me that I wondered if I were not the only blindfolded fighter in the ring, or if the man called Jackson hadn't succeeded in getting me after all.

Blindfolded, I could no longer control my motions. I had no dignity. I stumbled about like a baby or a drunken man. The smoke had become thicker and with each new blow it seemed to sear and further restrict my lungs. My saliva became like hot bitter glue. A glove connected with my head, filling my mouth with warm blood. It was everywhere. I could not tell if the moisture I felt upon my body was sweat or blood. A blow landed hard against the nape of my neck. I felt myself going over, my head hitting the floor. Streaks of blue light filled the black world behind the blindfold. I lay prone, pretending that I was knocked out, but felt myself seized by hands and yanked to my feet. "Get going, black boy! Mix it up!" My arms were like lead, my head smarting from blows. I managed to feel my way to the ropes and held on, trying to catch my breath. A glove landed in my mid-section and I went over again, feeling as though the smoke had become a knife jabbed into my guts. Pushed this way and that by the legs milling around me, I finally pulled erect and discovered that I could see the black, sweat-washed forms weaving in the smoky-blue atmosphere like drunken dancers weaving to the rapid drumlike thuds of blows.

Everyone fought hysterically. It was complete anarchy. Everybody fought everybody else. No group fought together for long. Two, three, four, fought one, then turned to fight each other, were themselves attacked. Blows landed below the belt and in the kidney, with the gloves open as well as closed, and with my eye partly opened now there was not so much terror. I moved carefully, avoiding blows, although not too many to attract attention, fighting from group to group. The boys groped about like blind, cautious crabs crouching to protect their mid-sections, their heads pulled in short against their shoulders, their arms stretched nervously before them, with their fists testing the smoke-filled air like the knobbed feelers of hypersensitive snails. In one corner I glimpsed a boy violently punching the air and heard him scream in pain as he smashed his hand against a ring post. For a second I saw him bent over holding his hand, then going down as a blow caught his unprotected head. I played one group against the other, slipping in and throwing a punch then stepping out of range while pushing the others into the melee to take the blows blindly aimed at me. The smoke was agonizing and there were no rounds, no bells at three minute intervals to relieve our exhaustion. The room spun round me, a swirl of lights, smoke, sweating bodies surrounded by tense white faces. I bled from both nose and mouth, the blood spattering upon my chest.

The men kept yelling, "Slug him, black boy! Knock his guts out!"

"Uppercut him! Kill him! Kill that big boy!" 25

Taking a fake fall, I saw a boy going down heavily beside me as though we were felled by a single blow, saw a sneaker-clad foot shoot into his groin as the two who had knocked him down stumbled upon him. I rolled out of range, feeling a twinge of nausea.

The harder we fought the more threatening the men became. And yet, I had begun to worry about my speech again. How would it go? Would they recognize my ability? What would they give me?

I was fighting automatically when suddenly I noticed that one after another of the boys was leaving the ring. I was surprised, filled with panic, as though I had been left alone with an unknown danger. Then I understood. The boys had arranged it among themselves. It was the custom for the two men left in the ring to slug it out for the winner's prize. I discovered this too late. When the bell sounded two men in tuxedoes leaped into the ring and removed the blindfold. I found myself facing Tatlock, the biggest of the gang. I felt sick at my stomach. Hardly had the bell stopped ringing in my ears than it clanged again and I saw him moving swiftly toward me. Thinking of nothing else to do I hit him smash on the nose. He kept coming, bringing the rank sharp violence of stale sweat. His face was a black blank of a face, only his eyes alive — with hate of me and aglow with a feverish terror from what had happened to us all. I became anxious. I wanted to deliver my speech and he came at me as though he meant to beat it out of me. I smashed him again and again, taking his blows as they came. Then on a sudden impulse I struck him lightly and as we clinched, I whispered, "Fake like I knocked you out, you can have the prize."

"I'll break your behind," he whispered hoarsely.

"For *them?*"

"For *me,* sonofabitch!"

They were yelling for us to break it up and Tatlock spun me half around with a blow, and as a joggled camera sweeps in a reeling scene, I saw the howling red faces crouching tense beneath the cloud of blue-gray smoke. For a moment the world wavered, unraveled, flowed, then my head cleared and Tatlock bounced before me. That fluttering shadow before my eyes was his jabbing left hand. Then falling forward, my head against his damp shoulder, I whispered,

"I'll make it five dollars more."

"Go to hell!"

But his muscles relaxed a trifle beneath my pressure and I breathed, "Seven?"

"Give it to your ma," he said, ripping me beneath the heart.

And while I still held him I butted him and moved away. I felt myself bombarded with punches. I fought back with hopeless desperation. I wanted to deliver my speech more than anything else in the world, because I felt that only these men could judge truly my ability, and now this stupid clown was ruining my chances. I began fighting carefully now, moving in to punch him and out again with my greater speed. A lucky blow to his chin and I had him going too — until I heard a loud voice yell, "I got my money on the big boy."

Hearing this, I almost dropped my guard. I was confused: Should I try to win against the voice out there? Would not this go against my speech, and was not this a moment for humility, for nonresistance? A blow to my head as I danced about sent my right eye popping like a jack-in-the-box and settled my dilemma. The room went red as I fell. It was a dream fall, my body languid and fastidious as to where to land, until the floor became impatient and smashed up to meet me. A moment later I came to. An hypnotic voice said FIVE, emphatically. And I lay there, hazily watching a dark red spot of my own blood shaping itself into a butterfly, glistening and soaking into the soiled gray world of the canvas.

When the voice drawled TEN I was lifted up and dragged to a chair. I sat dazed. My eye pained and swelled with each throb of my pounding heart and I wondered if now I would be allowed to speak, I was wringing wet, my mouth still bleeding. We were grouped along the wall now. The other boys ignored me as they congratulated Tatlock and speculated as to how much they would be paid. One boy whimpered over his smashed hand. Looking up front, I saw attendants in white jackets rolling the portable ring away and placing a small square rug in the vacant space surrounded by chairs. Perhaps, I thought, I will stand on the rug to deliver my speech.

Then the M.C. called to us, "Come on up here boys and get your money." We ran forward to where the men laughed and talked in their chairs, waiting. Everyone seemed friendly now.

"There it is on the rug," the man said. I saw the rug covered with coins of all dimensions and a few crumpled bills. But what excited me, scattered here and there, were the gold pieces.

"Boys, it's all yours," the man said. "You get all you grab."

"That's right, Sambo," a blond man said, winking at me confidentially.

I trembled with excitement, forgetting my pain. I would get the gold and the bills, I thought. I would use both hands. I would throw my body against the boys nearest me to block them from the gold.

"Get down around the rug now," the man commanded, "and don't anyone touch it until I give the signal."

"This ought to be good," I heard.

As told, we got around the square rug on our knees. Slowly the man raised his freckled hand as we followed it upward with our eyes.

I heard, "These niggers look like they're about to pray!"

Then, "Ready," the man said. "Go!"

I lunged for a yellow coin lying on the blue design of the carpet, touching it and sending a surprised shriek to join those rising around me. I tried frantically to remove my hand but could not let go. A hot, violent force tore through my body, shaking me like a wet rat. The rug was electrified. The hair bristled up on my head as I shook myself free. My muscles jumped, my nerves jangled, writhed. But I saw that this was not stopping the other boys. Laughing in fear and embarrassment, some were holding back and scooping up the coins knocked off by the painful contortions of the others. The men roared above us as we struggled.

"Pick it up, goddamnit, pick it up!" someone called like a bass-voiced parrot. "Go on, get it!"

I crawled rapidly around the floor, picking up the coins, trying to avoid the coppers and to get greenbacks and the gold. Ignoring the shock by laughing, as I brushed the coins off quickly, I discovered that I could contain the electricity — a contradiction, but it works. Then the men began to push us onto the rug. Laughing embarrassedly, we struggled out of their hands and kept after the coins. We were all wet and slippery and hard to hold. Suddenly I saw a boy lifted into the air, glistening with sweat like a circus seal, and dropped, his wet back landing flush upon the charged rug, heard him yell and saw him literally dance upon his back, his elbows beating a frenzied tattoo upon the floor, his muscles twitching like the flesh of a horse stung by many flies. When he finally rolled off, his face was gray and no one stopped him when he ran from the floor amid booming laughter.

"Get the money," the M.C. called. "That's good hard American cash!"

And we snatched and grabbed, snatched and grabbed. I was careful not to come too close to the rug now, and when I felt the hot whiskey breath descend upon me like a cloud of foul air I reached out and grabbed the leg of a chair. It was occupied and I held on desperately.

"Leggo, nigger! Leggo!"

The huge face wavered down to mine as he tried to push me free. But my body was slippery and he was too drunk. It was Mr. Colcord, who owned a chain of movie houses and "entertainment palaces." Each time he grabbed me I slipped out of his hands. It became a real struggle. I feared the rug more than I did the drunk, so I held on, surprising myself for a moment by trying to topple *him* upon the rug. It was such an enormous idea that I found myself actually carrying it out. I tried not to be obvious, yet when I grabbed his leg, trying to tumble him out of the chair, he raised up roaring with laughter, and, looking at me with soberness dead in the eye, kicked me viciously in the chest. The chair leg flew out of my hand and I felt myself going and rolled. It was as though I had rolled through a bed of hot coals. It seemed a whole century would pass before I would roll free, a century in which I was seared through the deepest levels of my body to the fearful breath within me and the breath seared and heated to the point of explosion. It'll all be over in a flash, I thought as I rolled clear. It'll all be over in a flash.

But not yet, the men on the other side were waiting, red faces swollen as though from apoplexy as they bent forward in their chairs. Seeing their fingers coming toward me I rolled away as a fumbled football rolls off the receiver's fingertips, back into the coals. That time I luckily sent the rug sliding out of place and heard the coins ringing against the floor and the boys scuffling to pick them up and the M.C. calling, "All right, boys, that's all. Go get dressed and get your money."

I was limp as a dish rag. My back felt as though it had been beaten with wires.

When we had dressed the M.C. came in and gave us each five dollars, except Tatlock, who got ten for being last in the ring. Then he told us to leave. I was not to get a chance to deliver my speech, I thought. I was going out into the dim alley in despair when I was stopped and told to go back. I returned to the ballroom, where the men were pushing back their chairs and gathering in groups to talk.

The M.C. knocked on a table for quiet. "Gentlemen," he said, "we almost forgot an important part of the program. A most serious part, gentlemen. This boy was brought here to deliver a speech which he made at his graduation yesterday . . ."

"Bravo!"

"I'm told that he is the smartest boy we've got out there in Greenwood. I'm told that he knows more big words than a pocket-sized dictionary."

Much applause and laughter.

"So now, gentlemen, I want you to give him your attention."

There was still laughter as I faced them, my mouth dry, my eye throbbing. I began slowly, but evidently my throat was tense, because they began shouting, "Louder! Louder!"

"We of the younger generation extol the wisdom of that great leader and educator," I shouted, "who first spoke these flaming words of wisdom: 'A ship lost at sea for many days suddenly sighted a friendly vessel. From the mast of the unfortunate vessel was seen a signal: "Water, water; we die of thirst!" The answer from the friendly vessel came back: "Cast down your bucket where you are." The captain of the distressed vessel, at last heeding the injunction, cast down his bucket, and it came up full of fresh sparkling water from the mouth of the Amazon River.'

And like him I say, and in his words, 'To those of my race who depend upon bettering their condition in a foreign land, or who underestimate the importance of cultivating friendly relations with the Southern white man, who is his next-door neighbor, I would say: "Cast down your bucket where you are" — cast it down in making friends in every manly way of the people of all races by whom we are surrounded . . .' "

I spoke automatically and with such fervor that I did not realize that the men were still talking and laughing until my dry mouth, filling up with blood from the cut, almost strangled me. I coughed, wanting to stop and go to one of the tall brass, sand-filled spittoons to relieve myself, but a few of the men, especially the superintendent, were listening and I was afraid. So I gulped it down, blood, saliva, and all, and continued. (What powers of endurance I had during those days! What enthusiasm! What a belief in the rightness of things!) I spoke even louder in spite of the pain. But still they talked and still they laughed, as though deaf with cotton in dirty ears. So I spoke with greater emotional emphasis. I closed my ears and swallowed blood until I was nauseated. The speech seemed a hundred times as long as before, but I could not leave out a single word. All had to be said, each memorized nuance considered, rendered. Nor was that all. Whenever I uttered a word of three or more syllables a group of voices would yell for me to repeat it. I used the phrase "social responsibility" and they yelled:

"What's that word you say, boy?"

"Social responsibility," I said.

"What?" 70

"Social . . ."

"Louder."

". . . responsibility."

"More!"

"Respon —" 75

"Repeat!"

"— sibility."

The room filled with the uproar of laughter until, no doubt, distracted by having to gulp down my blood, I made a mistake and yelled a phrase I had often seen denounced in newspaper editorials, heard debated in private.

"Social . . ."

"What?" they yelled.

". . . equality —" 80

The laughter hung smokelike in the sudden stillness. I opened my eyes, puzzled. Sounds of displeasure filled the room. The M.C. rushed forward. They shouted hostile phrases at me. But I did not understand.

A small dry mustached man in the front row blared out, "Say that slowly, son!"

"What, sir?"

"What you just said!"

"Social responsibility, sir," I said. 85

"You weren't being smart, were you, boy?" he said, not unkindly.

"No, sir!"

"You sure that about 'equality' was a mistake?"

"Oh, yes, sir," I said. "I was swallowing blood." 90

"Well, you had better speak more slowly so we can understand. We mean to do right by you, but you've got to know your place at all times. All right, now, go on with your speech."

I was afraid. I wanted to leave but I wanted also to speak and I was afraid they'd snatch me down.

"Thank you, sir," I said, beginning where I had left off, and having them ignore me as before.

Yet when I finished there was a thunderous applause. I was surprised to see the superintendent come forth with a package wrapped in white tissue paper, and, gesturing for quiet, address the men.

"Gentlemen, you see that I did not overpraise this boy. He makes a good 95
speech and some day he'll lead his people in the proper paths. And I don't have to tell you that that is important in these days and times. This is a good, smart boy, and so to encourage him in the right direction, in the name of the Board of Education I wish to present him a prize in the form of this . . ."

He paused, removing the tissue paper and revealing a gleaming calfskin brief case.

". . . in the form of this first-class article from Shad Whitmore's shop."

"Boy," he said, addressing me, "take this prize and keep it well. Consider it a badge of office. Prize it. Keep developing as you are and some day it will be filled with important papers that will help shape the destiny of your people."

I was so moved that I could hardly express my thanks. A rope of bloody saliva forming a shape like an undiscovered continent drooled upon the leather and I wiped it quickly away. I felt an importance that I had never dreamed.

"Open it and see what's inside," I was told. 100

My fingers a-tremble, I complied, smelling the fresh leather and finding an official-looking document inside. It was a scholarship to the state college for Negroes. My eyes filled with tears and I ran awkwardly off the floor.

I was overjoyed; I did not even mind when I discovered that the gold pieces I had scrambled for were brass pocket tokens advertising a certain make of automobile.

When I reached home everyone was excited. Next day the neighbors came to congratulate me. I even felt safe from grandfather, whose deathbed curse usually spoiled my triumphs. I stood beneath his photograph with my brief case in hand and smiled triumphantly into his stolid black peasant's face. It was a face that fascinated me. The eyes seemed to follow everywhere I went.

That night I dreamed I was at a circus with him and that he refused to laugh at the clowns no matter what they did. Then later he told me to open my brief case and read what was inside and I did, finding an official envelope stamped with the state seal; and inside the envelope I found another and another, endlessly, and I thought I would fall of weariness. "Them's years," he said. "Now open that one." And I did and in it I found an engraved document containing a short message in letters of gold. "Read it," my grandfather said. "Out loud!"

"To Whom It May Concern," I intoned. "Keep This Nigger-Boy Running." 105

I awoke with the old man's laughter ringing in my ears.

(It was a dream I was to remember and dream again for many years after. But at that time I had no insight into its meaning. First I had to attend college.) *[1947]*

≡ THINKING ABOUT THE TEXT

1. Some critics have seen the events at the smoker as symbolic or perhaps as an allegory of the plight of African Americans in the segregated South. Pick at least two specific events from the story. How are they meant to explain certain aspects of the African American experience before the civil rights movement of the 1960s?
2. Some readers are surprised by the bizarre and cruel behavior of the town's leaders. Are you? How do you explain what goes on there?
3. How do you interpret the narrator's dream (paras. 104–06)? Why would his grandfather be laughing?
4. Reread paragraphs 1 through 3. How is this opening section connected to the story? To the last paragraph? What might Ellison's narrator mean when he says in paragraph 1 that he is "an invisible man"?
5. The grandfather's deathbed advice in paragraph 2 causes quite a stir. In your own words, what is his advice? Why are his relatives surprised? What might be some alternatives for dealing with oppression? Which "solution" sounds like the one you would have promoted for our society during Ellison's boyhood?

BOOKER T. WASHINGTON
Atlanta Exposition Address (The Atlanta Compromise)

Recognized in his time as the major spokesman for his race, Booker T. Washington (1856–1915) is often seen today as an accommodationist whose insistence on gradual progress and vocational rather than intellectual education played into the hands of the white power structure, delaying racial equality. He founded and served as president of Tuskegee Institute, wrote twelve books (including the autobiographical Up from Slavery *in 1901), controlled much of the Negro press, and spoke in cities throughout the nation. His speech at the Atlanta Cotton States and International Exposition in 1895, in which he praised the South, condoned segregation and the glory of "common labor" for his race, and called for harmony and cooperation between the races, is often called "The Atlanta Compromise."*

One-third of the population of the South is of the Negro race. No enterprise seeking the material, civil, or moral welfare of this section can disregard this element of our population and reach the highest success. I but convey to you, Mr. President and Directors, the sentiment of the masses of my race when I say that in no way have the value and manhood of the American Negro been more fittingly and generously recognized than by the managers of this magnificent Exposition at every stage of its progress. It is a recognition that will do more to cement the friendship of the two races than any occurrence since the dawn of our freedom.

Not only this, but the opportunity here afforded will awaken among us a new era of industrial progress. Ignorant and inexperienced, it is not strange that in the first years of our new life we began at the top instead of at the bottom; that a seat in Congress or the state legislature was more sought than real estate or industrial skill; that the political convention or stump speaking had more attractions than starting a dairy farm or truck garden.

A ship lost at sea for many days suddenly sighted a friendly vessel. From the mast of the unfortunate vessel was seen a signal, "Water, water; we die of thirst!" The answer from the friendly vessel at once came back, "Cast down your bucket where you are." A second time the signal, "Water, water, send us water!" ran up from the distressed vessel, and was answered, "Cast down your bucket where you are." And a third and fourth signal for water was answered, "Cast down your bucket where you are." The captain of the distressed vessel, at last heeding the injunction, cast down his bucket, and it came up full of fresh, sparkling water from the mouth of the Amazon River. To those of my race who depend on bettering their condition in a foreign land or who underestimate the importance of cultivating friendly relations with the Southern white man, who is their next-door neighbor, I would say: "Cast down your bucket where you are" — cast it down in making friends in every manly way of the people of all races by whom we are surrounded.

Cast it down in agriculture, mechanics, in commerce, in domestic service, and in the professions. And in this connection it is well to bear in mind that whatever other sins the South may be called to bear, when it comes to business, pure and simple, it is in the South that the Negro is given a man's chance in the commercial world, and in nothing is this Exposition more eloquent than in emphasizing this chance. Our greatest danger is that in the great leap from slavery to freedom we may overlook the fact that the masses of us are to live by the productions of our hands, and fail to keep in mind that we shall prosper in proportion as we learn to dignify and glorify common labor and put brains and skill into the common occupations of life; shall prosper in proportion as we learn to draw the line between the superficial and the substantial, the ornamental gewgaws of life and the useful. No race can prosper till it learns that there is as much dignity in tilling a field as in writing a poem. It is at the bottom of life we must begin, and not at the top. Nor should we permit our grievances to overshadow our opportunities.

To those of the white race who look to the incoming of those of foreign birth 5
and strange tongue and habits for the prosperity of the South, were I permitted I would repeat what I say to my own race, "Cast down your bucket where you are." Cast it down among the eight millions of Negroes whose habits you know, whose fidelity and love you have tested in days when to have proved treacherous meant the ruin of your firesides. Cast down your bucket among these people who have, without strikes and labor wars, tilled your fields, cleared your forests, builded your railroads and cities, and brought forth treasures from the bowels

of the earth, and helped make possible this magnificent representation of the progress of the South. Casting down your bucket among my people, helping and encouraging them as you are doing on these grounds, and to education of head, hand, and heart, you will find that they will buy your surplus land, make blossom the waste places in your fields, and run your factories. While doing this, you can be sure in the future, as in the past, that you and your families will be surrounded by the most patient, faithful, law-abiding, and unresentful people that the world has seen. As we have proved our loyalty to you in the past, in nursing your children, watching by the sick-bed of your mothers and fathers, and often following them with tear-dimmed eyes to their graves, so in the future, in our humble way, we shall stand by you with a devotion that no foreigner can approach, ready to lay down our lives, if need be, in defense of yours, interlacing our industrial, commercial, civil, and religious life with yours in a way that shall make the interests of both races one. In all things that are purely social we can be as separate as the fingers, yet one as the hand in all things essential to mutual progress.

There is no defense or security for any of us except in the highest intelligence and development of all. If anywhere there are efforts tending to curtail the fullest growth of the Negro, let these efforts be turned into stimulating, encouraging, and making him the most useful and intelligent citizen. Effort or means so invested will pay a thousand per cent interest. These efforts will be twice blessed — "blessing him that gives and him that takes."

There is no escape through law of man or God from the inevitable: —

The laws of changeless justice bind
Oppressor with oppressed;
And close as sin and suffering joined
We march to fate abreast.

Nearly sixteen millions of hands will aid you in pulling the load upward, or they will pull against you the load downward. We shall constitute one-third and more of the ignorance and crime of the South, or one-third its intelligence and progress; we shall contribute one-third to the business and industrial prosperity of the South, or we shall prove a veritable body of death, stagnating, depressing, retarding every effort to advance the body politic.

Gentlemen of the Exposition, as we present to you our humble effort at an exhibition of our progress, you must not expect overmuch. Starting thirty years ago with ownership here and there in a few quilts and pumpkins and chickens (gathered from miscellaneous sources), remember the path that has led from these to the inventions and production of agricultural implements, buggies, steam-engines, newspapers, books, statuary, carving, paintings, the management of drug-stores and banks, has not been trodden without contact with thorns and thistles. While we take pride in what we exhibit as a result of our independent efforts, we do not for a moment forget that our part in this exhibition would fall far short of your expectations but for the constant help that has come to our educational life, not only from the Southern states, but especially from Northern philanthropists who have made their gifts a constant stream of blessing and encouragement.

The wisest among my race understand that the agitation of questions of social equality is the extremest folly, and that progress in the enjoyment of all the privileges that will come to us must be the result of severe and constant struggle rather than of artificial forcing. No race that has anything to contribute to the markets of the world is long in any degree ostracized. It is important and right that all privileges of the law be ours, but it is vastly more important that we be prepared for the exercises of these privileges. The opportunity to earn a dollar in a factory just now is worth infinitely more than the opportunity to spend a dollar in an opera-house. 10

In conclusion, may I repeat that nothing in thirty years has given us more hope and encouragement, and drawn us so near to you of the white race, as this opportunity offered by the Exposition; and here bending, as it were, over the altar that represents the results of the struggles of your race and mine, both starting practically empty-handed three decades ago, I pledge that in your effort to work out the great and intricate problem which God has laid at the doors of the South, you shall have at all times the patient, sympathetic help of my race; only let this be constantly in mind, that, while from representations in these buildings of the product of field, of forest, of mine, of factory, letters, and art, much good will come, yet far above and beyond material benefits will be that higher good, that, let us pray God, will come, in a blotting out of sectional differences and racial animosities and suspicions, in a determination to administer absolute justice, in a willing obedience among all classes to the mandates of law. This, this, coupled with our material prosperity, will bring into our beloved South a new heaven and a new earth. *[1895]*

THINKING ABOUT THE TEXT

1. Cite two passages from Washington's speech that would probably have had an impact on the African American characters in "Battle Royal."
2. Do you think Washington is right in saying, "No race can prosper till it learns that there is as much dignity in tilling a field as in writing a poem" (para. 4)?
3. Are you surprised that Washington pledges "the patient, sympathetic help of my race" as those whites in power "work out the great and intricate problem which God has laid at the doors of the South" (para. 11)? What might contemporary black leaders think of this attitude?

W. E. B. DU BOIS

Of Mr. Booker T. Washington

W. E. B. Du Bois (1868–1963) was a driving force in the movement for equality for people of color in America and throughout the world well into his nineties. He was born in Massachusetts soon after the Civil War, and his death in Africa coincided with the March on Washington in 1963. Du Bois was educated at Fisk, Berlin, and Harvard

Universities, receiving a Ph.D. from Harvard in 1895 for his dissertation on the history of the slave trade. He is best known for his work with the National Association for the Advancement of Colored People (NAACP), serving as editor of The Crisis *from 1910 to 1932. As a scholar, writer, and intellectual, Du Bois openly opposed policies such as those supported by Booker T. Washington that kept social, political, and educational opportunities from most African Americans.* The Souls of Black Folk *(1903), from which our reading is taken, is perhaps the most influential of his many writings.*

Easily the most striking thing in the history of the American Negro since 1876 is the ascendancy of Mr. Booker T. Washington. It began at the time when war memories and ideals were rapidly passing; a day of astonishing commercial development was dawning; a sense of doubt and hesitation overtook the freedmen's sons,—then it was that his leading began. Mr. Washington came, with a simple definite programme, at the psychological moment when the nation was a little ashamed of having bestowed so much sentiment on Negroes, and was concentrating its energies on Dollars. His programme of industrial education, conciliation of the South, and submission and silence as to civil and political rights, was not wholly original; the Free Negroes from 1830 up to wartime had striven to build industrial schools, and the American Missionary Association had from the first taught various trades; and Price° and others had sought a way of honorable alliance with the best of the Southerners. But Mr. Washington first indissolubly linked these things; he put enthusiasm, unlimited energy, and perfect faith into this programme, and changed it from a by-path into a veritable Way of Life. And the tale of the methods by which he did this is a fascinating study of human life.

It startled the nation to hear a Negro advocating such a programme after many decades of bitter complaint; it startled and won the applause of the South, it interested and won the admiration of the North; and after a confused murmur of protest, it silenced if it did not convert the Negroes themselves.

To gain the sympathy and cooperation of the various elements comprising the white South was Mr. Washington's first task; and this, at the time Tuskegee was founded, seemed, for a black man, well-nigh impossible. And yet ten years later it was done in the word spoken at Atlanta: "In all things purely social we can be as separate as the five fingers, and yet one as the hand in all things essential to mutual progress." This "Atlanta Compromise" is by all odds the most notable thing in Mr. Washington's career. The South interpreted it in different ways: the radicals received it as a complete surrender of the demand for civil and political equality; the conservatives, as a generously conceived working basis for mutual understanding. So both approved it, and today its author is certainly the most distinguished Southerner since Jefferson Davis, and the one with the largest personal following. . . .

Mr. Washington represents in Negro thought the old attitude of adjustment and submission; but adjustment at such a peculiar time as to make his programme

Price: Joseph C. Price (1854–1893), founder of Zion Wesley College and Livingstone College, was a prominent African American educator and championed liberal-arts education.

unique. This is an age of unusual economic development, and Mr. Washington's programme naturally takes an economic cast, becoming a gospel of Work and Money to such an extent as apparently almost completely to over-shadow the higher aims of life. Moreover, this is an age when the more advanced races are coming in closer contact with the less developed races, and the race-feeling is therefore intensified; and Mr. Washington's programme practically accepts the alleged inferiority of the Negro races. Again, in our own land, the reaction from the sentiment of war time has given impetus to race-prejudice against Negroes, and Mr. Washington withdraws many of the high demands of Negroes as men and American citizens. In other periods of intensified prejudice all the Negro's tendency to self-assertion has been called forth; at this period a policy of submission is advocated. In the history of nearly all other races and people the doctrine preached at such crises has been that manly self-respect is worth more than lands and houses, and that a people who voluntarily surrender such respect, or cease striving for it, are not worth civilizing.

In answer to this, it has been claimed that the Negro can survive only 5
through submission. Mr. Washington distinctly asks that black people give up, at least for the present, three things —

First, political power,
Second, insistence on civil rights,
Third, higher education of Negro youth, —

and concentrate all their energies on industrial education, the accumulation of wealth, and the conciliation of the South. This policy has been courageously and insistently advocated for over fifteen years, and has been triumphant for perhaps ten years. As a result of this tender of the palm-branch, what has been the return? In these years there have occurred:

1. The disfranchisement of the Negro.
2. The legal creation of a distinct status of civil inferiority for the Negro.
3. The steady withdrawal of aid from institutions for the higher training of the Negro.

These movements are not, to be sure, direct results of Mr. Washington's teachings; but his propaganda has, without a shadow of doubt, helped their speedier accomplishment. The question then comes: Is it possible, and probable, that nine millions of men can make effective progress in economic lines if they are deprived of political rights, made a servile caste, and allowed only the most meager chance for developing their exceptional men? If history and reason give any distinct answer to these questions, it is an emphatic *No*. . . .

In failing thus to state plainly and unequivocally the legitimate demands of their people, even at the cost of opposing an honored leader the thinking classes of American Negroes would shirk a heavy responsibility, — a responsibility to themselves, a responsibility to struggling masses, a responsibility to the darker races of men whose future depends so largely on this American experiment, but especially a responsibility to this nation, — this common Fatherland. It is wrong to encourage a man or a people in evil-doing; it is wrong to aid and abet a national crime simply because it is unpopular not to do so. The growing spirit of kindliness and reconciliation between the North and South after the frightful differences of a generation ago ought to be a source of deep congratulation to all, and especially to those whose mistreatment caused the war; but if that reconciliation is to be marked by the industrial slavery and civic death of those same black men, with permanent legislation into a position of inferiority, then those black men, if they are really men, are called upon by every consideration of patriotism and loyalty to oppose such a course by all civilized methods, even though such opposition involves disagreement with Mr. Booker T. Washington. We have no right to sit silently by while the inevitable seeds are sown for a harvest of disaster to our children, black and white.

First, it is the duty of black men to judge the South discriminatingly. The present generation of Southerners are not responsible for the past, and they should not be blindly hated or blamed for it. Furthermore, to no class is the indiscriminate endorsement of the recent course of the South toward Negroes more nauseating than to the best thought of the South. The South is not "solid"; it is a land in the ferment of social change, wherein forces of all kinds are fighting for supremacy; and to praise the ill the South is today perpetrating is just as wrong as to condemn the good. Discriminating and broad-minded criticism is what the South needs, — needs it for the sake of her own white sons and daughters, and for the insurance of robust, healthy mental and moral development.

Today even the attitude of the Southern whites toward the blacks is not, as so many assume, in all cases the same; the ignorant Southerner hates the Negro, the workingmen fear his competition, the money-makers wish to use him as a laborer, some of the educated see a menace in his upward development, while others, — usually the sons of the masters — wish to help him to rise. National opinion has enabled this last class to maintain the Negro common schools, and to protect the Negro partially in property, life, and limb. Through the pressure of the money-makers, the Negro is in danger of being reduced to semi-slavery, especially in the country districts; the workingmen, and those of the educated who fear the Negro, have united to disfranchise him, and some have urged his deportation; while the passions of the ignorant are easily aroused to lynch and abuse any black man. To praise this intricate whirl of thought and prejudice is nonsense, to inveigh indiscriminately against "the South" is unjust; but to use the same breath in praising Governor Aycock, exposing Senator Morgan, arguing with Mr. Thomas Nelson Page, and denouncing Senator Ben Tillman, is not only sane, but the imperative duty of thinking black men.

It would be unjust to Mr. Washington not to acknowledge that in several 10
instances he has opposed movements in the South which were unjust to the Negro; he sent memorials to the Louisiana and Alabama constitutional conventions, he has spoken against lynching, and in other ways has openly or silently set his influence against sinister schemes and unfortunate happenings. Notwithstanding this, it is equally true to assert that on the whole the distinct impression left by Mr. Washington's propaganda is, first, that the South is justified in its present attitude toward the Negro because of the Negro's degradation; secondly, that the prime cause of the Negro's failure to rise more quickly is his wrong education in the past; and, thirdly, that his future rise depends primarily on his own efforts. Each of these propositions is a dangerous half-truth. The supplementary

truths must never be lost sight of: first, slavery and race-prejudice are potent if not sufficient causes of the Negro's position; second, industrial and common-school training were necessarily slow in planting because they had to await the black teachers trained by higher institutions,—it being extremely doubtful if any essentially different development was possible, and certainly a Tuskegee was unthinkable before 1880; and, third, while it is a great truth to say that the Negro must strive and strive mightily to help himself, it is equally true that unless his striving be not simply seconded, but rather aroused and encouraged, by the initiative of the richer and wiser environing group, he cannot hope for great success.

In his failure to realize and impress this last point, Mr. Washington is especially to be criticized. His doctrine has tended to make the whites, North and South, shift the burden of the Negro problem to the Negro's shoulders and stand aside as critical and rather pessimistic spectators; when in fact the burden belongs to the nation, and the hands of none of us are clean if we bend not our energies to righting these great wrongs.

The South ought to be led, by candid and honest criticism, to assert her better self and do her full duty to the race she has cruelly wronged and is still wronging. The North — her copartner in guilt — cannot salve her conscience by plastering it with gold. We cannot settle this problem by diplomacy and suaveness, by "policy" alone. If worse come to worst, can the moral fiber of this country survive the slow throttling and murder of nine millions of men?

The black men of America have a duty to perform, a duty stern and delicate,—a forward movement to oppose a part of the work of their greatest leader. So far as Mr. Washington preaches Thrift, Patience, and Industrial Training for the masses, we must hold up his hands and strive with him, rejoicing in his honors and glorying in the strength of this Joshua called of God and of man to lead the headless host. But so far as Mr. Washington apologizes for injustice, North or South, does not rightly value the privilege and duty of voting, belittles the emasculating effects of caste distinctions, and opposes the higher training and ambition of our brighter minds,—so far as he, the South, or the Nation, does this,—we must unceasingly and firmly oppose them. By every civilized and peaceful method we must strive for the rights which the world accords to men, clinging unwaveringly to those great words which the sons of the Fathers would fain forget: "We hold these truths to be self-evident: that all men are created equal; that they are endowed by their Creator with certain unalienable rights; that among these are life, liberty, and the pursuit of happiness." *[1903]*

THINKING ABOUT THE TEXT

1. Du Bois is clearly upset with Washington. What is his main objection to the Atlanta Compromise? Do you agree with him?
2. Is the narrator of "Battle Royal" still under Washington's influence, or has the thinking of Du Bois made some inroads?
3. What might the grandfather in "Battle Royal" think of Du Bois's last paragraph?

GUNNAR MYRDAL

Social Equality

A Swedish economist who with his wife, Alva Myrdal (winner of the 1982 Nobel Peace Prize), established a model social-welfare system for Sweden in the 1930s, Gunnar Myrdal (1898–1987) was asked by the Carnegie Foundation in 1938 to study racism in the United States. "Social Equality" is an excerpt from the book that elaborated on the results of his study, An American Dilemma: The Negro Problem and Modern Democracy *(1944). In* Cultural Contexts for Ralph Ellison's "Invisible Man," *historian Eric Sundquist points out that for the white men in "Battle Royal," the term* social equality *would have included sexual relations and marriage between black men and white women, which was then an important cultural taboo.*

In his first encounter with the American Negro problem, perhaps nothing perplexes the outside observer more than the popular term and the popular theory of "no social equality." He will be made to feel from the start that it has concrete implications and a central importance for the Negro problem in America. But, nevertheless, the term is kept vague and elusive, and the theory loose and ambiguous. One moment it will be stretched to cover and justify every form of social segregation and discrimination, and, in addition, all the inequalities in justice, politics, and breadwinning. The next moment it will be narrowed to express only the denial of close personal intimacies and intermarriage. The very lack of precision allows the notion of "no social equality" to rationalize the rather illogical and wavering system of color caste in America.

The kernel of the popular theory of "no social equality" will, when pursued, be presented as a firm determination on the part of the whites to block amalgamation and preserve "the purity of the white race." The white man identifies himself with "the white race" and feels that he has a stake in resisting the dissipation of its racial identity. Important in this identification is the notion of "the absolute and unchangeable superiority of the white race." From this racial dogma will often be drawn the *direct* inference that the white man shall dominate in all spheres. But when the logic of this inference is inquired about, the inference will be made *indirect* and will be made to lead over to the danger of amalgamation, or, as it is popularly expressed, "intermarriage."

It is further found that the ban on intermarriage is focused on white women. For them it covers both formal marriage and illicit intercourse. In regard to white men it is taken more or less for granted that they would not stoop to marry Negro women, and that illicit intercourse does not fall under the same intense taboo. Their offspring, under the popular doctrine that maternity is more certain than paternity, become Negroes anyway, and the white race easily avoids pollution with Negro blood. To prevent "intermarriage" in this specific sense of sex relations between white women and Negro men, it is not enough to apply legal and social sanctions against it — so the popular theory runs. In using the danger of intermarriage as a defense for the whole caste system, it is assumed both that

Negro men have a strong desire for "intermarriage," and that white women would be open to proposals from Negro men, *if* they are not guarded from even meeting them on an equal plane. The latter assumption, of course, is never openly expressed, but is logically implicit in the popular theory. The conclusion follows that the whole system of segregation and discrimination is justified. Every single measure is defended as necessary to block "social equality" which in its turn is held necessary to prevent "intermarriage."

The basic role of the fear of amalgamation in white attitudes to the race problem is indicated by the popular magical concept of "blood." Educated white Southerners, who know everything about modern genetic and biological research, confess readily that they actually feel an irrational or "instinctive" repugnance in thinking of "intermarriage." These measures of segregation and discrimination are often of the type found in the true taboos, and in the notion "not to be touched" of primitive religion. The specific taboos are characterized, further, by a different degree of excitement which attends their violation and a different degree of punishment to the violator: the closer the act to sexual association, the more furious is the public reaction. Sexual association itself is punished by death and is accompanied by tremendous public excitement; the other social relations meet decreasing degrees of public fury. Sex becomes in this popular theory the principle around which the whole structure of segregation of the Negroes — down to disfranchisement and denial of equal opportunities on the labor market — is organized. The reasoning is this: "For, say what we will, may not all the equalities be ultimately based on potential social equality, and that in turn on intermarriage? Here we reach the real *crux* of the question." In cruder language, but with the same logic, the Southern man on the street responds to any plea for social equality: "Would you like to have your daughter marry a Negro?"

This theory of color caste centering around the aversion to amalgamation determines, as we have just observed, the white man's rather definite rank order of the various measures of segregation and discrimination against Negroes. The relative significance attached to each of those measures is dependent upon their degree of expediency or necessity — in the view of white people — as means of upholding the ban on "intermarriage." In this rank order, (1) the ban on intermarriage and other sex relations involving white women and colored men takes precedence before everything else. It is the end for which the other restrictions are arranged as means. Thereafter follow: (2) all sorts of taboos and etiquettes in personal contacts; (3) segregation in schools and churches; (4) segregation in hotels, restaurants, and theaters, and other public places where people meet socially; (5) segregation in public conveyances; (6) discrimination in public services; and, finally, inequality in (7) politics, (8) justice, and (9) breadwinning and relief.

The degree of liberalism on racial matters in the white South can be designated mainly by the point on this rank order where a man stops because he believes further segregation and discrimination are not necessary to prevent "intermarriage." We have seen that white liberals in the South of the present day, as a matter of principle, rather unanimously stand up against inequality in breadwinning, relief, justice, and politics. These fields of discrimination form the chief battleground and considerable changes in them are, as we have seen, on the way. When we ascend to the higher ranks which concern social relations in the narrow sense, we find the Southern liberals less prepared to split off from the majority opinion of the region. Hardly anybody in the South is prepared to go the whole way and argue that even the ban on intermarriage should be lifted. Practically all agree, not only upon the high desirability of preventing "intermarriage," but also that a certain amount of separation between the two groups is expedient and necessary to prevent it. Even the one who has his philosophical doubts on the point must, if he is reasonable, abstain from ever voicing them. The social pressure is so strong that it would be foolish not to conform. Conformity is a political necessity for having any hope of influence; it is, in addition, a personal necessity for not meeting social ostracism. . . .

The fixation on the purity of white womanhood, and also part of the intensity of emotion surrounding the whole sphere of segregation and discrimination, are to be understood as the backwashes of the sore conscience on the part of white men for their own or their compeers' relations with, or desires for, Negro women. These psychological effects are greatly magnified because of the puritan *milieu* of America and especially of the South. The upper class men in a less puritanical people could probably have indulged in sex relations with, and sexual day-dreams of, lower caste women in a more matter-of-course way and without generating so much pathos about white womanhood. The Negro people have to carry the burden not only of the white men's sins but also of their virtues. The virtues of the honest, democratic, puritan white Americans in the South are great, and the burden upon the Negroes becomes ponderous.

Our practical conclusion is that it would have cleansing effects on race relations in America, and particularly in the South, to have an open and sober discussion in rational terms of this ever present popular theory of "intermarriage" and "social equality," giving matters their factual ground, true proportions and logical relations. Because it is, to a great extent, an opportunistic rationalization, and because it refers directly and indirectly to the most touchy spots in American life and American morals, tremendous inhibitions have been built up against a detached and critical discussion of this theory. But such inhibitions are gradually overcome when, in the course of secularized education, people become rational about their life problems. It must never be forgotten that in our increasingly intellectualized civilization even the plain citizen feels an urge for truth and objectivity, and that this rationalistic urge is increasingly competing with the opportunistic demands for rationalization and escape.

There are reasons to believe that a slow but steady cleansing of the American mind is proceeding as the cultural level is raised. The basic racial inferiority doctrine is being undermined by research and education. For a white man to have illicit relations with Negro women is increasingly meeting disapproval. Negroes themselves are more and more frowning upon such relations. This all must tend to dampen the emotional fires around "social equality." Sex and race fears are, however, even today the main defense for segregation and, in fact, for the whole caste order. The question shot at the interviewer touching any point of this order is still: "Would you like to have your daughter (sister) marry a Negro?" *[1944]*

≡ THINKING ABOUT THE TEXT

1. Look back at the smoker section in "Battle Royal," especially when the narrator during his speech says "social equality" instead of "social responsibility." Why do you think there was a "sudden stillness" in the room (paras. 81–82)?
2. Based on his ideas about white sexual fears, how might Myrdal read the part of the smoker dealing with the naked dancer?
3. Myrdal writes that "conformity is a political necessity for having any hope of influence; it is, in addition, a personal necessity for not meeting social ostracism" (para. 6). Does this insight help your understanding of the world of the smoker?

≡ WRITING ABOUT ISSUES

1. Argue that the episode at the smoker is or is not evidence that the grandfather's advice in "Battle Royal" to " 'overcome 'em with yeses, undermine 'em with grins, agree 'em to death and destruction' " (para. 2) will not work.
2. Analyze the arguments of Washington and Du Bois in terms of the claims they both make, the assumptions they base their claims on, the evidence they use as support for their assumptions, and the effectiveness of their claims with the intended audience. Which writer do you find more persuasive?
3. Write a personal narrative detailing an experience either when you were the victim of bias because of your race, sex, age, religion, ethnicity, sexual preference, or any other personal dynamic or when you were part of a group that held biased views. Be specific about what happened, how you felt then, how you feel now, and what you learned from the experience.

From City to Country: Critical Commentaries on a Play

OSCAR WILDE, *The Importance of Being Earnest*

CRITICAL COMMENTARIES:

SOS ELTIS, From *Revising Wilde: Society and Subversion in the Plays of Oscar Wilde*

TIRTHANKAR BOSE, From "Oscar Wilde's Game of Being Earnest"

PATRICIA FLANAGAN BEHRENDT, From *Oscar Wilde: Eros and Aesthetics*

CHARLES ISHERWOOD, "A Stylish Monster Conquers at a Glance"

Many literary plots have centered on trips from city to country or vice versa. In traveling from one of these places to the other, characters often go through experiences that force them to reexamine their identities, relationships, assumptions, and goals. What they find in their new setting needn't be traumatic, of course; they may even fall in love. In the modern theater, one of the most celebrated and discussed plays about a journey from city to country is Oscar Wilde's 1895 comedy *The Importance of Being Earnest*. Acclaimed when it opened, it is still much performed today, with audience after audience relishing its wit. Meanwhile, more than ever, scholars of literature speculate about what Wilde hoped to convey through his script. They suspect that by subtitling the play "A Trivial Comedy for Serious People," he was signaling that major social criticisms lurked beneath its humorous surface. In part, these analysts of *Earnest* are influenced by their knowledge of what happened to Wilde soon after its premiere. Under England's repressive legal system of the time, he was criminally convicted for the homosexual affairs he had been conducting in secret. But to what extent, and in what ways, *is* the play autobiographical? The question lacks a clear answer; the result is continued debate. Here we encourage *you* to enter the conversation. We do so by presenting multiple lenses on Wilde's text: excerpts by three critics who have analyzed *Earnest*.

BEFORE YOU READ

In the United States or in another nation you know well, do you think urban communities and rural communities still differ significantly, or do you sense that they have grown pretty much alike? Identify specific features of these communities that come to your mind as you consider this question.

OSCAR WILDE

The Importance of Being Earnest

A Trivial Comedy for Serious People

Oscar Wilde (1854–1900) was born in Dublin, Ireland, but graduated from Oxford University in England and then moved to London, where he became one of the most acclaimed playwrights of his day. He was also well known in the United States, especially during a lecture tour he made there in 1882. Wilde wrote in other literary genres besides drama: verse, such as his 1881 book Poems*; fiction, most notably his novel* The Picture of Dorian Gray *(1891); and essays, such as "The Soul of Man under Socialism" and "The Decay of Lying" (both 1891). But his theatrical comedies are what chiefly comprise his literary legacy today. They include* Lady Windermere's Fan *(1892),* A Woman of No Importance *(1893), and* An Ideal Husband *(1895).* The Importance of Being Earnest*, his last and most performed play, debuted in 1895. Despite its immediate success, however, Wilde plunged into serious trouble with the law*

Heritage Images/Getty Images

that same year. Although married, he had been conducting an affair with Lord Alfred Douglas, in an era when homosexuality was officially a crime. When accused of this by Douglas's father, the Marquis of Queensberry, Wilde sued him for libel, but lost the case when the facts of his private life emerged. Wilde was then convicted of "gross indecency" and subsequently served two years in prison. During his confinement, he wrote an anguished autobiographical letter to Douglas, eventually published as "De Profundis." When Wilde was released in 1897, he was still notorious and also broke. He died four years later in Paris, after writing a poem about his prison ordeal entitled "The Ballad of Reading Gaol" (1898).

THE PERSONS OF THE PLAY

JOHN WORTHING, J.P., *of the Manor House, Woolton, Hertfordshire*
ALGERNON MONCRIEFF, *his friend*
REV. CANON CHASUBLE, *D.D., rector of Woolton*
MERRIMAN, *butler to Mr. Worthing*
LANE, *Mr. Moncrieff's manservant*
LADY BRACKNELL
HON. GWENDOLEN FAIRFAX, *her daughter*
CECILY CARDEW, *John Worthing's ward*
MISS PRISM, *her governess*

THE SCENES OF THE PLAY

ACT I: *Algernon Moncrieff's Flat in Half Moon Street, W.*
ACT II: *The Garden at the Manor House, Woolton*
ACT III: *Morning Room at the Manor House, Woolton*

ACT I

(Scene: Morning room in Algernon's flat in Half Moon Street. The room is luxuriously and artistically furnished. The sound of a piano is heard in the adjoining room. Lane is arranging afternoon tea on the table, and after the music has ceased, Algernon enters.)

ALGERNON: Did you hear what I was playing, Lane?

LANE: I didn't think it polite to listen, sir.

ALGERNON: I'm sorry for that, for your sake. I don't play accurately — anyone can play accurately — but I play with wonderful expression. As far as the piano is concerned, sentiment is my forte. I keep science for Life.

LANE: Yes, sir.

ALGERNON: And, speaking of the science of Life, have you got the cucumber sandwiches cut for Lady Bracknell?

LANE: Yes, sir. *(Hands them on a salver.°)*

ALGERNON (*inspects them, takes two, and sits down on the sofa*): Oh! — by the way, Lane, I see from your book that on Thursday night, when Lord Shoreham

salver: A flat tray, often made of silver.

and Mr. Worthing were dining with me, eight bottles of champagne are entered as having been consumed.

LANE: Yes, sir; eight bottles and a pint.

ALGERNON: Why is it that at a bachelor's establishment the servants invariably drink the champagne? I ask merely for information.

LANE: I attribute it to the superior quality of the wine, sir. I have often observed that in married households the champagne is rarely of a first-rate brand.

ALGERNON: Good heavens! Is marriage so demoralizing as that?

LANE: I believe it *is* a very pleasant state, sir. I have had very little experience of it myself up to the present. I have only been married once. That was in consequence of a misunderstanding between myself and a young person.

ALGERNON (*languidly*): I don't know that I am much interested in your family life, Lane.

LANE: No, sir; it is not a very interesting subject. I never think of it myself.

ALGERNON: Very natural, I am sure. That will do, Lane, thank you.

LANE: Thank you, sir. (*Lane goes out.*)

ALGERNON: Lane's views on marriage seem somewhat lax. Really, if the lower orders don't set us a good example, what on earth is the use of them? They seem, as a class, to have absolutely no sense of moral responsibility.

(Enter Lane.)

LANE: Mr. Ernest Worthing.

(Enter Jack. Lane goes out.)

ALGERNON: How are you, my dear Ernest? What brings you up to town?

JACK: Oh, pleasure, pleasure! What else should bring one anywhere? Eating as usual, I see, Algy!

ALGERNON (*Stiffly*): I believe it is customary in good society to take some slight refreshment at five o'clock. Where have you been since last Thursday?

JACK (*sitting down on the sofa*): In the country.

ALGERNON: What on earth do you do there?

JACK (*pulling off his gloves*): When one is in town one amuses oneself. When one is in the country one amuses other people. It is excessively boring.

ALGERNON: And who are the people you amuse?

JACK (*airily*): Oh, neighbors, neighbors.

ALGERNON: Got nice neighbors in your part of Shropshire?

JACK: Perfectly horrid! Never speak to one of them.

ALGERNON: How immensely you must amuse them! (*Goes over and takes sandwich.*) By the way, Shropshire is your country, is it not?

JACK: Eh? Shropshire? Yes, of course. Hallo! Why all these cups? Why cucumber sandwiches? Why such reckless extravagance in one so young? Who is coming to tea?

ALGERNON: Oh! merely Aunt Augusta and Gwendolen.

JACK: How perfectly delightful!

ALGERNON: Yes, that is all very well; but I am afraid Aunt Augusta won't quite approve of your being here.

JACK: May I ask why?

ALGERNON: My dear fellow, the way you flirt with Gwendolen is perfectly disgraceful. It is almost as bad as the way Gwendolen flirts with you.

JACK: I am in love with Gwendolen. I have come up to town expressly to propose to her.

ALGERNON: I thought you had come up for pleasure?—I call that business.

JACK: How utterly unromantic you are!

ALGERNON: I really don't see anything romantic in proposing. It is very romantic to be in love. But there is nothing romantic about a definite proposal. Why, one may be accepted. One usually is, I believe. Then the excitement is all over. The very essence of romance is uncertainty. If ever I get married, I'll certainly try to forget the fact.

JACK: I have no doubt about that, dear Algy. The Divorce Court was specially invented for people whose memories are so curiously constituted.

ALGERNON: Oh! there is no use speculating on that subject. Divorces are made in heaven—(*Jack puts out his hand to take a sandwich. Algernon at once interferes.*) Please don't touch the cucumber sandwiches. They are ordered specially for Aunt Augusta. (*Takes one and eats it.*)

JACK: Well, you have been eating them all the time.

ALGERNON: That is quite a different matter. She is my aunt. (*Takes plate from below.*) Have some bread and butter. The bread and butter is for Gwendolen. Gwendolen is devoted to bread and butter.

JACK (*advancing to table and helping himself*): And very good bread and butter it is too.

ALGERNON: Well, my dear fellow, you need not eat as if you were going to eat it all. You behave as if you were married to her already. You are not married to her already, and I don't think you ever will be.

JACK: Why on earth do you say that?

ALGERNON: Well, in the first place, girls never marry the men they flirt with. Girls don't think it right.

JACK: Oh, that is nonsense!

ALGERNON: It isn't. It is a great truth. It accounts for the extraordinary number of bachelors that one sees all over the place. In the second place, I don't give my consent.

JACK: Your consent!

ALGERNON: My dear fellow, Gwendolen is my first cousin. And before I allow you to marry her, you will have to clear up the whole question of Cecily. (*Rings bell.*)

JACK: Cecily! What on earth do you mean? What do you mean, Algy, by Cecily? I don't know anyone of the name of Cecily.

(*Enter Lane.*)

ALGERNON: Bring me that cigarette case Mr. Worthing left in the smoking room the last time he dined here.

LANE: Yes, sir. (*Lane goes out.*)

JACK: Do you mean to say you have had my cigarette case all this time? I wish to goodness you had let me know. I have been writing frantic letters to Scotland Yard about it. I was very nearly offering a large reward.

ALGERNON: Well, I wish you would offer one. I happen to be more than usually hard up.

JACK: There is no good offering a large reward now that the thing is found.

(Enter Lane with the cigarette case on a salver. Algernon takes it at once. Lane goes out.)

ALGERNON: I think that is rather mean of you, Ernest, I must say. (*Opens case and examines it.*) However, it makes no matter, for, now that I look at the inscription inside, I find that the thing isn't yours after all.

JACK: Of course it's mine. (*Moving to him.*) You have seen me with it a hundred times, and you have no right whatsoever to read what is written inside. It is a very ungentlemanly thing to read a private cigarette case.

ALGERNON: Oh! it is absurd to have a hard-and-fast rule about what one should read and what one shouldn't. More than half of modern culture depends on what one shouldn't read.

JACK: I am quite aware of the fact, and I don't propose to discuss modern culture. It isn't the sort of thing one should talk of in private. I simply want my cigarette case back.

ALGERNON: Yes; but this isn't your cigarette case. This cigarette case is a present from someone of the name of Cecily, and you said you didn't know anyone of that name.

JACK: Well, if you want to know, Cecily happens to be my aunt.

ALGERNON: Your aunt!

JACK: Yes. Charming old lady she is, too. Lives at Tunbridge Wells. Just give it back to me, Algy.

ALGERNON (*retreating to back of sofa*): But why does she call herself little Cecily if she is your aunt and lives at Tunbridge Wells? (*Reading.*) "From little Cecily with her fondest love."

JACK (*moving to sofa and kneeling upon it*): My dear fellow, what on earth is there in that? Some aunts are tall, some aunts are not tall. That is a matter that surely an aunt may be allowed to decide for herself. You seem to think that every aunt should be exactly like your aunt! That is absurd! For heaven's sake give me back my cigarette case.

(Follows Algernon round the room.)

ALGERNON: Yes. But why does your aunt call you her uncle? "From little Cecily, with her fondest love to her dear Uncle Jack." There is no objection, I admit, to an aunt being a small aunt, but why an aunt, no matter what her size may be, should call her own nephew her uncle, I can't quite make out. Besides, your name isn't Jack at all; it is Ernest.

JACK: It isn't Ernest; it's Jack.

ALGERNON: You have always told me it was Ernest. I have introduced you to everyone as Ernest. You answer to the name of Ernest. You look as if your name was Ernest. You are the most earnest looking person I ever saw in my life. It is perfectly absurd your saying that your name isn't Ernest. It's on your cards. Here is one of them (*taking it from case*) "Mr. Ernest Worthing, B.4, The Albany." I'll keep this as a proof that your name is Ernest if ever you attempt to deny it to me, or to Gwendolen, or to anyone else.

(Puts the card in his pocket.)

JACK: Well, my name is Ernest in town and Jack in the country, and the cigarette case was given to me in the country.

ALGERNON: Yes, but that does not account for the fact that your small Aunt Cecily, who lives at Tunbridge Wells, calls you her dear uncle. Come, old boy, you had much better have the thing out at once.

JACK: My dear Algy, you talk exactly as if you were a dentist. It is very vulgar to talk like a dentist when one isn't a dentist. It produces a false impression.

ALGERNON: Well, that is exactly what dentists always do. Now, go on! Tell me the whole thing. I may mention that I have always suspected you of being a confirmed and secret Bunburyist; and I am quite sure of it now.

JACK: Bunburyist? What on earth do you mean by a Bunburyist?

ALGERNON: I'll reveal to you the meaning of that incomparable expression as soon as you are kind enough to inform me why you are Ernest in town and Jack in the country.

JACK: Well, produce my cigarette case first.

ALGERNON: Here it is. (*Hands cigarette case.*) Now produce your explanation, and pray make it improbable.

(Sits on sofa.)

JACK: My dear fellow, there is nothing improbable about my explanation at all. In fact it's perfectly ordinary. Old Mr. Thomas Cardew, who adopted me when I was a little boy, made me in his will guardian to his granddaughter, Miss Cecily Cardew. Cecily, who addresses me as her uncle from motives of respect that you could not possibly appreciate, lives at my place in the country under the charge of her admirable governess, Miss Prism.

ALGERNON: Where is that place in the country, by the way?

JACK: That is nothing to you, dear boy. You are not going to be invited—I may tell you candidly that the place is not in Shropshire.

ALGERNON: I suspected that, my dear fellow! I have Bunburyed all over Shropshire on two separate occasions. Now, go on. Why are you Ernest in town and Jack in the country?

JACK: My dear Algy, I don't know whether you will be able to understand my real motives. You are hardly serious enough. When one is placed in the position of guardian, one has to adopt a very high moral tone on all subjects. It's one's duty to do so. And as a high moral tone can hardly be said to conduce very much to either one's health or one's happiness, in order to get up to town I have always pretended to have a younger brother of the name of Ernest, who lives in the Albany, and gets into the most dreadful scrapes. That, my dear Algy, is the whole truth pure and simple.

ALGERNON: The truth is rarely pure and never simple. Modern life would be very tedious if it were either and modern literature a complete impossibility!

JACK: That wouldn't be at all a bad thing.

ALGERNON: Literary criticism is not your forte, my dear fellow. Don't try it. You should leave that to people who haven't been at a university. They do it so well in the daily papers. What you really are is a Bunburyist. I was quite right in saying you were a Bunburyist. You are one of the most advanced Bunburyists I know.

JACK: What on earth do you mean?

ALGERNON: You have invented a very useful younger brother called Ernest, in order that you may be able to come up to town as often as you like. I have invented an invaluable permanent invalid called Bunbury, in order that I may be able to go down into the country whenever I choose. Bunbury is perfectly invaluable. If it wasn't for Bunbury's extraordinary bad health, for instance, I wouldn't be able to dine with you at Willis's tonight, for I have been really engaged to Aunt Augusta for more than a week.

JACK: I haven't asked you to dine with me anywhere tonight.

ALGERNON: I know. You are absurdly careless about sending out invitations. It is very foolish of you. Nothing annoys people so much as not receiving invitations.

JACK: You had much better dine with your Aunt Augusta.

ALGERNON: I haven't the smallest intention of doing anything of the kind. To begin with, I dined there on Monday, and once a week is quite enough to dine with one's own relations. In the second place, whenever I do dine there I am always treated as a member of the family, and sent down with° either no woman at all, or two. In the third place, I know perfectly well whom she will place me next to, tonight. She will place me next Mary Farquhar, who always flirts with her own husband across the dinner table. That is not very pleasant. Indeed, it is not even decent—and that sort of thing is enormously on the increase. The amount of women in London who flirt with their own husbands is perfectly scandalous. It looks so bad. It is simply washing one's clean linen in public. Besides, now that I know you to be a confirmed Bunburyist I naturally want to talk to you about Bunburying. I want to tell you the rules.

JACK: I'm not a Bunburyist at all. If Gwendolen accepts me, I am going to kill my brother, indeed I think I'll kill him in any case. Cecily is a little too much interested in him. It is rather a bore. So I am going to get rid of Ernest. And I strongly advise you to do the same with Mr.—with your invalid friend who has the absurd name.

ALGERNON: Nothing will induce me to part with Bunbury, and if you ever get married, which seems to me extremely problematic, you will be very glad to know Bunbury. A man who marries without knowing Bunbury has a very tedious time of it.

JACK: That is nonsense. If I marry a charming girl like Gwendolen, and she is the only girl I ever saw in my life that I would marry, I certainly won't want to know Bunbury.

sent down with: Assigned a woman to escort into the dining room for dinner.

ALGERNON: Then your wife will. You don't seem to realize, that in married life three is company and two is none.

JACK (*sententiously*): That, my dear young friend, is the theory that the corrupt French drama has been propounding for the last fifty years.

ALGERNON: Yes; and that the happy English home has proved in half the time.

JACK: For heaven's sake, don't try to be cynical. It's perfectly easy to be cynical.

ALGERNON: My dear fellow, it isn't easy to be anything nowadays. There's such a lot of beastly competition about. (*The sound of an electric bell is heard.*) Ah! that must be Aunt Augusta. Only relatives, or creditors, ever ring in that Wagnerian° manner. Now, if I get her out of the way for ten minutes, so that you can have an opportunity for proposing to Gwendolen, may I dine with you tonight at Willis's?

JACK: I suppose so, if you want to.

ALGERNON: Yes, but you must be serious about it. I hate people who are not serious about meals. It is so shallow of them.

(Enter Lane.)

LANE: Lady Bracknell and Miss Fairfax.

(Algernon goes forward to meet them. Enter Lady Bracknell and Gwendolen.)

LADY BRACKNELL: Good afternoon, dear Algernon, I hope you are behaving very well.

ALGERNON: I'm feeling very well, Aunt Augusta.

LADY BRACKNELL: That's not quite the same thing. In fact the two things rarely go together.

(Sees Jack and bows to him with icy coldness.)

ALGERNON (*to Gwendolen*): Dear me, you are smart!

GWENDOLEN: I am always smart! Aren't I, Mr. Worthing?

JACK: You're quite perfect, Miss Fairfax.

GWENDOLEN: Oh! I hope I am not that. It would leave no room for developments, and I intend to develop in many directions.

(Gwendolen and Jack sit down together in the corner.)

LADY BRACKNELL: I'm sorry if we are a little late Algernon, but I was obliged to call on dear Lady Harbury. I hadn't been there since her poor husband's death. I never saw a woman so altered; she looks quite twenty years younger. And now I'll have a cup of tea, and one of those nice cucumber sandwiches you promised me.

ALGERNON: Certainly, Aunt Augusta.

(Goes over to tea table.)

LADY BRACKNELL: Won't you come and sit here, Gwendolen?

GWENDOLEN: Thanks, Mama, I'm quite comfortable where I am.

Wagnerian: Referring to the operas of Richard Wagner (1813–1883), whose music was popularly thought to be loud.

ALGERNON (*picking up empty plate in horror*): Good heavens! Lane! Why are there no cucumber sandwiches? I ordered them specially.

LANE (*gravely*): There were no cucumbers in the market this morning, sir. I went down twice.

ALGERNON: No cucumbers?

LANE: No, sir. Not even for ready money.

ALGERNON: That will do, Lane, thank you.

LANE: Thank you, sir. (*Goes out.*)

ALGERNON: I am greatly distressed, Aunt Augusta, about there being no cucumbers, not even for ready money.

LADY BRACKNELL: It really makes no matter, Algernon. I had some crumpets with Lady Harbury, who seems to me to be living entirely for pleasure now.

ALGERNON: I hear her hair has turned quite gold from grief.

LADY BRACKNELL: It certainly has changed its color. From what cause I, of course, cannot say. (*Algernon crosses and hands tea.*) Thank you. I've quite a treat for you tonight, Algernon. I am going to send you down with Mary Farquhar. She is such a nice woman, and so attentive to her husband. It's delightful to watch them.

ALGERNON: I am afraid, Aunt Augusta, I shall have to give up the pleasure of dining with you tonight after all.

LADY BRACKNELL (*frowning*): I hope not, Algernon. It would put my table completely out. Your uncle would have to dine upstairs. Fortunately he is accustomed to that.

ALGERNON: It is a great bore, and, I need hardly say, a terrible disappointment to me, but the fact is I have just had a telegram to say that my poor friend Bunbury is very ill again. (*Exchanges glances with Jack.*) They seem to think I should be with him.

LADY BRACKNELL: It is very strange. This Mr. Bunbury seems to suffer from curiously bad health.

ALGERNON: Yes; poor Bunbury is a dreadful invalid.

LADY BRACKNELL: Well, I must say, Algernon, that I think it is high time that Mr. Bunbury made up his mind whether he was going to live or to die. This shilly-shallying with the question is absurd. Nor do I in any way approve of the modern sympathy with invalids. I consider it morbid. Illness of any kind is hardly a thing to be encouraged in others. Health is the primary duty of life. I am always telling that to your poor uncle, but he never seems to take much notice — as far as any improvement in his ailments goes. I should be much obliged if you would ask Mr. Bunbury, from me, to be kind enough not to have a relapse on Saturday, for I rely on you to arrange my music for me. It is my last reception, and one wants something that will encourage conversation, particularly at the end of the season when everyone has practically said whatever they had to say, which, in most cases, was probably not much.

ALGERNON: I'll speak to Bunbury, Aunt Augusta, if he is still conscious, and I think I can promise you he'll be all right by Saturday. Of course the music is a great difficulty. You see, if one plays good music, people don't listen, and if one plays bad music people don't talk. But I'll run over the program I've drawn out, if you will kindly come into the next room for a moment.

LADY BRACKNELL: Thank you, Algernon. It is very thoughtful of you. (*Rising, and following Algernon.*) I'm sure the program will be delightful, after a few expurgations. French songs I cannot possibly allow. People always seem to think that they are improper, and either look shocked, which is vulgar, or laugh, which is worse. But German sounds a thoroughly respectable language, and indeed, I believe is so. Gwendolen, you will accompany me.

GWENDOLEN: Certainly, Mama.

(Lady Bracknell and Algernon go into the music room. Gwendolen remains behind.)

JACK: Charming day it has been, Miss Fairfax.

GWENDOLEN: Pray don't talk to me about the weather Mr. Worthing. Whenever people talk to me about the weather, I always feel quite certain that they mean something else. And that makes me so nervous.

JACK: I do mean something else.

GWENDOLEN: I thought so. In fact, I am never wrong.

JACK: And I would like to be allowed to take advantage of Lady Bracknell's temporary absence—

GWENDOLEN: I would certainly advise you to do so. Mama has a way of coming back suddenly into a room that I have often had to speak to her about.

JACK (*nervously*): Miss Fairfax, ever since I met you I have admired you more than any girl—I have ever met since—I met you.

GWENDOLEN: Yes, I am quite aware of the fact. And I often wish that in public, at any rate, you had been more demonstrative. For me you have always had an irresistible fascination. Even before I met you I was far from indifferent to you. (*Jack looks at her in amazement.*) We live, as I hope you know Mr. Worthing, in an age of ideals. The fact is constantly mentioned in the more expensive monthly magazines, and has reached the provincial pulpits I am told; and my ideal has always been to love someone of the name of Ernest. There is something in that name that inspires absolute confidence. The moment Algernon first mentioned to me that he had a friend called Ernest, I knew I was destined to love you.

JACK: You really love me, Gwendolen?

GWENDOLEN: Passionately!

JACK: Darling! You don't know how happy you've made me.

GWENDOLEN: My own Ernest!

JACK: But you don't mean to say that you couldn't love me if my name wasn't Ernest?

GWENDOLEN: But your name is Ernest.

JACK: Yes, I know it is. But supposing it was something else? Do you mean to say you couldn't love me then?

GWENDOLEN (*glibly*): Ah! that is clearly a metaphysical speculation, and like most metaphysical speculations has very little reference at all to the actual facts of real life, as we know them.

JACK: Personally, darling, to speak quite candidly, I don't much care about the name of Ernest—I don't think the name suits me at all.

GWENDOLEN: It suits you perfectly. It is a divine name. It has a music of its own. It produces vibrations.

JACK: Well, really, Gwendolen, I must say that I think there are lots of other much nicer names. I think Jack, for instance, a charming name.

GWENDOLEN: Jack?—No, there is very little music in the name Jack, if any at all, indeed. It does not thrill. It produces absolutely no vibrations—I have known several Jacks, and they all, without exception, were more than usually plain. Besides, Jack is a notorious domesticity for John! And I pity any woman who is married to a man called John. She would probably never be allowed to know the entrancing pleasure of a single moment's solitude. The only really safe name is Ernest.

JACK: Gwendolen, I must get christened at once—I mean we must get married at once. There is no time to be lost.

GWENDOLEN: Married, Mr. Worthing?

JACK (*astounded*): Well—surely. You know that I love you, and you led me to believe, Miss Fairfax, that you were not absolutely indifferent to me.

GWENDOLEN: I adore you. But you haven't proposed to me yet. Nothing has been said at all about marriage. The subject has not even been touched on.

JACK: Well—may I propose to you now?

GWENDOLEN: I think it would be an admirable opportunity. And to spare you any possible disappointment, Mr. Worthing, I think it only fair to tell you quite frankly beforehand that I am fully determined to accept you.

JACK: Gwendolen!

GWENDOLEN: Yes, Mr. Worthing, what have you got to say to me?

JACK: You know what I have got to say to you.

GWENDOLEN: Yes, but you don't say it.

JACK: Gwendolen, will you marry me?

(Goes on his knees.)

GWENDOLEN: Of course I will, darling. How long you have been about it! I am afraid you have had very little experience in how to propose.

JACK: My own one, I have never loved anyone in the world but you.

GWENDOLEN: Yes, but men often propose for practice. I know my brother Gerald does. All my girlfriends tell me so. What wonderfully blue eyes you have, Ernest! They are quite, quite blue. I hope you will always look at me just like that, especially when there are other people present.

(Enter Lady Bracknell.)

LADY BRACKNELL: Mr. Worthing! Rise, sir, from this semirecumbent posture. It is most indecorous.

GWENDOLEN: Mama! (*He tries to rise; she restrains him.*) I must beg you to retire. This is no place for you. Besides, Mr. Worthing has not quite finished yet.

LADY BRACKNELL: Finished what, may I ask?

GWENDOLEN: I am engaged to Mr. Worthing, Mama.

(They rise together.)

LADY BRACKNELL: Pardon me, you are not engaged to anyone. When you do become engaged to someone, I, or your father, should his health permit him, will inform you of the fact. An engagement should come on a young girl as a surprise, pleasant or unpleasant, as the case may be. It is hardly a matter that she could be allowed to arrange for herself — And now I have a few questions to put to you, Mr. Worthing. While I am making these inquiries, you, Gwendolen, will wait for me below in the carriage.

GWENDOLEN (*reproachfully*): Mama!

LADY BRACKNELL: In the carriage, Gwendolen! (*Gwendolen goes to the door. She and Jack blow kisses to each other behind Lady Bracknell's back. Lady Bracknell looks vaguely about as if she could not understand what the noise was. Finally turns round.*) Gwendolen, the carriage!

GWENDOLEN: Yes, Mama.

(*Goes out, looking back at Jack.*)

LADY BRACKNELL (*sitting down*): You can take a seat, Mr. Worthing.

(*Looks in her pocket for notebook and pencil.*)

JACK: Thank you, Lady Bracknell, I prefer standing.

LADY BRACKNELL (*pencil and notebook in hand*): I feel bound to tell you that you are not down on my list of eligible young men, although I have the same list as the dear Duchess of Bolton has. We work together, in fact. However, I am quite ready to enter your name, should your answers be what a really affectionate mother requires. Do you smoke?

JACK: Well, yes, I must admit I smoke.

LADY BRACKNELL: I am glad to hear it. A man should always have an occupation of some kind. There are far too many idle men in London as it is. How old are you?

JACK: Twenty-nine.

LADY BRACKNELL: A very good age to be married at. I have always been of opinion that a man who desires to get married should know either everything or nothing. Which do you know?

JACK (*after some hesitation*): I know nothing, Lady Bracknell.

LADY BRACKNELL: I am pleased to hear it. I do not approve of anything that tampers with natural ignorance. Ignorance is like a delicate exotic fruit; touch it and the bloom is gone. The whole theory of modern education is radically unsound. Fortunately in England, at any rate, education produces no effect whatsoever. If it did, it would prove a serious danger to the upper classes, and probably lead to acts of violence in Grosvenor Square. What is your income?

JACK: Between seven and eight thousand a year.

LADY BRACKNELL (*makes a note in her book*): In land, or in investments?

JACK: In investments, chiefly.

LADY BRACKNELL: That is satisfactory. What between the duties expected of one during one's lifetime, and the duties exacted from one after one's death, land has ceased to be either a profit or a pleasure. It gives one position, and prevents one from keeping it up. That's all that can be said about land.

JACK: I have a country house with some land, of course, attached to it, about fifteen hundred acres, I believe; but I don't depend on that for my real income.

In fact, as far as I can make out, the poachers are the only people who make anything out of it.

LADY BRACKNELL: A country house! How many bedrooms? Well, that point can be cleared up afterwards. You have a town house, I hope? A girl with a simple, unspoiled nature, like Gwendolen, could hardly be expected to reside in the country.

JACK: Well, I own a house in Belgrave Square, but it is let by the year to Lady Bloxham. Of course, I can get it back whenever I like, at six months' notice.

LADY BRACKNELL: Lady Bloxham? I don't know her.

JACK: Oh, she goes about very little. She is a lady considerably advanced in years.

LADY BRACKNELL: Ah, nowadays that is no guarantee of respectability of character. What number in Belgrave Square?

JACK: 149.

LADY BRACKNELL (*shaking her head*): The unfashionable side. I thought there was something. However, that could easily be altered.

JACK: Do you mean the fashion, or the side?

LADY BRACKNELL (*sternly*): Both, if necessary, I presume. What are your politics?

JACK: Well, I am afraid I really have none. I am a Liberal Unionist.

LADY BRACKNELL: Oh, they count as Tories. They dine with us. Or come in the evening, at any rate. Now to minor matters. Are your parents living?

JACK: I have lost both my parents.

LADY BRACKNELL: Both? To lose one parent may be regarded as a misfortune—to lose *both* seems like carelessness. Who was your father? He was evidently a man of some wealth. Was he born in what the Radical papers call the purple of commerce, or did he rise from the ranks of the aristocracy?

JACK: I am afraid I really don't know. The fact is, Lady Bracknell, I said I had lost my parents. It would be nearer the truth to say that my parents seem to have lost me—I don't actually know who I am by birth. I was—well, I was found.

LADY BRACKNELL: Found!

JACK: The late Mr. Thomas Cardew, an old gentleman of a very charitable and kindly disposition, found me, and gave me the name of Worthing, because he happened to have a first-class ticket for Worthing in his pocket at the time. Worthing is a place in Sussex. It is a seaside resort.

LADY BRACKNELL: Where did the charitable gentleman who had a first-class ticket for this seaside resort find you?

JACK (*gravely*): In a handbag.

LADY BRACKNELL: A handbag?

JACK (*very seriously*): Yes, Lady Bracknell. I was in a handbag—a somewhat large, black leather handbag, with handles to it—an ordinary handbag in fact.

LADY BRACKNELL: In what locality did this Mr. James, or Thomas, Cardew come across this ordinary handbag?

JACK: In the cloakroom at Victoria Station. It was given to him in mistake for his own.

LADY BRACKNELL: The cloakroom at Victoria Station?

JACK: Yes. The Brighton line.

LADY BRACKNELL: The line is immaterial. Mr. Worthing, I confess I feel somewhat bewildered by what you have just told me. To be born, or at any rate bred, in a handbag, whether it had handles or not, seems to me to display a contempt for the ordinary decencies of family life that reminds one of the worst excesses of the French Revolution. And I presume you know what that unfortunate movement led to? As for the particular locality in which the handbag was found, a cloakroom at a railway station might serve to conceal a social indiscretion—has probably, indeed, been used for that purpose before now—but it could hardly be regarded as an assured basis for a recognized position in good society.

JACK: May I ask you then what you would advise me to do? I need hardly say I would do anything in the world to ensure Gwendolen's happiness.

LADY BRACKNELL: I would strongly advise you, Mr. Worthing, to try and acquire some relations as soon as possible, and to make a definite effort to produce at any rate one parent of either sex, before the season is quite over.

JACK: Well, I don't see how I could possibly manage to do that. I can produce the handbag at any moment. It is in my dressing room at home. I really think that should satisfy you, Lady Bracknell.

LADY BRACKNELL: Me, sir! What has it to do with me? You can hardly imagine that I and Lord Bracknell would dream of allowing our only daughter—a girl brought up with the utmost care—to marry into a cloakroom, and form an alliance with a parcel? Good morning, Mr. Worthing!

(Lady Bracknell sweeps out in majestic indignation.)

JACK: Good morning! (*Algernon, from the other room, strikes up the Wedding March. Jack looks perfectly furious, and goes to the door.*) For goodness' sake don't play that ghastly tune, Algy! How idiotic you are!

(The music stops, and Algernon enters cheerily.)

ALGERNON: Didn't it go off all right, old boy? You don't mean to say Gwendolen refused you? I know it is a way she has. She is always refusing people. I think it is most ill-natured of her.

JACK: Oh, Gwendolen is as right as a trivet. As far as she is concerned, we are engaged. Her mother is perfectly unbearable. Never met such a Gorgon°—I don't really know what a Gorgon is like, but I am quite sure that Lady Bracknell is one. In any case, she is a monster, without being a myth, which is rather unfair. I beg your pardon, Algy, I suppose I shouldn't talk about your own aunt in that way before you.

ALGERNON: My dear boy, I love hearing my relations abused. It is the only thing that makes me put up with them at all. Relations are simply a tedious pack of people, who haven't got the remotest knowledge of how to live, nor the smallest instinct about when to die.

JACK: Oh, that is nonsense!

ALGERNON: It isn't!

Gorgon: In Greek myth, one of three very ugly sisters who had, among other characteristics, serpents for hair.

JACK: Well, I won't argue about the matter. You always want to argue about things.

ALGERNON: That is exactly what things were originally made for.

JACK: Upon my word, if I thought that, I'd shoot myself — (*A pause.*) You don't think there is any chance of Gwendolen becoming like her mother in about a hundred and fifty years, do you Algy?

ALGERNON: All women become like their mothers. That is their tragedy. No man does. That's his.

JACK: Is that clever?

ALGERNON: It is perfectly phrased! and quite as true as any observation in civilized life should be.

JACK: I am sick to death of cleverness. Everybody is clever nowadays. You can't go anywhere without meeting clever people. The thing has become an absolute public nuisance. I wish to goodness we had a few fools left.

ALGERNON: We have.

JACK: I should extremely like to meet them. What do they talk about?

ALGERNON: The fools? Oh! about the clever people, of course.

JACK: What fools!

ALGERNON: By the way, did you tell Gwendolen the truth about your being Ernest in town, and Jack in the country?

JACK (*in a very patronizing manner*): My dear fellow, the truth isn't quite the sort of thing one tells to a nice sweet refined girl. What extraordinary ideas you have about the way to behave to a woman!

ALGERNON: The only way to behave to a woman is to make love to her if she is pretty, and to someone else if she is plain.

JACK: Oh, that is nonsense.

ALGERNON: What about your brother? What about the profligate Ernest?

JACK: Oh, before the end of the week I shall have got rid of him. I'll say he died in Paris of apoplexy. Lots of people die of apoplexy, quite suddenly, don't they?

ALGERNON: Yes, but it's hereditary, my dear fellow. It's a sort of thing that runs in families. You had much better say a severe chill.

JACK: You are sure a severe chill isn't hereditary, or anything of that kind?

ALGERNON: Of course it isn't!

JACK: Very well, then. My poor brother Ernest is carried off suddenly in Paris, by a severe chill. That gets rid of him.

ALGERNON: But I thought you said that — Miss Cardew was a little too much interested in your poor brother Ernest? Won't she feel his loss a good deal?

JACK: Oh, that is all right. Cecily is not a silly romantic girl, I am glad to say. She has got a capital appetite, goes on long walks, and pays no attention at all to her lessons.

ALGERNON: I would rather like to see Cecily.

JACK: I will take very good care you never do. She is excessively pretty, and she is only just eighteen.

ALGERNON: Have you told Gwendolen yet that you have an excessively pretty ward who is only just eighteen?

JACK: Oh! one doesn't blurt these things out to people. Cecily and Gwendolen are perfectly certain to be extremely great friends. I'll bet you anything you like that half an hour after they have met, they will be calling each other sister.

ALGERNON: Women only do that when they have called each other a lot of other things first. Now, my dear boy, if we want to get a good table at Willis's, we really must go and dress. Do you know it is nearly seven?

JACK (*irritably*): Oh! it always is nearly seven.

ALGERNON: Well, I'm hungry.

JACK: I never knew you when you weren't—

ALGERNON: What shall we do after dinner? Go to a theater?

JACK: Oh, no! I loathe listening.

ALGERNON: Well, let us go to the Club?

JACK: Oh, no! I hate talking.

ALGERNON: Well, we might trot round to the Empire° at ten?

JACK: Oh, no! I can't bear looking at things. It is so silly.

ALGERNON: Well, what shall we do?

JACK: Nothing!

ALGERNON: It is awfully hard work doing nothing. However, I don't mind hard work where there is no definite object of any kind.

(Enter Lane.)

LANE: Miss Fairfax.

(Enter Gwendolen. Lane goes out.)

ALGERNON: Gwendolen, upon my word!

GWENDOLEN: Algy, kindly turn your back. I have something very particular to say to Mr. Worthing.

ALGERNON: Really, Gwendolen, I don't think I can allow this at all.

GWENDOLEN: Algy, you always adopt a strictly immoral attitude towards life. You are not quite old enough to do that.

(Algernon retires to the fireplace.)

JACK: My own darling!

GWENDOLEN: Ernest, we may never be married. From the expression on Mama's face I fear we never shall. Few parents nowadays pay any regard to what their children say to them. The old-fashioned respect for the young is fast dying out. Whatever influence I ever had over Mama, I lost at the age of three. But although she may prevent us from becoming man and wife, and I may marry someone else, and marry often, nothing that she can possibly do can alter my eternal devotion to you.

JACK: Dear Gwendolen!

GWENDOLEN: The story of your romantic origin, as related to me by Mama, with unpleasing comments, has naturally stirred the deeper fibers of my nature. Your Christian name has an irresistible fascination. The simplicity of your

Empire: Empire Theatre, a London music hall that was also a rendezvous for prostitutes.

character makes you exquisitely incomprehensible to me. Your town address at the Albany I have. What is your address in the country?

JACK: The Manor House, Woolton, Hertfordshire.

(Algernon, who has been carefully listening, smiles to himself, and writes the address on his shirt cuff. Then picks up the Railway Guide.)

GWENDOLEN: There is a good postal service, I suppose? It may be necessary to do something desperate. That of course will require serious consideration. I will communicate with you daily.

JACK: My own one!

GWENDOLEN: How long do you remain in town?

JACK: Till Monday.

GWENDOLEN: Good! Algy, you may turn round now.

ALGERNON: Thanks, I've turned round already.

GWENDOLEN: You may also ring the bell.

JACK: You will let me see you to your carriage, my own darling?

GWENDOLEN: Certainly.

JACK (*to Lane, who now enters*): I will see Miss Fairfax out.

LANE: Yes, sir. *(Jack and Gwendolen go off.)*

(Lane presents several letters on a salver to Algernon. It is to be surmised that they are bills, as Algernon, after looking at the envelopes, tears them up.)

ALGERNON: A glass of sherry, Lane.

LANE: Yes, sir.

ALGERNON: Tomorrow, Lane, I'm going Bunburying.

LANE: Yes, sir.

ALGERNON: I shall probably not be back till Monday. You can put up my dress clothes, my smoking jacket, and all the Bunbury suits—

LANE: Yes, sir. (*Handing sherry.*)

ALGERNON: I hope tomorrow will be a fine day, Lane.

LANE: It never is, sir.

ALGERNON: Lane, you're a perfect pessimist.

LANE: I do my best to give satisfaction, sir.

(Enter Jack. Lane goes off.)

JACK: There's a sensible, intellectual girl! the only girl I ever cared for in my life. (*Algernon is laughing immoderately.*) What on earth are you so amused at?

ALGERNON: Oh, I'm a little anxious about poor Bunbury, that is all.

JACK: If you don't take care, your friend Bunbury will get you into a serious scrape some day.

ALGERNON: I love scrapes. They are the only things that are never serious.

JACK: Oh, that's nonsense, Algy. You never talk anything but nonsense.

ALGERNON: Nobody ever does.

(Jack looks indignantly at him, and leaves the room. Algernon lights a cigarette, reads his shirt cuff, and smiles.)

ACT II

(Scene: Garden at the Manor House. A flight of gray stone steps leads up to the house. The garden, an old-fashioned one, full of roses. Time of year, July. Basket chairs, and a table covered with books, are set under a large yew tree. Miss Prism discovered seated at the table. Cecily is at the back watering flowers.)

MISS PRISM (*calling*): Cecily, Cecily! Surely such a utilitarian occupation as the watering of flowers is rather Moulton's duty than yours? Especially at a moment when intellectual pleasures await you. Your German grammar is on the table. Pray open it at page fifteen. We will repeat yesterday's lesson.

CECILY (*coming over very slowly*): But I don't like German. It isn't at all a becoming language. I know perfectly well that I look quite plain after my German lesson.

MISS PRISM: Child, you know how anxious your guardian is that you should improve yourself in every way. He laid particular stress on your German, as he was leaving for town yesterday. Indeed, he always lays stress on your German when he is leaving for town.

CECILY: Dear Uncle Jack is so very serious! Sometimes he is so serious that I think he cannot be quite well.

MISS PRISM (*drawing herself up*): Your guardian enjoys the best of health, and his gravity of demeanor is especially to be commended in one so comparatively young as he is. I know no one who has a higher sense of duty and responsibility.

CECILY: I suppose that is why he often looks a little bored when we three are together.

MISS PRISM: Cecily! I am surprised at you. Mr. Worthing has many troubles in his life. Idle merriment and triviality would be out of place in his conversation. You must remember his constant anxiety about that unfortunate young man his brother.

CECILY: I wish Uncle Jack would allow that unfortunate young man, his brother, to come down here sometimes. We might have a good influence over him, Miss Prism. I am sure you certainly would. You know German, and geology, and things of that kind influence a man very much.

(Cecily begins to write in her diary.)

MISS PRISM (*shaking her head*): I do not think that even I could produce any effect on a character that according to his own brother's admission is irretrievably weak and vacillating. Indeed I am not sure that I would desire to reclaim him. I am not in favor of this modern mania for turning bad people into good people at a moment's notice. As a man sows so let him reap. You must put away your diary, Cecily. I really don't see why you should keep a diary at all.

CECILY: I keep a diary in order to enter the wonderful secrets of my life. If I didn't write them down I should probably forget all about them.

MISS PRISM: Memory, my dear Cecily, is the diary that we all carry about with us.

CECILY: Yes, but it usually chronicles the things that have never happened, and couldn't possibly have happened. I believe that Memory is responsible for nearly all the three-volume novels that Mudie° sends us.

MISS PRISM: Do not speak slightingly of the three-volume novel, Cecily. I wrote one myself in earlier days.

CECILY: Did you really, Miss Prism? How wonderfully clever you are! I hope it did not end happily? I don't like novels that end happily. They depress me so much.

MISS PRISM: The good ended happily, and the bad unhappily. That is what Fiction means.

CECILY: I suppose so. But it seems very unfair. And was your novel ever published?

MISS PRISM: Alas! no. The manuscript unfortunately was abandoned. I use the word in the sense of lost or mislaid. To your work, child, these speculations are profitless.

CECILY (*smiling*): But I see dear Dr. Chasuble coming up through the garden.

MISS PRISM (*rising and advancing*): Dr. Chasuble! This is indeed a pleasure.

(Enter Canon Chasuble.)

CHASUBLE: And how are we this morning? Miss Prism, you are, I trust, well?

CECILY: Miss Prism has just been complaining of a slight headache. I think it would do her so much good to have a short stroll with you in the park, Dr. Chasuble.

MISS PRISM: Cecily, I have not mentioned anything about a headache.

CECILY: No, dear Miss Prism, I know that, but I felt instinctively that you had a headache. Indeed I was thinking about that, and not about my German lesson, when the Rector came in.

CHASUBLE: I hope, Cecily, you are not inattentive.

CECILY: Oh, I am afraid I am.

CHASUBLE: That is strange. Were I fortunate enough to be Miss Prism's pupil, I would hang upon her lips. (*Miss Prism glares.*) I spoke metaphorically.—My metaphor was drawn from bees. Ahem! Mr. Worthing, I suppose, has not returned from town yet?

MISS PRISM: We do not expect him till Monday afternoon.

CHASUBLE: Ah yes, he usually likes to spend his Sunday in London. He is not one of those whose sole aim is enjoyment, as, by all accounts, that unfortunate young man his brother seems to be. But I must not disturb Egeria° and her pupil any longer.

MISS PRISM: Egeria? My name is Laetitia, Doctor.

CHASUBLE (*bowing*): A classical allusion merely, drawn from the Pagan authors. I shall see you both no doubt at Evensong?

MISS PRISM: I think, dear Doctor, I will have a stroll with you. I find I have a headache after all, and a walk might do it good.

CHASUBLE: With pleasure, Miss Prism, with pleasure. We might go as far as the schools and back.

Mudie: A well-known lending library of the time, established by Charles Edward Mudie.
Egeria: Roman goddess of water.

MISS PRISM: That would be delightful. Cecily, you will read your Political Economy in my absence. The chapter on the Fall of the Rupee° you may omit. It is somewhat too sensational. Even these metallic problems have their melodramatic side.

(Goes down the garden with Dr. Chasuble.)

CECILY (*picks up books and throws them back on table*): Horrid Political Economy! Horrid Geography! Horrid, horrid German!

(Enter Merriman with a card on a salver.)

MERRIMAN: Mr. Ernest Worthing has just driven over from the station. He has brought his luggage with him.

CECILY (*takes the card and reads it*): "Mr. Ernest Worthing, B.4, The Albany, W." Uncle Jack's brother! Did you tell him Mr. Worthing was in town?

MERRIMAN: Yes, Miss. He seemed very much disappointed. I mentioned that you and Miss Prism were in the garden. He said he was anxious to speak to you privately for a moment.

CECILY: Ask Mr. Ernest Worthing to come here. I suppose you had better talk to the housekeeper about a room for him.

MERRIMAN: Yes, Miss. (*Merriman goes off.*)

CECILY: I have never met any really wicked person before. I feel rather frightened. I am so afraid he will look just like everyone else.

(Enter Algernon, very gay and debonair.)

He does!

ALGERNON (*raising his hat*): You are my little cousin Cecily, I'm sure.

CECILY: You are under some strange mistake. I am not little. In fact, I believe I am more than usually tall for my age. (*Algernon is rather taken aback.*) But I am your cousin Cecily. You, I see from your card, are Uncle Jack's brother, my cousin Ernest, my wicked cousin Ernest.

ALGERNON: Oh! I am not really wicked at all, Cousin Cecily. You mustn't think that I am wicked.

CECILY: If you are not, then you have certainly been deceiving us all in a very inexcusable manner. I hope you have not been leading a double life, pretending to be wicked and being really good all the time. That would be hypocrisy.

ALGERNON (*looks at her in amazement*): Oh! Of course I have been rather reckless.

CECILY: I am glad to hear it.

ALGERNON: In fact, now you mention the subject, I have been very bad in my own small way.

CECILY: I don't think you should be so proud of that, though I am sure it must have been very pleasant.

ALGERNON: It is much pleasanter being here with you.

CECILY: I can't understand how you are here at all. Uncle Jack won't be back till Monday afternoon.

Fall of the Rupee: Reference to the Indian rupee, whose steady deflation between 1873 and 1893 caused the Indian government finally to close the mints.

ALGERNON: That is a great disappointment. I am obliged to go up by the first train on Monday morning. I have a business appointment that I am anxious—to miss.

CECILY: Couldn't you miss it anywhere but in London?

ALGERNON: No: the appointment is in London.

CECILY: Well, I know, of course, how important it is not to keep a business engagement, if one wants to retain any sense of the beauty of life, but still I think you had better wait till Uncle Jack arrives. I know he wants to speak to you about your emigrating.

ALGERNON: About my what?

CECILY: Your emigrating. He has gone up to buy your outfit.

ALGERNON: I certainly wouldn't let Jack buy my outfit. He has no taste in neckties at all.

CECILY: I don't think you will require neckties. Uncle Jack is sending you to Australia.

ALGERNON: Australia! I'd sooner die.

CECILY: Well, he said at dinner on Wednesday night, that you would have to choose between this world, the next world, and Australia.

ALGERNON: Oh, well! The accounts I have received of Australia and the next world are not particularly encouraging. This world is good enough for me, Cousin Cecily.

CECILY: Yes, but are you good enough for it?

ALGERNON: I'm afraid I'm not that. That is why I want you to reform me. You might make that your mission, if you don't mind, Cousin Cecily.

CECILY: I'm afraid I've no time, this afternoon.

ALGERNON: Well, would you mind my reforming myself this afternoon?

CECILY: It is rather quixotic° of you. But I think you should try.

ALGERNON: I will. I feel better already.

CECILY: You are looking a little worse.

ALGERNON: That is because I am hungry.

CECILY: How thoughtless of me. I should have remembered that when one is going to lead an entirely new life, one requires regular and wholesome meals. Won't you come in?

ALGERNON: Thank you. Might I have a buttonhole° first? I never have any appetite unless I have a buttonhole first.

CECILY: A Maréchal Niel?°

ALGERNON: No, I'd sooner have a pink rose.

CECILY: Why? *(Cuts a flower.)*

ALGERNON: Because you are like a pink rose, Cousin Cecily.

CECILY: I don't think it can be right for you to talk to me like that. Miss Prism never says such things to me.

quixotic: Foolishly impractical, from the idealistic hero of Cervantes' Don Quixote.
buttonhole: Boutonniere.
Maréchal Niel: A yellow rose named for a French military hero, i.e., a rose appropriate for a man.

ALGERNON: Then Miss Prism is a shortsighted old lady. (*Cecily puts the rose in his buttonhole.*) You are the prettiest girl I ever saw.

CECILY: Miss Prism says that all good looks are a snare.

ALGERNON: They are a snare that every sensible man would like to be caught in.

CECILY: Oh! I don't think I would care to catch a sensible man. I shouldn't know what to talk to him about.

(*They pass into the house. Miss Prism and Dr. Chasuble return.*)

MISS PRISM: You are too much alone, dear Dr. Chasuble. You should get married. A misanthrope I can understand—a womanthrope, never!

CHASUBLE (*with a scholar's shudder*): Believe me, I do not deserve so neologistic a phrase. The precept as well as the practice of the Primitive Church was distinctly against matrimony.

MISS PRISM (*sententiously*): That is obviously the reason why the Primitive Church has not lasted up to the present day. And you do not seem to realize, dear Doctor, that by persistently remaining single, a man converts himself into a permanent public temptation. Men should be more careful; this very celibacy leads weaker vessels astray.

CHASUBLE: But is a man not equally attractive when married?

MISS PRISM: No married man is ever attractive except to his wife.

CHASUBLE: And often, I've been told, not even to her.

MISS PRISM: That depends on the intellectual sympathies of the woman. Maturity can always be depended on. Ripeness can be trusted. Young women are green. (*Dr. Chasuble starts.*) I spoke horticulturally. My metaphor was drawn from fruits. But where is Cecily?

CHASUBLE: Perhaps she followed us to the schools.

(*Enter Jack slowly from the back of the garden. He is dressed in the deepest mourning, with crepe hatband and black gloves.*)

MISS PRISM: Mr. Worthing!

CHASUBLE: Mr. Worthing?

MISS PRISM: This is indeed a surprise. We did not look for you till Monday afternoon.

JACK (*shakes Miss Prism's hand in a tragic manner*): I have returned sooner than I expected. Dr. Chasuble, I hope you are well?

CHASUBLE: Dear Mr. Worthing, I trust this garb of woe does not betoken some terrible calamity?

JACK: My brother.

MISS PRISM: More shameful debts and extravagance?

CHASUBLE: Still leading his life of pleasure?

JACK (*shaking his head*): Dead!

CHASUBLE: Your brother Ernest dead?

JACK: Quite dead.

MISS PRISM: What a lesson for him! I trust he will profit by it.

CHASUBLE: Mr. Worthing, I offer you my sincere condolence. You have at least the consolation of knowing that you were always the most generous and forgiving of brothers.

JACK: Poor Ernest! He had many faults, but it is a sad, sad blow.

CHASUBLE: Very sad indeed. Were you with him at the end?

JACK: No. He died abroad, in Paris, in fact. I had a telegram last night from the manager of the Grand Hotel.

CHASUBLE: Was the cause of death mentioned?

JACK: A severe chill, it seems.

MISS PRISM: As a man sows, so shall he reap.

CHASUBLE (*raising his hand*): Charity, dear Miss Prism, charity! None of us are perfect. I myself am peculiarly susceptible to drafts. Will the interment take place here?

JACK: No. He seemed to have expressed a desire to be buried in Paris.

CHASUBLE: In Paris! (*Shakes his head.*) I fear that hardly points to any very serious state of mind at the last. You would no doubt wish me to make some slight allusion to this tragic domestic affliction next Sunday. (*Jack presses his hand convulsively.*) My sermon on the meaning of the manna in the wilderness can be adapted to almost any occasion, joyful, or, as in the present case, distressing. (*All sigh.*) I have preached it at harvest celebrations, christenings, confirmations, on days of humiliation and festal days. The last time I delivered it was in the Cathedral, as a charity sermon on behalf of the Society for the Prevention of Discontent among the Upper Orders. The Bishop, who was present, was much struck by some of the analogies I drew.

JACK: Ah! that reminds me, you mentioned christenings I think, Dr. Chasuble? I suppose you know how to christen all right? (*Dr. Chasuble looks astounded.*) I mean, of course, you are continually christening, aren't you?

MISS PRISM: It is, I regret to say, one of the Rector's most constant duties in this parish. I have often spoken to the poorer classes on the subject. But they don't seem to know what thrift is.

CHASUBLE: But is there any particular infant in whom you are interested, Mr. Worthing? Your brother was, I believe, unmarried, was he not?

JACK: Oh yes.

MISS PRISM (*bitterly*): People who live entirely for pleasure usually are.

JACK: But it is not for any child, dear Doctor. I am very fond of children. No! the fact is, I would like to be christened myself, this afternoon, if you have nothing better to do.

CHASUBLE: But surely, Mr. Worthing, you have been christened already?

JACK: I don't remember anything about it.

CHASUBLE: But have you any grave doubts on the subject?

JACK: I certainly intend to have. Of course I don't know if the thing would bother you in any way, or if you think I am a little too old now.

CHASUBLE: Not at all. The sprinkling, and, indeed, the immersion of adults is a perfectly canonical practice.

JACK: Immersion!

CHASUBLE: You need have no apprehensions. Sprinkling is all that is necessary, or indeed I think advisable. Our weather is so changeable. At what hour would you wish the ceremony performed?

JACK: Oh, I might trot round about five if that would suit you.

CHASUBLE: Perfectly, perfectly! In fact I have two similar ceremonies to perform at that time. A case of twins that occurred recently in one of the outlying cottages on your own estate. Poor Jenkins the carter, a most hardworking man.

JACK: Oh! I don't see much fun in being christened along with other babies. It would be childish. Would half-past five do?

CHASUBLE: Admirably! Admirably! (*Takes out watch.*) And now, dear Mr. Worthing, I will not intrude any longer into a house of sorrow. I would merely beg you not to be too much bowed down by grief. What seem to us bitter trials are often blessings in disguise.

MISS PRISM: This seems to me a blessing of an extremely obvious kind.

(Enter Cecily from the house.)

CECILY: Uncle Jack! Oh, I am pleased to see you back. But what horrid clothes you have got on! Do go and change them.

MISS PRISM: Cecily!

CHASUBLE: My child! my child!

(Cecily goes towards Jack; he kisses her brow in a melancholy manner.)

CECILY: What is the matter, Uncle Jack? Do look happy! You look as if you had toothache, and I have got such a surprise for you. Who do you think is in the dining room? Your brother!

JACK: Who?

CECILY: Your brother Ernest. He arrived about half an hour ago.

JACK: What nonsense! I haven't got a brother.

CECILY: Oh, don't say that. However badly he may have behaved to you in the past he is still your brother. You couldn't be so heartless as to disown him. I'll tell him to come out. And you will shake hands with him, won't you, Uncle Jack?

(Runs back into the house.)

CHASUBLE: These are very joyful tidings.

MISS PRISM: After we had all been resigned to his loss, his sudden return seems to me peculiarly distressing.

JACK: My brother is in the dining room? I don't know what it all means. I think it is perfectly absurd.

(Enter Algernon and Cecily hand in hand. They come slowly up to Jack.)

JACK: Good heavens! *(Motions Algernon away.)*

ALGERNON: Brother John, I have come down from town to tell you that I am very sorry for all the trouble I have given you, and that I intend to lead a better life in the future.

(Jack glares at him and does not take his hand.)

CECILY: Uncle Jack, you are not going to refuse your own brother's hand?

JACK: Nothing will induce me to take his hand. I think his coming down here disgraceful. He knows perfectly well why.

CECILY: Uncle Jack, do be nice. There is some good in everyone. Ernest has just been telling me about his poor invalid friend Mr. Bunbury whom he goes to visit so often. And surely there must be much good in one who is kind to an invalid, and leaves the pleasures of London to sit by a bed of pain.

JACK: Oh! he has been talking about Bunbury has he?

CECILY: Yes, he has told me all about poor Mr. Bunbury, and his terrible state of health.

JACK: Bunbury! Well, I won't have him talk to you about Bunbury or about anything else. It is enough to drive one perfectly frantic.

ALGERNON: Of course I admit that the faults were all on my side. But I must say that I think that Brother John's coldness to me is peculiarly painful. I expected a more enthusiastic welcome, especially considering it is the first time I have come here.

CECILY: Uncle Jack, if you don't shake hands with Ernest I will never forgive you.

JACK: Never forgive me?

CECILY: Never, never, never!

JACK: Well, this is the last time I shall ever do it.

(Shakes hands with Algernon and glares.)

CHASUBLE: It's pleasant, is it not, to see so perfect a reconciliation? I think we might leave the two brothers together.

MISS PRISM: Cecily, you will come with us.

CECILY: Certainly, Miss Prism. My little task of reconciliation is over.

CHASUBLE: You have done a beautiful action today, dear child.

MISS PRISM: We must not be premature in our judgments.

CECILY: I feel very happy. *(They all go off.)*

JACK: You young scoundrel, Algy, you must get out of this place as soon as possible. I don't allow any Bunburying here.

(Enter Merriman.)

MERRIMAN: I have put Mr. Ernest's things in the room next to yours, sir. I suppose that is all right?

JACK: What?

MERRIMAN: Mr. Ernest's luggage, sir. I have unpacked it and put it in the room next to your own.

JACK: His luggage?

MERRIMAN: Yes, sir. Three portmanteaus, a dressing case, two hatboxes, and a large luncheon basket.

ALGERNON: I am afraid I can't stay more than a week this time.

JACK: Merriman, order the dog cart at once. Mr. Ernest has been suddenly called back to town.

MERRIMAN: Yes, sir. *(Goes back into the house.)*

ALGERNON: What a fearful liar you are, Jack. I have not been called back to town at all.

JACK: Yes, you have.

ALGERNON: I haven't heard anyone call me.

JACK: Your duty as a gentleman calls you back.

ALGERNON: My duty as a gentleman has never interfered with my pleasures in the smallest degree.

JACK: I can quite understand that.

ALGERNON: Well, Cecily is a darling.

JACK: You are not to talk of Miss Cardew like that. I don't like it.

ALGERNON: Well, I don't like your clothes. You look perfectly ridiculous in them. Why on earth don't you go up and change? It is perfectly childish to be in deep mourning for a man who is actually staying for a whole week in your house as a guest. I call it grotesque.

JACK: You are certainly not staying with me for a whole week as a guest or anything else. You have got to leave—by the four-five train.

ALGERNON: I certainly won't leave you so long as you are in mourning. It would be most unfriendly. If I were in mourning you would stay with me, I suppose. I should think it very unkind if you didn't.

JACK: Well, will you go if I change my clothes?

ALGERNON: Yes, if you are not too long. I never saw anybody take so long to dress, and with such little result.

JACK: Well, at any rate, that is better than being always overdressed as you are.

ALGERNON: If I am occasionally a little overdressed, I make up for it by being always immensely overeducated.

JACK: Your vanity is ridiculous, your conduct an outrage, and your presence in my garden utterly absurd. However, you have got to catch the four-five, and I hope you will have a pleasant journey back to town. This Bunburying, as you call it, has not been a great success for you.

(Goes into the house.)

ALGERNON: I think it has been a great success. I'm in love with Cecily, and that is everything.

(Enter Cecily at the back of the garden. She picks up the can and begins to water the flowers.)

But I must see her before I go, and make arrangements for another Bunbury. Ah, there she is.

CECILY: Oh, I merely came back to water the roses. I thought you were with Uncle Jack.

ALGERNON: He's gone to order the dog cart for me.

CECILY: Oh, is he going to take you for a nice drive?

ALGERNON: He's going to send me away.

CECILY: Then have we got to part?

ALGERNON: I am afraid so. It's a very painful parting.

CECILY: It is always painful to part from people whom one has known for a very brief space of time. The absence of old friends one can endure with equanimity. But even a momentary separation from anyone to whom one has just been introduced is almost unbearable.

ALGERNON: Thank you.

(Enter Merriman.)

MERRIMAN: The dog cart is at the door, sir.

(Algernon looks appealingly at Cecily.)

CECILY: It can wait, Merriman — for — five minutes.

MERRIMAN: Yes, miss. *(Exit Merriman.)*

ALGERNON: I hope, Cecily, I shall not offend you if I state quite frankly and openly that you seem to me to be in every way the visible personification of absolute perfection.

CECILY: I think your frankness does you great credit, Ernest. If you will allow me I will copy your remarks into my diary.

(Goes over to table and begins writing in diary.)

ALGERNON: Do you really keep a diary? I'd give anything to look at it. May I?

CECILY: Oh no. (*Puts her hand over it.*) You see, it is simply a very young girl's record of her own thoughts and impressions, and consequently meant for publication. When it appears in volume form I hope you will order a copy. But pray, Ernest, don't stop. I delight in taking down from dictation. I have reached "absolute perfection." You can go on. I am quite ready for more.

ALGERNON (*somewhat taken aback*): Ahem! Ahem!

CECILY: Oh, don't cough, Ernest. When one is dictating one should speak fluently and not cough. Besides, I don't know how to spell a cough.

(Writes as Algernon speaks.)

ALGERNON (*speaking very rapidly*): Cecily, ever since I first looked upon your wonderful and incomparable beauty, I have dared to love you wildly, passionately, devotedly, hopelessly.

CECILY: I don't think that you should tell me that you love me wildly, passionately, devotedly, hopelessly. Hopelessly doesn't seem to make much sense, does it?

ALGERNON: Cecily!

(Enter Merriman.)

MERRIMAN: The dog cart is waiting, sir.

ALGERNON: Tell it to come round next week, at the same hour.

MERRIMAN (*looks at Cecily, who makes no sign*): Yes, sir.

(Merriman retires.)

CECILY: Uncle Jack would be very much annoyed if he knew you were staying on till next week, at the same hour.

ALGERNON: Oh, I don't care about Jack. I don't care for anybody in the whole world but you. I love you, Cecily. You will marry me, won't you?

CECILY: You silly boy! Of course. Why, we have been engaged for the last three months.

ALGERNON: For the last three months?

CECILY: Yes, it will be exactly three months on Thursday.

ALGERNON: But how did we become engaged?

CECILY: Well, ever since dear Uncle Jack first confessed to us that he had a younger brother who was very wicked and bad, you of course have formed the chief topic of conversation between myself and Miss Prism. And of course a man who is much talked about is always very attractive. One feels there must be something in him after all. I daresay it was foolish of me, but I fell in love with you, Ernest.

ALGERNON: Darling! And when was the engagement actually settled?

CECILY: On the 14th of February last. Worn out by your entire ignorance of my existence, I determined to end the matter one way or the other, and after a long struggle with myself I accepted you under this dear old tree here. The next day I bought this little ring in your name, and this is the little bangle with the true lovers' knot I promised you always to wear.

ALGERNON: Did I give you this? It's very pretty, isn't it?

CECILY: Yes, you've wonderfully good taste, Ernest. It's the excuse I've always given for your leading such a bad life. And this is the box in which I keep all your dear letters.

(Kneels at table, opens box, and produces letters tied up with blue ribbon.)

ALGERNON: My letters! But my own sweet Cecily, I have never written you any letters.

CECILY: You need hardly remind me of that, Ernest. I remember only too well that I was forced to write your letters for you. I wrote always three times a week, and sometimes oftener.

ALGERNON: Oh, do let me read them, Cecily!

CECILY: Oh, I couldn't possibly. They would make you far too conceited. (*Replaces box.*) The three you wrote me after I had broken off the engagement are so beautiful, and so badly spelled, that even now I can hardly read them without crying a little.

ALGERNON: But was our engagement ever broken off?

CECILY: Of course it was. On the 22nd of last March. You can see the entry if you like. (*Shows diary.*) "Today I broke off my engagement with Ernest. I feel it is better to do so. The weather still continues charming."

ALGERNON: But why on earth did you break it off? What had I done? I had done nothing at all. Cecily, I am very much hurt indeed to hear you broke it off. Particularly when the weather was so charming.

CECILY: It would hardly have been a really serious engagement if it hadn't been broken off at least once. But I forgave you before the week was out.

ALGERNON (*crossing to her, and kneeling*): What a perfect angel you are, Cecily.

CECILY: You dear romantic boy. (*He kisses her; she puts her fingers through his hair.*) I hope your hair curls naturally, does it?

ALGERNON: Yes, darling, with a little help from others.

CECILY: I am so glad.

ALGERNON: You'll never break off our engagement again, Cecily?

CECILY: I don't think I could break it off now that I have actually met you. Besides, of course, there is the question of your name.

ALGERNON (*nervously*): Yes, of course.

CECILY: You must not laugh at me, darling, but it had always been a girlish dream of mine to love someone whose name was Ernest. (*Algernon rises, Cecily also.*) There is something in that name that seems to inspire absolute confidence. I pity any poor married woman whose husband is not called Ernest.

ALGERNON: But, my dear child, do you mean to say you could not love me if I had some other name?

CECILY: But what name?

ALGERNON: Oh, any name you like — Algernon — for instance —

CECILY: But I don't like the name of Algernon.

ALGERNON: Well, my own dear, sweet, loving little darling, I really can't see why you should object to the name of Algernon. It is not at all a bad name. In fact, it is rather an aristocratic name. Half of the chaps who get into the Bankruptcy Court are called Algernon. But seriously, Cecily — (*moving to her*) — if my name was Algy, couldn't you love me?

CECILY (*rising*): I might respect you, Ernest, I might admire your character, but I fear that I should not be able to give you my undivided attention.

ALGERNON: Ahem! Cecily! (*Picking up hat.*) Your Rector here is, I suppose, thoroughly experienced in the practice of all the rites and ceremonials of the Church?

CECILY: Oh yes. Dr. Chasuble is a most learned man. He has never written a single book, so you can imagine how much he knows.

ALGERNON: I must see him at once on a most important christening — I mean on most important business.

CECILY: Oh!

ALGERNON: I shan't be away more than half an hour.

CECILY: Considering that we have been engaged since February the 14th, and that I only met you today for the first time, I think it is rather hard that you should leave me for so long a period as half an hour. Couldn't you make it twenty minutes?

ALGERNON: I'll be back in no time.

(Kisses her and rushes down the garden.)

CECILY: What an impetuous boy he is! I like his hair so much. I must enter his proposal in my diary.

(Enter Merriman.)

MERRIMAN: A Miss Fairfax has just called to see Mr. Worthing. On very important business Miss Fairfax states.

CECILY: Isn't Mr. Worthing in his library?

MERRIMAN: Mr. Worthing went over in the direction of the Rectory some time ago.

CECILY: Pray ask the lady to come out here; Mr. Worthing is sure to be back soon. And you can bring tea.

MERRIMAN: Yes, miss. (*Goes out.*)

CECILY: Miss Fairfax! I suppose one of the many good elderly women who are associated with Uncle Jack in some of his philanthropic work in London.

I don't quite like women who are interested in philanthropic work. I think it is so forward of them.

(Enter Merriman.)

MERRIMAN: Miss Fairfax.

(Enter Gwendolen. Exit Merriman.)

CECILY (*advancing to meet her*): Pray let me introduce myself to you. My name is Cecily Cardew.

GWENDOLEN: Cecily Cardew? (*Moving to her and shaking hands.*) What a very sweet name! Something tells me that we are going to be great friends. I like you already more than I can say. My first impressions of people are never wrong.

CECILY: How nice of you to like me so much after we have known each other such a comparatively short time. Pray sit down.

GWENDOLEN (*still standing up*): I may call you Cecily, may I not?

CECILY: With pleasure!

GWENDOLEN: And you will always call me Gwendolen, won't you?

CECILY: If you wish.

GWENDOLEN: Then that is all quite settled, is it not?

CECILY: I hope so.

(A pause. They both sit down together.)

GWENDOLEN: Perhaps this might be a favorable opportunity for my mentioning who I am. My father is Lord Bracknell. You have never heard of Papa, I suppose?

CECILY: I don't think so.

GWENDOLEN: Outside the family circle, Papa, I am glad to say, is entirely unknown. I think that is quite as it should be. The home seems to me to be the proper sphere for the man. And certainly once a man begins to neglect his domestic duties he becomes painfully effeminate, does he not? And I don't like that. It makes men so very attractive. Cecily, Mama, whose views on education are remarkably strict, has brought me up to be extremely shortsighted; it is part of her system, so do you mind my looking at you through my glasses?

CECILY: Oh! not at all, Gwendolen. I am very fond of being looked at.

GWENDOLEN (*after examining Cecily carefully through a lorgnette*): You are here on a short visit I suppose?

CECILY: Oh no! I live here.

GWENDOLEN (*severely*): Really? Your mother, no doubt, or some female relative of advanced years, resides here also?

CECILY: Oh no! I have no mother, nor, in fact, any relations.

GWENDOLEN: Indeed?

CECILY: My dear guardian, with the assistance of Miss Prism, has the arduous task of looking after me.

GWENDOLEN: Your guardian?

CECILY: Yes, I am Mr. Worthing's ward.

GWENDOLEN: Oh! It is strange he never mentioned to me that he had a ward. How secretive of him! He grows more interesting hourly. I am not sure, however, that the news inspires me with feelings of unmixed delight. (*Rising and going to her.*) I am very fond of you, Cecily; I have liked you ever since I met you! But I am bound to state that now that I know that you are Mr. Worthing's ward, I cannot help expressing a wish you were — well just a little older than you seem to be — and not quite so very alluring in appearance. In fact, if I may speak candidly —

CECILY: Pray do! I think that whenever one has anything unpleasant to say, one should always be quite candid.

GWENDOLEN: Well, to speak with perfect candor, Cecily, I wish that you were fully forty-two, and more than usually plain for your age. Ernest has a strong upright nature. He is the very soul of truth and honor. Disloyalty would be as impossible to him as deception. But even men of the noblest possible moral character are extremely susceptible to the influence of the physical charms of others. Modern, no less than Ancient History, supplies us with many most painful examples of what I refer to. If it were not so, indeed, History would be quite unreadable.

CECILY: I beg your pardon, Gwendolen, did you say Ernest?

GWENDOLEN: Yes.

CECILY: Oh, but it is not Mr. Ernest Worthing who is my guardian. It is his brother — his elder brother.

GWENDOLEN (*sitting down again*): Ernest never mentioned to me that he had a brother.

CECILY: I am sorry to say they have not been on good terms for a long time.

GWENDOLEN: Ah! that accounts for it. And now that I think of it I have never heard any man mention his brother. The subject seems distasteful to most men. Cecily, you have lifted a load from my mind. I was growing almost anxious. It would have been terrible if any cloud had come across a friendship like ours, would it not? Of course you are quite, quite sure that it is not Mr. Ernest Worthing who is your guardian?

CECILY: Quite sure. (*A pause.*) In fact, I am going to be his.

GWENDOLEN (*inquiringly*): I beg your pardon?

CECILY (*rather shy and confidingly*): Dearest Gwendolen, there is no reason why I should make a secret of it to you. Our little county newspaper is sure to chronicle the fact next week. Mr. Ernest Worthing and I are engaged to be married.

GWENDOLEN (*quite politely, rising*): My darling Cecily, I think there must be some slight error. Mr. Ernest Worthing is engaged to me. The announcement will appear in the *Morning Post* on Saturday at the latest.

CECILY (*very politely, rising*): I am afraid you must be under some misconception. Ernest proposed to me exactly ten minutes ago. (*Shows diary.*)

GWENDOLEN (*examines diary through her lorgnette carefully*): It is certainly very curious, for he asked me to be his wife yesterday afternoon at 5:30. If you would care to verify the incident, pray do so. (*Produces diary of her own.*) I never travel without my diary. One should always have something sensational to read in the train. I am so sorry, dear Cecily, if it is any disappointment to you, but I am afraid *I* have the prior claim.

CECILY: It would distress me more than I can tell you, dear Gwendolen, if it caused you any mental or physical anguish, but I feel bound to point out that since Ernest proposed to you he clearly has changed his mind.

GWENDOLEN (*meditatively*): If the poor fellow has been entrapped into any foolish promise I shall consider it my duty to rescue him at once, and with a firm hand.

CECILY (*thoughtfully and sadly*): Whatever unfortunate entanglement my dear boy may have got into, I will never reproach him with it after we are married.

GWENDOLEN: Do you allude to me, Miss Cardew, as an entanglement? You are presumptuous. On an occasion of this kind it becomes more than a moral duty to speak one's mind. It becomes a pleasure.

CECILY: Do you suggest, Miss Fairfax, that I entrapped Ernest into an engagement? How dare you? This is no time for wearing the shallow mask of manners. When I see a spade I call it a spade.

GWENDOLEN (*satirically*): I am glad to say that I have never seen a spade. It is obvious that our social spheres have been widely different.

(Enter Merriman, followed by the Footman. He carries a salver, tablecloth, and plate stand. Cecily is about to retort. The presence of the servants exercises a restraining influence, under which both girls chafe.)

MERRIMAN: Shall I lay tea here as usual, miss?

CECILY (*sternly, in a calm voice*): Yes, as usual.

(Merriman begins to clear table and lay cloth. A long pause. Cecily and Gwendolen glare at each other.)

GWENDOLEN: Are there many interesting walks in the vicinity, Miss Cardew?

CECILY: Oh! Yes! a great many. From the top of one of the hills quite close one can see five counties.

GWENDOLEN: Five counties! I don't think I should like that. I hate crowds.

CECILY (*sweetly*): I suppose that is why you live in town?

(Gwendolen bites her lip, and beats her foot nervously with her parasol.)

GWENDOLEN (*looking round*): Quite a well-kept garden this is, Miss Cardew.

CECILY: So glad you like it, Miss Fairfax.

GWENDOLEN: I had no idea there were any flowers in the country.

CECILY: Oh, flowers are as common here, Miss Fairfax, as people are in London.

GWENDOLEN: Personally I cannot understand how anybody manages to exist in the country, if anybody who is anybody does. The country always bores me to death.

CECILY: Ah! This is what the newspapers call agricultural depression, is it not? I believe the aristocracy are suffering very much from it just at present. It is almost an epidemic amongst them, I have been told. May I offer you some tea, Miss Fairfax?

GWENDOLEN (*with elaborate politeness*): Thank you. (*Aside.*) Detestable girl! But I require tea!

CECILY (*sweetly*): Sugar?

GWENDOLEN (*superciliously*): No, thank you. Sugar is not fashionable anymore.

(Cecily looks angrily at her, takes up the tongs, and puts four lumps of sugar into the cup.)

CECILY (*severely*): Cake or bread and butter?

GWENDOLEN (*in a bored manner*): Bread and butter, please. Cake is rarely seen at the best houses nowadays.

CECILY (*cuts a very large slice of cake, and puts it on the tray*): Hand that to Miss Fairfax.

(Merriman does so, and goes out with Footman. Gwendolen drinks the tea and makes a grimace. Puts down cup at once, reaches out her hand to the bread and butter, looks at it, and finds it is cake. Rises in indignation.)

GWENDOLEN: You have filled my tea with lumps of sugar, and though I asked most distinctly for bread and butter, you have given me cake. I am known for the gentleness of my disposition, and the extraordinary sweetness of my nature, but I warn you, Miss Cardew, you may go too far.

CECILY (*rising*): To save my poor, innocent, trusting boy from the machinations of any other girl there are no lengths to which I would not go.

GWENDOLEN: From the moment I saw you I distrusted you. I felt that you were false and deceitful. I am never deceived in such matters. My first impressions of people are invariably right.

CECILY: It seems to me, Miss Fairfax, that I am trespassing on your valuable time. No doubt you have many other calls of a similar character to make in the neighborhood.

(Enter Jack.)

GWENDOLEN (*catching sight of him*): Ernest! My own Ernest!

JACK: Gwendolen! Darling! (*Offers to kiss her.*)

GWENDOLEN (*drawing back*): A moment! May I ask if you are engaged to be married to this young lady? (*Points to Cecily.*)

JACK (*laughing*): To dear little Cecily! Of course not! What could have put such an idea into your pretty little head?

GWENDOLEN: Thank you. You may!

(*Offers her cheek.*)

CECILY (*very sweetly*): I knew there must be some misunderstanding, Miss Fairfax. The gentleman whose arm is at present round your waist is my dear guardian, Mr. John Worthing.

GWENDOLEN: I beg your pardon?

CECILY: This is Uncle Jack.

GWENDOLEN (*receding*): Jack! Oh!

(Enter Algernon.)

CECILY: Here is Ernest.

ALGERNON (*goes straight over to Cecily without noticing anyone else*): My own love! *(Offers to kiss her.)*

CECILY (*drawing back*): A moment, Ernest! May I ask you—are you engaged to be married to this young lady?

ALGERNON (*looking round*): To what young lady? Good heavens! Gwendolen!

CECILY: Yes! to good heavens, Gwendolen, I mean to Gwendolen.

ALGERNON (*laughing*): Of course not! What could have put such an idea into your pretty little head?

CECILY: Thank you. (*Presenting her cheek to be kissed.*) You may. *(Algernon kisses her.)*

GWENDOLEN: I felt there was some slight error, Miss Cardew. The gentleman who is now embracing you is my cousin, Mr. Algernon Moncrieff.

CECILY (*breaking away from Algernon*): Algernon Moncrieff! Oh!

(The two girls move towards each other and put their arms round each other's waists as if for protection.)

CECILY: Are you called Algernon?

ALGERNON: I cannot deny it.

CECILY: Oh!

GWENDOLEN: Is your name really John?

JACK (*standing rather proudly*): I could deny it if I liked. I could deny anything if I liked. But my name certainly is John. It has been John for years.

CECILY (*to Gwendolen*): A gross deception has been practiced on both of us.

GWENDOLEN: My poor wounded Cecily!

CECILY: My sweet wronged Gwendolen!

GWENDOLEN (*slowly and seriously*): You will call me sister, will you not?

(They embrace. Jack and Algernon groan and walk up and down.)

CECILY (*rather brightly*): There is just one question I would like to be allowed to ask my guardian.

GWENDOLEN: An admirable idea! Mr. Worthing, there is just one question I would like to be permitted to put to you. Where is your brother Ernest? We are both engaged to be married to your brother Ernest, so it is a matter of some importance to us to know where your brother Ernest is at present.

JACK (*slowly and hesitatingly*): Gwendolen—Cecily—it is very painful for me to be forced to speak the truth. It is the first time in my life that I have ever been reduced to such a painful position, and I am really quite inexperienced in doing anything of the kind. However I will tell you quite frankly that I have no brother Ernest. I have no brother at all. I never had a brother in my life, and I certainly have not the smallest intention of ever having one in the future.

CECILY (*surprised*): No brother at all?

JACK (*cheerily*): None!

GWENDOLEN (*severely*): Had you never a brother of any kind?

JACK (*pleasantly*): Never. Not even of any kind.

GWENDOLEN: I am afraid it is quite clear, Cecily, that neither of us is engaged to be married to anyone.

CECILY: It is not a very pleasant position for a young girl suddenly to find herself in. Is it?

GWENDOLEN: Let us go into the house. They will hardly venture to come after us there.

CECILY: No, men are so cowardly, aren't they?

(They retire into the house with scornful looks.)

JACK: This ghastly state of things is what you call Bunburying, I suppose?

ALGERNON: Yes, and a perfectly wonderful Bunbury it is. The most wonderful Bunbury I have ever had in my life.

JACK: Well, you've no right whatsoever to Bunbury here.

ALGERNON: That is absurd. One has a right to Bunbury anywhere one chooses. Every serious Bunburyist knows that.

JACK: Serious Bunburyist! Good heavens!

ALGERNON: Well, one must be serious about something, if one wants to have any amusement in life. I happen to be serious about Bunburying. What on earth you are serious about I haven't got the remotest idea. About everything, I should fancy. You have such an absolutely trivial nature.

JACK: Well, the only small satisfaction I have in the whole of this wretched business is that your friend Bunbury is quite exploded. You won't be able to run down to the country quite so often as you used to do, dear Algy. And a very good thing too.

ALGERNON: Your brother is a little off color, isn't he, dear Jack? You won't be able to disappear to London quite so frequently as your wicked custom was. And not a bad thing either.

JACK: As for your conduct towards Miss Cardew, I must say that your taking in a sweet, simple, innocent girl like that is quite inexcusable. To say nothing of the fact that she is my ward.

ALGERNON: I can see no possible defense at all for your deceiving a brilliant, clever, thoroughly experienced young lady like Miss Fairfax. To say nothing of the fact that she is my cousin.

JACK: I wanted to be engaged to Gwendolen, that is all. I love her.

ALGERNON: Well, I simply wanted to be engaged to Cecily. I adore her.

JACK: There is certainly no chance of your marrying Miss Cardew.

ALGERNON: I don't think there is much likelihood, Jack, of you and Miss Fairfax being united.

JACK: Well, that is no business of yours.

ALGERNON: If it was my business, I wouldn't talk about it. (*Begins to eat muffins.*) It is very vulgar to talk about one's business. Only people like stockbrokers do that, and then merely at dinner parties.

JACK: How you can sit there, calmly eating muffins when we are in this horrible trouble. I can't make out. You seem to me to be perfectly heartless.

ALGERNON: Well, I can't eat muffins in an agitated manner. The butter would probably get on my cuffs. One should always eat muffins quite calmly. It is the only way to eat them.

JACK: I say it's perfectly heartless your eating muffins at all, under the circumstances.

ALGERNON: When I am in trouble, eating is the only thing that consoles me. Indeed, when I am in really great trouble, as anyone who knows me intimately will tell you, I refuse everything except food and drink. At the present moment I am eating muffins because I am unhappy. Besides, I am particularly fond of muffins.

(Rising.)

JACK (*rising*): Well, that is no reason why you should eat them all in that greedy way.

(Takes muffins from Algernon.)

ALGERNON (*offering tea cake*): I wish you would have tea cake instead. I don't like tea cake.

JACK: Good heavens! I suppose a man may eat his own muffins in his own garden.

ALGERNON: But you have just said it was perfectly heartless to eat muffins.

JACK: I said it was perfectly heartless of you, under the circumstances. That is a very different thing.

ALGERNON: That may be, but the muffins are the same.

(He seizes the muffin dish from Jack.)

JACK: Algy, I wish to goodness you would go.

ALGERNON: You can't possibly ask me to go without having some dinner. It's absurd. I never go without my dinner. No one ever does, except vegetarians and people like that. Besides I have just made arrangements, with Dr. Chasuble to be christened at a quarter to six under the name of Ernest.

JACK: My dear fellow, the sooner you give up that nonsense the better. I made arrangements this morning with Dr. Chasuble to be christened myself at 5:30, and I naturally will take the name of Ernest. Gwendolen would wish it. We can't both be christened Ernest. It's absurd. Besides, I have a perfect right to be christened if I like. There is no evidence at all that I ever have been christened by anybody. I should think it extremely probable I never was, and so does Dr. Chasuble. It is entirely different in your case. You have been christened already.

ALGERNON: Yes, but I have not been christened for years.

JACK: Yes, but you have been christened. That is the important thing.

ALGERNON: Quite so. So I know my constitution can stand it. If you are not quite sure about your ever having been christened, I must say I think it rather dangerous your venturing on it now. It might make you very unwell. You can hardly have forgotten that someone very closely connected with you was very nearly carried off this week in Paris by a severe chill.

JACK: Yes, but you said yourself that a severe chill was not hereditary.

ALGERNON: It usen't to be, I know—but I daresay it is now. Science is always making wonderful improvements in things.

JACK (*picking up the muffin dish*): Oh, that is nonsense; you are always talking nonsense.

ALGERNON: Jack, you are at the muffins again! I wish you wouldn't. There are only two left. (*Takes them.*) I told you I was particularly fond of muffins.

JACK: But I hate tea cake.

ALGERNON: Why on earth then do you allow tea cake to be served up for your guests? What ideas you have of hospitality!

JACK: Algernon! I have already told you to go. I don't want you here. Why don't you go!

ALGERNON: I haven't quite finished my tea yet! and there is still one muffin left.

(Jack groans, and sinks into a chair. Algernon still continues eating.)

ACT III

(Scene: Morning room at the Manor House. Gwendolen and Cecily are at the window, looking out into the garden.)

GWENDOLEN: The fact that they did not follow us at once into the house, as anyone else would have done, seems to me to show that they have some sense of shame left.

CECILY: They have been eating muffins. That looks like repentance.

GWENDOLEN (*after a pause*): They don't seem to notice us at all. Couldn't you cough?

CECILY: But I haven't got a cough.

GWENDOLEN: They're looking at us. What effrontery!

CECILY: They're approaching. That's very forward of them.

GWENDOLEN: Let us preserve a dignified silence.

CECILY: Certainly. It's the only thing to do now.

(Enter Jack followed by Algernon. They whistle some dreadful popular air from a British opera.)

GWENDOLEN: This dignified silence seems to produce an unpleasant effect.

CECILY: A most distasteful one.

GWENDOLEN: But we will not be the first to speak.

CECILY: Certainly not.

GWENDOLEN: Mr. Worthing, I have something very particular to ask you. Much depends on your reply.

CECILY: Gwendolen, your common sense is invaluable. Mr. Moncrieff, kindly answer me the following question. Why did you pretend to be my guardian's brother?

ALGERNON: In order that I might have an opportunity of meeting you.

CECILY (*to Gwendolen*): That certainly seems a satisfactory explanation, does it not?

GWENDOLEN: Yes, dear, if you can believe him.

CECILY: I don't. But that does not affect the wonderful beauty of his answer.

GWENDOLEN: True. In matters of grave importance, style, not sincerity is the vital thing. Mr. Worthing, what explanation can you offer to me for pretending to have a brother? Was it in order that you might have an opportunity of coming up to town to see me as often as possible?

JACK: Can you doubt it, Miss Fairfax?

GWENDOLEN: I have the gravest doubts upon the subject. But I intend to crush them. This is not the moment for German skepticism. (*Moving to Cecily.*) Their explanations appear to be quite satisfactory, especially Mr. Worthing's. That seems to me to have the stamp of truth upon it.

CECILY: I am more than content with what Mr. Moncrieff said. His voice alone inspires one with absolute credulity.

GWENDOLEN: Then you think we should forgive them?

CECILY: Yes. I mean no.

GWENDOLEN: True! I had forgotten. There are principles at stake that one cannot surrender. Which of us should tell them? The task is not a pleasant one.

CECILY: Could we not both speak at the same time?

GWENDOLEN: An excellent idea! I nearly always speak at the same time as other people. Will you take the time from me?

CECILY: Certainly.

(Gwendolen beats time with uplifted finger.)

GWENDOLEN AND CECILY (*speaking together*): Your Christian names are still an insuperable barrier. That is all!

JACK AND ALGERNON (*speaking together*): Our Christian names! Is that all? But we are going to be christened this afternoon.

GWENDOLEN (*to Jack*): For my sake you are prepared to do this terrible thing?

JACK: I am!

CECILY (*to Algernon*): To please me you are ready to face this fearful ordeal?

ALGERNON: I am!

GWENDOLEN: How absurd to talk of the equality of the sexes! Where questions of self-sacrifice are concerned, men are infinitely beyond us.

JACK: We are! (*Clasps hands with Algernon.*)

CECILY: They have moments of physical courage of which we women know absolutely nothing.

GWENDOLEN (*to Jack*): Darling!

ALGERNON (*to Cecily*): Darling!

(They fall into each other's arms.)

(Enter Merriman. When he enters he coughs loudly, seeing the situation.)

MERRIMAN: Ahem! Ahem! Lady Bracknell!

JACK: Good heavens!

(Enter Lady Bracknell. The couples separate, in alarm. Exit Merriman.)

LADY BRACKNELL: Gwendolen! What does this mean?

GWENDOLEN: Merely that I am engaged to be married to Mr. Worthing, Mama.

LADY BRACKNELL: Come here. Sit down. Sit down immediately. Hesitation of any kind is a sign of mental decay in the young, of physical weakness in the old. (*Turns to Jack.*) Apprised, sir, of my daughter's sudden flight by her trusty maid, whose confidence I purchased by means of a small coin, I followed her at once by a luggage train. Her unhappy father is, I am glad to say, under the impression that she is attending a more than usually lengthy lecture by the University Extension Scheme on the influence of a permanent income on thought. I do not propose to undeceive him. Indeed I have never undeceived him on any question. I would consider it wrong. But of course, you will clearly understand that all communication between yourself and my daughter must cease immediately from this moment. On this point, as indeed on all points, I am firm.

JACK: I am engaged to be married to Gwendolen, Lady Bracknell!

LADY BRACKNELL: You are nothing of the kind, sir. And now, as regards Algernon!—Algernon!

ALGERNON: Yes, Aunt Augusta.

LADY BRACKNELL: May I ask if it is in this house that your invalid friend Mr. Bunbury resides?

ALGERNON (*stammering*): Oh! No! Bunbury doesn't live here. Bunbury is somewhere else at present. In fact, Bunbury is dead.

LADY BRACKNELL: Dead! When did Mr. Bunbury die? His death must have been extremely sudden.

ALGERNON (*airily*): Oh! I killed Bunbury this afternoon. I mean poor Bunbury died this afternoon.

LADY BRACKNELL: What did he die of?

ALGERNON: Bunbury? Oh, he was quite exploded.

LADY BRACKNELL: Exploded! Was he the victim of a revolutionary outrage? I was not aware that Mr. Bunbury was interested in social legislation. If so, he is well punished for his morbidity.

ALGERNON: My dear Aunt Augusta, I mean he was found out! The doctors found out that Bunbury could not live, that is what I mean—so Bunbury died.

LADY BRACKNELL: He seems to have had great confidence in the opinion of his physicians. I am glad, however, that he made up his mind at the last to some definite course of action, and acted under proper medical advice. And now that we have finally got rid of this Mr. Bunbury, may I ask, Mr. Worthing, who is that young person whose hand my nephew Algernon is now holding in what seems to me a peculiarly unnecessary manner?

JACK: That lady is Miss Cecily Cardew, my ward.

(Lady Bracknell bows coldly to Cecily.)

ALGERNON: I am engaged to be married to Cecily, Aunt Augusta.

LADY BRACKNELL: I beg your pardon?

CECILY: Mr. Moncrieff and I are engaged to be married, Lady Bracknell.

LADY BRACKNELL (*with a shiver, crossing to the sofa and sitting down*): I do not know whether there is anything peculiarly exciting in the air of this particular part of Hertfordshire, but the number of engagements that go on seems to me considerably above the proper average that statistics have laid down for our guidance. I think some preliminary inquiry on my part would not be out of place. Mr. Worthing, is Miss Cardew at all connected with any of the larger railway stations in London? I merely desire information. Until yesterday I had no idea that there were any families or persons whose origin was a Terminus. *(Jack looks perfectly furious, but restrains himself.)*

JACK *(in a clear, cold voice)*: Miss Cardew is the granddaughter of the late Mr. Thomas Cardew of 149, Belgrave Square, S. W.; Gervase Park, Dorking, Surrey; and the Sporran, Fifeshire, N.B.

LADY BRACKNELL: That sounds not unsatisfactory. Three addresses always inspire confidence, even in tradesmen. But what proof have I of their authenticity?

JACK: I have carefully preserved the Court Guides of the period. They are open to your inspection, Lady Bracknell.

LADY BRACKNELL *(grimly)*: I have known strange errors in that publication.

JACK: Miss Cardew's family solicitors are Messrs. Markby, Markby, and Markby.

LADY BRACKNELL: Markby, Markby, and Markby? A firm of the very highest position in their profession. Indeed I am told that one of the Mr. Markbys is occasionally to be seen at dinner parties. So far I am satisfied.

JACK *(very irritably)*: How extremely kind of you, Lady Bracknell! I have also in my possession, you will be pleased to hear, certificates of Miss Cardew's birth, baptism, whooping cough, registration, vaccination, confirmation, and the measles; both the German and the English variety.

LADY BRACKNELL: Ah! A life crowded with incident I see; though perhaps somewhat too exciting for a young girl. I am not myself in favor of premature experiences. *(Rises, looks at her watch.)* Gwendolen! the time approaches for our departure. We have not a moment to lose. As a matter of form, Mr. Worthing, I had better ask you if Miss Cardew has any little fortune?

JACK: Oh! about a hundred and thirty thousand pounds in the Funds. That is all. Good-bye, Lady Bracknell. So pleased to have seen you.

LADY BRACKNELL *(sitting down again)*: A moment, Mr. Worthing. A hundred and thirty thousand pounds! And in the Funds! Miss Cardew seems to me a most attractive young lady, now that I look at her. Few girls of the present day have any really solid qualities, any of the qualities that last, and improve with time. We live, I regret to say, in an age of surfaces. *(To Cecily.)* Come over here, dear. *(Cecily goes across.)* Pretty child! your dress is sadly simple, and your hair seems almost as Nature might have left it. But we can soon alter all that. A thoroughly experienced French maid produces a really marvelous result in a very brief space of time: I remember recommending one to young Lady Lancing, and after three months her own husband did not know her.

JACK *(aside)*: And after six months nobody knew her.

LADY BRACKNELL *(glares at Jack for a few moments. Then bends, with a practiced smile, to Cecily)*: Kindly turn round, sweet child. *(Cecily turns completely round.)* No, the side view is what I want. *(Cecily presents her profile.)* Yes, quite as I expected. There are distinct social possibilities in your profile. The two weak points in our age are its want of principle and its want of profile. The chin a little higher, dear. Style largely depends on the way the chin is worn. They are worn very high, just at present. Algernon!

ALGERNON: Yes, Aunt Augusta!

LADY BRACKNELL: There are distinct social possibilities in Miss Cardew's profile.

ALGERNON: Cecily is the sweetest, dearest, prettiest girl in the whole world. And I don't care twopence about social possibilities.

LADY BRACKNELL: Never speak disrespectfully of Society, Algernon. Only people who can't get into it do that. (*To Cecily.*) Dear child, of course you know that Algernon has nothing but his debts to depend upon. But I do not approve of mercenary marriages. When I married Lord Bracknell I had no fortune of any kind. But I never dreamed for a moment of allowing that to stand in my way. Well, I suppose I must give my consent.

ALGERNON: Thank you, Aunt Augusta.

LADY BRACKNELL: Cecily, you may kiss me!

CECILY (*kisses her*): Thank you, Lady Bracknell.

LADY BRACKNELL: You may also address me as Aunt Augusta for the future.

CECILY: Thank you, Aunt Augusta.

LADY BRACKNELL: The marriage, I think, had better take place quite soon.

ALGERNON: Thank you, Aunt Augusta.

CECILY: Thank you, Aunt Augusta.

LADY BRACKNELL: To speak frankly, I am not in favor of long engagements. They give people the opportunity of finding out each other's character before marriage, which I think is never advisable.

JACK: I beg your pardon for interrupting you, Lady Bracknell, but this engagement is quite out of the question. I am Miss Cardew's guardian, and she cannot marry without my consent until she comes of age. That consent I absolutely decline to give.

LADY BRACKNELL: Upon what grounds may I ask? Algernon is an extremely, I may almost say an ostentatiously, eligible young man. He has nothing, but he looks everything. What more can one desire?

JACK: It pains me very much to have to speak frankly to you, Lady Bracknell, about your nephew, but the fact is that I do not approve at all of his moral character. I suspect him of being untruthful.

(Algernon and Cecily look at him in indignant amazement.)

LADY BRACKNELL: Untruthful! My nephew Algernon? Impossible! He is an Oxonian.°

JACK: I fear there can be no possible doubt about the matter. This afternoon, during my temporary absence in London on an important question of romance, he obtained admission to my house by means of the false pretense of being my brother. Under an assumed name he drank, I've just been informed by my butler, an entire pint bottle of my Perrier-Jouët, Brut, '89; a wine I was specially reserving for myself. Continuing his disgraceful deception, he succeeded in the course of the afternoon in alienating the affections of my only ward. He subsequently stayed to tea, and devoured every single muffin. And what makes his conduct all the more heartless is, that he was perfectly well

Oxonian: Educated at Oxford University.

aware from the first that I have no brother, that I never had a brother, and that I don't intend to have a brother, not even of any kind. I distinctly told him so myself yesterday afternoon.

LADY BRACKNELL: Ahem! Mr. Worthing, after careful consideration I have decided entirely to overlook my nephew's conduct to you.

JACK: That is very generous of you, Lady Bracknell. My own decision, however, is unalterable. I decline to give my consent.

LADY BRACKNELL (*to Cecily*): Come here, sweet child. (*Cecily goes over.*) How old are you, dear?

CECILY: Well, I am really only eighteen, but I always admit to twenty when I go to evening parties.

LADY BRACKNELL: You are perfectly right in making some slight alteration. Indeed, no woman should ever be quite accurate about her age. It looks so calculating—(*In a meditative manner.*) Eighteen but admitting to twenty at evening parties. Well, it will not be very long before you are of age and free from the restraints of tutelage. So I don't think your guardian's consent is, after all, a matter of any importance.

JACK: Pray excuse me, Lady Bracknell, for interrupting you again, but it is only fair to tell you that according to the terms of her grandfather's will Miss Cardew does not come legally of age till she is thirty-five.

LADY BRACKNELL: That does not seem to me to be a grave objection. Thirty-five is a very attractive age. London society is full of women of the very highest birth who have, of their own free choice, remained thirty-five for years. Lady Dumbleton is an instance in point. To my own knowledge she has been thirty-five ever since she arrived at the age of forty, which was many years ago now. I see no reason why our dear Cecily should not be even still more attractive at the age you mention than she is at present. There will be a large accumulation of property.

CECILY: Algy, could you wait for me till I was thirty-five?

ALGERNON: Of course I could, Cecily. You know I could.

CECILY: Yes, I felt it instinctively, but I couldn't wait all that time. I hate waiting even five minutes for anybody. It always makes me rather cross. I am not punctual myself, I know, but I do like punctuality in others, and waiting, even to be married, is quite out of the question.

ALGERNON: Then what is to be done, Cecily?

CECILY: I don't know, Mr. Moncrieff.

LADY BRACKNELL: My dear Mr. Worthing, as Miss Cardew states positively that she cannot wait till she is thirty-five—a remark which I am bound to say seems to me to show a somewhat impatient nature—I would beg of you to reconsider your decision.

JACK: But my dear Lady Bracknell, the matter is entirely in your own hands. The moment you consent to my marriage with Gwendolen, I will most gladly allow your nephew to form an alliance with my ward.

LADY BRACKNELL (*rising and drawing herself up*): You must be quite aware that what you propose is out of the question.

JACK: Then a passionate celibacy is all that any of us can look forward to.

LADY BRACKNELL: That is not the destiny I propose for Gwendolen. Algernon, of course, can choose for himself. (*Pulls out her watch.*) Come, dear; (*Gwendolen rises*) we have already missed five, if not six, trains. To miss any more might expose us to comment on the platform.

(Enter Dr. Chasuble.)

CHASUBLE: Everything is quite ready for the christenings.

LADY BRACKNELL: The christenings, sir! Is not that somewhat premature?

CHASUBLE (*looking rather puzzled, and pointing to Jack and Algernon*): Both these gentlemen have expressed a desire for immediate baptism.

LADY BRACKNELL: At their age? The idea is grotesque and irreligious! Algernon, I forbid you to be baptized. I will not hear of such excesses. Lord Bracknell would be highly displeased if he learned that that was the way in which you wasted your time and money.

CHASUBLE: Am I to understand then that there are to be no christenings at all this afternoon?

JACK: I don't think that, as things are now, it would be of much practical value to either of us, Dr. Chasuble.

CHASUBLE: I am grieved to hear such sentiments from you, Mr. Worthing. They savor of the heretical views of the Anabaptists,° views that I have completely refuted in four of my unpublished sermons. However, as your present mood seems to be one peculiarly secular, I will return to the church at once. Indeed, I have just been informed by the pew opener that for the last hour and a half Miss Prism has been waiting for me in the vestry.

LADY BRACKNELL (*starting*): Miss Prism! Did I hear you mention a Miss Prism?

CHASUBLE: Yes, Lady Bracknell. I am on my way to join her.

LADY BRACKNELL: Pray allow me to detain you for a moment. This matter may prove to be one of vital importance to Lord Bracknell and myself. Is this Miss Prism a female of repellent aspect, remotely connected with education?

CHASUBLE (*somewhat indignantly*): She is the most cultivated of ladies, and the very picture of respectability.

LADY BRACKNELL: It is obviously the same person. May I ask what position she holds in your household?

CHASUBLE (*severely*): I am a celibate, madam.

JACK (*interposing*): Miss Prism, Lady Bracknell, has been for the last three years Miss Cardew's esteemed governess and valued companion.

LADY BRACKNELL: In spite of what I hear of her, I must see her at once. Let her be sent for.

CHASUBLE (*looking off*): She approaches; she is nigh.

(Enter Miss Prism hurriedly.)

MISS PRISM: I was told you expected me in the vestry, dear Canon. I have been waiting for you there for an hour and three-quarters.

Anabaptists: A religious sect founded in the sixteenth century and advocating adult baptism and church membership for adults only.

(Catches sight of Lady Bracknell who has fixed her with a stony glare. Miss Prism grows pale and quails. She looks anxiously round as if desirous to escape.)

LADY BRACKNELL (*in a severe, judicial voice*): Prism! (*Miss Prism bows her head in shame.*) Come here, Prism! (*Miss Prism approaches in a humble manner.*) Prism! Where is that baby? (*General consternation. The Canon starts back in horror. Algernon and Jack pretend to be anxious to shield Cecily and Gwendolen from hearing the details of a terrible public scandal.*) Twenty-eight years ago, Prism, you left Lord Bracknell's house, Number 104, Upper Grosvenor Street, in charge of a perambulator that contained a baby, of the male sex. You never returned. A few weeks later, through the elaborate investigations of the Metropolitan police, the perambulator was discovered at midnight, standing by itself in a remote corner of Bayswater. It contained the manuscript of a three-volume novel of more than usually revolting sentimentality. (*Miss Prism starts in involuntary indignation.*) But the baby was not there! (*Everyone looks at Miss Prism.*) Prism! Where is that baby?

(A pause.)

MISS PRISM: Lady Bracknell, I admit with shame that I do not know. I only wish I did. The plain facts of the case are these. On the morning of the day you mention, a day that is forever branded on my memory, I prepared as usual to take the baby out in its perambulator. I had also with me a somewhat old, but capacious handbag in which I had intended to place the manuscript of a work of fiction that I had written during my few unoccupied hours. In a moment of mental abstraction, for which I never can forgive myself, I deposited the manuscript in the bassinette, and placed the baby in the handbag.

JACK (*who has been listening attentively*): But where did you deposit the handbag?

MISS PRISM: Do not ask me, Mr. Worthing.

JACK: Miss Prism, this is a matter of no small importance to me. I insist on knowing where you deposited the handbag that contained that infant.

MISS PRISM: I left it in the cloakroom of one of the larger railway stations in London.

JACK: What railway station?

MISS PRISM (*quite crushed*): Victoria. The Brighton line.

(Sinks into a chair.)

JACK: I must retire to my room for a moment. Gwendolen, wait here for me.

GWENDOLEN: If you are not too long, I will wait here for you all my life.

(Exit Jack in great excitement.)

CHASUBLE: What do you think this means, Lady Bracknell?

LADY BRACKNELL: I dare not even suspect, Dr. Chasuble. I need hardly tell you that in families of high position strange coincidences are not supposed to occur. They are hardly considered the thing.

(Noises heard overhead as if someone was throwing trunks about. Everyone looks up.)

CECILY: Uncle Jack seems strangely agitated.

CHASUBLE: Your guardian has a very emotional nature.

LADY BRACKNELL: This noise is extremely unpleasant. It sounds as if he was having an argument. I dislike arguments of any kind. They are always vulgar, and often convincing.

CHASUBLE (*looking up*): It has stopped now.

(The noise is redoubled.)

LADY BRACKNELL: I wish he would arrive at some conclusion.

GWENDOLEN: This suspense is terrible. I hope it will last.

(Enter Jack with a handbag of black leather in his hand.)

JACK (*rushing over to Miss Prism*): Is this the handbag, Miss Prism? Examine it carefully before you speak. The happiness of more than one life depends on your answer.

MISS PRISM (*calmly*): It seems to be mine. Yes, here is the injury it received through the upsetting of a Gower Street omnibus in younger and happier days. Here is the stain on the lining caused by the explosion of a temperance beverage, an incident that occurred at Leamington. And here, on the lock, are my initials. I had forgotten that in an extravagant mood I had had them placed there. The bag is undoubtedly mine. I am delighted to have it so unexpectedly restored to me. It has been a great inconvenience being without it all these years.

JACK (*in a pathetic voice*): Miss Prism, more is restored to you than this handbag. I was the baby you placed in it.

MISS PRISM (*amazed*): You?

JACK (*embracing her*): Yes—mother!

MISS PRISM (*recoiling in indignant astonishment*): Mr. Worthing! I am unmarried!

JACK: Unmarried! I do not deny that is a serious blow. But after all, who has the right to cast a stone against one who has suffered? Cannot repentance wipe out an act of folly? Why should there be one law for men, and another for women? Mother, I forgive you. (*Tries to embrace her again.*)

MISS PRISM (*still more indignant*): Mr. Worthing, there is some error. (*Pointing to Lady Bracknell.*) There is the lady who can tell you who you really are.

JACK (*after a pause*): Lady Bracknell, I hate to seem inquisitive, but would you kindly inform me who I am?

LADY BRACKNELL: I am afraid that the news I have to give you will not altogether please you. You are the son of my poor sister, Mrs. Moncrieff, and consequently Algernon's elder brother.

JACK: Algy's elder brother! Then I have a brother after all. I knew I had a brother! I always said I had a brother! Cecily,—how could you have ever doubted that I had a brother. (*Seizes hold of Algernon.*) Dr. Chasuble, my unfortunate brother. Miss Prism, my unfortunate brother. Gwendolen, my unfortunate brother. Algy, you young scoundrel, you will have to treat me with more respect in the future. You have never behaved to me like a brother in all your life.

ALGERNON: Well, not till today, old boy, I admit. I did my best, however, though I was out of practice.

(Shakes hands.)

GWENDOLEN (*to Jack*): My own! But what own are you? What is your Christian name, now that you have become someone else?

JACK: Good heavens!—I had quite forgotten that point. Your decision on the subject of my name is irrevocable, I suppose?

GWENDOLEN: I never change, except in my affections.

CECILY: What a noble nature you have, Gwendolen!

JACK: Then the question had better be cleared up at once. Aunt Augusta, a moment. At the time when Miss Prism left me in the handbag, had I been christened already?

LADY BRACKNELL: Every luxury that money could buy, including christening, had been lavished upon you by your fond and doting parents.

JACK: Then I was christened! That is settled. Now, what name was I given? Let me know the worst.

LADY BRACKNELL: Being the eldest son you were naturally christened after your father.

JACK (*irritably*): Yes, but what was my father's Christian name?

LADY BRACKNELL (*meditatively*): I cannot at the present moment recall what the General's Christian name was. But I have no doubt he had one. He was eccentric, I admit. But only in later years. And that was the result of the Indian climate, and marriage, and indigestion, and other things of that kind.

JACK: Algy! Can't you recollect what our father's Christian name was?

ALGERNON: My dear boy, we were never even on speaking terms. He died before I was a year old.

JACK: His name would appear in the Army Lists of the period, I suppose, Aunt Augusta?

LADY BRACKNELL: The General was essentially a man of peace, except in his domestic life. But I have no doubt his name would appear in any military directory.

JACK: The Army Lists of the last forty years are here. These delightful records should have been my constant study. (*Rushes to bookcase and tears the books out.*) M. Generals—Mallam, Maxbohm, Magley, what ghastly names they have—Markby, Migsby, Mobbs, Moncrieff! Lieutenant 1840, Captain, Lieutenant-Colonel, Colonel, General 1869, Christian names, Ernest John. (*Puts book very quietly down and speaks quite calmly.*) I always told you, Gwendolen, my name was Ernest, didn't I? Well, it is Ernest after all. I mean it naturally is Ernest.

LADY BRACKNELL: Yes, I remember now that the General was called Ernest. I knew I had some particular reason for disliking the name.

GWENDOLEN: Ernest! My own Ernest! I felt from the first that you could have no other name!

JACK: Gwendolen, it is a terrible thing for a man to find out suddenly that all his life he has been speaking nothing but the truth. Can you forgive me?

GWENDOLEN: I can. For I feel that you are sure to change.

JACK: My own one!

CHASUBLE (*to Miss Prism*): Laetitia! (*Embraces her.*)

MISS PRISM (*enthusiastically*): Frederick! At last!

ALGERNON: Cecily! (*Embraces her.*) At last!

JACK: Gwendolen! (*Embraces her.*) At last!

LADY BRACKNELL: My nephew, you seem to be displaying signs of triviality.

JACK: On the contrary, Aunt Augusta, I've now realized for the first time in my life the vital Importance of Being Earnest. *[1895]*

☰ THINKING ABOUT THE TEXT

1. Are city and country significantly different "worlds" in this play, or do they seem basically the same? Refer to specific elements of both settings.
2. To a great extent, the play's humor results from the characters saying things that challenge conventional wisdom. What are some examples? Another comic element is the speed with which characters make major decisions. What are some of these moments?
3. In what ways other than biological are Jack and Algernon "brothers"? Gwendolen and Cecily "sisters"?
4. In what respects, if any, does this play seem "modern" to you? Define what you mean by the term. In what respects, if any, do you think it relies on age-old theatrical conventions?
5. If you were staging or filming this play, whom would you cast in its major roles? Why?

SOS ELTIS

From *Revising Wilde: Society and Subversion in the Plays of Oscar Wilde*

Sos Eltis is a Tutorial Fellow in English at Oxford University's Brasenose College. She has written numerous academic articles as well as Acts of Desire: Women and Sex on Stage, 1800–1930 *(2013). The excerpt below comes from her 1996 book about Oscar Wilde's plays. She emphasizes how* The Importance of Being Earnest *affirms the spirit of anarchy.*

The Importance of Being Earnest was to all appearances a conventional nineteenth-century farce. As with Wilde's previous plays, most of the basic ingredients of the plot were familiar from innumerable other farces: misplaced parents, forbidden engagements, false identities, overbearing mothers, and the copious consumption of food were all clichés of the comic stage. Yet Wilde used his material to highly unconventional ends, for the world of *Earnest* is an anarchic one.

All farce contains an element of anarchy. Pinero's° farces are a perfect example of controlled comic chaos, where a figure of authority — schoolmistress, magistrate, or dean — disrupts the proper order by pursuing improper pastimes — singing comic operas, drinking after hours, or betting on horses. The disruption spreads as respectable persons are forced to lie, steal, and assume

Pinero: Sir Arthur Wing Pinero (1855–1934), English actor, stage director, and dramatist whose comedies include The Schoolmistress (1886), The Magistrate (1885), and Dandy Dick (1887).

false identities to cover up their indiscretions. Yet, ultimately, law, order, and the *status quo* are re-established. The disorder is short-lived and the only after-effects are that the errant figures of authority have been led to a more sympathetic understanding of human error. The spirit of anarchy is constantly opposed by the ruling spirit of civilized society, and civilized society eventually achieves an impressive victory. In Wilde's farce, however, there is no division between chaos and order, fact and fiction. It is not a civilized society temporarily disrupted, but a perfect anarchic state in which the characters live, luxuriating in its benevolent lack of rules, morals, and principles. . . .

. . . *The Importance of Being Earnest* is remarkable less for any specific satire within it than for the fact that the play itself is the perfect realization of all Wilde's anarchist ideals; it is the society of "The Soul of Man under Socialism" made real°. In his political essay Wilde condemns all authority as degrading; in *Earnest* he reduces all authority to an absurdity. It is a utopia where all attempts to assert authority are doomed to failure. Its characters are free to realize themselves perfectly, for there are no harsh laws to intervene. It is an idyll of wish-fulfilment, where Cecily has only to dream she is engaged to Ernest for it to come true. Jack declares he is called Ernest and, sure enough, he is. Algy pretends to be Jack's younger brother, and by the end of the afternoon, this fantasy too has materialized. Nothing stands in the way of their self-creation, for reality itself is infinitely adaptable. So, when Lady Bracknell pronounces that Jack lives on the unfashionable side of Belgrave Square, the solution is simple:

> LADY BRACKNELL. I thought there was something. However, that could easily be altered.
>
> JACK. Do you mean the fashion, or the side?
>
> LADY BRACKNELL. Both, if necessary, I presume.

In this magical world, the perfect state of anarchy is realized, for the individual may pursue "The Soul of Man," his own desires without obstructing those of his neighbor. Wilde declared: "Selfishness is not living as one wishes to live, it is asking others to live as one wishes to live. And unselfishness is letting other people's lives alone, not interfering with them." So Gwendolen, Jack, Algy, and Cecily forge ahead, oblivious to anyone else's desires, and yet, in spite of Jack's determination to forbid Cecily's marriage unless he be allowed to marry Gwendolen, each achieves his or her goal without interfering with the others. Even Lady Bracknell, the one character who seeks to impose her own standards on everyone else, is transformed from a gorgon into the play's fairy godmother: contrary to her intentions, she finds herself playing the *dea ex machina* and granting the other characters' wishes.

This anarchic freedom, in which the characters are at liberty to create themselves, once again separates *Earnest* from other, more conventional, farces. The double lives led by Algernon, Jack, Cecily (through her diary), and even Miss Prism

The Soul of Man: Wilde expounded a social anarchist philosophy in his 1891 essay "The Soul of Man under Socialism."

(via her abandoned three-volume novel) are another means by which they liberate themselves from the formal strictures of society. Characters have assumed false identities in almost every farce ever written. In Brandon Thomas's extremely popular *Charley's Aunt* (1892), for example, the unfortunate Lord Fancourt Babberley is forced by friends to assume the guise of Charley's aunt from Brazil, in order to provide a chaperon for their female guests. The young students spend the next three acts desperately trying to sustain the pretense in the face of innumerable complications. In the last act Fancourt Babberley is released from the constrictions of his disguise and returned to his true identity. No such unmasking ends *The Importance of Being Earnest*; Cecily, Algy, and Jack become their own fantastic doubles, permanently granted the freedom which their fictions allowed them. Wilde, whose own sexuality was outlawed by the rigid and inhuman legislation of Victorian society, had created a fantasy world in which such laws had no power and double lives like his own no longer had to be kept secret. *[1996]*

TIRTHANKAR BOSE

From "*Oscar Wilde's Game of Being Earnest*"

Tirthankar Bose taught English at Simon Fraser University in Canada. The following excerpt comes from his article on The Importance of Being Earnest *that appeared in the Spring 1978 issue of the journal* Modern Drama. *As the article's title suggests, Bose sees the play's characters as playing games with one another.*

What we observe is a reversion to an ancient archetype of mating behaviour. A common custom of tribal societies is that a suitor must prove his love, and more important, his manhood, by performing some extraordinary feat or by presenting some precious gift. This custom is precisely the demand that the girls make upon the men. This sense, implicit at first, becomes explicit and unambiguous at the end, when the girls term the men's decision to be re-christened "this terrible thing" and "this fearful ordeal," and reward them for their "self-sacrifice" and "physical courage" (Act III). The utterly nonsensical nature of the issue is of course the basis of laughter, and it can be sustained only within a very special framework of character conception, a framework made up of centuries-old male notions of female willfulness. What gives satiric edge to the laughter is the ambivalence of that framework in conforming both to the nineteenth-century mores and to the behavioral archetypes of the species.

As a theatrical image, the ritual of courtship is singularly effective. The men approach the girls and are rejected. Then, through a sequence of question and response, they are accepted, only to be rejected again through a second sequence of question and response; they are then given a task of symbolic value, and on its performance (actually on the mere promise of performance, as in codified rituals) they are finally accepted. All verbal exchanges, gestures, and movements of which the ritual is composed require total stylization through exact matching and counterpoise. Each group uses the same language, goes through the same motions, and strikes the same attitudes. As examples of counterpoising, we may cite several pieces of the stage action. While Gwendolen and Cecily embrace and stand still and silent, Jack and Algy "*groan and walk up and down*" (stage direction, Act II). To Gwendolen's "severe" question, "Had you never a brother of any kind?" Jack returns the cheery answer, "Never" (*Ibid.*). When Cecily and Gwendolen "*preserve a dignified silence,*" Jack and Algernon "*whistle some dreadful popular air from a British opera*" (stage direction, Act III). The whole sequence comes to an operatic finale as the girls, "*speaking together,*" say—while Gwendolen "*beats time with uplifted finger*"—"Your Christian names are still an insuperable barrier! That is all!" The men reply, "*speaking together,*" "Our Christian names! Is that all?" And soon thereafter they "*fall into each other's arms*" (Act III).

Structurally, then, the play may be seen as a societal model simulating a courtship ritual which identifies the sexual drive of man as the controlling force in social relationships. Such an understanding could conceivably enrich a production of the play by replacing the evanescent world of the comedy of manners with the more durable framework of anthropological archetypes. But conspicuous as the ritual format is, it is possible to perceive the superimposition on it of yet another kind of archetypal design, that of a game of combat. *Earnest* begins, like most plays, with situations involving conflicts of interest; but it reveals its game characteristics in the layout of the situations. The design is made up of matched elements, the strategy of matching not confined to a specific sequence of action but determining to an ever-increasing degree the unfolding of the entire action. It is thus the real principle of structure. Conflicts arise between Jack and Algernon, and between Jack and Lady Bracknell. These situations are matched against each other. Jack obstructs Algernon while Lady Bracknell obstructs Jack. The object of the game is constant: to capture a closely guarded woman. The strategies are the same: the attacker pretends to be someone else; the defender refuses to move out of his square. This growing similarity between the two lines of play naturally brings them together and leads them to a joint climax in the second and the third acts when, after a mêlée, viable partnerships are formed. This part of the game makes deliberate use of a courtship format, for that is what the actual life situation requires. The game situation is: pursuit, capture, surrender, confrontation, reversed surrender, coalition. The men pursue and seize the women who, after a momentary surrender, confront the men with the discovery of their vulnerability, that is, their pretended identity. The men surrender to the women's demands by consenting to be re-christened, and partnerships are formed. Now we enter the second phase of the game in which the initial situation matches that of the first act: Lady Bracknell obstructs Jack and Jack obstructs Algernon. At the same time, Lady Bracknell is a supplicant before Jack just as he is before her. Both as opponents and supplicants, Jack and Lady Bracknell are evenly matched, and under these conditions the game has to end in a draw. Miss Prism, a new player, now enters the game and alters its balance by strengthening Jack, whereupon he demolishes all opposition, the conflict relating to him ends, and the new circumstances in turn terminate Algernon's problem. *[1978]*

PATRICIA FLANAGAN BEHRENDT

From *Oscar Wilde: Eros and Aesthetics*

Before retiring, Patricia Flanagan Behrendt taught theater arts at the University of Nebraska in Lincoln. She has also served as editor of the journal American Theatre. *In this except from her 1991 book on Oscar Wilde, she joins several other Wilde scholars in hypothesizing that* The Importance of Being Earnest *touches on issues related to homosexuality.*

While *The Importance of Being Earnest* perpetuates the dandy's vision of the ridiculousness of relations between men and women as it had been put forth in the earlier plays, it simultaneously reveals a matrix of allusions to the complex problems of homosexual identity. The title, which is traditionally interpreted as a pun on the importance of being Ernest as well as earnest, embodies a pun of a far more significant nature. Karl Heinrich Ulrichs (1825–95), a German sexologist who studied the phenomenon of homosexuality, applied the term *Urning* to males with homosexual tendencies, a condition which he felt reflected a female spirit in a male body. Proof that Wilde was familiar with one English equivalent of Urning—Uranian—is his use of the term in a letter to Robert Ross (*Letters*, 705). More important, however, considering Wilde's expertise in French and his familiarity with things French, is the fact that, while the English equivalent of *Urning* is Uranian, the French equivalent is *Uraniste*—a term whose pronunciation clearly suggests the name Ernest. The fact that Wilde was probably familiar with the French term suggests that the title of his play may not only propose the importance of being Ernest or earnest but may also propose the importance of being *Uraniste* as well—a sentiment which refers to the intellectually superior role that Wilde had assigned to his dandies throughout his work, to the private delight of the coterie of the green carnation.°

The play's concerns with complex problems of identity, suggested by the title, are encoded within further references to homosexuality. For example . . . Algernon's conversation with the butler, Lane, in the opening moments of the play is significant in relation to his own piano playing. Algernon asks Lane if he has heard what he was playing. Lane replies, "I didn't think it polite to listen, sir." For the Victorian audience, Lane's is the seemingly guarded response of the domestic servant expressing his detached view of the household activities. However, the fact that the term "musical" was an 1890s code word for homosexuality illuminates quite another aspect of the scene. When Lane announces that he did not think it polite to acknowledge Algernon's musicianship, he represents through encoded verbal allusion Victorian society's refusal to acknowledge behaviors which it knows exist and which affront its moral codes and assumptions, even when that society and its attitudes are challenged directly, as Algernon challenges Lane. In order to maintain his detached role as one who supposedly does not observe beyond his station. Lane is forced into the hypocritical and absurd

coterie of the green carnation: Followers of Wilde wore this flower, which they dyed green.

position of denying his own senses. In his witty exchange with Lane, Algernon affirms the power of dandy language to manipulate characters into revealing the inherent absurdity of their poses by saying (or doing) things which they know contradict a reality which they otherwise acknowledge.

For the Victorian audience in general, the subsequent events of the play ostensibly concern merely the humorous frustrations of two couples on the complicated route to marriage. However, while appearing to poke fun at courtship, Wilde's play depicts the destructive effects of Jack's pursuit of marriage on his initially stable sense of personal identity. The conversation between Jack and Algernon in the opening scene reveals that Jack has been maintaining a complicated existence, successfully balancing two identities. In the country he is the country gentleman, Jack Worthing, who is responsible enough to have been made guardian to his own benefactor's granddaughter. In the city, however, where he casts off responsibility in favor of the pursuit of pleasure, he calls himself Ernest Worthing. Jack's situation is under control until he announces to Algernon that he has come to town to propose to Algernon's cousin Gwendolyn. Algernon suggests that proposals of marriage constitute business rather than pleasure, a conclusion which recalls Wilde's earlier associations of marriage with ulterior motives and secret pursuits. After discovering Jack's intentions, Algernon who has known Jack only as Ernest reveals that he has found a cigarette case left behind by Jack (Ernest) during an earlier visit and inscribed "To Uncle Jack from his ward Cecily (*sic*)." From this development, Algernon learns not only of Jack's double identity—as Ernest in town and Jack in the country—but also of the fact that Jack pretends that Ernest is a profligate younger brother who lives "in the Albany and gets into the most dreadful scrapes." At this point Algernon upsets Jack's satisfaction with his compartmentalized existence by accusing him of being a Bunburyist. The term, he says, comes from the name of his own imaginary invalid friend whom he "visits" when he wants to get out of other obligations. Algernon refers to himself as one who has "Bunburyed all over Shropshire." The phrase blatantly calls forth the image of a promiscuous sodomite and foreshadows the epithet "somdomite" [*sic*] applied to Wilde by Lord Alfred Douglas's father, the Marquis of Queensberry, only weeks after the play opened.

Infuriated by Algernon's suggestion that he is a hypocrite, Jack concludes that, if Gwendolyn accepts him, he will kill off Ernest. Algernon questions the wisdom of eliminating Ernest and adds his own doubts about Jack's identity as a married man. He says, ". . . if you ever get married, which seems to me extremely problematic, you will be very glad to know Bunbury. A man who marries without knowing Bunbury has a very tedious time of it." The subtext of these otherwise humorous lines concerns the fact that from the moment Jack announces his intention to marry Gwendolyn, his identity becomes the subject of greater and greater confusion. Having revealed his double identity as his imaginary younger brother which Algernon recognizes as his alter ego, Jack is forced into the position of defending his identity and his sense of himself against the accusation that he is a Bunburyist. The important aspect of his ardent self-defense is that Algernon's initial recognition that Jack is a Bunburyist—because he has a second identity as "Ernest" designed to mask certain activities—will prove to be true at the end of the play when Jack discovers that his name really is Ernest. In other words, within the context of the play, once Jack announces his pursuit of marriage, his understanding of his own identity undergoes a process of deconstruction until he realizes that he is exactly the person whom he most denied being in the opening scene. This reinforces our understanding of Algernon's intellectual superiority, since what he has predicted is proved in fact to be true.

The second assault upon Jack's identity occurs when he proposes to Gwen- 5
dolyn in the next scene. She announces that her "ideal has always been to love someone of the name of Ernest." To his horror, Jack discovers that she will love only someone who bears the name of the very identity that he was going to "kill off" if she agreed to marry him. Given the homosexual connotation of musicality, an ironic note is added when she says that Ernest "is a divine name. It has a music of its own." To further undermine Jack's sense of himself, she repudiates his suggestion that Jack or John might be acceptable. She adds, "I pity any woman who is married to a man called John. She would probably never be allowed to know the entrancing pleasure of a single moment's solitude. The only really safe name is Ernest." In these complicated lines, Gwendolyn is already intimating, prior to marriage, that she anticipates the need for solitude and that she would prefer a certain level of uninterest in a husband. Moments earlier she had told Jack that she would prefer that he be more demonstrative toward her in public, implying that the public manifestations of their engagement are more important than their relationship in private. One begins to suspect that, when Gwendolyn speaks of "the only really safe" husband, she is referring to one who will affect a high level of uninterest in her behind closed doors while putting up a facade of attentiveness in public.

Since it is the sexual aspect of marriage that is conducted in private, and since Gwendolyn seems to prefer an uninterested husband in private, we can assume that she is implying that she would prefer a husband with only limited interest in the sexual sphere of marriage. Since Wilde has already given the name Ernest overtones of homosexuality by having Gwendolyn observe that it has "music of its own," we might wonder if Wilde is not implying that Gwendolyn's own subconscious idea of "the ideal husband" is one who wears the attentive mask of the devoted husband in public but has no intention of making sexual demands in private. In such a situation, which would have appeared ideal to Wilde himself, both parties are free to pursue their own interests, protected from public scrutiny by the conventional facade of marriage.

The idea that Gwendolyn is attracted specifically to men of questionable sexual preferences is substantiated in the second act, when she suggests that "once a man begins to neglect his domestic duties he becomes painfully effeminate, does he not? And I don't like that." Since "effeminate" is also a code word homosexuality in the period, Gwendolyn would appear to be signalling her antipathy toward the type until she adds the seemingly paradoxical statement that being painfully effeminate "makes men so very attractive." The attraction that the effeminate man would hold for Gwendolyn would be his lack of sexual interest in her. Once again Wilde introduces the theme of the dandy who is both attractive to women and yet sexually uninterested in them as a woman's own vision of "the ideal husband." While Jack's discovery at the end of the play that he is actually Ernest makes him an ideal husband for Gwendolyn according to Lady Bracknell's standards, it is Jack's discovery of his identity as Ernest "the Bunburyist" that makes him an ideal husband by Wilde's standards.

The first two scenes of the play reveal Jack's deteriorating sense of identity in the wake of his announcement of his intention to marry Gwendolyn. While Algernon accuses Jack of not being who he pretends to be, Gwendolyn believes Jack to be the very person that he is not. What he has denied himself to Algernon to be — that he is Ernest and therefore a Bunburyist — he must become in order to please Gwendolyn. Under the cover of humor, Wilde once again reveals that marriage results in compromising one's identity. Most important, it is the dandy, Algernon, who, like Cecil Graham in conversation with Lord Darlington,° aggressively challenges the wisdom of Jack's pursuit of a woman by predicting that it will be "extremely problematic." The dandy's insight is correct, as usual.

After his interview with Algernon and Gwendolyn, Jack is confronted by Lady Bracknell, Algernon's aunt and soon to be revealed as Jack's aunt as well. She demands that Jack find some respectable relations if he intends to be considered a serious suitor for Gwendolyn. Lady Bracknell is the voice of authority whom everyone must please. Her description of her own marriage reveals that she dominates her husband to the point of making him eat upstairs when his presence will create an uneven table at dinner. When Wilde has Jack ask Algernon if Gwendolyn will become like her mother in a hundred years, he foreshadows Jack's grim destiny, for which Bunburying is the only recourse according to Algernon. After all, Gwendolyn has already revealed her ability to dominate Jack by making it impossible for him even to expose the simple fact that his name is not Ernest.

10 The fact that Lady Bracknell has usurped the traditionally masculine role of dominating the household and of granting permission for Gwendolyn to marry accounts for the tendency to cast a man in her role, thereby revealing the hypocrisy of marriage in which the woman has absorbed the role of the male. Additional humor is added to the blurring of Lady Bracknell's gender by her designation as the "aunt." The word "aunt" or "auntie" was typical 1890s slang for a homosexual among homosexuals.

In terms of the structure of the play, Algernon's condemning remarks in the first scene about the unattractiveness of marriage pass at first as witty cynicism but are proved to be absolutely true to the reality of the play. The play is designed to reveal the truth, of Algernon's warning to Jack in the opening scene that a second identity — which makes Jack a Bunburyist — is essential to marital happiness. Jack discovers as the play progresses that in order to achieve the happiness of being accepted by Gwendolyn he must become Ernest, his Bunbury alter ego. The complication reveals that the dandy knows the other characters better than they know themselves.

Cecil Graham; Lord Darlington: Characters in the Oscar Wilde play *Lady Windermer's Fan.*

In the tradition of Wilde's plays, the comedy ends in the country setting with Jack and Algernon engaged to marry Gwendolyn and Cecily respectively. Echoing the relationship between Lord Goring and Lord Chiltern in *An Ideal Husband*, Algernon's possessive interests in Jack's affairs have led him to the country to meet Jack's ward, to whom he becomes engaged. The country setting is significant in that it is always associated in Wilde's works with impulsive actions. Just as Lord Goring's marriage to Mabel ensures his access to Chiltern, Algernon's engagement to Jack's ward ensures Algernon's access to Jack. Wilde cements their ties when Jack's discovery that his name is Ernest results also in the discovery that he is Algernon's older brother. Part of the vanity of Algernon's intense interest in Jack, therefore, stems from the fact that he clearly sees himself reflected in Jack, like Narcissus° yearning for his own image in the pool. His attention to Jack is a typical measure of dandy self-centeredness. However, since Algernon has already indicated that he will never give up Bunburying and since Jack has discovered that he *is* a Bunburyist, we see that the two are one of a kind and have merely capitulated to the compromises required for marriage. Their future is filled with the promise of hypocrisy heaped upon hypocrisy behind the mask of domestic tranquility. As in each of the plays, the role of the dandy is to expose the chilling—if not morbid—nature of heterosexual relations while revealing genuine good will, affection, human bonding, fun, and intellectual exchange which are played out between men. *[1991]*

MAKING COMPARISONS

1. While reading the play, did you look at it as Eltis, Bose, and Behrendt do? Why, or why not? Do you find one of these interpretations more illuminating than the others? Explain.
2. Are the lenses that Eltis, Bose, and Behrendt use compatible with one another? Is it possible for a reader of the play to agree with all three of these critics? Why, or why not?
3. Find three recent reviews of *Earnest* and compare their perspective to those presented here.

WRITING ABOUT ISSUES

1. Choose a bit of dialogue—perhaps one line, perhaps a few—that for you conveys much of what is important about the journey from city to country in *The Importance of Being Earnest*. Then, write an essay explaining why the dialogue you have selected is significant.
2. How useful is knowledge of Wilde's life for an understanding of *The Importance of Being Earnest*? Write an essay that answers this question by referring to Behrendt and at least one other critic.

Narcissus: A famous youth in Greek mythology who fell in love with his own reflection when he looked in a pool.

3. Suppose that you are the casting director of a new production of *The Importance of Being Earnest*. What would you say to someone who argues that casting a star as Lady Bracknell – whether the star is a man or a woman – risks making that character seem more important than she actually is? Write an essay that states and supports your response.
4. Choose a specific film – perhaps a romantic comedy – that seems less original to you than it did before you read *The Importance of Being Earnest*. How does your new knowledge of Wilde's play make the movie seem less fresh? Answer in an essay.

Crossing Boundaries: Essays

RICHARD RODRIGUEZ, "Aria"

JOSE ANTONIO VARGAS, "My Life as an Undocumented Immigrant"

Although both Richard Rodriguez and Jose Antonio Vargas grew up in immigrant families around San Francisco, their responses to the cultural and language boundaries each had to negotiate were quite different. Rodriguez agonized over his childhood fluency in English. He felt Spanish was the comforting and solidifying language of family life. As he learned the public language of the majority, he felt his family life changed. In a way, his growing proficiency in English and gradual socialization into American culture distanced him from the family life he so loved as a child. His progress was also a loss. Despite this sense of loss, Rodriguez opposes bilingual education and affirmative action and favors immersing students in English. As a result of this controversial position against students using their native languages in school, he was widely criticized as a traitor to Mexican Americans. Caught between two cultures, not belonging completely in either, Rodriguez claims he is "a comic victim of two cultures."

Jose Vargas also has a foothold in both cultures, but he seems not to have suffered the emotional family turmoil that Rodriguez recounts. Vargas has assimilated into American culture with eloquence and excellence. His problem is a technical one. As he explains, "I am an American. I just don't have the right papers." Vargas's essay tells of his attempts to cross the boundary from immigrant to American citizen without official approval. That he is so successful is in itself an example of the American Dream.

BEFORE YOU READ

Recall incidents from your past when you felt you had to cross or negotiate various boundaries. How did you feel? Recall stories or films about people crossing boundaries, whether geographical, linguistic, class, religious, or other. How did you respond?

RICHARD RODRIGUEZ

Aria

A native of San Francisco, California, Richard Rodriguez (b. 1944) is the son of Mexican immigrants. Until he entered school at the age of six, he spoke primarily Spanish. His 1982 memoir, Hunger of Memory, *describes how English-language instruction distanced him from his parents' native culture. Rodriguez went on to attend Stanford University and the University of California at Berkeley, where he earned a doctorate in English Renaissance literature. He is also the author of* Days of Obligation: An Argument with My Mexican Father *(1992) and* Brown: The Last Discovery of America

(2002). His essay "The God of the Desert" was published in The Best American Essays 2009. *Currently Rodriguez is a contributing editor for* Harper's *magazine and a commentator on public television's* NewsHour.

1

I remember to start with that day in Sacramento—a California now nearly thirty years past—when I first entered a classroom, able to understand some fifty stray English words.

The third of four children, I had been preceded to a neighborhood Roman Catholic school by an older brother and sister. But neither of them had revealed very much about their classroom experiences. Each afternoon they returned, as they left in the morning, always together, speaking in Spanish as they climbed the five steps of the porch. And their mysterious books, wrapped in shopping-bag paper, remained on the table next to the door, closed firmly behind them.

An accident of geography sent me to a school where all my classmates were white, many the children of doctors and lawyers and business executives. All my classmates certainly must have been uneasy on that first day of school—as most children are uneasy—to find themselves apart from their families in the first institution of their lives. But I was astonished.

The nun said, in a friendly but oddly impersonal voice, "Boys and girls, this is Richard Rodriguez." (I heard her sound out: *Rich-heard Road-ree-guess.*) It was the first time I had heard anyone name me in English. "Richard," the nun repeated more slowly, writing my name down in her black leather book. Quickly I turned to see my mother's face dissolve in a watery blur behind the pebbled glass door.

Many years later there is something called bilingual education—a scheme pro- 5
posed in the late 1960s by Hispanic-American social activists, later endorsed by a congressional vote. It is a program that seeks to permit non-English-speaking children, many from lower-class homes, to use their family language as the language of school. (Such is the goal its supporters announce.) I hear them and am forced to say no: it is not possible for a child—any child—ever to use his family's language in school. Not to understand this is to misunderstand the public uses of schooling and to trivialize the nature of intimate life—a family's "language."

Memory teaches me what I know of these matters; the boy reminds the adult. I was a bilingual child, a certain kind—socially disadvantaged—the son of working-class parents, both Mexican immigrants.

In the early years of my boyhood, my parents coped very well in America. My father had steady work. My mother managed at home. They were nobody's victims. Optimism and ambition led them to a house (our home) many blocks from the Mexican south side of town. We lived among *gringos* and only a block from the biggest, whitest houses. It never occurred to my parents that they couldn't live wherever they chose. Nor was the Sacramento of the fifties bent on teaching them a contrary lesson. My mother and father were more annoyed than intimidated by those two or three neighbors who tried initially to make us unwelcome. ("Keep your brats away from my sidewalk!") But despite all they achieved, perhaps because they had so much to achieve, any deep feeling of ease, the confidence of "belonging" in public was withheld from them both. They regarded the people at work, the faces in crowds, as very distant from us. They were the others, *los gringos.* That term was interchangeable in their speech with another, even more telling, *los americanos.*

I grew up in a house where the only regular guests were my relations. For one day, enormous families of relatives would visit and there would be so many people that the noise and the bodies would spill out to the backyard and front porch. Then, for weeks, no one came by. (It was usually a salesman who rang the doorbell.) Our house stood apart. A gaudy yellow in a row of white bungalows. We were the people with the noisy dog. The people who raised pigeons and chickens. We were the foreigners on the block. A few neighbors smiled and waved. We waved back. But no one in the family knew the names of the old couple who lived next door; until I was seven years old, I did not know the names of the kids who lived across the street.

In public, my father and mother spoke a hesitant, accented, not always grammatical English. And they would have to strain—their bodies tense—to catch the sense of what was rapidly said by *los gringos.* At home they spoke Spanish. The language of their Mexican past sounded in counterpoint to the English of public society. The words would come quickly, with ease. Conveyed through those sounds was the pleasing, soothing, consoling reminder of being at home.

During those years when I was first conscious of hearing, my mother and 10
father addressed me only in Spanish; in Spanish I learned to reply. By contrast, English (*inglés*), rarely heard in the house, was the language I came to associate with *gringos.* I learned my first words of English overhearing my parents speak to strangers. At five years of age, I knew just enough English for my mother to trust me on errands to stores one block away. No more.

I was a listening child, careful to hear the very different sounds of Spanish and English. Wide-eyed with hearing, I'd listen to sounds more than words. First, there were English (*gringo*) sounds. So many words were still unknown that when the butcher or the lady at the drugstore said something to me, exotic polysyllabic sounds would bloom in the midst of their sentences. Often, the speech of people in public seemed to me very loud, booming with confidence. The man behind the counter would literally ask, "What can I do for you?" But by being so firm and so clear, the sound of his voice said that he was a *gringo*; he belonged in public society.

I would also hear then the high nasal notes of middle-class American speech. The air stirred with sound. Sometimes, even now, when I have been traveling abroad for several weeks, I will hear what I heard as a boy. In hotel lobbies or airports, in Turkey or Brazil, some Americans will pass, and suddenly I will hear it again—the high sound of American voices. For a few seconds I will hear it with pleasure, for it is now the sound of *my* society—a reminder of home. But inevitably—already on the flight headed for home—the sound fades with repetition. I will be unable to hear it anymore.

When I was a boy, things were different. The accent of *los gringos* was never pleasing nor was it hard to hear. Crowds at Safeway or at bus stops would be noisy with sound. And I would be forced to edge away from the chirping chatter above me.

I was unable to hear my own sounds, but I knew very well that I spoke English poorly. My words could not stretch far enough to form complete thoughts. And the words I did speak I didn't know well enough to make into distinct sounds. (Listeners would usually lower their heads, better to hear what I was trying to say.) But it was one thing for *me* to speak English with difficulty. It was more troubling for me to hear my parents speak in public: their high-whining vowels and guttural consonants; their sentences that got stuck with "eh" and "ah" sounds; the confused syntax; the hesitant rhythm of sounds so different from the way *gringos* spoke. I'd notice, moreover, that my parents' voices were softer than those of *gringos* we'd meet.

15 I am tempted now to say that none of this mattered. In adulthood I am embarrassed by childhood fears. And in a way, it didn't matter very much that my parents could not speak English with ease. Their linguistic difficulties had no serious consequences. My mother and father made themselves understood at the county hospital clinic and at government offices. And yet, in another way, it mattered very much—it was unsettling to hear my parents struggle with English. Hearing them, I'd grow nervous, my clutching trust in their protection and power weakened.

There were many times like the night at a brightly lit gasoline station (a blaring white memory) when I stood uneasily, hearing my father. He was talking to a teenaged attendant. I do not recall what they were saying, but I cannot forget the sounds my father made as he spoke. At one point his words slid together to form one word—sounds as confused as the threads of blue and green oil in the puddle next to my shoes. His voice rushed through what he had left to say. And, toward the end, reached falsetto notes, appealing to his listener's understanding. I looked away to the lights of passing automobiles. I tried not to hear anymore. But I heard only too well the calm, easy tones in the attendant's reply. Shortly afterward, walking toward home with my father, I shivered when he put his hand on my shoulder. The very first chance that I got, I evaded his grasp and ran on ahead into the dark, skipping with feigned boyish exuberance.

But then there was Spanish. *Español*: my family's language. *Español*: the language that seemed to me a private language. I'd hear strangers on the radio and in the Mexican Catholic church across town speaking in Spanish, but I couldn't really believe that Spanish was a public language, like English. Spanish speakers, rather, seemed related to me, for I sensed that we shared—through our language—the experience of feeling apart from *los gringos*. It was thus a ghetto Spanish that I heard and I spoke. Like those whose lives are bound by a barrio, I was reminded by Spanish of my separateness from *los otros, los gringos* in power. But more intensely than for most barrio children—because I did not live in a barrio—Spanish seemed to me the language of home. (Most days it was only at home that I'd hear it.) It became the language of joyful return.

A family member would say something to me and I would feel myself specially recognized. My parents would say something to me and I would feel embraced by the sounds of their words. Those sounds said: *I am speaking with ease in Spanish. I am addressing you in words I never use with* los gringos. *I recognize you as someone special, close, like no one outside. You belong with us. In the family.*

(*Ricardo.*)

At the age of five, six, well past the time when most other children no longer 20
easily notice the difference between sounds uttered at home and words spoken in public, I had a different experience. I lived in a world magically compounded of sounds. I remained a child longer than most; I lingered too long, poised at the edge of language — often frightened by the sounds of *los gringos*, delighted by the sounds of Spanish at home. I shared with my family a language that was startlingly different from that used in the great city around us.

For me there were none of the gradations between public and private society so normal to a maturing child. Outside the house was public society; inside the house was private. Just opening or closing the screen door behind me was an important experience. I'd rarely leave home all alone or without reluctance. Walking down the sidewalk, under the canopy of tall trees, I'd warily notice the — suddenly — silent neighborhood kids who stood warily watching me. Nervously, I'd arrive at the grocery store to hear there the sounds of the *gringo* — foreign to me — reminding me that in this world so big, I was a foreigner. But then I'd return. Walking back toward our house, climbing the steps from the sidewalk, when the front door was open in summer, I'd hear voices beyond the screen door talking in Spanish. For a second or two, I'd stay, linger there, listening. Smiling, I'd hear my mother call out, saying in Spanish (words): "Is that you, Richard?" All the while her sounds would assure me: *You are home now; come closer; inside. With us.*

"*Sí,*" I'd reply.

Once more inside the house I would resume (assume) my place in the family. The sounds would dim, grow harder to hear. Once more at home, I would grow less aware of that fact. It required, however, no more than the blurt of the doorbell to alert me to listen to sounds all over again. The house would turn instantly still while my mother went to the door. I'd hear her hard English sounds. I'd wait to hear her voice return to soft-sounding Spanish, which assured me, as surely as did the clicking tongue of the lock on the door, that the stranger was gone.

Plainly, it is not healthy to hear such sounds so often. It is not healthy to distinguish public words from private sounds so easily. I remained cloistered by sounds, timid and shy in public, too dependent on voices at home. And yet it needs to be emphasized: I was an extremely happy child at home. I remember many nights when my father would come back from work, and I'd hear him call out to my mother in Spanish, sounding relieved. In Spanish, he'd sound light and free notes he never could manage in English. Some nights I'd jump up just at hearing his voice. With *mis hermanos* I would come running into the room where he was with my mother. Our laughing (so deep was the pleasure!) became screaming. Like others who know the pain of public alienation, we transformed the knowledge of our public separateness and made it consoling — the reminder of intimacy. Excited, we joined our voices in a celebration of sounds. *We are speaking now the way we never speak out in public. We are alone — together,* voices sounded, surrounded to tell me. Some nights, no one seemed willing to loosen the hold sounds had on us. At dinner, we invented new words. (Ours sounded Spanish, but made sense only to us.) We pieced together new words by taking, say, an English verb and giving it Spanish endings. My mother's instructions at bedtime would be lacquered with mock-urgent tones. Or a word like *sí* would become, in several notes, able to convey added measures of feeling. Tongues explored the edges of words, especially the fat vowels. And we happily sounded that military drum roll, the twirling roar of the Spanish *r*. Family language: my family's sounds. The voices of my parents and sisters and brother. Their voices insisting: *You belong here. We are family members. Related. Special to one another. Listen!* Voices singing and sighing, rising, straining, then surging, teeming with pleasure that burst syllables into fragments of laughter. At times it seemed there was steady quiet only when, from another room, the rustling whispers of my parents faded and I moved closer to sleep.

2

25 Supporters of bilingual education today imply that students like me miss a great deal by not being taught in their family's language. What they seem not to recognize is that, as a socially disadvantaged child, I considered Spanish to be a private language. What I needed to learn in school was that I had the right—and the obligation—to speak the public language of *los gringos*. The odd truth is that my first-grade classmates could have become bilingual, in the conventional sense of that word, more easily than I. Had they been taught (as upper-middle-class children are often taught early) a second language like Spanish or French, they could have regarded it simply as that: another public language. In my case such bilingualism could not have been so quickly achieved. What I did not believe was that I could speak a single public language.

Without question, it would have pleased me to hear my teachers address me in Spanish when I entered the classroom. I would have felt much less afraid. I would have trusted them and responded with ease. But I would have delayed—for how long postponed?—having to learn the language of public society. I would have evaded—and for how long could I have afforded to delay?—learning the great lesson of school, that I had a public identity.

Fortunately, my teachers were unsentimental about their responsibility. What they understood was that I needed to speak a public language. So their voices would search me out, asking me questions. Each time I'd hear them, I'd look up in surprise to see a nun's face frowning at me. I'd mumble, not really meaning to answer. The nun would persist, "Richard, stand up. Don't look at the floor. Speak up. Speak to the entire class, not just to me!" But I couldn't believe that the English language was mine to use. (In part, I did not want to believe it.) I continued to mumble. I resisted the teacher's demands. (Did I somehow suspect that once I learned public language my pleasing family life would be changed?) Silent, waiting for the bell to sound, I remained dazed, diffident, afraid.

Because I wrongly imagined that English was intrinsically a public language and Spanish an intrinsically private one, I easily noted the difference between classroom language and the language of home. At school, words were directed to a general audience of listeners. ("Boys and girls.") Words were meaningfully ordered. And the point was not self-expression alone but to make oneself understood by many others. The teacher quizzed: "Boys and girls, why do we use that word in this sentence? Could we think of a better word to use there? Would the sentence change its meaning if the words were differently arranged? And wasn't there a better way of saying much the same thing?" (I couldn't say. I wouldn't try to say.)

Three months. Five. Half a year passed. Unsmiling, ever watchful, my teachers noted my silence. They began to connect my behavior with the difficult progress my older sister and brother were making. Until one Saturday morning three nuns arrived at the house to talk to our parents. Stiffly, they sat on the blue living room sofa. From the doorway of another room, spying the visitors, I noted the incongruity — the clash of two worlds, the faces and voices of school intruding upon the familiar setting of home. I overheard one voice gently wondering, "Do your children speak only Spanish at home, Mrs. Rodriguez?" While another voice added, "That Richard especially seems so timid and shy."

That Rich-heard! 30

With great tact the visitors continued, "Is it possible for you and your husband to encourage your children to practice their English when they are home?" Of course, my parents complied. What would they not do for their children's well-being? And how could they have questioned the Church's authority which those women represented? In an instant, they agreed to give up the language (the sounds) that had revealed and accentuated our family's closeness. The moment after the visitors left, the change was observed. "*Ahora*, speak to us *en inglés*," my father and mother united to tell us.

At first, it seemed a kind of game. After dinner each night, the family gathered to practice "our" English. (It was still then *inglés*, a language foreign to us, so we felt drawn as strangers to it.) Laughing, we would try to define words we could not pronounce. We played with strange English sounds, often overanglicizing our pronunciations. And we filled the smiling gaps of our sentences with familiar Spanish sounds. But that was cheating, somebody shouted. Everyone laughed. In school, meanwhile, like my brother and sister, I was required to attend a daily tutoring session. I needed a full year of special attention. I also needed my teachers to keep my attention from straying in class by calling out, *Rich-heard* — their English voices slowly prying loose my ties to my other name, its three notes, *Ri-car-do*. Most of all I needed to hear my mother and father speak to me in a moment of seriousness in broken — suddenly heartbreaking — English. The scene was inevitable: one Saturday morning I entered the kitchen where my parents were talking in Spanish. I did not realize that they were talking in Spanish however until, at the moment they saw me, I heard their voices change to speak English. Those *gringo* sounds they uttered startled me. Pushed me away. In that moment of trivial misunderstanding and profound insight, I felt my throat twisted by unsounded grief. I turned quickly and left the room. But I had no place to escape to with Spanish. (The spell was broken.) My brother and sisters were speaking English in another part of the house.

Again and again in the days following, increasingly angry, I was obliged to hear my mother and father: "Speak to us *en inglés.*" (*Speak.*) Only then did I determine to learn classroom English. Weeks after, it happened: one day in school I raised my hand to volunteer an answer. I spoke out in a loud voice. And I did not think it remarkable when the entire class understood. That day, I moved very far from the disadvantaged child I had been only days earlier. The belief, the calming assurance that I belonged in public, had at last taken hold.

Shortly after, I stopped hearing the high and loud sounds of *los gringos*. A more and more confident speaker of English, I didn't trouble to listen to *how* strangers sounded, speaking to me. And there simply were too many English-speaking people in my day for me to hear American accents anymore. Conversations quickened. Listening to persons who sounded eccentrically pitched voices, I usually noted their sounds for an initial few seconds before I concentrated on *what* they were saying. Conversations became content-full. Transparent. Hearing someone's *tone* of voice — angry or questioning or sarcastic or happy or sad — I didn't distinguish it from the words it expressed. Sound and word were thus tightly wedded. At the end of a day, I was often bemused, always relieved, to realize how "silent," though crowded with words, my day in public had been. (This public silence measured and quickened the change in my life.)

At last, seven years old, I came to believe what had been technically true 35
since my birth: I was an American citizen.

But the special feeling of closeness at home was diminished by then. Gone was the desperate, urgent, intense feeling of being at home; rare was the experience of feeling myself individualized by family intimates. We remained a loving family, but one greatly changed. No longer so close; no longer bound tight by the pleasing and troubling knowledge of our public separateness. Neither my older brother nor sister rushed home after school anymore. Nor did I. When I arrived home there would often be neighborhood kids in the house. Or the house would be empty of sounds.

Following the dramatic Americanization of their children, even my parents grew more publicly confident. Especially my mother. She learned the names of all the people on our block. And she decided we needed to have a telephone installed in the house. My father continued to use the word *gringo*. But it was no longer charged with the old bitterness or distrust. (Stripped of any emotional content, the word simply became a name for those Americans not of Hispanic descent.) Hearing him, sometimes, I wasn't sure if he was pronouncing the Spanish word *gringo* or saying gringo in English.

Matching the silence I started hearing in public was a new quiet at home. The family's quiet was partly due to the fact that, as we children learned more and more English, we shared fewer and fewer words with our parents. Sentences needed to be spoken slowly when a child addressed his mother or father. (Often the parent wouldn't understand.) The child would need to repeat himself. (Still the parent misunderstood.) The young voice, frustrated, would end up saying, "Never mind" — the subject was closed. Dinners would be noisy with the clinking of knives and forks against dishes. My mother would smile softly between her remarks; my father at the other end of the table would chew and chew at his food, while he stared over the heads of his children.

My *mother*! My *father*! After English became my primary language, I no longer knew what words to use in addressing my parents. The old Spanish words (those tender accents of sound) I had used earlier — *mamá* and *papá* — I couldn't use anymore. They would have been too painful reminders of how much had changed in my life. On the other hand, the words I heard neighborhood kids call *their* parents seemed equally unsatisfactory. *Mother* and *Father*; *Ma, Papa, Pa, Dad, Pop* (how I hated the all-American sound of that last word especially) — all these terms I felt were unsuitable, not really terms of address for *my* parents. As a result, I never used them at home. Whenever I'd speak to my parents, I would try to get their attention with eye contact alone. In public conversations, I'd refer to "my parents" or "my mother and father."

My mother and father, for their part, responded differently, as their children 40
spoke to them less. She grew restless, seemed troubled and anxious at the scarcity of words exchanged in the house. It was she who would question me about my day when I came home from school. She smiled at small talk. She pried at the edges of my sentences to get me to say something more. (What?) She'd join conversations she overheard, but her intrusions often stopped her children's talking. By contrast, my father seemed reconciled to the new quiet. Though his English improved somewhat, he retired into silence. At dinner he spoke very little. One night his children and even his wife helplessly giggled at his garbled English pronunciation of the Catholic Grace before Meals. Thereafter he made his wife recite the prayer at the start of each meal, even on formal occasions, when there were guests in the house. Hers became the public voice of the family. On official business, it was she, not my father, one would usually hear on the phone or in stores, talking to strangers. His children grew so accustomed to his silence that, years later, they would speak routinely of his shyness. (My mother would often try to explain: both his parents died when he was eight. He was raised by an uncle who treated him like little more than a menial servant. He was never encouraged to speak. He grew up alone. A man of few words.) But my father was not shy, I realized, when I'd watch him speaking Spanish with relatives. Using Spanish, he was quickly effusive. Especially when talking with other men, his voice would spark, flicker, flare alive with sounds. In Spanish, he expressed ideas and feelings he rarely revealed in English. With firm Spanish sounds, he conveyed confidence and authority English would never allow him.

The silence at home, however, was finally more than a literal silence. Fewer words passed between parent and child, but more profound was the silence that resulted from my inattention to sounds. At about the time I no longer bothered to listen with care to the sounds of English in public, I grew careless about listening to the sounds family members made when they spoke. Most of the time I heard someone speaking at home and didn't distinguish his sounds from the words people uttered in public. I didn't even pay much attention to my parents' accented and ungrammatical speech. At least not at home. Only when I was with them in public would I grow alert to their accents. Though, even then, their sounds caused me less and less concern. For I was increasingly confident of my own public identity.

I would have been happier about my public success had I not sometimes recalled what it had been like earlier, when my family had conveyed its intimacy through a set of conveniently private sounds. Sometimes in public, hearing a stranger, I'd hark back to my past. A Mexican farmworker approached me downtown to ask directions to somewhere. "*¿Hijito . . . ?*" he said. And his voice summoned deep longing. Another time, standing beside my mother in the visiting room of a Carmelite convent, before the dense screen which rendered the nuns shadowy figures, I heard several Spanish-speaking nuns — their busy, singsong overlapping voices — assure us that yes, yes, we were remembered, all our family was remembered in their prayers. (Their voices echoed faraway family sounds.) Another day, a dark-faced old woman — her hand light on my shoulder — steadied herself against me as she boarded a bus. She murmured something I couldn't quite comprehend. Her Spanish voice came near, like the face of a never-before-seen relative in the instant before I was kissed. Her voice, like so many of the Spanish voices I'd hear in public, recalled the golden age of my youth. Hearing Spanish then, I continued to be a careful, if sad, listener to sounds. Hearing a Spanish-speaking family walking behind me, I turned to look. I smiled for an instant, before my glance found the Hispanic-looking faces of strangers in the crowd going by.

Today I hear bilingual educators say that children lose a degree of "individuality" by becoming assimilated into public society. (Bilingual schooling was popularized in the seventies, that decade when middle-class ethnics began to resist the process of assimilation — the American melting pot.) But the bilingualists simplistically scorn the value and necessity of assimilation. They do not seem to realize that there are *two* ways a person is individualized. So they do not realize that while one suffers a diminished sense of *private* individuality by becoming assimilated into public society, such assimilation makes possible the achievement of *public* individuality.

The bilingualists insist that a student should be reminded of his difference from others in mass society, his heritage. But they equate mere separateness with individuality. The fact is that only in private — with intimates — is separateness from the crowd a prerequisite for individuality. (An intimate draws me apart, tells me that I am unique, unlike all others.) In public, by contrast, full individuality is achieved, paradoxically, by those who are able to consider themselves members of the crowd. Thus it happened for me: only when I was able to think of myself as an American, no longer an alien in *gringo* society, could I seek the rights and opportunities necessary for full public individuality. The social and political advantages I enjoy as a man result from the day that I came to believe that my name, indeed, is *Rich-heard Road-ree-guess*. It is true that my public society today is often impersonal. (My public society is usually mass society.) Yet despite the anonymity of the crowd and despite the fact that the individuality I achieve in public is often tenuous — because it depends on my being one in a crowd — I celebrate the day I acquired my new name. Those middle-class ethnics who scorn assimilation seem to me filled with decadent self-pity, obsessed by the burden of public life. Dangerously, they romanticize public separateness and they trivialize the dilemma of the socially disadvantaged.

My awkward childhood does not prove the necessity of bilingual education. 45
My story discloses instead an essential myth of childhood — inevitable pain. If I rehearse here the changes in my private life after my Americanization, it is finally to emphasize the public gain. The loss implies the gain: the house I returned to each afternoon was quiet. Intimate sounds no longer rushed to the door to greet me. There were other noises inside. The telephone rang. Neighborhood kids ran past the door of the bedroom where I was reading my schoolbooks — covered with shopping-bag paper. Once I learned public language, it would never again be easy for me to hear intimate family voices. More and more of my day was spent hearing words. But that may only be a way of saying that the day I raised my hand in class and spoke loudly to an entire roomful of faces, my childhood started to end. *[1982]*

THINKING ABOUT THE TEXT

1. What distinctions does Rodriguez make between the "private" and "public" worlds of his childhood? Ultimately, he brings up the possibility of "*public* individuality" (para. 43). What does he mean by this? Does this concept make sense to you?
2. What, according to Rodriguez, were the changes he experienced? With what tone does he recall these changes? Consider in particular the way he describes his changing relationship to his parents.
3. Do you agree with Rodriguez that the changes he went through were necessary? To what extent is your answer influenced by your own social position?
4. Rodriguez declares, "Those middle-class ethnics who scorn assimilation seem to me filled with decadent self-pity, obsessed by the burden of public life. Dangerously, they romanticize public separateness and they trivialize the dilemma of the socially disadvantaged" (para. 44). Evaluate this claim. Would you say that you are a "middle-class ethnic"? Why, or why not?
5. Rodriguez suggests that a student must speak up in class to succeed in school. Do you agree? Rodriguez indicates that matters of language play a crucial role in a child's education. Have you found this true? Be specific.

JOSE ANTONIO VARGAS

My Life as an Undocumented Immigrant

Jose Antonio Vargas (b. 1981) is a journalist, filmmaker, and immigrant activist. He was born in the Philippines and at the age of twelve was sent to the United States to live with his grandparents, but without official authorization. He became interested in journalism in high school and became a copy boy with the San Francisco Chronicle. *After graduating from San Francisco State University, he began writing at the* Washington Post. *Vargas was part of a team working on the story of the Virginia Tech shootings that earned him a Pulitzer Prize. In 2009 he joined the staff of the* Huffington Post. *The following essay was published in the* New York Times Sunday Magazine *and won the June 2011 Sidney Award as an "outstanding piece of socially conscious journalism." He continues to be an activist for immigrant issues.*

One August morning nearly two decades ago, my mother woke me and put me in a cab. She handed me a jacket. "*Baka malamig doon*" were among the few words she said. ("It might be cold there.") When I arrived at the Philippines' Ninoy Aquino International Airport with her, my aunt, and a family friend, I was introduced to a man I'd never seen. They told me he was my uncle. He held my hand as I boarded an airplane for the first time. It was 1993, and I was twelve.

My mother wanted to give me a better life, so she sent me thousands of miles away to live with her parents in America—my grandfather (*Lolo* in Tagalog) and grandmother (*Lola*). After I arrived in Mountain View, California, in the San Francisco Bay Area, I entered sixth grade and quickly grew to love my new home, family, and culture. I discovered a passion for language, though it was hard to learn the difference between formal English and American slang. One of my early memories is of a freckled kid in middle school asking me, "What's up?" I replied, "The sky," and he and a couple of other kids laughed. I won the eighth-grade spelling bee by memorizing words I couldn't properly pronounce. (The winning word was "indefatigable.")

One day when I was sixteen, I rode my bike to the nearby D.M.V. office to get my driver's permit. Some of my friends already had their licenses, so I figured it was time. But when I handed the clerk my green card as proof of U.S. residency, she flipped it around, examining it. "This is fake," she whispered. "Don't come back here again."

Confused and scared, I pedaled home and confronted Lolo. I remember him sitting in the garage, cutting coupons. I dropped my bike and ran over to him, showing him the green card. "*Peke ba ito?*" I asked in Tagalog. ("Is this fake?") My grandparents were naturalized American citizens—he worked as a security guard, she as a food server—and they had begun supporting my mother and me financially when I was three, after my father's wandering eye and inability to properly provide for us led to my parents' separation. Lolo was a proud man, and I saw the shame on his face as he told me he purchased the card, along with other fake documents, for me. "Don't show it to other people," he warned.

I decided then that I could never give anyone reason to doubt I was an American. 5
I convinced myself that if I worked enough, if I achieved enough, I would be rewarded with citizenship. I felt I could earn it.

I've tried. Over the past fourteen years, I've graduated from high school and college and built a career as a journalist, interviewing some of the most famous people in the country. On the surface, I've created a good life. I've lived the American dream.

But I am still an undocumented immigrant. And that means living a different kind of reality. It means going about my day in fear of being found out. It means rarely trusting people, even those closest to me, with who I really am. It means keeping my family photos in a shoebox rather than displaying them on shelves in my home, so friends don't ask about them. It means reluctantly, even painfully, doing things I know are wrong and unlawful. And it has meant relying on a sort of twenty-first-century underground railroad of supporters, people who took an interest in my future and took risks for me.

Last year I read about four students who walked from Miami to Washington to lobby for the Dream Act, a nearly decade-old immigration bill that would provide a path to legal permanent residency for young people who have been educated in this country. At the risk of deportation—the Obama administration has deported almost 800,000 people in the last two years—they are speaking out. Their courage has inspired me.

There are believed to be 11 million undocumented immigrants in the United States. We're not always who you think we are. Some pick your strawberries or care for your children. Some are in high school or college. And some, it turns out, write news articles you might read. I grew up here. This is my home. Yet even though I think of myself as an American and consider America my country, my country doesn't think of me as one of its own.

10 My first challenge was the language. Though I learned English in the Philippines, I wanted to lose my accent. During high school, I spent hours at a time watching television (especially *Frasier*, *Home Improvement*, and reruns of *The Golden Girls*) and movies (from *Goodfellas* to *Anne of Green Gables*), pausing the VHS to try to copy how various characters enunciated their words. At the local library, I read magazines, books, and newspapers—anything to learn how to write better. Kathy Dewar, my high-school English teacher, introduced me to journalism. From the moment I wrote my first article for the student paper, I convinced myself that having my name in print—writing in English, interviewing Americans—validated my presence here.

The debates over "illegal aliens" intensified my anxieties. In 1994, only a year after my flight from the Philippines, Governor Pete Wilson was re-elected in part because of his support for Proposition 187, which prohibited undocumented immigrants from attending public school and accessing other services. (A federal court later found the law unconstitutional.) After my encounter at the D.M.V. in 1997, I grew more aware of anti-immigrant sentiments and stereotypes: *they don't want to assimilate, they are a drain on society*. They're not talking about me, I would tell myself. I have something to contribute.

To do that, I had to work—and for that, I needed a Social Security number. Fortunately, my grandfather had already managed to get one for me. Lolo had always taken care of everyone in the family. He and my grandmother emigrated legally in 1984 from Zambales, a province in the Philippines of rice fields and bamboo houses, following Lolo's sister, who married a Filipino American serving in the American military. She petitioned for her brother and his wife to join her. When they got here, Lolo petitioned for his two children—my mother and her younger brother—to follow them. But instead of mentioning that my mother was a married woman, he listed her as single. Legal residents can't petition for their married children. Besides, Lolo didn't care for my father. He didn't want him coming here too.

But soon Lolo grew nervous that the immigration authorities reviewing the petition would discover my mother was married, thus derailing not only her chances of coming here but those of my uncle as well. So he withdrew her petition. After my uncle came to America legally in 1991, Lolo tried to get my mother here through a tourist visa, but she wasn't able to obtain one. That's when she decided to send me. My mother told me later that she figured she would follow me soon. She never did.

The "uncle" who brought me here turned out to be a coyote,° not a relative, my grandfather later explained. Lolo scraped together enough money—I eventually learned it was $4,500, a huge sum for him—to pay him to smuggle me here under a fake name and fake passport. (I never saw the passport again after the flight and have always assumed that the coyote kept it.) After I arrived in America, Lolo obtained a new fake Filipino passport, in my real name this time, adorned with a fake student visa, in addition to the fraudulent green card.

Using the fake passport, we went to the local Social Security Administration 15
office and applied for a Social Security number and card. It was, I remember, a quick visit. When the card came in the mail, it had my full, real name, but it also clearly stated: "Valid for work only with I.N.S. authorization."

When I began looking for work, a short time after the D.M.V. incident, my grandfather and I took the Social Security card to Kinko's, where he covered the "I.N.S. authorization" text with a sliver of white tape. We then made photocopies of the card. At a glance, at least, the copies would look like copies of a regular, unrestricted Social Security card.

Lolo always imagined I would work the kind of low-paying jobs that undocumented people often take. (Once I married an American, he said, I would get my real papers, and everything would be fine.) But even menial jobs require documents, so he and I hoped the doctored card would work for now. The more documents I had, he said, the better.

While in high school, I worked part time at Subway, then at the front desk of the local Y.M.C.A., then at a tennis club, until I landed an unpaid internship at the *Mountain View Voice*, my hometown newspaper. First I brought coffee and helped around the office; eventually I began covering city-hall meetings and other assignments for pay.

For more than a decade of getting part-time and full-time jobs, employers have rarely asked to check my original Social Security card. When they did, I showed the photocopied version, which they accepted. Over time, I also began checking the citizenship box on my federal I-9 employment eligibility forms. (Claiming full citizenship was actually easier than declaring permanent resident "green card" status, which would have required me to provide an alien registration number.)

coyote: A person who smuggles undocumented aliens across the border into the United States, usually for a fee.

This deceit never got easier. The more I did it, the more I felt like an impostor, 20
the more guilt I carried — and the more I worried that I would get caught. But I kept doing it. I needed to live and survive on my own, and I decided this was the way.

Mountain View High School became my second home. I was elected to represent my school at school-board meetings, which gave me the chance to meet and befriend Rich Fischer, the superintendent for our school district. I joined the speech and debate team, acted in school plays, and eventually became co-editor of the *Oracle*, the student newspaper. That drew the attention of my principal, Pat Hyland. "You're at school just as much as I am," she told me. Pat and Rich would soon become mentors, and over time, almost surrogate parents for me.

After a choir rehearsal during my junior year, Jill Denny, the choir director, told me she was considering a Japan trip for our singing group. I told her I couldn't afford it, but she said we'd figure out a way. I hesitated, and then decided to tell her the truth. "It's not really the money," I remember saying. "I don't have the right passport." When she assured me we'd get the proper documents, I finally told her. "I can't get the right passport," I said. "I'm not supposed to be here."

She understood. So the choir toured Hawaii instead, with me in tow. (Mrs. Denny and I spoke a couple of months ago, and she told me she hadn't wanted to leave any student behind.)

Later that school year, my history class watched a documentary on Harvey Milk, the openly gay San Francisco city official who was assassinated. This was 1999, just six months after Matthew Shepard's body was found tied to a fence in Wyoming. During the discussion, I raised my hand and said something like: "I'm sorry Harvey Milk got killed for being gay. . . . I've been meaning to say this. . . . I'm gay."

I hadn't planned on coming out that morning, though I had known that I 25
was gay for several years. With that announcement, I became the only openly gay student at school, and it caused turmoil with my grandparents. Lolo kicked me out of the house for a few weeks. Though we eventually reconciled, I had disappointed him on two fronts. First, as a Catholic, he considered homosexuality a sin and was embarrassed about having "*ang apo na bakla*" ("a grandson who is gay"). Even worse, I was making matters more difficult for myself, he said. I needed to marry an American woman in order to gain a green card.

Tough as it was, coming out about being gay seemed less daunting than coming out about my legal status. I kept my other secret mostly hidden.

While my classmates awaited their college acceptance letters, I hoped to get a full-time job at the *Mountain View Voice* after graduation. It's not that I didn't want to go to college, but I couldn't apply for state and federal financial aid. Without that, my family couldn't afford to send me.

But when I finally told Pat and Rich about my immigration "problem" — as we called it from then on — they helped me look for a solution. At first, they even wondered if one of them could adopt me and fix the situation that way, but a lawyer Rich consulted told him it wouldn't change my legal status because I was too old. Eventually they connected me to a new scholarship fund for high-potential students who were usually the first in their families to attend college. Most important, the fund was not concerned with immigration status. I was among the first recipients, with the scholarship covering tuition, lodging, books, and other expenses for my studies at San Francisco State University.

As a college freshman, I found a job working part time at the *San Francisco Chronicle*, where I sorted mail and wrote some freelance articles. My ambition was to get a reporting job, so I embarked on a series of internships. First I landed at the *Philadelphia Daily News*, in the summer of 2001, where I covered a drive-by shooting and the wedding of the 76ers star Allen Iverson. Using those articles, I applied to the *Seattle Times* and got an internship for the following summer.

But then my lack of proper documents became a problem again. The *Times*'s 30
recruiter, Pat Foote, asked all incoming interns to bring certain paperwork on their first day: a birth certificate, or a passport, or a driver's license plus an original Social Security card. I panicked, thinking my documents wouldn't pass muster. So before starting the job, I called Pat and told her about my legal status. After consulting with management, she called me back with the answer I feared: I couldn't do the internship.

This was devastating. What good was college if I couldn't then pursue the career I wanted? I decided then that if I was to succeed in a profession that is all about truth-telling, I couldn't tell the truth about myself.

After this episode, Jim Strand, the venture capitalist who sponsored my scholarship, offered to pay for an immigration lawyer. Rich and I went to meet her in San Francisco's financial district.

I was hopeful. This was in early 2002, shortly after Senators Orrin Hatch, the Utah Republican, and Dick Durbin, the Illinois Democrat, introduced the Dream Act—Development, Relief, and Education for Alien Minors. It seemed like the legislative version of what I'd told myself: If I work hard and contribute, things will work out.

But the meeting left me crushed. My only solution, the lawyer said, was to go back to the Philippines and accept a ten-year ban before I could apply to return legally.

If Rich was discouraged, he hid it well. "Put this problem on a shelf," he told 35
me. "Compartmentalize it. Keep going."

And I did. For the summer of 2003, I applied for internships across the country. Several newspapers, including the *Wall Street Journal*, the *Boston Globe*, and the *Chicago Tribune*, expressed interest. But when the *Washington Post* offered me a spot, I knew where I would go. And this time, I had no intention of acknowledging my "problem."

The *Post* internship posed a tricky obstacle: It required a driver's license. (After my close call at the California D.M.V., I'd never gotten one.) So I spent an afternoon at the Mountain View Public Library, studying various states' requirements. Oregon was among the most welcoming—and it was just a few hours' drive north.

Again, my support network came through. A friend's father lived in Portland, and he allowed me to use his address as proof of residency. Pat, Rich, and Rich's longtime assistant, Mary Moore, sent letters to me at that address. Rich taught me how to do three-point turns in a parking lot, and a friend accompanied me to Portland.

The license meant everything to me—it would let me drive, fly, and work. But my grandparents worried about the Portland trip and the Washington internship. While Lola offered daily prayers so that I would not get caught, Lolo told me that I was dreaming too big, risking too much.

I was determined to pursue my ambitions. I was twenty-two, I told them, 40
responsible for my own actions. But this was different from Lolo's driving a confused teenager to Kinko's. I knew what I was doing now, and I knew it wasn't right. But what was I supposed to do?

I was paying state and federal taxes, but I was using an invalid Social Security card and writing false information on my employment forms. But that seemed better than depending on my grandparents or on Pat, Rich, and Jim—or returning to a country I barely remembered. I convinced myself all would be O.K. if I lived up to the qualities of a "citizen": hard work, self-reliance, love of my country.

At the D.M.V. in Portland, I arrived with my photocopied Social Security card, my college I.D., a pay stub from the *San Francisco Chronicle*, and my proof of state residence—the letters to the Portland address that my support network had sent. It worked. My license, issued in 2003, was set to expire eight years later, on my thirtieth birthday, on February 3, 2011. I had eight years to succeed professionally, and to hope that some sort of immigration reform would pass in the meantime and allow me to stay.

It seemed like all the time in the world.

My summer in Washington was exhilarating. I was intimidated to be in a major newsroom but was assigned a mentor—Peter Perl, a veteran magazine writer—to help me navigate it. A few weeks into the internship, he printed out one of my articles, about a guy who recovered a long-lost wallet, circled the first two paragraphs, and left it on my desk. "Great eye for details—awesome!" he wrote. Though I didn't know it then, Peter would become one more member of my network.

At the end of the summer, I returned to the *San Francisco Chronicle*. My plan 45
was to finish school—I was now a senior—while I worked for the *Chronicle* as a reporter for the city desk. But when the *Post* beckoned again, offering me a full-time, two-year paid internship that I could start when I graduated in June 2004, it was too tempting to pass up. I moved back to Washington.

About four months into my job as a reporter for the *Post*, I began feeling increasingly paranoid, as if I had "illegal immigrant" tattooed on my forehead—and in Washington, of all places, where the debates over immigration seemed never-ending. I was so eager to prove myself that I feared I was annoying some colleagues and editors—and worried that any one of these professional journalists could discover my secret. The anxiety was nearly paralyzing. I decided I had to tell one of the higher-ups about my situation. I turned to Peter.

By this time, Peter, who still works at the *Post*, had become part of management as the paper's director of newsroom training and professional development.

One afternoon in late October, we walked a couple of blocks to Lafayette Square, across from the White House. Over some twenty minutes, sitting on a bench, I told him everything: the Social Security card, the driver's license, Pat and Rich, my family.

Peter was shocked. "I understand you 100 times better now," he said. He told me that I had done the right thing by telling him, and that it was now our shared problem. He said he didn't want to do anything about it just yet. I had just been hired, he said, and I needed to prove myself. "When you've done enough," he said, "we'll tell Don and Len together." (Don Graham is the chairman of the Washington Post Company; Leonard Downie Jr. was then the paper's executive editor.) A month later, I spent my first Thanksgiving in Washington with Peter and his family.

In the five years that followed, I did my best to "do enough." I was promoted to staff writer, reported on video-game culture, wrote a series on Washington's H.I.V./AIDS epidemic, and covered the role of technology and social media in the 2008 presidential race. I visited the White House, where I interviewed senior aides and covered a state dinner—and gave the Secret Service the Social Security number I obtained with false documents.

50 I did my best to steer clear of reporting on immigration policy but couldn't always avoid it. On two occasions, I wrote about Hillary Clinton's position on driver's licenses for undocumented immigrants. I also wrote an article about Senator Mel Martinez of Florida, then the chairman of the Republican National Committee, who was defending his party's stance toward Latinos after only one Republican presidential candidate—John McCain, the coauthor of a failed immigration bill—agreed to participate in a debate sponsored by Univision, the Spanish-language network.

It was an odd sort of dance: I was trying to stand out in a highly competitive newsroom, yet I was terrified that if I stood out too much, I'd invite unwanted scrutiny. I tried to compartmentalize my fears, distract myself by reporting on the lives of other people, but there was no escaping the central conflict in my life. Maintaining a deception for so long distorts your sense of self. You start wondering who you've become, and why.

In April 2008, I was part of a *Post* team that won a Pulitzer Prize for the paper's coverage of the Virginia Tech shootings a year earlier. Lolo died a year earlier, so it was Lola who called me the day of the announcement. The first thing she said was, "*Anong mangyayari kung malaman ng mga tao?*"

What will happen if people find out?

I couldn't say anything. After we got off the phone, I rushed to the bathroom on the fourth floor of the newsroom, sat down on the toilet, and cried.

In the summer of 2009, without ever having had that follow-up talk with top *Post* management, I left the paper and moved to New York to join the *Huffington Post*. I met Arianna Huffington at a Washington Press Club Foundation dinner I was covering for the *Post* two years earlier, and she later recruited me to join her news site. I wanted to learn more about Web publishing, and I thought the new job would provide a useful education.

Still, I was apprehensive about the move: many companies were already using E-Verify, a program set up by the Department of Homeland Security that checks if prospective employees are eligible to work, and I didn't know if my new employer was among them. But I'd been able to get jobs in other newsrooms, I figured, so I filled out the paperwork as usual and succeeded in landing on the payroll.

While I worked at the *Huffington Post*, other opportunities emerged. My H.I.V./AIDS series became a documentary film called "The Other City," which opened at the Tribeca Film Festival last year and was broadcast on Showtime. I began writing for magazines and landed a dream assignment: profiling Facebook's Mark Zuckerberg for *The New Yorker*.

The more I achieved, the more scared and depressed I became. I was proud of my work, but there was always a cloud hanging over it, over me. My old eight-year deadline—the expiration of my Oregon driver's license—was approaching.

After slightly less than a year, I decided to leave the *Huffington Post*. In part, this was because I wanted to promote the documentary and write a book about online culture—or so I told my friends. But the real reason was, after so many years of trying to be a part of the system, of focusing all my energy on my professional life, I learned that no amount of professional success would solve my problem or ease the sense of loss and displacement I felt. I lied to a friend about why I couldn't take a weekend trip to Mexico. Another time I concocted an excuse for why I couldn't go on an all-expenses-paid trip to Switzerland. I have been unwilling, for years, to be in a long-term relationship because I never wanted anyone to get too close and ask too many questions. All the while, Lola's question was stuck in my head: What will happen if people find out?

60 Early this year, just two weeks before my thirtieth birthday, I won a small reprieve: I obtained a driver's license in the state of Washington. The license is valid until 2016. This offered me five more years of acceptable identification—but also five more years of fear, of lying to people I respect and institutions that trusted me, of running away from who I am.

I'm done running. I'm exhausted. I don't want that life anymore.

So I've decided to come forward, own up to what I've done, and tell my story to the best of my recollection. I've reached out to former bosses and employers and apologized for misleading them—a mix of humiliation and liberation coming with each disclosure. All the people mentioned in this article gave me permission to use their names. I've also talked to family and friends about my situation and am working with legal counsel to review my options. I don't know what the consequences will be of telling my story.

I do know that I am grateful to my grandparents, my Lolo and Lola, for giving me the chance for a better life. I'm also grateful to my other family—the support network I found here in America—for encouraging me to pursue my dreams.

It's been almost eighteen years since I've seen my mother. Early on, I was mad at her for putting me in this position, and then mad at myself for being angry and ungrateful. By the time I got to college, we rarely spoke by phone. It became too painful; after a while it was easier to just send money to help support her and my two half-siblings. My sister, almost two years old when I left, is almost twenty now. I've never met my fourteen-year-old brother. I would love to see them.

Not long ago, I called my mother. I wanted to fill the gaps in my memory about that August morning so many years ago. We had never discussed it. Part of me wanted to shove the memory aside, but to write this article and face the facts of my life, I needed more details. Did I cry? Did she? Did we kiss goodbye?

My mother told me I was excited about meeting a stewardess, about getting on a plane. She also reminded me of the one piece of advice she gave me for blending in: If anyone asked why I was coming to America, I should say I was going to Disneyland. *[2011]*

WRITING ABOUT THE TEXT

1. Who is the audience for this essay? What response do you think Vargas wants? What likely response will he get? What is your response to this confession?
2. Why does Vargas mention the incident where he asserts that he is gay? Do you think this will make him more or less sympathetic?
3. Comment on the tension between Vargas telling the truth and fulfilling his dream. Mention at least three specific examples and say why you think he made the right or wrong choice.
4. If this essay were to be considered an attempt at persuasion, point out two or three incidents and say why you think they are persuasive.
5. Why do you think Vargas opens and closes with accounts of his mother? What significance do you think should be attributed to Vargas's mention of Disneyland in the last sentence?

MAKING COMPARISONS

1. Compare Rodriguez's and Vargas's childhood views of English.
2. Rodriguez has generally been criticized by the immigrant activists, while Vargas has been praised. Point to attitudes in these two essays that might account for such a difference.
3. What lessons have Rodriguez's and Vargas's childhoods taught them?

WRITING ABOUT ISSUES

1. Argue that either Rodriguez or Vargas has more successfully crossed the boundary between immigrant and mainstream culture.
2. Write an essay that argues that Vargas should or should not be allowed to become an American citizen.
3. There is a complex and emotional debate in Congress over illegal immigrants. What seem to you to be the most cogent arguments on both sides? Explain why.
4. Locate Vargas's cover story for *Time* (June 15, 2012) on undocumented immigrants and argue that he does or does not offer a compelling solution.

Traumatic Journeys: Across Genres

WILFRED OWEN, "Dulce et Decorum Est" (poem)

MICHAEL HERR, "Scream a Lot" (essay)

THOMAS LUX, "The People of the Other Village" (poem)

Perhaps no one depicts the graphic horrors of war more effectively than Wilfred Owen, one of several talented poets who wrote of the gruesome horrors of trench warfare during World War I. He was tragically shot in the head one week before the end of the war. We know now that many thousands of soldiers who were forced to witness the mutilation and death of their comrade returned home with posttraumatic stress disorder (PTSD), although it was then called "shell shock" by those who thought the percussion of the bombs affected emotional stability. Incredibly, many military leaders at this time saw the symptoms of these men as the result of moral weakness. It was not until thousands of Vietnam soldiers returned home with severe psychological wounds that the cause of their alienation and depression was fully acknowledged as a valid psychological disorder with devastating and often deadly consequences. Both Owen and Herr describe conditions that would traumatize ordinary, healthy people. Trauma studies in recent years have also found that sexual and domestic abuse and political terror can induce the same symptoms in victims as the ravages of war. Thomas Lux's poem describes the kind of loss of humanity that often occurs in traumatized people battered by constant brutality and terror.

WILFRED OWEN

Dulce et Decorum Est

English poet and soldier Wilfred Owen (1893–1918) is regarded as the best war poet of World War I, known for his frank and disturbingly realistic depictions of the horrors of trench and gas warfare. He attended what is now the University of Reading for a while and taught at the Berlitz School of Languages in Bordeaux. He enlisted in the war in 1915 and was commissioned as a second lieutenant. He was wounded and suffered "shell shock." He was sent home but returned to the front and was killed one week before the Armistice. He is often linked with his mentor and fellow poet Siegfried Sassoon, who inspired Owen's gritty realism and his focus on showing the "the pity of war."

Bent double, like old beggars under sacks,
Knock-kneed, coughing like hags, we cursed through sludge,
Till on the haunting flares we turned our backs
And towards our distant rest began to trudge.
Men marched asleep. Many had lost their boots
But limped on, blood-shod. All went lame; all blind;
Drunk with fatigue; deaf even to the hoots
Of disappointed shells that dropped behind.

Officer Cadet Owen in July 1916
scrupulously – too scrupulously, Harold thought – parted down th
middle. Wilfred detected disapproval and said:

Fotosearch/Getty Images

GAS! Gas! Quick, boys! — An ecstasy of fumbling,
Fitting the clumsy helmets just in time;
But someone still was yelling out and stumbling
And floundering like a man in fire or lime. —
Dim, through the misty panes and thick green light
As under a green sea, I saw him drowning.

In all my dreams, before my helpless sight,
He plunges at me, guttering, choking, drowning.

If in some smothering dreams you too could pace
Behind the wagon that we flung him in,
And watch the white eyes writhing in his face,
His hanging face, like a devil's sick of sin;
If you could hear, at every jolt, the blood
Come gargling from the froth-corrupted lungs,
Obscene as cancer, bitter as the cud
Of vile, incurable sores on innocent tongues, —
My friend, you would not tell with such high zest
To children ardent for some desperate glory,
The old Lie: Dulce et decorum est
Pro patria mori.

[1920]

THINKING ABOUT THE TEXT

1. What does the Latin quote that ends the poem (and from which its title is taken) mean? Why do you think Owen chose Latin?
2. Which images seem particularly gruesome to you? What do you think Owen's purpose is in being so graphic?
3. Most poets don't directly address the reader. Owen does, making a request, hoping the reader will do something. What is it? Do you agree with him? In what ways is this poem an act of persuasion? Is it effective?
4. What statement about war do you think Owen would agree with?
5. In the opening lines of the last stanza, Owen seems to be saying that if you experienced war, it would change your mind. Do you think there are other ways to convince people of war's horrors?

MICHAEL HERR

Scream a Lot

Michael Herr (b. 1940) was a correspondent during the Vietnam War for Esquire *magazine.* Dispatches, *a memoir of that experience, won high praise from critics and readers. John le Carré, the spy novelist, said it was "the best book I have ever read on men and war in our time." The following is an excerpt from that memoir. Herr also worked on the films* Full Metal Jacket *with Stanley Kubrick and* Apocalypse Now *with Francis Ford Coppola. His other books are* Walter Winchell: A Novel *(1990) and* Kubrick *(2000).*

You could make all the ritual moves, carry your lucky piece, wear your magic jungle hat, kiss your thumb knuckle smooth as stones under running water, the Inscrutable Immutable was still out there, and you kept on or not at its pitiless discretion. All you could say that wasn't fundamentally lame was something like, "He who bites it this day is safe from the next," and that was exactly what nobody wanted to hear.

After enough time passed and memory receded and settled, the name itself became a prayer, coded like all prayer to go past the extremes of petition and gratitude: Vietnam Vietnam Vietnam, say again, until the word lost all its old loads of pain, pleasure, horror, guilt, nostalgia. Then and there, everyone was just trying to get through it, existential crunch, no atheists in foxholes like you wouldn't believe. Even bitter refracted faith was better than none at all, like the black Marine I'd heard about during heavy shelling at Con Thien who said, "Don't worry, baby, God'll think of something."

Flip religion, it was so far out, you couldn't blame anybody for believing anything. Guys dressed up in Batman fetishes, I saw a whole squad like that, it gave them a kind of dumb esprit. Guys stuck the ace of spades in their helmet bands, they picked relics off of an enemy they'd killed, a little transfer of

Dudley Reed/Contour

power; they carried around five-pound Bibles from home, crosses, St. Christophers, mezuzahs, locks of hair, girlfriends' underwear, snaps of their families, their wives, their dogs, their cows, their cars, pictures of John Kennedy, Lyndon Johnson, Martin Luther King, Huey Newton, the Pope, Che Guevara, the Beatles, Jimi Hendrix, wiggier than cargo cultists. One man was carrying an oatmeal cookie through his tour, wrapped up in foil and plastic and three pair of socks. He took a lot of shit about it ("When you go to sleep we're gonna eat your . . . cookie"), but his wife had baked it and mailed it to him, he wasn't kidding.

On operations you'd see men clustering around the charmed grunt that many outfits created who would take himself and whoever stayed close enough through a field of safety, at least until he rotated home or got blown away, and then the outfit would hand the charm to someone else. If a bullet creased your head or you'd stepped on a dud mine or a grenade rolled between your feet and just lay there, you were magic enough. If you had any kind of extra-sense capacity, if you could smell VC° or their danger the way hunting guides smelled the coming weather, if you had special night vision, or great ears, you were magic too; anything bad that happened to you could leave the men in your outfit pretty depressed. I met a man in the Cav . . . one afternoon, sound asleep in a huge tent with thirty cots inside, all empty but his, when some mortar rounds came in, tore the tent down to canvas slaw and put frags through every single cot but his, he was still high out of his mind from it, speedy, sure and lucky. The Soldier's

VC: Military jargon for Viet Cong, or Vietnamese Communists.

Prayer came in two versions: Standard, printed on a plastic-coated card by the Defense Department, and Standard Revised, impossible to convey because it got translated outside of language, into chaos—screams, begging, promises, threats, sobs, repetitions of holy names until their throats were cracked and dry, until some men had bitten through their collar points and rifle straps and even their dog-tag chains.

5 Varieties of religious experience, good news and bad news; a lot of men found their compassion in the war, some found it and couldn't live with it, war-washed shutdown of feeling, . . . People retreated into positions of hard irony, cynicism, despair, some saw the action and declared for it, only heavy killing could make them feel so alive. And some just went insane, followed the black-light arrow around the bend and took possession of the madness that had been waiting there in trust for them for eighteen or twenty-five or fifty years. Every time there was combat you had a license to go maniac, everyone snapped over the line at least once there and nobody noticed, they hardly noticed if you forgot to snap back again.

One afternoon at Khe Sanh a Marine opened the door of a latrine and was killed by a grenade that had been rigged on the door. The Command tried to blame it on a North Vietnamese infiltrator, but the grunts knew what had happened: "Like a gook is really gonna tunnel all the way in here to booby-trap a shithouse, right? Some guy just flipped out is all." And it became another one of those stories that moved across the DMZ,° making people laugh and shake their heads and look knowingly at each other, but shocking no one. They'd talk about physical wounds in one way and psychic wounds in another, each man in a squad would tell you how crazy everyone else in the squad was, everyone knew grunts who'd gone crazy in the middle of a firefight, gone crazy on patrol, gone crazy back at camp, gone crazy on R&R, gone crazy during their first month home. Going crazy was built into the tour, the best you could hope for was that it didn't happen around you, the kind of crazy that made men empty clips into strangers or fix grenades on latrine doors. That was *really* crazy; anything less was almost standard, as standard as the vague prolonged stares and involuntary smiles, common as ponchos or 16's or any other piece of war issue. If you wanted someone to know you'd gone insane you really had to sound off like you had a pair, "Scream a lot, and all the time." *[1977]*

THINKING ABOUT THE TEXT

1. What do you think Herr means by the "Inscrutable Immutable" (para. 1)?
2. Explain the significance of Herr's statement, "You couldn't blame anybody for believing anything" (para. 3).
3. Explain what you think is the significance of some of the concrete things the soldiers carried. Do you or anyone you know carry comparable things? Why?

DMZ: Military jargon for demilitarized zone.

4. Which specific passages are the most convincing about the horrors of war? Explain.
5. What is Herr's point of view in this selection, that is, is he journalistically neutral, sympathetic, critical? Explain.

MAKING COMPARISONS

1. Which passage in Herr is closes to the theme of Owen's poem?
2. Compare some of the imagery in Herr to that in Owen. How effective are these images in conveying the traumatic context?
3. How would you describe the intention of Owen and Herr? Do they have similar goals?

THOMAS LUX

The People of the Other Village

Thomas Lux (1946–2017) was born in Northampton, Massachusetts, and attended Emerson College in Boston. During his life he wrote numerous volumes of poetry, including The Street of Clocks *(2001) and* The Cradle Place: Poems *(2004), and he was the recipient of many prestigious grants and prizes. His most recent collection is* To the Left of Time *(2016). He taught at Sarah Lawrence College; the University of California, Irvine; Emerson College; and Georgia Tech in Atlanta, where he served as the Bourne Chair in poetry until his death. The following poem is from* New and Selected Poems *(1997).*

Jim Spellman/Getty Images

hate the people of this village
and would nail our hats
to our heads for refusing in their presence to remove them
or staple our hands to our foreheads
for refusing to salute them
if we did not hurt them first: mail them packages of rats,
mix their flour at night with broken glass.
We do this, they do that.
They peel the larynx from one of our brothers' throats.
We devein one of their sisters.
The quicksand pits they built were good.
Our amputation teams were better.
We trained some birds to steal their wheat.
They sent to us exploding ambassadors of peace.
They do this, we do that.
We canceled our sheep imports.
They no longer bought our blankets.
We mocked their greatest poet
and when that had no effect
we parodied the way they dance
which did cause pain, so they, in turn, said our God
was leprous, hairless.
We do this, they do that.
Ten thousand (10,000) years, ten thousand
(10,000) brutal, beautiful years. *[1997]*

THINKING ABOUT THE TEXT

1. "We do this, they do that" (line 8 and line 23) and its reverse (line 15) is a kind of refrain suggesting the poem's theme. What is that theme and how accurate a statement about human nature do you think this is?
2. Conflicts between villages/cities/countries are often rooted in religious, ethnic, racial, or political differences. Does Lux hint at these or is he deliberately vague?
3. Lux is known for blending irony and humor with serious subjects. Are some of the grotesque details of the disputes meant as gallows humor? What effect do these graphic details have?
4. What is Lux's intention in this poem? Is it, for example, a plea for tolerance? Is it a bitter indictment of humanity? Or something else?
5. What is the significance of the seemingly incongruous "beautiful" in the last line?

WRITING ABOUT ISSUES

1. Write an essay that judges the effectiveness of the three texts here as anti-war documents.
2. Write an essay that researches the history of trauma during World War I and compare it to recent ideas of PTSD during the wars in Iraq and Afghanistan.
3. Research ideas about trauma. Look especially at Judith Herman (*Trauma and Recovery*). Write an essay that relates the three texts here to her ideas.
4. Read Owen's "Anthem for a Doomed Youth" and Sassoon's "Aftermath" and compare these war poems to "Dulce et Decorum Est."

Acknowledgments *(continued from page vi)*

Chad Abushnab, "Dead Town." *The Hopkins Review* 9:4 (2016), 483. Copyright © 2016 Chad Abushnab. Reprinted with permission of Johns Hopkins University Press.

James Eli Adams. "Narrating Nature: Darwin" from *A History of Victorian Literature* by James Eli Adams. Copyright © 2012 by James Eli Adams. Reprinted by permission of the author.

Amin Ahmad, "I Belong Here," first published in *The Sun*, January 2010. Reprinted by permission of the author.

Ryūnosuke Akutagawa, "In a Bamboo Grove," copyright © by Jay Rubin; from *Rashomon and Seventeen Other Stories* (Penguin Classics Deluxe Edition) by Ryūnosuke Akutagawa, translated by Jay Rubin. Used by permission of Penguin Books, an imprint of Penguin Publishing Group, a division of Penguin Random House LLC and of Penguin Books UK. All rights reserved.

Caroline Alexander, "The Shock of War" from *Smithsonian* Magazine, September 2010. Reprinted by permission of the author.

Sherman Alexie, "Capital Punishment," from *The Summer of Black Widows*. Copyright © 1996 by Sherman Alexie. Reprinted by permission of Hanging Loose Press.

Allison Alsup, "Old Houses" first published in *New Orleans Review* 38.1 (2014). Reprinted by permission of the author.

W. H. Auden, "Funeral Blues" copyright © 1940 and renewed 1968 by W. H. Auden; from *W.H. Auden Collected Poems* by W. H. Auden. Used by permission of Random House, an imprint and division of Penguin Random House LLC and of Curtis Brown, Ltd.

W. H. Auden, "Refugee Blues," from *The Guardian: From Collected Shorter Poems 1927–1957* by W. H. Auden. Copyright © 1940 by W. H. Auden, renewed. Reprinted by permission of Curtis Brown, Ltd.

Steven Gould Axelrod, *Sylvia Plath: The Wound and the Cure of Words*. pp. 1–8. Copyright © 1990 Johns Hopkins University Press. Reprinted with permission of Johns Hopkins University Press.

Jimmy Santiago Baca, "So Mexicans Are Taking Jobs from Americans," from *Immigrants in Our Own Land*, copyright © 1979 by Jimmy Santiago Baca. Reprinted by permission of New Directions Publishing Corp.

Toni Cade Bambara, "The Lesson," copyright © 1972 by Toni Cade Bambara; from *Gorilla, My Love* by Toni Cade Bambara. Used by permission of Random House, an imprint and division of Penguin Random House LLC. All rights reserved.

Stephen C. Bandy, excerpt from "'One of My Babies': The Misfit and the Grandmother." Originally published in *Studies in Short Fiction*, 33.1, winter 1996. Copyright © 1996 by Stephen C. Bandy. Reproduced with permission of the author.

Robin Becker, "Morning Poem" from *Backtalk*. Copyright © 1982 by Robin Becker. Reprinted with the permission of The Permissions Company, Inc., on behalf of Alice James Books, www.alicejamesbooks.org.

Patricia Flanagan Behrendt. Excerpt from *Oscar Wilde: Eros and Aesthetics* by Patricia Flanagan Behrendt, pp. 172–178, 1991, St. Martin's Press, N.Y. Copyright © 1991 by Patricia Flanagan Behrendt. Reproduced with permission of Springer Nature.

Millicent Bell. "Othello's Jealousy" from the *Yale Review* 85.2 (April 1997). Copyright © 1997 by Yale University. Reprinted with permission of Blackwell Publishing Ltd.

Abdelkader Benali, "From Teenage Angst to Jihad" from *The New York Times*, January 13, 2015. Reprinted by permission of the author.

Emily Bernard. "Scar Tissue," *American Scholar* 80.4 (Autumn 2011). Copyright © 2011 by Emily Bernard. Reprinted by permission of the author.

Richard Blanco, "Queer Theory: According to My Grandmother" from *Looking for the Gulf Motel*, by Richard Blanco, Copyright © 2012. Reprinted by permission of the University of Pittsburgh Press.

Robert Blecker, "With Death Penalty, Let Punishment Truly Fit the Crime" from *CNN.com*, August 22, 2013, © 2013 Turner Broadcast Systems. All rights reserved. Used by permission and protected by the Copyright Laws of the United States. The printing, copying, redistribution, or retransmission of this Content without express written permission is prohibited.

Tirthankar Bose, excerpt from "Oscar Wilde's Game of Being Earnest," from *MODERN DRAMA, 21.1* (spring 1978): 81–86. Copyright © 1978 by Tirthankar Bose. Reproduced with permission of the author.

Brian Boyd, excerpt from *Vladimir Nabokov: The American Years.* Copyright © 1991. Reprinted with permission of Princeton University Press; permission conveyed through Copyright Clearance Center, Inc.

T. C. Boyle, "Balto" from *Wild Child: and Other Stories* by T. C. Boyle, copyright © 2010 by T. Coraghessan Boyle. Used by permission of Viking Books, an imprint of Penguin Publishing Group, a division of Penguin Random House LLC. All rights reserved.

David Brooks, "The Child in the Basement" from *The New York Times*, January 13, 2015. Copyright © 2015 The New York Times. All rights reserved. Used by permission and protected by the Copyright Laws of the United States. The printing, copying, redistribution, or retransmission of this Content without express written permission is prohibited.

Lynda K. Bundtzen, excerpt from *Plath's Incarnations: Women and the Creative Process.* Copyright © 1989. Republished with permission of the University of Michigan Press; permission conveyed through Copyright Clearance Center, Inc.

Octavia Butler, "Human Evolution" from *Imago* by Octavia E. Butler. Copyright © 2009 by Octavia E. Butler. Reprinted by permission of Grand Central Publishing.

Steven Camarota, "Unskilled Workers Lose Out to Immigrants." Reprinted by permission of the author.

Angela Carter, "The Company of Wolves" from *The Bloody Chamber* by Angela Carter. Copyright © Angela Carter 1979. Reproduced by permission of The Estate of Angela Carter c/o Rogers, Coleridge, & White, Ltd., 20 Powis Mews, London W11 1JN.

Raymond Carver, "What We Talk About When We Talk About Love" from *What We Talk About When We Talk About Love: Stories* by Raymond Carver, copyright © 1974, 1976, 1978, 1980, 1981 by Tess Gallagher. Used by permission of Alfred A. Knopf, an imprint of Knopf Doubleday Publishing Group, a division of Penguin Random House LLC. All rights reserved.

Victoria Chang, "Edward Hopper's Conference at Night," from "The Boss" by Victoria Chang, August 2013. First appeared in the *Missouri Review*, December 13, 2011. [http://www.missourireview.com/archives/victoria-chang-edward-hoppers-conference-at-night/] Copyright © 2011 by Victoria Chang. Reproduced with permission of the author.

John Cheever, "Reunion" from *The Stories of John Cheever*, copyright © 1978 by John Cheever. Used by permission of Alfred A. Knopf, an imprint of Knopf Doubleday Publishing Group, a division of Penguin Random House LLC. All rights reserved.

Ted Chiang, "The Great Silence" from *Untitled Collection* by Ted Chiang, copyright © 2019 by Ted Chiang. Used by permission of Alfred A. Knopf, an imprint of the Knopf Doubleday Publishing Group, a division of Penguin Random House LLC. All rights reserved.

Chyrstos, "Today was a Bad Day Like TB." Copyright © 1993 Chrystos. Used by permission of the author.

Arthur Clarke, "The Nine Billion Names of God." Reprinted by permission of the author and the author's agents, Scott Galen Ghosh Literary Agency, Inc.

Lucille Clifton, "forgiving my father." Copyright © 1980 by Lucille Clifton. First appeared in *two-head woman*, published by the University of Massachusetts Press. Now appears in *The Collected Poems of Lucille Clifton 1965–2010* by Lucille Clifton, published by BOA Editions. Reprinted by permission of Curtis Brown, Ltd.

Judith Ortiz Cofer, "Claims" from *Reaching for the Mainland & Selected New Poems* by Judith Ortiz Cofer, 1995. Reprinted by permission of Bilingual Press/Editorial Bilingue, Arizona State University, Tempe, AZ.

Roger Cohen, "Why ISIS Trumps Freedom" from *The New York Times*, August 15, 2015. Copyright © 2015 The New York Times. All rights reserved. Used by permission and protected by the Copyright Laws of the United States. The printing, copying, redistribution, or retransmission of this Content without express written permission is prohibited.

Countee Cullen. "Incident" from *Color* by Countee Cullen. Copyright © 1925 by Harper & Brothers; copyright renewed 1952 by Ida M. Cullen. Copyrights held by the Amistad Research Center, Tulane University, administered by Thompson and Thompson, Brooklyn, NY.

e. e. cummings, "somewhere I have never travelled, gladly beyond." Copyright 1931, © 1959, 1991 by the Trustees for the E. E. Cummings Trust. Copyright © 1979 George James Firmage, from *Complete Poems: 1904–1962* by E. E. Cummings, edited by George James Firmage. Used by permission of Liveright Publishing Corporation.

Meghan Daum, "Jaycee Dugard and the Feel Good Imperative." Copyright © 2011 by Meghan Daum. All Rights Reserved. "Jaycee Dugard and the Feel Good Imperative" was originally published by the *Los Angeles Times* (July 2011). Reprinted by permission of the author.

Edward J. Delaney. "Clean." First published in *The Atlantic*, November 2012. Copyright © 2012 by Edward J. Delaney. Reprinted by permission of the Ann Rittenberg Literary Agency, Inc.

Toi Derricotte, "Black Boys Play the Classics" from *Tender*, copyright © 1997. Reprinted by permission of the University of Pittsburgh Press.

John Desmond, "Flannery O'Connor's Misfit and The Mystery of Evil" in Renascence: Essays on Values in Literature, Volume 56, Issue 2, Winter 2004, pp.129–137. Reprinted by permission of The Philosophy Documentation Center.

Emily Dickinson, "Because I could not stop for Death" from *The Poems of Emily Dickinson*, edited by Thomas H. Johnson, Cambridge, Mass.: The Belknap Press of Harvard University Press, copyright © 1951, 1955 by the President and Fellows of Harvard College. Copyright © renewed 1979, 1983 by the President and Fellows of Harvard College. Copyright © 1914, 1918, 1919, 1924, 1929, 1930, 1932, 1935, 1937, 1942 by Martha Dickinson Bianchi. Copyright © 1952, 1957, 1958, 1963, 1965 by Mary L. Hampson.

Emily Dickinson, "My Life had stood—a Loaded Gun" from *The Poems of Emily Dickinson*, edited by Thomas H. Johnson, Cambridge, Mass.: The Belknap Press of Harvard University Press, Copyright © 1951, 1955 by the President and Fellows of Harvard College. Copyright © renewed 1979, 1983 by the President and Fellows of Harvard College. Copyright © 1914, 1918, 1919, 1924, 1929, 1930, 1932, 1935, 1937, 1942 by Martha Dickinson Bianchi. Copyright © 1952, 1957, 1958, 1963, 1965 by Mary L. Hampson.

Emily Dickinson, "Success is counted sweetest" from *The Poems of Emily Dickinson*, edited by Thomas H. Johnson, Cambridge, Mass.: The Belknap Press of Harvard University Press, Copyright © 1951, 1955 by the President and Fellows of Harvard College. Copyright © renewed 1979, 1983 by the President and Fellows of Harvard College. Copyright © 1914, 1918, 1919, 1924, 1929, 1930, 1932, 1935, 1937, 1942 by Martha Dickinson Bianchi. Copyright © 1952, 1957, 1958, 1963, 1965 by Mary L. Hampson.

Emily Dickinson, "Tell all the Truth but tell it slant—" from *The Poems of Emily Dickinson*, edited by Thomas H. Johnson, Cambridge, Mass.: The Belknap Press of Harvard University Press, Copyright © 1951, 1955 by the President and Fellows of Harvard College. Copyright © renewed 1979, 1983 by the President and Fellows of Harvard College. Copyright © 1914, 1918, 1919, 1924, 1929, 1930, 1932, 1935, 1937, 1942 by Martha Dickinson Bianchi. Copyright © 1952, 1957, 1958, 1963, 1965 by Mary L. Hampson.

David Dominguez. "Wedding Portrait" from *The Ghost of Cesar Chavez: Poems.* Copyright © 2010 by David Dominguez. Reprinted by permission of C&R Press.

Andre Dubus, "Killings" from *Finding a Girl in America* by Andre Dubus. Reprinted by permission of David R. Godine, Publisher, Inc. Copyright © 1980 by Andrew Dubus.

John R. Ehrenfeld, "The Error of Trying to Measure Good and Bad." Reprinted by permission of Flourishing by Design.

T. S. Eliot, "The Love Song of J. Alfred Prufrock" from *Collected Poems 1909–1962* by T. S. Eliot. Reprinted by permission of Faber & Faber LTD.

Ralph Ellison, "Chapter 1 [Battle Royal]," copyright © 1948 and renewed 1976 by Ralph Ellison; from *Invisible Man*. Used by permission of Random House, an imprint and division of Penguin Random House LLC. All rights reserved.

Sol Eltis, excerpt from *Revising Wilde: Society and Subversion in the Plays of Oscar Wilde* by Eltis (1996) 775w from pp. 194–196. By permission of Oxford University Press.

Maria Enchautegui, "Immigrants Are Replacing, Not Displacing, Workers." Reprinted by permission of the author.

William Faulkner, "A Rose for Emily," copyright © 1930 and renewed 1958 by William Faulkner; from *Collected Stories of William Faulkner* by William Faulkner. Used by permission of Random House, an imprint and division of Penguin Random House LLC and of W. W. Norton & Company. All rights reserved.

Lawrence Ferlinghetti, "Short Story on a Painting of Gustav Klimt," from *Endless Life*, copyright © 1976 by Lawrence Ferlinghetti. Reprinted by permission of New Directions Publishing Corp.

Ida Fink, "The Table." Originally published in the Polish Language as *Skrawek Czasu* by Aneks Publishers, London. Copyright © 1983 by Ida Fink. English translation first published by Pantheon Books, a division of Random House Inc., in 1987; copyright © by Random House. Northwestern University Press edition published 1995 by arrangement with Ida Fink. All rights reserved.

Brooke Lea Foster, "The Persistent Myth of the Narcissistic Millennial." Copyright © 2014 The Atlantic Media Co., as first published in *The Atlantic* Magazine. All rights reserved. Distributed by Tribune Content Agency, LLC.

Michel Foucault, "Panopticism" from *Discipline & Punish: The Birth of the Prison* by Michel Foucault. English translation copyright © 1977 by Alan Sheridan. Originally published in French as *Surveiller et Punir*. Copyright © 1975 by Editions Gallimard. Reprinted by permission of Georges Borchardt, Inc., for Editions Gallimard.

Robert Frost, "Acquainted with the Night" from the book *The Poetry of Robert Frost* edited by Edward Connery Lathem. Copyright © 1916, 1923, 1928, 1969 by Henry Holt and Company. Copyright © 1944, 1951, 1956 by Robert Frost. Reprinted by permission of Henry Holt and Company. All rights reserved.

Robert Frost, "Birches" from the book *The Poetry of Robert Frost* edited by Edward Connery Lathem. Copyright © 1916, 1923, 1928, 1969 by Henry Holt and Company. Copyright © 1944, 1951, 1956 by Robert Frost. Reprinted by permission of Henry Holt and Company. All rights reserved.

Robert Frost, "Stopping by Woods on a Snowy Evening" from the book *The Poetry of Robert Frost* edited by Edward Connery Lathem. Copyright © 1916, 1923, 1928, 1969 by Henry Holt and Company. Copyright © 1944, 1951, 1956 by Robert Frost. Reprinted by permission of Henry Holt and Company. All rights reserved.

Rivka Galchen, "Usl at the Stadium" from *The New Yorker*, October 12, 2015. Copyright © 2015 by Rivka Galchen. All rights not specifically granted herein are hereby reserved to the Licensor.

Deborah Garrison, "Worked Late on a Tuesday Night" from *A Working Girl Can't Win: And Other Poems*, copyright © 1998 by Deborah Garrison. Used by permission of Random House, an imprint and division of Penguin Random House LLC. All rights reserved.

Karen Gershon, "Race," from *Collected Poems* by Karen Gershon, published by Macmillan, Papermac, 1990. Copyright © 1990 by Stella Tripp. Reproduced with permission of Stella Tripp for the Estate of Karen Gershon.

Dagoberto Gilb, "Uncle Rock" from *Before the End, After the Beginning: Stories* by Dagoberto Gilb. Copyright © 2011 by Dagoberto Gilb. Reprinted by permission of the author.

Christopher Gilbert, "On the Way Back Home" from *Turning into Dwelling*. Copyright © 2015 by the Estate of Christopher Gilbert. Reprinted with the permission of The Permissions Company, Inc., on behalf of Graywolf Press, Minneapolis, Minnesota, www.graywolfpress.org.

Sandra Gilbert, "Jacob Lawrence's 'They Were Very Poor'" from *Field* #92 (Spring 2015). Reprinted by permission of Oberlin College Press.

Nikki Giovanni, "Legacies" from *My House* by Nikki Giovanni. Copyright © 1972 by Nikki Giovanni, Renewed 2000 by Nikki Giovanni. Reprinted by permission of HarperCollins Publishers.

Wayne Goodman, from "Forum: High Pressure: Psychosis, Performance, Schizophrenia, Literature" from *Anatomy of a Short Story*, edited by Yuri Leving. Copyright © 2012. Reprinted by permission of Continuum Publishing, an imprint of Bloomsbury Publishing Inc.

Michael S. Harper, "Discovery," from *Songlines in Michaeltree: New and Collected Poems*. Copyright © 2000 by Michael S. Harper. Reproduced with permission of University of Illinois Press.

Robert Hayden, "Those Winter Sundays." Copyright © 1966 by Robert Hayden, from *Collected Poems of Robert Hayden* by Robert Hayden, edited by Frederick Glaysher. Used by permission of Liveright Publishing Corporation.

Seamus Heaney. "Punishment" from *Opened Ground: Selected Poems 1966–1996* by Seamus Heaney. Copyright © 1998 by Seamus Heaney. Reprinted by permission of Farrar, Straus and Giroux, LLC and Faber and Faber Ltd.

Ernest Hemingway, "Soldier's Home." Reprinted with permission of Simon & Schuster, Inc. All rights reserved.

Leicester Hemingway, excerpts from *My Brother, Ernest Hemingway.* Reprinted by permission of Pineapple Press, Inc.

Essex Hemphill, "Commitments" from *Ceremonies: Prose and Poetry* by Essex Hemphill. Copyright © 1992 by Essex Hemphill. Reprinted by permission of the Frances Goldin Literary Agency.

David Hernandez, "Words Without Thoughts Never to Heaven Go" from *Southern Review,* Vol. 52, no. 2 (Spring 2016). Reprinted by permission of the author.

Michael Herr, "Breathing In" from *Dispatches,* copyright © 1977 by Michael Herr. Used by permission of Alfred A. Knopf, an imprint of Knopf Doubleday Publishing Group, a division of Penguin Random House LLC. All rights reserved.

Edward Hirsch, "Execution," from *The Night Parade,* copyright © 1989 by Edward Hirsch. Used by permission of Alfred A. Knopf, an imprint of Knopf Doubleday Publishing Group, a division of Penguin Random House LLC. All rights reserved.

Tony Hoagland, "What Narcissism Means to Me" from *What Narcissism Means to Me.* Copyright © 2003 by Tony Hoagland. Reprinted with the permission of The Permissions Company, Inc., on behalf of Graywolf Press, Minneapolis, Minnesota, www.graywolfpress.org.

Linda Hogan, "Heritage" from *Calling Myself Home* by Linda Hogan. First appeared in *Red Clay* by Linda Hogan. Copyright © 1991 by Linda Hogan. Reprinted by permission of the author.

Langston Hughes, "Harlem" from *The Collected Poems of Langston Hughes* by Langston Hughes, edited by Arnold Rampersad with David Roessel, Associate Editor, copyright © 1994 by the Estate of Langston Hughes. Used by permission of Alfred A. Knopf, a division of Knopf Doubleday Publishing Group, an imprint of Penguin Random House LLC and of Harold Ober Associates Incorporated. All rights reserved.

Langston Hughes, "Open Letter to the South" from *The Collected Poems of Langston Hughes* by Langston Hughes, edited by Arnold Rampersad with David Roessel, Associate Editor, copyright © 1994 by the Estate of Langston Hughes. Used by permission of Alfred A. Knopf, a division of Knopf Doubleday Publishing Group, an imprint of Penguin Random House LLC and of Harold Ober Associates Incorporated. All rights reserved.

Langston Hughes, "Theme for English B" from *The Collected Poems of Langston Hughes* by Langston Hughes, edited by Arnold Rampersad with David Roessel, Associate Editor, copyright © 1994 by the Estate of Langston Hughes. Used by permission of Alfred A. Knopf, a division of Knopf Doubleday Publishing Group, an imprint of Penguin Random House LLC and of Harold Ober Associates Incorporated. All rights reserved.

Lynda Hull, "Night Waitress" from *Collected Poems.* Copyright © 1986 by Lynda Hull. Reprinted with the permission of The Permissions Company, Inc., on behalf of Graywolf Press, Minneapolis, Minnesota, www.graywolfpress.org.

James M. Hutchinson, excerpts from *Ernest Hemingway: A New Life*. Copyright © 2016 The Pennsylvania State University. Reprinted by permission of The Pennsylvania State University Press.

Luisa Igloria, "Regarding History," from *Trill & Mordent*. Copyright © 2005 by WordTech Communications, LLC. Reproduced with permission of WordTech Editions, Cincinnati, Ohio, USA.

Shirley Jackson. "The Lottery" from *The Lottery* by Shirley Jackson. Copyright © 1948, 1949 by Shirley Jackson. Copyright renewed 1976, 1977 by Laurence Hyman, Barry Hyman, Mrs. Sarah Webster, and Mrs. Joanne Schnurer. Reprinted by permission of Farrar, Straus and Giroux, LLC.

Jennifer Jacquet, "The 7 Habits of Highly Effective Shaming," from *Is Shame Necessary?: New Uses for an Old Tool,* copyright © 2015 by Jennifer Jacquet. Used by permission of Pantheon Books, an imprint of Knopf Doubleday Publishing Group, a division of Penguin Random House LLC. All rights reserved.

Ha Jin, "Saboteur" from *The Bridegroom: Stories*, copyright © 2000 by Ha Jin. Used by permission of Pantheon Books, an imprint of Knopf Doubleday Publishing Group, a division of Penguin Random House LLC. All rights reserved.

June Jordan, "Many Rivers to Cross" from *On Call: Political Essays*, South End Press, Boston, 1985. Copyright © 1985, 2017 June H. Jordan Literary Estate. Reprinted by permission. www.junejordan.com

Tim Kendall, Excerpt from "The Theatrical Comeback: Repetition of Performance in *Ariel*" from *Sylvia Plath: A Critical Study* by Tim Kendall. Copyright © 2001 by Tim Kendall. Reprinted by permission of Faber and Faber, Inc., an affiliate of Farrar, Straus and Giroux, LLC and Faber and Faber Ltd.

X. J. Kennedy, "Death of a Window Washer." *In a Prominent Bar in Secaucus: New and Selected Poems, 1955–2007*. p. 168. Copyright © 2007 X. J. Kennedy. Reprinted with permission of Johns Hopkins University Press.

Jamaica Kincaid, "Girl" from *At the Bottom of the River* by Jamaica Kincaid. Copyright © 1983 by Jamaica Kincaid. Reprinted by permission of Farrar, Straus and Giroux, LLC.

Maxine Hong Kingston, "No Name Woman" from *The Woman Warrior: Memoirs of a Girlhood Among Ghosts*, copyright © 1975, 1976 by Maxine Hong Kingston. Used by permission of Alfred A. Knopf, an imprint of Knopf Doubleday Publishing Group, a division of Penguin Random House LLC. All rights reserved.

Laura Kipnis. "Love in the 21st Century—Against Love," *New York Times*, October 14, 2001. Reprinted by permission of the author.

Yusef Komunyakaa, "Blackberries" from *Pleasure Dome: New and Collected Poems*. Copyright © 2001 by Yusef Komunyakaa. Published by Wesleyan University Press. Used by permission.

Geeta Kothari, "If You Are What You Eat, Then What Am I?" from *The Kenyon Review*, Winter 1999, Vol. 21, No. 1. Reprinted by permission of the author.

Maxine Kumin, "Woodchucks" from *Selected Poems 1960–1990*. Copyright © 1972, 1997 by Maxine Kumin. Used by permission of W. W. Norton & Company, Inc.

Hanif Kureishi, from *Love in a Blue Time* by Hanif Kureishi. Copyright © 1997 by Hanif Kureishi. Reprinted with the permission of Scribner, a division of Simon & Schuster, Inc. All rights reserved.

Li-Young Lee, "My Father, in Heaven, is Reading Out Loud" from *The City in Which I Love You*. Copyright © 1990 by Li-Young Lee. Reprinted with the permission of The Permissions Company, Inc., on behalf of BOA Editions, Ltd., www.boaeditions.org.

Ursula LeGuin, "The Ones Who Walk Away from Omelas." Copyright © 1973 by Ursula K. LeGuin. First appeared in "New Dimension 3" in 1973, and then in *The Wind's Twelve Quarters*, published by HarperCollins in 1975. Reprinted by permission of Curtis Brown, Ltd.

Philip Levine, "What Work Is" from *What Work Is*, copyright © 1991 by Philip Levine. Used by permission of Alfred A. Knopf, an imprint of Knopf Doubleday Publishing Group, a division of Penguin Random House LLC. All rights reserved.

Audre Lorde, "Who Said It Was Simple" from *The Collected Poems of Audre Lorde*. Copyright © 1973 by Audre Lorde. Used by permission of W. W. Norton & Company, Inc.

Peter Ludlow, "The Banality of Systemic Evil" from *The New York Times*, September 15, 2013. Copyright © 2013 The New York Times. All rights reserved. Used by permission and protected by the Copyright Laws of the United States. The printing, copying, redistribution, or retransmission of this Content without express written permission is prohibited.

Thomas Lux "The People of the Other Village" from *Split Horizon: Poems* by Thomas Lux. Copyright © 1994 by Thomas Lux. Reprinted by permission of Houghton Mifflin Harcourt Publishing Company. All rights reserved.

Maurice Manning, "The Hill People" from *The Gone and the Going Away* by Maurice Manning. Copyright © 2013 by Maurice Manning. Reprinted by permission of Houghton Mifflin Harcourt Publishing Company. All rights reserved.

Edna St. Vincent Millay, "What My Lips Have Kissed, and Where, and Why" from *Collected Poems.* Copyright © 1923, 1951 by Edna St. Vincent Millay and Norma Millay Ellis. Reprinted with the permission of The Permissions Company, Inc., on behalf of Holly Peppe, Literary Executor, The Millay Society, www.millay.org.

May Miller. "The Scream" from *Dust of Uncertain Journey* by May Miller (Detroit: Lotus Press, 1975). Copyright © 1975. Reprinted by permission of Lotus Press.

Susan Minot, "My Husband's Back." Copyright © 2005 by Susan Minot. Originally appeared in *The New Yorker* (August 25, 2005). Reprinted by permission of Georges Borchardt, Inc., on behalf of the author.

Pat Mora, "Legal Alien," reprinted with permission of the publisher of "Chants" by Pat Mora (copyright © 1994 Arte Publico Press-University of Houston).

Don Moser, "The Pied Piper of Tuscon" from *Life* Magazine, March 4, 1966. Copyright © 1966 Time, Inc. All rights reserved. Printed from LIFE and published with permission of Time Inc. Reproduction in any manner in any language in whole or in part without written permission is prohibited.

Jeffrie G. Murphy. "Jealousy, Shame, and the Rival," *Philosophical Studies* 108.1 (March 1, 2002), pages 143–50. © 2002 Kluwer Academic Publishers. With permission of Springer.

Gunnar Myrdal, "Social Equality" pages 67–71 from *An American Dilemma: The Negro Problem and Modern Democracy* by Gunnar Myrdal. Copyright © 1944, 1962 by Harper & Row, Publishers, Inc. Reprinted by permission of HarperCollins Publishers.

Vladimir Nabokov, "Signs and Symbols" from *The Stories of Vladimir Nabokov,* copyright © 1995 by Dmitri Nabokov. Used by permission of Alfred A. Knopf, an imprint of Knopf Doubleday Publishing Group, a division of Penguin Random House LLC. All rights reserved.

Lynn Nottage. *POOF!* Published in *Crumbs from the Table of Joys and Other Plays* by Lynn Nottage. Copyright © 1993, 2004 by Lynn Nottage. Published by Theatre Communications Group. Used by permission of Theatre Communications Group.

Naomi Shihab Nye, "Blood" from *19 Varieties of Gazelle: Poems of the Middle East* by Naomi Shihab Nye. Text copyright © 2002 Naomi Shihab Nye. Used by permission of HarperCollins Publishers.

Joyce Carol Oates, "Smooth Talk: Short Story Into Film." Reprinted by permission of John Hawkins and Associates, Inc. Copyright © 1988 Joyce Carol Oates.

Joyce Carol Oates. "Where Are You Going, Where Have You Been?" from *(Woman) Writer: Occasions and Opportunities* by Joyce Carol Oates. Copyright © 1988 by The Ontario Review, Inc. Reprinted by permission of HarperCollins Publishers, Inc.

Tim O'Brien, "The Things They Carried" from *The Things They Carried* by Tim O'Brien. Copyright © 1990 by Tim O'Brien. Reprinted by permission of Houghton Mifflin Harcourt Publishing Company. All rights reserved.

Flannery O'Connor, "A Good Man is Hard to Find" from *A Good Man is Hard to Find and Other Stories* by Flannery O'Connor. Copyright © 1953 by Flannery O'Connor. Copyright © Renewed 1981 by Regina O'Connor. Reprinted by permission of Houghton Mifflin Harcourt Publishing Company. All rights reserved.

Flannery O'Connor. Excerpt from "On Her Own Work" in *Mystery and Manners* by Flannery O'Connor, edited by Sally and Robert Fitzgerald. Copyright © 1969 by the Estate of Mary Flannery O'Connor. Reprinted by permission of Farrar, Straus and Giroux, LLC.

Charles Ogletree, "Condemned to Die Because He's Black" from *The New York Times,* August 1, 2013. Copyright © 2013 The New York Times. All rights reserved. Used by permission and protected by the Copyright Laws of the United States. The printing, copying, redistribution, or retransmission of this Content without express written permission is prohibited.

Dwight Okita. "In Response to Executive Order 9066" from *Crossing with the Light* by Dwiight Okita. Copyright © 1992 by Dwight Okita. Reprinted by permission of the author.

Sharon Olds, "Summer Solstice, New York City" from *The Gold Cell,* copyright © 1987 by Sharon Olds. Used by permission of Alfred A. Knopf, an imprint of Knopf Doubleday Publishing Group, a division of Penguin Random House LLC. All rights reserved.

Mary Oliver, "Singapore" from *House of Light* by Mary Oliver. Published by Beacon Press, Boston. Copyright © 1990 by Mary Oliver. Reprinted by permission of The Charlotte Sheedy Literary Agency Inc.

Mary Oliver, "When Death Comes" from *New & Selected Poems, vol. 1* by Mary Oliver. Published by Beacon Press, Boston. Copyright © 1992 by Mary Oliver. Reprinted by permission of The Charlotte Sheedy Literary Agency Inc.

Tillie Olsen, "I Stand Here Ironing" reproduced from *Tell Me a Riddle, Requa I, and Other Works*, by Tillie Olsen, with a foreword by Laurie Olsen and an introduction by Rebekah Edwards, by permission of the University of Nebraska Press. Copyright © 2013 by the Tillie Olsen Estate.

Meghan O'Rourke, "The Marriage Trap" from *Slate*, September 3, 2003. Copyright © 2003 The Slate Group. All rights reserved. Used by permission and protected by the Copyright Laws of the United States. The printing, copying, redistribution, or retransmission of this Content without express written permission is prohibited.

Daniel Orozco, "Orientation" from *Orientation and Other Stories* by Daniel Orozco. Copyright © 2011 by Daniel Orozco. Reprinted by permission of Faber and Faber, Inc., an affiliate of Farrar, Straus and Giroux, LLC.

Linda Pastan, "Ethics" from *Waiting for My Life*. Copyright © 1981 by Linda Pastan. Used by permission of W.W. Norton & Company, Inc.

Don Paterson, "Two Trees" from *Rain* by Don Paterson. Copyright © 2009 by Don Paterson. Reprinted by permission of Farrar, Straus and Giroux, LLC and of the author c/o Rogers, Coleridge & White, LTD., 20 Powis Mews, London W11 1JN.

Rolando Perez. "Office at Night" from *The Lining of Our Souls: Excursions into Selected Paintings of Edward Hopper* by Rolando Perez. Cool Grove Press. Copyright © 2002. Reprinted by permission of Cool Grove Publishing.

Sylvia Plath, "Daddy" from *The Collected Poems of Sylvia Plath*, edited by Ted Hughes. Copyright © 1960, 1965, 1971, 1981 by the Estate of Sylvia Plath. Reprinted by permission of HarperCollins Publishers and Faber and Faber Ltd.

Minnie Bruce Pratt, "Two Small-Sized Girls" from *Crime Against Nature*. Copyright © Minnie Bruce Pratt. Reprinted by permission of the author.

Kirsten Valdez Quade, "The Manzanos" from *Night at the Fiestas: Stories*. Copyright © 2015 by Kirstin Valdez Quade. Used by permission of W. W. Norton & Company.

Ruth Reichl, "Chapter 1: The Queen of Mold" and "Miriam Reichl's Corned Beef Ham Recipe" from *Tender at the Bone: Growing Up at the Table*, copyright © 1998, 2010 by Ruth Reichl. Used by permission of Random House, an imprint and division of Penguin Random House LLC. All rights reserved.

Adrienne Rich. "Diving into the Wreck" from *Later Poems: Selected and New, 1971–2012* by Adrienne Rich. Copyright © 2013 by the Adrienne Rich Literary Trust. Copyright © 1973 by W. W. Norton & Company, Inc. Used by permission of W. W. Norton & Company, Inc.

Alberto Ríos, "Mi Abuelo" from *Whispering to Fool the Wind* by Alberto Ríos. Copyright © 1982 by Alberto Ríos. Reprinted by permission of the author.

Richard Rodriguez, "Aria: A Memoir of a Bilingual Childhood." Copyright © 1981 by Richard Rodriguez. Originally appeared in *The American Scholar* (Winter 1981). Reprinted by permission of Georges Borchardt, Inc., on behalf of the author.

Theodore Roethke, "My Papa's Waltz." Copyright © 1942 by Hearst Magazines, Inc. Reprinted from *Collected Poems* by Theodore Roethke. Used by permission of Doubleday, an imprint of Knopf Doubleday Publishing Group, a division of Penguin Random House LLC. All rights reserved.

Jon Ronson, "How One Stupid Tweet Blew up Justine Sacco's Life" from *The New York Times*, February 15, 2015, copyright © 2015 The New York Times. All rights reserved. Used by permission and protected by the Copyright Laws of the United States. The printing, copying, redistribution, or retransmission of this Content without express written permission is prohibited.

Joanna Russ, "When It Changed" from *Again, Dangerous Visions*. Copyright © 1972 by the Estate of Joanna Russ. Reprinted by permission of the Diana Finch Literary Agency.

Karen Russell, "The Bog Girl" from *The New Yorker*, June 20, 2016. Copyright © 2016 by Karen Russell. Reprinted with permission of the Denise Shannon Literary Agency, Inc. All rights reserved.

Susanna Rustin, "*A Doll's House* Is More Relevant Than Ever" from *The Guardian*, August 10, 2013. Copyright Guardian News & Media Ltd 2017. Reprinted by permission of Guardian News & Media Ltd.

Nelly Sachs. "Chorus of the Rescued" from *O The Chimneys* by Nelly Sachs, translated by Michael Roloff. Translation copyright © 1967, renewed 1995 by Farrar, Straus and Giroux, LLC. Reprinted by permission of Farrar, Straus and Giroux, LLC.

Philip Schultz, "Greed." Copyright © 2013 by Philip Schultz. Originally appeared in *Poetry Magazine* (July/August 2013). Reprinted by permission of Georges Borchardt, Inc., on behalf of the author.

David Sedaris, "Tasteless." First published in *The New Yorker* and reprinted by permission of Don Congdon Associates, Inc. Copyright © 2007 by David Sedaris.

Anne Sexton, "After Auschwitz" from *The Awful Rowing Toward God* by Anne Sexton. Copyright © 1975 by Loring Conant, Jr., Executor of the Estate of Anne Sexton. Reprinted by permission of Houghton Mifflin Harcourt Publishing Company and SLL/Sterling Lord Literistic, Inc. All rights reserved.

William Shakespeare, *Othello.* "Notes and Commentary" by Gerald Eades Bentley and Entire Play from *Othello* by William Shakespeare, edited by Gerald Eades Bentley, copyright © 1958, 1970 by Penguin Random House LLC. Used by permission of Penguin Books, an imprint of Penguin Publishing Group, a division of Penguin Random House LLC. All rights reserved.

Bruce Shapiro, "One Violent Crime," from *The Nation*, April 3, 1995. Copyright © 1995 by Bruce Shapiro. Reproduced with permission of the author.

Leslie Marmon Silko, "Yellow Woman" from *Storyteller*, copyright © 1981, 2012 by Leslie Marmon Silko. Used by permission of Viking Books, an imprint of Penguin Publishing Group, a division of Penguin Random House LLC. All rights reserved.

Emily Esfahani Smith and Jennifer Aaker, "Millenial Seachers" from *The New York Times*, December 1, 2013. Copyright © 2013 The New York Times. All rights reserved. Used by permission and protected by the Copyright Laws of the United States. The printing, copying, redistribution, or retransmission of this Content without express written permission is prohibited.

Stevie Smith, "Not Waving But Drowning," from *Collected Poems of Stevie Smith*, copyright © 1957 by Stevie Smith. Reprinted by permission of New Directions Publishing Corp.

Sophocles, *Antigone*, translated by Elizabeth Wyckoff, from *The Complete Greek Tragedies: Sophocles I*, 3rd edition, edited by Mark Griffith and Glenn W. Most. Copyright © 1954, 2013 by The University of Chicago. Reprinted by permission of The University of Chicago Press.

Gary Soto, "Behind Grandma's House" from *New and Selected Poems* by Gary Soto. Copyright © 1995 by Gary Soto. Used with permission of Chronicle Books LLC, San Francisco. Visit ChronicleBooks.com.

Gabriel Spera, "My Ex-Husband" from *Poetry* 149, #5. Copyright © 1992 by Gabriel Spera. Reproduced with permission of the author.

William Stafford, "Traveling Through the Dark" from *The Way It Is: New and Selected Poems.* Copyright © 1998 by the Estate of William Stafford. Reprinted with the permission of The Permissions Company, Inc., on behalf of Graywolf Press, Minneapolis, Minnesota, www.graywolfpress.org.

Martha Stephens. Excerpt from *The Question of Flannery O'Connor* by Martha Stephens. Copyright © 1973. Reprinted by permission of Louisiana State University Press.

Amy Tan, "Two Kinds" from *The Joy Luck Club*, copyright © 1989 by Amy Tan. Used by permission of G. P. Putnam's Sons, an imprint of Penguin Publishing Group, a division of Penguin Random House LLC. All rights reserved.

Dylan Thomas, "Do Not Go Gentle Into That Good Night" from *The Poems of Dylan Thomas*, copyright © 1952 by Dylan Thomas. Reprinted by permission of New Directions Publishing Corp.

Jeffrey Toobin, "Edward Snowden's Real Impact" from *The New Yorker*, August 19, 2013. © Conde Nast. Reprinted with permission of Conde Nast.

Natasha Trethewey, "Incident" from *Native Guard: Poems* by Natasha Trethewey. Copyright © 2006 by Natasha Trethewey. Reprinted by permission of Houghton Mifflin Harcourt Publishing Company. All rights reserved.

John Updike, "A & P" from *Pigeon Feathers and Other Stories* by John Updike, copyright © 1962, copyright renewed 1990 by John Updike. Used by permission of Alfred A. Knopf, an imprint of Knopf Doubleday Publishing Group, a division of Penguin Random House LLC. All rights reserved.

Jose Antonio Vargas, "My Life as an Undocumented Immigrant" from *The New York Times*, June 26, 2011. Copyright © 2011 The New York Times. All rights reserved. Used by permission and protected by the Copyright Laws of the United States. The printing, copying, redistribution, or retransmission of this Content without express written permission is prohibited.

Kurt Vonnegut, "Harrison Bergeron," copyright © 1961 by Kurt Vonnegut, copyright © renewed 1989 by Kurt Vonnegut; from *Welcome to the Monkey House* by Kurt Vonnegut. Used by permission of Dell Publishing, an imprint of Random House, a division of Penguin Random House LLC. All rights reserved.

Derek Walcott, "Love After Love" from *Collected Poems 1948–1984* by Derek Walcott. Copyright © 1986 by Derek Walcott. Reprinted by permission of Farrar, Straus and Giroux, LLC.

Alice Walker, "Everyday Use" from *In Love & Trouble: Stories of Black Women* by Alice Walker. Copyright © 1973 and renewed 2001 by Alice Walker. Reprinted by permission of Houghton Mifflin Harcourt Publishing Company and the Joy Harris Literary Agency, Inc. All rights reserved.

David Foster Wallace, "Good People" from *The New Yorker*, February 5, 2007. Reprinted by permission of the Hill Nadell Literary Agency on behalf of the David Foster Wallace Literary Trust.

Alexander Weinstein, "Rocket Night" from *Children of the New World*. First published in *Southern Indiana Review* (Spring 2013). Reprinted by permission of Farrar, Straus and Giroux, LLC.

Eudora Welty, "A Worn Path" from *A Curtain of Green and Other Stories* by Eudora Welty. Copyright © 1941 and renewed 1969 by Eudora Welty. Reprinted by permission of Houghton Mifflin Harcourt Publishing Company and of Russell & Volkening as agents for the author. All rights reserved.

Colson Whitehead, "How 'You Do You' Perfectly Captures Our Narcissistic Culture" from *The New York Times*, April 5, 2015. Copyright © 2015 The New York Times. All rights reserved. Used by permission and protected by the Copyright Laws of the United States. The printing, copying, redistribution, or retransmission of this Content without express written permission is prohibited.

Ted Widmer, "The Immigration Dividend" from *The New York Times*, October 6, 2015. Copyright © 2015 The New York Times. All rights reserved. Used by permission and protected by the Copyright Laws of the United States. The printing, copying, redistribution, or retransmission of this Content without express written permission is prohibited.

George F. Will, "Capital Punishment's Flow Death" from *The Washington Post*, May 20, 2015. Copyright © 2015 The Washington Post. All rights reserved. Used by permission and protected by the Copyright Laws of the United States. The printing, copying, redistribution, or retransmission of this Content without express written permission is prohibited.

Michael Wood, from "Consulting the Oracle" from *Essays in Criticism*, Vol. XLIII, no. 2 (April 1993), pp. 93–110. Reprinted by permission of Oxford University Press.

James Wright, "Lying in a Hammock at William Duffy's Farm in Pine Island, Minnesota" from *Collected Poems*. Copyright © 1971 by James Wright. Reprinted by permission of Wesleyan University Press.

William Butler Yeats, "Sailing to Byzantium" from *The Collected Works of W.B. Yeats, Volume 1: The Poems, Revised* by W. B. Yeats, edited by Richard J. Finneran. Copyright © 1928 by The Macmillan Company, renewed 1956 by Georgie Yeats. Reprinted with the permission of Scribner, a division of Simon & Schuster, Inc. All rights reserved.

Index of Authors, Titles, First Lines, and Key Terms

Key terms page numbers are in bold.